T0202957

Lecture Notes in Computer Science　　11464

Commenced Publication in 1973
Founding and Former Series Editors:
Gerhard Goos, Juris Hartmanis, and Jan van Leeuwen

More information about this series at http://www.springer.com/series/7410

Robert H. Deng · Valérie Gauthier-Umaña ·
Martín Ochoa · Moti Yung (Eds.)

Applied Cryptography and Network Security

17th International Conference, ACNS 2019
Bogota, Colombia, June 5–7, 2019
Proceedings

 Springer

Editors
Robert H. Deng (iD)
Singapore Management University
Singapore, Singapore

Valérie Gauthier-Umaña (iD)
Universidad del Rosario
Bogota, Colombia

Martín Ochoa (iD)
Cyxtera Technologies
Bogota, Colombia

Moti Yung
Columbia University
New York, NY, USA

ISSN 0302-9743   ISSN 1611-3349   (electronic)
Lecture Notes in Computer Science
ISBN 978-3-030-21567-5   ISBN 978-3-030-21568-2   (eBook)
https://doi.org/10.1007/978-3-030-21568-2

LNCS Sublibrary: SL4 – Security and Cryptology

This Springer imprint is published by the registered company Springer Nature Switzerland AG
The registered company address is: Gewerbestrasse 11, 6330 Cham, Switzerland

Preface

We are pleased to present the proceedings of the 17th International Conference on Applied Cryptography and Network Security (ACNS 2019) held during June 5–7 2019, in Bogotá, Colombia. The local organization was in the capable hands of Professors Valérie Gauthier-Umaña from Universidad del Rosario, Colombia, and Martín Ochoa, Universidad del Rosario and Cyxtera Technologies, and we are deeply indebted to them for their generous support and leadership to ensure the success of the conference.

We received 111 submissions from all over the world. This year's Program Committee (PC) consisted of 56 members with diverse background and broad research interests. The review process was double-blind and rigorous. The selection of the program was challenging; in the end some high-quality papers had to be rejected owing to lack of space. After the review process concluded, 29 papers were accepted to be presented at the conference and included in the proceedings, representing an acceptance rate of about 26%.

Among those papers, ten were co-authored and presented by full-time students. From this subset, we awarded two Best Student Paper Awards, to Matthias J. Kannwischer (co-authored with Joost Rijneveld and Peter Schwabe) for the paper "Faster Multiplication in $\mathbb{Z}_{2^m}[x]$ on Cortex-M4 to Speed up NIST PQC Candidates" and Zhengzhong Jin (co-authored with Yunlei Zhao) for the work "Practical Key Establishment from Lattice." These papers received very positive comments by the reviewers and we appreciated their theoretical and practical contributions in the post-quantum cryptography field. To them also goes a monetary prize of 500 euro each, generously sponsored by Springer.

This year we had two outstanding keynote talks: "Toward Secure High-Performance Computer Architectures" presented by Prof. Srini Devadas, MIT, and "Foundational Aspects of Blockchain Protocols" by Prof. Juan Garay, Texas A&M University. To Srini and Juan, our deepest gratitude for their excellent presentations.

We had a strong program along with a workshop track in parallel with the main event, providing a forum to address specific topics at the forefront of cybersecurity research. The papers presented at those sessions will be published in separate proceedings.

ACNS 2019 was made possible by the joint efforts of many individuals and organizations. We sincerely thank the authors of all submissions. We are grateful to all the PC members for their great effort in reading, commenting, debating, and finally selecting the papers. We also thank all the external reviewers for assisting the PC in their particular areas of expertise. Finally, we thank everyone else, speakers and session chairs, for their contribution to the program of ACNS 2019.

We would also like to thank the sponsors for their generous support: Universidad del Rosario, the Fellows program from ICETEX, Cyxtera Technologies, Google and Springer.

June 2019   Robert Deng
                                                              Moti Yung

Organization

ACNS 2019

Applied Cryptography and Network Security 2019

June 5–7, 2019
Universidad del Rosario
Bogotá, Colombia

General Chairs

Valérie Gauthier-Umaña   Universidad del Rosario, Colombia
Martín Ochoa   Cyxtera Technologies, Colombia

Program Committee Chairs

Robert Deng   Singapore Management University, Singapore
Moti Yung   Google and Columbia University, USA

Program Committee

Michel Abdalla   ENS and CNRS, France
Man Ho Au   The Hong Kong Polytechnic University, SAR China
Joonsang Baek   University of Wollongong, Australia
Alex Biryukov   University of Luxembourg, Luxembourg
Pino Caballero-Gil   University of La Laguna
Alvaro Cardenas   The University of Texas at Dallas, USA
Liqun Chen   University of Surrey, UK
Xiaofeng Chen   Xidian University, China
Sherman S. M. Chow   The Chinese University of Hong Kong, SAR China
Mauro Conti   University of Padua, Italy
Robert Deng   Singapore Management University, Singapore
Xuhua Ding   Singapore Management University, Singapore
Benjamin Dowling   Royal Holloway University of London, UK
Sara Foresti   University of Milan, Italy
Debin Gao   Singapore Management University, Singapore
Joaquin Garcia-Alfaro   Telecom SudParis, France
Maria Isabel Gonzalez   Universidad Rey Juan Carlos, Spain
Shoichi Hirose   University of Fukui, Japan
Xinyi Huang   Fujian Normal University, China
Stefan Katzenbeisser   TU Darmstadt, Germany
Hiroaki Kikuchi   Meiji University, Japan
Mirosław Kutyłowski   Wrocław University of Technology, Poland

Junzuo Lai	Jinan University, China
Shujun Li	University of Kent, UK
Yingjiu Li	Singapore Management University, Singapore
Joseph Liu	Monash University, Australia
Javier Lopez	University of Malaga, Spain
Di Ma	University of Michigan, USA
Mark Manulis	University of Surrey, UK
Takahiro Matsuda	National Institute of Advanced Industrial Science and Technology (AIST)
Sjouke Mauw	University of Luxembourg, Luxembourg
Martín Ochoa	Cyxtera Technologies, Colombia
Panos Papadimitratos	KTH Royal Institute of Technology, Sweden
Thomas Peters	Université catholique de Louvain, Belgium
Bertram Poettering	Royal Holloway, University of London, UK
Christina Pöpper	New York University Abu Dhabi
Zhan Qin	State University of New York at Buffalo, USA
Ruben Rios	University of Malaga, Spain
Francisco Rodríguez	CINVESTAV-IPN, Mexico
Sushmita Ruj	Indian Statistical Institute, India
Giovanni Russello	The University of Auckland, New Zealand
Chunhua Su	University of Aizu, Japan
Hung-Min Sun	National Tsing Hua University, Taiwan
Qiang Tang	Cornell University, USA
Juan Tapiador	Universidad Carlos III de Madrid, Spain
Nils Ole Tippenhauer	CISPA, Germany
Cong Wang	City University of Hong Kong, SAR China
Jian Weng	Jinan University, China
Qianhong Wu	Beihang University, China
Toshihiro Yamauchi	Okayama University, Japan
Guomin Yang	University of Wollongong, Australia
Tsz Hon Yuen	The University of Hong Kong, SAR China
Moti Yung	Google and Columbia University, USA
Santiago Zanella-Béguelin	Microsoft, UK
Kehuan Zhang	The Chinese University of Hong Kong, SAR China
Jianying Zhou	Singapore University of Technology and Design, Singapore

Additional Reviewers

Alcaraz, Cristina
Armour, Marcel
Beierle, Christof
Bernieri, Giuseppe
Bobowski, Adam

Caballero-Gil, Cándido
Cecconello, Stefano
Chatterjee, Ayantika
Chen, Jie
Chen, Long

Chenu-de La Morinerie, Mathilde
Cui, Shujie
Cuvelier, Edouard
Dai, Elim

Dai, Xiaopeng
Deo, Amit
Dragan, Catalin
El Kassem, Nada
Feher, Daniel
Fuchsbauer, Georg
Galbraith, Steven
Gangwal, Ankit
Gardham, Daniel
Groszschaedl, Johann
Guo, Chun
Gębala, Maciej
Hosoyamada, Akinori
Jonker, Hugo
Katsumata, Shuichi
Kim, Jongkil
Kitagawa, Fuyuki
Kiyoshima, Susumu
Li, Dawei
Li, Zengpeng
Libert, Benoit
Lin, Chengjun
Liu, Jianghua
Liu, Yixin
Lu, Yuan
Ma, Haoyu

Ma, Jack P. K.
Ng, Ka-Lok
Nuida, Koji
Pan, Jing
Perez Del Pozo, Angel L.
Pijnenburg, Jeroen
Rivero-García, Alexandra
Rodríguez-Pérez, Nayra
Roy, Partha Sarathi
Roşie, Răzvan
Rubio, Juan E.
Rubio-Hernan, Jose
Santos-González, Iván
Sato, Masaya
Schuldt, Jacob
Sengupta, Binanda
Shaft, Brian
Smith, Zach
Song, Yongcheng
Suárez Corona, Adriana
Suárez-Armas, Jonay
Syga, Piotr
Tang, Qiang
Tian, Yangguang
Tikhomirov, Sergei
Vazquez Sandoval, Itzel

Villar, Jorge
Vitto, Giuseppe
Wang, Hongbing
Wang, Jiafan
Wang, Jianfeng
Wang, Qingju
Weng, Jiasi
Wszola, Marta
Xie, Congge
Xu, Dongqing
Xu, Shengmin
Xue, Haiyang
Yamada, Shota
Yamakawa, Takashi
Yang, Rupeng
Yang, Shao-Jun
Yang, Yaxi
Yang, Zheng
Yu, Ruyun
Yu, Zuoxia
Zhang, Xiaoqian
Zhang, Xiaoyu
Zhao, Yongjun
Zhu, Yan

Contents

Theory of Cryptographic Implementations

Privacy Preserving Techniques

Integrity and Cryptanalysis

Rate-Optimizing Compilers
for Continuously Non-malleable Codes

Sandro Coretti[1], Antonio Faonio[2], and Daniele Venturi[3(✉)]

[1] IOHK, Hong Kong, China
[2] IMDEA Software Institute, Madrid, Spain
[3] Department of Computer Science, Sapienza University of Rome, Rome, Italy
venturi@di.uniroma1.it

Abstract. We study the *rate* of so-called *continuously* non-malleable codes, which allow to encode a message in such a way that (possibly adaptive) continuous tampering attacks on the codeword yield a decoded value that is unrelated to the original message. Our results are as follows:
- For the case of bit-wise independent tampering, we establish the existence of rate-one continuously non-malleable codes with information-theoretic security, in the plain model.
- For the case of split-state tampering, we establish the existence of rate-one continuously non-malleable codes with computational security, in the (non-programmable) random oracle model. We further exhibit a rate-1/2 code and a rate-one code in the common reference string model, but the latter only withstands *non-adaptive* tampering. It is well known that computational security is inherent for achieving continuous non-malleability in the split-state model (even in the presence of non-adaptive tampering).

Continuously non-malleable codes are useful for protecting *arbitrary* cryptographic primitives against related-key attacks, as well as for constructing non-malleable public-key encryption schemes. Our results directly improve the efficiency of these applications.

1 Introduction

1.1 Background

The beautiful concept of non-malleable codes [24] has recently emerged at the intersection between cryptography and information theory. Given a function family $\mathcal{F}$, such codes allow to encode a k-bit value s into an n-bit codeword c, such that, for each $f \in \mathcal{F}$, it is unlikely that $f(c)$ encodes a value $\tilde{s}$ that is related to s. On the theoretical side, being a weaker guarantee than error correction/detection, non-malleability is achievable for very rich families $\mathcal{F}$; on the practical side, non-malleable codes have interesting applications to cryptography.

S. Coretti—Supported by NSF grants 1314568 and 1619158. Work done while author was at New York University.

A. Faonio—Supported by the Spanish Ministry of Economy under the projects Dedetis (ref. TIN2015-70713-R) and Datamantium (ref. RTC-2016-4930-7), and by the Madrid Regional Government under project N-Greens (ref. S2013/ICE-2731).

© Springer Nature Switzerland AG 2019
R. H. Deng et al. (Eds.): ACNS 2019, LNCS 11464, pp. 3–23, 2019.
https://doi.org/10.1007/978-3-030-21568-2_1

Continuous Non-malleability. In the original definition of non-malleable codes, the property of non-malleability is guaranteed as long as a *single*, possibly adversarial, function $f \in \mathcal{F}$ is applied to a target codeword. All bets are off, instead, if an adversary can tamper *multiple* times with the *same* codeword. While "one-time" non-malleability is already sufficient in some cases, it comes with some shortcomings, among which, for instance, the fact that in applications, after a decoding takes place, we always need to re-encode the message using fresh randomness; the latter might be problematic, as such a re-encoding procedure needs to take place in a tamper-proof environment.

Motivated by these limitations, Faust *et al.* [29] introduced a natural extension of non-malleable codes where the adversary is allowed to tamper a target codeword by specifying polynomially-many functions $f_j \in \mathcal{F}$; in case the functions can be chosen adaptively, depending on the outcome of previous queries, we speak of adaptive tampering, and otherwise we say that tampering is non-adaptive. As argued in [29], such *continuously* non-malleable codes allow to overcome several limitations of one-time non-malleable codes, and further yield new applications where continuous non-malleability is essential [17,19,29,30].

Bit-Wise and Split-State Tampering. Since non-malleable codes do not involve secret keys, it is impossible to achieve (even one-time) non-malleability against all efficient families of functions $\mathcal{F}$. (In fact, whenever the encoding and decoding algorithms belong to $\mathcal{F}$, it is always possible to decode the target codeword, obtain the message, and encode a related value.) For this reason, research on non-malleable codes has focused on obtaining (continuous) non-malleability for limited, yet interesting, particular families. Two prominent examples, which are also the focus of this work, are described below:

- **Bit-wise independent tampering:** Here, each function $f \in \mathcal{F}^n_{\mathsf{bit}}$ is specified as a tuple $f := (f_1, \ldots, f_n)$, where each f_i is an arbitrary map determining whether the i-th bit of the codeword should be kept, flipped, set to zero, or set to one. Continuously non-malleable codes for bit-wise independent tampering, with information-theoretic security, exist in the plain model [19] (i.e., without assuming a trusted setup).
- **Split-state tampering:** Here, each function $f \in \mathcal{F}^{n_0,n_1}_{\mathsf{split}}$ is specified as a pair $f := (f_0, f_1)$, where $n = n_0 + n_1$, and f_0 and f_1 are arbitrary functions to be applied, respectively, to the first n_0 bits and to the last n_1 bits of the codeword. Continuously non-malleable codes for split-state tampering, with computational security, were constructed in the common reference string (CRS) model [26,29] (i.e., assuming a trusted setup), and very recently in the plain model [43] (assuming injective one-way functions).

It is well known that continuous non-malleability is impossible in the split-state model with information-theoretic security, even for non-adaptive tampering [29]. Furthermore, non-adaptive continuous non-malleability for both the above families requires a special "self-destruct" capability that instructs the decoding algorithm to always output the symbol $\perp$ (meaning "decoding error") after the first invalid codeword is decoded, otherwise generic attacks are possible [29,32].

An important parameter of non-malleable codes is their *rate*, defined as the asymptotic ratio between the length of the message to the length of its encoding, as the message length goes to infinity. The optimal rate is one, whereas a code has rate zero if the length of the codeword is super-linear in the length of the message. Non-malleable codes with optimal rate for bit-wise independent tampering [8] (with information-theoretic security) and split-state tampering [1] (with computational security), were recently constructed. To the best of our knowledge, however, the achievable rate for *continuously* non-malleable codes for the same families is poorly understood.

1.2 Our Contributions

In this paper, we make significant progress towards characterizing the achievable rate for continuously non-malleable codes in the bit-wise independent and split-state tampering model.

Split-State Tampering. In Sect. 3, we give three constructions of continuously non-malleable codes in the split-state model, with a natural trade-off in terms of efficiency, security, and assumptions. In particular, we show:

Theorem 1 (Informal). *There exists a continuously non-malleable code in the split-state model in the following settings:*

(i) *With rate 1 and with security against* non-adaptive *tampering in the common reference string model, assuming collision-resistant hash functions and non-interactive zero-knowledge proofs.*

(ii) *With rate 1/2 and with computational security against* adaptive *tampering in the common reference string model, assuming collision-resistant hash functions and non-interactive zero-knowledge proofs.*

(iii) *With rate 1 and with computational security against* adaptive *tampering in the non-programmable random oracle model.*

Recall that computational security is inherent for continuous non-adaptive non-malleability in the split-state model, even in the random oracle model.

Bit-Wise Independent Tampering. In Sect. 4, we show a similar result for the case of bit-wise independent tampering, unconditionally:

Theorem 2 (Informal). *There exists a rate-one continuously non-malleable code against bit-wise independent tampering, achieving information-theoretic security against adaptive tampering in the plain model.*

From a technical perspective, the above theorems are proved by exhibiting so-called rate compilers. A rate compiler is a black-box transformation from a rate-zero non-malleable code Σ for some family $\mathcal{F}$ into a non-malleable code Σ' for the same family and with improved rate. In fact, we show that the rate compilers constructed in [1,8] already work, with some tweaks, in the continuous case. We stress, however, that while the constructions we analyze are similar to previous work, our security proofs differ significantly from the non-continuous case, and require several new ideas. We refer the reader directly to Sects. 3 and 4 for an overview of the main technical challenges we had to overcome.

1.3   Related Work

Several constructions of non-malleable codes for bit-wise [4,7,8,17,19,24] and split-state [1–3,5,6,12,16,20,23–26,29,39,40,43] tampering appear in the literature; out of those, only a few achieve continuous non-malleability [6,17,19,26, 29,37,43].[1] Non-malleable codes also exist for a plethora of alternative models, including bit-wise tampering composed with permutations [7,8,16], circuits of polynomial size [15,24,31], constant-state tampering [4,14,38], block-wise tampering [11], functions with few fixed points and high entropy [37], space-bounded algorithms [10,28], and bounded-depth circuits [9,13].

The capacity (i.e., the best achievable rate) of information-theoretic non-malleable coding was first studied by Cheraghchi and Guruswami [15], who established that $1 - \alpha$ is the maximum rate for function families which are only allowed to tamper the first αn bits of the codeword. This translates into a lower bound of $1/2$ for the case of split-state tampering, and we also know that computational assumptions, in particular one-way functions, are necessary to go beyond the $1/2$ barrier [1].

Non-malleable codes find applications to cryptography, in particular for protecting arbitrary cryptographic primitives against related-key attacks [24]. In this context, continuous non-malleability is a plus [29,30]. Additional applications include constructions of non-malleable commitments [34], interactive proof systems [33], and domain extenders for public-key non-malleable encryption [17,19,41] and commitments [7].

2   Preliminaries

2.1   Notation

For a string x, we denote respectively its length by $|x|$ and the i-th bit by x_i; if $\mathcal{X}$ is a set, $|\mathcal{X}|$ represents the number of elements in $\mathcal{X}$. When x is chosen randomly in $\mathcal{X}$, we write $x \leftarrow_\$ \mathcal{X}$. When A is an algorithm, we write $y \leftarrow_\$ \mathsf{A}(x)$ to denote a run of A on input x and output y; if A is randomized, then y is a random variable and $\mathsf{A}(x; r)$ denotes a run of A on input x and randomness r. An algorithm A is *probabilistic polynomial-time* (PPT) if A is randomized and for any input $x, r \in \{0,1\}^*$ the computation of $\mathsf{A}(x; r)$ terminates in a polynomial number of steps (in the size of the input). Given two strings $x, y \in \{0,1\}^n$, we define the Hamming distance $\Delta(x, y) := \sum_{i \in [n]}(x_i + y_i \mod 2)$, where the sum is over the integers.

---

[1] Strictly speaking, [6] only achieves continuous non-malleability for the weaker case of persistent tampering (where each tampering function is applied to the output of the previous tampering function).

Negligible Functions. We denote with $\lambda \in \mathbb{N}$ the security parameter. A function $\nu : \mathbb{N} \to [0,1]$ is negligible in the security parameter (or simply negligible) if it vanishes faster than the inverse of any polynomial in λ. We sometimes write $\nu(\lambda) \in \texttt{negl}(\lambda)$ to denote that $\nu(\lambda)$ is negligible.

Random Variables. For a random variable $\mathbf{X}$, we write $\mathbb{P}\left[\mathbf{X} = x\right]$ for the probability that $\mathbf{X}$ takes on a particular value $x \in \mathcal{X}$ (with $\mathcal{X}$ being the set where $\mathbf{X}$ is defined). The statistical distance between two random variables $\mathbf{X}$ and $\mathbf{X}'$ defined over the same set $\mathcal{X}$ is defined as $\mathbb{SD}\left(\mathbf{X}; \mathbf{X}'\right) = \frac{1}{2}\sum_{x \in \mathcal{X}} |\mathbb{P}\left[\mathbf{X} = x\right] - \mathbb{P}\left[\mathbf{X}' = x\right]|$.

Given two ensembles $\mathbf{X} = \{\mathbf{X}_\lambda\}_{\lambda \in \mathbb{N}}$ and $\mathbf{Y} = \{\mathbf{Y}_\lambda\}_{\lambda \in \mathbb{N}}$, we write $\mathbf{X} \equiv \mathbf{Y}$ to denote that they are identically distributed, $\mathbf{X} \approx_s \mathbf{Y}$ to denote that they are statistically close, i.e. $\mathbb{SD}\left(\mathbf{X}_\lambda; \mathbf{X}'_\lambda\right) \in \texttt{negl}(\lambda)$, and $\mathbf{X} \approx_c \mathbf{Y}$ to denote that they are computationally indistinguishable, i.e., for all PPT distinguishers D:

$$|\mathbb{P}\left[D(\mathbf{X}_\lambda) = 1\right] - \mathbb{P}\left[D(\mathbf{Y}_\lambda) = 1\right]| \in \texttt{negl}(\lambda).$$

2.2 Non-malleable Codes

We start by recalling the standard notion of a coding scheme in the common reference string (CRS) model.[2]

Definition 1 (Coding scheme). *Let* $k(\lambda) = k \in \mathbb{N}$ *and* $n(\lambda) = n \in \mathbb{N}$ *be functions of the security parameter* $\lambda \in \mathbb{N}$*. A* (k,n)*-code is a tuple of algorithms* $\Sigma = (\mathsf{Init}, \mathsf{Enc}, \mathsf{Dec})$ *specified as follows: (1) The randomized algorithm* Init *takes as input the security parameter* $\lambda \in \mathbb{N}$*, and outputs a CRS* $\omega \in \{0,1\}^{p(\lambda)}$*, where* $p(\lambda) \in \texttt{poly}(\lambda)$*; (2) The randomized algorithm* Enc *takes as input a value* $s \in \{0,1\}^k$*, and outputs a codeword* $c \in \{0,1\}^n$*; (3) The deterministic decoding algorithm* Dec *takes as input a codeword* $c \in \{0,1\}^n$*, and outputs a value* $s \in \{0,1\}^k \cup \{\bot\}$ *(where* $\bot$ *denotes an invalid codeword).*

We say that Σ *satisfies correctness if for all* $\omega \in \{0,1\}^{p(\lambda)}$ *output by* $\mathsf{Init}(1^\lambda)$*, and for all values* $s \in \{0,1\}^k$ *the following holds:* $\mathbb{P}[\mathsf{Dec}(\omega, \mathsf{Enc}(\omega, s)) = s] = 1$.

An important parameter of a coding scheme is its *rate*, i.e. the asymptotic ratio of the length of a message to the length of its encoding (in bits), as the message length increases to infinity. More formally, $\rho(\Sigma) := \inf_{\lambda \in \mathbb{N}} \lim_{k \to \infty} \frac{k(\lambda)}{n(\lambda)}$. The best rate possible is 1; if the length of the encoding is super-linear in the length of the message, the rate is 0.

Non-malleability. Let $\mathcal{F}$ be a family of functions $\mathcal{F} := \{f : \{0,1\}^n \to \{0,1\}^n\}$. The notion of $\mathcal{F}$-non-malleability [24] captures the intuition that any modification of a given target encoding via functions $f \in \mathcal{F}$ yields a codeword that either decodes to the same message as the original codeword, or to a completely unrelated value.

---

[2] Such codes are sometimes also called non-explicit. Explicit codes are obtained by enforcing algorithm Init to output the empty string.

$$\begin{array}{ll}
\textbf{Real}_{\Sigma,\mathsf{A},\mathcal{F}}(\lambda): & \textbf{Simu}_{\mathsf{S},\mathsf{A},\mathcal{F}}(\lambda): \\
\hline
\omega \leftarrow\!\!{\scriptstyle\$}\ \mathsf{Init}(1^\lambda) & (\omega,\sigma) \leftarrow\!\!{\scriptstyle\$}\ \mathsf{S}_0(1^\lambda) \\
(s,\alpha_0) \leftarrow\!\!{\scriptstyle\$}\ \mathsf{A}_0(\omega) & (s,\alpha_0) \leftarrow\!\!{\scriptstyle\$}\ \mathsf{A}_0(\omega) \\
c \leftarrow\!\!{\scriptstyle\$}\ \mathsf{Enc}(\omega,s) & \alpha_1 \leftarrow\!\!{\scriptstyle\$}\ \mathsf{A}_1^{\mathcal{O}_{\mathsf{sim}}(\mathsf{S}_1,\sigma,s,\cdot)}(\alpha_0) \\
\alpha_1 \leftarrow\!\!{\scriptstyle\$}\ \mathsf{A}_1^{\mathcal{O}_{\mathsf{maul}}(\omega,c,\cdot)}(\alpha_0) & \text{Return } \alpha_1 \\
\text{Return } \alpha_1 &
\end{array}$$

Oracle $\mathcal{O}_{\mathsf{sim}}(\mathsf{S}_1,\sigma,s,\cdot)$:

Upon $f \in \mathcal{F}$:
$\quad \tilde{s} \leftarrow\!\!{\scriptstyle\$}\ \mathsf{S}_1(\sigma,f)$
$\quad$ If $(\tilde{s} = \diamond)$, then $\tilde{s} \leftarrow s$
$\quad$ If $\tilde{s} = \bot$, self-destruct
$\quad$ Return $\tilde{s}$

Oracle $\mathcal{O}_{\mathsf{maul}}(\omega,c,\cdot)$:

Upon $f \in \mathcal{F}$:
$\quad \tilde{c} = f(c)$
$\quad \tilde{s} = \mathsf{Dec}(\omega,\tilde{c})$
$\quad$ If $\tilde{s} = \bot$, self-destruct
$\quad$ Return $\tilde{s}$

Fig. 1. Experiments defining continuously non-malleable codes. The self-destruct command causes the tamper oracles $\mathcal{O}_{\mathsf{maul}}$ and $\mathcal{O}_{\mathsf{sim}}$ to return $\bot$ on all subsequent queries.

The definition below formalizes the above intuition in a more general setting where non-malleability is required to hold against (fully adaptive) adversaries that can maul the original encoding several times. This is often referred to as *continuous* non-malleability [29]. Roughly speaking, security is defined by comparing two experiments (cf. Fig. 1). In the "real experiment", the adversary tampers continuously with a target encoding of a chosen message (possibly dependent on the CRS);[3] for each tampering attempt, represented by a function $f \in \mathcal{F}$, the adversary learns the outcome corresponding to the decoding of the modified codeword. In the "simulated experiment", the view of the adversary is faked by a simulator which is completely oblivious of the message being encoded; importantly, the simulator is allowed to return a special symbol $\diamond$ meaning that (it believes) the tampering function yields a modified codeword which decodes to the original message. Both experiments self-destruct upon the first occurrence of $\bot$, i.e., they answer all subsequent queries by $\bot$.

Definition 2 (Continuous non-malleability). *Let $\Sigma = (\mathsf{Init}, \mathsf{Enc}, \mathsf{Dec})$ be a (k,n)-code in the CRS model. We say that Σ is continuously $\mathcal{F}$-non-malleable if for all PPT adversaries $\mathsf{A} := (\mathsf{A}_0, \mathsf{A}_1)$ there exists a simulator $\mathsf{S} := (\mathsf{S}_0, \mathsf{S}_1)$ such that*

$$\{\textbf{Real}_{\Sigma,\mathsf{A},\mathcal{F}}(\lambda)\}_{\lambda\in\mathbb{N}} \approx_c \{\textbf{Simu}_{\mathsf{S},\mathsf{A},\mathcal{F}}(\lambda)\}_{\lambda\in\mathbb{N}},$$

where the experiments $\textbf{Real}_{\Sigma,\mathsf{A},\mathcal{F}}(\lambda)$ and $\textbf{Simu}_{\mathsf{S},\mathsf{A},\mathcal{F}}(\lambda)$ are defined in Fig. 1.

Remark 1 (Non-adaptive tampering). We model non-adaptive tampering by allowing the adversary A_1 to submit a *single* query $(f_j)_{j\in[q]}$ to the oracle $\mathcal{O}_{\mathsf{maul}}$, for some polynomial $q(\lambda) \in \mathsf{poly}(\lambda)$. Upon input such a query, the oracle computes $\tilde{c}_j = f_j(c)$, and returns $\tilde{s}_j = \mathsf{Dec}(\omega,\tilde{c}_j)$ for all $j \in [q]$ (up to self-destruct). In this case, we say that Σ is *non-adaptively* continuously $\mathcal{F}$-non-malleable.

---

[3] Importantly, each tampering function is applied to the original coding; this setting is sometimes known as *non-persistent* tampering.

Tampering Families. We are particularly interested in the following tampering families.

- **Split-state tampering:** This is the family of functions $\mathcal{F}_{\text{split}}^{n_0,n_1} := \{(f_0, f_1) : f_0 : \{0,1\}^{n_0} \rightarrow \{0,1\}^{n_0}, f_1 : \{0,1\}^{n_1} \rightarrow \{0,1\}^{n_1}\}$, for some fixed $n_0(\lambda) = n_0 \in \mathbb{N}$ and $n_1(\lambda) = n_1 \in \mathbb{N}$ such that $n_0 + n_1 = n$. Given an input codeword $c = (c_0, c_1)$, tampering with a function $(f_0, f_1) \in \mathcal{F}_{\text{split}}^{n_0,n_1}$ results in a modified codeword $\tilde{c} = (f_0(c_0), f_1(c_1))$, where c_0 (resp., c_1) consists of the first n_0 (resp., the last n_1) bits of c.
- **Bit-wise independent tampering:** This is the family of functions $\mathcal{F}_{\text{bit}}^n := \{(f_1, \ldots, f_n) : \forall i \in [n], f_i : \{0,1\} \rightarrow \{0,1\}\}$. Given an input codeword $c = (c_1, \ldots, c_n)$, tampering with a function $f \in \mathcal{F}_{\text{bit}}^n$ results in a modified codeword $\tilde{c} = (f_1(c_1), \ldots, f_n(c_n))$, where each f_i is any of the following functions: (i) $f_i(x) = x$ (keep); (ii) $f_i(x) = 1 \oplus x$ (flip); (iii) $f_i(x) = 0$ (zero); (iv) $f_i(x) = 1$ (one).

2.3 Authenticated Encryption

A secret-key encryption (SKE) scheme is a tuple of algorithms $\Pi := (\mathsf{KGen}, \mathsf{AEnc}, \mathsf{ADec})$ specified as follows: (1) The randomized algorithm KGen takes as input the security parameter $\lambda \in \mathbb{N}$, and outputs a uniform key $\kappa \leftarrow_{\$} \{0,1\}^d$; (2) The randomized algorithm AEnc takes as input a key $\kappa \in \{0,1\}^d$, a message $\mu \in \{0,1\}^k$, and outputs a ciphertext $\gamma \in \{0,1\}^m$; (3) The deterministic algorithm ADec takes as input a key $\kappa \in \{0,1\}^d$, a ciphertext $\gamma \in \{0,1\}^m$, and outputs a value $\mu \in \{0,1\}^k \cup \{\bot\}$ (where $\bot$ denotes an invalid ciphertext). The values $d(\lambda), k(\lambda), m(\lambda)$ are all polynomials in the security parameter $\lambda \in \mathbb{N}$, and sometimes we call Π a (d, k, m)-SKE scheme.

We say that Π meets correctness if for all $\kappa \in \{0,1\}^d$, and all messages $\mu \in \{0,1\}^k$, we have that $\mathbb{P}[\mathsf{ADec}(\kappa, \mathsf{AEnc}(\kappa, \mu)) = \mu] = 1$ (over the randomness of AEnc). As for security, an authenticated SKE scheme should satisfy two properties (see below for formal definitions). The first property, usually known as *semantic security*, says that it is hard to distinguish the encryptions of any two (adversarially chosen) messages. The second property, usually called *authenticity*, says that, without knowing the secret key, it is hard to produce a valid ciphertext (i.e., a ciphertext that does not decrypt to $\bot$).

Definition 3 (Security of SKE). *We say that $\Pi = (\mathsf{KGen}, \mathsf{AEnc}, \mathsf{ADec})$ is a secure authenticated SKE scheme if the following holds for the games of Fig. 2:*

- *For all PPT adversaries* A, *we have* $\mathbb{P}\left[\mathbf{G}_{\Pi,\mathsf{A}}^{\text{auth}}(\lambda) = 1\right] \in \mathsf{negl}(\lambda)$;
- $\left\{\mathbf{G}_{\Pi,\mathsf{A}}^{\text{ind}}(\lambda, 0)\right\}_{\lambda \in \mathbb{N}} \approx_c \left\{\mathbf{G}_{\Pi,\mathsf{A}}^{\text{ind}}(\lambda, 1)\right\}_{\lambda \in \mathbb{N}}.$

Note that since both authenticity and semantic security are one-time properties, in principle, information-theoretic constructions with such properties are possible when $d \leq k$. However, we are interested in constructions where $k > d$, for which the existence of one-way functions is a necessary assumption.

$$\begin{array}{ll} \mathbf{G}_{\Pi,\mathsf{A}}^{\mathsf{ind}}(\lambda, b): & \mathbf{G}_{\Pi,\mathsf{A}}^{\mathsf{auth}}(\lambda): \\ \hline \kappa \leftarrow\!\!{}_\$ \{0,1\}^d & \kappa \leftarrow\!\!{}_\$ \{0,1\}^d \\ (\mu_0, \mu_1, \alpha) \leftarrow\!\!{}_\$ \mathsf{A}_0(1^\lambda) & (\mu, \alpha) \leftarrow\!\!{}_\$ \mathsf{A}_0(1^\lambda) \\ \gamma \leftarrow\!\!{}_\$ \mathsf{AEnc}(\kappa, \mu_b) & \gamma \leftarrow\!\!{}_\$ \mathsf{AEnc}(\kappa, \mu) \\ \text{Return } \mathsf{A}_1(\gamma, \alpha) & \gamma' \leftarrow\!\!{}_\$ \mathsf{A}_1(\gamma, \alpha) \\ & \text{Return 1 iff:} \\ & \quad \text{(i) } \gamma' \neq \gamma; \text{ and} \\ & \quad \text{(ii) } \mathsf{ADec}(\kappa, \gamma') \neq \bot. \end{array}$$

Fig. 2. Experiments defining security of SKE.

2.4   Error-Correcting Sharing Schemes

Intuitively, an error-correcting sharing scheme is an error-correcting code satisfying some form of privacy.

Definition 4 (Error-correcting sharing scheme). *A (k, n, T, D) error correcting sharing scheme (ECSS) is a triple of algorithms* (Enc, Dec, ECorr), *where* Enc $: \{0,1\}^k \to \{0,1\}^n$ *is probabilistic,* Dec $: \{0,1\}^n \to \{0,1\}^k$, *and* ECorr $: \{0,1\}^n \to \{0,1\}^n \cup \{\bot\}$, *with the following properties:*

- **Correctness:** *For all $s \in \{0,1\}^k$,* Dec(Enc(s)) $= 1$ *with probability 1 (over the randomness of* Enc*).*
- **Privacy:** *For all $s \in \{0,1\}^k$, any subset of up to T bits of* Enc(s) *are distributed uniformly and independently (over the randomness of* Enc*).*
- **Distance:** *Any two codewords in the range of* Enc *have Hamming distance at least D.*
- **Error correction:** *For any codeword c in the range of* Enc *and any $\tilde{c} \in \{0,1\}^n$,* ECorr($\tilde{c}$) $= c$ *if their Hamming distance is less than $D/2$, and* ECorr($\tilde{c}$) $= \bot$ *otherwise.*

3   Split-State Tampering

In this section, we study several rate-optimizing compilers for continuously non-malleable codes in the split-state setting. As a starting point, in Sect. 3.1, we prove that, under certain assumptions on the initial rate-zero code, the compiler of Aggarwal *et al.* [1] actually achieves continuous security against *non-adaptive* tampering. Unfortunately, as we show in the full version [18], the limitation of non-adaptive security is inherent for this particular construction.

Motivated by this limitation, we propose two variants of the rate compiler from [1] that guarantee continuous security in the presence of adaptive tampering attacks. The first variant, which is described in Sect. 3.2, achieves rate $1/2$. The second variant, which is described in Sect. 3.3, achieves rate one in the (non-programmable) random oracle model.

3.1 Rate-One Compiler (Non-adaptive Tampering)

Let $\Sigma = (\mathsf{Init}, \mathsf{Enc}, \mathsf{Dec})$ be a rate-zero (d, n)-code, and $\Pi = (\mathsf{KGen}, \mathsf{AEnc}, \mathsf{ADec})$ be a (d, k, m)-SKE scheme. Consider the following construction of a (k, n')-code $\Sigma' = (\mathsf{Init}', \mathsf{Enc}', \mathsf{Dec}')$, where $n' := m + n$.

$\mathsf{Init}'(1^\lambda)$: Upon input $\lambda \in \mathbb{N}$, return the same as $\mathsf{Init}(1^\lambda)$.

$\mathsf{Enc}'(\omega, s)$: Upon input ω and a value $s \in \{0, 1\}^k$, sample $\kappa \leftarrow\!\!\$ \{0, 1\}^d$, compute $c \leftarrow\!\!\$ \mathsf{Enc}(\omega, \kappa)$ and $\gamma \leftarrow\!\!\$ \mathsf{AEnc}(\kappa, s)$; return $c' := c\|\gamma$.

$\mathsf{Dec}'(\omega, c')$: Parse $c' := c\|\gamma$, and let $\tilde{\kappa} = \mathsf{Dec}(\omega, c)$. If $\tilde{\kappa} = \bot$, return $\bot$ and self-destruct; else let $\tilde{s} = \mathsf{ADec}(\tilde{\kappa}, \gamma)$. If $\tilde{s} = \bot$, return $\bot$ and self-destruct; else return $\tilde{\mu}$.

Roughly speaking, the compiler uses the underlying (rate-zero) code to encode a uniform key for the authenticated encryption scheme; such a key is then used to encrypt the message, and the resulting ciphertext is appended to the encoding of the key. The decoding algorithm, naturally decodes the encoding of the key, and hence uses the resulting key to decrypt the ciphertext.

Augmented Continuous Non-malleability. Assume that Σ is non-malleable in the split-state setting, where the encoding c is split in two halves c_0 and c_1 (consisting of n_0 and n_1 bits, respectively) that can be modified arbitrarily (yet independently). Intuitively, we would like to show that Σ' is continuously non-malleable against the class of split-state functions that modifies $c_0' := c_0$ and $c_1' := (c_1, \gamma)$ independently.

The difficulty, originally observed in [1], is that, although (c_0, c_1) is a non-malleable encoding of κ (as long as c_0 and c_1 are mauled independently), the adversary could attempt to (independently) modify c_1' and c_0' yielding shares $\tilde{c}_1' := (\tilde{c}_1, \tilde{\gamma})$ and $\tilde{c}_0'$ such that $(\tilde{c}_0, \tilde{c}_1)$ decodes to a key $\tilde{\kappa}$ which is unrelated to κ, yet decrypting $\tilde{\gamma}$ with $\tilde{\kappa}$ results in a message $\tilde{s}$ that is related to s.

A similar difficulty, of course, appears in the continuous setting. In order to overcome this obstacle, inspired by the approach taken in [1], we define a notion of *augmented* continuous non-malleability. Such a notion is a stronger form of continuous non-malleability where, in the "real experiment" after A is done with tampering queries, it is additionally given one share of the *original* encoding (say, c_1). In turn, the "ideal experiment" features a sort of "canonical" simulator S that at the beginning of the simulation computes an encoding $\hat{c} := (\hat{c}_0, \hat{c}_1)$ of, say, the all-zero string; hence, the dummy encoding $\hat{c}$ is used to answer tampering queries from A, and, after the adversary is done with tampering queries, the simulator returns $\hat{c}_1$ to A. The formal definition appears below.

Definition 5 (Augmented continuous non-malleability). *Let* $\Sigma = (\mathsf{Init}, \mathsf{Enc}, \mathsf{Dec})$ *be a* (k, n)-*code in the CRS model, and let* $n_0(\lambda) = n_0 \in \mathbb{N}$ *and* $n_1(\lambda) = n_1 \in \mathbb{N}$ *be such that* $n = n_0 + n_1$. *We say that* Σ *is* augmented *continuously* $\mathcal{F}_{\mathsf{split}}^{n_0, n_1}$-*non-malleable if for all PPT adversaries* $\mathsf{A} := (\mathsf{A}_0, \mathsf{A}_1, \mathsf{A}_2)$ *there exists a simulator* $\mathsf{S} := (\mathsf{S}_0, \mathsf{S}_1)$ *such that*

$$\left\{ \mathbf{Real}_{\Sigma, \mathsf{A}, \mathcal{F}_{\mathsf{split}}^{n_0, n_1}}^+ (\lambda, n_0, n_1) \right\}_{\lambda \in \mathbb{N}} \approx_c \left\{ \mathbf{Simu}_{\mathsf{S}, \mathsf{A}, \mathcal{F}_{\mathsf{split}}^{n_0, n_1}}^+ (\lambda, n_0, n_1) \right\}_{\lambda \in \mathbb{N}}, \quad (1)$$

$$\mathbf{Real}^{+}_{\Sigma,\mathsf{A},\mathcal{F}^{n_0,n_1}_{\mathsf{split}}}(\lambda, n_0, n_1): \qquad \mathbf{Simu}^{+}_{\mathsf{S},\mathsf{A},\mathcal{F}^{n_0,n_1}_{\mathsf{split}}}(\lambda, n_0, n_1):$$

$\mathbf{Real}^{+}_{\Sigma,\mathsf{A},\mathcal{F}^{n_0,n_1}_{\mathsf{split}}}(\lambda, n_0, n_1):$	$\mathbf{Simu}^{+}_{\mathsf{S},\mathsf{A},\mathcal{F}^{n_0,n_1}_{\mathsf{split}}}(\lambda, n_0, n_1):$
$\omega \leftarrow\!\!{\scriptstyle\$}\ \mathsf{Init}(1^\lambda)$	$(\omega, \sigma, \hat{c}_1) \leftarrow\!\!{\scriptstyle\$}\ \mathsf{S}_0(1^\lambda)$
$(s, \alpha_0) \leftarrow\!\!{\scriptstyle\$}\ \mathsf{A}_0(\omega)$	$(s, \alpha_0) \leftarrow\!\!{\scriptstyle\$}\ \mathsf{A}_0(\omega)$
$c \leftarrow\!\!{\scriptstyle\$}\ \mathsf{Enc}(\omega, s)$	$\alpha_1 \leftarrow\!\!{\scriptstyle\$}\ \mathsf{A}_1^{\mathcal{O}_{\mathsf{sim}}(\mathsf{S}_1,\sigma,\hat{c}_1,s,\cdot)}(\alpha_0)$
$c_1 \leftarrow (c[n_0 + 1], \dots, c[n])$	$\alpha_2 \leftarrow\!\!{\scriptstyle\$}\ \mathsf{A}_2(\alpha_1, \hat{c}_1)$
$\alpha_1 \leftarrow\!\!{\scriptstyle\$}\ \mathsf{A}_1^{\mathcal{O}_{\mathsf{maul}}(\omega,c,\cdot)}(\alpha_0)$	Return α_2
$\alpha_2 \leftarrow\!\!{\scriptstyle\$}\ \mathsf{A}_2(\alpha_1, c_1)$	
Return α_2	
	Oracle $\mathcal{O}_{\mathsf{sim}}(\mathsf{S}_1, \sigma, \hat{c}_1, s, \cdot):$
Oracle $\mathcal{O}_{\mathsf{maul}}(\omega, c, \cdot):$	Upon $(f_0, f_1) \in \mathcal{F}^{n_0,n_1}_{\mathsf{split}}:$
Upon $(f_0, f_1) \in \mathcal{F}^{n_0,n_1}_{\mathsf{split}}:$	$\tilde{s} \leftarrow\!\!{\scriptstyle\$}\ \mathsf{S}_1(\sigma, (f_0, f_1), \hat{c}_1)$
$\tilde{c} = (f_0(c_0), f_1(c_1))$	If $(\tilde{s} = \diamond)$, then $\tilde{s} \leftarrow s$
$\tilde{s} = \mathsf{Dec}(\omega, \tilde{c})$	If $\tilde{s} = \bot$, self-destruct
If $\tilde{s} = \bot$, self-destruct	Return $\tilde{s}$
Return $\tilde{s}$	

Fig. 3. Experiments defining *augmented* continuously non-malleable codes.

where the experiments $\mathbf{Real}^{+}_{\Sigma,\mathsf{A},\mathcal{F}^{n_0,n_1}_{\mathsf{split}}}$ and $\mathbf{Simu}^{+}_{\mathsf{S},\mathsf{A},\mathcal{F}^{n_0,n_1}_{\mathsf{split}}}$ are defined in Fig. 3.

Security Analysis. In the full version [18], we prove the following result.

Theorem 3. *Assume that Σ is an* augmented *continuously $\mathcal{F}^{n_0,n_1}_{\mathsf{split}}$-non-malleable (d,n)-code, and that Π is a secure authenticated (d,k,m)-SKE scheme. Then Σ' as defined in Sect. 3.1 is a non-adaptively* continuously $\mathcal{F}^{n_0,n_1+m}_{\mathsf{split}}$-non-malleable $(k, m+n)$-code.*

Remark 2. Similarly to [1], the analysis actually shows that the code Σ' also preserves *augmented* continuous non-malleability (and not just continuous non-malleability). However, since our goal is to construct continuously non-malleable codes (in the standard sense), we do not give the proof for the augmented case.

We also stress that it suffices to start from an augmented code Σ' that is *non-adaptively* continuously non-malleable. However, we rely on the stronger assumption of full adaptivity in order to simplify the exposition, and because, looking ahead, our instantiation from Sect. 5.1 achieves this property.

Proof Intuition. We sketch the main ideas behind the security proof. We need to describe a simulator S' that can emulate arbitrary non-adaptive split-state tampering with a target encoding $c' := (c_0, (c_1, \gamma))$ of a message s, without knowing s. Roughly, S' does the following.

- At the beginning, run the simulator S_0^+ of the underlying augmented non-malleable code, obtaining a fake CRS ω and a simulated right share $\hat{c}_1$.
- Sample a key κ for the authenticated encryption scheme, and define γ as an encryption of 0^k under the sampled key.

- Upon receiving a sequence of non-adaptive tampering queries $(f'_{0,j}, f'_{1,j})_{j \in [q]}$ behave as follows for each $j \in [q]$:
  - Invoke the simulator S_1^+ of the underlying augmented non-malleable code upon $(f'_{0,j}, f'_{1,j}, \hat{c}_1)$, obtaining a simulated decoded key $\tilde{\kappa}_j \in \{\diamond, \bot\} \cup \{0,1\}^d$.
  - Compute the mauled ciphertext $\tilde{\gamma}_j$ by applying $f'_{1,j}$ on $(\hat{c}_1, \gamma)$.
- For each key $\tilde{\kappa}_j$:
  - If $\tilde{\kappa}_j = \bot$ set $\tilde{s}_j := \bot$.
  - Else if $\tilde{\kappa}_j = \diamond$, set $\tilde{s}_j := \bot$ in case $\tilde{\gamma}_j$ is different from the original ciphertext γ, and otherwise set $\tilde{s} := \diamond$.
  - Else set $\tilde{s}_j$ as the decryption of $\tilde{\gamma}_j$ under $\tilde{\kappa}_j$.
  - Simulate a self-destruct by taking the minimum index j^* such that either $\tilde{\kappa}_{j^*} = \bot$ or $\tilde{s}_{j^*} = \bot$, and overwrite all values $\tilde{s}_{j^*+1}, \ldots, \tilde{s}_q$ with $\bot$.
- Return $\tilde{s}_1, \ldots, \tilde{s}_q$.

In order to prove that the above simulation is indeed correct, we define a sequence of hybrid experiments starting with the real experiment (where the adversary A' tampers non-adaptively with a target encoding computed using Σ') and ending with the ideal experiment (where the above simulator is used to answer A''s tampering queries). In the first hybrid, we change the way a non-adaptive tampering query $(f'_{0,j}, f'_{1,j})_{j \in [q]}$ is answered. In particular, given each $(f'_{0,j}, f'_{1,j})$, we run the augmented simulator S_1^+ upon $(f_{0,j}, f_{1,j})$, where $f_{0,j}$ is identical to $f'_{0,j}$, whereas $f_{1,j}$ is obtained by hard-wiring the ciphertext γ (encrypting the real message s) into $f'_{1,j}$. This allows us to get a mauled key $\tilde{\kappa}_j$ that is then used to decrypt the ciphertext $\tilde{\gamma}_j$ defined by applying the function $f'_{1,j}$ on $(\hat{c}_1, \gamma)$, where $\hat{c}_1$ is the right share of an encoding produced at the beginning of the experiment by running the augmented simulator S_0^+.

The most interesting part of the proof is to show that the real experiment and the above hybrid are computationally indistinguishable; here, the augmented non-malleability of the underlying code Σ plays a crucial role. For the purpose of this proof sketch, we only focus on this particular step of the proof, and refer the reader to the full proof for the analysis of the other hybrids. The main challenge is to reduce the attacker A' against Σ' to an attacker A against Σ. In fact, the attacker A' expects to attack a target encoding of the form $(c_0, (c_1, \gamma))$, whereas the attacker A can only tamper with (c_0, c_1). This issue is resolved by having A encrypt the value s chosen by A' under a uniformly random key κ for the authenticated encryption, and by mapping each pair of tampering functions $(f'_{0,j}, f'_{1,j})$ into a pair $(f_{0,j}, f_{1,j})$ such that $f_{0,j} := f'_{0,j}$ and $f_{1,j}(\cdot) := f'_{1,j}(\cdot, \gamma)$ (i.e., the ciphertext γ is hard-wired into the right tampering function).

The above trick allows the reduction to obtain a mauled key $\tilde{\kappa}_j \in \{\diamond, \bot\} \cup \{0,1\}^d$ that is either distributed as in the real experiment (where decoding takes place) or as in the hybrid experiment (where the augmented simulator S_1^+ is used). Unfortunately, this information alone is not sufficient to complete the simulation; in fact, the reduction would need to use the key $\tilde{\kappa}_j$ to decrypt the mauled ciphertext $\tilde{\gamma}_j$ which is obtained by applying the function $f'_{1,j}$ upon input the ciphertext γ and either the real share c_1 (in the real experiment) or the simulated share $\hat{c}_1$ (in the hybrid experiment). Now, if A' were fully adaptive, the reduction would get to know the right share of the encoding only after the last tampering query, which makes it difficult to complete the reduction. Here is where we rely on the fact that tampering is non adaptive, as in this case A' specifies all functions $(f'_{0,j}, f'_{1,j})_{j \in [q]}$ in one go, which in turn allows A to specify $(f_{0,j}, f_{1,j})_{j \in [q]}$ as defined above, obtain all values $(\tilde{\kappa}_j)_{j \in [q]}$ together with the right share (i.e., either c_1 or $\hat{c}_1$), compute the ciphertexts $(\tilde{\gamma}_j)_{j \in [q]}$, and finally complete the simulation.

3.2   Rate-1/2 Compiler (Adaptive Tampering)

We now explain how to slightly modify the compiler from Sect. 3.1 in order to get adaptive security, at the price or reducing the rate of the compiled code to $1/2$. The main difference is that the authenticated ciphertext γ is stored in both halves of the target codeword, i.e. a codeword is now a tuple $(c_0\|\gamma_0, c_1\|\gamma_1)$ where $\gamma_0 = \gamma_1 := \gamma$, and the decoding algorithm additionally checks that, indeed, the two ciphertexts γ_0, γ_1 are the same.

Intuitively, an adaptive adversary cannot store useful information about the inner encoding c_1 in the part of the codeword that stores γ_1. The idea is that in such a case, the same information must be guessed on the other side and overwritten in $\tilde{\gamma}_1$, as otherwise the decoding algorithm would output $\bot$ with consequent self-destruct; but then the adversary could have guessed this information directly, even without the need of a tampering oracle.

Note that the adversary might still be able to learn some partial information about the inner encoding, however, we show that this is not a problem as long as the underlying rate-0 continuously non-malleable code satisfies the additional property of being leakage resilient [5,29,40]. (Augmented non-malleability is not required here.) We defer the formal analysis to the full version of this paper [18].

3.3   Rate-One Compiler (Adaptive Tampering)

We give yet another twist of the rate-optimizing compiler from Sect. 3.1, in order to achieve optimal rate in the (non-programmable) random oracle model. The main idea is to store the ciphertext γ on one share of the codeword, say the right share, as before, and to add the hash of γ on the left share. Specifically, a codeword is now a tuple $(c_0\|h, c_1\|\gamma)$ where $h = H(\gamma)$, and the decoding additionally checks that indeed the value h is equal to $H(\gamma)$. The intuition is that having $H(\gamma)$ in one share is equivalent to having γ itself, as in the random oracle model the value $H(\gamma)$ can be seen as a "handle" for the value γ.

Non-malleability in the Random Oracle Model. We start by explaining what it means to construct a continuously non-malleable code in the (non-programmable) random oracle model. First, the construction itself might make use of the random oracle, so that a code is now a tuple $\Sigma = (\mathsf{Init}^H, \mathsf{Enc}^H, \mathsf{Dec}^H)$ where all algorithms can additionally make random-oracle queries (as in the code sketched above). Second, the adversary A is allowed to make random-oracle queries, and to specify split-state tampering functions of the form $f := (f_0, f_1)$, such that f_0 and f_1 can additionally query the random oracle.

When defining non-malleability in the random oracle model, we also assume that the simulator can query the random oracle. We restrict to simulators that simply observe the random oracle queries made by the tampering functions, but do not *program* them, i.e. the so-called non-programmable random oracle model.

Proof Intuition. We now give an informal argument for the security of the above construction. We do so by showing a reduction to the continuous non-malleability of the code from Sect. 3.2; in order to simplify the exposition, we sketch the analysis in the programmable random oracle model, where the reduction/simulator is further allowed to program the random oracle. In the full version of this paper [18], we give a (slightly more complicated) direct proof that does not require to program the random oracle.

Let A be an adaptive adversary against the security of the rate-one code; we build an adversary B against the security of the rate-1/2 code. Adversary B simply emulates A, keeping a list $\mathcal{Q}_{H,A}$ of all the random-oracle queries made by A. Upon input a split-state tampering query (f_0, f_1) from A, adversary B specifies its own tampering function (f_0', f_1') as follows:

Tampering function $f_0'(c_0\|\gamma_0)$:

  - Compute $h = H(\gamma)$, then execute $f_0(c_0\|h)$.
  - Keep a list $\mathcal{Q}_{H,f}$ of all the queries made by f_0 to the random oracle.
  - Eventually, f_0 outputs $(\tilde{c}_0\|\tilde{h})$, try to find a value $\tilde{\gamma} \in \mathcal{Q}_{H,A} \cup \mathcal{Q}_{H,f}$ such that $H(\tilde{\gamma}) = \tilde{h}$; if such value is found output $(\tilde{c}_0\|\tilde{\gamma})$ else output $\perp$.

Tampering function $f_1'(c_1\|\gamma_1)$:

  - Run $f_1(c_1\|\gamma_1)$.

One can show that B simulates almost perfectly the tampering experiment with A. In fact, the only bad event is when the hash of $\tilde{\gamma}$ as computed by f_1 is equal to $\tilde{h}$, but $\tilde{\gamma}$ has never been queried to H. However, if the adversary A or the tampering function f_0 do not query the random oracle with $\tilde{\gamma}$, then the bad event happens only with probability $2^{-\lambda}$.

In the above description, we did not specify how the reduction treats random-oracle queries asked by the tampering functions f_0 and f_1. The latter can be done by replacing the random oracle H with the evaluation of a pseudorandom function F (with random key κ' sampled by the reduction) which we can hard-code in the description of (f_0', f_1'). This allows to simulate random-oracle queries consistently, but requires to program the random oracle.

4   Bit-Wise Tampering

The compiler from Sect. 3 automatically implies a rate-compiler for continuously non-malleable codes tolerating bit-wise independent tampering (as $\mathcal{F}^n_{\text{bit}} \subset \mathcal{F}^{n_0,n_1,n}_{\text{split}}$) in the computational setting. However, since continuously non-malleable codes for bit-wise tampering also exist unconditionally [19], it might be possible to obtain such codes with optimal rate in the information-theoretic setting. This section shows that this is indeed possible, by extending the analysis of the compiler from Agrawal *et al.* [8] to the continuous case.

4.1 Description of the Compiler

The compiler combines a low-rate continuously non-malleable code (CNMC) Σ' against $\mathcal{F}^n_{\text{bit}}$ with an error-correcting secret-sharing scheme (ECSS) Π with high rate (cf. Sect. 2.4). The main idea of the compiler is to carefully introduce random errors into an encoding of a message s under Π and record these errors in a tag τ, which is encoded with Σ'.

Specifically, let $\Pi = (\text{Enc}, \text{Dec}, \text{ECorr})$ be a (k, n, T, D)-ECSS and $\Sigma' = (\text{Init}', \text{Enc}', \text{Dec}')$ be a continuously $\mathcal{F}^{n'}_{\text{bit}}$-non-malleable (k', n')-code. Let $E \leq n$ be a parameter to be set later. Consider the following construction[4] of a (k, n'')-code $\Sigma'' = (\text{Init}'', \text{Enc}'', \text{Dec}'')$, where $n'' := n + n'$.

$\text{Init}''(1^\lambda)$: Upon input $\lambda \in \mathbb{N}$, return $\text{Init}'(1^\lambda)$.

$\text{Enc}''(\omega, s)$: Upon input ω and a message $s \in \{0,1\}^k$:
    (a) Choose a set $\mathcal{I} = \{i_1, \ldots, i_E\} \subseteq [n]$ of cardinality E and a string $\xi = (\xi_{i_1}, \ldots, \xi_{i_E}) \in \{0,1\}^E$ uniformly at random and let $\tau = (\mathcal{I}, \xi)$.[5]
    (b) Compute $a \leftarrow_{\$} \text{Enc}(s)$ and, for $i \in [n]$, let

$$c_i^{(1)} = \begin{cases} \xi_i & \text{if } i \in \mathcal{I}, \\ a_i & \text{otherwise.} \end{cases}$$

    (a) Compute $c^{(2)} \leftarrow_{\$} \text{Enc}'(\omega, \tau)$ and return $c = (c^{(1)}, c^{(2)})$.

$\text{Dec}''(\omega, \tilde{c})$: Upon input ω and $\tilde{c} = (\tilde{c}^{(1)}, \tilde{c}^{(2)})$,
    (a) Compute $\tau^* = \text{Dec}'(\omega, \tilde{c}^{(2)})$. If $\tau^* = \bot$, return $\bot$.
    (b) Let $a^* = \text{ECorr}(\tilde{c}^{(1)})$. If $a^* = \bot$, return $\bot$.
    (c) Let $\tau^* = (\mathcal{I}^*, \xi^*)$ with $\mathcal{I}^* = \{i_1, \ldots, i_E\}$ and $\xi^* = (\xi^*_{i_1}, \ldots, \xi^*_{i_E})$. Define $c^* = (c^*_1, \ldots, c^*_n)$ as

$$c^*_i = \begin{cases} \xi^*_i & \text{if } i \in \mathcal{I}, \\ a^*_i & \text{otherwise.} \end{cases} \tag{2}$$

    If $c^* \neq \tilde{c}^{(1)}$, output $\bot$.
    (d) Return $\text{Dec}(a^*)$.

---

[4] While we describe the compiler in the CRS model, our instantiation in Sect. 5.2 does not require any trusted setup.
[5] Note that the bits of ξ are indexed by the elements of $\mathcal{I}$.

4.2 Security Analysis

In the full version [18], we prove the following result (cf. also Sect. 5.2 for a concrete instantiation).

Theorem 4. *Let Π be a (k, n, T, D)-ECSS with rate $\rho = k/n$ and $T = \omega(\log n)$, and let Σ' be a continuously $\mathcal{F}_{\text{bit}}^{n'}$-non-malleable code with rate ρ'. Then, for any E satisfying*

$$\frac{n \cdot \omega(\log n)}{D} = E < \frac{D}{4},$$

Σ'' is is a continuously $\mathcal{F}_{\text{bit}}^{n+n'}$-non-malleable code with rate $\rho'' = \frac{k}{\rho^{-1}k + 2\rho'^{-1}E}$.

Proof Intuition. We start with the real security experiment for code Σ'' and consider a series of hybrid experiments $\mathbf{H}_1, \mathbf{H}_2, \mathbf{H}_3$ such that a simulation strategy for the ideal experiment is immediately apparent in $\mathbf{H}_3$.

The first hybrid $\mathbf{H}_1$ changes the way the tampered tag τ^* is computed when $\mathcal{O}_{\text{maul}}$ answers a tamper query f: Instead of computing it from a tampered encoding $f^{(2)}(c^{(2)})$, the simulator S_1' for the underlying non-malleable code Σ' is invoked to determine the outcome of applying f. The indistinguishability of the real experiment and $\mathbf{H}_1$ follows directly from the security of Σ'.

Once the switch to $\mathbf{H}_1$ has been made, the right part $f^{(2)}$ of a tamper function $f = (f^{(1)}, f^{(2)})$ can have one of three effects on the tag τ^*, which lead to the definition of the second hybrid $\mathbf{H}_2$:

1. $\tau^* = \bot$, in which case the outcome of tampering with f is $\bot$ as well.
2. τ^* is equal to the original tag τ. Thus, if the attacker changes too many bits of the left-hand side encoding $c^{(1)}$, the result will almost surely be $\bot$ since the changes are likely to be inconsistent with the parts of $c^{(1)}$ recorded in the tag and are independent of it. Correspondingly, $\mathbf{H}_2$ is defined to *always* answer such tamper queries by $\bot$. If there are only few changes on the left-hand side, $\mathbf{H}_2$ proceeds as $\mathbf{H}_1$.
3. τ^* is independent of the original tag. Thus, if the attacker overrides too few bits of $c^{(1)}$, the random errors in $c^{(1)}$ are highly unlikely to match the corresponding bits in τ^* or not to be detected by the error correction. Correspondingly, $\mathbf{H}_2$ is defined to *always* answers such tamper queries by $\bot$. If there are many overrides on the left-hand side, $\mathbf{H}_2$ proceeds as $\mathbf{H}_1$.

To show that hybrids $\mathbf{H}_1$ and $\mathbf{H}_2$ are indistinguishable, one first argues, drawing on an idea from [17], that for every adaptive strategy, there is an equally good non-adaptive one.[6] The advantage of non-adaptive attackers is bounded by using a simple concentration bound to argue that it is highly unlikely that the query types described above are not caught by comparing the left-hand side to the tag or by performing error correction.

Returning to the case distinction above, it remains to consider the two cases where $\mathbf{H}_1$ was not changed:

---

[6] Recall that a non-adaptive attacker submits all tamper queries at once.

1. Suppose τ^* is equal to the original tag τ and the tamper function changes only a few bits on the left-hand side. In such a case, it can be shown that the result of the tampering is either the original message s or $\bot$. The key observation here is that in order to determine which is the case, one needs merely to find out whether the tamper function "guesses" the bits of $c^{(1)}$ it overrides correctly.
2. Suppose τ^* is independent of the original tag and the tamper function overrides most of the bits on the left-hand side. In this case, it can be argued that the outcome of the tampering is either $\bot$ or a *unique* message, stemming from a unique encoding $\tilde{a}$. To see which is the case, one need only determine if the positions that are not overridden by the tampering function match $\tilde{a}$.

This process can be abstracted as a guessing game for a randomly generated encoding a of s, where the game ends in a self-destruct as soon as an incorrect guess is made. The self-destruct property allows to argue that the guessing game for a generated as an encoding for s is indistinguishable from the guessing game for, say, the all-zero message (by privacy of the ECSS). Correspondingly, hybrid $\mathbf{H}_3$ is defined to work as $\mathbf{H}_2$, except that it works on an encoding of the all-zero message. The indistinguishability of the hybrids follows directly from the indistinguishability of the guessing games. Since hybrid $\mathbf{H}_3$ is independent of the originally encoded message, it is straight-forward to design a simulation strategy.

5   Instantiating the Compilers

5.1   Split-State Model

Rate-One Code (Non-adaptive Tampering). In order to instantiate the compiler from Sect. 3.1, we need to exhibit an augmented continuously non-malleable code in the split-state model. Below, we give a short description of such a code, highlighting the main technical challenges. We assume the reader is familiar with the concept of zero-knowledge proofs.

The Code. The encoding scheme is a variation of the code from [29]. Given a k-bit string s, its encoding has the form $(c_0, c_1) = ((c'_0, h_1, \pi_1), (c'_1, h_0, \pi_0))$, where h_0 (resp. h_1) is a collision-resistant hashing of c'_0 (resp. c'_1), π_0 (resp. π_1) is a NIZK proof of knowledge of a pre-image of the hash value h_0 (resp. h_1), and (c'_0, c'_1) is a leakage-resilient encoding [21] of the input.[7] The decoding algorithm first checks the validity of the proofs locally on the left and right share, and then it makes sure that h_0 (resp. h_1) is indeed the hash of c'_0 (resp. c'_1); if any of the checks fails, it returns $\bot$, and else it decodes (c'_0, c'_1) using the decoding procedure of the leakage-resilient code.

The security proof differs significantly from that of [29]. In particular, we exploit the following additional properties of the leakage-resilient code: (1) It

---

[7] Such an encoding roughly guarantees that ℓ bits of independent leakage from c'_0 and c'_1 do not reveal anything on the encoded message.

should tolerate so-called noisy leakage [22,27,42], meaning that the parameter ℓ is an upper bound on the average min-entropy gap induced by the leakage (and not its bit-length). (2) Indistinguishability should hold even if the distinguisher is given one of the two shares of the target codeword, at the end of the experiment; this property is the one that allows to show *augmented* non-malleability. (3) For all messages, the distributions corresponding to the two shares c_0', c_1' of an encoding are almost independent. Properties (2) was already used in [29], whereas properties (1) and (3) are easily seen to be met by known constructions.

Simulator. The (augmented) code simulator roughly works as follows. It starts by sampling a dummy encoding (c_0', c_1') of the message 0^k under the leakage-resilient code, and hence it computes the hash values h_0, h_1 and simulates the zero-knowledge proofs π_0, π_1; this defines a simulated codeword $(c_0, c_1) = ((c_0', h_1, \pi_1), (c_1', h_0, \pi_0))$. Thus, given a tampering query (f_0, f_1), we design a special simulation strategy that outputs a candidate decoded message acting only either on $(f_0, (c_0', h_1, \pi_1))$ or on $(f_1, (c_1', h_0, \pi_0))$. Let $\tilde{s}_0$ and $\tilde{s}_1$ be such candidate messages. Finally, as long as $\tilde{s}_0 = \tilde{s}_1$ the simulator outputs $\tilde{s}_0$, and otherwise it outputs $\bot$ and self-destructs.

Intuitively, we want to make a reduction to the security of the leakage-resilient code in order to switch the dummy encoding of 0^k with an encoding of the real message. In such a reduction, the values $\tilde{s}_0$ and $\tilde{s}_1$ are obtained via leakage queries, and thus the main challenge is to argue that such leakage is allowed. Take for instance the left share. The main observation is that, as long as $\tilde{s}_0 = \tilde{s}_1$, then the leakage on c_0' reveals no additional information beyond what is revealed by c_1' and the hash of c_0'. In fact, since $\tilde{s}_0 = \tilde{s}_1$, the leakage performed on c_0' could have been also performed on c_1' (as the leaked values are the same!), and furthermore, by property (3) above and by the fact that the hash is short, those values do not reduce the min-entropy of c_0' by too much. On the other hand, if $\tilde{s}_0 \neq \tilde{s}_1$, the amount of leakage can be naively[8] bounded by $2k$, but notice that this happens only once, since the simulator self-destructs after the first $\bot$ is obtained.

Further Optimizations. Along the way, we were also able to improve the parameters w.r.t. the original proof given by [29]. In particular, the leakage parameter we require from the underlying leakage-resilient code is $\ell' \in O(\lambda)$ instead that $\ell' \in \Omega(\lambda \log \lambda)$ in the original proof. This improvement also yields better efficiency in terms of computational complexity for the zero-knowledge proof system (e.g., when using the Groth-Sahai proof system [35,36]). The details are deferred to the full version of this paper.

Putting it Together. Summarizing the above discussion, assuming collision-resistant hash functions and non-interactive zero-knowledge proofs, we have obtained a *rate-optimal* continuously non-malleable code with computational security against *non-adaptive* split-state tampering in the common reference string model, as stated in item (i) of Theorem 1.

---

[8] The leakage parameter can be improved to $O(\lambda)$ by leaking a hash of the message.

Rate-1/2 Code (Adaptive Tampering). In order to instantiate the compiler from Sect. 3.2, we need a leakage-resilient continuously non-malleable code in the split-state model. Luckily, the above construction inherits leakage resilience from the underlying leakage-resilient code.

Hence, assuming collision-resistant hash functions and non-interactive zero-knowledge proofs, we have obtained a rate-1/2 continuously non-malleable code with computational security against *adaptive* split-state tampering in the common reference string model, as stated in item (ii) of Theorem 1.

Rate-One Code (Adaptive Tampering). Finally, we can instantiate the compiler from Sect. 3.3 under the same assumptions of the previous code, i.e. all we need is a leakage-resilient continuously non-malleable code in the split-state model. Here, we can further simplify the above construction by relying on the random oracle heuristic, and consider codewords of the form $(c_0, c_1) = ((c_0', h_1), (c_1', h_0))$, where h_0 (resp. h_1) is computed by hashing c_0' (resp. c_1') via a random oracle. One can prove that this construction achieves (computational) continuous non-malleability in the split-state model.

Hence, we have obtained a *rate-optimal* continuously non-malleable code with computational security against *adaptive* split-state tampering in the (non-programmable) random oracle model, as stated in item (iii) of Theorem 1.

5.2   Bit-Wise Independent Model

The ECSS for the $\mathcal{F}_{\mathrm{bit}}^n$-compiler can be instantiated using share packing, as shown in [8]. This results in a (k, n, T, D)-ECSS with $T = D = \tilde{\Theta}(n^{3/4})$ and $n = (1 + o(1))k$, which in turn allows to choose, e.g., $E = n^{1/4+\gamma}$ for any $\gamma > 0$.

The low-rate CNMC Σ' can be instantiated, e.g., by the codes of [16,19]. Note that such codes are in the plain model (i.e., algorithm Init' returns the empty string), and thus Theorem 4 yields a rate-optimal continuously non-malleable code with information-theoretic security against adaptive bit-wise independent tampering, and without trusted setup, as stated in Theorem 2.

6   Conclusions

We have provided several constructions of rate-optimizing compilers for continuously non-malleable codes in the bit-wise independent and split-state tampering models. While in the former case our compiler is optimal both in terms of rate and assumptions (in fact, the result is unconditional), in the latter case we only get rate-optimal codes for the case of non-adaptive tampering and assuming trusted setup, and in the random oracle model. Thus, the main problem left open by our work is whether rate-one continuously non-malleable codes for the split-state model, with adaptive security and without random oracles, actually exist (with or without trusted setup).

References

1. Aggarwal, D., Agrawal, S., Gupta, D., Maji, H.K., Pandey, O., Prabhakaran, M.: Optimal computational split-state non-malleable codes. In: Kushilevitz, E., Malkin, T. (eds.) TCC 2016. LNCS, vol. 9563, pp. 393–417. Springer, Heidelberg (2016). https://doi.org/10.1007/978-3-662-49099-0_15
2. Aggarwal, D., Dodis, Y., Kazana, T., Obremski, M.: Non-malleable reductions and applications. In: ACM STOC, pp. 459–468 (2015)
3. Aggarwal, D., Dodis, Y., Lovett, S.: Non-malleable codes from additive combinatorics. In: ACM STOC, pp. 774–783 (2014)
4. Aggarwal, D., Dottling, N., Nielsen, J.B., Obremski, M., Purwanto, E.: Continuous non-malleable codes in the 8-split-state model. Cryptology ePrint Archive, Report 2017/357 (2017). https://eprint.iacr.org/2017/357
5. Aggarwal, D., Dziembowski, S., Kazana, T., Obremski, M.: Leakage-resilient non-malleable codes. In: Dodis, Y., Nielsen, J.B. (eds.) TCC 2015. LNCS, vol. 9014, pp. 398–426. Springer, Heidelberg (2015). https://doi.org/10.1007/978-3-662-46494-6_17
6. Aggarwal, D., Kazana, T., Obremski, M.: Inception makes non-malleable codes stronger. In: Kalai, Y., Reyzin, L. (eds.) TCC 2017. LNCS, vol. 10678, pp. 319–343. Springer, Cham (2017). https://doi.org/10.1007/978-3-319-70503-3_10
7. Agrawal, S., Gupta, D., Maji, H.K., Pandey, O., Prabhakaran, M.: Explicit non-malleable codes against bit-wise tampering and permutations. In: Gennaro, R., Robshaw, M. (eds.) CRYPTO 2015. LNCS, vol. 9215, pp. 538–557. Springer, Heidelberg (2015). https://doi.org/10.1007/978-3-662-47989-6_26
8. Agrawal, S., Gupta, D., Maji, H.K., Pandey, O., Prabhakaran, M.: A rate-optimizing compiler for non-malleable codes against bit-wise tampering and permutations. In: Dodis, Y., Nielsen, J.B. (eds.) TCC 2015. LNCS, vol. 9014, pp. 375–397. Springer, Heidelberg (2015). https://doi.org/10.1007/978-3-662-46494-6_16
9. Ball, M., Dachman-Soled, D., Kulkarni, M., Malkin, T.: Non-malleable codes for bounded depth, bounded fan-in circuits. In: Fischlin, M., Coron, J.-S. (eds.) EUROCRYPT 2016. LNCS, vol. 9666, pp. 881–908. Springer, Heidelberg (2016). https://doi.org/10.1007/978-3-662-49896-5_31
10. Ball, M., Dachman-Soled, D., Kulkarni, M., Malkin, T.: Non-malleable codes from average-case hardness: AC^0, decision trees, and streaming space-bounded tampering. In: Nielsen, J.B., Rijmen, V. (eds.) EUROCRYPT 2018. LNCS, vol. 10822, pp. 618–650. Springer, Cham (2018). https://doi.org/10.1007/978-3-319-78372-7_20
11. Chandran, N., Goyal, V., Mukherjee, P., Pandey, O., Upadhyay, J.: Block-wise non-malleable codes. In: ICALP, pp. 31:1–31:14 (2016)
12. Chandran, N., Kanukurthi, B., Raghuraman, S.: Information-theoretic local non-malleable codes and their applications. In: Kushilevitz, E., Malkin, T. (eds.) TCC 2016. LNCS, vol. 9563, pp. 367–392. Springer, Heidelberg (2016). https://doi.org/10.1007/978-3-662-49099-0_14
13. Chattopadhyay, E., Li, X.: Non-malleable codes and extractors for small-depth circuits, and affine functions. In: ACM STOC, pp. 1171–1184 (2017)
14. Chattopadhyay, E., Zuckerman, D.: Non-malleable codes against constant split-state tampering. In: IEEE FOCS, pp. 306–315 (2014)
15. Cheraghchi, M., Guruswami, V.: Capacity of non-malleable codes. In: Innovations in Theoretical Computer Science, pp. 155–168 (2014)

16. Cheraghchi, M., Guruswami, V.: Non-malleable coding against bit-wise and split-state tampering. In: Lindell, Y. (ed.) TCC 2014. LNCS, vol. 8349, pp. 440–464. Springer, Heidelberg (2014). https://doi.org/10.1007/978-3-642-54242-8_19

17. Coretti, S., Dodis, Y., Tackmann, B., Venturi, D.: Non-malleable encryption: simpler, shorter, stronger. In: Kushilevitz, E., Malkin, T. (eds.) TCC 2016. LNCS, vol. 9562, pp. 306–335. Springer, Heidelberg (2016). https://doi.org/10.1007/978-3-662-49096-9_13

18. Coretti, S., Faonio, A., Venturi, D.: Rate-optimizing compilers for continuously non-malleable codes. IACR Cryptology ePrint Archive, vol. 2019, p. 55 (2019). https://eprint.iacr.org/2019/055

19. Coretti, S., Maurer, U., Tackmann, B., Venturi, D.: From single-bit to multi-bit public-key encryption via non-malleable codes. In: Dodis, Y., Nielsen, J.B. (eds.) TCC 2015. LNCS, vol. 9014, pp. 532–560. Springer, Heidelberg (2015). https://doi.org/10.1007/978-3-662-46494-6_22

20. Dachman-Soled, D., Liu, F.-H., Shi, E., Zhou, H.-S.: Locally decodable and updatable non-malleable codes and their applications. In: Dodis, Y., Nielsen, J.B. (eds.) TCC 2015. LNCS, vol. 9014, pp. 427–450. Springer, Heidelberg (2015). https://doi.org/10.1007/978-3-662-46494-6_18

21. Davì, F., Dziembowski, S., Venturi, D.: Leakage-resilient storage. In: Garay, J.A., De Prisco, R. (eds.) SCN 2010. LNCS, vol. 6280, pp. 121–137. Springer, Heidelberg (2010). https://doi.org/10.1007/978-3-642-15317-4_9

22. Dodis, Y., Haralambiev, K., López-Alt, A., Wichs, D.: Cryptography against continuous memory attacks. In: FOCS, pp. 511–520 (2010)

23. Dziembowski, S., Kazana, T., Obremski, M.: Non-malleable codes from two-source extractors. In: Canetti, R., Garay, J.A. (eds.) CRYPTO 2013. LNCS, vol. 8043, pp. 239–257. Springer, Heidelberg (2013). https://doi.org/10.1007/978-3-642-40084-1_14

24. Dziembowski, S., Pietrzak, K., Wichs, D.: Non-malleable codes. In: Innovations in Computer Science, pp. 434–452 (2010)

25. Faonio, A., Nielsen, J.B.: Non-malleable codes with split-state refresh. In: Fehr, S. (ed.) PKC 2017. LNCS, vol. 10174, pp. 279–309. Springer, Heidelberg (2017). https://doi.org/10.1007/978-3-662-54365-8_12

26. Faonio, A., Nielsen, J.B., Simkin, M., Venturi, D.: Continuously non-malleable codes with split-state refresh. In: Preneel, B., Vercauteren, F. (eds.) ACNS 2018. LNCS, vol. 10892, pp. 121–139. Springer, Cham (2018). https://doi.org/10.1007/978-3-319-93387-0_7

27. Faonio, A., Nielsen, J.B., Venturi, D.: Fully leakage-resilient signatures revisited: graceful degradation, noisy leakage, and construction in the bounded-retrieval model. Theor. Comput. Sci. **660**, 23–56 (2017)

28. Faust, S., Hostáková, K., Mukherjee, P., Venturi, D.: Non-malleable codes for space-bounded tampering. In: Katz, J., Shacham, H. (eds.) CRYPTO 2017. LNCS, vol. 10402, pp. 95–126. Springer, Cham (2017). https://doi.org/10.1007/978-3-319-63715-0_4

29. Faust, S., Mukherjee, P., Nielsen, J.B., Venturi, D.: Continuous non-malleable codes. In: Lindell, Y. (ed.) TCC 2014. LNCS, vol. 8349, pp. 465–488. Springer, Heidelberg (2014). https://doi.org/10.1007/978-3-642-54242-8_20

30. Faust, S., Mukherjee, P., Nielsen, J.B., Venturi, D.: A tamper and leakage resilient von neumann architecture. In: Katz, J. (ed.) PKC 2015. LNCS, vol. 9020, pp. 579–603. Springer, Heidelberg (2015). https://doi.org/10.1007/978-3-662-46447-2_26

31. Faust, S., Mukherjee, P., Venturi, D., Wichs, D.: Efficient non-malleable codes and key-derivation for poly-size tampering circuits. In: Nguyen, P.Q., Oswald, E. (eds.) EUROCRYPT 2014. LNCS, vol. 8441, pp. 111–128. Springer, Heidelberg (2014). https://doi.org/10.1007/978-3-642-55220-5_7

32. Gennaro, R., Lysyanskaya, A., Malkin, T., Micali, S., Rabin, T.: Algorithmic tamper-proof (ATP) security: theoretical foundations for security against hardware tampering. In: Naor, M. (ed.) TCC 2004. LNCS, vol. 2951, pp. 258–277. Springer, Heidelberg (2004). https://doi.org/10.1007/978-3-540-24638-1_15

33. Goyal, V., Jain, A., Khurana, D.: Non-malleable multi-prover interactive proofs and witness signatures. Cryptology ePrint Archive, Report 2015/1095 (2015). https://eprint.iacr.org/2015/1095

34. Goyal, V., Pandey, O., Richelson, S.: Textbook non-malleable commitments. In: ACM STOC, pp. 1128–1141 (2016)

35. Groth, J., Ostrovsky, R., Sahai, A.: New techniques for noninteractive zero-knowledge. J. ACM 59(3), 11:1–11:35 (2012)

36. Groth, J., Sahai, A.: Efficient noninteractive proof systems for bilinear groups. SIAM J. Comput. 41(5), 1193–1232 (2012)

37. Jafargholi, Z., Wichs, D.: Tamper detection and continuous non-malleable codes. In: Dodis, Y., Nielsen, J.B. (eds.) TCC 2015. LNCS, vol. 9014, pp. 451–480. Springer, Heidelberg (2015). https://doi.org/10.1007/978-3-662-46494-6_19

38. Kanukurthi, B., Obbattu, S.L.B., Sekar, S.: Four-state non-malleable codes with explicit constant rate. In: Kalai, Y., Reyzin, L. (eds.) TCC 2017. LNCS, vol. 10678, pp. 344–375. Springer, Cham (2017). https://doi.org/10.1007/978-3-319-70503-3_11

39. Li, X.: Improved non-malleable extractors, non-malleable codes and independent source extractors. In: ACM STOC, pp. 1144–1156 (2017)

40. Liu, F.-H., Lysyanskaya, A.: Tamper and leakage resilience in the split-state model. In: Safavi-Naini, R., Canetti, R. (eds.) CRYPTO 2012. LNCS, vol. 7417, pp. 517–532. Springer, Heidelberg (2012). https://doi.org/10.1007/978-3-642-32009-5_30

41. Matsuda, T., Hanaoka, G.: An asymptotically optimal method for converting bit encryption to multi-bit encryption. In: Iwata, T., Cheon, J.H. (eds.) ASIACRYPT 2015. LNCS, vol. 9452, pp. 415–442. Springer, Heidelberg (2015). https://doi.org/10.1007/978-3-662-48797-6_18

42. Naor, M., Segev, G.: Public-key cryptosystems resilient to key leakage. SIAM J. Comput. 41(4), 772–814 (2012)

43. Ostrovsky, R., Persiano, G., Venturi, D., Visconti, I.: Continuously non-malleable codes in the split-state model from minimal assumptions. In: Shacham, H., Boldyreva, A. (eds.) CRYPTO 2018. LNCS, vol. 10993, pp. 608–639. Springer, Cham (2018). https://doi.org/10.1007/978-3-319-96878-0_21

Re: What's Up Johnny?
Covert Content Attacks on Email End-to-End Encryption

Jens Müller[1]([⊠]), Marcus Brinkmann[1], Damian Poddebniak[2],
Sebastian Schinzel[2], and Jörg Schwenk[1]

[1] Ruhr University Bochum, Bochum, Germany
{jens.a.mueller,marcus.brinkmann,joerg.schwenk}@rub.de
[2] Münster University of Applied Sciences, Münster, Germany
{damian.poddebniak,schinzel}@fh-muenster.de

Abstract. We show practical attacks against OpenPGP and S/MIME
encryption and digital signatures in the context of email. Instead of targeting the underlying cryptographic primitives, our attacks abuse legitimate features of the MIME standard and HTML, as supported by email
clients, to deceive the user regarding the actual message content. We
demonstrate how the attacker can unknowingly abuse the user as a
decryption oracle by replying to an unsuspicious looking email. Using
this technique, the plaintext of hundreds of encrypted emails can be
leaked at once. Furthermore, we show how users could be tricked into
signing arbitrary text by replying to emails containing CSS conditional
rules. An evaluation shows that 17 out of 19 OpenPGP-capable email
clients, as well as 21 out of 22 clients supporting S/MIME, are vulnerable to at least one attack. We provide different countermeasures and
discuss their advantages and disadvantages.

Keywords: PGP · S/MIME · Decryption oracles · Signing oracles

1 Introduction

Email was designed as a plaintext protocol, which allows eavesdroppers to read or
modify the communication on the channel. While it is common today that traffic
between mailservers is TLS encrypted,[1] transport encryption is not sufficient to
protect against strong attackers, such as a man-in-the-middle (MitM) within the
infrastructure (e.g., a dishonest mail server operator), or an attacker who gains
access to leaked user emails. OpenPGP [2] and S/MIME [8] are the two major
standards used in such scenarios and provide end-to-end cryptographic protection. Both standards are designed to guarantee confidentiality, integrity, and
authenticity of messages, even in hostile environments such as a compromised
or untrustworthy mail server by encrypting and digitally signing emails.

---

[1] According to Google's transparency report, 88% of the email traffic was TLS
encrypted in the fourth quarter of 2018: https://transparencyreport.google.com/
safer-email/.

© Springer Nature Switzerland AG 2019
R. H. Deng et al. (Eds.): ACNS 2019, LNCS 11464, pp. 24–42, 2019.
https://doi.org/10.1007/978-3-030-21568-2_2

Research Question. Both standards are based on asymmetric encryption; only the user has access to the private key and, therefore, can decrypt messages encrypted with the public key or sign messages. However, email usage involves interaction with multiple communication partners, including potentially dishonest parties. Example: a mail server operator, Eve, who is in possession of the ciphertext messages sent from Alice to Bob can simply re-send the encrypted message from her address and have Bob decrypt it.[2] If Bob simply replied to Eve while quoting the original message, he would leak the plaintext of his communication with Alice. Such message takeover attacks under a new identity are well-known issues in email end-to-end encryption (see [5,6]). However, they are generally considered an acceptable risk because it is assumed that given the context of the message (e.g., *"Hi Bob, [...] Yours, Alice"*) Bob can tell that this message is not originally from Eve and could easily discover the deception.

Therefore, the research question arises: *Is it possible to hide the original text to trick a user into unintentionally acting as a decryption oracle?* A schematic illustration of such an attack is given in Fig. 1.

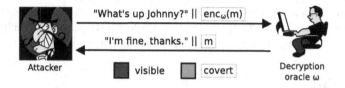

Fig. 1. Covert content attacks against email encryption.

Contributions. In this work, we show simple, yet practical, attacks against email encryption and digital signatures, and discuss the countermeasures. We demonstrate how an attacker can wrap ciphertext into a specially crafted email which looks benign but leaks the plaintext of hundreds of encrypted emails at once if replied to. Furthermore, we show how to turn the victim into a signing oracle by having him sign quoted covert content. The attacker can put this content into a different context based on CSS conditional rules, resulting in arbitrary text to be displayed as correctly signed by the victim. Our evaluation shows that 17 out of 19 OpenPGP capable email clients, as well as 21 out of 22 clients supporting S/MIME are vulnerable to at least one attack. Our attacks raise concerns about the overall security of encryption and digital signatures in the context of email, even though the security guarantees of the cryptography behind them remains untouched.

---

[2] Note that digital signatures do not prevent this attack because Eve can strip them and re-sign the message under her identity as discussed in Sect. 8.1 of this paper.

Responsible Disclosure. We reported our attacks to the affected vendors and proposed appropriate countermeasures. Our findings regarding email end-to-end encryption resulted in CVE-2019-10731 to CVE-2019-10741. Our attacks on digital signatures are documented as CVE-2019-10726 to CVE-2019-10730.

2   Background

In this section, we provide the fundamentals and the historical context of the OpenPGP and S/MIME encryption schemes, as well as MIME and HTML email.

2.1   OpenPGP

Pretty Good Privacy (PGP) was invented in 1991 by Phil Zimmermann and played a major political role in the 'crypto wars' of the mid-1990s. Until today, it has a high reputation among activists, journalists, and privacy enthusiasts. PGP was standardized as OpenPGP in RFC4880 which comes in two flavors: For PGP/Inline, the plaintext in the email body is simply replaced by its encrypted counterpart. This is done separately for each body part (or attachment) in case of multipart emails. For PGP/MIME, the whole MIME structure including all body parts is encrypted into a single part of content type *multipart/encrypted*.

2.2   S/MIME

In the late 1990s, S/MIME was specified as an Internet standard for email encryption and digital signatures based on X.509 public key certificates and a PKI. Besides having a more centralized trust model than OpenPGP, both standards have a lot in common. S/MIME and OpenPGP are both hybrid cryptosystems, consisting of a symmetric cipher such as AES and an asymmetric cipher like RSA. S/MIME encrypts the whole MIME structure into a single body part of content type *application/pkcs7-mime*. It is supported natively by various mail clients and used in business environments and organizations, such as universities.

2.3   MIME Email

Historically, RFC822 email was limited to ASCII messages. This did not fit the needs of users to send other file formats such as binary data. Therefore, in 1992 Multipurpose Internet Mail Extensions (MIME) were born, enabling emails that consist of multiple parts of various content types. An example HTML email with inline images, additional text parts, and a PDF attachment is given in Fig. 2.

   In the context of end-to-end encryption, the flexibility of multipart mails can be dangerous. Neither OpenPGP nor the S/MIME standard cover the edge-case of partially encrypted messages: e.g., ciphertexts can be wrapped as a sub-part within the MIME tree, which is the foundation of our attacks on encryption.

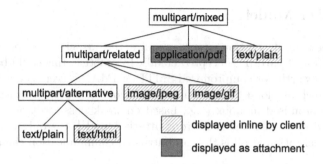

Fig. 2. Exemplary MIME tree of a multipart email.

2.4 HTML Email

HTML in emails was introduced by Netscape in 1995 to format messages, e.g., to provide bold or colored text. It competed with the *text/enriched* MIME type as defined in RFC1563 and Microsoft's proprietary Rich Text Format (RTF). HTML email was eventually adopted by the general public, despite opposition by tech enthusiasts (as expressed, e.g., in the ASCII ribbon campaign). Today most mail clients support HTML emails by default.[3] However, until today, there is no standard that defines which HTML elements should be enabled in email. For example, some email clients even execute script tags within emails (see [7]).

3 Related Work

In 2000 Katz, Schneier, and Jallad [5,6] presented chosen-ciphertext attacks against OpenPGP and S/MIME, in which they make use of the malleability feature of CFB and CBC mode to modify encrypted messages resulting in 'garbage' plaintext. A victim replying to the garbled plaintext unwittingly acts as a decryption oracle, allowing the receiver to reconstruct the original plaintext. Recently, Poddebniak et al. [7] demonstrated that the malleability of CFB/CBC can be used to modify encrypted emails such that their plaintext is automatically exfiltrated to the attacker when opened in a vulnerable email client, using HTML and other backchannels. They, furthermore, showed that some email clients concatenate encrypted and unencrypted MIME parts, allowing an attacker to leak the plaintext of OpenPGP and S/MIME encrypted messages by loading them as the resource of a remote URL. Message takeover attacks for signed emails have been discussed by Davis [3] in 2001. He showed that a signed message "Let's break up" from Bob to Eve can simply be re-send by Eve to scare Alice (Bob's new girlfriend). Furthermore, Davis demonstrated that signatures can simply be removed in many scenarios and the message can be re-signed by the attacker. In 2017, Ribeiro [9] showed that the displayed content of signed HTML emails can be changed subsequently if the mail client fetches external CSS stylesheets.

---

[3] According to an email marketing statistics and metrics study conducted by Juniper Research, 97% of all email clients used in 2007 supported HTML messages.

4   Attacker Model

Attacks based on decryption oracles require the attacker to *somehow* have obtained PGP or S/MIME encrypted emails. In practice, this could be achieved via an untrustworthy or compromised SMTP or IMAP server, via a third party component such as cloud-based antivirus solutions scanning transiting emails, or via a compromised mailbox (e.g., based on weak passwords or XSS on the webmail service). While this is a strong attacker model, the only reason to use end-to-end encryption at all is that an untrusted communication channel is presumed.

After having obtained ciphertext messages, the attacker, Eve, can re-send them in her own name to one of the original communication parties, Alice or Bob. Note that both can act as a decryption oracle because emails are usually encrypted with the public key of both, the sender and the receiver, as both parties want to be able to decrypt it later. Eve can perform additional changes to the encrypted messages such as wrapping them within a multipart mail. In addition, Eve may apply social engineering to lure the victim – Alice or Bob – into replying to her (benign-looking) message. Note that this is a weak requirement as it is a basic function of email to reply to communication partners, even previously unknown ones. It is clear that the security of a cryptographic protocol should not be dependent on the assumption that no communication is made. Signing oracle-based attacks only require the victim to reply to a benign-looking email.

5   Decryption Oracles

Replying to a decrypted email and quoting the original message can leak the plaintext to a third party in case the *From:* or *Reply-To:* header had been replaced with the attacker's email address. Such message takeover attacks under a new identity are well-known (see [5,6]). However, they can often be detected based on the message content. It is generally assumed that trained users should get suspicious and discover the deception instead of replying to 'out of context' messages. In this paper we show how to hide the original plaintext and instead show a meaningful message, asking the user to reply and, therefore, leak the (hidden) plaintext. We do this by abusing the MIME standard in combination

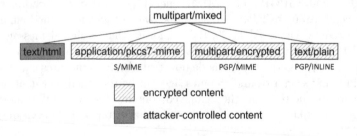

Fig. 3. MIME tree of a partially encrypted email.

with HTML email. Encrypted messages can themselves be a sub-part within a MIME tree which may include further non-encrypted parts. Even though there are hardly meaningful use cases for such 'partially encrypted' emails, they are a valid feature. This allows an attacker to integrate captured ciphertext messages into a MIME tree under her control and re-send this new email to the victim (i.e., the original sender or receiver). A MIME tree containing an attacker-controlled message, as well as S/MIME and OpenPGP encrypted parts, is given in Fig. 3.

Plaintext Merged with Attacker's Text. If a client receives a multipart email, it decrypts the ciphertext parts and afterwards merges all ASCII and HTML parts into a single document which is quoted upon replying.[4] This implementation approach of the MIME standard can be considered dangerous: Eve can prepend her own message, followed by a lot of newlines, to the captured ciphertext part. If Alice replies without scrolling down she unintentionally acts as a decryption oracle and leaks the plaintext. Other obfuscation techniques include hiding the ciphertext somewhere between the attacker's message parts: Emails, especially forwarded mails, can contain a long conversation history and top-posting without reading the whole conversation history is common user behavior. A user replying to a 'mixed content' conversation can thereby leak the plaintext of encrypted messages wrapped within the attacker-controlled text.

Plaintext Hidden Using HTML and CSS. In the context of HTML email, mixed content attacks are more serious than in ASCII emails. An attacker who can inject her own HTML/CSS code into the same document where the plaintext is displayed can completely hide it, e.g., by wrapping it within an iframe. An example email is given in Fig. 4. The result for Apple Mail is shown in Fig. 5.

Note that a closing `</iframe>` tag is not required. However, it could easily be added by placing another attacker-controlled *text/html* part at the end of the message. Iframes are just one way to hide the original plaintext. Other options include wrapping it into HTML comments or other elements such as `<audio>` or `<canvas>` which do not display the content between opening and closing tags – while it is still kept when replying to the email. Other, more advanced, techniques to hide the plaintext using CSS properties are shown for attacks on signatures in Sect. 6. A comprehensive list of CSS blinding options is given in Table 1.

---

[4] There are alternative ways to handle multipart messages. The email client "The Bat!" shows a new tab for each body part, while Outlook only displays the very first part. However, a majority of the evaluated clients follows the described approach.

```
1   From: eve@evil.com
2   To: johnny@good.com
3   Content-Type: multipart/mixed; boundary="BOUNDARY"
4
5   --BOUNDARY
6   Content-Type: text/html
7
8   <b>Hello Johnny,</b>
9   I'm interested in your work. Could you explain to me how...
10  <iframe height="1" frameborder="0">
11  --BOUNDARY
12  Content-Type: application/pkcs7-mime; smime-type=enveloped-data
13  Content-Transfer-Encoding: base64
14
15  [... ciphertext ...]
16  --BOUNDARY--
```

(a) Attacker-prepared multipart email received by victim's mail client.

```
1                                          1   Dear Eve, ...
2                                          2
3                                          3   On 01/05/19 08:27, Eve wrote:
4   <b>Hello Johnny,</b>                   4   > <b>Hello Johnny,</b>
5   I'm interested in your work. Could you...  5   > I'm interested in your work. Could you...
6   <iframe height="1" frameborder="0">    6   <iframe height="1" frameborder="0">
7   Secret message, for Johnny's eye only... 7   Secret message, for Johnny's eye only...
```

(b) HTML code after decryption.   (c) HTML code in reply message.

Fig. 4. Email structure to hide S/MIME ciphertext in an invisible *iframe*. After decryption the plaintext will be included as 'covert content' in the quoted reply.

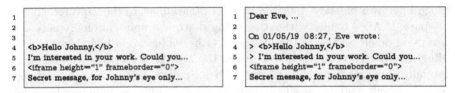

(a) Johnny receives a benign-looking email from Eve.

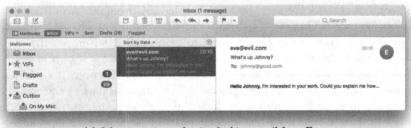

(b) Johnny replies to Eve.   (c) Eve obtains the plaintext.

Fig. 5. Covert content attack using Apple Mail as S/MIME decryption oracle.

Breaking Mixed-Content Isolation with References. In cases where multiple MIME parts are not automatically concatenated by the client, this behavior can be enforced by creating a *multipart/related* email structure referencing the ciphertext via *cid:* URI schemes (see RFC2392). Such Content-ID resource locators are typically used to embed and display inline images within HTML emails. They are generally seen as more compatible than referencing remote images which are blocked in most email clients for privacy reasons. In the example email given in Fig. 6, the attacker's *text/html* part includes the ciphertext as an 'image'. Because the resulting plaintext is not a valid image file, it cannot be displayed by the client. However, the decrypted inline 'image' is included in reply emails, therefore leaking the plaintext. A resulting screenshot of the wrapped PGP/MIME message being opened in Thunderbird is given in Fig. 10 in the appendix. The attacker is not limited to images; the plaintext can also be referenced as the content of an *iframe, object, embed,* and other elements.

```
1   From: eve@evil.com
2   To: johnny@good.com
3   Content-Type: multipart/related; boundary="BOUNDARY"
4
5   --BOUNDARY
6   Content-Type: text/html
7
8   What's up Johnny?
9   <img src="cid:target" width="1" height="1">
10  <style>fieldset , br{display:none}</style>
11
12  --BOUNDARY
13  Content-ID: <target>
14  Content-Type: multipart/encrypted; protocol="application/pgp-encrypted"; boundary="PGPMIME"
15
16  --PGPMIME
17  Content-Type: application/pgp-encrypted
18
19  Version: 1
20  --PGPMIME
21  Content-Type: application/octet-stream; name="encrypted.asc"
22  Content-Disposition: inline; filename="encrypted.asc"
23
24  -----BEGIN PGP MESSAGE-----
25  [... ciphertext ...]
26  -----END PGP MESSAGE-----
27  --PGPMIME--
28  --BOUNDARY--
```

Fig. 6. Email structure to hide PGP/MIME ciphertext in a referenced 'image'.

Note that the attack does not require a 'partially encrypted' email because Eve can also encrypt her malicious parts with the victim's public PGP key or S/MIME certificate. The attack is even successful if the victim replies to Eve with an encrypted email because Eve's public key is used for re-encryption. These attacks apply not only for single ciphertext messages in the middle part of a multipart email, but hundreds of encrypted emails can be hidden as sub-parts and their plaintext can be leaked with a single reply.[5] Furthermore, the attack

---

[5] At some point, the SMTP server may enforce a resource limit, e.g., 25 MB for Gmail.

does not require an active MitM, but rather, the obtained ciphertext could be years-old. For example, a nation-state actor could have captured a target user's encrypted emails over years and later decides to expose them by sending a single benign-looking email which lures the user into replying. While the attacks use email to exfiltrate the plaintext, their scope is not limited to exfiltrating decrypted emails. The attacks also work with non-email ciphertexts such as PGP encrypted files. Covert content attacks are independent of the applied encryption scheme, even though email clients and crypto plugins may handle multipart messages differently, depending on whether S/MIME and OpenPGP is used. While the attacks require user interaction, they do not require any 'unusual' behavior, but instead normal usage of email as a communication medium. They also do not require complex cryptographic attacks like the CBC gadgets discussed in [7].

6   Signing Oracles

Digital signatures should guarantee integrity, authenticity, and non-repudiation of messages. To give an example, Johnny could be a commander-in-chief who takes information security seriously. All his emails are digitally signed, making it hard to impersonate him in order to send forged statements or instructions. The goal of our attacker Eve is to start false-flag warfare. Therefore, she needs to obtain a digitally signed 'declaration of war' which she can forward to the armed forces. Every time Johnny replies to a message he already acts – to a certain extent – as a signing oracle when quoting the original text. For example, consider the following message from Eve to Johnny:

```
1  I hereby declare war.
```

Johnny replies with a signed message, thereby quoting the original text:

```
1  Sorry Eve, You can't do that.
2
3  On 01/05/19 09:42, Eve wrote:
4  > I hereby declare war.
```

In the reply, commander Johnny unintentionally signed Eve's quoted text. Certainly, given the message context and the quote prefix (>...) it is clear that declaring war is not his intention. However, Eve can try to hide her malicious content using *CSS blinding options* while a benign text message, such as *"What's up Johnny?"*, is added to be shown. Similarly, the benign text can be hidden while showing the malicious content, based on *CSS conditional rules* which are satisfied only for a third party. If Johnny replies to such a specially-crafted HTML/CSS email, he signs arbitrary covert content along with visible content. This signed message can then be forwarded by Eve to a third party (e.g., the armed forces) where it displays the previously hidden malicious content *"I hereby declare war"*, while hiding the benign content. A schematic illustration of such covert content attacks on email signatures is given in Fig. 7.

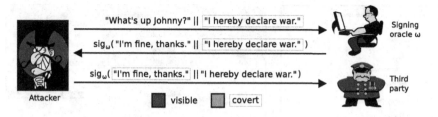

Fig. 7. Covert content attacks against email signatures.

A simple HTML email containing conditional CSS code to display different content based on the device's screen resolution is given in Fig. 8. It can be used to obtain a signed email from a mobile device, where a benign message is shown. The reply message instead displays a (signed) declaration of war when shown on a desktop mail client. A screenshot of the attack using iOS Mail as a signing oracle and the resulting signed email shown in Thunderbird is given in Fig. 9.

```
1   From: eve@evil.com
2   To: johnny@good.com
3   Content-Type: text/html
4
5   <style>
6   /* hide malicious content on mobile devices */
7   @media (max-device-width: 834px) {
8   .covert {visibility: hidden;}
9   }
10  /* but show on desktop/large-screen devices */
11  @media (min-device-width: 835px) {
12  * {visibility: hidden;}
13  .covert {visibility: visible !important; position: absolute; top: 8px; left: 8px;}
14  }
15  </style>
16
17  What's up Johnny?
18  <div class="covert" style="visibility: hidden">I hereby declare war.</div>
```

(a) Attacker-prepared HTML/CSS email sent to Johnny.

```
1   What's up Johnny?
```

(b) Content seen by Johnny on his mobile email client.

```
1   I'm fine, thanks.
2
3   On 01/05/19 09:53, Eve wrote:
4   > What's up Johnny?
```

(c) Content seen by Johnny when replying to the message.

```
1   I hereby declare war.
```

(d) Signed content seen by a third party on a desktop client.

Fig. 8. Malicious HTML/CSS email to obtain a signed 'declaration of war'.

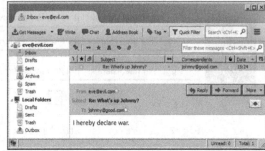

(a) Johnny replies to Eve's email.   (b) Eve obtains a signed reply email for arbitrary text.

Fig. 9. Covert content attack abusing iOS Mail as S/MIME signing oracle.

In the given example, email clients with a screen width of less than 835px (e.g., a mobile phone or tablet) show a different text than desktop mail clients based on the @media conditional rule. If the email client includes this conditional CSS in the reply message it can be misused as a signing oracle, therefore allowing the attacker to obtain signed messaged for arbitrary (displayed) content.

Conditional Rules. The W3C specifies CSS conditional rules [11] like @media, which allow different formatting based on conditions such as screen width or orientation. For example, a different text can be shown whether a mobile phone is held in portrait or landscape mode, or whether the document is displayed on a screen or printed out. Besides media queries, we can show different text in different email clients using the @support conditional rule, which applies formatting based on CSS feature support in the client. For example, an email can be shown in red if two property-value pairs are supported:

```
1 @supports (property1: value1) and (property2: value2) {* {color:red}}
```

We assembled a list of over 1,000 CSS property-value pairs to fingerprint the features supported by clients. This allows us to selectively enable certain CSS code for every client that interprets the @support rule. A further conditional rule introduced by Mozilla is @document. It allows CSS code to be executed based on the document location. In the context of email clients, this even allows us to show different text for each user because the location contains an *imap://* URI scheme with the email address. For example, to apply a red color solely for the emails of *general@good.com* the following CSS code can be used:

```
1 @-moz-document url-prefix("imap://general@good.com") {* {color:red}}
```

In case CSS conditional rules are not supported, email clients may support their own proprietary conditional statements. For example, Outlook interprets HTML and CSS code within `<!--[if mso]>...<![endif]-->`, while other clients will ignore it. A listing of other conditional features is given in Fig. 11 in the appendix.

Blinding Options. We identified seven CSS properties which can be used for covert content attacks, as shown in Table 1. However, this list is unlikely to be complete because CSS is very complex and offers more possibilities to hide text.

Table 1. CSS properties to hide text.

Property	Show	Hide
display:	initial;	none;
visibility:	visible;	hidden;
opacity:	1;	0;
clip-path:	initial;	polygon(0px 0px, 0px 0px, 0px 0px, 0px 0px);
position:	static;	absolute; top: -9999px; left: -9999px;
color:	initial;	transparent;
font-size:	initial;	0;

The proposed attacks allow an attacker to obtain valid signatures for arbitrary content to be displayed. This can be used to trick a third party, which relies on the authenticity and integrity of signed messages, to perform certain actions (such as starting a war). A forensic analysis can reveal the deception, but then it may already be too late (i.e., war is already declared). Note that the covert content attacks to obtain signatures do not require any MIME wrapping, but rather depend on HTML emails, and on support for (internal) CSS styles.

7   Evaluation

To evaluate the proposed attacks, we selected 19 widely-used email clients with OpenPGP support and 22 clients supporting S/MIME from a comprehensive list of over 50 email clients assembled from public software directories for all major platforms (Windows, Linux, macOS, Android, iOS, and Web). Email clients were excluded if they were not updated for several years, or if the cost to obtain them would be prohibitive (e.g., appliances). All clients were tested in the default settings with an additional PGP or S/MIME plugin installed where required. The results from the tested clients regarding covert content attacks, (i.e., tricking a user into acting as an oracle for decryption or signing) are shown in Table 2.

All tested email clients quote the original message when replying, which is the precondition for our attacks. Of the overall tested 24 clients, 20 display HTML emails in the default settings without any additional user interaction, but only 16 clients reply with HTML formatted content. While only five clients download external CSS style sheets by default, all HTML capable clients support internal and/or inline CSS, and at least one blinding option to hide text. All but two HTML capable clients support conditional rules or other features to conditionally show or hide text. Full details on HTML and CSS support for the various tested email clients are given in Table 3 in the appendix.

Table 2. Evaluation of covert content attacks on email encryption and signatures

		Support		Decryption		Signatures	
		S/MIME	**PGP**	**S/MIME**	**PGP**	**S/MIME**	**PGP**
Windows	Thunderbird (52.5.2)	native	Enigmail	●	●	●	●
	Outlook 2016 (16.0.4266)	native	GpgOL	○	○	◑	◑
	Win. 10 Mail (17.8730)	native	–	○	–	◑	–
	Win. Live Mail (16.4.3528)	native	–	○	–	●	–
	The Bat! (8.2.0)	native	GnuPG	○	○	○	○
	Postbox (5.0.20)	native	Enigmail	●	●	●	●
	eM Client (7.1.31849.0)	native	native	○	○	◑	◑
Linux	KMail (5.2.3)	native	GPGME	◐	◐	○	○
	Evolution (3.22.6)	native	GnuPG	◐	◐	◑	◑
	Trojitá (0.7-278)	native	GPGME	◐	◐	◑	◑
	Claws (3.14.1)	plugin	GPG plugin	◐	◐	○	○
	Mutt (1.7.2)	native	GPGME	◐	◐	○	○
macOS	Apple Mail (11.2)	native	GPGTools	●	●	◑	◑
	MailMate (1.10)	native	GPGTools	●	●	●	●
	Airmail (3.5.3)	plugin	GPG-PGP	●	●	●	●
iOS	Mail App (11.2.2)	native	–	●	–	●	–
Android	K-9 Mail (5.403)	–	OpenKeychain	–	○	–	●
	R2Mail2 (2.30)	native	native	○	●	◑	◑
	MailDroid (4.81)	Flipdog	Flipdog	○	○	●	●
	Nine (4.1.3a)	native	–	○	–	●	–
Web	Exchange/OWA (15.1.1034)	plugin	–	○	–	●	–
	Roundcube (1.3.4)	plugin	Enigma	–	◐	◑	◑
	Horde/IMP (6.2.21)	native	GnuPG	○	○	◑	◑
	Mailpile (1.0.0rc2)	–	GnuPG	–	○	–	○

decryption oracles { ● Plaintext can be completely hidden ● Covert rules are kept in reply message } signing oracles
◐ Plaintext merged with attacker-text ◑ Covert rules only for received message
– Cryptosystem not available ○ No vulnerabilities found

7.1 Decryption Oracles

All email clients, excluding Microsoft products and "The Bat!", merge multiple ASCII text or HTML parts into a single document when replying, making them potentially vulnerable to covert content attacks. However, not all clients decrypt ciphertext sub-parts within the MIME tree, thereby disabling the attack. From discussions with application developers, we learned that this was initially *not* meant as a security precaution. Instead, the case of partially encrypted messages was simply not considered in the implementation of S/MIME or the PGP plugin. As a consequence, clients that are more feature complete, have higher compatibility, and require a larger implementation effort are more likely to be misused as decryption oracles. We consider clients as vulnerable if the plaintext of encrypted messages can either be completely hidden, or if it is concatenated with attacker-controlled text.

For seven clients, including popular applications such as Apple Mail or Thunderbird, we could completely hide the ciphertext within a multipart mail using HTML/CSS and show arbitrary content instead. A user replying to such a benign-looking email unknowingly leaks the plaintext of up to hundreds of encrypted emails at once. For another six vulnerable clients, HTML formatted replies are deactivated in the default settings or not supported at all. In such cases, our attacks are limited because the decrypted message cannot be completely hidden. However, it can be appended to the attacker's text, separated by a lot of newlines, or wrapped somewhere within the conversation history. All affected clients, except R2Mail2, show consistent behavior, independently of whether S/MIME or OpenPGP is used as encryption scheme.

7.2 Signing Oracles

We classify clients as vulnerable not only if they can act as a signing oracle, but also if they show different text for signed messages based on conditional CSS. Both vulnerabilities are required for the attack, but they do not need to exist in the same client. In fact, because the targeted users (e.g., *Johnny* and *General*) in each of these cases are different, they are likely to use different clients.

Ten clients, including popular applications such as Thunderbird, K-9 Mail, the iOS Mail App, and Outlook Web Application (OWA), the GUI for Microsoft Exchange, keep the original `<style>` element in replies, allowing an attacker to misuse them as signing oracles.[6] Of the remaining clients, six convert internal CSS style information into inline styles when replying and eight clients reply to HTML emails with ASCII text in the default settings. Once a signed email with conditional CSS has been obtained, it can be used to trick 18 of the 20 clients displaying HTML in the default settings (all but Mailpile and "The Bat!") as well as the HTML-to-text converter used by Horde/IMP into selectively showing/hiding certain text. We could observe the same behavior for all email clients, independent of the applied encryption scheme.

8 Countermeasures

Building a secure encryption protocol on top of email is very challenging. There are many pitfalls and edge-cases to be considered. In this section, we provide best practices to counter the attacks previously described. These practices should be of help to guide implementations of OpenPGP or S/MIME capable clients.

8.1 Decryption Oracles

All-or-Nothing Encryption. Partially encrypted messages can be considered harmful. Therefore, email clients *must not* decrypt emails unless they contain a single encrypted part (i.e., the root node in the MIME tree). This can be standardized and enforced for S/MIME and PGP/MIME. For PGP/Inline however, the only way to send a multipart message is to separately encrypt each part. Unfortunately, every PGP/MIME message can be interpreted in the context of a PGP/Inline message (i.e., a downgrade attack). Hence, email clients supporting PGP/Inline *must* enforce a strict separation between multiple body parts,

---

[6] It must be noted that for two clients, MailMate and Airmail, some additional effort was required to bypass filters which would otherwise strip internal CSS styles.

for example, by opening each part in a separate window or tab. When replying to multipart messages, only the very first body part may be quoted and, therefore, included in the reply to prevent unintended leakage of covert plaintext content.

Accepting ASCII Text Only. Active content such as HTML within emails is dangerous. Disabling HTML prevents most attacks described in this work. Unfortunately, this does not meet today's usage of email. HTML email has become the norm and in ten of the tested email clients – for example, in Apple Mail and iOS Mail – there is not even an option to disable HTML for incoming emails. For Thunderbird with HTML disabled, we furthermore discovered a technique to escalate into HTML context using specially crafted *mailto:* links. It must be additionally noted that modern email clients also display *text/plain* emails within an HTML widget component. One major problem is that no definition for 'HTML email' exists. A standard describing a 'safe' subset of HTML which can be used in emails to allow basic formatting, but forbid potentially harmful features, would be a step in the right direction and is considered as future work.

Enforcing Digital Signatures. In theory, signed emails offer protection against covert content attacks. If Bob received an email originating from Eve, but one message part was signed by Alice, he may get suspicious and not reply to Eve. In practice, email clients miserably fail when it comes to verifying signatures for multipart messages. Our tests show that most email clients either do not show a signature at all for partially signed messages, or show the first available signature in the MIME tree – which can originate from Eve because she can simply re-sign the message. Even in cases where the client explicitly shows inline information regarding which part is signed, we managed to hide the signature information itself using CSS. Moreover, S/MIME signatures can be stripped by targeted modifications of the CBC-ciphertext as shown by Strenzke [10]. Nevertheless, digital signatures – if done right – can enhance message authenticity and integrity. For example, a company could set up a policy to discard all incoming messages if they do not contain exactly one single sign-then-encrypt message part, including signed email headers which can be enforced using extensions such as Memory Hole for OpenPGP [4] or Secure Header Fields for S/MIME [1].

It is important to note that the described countermeasures must be implemented by *all* involved parties. Usually, a user has no control over the security precautions taken by his communication partners. In the context of email end-to-end encryption, this is problematic because both the sender and the receiver can act as a decryption oracle for captured ciphertext. Even if Bob discarded partially encrypted messages and disabled HTML, Alice may still be vulnerable.

8.2   Signing Oracles

Dropping CSS Support. Conditional CSS makes it easy for an attacker to hide certain text within a signed message while showing different text. Ideally, clients would ignore CSS in received emails. However, this is an unrealistic scenario given today's usage of email, especially in a business context, where it is expected that emails can have any sort of formatting – technically implemented with CSS. Sanitizing conditional CSS rules and properties which can be used to hide content is feasible, but it may be insufficient as web technologies are constantly evolving. Nevertheless, it is important to display digitally signed content equally to all viewers. The S/MIME and OpenPGP standards, which are from a time-period where messages were ASCII text, fail to address this and should be extended.

Only ASCII Text in Replies. It should not harm the user experience if mail clients converted quoted messages into ASCII text when replying to an email. Eight of the tested clients (e.g., Roundcube) are actually doing this. Thus, we recommend that security-focused mail clients should adopt this behavior. They *must not* sign any quoted HTML/CSS input from the original message, so that they cannot be misused as signing oracles.

9   Conclusion

Email is complex. The MIME standard and HTML, as supported by modern email clients, provide a high level of flexibility and allow arbitrary wrapping, nesting, and hiding of encrypted or to-be-signed content. This complexity and the conjoined attack surface are not dealt with in the security considerations of the OpenPGP and S/MIME standards, which primarily focus on cryptographic algorithms and their parameters such as key sizes. However, relying on the security of cryptographic primitives, such as AES or ECDH, is not enough for secure email end-to-end encryption and signatures. The developers of email clients have to handle a plethora of critical edge-cases – without being able to consult any published best practices. Our work aims to close this research gap. We reveal implementation pitfalls in the "no man's land" between cryptography and email, as used today, and give guidance and best practices in order to improve the security of S/MIME and OpenPGP capable email clients.

Acknowledgements. The authors thank Juraj Somorovsky for his valuable feedback and insightful discussions. Jens Müller was supported by the research training group 'Human Centered System Security' sponsored by the state of North-Rhine Westfalia. In addition, this work was supported by the German Research Foundation (DFG) within the framework of the Excellence Strategy of the Federal Government and the States – EXC 2092 CASA.

A   Screenshots of Decryption Oracles

A.1   Plaintext Hidden in a Referenced Inline 'Image'

Figure 10 depicts a covert content attack against Thunderbird/Enigmail based
on the example email given in Fig. 6. The ciphertext is hidden in an embedded
'image' file, referenced from the attacker's part via a *cid:* URI scheme. The
OpenPGP plugin – Enigmail – detects the 'image' as PGP/MIME content and
decrypts it. The decrypted 'image' is then Base64 encoded by Thunderbird and
included in the reply message, therefore leaking the plaintext.

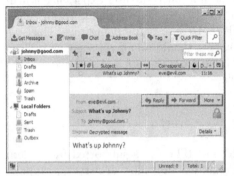

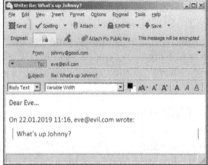

(a) Johnny receives a benign-looking
email with an embedded invisible 'image'
which contains PGP/MIME ciphertext.

(b) Johnny replies to Eve, thereby unknowingly leaking the plaintext within
the invisible inline image.

(c) Eve obtains the reply email, including
the Base64 encoded 'image' which contains the plaintext.

(d) Eve decodes the Base64 encoded
data, resulting in the original plaintext
MIME message.

Fig. 10. Convert content attack using Thunderbird as PGP decryption oracle.

B   HTML/CSS Email Support

Table 3. HTML and CSS support in various email clients.

		HTML		CSS styles			blinding options							conditional rules			
		view	reply	external	internal	inline	display	visibility	opacity	clip-path	position	color	font-size	@media	@supports	@document	other
Windows	Thunderbird	●	●	◐	●	●	●	●	●	●	●	●	●	●	●	●	●
	Outlook 2016	●	●	◐	●	●	●	○	○	○	○	●	●	○	○	○	●
	Win. 10 Mail	●	●	◐	●	●	●	○	○	○	○	●	●	○	○	○	●
	W. Live Mail	●	●	●	●	●	●	●	○	○	●	●	●	○	○	○	●
	The Bat!	●	●	○	●	●	○	○	○	○	○	●	○	○	○	○	○
	Postbox	●	●	◐	●	●	●	●	○	○	●	●	●	●	○	●	○
	eM Client	●	●	◐	●	●	●	●	○	○	●	●	●	●	●	○	○
Linux	KMail	◐	●	○	◐	◐	◐	◐	◐	○	◐	◐	◐	◐	○	○	○
	Evolution	●	◐	◐	●	●	●	●	●	○	●	●	●	●	●	○	○
	Trojitá	●	○	◐	●	●	●	●	●	○	●	●	●	●	○	○	○
	Claws	○	○	○	○	○	○	○	○	○	○	○	○	○	○	○	○
	Mutt	○	○	○	○	○	○	○	○	○	○	○	○	○	○	○	○
Mac	Apple Mail	●	●	●	●	●	●	●	●	○	●	●	●	●	●	○	○
	MailMate	●	●	◐	●	●	●	●	●	○	●	●	●	●	●	○	○
	Airmail	●	●	●	●	○	●	●	●	○	●	●	●	●	●	○	○
iOS	Mail App	●	●	●	●	●	●	●	●	○	●	●	●	●	●	○	○
Android	K-9 Mail	●	●	○	●	●	●	●	●	○	●	●	●	●	○	○	○
	R2Mail2	●	○	○	●	○	●	●	●	○	●	●	●	●	○	○	○
	MailDroid	●	●	◐	●	●	●	●	●	○	●	●	●	●	○	○	○
	Nine	●	●	●	●	●	●	●	●	○	●	●	●	●	○	○	○
Web	Exchange/OWA	●	●	○	●	●	●	●	○	○	○	●	●	○	○	○	●
	Roundcube	●	◐	○	●	●	●	●	●	●	●	●	●	●	●	●	○
	Horde/IMP	◐	◐	○	◐	◐	◐	◐	◐	◐	◐	◐	◐	◐	◐	◐	○
	Mailpile	●	○	○	○	●	●	●	●	●	●	●	●	○	○	○	○

○ Not supported by client   ● Supported in default settings   ◐ Supported in non-default settings

C   Other Conditional Features

```
1   <html><head>
2   <!--[if IE]><style>.wlm {color: red;}</style><![endif]-->    <!-- Windows Live Mail -->
3   <!--[if mso]><style>.ol {color: red;}</style><![endif]-->    <!-- Outlook / W10Mail -->
4   <style>
5   .ExternalClass .owa, [owa] .owa {color: red;}               /* Exchange (OWA) */
6   .moz-text-html .tb {color: red;}                            /* Thunderbird */
7   </style>
8   </head>
9   <body>
10  <div class="wlm"> RED text only in Windows Live Mail </div>
11  <div class="ol"> RED text only in Outlook / W10Mail </div>
12  <div class="owa"> RED text only in Exchange (OWA)     </div>
13  <div class="tb"> RED text only in Thunderbird        </div>
14  </body></html>
```

Fig. 11. Proprietary features and CSS to target only certain clients.

References

1. Cailleux, L., Bonatti, C.: Securing Header Fields with S/MIME, April 2015. http://tools.ietf.org/rfc/rfc7508.txt, RFC7508

2. Callas, J., Donnerhacke, L., Finney, H., Thayer, R.: OpenPGP Message Format, November 1998. http://tools.ietf.org/rfc/rfc2440.txt, RFC2440
3. Davis, D.: Defective sign & encrypt in S/MIME, PKCS#7, MOSS, PEM, PGP, and XML. In: Proceedings of the General Track: 2001 USENIX Annual Technical Conference, pp. 65–78. USENIX Association, Berkeley (2001). http://dl.acm.org/citation.cfm?id=647055.715781
4. Gillmor, D.K.: Memory Hole spec and documentation (2014). https://github.com/autocrypt/memoryhole
5. Jallad, K., Katz, J., Schneier, B.: Implementation of chosen-ciphertext attacks against PGP and GnuPG. In: Chan, A.H., Gligor, V. (eds.) ISC 2002. LNCS, vol. 2433, pp. 90–101. Springer, Heidelberg (2002). https://doi.org/10.1007/3-540-45811-5_7
6. Katz, J., Schneier, B.: A chosen ciphertext attack against several e-mail encryption protocols. In: Proceedings of the 9th Conference on USENIX Security Symposium, SSYM 2000, vol. 9, p. 18. USENIX Association, Berkeley (2000). http://dl.acm.org/citation.cfm?id=1251306.1251324
7. Poddebniak, D., et al.: Efail: breaking S/MIME and OpenPGP email encryption using exfiltration channels. In: 27th USENIX Security Symposium (USENIX Security 18), pp. 549–566. USENIX Association, Baltimore (2018). https://www.usenix.org/conference/usenixsecurity18/presentation/poddebniak
8. Ramsdell, B.: S/MIME Version 3 Message Specification, June 1999. http://tools.ietf.org/rfc/rfc2633.txt, RFC2633
9. Ribeiro, F.: The Ropemaker Email Exploit (2017)
10. Strenzke, F.: Improved Message Takeover Attacks against S/MIME, February 2016. https://cryptosource.de/posts/smime_mta_improved_en.html
11. W3C: CSS Conditional Rules Module Level 3 (2013). https://www.w3.org/TR/css3-conditional/

Cryptanalysis of ForkAES

Subhadeep Banik[1], Jannis Bossert[2], Amit Jana[3], Eik List[2], Stefan Lucks[2],
Willi Meier[4], Mostafizar Rahman[3], Dhiman Saha[5], and Yu Sasaki[6]([✉])

[1] EPFL, Lausanne, Switzerland
subhadeep.banik@epfl.ch
[2] Bauhaus-Universität Weimar, Weimar, Germany
{jannis.bossert,eik.list,stefan.lucks}@uni-weimar.de
[3] CSRU, Indian Statistical Institute, Kolkata, India
janaamit001@gmail.com, mrahman454@gmail.com
[4] FHNW, Windisch, Switzerland
willi.meier@fhnw.ch
[5] IIT Bhilai, Raipur, India
dhiman@iitbhilai.ac.in
[6] NTT Secure Platform Laboratories, Tokyo, Japan
yu.sasaki.sk@hco.ntt.co.jp

Abstract. Forkciphers are a new kind of primitive proposed recently by Andreeva et al. for efficient encryption and authentication of small messages. They fork the middle state of a cipher and encrypt it twice under two smaller independent permutations. Thus, forkciphers produce two output blocks in one primitive call.

Andreeva et al. proposed ForkAES, a tweakable AES-based forkcipher that splits the state after five out of ten rounds. While their authenticated encrypted schemes were accompanied by proofs, the security discussion for ForkAES was not provided, and founded on existing results on the AES and KIASU-BC. Forkciphers provide a unique interface called reconstruction queries that use one ciphertext block as input and compute the respective other ciphertext block. Thus, they deserve a careful security analysis.

This work fosters the understanding of the security of ForkAES with three contributions: (1) We observe that security in reconstruction queries differs strongly from the existing results on the AES. This allows to attack nine out of ten rounds with differential, impossible-differential and yoyo attacks. (2) We observe that some forkcipher modes may lack the interface of reconstruction queries, so that attackers must use encryption queries. We show that nine rounds can still be attacked with rectangle and impossible-differential attacks. (3) We present forgery attacks on the AE modes proposed by Andreeva et al. with nine-round ForkAES.

Keywords: Symmetric-key cryptography · Cryptanalysis ·
Tweakable block cipher · Impossible differential · Boomerang · Yoyo ·
AE

© Springer Nature Switzerland AG 2019
R. H. Deng et al. (Eds.): ACNS 2019, LNCS 11464, pp. 43–63, 2019.
https://doi.org/10.1007/978-3-030-21568-2_3

1   Introduction

The fast distribution of resource-constrained devices demands efficient encryption and authentication of short messages. Forkciphers are a recent proposal by Andreeva et al. [1] to address this purpose. Like classical (tweakable) block ciphers, they encrypt a plaintext block under a secret key; In contrast, however, forkciphers compute two ciphertext blocks from the same input. To boost the performance, the state in the middle of the computation is forked, and both ciphertext blocks are computed separately only from the middle. Therefore, the construction can share some computations and has to encrypt only twice over the bottom rounds. Thus, efficient AE schemes can obtain a ciphertext and tag efficiently for messages whose size is at most a block. Owing to this construction, forkciphers provide a new interface called *reconstruction* that takes one of the ciphertext blocks as input and returns the other one.

As instance of particular interest, Andreeva et al. [1] proposed ForkAES, which employs the original key schedule and round function of the AES-128. Moreover, ForkAES is a tweakable block cipher that adopts the concept from KIASU-BC [15]: in every round where the round key is XORed to the state, an additional 64-bit public tweak T is XORed to the topmost two state rows. ForkAES encrypts the plaintext P over the first five rounds exactly as in the KIASU-BC; though, it forks the middle state X and produces from it a ciphertext C_0 exactly as KIASU-BC with the round keys K^5 through K^{10} plus a second ciphertext C_1 under six further round keys K^{11} through K^{16}.

EXISTING SECURITY ARGUMENTS. The adoption of the AES round function and the tweak process from KIASU-BC allowed to profit from existing results, e.g., for the resistance against differential and linear cryptanalysis. Andreeva et al. also considered meet-in-the-middle attacks briefly; concerning further attacks, they stated that: "the security of our forkcipher design can be reduced to the security of the AES and KIASU ciphers for further type of attacks" [1, Sect 3.2]. However, the structure of ForkAES may allow new attack angles, and it appeared to be a highly interesting task for the community to study ForkAES deeply.

CONTRIBUTION. This work analyzes attack vectors on forkciphers and ForkAES in depth. We generalize it to ForkAES-r_t-r_{b_0}-r_{b_1}, where r_t, r_{b_0} and r_{b_1} denote the number of rounds from P to X, from X to C_0, and from X to C_1, respectively; e.g., ForkAES-5-5-5 means the original ForkAES. While we consider only the case $r_{b_0} = r_{b_1}$, we indicate by ForkAES-*-r_{b_0}-r_{b_1} if r_t can be any non-negative integer.

First, we observe that the security of the reconstruction of forkciphers is very different from the encryption and decryption of the conventional AES since the first half of the computation uses the inverse of the round function whereas the second half employs the ordinary round function. We exploit this property by introducing *reflection differential trails* that allow to attack nine rounds (ForkAES-5-4-4) with a low complexity. We also present impossible-differential [4,7-9,12,17] and yoyo [3,20] attacks as well as forgery attacks for the AE mode by exploiting the reflection feature.

Second, we consider the restricted case where the reconstruction interface is unavailable. This is natural for some usages. For example, Andreeva et al. [1] suggested to replace the standard CTR mode with forkciphers; two ciphertext blocks of forkciphers can halve the number of primitive calls to generate the same key-stream length. In such settings, reconstruction (and even decryption) queries of forkciphers are not exploitable by adversaries. We show that even in such environments, attacks can reach nine rounds by a rectangle [5,6,10,18,22] and an impossible-differential attack. Those attacks also exploit the forking step, which produces rectangle quartets from pairs of plaintexts.

Our attacks do not endanger the security of the full ForkAES; however, they contradict some of the designer's claims as they cover one round more than attacks for KIASU-BC [13,21]. More importantly, the forking principle exposes reflection properties in reconstruction queries (Table 1).

Table 1. Comparison of Attacks. CP and CR denote chosen plaintexts and chosen reconstruction queries, respectively. Due to the limited space, two attacks are omitted and are detailed in the full version of this work [2].

Construction	Attack type	Data		Time		Mem.	Section
				Encs.	MAs		
Encryption queries							
ForkAES-*-4-4	Rectangle	2^{85}	CP	$2^{88.5}$	$2^{92.4}$	$2^{86.4}$	Sect. 6
ForkAES-*-4-4	Impossible Diff	$2^{70.2}$	CP	$2^{75.4}$	$2^{110.2}$	2^{100}	Sect. 7
Reconstruction queries							
ForkAES-*-4-4	Reflection Diff	2^{35}	CR	2^{28}	2^{35}	2^{33}	Sect. 3
ForkAES-*-4-4	Impossible Diff	$2^{39.4}$	CR	2^{47}	2^{47}	2^{35}	Sect. 4
ForkAES-*-3-3	Yoyo	$2^{14.5}$	CR	$2^{14.5}$	2^{29}	2^{29}	Sect. 5
ForkAES-*-4-4	Imp.-diff. Yoyo	$2^{122.83}$	CR	$2^{122.83}$	–	$O(1)$	[2, App. D]
Forgery attacks on AE modes							
PAEF-ForkAES-*-4-4	Reflection Diff	2^{92}	CR	2^{92}	–	$O(1)$	[2, App. C]

OUTLINE. Next, we briefly revisit the necessary details on the AES, KIASU-BC, and ForkAES. Sections 3–5 detail our attacks based on reflection queries and Sects. 6 and 7 describe our attacks based on encryption queries. Due to space limitations, those sections contain only a representative description of an attack each; detailed results can be found in the full version of this work [2].

2 Preliminaries

GENERAL NOTATION. We assume, the reader is familiar with the concepts of block ciphers and their analysis. Most of the time, we consider bit strings of fixed length. We mostly use uppercase letters (e.g., X) for bit strings, lowercase letters for indices (x), and calligraphic letters for sets ($\mathcal{X}$). For some positive integer n, we interpret bit strings $X \in \{0,1\}^n$ as vector elements of $\mathbb{F}_2^n$, where addition is the bit-wise XOR, denoted by $\oplus$. Moreover, the AES works on byte vectors or byte matrices, i.e., 16-element vectors in $\mathbb{F}_{2^8}$. So, we interpret byte matrices of r rows and c columns as elements of $\mathbb{F}_{2^8}^{r \times c}$.

FORKCIPHERS. Let $\mathcal{B}$, $\mathcal{K}$, and $\mathcal{T}$ be non-empty sets or spaces. A tweakable fork-cipher $\widetilde{E}$ is a tuple of three deterministic algorithms: An encryption algorithm $\widetilde{E} : \mathcal{K} \times \mathcal{T} \times \mathcal{B} \to (\mathcal{B})^2$; a decryption algorithm $\widetilde{D} : \mathcal{K} \times \mathcal{T} \times \mathcal{B} \times \{0,1\} \to \mathcal{B}$; and a tag-reconstruction algorithm $\widetilde{R} : \mathcal{K} \times \mathcal{T} \times \mathcal{B} \times \{0,1\} \to \mathcal{B}$. The encryption produces $\widetilde{E}_K^T(P) = (C_0 \,\|\, C_1)$. We define $\widetilde{E}_K^T(P)[0] = C_0$ and $\widetilde{E}_K^T(P)[1] = C_1$ Decryption and tag reconstruction take a bit b s. t. it holds $\widetilde{D}_K^{T,b}(\widetilde{E}_K^T(P)[b]) = P$, for all $K, T, P, b \in \mathcal{K} \times \mathcal{T} \times \mathcal{B} \times \{0,1\}$. The tag-reconstruction takes K, T, C_b, and b as input, and produces $C_{b \oplus 1}$. The ideal tweakable forked permutation $\widetilde{\Pi}$ encrypts messages P under two independent permutations $\widetilde{\pi}_0, \widetilde{\pi}_1 : \mathcal{T} \times \mathcal{B} \to \mathcal{B}$, and outputs $(C_0 \,\|\, C_1)$ as $C_b \leftarrow \widetilde{\pi}_b(P)$, for $b \in \{0,1\}$.

THE AES-128 is a substitution-permutation network over 128-bit inputs, which transforms the input through ten rounds consisting of SubBytes (SB), ShiftRows (SR), MixColumns (MC), and a round-key addition with a round key K^i. At the start, a whitening key K^0 is XORed to the state; the final round omits the MixColumns operation. We write S^i for the state after Round i, and $S^i[j]$ for the j-th byte, for $0 \le i \le 10$ and $0 \le j \le 15$. Further, we use $S^{r,\mathsf{SB}}$, $S^{r,\mathsf{SR}}$, and $S^{r,\mathsf{MC}}$ for the states in the r-th round directly after the SubBytes, ShiftRows, and MixColumns operations, respectively. The byte ordering is given by:

$$\begin{bmatrix} 0 & 4 & 8 & 12 \\ 1 & 5 & 9 & 13 \\ 2 & 6 & 10 & 14 \\ 3 & 7 & 11 & 15 \end{bmatrix}.$$

We adopt a similar convention for the round keys K^i and their bytes $K^i[j]$, for $0 \le i \le 16$; for both, we also use often a matrix-wise indexing of the bytes from $0,0$ to $3,3$. More details can be found in [11,19].

KIASU-BC [15] is a tweakable block cipher that differs from the AES-128 only in the fact that it XORs a public 64-bit tweak T to the topmost two rows of the state whenever a round key is XORed. We denote the tweak by T and by $T[j]$, $0 \le j \le 7$, the bytes of T. The bytes are ordered as

$$\begin{bmatrix} 0 & 2 & 4 & 6 \\ 1 & 3 & 5 & 7 \end{bmatrix}.$$

FORKAES is a forkcipher based on KIASU-BC. It forks the state after five rounds and transforms it twice to two ciphertexts C_0 and C_1. We denote the states of the first branch by $X^i =^{\mathrm{def}} S^i$, for $5 \le i \le 10$, where $X^5 = S^5$ and $X^{10} = C_0$. Moreover, we denote the states of the second branch by Y^i, for $5 \le i \le 10$, where $Y^5 = S^5$ and $Y^{10} = C_1$. We will also write R for the sequence

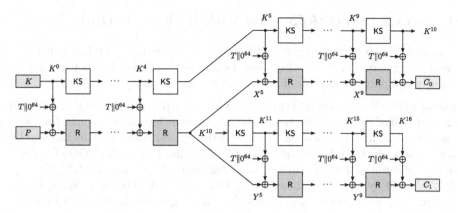

Fig. 1. ForkAES. R is the AES-128 round function; KS a round of its key schedule. (Color figure online)

MC∘SR∘SB. and KS for an iteration of the AES-128 key schedule. A schematic illustration is given in Fig. 1, and more details can be found in [1]. We will sometimes reorder the linear operations, e.g., swap MixColumns, ShiftRows, and the key addition. We will write $\widetilde{K}^r = \mathsf{MC}^{-1}(K^r)$ and $\widehat{K}^r = \mathsf{SR}^{-1}(\mathsf{MC}^{-1}(K^r))$ for the transformed round keys.

SUBSPACES OF THE AES. We adopt the notion of AES subspaces from Grassi et al. [14]. Given a vector space $\mathcal{W}$ and a subspace $\mathcal{V} \subseteq \mathcal{W}$; if a is an element of $\mathcal{W}$, then, a coset $\mathcal{V} \oplus a =^{\mathrm{def}} \{v \oplus a | \forall v \in \mathcal{V}\}$ is a subset of $\mathcal{V}$ in $\mathcal{W}$. We consider vectors and vector spaces over $\mathbb{F}_{2^8}^{4\times4}$, and denote by $\{e_{0,0}, \ldots, e_{3,3}\}$ the unit vectors of $\mathbb{F}_{2^8}^{4\times4}$, i.e., $e_{i,j}$ has a single 1 in the i-th row and j-th column. For a vector space $\mathcal{V}$ and a function $F : \mathbb{F}_{2^8}^{4\times4} \to \mathbb{F}_{2^8}^{4\times4}$, we let $F(\mathcal{V}) =^{\mathrm{def}} \{F(v) | v \in \mathcal{V}\}$. For a subset $\mathcal{I} \subseteq \{1, 2, \ldots, n\}$ and a subset of vector spaces $\{\mathcal{V}_1, \mathcal{V}_2, \ldots, \mathcal{V}_n\}$, we define $\mathcal{V}_\mathcal{I} =^{\mathrm{def}} \bigoplus_{i \in \mathcal{I}} \mathcal{V}_i$. We adopt the definitions by Grassi et al. of four families of subspaces for the AES, for $i \in \{0, 1, 2, 3\}$:

- the column spaces $\mathcal{C}_i$ as $\mathcal{C}_i = \langle e_{0,i}, e_{1,i}, e_{2,i}, e_{3,i}\rangle$,
- the diagonal spaces $\mathcal{D}_i$ as $\mathcal{D}_i = \mathsf{SR}^{-1}(\mathcal{C}_i)$,
- the inverse-diagonal spaces $\mathcal{ID}_i$ as $\mathcal{ID}_i = \mathsf{SR}(\mathcal{C}_i)$, and
- the mixed spaces $\mathcal{M}_i$ as $\mathcal{M}_i = \mathsf{MC}(\mathcal{ID}_i)$.

The S-box $\mathsf{S} : \mathbb{F}_{2^8} \to \mathbb{F}_{2^8}$ of the AES has a few well-analyzed properties; here, we briefly recall one that will be relevant in our later attacks.

Property 1. Let $\alpha, \beta \in \mathbb{F}_{2^8} \setminus \{0^8\}$. For $F \in \{\mathsf{S}, \mathsf{S}^{-1}\}$, it holds that $|\{x : \mathsf{F}(x) \oplus \mathsf{F}(x \oplus \alpha) = \beta\}|$ equals four in one, two in 126, and zero in 129 cases. So, for any differential $\alpha \to \beta$, there exists approximately one input x on average that satisfies the differential.

3   Attack on **ForkAES**-∗-4-4 with Reflection Trails

Our attacks can work for arbitrary value of r_t. Then the round-key indices for two forking parts depend on the value of r_t. To avoid making the analysis unnecessarily complex, we explain our attacks by using the case with $r_t = 5$.

OBSERVATIONS FOR RECONSTRUCTION QUERIES. Recall that the first half and the last half of the reconstruction is the inverse and the ordinary round function, respectively. This motivates us to consider the reflection property introduced by Kara [16] against the block cipher GOST. The final 16 rounds of GOST consist of an eight-round Feistel network with the round keys in order K^0, K^1, ..., K^7, followed by eight rounds with K^7, K^6, ..., K^0 in this order. Since Feistel networks are involutions, this enables the following so-called *reflection property*.

Proposition 1 (Reflection Property). When an input value V achieves a symmetric state after eight rounds, i.e. left branch value is identical with right branch value, the output of the final eight rounds will be V.

The reflection property is strong, but possesses limitations: there must not exist round constants, the round keys must be ordered inverted in the first and second chunks, and the target function must be an involution.

This paper considers a differential version of the reflection property. To be more general, the same concept applies if we build trails that are invariant w.r.t. XOR. Suppose, a round function F consists of an arbitrary bijective function, an XOR with a round constant c_i, and an XOR with a round key K^i. Consider $2r$ rounds, where the first r rounds apply F and the final r rounds apply F^{-1}. The round keys $K^i, i = 1, 2, \ldots, 2r$ as well as the round constants $c_i, i = 1, 2, \ldots, 2r$ can differ individually. Then, we have the following property.

Proposition 2 (Reflection Differential Trails). If there exists a differential for the r-round transformation F^r that propagates a difference ΔI to ΔO with probability p, there exists a differential for the $2r$-round transformation $(F^{-1})^r \circ F^r$ that propagates a difference ΔI to ΔI with probability at least p^2. This property holds for any choice of round keys and constants in the $2r$ rounds.

Reflection trails can be applied to reconstruction queries of forkciphers where C_1 (resp. C_0) is computed from C_0 (resp. C_1). The first and last halves of a reconstruction query are back- and forward computations of the same round function, and different round keys and round constants do not impact the property.

Reflection trails are particularly useful for the AES, which achieves full diffusion in only two rounds. There, a single active byte propagates to $1 \xrightarrow{F^{-1}} 4 \xrightarrow{F^{-1}} 16$ active bytes. In contrast, it propagates as $1 \xrightarrow{F^{-1}} 4 \xrightarrow{\text{reflect}} 4 \xrightarrow{F} 1$ in the reflection trail, where $\xrightarrow{F}$ and $\xrightarrow{F^{-1}}$ denote the propagation of the number of active S-boxes with F and F^{-1}, respectively, and $\xrightarrow{\text{reflect}}$ denotes the duplication of the state by forkciphers. This idea allows us to build long differential trails.

It is notable that the designers of ForkAES did not expect the existence of reflection trails. In fact, based on the property that the maximum probability of

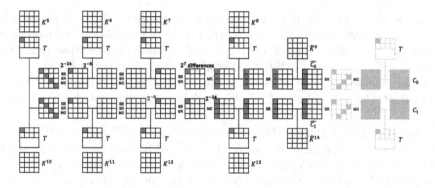

Fig. 2. Truncated differentials for ForkAES-∗-4-4. (Color figure online)

differential characteristics for four-round AES is 2^{-150}, the designers claim as *"Since our* ForkAES *design uses the* AES *round function, we can easily deduce that our design will provide enough security in this setting after four rounds against differential attacks in the single-key model."* [1, Sect. 3.2]

The combination of the reflection trail and a KIASU-like tweak injection yields further efficient differential trails. Tweak difference allows an attacker to create a blank round, and the reflection trail increases the number of blank rounds to 2. Indeed, the reflection trail with $4 \xrightarrow{F^{-1}} 1 \xrightarrow{F^{-1}} 0 \xrightarrow{F^{-1}} 4 \xrightarrow{\text{reflect}} 4 \xrightarrow{F} 0 \xrightarrow{F} 1 \xrightarrow{F} 4$ bytes enables the attacker to build a very efficient trail.

THE DIFFERENTIAL TRAIL AND PROBABILITY. The linear computations in the last round do not affect the security. Hence, we introduce the equivalent cipher-text $\widehat{C}_0 := \mathsf{SR}^{-1} \circ \mathsf{MC}^{-1}(C_0 \oplus T)$ and equivalent key $\widehat{K}^9 := \mathsf{SR}^{-1} \circ \mathsf{MC}^{-1}(K^9)$. $\widehat{C}_1$ and $\widehat{K}^{14}$ can be defined similarly. Refer to Fig. 2 for the differential trail, where we append one round to the above-mentioned trail in reconstruction queries. The attacker queries C_1 and obtains C_0.

The number of active bytes injected by $\widehat{C}_1$ must shrink to one during the inverse of MixColumns and must be canceled by the tweak difference, which occurs with probability 2^{-32}. In Round 6, the four-byte difference in a diagonal position must shrink to one-byte difference and be canceled by the tweak difference. This also occurs with probability 2^{-32}. So, the total probability of this trail is 2^{-64}.

ATTACK PROCEDURE. During the attack, the tweak difference is fixed.

1. Choose tweaks T and T' with the fixed difference. For each pair T, T', choose 2^{32} distinct values for the first column of $\widehat{C}_1$. Fix the other 12 bytes to arbitrary values and compute the corresponding C_1 offline and query them to obtain the corresponding C_0. Compute the corresponding $\widehat{C}_0$ offline. Hence, we obtain 2^{32} choices of $\widehat{C}_0$ with T and 2^{32} choices of $\widehat{C}_0$ with T'.
2. From 2^{64} pairs of $\widehat{C}_0$ between different tweaks, pick the one with 12 inactive bytes in the Columns 2, 3, and 4 of $\widehat{C}_0$. We expect one right pair.

3. For the right pair, obtain 2^7 key candidates of the first column of $\widehat{K}^9$, which has 1 active byte in the top byte after the inverse of MixColumns and moreover the difference should be one of the 2^7 choices that can be output from the tweak difference after the S-box. This step is colored by red in Fig. 2.

4. Iterate the steps above by shifting the active-byte positions to obtain 2^7 candidates for each column of $\widehat{K}^9$. 2^{28} candidates are then tested exhaustively.

COMPLEXITY EVALUATION. The data complexity is $4 \cdot (2^{33} + 2^{33}) = 2^{35}$ reconstruction queries. The memory complexity is 2^{33} AES states to store 2^{33} values of $\widehat{C}_0$. The time complexity is 2^{19} memory access to queried data and 2^{28} encryptions for the last exhaustive search. Note that in Step (3), there are 2^7 choices of the input difference to the last SubBytes and the output difference from this SubBytes are fixed to the ciphertext difference of the right pair. For the AES S-box, a randomly chosen pair of input and output differences can be propagated with probability about 2^{-1}, and once they can be propagated, the number of solutions is about 2. Therefore, $2^7 \times (2^{-1})^4$ pairs can be propagated for all the 4 bytes, and the number of total solutions is $2^7 \times (2^{-1})^4 \cdot 2^4 = 2^7$. So, 2^7 candidates of one column of $\widehat{K}^9$ can be obtained with 2^7 computations.

EXPERIMENTAL VERIFICATION. We implemented the attack on ForkAES-*-3-3 which removed the last rounds of the above attack. ForkAES-*-3-3 can be attacked with $(Data, Time, Memory) = (2^{19}, 2^{28}, 2^{17})$. This implementation in Java demonstrates its validity.

4   Impossible-Differential Attack with Reflection Trails

This section describes an impossible-differential distinguisher on ForkAES-*-4-4 with reconstruction queries; we will extend it for key recovery.

DISTINGUISHER. The impossible differential distinguisher is as follows.

$$1 \xrightarrow{F^{-1}} 0 \xrightarrow{F^{-1}} 4 \xrightarrow{\text{reflect}} 4 \xrightarrow{F} ? \xrightarrow{F} ? \xleftrightarrow{\text{impossible}} ? \xrightarrow{F} ? \xrightarrow{F} 12. \qquad (1)$$

The positions of active bytes are illustrated in Fig. 3. The fact that those trails are satisfied with probability zero is explained as follows.

- **Trail from Y^7:** After the tweak injection along with K^6, any number of bytes can be active in the leftmost column. They are moved to different columns by the following ShiftRows operation. After MixColumns, each column is either fully active or fully inactive.

- **Trail from $\widehat{C}_0$:** After the inverse of MixColumns and ShiftRows, at least one inverse diagonal is inactive. Moreover, at least three bytes are active in the state. The subsequent tweak injection (along with K^7), never affects the inactive inverse diagonal. It may cancel one active byte in the state, but does not impact the analysis. In summary, we have the following two properties.

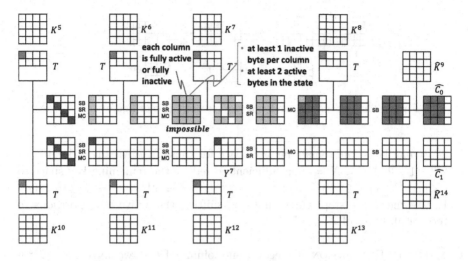

Fig. 3. Impossible-differential distinguisher. (Color figure online)

1. There is at least one inactive byte for each column.
2. The number of active bytes is at least two.

The case that the trail from Y^7 has no active byte is impossible, because the trail from $\widehat{C}_0$ ensures at least three active bytes. The case that the trail from Y^7 has at least 1 fully active column is impossible because the trail from $\widehat{C}_0$ ensures at least one inactive byte for each column. Hence, any trail from Y^7 is impossible to propagate to the difference of $\widehat{C}_0$.

The inactive column position at $\widehat{C}_0$ is the rightmost (4th) column in Fig. 3, but it can also be located in the second or third column position. It cannot be located in the leftmost (first) column because of the tweak difference.

KEY RECOVERY. We append key recovery rounds for the trail in Fig. 3 as depicted in Fig. 4. Suppose, we have a pair of outputs with only a single active column at $\widehat{C}_1$. Then, only five (equivalent-)key bytes must be guessed.

ATTACK PROCEDURE. During the attack, the tweak difference is fixed.

1. Choose two tweaks T, T' having the fixed difference. For each of T, T', choose 2^{32} distinct values for the active 4-byte values of $\widehat{C}_1$ and fix the other 12 bytes to arbitrary value, say 0. After making 2^{33} reconstruction queries, we obtain 2^{32} choices of $\widehat{C}_0$ associated with T and with T'.
2. From 2^{64} pairs of $\widehat{C}_0$ with different tweaks, pick one with at least one inactive column in Columns 2, 3, or 4 at $\widehat{C}_0$. We expect $3 \cdot 2^{64-32} = 2^{33.58}$ pairs.
3. For each picked pair, derive 2^7 wrong candidates of the top-left byte of $\widehat{K}^{13}$ and the leftmost column of $\widehat{K}^{14}$ by trying 2^7 possible differences in the middle rounds. After evaluating $2^{33.58}$ pairs, we obtain $2^{40.58}$ wrong-key candidates.
4. Iterate the steps above $2^{4.42}$ times by changing the fixed 12 bytes of $\widehat{C}_1$. We obtain $2^{40.58+4.42} = 2^{45}$ wrong candidates of the 5 key bytes. After obtaining

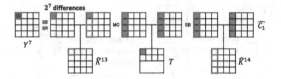

Fig. 4. The appended rounds for key recovery. (Color figure online)

2^N wrong keys, the remaining key space for those five bytes is estimated as $2^{40} \cdot (1 - 2^{-40})^{2^N}$. $N = 45$ is sufficient to reduce the remaining key space to 1 since $2^{40} \cdot (1 - 2^{-40})^{2^{45}} = 2^{40} \cdot (1 - 2^{-40})^{2^{40} \cdot 2^5} = 2^{40} \cdot e^{-2^5} = 2^{-6.17} < 1$.

5. Iterate the above steps three times by shifting the active byte positions to recover all bytes of $\widehat{K}^{14}$.

COMPLEXITY EVALUATION. To recover one column of $\widehat{K}^{14}$, we make $2^{4.42} \cdot (2^{32} + 2^{32}) = 2^{37.42}$ reconstruction queries. The data complexity to recover all bytes of $\widehat{K}^{14}$ is $4 \cdot 2^{37.42} = 2^{39.42}$.

To recover one column of $\widehat{K}^{14}$, we spend 2^{45} encryptions to discard 2^{45} wrong-key candidates. The time complexity to recovery all bytes of $\widehat{K}^{14}$ is $4 \cdot 2^{45} = 2^{47}$.

For the memory complexity, we use the 40-bit counter to record wrong-key candidates, which is equivalent to 2^{33} AES states. To recover 1 column of $\widehat{K}^{14}$, we also need to store 2^{33} $\widehat{C}_0$ and 2^{34} pairs satisfying the differences. Hence, the memory complexity is $2^{33} + 2^{33} + 2^{34} = 2^{35}$ AES states.

5 Yoyo Key-Recovery Attack on ForkAES-*-3-3

The yoyo game was introduced by Biham et al. against Skipjack [3]. Rønjom et al. [20] reported deterministic distinguishers for two generic Substitution-Permutation (SP) rounds. We review existing work in Appendix A. Here, we observe that, during reconstruction queries, two-round decryption and two-round encryption can be computed independently for each column, which we call a *MegaSBox*.

MEGASBOX IN FORKAES. Refer to Fig. 5 for the MegaSBox construction of ForkAES. Consider any inverse diagonal in $Y^{6,\mathsf{SR}}$. After SR^{-1} and SB^{-1}, the MegaSBox aligns to a column. After MC^{-1}, the column remains independent of the other columns. The inverses of SR and SB align the bytes back into a diagonal. After the reflection, the same operations are applied to these four bytes; after SR, those bytes align to an inverse diagonal in $X^{6,\mathsf{SR}}$. Clearly, the value in this inverse diagonal depends only on the same inverse diagonal in $Y^{6,\mathsf{SR}}$. This can be considered as a MegaSBox with 32-bit input (inverse diagonals). The transition from $Y^{6,\mathsf{SR}}$ to $X^{6,\mathsf{SR}}$ can be depicted in terms of 4 parallel MegaSBoxes. To be explicit, for $x \in \{0,1\}^{32}$, the computation of MegaSbox is defines as $\mathsf{MegaSBox}(x) := \mathsf{SR} \circ \mathsf{SB} \circ \mathsf{ATK} \circ \mathsf{MC} \circ \mathsf{SR} \circ \mathsf{SB} \circ \mathsf{ATK} \circ \mathsf{ATK}^{-1} \circ \mathsf{SB}^{-1} \circ \mathsf{SR}^{-1} \circ \mathsf{MC}^{-1} \circ \mathsf{ATK}^{-1} \circ \mathsf{SB}^{-1} \circ \mathsf{SR}^{-1}(x)$, where ATK denotes the addition of a round key and a tweak.

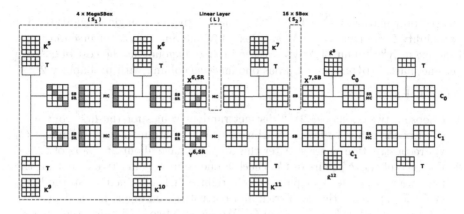

Fig. 5. MegaSBox of ForkAES

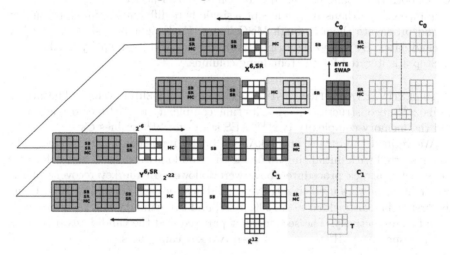

Fig. 6. Yoyo Key Recovery for ForkAES-∗-3-3. (Color figure online)

KEY-RECOVERY ATTACK. For applying the Yoyo game on ForkAES-∗-3-3, $S_1 \cdot L \cdot S_2$ needs to be identified. Referring to Fig. 5, following MC and SB of $X^{6,\mathsf{SR}}$ can be regarded as L and S_2 layers respectively. Four MegaSBoxes act as S_1 layer. Thus the operations from $Y^{6,\mathsf{SR}}$ to $X^{7,\mathsf{SB}}$ constitute the $S_1 \cdot L \cdot S_2$ construction. We choose a pair of texts (x_1, x_2) in $Y^{6,\mathsf{SR}}$ and compute $X^{7,\mathsf{SB}}$; bytes are swapped among the texts in $X^{7,\mathsf{SB}}$ and their corresponding values in $Y^{6,\mathsf{SR}}$ are calculated as (x'_1, x'_2). Theorem 1 in Appendix A ensures that $\nu(x_1 \oplus x_2) = \nu(x'_1 \oplus x'_2)$.[1] Refer to Fig. 6 for the attack. It starts with activating one column at $\widehat{C}_1$ for a pair of texts and queries the reconstruction algorithm for a pair of $\widehat{C}_0$. We

---

[1] ν is a so-called zero-differential pattern that denotes the position of inactive words. Refer to Appendix A for more precise definition.

use the propagation $4 \xrightarrow{\text{MC}^{-1}} 1$ in $Y^{6,\text{SR}}$, which activates a single MegaSBox with probability 2^{-22}. Due to the MegaSBox, only one SuperSbox (inverse diagonal) is active in $X^{6,\text{SR}}$. Out of 4 bytes of the inverse diagonal, at the cost of 2^{-6}, we get one inactive byte. Thus, $\widehat{C}_0$ has one inactive column with probability 2^{-28}.

ATTACK PROCEDURE.

1. Choose a tweak; choose $2^{14.5}$ distinct random values for the first column of $\widehat{C}_1$. Fix the other 12 bytes to arbitrary value. Obtain the corresponding $\widehat{C}_0$ via reconstruction queries. After this step, we have about 2^{28} pairs of $\widehat{C}_0$.
2. For each of the 2^{28} pairs of $\widehat{C}_0$, check if one column is inactive or not for the pair; we expect one right pair. Once a right pair is obtained, swap the bytes at $\widehat{C}_0$ for applying the yoyo trick and reconstruction algorithm is queried to get a pair which is fully active in $\widehat{C}_1$. We retrieve two such pairs (right pairs).
3. For both right pairs, obtain $\widehat{K}^{12}$ that have only 1 active byte in the first column, e.g., by exhaustively guessing a single-byte difference before MixColumns and propagate them through MixColumns. Each right pair suggests 2^{10} key candidates. By analyzing 2 right pairs, the key will be uniquely fixed.
4. Step 3 is iterated for the remaining columns.

COMPLEXITY EVALUATION AND EXPERIMENTAL VERIFICATION. The attack needs $2^{14.5}$ reconstruction queries; its time complexity is $2^{14.5}$ memory accesses, and the memory complexity is $2^{14.5}$ AES states for $2^{14.5}$ values $\widehat{C}_0$.

We verified the attack on ForkAES-*-3-3 by implementing it in Java. The attack started with initializing an oracle that randomly chooses a key, before the steps in the attack procedure above were followed. In the key-recovery phase, two right pairs were used to retrieve candidates for each column of $\widehat{K}^{12}$. Using the first right pair yielded 976, 1296, 1008, and 976 candidates for Column 0, 1, 2, and 3, respectively. The second right pair reduced the candidates to 1, 1, 2, and 1, respectively. Hence, we obtained two key candidates.

6   Rectangle Attack with Encryption Queries

This section describes a rectangle attack on ForkAES-*-4-4; for concreteness, we exemplify it for five top rounds. Briefly spoken, boomerangs and rectangles are types of differential cryptanalysis where a given cipher E is split into sub-ciphers $E = E_2 \circ E_m \circ E_1$ such that there exist a differential $\alpha \to \beta$ with probability p over E_1, a middle trail $\beta \to \gamma$ with probability r, and a differential $\gamma \to \delta$ with probability q over E_2. Note that, we approximate the middle part E_m to be empty for our attack. The differentials are often referred to as upper and lower differentials or trails. The probability of a correct quartet is often approximated by $r(pq)^2$ since the trails must hold for both pairs.

We consider two tuples (P, T) and (P', T') that are encrypted to (C_0, C_1) and (C'_0, C'_1), respectively. We denote by $\Delta X^r = X^r \oplus X'^r$ their differences between the states after Round r that lead to C_0, and by $\Delta Y^r = Y^r \oplus Y'^r$ the differences in the states that lead to C_1. For clarity, we define that the fork from

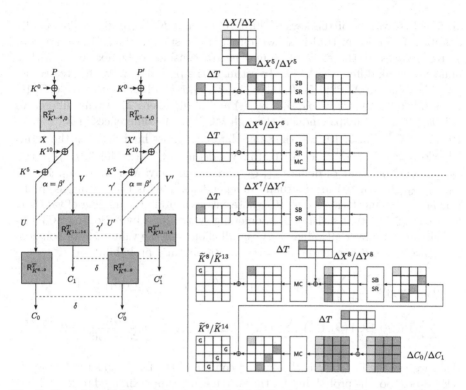

Fig. 7. Overview (**left**) and bottom trail (**right**) of our rectangle attack. The key recovery covers the parts below the dashed horizontal line and guesses the bytes with G. (Color figure online)

X to C_0 employs the round keys K^5 through K^9, and the fork from Y to C_1 uses K^{10} through K^{14}. An overview is depicted on the left side of Fig. 7. There, $R^T_{K^{i..j}}$ means the round sequence $R^T_{K^j} \circ \cdots \circ R^T_{K^i}$. We construct 2^8 sets of 2^s plaintext-tweak tuples. The sets differ in $T[0]$; all plaintexts in a set share the same tweak. So, we can combine 2^s texts (tuples of C_0, C_1) of Set i with 2^s texts of Set j, for $i \neq j$, or $2^s \cdot \binom{2^8}{2} \simeq 2^{2s+15}$ pairs (quartets of C_0, C_1, C'_0, C'_1).

THE TOP DIFFERENTIAL. In contrast to the pure AES or to KIASU-BC, the forking step guarantees that the difference between the inputs to Rounds 6 and 10 is equal for each plaintext. So, the top differential reduces to the key addition, that is, the XOR with K^5 for the branch that encrypts from X to C_0, and to the XOR with K^{10} for the branch that encrypts from Y to C_1. So, $\alpha = \beta = K^5 \oplus K^{10}$ holds with probability one for each pair. The adversary collects pairs and waits that the difference at the beginning of the bottom trail occurs, whose probability can be approximated by 2^{-128}. From approximately 2^{2s+15} pairs, we expect 2^{2s-113} to have a specific difference γ at the forking step.

FOR THE MIDDLE PHASE AND THE BOTTOM DIFFERENTIAL, we use two simplifying assumptions: (1) all differences after five rounds are equally possible; (2)

all four-byte values of the keys $K^5[0, 5, 10, 15]$ and $K^{10}[0, 5, 10, 15]$ are equally possible. The bottom trail is shown on the right side of Fig. 7. There are four active S-boxes at the start of Round 6. We consider only text pairs with a non-zero tweak difference $\Delta T[0]$. To estimate the probability, we iterate over all possible values of $X^{6,\text{SB}}[0, 5, 10, 15] = (\bar{x}_0, \bar{x}_1, \bar{x}_2, \bar{x}_3)$, all differences $K^5[0, 5, 10, 15] \oplus K^{10}[0, 5, 10, 15] = (\beta_0, \beta_1, \beta_2, \beta_3)$ and all non-zero 255 tweak differences $\Delta T[0] \neq 0$; $\Delta T[0]$ maps uniquely through MC^{-1} to the differences in $X^{6,\text{SB}}[0, 5, 10, 15] \oplus X'^{6,\text{SB}}[0, 5, 10, 15]$; the same difference must hold between the terms $Y^{6,\text{SB}}[0, 5, 10, 15] \oplus Y'^{6,\text{SB}}[0, 5, 10, 15]$. We define $\text{MC}^{-1}((\Delta T[0], 0, 0, 0)) = (\zeta_0, \zeta_1, \zeta_2, \zeta_3)$. Note that ζ_0 defines ζ_1, ζ_2, and ζ_3 uniquely. Moreover, $(\bar{x}_0, \bar{x}_1, \bar{x}_2, \bar{x}_3, \zeta_0, \beta_0, \beta_1, \beta_2, \beta_3)$ are mutually independent. This is the setting as in the Boomerang-connectivity Table [10] whose entries contain the number of values x_i for a pair (ζ_i, β_i) that satisfy the boomerang switch for a byte. So, the BCT values already sum over all values x_i. Over all choices of the values $\bar{x}_i$, all non-zero differences ζ_i, and non-zero differences β_i, we obtain a probability of

$$\frac{1}{255 \cdot (256)^8} \sum_{\zeta_0 \neq 0} \sum_{\beta_0} (\Pr[\zeta_0] \cdot \Pr[\beta_0] \cdot \text{BCT}(\beta_0, \zeta_0)) \cdot \sum_{\beta_1} (\Pr[\beta_1] \cdot \text{BCT}(\beta_1, \zeta_1)) \cdot$$

$$\sum_{\beta_2} (\Pr[\beta_2] \cdot \text{BCT}(\beta_2, \zeta_2)) \cdot \sum_{\beta_3} (\Pr[\beta_3] \cdot \text{BCT}(\beta_3, \zeta_3)) = \frac{(520)^4}{255 \cdot 256^8} \simeq 2^{-35.905}.$$

Here, we use the fact that each row and column of the BCT sums to 520 for the AES S-box. So, the probability for the switch can be approximated by $2^{-36} \cdot 2^{-128}$ for hitting our difference between two queries. The remainder in the bottom trail holds with probability 1. Thus, we can expect about 2^{2s-149} correct pairs.

OFFLINE PREPARATIONS. We define a linear map $F : \mathbb{F}_{2^8}^{4 \times 4} \rightarrow \mathbb{F}_{2^8}^{12}$ that returns the value of the 12 inactive bytes in $\Delta X^{9,\text{SR}}$. So, we can identify pairs (C_i, C_i') with our desired difference from collisions between $F(\text{MC}^{-1}(T \oplus C_b)) = F(\text{MC}^{-1}(T' \oplus C_b'))$ with two evaluations of F per text instead of comparing all differences.

We can perform another offline step for saving effort later. Let $x = X^{9,\text{SB}}[0, 7, 10, 13]$, $x' = X'^{9,\text{SB}}[0, 7, 10, 13]$, $k^8 = \widetilde{K}^8[0]$, and $k^9 = \widetilde{K}^9[0, 7, 10, 13]$ be short forms. We construct a hash map $\mathcal{H} : \mathbb{F}_{2^8} \times \mathbb{F}_{2^8} \times \mathbb{F}_{2^8}^4 \times \mathbb{F}_{2^8}^4 \rightarrow (\mathbb{F}_{2^8}^5)^*$ such that for all inputs $(T[0], T'[0], x, x')$, $\mathcal{H}$ returns exactly those keys (k^8, k^9) that map x and x' to a zero difference at $\Delta X^{7,\text{MC}}$. The trail contains 32 bit conditions that have to be fulfilled; thus, $\mathcal{H}$ maps to approximately 2^8 suggestions of 40 key bits on average. $\mathcal{H}$ can be used also to obtain suggestions for $\widetilde{K}^{13}[0]$ and $\widetilde{K}^{14}[0, 7, 10, 13]$ from inputs $Y^{9,\text{SB}}[0, 7, 10, 13]$, $Y'^{9,\text{SB}}[0, 7, 10, 13]$, $T[0]$, and $T'[0]$.

ATTACK STEPS. The steps are as follows:

1. Initialize an empty list $\mathcal{Q}$. Initialize two zeroed lists of byte counters for 40 key bits each: $\mathcal{K}$ for $(\widetilde{K}^8[0], \widetilde{K}^9[0, 7, 10, 13])$, and $\mathcal{L}$ for $(\widetilde{K}^{13}[0], \widetilde{K}^{14}[0, 7, 10, 13])$.
2. Precompute $\mathcal{H}$.
3. Choose an arbitrary base tweak $T \in \mathbb{F}_{2^8}^{2 \times 4}$. Construct 2^8 sets $\mathcal{S}^i$. For each set, choose 2^s plaintexts P such that all texts in a set use the same tweak value

T. Ask for their 2^{s+8} encryptions (T, C_0, C_1), invert the final tweak addition, and the final MixColumns operation for each output tuple (C_0, C_1).

4. We define $Q_b = F(\mathsf{MC}^{-1}(T \oplus C_b))$, for $b \in \{0, 1\}$. For all ciphertexts, compute Q_0 and Q_1 from C_0 and C_1 and store (T, C_0, C_1, Q_0, Q_1) into buckets of $\mathcal{Q}$.

5. Focus on pairs of tuples (T, C_0, C_1, Q_0, Q_1) and $(T', C_0', C_1', Q_0', Q_1')$ if $T[0] \neq T'[0]$, $C_0 = C_0'$ and $C_1 = C_1'$. We call such pairs of tuples with our desired property **correct pairs**. Discard all tuples that do not form correct pairs.

6. For each correct pair, lookup in $\mathcal{H}$ the suggestions of the 40 key bits $\widetilde{K}^8[0]$ and $\widetilde{K}^9[0, 7, 10, 13]$ from $T[0]$, $T'[0]$, $X^{9,\mathsf{SB}}[0, 7, 10, 13]$, and $X'^{9,\mathsf{SB}}[0, 7, 10, 13]$. We expect 2^8 suggestions on average. For each suggested key candidate, increment its corresponding counter in $\mathcal{K}$.

7. Similarly, for each correct pair, lookup in $\mathcal{H}$ the suggestions for the 40 key bits $\widetilde{K}^{13}[0]$ and $\widetilde{K}^{14}[0, 7, 10, 13]$. We expect 2^8 suggestions on average. For each suggestion, increment the corresponding counter in $\mathcal{L}$.

8. Output the keys in $\mathcal{K}$ and $\mathcal{L}$ in descending order of their counters.

9. While the adversary has 80 key bits, the key schedule may render it more performant to start from the 40 bits of either $\widetilde{K}^8[0]$, $\widetilde{K}^9[0, 7, 10, 13]$ or $\widetilde{K}^{13}[0]$, $\widetilde{K}^{14}[0, 7, 10, 13]$ and search the 88 remaining key bits with the given data.

COMPLEXITY. From 2^8 sets of 2^s texts each, we expect 2^{2s-149} correct pairs; $s = 77$ yields 2^5 correct pairs on average, and needs 2^{85} plaintext-tweak tuples. The time complexity consists of the following terms:

- $\mathcal{H}$ can be precomputed in Step (2) by decrypting one column over 2 rounds 2^{80} times, which yields at most $2/13 \cdot 1/4 \cdot 2^{80} \simeq 2^{75.3}$ encryption equivalents.
- Step (3) needs 2^{s+8} encryptions of 13 AES rounds each.
- Step (4) employs $2 \cdot 2^{s+8}$ evaluations of F and $2 \cdot 2^{s+8} \cdot (s + 8)$ memory accesses (MAs). This step yields $2^{2s+15} \cdot 2^{-192} = 2^{2s-177}$ wrong pairs plus 2^{2s-149} correct pairs on average.
- Step (6) does not need $\mathcal{H}$, but can test the keys on-the-fly, for $2 \cdot 2^5$ states of 2^{40} keys, of $1/4$ of the state through two out of 13 rounds. Each surviving pair requires $2 \cdot 2^8$ MAs to $\mathcal{H}$ plus $2 \cdot 2^8$ MAs to $\mathcal{K}$ and $\mathcal{L}$ on average. We expect an average sum of all counters of $2^8 \cdot 2^{2s-149} = 2^{13}$ in each of both lists, distributed normally over the keys. For $s = 77$, we expect $(2^{-23} \cdot 2^8) + 2^5 \cdot 2^8 \simeq 2^{13}$ counters over the 40 key bits on average.

We can expect that the correct keys have a significantly higher number of counts. So, we obtain about $2^{75.3} + 2 \cdot 2^5 \cdot 2^{40} \cdot \frac{1}{4} \cdot \frac{2}{13} + 2^{s+8} + 2 \cdot 2^{s+8} + 2^{88} \simeq 2^{88.5}$ Encryptions and $2 \cdot 2^{s+8} \cdot (s+8) + 2 \cdot 2^{2s-177} \cdot 2 \cdot 2^8 + 2 \cdot 2^5 \cdot 2^8 \simeq 2^{92.4}$ MAs. The attack needs 2^{80} byte counters for the keys; $\mathcal{Q}$ needs $2^{s+8} \cdot (2 \cdot 16 + 8) < 2^{s+13.33} \simeq 2^{90.4}$ bytes of memory, or $2^{86.4}$ states, which dominates the memory complexity.

7   Impossible-Differential Attack with Encryption Queries

IMPOSSIBLE DIFFERENTIALS. This section outlines an impossible-differential attack on ForkAES-*-4-4. Again, we describe it for five top rounds. The high-level

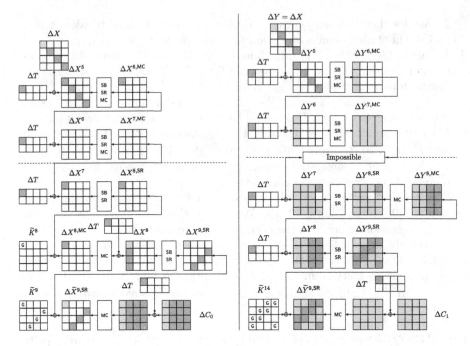

Fig. 8. Left: The trail $\Delta C_0 \to \Delta X$. **Right:** One variant of an impossible trail $\Delta C_1 \not\to \Delta Y$. White bytes are inactive, light-blue bytes possibly active, and dark-blue bytes are active. Parts below the dashed horizontal lines are considered in the on-line phase. (Color figure online)

idea is straight-forward: The adversary queries plaintexts under tweaks that differ only in $T[0]$ and waits for tuples $(C_{i,0}, T_i)$ and $(C_{j,0}, T_j)$. It inverts the final MC^{-1} operation and tweak addition, and uses the ciphertexts only if their difference $\Delta \widetilde{C}_0$ (before MC) activates only the inverse diagonal $\mathcal{ID}_0$, as given in the left side of Fig. 8. It deduces those key bytes $\widetilde{K}^9[0, 7, 10, 13]$ and $\widetilde{K}^8[0]$ that lead to a zero difference in $\Delta X^{7,\mathsf{MC}}$, i.e., that cancel after the tweak XOR at the end of Round 7. Then, there is a zero difference through the inverse Round 7, which leads to a single active byte in $\Delta X^{6,\mathsf{MC}}$, and to a single active diagonal at the start of Round 6. Again, see the left side of Fig. 8. The second trail decrypts ΔC_1 backwards to $\Delta Y = \Delta X$. So, at least one of the following cases must hold:

(1) ΔY^7 has at least one fully active column: $\Delta Y^7 \in \mathcal{C}_i$.
(2) Bytes $\Delta Y^7[1, 2, 3]$ are active.
(3) $\Delta C_1 \in \mathcal{M}_0$, i.e., is in the mixed space, generated by $\Delta Y^{9,\mathsf{SR}} \in \mathcal{ID}_0$.

In Case (3), the ΔY trail is similar to the ΔX trail. So, we have a distinguisher similar to the rectangle distinguisher described in Sect. 6. However, this section tries to exploit a different distinguisher with lower data complexity and does not have to wait for such an event. In the Cases (1) and (2), the Columns 1 to 3 of ΔY^7 are either completely active or completely inactive. Thus, the adversary can guess eight bytes of $\widetilde{K}^{14}$ that are mapped to one of those columns and can filter out all key guesses where one of those columns would become partially active.

OFFLINE PREPARATIONS. We define $\widetilde{X}^{r,\mathsf{SR}} \stackrel{\text{def}}{=} \mathsf{SR}(\mathsf{SB}(X^{r-1})) \oplus \widetilde{K}^r$, and $\widetilde{Y}^{r,\mathsf{SR}}$, $\widetilde{X'}^{r,\mathsf{SR}}$, and $\widetilde{Y'}^{r,\mathsf{SR}}$ analogously. Again, we can define a linear map F of rank 96 such that $F(\mathsf{MC}^{-1}(\Delta C_0 \oplus \Delta T)) = 0$ so that we can identify pairs with our desired difference from collisions in $\Delta \widetilde{X}^{9,\mathsf{SR}}$. We construct a hash map $\mathcal{H}_0 : \mathbb{F}_{2^8} \times \mathbb{F}_{2^8} \times \mathbb{F}_{2^8}^4 \times \mathbb{F}_{2^8}^4 \to (\mathbb{F}_{2^8}^5)^*$ that maps $x = (T[0], T'[0], \widetilde{X}^{9,\mathsf{SR}}[0,7,10,13], \widetilde{X'}^{9,\mathsf{SR}}[0,7,10,13])$ to all five-byte keys that yield $\Delta X^{7,\mathsf{MC}} = 0$. We construct a second hash map $\mathcal{H}_1 : \mathbb{F}_{2^8}^8 \times \mathbb{F}_{2^8}^8 \to (\mathbb{F}_{2^8}^8)^*$. For all inputs $x = (\widetilde{Y}^{9,\mathsf{SR}}[2,3,5,6,8,9,12,15], \widetilde{Y'}^{9,\mathsf{SR}}[2,3,5,6,8,9,12,15])$, $\mathcal{H}_1(x)$ returns exactly the keys $\widetilde{K}^{14}[2,3,5,6,8,9,12,15]$ that yield one of the impossible differentials in $\Delta Y^{8,\mathsf{SR}}$.

$\mathcal{H}_1$ does not need the tweak as input since the final tweak addition, MixColumns, and ShiftRows can be inverted before the lookup in $\mathcal{H}_1$; the tweak addition at the end of Round 8 does not affect the difference in $\Delta Y^{8,\mathsf{SR}}$. Note that $\mathcal{H}_1$ can be built more efficiently from several smaller lookup tables since the columns can be computed independently from each other.

There exist four combinations of bytes $\Delta Y^{8,\mathsf{SR}}[i,j]$ with $(i,j) \in \{(8,15),$ $(9,12), (10,13), (11,14)\}$ and two options if Byte i or Byte j is active. Among 2^{32} difference inputs to MC^{-1}, 2^{24} are mapped to an output difference with a zero-difference byte at a fixed index. On the other hand, $2^{32} - 2^{24}$ inputs yield a non-zero difference at a given byte index. Thus, given an input $Y^{9,\mathsf{SB}}$, $\mathcal{H}_1$ returns $4 \cdot 2$ combinations of $2^{24} \cdot (2^{32} - 2^4) \simeq 2^{56}$ keys that yield the impossible differential. This can be evaluated with $4 \cdot 2$ calls to two 32-bit tables each, or 16 tables that map 32 state bits to 2^{32} or 2^{24} keys. So, $\mathcal{H}_1$ needs $8 \cdot 2^{32} \cdot 2^{32} \cdot 4$ bytes $+ 8 \cdot 2^{32} \cdot 2^{24} \cdot 4$ bytes $\simeq 2^{72}$ bytes of memory. The tables can be computed with at most $16 \cdot 2^{32} \cdot 2^{32}$ quarter-rounds of the AES, which is at most $16/13 \cdot 2^{64} \simeq 2^{64.3}$ equivalents of ForkAES-5-4-4.

ATTACK PROCEDURE. The steps in the attack are as follows:

1. Initialize two empty lists $\mathcal{Q}$ and $\mathcal{K}$; the latter will hold all 13-byte keys $\widetilde{K}^8[0]$, $\widetilde{K}^9[0,7,10,13]$, and $\widetilde{K}^{14}[2,3,5,6,8,9,12,15]$.
2. Choose an arbitrary base tweak $T \in \mathbb{F}_{2^8}^{2 \times 4}$. Construct 2^8 sets $\mathcal{S}^i$ from iterating over $T[0]$. For each set, choose 2^s plaintexts P. All texts in a set use the same tweak T^i with $T^i[0] = i$. Ask for their 2^{s+8} encryptions (T, C_0, C_1).
3. For each ciphertext, invert the final tweak addition, the final MC operation, and process all ciphertexts by F: $Q_b = F(\mathsf{MC}^{-1}(C_b \oplus T))$, for $b \in \{0,1\}$. Store (T, C_0, C_1, Q_0, Q_1) into buckets of $\mathcal{Q}$.
4. Only consider pairs of tuples (T, C_0, C_1, Q_0, Q_1) and $(T', C_0', C_1', Q_0', Q_1')$ if $T \neq T'$ and $Q_0 = Q_0'$. Discard all other tuples. We call pairs of tuples with our desired property **correct pairs**.
5. For each correct pair, derive from $\mathcal{H}_0$ the key candidates $\widetilde{K}^8[0]$ and $\widetilde{K}^9[0,7,10,13]$ that yield a zero difference in $\Delta X^{7,\mathsf{MC}}$. Further derive from $\mathcal{H}_1$ all

key candidates for $\widetilde{K}^{14}[2,3,5,6,8,9,12,15]$ that yield one of the impossible differentials. Remove those candidates from $\mathcal{K}$.

6. Output the 13-byte key candidates remaining in $\mathcal{K}$.

CONDITIONS AND COMPLEXITIES. The adversary queries 2^8 sets of 2^s texts each and guesses 13 key bytes in total: $\widetilde{K}^9[0,7,10,13]$, $\widetilde{K}^8[0]$, and $\widetilde{K}^{14}[2,3,5,6,8,9,12,15]$, i.e., 104 key bits. The attack requires pairs with $\Delta C_0 \in \mathcal{M}_0$, which occurs with probability of approximately $p \simeq 2^{-96}$. We can assume that $(\Delta C_0, \Delta C_1) \in \mathcal{M}_0 \times \mathcal{M}_0$ never occurs by accident; while it could theoretically still occur and could be exploited, we consider a different distinguisher here.

The probability that a key $\widetilde{K}^9[0,7,10,13]$ reduces the four active bytes in $\Delta X^{9,\mathsf{SR}}$ to a single active byte in $\Delta X^{8,\mathsf{MC}}[0]$ is 2^{-24}, and its difference is $\Delta T[0]$ in ΔX^7 with probability 2^{-8}. So, a key in the ΔX trail yields our desired differential with a probability of about 2^{-32}. There are four options which columns in ΔY^7 become partially active, and two options for the order which of the two known bytes in this column are active/inactive. The probability for one inactive byte is $(2^{-8} - 1) \cdot (1 - 2^{-8}) \simeq 2^{-8}$; so, a key yields the impossible differential in $\Delta Y^{7,\mathsf{MC}}$ with probability approximately $2^{-32} \cdot 2^{-8} \cdot 4 \cdot 2 \simeq 2^{-37}$.

In the framework by Boura et al. [9], this can be represented as 37 bit conditions that have to be fulfilled to filter a key from a given correct pair. The probability for a wrong key to survive is $p_{\mathsf{survive}} = (1 - 2^{-37})^N$, where N is the number of correct pairs. For 2^{104} keys, $p_{\mathsf{survive}} \leq 2^{-104}$ would allow us to filter all keys to only the correct key, plus at most a few more false positives. For this purpose, we need $N \geq 2^{43.2}$ pairs with 12 inactive bytes in $\Delta \widetilde{X}^{9,\mathsf{SR}}$, which yields $2^{43.2} \cdot 2^{12.8} = 2^{139.2}$ necessary pairs. From 2^s structures, we can construct about 2^{2s+15} pairs, which gives $s = 62.1$ or $C_N = 2^{s+8} = 2^{70.1}$ queries. The computational complexity is composed of the following terms:

- Precompute $\mathcal{H}_0$ with 2^{80} times twice a quarter round of the AES, which can be approximated by $2^{80} \cdot 2/13 \cdot 1/4 \simeq 2^{75.3}$ encryption equivalents.
- Precompute $\mathcal{H}_1$ with at most $2^{64.3}$ encryption equivalents.
- Encrypt 2^{s+8} plaintext-tweak tuples.
- Invert $2^{s+8} \cdot 2$ times the final tweak addition, MixColumns, and ShiftRows operation, which can be overestimated by $2^{70.1} \cdot 2 \cdot 1/13 \approx 2^{67.5}$ encryptions.
- Apply F to all states C_0, which is at most 2^{s+8} ForkAES computations, or $2^{70.1} \cdot 2 \simeq 2^{70.1}$ encryptions. Moreover, we need $2 \cdot 2^{s+8} \cdot (s+8) = 2 \cdot 70.1 \cdot 2^{70.1} \simeq 2^{77.3}$ MAs on average with an efficient data structure. We obtain about $2^{2s+15-96} \sim 2^{2s-81} = 2^{43.2}$ remaining pairs.
- For each of the $2^{43.2}$ pairs allows to filter keys. Since we have 37 bit conditions, each pair allows to filter $2^{104-37} = 2^{67}$ keys on average from $\mathcal{H}_0$ and $\mathcal{H}_1$ with two MAs each and remove them from $\mathcal{K}$.
- Our attack aims at recovering 104 bits of $\widetilde{K}^9$ and $\widetilde{K}^{14}$. So, the final term for recovering 64 remaining key bits of $\widetilde{K}^{14}$ can be estimated by 2^{64} encryptions.

The time complexity can be bounded by about $2^{75.3} + 2^{64.3} + 2^{70.1} + 2^{67.5} + 2^{70.1} + 2^{64} \simeq 2^{75.4}$ encryptions and $2 \cdot 2^{70.1} + 2^{77.3} + 2^{43.2} \cdot 2 + 2^{43.2} \cdot 2^{67} \simeq 2^{110.2}$ MAs.

The attack needs $2^{80} \cdot 2^8 \cdot 40$ bits for $\mathcal{H}_0$, at most 2^{72} bytes for the components of $\mathcal{H}_1$, $2^{s+8} = 2^{70.2} \cdot (2 \cdot 16 + 8) < 2^{s+14} = 2^{76.2}$ bytes for $\mathcal{Q}$, and 2^{104} byte counters or (2^{100} states) for $\mathcal{K}$; the latter term dominates the memory complexity.

Acknowledgments.. Parts of this work have been initiated during the group sessions of the 8th Asian Workshop on Symmetric Cryptography (ASK 2018) held at the Indian Statistical Institute in Kolkata. We would also like to thank the anonymous reviewers and the designers of ForkAES for their helpful comments. Subhadeep Banik is supported by the Ambizione Grant PZ00P2_179921, awarded by the Swiss National Science Foundation.

A   Previous Yoyo Game

The yoyo game was introduced by Biham et al. for the cryptanalysis of Skipjack [3]. Recently, Rønjom et al. [20] reported a deterministic distinguisher for two generic Substitution-Permutation (SP) rounds. This result has been applied to eight-round ForkAES to perform a key-recovery attack. Let us look at some definitions originally introduced in [20]. Let $F : \mathbb{F}_q^n \to \mathbb{F}_q^n$ be a generic permutation where $q = 2^k$. Then, F is given by $F = S \circ L \circ S \circ L \circ S$, where S is a concatenation of n parallel S-Boxes on n individual *words* from $\mathbb{F}_q$ and L denotes the linear layer over $\mathbb{F}_q^n$. A vector of words $\alpha = (\alpha_0, \alpha_1, \cdots, \alpha_{n-1}) \in \mathbb{F}_q^n$ forms the *states*. The Zero-difference Pattern is defined as:

Definition 1 (Zero-difference Pattern [20]). Let, $\alpha \in \mathbb{F}_q^n$ for $q = 2^k$. The Zero-difference Pattern for α is $\nu(\alpha) = (z_0, z_1, ..., z_{n-1})$, where $\nu(\alpha)$ takes values in $\mathbb{F}_2^n$ and $z_i = 1$ if $\alpha_i = 0$ or $z_i = 0$ otherwise.

The weight $wt(\nu(\alpha))$ refers to the number of active words in α. The Yoyo game depends then on the swapping of words among the texts. The following definition describes the swapping mechanism.

Definition 2 (Word Swapping [20]). Let, $\alpha, \beta \in \mathbb{F}_q^n$ be two states and $v \in \mathbb{F}_2^n$ be a vector, then $\rho^v(\alpha, \beta)$ is a new state in $\mathbb{F}_q^n$ created from α, β by swapping components among them. The i-th component of $\rho^v(\alpha, \beta) = \alpha_i$ if $v_i = 1$ and $\rho^v(\alpha, \beta) = \beta_i$ otherwise.

YOYO DISTINGUISHER FOR TWO GENERIC SP ROUNDS. Two generic SP rounds can be written as $G_2 = L \circ S \circ L \circ S$ where the final L layer can be omitted since it does not affect the security. Also, the substitution layers do not have to be equal. After modification, $G_2 = S_1 \circ L \circ S_2$. The deterministic distinguisher for two generic SP rounds is described by the following theorem.

Theorem 1 (The Yoyo Game [20]). Let, $p^0, p^1 \in \mathbb{F}_q^n$, $c^0 = G_2(p^0)$ and $c^1 = G_2(p^1)$. For any vector $v \in \mathbb{F}_2^n$, $c'^0 = \rho^v(c^0, c^1)$ and $c'^1 = \rho^v(c^1, c^0)$. Then

$$\nu(G_2^{-1}(c'^0) \oplus G_2^{-1}(c'^1)) = \nu(p'^0 \oplus p'^1) = \nu(p^0 \oplus p^1).$$

References

1. Andreeva, E., Reyhanitabar, R., Varici, K., Vizár, D.: Forking a blockcipher for authenticated encryption of very short messages. IACR Archive (2018). https://eprint.iacr.org/2018/916, Version: 20180926:123554
2. Banik, S., et al.: Cryptanalysis of ForkAES. Cryptology ePrint Archive, Report 2019/289 (2019). https://eprint.iacr.org/2019/289
3. Biham, E., Biryukov, A., Dunkelman, O., Richardson, E., Shamir, A.: Initial observations on skipjack: cryptanalysis of skipjack-3XOR. In: Tavares, S., Meijer, H. (eds.) SAC 1998. LNCS, vol. 1556, pp. 362–375. Springer, Heidelberg (1999). https://doi.org/10.1007/3-540-48892-8_27
4. Biham, E., Biryukov, A., Shamir, A.: Cryptanalysis of skipjack reduced to 31 rounds using impossible differentials. In: Stern, J. (ed.) EUROCRYPT 1999. LNCS, vol. 1592, pp. 12–23. Springer, Heidelberg (1999). https://doi.org/10.1007/3-540-48910-X_2
5. Biham, E., Dunkelman, O., Keller, N.: The rectangle attack - rectangling the serpent. In: Pfitzmann, B. (ed.) EUROCRYPT 2001. LNCS, vol. 2045, pp. 340–357. Springer, Heidelberg (2001). https://doi.org/10.1007/3-540-44987-6_21
6. Biham, E., Dunkelman, O., Keller, N.: New results on boomerang and rectangle attacks. In: Daemen, J., Rijmen, V. (eds.) FSE 2002. LNCS, vol. 2365, pp. 1–16. Springer, Heidelberg (2002). https://doi.org/10.1007/3-540-45661-9_1
7. Blondeau, C.: Accurate Estimate of the Advantage of Impossible Differential Attacks. IACR Trans. Symmetric Cryptol. **2017**(3), 169–191 (2017)
8. Boura, C., Lallemand, V., Naya-Plasencia, M., Suder, V.: Making the impossible possible. J. Cryptol. **31**(1), 101–133 (2018)
9. Boura, C., Naya-Plasencia, M., Suder, V.: Scrutinizing and improving impossible differential attacks: applications to CLEFIA, Camellia, LBlock and SIMON. In: Sarkar, P., Iwata, T. (eds.) ASIACRYPT 2014. LNCS, vol. 8873, pp. 179–199. Springer, Heidelberg (2014). https://doi.org/10.1007/978-3-662-45611-8_10
10. Cid, C., Huang, T., Peyrin, T., Sasaki, Y., Song, L.: Boomerang connectivity table: a new cryptanalysis tool. In: Nielsen, J.B., Rijmen, V. (eds.) EUROCRYPT 2018. LNCS, vol. 10821, pp. 683–714. Springer, Cham (2018). https://doi.org/10.1007/978-3-319-78375-8_22
11. Daemen, J., Rijmen, V.: The Design of Rijndael: AES - The Advanced Encryption Standard. Springer, Heidelberg (2002). https://doi.org/10.1007/978-3-662-04722-4
12. Derbez, P.: Note on impossible differential attacks. In: Peyrin, T. (ed.) FSE 2016. LNCS, vol. 9783, pp. 416–427. Springer, Heidelberg (2016). https://doi.org/10.1007/978-3-662-52993-5_21
13. Dobraunig, C., List, E.: Impossible-differential and boomerang cryptanalysis of round-reduced Kiasu-BC. In: Handschuh, H. (ed.) CT-RSA 2017. LNCS, vol. 10159, pp. 207–222. Springer, Cham (2017). https://doi.org/10.1007/978-3-319-52153-4_12
14. Grassi, L., Rechberger, C., Rønjom, S.: Subspace trail cryptanalysis and its applications to AES. IACR Trans. Symmetric Cryptol. **2016**(2), 192–225 (2016)
15. Jean, J., Nikolić, I., Peyrin, T.: Tweaks and keys for block ciphers: the TWEAKEY framework. In: Sarkar, P., Iwata, T. (eds.) ASIACRYPT 2014. LNCS, vol. 8874, pp. 274–288. Springer, Heidelberg (2014). https://doi.org/10.1007/978-3-662-45608-8_15

16. Kara, O.: Reflection cryptanalysis of some ciphers. In: Chowdhury, D.R., Rijmen, V., Das, A. (eds.) INDOCRYPT 2008. LNCS, vol. 5365, pp. 294–307. Springer, Heidelberg (2008). https://doi.org/10.1007/978-3-540-89754-5_23
17. Knudsen, L.: DEAL - a 128-bit block cipher. Complexity **258**(2), 216 (1998)
18. Murphy, S.: The return of the cryptographic boomerang. IEEE Trans. Inf. Theory **57**(4), 2517–2521 (2011)
19. National Institute of Standards and Technology. FIPS 197. National Institute of Standards and Technology, November, pp. 1–51 (2001)
20. Rønjom, S., Bardeh, N.G., Helleseth, T.: Yoyo tricks with AES. In: Takagi, T., Peyrin, T. (eds.) ASIACRYPT 2017. LNCS, vol. 10624, pp. 217–243. Springer, Cham (2017). https://doi.org/10.1007/978-3-319-70694-8_8
21. Tolba, M., Abdelkhalek, A., Youssef, A.M.: A meet in the middle attack on reduced round Kiasu-BC. IEICE Trans. Fundam. Electron. Commun. Comput. Sci. **E99-A**(10), 21–34 (2016)
22. Wagner, D.: The boomerang attack. In: Knudsen, L. (ed.) FSE 1999. LNCS, vol. 1636, pp. 156–170. Springer, Heidelberg (1999). https://doi.org/10.1007/3-540-48519-8_12

Digital Signature and MAC

Short Lattice-Based One-out-of-Many Proofs and Applications to Ring Signatures

Muhammed F. Esgin[1,2]($\boxtimes$), Ron Steinfeld[1], Amin Sakzad[1], Joseph K. Liu[1], and Dongxi Liu[2]

[1] Faculty of Information Technology, Monash University, Melbourne, Australia
{Muhammed.Esgin,Ron.Steinfeld,Amin.Sakzad,Joseph.Liu}@monash.edu
[2] Data61, CSIRO, Marsfield, Australia
Dongxi.Liu@data61.csiro.au

Abstract. In this work, we construct a short one-out-of-many proof from (module) lattices, allowing one to prove knowledge of a secret associated with one of the public values in a set. The proof system builds on a combination of ideas from the efficient proposals in the discrete logarithm setting by Groth and Kohlweiss (EUROCRYPT '15) and Bootle et al. (ESORICS '15), can have logarithmic communication complexity in the set size and does not require a trusted setup.

Our work resolves an open problem mentioned by Libert et al. (EUROCRYPT '16) of how to efficiently extend the above discrete logarithm proof techniques to the lattice setting. To achieve our result, we introduce new technical tools for design and analysis of algebraic lattice-based zero-knowledge proofs, which may be of independent interest.

Using our proof system as a building block, we design a short ring signature scheme, whose security relies on "post-quantum" lattice assumptions. Even for a very large ring size such as 1 billion, our ring signature size is only 3 MB for 128-bit security level compared to 216 MB in the best existing lattice-based result by Libert et al. (EUROCRYPT '16).

Keywords: Lattice-based cryptography · Zero-knowledge proof · Ring signature

1 Introduction

In the last decade, lattice-based cryptography has seen a great interest with many new applications developed rapidly. Although it offers solutions even to problems which long seemed elusive, there is still a gap in some areas where lattice-based cryptographic proposals are not efficient enough for practical use and even fall far behind their number theoretic counterparts in terms of efficiency. One important example for such a case is zero-knowledge proofs (ZKPs). It seems that lattice-based cryptography does not agree well with ZKPs and extending the existing number theoretic proposals to the lattice setting is quite challenging.

© Springer Nature Switzerland AG 2019
R. H. Deng et al. (Eds.): ACNS 2019, LNCS 11464, pp. 67–88, 2019.
https://doi.org/10.1007/978-3-030-21568-2_4

A particular example is one-out-of-many proofs where the prover's goal is to prove knowledge of an opening of a commitment within a set of commitments without revealing which one he has. Groth and Kohlweiss [15] and Bootle et al. [7] gave very efficient constructions with logarithmic (log) communication complexity in the size of the set of commitments based on decisional Diffie-Hellman assumption. Their protocols also lead to very efficient ring signatures without trusted setup[1], where a signatory signs a message on behalf of a group of users (referred as a *ring*). The idea behind obtaining a ring signature from a one-out-of-many proof works as follows. Users commit to their secret keys, resulting in the users' public keys. Then, the signatory proves (in a non-interactive fashion using Fiat-Shamir heuristic) that he knows an opening (i.e., the secret key) of one of the commitments (i.e., the corresponding public keys) used to create the ring signature. Ring signatures are important tools used in e-voting systems and cryptocurrencies to provide anonymity. Especially in the case of cryptocurrencies, an important aspect is the ring signature size, which makes the schemes in [7,15] very attractive on a large scale. However, these proposals in [7,15] do not offer post-quantum security as they are in the discrete logarithm (DL) setting.

On the side of lattice-based cryptography, a promising candidate for post-quantum security, efficient designs targeting the same problems do not currently exist. There has not been a successful extension of the ideas in [7,15] to the lattice setting, and other approaches proposed so far resulted in very inefficient schemes that are far from offering practical usability. To illustrate, while [7] gives constructions in the order of a few KB even for very large ring sizes, the current shortest log-sized ring signature from lattices by Libert et al. [18] results in a ring signature of size 75 MB for around a thousand ring members and a security level of 128 bits. It is therefore tempting to realise the ideas in [7,15] using lattice-based techniques, but, as we discuss next, this is far from trivial. In this work, we tackle this problem and design short one-out-of-many proofs and ring signatures from (module) lattices by introducing new tools for the design and analysis of algebraic lattice-based ZKPs (see Sect. 3).

For some practical applications, one requires *linkability* between ring signatures generated using the same secret key. This is often referred to as a *linkable ring signature* [20], which is useful in e-voting systems (e.g., see [11]) and blockchain confidential transactions (e.g., see [24,26,27]). Our ring signature can be extended to provide linkability using the same techniques as in [4,29].

1.1 Technical Difficulties

The starting point of our protocol is the works by Groth and Kohlweiss [15] and Bootle et al. [7], instantiated using Pedersen commitment as a core ingredient. As also noted in [18] and [4], it is not straightforward to design lattice-based one-out-of-many proofs and ring signatures from the ideas in [7,15]. One can see [29] for an attempt to design a (linkable) lattice-based ring signature based

---

[1] There are some constructions of ring signatures that give a constant size signature but require a trusted setup.

on [15]. The authors of [29] claim that the anonymity and unforgeability of their scheme follow from the framework of [15], provided that a perfectly hiding and computationally binding commitment scheme is used. However, as we show here, there are many issues to be addressed if one aims to use the ideas from [7,15] in the lattice setting, whereas [29] did not go into details of how these issues are to be solved. To begin with, the *valid* input space of lattice-based commitment schemes is a proper subset of $\mathbb{Z}_q^v$ for some $v \geq 1$ (or the underlying polynomial ring $R_q^v = \mathbb{Z}_q[X]/(X^d + 1)$ in the case of ring variants) consisting of vectors of *small* elements unlike their number-theoretic counterparts such as Pedersen commitment accepting any element in $\mathbb{Z}_q^v$. This restriction prevents straightforward adaptation of number-theoretic results, and in fact there is a crucial difference between the relations of the lattice-based and DDH-based one-out-of-many proofs (see Remark 1 in Sect. 4). Furthermore, extending [15] alone does not yield *efficient* lattice-based ring signatures even if the security issues in the lattice setting are addressed properly.

Let us briefly discuss the main technical difficulties our new techniques enable us to overcome in extending [7,15] to the lattice setting. We denote the public set size for one-out-of-many proof (or the ring size for the ring signature) by N, and $C = \mathrm{Com}_{ck}(m \; ; \; r)$ as a commitment to a message m with randomness r using a commitment key ck. A pair of *acceptable* values (m', r') such that $C = \mathrm{Com}_{ck}(m' \; ; \; r')$ is called an opening of C. The reader unfamiliar with the general concepts of Σ-protocols is referred to Sect. 2.3.

1. **Growth of extracted witness size:** As mentioned previously, lattice-based commitment schemes accept only elements of bounded size as valid openings. We show that the sizes of extracted witnesses, which will be openings of some commitments, grow rapidly with the size of challenge difference inverses in the framework of [7,15] (see Sect. 3.2). In particular, we show that if one works over a ring $R_q = \mathbb{Z}_q[X]/(X^d + 1)$, the growth can be made to be of the form $\Gamma = d^{\log N}$ (see Sect. 5). Letting $d = 2^{10}$ with $N = 2^{20}$ users, Γ (and, in turn, q) reaches 200 bits without any additional considerations.

2. **(Small) challenge space size:** In connection with the above difficulty, we need to find a challenge space where the sizes of challenge difference inverses are guaranteed to be small. Unfortunately, we cannot find such a space with exponentially many elements, restricting us to a small challenge space. A simple (commonly used) possible option is to use binary challenges. However, the scheme presented in [7] requires at least 3 distinct challenges to extract a witness, making that option ineligible. In fact, the main protocols in [7,15] even require up to $\log_2 N + 1$ challenges for witness extraction, which means that several *forkings* are required in the unforgeability proof of the ring signature. This fact combined with a small challenge space causes major issues in the unforgeability proof (see proof of Theorem 3). For example, one cannot simply rely on a commonly used Forking Lemma from [9].

3. **Proof of commitment to a binary value over R_q:** When working over the ring $R_q = \mathbb{Z}_q[X]/(X^d + 1)$, the following statement, which is typically used to prove that a value is binary, does not necessarily hold: $x(x - 1) = 0$

$\implies x \in \{0,1\}$. This is because there exist zero divisors in R_q (unlike the field $\mathbb{Z}_q$ used in DL-based schemes). Hence, straightforward proofs of $x(x-1) = 0$ does not guarantee that x is binary (see Sect. 3.1).

4. **Soundness gap:** In common with some other lattice-based proofs, our protocol has the so-called *soundness gap* unlike DL-based schemes. That is, the extractor recovers the openings of $\gamma \cdot \text{Com}_{ck}(m ; r)$ instead of the actual commitments of the form $\text{Com}_{ck}(m ; r)$. This makes things more complicated in the soundness proofs (see the proofs of Theorems 1 and 2) and requires one to be careful in protocol's application to a ring signature as the extractor is never guaranteed to recover the openings of the actual commitments used in the protocol (see the proof of Theorem 3).

1.2   Our Contributions

New Technical Tools for Algebraic Protocols and Design of Short Lattice-Based One-out-of-Many Proofs and Ring Signatures. By now, it is clear that extending the works [7,15] to the lattice setting is far from being trivial, which was indeed stated as an open problem in [4,18]. Our main contributions in this work are the introduction of new technical tools for the design and analysis of algebraic protocols from lattices (Sect. 3) and the design of short (sublinear-sized) one-out-of-many proofs and ring signature schemes from (module) lattices (Sects. 5 and 6). It is worth emphasising that our proposal is not a direct adaptation of either [15] or [7], but rather carefully combines ideas from both in a way suitable in the lattice scenario, and also that the technical difficulties mentioned in Sect. 1.1 do not allow straightforward extension of [15] or [7].

As shown in Table 1, our ring signature achieves a dramatic improvement in terms of length over the shortest existing log-sized result from lattices by Libert et al. [18], where the improvement is almost two orders of magnitude.[2] Moreover, an important feature of our constructions is that a modulus q of a special form (such as $q \equiv 17 \mod 32$ as in [12]) is not required, which allows the use of fast computation algorithms such as Number Theoretic Transform (NTT).

A series of previous proposals of group/ring signatures (e.g., [17–19]) rely on combinatorial Stern-like protocols [25]. Even though these protocols offer a range of functionalities, all of them have very long signature sizes that seem too large for practical use. Our new technical tools developed in Sect. 3 introduce new directions for efficient applications of algebraic lattice-based techniques to areas where lattice-based proposals fall behind their number-theoretic counterparts. The protocol structure, for whose construction our new tools provide efficient techniques, is also involved in advanced ZKPs such as arithmetic circuit arguments [8] and Bulletproofs [10]. Hence, our new tools may be of independent interest, especially for the extension of other advanced ZKPs in the DL setting

---

[2] Our scheme, like [18], is only analyzed in the classical random oracle model (ROM) (rather than quantum ROM). Also, note that the linear-sized ring signature schemes are inherently long for large ring sizes.

Table 1. Comparison of ring signature sizes at $\lambda = 128$-bit security with N ring members. For [18], we use the same system parameters given in [18] for 80-bit security, but only increase the number of protocol repetitions to reach 2^{-128} soundness error. See Sect. 6.1 for detailed parameter setting.

N	2^6	2^8	2^{10}	2^{12}	2^{16}	2^{20}	2^{30}
[18] (sign. size in KB)	47294	61438	75582	89726	118014	146303	217023
Our work (sign. size in KB)	774	881	1021	1178	1487	1862	3006

to the lattice setting. In fact, the issues in [29] can be fixed using our techniques, but the revised scheme is unlikely to be more efficient than our work.

Exploiting Module Variants of Standard Lattice Assumptions for Efficiency Purposes. Another contribution of our work is to show that the use of Module-SIS (M-SIS) problem [16] (over SIS or Ring-SIS) opens the door for significant efficiency improvements by allowing us to tradeoff extracted witness size growth (and hence signature length) against computational efficiency. To the best of our knowledge, this is the first time a lattice-based ZKP has been instantiated based on M-SIS to gain such an efficiency improvement.[3]

In the Ring-LWE setting, *monomial challenges*, $X^i \in R = \mathbb{Z}[X]/(X^d+1)$, was introduced in [5] to enable a challenge space of size $2d$ with the property that the doubled inverse of the difference of such challenges have small norm. The three methods introduced in Sect. 3 provide an in-depth analysis of the use of monomial challenges in a more generalized setting of $(k + 1)$-special sound protocols. We believe that the combination of using monomial challenges together with M-SIS to fine-tune the parameters for efficiency purposes holds great potential to be investigated through further research in lattice-based cryptography.

Paper Organization. Section 2 discusses some preliminaries. Our new tools for the design and analysis of algebraic protocols from lattices are introduced in Sect. 3. Sections 4 and 5 cover our binary proof and one-out-of-many proof, respectively. Our compact lattice-based ring signature is then provided in Sect. 6. More detailed related work, rigorous definitions of ring signatures and the full proofs of our new results are available in the full version [14].

2   Preliminaries

We use the standard notations and let $R = \mathbb{Z}[X]/(X^d + 1)$ and $R_q = \mathbb{Z}_q[X]/(X^d + 1)$ for a power-of-two $d > 1$ and odd prime q. S_c defines the set of all polynomials in R with infinity norm at most $c \in \mathbb{Z}^+$. We write $p \leftarrow S^{md}$ to indicate that $p \in R^m$ is a vector of m polynomials where each coefficient is sampled from a set S (i.e., md coefficients are sampled in total).

---

[3] M-SIS is used usually (e.g. in [12]) to fix the ring dimension d and to avoid the need for a change of it to accommodate new security parameters. It does not have a significant effect on efficiency due to extracted witness norm unlike in our case.

For $f \in R$ and $\boldsymbol{p} \in R^m$, $\mathrm{Rot}(f)$ and $\mathrm{Coeff}(\boldsymbol{p})$ denote the representative matrix of f and the md-dimensional coefficient vector of $\boldsymbol{p}$, respectively.

2.1   Module-SIS, Module-LWE Problems and Commitment Scheme

In our schemes, we work over a ring R_q and rely on the hardness of Module-SIS (M-SIS)[4] and Module-LWE (M-LWE) problems [16] defined below.

Definition 1 (M-SIS$_{n,m,q,\theta}$). *Let $R_q = \mathbb{Z}_q[X]/(X^d + 1)$. Given $\boldsymbol{A} = [\, \boldsymbol{I}_n \,\|\, \boldsymbol{A}' \,] \in R_q^{n \times m}$ where each component of $\boldsymbol{A}'$ is chosen independently from the uniform distribution, find $\boldsymbol{z} \in R_q^m$ such that $\boldsymbol{A}\boldsymbol{z} = \boldsymbol{0} \bmod q$ and $0 < \|\boldsymbol{z}\| \leq \theta$.*

For simplicity, we consider a special case of M-LWE problem where each error and secret key coefficient is sampled uniformly from $\{-\mathcal{B}, \dots, \mathcal{B}\}$ for some $\mathcal{B} \in \mathbb{Z}^+$. A more special case of $\mathcal{B} = 1$ is commonly practised in recent lattice-based proposals [3,13,22], and our results can be easily extended to a case with a discrete Gaussian distribution.

Definition 2 (M-LWE$_{n,m,q,\mathcal{B}}$). *Let $R_q = \mathbb{Z}_q[X]/(X^d + 1)$ and $\boldsymbol{s} \leftarrow S_{\mathcal{B}}^n$ be a secret key. Define $\mathrm{LWE}_{q,s}$ as the distribution obtained by sampling $e \leftarrow S_{\mathcal{B}}$, $\boldsymbol{a} \leftarrow R_q^n$ and returning $(\boldsymbol{a}, \langle \boldsymbol{a}, \boldsymbol{s} \rangle + e)$. Given m samples from either $\mathrm{LWE}_{q,s}$ or $\mathcal{U}(R_q^n, R_q)$, the problem asks to distinguish which is the case.*

We use the following lattice-based commitment scheme that allows commitment to multiple messages, and is additively homomorphic. Following the standard notions, *hiding* property requires that it is hard to distinguish between commitments to two distinct message-randomness pairs, and *strong binding* property (which is stronger than the standard binding property) dictates that it is hard to find two distinct *valid* openings (message-randomness pairs) of a commitment. In common with similar lattice-based commitment schemes (see, e.g., [3] for more discussion), the opening algorithm of the commitment scheme has an additional input $y \in R_q$, called the relaxation factor, and the opening message-randomness pair is required to have a bounded norm. The latter is needed to relate the binding property to the M-SIS problem (as given in Lemma 1). Thus, we introduce a parameter $T_{\mathrm{com}} \in \mathbb{R}^+$ and say T_{com}-binding where T_{com} serves as an upperbound on the norm of a valid opening message-randomness pair.

- CKeygen(1^λ): Pick $\boldsymbol{G}_r' \leftarrow R_q^{n \times (m-n)}$, $\boldsymbol{G}_m \leftarrow R_q^{n \times v}$ and set $\boldsymbol{G}_r = [\, \boldsymbol{I}_n \,\|\, \boldsymbol{G}_r' \,]$. Output $ck = \boldsymbol{G} = [\, \boldsymbol{G}_r \,\|\, \boldsymbol{G}_m \,] \in R_q^{n \times (m+v)}$.
- Commit$_{ck}(\boldsymbol{m})$: Pick $\boldsymbol{r} \leftarrow S_{\mathcal{B}}^m$. Output $\mathrm{Com}_{ck}(\boldsymbol{m} \,;\, \boldsymbol{r}) = \boldsymbol{G} \cdot (\boldsymbol{r}, \boldsymbol{m}) = \boldsymbol{G}_r \cdot \boldsymbol{r} + \boldsymbol{G}_m \cdot \boldsymbol{m}$.
- Open$_{ck}(C, (y, \boldsymbol{m}', \boldsymbol{r}'))$: For $y \in R_q$, if $\mathrm{Com}_{ck}(\boldsymbol{m}' \,;\, \boldsymbol{r}') = yC$ and $\|(\boldsymbol{r}', \boldsymbol{m}')\| \leq T_{\mathrm{com}}$, return 1. Otherwise, return 0.

Lemma 1. *The commitment scheme defined above is computationally hiding if M-LWE$_{m-n,n,q,\mathcal{B}}$ is hard. It is also computationally strong T_{com}-binding with respect to the same relaxation factor y if M-SIS$_{n,m+v,q,2T_{com}}$ problem is hard.*

---

[4] As in [3], we define M-SIS in "Hermite normal form", which is equivalent to M-SIS with completely random $\boldsymbol{A}$.

2.2 Technical Definitions and General Lemmas

For a rank-n matrix S, we denote the discrete Gaussian distribution (centered at zero) with parameter S (and covariance matrix $S^\top S$) by $\mathcal{D}_S^n$, and by $\mathcal{D}_s^n$ if $S = sI_n$. We denote by D_σ^n the discrete normal distribution with standard deviation σ, defined as $\mathcal{D}_s^n$ with $s = \sigma\sqrt{2\pi}$.

Fact 1 (A result of [1, Fact 2]). *For an invertible $n \times n$ matrix X, $X \cdot \mathcal{D}_S^n = \mathcal{D}_{SX^\top}^n$. That is, the distribution induced by sampling $v \leftarrow \mathcal{D}_S^n$ and outputting $y = Xv$ is the same as $\mathcal{D}_{SX^\top}^n$.*

As defined in [23], for a lattice L and real $\epsilon > 0$, the *smoothing parameter*, $\eta_\epsilon(L)$, of L is the smallest s such that $\rho_{1/s}(L^* \setminus \{0\}) \le \epsilon$ where L^* is the "dual lattice". We skip the details, but for our purposes the following facts are enough.

Fact 2 ([23, Lemma 3.3]). *$\eta_\epsilon(\mathbb{Z}^n) < 6$ for $\epsilon = 2^{-128}$ and any $1 \le n \le 2^{32}$.*

Lemma 2 ([1, Lemma 3]). *Let $\sigma_1(S)$ and $\sigma_n(S)$ be the largest and the least singular values of a rank-n matrix S, respectively. If $\sigma_n(S) \ge \eta_\epsilon(\mathbb{Z}^n)$,*

$$\Pr_{v \leftarrow \mathcal{D}_S^n}\left[\, \|v\| \ge \sigma_1(S)\sqrt{n}\, \right] \le \frac{1+\epsilon}{1-\epsilon} \cdot 2^{-n}.$$

The lemma below recalls the norm bound of monomial challenge differences.

Lemma 3 ([5, Lemma 3.1]). *For $0 \le i, j \le 2d-1$, all the coefficients of $2(X^i - X^j)^{-1} \in R$ are in $\{-1, 0, 1\}$. This implies that $\left\|2(X^i - X^j)^{-1}\right\| \le \sqrt{d}$.*

Finally, we summarize the rejection sampling technique from [21].

Algorithm 1. $\text{Rej}(z, c, \phi, K)$

1: $\sigma = \phi K$; $\mu(\phi) = e^{12/\phi + 1/(2\phi^2)}$; $u \leftarrow [0, 1)$
2: **if** $u > (\frac{1}{\mu(\phi)}) \cdot \exp\left(\frac{-2\langle z, c\rangle + \|c\|^2}{2\sigma^2}\right)$ **then return** 0   ▷ indicates 'abort protocol'.
3: **else return** 1

2.3 Σ-protocols

Σ-protocols are a type of zero-knowledge proofs between two parties: the prover and the verifier. A language $\mathcal{L} \subseteq \{0,1\}^*$ is said to have a witness relationship $\mathcal{R} \subseteq \{0,1\}^* \times \{0,1\}^*$ provided $v \in \mathcal{L}$ if and only if there exists $w \in \{0,1\}^*$ such that $(v, w) \in \mathcal{R}$. The quantity w is referred to as a witness for v. The definition of Σ-protocols from [5] generalises the well-known notion of Σ-protocols. We further extend it to allow $(k+1)$-special soundness as in [7,15].

Definition 3 (Extension of Definition 2.5 in [5]). *Let $(\mathcal{P}, \mathcal{V})$ be a two-party protocol where $\mathcal{V}$ is a PPT algorithm, and $\mathcal{L}, \mathcal{L}'$ be languages with witness relations $\mathcal{R}, \mathcal{R}'$ with $\mathcal{R} \subseteq \mathcal{R}'$. Then, $(\mathcal{P}, \mathcal{V})$ is called a Σ-protocol for $\mathcal{R}, \mathcal{R}'$ with completeness error α, a challenge set $\mathcal{C}$, public input v and private input w, if it satisfies the following conditions:*

- **Three-move form:** *The protocol has the following form. On input (v, w), $\mathcal{P}$ computes initial commitment t and sends it to $\mathcal{V}$. On input v, $\mathcal{V}$ draws a challenge $x \leftarrow \mathcal{C}$ and sends it to $\mathcal{P}$. The prover sends a response s to $\mathcal{V}$. The verifier accepts or rejects depending on the protocol transcript (t, x, s). The transcript (t, x, s) is called accepting if the verifier accepts the protocol run.*
- **Completeness:** *Whenever $(v, w) \in \mathcal{R}$, the honest verifier accepts with probability at least $1 - \alpha$ when interacting with an honest prover.*
- $(k + 1)$**-special soundness:** *There exists a PPT algorithm $\mathcal{E}$ (called the extractor) which takes $(k + 1)$ accepting transcripts $(t, x_0, s_0), \ldots, (t, x_k, s_k)$ with pairwise distinct x_i's $(0 \leq i \leq k)$ as inputs, and outputs w' satisfying $(v, w') \in \mathcal{R}'$. We call this procedure witness extraction, and say that the protocol has a soundness error $\frac{k}{|\mathcal{C}|}$.[5]*
- **Special honest-verifier zero-knowledge (SHVZK):** *There exists a PPT algorithm $\mathcal{S}$ (called the simulator) that takes $v \in \mathcal{L}$ and $x \in \mathcal{C}$ as inputs, and outputs (t, s) such that (t, x, s) is indistinguishable from an accepting protocol transcript generated by a real protocol run.*

3   New Technical Tools for Lattice-Based Proofs

In this section, we present a collection of technical tools we use in our constructions. These new tools may be of independent interest for future works on algebraic lattice-based zero-knowledge proofs and signatures.

3.1   Proving a Value Binary in R_q

We show a lemma that, in particular, enables us to guarantee that $b \in R_q$ is a bit when the equation $b \cdot (1 - b) = 0$ holds over R_q. Our lemma does not put any additional assumption on q but its size, which enables one to use fast computation algorithms such as the number-theoretic transform (NTT) with $q \equiv 1 \bmod 2d$. In particular, we do not need number theoretic conditions on q that makes NTT less efficient. For example, such a condition is imposed in [12] to ensure the invertibility of small elements in R_q.

Lemma 4. *For $b \in R_q$, if $b \cdot (\alpha - b) = 0$ over R_q for some positive integer α, and $\|b\| + \alpha < \sqrt{q}$, then $b \in \{0, \alpha\}$.*

---

[5] We refer to Sect. 2.2 of [6] for further discussion on soundness error.

3.2 Bounding the Extracted Witness Norm for Monomial Challenges

Consider a Σ-protocol where the prover's initial commitments are $A_0, A_1, \ldots, A_k$ ($k \geq 1$), and he responds with $(\boldsymbol{f}_x, \boldsymbol{r}_x)$ for a given challenge x by the verifier. Then, the verifier checks whether $A_0 + A_1 x + A_2 x^2 + \cdots + A_k x^k = \mathrm{Com}(\boldsymbol{f}_x; \boldsymbol{r}_x)$ holds where Com is a homomorphic commitment scheme. Now, suppose A_k is the commitment of prover's witness and that the extractor obtains $k + 1$ accepting protocol transcripts for the same initial commitments, represented as follows.

$$
\begin{pmatrix}
1 & x_0 & x_0^2 & \cdots & x_0^k \\
1 & x_1 & x_1^2 & \cdots & x_1^k \\
\vdots & \vdots & \vdots & \vdots & \vdots \\
1 & x_k & x_k^2 & \cdots & x_k^k
\end{pmatrix}
\cdot
\begin{pmatrix}
A_0 \\ A_1 \\ \vdots \\ A_k
\end{pmatrix}
=
\begin{pmatrix}
\mathrm{Com}(\boldsymbol{f}_{x_0}; \boldsymbol{r}_{x_0}) \\
\mathrm{Com}(\boldsymbol{f}_{x_1}; \boldsymbol{r}_{x_1}) \\
\vdots \\
\mathrm{Com}(\boldsymbol{f}_{x_k}; \boldsymbol{r}_{x_k})
\end{pmatrix}.
$$

Here, the matrix on the very left is a Vandermonde matrix $\boldsymbol{V}$, and the extractor can recover a *possible* opening of A_k via multiplying both sides by $\boldsymbol{V}^{-1}$, if exists, due to the homomorphic properties of the commitment scheme. We observe from [28] that the inverse matrix $\boldsymbol{V}^{-1}$ has the following form:

$$
\begin{pmatrix}
\frac{*}{(x_0-x_1)(x_0-x_2)\cdots(x_0-x_k)} & \frac{*}{(x_0-x_1)(x_1-x_2)\cdots(x_1-x_k)} & \cdots & \frac{*}{(x_0-x_k)(x_1-x_k)\cdots(x_{k-1}-x_k)} \\
\frac{*}{(x_0-x_1)(x_0-x_2)\cdots(x_0-x_k)} & \frac{*}{(x_0-x_1)(x_1-x_2)\cdots(x_1-x_k)} & \cdots & \frac{*}{(x_0-x_k)(x_1-x_k)\cdots(x_{k-1}-x_k)} \\
\vdots & \vdots & \vdots & \vdots \\
\frac{1}{(x_0-x_1)(x_0-x_2)\cdots(x_0-x_k)} & \frac{-1}{(x_0-x_1)(x_1-x_2)\cdots(x_1-x_k)} & \cdots & \frac{(-1)^k}{(x_0-x_k)(x_1-x_k)\cdots(x_{k-1}-x_k)}
\end{pmatrix}, \quad (1)
$$

where $*$ denotes some element in the domain. Our protocol as well as the protocols in [7,15] have this structure and, therefore, the Vandermonde matrix inverse plays a crucial role in the witness extraction. In particular, if we denote the entries in the last row of $\boldsymbol{V}^{-1}$ by $\alpha_0, \ldots, \alpha_k$ (from left to right), we have

$$
A_k = \sum_{j=0}^{k} \alpha_j \mathrm{Com}(\boldsymbol{f}_{x_j}; \boldsymbol{r}_{x_j}) = \mathrm{Com}\left(\sum_{j=0}^{k} \alpha_j \boldsymbol{f}_{x_j}; \sum_{j=0}^{k} \alpha_j \boldsymbol{r}_{x_j} \right) =: \mathrm{Com}(\boldsymbol{m}_{\mathrm{ext}}; \boldsymbol{r}_{\mathrm{ext}}).
$$

$$(2)$$

These arguments tell us that we need to make sure $\boldsymbol{V}^{-1}$ exists in the first place, which follows from the invertibility of pairwise differences of challenges. What is more important in the case of lattice-based proofs is that α_j's (and, in general, the entries in $\boldsymbol{V}^{-1}$) must have small norm so that extracted witness (particularly, $(\boldsymbol{m}_{\mathrm{ext}}; \boldsymbol{r}_{\mathrm{ext}})$) is a *valid* opening (of A_k). To that end, we can make use of Lemma 3 to bound the entries in $\boldsymbol{V}^{-1}$, which brings us to our first method below. In the rest, we focus on the last row of $\boldsymbol{V}^{-1}$, which is enough for our purposes, but our results can be extended to the cases related to the other entries of $\boldsymbol{V}^{-1}$.

Method 1. Taking the first entry α_0 as an example, we have

$$
2^k \alpha_0 = \frac{2^k}{(x_0 - x_1)(x_0 - x_2) \cdots (x_0 - x_k)} = \frac{2}{x_0 - x_1} \cdot \frac{2}{x_0 - x_2} \cdots \frac{2}{x_0 - x_k}.
$$

For monomial challenges, using standard norm relations in R and Lemma 3, we get

$$\left\| 2^k \alpha_0 \right\| = \left\| \prod_{i=1}^{k} \frac{2}{x_0 - x_i} \right\| \leq \left(\sqrt{d} \right)^{k-1} \prod_{i=1}^{k} \left\| 2(x_0 - x_i)^{-1} \right\| \leq \left(\sqrt{d} \right)^{k-1} \left(\sqrt{d} \right)^k = d^{k-0.5}.$$

Since all the entries in the last row have a similar form and the bound does not depend on the particular choice of monomials, the same bound holds for all entries in the last row of V^{-1}. Note that V^{-1} exists over R_q for odd q (though may not have small entries) since 2 is invertible for such q. We summarise these results in the following lemma, whose proof follows from the above discussion.

Lemma 5. *For* $k \in \mathbb{Z}^+$, *let* $x_i = X^{\omega_i} \in R = \mathbb{Z}[X]/(X^d + 1)$ *for* $0 \leq \omega_i \leq 2d - 1$ *and* $0 \leq i \leq k$. *Define the Vandermonde matrix* V *of dimension* $k + 1$ *where* i-*th row is the vector* $(1, x_i, x_i^2, \ldots, x_i^k)$. *Then,* V *is invertible over* R_q *for odd* q, *and for any entry* α_j ($0 \leq j \leq k$) *in the last row of* V^{-1}, *we have* $\left\| 2^k \alpha_j \right\| \leq d^{k-0.5}$.

Using Lemma 5, we can now summarise the main result of Method 1.

Lemma 6. *For the extracted opening* $(m_{\text{ext}}, r_{\text{ext}})$ *of* A_k *in* (2), *we have*

$$\left\| 2^k r_{\text{ext}} \right\| \leq (k+1) \cdot d^k \cdot \max_{0 \leq j \leq k} \left\| r_{x_j} \right\| \quad \text{and} \quad \left\| 2^k m_{\text{ext}} \right\| \leq (k+1) \cdot d^k \cdot \max_{0 \leq j \leq k} \left\| f_{x_j} \right\|.$$

This initial attempt succeeds, but the result may not be optimal. Thus, we deepen our analysis to get a tighter bound.

Method 2. We observe that all entries in V^{-1} are constructed by challenge values, which are public. Therefore, independent of a protocol run, anyone can take a set of challenges and compute, in particular, $\left\| 2^k \alpha_j \right\|$ for any entry α_j in the last row of V^{-1}. The important part here is that one can indeed iterate through all the possible challenge sets (to be used in witness extraction) *if* the challenge space size and k are not too large. This means anyone can compute a global bound $\mathbb{B}_{d,k}$ on $\left\| 2^k \alpha_j \right\|$ for any given k and d independent of the index j and the challenges used in the witness extraction.

Observing from (1), the total search space will be of size at most $(k+1) \cdot |\mathcal{C}|^{k+1}$ where $|\mathcal{C}| = 2d$ denotes the monomial challenge space size. However, note that, assuming w.l.o.g. $i > j$,

$$\left\| (X^i - X^j)^{-1} \right\| = \left\| X^{2d-i}(1 - X^{j-i})^{-1} \right\| = \left\| (1 - X^{j-i})^{-1} \right\| \tag{3}$$

since multiplication by a monomial in R simply performs a nega-cyclic rotation of the coefficients. Therefore, for any given k, it is enough to iterate through all subsets of $\{1, \ldots, 2d-1\}$ of size k, and compute $\left\| \prod_{\omega \in U_k} 2(1 - X^\omega)^{-1} \right\|$ for such a given subset U_k. As a result, the search space size is reduced to $\binom{|\mathcal{C}|-1}{k}$. In our parameter setting for practical ring sizes of $N \leq 2^{20}$, we have $k \leq 3$. Therefore, for example, for $d = 64$ and $k = 3$, this requires only $\binom{127}{3} < 2^{18.4}$ iterations to be performed only ever once. Below is the result of Method 2 where the proof follows via bounding $\max_{0 \leq j \leq k} \left\| 2^k \alpha_j \right\|$ by $\mathbb{B}_{d,k}$ instead of $d^{k-0.5}$ as in Lemma 5.

Lemma 7. *For the extracted opening* $(\boldsymbol{m}_{\mathrm{ext}}, \boldsymbol{r}_{\mathrm{ext}})$ *of* A_k *in* (2)*, and any given* d *and* k*, there exists a constant* $\mathbb{B}_{d,k} \leq d^{k-0.5}$ *and an algorithm to compute* $\mathbb{B}_{d,k}$ *with a running time at most* $(k-1) \cdot \binom{2d-1}{k}$ *polynomial multiplications in* R_q *and* $\binom{2d-1}{k}$ *Euclidean norm computations of degree* d *polynomials such that*

$$\left\| 2^k \boldsymbol{r}_{\mathrm{ext}} \right\| \leq (k+1) \cdot \sqrt{d} \cdot \mathbb{B}_{d,k} \cdot \max_{0 \leq j \leq k} \left\| \boldsymbol{r}_{x_j} \right\|, \ and \tag{4}$$

$$\left\| 2^k \boldsymbol{m}_{\mathrm{ext}} \right\| \leq (k+1) \cdot \sqrt{d} \cdot \mathbb{B}_{d,k} \cdot \max_{0 \leq j \leq k} \left\| \boldsymbol{f}_{x_j} \right\|. \tag{5}$$

Method 3. The above two methods give us ways to bound the extracted witness length independent of a protocol run. The question now is "How much additional information can we use from a protocol run?"

Assume that the prover's response follows a discrete Gaussian distribution, i.e., $\boldsymbol{r}_x \leftarrow \mathcal{D}_s^{md}$ for some $s \in \mathbb{R}^+, m \in \mathbb{Z}^+$. Instead of bounding $\left\| 2^k \alpha_j \right\|$, we bound $\left\| 2^k \alpha_j \boldsymbol{r}_{x_j} \right\|$ for all j's. The product $2^k \alpha_j \boldsymbol{r}_{x_j}$ can be represented as $(\mathrm{Rot}(2^k \alpha_j) \otimes \boldsymbol{I}_m) \cdot \mathrm{Coeff}(\boldsymbol{r}_{x_j}) = \mathrm{Coeff}(2^k \alpha_j \boldsymbol{r}_{x_j})$ where $\otimes$ denotes the Kronecker product. Let us denote $\boldsymbol{R}_j = \mathrm{Rot}(2^k \alpha_j) \otimes \boldsymbol{I}_m$. Since $\mathrm{Coeff}(\boldsymbol{r}_{x_j}) \leftarrow \mathcal{D}_s^{md}$, by Fact 1, we have $\boldsymbol{R}_j \cdot \mathrm{Coeff}(\boldsymbol{r}_{x_j}) \in \mathcal{D}_{s \boldsymbol{R}_j^\top}^{md}$. Hence, by Lemma 2, with high probability, we get

$$\left\| \mathrm{Coeff}(2^k \alpha_j \boldsymbol{r}_{x_j}) \right\| = \left\| \boldsymbol{R}_j \cdot \mathrm{Coeff}(\boldsymbol{r}_{x_j}) \right\| \leq \sigma_1(s \boldsymbol{R}_j^\top) \sqrt{md} = \sigma_1(\boldsymbol{R}_j) s \sqrt{md}, \tag{6}$$

if $\sigma_n(s \boldsymbol{R}_j^\top) \geq \eta_\epsilon(\mathbb{Z}^{md})$, which can be easily satisfied as shown in the proof of Lemma 8. We can now summarize the main result of Method 3 as below.

Lemma 8. *Let* $\boldsymbol{r}_{\mathrm{ext}} = \sum_{j=0}^k \alpha_j \boldsymbol{r}_{x_j}$ *be the randomness opening of* A_k *as in* (2)*. Assume that* $s \geq 6$*,* $d \in \{4, 8, \ldots, 512\}$ *and* $md \leq 2^{32}$*. If* $\boldsymbol{r}_{x_j} \leftarrow \mathcal{D}_s^{md}$ *for all* $0 \leq j \leq k$*, then with probability at least* $1 - \frac{1+\epsilon}{1-\epsilon} 2^{-md}$ *for* $\epsilon = 2^{-128}$*,*

$$\left\| 2^k \boldsymbol{r}_{\mathrm{ext}} \right\| \leq (k+1) \cdot \max_{0 \leq j \leq k} \sigma_1(\boldsymbol{S}_j) \cdot s \sqrt{md}, \tag{7}$$

where $\boldsymbol{S}_j = \mathrm{Rot}(2^k \alpha_j)$ *for* $j = 0, \ldots, k$*.*

Similar to the idea in Method 2, one can iterate through all $\boldsymbol{S}_j$'s and compute a global bound $\mathbb{S}_{d,k}$ on possible $\sigma_1(\boldsymbol{S}_j)$'s for a given d and k. When $\boldsymbol{r}_{x_j} \leftarrow \mathcal{D}_s^{md}$, we have $\left\| \boldsymbol{r}_{x_j} \right\| \leq s \sqrt{md}$ (up to a small constant factor) by Lemma 2. As a result, we may reduce the comparison of the three methods to the comparison of the values d^k (Method 1), $\mathbb{B}'_{d,k} = \sqrt{d} \cdot \mathbb{B}_{d,k}$ (Method 2) and $\mathbb{S}_{d,k}$ (Method 3).

However, there is an important detail in Method 3: it only works when the prover's response follows a discrete Gaussian distribution and the verifier cannot simply check if that is the case. To solve this problem, we introduce a new tool called, Pseudo Witness Extraction in Algorithm 2. If Algorithm 2 is used in the protocol's verification with an input bound β, then $\left\| 2^k \boldsymbol{r}_{\mathrm{ext}} \right\| \leq (k+1)\beta$ must hold. Therefore, when the prover's responses $\boldsymbol{r}_{x_j}$'s are from $\mathcal{D}_s^{md}$, setting $\beta = \mathbb{S}_{d,k} s \sqrt{md}$ ensures both that an honest prover's proof will be accepted and also that the extracted randomness will satisfy the norm-bound as in Lemma 8.

Algorithm 2. Pseudo-witness-extraction

1: **Input:** a vector r; a challenge $x_0 \in \mathcal{C}$; an integer $k \geq 1$; a norm bound $\beta \in \mathbb{R}^+$
2: **for each** k-tuple $(x_1, \ldots, x_k) \in \mathcal{C}^k$ s.t. $x_0 \neq x_1 \neq \cdots \neq x_k$ **do**
3:    $r_{\text{p-ext}} = \left[\prod_{j=1}^{k} 2(x_0 - x_j)^{-1} \right] \cdot r$
4:    **if** $\|r_{\text{p-ext}}\| > \beta$ **then return** False
5: **end for**
6: **return** True

In Table 2, we provide a comparison between the three methods introduced.[6] As can be seen from the table, as k increases, the advantage of Methods 2 and 3 over Method 1 grows larger. There are also obvious patterns that can be observed from the table such as $\mathbb{S}_{d,k}/\mathbb{B}'_{d,k} \approx \sqrt{2}$ for any d and k. We leave the investigation of these behaviours as an open problem. For larger values of k, for which it is infeasible to search the whole space, one can use the theoretical bounds on the norm of a product of polynomials to upper-bound $\mathbb{B}_{d,k}$ (as $\mathbb{B}_{d,k}$ is an upperbound on the norm of a product of polynomials) and the theoretical bounds on the singular value of a product of matrices to upper-bound $\mathbb{S}_{d,k}$ (as $\mathbb{S}_{d,k}$ is an upperbound on the singular value of a product of matrices). These still give better results over Method 1.

Table 2. Comparison of Methods 1, 2 and 3. * indicates that only a subset of the whole search space has been iterated through.

	$k = 2$			$k = 3$			$k = 4$		
d	$\log(d^k)$	$\log(\mathbb{B}'_{d,k})$	$\log(\mathbb{S}_{d,k})$	$\log(d^k)$	$\log(\mathbb{B}'_{d,k})$	$\log(\mathbb{S}_{d,k})$	$\log(d^k)$	$\log(\mathbb{B}'_{d,k})$	$\log(\mathbb{S}_{d,k})$
32	10	9.21	8.70	15	12.55	12.05	20	15.90	15.40
64	12	11.21	10.70	18	15.55	15.05	24	19.90	19.40
128	14	13.21	12.70	21	18.55	18.05*	28	23.90*	23.40*

4 Σ-protocol for Commitment to a Sequence of Bits

In this section, we describe a lattice-based Σ-protocol showing that a commitment B opens to sequences of binary values where the Hamming weight of each sequence is exactly one. Let $N = \beta^k > 1$ and $r, \hat{r} \in R_q^m$, and define the relations to be proved in Definition 4.

Definition 4. *For positive real numbers T and $\hat{T}$, we define the following relations to be used in Protocol 1.*

---

[6] A more detailed table is available in the full version of the manuscript [14].

$$\mathcal{R}_{\mathrm{bin}}(\mathcal{T}) = \left\{ \begin{array}{c} ((ck, B), (b_{0,0}, \ldots, b_{k-1,\beta-1}, r)) \; : \; \|r\| \leq \mathcal{T} \; \wedge \; (b_{j,i} \in \{0,1\} \; \forall j, i) \\ \wedge \; B = \mathrm{Com}_{ck}(b_{0,0}, \ldots, b_{k-1,\beta-1} \; ; \; r) \; \wedge \; (\sum_{i=0}^{\beta-1} b_{j,i} = 1 \; \forall j) \end{array} \right\}.$$

$$\mathcal{R}'_{\mathrm{bin}}(\hat{\mathcal{T}}) = \left\{ \begin{array}{c} ((ck, B), (b_{0,0}, \ldots, b_{k-1,\beta-1}, \hat{r})) \; : \; \|\hat{r}\| \leq \hat{\mathcal{T}} \; \wedge \; (b_{j,i} \in \{0,1\} \; \forall j, i) \\ \wedge \; 2B = \mathrm{Com}_{ck}(2b_{0,0}, \ldots, 2b_{k-1,\beta-1} \; ; \; \hat{r}) \; \wedge \; (\sum_{i=0}^{\beta-1} b_{j,i} = 1 \; \forall j) \end{array} \right\}.$$

Remark 1. The conditions on the norms of r and $\hat{r}$ in the relations $\mathcal{R}_{\mathrm{bin}}$ and $\mathcal{R}'_{\mathrm{bin}}$ play a very crucial role, and is one of the main differences of a lattice-based zero-knowledge proof over its number-theoretic counterpart. Without that control, one cannot easily tie the security of the protocol to a hard lattice problem.

In the protocol, we first prove that each value in the sequences is binary, and then that the sum of each sequence equals one. This guarantees that there is only a single 1 in each sequence. The idea behind proving a value binary works as follows. Let b be the value we want to prove binary. Given a challenge x, the value b is multiplied by x and the resulting value is masked by a as $f = x \cdot b + a$ in the protocol (Step 10 in Protocol 1). Now observe that $f \cdot (x - f) = b(1 - b) \cdot x^2 + a(1 - 2b) \cdot x - a^2$ and proving that the coefficient of x^2 is zero implies that $b(1 - b) = 0$. Then, using Lemma 4, for a sufficiently large q, this statement over R_q implies that b is binary.

Similar to [5], we make use of an auxiliary commitment scheme aCom (which is assumed to be hiding and binding) in order to be able to simulate aborts in the proof of zero-knowledge property.[7] One can treat aCom as a random oracle. However, if aCom is computationally binding, then the soundness of the protocol holds under the respective assumption and similarly if it is computationally hiding [5]. The protocol is described in Protocol 1, which will later be used in the one-out-of-many proof. The parameters ϕ_1, ϕ_2 control the acceptance rate of two-step rejection sampling and can be adjusted as desired. The following summarizes the result of Protocol 1.

Theorem 1. *For* $T = (2d + 2) \left(5^4 \phi_1^4 d^3 k^3 \beta(\beta - 1) + 12\phi_2^2 \mathcal{B}^2 m^2 d^2\right)^{1/2}$, *assume that the commitment scheme is* T-*binding and also hiding (i.e.,* M-LWE$_{m-n,n,q,\mathcal{B}}$ *is hard). Let* $d \geq 7$, $md \geq 86$, *and* $q > (10\phi_1 d\sqrt{kd(\beta - 1)} + 2)^2$. *Then, Protocol 1 is a 3-special sound* Σ-*protocol (as in Definition 3) for relations* $\mathcal{R}_{\mathrm{bin}}(\mathcal{B}\sqrt{md})$ *and* $\mathcal{R}'_{\mathrm{bin}}(4\sqrt{2}\phi_2\mathcal{B}md^2)$ *with soundness error* $1/d$ *and a completeness error* $1 - 1/(\mu(\phi_1)\mu(\phi_2))$.

Remark 2. The way the rejection sampling is done in Protocol 1 allows us to sample $f_{j,i}$'s from a narrower distribution, and to make their norm smaller. This as a result weakens the condition on the size of q.

---

[7] In protocol's application to a ring signature (and for other applications in general), simulation of aborts is not needed as the protocol is made non-interactive.

$\mathcal{P}_{\mathrm{bin}}(ck, B, (\{b_{j,i}\}_{j,i=0}^{k-1,\beta-1}; \boldsymbol{r}))$	$\mathcal{V}_{\mathrm{bin}}(ck, B)$

1: $a_{0,1}, \ldots, a_{k-1,\beta-1} \leftarrow D_{\phi_1\sqrt{k}}^d$

2: $\boldsymbol{r}_c \leftarrow \{-\mathcal{B}, \ldots, \mathcal{B}\}^{md}$

3: $\boldsymbol{r}_a, \boldsymbol{r}_d \leftarrow D_{\phi_2\mathcal{B}\sqrt{2md}}^{md}$

4: **for** $j = 0, \ldots, k-1$ **do**

5: $\quad a_{j,0} = -\sum_{i=1}^{\beta-1} a_{j,i}$

6: $A = \mathrm{Com}_{ck}(a_{0,0}, \ldots, a_{k-1,\beta-1} \; ; \; \boldsymbol{r}_a)$

7: $C = \mathrm{Com}_{ck}(\{a_{j,i}(1 - 2b_{j,i})\}_{j,i=0}^{k-1,\beta-1} \; ; \; \boldsymbol{r}_c)$

8: $D = \mathrm{Com}_{ck}(-a_{0,0}^2, \ldots, -a_{k-1,\beta-1}^2 \; ; \; \boldsymbol{r}_d)$

9: $(c_a, d_a) = \mathrm{aCom}(A, C, D)$

$$\xrightarrow{\quad\quad c_a \quad\quad}$$

$$\xleftarrow{\quad x := X^\omega \quad} \quad \omega \leftarrow \{0, \ldots, 2d-1\}$$

10: $f_{j,i} = x \cdot b_{j,i} + a_{j,i} \; \forall j, \forall i \neq 0$

$\boldsymbol{f}_1 := (f_{0,1}, \ldots, f_{k-1,\beta-1}), \boldsymbol{b}_1 := (b_{0,1}, \ldots, b_{k-1,\beta-1})$

11: $\mathrm{Rej}(\boldsymbol{f}_1, x\boldsymbol{b}_1, \phi_1, \sqrt{k})$

12: $\boldsymbol{z}_b = x \cdot \boldsymbol{r} + \boldsymbol{r}_a$

13: $\boldsymbol{z}_c = x \cdot \boldsymbol{r}_c + \boldsymbol{r}_d$

14: $\mathrm{Rej}((\boldsymbol{z}_b, \boldsymbol{z}_c), x(\boldsymbol{r}, \boldsymbol{r}_c), \phi_2, \mathcal{B}\sqrt{2md})$

Return $\perp$ if aborted.

$$\xrightarrow{\begin{array}{c} f_{0,1}, \ldots, f_{k-1,\beta-1}, \\ d_a, A, C, D, \boldsymbol{z}_b, \boldsymbol{z}_c \end{array}}$$

1: **for** $j = 0, \ldots, k-1$ **do**

2: $\quad f_{j,0} = x - \sum_{i=1}^{\beta-1} f_{j,i}$

3: $(c_a, d_a) \stackrel{?}{=} \mathrm{aCom}(A, C, D)$

4: $\|f_{j,i}\| \stackrel{?}{\leq} 5\phi_1\sqrt{dk} \; \forall j, \forall i \neq 0$

5: $\|f_{j,0}\| \stackrel{?}{\leq} 5\phi_1\sqrt{dk(\beta-1)} \; \forall j$

6: $\|\boldsymbol{z}_b\|, \|\boldsymbol{z}_c\| \stackrel{?}{\leq} 2\sqrt{2}\phi_2\mathcal{B}md$

$\quad \boldsymbol{f} := (f_{0,0}, \ldots, f_{k-1,\beta-1})$

$\quad \boldsymbol{g} := \{f_{j,i}(x - f_{j,i})\}_{j,i=0}^{k-1,\beta-1}$

7: $xB + A \stackrel{?}{=} \mathrm{Com}_{ck}(\boldsymbol{f} \; ; \; \boldsymbol{z}_b)$

8: $xC + D \stackrel{?}{=} \mathrm{Com}_{ck}(\boldsymbol{g} \; ; \; \boldsymbol{z}_c)$

Protocol 1: Lattice-based Σ-protocol for $\mathcal{R}_{\mathrm{bin}}$ and $\mathcal{R}'_{\mathrm{bin}}$.

5   Lattice-Based One-out-of-Many Protocol

We are now ready to describe our main protocol. Let $\delta_{j,i}$ denote the Kronecker's delta such that $\delta_{j,i} = 1$ if $j = i$, and $\delta_{j,i} = 0$ otherwise. The prover's goal in the protocol is to show that he knows the randomness within a commitment to zero among a list of N commitments. (Note that the commitments other than the prover's need not be commitments to zero, i.e., there is no need to assume that they are well-formed). Similar to the previous works [7,15], we assume that the number of commitments satisfy $N = \beta^k$, which can be realised by using the same commitment multiple times until such an N is reached. Let c_ℓ be the prover's commitment for $0 \leq \ell \leq N - 1$, and $L = \{c_0, \ldots, c_{N-1}\}$ be the list of all commitments. The main idea is to prove knowledge of the index ℓ such that $\sum_{i=0}^{N-1} \delta_{\ell,i} c_i$ is a commitment to zero. Note that $\delta_{\ell,i} = \prod_{j=0}^{k-1} \delta_{\ell_j,i_j}$ where $\ell = (\ell_0, \ldots, \ell_{k-1})$ and $i = (i_0, \ldots, i_{k-1})$ are representations in base β. The relations for the protocol are given in Definition 5.

Definition 5. *For positive real numbers T and $\hat{T}$, we define the following relations to be used in Protocol 2.*

$$\mathcal{R}_{1/\mathrm{N}}(T) = \left\{ \begin{array}{l} ((ck, (c_0, \ldots, c_{N-1})), (\ell, r)) \; : \; (c_i \in R_q^n \; \forall i \in [0, N-1]) \wedge \\ \ell \in \{0, \ldots, N-1\} \wedge \|r\| \leq T \wedge c_\ell = \mathrm{Com}_{ck}(\mathbf{0} \; ; \; r) \end{array} \right\}.$$

$$\mathcal{R}'_{1/\mathrm{N}}(\hat{T}) = \left\{ \begin{array}{l} ((ck, (c_0, \ldots, c_{N-1})), (\ell, \hat{r})) \; : \; (c_i \in R_q^n \; \forall i \in [0, N-1]) \wedge \\ \ell \in \{0, \ldots, N-1\} \wedge \|\hat{r}\| \leq \hat{T} \wedge 2^k c_\ell = \mathrm{Com}_{ck}(\mathbf{0} \; ; \; \hat{r}) \end{array} \right\}.$$

For each $0 \leq j \leq k - 1$, the prover commits to a sequence $(\delta_{\ell_j, 0}, \ldots, \delta_{\ell_j, \beta - 1})$ and proves that it is a binary sequence with Hamming weight one using Protocol 1. As given in Protocol 1, the prover responds with $f_{j,i} = x \cdot \delta_{\ell_j, i} + a_{j,i}$ upon receiving a challenge x. Now, let us concentrate on the product $\prod_{j=0}^{k-1} f_{j, i_j} =: p_i(x)$. Observe that for all $i \in \{0, \ldots, N-1\}$,

$$p_i(x) = \prod_{j=0}^{k-1} \left(x\delta_{\ell_j, i_j} + a_{j, i_j} \right) = \prod_{j=0}^{k-1} x\delta_{\ell_j, i_j} + \sum_{j=0}^{k-1} p_{i,j} x^j = \delta_{\ell, i} x^k + \sum_{j=0}^{k-1} p_{i,j} x^j, \quad (8)$$

for some coefficients $p_{i,j}$'s depending on ℓ and $a_{j,i}$, which means that $p_{i,j}$'s can be computed by the prover before receiving a challenge. Now, since $\delta_{\ell,i} = 1$ if and only if $i = \ell$, the only p_i of degree k is p_ℓ. Then, the idea is to send some E_j's in the initial message, which will later be used by the verifier to cancel out the coefficients of low order terms $1, x, \ldots, x^{k-1}$, and the coefficient of x^k will be $\sum_{i=0}^{N-1} \delta_{\ell,i} c_i = c_\ell$, which corresponds to the prover's commitment. The full protocol is described in Protocol 2. We summarize the results of Protocol 2 below.

Theorem 2. *For $T = (2d + 2) \left(5^4 \phi_1^4 d^3 k^3 \beta(\beta - 1) + 12\phi_2^2 \mathcal{B}^2 m^2 d^2\right)^{1/2}$, assume that the commitment scheme is T-binding and also hiding (i.e., M-LWE$_{m-n,n,q,\mathcal{B}}$ is hard). Let $d \geq 7$, $md \geq 86$, and $q > (10\phi_1 d\sqrt{dk(\beta - 1)} + 2)^2$. Then, Protocol 2 is a $(k' + 1)$-special sound Σ-protocol (as in Definition 3) for the relations*

$\mathcal{R}_{1/N}(\mathcal{B}\sqrt{md})$ and $\mathcal{R}'_{1/N}(2\sqrt{3}\phi_2\mathcal{B}md \cdot (k+1) \cdot d^k)$ with a soundness error $\frac{k'}{2d}$ and a completeness error $1 - 1/(\mu(\phi_1)\mu(\phi_2))$ where $k' = \max\{2, k\}$.

Proof (Theorem 2). Completeness and SHVZK are available in the full version.
$(k'+1)$-**special soundness:** Given $(k+1)$ distinct challenges $x_0, \ldots, x_k$, by the binding property of aCom, we have $(k + 1)$ accepting responses with the same $(A, B, C, D, \{E_j\})$. Suppose that $((f_{j,i}^{(0)}, z^{(0)}), \ldots, (f_{j,i}^{(k)}, z^{(k)}))$ are produced and $k > 1$. We first use 3-special soundness of Protocol 1 to extract openings $\hat{b}_{j,i}$ and $\hat{a}_{j,i}$ of $2B$ and $2A$, respectively. We can also obtain $b_{j,i}$ such that $\hat{b}_{j,i} = 2b_{j,i}$, and it is guaranteed that $b_{j,i} \in \{0, 1\}$ and $\sum_{i=0}^{\beta-1} b_{j,i} = 1$. From here, we can obtain the digits ℓ_j by choosing $\ell_j = i^*$ for which $b_{j,i^*} = 1$. Then, we construct the index ℓ as $\ell = \sum_{j=0}^{k-1} \beta^j \ell_j$.

Using $b_{j,i}$ and $\hat{a}_{j,i}$, we can compute $\hat{p}_i(x) = 2^k \prod_{j=0}^{k-1} f_{j,i_j} = \prod_{j=0}^{k-1} 2f_{j,i_j} = \prod_{j=0}^{k-1}(x \cdot 2b_{j,i_j} + \hat{a}_{j,i_j})$. Note that $\hat{p}_\ell(x)$ is the only such polynomial of degree k in x by the construction of ℓ. Thus, the last verification step, when both sides are multiplied by 2^k, can be rewritten as $\sum_{i=0}^{N-1} \hat{p}_i(x)c_i - \sum_{j=0}^{k-1} 2^k E_j x^j = \text{Com}_{ck}(\mathbf{0} \; ; \; 2^k \mathbf{z})$. Separating the term of degree k with respect to x, we get

$$x^k \cdot 2^k c_\ell + \sum_{j=0}^{k-1} \tilde{E}_j x^j = \text{Com}_{ck}(\mathbf{0} \; ; \; 2^k \mathbf{z}), \qquad (9)$$

where $\tilde{E}_j$'s are the coefficients of the monomials x^j of degree strictly less than k. Now, we know that (9) holds for distinct challenges $x_0, \ldots, x_k$, which can be represented as a system of equations where $x_0, \ldots, x_k$ form a Vandermonde matrix $\mathbf{V}$ as in Sect. 3.2. From the discussion in Sect. 3.2, $\mathbf{V}$ is invertible and we can obtain a linear combination $\alpha_0, \ldots, \alpha_k$ of copies of (9) with respect to different challenges that produces the vector $(0, \ldots, 0, 1)$. This gives

$$2^k c_\ell = \sum_{e=0}^{k} \alpha_e \left(x_e^k \cdot 2^k c_\ell + \sum_{j=0}^{k-1} \tilde{E}_j x_e^j \right) = \text{Com}_{ck}(\mathbf{0} \; ; \; 2^k \sum_{e=0}^{k} \alpha_e \mathbf{z}^{(e)}). \quad (10)$$

An opening of $2^k c_\ell$ to the message $\mathbf{0}$ with randomness $\mathbf{r}_{\text{ext}} = 2^k \sum_{e=0}^{k} \alpha_e \mathbf{z}^{(e)}$ is obtained. The bound on the norm of $\mathbf{r}_{\text{ext}}$ for $\mathcal{R}'_{1/N}$ follows easily by Lemma 6.

Finally, we assumed that $k > 1$. If $k = 1$, then we still need at least 3 challenges to be able to prove special soundness due to the 3-special soundness of Protocol 1. Thus, Protocol 2 is $(k'+1)$-special sound for $k' = \max\{2, k\}$, and since $|\mathcal{C}| = 2d$, the soundness error is $k'/2d$. $\qquad \square$

It is easy to see from the definition of $\mathcal{R}'_{1/N}$ that the norm of the extracted randomness, and thus the size of q, grows with $d^k = d^{\log_\beta N}$. If one is to rely on Ring-SIS and use a base $\beta = 2$, then this growth would be very rapid, yielding a very inefficient scheme. This justifies our choice of working with M-SIS problem and choosing large base values β as given in Sect. 6.1. As discussed in Sect. 3.2, the bound on $\|\mathbf{r}_{\text{ext}}\|$ can be tightened using Methods 2 or 3.

$\mathcal{P}(ck, (c_0, \ldots, c_{N-1}), (\ell, \boldsymbol{r}))$	$\mathcal{V}(ck, (c_0, \ldots, c_{N-1}))$

1: $\boldsymbol{r}_b \leftarrow \{-\mathcal{B}, \ldots, \mathcal{B}\}^{md}$

2: $\boldsymbol{\delta} = (\delta_{\ell_0,0}, \ldots, \delta_{\ell_{k-1},\beta-1})$

3: $B = \mathrm{Com}_{ck}(\boldsymbol{\delta} \; ; \; \boldsymbol{r}_b)$

4: $A, C, D, \boldsymbol{r}_c \leftarrow \mathcal{P}_{\mathrm{bin}}(ck, B, (\boldsymbol{\delta}, \boldsymbol{r}_b))[1-8]$

5: **for** $j = 0, \ldots, k-1$ **do**

6: $\quad \boldsymbol{\rho}_j \leftarrow D^{md}_{\phi_2 \mathcal{B}\sqrt{3md/k}}$

7: $\quad E_j = \displaystyle\sum_{i=0}^{N-1} p_{i,j} c_i + \mathrm{Com}_{ck}(\boldsymbol{0} \; ; \; \boldsymbol{\rho}_j)$

using $p_{i,j}$'s from (8)

8: $(c_a, d_a) = a\mathrm{Com}(A, B, C, D, \{E_j\})$

$$\xrightarrow{\quad\quad c_a \quad\quad}$$

$$\xleftarrow{\quad x = X^\omega \quad} \quad \omega \leftarrow \{0, \ldots, 2d-1\}$$

9: $\boldsymbol{f}_1, \boldsymbol{z}_b, \boldsymbol{z}_c \leftarrow \mathcal{P}_{\mathrm{bin}}(x)[10-13]$

10: $\boldsymbol{z} = x^k \cdot \boldsymbol{r} - \displaystyle\sum_{j=0}^{k-1} x^j \cdot \boldsymbol{\rho}_j$

11: $\mathrm{Rej}((\boldsymbol{z}, \boldsymbol{z}_b, \boldsymbol{z}_c), (x^k \boldsymbol{r}, x\boldsymbol{r}_b, x\boldsymbol{r}_c), \phi_2, \mathcal{B}\sqrt{3md})$

Return $\perp$ if aborted.

$$\xrightarrow{\quad d_a, \boldsymbol{f}_1, B, \boldsymbol{z}, \{E_j\}_{j=0}^{k-1} \quad} \\ \boldsymbol{R} := (A, C, D, \boldsymbol{z}_b, \boldsymbol{z}_c)$$

1: $\mathcal{V}_{\mathrm{bin}}(ck, B, x, \boldsymbol{f}_1, \boldsymbol{R})[1,2,6,7] \overset{?}{=} 1$

2: $(c_a, d_a) \overset{?}{=} a\mathrm{Com}(A, B, C, D, \{E_j\})$

3: $\|f_{j,i}\| \overset{?}{\leq} 5\phi_1\sqrt{dk} \quad \forall j, \forall i \neq 0$

4: $\|f_{j,0}\| \overset{?}{\leq} 5\phi_1\sqrt{dk(\beta-1)} \quad \forall j$

5: $\|\boldsymbol{z}\|, \|\boldsymbol{z}_b\|, \|\boldsymbol{z}_c\| \overset{?}{\leq} 2\sqrt{3}\phi_2 \mathcal{B}md$

6: $\displaystyle\sum_{i=0}^{N-1} \left(\prod_{j=0}^{k-1} f_{j,i_j} \right) c_i - \sum_{j=0}^{k-1} E_j x^j$
$$\overset{?}{=} \mathrm{Com}_{ck}(\boldsymbol{0} \; ; \; \boldsymbol{z})$$
for $i = (i_0, \ldots, i_{k-1})$.

Protocol 2: Lattice-based Σ-protocol for $\mathcal{R}_{1/\mathrm{N}}$ and $\mathcal{R}'_{1/\mathrm{N}}$.

$\mathcal{P}_{\mathrm{bin}}(ck, B, (\boldsymbol{\delta}, \boldsymbol{r}_b))[1-8]$ denotes running the same steps from 1 to 8 done by $\mathcal{P}_{\mathrm{bin}}$ in Protocol 1. Similar notation is used for $\mathcal{V}_{\mathrm{bin}}$. $\boldsymbol{r}_a$ and $\boldsymbol{r}_d$ in $\mathcal{P}_{\mathrm{bin}}(ck, B, (\boldsymbol{\delta}, \boldsymbol{r}_b))[1-8]$ are drawn from $D^{md}_{\phi_2 \mathcal{B}\sqrt{3md}}$ instead of $D^{md}_{\phi_2 \mathcal{B}\sqrt{2md}}$ as the rejection sampling is now done on a $(3md)$-dimensional vector.

6   Lattice-Based Ring Signature

Let $N = \beta^k$ for $2 \leq \beta \leq N$, and n, m be fixed positive integers. As a single run of Protocol 2 does not provide a small enough soundness error, suppose that r non-aborting executions of Protocol 2 gives negligible soundness error of $2^{-\lambda}$.

Recall that a single run of Protocol 2 produces an accepting transcript with probability $1/(\mu(\phi_1)\mu(\phi_2))$. Therefore, when it is repeated r times, the overall acceptance rate reduces to $1/(\mu(\phi_1)\mu(\phi_2))^r$, which is too small. Therefore, we introduce the tweaks below to Protocol 2 in order to get an overall completeness error of $1 - 1/(\mu(\phi_1)\mu(\phi_2))$ for the r-repeated protocol.

Tweaks for r-repeated Protocol. First, we apply the rejection sampling to r-concatenated vectors at once. That is, it is applied on $(\boldsymbol{f}_1^1, \ldots, \boldsymbol{f}_1^r)$ and $(\boldsymbol{z}^1, \boldsymbol{z}_b^1, \boldsymbol{z}_c^1, \ldots, \boldsymbol{z}^r, \boldsymbol{z}_b^r, \boldsymbol{z}_c^r)$. Thus, we need to sample $f_{j,i} \leftarrow D_{12\sqrt{kr}}^d$ $(i \neq 0)$ and $\boldsymbol{z}, \boldsymbol{z}_b, \boldsymbol{z}_c \leftarrow D_{12\mathcal{B}\sqrt{3mdr}}^{md}$, and hence require $q > (10\phi_1 d\sqrt{dkr(\beta - 1)} + 2)^2$ as in Assumption 1. Furthermore, since the extracted randomness norm will be larger, the relation $\mathcal{R}_{1/N}'$ becomes $\mathcal{R}_{1/N}'(24\sqrt{3}r\mathcal{B}md \cdot (k + 1) \cdot d^k)$ and the commitment scheme is required to be binding in a larger domain. Therefore, the commitment scheme is set to be T_1-binding for $T_1 = (2d + 2)\left(5^4\phi_1^4 d^3 k^3 \beta(\beta - 1)r^2 + 12\phi_2^2\mathcal{B}^2 m^2 d^2 r\right)^{1/2}$.

Note that these tweaks do not affect the soundness error of individual protocol runs as the extraction still works with $k + 1$ accepting transcripts. Only the extracted witness norm is increased since the bound on $\|\boldsymbol{z}\|$ changes from $24\sqrt{3}\mathcal{B}md$ to $24\sqrt{3r}\mathcal{B}md$ in Protocol 2.

Construction. We now describe our lattice-based ring signature, which similarly builds on the one-out-of-many proof as in [7,15]. First, we summarise the assumptions on the parameters, and also let $CMT = (A, B, C, D, \{E_j\}_{j=0}^{k-1})$ and $RSP = (\{f_{j,i}\}_{j=0,i=1}^{k-1,\beta-1}, \boldsymbol{z}, \boldsymbol{z}_b, \boldsymbol{z}_c)$ be the corresponding values from Protocol 2.

Assumption 1. *Assume $d \geq 7$, $md \geq 86$ and $q > (10\phi_1 d\sqrt{dkr(\beta - 1)} + 2)^2$.*

- **RSetup(1^λ):** Run $\boldsymbol{G} \leftarrow \mathsf{CKeygen}(1^\lambda)$ and pick a hash function $H : \{0,1\}^* \to \mathcal{C}^r$ for $\mathcal{C} = \{X^\omega : \omega \in [0, 2d - 1]\}$. Return $ck = \boldsymbol{G}$ and H as $pp = (ck, H)$.
- **RKeygen(pp):** Run $\boldsymbol{r} \leftarrow S_\mathcal{B}^m$, $c = \mathsf{Com}_{ck}(\boldsymbol{0} \; ; \; \boldsymbol{r})$ and return $(pk, sk) = (c, \boldsymbol{r})$.
- **RSign$_{pp,sk}(\mathcal{M}, L)$:** Parse $L = (c_0, \ldots, c_{N-1})$ with $c_\ell = \mathsf{Com}_{ck}(\boldsymbol{0} \; ; \; sk)$ where $\ell \in \{0, \ldots, N - 1\}$. Continue as follows.
  1. Generate $(CMT_1, \ldots, CMT_r)$ by running $\mathcal{P}(ck, (c_0, \ldots, c_{N-1}), (\ell, sk))[1 - 7]$ r-times in parallel with the described modifications.
  2. Compute $\boldsymbol{x} = (x_1, \ldots, x_r) = H(ck, \mathcal{M}, L, (CMT_1, \ldots, CMT_r))$.
  3. Compute RSP_i by running $\mathcal{P}(x_i)[9 - 11]$ with CMT_i for all $i \in \{1, \ldots, r\}$.
  4. If $RSP_i \neq\, \perp$ for all $i \in \{1, \ldots, r\}$, return $\sigma = (\{CMT_i\}_{i=1}^r, \boldsymbol{x}, \{RSP_i\}_{i=1}^r)$.
  2. Otherwise go to Step 1.
- **RVerify$_{pp}(\mathcal{M}, L, \sigma)$:** Parse $\sigma = (\{CMT_i\}_{i=1}^r, \boldsymbol{x}, \{RSP_i\}_{i=1}^r)$, $\boldsymbol{x} = (x_1, \ldots, x_r)$ and $L = (c_0, \ldots, c_{N-1})$. Proceed as follows.

1. If $x \neq H(ck, \mathcal{M}, L, (CMT_1, \ldots, CMT_r))$, return 0.
2. For each $i \in \{1, \ldots, r\}$:
   (a) Run Protocol 2's verification with CMT_i, x_i and RSP_i except Step 2.
   (b) If verification fails, return 0.
3. Return 1.

We can remove A, D, E_0 from the signature as they are uniquely determined by the remaining components, and Step 1 in **RVerify** ensures the relevant protocol verification steps hold. This is a standard technique and we skip the details.

The correctness and anonymity properties of the ring signature follow from the completeness and zero-knowledge properties of Protocol 2, respectively. In particular, the expected number of iterations in **RSign** is $\mu(\phi_1)\mu(\phi_2)$, which is upper-bounded by 3 in the parameter setting. However, the unforgeability proof of the ring signature is not straightforward due to the small challenge space and soundness gap issues. A detailed proof is available in the full version [14].

Theorem 3. *If Assumption 1 holds and the commitment scheme defined in Sect. 2.1 is T'-binding where $T' = \max\{T_1, \sqrt{(24\sqrt{3r} \cdot m\mathcal{B}(k+1)d^{k+1})^2 + 2^{2k}}\}$ for T_1 described with the tweaks, then the ring signature scheme described is unforgeable with respect to insider corruption in the random oracle model.*

6.1   Parameter Setting

First, we set $\phi_1 = \phi_2 = 22$ to get an acceptance rate of more than $1/3$ for the two-step rejection sampling. Such an acceptance rate is greater than or equal to the most commonly used ones such as those in [3,4,12,21] and the expected number of iterations in **RSign** is 3 in this case. Also, we ensure that the commitment scheme T'-binding as in Theorem 3. Method 2 is used to bound the extracted witness norm, which does not require the use of Algorithm 2 in the protocol's verification. For (d, k) pairs in Table 3, the exact value of $\mathbb{B}_{d,k}$ is computed by

Table 3. Parameters and sizes of our lattice-based ring signature for a root Hermite factor $\delta \leq 1.0045$. The signature sizes are rounded to the nearest integer.

N	64	256	1024	4096	$\sim 2^{16}$	$\sim 2^{20}$	2^{30}
(n, m)	$(5, 13)$	$(5, 13)$	$(11, 25)$	$(21, 50)$	$(20, 51)$	$(40, 101)$	$(41, 106)$
$(d, \log q)$	$(256, 50)$	$(256, 53)$	$(128, 46)$	$(64, 47)$	$(64, 50)$	$(32, 49)$	$(32, 52)$
(k, β)	$(2, 8)$	$(2, 16)$	$(2, 32)$	$(2, 64)$	$(3, 41)$	$(3, 102)$	$(5, 64)$
r	16	16	19	22	24	29	35
λ	128.0	128.0	133.0	132.0	129.96	128.04	128.73
Signature size (KB)	774	881	1021	1178	1487	1862	3006
User PK size (KB)	7.81	8.28	7.91	7.71	7.81	7.66	8.33
User SK size (KB)	0.81	0.81	0.78	0.78	0.80	0.79	0.83

iterating through the whole search space. We also set $\mathcal{B} = 1$ as in previous works [3,13,22], and make sure that M-LWE$_{m-n,n,q,1}$ is hard using Albrecht et al.'s estimator [2]. The root Hermite factor δ is at most 1.0045 for both M-SIS and M-LWE security estimations. Finally, Assumption 1 is ensured to hold.

Acknowledgements. The work of Ron Steinfeld and Amin Sakzad was supported in part by ARC grant DP150100285. Ron Steinfeld and Joseph K. Liu were also supported in part by ARC grant DP180102199.

References

1. Agrawal, S., Gentry, C., Halevi, S., Sahai, A.: Discrete Gaussian leftover hash lemma over infinite domains. In: Sako, K., Sarkar, P. (eds.) ASIACRYPT 2013. LNCS, vol. 8269, pp. 97–116. Springer, Heidelberg (2013). https://doi.org/10.1007/978-3-642-42033-7_6
2. Albrecht, M.R., Player, R., Scott, S.: On the concrete hardness of learning with errors. J. Math. Cryptol. **9**(3), 169–203 (2015)
3. Baum, C., Damgård, I., Lyubashevsky, V., Oechsner, S., Peikert, C.: More efficient commitments from structured lattice assumptions. In: Catalano, D., De Prisco, R. (eds.) SCN 2018. LNCS, vol. 11035, pp. 368–385. Springer, Cham (2018). https://doi.org/10.1007/978-3-319-98113-0_20
4. Baum, C., Lin, H., Oechsner, S.: Towards practical lattice-based one-time linkable ring signatures. In: Naccache, D., et al. (eds.) ICICS 2018. LNCS, vol. 11149, pp. 303–322. Springer, Cham (2018). https://doi.org/10.1007/978-3-030-01950-1_18
5. Benhamouda, F., Camenisch, J., Krenn, S., Lyubashevsky, V., Neven, G.: Better zero-knowledge proofs for lattice encryption and their application to group signatures. In: Sarkar, P., Iwata, T. (eds.) ASIACRYPT 2014. LNCS, vol. 8873, pp. 551–572. Springer, Heidelberg (2014). https://doi.org/10.1007/978-3-662-45611-8_29
6. Benhamouda, F., Krenn, S., Lyubashevsky, V., Pietrzak, K.: Efficient zero-knowledge proofs for commitments from learning with errors over rings. In: Pernul, G., Ryan, P.Y.A., Weippl, E. (eds.) ESORICS 2015. LNCS, vol. 9326, pp. 305–325. Springer, Cham (2015). https://doi.org/10.1007/978-3-319-24174-6_16
7. Bootle, J., Cerulli, A., Chaidos, P., Ghadafi, E., Groth, J., Petit, C.: Short accountable ring signatures based on DDH. In: Pernul, G., Ryan, P.Y.A., Weippl, E. (eds.) ESORICS 2015. LNCS, vol. 9326, pp. 243–265. Springer, Cham (2015). https://doi.org/10.1007/978-3-319-24174-6_13
8. Bootle, J., Cerulli, A., Chaidos, P., Groth, J., Petit, C.: Efficient zero-knowledge arguments for arithmetic circuits in the discrete log setting. In: Fischlin, M., Coron, J.-S. (eds.) EUROCRYPT 2016. LNCS, vol. 9666, pp. 327–357. Springer, Heidelberg (2016). https://doi.org/10.1007/978-3-662-49896-5_12
9. Brickell, E., Pointcheval, D., Vaudenay, S., Yung, M.: Design validations for discrete logarithm based signature schemes. In: Imai, H., Zheng, Y. (eds.) PKC 2000. LNCS, vol. 1751, pp. 276–292. Springer, Heidelberg (2000). https://doi.org/10.1007/978-3-540-46588-1_19
10. Bünz, B., Bootle, J., Boneh, D., Poelstra, A., Wuille, P., Maxwell, G.: Bulletproofs: short proofs for confidential transactions and more. In: S&P. IEEE (2018)
11. Chow, S.S.M., Liu, J.K., Wong, D.S.: Robust receipt-free election system with ballot secrecy and verifiability. In: NDSS. The Internet Society (2008)

12. del Pino, R., Lyubashevsky, V., Neven, G., Seiler, G.: Practical quantum-safe voting from lattices. In: CCS, pp. 1565–1581. ACM (2017)
13. del Pino, R., Lyubashevsky, V., Seiler, G.: Lattice-based group signatures and zero-knowledge proofs of automorphism stability. In: CCS, pp. 574–591. ACM (2018)
14. Esgin, M.F., Steinfeld, R., Sakzad, A., Liu, J.K., Liu, D.: Short lattice-based one-out-of-many proofs and applications to ring signatures. Cryptology ePrint Archive, Report 2018/773 (2018). https://eprint.iacr.org/2018/773
15. Groth, J., Kohlweiss, M.: One-out-of-many proofs: or how to leak a secret and spend a coin. In: Oswald, E., Fischlin, M. (eds.) EUROCRYPT 2015. LNCS, vol. 9057, pp. 253–280. Springer, Heidelberg (2015). https://doi.org/10.1007/978-3-662-46803-6_9
16. Langlois, A., Stehlé, D.: Worst-case to average-case reductions for module lattices. Des. Codes Crypt. **75**(3), 565–599 (2015)
17. Libert, B., Ling, S., Mouhartem, F., Nguyen, K., Wang, H.: Signature schemes with efficient protocols and dynamic group signatures from lattice assumptions. In: Cheon, J.H., Takagi, T. (eds.) ASIACRYPT 2016. LNCS, vol. 10032, pp. 373–403. Springer, Heidelberg (2016). https://doi.org/10.1007/978-3-662-53890-6_13
18. Libert, B., Ling, S., Nguyen, K., Wang, H.: Zero-knowledge arguments for lattice-based accumulators: logarithmic-size ring signatures and group signatures without trapdoors. In: Fischlin, M., Coron, J.-S. (eds.) EUROCRYPT 2016. LNCS, vol. 9666, pp. 1–31. Springer, Heidelberg (2016). https://doi.org/10.1007/978-3-662-49896-5_1
19. Ling, S., Nguyen, K., Wang, H., Xu, Y.: Lattice-based group signatures: achieving full dynamicity with ease. In: Gollmann, D., Miyaji, A., Kikuchi, H. (eds.) ACNS 2017. LNCS, vol. 10355, pp. 293–312. Springer, Cham (2017). https://doi.org/10.1007/978-3-319-61204-1_15
20. Liu, J.K., Wei, V.K., Wong, D.S.: Linkable spontaneous anonymous group signature for ad hoc groups. In: Wang, H., Pieprzyk, J., Varadharajan, V. (eds.) ACISP 2004. LNCS, vol. 3108, pp. 325–335. Springer, Heidelberg (2004). https://doi.org/10.1007/978-3-540-27800-9_28
21. Lyubashevsky, V.: Lattice signatures without trapdoors. In: Pointcheval, D., Johansson, T. (eds.) EUROCRYPT 2012. LNCS, vol. 7237, pp. 738–755. Springer, Heidelberg (2012). https://doi.org/10.1007/978-3-642-29011-4_43
22. Lyubashevsky, V., Neven, G.: One-shot verifiable encryption from lattices. In: Coron, J.-S., Nielsen, J.B. (eds.) EUROCRYPT 2017. LNCS, vol. 10210, pp. 293–323. Springer, Cham (2017). https://doi.org/10.1007/978-3-319-56620-7_11
23. Micciancio, D., Regev, O.: Worst-case to average-case reductions based on Gaussian measures. SIAM J. Comput. **37**(1), 267–302 (2007). Preliminary version in FOCS 2004
24. Noether, S.: Ring signature confidential transactions for monero. Cryptology ePrint Archive, Report 2015/1098 (2015). https://eprint.iacr.org/2015/1098
25. Stern, J.: A new paradigm for public key identification. IEEE Trans. Inf. Theory **42**(6), 1757–1768 (1996)
26. Sun, S.-F., Au, M.H., Liu, J.K., Yuen, T.H.: RingCT 2.0: a compact accumulator-based (linkable ring signature) protocol for blockchain cryptocurrency Monero. In: Foley, S.N., Gollmann, D., Snekkenes, E. (eds.) ESORICS 2017. LNCS, vol. 10493, pp. 456–474. Springer, Cham (2017). https://doi.org/10.1007/978-3-319-66399-9_25

27. Alberto Torres, W.A., et al.: Post-quantum one-time linkable ring signature and application to ring confidential transactions in blockchain (lattice ringCT v1.0). In: Susilo, W., Yang, G. (eds.) ACISP 2018. LNCS, vol. 10946, pp. 558–576. Springer, Cham (2018). https://doi.org/10.1007/978-3-319-93638-3_32

28. Turner, L.R.: Inverse of the Vandermonde matrix with applications. Technical report NASA-TN-D-3547, Lewis Research Center, NASA (1966)

29. Zhang, H., Zhang, F., Tian, H., Au, M.H.: Anonymous post-quantum cryptocash. Cryptology ePrint Archive, Report 2017/716 (2017). https://eprint.iacr.org/2017/716 (To appear in FC 2018)

Hierarchical Attribute-Based Signatures: Short Keys and Optimal Signature Length

Daniel Gardham$^{(\boxtimes)}$ and Mark Manulis

Surrey Centre for Cyber Security, University of Surrey, Guildford, UK
d.gardham@surrey.ac.uk, mark@manulis.eu

Abstract. With Attribute-based Signatures (ABS) users can simultaneously sign messages and prove compliance of their attributes, issued by designated attribute authorities, with some verification policy. Neither signer's identity nor possessed attributes are leaked during the verification process, making ABS schemes a handy tool for applications requiring privacy-preserving authentication. Earlier ABS schemes lacked support for hierarchical delegation of attributes (across tiers of attribute authorities down to the signers), a distinct property that has made traditional PKIs more scalable and widely adoptable.

This changed recently with the introduction of Hierarchical ABS (HABS) schemes, where support for attribute delegation was proposed in combination with stronger privacy guarantees for the delegation paths (path anonymity) and new accountability mechanisms allowing a dedicated tracing authority to identify these paths (path traceability) and the signer, along with delegated attributes, if needed. Yet, current HABS construction is generic with inefficient delegation process resulting in suboptimal signature lengths of order $O(k^2|\Psi|)$ where Ψ is the policy size and k the height of the hierarchy.

This paper proposes a direct HABS construction in bilinear groups that significantly improves on these bounds and satisfies the original security and privacy requirements. At the core of our HABS scheme is a new delegation process based on the length-reducing homomorphic trapdoor commitments to group elements for which we introduce a new delegation technique allowing step-wise commitments to additional elements without changing the length of the original commitment and its opening. While also being of independent interest, this technique results in shorter HABS keys and achieves the signature-length growth of $O(k|\Psi|)$ which is optimal due to the path-traceability requirement.

1 Introduction

Attribute-based Signatures, first introduced in [30] and [31], provide privacy-preserving mechanisms for authenticating messages. An ABS signature assures the verifier that the signer owns a set of attributes that satisfy the signing policy without leaking their identity, nor the set of attributes used. Traditional

© Springer Nature Switzerland AG 2019
R. H. Deng et al. (Eds.): ACNS 2019, LNCS 11464, pp. 89–109, 2019.
https://doi.org/10.1007/978-3-030-21568-2_5

ABS schemes considered two security properties, user privacy and unforgeability. Informally, a user is anonymous if an ABS signature does not leak their identity, nor the set of attributes used to satisfy the signing policy, while unforgeability requires that a signer cannot produce a signature conforming to a policy for which he does not own a set of suitable attributes. Later constructions [14,16,20] offered more advanced functionality with an additional property of traceability which holds signers accountable by allowing a dedicated tracing authority to identity them if required.

The vast majority of existing ABS schemes [5,13,14,16,20,32,33,35] are non-interactive, in the standard model and is based on bilinear maps and Groth-Sahai proofs [21], with the exception of [23], which uses RSA setting and the random oracle model, and the recent schemes in [15,38] which rely on lattices. Interactive ABS schemes, e.g. [27], where policies must be chosen by verifiers ahead of the signing phase have also been proposed. In general, signing polices can have varying levels of flexibility and range from threshold policies [30], to monotone boolean predicates [14,20], and generalised circuits [35]. Typically, more restrictive policies allow for more efficient constructions. Policy-based Signatures (PBS) [5] can be viewed as a generalisation of ABS schemes, albeit their security is currently proven in a single-user setting without addressing stronger non-frameability requirement of more recent ABS schemes [12,14,20].

Hierarchical Attribute-Based Signature and Their Limitations. Hierarchical Attribute-based Signatures (HABS), recently introduced in [12], extend traditional ABS schemes by permitting controlled delegation of attributes from a root authority (RA) over possibly multiple intermediate authorities (IAs) down to the users. In this way HABS aims to close the gap between ABS and traditional PKIs where hierarchical delegation can be achieved at low cost. In HABS, IAs can delegate attributes to any authority in the scheme and users can acquire attributes from any authority in the hierarchy that is authorised to issue them. In addition to strong non-frameability property in a multi-user setting, the authors extend traditional ABS privacy guarantees to protect not only the identity of the signer but also the identities of all intermediate authorities in the delegation path, as part of their new path-anonymity property. Traditional traceability property of ABS schemes has also been extended to hold not only signers but also intermediate authorities accountable for their actions, through the new notion of path-traceability where a dedicated tracing authority can reveal the entire delegation path, along with delegated attributes.

We observe that the HABS scheme in [12] is generic, based on standard cryptographic primitives, i.e., public key encryption, one-time signature, tag-based signature, and non-interactive zero-knowledge proofs. Its delegation process is handled using a tag-based signature (TBS) where an authority at level i produces a TBS signature, using attribute as a tag, on the public key of authority j together with all public keys appearing previously in the delegation path. As part of its HABS signature the signer proves knowledge of each TBS at every delegation of each attribute that is required to satisfy the policy. Clearly this delegation process is highly inefficient. Not only does an additional signature need to be verified per delegation (and per attribute), the size of the signature grows linearly in the distance from the root authority. Thus, per attribute, verification of the delegation path is of order $O(k^2)$.

Other Related Work. Attribute-based signatures can be seen as a generalisation of group [11] and ring [34] signatures, in which case identities are viewed as attributes and policies can only contain disjunction over them. The notion of hierarchical delegation in these, more restricted, primitives have been explored in [37] and [29] respectively. Attribute delegation has been widely investigated in anonymous credentials [9, 10]. Maji et al. [31] give discussion that ACs are a more powerful primitive than ABS but with efficiency drawbacks, as attribute acquisition typically requires expensive zero-knowledge proofs. Note that in HABS intermediate authorities may know each other, and so as discussed in [12], there is no need to hide their identities from each other during the delegation phase, which in turn helps to omit costly proofs and make this phase more efficient than in the case of ACs. Regardless, we note that ACs with hierarchical delegation have been proposed [4]. Further, a homomorphic ABS scheme [25] has been used to construct non-delegatable anonymous credentials. In this setting, a signer obtains attributes directly from the (multiple) root authorities where combining attributes from different issuers requires an online collaboration. Anonymous Proxy Signatures [17] also allow for verification of anonymous delegation paths back to a root authority. However, tasks that are delegated, when viewed as attributes, remain in the clear and are required for verification of the proxy signature. Homomorphic Signatures [38] have been claimed to be equivalent to Attribute-based Signatures, however this equality has been shown to hold in the weaker security setting that only considers a solitary user. In which, it is impossible to capture the notion of collusion and non-frameability. Finally, we note functional signatures [3, 8] also allow for delegation of signing rights. Here, however, keys are dependent on the function f and can only sign on messages that fall within the range. For an attribute-based scheme, this would require keys for each possible combination of attributes a user obtains.

Contribution. We address the suboptimal efficiency of the so-far only (generic) HABS construction [12] and propose a scheme with a completely new delegation mechanism which no longer relies on the consecutive issue of tag-based signatures from higher-level to lower-level authorities on the delegation path. The main novelty in our approach is a smart use of the length-reducing homomorphic trapdoor commitment scheme to multiple group elements from [21] which we extend with delegation capabilities. At a high level, at each delegation the issuing intermediate authority amends the current trapdoor opening such that the existing commitment incorporates the public key of the next-level authority or user to whom the attribute is delegated. With this new delegation mechanism we are able to significantly reduce the lengths of HABS keys and achieve the optimal growth of $O(k|\Psi|)$ for the length of HABS signatures, depending on the length k of the delegation path and size $|\Psi|$ of the signing policy. In particular, verifying delegation of an attribute along the path takes $O(k)$ steps (as opposed to $O(k^2)$ in [12]). We use the original security model from [12] to show that our construction satisfies the required properties of path anonymity, path traceability, and non-frameability, in the standard model under standard assumptions in bilinear groups and an additional assumption which we justify using the generic group model [36]. Our efficiency improvement claims over [12] are reinforced in a detailed comparison between the two schemes.

2 HABS Model: Entities and Definitions

We start with the description of entities within the HABS ecosystem.

Attribute Authorities. The set of Attribute Authorities (AA) comprises the Root Authority (RA) and Intermediate Authorities (IAs). All AAs can delegate attributes to lower-level IAs and users. The RA is at the top of the hierarchy and upon setup, defines the universe of attributes $\mathbb{A}$. With its key pair (ask_0, apk_0), the RA can delegate a subset of attributes to IAs which hold their own key pairs (ask_i, apk_i), $i > 0$. IAs can further delegate/issue attributes to any end user (aka. signer). In this way a dynamically expandable HABS hierarchy can be established.

Users. Users join the scheme by creating their own key pair (usk, upk), and are issued attributes by possibly multiple AAs.

By Ψ we denote a predicate for some signing policy. A policy-conforming user can use usk to create a HABS signature, provided their issued set of attributes A satisfies the policy, i.e. $\Psi(A') = 1$ for some $A' \subseteq A$. Users are unable to delegate attributes further and thus can be viewed as the lowest tier of the hierarchy. To account for this, when an attribute is delegated to a user a dedicated symbol $\star$ will be used in addition to upk to mark the end of the delegation path.

Warrants. An IA or user, upon joining the HABS scheme, receives a *warrant* **warr** that consists of all their delegated attributes $a \in \mathbb{A}$ and a list of all AAs in each of the delegation paths. Warrants can be updated at any time, i.e. if the owner is issued a new attribute, by appending a new entry with the list of authorities on the delegation path. We use the notation |**warr**| to denote the size of the warrant, i.e. the number of attributes stored in the warrant **warr**, and we use |**warr**[a]| to denote the length of the delegation path of the attribute $a \in \mathbb{A}$. Upon signing, the user submits a reduced warrant for an attribute set $A' \subseteq A$ that satisfies $\Psi(A') = 1$.

Tracing Authority. The tracing authority (TA) is independent of the hierarchy. Upon receiving a valid HABS signature, it can identify the signer and all authorities on the delegation paths for attributes that the signer used to satisfy the signing policy. The tracing authority can output a publicly verifiable proof $\hat{\pi}$ that the path was identified correctly. The existence of such tracing authority improves the accountability of signers and IAs from possible misbehaviour.

Definition 1 (Hierarchical ABS Scheme [12]). *A scheme* HABS := (Setup, KGen, AttIssue, Sign, Verify, Trace, Judge) *consists of the following seven processes:*

- Setup(1^λ) *is the initialisation process where based on some security parameter* $\lambda \in \mathbb{N}$, *the public parameters* pp *of the scheme are defined, and the root and tracing authority independently generate their own key pair, i.e. RA's* (ask_0, apk_0) *and TA's* (tsk, tpk). *In addition, RA defines the universe* $\mathbb{A}$ *of attributes, and a label* $\star$ *for users. We stress that due to dynamic hierarchy, the system can be initialised by publishing* (pp, apk_0, tpk) *with* $\mathbb{A}$ *and* $\star$ *contained in* pp.
- KGen(pp) *is a key generation algorithm executed independently by intermediate authorities and users. Each entity generates its own key pair, i.e.,* (ask_i, apk_i) *for* $i > 0$ *or* (usk, upk).
- AttIssue (ask_i, $\textbf{warr}_i$, A, $\{apk_j | upk_j\}$) *is an algorithm that is used to delegate attributes to an authority with* apk_j *or issue them to the user with* upk. *On input of an authority's secret key* ask_i, $i \in \mathbb{N}_0$, *its warrant* $\textbf{warr}_i$, *a subset of attributes* A *from* $\textbf{warr}_i$, *and the public key of the entity to which attributes are delegated or issued, it outputs a new warrant for that entity.*
- Sign (($usk, \textbf{warr}$), m, Ψ) *is the signing algorithm. On input of the signer's* usk *and (possibly reduced)* $\textbf{warr}$, *a message* m *and a predicate* Ψ *it outputs a signature* σ.
- Verify (apk_0, (m, Ψ, σ)) *is a deterministic algorithm that outputs 1 if a candidate signature* σ *on a message* m *is valid with respect to the predicate* Ψ *and 0 otherwise.*
- Trace (tsk, apk_0, (m, Ψ, σ)) *is an algorithm executed by the TA on input of its private key* tsk *and outputs either a triple* ($upk, \textbf{warr}, \hat{\pi}$) *if the tracing is successful or* $\bot$ *to indicate its failure. Note that* $\textbf{warr}$ *contains attributes and delegation paths that were used by the signer.*
- Judge (tpk, apk_0, (m, Ψ, σ), ($upk, \textbf{warr}, \hat{\pi}$)) *is a deterministic algorithm that checks a candidate triple* ($upk, \textbf{warr}, \hat{\pi}$) *from the tracing algorithm and outputs 1 if the triple is valid and 0 otherwise.*

A HABS scheme must have the *correctness* property ensuring that any signature σ generated based on an honestly issued warrant will verify and trace correctly. The output ($upk, \textbf{warr}, \hat{\pi}$) of the tracing algorithm on such signatures will be accepted by the public judging algorithm with overwhelming probability.

2.1 Security Properties

Our security definitions resemble the requirements of *path anonymity*, *path traceability*, and *non-frameability* from [12]. We recall the associated game-based definitions assuming probabilistic polynomial time (PPT) adversaries interacting with HABS entities through the following set of oracles (Fig. 1):

- O_{Reg}: $\mathcal{A}$ registers new IAs and users through this registration oracle, for which a key pair will be generated and added to *List*. The public key is given to the adversary. Initially, the entity is considered honest, and so the public key is also added to the list HU.

- O_{Corr}: This oracle allows $\mathcal{A}$ to corrupt registered users or IAs. Upon input of a public key, the corresponding private key is given as output if it exists in $List$. The public key is removed from HU so the oracle keeps track of corrupt entities.
- O_{Att}: $\mathcal{A}$ uses this oracle to ask an attribute authority to delegate attributes to either an IA or to the user. In particular, the adversary has control over which attributes are issued and the oracle outputs a warrant **warr** if both parties are registered, otherwise it outputs $\perp$.
- O_{Sig}: $\mathcal{A}$ can ask for a HABS signature from a registered user. The adversary provides the warrant (and implicitly the attributes used), signing policy, message and the public key of the signer. If the attribute set satisfies the policy, and the public key is contained in HU then the signature will be given to $\mathcal{A}$, otherwise $\perp$ is returned.
- O_{Tr}: s $\mathcal{A}$ can ask the TA trace a HABS signature (provided by the adversary) to the output is returned. The TA does verification checks on the signature and upon failure, will return $\perp$.

$O_{\text{Reg}}(\,\cdot\,)$ with $(\,\cdot\,) = (\,i\,)$ and $i \notin HU$

1: $(sk_i, pk_i) \leftarrow \text{KGen}(pp)$
2: $List \leftarrow List \cup \{(i, pk_i, sk_i)\}$
3: $HU \leftarrow HU \cup \{i\}$
4: **return** pk_i

$O_{\text{Corr}}(\,\cdot\,)$ with $(\,\cdot\,) = (\,i\,)$

1: **if** $i \in HU$ **then**
2:    $HU \leftarrow HU - \{i\}$
3: **return** sk_i from $List$

$O_{\text{Tr}}(\,\cdot\,)$ with $(\,\cdot\,) = (m, \Psi, \sigma)$

1: **return** $\text{Trace}(tsk, apk_0, (m, \Psi, \sigma))$

$O_{\text{Att}}(\,\cdot\,)$

$(\,\cdot\,) = (i, \textbf{warr}_i, a, \{apk_j | upk_j\})$
1: $L := \{a | (a, pk_a, sk_a) \in List\}$
2: **if** $i \in L \wedge j \in L$ **then**
3:    $\text{warr} \leftarrow \text{AttIssue}(ask_i,$
       $\textbf{warr}_i, a, \{apk_j | upk_j\})$
4:    **return warr**
5: **return** $\perp$

$O_{\text{Sig}}(\,\cdot\,)$ with $(\,\cdot\,) = (i, \textbf{warr}, m, \Psi)$

1: $A \leftarrow \{a | a \in \textbf{warr}\}$
2: **if** $i \in HU \wedge \Psi(A)$ **then**
3:    $\sigma \leftarrow \text{Sign}((usk_i, \textbf{warr}), m, \Psi)$
4:    **return** σ
5: **return** $\perp$

Fig. 1. Oracles used in the HABS security experiments.

Path Anonymity. This property extends the anonymity guarantees of traditional ABS schemes and hides not only the identity of the signer but also the identities of all intermediate authorities on delegation paths for attributes included into the signer's warrant. Path anonymity, as defined in Fig. 2, also ensures that signatures produced by the same signer remain unlinkable. The corresponding experiment requires the adversary to distinguish which warrant and private key were used in the generation of the challenge HABS signature σ_b. In the first phase, $\mathcal{A}_1$ generates a hierarchy of authorities and users, utilising the RA's secret key ask_0. If the warrants created by $\mathcal{A}_1$ are of the same size, a challenge HABS signature σ_b is produced on the randomly chosen user-warrant pair. In the second phase, with access to the tracing oracle, the adversary $\mathcal{A}_2$ must be able to guess the challenge bit b.

Definition 2 (Path Anonymity [12]**).** *A HABS scheme offers path anonymity if no PPT adversary adv can distinguish between* $\mathbf{Exp}^{pa-0}_{HABS,\mathcal{A}}$ *and* $\mathbf{Exp}^{pa-1}_{HABS,\mathcal{A}}$ *defined in Fig. 2, i.e., the following advantage is negligible in λ:*

$$\mathrm{Adv}^{pa}_{HABS,\mathcal{A}}(\lambda) = |\mathrm{Pr}[\mathrm{Exp}^{pa-0}_{HABS,\mathcal{A}}(\lambda) = 1] - |\mathrm{Pr}[\mathbf{Exp}^{pa-1}_{HABS,\mathcal{A}}(\lambda) = 1]|.$$

$\mathbf{Exp}^{pa\text{-}b}_{HABS,\mathcal{A}}(\lambda)$

1 : $(pp, ask_0, tsk) \leftarrow \mathtt{Setup}(1^\lambda)$

2 : $(st, (usk_0, \mathbf{warr}_0), (usk_1, \mathbf{warr}_1), m, \Psi) \leftarrow \mathcal{A}_1(pp, ask_0 : O_{\mathrm{Reg}}, O_{\mathrm{Corr}}, O_{\mathrm{Tr}})$

3 : **if** $|\mathbf{warr}_0| = |\mathbf{warr}_1|$ **then**

4 : $\sigma_0 \leftarrow \mathtt{Sign}((usk_0, \mathbf{warr}_0), m, \Psi),\ \sigma_1 \leftarrow \mathtt{Sign}((usk_1, \mathbf{warr}_1), m, \Psi)$

5 :   **if** $\mathtt{Verify}(apk_0, (m, \Psi, \sigma_0)) = 1$ and $\mathtt{Verify}(apk_0, (m, \Psi, \sigma_1)) = 1$ **then**

6 : $b' \leftarrow \mathcal{A}_2(st, \sigma_b : O_{\mathrm{Tr}})$

7 :   **return** $b' \wedge \mathcal{A}2$ did not query $O_{\mathrm{Tr}}(tsk, (m, \Psi, \sigma_b))$

8 : **return** 0

Fig. 2. Path-anonymity experiment

Non-frameability. This property, formalised in Fig. 3, captures the notion of unforgeability, i.e., that no PPT adversary can create a HABS signature without having an honestly issued warrant that satisfies the policy, and in particular, they cannot create one on behalf of an user for which the secret key is not known. The adversary wins if either he produces a valid HABS signature, or is able to perform delegation for at least one attribute on behalf of any honest authority anywhere in the delegation path.

Definition 3 (Non-Frameability [12]**).** *A HABS scheme is non-frameable, if no PPT adversary $\mathcal{A}$ can win the experiment* $\mathbf{Exp}^{nf}_{HABS,\mathcal{A}}$ *defined in Fig. 3, i.e., the following advantage is negligible in λ:*

$$\mathbf{Adv}^{nf}_{HABS,\mathcal{A}}(\lambda) = |\mathrm{Pr}[\mathbf{Exp}^{nf}_{HABS,\mathcal{A}}(\lambda) = 1]|.$$

$\mathbf{Exp}^{\text{nf}}_{HABS,\mathcal{A}}(\lambda)$

---

1 : $\text{pp} \leftarrow \text{Setup}(1^\lambda), ask_0 \leftarrow \text{KGen}(1^\lambda), tsk \leftarrow \text{TKGen}(1^\lambda)$

2 : $((\sigma, m, \Psi), (upk_j, \mathbf{warr}, \hat{\pi})) \leftarrow \mathcal{A}(\text{pp}, ask_0, tsk : O_{\text{Att}}, O_{\text{Sig}}, O_{\text{Corr}}, O_{\text{Reg}})$

3 : **if** $\text{Verify}(apk_0, (m, \Psi, \sigma)) \wedge \text{Judge}(tpk, apk_0, (m, \Psi, \sigma), (upk_j, \mathbf{warr}, \hat{\pi}))$ **then**

4 :   **if** $j \in HU \wedge \mathcal{A}$ did not query $O_{\text{Sig}}((usk_j, \mathbf{warr}), m, \Psi)$ **then,**   **return** 1

5 :   **if** $\exists a.\ a \in \mathbf{warr} \implies (apk_0, apk_1, \ldots, apk_n, upk_j, \star) = \mathbf{warr}[a] \wedge$

6 : $((\exists i \in [0, n-1].\ \mathcal{A} \text{ did not query } O_{\text{Att}}(i, \ \cdot\ , a, apk_{i+1}) \wedge i \in HU) \vee$

7 : $(\mathcal{A} \text{ did not query } O_{\text{Att}}(n, \ \cdot\ , a, upk_j) \wedge n \in HU)\ )$ **then, return** 1

8 : **return** 0

Fig. 3. Non-frameability experiment

$\mathbf{Exp}^{\text{tr}}_{\text{HABS},\mathcal{A}}(\lambda)$

---

1 : $\text{pp} \leftarrow \text{Setup}(1^\lambda), ask_0 \leftarrow \text{KGen}(1^\lambda), tsk \leftarrow \text{TKGen}(1^\lambda)$

2 : $((\sigma, m, \Psi), (upk, \mathbf{warr}, \hat{\pi})) \leftarrow \mathcal{A}(\text{pp}, tsk : O_{\text{Att}}, O_{\text{Corr}}, O_{\text{Reg}})$

3 : **if** $\text{Verify}(apk_0, (m, \Psi, \sigma))$ **then**

4 :   **if** $\text{Trace}(tsk, (m, \Psi, \sigma)) = \perp$ **then,**   **return** 1

5 :   **if** $\text{Judge}(tpk, apk_0, (m, \Psi, \sigma), (upk, \mathbf{warr}, \hat{\pi})) \wedge$

6 : $(\exists a.\ a \in \mathbf{warr} \implies (apk_0, apk_1, \ldots, apk_n, upk, \star) = \mathbf{warr}[a] \wedge$

7 : $(\ (\exists i \in [0, n-1].\ i \in HU \wedge (i+1, apk_{i+1}, ask_{i+1}) \notin List) \vee$

8 : $(n \in HU \wedge (\ \cdot\ , upk, usk) \notin List)\ )\ )$ **then,**   **return** 1

9 : **return** 0

Fig. 4. Path-traceability experiment

Path Traceability. This property, formalised in Fig. 4, ensures that any valid HABS signature can be traced (by the tracing authority) to the signer and the set of authorities that were involved in the issue of attributes used to produce the signature. The adversary is required to output either a HABS signature that verifies but cannot be traced, or one in which the tracing algorithm outputs a warrant for which at least one IA or the user is unknown to the experiment, i.e., were not previously registered in *List*. The attribute-issuing oracle checks that both entities are registered to prevent the trivial attack where adversary asks the oracle to delegate to an unregistered entity.

Definition 4 (Path Traceability [12]). *A HABS scheme offers path traceability if no PPT adversary $\mathcal{A}$ can win the experiment $\mathbf{Exp}^{\text{tr}}_{\text{HABS},\mathcal{A}}$ defined in Fig. 4, i.e., the following advantage is negligible in λ:*

$$\mathbf{Adv}^{\text{tr}}_{HABS,\mathcal{A}}(\lambda) = |\Pr[\mathbf{Exp}^{\text{tr}}_{HABS,\mathcal{A}}(\lambda) = 1]|.$$

3 Our Short HABS Construction

We start with the description of the underlying hardness assumptions and building blocks.

3.1 Underlying Hardness Assumptions

In addition to widely used hardness assumptions in the asymmetric bilinear group setting generated by $\mathcal{BG}(1^\lambda)$, namely q-Srong Diffie-Hellman (q-SDH) [7], Symmetric eXternal Diffie-Hellman (SXDH) [1] and Simultaneous Decision LINear (SDLIN) [26] assumptions, which we do not recall here, our scheme requires the following interactive assumption, which we prove to hold in the generic group model [24,36]. We equip the adversary with an oracle $\mathcal{O}_{X_0,Y_0}$ and assume that it is hard to produce group elements that satisfy the verification equations for an input that has not been queried to the oracle. We note that on input of (X,Y), the oracle can compute each component without knowledge the discrete logarithm of X or Y as it has access to r,s,t_1,t_2.

Assumption 1. *Let* $pp := (p, \mathbb{G}_1, \mathbb{G}_2, \mathbb{G}_T, e, g_1, g_2) \leftarrow \mathcal{BG}(1^\lambda)$. *The adversary* $\mathcal{A}$ *has access to the oracle* $\mathcal{O}_{X_0,Y_0}(\cdot, \cdot)$ *which on input* (X, Y) *returns* $(A, B, T_1, T_2, T_3, T_4) := (h_2^{x_0 t_1} h_5^{x_0 t_2} h_2^{x t_1} h_5^{y t_1}, h_5^{y_0 t_1} h_4^{y_0 t_2} h_5^{x t_2} h_4^{y t_2}, f_1^{t_1}, f_2^{t_2}, g_2^{t_1}, g_2^{t_2})$ *for* $t_1, t_2 \leftarrow \mathbb{Z}_p^*$. *We assume that for all p.p.t. adversaries* $\mathcal{A}$, *the following probability is negligible in* λ.

$$Adv_{\mathcal{A}}^{\mathsf{Assump1}}(\lambda) :=$$
$$Pr \begin{bmatrix} x_0, y_0, r, s \leftarrow \mathbb{Z}_p^*; h_1 := g_1^s, h_2 := g_1^{s^2}, h_3 := g_1^r, h_4 := g_1^{r^2}, h_5 := g_1^{rs} \\ f_1 := g_2^s, f_2 := g_2^r, X_0 := h_1^{x_0}; Y_0 := h_3^{y_0}; \\ (\hat{A}, \hat{B}, \hat{T}_1, \hat{T}_2, \hat{T}_3, \hat{T}_4, \hat{X}, \hat{Y}) \leftarrow \mathcal{A}^{\mathcal{O}_{X_0,Y_0}}(pp, X_0, Y_0, h_1, h_2, h_3, h_4, h_5, f_1, f_2) : \\ e(\hat{A}, g_2) = e(X_0, \hat{T}_1 \hat{T}_2)e(\hat{X}\hat{Y}, \hat{T}_1) \ \wedge \ e(\hat{B}, g_2) = e(Y_0, \hat{T}_1 \hat{T}_2)e(\hat{X}\hat{Y}, \hat{T}_2) \\ \wedge \ e(g_1, \hat{T}_1 \hat{T}_2) = e(h_1, \hat{T}_3)e(h_3, \hat{T}_4) \quad \text{where } (\hat{X}, \hat{Y}) \text{ was not queried.} \end{bmatrix}$$

Theorem 1. *Let* $\mathcal{A}$ *denote an adversary in the generic group model against Assumption 1.* $\mathcal{A}$ *has access to oracles for which he makes* q_G *group queries,* q_P *pairing queries, and* q_O *oracle queries. The probability* ϵ *of* $\mathcal{A}$ *winning the game for Assumption 1 is bounded by* $\epsilon \le 5(q_G + q_P + 6q_O + 11)^2/p$, *where* p *is the prime order of the generic groups.*

Proof. See full version [19].

3.2 Cryptographic Building Blocks

The following building blocks will be used in our HABS construction.

Tag-Based Encryption. A TBE scheme has the same algorithms as a traditional public key encryption scheme, except that its encryption and decryption procedures take an extra tag t as input. A correctly formed TBE ciphertext C will fail to decrypt if the tag used as input to the decryption algorithm is different from the one used upon encryption. We adopt the TBE scheme from [26] which relies on the SDLIN assumption. It offers selective-tag witness-indistinguishable chosen-ciphertext (st-IND-CCA) security, where an adversary is unable to distinguish between two ciphertexts under the same tag t of their choosing. Kiltz [28] showed that a st-IND-CCA TBE scheme combined with a strongly unforgeable one-time signature, where the one-time verification key is used as the tag, gives rise to an IND-CCA2 secure PKE. Our scheme uses this approach.

One-Time Signature. For the OTS, we use the strongly unforgeable BBS one-time signature scheme from [7]. It consist of three algorithms (KeyGen, Sig, Ver) with a verification key in $\mathbb{G}^2 \times \mathbb{Z}_p^*$ and the corresponding signing key in $\mathbb{Z}_p^{*2}$.

Groth-Sahai Proofs. We use the Groth-Sahai proof system [22] to construct the required non-interactive zero-knowledge proofs NIZK. A GS proof, which consists of five algorithms (Setup, Prove, Verify, SimSetup, SimProve), allows proving relations involving multi-linear, quadratic, and pairing-based equations. We use GS proofs in the asymmetric bilinear group setting with Type-3 curves [18], i.e., where there is no computable isomorphism between $\mathbb{G}_1$ and $\mathbb{G}_2$, in which case their security is based on the SXDH assumption [7].

Homomorphic Trapdoor Commitments to Group Elements. The key to our short HABS scheme is the length-reducing homomorphic trapdoor commitment scheme by Groth [21], adopted in our new delegation mechanism. With the HTC scheme, defined by four algorithms (Setup, KeyGen, Commit, Trapdoor), one can use the trapdoor key tk to open a constant-length commitment (c, d) to arbitrary group elements with respect to a commitment key. We observe that due to its construction this HTC scheme has an interesting property that allows a commitment to group elements step-wise, i.e. an opening (a_i, b_i) to elements $g_1, \ldots, g_i$ can be transformed into an opening (a_{i+1}, b_{i+1}) for an extended set of elements $g_1, \ldots, g_{i+1}$ without knowledge of the secret commitment key, i.e., without jeopardising the binding property for the already committed group elements. In our HABS scheme such step-wise extension of an initial commitment (c, d) produced by the root authority allows intermediate authorities, upon delegation, to embed public keys of next-level authorities or users, along with the delegated attribute, by providing appropriate modification to the opening of (c, d), that is without changing its value nor increasing its length. Proving ownership of a delegated attribute amounts to presenting an opening (a, b) for the commitment (c, d) to the attribute and the list of public keys of authorities on the delegation path, i.e., $apk_0, \ldots, upk, \star$. In our scheme we use the asymmetric variant of Groth's HTC scheme with security based on the XDLIN assumption [1].

3.3 Specification of Our HABS Scheme

We start with a high-level intuition behind our HABS construction and provide detailed specification in Figs. 5, 6, and 7.

High-Level Overview. As part of the setup process public parameters pp of the scheme are generated. They include the security parameter λ, the description of bilinear groups $(\mathbb{G}_1, \mathbb{G}_2, \mathbb{G}_T)$, the trapdoor key tk for the HTC scheme, the initial 'dummy' HTC commitment (c, d) with an opening (a_0, b_0), and the description of the attribute universe $\mathbb{A}$. The independent tracing authority TA generates the TBE key-pair $(tsk, tpk) := ((\eta_1, \eta_2), (V_1, V_2, V_3, V_4))$ with tpk included into pp. For simplicity we describe the setup phase as a single process involving computations performed by the RA and TA. We stress, however, that generation of $h_1, ..., h_5, f_1, f_2$ must be trusted in that no entity knows the corresponding exponents.

Setup(λ)

0 : $(\mathbb{G}_1, \mathbb{G}_2, \mathbb{G}_T, g_1, g_2, e, p) \leftarrow \mathcal{BG}(1^\lambda)$

1 : Sample $r, s \leftarrow \mathbb{Z}_p^*$

2 : $h_1 := g_1^s, h_2 := g_1^{s^2}, h_3 := g_1^r,$

   $h_4 := g_1^{r^2}, h_5 := g_1^{rs}$

3 : $f_1 := g_2^s, f_2 := g_2^r$

4 : Define $\mathcal{H}_1 : \mathbb{A} \to \mathbb{Z}_p^*,$

   $\mathcal{H}_2 : \{0, 1\}^* \to \mathbb{Z}_p^*, \mathcal{H}_3 : \{0, 1\}^* \to \mathbb{Z}_p^*$

5 : Sample $\tilde{g}_1 \leftarrow \mathbb{G}_1, \tilde{g}_2 \leftarrow \mathbb{G}_2$

6 : Compute $\zeta \leftarrow e(\tilde{g}_1, \tilde{g}_2)$

7 : $(tsk, tpk) \leftarrow$ TKGen

8 : $w_1 \leftarrow$ NIZK$_1$.Setup

9 : $w_2 \leftarrow$ NIZK$_2$.Setup

10 : Define attribute universe $\mathbb{A}$

11 : Sample $m_r, m_s, n_r, n_s \leftarrow \mathbb{Z}_p^*$

12 : Sample $a_0, b_0 \leftarrow \mathbb{G}_1$

13 : Compute $g_r \leftarrow g_2^{m_r}, g_s \leftarrow g_2^{m_s},$

   $h_r \leftarrow g_2^{n_r}, h_s \leftarrow g_2^{n_s}$

14 : Compute $c := e(a_0, g_r)e(b_0, g_s)$

   $d := e(a_0, h_r)e(b_0, h_s)$

15 : Compute $\Delta := m_r n_s - n_r m_s$

16 : $\alpha := n_s/\Delta, \beta := -m_s/\Delta,$

   $\gamma := -n_r/\Delta, \delta := m_r/\Delta$

17 : $tk := (m_r, m_s, n_r, n_s, \alpha, \beta, \gamma, \delta)$

18 : pp := $(\mathcal{G}, c, d, a_0, b_0, tk, \mathcal{H}_1, \mathcal{H}_2,$

   $\mathcal{H}_3, \zeta, \tilde{g}_1, \tilde{g}_2, tpk, \mathbb{A}, w_1, w_2)$

   for $\mathcal{G} := (\mathbb{G}_1, \mathbb{G}_2, \mathbb{G}_T, g_1, g_2, e, p$

   $h_1, h_2, h_3, h_4, h_5, f_1, f_2)$

19 : **return** pp

Fig. 5. Setup algorithm of our HABS construction.

In our scheme, all attribute authorities and users generate their own private/public key pairs (ask_i, apk_i) and (usk, upk) respectively, of the form $\{(x, y), (X, Y, Z, \hat{Z})\}$. While only X and Y are used in the verification of attribute delegation which we prove in the signature, the components $(Z, \hat{Z})$ are used in the issuing phase. To ensure an authority creates a delegation that opens to (X, Y), we insist that the validity of a public key is checked prior to delegation. This is done by evaluating $e(XY, h_1) = e(Z, g_2)$ and $e(XY, h_3) = e(\hat{Z}, g_2)$. IAs and users obtain attributes from existing authorities at a higher level in the hierarchy. Ownership of a valid key-pair (ask_i, apk_i) allows authorities to delegate attributes further down the hierarchy and to the users, by manipulating the opening of the initial commitment (c, d).

With the trapdoor key tk an authority can create an opening (a_i, b_i) for (c, d) to the path that includes delegate's public key e.g. apk_j. Rather than opening directly, the issuer first creates randomisation tokens $T_1, T_2, T_3, T_4 \in \mathbb{G}_2$ and opens to these instead. It then uses T_1 and T_2 as *one-time* commitment keys to open to apk_j and the delegated attribute att, that is hashed into the message space using $g^{\mathcal{H}_1(att)}$. The randomisation tokens T_1 and T_2 are used to prevent forgeries (where the adversary combines multiple openings and in doing so, forges an opening to a new public key) whereas T_3 and T_4 are used to verify the well-formedness of T_1 and T_2, by evaluating $e(g_1, T_1 T_2) = e(h_1, T_4) e(h_3, T_3)$. The issuing authority updates the (possibly empty) warrant with opening (a_i, b_i), his public key apk_i and the randomisation tokens (T_1, T_2, T_3, T_4). As tk is part of public parameters, any IA in the hierarchy is able to perform the delegation procedure, where it receives (a_{i-1}, b_{i-1}) from its issue and generates (a_i, b_i) for the next delegation. When delegating to users, an issuing IA will open (c, d) to a designated element $\star \in \mathbb{G}$, in addition to the user's public key upk and the attribute att. A warrant contains the trapdoor opening and a list of all public keys of AAs that appear in the delegation path for any issued attribute.

Upon signing, the user first generates an OTS key-pair $(otssk, otsvk) := \{(k_1, k_2), (K_1, K_2, \kappa)\}$ and an opening to $\mathcal{H}_3(otsvk)$ by modifying the opening (a_0, b_0) using his public key upk and the trapdoor key tk. The reduced **warr** along with upk are encrypted in a TBE ciphertext under the TA's public key tpk and tag $\mathcal{H}_3(otsvk)$. The signing policy Ψ is modelled as a monotone span program, with labelling function ρ that maps rows from $\mathbf{S}$ to the

---

KGen(pp)

0 :   Sample $x, y \leftarrow \mathbb{Z}_p^*$

1 : $X := h_1^x, Y := h_3^y,$

2 : $Z := h_2^x h_5^y, \hat{Z} := h_5^x h_4^y$

3 : $pk := (X, Y, Z, \hat{Z}),$

4 : $sk := (pk, x, y)$

5 :   **return** (pk, sk)

TKGen(pp)

0 :   Sample $\eta_1, \eta_2 \leftarrow \mathbb{Z}_p^*$

1 :   Compute $V_1 := g_1^{\eta_1}, V_2 := g_1^{\eta_2}$

2 :   Sample $V_3, V_4 \leftarrow \mathbb{G}_2$

3 : $tpk := (V_1, V_2, V_3, V_4)$

4 : $tsk := (tpk, \eta_1, \eta_2)$

5 :   **return** (tsk, tpk)

AttIssue$(ask_i, \{apk_j | upk\}, att, a_i, b_i, \mathbf{warr})$

0 :   Parse $\{apk_j | upk\}$ as $(X_j, Y_j, Z_j, \hat{Z}_j)$

1 :   Verify $e(XY, h_1) = e(Z, g_2)$

      and $e(XY, h_3) = e(\hat{Z}, g_2)$

2 :   Sample $t_1, t_2 \leftarrow \mathbb{Z}_p^*$

3 : $T_1 := f_1^{t_1}, T_2 := f_2^{t_2}, T_3 := g_2^{t_1}, T_4 := g_2^{t_2}$

4 : $\tilde{a} \leftarrow a_i^{m_r} b_i^{m_s} (h_2^{t_1} h_5^{t_2})^{-x_i} (Z_j h_1^{\mathcal{H}_1(att)})^{-t_1}$

      $\tilde{b} \leftarrow a_i^{n_r} b_i^{n_s} (h_5^{t_1} h_4^{t_2})^{-y_i} (\hat{Z}_j h_3^{\mathcal{H}_1(att)})^{-t_2}$

5 : $(a_{i+1}, b_{i+1}) := (\tilde{a}^\alpha \tilde{b}^\beta, \tilde{a}^\gamma \tilde{b}^\delta)$

6 :   **warr** $= \mathbf{warr} \cup \{apk_i, T_1, T_2\}$

7 :   **return** $(a_{i+1}, b_{i+1}, \mathbf{warr})$

Fig. 6. Key generation and issue of attributes in our HABS construction.

attribute set $\mathbb{A}$. The signer proves that this set satisfies Ψ by computing a vector $\mathbf{z}$ such that $\mathbf{z}\mathbf{S} = [1, 0, ..., 0]$, where any non-zero entry $\mathbf{z}_i$ implies $\rho(i) \in \mathbf{warr}$. A NIZK proof π is then computed using Groth-Sahai framework with witness $(upk, \mathbf{warr}, \mathbf{z}, \tilde{r}, \tilde{s})$ for the following relation:

$$((a, b), \mathbf{warr}, upk, \mathbf{z}), (\Psi, otsvk, apk_0, C, tpk) : \mathbf{z}S = [1, 0, ..., 0]$$
$$\wedge \ (\forall i. \ \mathbf{z}_i \neq 0 \implies att_i = \rho(i) \ \wedge \ (apk_{i_1}, ..., apk_{i_n}, apk_{i_{n+1}} := upk) \in C$$
$$\wedge \ c^{|\mathbf{warr}|+1} = e(a, g_r)e(b, g_s)e(X, g_2^{\mathcal{H}_3(otsvk)})$$
$$\Pi_i \Pi_{n=0}^{k} e(X_{i_n}, T_{1,i_n} T_{2,i_n}) e(X_{i_{n+1}} Y_{i_{n+1}} g_1^{\mathcal{H}_1(att)}, T_{1,i_n})$$
$$\wedge \ d^{|\mathbf{warr}|+1} = e(a, h_r)e(b, h_s)e(Y, g_2^{\mathcal{H}_3(otsvk)})$$
$$\Pi_i \Pi_{n=0}^{k} e(Y_{i_n}, T_{1,i_n} T_{2,i_n}) e(X_{i_{n+1}} Y_{i_{n+1}} g_1^{\mathcal{H}_1(att)}, T_{2,i_n})$$
$$\wedge \ e(g_1, \Pi_i \Pi_{n=0}^{k} T_{1,i_n} T_{2,i_n}) = e(h_1, \Pi_i \Pi_{n=0}^{n} T_{4,i_n}) e(h_3, \Pi_i \Pi_{n=0}^{k} T_{3,i_n}).$$

Sign$(usk, m, \Psi, \{att_j, a_j, b_j, \mathbf{warr}_j\}_{j \in J})$

0 : $(k_1, k_2, k_3) \leftarrow \mathbb{Z}_p^*$

1 : $otsvk := (\tilde{g}_2^{k_1}, \tilde{g}_2^{k_2}, k_3)$

2 : Compute $\mathbf{z}$ s.t. $\mathbf{z}S = [1, 0, ..., 0]$

3 : $T_1 := f_1^{t_1}, T_2 := f_2^{t_2},$
   $T_3 := g_2^{t_1}, T_4 := g_2^{t_2}$

4 : $a' \leftarrow a_i^{m_r} b_i^{m_s} (h_2^{t_1} h_5^{t_2})^{-x} h_1^{-t_1 \mathcal{H}_3(otsvk)}$
   $b' \leftarrow a_i^{n_r} b_i^{n_s} (h_5^{t_1} h_4^{t_2})^{-y} h_3^{-t_2 \mathcal{H}_3(otsvk)}$

5 : $(a', b') := (\tilde{a}^\alpha \tilde{b}^\beta, \tilde{a}^\gamma \tilde{b}^\delta)$

6 : $(a, b) = (a' \cdot \Pi a_j, b' \cdot \Pi b_j)$

7 : $C \leftarrow$ TBE.Enc$(tpk, \mathbf{warr}, upk,$
   $a, b, \{\mathcal{H}_1(otsvk)\})$

8 : $\pi \leftarrow$ NIZK$_1$.Prove$((upk, \mathbf{z}, \mathbf{warr}, a, b) :$
   $(C, otsvk, tpk, apk_0, \Psi) \in \mathcal{R})$

9 : $H \leftarrow \mathcal{H}_2(\pi || C || \Psi || m || otsvk)$

10 : $\sigma_o \leftarrow \tilde{g}_1^{1/(k_1 + H + k_2 k_3)}$

11 : **return** $(\sigma_o, C, \pi, otsvk)$

Verify(pk, σ, m, Ψ)

0 : Parse σ as $(ots, \pi, otsvk)$

1 : $H \leftarrow \mathcal{H}_2(\pi || C || \Psi || m || otsvk)$

2 : **return** NIZK.Verify(π)
   $\wedge \ e(\sigma_o, \tilde{g}_2^{k_1} \cdot \tilde{g}_2^H \cdot \tilde{g}_2^{k_2 k_3}) = \zeta$

Trace(tsk, σ, m, Ψ)

0 : **if** Verify$(\sigma, m, \Psi) = 1$ **then**

1 : $\mathbf{warr} \leftarrow$ TBE.Dec(tsk, C, t)
   for $t = \mathcal{H}_1(otsvk)$

2 : $\hat{\pi} \leftarrow$ NIZK$_2$.Prove$(tsk :$
   $(otsvk, C, tpk, (apk_0, \mathbf{warr})))$

3 : **return** $(\mathbf{warr}, \hat{\pi})$

Judge$(tpk, \mathbf{warr}, \sigma)$

0 : Verify$(ask_0, (\sigma, m, \Psi))$
   $\wedge \ $ NIZK$_2$.Verify(π_2)

Fig. 7. Sign, Verify, Trace and Judge algorithms of our HABS construction.

The message m and policy Ψ are then bound to this proof and ciphertext by hashing $\mathcal{H}_2(\pi, C, \Psi, m)$, before an OTS signature σ_o is produced with $otssk$. The resulting signature is verified with respect to the public parameters of the scheme, and the RA's public key apk_0 by verifying the OTS signature and the NIZK proof.

As part of the tracing procedure, executed by TA with knowledge of tsk, the ciphertext C is decrypted to obtain the warrant $\mathbf{warr}$, signer's public key upk, and the opening (a, b). A publicly verifiable NIZK proof $\hat{\pi}$ is created with witness tsk for the statement $(otsvk, C, tpk, (apk_0, \mathbf{warr}))$ and relation:

$$\text{TBE.Dec}(tsk, C, \mathcal{H}_3(otsvk)) = (upk, \mathbf{warr}, a, b).$$

We give a detailed construction for the Groth-Sahai proofs NIZK_1 and NIZK_2 in Appendix D.

3.4   Security Analysis

In this section we prove that our construction meets HABS security properties of path anonymity, non-frameability and path traceability.

Lemma 1. *The HABS construction from Figs. 5, 6 and 7 offers path anonymity, if SXDH, SDLIN and q-SDH hold in $\mathcal{G}$.*

Proof. We follow a game-based approach and show that the advantage of the PPT adversary $\mathcal{A}$ in the path-anonymity experiment for the HABS construction from Figs. 5, 6 and 7, is bounded by the advantages of the constructed adversaries for the underlying primitives. We assume that adversary $\mathcal{A}$ asks n user registration queries and the probability for sampling one of these users is $1/n$.

Game G_0: This game is defined to the be the experiment $\mathbf{Exp}^{\text{pa-}b}_{\text{HABS},\mathcal{A}}(\lambda)$ in Fig. 2, where the 2-stage adversary $\mathcal{A} = (\mathcal{A}_1, \mathcal{A}_2)$ is required to distinguish between the HABS signatures $\sigma_0 = (\sigma^0_o, C_0, \pi_0, otsvk_0)$ and $\sigma_1 = (\sigma^1_o, C_1, \pi_1, otsvk_1)$.
Game G_1: We define the game G_1 as G_0 where the check "$\mathcal{A}_2$ did not query $O_{\text{Tr}}(m, \Psi, \sigma_b)$" is enforced by the O_{Tr} oracle available to $\mathcal{A}_2$, which aborts the game if this is the case. The probability from G_0 to G_1 is preserved.
Game G_2: The game G_2 is obtained from G_1 where, on the output of O_{Tr}, we replace the NIZK_2 proof $\hat{\pi}$ with $\hat{\pi}'$ from the simulator $\text{NIZK}_2.\text{SimProve}$. We also replace Setup by SimSetup for NIZK_2. This prevents the case where $\mathcal{A}$ may "extract" tsk from NIZK_2 proofs. Thus, for all future O_{Tr} oracle calls we use the simulated NIZK_2 proof. The probability that $\mathcal{A}$ can distinguish between these two games is bounded by the advantage of the zero-knowledge adversary $\mathcal{B}_{nizk2}$ for NIZK_2. For our instantiation of GS proofs, this is reduced to the SXDH assumption [22].
Game G_3: Let G_3 be the game obtained from G_2 where we replace the proof π_b from the challenge signature $\sigma_b = (\sigma_{o,b}, C_b, \pi_b, otsvk_b)$ with the simulated proof π'_b by calling $\text{NIZK}_1.\text{Sim}$ on $(C_b, otsvk_b, tpk, apk_0, \Psi)$. Additionally, we replace $\text{NIZK}_1.\text{Setup}$ by $\text{NIZK}_1.\text{SimSetup}$. The probability that $\mathcal{A}$ can distinguish between games G_2 and G_3 is bounded by the advantage of the zero-knowledge adversary $\mathcal{B}_{nizk1}$ for NIZK_1 proof. Similarly, this property is implied by SXDH.
Game G_4: Game G_4 only differs from game G_3 in that we abort if $\mathcal{A}_2$ queries $O_{\text{Tr}}(m, \Psi, (\sigma_o, C_b, \pi, otsvk_b))$. The adversary $\mathcal{A}$ is only able to distinguish between these games if it can produce a valid OTS signature σ_o for the message (C_b, π, m, Ψ) and public key $otsvk_b$, without knowledge of the secret key $otssk_b$. Thus, the capabilities of the adversary $\mathcal{A}$ to distinguish between these

two games is bounded by the advantage of the adversary $\mathcal{B}_{ots}$ against the strong unforgeability of the OTS scheme, which is reduced to the q-SDH assumption [7].

Game G_5: Game G_5 is defined to be G_4, except we additionally do a check for any queries $\mathcal{A}_2$ makes do not contain the challenge ciphertext, that is $O_{\mathrm{Tr}}(m, \Psi, (\sigma_o, C_b, \pi, otsvk))$. If so the game is aborted. The output of O_{Tr} is for G_4 and G_5 is the same, as the oracle returns $\perp$ if the tag $otsvk_b$ for C is different from $otsvk$ received as input. Hence, the probability is preserved.

Game G_6: The game G_6 is the same as G_5, except that we move the OTS key generation from the signature generation phase into the setup of the experiment. Note that only one key pair needs to be created in this game since the adversary only sees the challenge signature. This step is necessary to utilise the st-IND-CCA property of the TBE scheme. The probability is unchanged from game G_5 to G_6.

Game G_7: Let G_7 be the game obtained from G_6 where the TBE ciphertext C_b from the challenge signature $\sigma_b = (\sigma_o^b, C_b, \pi_b', otsvk_b)$ is replaced with the C_0. The adversary $\mathcal{A}$ is unable to query a ciphertext $C' \neq C_b$ for the same tag $\mathcal{H}_3(otsvk)$ as a result of game G_4. Further, any query to the oracle for a tag $t' \neq \mathcal{H}_3(otsvk)$ will also fail as decryption of C_b is dependent on the correct tag. Thus, the ability of the adversary $\mathcal{A}_2$ to distinguish between the ciphertexts C_0 and C_b is bounded by the advantage of the st-IND-CCA adversary $\mathcal{B}_{ind}$. For out instantiation, this property of TBE is implied by SDLIN [26].

The experiment G_7 provides $\mathcal{A}$ with the same challenge signature independent of b that $\mathcal{A}$ is asked to guess. Additionally, due to the zero-knowledge property of NIZK$_2$ used in G_1, $\mathcal{A}$ does not have access to tsk. Therefore, the probability that the adversary wins game G_7 is $1/2$ and hence the advantage of $\mathcal{A}$ to win this experiment is 0.   □

Lemma 2. *The HABS construction from Figs. 5, 6 and 7 is non-frameable, if $\mathcal{H}_1, \mathcal{H}_2$ and $\mathcal{H}_3$ are second-preimage resistant hash functions, and q-SDH, SXDH and Assumption 1 hold in $\mathcal{G}$.*

Proof. We begin by first splitting the non-frameability experiment from Fig. 3 into two experiments based on the winning condition of the adversary $\mathcal{A}$. The first **Exp$_1$**, defined in Fig. 8, captures the probability of the adversary $\mathcal{A}$ to create a forged HABS signature. The second experiment **Exp$_2$** is the same as **Exp$_1$** except that the event "$j \in HU \wedge \mathcal{A}$ did not query $O_{\mathrm{Sig}}((usk_j, \mathbf{warr}), \Psi, m)$" is replaced with

"$\exists a. \ a \in \mathbf{warr} \implies (apk_0, apk_1, \ldots, apk_n, upk_j, \star) = \mathbf{warr}[a] \wedge$
(($\exists 0 \leq i \leq n - 1. \ \mathcal{A}$ did not call $O_{\mathrm{Att}}(i, \cdot, a, apk_{i+1}) \wedge i \in HU$) $\vee$
($\mathcal{A}$ did not call $O_{\mathrm{Att}}(n, \cdot, a, upk_u) \wedge n \in HU$))"

We capture the probability of winning the non-frameability experiment by the probability that $\mathcal{A}$ wins either **Exp$_1$** or **Exp$_2$**.

We first bound the advantage of the adversary for the experiment **Exp$_1$**. Intuitively, we consider the output of the adversary and argue that each component must coincide with a call to the signing oracle. The forgery is denoted by

---

Exp$_1$ - The **Exp$_{\text{HABS},\mathcal{A}}^{\text{nf}}$**$(\lambda)$ where $\mathcal{A}$ did not query $O_{\text{Sig}}((usk, \mathbf{warr}), \Psi, \mathsf{m})$

1 : $(\mathsf{pp}, ask_0, tsk) \leftarrow \mathsf{Setup}(1^\lambda)$

2 : $((\mathsf{m}, \Psi, \sigma), (upk_j, \mathbf{warr}, (\pi, \sigma_s))) \leftarrow \mathcal{A}(\mathsf{pp}, ask_0, tsk : O_{\text{Att}}, O_{\text{Sig}}, O_{\text{Corr}}, O_{\text{Reg}})$

3 : $(\sigma_o, \mathrm{C}, \pi, otsvk) = \sigma$

4 :   **if** $\mathsf{NIZK}_1.\mathsf{Verify}((\mathrm{C}, otsvk, tpk, apk_0, \Psi), \pi) \wedge$

5 : $\mathsf{OTS}.\mathsf{Verify}(otsvk, (\mathsf{m}, \Psi, \mathrm{C}, \pi), \sigma_o) \wedge$

6 : $\mathsf{NIZK}_2.\mathsf{Verify}(tpk, (otsvk, \mathrm{C}, upk_j, \mathbf{warr}, \sigma_s), \hat{\pi}) \wedge$

7 : $j \in HU \wedge$

8 : $\mathcal{A}$ did not query $O_{\text{Sig}}((usk_j, \mathbf{warr}), \Psi, \mathsf{m})$ **then**

9 :   **return** 1

10 : **return** 0

Fig. 8. Experiment **Exp$_1$**

$(upk', \mathbf{warr}', m', \Psi'), (\sigma'_o, \mathrm{C}', \pi', otsvk')$. We take each element of the tuple $(upk_j, \mathbf{warr}, m, \Psi)$ and try to reason about its relation with their prime counterpart.

Given n calls to the registration oracle, we model the probability the adversary can guess which oracle constructs the keys for a particular user uniformly, i.e. is equal to $1/n$.

Game G_0. This game is defined as **Exp$_1$** where the query restriction "$\mathcal{A}$ did not query $O_{\text{Sig}}((usk_j, \mathbf{warr}), m, \Psi)$" in instead enforced by a membership check $(upk_u, \mathbf{warr}, m, \Psi) \notin SigL$ for the list $SigL$. We also introduce the list $SigLO$ that stores the input and output of the O_{Sig} oracle. Both lists are initialised empty at the beginning of the experiment, and are updated with the inputs, and additionally, the outputs of the O_{Sig} oracle, respectively. The probability is preserved between **Exp$_1$** and G_0.

Game G_1. This game is defined exactly as G_0 with the exception of an additional check that the opening (a, b) for (c, d) contains the path $e(X_i, g^{\mathcal{H}_3(otsvk)})$ and $e(Y_i, g^{\mathcal{H}_3(otsvk)})$, respectively. The success probability of a soundness adversary for NIZK_1 bounds the distinguishability of G_1 from G_0. That is, $\mathcal{A}$ can only distinguish between these two games if it is able to generate a valid NIZK_1 proof for a false statement, namely that (a, b) does not open to $g^{\mathcal{H}_3(otsvk)}$. Soundness for our instantiation of NIZK_1 is implied by the SXDH assumption [22].

Game G_2. The game G_2 is obtained from G_1 by adding the condition $(upk_j, \star, \star, \star) \notin SigL$. The adversary in G_2 managed to create a valid opening (a, b) for upk_u to $g^{\mathcal{H}_3(otsvk)}$, without having access to the user's secret key usk_j (since $j \in HU$). The capabilities of $\mathcal{A}$ in this experiment are upper-bounded by the advantage of an adversary against Assumption 1 and the second-preimage property of $\mathcal{H}_3$.

Game G_3. Game G_3 is defined to be Game G_1, but where $\mathcal{A}$ made at least one signing query that contains user upk_j. Therefore, there exists $((upk_j, \mathbf{warr}', m', \Psi'), (\sigma'_o, \mathrm{C}', \pi', otsvk')) \in SigL$ with $(\mathbf{warr}, m, \Psi) \neq (\mathbf{warr}', m', \Psi')$ as $(upk_j,$

warr, $m, \Psi) \notin SigL$ but $(upk_j, \mathbf{warr}', m', \Psi') \in SigL$. The probability is preserved between G_1 and G_3.

Game G_4. We define G_4 as the game G_3 where $otsvk \neq otsvk'$. In this case, the adversary $\mathcal{A}$ is able to provide a forged opening to $g^{\mathcal{H}(otsvk')}$ without knowledge of usk_j. This is similar to the method of computing the bound for G_2, except that now $\mathcal{A}$ asks signature queries for upk. It is also bounded by an adversary against Assumption 1.

Game G_5. We define game G_5 as the game G_3 where $(m, \Psi) \neq (m', \Psi')$. At this point, we have $otsvk = otsvk'$ and $upk = upk_j$ for some j. Thus, if $\mathcal{A}$ can distinguish between G_5 and G_3 then it is able to provide a forgery for the OTS scheme by signing a message that contains (m', Ψ') without knowledge of $otssk$, or break the second preimage property of $\mathcal{H}_2$.

Game G_6. We define game G_6 as the game G_5 where $(m, \Psi) = (m', \Psi')$. Because of the $(\mathbf{warr}, m, \Psi) \neq (\mathbf{warr}', m', \Psi')$ restriction, we have $\mathbf{warr}' \neq \mathbf{warr}$. The correctness property of the encryption scheme TBE that builds C' now implies C $\neq$ C' under the tag $t = \mathcal{H}_3(otsvk)$. The probability that the adversary can distinguish between G_6 and G_5 is upper-bounded by an adversary $\mathcal{B}'_{cor}$ against the correctness of TBE, which is implied by the SDLIN assumption [26].

Game G_7. Let G_7 is the same as G_6 but with C $\neq$ C'. Assuming second-preimage resistance of $\mathcal{H}_2$, the adversary $\mathcal{A}$ managed to create a forged OTS signature without knowledge of $otssk$. Therefore, the probability of success for adversary $\mathcal{A}$ in this game is bounded by the advantage of an OTS-forger $\mathcal{B}'_{ots}$. The q-SDH assumption implies the BBS signature is strongly unforgeable [7].

From the sequence of games $G_0, \ldots, G_7$, it follows that the probability of $\mathbf{Exp}_1$ is bounded by the unforgeability of OTS, zero-knowledge of NIZK$_1$, correctness of TBE, and computational hardness of Assumption 1.

The experiment $\mathbf{Exp}_2$ captures the case where the adversary $\mathcal{A}$ is able to provide a forged delegation for an honest authority apk_i and some attribute att. In this case, $\mathcal{A}$ is bounded by the hardness of Assumption 1 and the second preimage property of $\mathcal{H}_1$.

Lemma 3. *The HABS construction from Figs. 5, 6 and 7 offers path traceability, if SXDH, SDLIN and Assumption 1 hold in $\mathcal{G}$.*

Proof. See full version [19].

Theorem 2. *The HABS scheme in Figs. 5, 6 and 7 offers path-anonymity, non-frameability and path-traceability if $\mathcal{H}_1$, $\mathcal{H}_2$ and $\mathcal{H}_3$ are second-preimage resistant hash functions and SXDH, SDLIN, q-SDH and Assumption 1 hold in $\mathcal{G}$.*

Proof. The result follows from Lemmas 1, 2 and 3. □

4   Efficiency Comparison

We first compare the warrant sizes for our scheme and [12]. For a single attribute, an authority at level 1 (with respect to the root authority at level 0) has a warrant size of 6 group elements (of the form $\mathbb{G}_1^2 \times \mathbb{G}_2^4$). Further delegation to level 2 adds a further 6 elements in $\mathbb{G}_1^2 \times \mathbb{G}_2^4$. A delegation from the root authority contains the opening (a, b) (as part of the 6 elements) which is updated by subsequent delegations, however the warrant must now also contain the issuers public key (X_i, Y_i) in $\mathbb{G}_1^2$. This generalises, and for a user at level k, the size of the warrant is $6k$ for a single attribute. Likewise, if we extend the number of attributes in the warrant to $|A|$, each of which has a delegation path of length k, then the warrant has $6k|A|$ group elements.

In contrast, for a single attribute issued to a level-1 entity, the warrant in [12] contains $7\lceil \frac{12+2m}{m-2} \rceil$ group elements, where m is the size of the message space used in the TBS instantiation. A level-2 delegation increases this to $7\lceil \frac{24+4m}{m-2} \rceil + 2m + 12$ elements, and this generalises for a single attribute that is issued to a level k entity to $7\lceil \frac{k(12+2m)}{m-2} \rceil + (k-1)(2m+12)$ elements. Similarly, a warrant that contains $|A|$ attributes adds a linear factor of $|A|$ to this term. To give a concrete comparison, a user with 3 attributes at level 4 of the hierarchy would have a warrant containing 72 group elements in our scheme, as opposed to 208 elements for an optimal choice of m (i.e., $m = 10$) in the scheme from [12]. Since m would be chosen in advance during the setup phase, the warrant would unlikely reach its optimal bound and for any suboptimal choice of m, the warrant grows linearly in this parameter.

Next, in Table 1 we compare the sizes of public keys (of users and authorities) and the lengths of signatures generated by our scheme and [12]. By β we denote the size of the span program representing the policy Ψ. As before k is the maximum length of a delegation path, $|\Psi|$ is the number of attributes needed to satisfy the signing policy, and m is the size of the message space for the TBS scheme used in [12].

Table 1. Comparison of key and signature sizes.

		Dragan et al. [12]		This Work		
		G	$\mathbb{Z}_p$	$\mathbb{G}_1$	$\mathbb{G}_2$	$\mathbb{Z}_p$
Public Keys	upk	14	-	4	-	-
	apk	$12+2m$		4	-	-
Sig.	ots	3	1	2	1	1
	C	$\frac{5(6+m)k(k-1)|\Psi|}{(m-2)} + 110$	-	$6(2k-1)|\Psi| + 12$	$4(2k-1)|\Psi| + 8$	-
	π	$\frac{28(6+m)k(k-1)|\Psi|}{(m-2)} + 18$	2β	8	$2k|\Psi| + 8$	β

In addition to being more efficient and shorter than [12], our scheme, in fact, produces HABS signatures of *optimal* length, from the asymptotic point of view. The need to provide path traceability, where the TA must be able to reveal the entire delegation path along with delegated attributes from a valid HABS signature implies the $O(k|\Psi|)$ growth of its length. This means that in order to reduce this bound path-tracability property would need to be relaxed.

Finally, our scheme brings a few other efficiency improvements. The use of Type-3 pairings results in fewer group elements and the possibility to achieve the same level security for a smaller choice of the prime p [18], which would give rise to smaller groups and faster operations than in the symmetric setting. In addition, we can adopt batch verification techniques available for Groth-Sahai proofs [6] to speed up the computations.

5   Conclusion

We proposed a direct construction of Hierarchical Attribute-based Signatures (HABS) with a new delegation process based on length-reducing homomorphic trapdoor commitments. Our HABS scheme significantly reduces the lengths of warrants, public keys and signatures in comparison to the so-far only known (generic) HABS construction. Moreover, due to the need to support the path-traceability requirement, our HABS scheme achieves optimal signature length growth of $O(k|\Psi|)$ for delegations paths of size k and signing policies of size $|\Psi|$. Our technique of step-wise embedding of new group elements into the homomorphic trapdoor commitment can be considered to be of independent interest, e.g., it could add support for delegation to other privacy-preserving signature schemes that rely on homomorphic trapdoor commitments, e.g. [2].

Acknowledgements. Daniel Gardham was supported by the UK Government PhD studentship scheme. Mark Manulis was supported by the EPSRC project TAPESTRY (EP/N02799X). The authors thank the anonymous reviewers of ACNS 2019 for their valuable comments.

References

1. Abe, M., Chase, M., David, B., Kohlweiss, M., Nishimaki, R., Ohkubo, M.: Constant-size structure-preserving signatures: generic constructions and simple assumptions. J. Cryptol. **29**, 833–878 (2016)
2. Abe, M., Haralambiev, K., Ohkubo, M.: Signing on elements in bilinear groups for modular protocol design. IACR Cryptology ePrint Archive, p. 133 (2010)
3. Backes, M., Meiser, S., Schröder, D.: Delegatable functional signatures. In: Cheng, C.-M., Chung, K.-M., Persiano, G., Yang, B.-Y. (eds.) PKC 2016. LNCS, vol. 9614, pp. 357–386. Springer, Heidelberg (2016). https://doi.org/10.1007/978-3-662-49384-7_14
4. Belenkiy, M., Camenisch, J., Chase, M., Kohlweiss, M., Lysyanskaya, A., Shacham, H.: Randomizable proofs and delegatable anonymous credentials. In: Halevi, S. (ed.) CRYPTO 2009. LNCS, vol. 5677, pp. 108–125. Springer, Heidelberg (2009). https://doi.org/10.1007/978-3-642-03356-8_7
5. Bellare, M., Fuchsbauer, G.: Policy-based signatures. In: Krawczyk, H. (ed.) PKC 2014. LNCS, vol. 8383, pp. 520–537. Springer, Heidelberg (2014). https://doi.org/10.1007/978-3-642-54631-0_30
6. Blazy, O., Fuchsbauer, G., Izabachène, M., Jambert, A., Sibert, H., Vergnaud, D.: Batch Groth–Sahai. In: Zhou, J., Yung, M. (eds.) ACNS 2010. LNCS, vol. 6123, pp. 218–235. Springer, Heidelberg (2010). https://doi.org/10.1007/978-3-642-13708-2_14
7. Boneh, D., Boyen, X.: Short signatures without random oracles. In: Cachin, C., Camenisch, J.L. (eds.) EUROCRYPT 2004. LNCS, vol. 3027, pp. 56–73. Springer, Heidelberg (2004). https://doi.org/10.1007/978-3-540-24676-3_4

8. Boyle, E., Goldwasser, S., Ivan, I.: Functional signatures and pseudorandom functions. In: Krawczyk, H. (ed.) PKC 2014. LNCS, vol. 8383, pp. 501–519. Springer, Heidelberg (2014). https://doi.org/10.1007/978-3-642-54631-0_29

9. Camenisch, J., Lysyanskaya, A.: A signature scheme with efficient protocols. In: Cimato, S., Persiano, G., Galdi, C. (eds.) SCN 2002. LNCS, vol. 2576, pp. 268–289. Springer, Heidelberg (2003). https://doi.org/10.1007/3-540-36413-7_20

10. Chaum, D.: Security without identification: transaction systems to make big brother obsolete. Commun. ACM **28**(10), 1030–1044 (1985)

11. Chaum, D., van Heyst, E.: Group signatures. In: Davies, D.W. (ed.) EUROCRYPT 1991. LNCS, vol. 547, pp. 257–265. Springer, Heidelberg (1991). https://doi.org/10.1007/3-540-46416-6_22

12. Drăgan, C.-C., Gardham, D., Manulis, M.: Hierarchical attribute-based signatures. In: Camenisch, J., Papadimitratos, P. (eds.) CANS 2018. LNCS, vol. 11124, pp. 213–234. Springer, Cham (2018). https://doi.org/10.1007/978-3-030-00434-7_11

13. El Kaafarani, A., Ghadafi, E.: Attribute-based signatures with user-controlled linkability without random oracles. In: O'Neill, M. (ed.) IMACC 2017. LNCS, vol. 10655, pp. 161–184. Springer, Cham (2017). https://doi.org/10.1007/978-3-319-71045-7_9

14. El Kaafarani, A., Ghadafi, E., Khader, D.: Decentralized traceable attribute-based signatures. In: Benaloh, J. (ed.) CT-RSA 2014. LNCS, vol. 8366, pp. 327–348. Springer, Cham (2014). https://doi.org/10.1007/978-3-319-04852-9_17

15. El Kaafarani, A., Katsumata, S.: Attribute-based signatures for unbounded circuits in the ROM and efficient instantiations from lattices. In: Abdalla, M., Dahab, R. (eds.) PKC 2018. LNCS, vol. 10770, pp. 89–119. Springer, Cham (2018). https://doi.org/10.1007/978-3-319-76581-5_4

16. Escala, A., Herranz, J., Morillo, P.: Revocable attribute-based signatures with adaptive security in the standard model. In: Nitaj, A., Pointcheval, D. (eds.) AFRICACRYPT 2011. LNCS, vol. 6737, pp. 224–241. Springer, Heidelberg (2011). https://doi.org/10.1007/978-3-642-21969-6_14

17. Fuchsbauer, G., Pointcheval, D.: Anonymous proxy signatures. In: Ostrovsky, R., De Prisco, R., Visconti, I. (eds.) SCN 2008. LNCS, vol. 5229, pp. 201–217. Springer, Heidelberg (2008). https://doi.org/10.1007/978-3-540-85855-3_14

18. Galbraith, S.D., Paterson, K.G., Smart, N.P.: Pairings for cryptographers. Discrete Appl. Math. **156**(16), 3113–3121 (2008)

19. Gardham, D., Manulis, M.: Hierarchical attribute-based signatures: short keys and optimal signature length. Cryptology ePrint Archive, Report 2019/382 (2019). https://eprint.iacr.org/2019/382

20. Ghadafi, E.: Stronger security notions for decentralized traceable attribute-based signatures and more efficient constructions. In: Nyberg, K. (ed.) CT-RSA 2015. LNCS, vol. 9048, pp. 391–409. Springer, Cham (2015). https://doi.org/10.1007/978-3-319-16715-2_21

21. Groth, J.: Homomorphic Trapdoor Commitments to Group Elements. Cryptology ePrint Archive, Report 2009/007 (2009)

22. Groth, J., Sahai, A.: Efficient non-interactive proof systems for bilinear groups. In: Smart, N. (ed.) EUROCRYPT 2008. LNCS, vol. 4965, pp. 415–432. Springer, Heidelberg (2008). https://doi.org/10.1007/978-3-540-78967-3_24

23. Herranz, J.: Attribute-based signatures from RSA. TCS **527**, 73–82 (2014)

24. Jager, T., Rupp, A.: The semi-generic group model and applications to pairing-based cryptography. In: Abe, M. (ed.) ASIACRYPT 2010. LNCS, vol. 6477, pp. 539–556. Springer, Heidelberg (2010). https://doi.org/10.1007/978-3-642-17373-8_31

25. Kaaniche, N., Laurent, M., Rocher, P.-O., Kiennert, C., Garcia-Alfaro, J.: PCS, a privacy-preserving certification scheme. In: Data Privacy Management, Cryptocurrencies and Blockchain Technology, pp. 239–256 (2017)

26. Kakvi, S.A.: Efficient fully anonymous group signatures based on the Groth group signature scheme. Master's thesis, University College London (2010)

27. Khader, D., Chen, L., Davenport, J.H.: Certificate-free attribute authentication. In: Parker, M.G. (ed.) IMACC 2009. LNCS, vol. 5921, pp. 301–325. Springer, Heidelberg (2009). https://doi.org/10.1007/978-3-642-10868-6_18

28. Kiltz, E.: Chosen-ciphertext security from tag-based encryption. In: Halevi, S., Rabin, T. (eds.) TCC 2006. LNCS, vol. 3876, pp. 581–600. Springer, Heidelberg (2006). https://doi.org/10.1007/11681878_30

29. Krzywiecki, Ł., Sulkowska, M., Zagórski, F.: Hierarchical ring signatures revisited – unconditionally and perfectly anonymous schnorr version. In: Chakraborty, R.S., Schwabe, P., Solworth, J. (eds.) SPACE 2015. LNCS, vol. 9354, pp. 329–346. Springer, Cham (2015). https://doi.org/10.1007/978-3-319-24126-5_19

30. Li, J., Au, M.H., Susilo, W., Xie, D., Ren, K.: Attribute-based signature and its applications. In: ACM ASIACCS 2010, pp. 60–69. ACM (2010)

31. Maji, H.K., Prabhakaran, M., Rosulek, M.: Attribute-based signatures. In: Kiayias, A. (ed.) CT-RSA 2011. LNCS, vol. 6558, pp. 376–392. Springer, Heidelberg (2011). https://doi.org/10.1007/978-3-642-19074-2_24

32. Okamoto, T., Takashima, K.: Decentralized attribute-based signatures. In: Kurosawa, K., Hanaoka, G. (eds.) PKC 2013. LNCS, vol. 7778, pp. 125–142. Springer, Heidelberg (2013). https://doi.org/10.1007/978-3-642-36362-7_9

33. Okamoto, T., Takashima, K.: Efficient attribute-based signatures for non-monotone predicates in the standard model. In: Catalano, D., Fazio, N., Gennaro, R., Nicolosi, A. (eds.) PKC 2011. LNCS, vol. 6571, pp. 35–52. Springer, Heidelberg (2011). https://doi.org/10.1007/978-3-642-19379-8_3

34. Rivest, R.L., Shamir, A., Tauman, Y.: How to leak a secret. In: Boyd, C. (ed.) ASIACRYPT 2001. LNCS, vol. 2248, pp. 552–565. Springer, Heidelberg (2001). https://doi.org/10.1007/3-540-45682-1_32

35. Sakai, Y.: Practical attribute-based signature schemes for circuits from bilinear map. IET Inf. Secur. **12**, 184–193 (2018)

36. Shoup, V.: Lower bounds for discrete logarithms and related problems. In: Fumy, W. (ed.) EUROCRYPT 1997. LNCS, vol. 1233, pp. 256–266. Springer, Heidelberg (1997). https://doi.org/10.1007/3-540-69053-0_18

37. Trolin, M., Wikström, D.: Hierarchical group signatures. In: Caires, L., Italiano, G.F., Monteiro, L., Palamidessi, C., Yung, M. (eds.) ICALP 2005. LNCS, vol. 3580, pp. 446–458. Springer, Heidelberg (2005). https://doi.org/10.1007/11523468_37

38. Tsabary, R.: An equivalence between attribute-based signatures and homomorphic signatures, and new constructions for both. In: Kalai, Y., Reyzin, L. (eds.) TCC 2017. LNCS, vol. 10678, pp. 489–518. Springer, Cham (2017). https://doi.org/10.1007/978-3-319-70503-3_16

Raptor: A Practical Lattice-Based (Linkable) Ring Signature

Xingye Lu[1], Man Ho Au[1]([⊠]), and Zhenfei Zhang[2]

[1] The Hong Kong Polytechnic University, Hung Hom, Hong Kong
xingye.lu@connect.polyu.hk, mhaau@polyu.edu.hk
[2] Algorand, Boston, USA
zhenfei@algorand.com

Abstract. We present RAPTOR, the first practical lattice-based (linkable) ring signature scheme with implementation. RAPTOR is as fast as classical solutions; while the size of the signature is roughly 1.3 KB per user. Prior to our work, all existing lattice-based solutions are analogues of their discrete-log or pairing-based counterparts. We develop a generic construction of (linkable) ring signatures based on the well-known generic construction from Rivest et al., which is not fully compatible with lattices. Our generic construction is provably secure in random oracle model. We also give instantiations from both standard lattice, as a proof of concept, and NTRU lattice, as an efficient instantiation. We show that the latter construction, called RAPTOR, is almost as efficient as the classical RST ring signatures and thus may be of practical interest.

1 Introduction

The notion of ring signatures was put forth by Rivest, Shamir and Tauman in 2001 [46]. It is a special type of group signature [16,18] where a signer is able to produce a signature on behalf of a group of potential signers. Unlike group signatures, there is no central party to manage group membership nor capable of revealing identity of the generator of the signature. In a typical use case of ring signatures, each user is associated with a public key and a group is formed spontaneously by collecting users' public keys. It is a very attractive property as it enables anonymity: the signer hides its identity within the group, and there is no trusted third party that is capable of revocation.

Ring signatures offer very strong anonymity. In particular, signatures created by the same signer are unlinkable. Observing that in some real-world applications, such as electronic voting, unlinkability can be undesirable, Liu, Wei and Wong [36] put forth the notion of linkable ring signatures. In such a scheme, the identity of the signer remains anonymous. In the meantime, two signatures created by the same signer can be linked.

Z. Zhang—This work was done when with OnBoard Security.
This work is supported by Innovation and Technology Funding under project ITS/356/17 and National Natural Science Foundation of China under project 61602396.

R. H. Deng et al. (Eds.): ACNS 2019, LNCS 11464, pp. 110–130, 2019.
https://doi.org/10.1007/978-3-030-21568-2_6

The properties of linkability and signer anonymity are very desirable in various real world applications, including, but not limited to, e-cash, e-voting, and ad-hoc authentication. For example, in the e-cash scenario, a linkable ring signature allows the spender to remain anonymous, while making it possible for the bank to identify double spenders. To date, linkable ring signature has become a mainstream solution to protect sender privacy in cryptocurrency transaction [43].

All linkable ring signatures deployed in practice are based on number-theoretic assumptions and thus vulnerable to quantum computers [48]. Even though quantum computers are still in their infancy, many believed that general purpose quantum computers will inevitably arrive, by when the exiting classical ring signatures will lose their anonymity and/or unforgeability.

Lattice-based cryptography is one of the most promising families of candidates [42] to the quantum apocalypse. Besides resistance to quantum attacks, problems in lattice-based cryptography exhibit an additional properties, namely, breaking a random instance of a lattice problem is as hard as solving the worst-case instance.

To date, there exist a number of lattice-based ring signature schemes and lattice-based linkable ring signature schemes [2,4,11,15,25,34]. While some of them are asymptotically efficient, they are hardly practical. In particular, to the best of our knowledge, none of these constructions come with an implementation.

1.1 Related Work

Classical Ring Signatures. We review the existing constructions of (linkable) ring signatures. The generic construction introduced by Rivest, Shamir and Tauman [46] in 2001 (RST). This generic construction is based on one-way trapdoor permutations along with a block cipher. It can be instantiated from the RSA assumption. In 2004, Abe, Ohkubo and Suzuku [1] (AOS) proposed a new generic construction which allows discrete-log type of keys. This generic construction can make use of hash-and-sign signature or any three-move sigma-protocol-based signature. It can be instantiated from RSA or discrete-log assumptions. Both of the RST and AOS constructions are secure in the random oracle model and the signature sizes are linear to the ring size. To achieve the security in standard model, Bender, Katz and Morselli [12] (BKM) presented a ring signature scheme which adopts a public-key encryption scheme, a signature scheme and a ZAP protocol for any language in $\mathcal{NP}$ [24]. Even though BKM construction is secure in standard model, the signature size is still linear in the number of group members and the generic ZAPs are actually quite impractical. Shacham and Waters [47] then proposed a more efficient linear-size ring signature scheme without random oracle from bilinear pairing.

To reduce the signature size, Dodis et al. proposed the first ring signature scheme with constant signature size in 2004 [20]. It relies on accumulator with one-way domain and is secure in the random oracle model. The first sub-linear size ring signature without random oracle model is due to Chandran, Groth and Sahai [17]. This scheme has signature size $\mathcal{O}(\sqrt{\ell})$ where ℓ is the number of users in the ring. All of the above sub-linear size constructions are secure in the common reference string model that requires a trusted setup. The first sub-linear ring signature without relying on a trusted setup is due to Groth and Kohlweiss [28]. It features logarithmic size signature and is secure in the random oracle model.

Classical Linkable Ring Signatures. Since the first proposal of linkable ring signature [36], we have seen a sequence of work [8,35,50,52] that provides different features. In 2005, Tsang and Wei [52] extends the genric ring signature introduced by Dodis et al. [20] to a linkable version, which also features constant signature size and is secure in the random oracle model. Au et al. [8] presented a new security model for linkable ring signatures and a new short linkable ring signature scheme that is secure in this strengthened model. In 2014, Liu et al. [35] presented the first linkable ring signature scheme achieving unconditional anonymity. Sun et al. [50] proposed a new generic linkable ring signature to construct RingCT 2.0 for Monero. There are also schemes with special properties such as identity-based linkable ring signatures [10,51] and certificate-based linkable ring signatures [9].

Lattice-Based Ring Signatures. For ring signatures in the lattice setting, Brakerski and Kalai [15] proposed a generic ring signature scheme in the standard model. This generic construction is based on a new primitive called ring trapdoor functions. They instantiated this function based on the inhomogeneous short integer solution problem (ISIS). However, the resulting scheme is only secure under a weak definition. To achieve full security, an inefficient transformation is needed. Melchor et al. [2] transforms Lyubashevsky's lattice-based signature [39] into a ring signature. As the authors pointed out themselves, their scheme is "pretty unpractical". In 2016, Libert et al. [34] presented a lattice-based accumulator. With the accumulator and a lattice-based zero-knowledge proof system, they build a ring signature scheme that features logarithmic signature size. However, the zero-knowledge arguments applied in the accumulator is very inefficient. The state-of-the-art is the lattice-based ring signature scheme proposed by Esgin et al. [25]. They adapt the efficient one-out-of-many proof [14,28] to build a lattice-based ring signature scheme. Same as [25,34] is also a logarithmic size ring signature scheme and is secure in the random oracle model.

Lattice-Based Linkable Ring Signatures. The first lattice-based linkable ring signature scheme was proposed by Torres et al. in 2018 [4]. It can be seen as an instantiation of the AOS framework from the lattice-based BLISS signature [21], with adaption to introduce linkability. The signature size is linear to the number of members in the ring and is reported to be 51 KB per ring member. In the same year, Baum, Lin and Oechsner [11] construct another lattice-based linkable ring signature scheme following a very similar ideal to [4]. The signature size for [11] is claimed to be around 10.3 KB per user. The main difference between these two work is the way to achieve linkability. We are not aware of any implementation of these work.

For the existing lattice-based (linkable) ring signature schemes, we are not aware of these constructions come with any implementation. In terms of performance, lattice-based (linkable) ring signatures [2,4,11] are all based on the lattice-based sigma-protocol-based signature and thus involve additional overhead in the form of rejection sampling which affects the performance of the signature scheme. As mentioned above, the inefficiency of the underlying zero-knowledge proof system makes [34] quite impractical. In this paper, we not only present a practical and efficient lattice-based (linkable) ring signature scheme but also implement it on a typical laptop and provide the performance.

1.2 Our Contribution

We present RAPTOR, the first lattice-based (linkable) ring signature with implementation. It gets its name as it is the next generation of FALCON [26] that features a "stealth" mode. RAPTOR is secure in the random oracle model, based on some widely-accepted lattice assumptions. We also present a less efficient version that is based on standard lattice problems. We implement RAPTOR, and its performance on a typical laptop is shown in Table 1(a) and (b). The experimental setting is presented in Sect. 5.

Table 1. Performance

(a) RAPTOR-512

Users	5	10	50
KeyGen	29 ms	29 ms	29 ms
Sign	6 ms	9.5 ms	40 ms
verification	3 ms	6.5 ms	32 ms
PK	0.9 KB	0.9 KB	0.9 KB
SK	4.1 KB	4.1 KB	4.1 KB
Signature	6.3 KB	12.7 KB	63.3 KB

(b) Linkable RAPTOR-512

Users	5	10	50
KeyGen	57 ms	57 ms	57 ms
Sign	10.7 ms	17.4 ms	61 ms
verification	5.2 ms	11 ms	50 ms
PK	0.9 KB	0.9 KB	0.9 KB
SK	9.1 KB	9.1 KB	9.1 KB
Signature	7.8 KB	14.2 KB	64.8 KB

Our solution is in a sense optimal for the family of solutions where the signatures are linear in terms of users: in our construction, the signature consists of a lattice vector and a random nonce of 2λ bits per user. The best theoretical work in linear size is due to [11], where the signature size is claimed to be 82.5 KB with a ring size of 8. Comparing with the state-of-the-art [25] with sublinear signature size, our work is still comparing favourably for ring signature size $\lesssim 1000$. As a remark, a common use case of linkable a ring signature, privacy protection for cryptocurrency, often uses a ring size less than 20 and thus Raptor is more preferable in this setting. The signature size of [25] is reported to be 930 KB with 2^6 users in the ring and 1409 KB with 2^{10} users in the ring. The comparison of signature size of our RAPTOR and other existing lattice-based (linkable) ring signature scheme is shown in Table 2.

Table 2. Comparison of lattice-based (linkable) ring signature at security level $\lambda = 100$. Signature size increases with ring size (i.e. number of public keys in the ring).

	[34]	[4]	[11]	[25]	RAPTOR	(linkable) RAPTOR
Signature size growth	Logarithm	Linear	Linear	Logarithm	Linear	Linear
Linkability	×	✓	✓	×	×	✓
Implementation	×	×	×	×	✓	✓
Signature size with 2^6 users	$\approx$ 37 MB	$\approx$ 649 KB	$\approx$ 585 KB	930 KB	80.6 KB	82.7 KB
with 2^8 users	$\approx$ 48.1 MB	$\approx$ 2474 KB	$\approx$ 2340 KB	1132 KB	332.6 KB	326.5 KB
with 2^{10} users	$\approx$ 59.1 MB	$\approx$ 9770 KB	$\approx$ 9360 KB	1409 KB	1290.2 KB	1301.9KB
with 2^{12} users	$\approx$ 70.2 MB	$\approx$ 39 MB	$\approx$ 37.4 MB	1492 KB	5161 KB	5203.3 KB

In terms of security, (linkable) RAPTOR is backed by a new generic framework that is provably secure in the random oracle model, under the assumption based on RST construction. Instead of relying on one-way trapdoor permutation, the new generic framework is based on a new primitive called Chameleon Hash Plus (CH^+) which can be instantiated from lattice setting (e.g. NTRU). Our generic construction can additionally transform any ring signature into a one-time linkable ring signature.

Nonetheless, when CH^+ is instantiated with a standard lattice problem (i.e., the short integer solution problem), we base the security of (linkable) ring signature on the worst-case lattice problems that are conjectured to be hard against quantum computers. In practice, one often resorts to NTRU lattices [31] for better efficiency. Our (linkable) RAPTOR scheme is such a case, where the CH^+ function is instantiated from the pre-image samplable function of FALCON [26].

1.3   Overview of Our Construction

Before presenting a high-level description of our construction, we first discuss the subtlety of instantiating the RST generic construction from lattices. Recall that the building block of RST ring signatures is one-way trapdoor permutation. While trapdoor functions can be built from lattices, they are not permutations by themselves and therefore cannot be applied directly. Consequently, all existing linear-size lattice-based constructions opt for the AOS framework, which can be built from any sigma-protocol based signatures. Indeed, [4,11] can be seen as instantiations from this framework. On the other hand, we identify essential properties required by the underlying building blocks in the RST framework. The result is a type of trapdoor function that we called Chameleon hash plus (CH^+), a construct that is similar to Chameleon hash functions.

Building Block: CH^+ The main building block for our generic constructions is a chameleon hash plus (CH^+) function. We recall the notion of chameleon hash function which was first formalized by Krawczyk and Rabin in 2000 [32]. Chameleon hash functions are randomized collision-resistant hash functions with an additional property that each hash key is equipped with a trapdoor. With the trapdoor, one can easily find collisions for any input. More specifically, on input a trapdoor tr corresponding to some chameleon hash key hk, two messages

m, m' and a randomness r, one can efficiently compute another randomness r' such that $\mathsf{Hash}(\mathsf{hk}, m, r) = \mathsf{Hash}(\mathsf{hk}, m', r')$.

Our CH^+ consists of four algorithms, namely, SetUp, $\mathsf{TrapGen}$, Hash and Inv. See Sect. 3.1 for details. Similar to a chameleon hash, without the trapdoor, CH^+ needs to be one-way and collision-resistant. There are two main difference in CH^+: 1. to compute new randomness r' for any given message m', only the hash value, $C = \mathsf{Hash}(\mathsf{hk}, m, r)$, is needed; whereas both the original message m and randomness r are required in a classical Chameleon hash; 2. optionally, there exists a system parameter $\mathsf{param}^{\mathsf{ch}}$ as an implicit input to all CH^+ operations.

Our Generic Construction of Ring Signatures. We describe how we can build a ring signature from CH^+. We assume $\mathsf{param}^{\mathsf{ch}}$ is available at the setup. In the key generation procedure, a signer runs algorithm $\mathsf{TrapGen}$ to obtain hash key hk and its trapdoor tr. Signer's public key and secret key will be hk and tr, respectively.

Suppose a signer, S_π, with public and secret keys $(\mathsf{hk}_\pi, \mathsf{sk}_\pi)$, tries to sign message μ on behalf of a group of signer $\{S_1, \cdots, S_\ell\}$ ($\pi \in \{1, \cdots, \ell\}$), S_π first collects all the public keys of the group of signers $\{\mathsf{hk}_1, \cdots, \mathsf{hk}_\ell\}$. Next, for $i \neq \pi$, S_π randomly samples message m_i, randomness r_i and computes hash output $C_i = \mathsf{Hash}(\mathsf{hk}_i, m_i, r_i)$; for $i = \pi$, i.e., the signer himself, S_π samples a C_π.

S_π further sets $C^* = \mathcal{H}(\mu, C_1, \cdots, C_\ell, \mathsf{hk}_1, \cdots, \mathsf{hk}_\ell)$ where μ is the message to be signed and $\mathcal{H}$ is a collision-resistant hash function. It then computes m_π which satisfies $m_1 \oplus \cdots \oplus m_\ell = C^*$ and uses the trapdoor to find an r_π such that $c_\pi = \mathsf{Hash}(\mathsf{hk}_\pi, m_\pi, r_\pi)$. The signature for S_π on μ is $\{(m_1, r_1), \cdots, (m_\ell, r_\ell)\}$. Note that without the trapdoor, it is hard to find such a randomness r_π since CH^+ is one-way and collision-resistant.

To verify the signature, one can first compute $C_i = \mathsf{Hash}(\mathsf{hk}_i, m_i, r_i)$ for $i = 1, \cdots, \ell$. Then check whether $m_1 \oplus \cdots \oplus m_\ell$ is equivalent to $\mathcal{H}(\mu, C_1, \cdots, C_\ell, \mathsf{hk}_1, \cdots, \mathsf{hk}_\ell)$. If so, the verifier accepts the signature as signed by one of the group members.

Our Generic Construction of Linkable Ring Signatures. Linkable ring signature scheme allows others to link two signatures sharing the same signer. At a high level, we will use a tag to achieve this property. The tag is a representative of the signer's identity for each signature. Signatures that share a same tag are linked. It is natural to enforce that each signer only obtains one unique tag; and this tag cannot be forged, or transferred from/to another user. We use a one-time signature[1] to achieve those properties.

During the key generation procedure, in addition to a hk and its trapdoor tr, the signer also generates a pair of public key and secret key $(\mathsf{opk}, \mathsf{osk})$ for a one-time signature. The signer then masks hk by $\mathcal{H}(\mathsf{opk})$ and obtains a masked hash key hk'. The unique tag for the signer will be the public key opk. In the end, the signer sets hk' as public key and $(\mathsf{tr}, \mathsf{opk}, \mathsf{osk})$ as secret key.

---

[1] Here we will only use the public key once; the actual signature scheme does not necessarily need to be a one-time signature scheme.

When the signer S_π signs a message μ on behalf of a group of signers $\{S_1, \cdots, S_\ell\}$ $(\pi \in \{1, \cdots, \ell\})$, it will collect the public keys of the group $\{\mathsf{hk}_1', \cdots, \mathsf{hk}_\ell'\}$ as usual. For each public key hk_i' in the group, S_π computes $\mathsf{hk}_i'' = \mathsf{hk}_i' \oplus \mathcal{H}(\mathsf{opk})$. A new list of "public keys", $\{\mathsf{hk}_1'', \cdots, \mathsf{hk}_\ell''\}$, is then formed. Note that hk_π'' is equivalent to the original hk_π. Next, the signer S_π invokes the (none linkable) ring signature with keys $\{\mathsf{hk}_1'', \cdots, \mathsf{hk}_\ell''\}$, a trapdoor tr_π and a message μ, and obtains a (none linkable) ring signature $\sigma_R = \{(m_1, r_1), \cdots, (m_\ell, r_\ell)\}$ on μ. Finally, S_π signs μ, σ_R using osk_π and gets a one-time signature sig. The linkable ring signature produced by S_π will be $\{\sigma_R, \mathsf{opk}_\pi, sig\}$. As for verification, in addition to verifying σ_R, one should also check whether sig is a valid signature on μ and σ_R under opk_π.

1.4 Organization

In Sect. 2, we introduce our notation, hardness assumptions in lattice, lattice-based preimage sampleable functions and syntax for (linkable) ring signature. We state the new primitive CH^+, and our new generic construction of (linkable) ring signature based on CH^+ in Sect. 3. We then instantiate CH^+ from standard lattice and NTRU in Sects. 4.1 and 4.2 respectively. We also give the full description of our linkable RAPTOR in Sect. 4.3. In the last section, we present the implementation result along with its parameter.

2 Preliminary

2.1 Notation

Elements in $\mathbb{Z}_q$ are represented by integers in $[-\frac{q}{2}, \frac{q}{2})$. For a ring $\mathcal{R}$ we define $\mathcal{R}_q$ to be the quotient ring $\mathbb{Z}_q[x]/(x^n + 1)$ with n being a power of 2 and q being a prime. Column vectors in $\mathbb{Z}_q^m$ and elements in $\mathcal{R}_q$ are denoted by lower-case bold letters (e.g. $\mathbf{x}$). Matrices are denoted by upper-case bold letters (e.g. $\mathbf{X}$). We use $\hat{\mathbf{x}}$ to denote a column vector with entries from the ring.

For distribution D, $x \leftarrow_\$ D$ means sampling x according to distribution D. $\|\mathbf{v}\|_1$ is the ℓ_1 norm of vector $\mathbf{v}$ and $\|\mathbf{v}\|$ is the ℓ_2 norm of $\mathbf{v}$. For $\hat{\mathbf{v}} = (\mathbf{v}_1, \cdots, \mathbf{v}_n)^T$, we define $\|\hat{\mathbf{v}}\| = \sqrt{\sum_{i=1}^n \|\mathbf{v}_i\|^2}$.

The continuous normal distribution over $\mathbb{R}^n$ centered at $\mathbf{v}$ with standard deviation σ is defined as $\rho_{\mathbf{v},\sigma}^n(\mathbf{x}) = (\frac{1}{\sqrt{2\pi\sigma^2}})^n e^{\frac{-\|\mathbf{x}-\mathbf{v}\|^2}{2\sigma^2}}$. For simplicity, when $\mathbf{v}$ is the zero vector, we use $\rho_\sigma^n(\mathbf{x})$.

The discrete normal distribution over $\mathbb{Z}^n$ centered at $\mathbf{v} \in \mathbb{Z}^n$ with standard deviation σ is defined as $D_{\mathbf{v},\sigma}^n(\mathbf{x}) = \frac{\rho_{\mathbf{v},\sigma}^n(\mathbf{x})}{\rho_{\mathbf{v},\sigma}^n(\mathbb{Z}^n)}$.

We define the exclusive-or operation of two matrix $\mathbf{X}^{(1)} \in \mathbb{Z}_q^{n \times m}$ and $\mathbf{X}^{(2)} \in \mathbb{Z}_q^{n \times m}$, $\mathbf{X}^{(1)} \oplus \mathbf{X}^{(2)}$, as:

$$\begin{bmatrix} \mathsf{b}_q(x_{11}^{(1)}) \oplus \mathsf{b}_q(x_{11}^{(2)}) & \cdots & \mathsf{b}_q(x_{1m}^{(1)}) \oplus \mathsf{b}_q(x_{1m}^{(2)}) \\ \vdots & \ddots & \vdots \\ \mathsf{b}_q(x_{n1}^{(1)}) \oplus \mathsf{b}_q(x_{n1}^{(2)}) & \cdots & \mathsf{b}_q(x_{nm}^{(1)}) \oplus \mathsf{b}_q(x_{nm}^{(2)}) \end{bmatrix}$$

where $b_q(x)$ means that transform a value $x \in \mathbb{Z}_q$ to its binary representation. $b_q(.)$ can be efficiently computed.

2.2 Lattices and Hardness Assumptions

A lattice in m-dimension Euclidean space $\mathbb{R}^m$ is a discrete set

$$\Lambda(\mathbf{b}_1, \cdots, \mathbf{b}_n) = \left\{ \sum_{i=1}^{n} x_i \mathbf{b}_i | x_i \in \mathbb{Z} \right\}$$

of all integral combinations of n linear independent vectors $\mathbf{b}_1, \cdots, \mathbf{b}_n$ in $\mathbb{R}^m$ ($m \leq n$). We call matrix $\mathbf{B} = [\mathbf{b}_1, \cdots, \mathbf{b}_n] \in \mathbb{R}^{m \times n}$ a basis of lattice Λ. Using matrix notation, a lattice can be defined as $\Lambda(\mathbf{B}) = \{\mathbf{B}\mathbf{x} | \mathbf{x} \in \mathbb{Z}^n\}$.

The discrete Gaussian distribution of a lattice Λ, parameter s and center $\mathbf{v}$ is defined as $D_{\Lambda, \mathbf{v}, s}(\mathbf{x}) = \frac{\rho_{\mathbf{v},s}(\mathbf{x})}{\rho_{\mathbf{v},s}(\Lambda)}$.

Lemma 1 ([39] *Lemma 4.4*). *For positive real number $s > 0$, we have*

1. $\Pr_{\mathbf{x} \leftarrow D_s^m}[\|\mathbf{x}\| \leq 2\sqrt{m}s] \geq 1 - 2^{-m}$;
2. $\Pr_{\mathbf{x} \leftarrow D_s^m}[\|\mathbf{x}\| \leq k\sqrt{m}s] \geq 1 - k^m e^{\frac{m}{2}(1-k^2)}$.

Definition 1. *Let $m \geq n \geq 1$ and $q \geq 2$. For arbitrary matrix $\mathbf{A} \in \mathbb{Z}_q^{n \times m}$ and vector $\mathbf{u} \in \mathbb{Z}_q^n$ define m-dimensional full-rank integer lattices and its shift:*

$$\Lambda^\perp(\mathbf{A}) = \{\mathbf{z} \in \mathbb{Z}^m : \mathbf{A}\mathbf{z} = \mathbf{0} \mod q\},$$

$$\Lambda_{\mathbf{u}}^\perp(\mathbf{A}) = \{\mathbf{z} \in \mathbb{Z}^m : \mathbf{A}\mathbf{z} = \mathbf{u} \mod q\}.$$

Short Integer Solution (SIS) problem and Inhomogeneous Short Integer Solution (ISIS) problem are two average-case hard problems frequently used in lattice-based cryptography constructions.

Definition 2 ($\text{SIS}_{q,n,m,\beta}$ problem). *Given a uniformly chosen matrix $\mathbf{A} \in \mathbb{Z}_q^{n \times m}$, find $\mathbf{x} \in \Lambda^\perp(\mathbf{A})$ and $0 < \|\mathbf{x}\| \leq \beta$.*

Definition 3 ($\text{ISIS}_{q,n,m,\beta}$ problem). *Given a uniformly chosen matrix $\mathbf{A} \in \mathbb{Z}_q^{n \times m}$ and vector $\mathbf{u} \in \mathbb{Z}_q^n$, find $\mathbf{x} \in \Lambda_{\mathbf{u}}^\perp(\mathbf{A})$ and $0 < \|\mathbf{x}\| \leq \beta$.*

According to [27], if $q \geq \omega(\sqrt{n \log n})\beta$ and $m, \beta = poly(n)$, then $\text{SIS}_{q,n,m,\beta}$ and $\text{ISIS}_{q,n,m,\beta}$ are at least as hard as a standard worst-case lattice problem SIVP_γ (Shortest Independent Vector Problem) with $\gamma = \tilde{O}(\beta n)$. Similarly, R-SIS (R-ISIS) problems are defined as an analogue of SIS (ISIS) problem in ideal lattices.

Definition 4 (R-$\text{SIS}_{q,m,\beta}$ problem). *Given a uniformly chosen vector $\hat{\mathbf{a}} \in \mathcal{R}_q^m$, find $\hat{\mathbf{x}} \in \mathcal{R}^m$ such that $\hat{\mathbf{a}}^T \cdot \hat{\mathbf{x}} = 0$ and $0 < \|\hat{\mathbf{x}}\| \leq \beta$.*

Definition 5 (R-ISIS$_{q,m,\beta}$ problem). *Given a uniformly chosen vector* $\hat{\mathbf{a}} \in \mathcal{R}_q^m$ *and a ring element* $\mathbf{u} \in \mathcal{R}_q$, *find* $\hat{\mathbf{x}} \in \mathcal{R}^m$ *such that* $\hat{\mathbf{a}}^T \cdot \hat{\mathbf{x}} = \mathbf{u}$ *and* $0 < \|\hat{\mathbf{x}}\| \leq \beta$.

The R-SIS problem was concurrently introduced in [40,45]. According to [40], the R-SIS$_{q,m,\beta}$ is as hard as the SVP$_\gamma$ (Shortest Vector Problem) for $\gamma = \tilde{O}(n\beta)$ in all lattice that are ideals in $\mathcal{R}$ if $\mathcal{R} = \mathbb{Z}[x]/(x^n + 1)$, where n is a power of 2.

Definition 6 (NTRU assumption). *Let* $\mathbf{a} = \mathbf{g}/\mathbf{f}$ *over* $\mathcal{R}_q$ *where* $\|\mathbf{f}, \mathbf{g}\|_1$ *is bounded by some parameter* $\beta < q$. *The NTRU assumption says it is hard to distinguish* $\mathbf{a}$ *from a uniformly random element from* $\mathcal{R}_q$.

Over the years, there has been a few different versions of the NTRU assumption [31,37,49]. Here we use a decisional version that is most convenient for our proof. Note that this assumption holds as long as GapSVP problem is hard for NTRU lattices.

2.3 Preimage Sampleable Functions and Falcon

Generating a 'hard' public basis $\mathbf{A}$ (chosen at random from some appropriate distribution) of some lattice Λ, together with a 'good' trapdoor basis $\mathbf{T}$ has been studied since the work of Ajtai [3]. In 2008, Gentry, Peikert and Vaikuntanathan [27] construct a preimage sampleable function using the 'hard' public basis and trapdoor basis, and apply it as a building block to lattice-based signature schemes. This celebrated work (referred to as the GPV framework) is followed by a sequence of improvements. Alwen and Peikert [7] is able to generate a shorter trapdoor, compared to [27]; while Peikert [44] provides a parallelizable algorithm to sample preimages. To the best of our knowledge, the most efficient construction following this direction while maintaining a security proof is due to Micciancio and Peikert [41]. Here we re-state one of their results.

Theorem 1 ([41], Theorem 5.1). *There exists an efficient algorithm* GenBasis $(1^n, 1^m, q)$ *that given any integers* $n \leq 1$, $q \leq 2$, *and sufficiently large* $m = O(n \log q)$, *outputs a parity-check matrix* $\mathbf{A} \in \mathbb{Z}_q^{n \times m}$ *and a 'trapdoor'* $\mathbf{T}$ *such that the distribution of* $\mathbf{A}$ *is* negl(n)-*far from uniform. Moreover, there is an efficient algorithm* PreSample. *With overwhelming probability over all random choices, for any* $\mathbf{u} \in \mathbb{Z}_q^n$ *and large enough* $s = O(\sqrt{n \log q})$, PreSample$(\mathbf{A}, \mathbf{T}, \mathbf{u}, s)$ *samples from a distribution within* negl(n) *statistical distance of* $D_{\Lambda_{\mathbf{u}}^{\perp}(\mathbf{A}), s \cdot \omega(\sqrt{\log n})}$.

On the other hand, the most efficient GPV construction in practice is due to Prest et al. [22,26] using NTRU lattices [31]. The corresponding signature scheme is named FALCON [26].

FALCON is a candidate lattice-based signature scheme to the NIST postquantum standardization process [42]. It is the resurrection of NTRUSign [30] with the aforementioned GPV framework for transcript security [22,27], and a fast Fourier sampling for efficiency [23]. It is by far the most practical candidates among all submitted proposals, in terms of the combined sizes of public keys and signatures; and the only solution that provides a preimage sampleable function. In terms of security,

- FALCON stems from the provable secure GPV construction [27], under the (quantum) random oracle model [13];
- although the parameters in FALCON does not support GPV's security proof, they are robust against best known attacks[2].

Falcon Signature Scheme. We now give the high level description of FALCON signature scheme. The detail of the scheme can be found in [26]. Here we assume the signature scheme works over a polynomial ring $\mathcal{R}_q := \mathbb{Z}_q[x]/(x^n + 1)$.

- FALCON.KeyGen(1^λ) $\to$ $(\mathbf{a}, \mathbf{T})$: this algorithm takes security parameter 1^λ as input and chooses random $\mathbf{f}$ and $\mathbf{g}$ polynomials $(\mathbf{f}, \mathbf{g} \in \mathcal{R}_q)$ using an appropriate distribution. The public key will be set as $\mathbf{a} = \mathbf{g}/\mathbf{f}$ and the secret key $\mathbf{T} := \begin{bmatrix} \mathbf{f} & \mathbf{g} \\ \bar{\mathbf{f}} & \bar{\mathbf{g}} \end{bmatrix}$ is the trapdoor of $\mathbf{a}$. $\bar{\mathbf{f}}$ and $\bar{\mathbf{g}}$ satisfy $\mathbf{f}\bar{\mathbf{g}} - \mathbf{g}\bar{\mathbf{f}} = q \mod (x^n + 1)$ and $\mathbf{f}, \mathbf{g}, \bar{\mathbf{f}}, \bar{\mathbf{g}}$ should be short.
- FALCON.Sign($\mathbf{a}, \mathbf{T}; \mu$) $\to$ $(\mathbf{r}_0, \mathbf{r}_1)$: the signing algorithm first hashes the message μ into a polynomial $\mathbf{c} \in \mathcal{R}_q$. Then it uses the short trapdoor $\mathbf{T}$ to produce a pair of short polynomials $(\mathbf{r}_0, \mathbf{r}_1)$ such that $\mathbf{r}_0 + \mathbf{a}\mathbf{r}_1 = \mathbf{c}$.
- FALCON.Verify($\mathbf{a}, (\mathbf{r}_0, \mathbf{r}_1), \mu$) $\to$ $0/1$: this algorithm verifies that $(\mathbf{r}_0, \mathbf{r}_1)$ is a pair of appropriately short polynomials and $\mathbf{c} = \mathbf{r}_0 + \mathbf{a}\mathbf{r}_1$ where $\mathbf{c}$ is the hash of message μ. If all pass, output 1; otherwise, output 0.

2.4   Syntax

In this section, we are going to introduce the syntax of ring signature and linkable ring signature.

Ring Signature. A ring signature scheme usually is a tuple of four algorithms (**Setup, KeyGen, Signing, Verification**):

- **Setup**(1^λ)$\to$ param: On input security parameter 1^λ, this algorithm generates system parameter param. We assume param is an implicit input to all the algorithms listed below.
- **KeyGen**$\to$ (sk, pk): By taking system parameter param, this key generation algorithm generates a private signing key sk and a public verification key pk.
- **Signing**(sk, μ, L_{pk}) $\to$ σ: On input message μ, a list of user public keys L_{pk}, and signing key sk of one of the public keys in L_{pk}, the signing algorithm outputs a ring signature σ on μ.
- **Verification**($\mu, \sigma, L_{\mathsf{pk}}$)$\to$ *accept/reject*: On input message μ, signature σ and list of user public keys L_{pk}, the verification algorithm outputs *accept* if σ is legitimately created; *reject*, otherwise.

Correctness: the scheme is correct if signatures generated according to above specification are always accepted during verification.

---

[2] In practical lattice-based cryptography, it is common to derive parameters from best known attacks other than security proofs. For example, see [5,6].

Linkable Ring Signature. A linkable ring signature scheme usually consists of five algorithms, namely, (**Setup, KeyGen, Signing, Verification, Link**):

- **Setup**$(1^\lambda) \rightarrow$ param: On input the security parameter 1^λ, this algorithm generates the system parameter param. We assume param is an implicit input to all the algorithms listed below.
- **KeyGen**$\rightarrow$ (sk, pk): By taking the system parameter param, this key generation algorithm generates a private signing key sk and a public verification key pk.
- **Signing**(sk, μ, L_{pk}) $\rightarrow \sigma$: On input a message μ, a list of user public keys L_{pk}, and a signing key sk of one of the public keys in L_{pk}, the signing algorithm outputs a ring signature σ on μ.
- **Verification**$(\mu, \sigma, L_{pk}) \rightarrow accept/reject$: On input a message μ, a signature σ and a list of user public keys L_{pk}, the verification algorithm outputs $accept$ if σ is legitimately created. Otherwise, output $reject$.
- **Link** (σ_1, σ_2, μ_1, μ_2, $L_{pk}^{(1)}$, $L_{pk}^{(2)}$) $\rightarrow linked/unlinked$: This algorithm takes two messages μ_1, μ_2 and their signatures σ_1 and σ_2 as input, output $linked$ or $unlinked$.

Correctness: the scheme is correct if: signatures signed as above is always accepted during verification; and two legally signed signatures are linked if and only if they share a same signer.

Due to page limitation, we omit the detailed security requirements for (linkable) ring signature. Usually, a ring signature scheme is said to be secure if the scheme is anonymous and unforgeable. A linkable ring signature scheme is said to be secure if the scheme is anonymous, linkable, nonslanderable and unforgeable. The detailed security requirements can be found in full version [38].

3   Our Generic Constructions

In this section, we present our generic construction of CH^+ and our (linkable) ring signature scheme based on CH^+.

3.1   Chameleon Hash Plus

CH^+ can be considered as a variant of Chameleon hash functions. A CH^+ consists of four algorithms, namely, SetUp, TrapGen, Hash and Inv, as follow:

- SetUp$(1^\lambda) \rightarrow$ param^{ch}: On input security parameter 1^λ, this algorithm generates system parameter param^{ch}. param^{ch} will be an implicit input to Hash and Inv.
- TrapGen$(1^\lambda) \rightarrow$ (hk, tr): This algorithm takes security parameter 1^λ as input and returns a pair (hk, tr) where hk and tr are respectively a hash key and a trapdoor.
- Hash(hk, m, r) $\rightarrow C$: On input hash key hk, message m and randomness r, this algorithm returns hash output C.

- $\mathsf{Inv}(\mathsf{hk}, \mathsf{tr}, C, m') \to r'$: On input hash key hk, trapdoor tr, hash output C and message m', this algorithm returns randomness r' s.t. $\mathsf{Hash}(\mathsf{hk}, m', r') = C$.

We require CH^+ to satisfy following requirements:

1. CH^+ should be one-way and collision resistant. In other words, for all PPT $\mathcal{A}$, there exists a negligible function $\mathsf{negl}(\lambda)$ such that

$$\Pr[\{(m_0, r_0), (m_1, r_1)\} \leftarrow \mathcal{A}(1^\lambda, \mathsf{hk}, \mathsf{param}^{\mathsf{ch}}) : (m_0, r_0) \neq$$

$$(m_1, r_1) \wedge \mathsf{Hash}(\mathsf{hk}, m_0, r_0) = \mathsf{Hash}(\mathsf{hk}, m_1, r_1)] = \mathsf{negl}(\lambda);$$

$$\Pr[(m, r) \leftarrow \mathcal{A}(1^\lambda, C, \mathsf{hk}, \mathsf{param}^{\mathsf{ch}}) : \mathsf{Hash}(\mathsf{hk}, m, r) = C] = \mathsf{negl}(\lambda).$$

2. For hash key hk generated from $\mathsf{TrapGen}$, assuming the range of hk is R_{hk}, the distribution of hk should be either statistically close to uniform in R_{hk}; or computationally close to the uniform distribution with an additional property that the probability a randomly sampled $\bar{\mathsf{hk}} \leftarrow_\$ R_{\mathsf{hk}}$ has a trapdoor is negligible.
3. For r' generated from Inv, the distribution of r' should be with $\mathsf{negl}(\lambda)$ distance from the distribution where r is sampled from.

3.2 A New Framework for Ring Signatures

Our ring signature is constructed as follows:

- **Setup**$(1^\lambda) \to \mathsf{param}$: On input the security parameter 1^λ, this algorithm chooses a hash function $\mathcal{H} : \{*\} \to R_C$. It also runs $\mathsf{SetUp}(1^\lambda) \to \mathsf{param}^{\mathsf{ch}}$.
- **KeyGen** $\to (\mathsf{sk}, \mathsf{pk})$: This algorithm generates $(\mathsf{hk}, \mathsf{tr}) \leftarrow \mathsf{TrapGen}(1^\lambda)$. Then it sets public key $\mathsf{pk} = \mathsf{hk}$ and secret key $\mathsf{sk} = \mathsf{tr}$.
- **Signing**$(\mathsf{sk}_\pi, \mu, L_{\mathsf{pk}}) \to \sigma$: On input a message μ, a list of user public keys $L_{\mathsf{pk}} = \{\mathsf{pk}_1, \cdots, \mathsf{pk}_\ell\}$, and a signing key $\mathsf{sk}_\pi = \mathsf{tr}_\pi$ of $\mathsf{pk}_\pi = \mathsf{hk}_\pi \in L_{\mathsf{pk}}$, the signing algorithm runs as follow:
  1. For $i \in [1, \cdots, \ell]$ and $i \neq \pi$, pick m_i and r_i at random. Compute $C_i = \mathsf{Hash}(\mathsf{hk}_i, m_i, r_i)$. For $i = \pi$, pick C_π at random from its possible range R_C.
  2. Compute m_π such that $m_1 \oplus \cdots \oplus m_\pi \oplus \cdots \oplus m_n = \mathcal{H}(\mu, C_1, \cdots, C_\ell, L_{\mathsf{pk}})$.
  3. Given m_π and C_π, invoke $\mathsf{Inv}(\mathsf{hk}_\pi, \mathsf{tr}_\pi, C_\pi, m_\pi) \to r_\pi$.
  The ring signature of μ and L_{pk} is $\sigma = \{(m_1, r_1), \cdots, (m_\ell, r_\ell)\}$.

- **Verification**$(\mu, \sigma, L_{\mathsf{pk}}) \to accept/reject$: On input a message μ, a signature σ and a list of user public keys L_{pk}, the verification algorithm first phrases $\sigma = \{(m_1, r_1), \cdots, (m_\ell, r_\ell)\}$. It then checks whether each pair of (m_i, r_i) satisfies $C_i = \mathsf{Hash}(\mathsf{hk}_i, m_i, r_i)$ for all $i \in [1, \cdots, \ell]$ and whether $m_1 \oplus \cdots \oplus m_\ell = \mathcal{H}(\mu, C_1, \cdots, C_\ell, L_{\mathsf{pk}})$. If yes, output $accept$. Otherwise, output $reject$.

3.3 A New Framework for Linkable Ring Signatures

Our linkable ring signature is constructed as follows:

- **Setup**$(1^\lambda) \to$ param: On input the security parameter 1^λ, this algorithm chooses two hash functions $\mathcal{H}$ and $\mathcal{H}_1$. It also runs $\mathsf{SetUp}(1^\lambda) \to$ param^{ch} and selects a one-time signature scheme $\Pi^{OTS} = \{\mathsf{OKeygen}, \mathsf{OSign}, \mathsf{OVer}\}$.
- **KeyGen** $\to$ (sk, pk): This algorithm first generates (hk, tr) $\leftarrow$ TrapGen(1^λ). It also generates a pair of Π^{OTS} public key and secret key (opk, osk) $\leftarrow$ OKeygen(1^λ) and computes mk $= \mathcal{H}_1(\mathsf{opk})$. It then computes hk$' = $ hk $\oplus$ mk. Finally, it sets public key pk $=$ hk$'$ and secret key sk $= \{\mathsf{tr}, \mathsf{opk}, \mathsf{osk}\}$.
- **Signing**$(\mathsf{sk}_\pi, \mu, L_{\mathsf{pk}}) \to \sigma$: On input a message μ, a list of user public keys $L_{\mathsf{pk}} = \{\mathsf{pk}_1, \cdots, \mathsf{pk}_\ell\}$, and a signing key $\mathsf{sk}_\pi = \{\mathsf{tr}_\pi, \mathsf{opk}_\pi, \mathsf{osk}_\pi\}$ of $\mathsf{pk}_\pi = $ hk$'_\pi \in L_{\mathsf{pk}}$, the signing algorithm runs as follow:
  1. Compute $\mathsf{mk}_\pi = \mathcal{H}_1(\mathsf{opk}_\pi)$.
  2. For $i \in [1, \cdots, n]$ and $i \neq \pi$, pick m_i and r_i at random. Compute hk$_i = $ hk$'_i \oplus \mathsf{mk}_\pi$ and $C_i = \mathsf{Hash}(\mathsf{hk}_i, m_i, r_i)$. For $i = \pi$, pick C_π at random.
  3. Compute m_π such that $m_1 \oplus \cdots \oplus m_\pi \oplus \cdots \oplus m_\ell = \mathcal{H}(\mu, C_1, \cdots, C_\ell, L_{\mathsf{pk}})$.
  4. Given m_π and C_π, compute $r_\pi \leftarrow \mathsf{Inv}(\mathsf{hk}_\pi, \mathsf{tr}_\pi, C_\pi, m_\pi)$.
  5. Compute one-time signature $sig = \mathsf{OSign}(\mathsf{osk}_\pi; (m_1, r_1), \cdots, (m_\ell, r_\ell), L_{\mathsf{pk}}, \mathsf{opk}_\pi)$.

  The linkable ring signature of μ and L_{pk} is $\sigma = \{(m_1, r_1), \cdots, (m_\ell, r_\ell), \mathsf{opk}_\pi, sig\}$.

- **Verification**$(\mu, \sigma, L_{\mathsf{pk}}) \to accept/reject$: On input a message μ, a signature σ and a list of user public keys $L_{\mathsf{pk}} = \{\mathsf{hk}'_1, \cdots, \mathsf{hk}'_\ell\}$, the verification algorithm first phrases $\sigma = \{(m_1, r_1), \cdots, (m_\ell, r_\ell), \mathsf{opk}, sig\}$. This algorithm runs as follow:
  1. It first computes mk $= \mathcal{H}_1(\mathsf{opk})$. It also computes hk$_i = $ hk$'_i \oplus$ mk and $C_i = \mathsf{Hash}(\mathsf{hk}_i, m_i, r_i)$ for all $i \in [1, \cdots, \ell]$;
  2. It checks whether $m_1 \oplus \cdots \oplus m_\ell = \mathcal{H}(\mu, C_1, \cdots, C_\ell, L_{\mathsf{pk}})$;
  3. Verify the signature via $\mathsf{OVer}(\mathsf{opk}; sig; (m_1, r_1), \cdots, (m_\ell, r_\ell), L_{\mathsf{pk}}, \mathsf{opk})$.

  If all pass, output *accept*. Otherwise, output *reject*.

- **Link**$(\sigma_1, \sigma_2, \mu_1, \mu_2, L_{\mathsf{pk}}^{(1)}, L_{\mathsf{pk}}^{(2)}) \to linked/unlinked$: On input two message signature pairs (μ_1, σ_1) and (μ_2, σ_2), this algorithm first checks the validity of signatures σ_1 and σ_2. If **Verification**$(\mu_1, \sigma_1, L_{\mathsf{pk}}^{(1)}) \to accept$ and **Verification**$(\mu_2, \sigma_2, L_{\mathsf{pk}}^{(2)}) \to accept$, it phrases $\sigma_1 = \{(m_1^{(1)}, r_1^{(1)}), \cdots, (m_\ell^{(1)}, r_\ell^{(1)}), \mathsf{opk}_1, sig_1\}$ and $\sigma_2 = \{(m_1^{(2)}, r_1^{(2)}), \cdots, (m_\ell^{(2)}, r_\ell^{(2)}), \mathsf{opk}_2, sig_2\}$. The algorithm outputs *linked* if $\mathsf{opk}_1 = \mathsf{opk}_2$. Otherwise, output *unlinked*.

Our generic ring signature scheme and linkable signature scheme are both secure under random oracle model. Due to page limitation, the security proof of our generic constructions is omitted. The detailed security proof can be found in full version [38].

4 Instantiation

In this section, we will show how to build CH^+ from standard lattice problems and from NTRU assumptions.

4.1 Instantiation of CH^+ from Standard Lattice

Here we present our first instantiation of CH^+ from standard lattice.

$SetUp(1^\lambda) \to H$: On input the security parameter 1^λ, this algorithm randomly samples a matrix $H \leftarrow_\$ \mathbb{Z}_q^{n \times k}$. The matrix H will be an implicit input to Hash and Inv algorithm.

$TrapGen(1^\lambda) \to (A, T)$: This algorithm runs $GenBasis(1^n, 1^m, q) \to (A, T)$ where $A \in \mathbb{Z}_q^{n \times m}$ is a parity-check matrix and T is a 'good' trapdoor basis of $\Lambda^\perp(A)$.

$Hash(A, b, r) \to c$: On input hash key A, binary message vector $b \in \{0, 1\}^k$ and randomness vector $r \leftarrow D_s^m$, this algorithm computes $c = Hb + Ar$ and returns c.

$Inv(A, T, c, b') \to r'$: On input hash key $A \in \mathbb{Z}_q^{n \times m}$ and its trapdoor T, a vector $c \in \mathbb{Z}_q^n$, a binary vector $b' \in \{0, 1\}^k$, it computes $u = c - Hb'$ and $r' = PreSample(A, T, u, s')$ where $s = s'\omega(\sqrt{\log n})$.

Now we argue that this instantiation satisfies our requirements of CH^+ in Sect. 3.1.

- Our instantiation is collision resistant and one-way if $SIS_{q,n,m',\beta}$ and $ISIS_{q,n,m',\beta}$ are hard for $m' = m + k$, $\beta = \sqrt{8ms^2 + 2k}$ and $\beta = \sqrt{4ms^2 + k}$ respectively.
- For the second requirement, according to Theorem 1, we have the distribution of parity-check matrix $A \in \mathbb{Z}_q^{n \times m}$ generated from GenBasis algorithm is within $negl(n)$ far from uniform. Thus, the distribution of A is statistically close to uniform in $\mathbb{Z}_q^{n \times m}$. Our instantiation satisfies the second requirement.
- For the third requirement, this instantiation requires that randomness vector r is sampled from Gaussian distribution D_s^m. According to Theorem 1, if we set deviation s appropriately (i.e., greater than the smooth parameter of T, see [27]), the random vector r' sampled by algorithm Inv is within $negl(n)$ statistical distance of D_s^m. Thus our instantiation satisfies the third requirement.

4.2 Instantiation of CH^+ from NTRU

The FALCON-based CH^+ scheme consists of following algorithms:

$SetUp(1^\lambda) \to (h, D_b, D_r)$: On input the security parameter 1^λ, this algorithm firstly sets up the polynomial ring $\mathcal{R}_q$ and samples $h \leftarrow_\$ \mathcal{R}_q$. It also sets related distributions:

- D_b: a uniform distribution over $\mathcal{R}_q$ with binary coefficients;
- D_r: a discrete Gaussian distribution over $\mathcal{R}_q \times \mathcal{R}_q$.

TrapGen(1^λ) $\rightarrow$ $(\mathbf{a}, \mathbf{T})$: This algorithm takes security parameter 1^λ as input and then runs FALCON key generation function to obtain a tuple $(\mathbf{a}, \mathbf{T})$ where the public description of CH^+, namely, $\mathbf{a} = \mathbf{g}/\mathbf{f}$ is computationally indistinguishable from uniform over $\mathcal{R}_q$ under NTRU assumption; $\mathbf{T} := \begin{bmatrix} \mathbf{f} & \mathbf{g} \\ \bar{\mathbf{f}} & \bar{\mathbf{g}} \end{bmatrix}$ is the trapdoor of $\mathbf{a}$.

Hash($\mathbf{a}, \mathbf{b}, \mathbf{r}$) $\rightarrow$ $\mathbf{c}$: On input a hash key $\mathbf{a}$, a binary message string $\mathbf{b} \in D_{\mathbf{b}}$ and randomness $\mathbf{r} := (\mathbf{r}_0, \mathbf{r}_1) \in D_{\mathbf{r}}$, this algorithm returns a hash output $\mathbf{c} := \mathbf{r}_0 + \mathbf{a}\mathbf{r}_1 + \mathbf{h}\mathbf{b} \in \mathcal{R}_q$.

Inv($\mathbf{a}, \mathbf{T}, \mathbf{c}, \mathbf{b}'$) $\rightarrow$ $\mathbf{r}'$: On input hash key $\mathbf{a}$, its trapdoor $\mathbf{T}$, a ring element $\mathbf{c}$ and a binary message $\mathbf{b}'$, this algorithm first computes $\mathbf{u} = \mathbf{c} - \mathbf{b}'\mathbf{h}$. It then generates a falcon signature $\mathbf{r}' := (\mathbf{r}_0', \mathbf{r}_1')$ on $\mathbf{u}$ such that $\mathbf{r}_0' + \mathbf{r}_1'\mathbf{a} = \mathbf{u}$. It returns $\mathbf{r}' \in D_{\mathbf{r}}$ such that Hash($\mathbf{a}, \mathbf{b}', \mathbf{r}'$) $= \mathbf{c}$. The distribution of $\mathbf{r}'$ will be identical to the distribution of $\mathbf{r}$ used in Hash due to the property of GPV sampler.

This instantiation satisfies our requirements of CH^+ in Sect. 3.1.

- The one-wayness and collision resistance of this instantiation is based on NTRU assumption, R-SIS and R-ISIS. According to NTRU assumption, $\mathbf{a}$ is computationally close to uniform. For a R-SIS$_{3,q,\beta}$ problem instance[3] $\{\mathbf{e}_1, \mathbf{e}_2, \mathbf{e}_3\}$, we can compute $\{1, \mathbf{a}', \mathbf{h}'\} = \{\frac{\mathbf{e}_1}{\mathbf{e}_1}, \frac{\mathbf{e}_2}{\mathbf{e}_1}, \frac{\mathbf{e}_3}{\mathbf{e}_1}\}$. $\mathbf{a}'$ should be indistinguishable with a real hash key $\mathbf{a}$. By obtaining a collision $\{\mathbf{r}_0^{(0)}, \mathbf{r}_1^{(0)}, \mathbf{b}^{(0)}\}$, $\{\mathbf{r}_0^{(1)}, \mathbf{r}_1^{(1)}, \mathbf{b}^{(1)}\}$ on hash key $\mathbf{a}'$ and public parameter $\mathbf{h}'$. We have

$$((\mathbf{r}_0^{(0)} - \mathbf{r}_0^{(1)}) + \mathbf{a}'(\mathbf{r}_1^{(0)} - \mathbf{r}_1^{(1)}) + \mathbf{h}'(\mathbf{b}^{(0)} - \mathbf{b}^{(1)})) = 0.$$

We find a solution to the problem instance $\{\mathbf{e}_1, \mathbf{e}_2, \mathbf{e}_3\}$. We can use the similar way to argue the one-wayness of NTRU instantiation.
- Under NTRU assumption, FALCON public key is computationally indistinguishable from uniform; and the probability that a uniform sampled ring element $\bar{\mathbf{a}} \leftarrow_\$ \mathcal{R}_q$ having a FALCON trapdoor is negligible.
- FALCON is essentially a GPV sampler over NTRU. Therefore, according to Theorem 1, if the deviation s of $D_{\mathbf{r}}$ is greater than the smoothing parameter, then $\mathbf{r}'$ generated by algorithm Inv will be within $\mathsf{negl}(n)$ statistical distance of $D_{\Lambda_{\mathbf{u}}^\perp(\mathbf{a}), s}$. Thus our instantiation satisfies the third requirement.

4.3 Full Description of Linkable Raptor

Here we present the full description of linkable RAPTOR. FALCON works over a polynomial ring $\mathcal{R}_q := \mathbb{Z}_q[x]/(x^n + 1)$ for $n \in \{512, 1024\}$ and $q = 12289$. There is a third parameter set with a different, more complicated polynomial ring. For simplicity, we omit this parameter set. For easiness of implementation, we will also use FALCON to instantiate Π^{OTS}.

Setup(1^λ) $\rightarrow$ param: On input the security parameter 1^λ, this algorithm chooses a hash function $\mathcal{H}: \{*\} \rightarrow \{0,1\}^n$, a suitable $\mathcal{R}_q$ and distributions $D_{\mathbf{b}}, D_{\mathbf{r}}$ for the

---

[3] We require at least one of the three elements is invertible over $\mathcal{R}_q$. For FALCON-512, the probability is $(1 - 1/q)^N \approx 96\%$.

security level, where $D_{\mathbf{b}} := \{0,1\}^{256}$, $D_{\mathbf{r}} := \mathcal{D}^2_{\mathcal{R}_q,\eta}$, $\mathcal{D}_{\mathcal{R}_q,\eta}$ is a discrete Gaussian distribution over $\mathcal{R}_q$ with deviation η, and $\eta \approx 1.17\sqrt{q}$ is the smooth parameter. It also picks a public polynomial $\mathbf{h} \leftarrow_\$ \mathcal{R}_q$ at random as $\mathsf{param}^{\mathsf{ch}}$. It also chooses a hash function $\mathcal{H}_1 \colon \{*\} \to \mathcal{R}_q$.

KeyGen$\to$ (sk, pk): This algorithm firstly generates $(\mathbf{a}, \mathbf{f}, \mathbf{g}, \bar{\mathbf{f}}, \bar{\mathbf{g}}) \leftarrow$ FAL-CON.KeyGen (param), and $(\mathbf{a}_{ots}, \mathbf{f}_{ots}, \mathbf{g}_{ots}, \bar{\mathbf{f}}_{ots}, \bar{\mathbf{g}}_{ots}) \leftarrow$ FALCON.KeyGen(param). Then it sets $\mathbf{a}' := \mathbf{a} + \mathcal{H}_1(\mathbf{a}_{ots}) \bmod q$.

The public key pk $= \mathbf{a}'$ and secret key sk $= \{\mathbf{f}, \mathbf{g}, \bar{\mathbf{f}}, \bar{\mathbf{g}}, \mathbf{f}_{ots}, \mathbf{g}_{ots}, \bar{\mathbf{f}}_{ots}, \bar{\mathbf{g}}_{ots}, \mathbf{a}_{ots}\}$.

Signing(sk$_\pi, \mu, L_{\mathsf{pk}}$, param) $\to \sigma$: On input message μ, list of user public keys $L_{\mathsf{pk}} = \{\mathsf{pk}_1, \cdots, \mathsf{pk}_\ell\}$, and signing key sk$_\pi = \{\mathbf{f}_\pi, \mathbf{g}_\pi, \bar{\mathbf{f}}_\pi, \bar{\mathbf{g}}_\pi, \mathbf{f}_{ots}, \mathbf{g}_{ots}, \bar{\mathbf{f}}_{ots}, \bar{\mathbf{g}}_{ots}, \mathbf{a}_{ots}\}$ of $\mathsf{pk}_\pi = \mathbf{a}'_\pi$, and the system parameter param, the signing algorithm runs as follow:

1. For $i \in [1, \cdots, \ell]$, compute $\mathbf{a}_i = \mathbf{a}'_i - \mathcal{H}_1(\mathbf{a}_{ots}) \bmod q$.
2. For $i \in [1, \cdots, \ell]$ and $i \neq \pi$, picks $\mathbf{b}_i \leftarrow_\$ \{0,1\}^{256}$ and $(\mathbf{r}_{i,0}, \mathbf{r}_{i,1}) \leftarrow \mathcal{D}^2_{\mathcal{R}_q,\eta}$. Compute $\mathbf{c}_i = \mathbf{r}_{i,0} + \mathbf{a}_i \mathbf{r}_{i,1} + \mathbf{h}_i \mathbf{b}_i$.
3. For $i = \pi$, pick $\mathbf{c}_\pi \leftarrow_\$ \mathcal{R}_q$.
4. Compute $\mathbf{b}_\pi$ such that $\mathbf{b}_1 \oplus \cdots \oplus \mathbf{b}_\pi \oplus \cdots \oplus \mathbf{b}_\ell = \mathcal{H}(\mu, \mathbf{c}_1, \cdots, \mathbf{c}_\ell)$.
5. Set $\mathbf{u}_\pi = \mathbf{c}_\pi - \mathbf{h}\mathbf{b}_\pi$.
6. Set $(\mathbf{r}_{\pi,0}, \mathbf{r}_{\pi,1}) =$ FALCON.sign$(\mathbf{a}_\pi, (\mathbf{f}_\pi, \mathbf{g}_\pi, \bar{\mathbf{f}}_\pi, \bar{\mathbf{g}}_\pi); \mathbf{u}_\pi)$ such that $\mathbf{r}_{\pi,0} + \mathbf{r}_{\pi,1}\mathbf{a}_\pi = \mathbf{u}_\pi$.
7. Compute $sig :=$ FALCON.sign $(\mathbf{a}_{ots}, (\mathbf{f}_{ots}, \mathbf{g}_{ots}, \bar{\mathbf{f}}_{ots}, \bar{\mathbf{g}}_{ots}); (\{\mathbf{r}_{i,0}, \mathbf{r}_{i,1}, \mathbf{b}_i\}^\ell_{i=1}, \{\mathbf{a}'_i\}^\ell_{i=1}, \mathbf{a}_{ots}))$.

The ring signature of μ and L_{pk} is $\sigma = \{\{\mathbf{r}_{i,0}, \mathbf{r}_{i,1}, \mathbf{b}_i\}^\ell_{i=1}, \mathbf{a}_{ots}, sig\}$.

Verification$(\mu, \sigma, L_{\mathsf{pk}}) \to accept/reject$: On input message μ, signature σ and a list of user public keys L_{pk}, the verification algorithm performs as follows:

1. phrases $\sigma = \{\{\mathbf{r}_{i,0}, \mathbf{r}_{i,1}, \mathbf{b}_i\}^\ell_{i=1}, \mathbf{a}_{ots}, sig\}$;
2. For $i \in [1, \cdots, \ell]$, compute $\mathbf{a}_i = \mathbf{a}'_i - \mathcal{H}_1(\mathbf{a}_{ots}) \bmod q$;
3. checks whether for each tuple of $(\mathbf{r}_{i,0}, \mathbf{r}_{i,1}, \mathbf{b}_i)$, $\|\mathbf{r}_{i,0}\|, \|\mathbf{r}_{i,1}\| \leq B_1$ and $\mathbf{b}_i \in D_{\mathbf{b}}$; outputs $reject$ if not.
4. computes $\mathbf{c}_i = \mathbf{r}_{i,0} + \mathbf{a}_i \mathbf{r}_{i,1} + \mathbf{h}_i \mathbf{b}_i$ for all $i \in [1, \cdots, \ell]$ and checks whether $\mathbf{b}_1 \oplus \cdots \oplus \mathbf{b}_\ell = \mathcal{H}(\mu, \mathbf{c}_1, \cdots, \mathbf{c}_\ell)$; outputs $reject$ if not.
5. verifies sig is a signature for $(\{\mathbf{r}_{i,0}, \mathbf{r}_{i,1}, \mathbf{b}_i\}^\ell_{i=1}, \{\mathbf{a}'_i\}^\ell_{i=1}, \mathbf{a}_{ots})$ with public key $\mathbf{a}_{ots}$; outputs $reject$ if fails.
6. outputs $accept$.

Link$(\sigma_1, \sigma_2, \mu_1, \mu_2, L^{(1)}_{\mathsf{pk}}, L^{(2)}_{\mathsf{pk}}) \to linked/unlinked$: On input two message signature pairs (μ_1, σ_1) and (μ_2, σ_2), this algorithm first checks the validity of signatures σ_1 and σ_2. It then phrases $\sigma_1 = \{\{\mathbf{r}^{(1)}_{i,0}, \mathbf{r}^{(1)}_{i,1}, \mathbf{b}^{(1)}_i\}^\ell_{i=1}, \mathbf{a}^{(1)}_{ots}, sig_1\}$ and $\sigma_2 = \{\{\mathbf{r}^{(2)}_{i,0}, \mathbf{r}^{(2)}_{i,1}, \mathbf{b}^{(2)}_i\}^{\ell'}_{i=1}, \mathbf{a}^{(2)}_{ots}, sig_2\}$. This algorithm outputs $linked$ if $\mathbf{a}^{(1)}_{ots} = \mathbf{a}^{(2)}_{ots}$. Otherwise, output $unlinked$.

For a legitimately produced ring signature σ, each $(\mathbf{r}_{i,0}, \mathbf{r}_{i,1})$ pair should be distributed according to $\mathcal{D}^2_{\mathcal{R}_q,\eta}$, thus the acceptance bound B_1 of $\mathbf{r}_{i,0}, \mathbf{r}_{i,1}$ should be $\nu\eta\sqrt{n}$ where ν is set such that $\|\mathbf{r}_{i,0}\|, \|\mathbf{r}_{i,1}\| \leq B_1$ with probability $1 - 2^{-100}$ according to Lemma 1.

Note that in this implementation we use additions and subtractions over the $\mathcal{R}_q$ instead of bit-wise XOR operations. Under the random oracle model $\mathcal{H}_1(\mathbf{a}_{ots})$ will output a random ring element. This creates a perfect one-time mask that assures $\mathbf{a}'$ is indistinguishable from random.

5   Parameters and Implementation

Here we give some parameter figures for RAPTOR-512, instantiated with FALCON-512. Our RAPTOR-512 uses a signature size of $(617 \times 2 + 32)\ell \approx 1.26\ell$ kilo bytes, where ℓ is the number of users in a signature. This is because, for each tuple $\{\mathbf{r}_{i,0}, \mathbf{r}_{i,1}, \mathbf{b}_i\}$ within a ring signature, we need a pair of $\mathbf{r}_{i,0}$ and $\mathbf{r}_{i,1}$, each of 617 bytes, and an additional 32 bytes for $\mathbf{b}_i$ to avoid any search attacks [29]. This parameter set yields 114 bits security against classical attackers, and 103 bits security against quantum attackers, under the BKZ2.0 framework [19] with (quantum) sieving algorithm [6,33].

As for linkable RAPTOR-512, we need an additional FALCON public key and signature which is of size $897 + 617 \approx 1.5$ kilo bytes. This accounts for a total of $(1.3\ell + 1.5)$ kilo bytes.

For conservative purpose, one may also choose FALCON-1024 for better security, which results in a signature size of 2.5ℓ kilo bytes for RAPTOR-1024, and $(2.5\ell + 3)$ kilo bytes for linkable RAPTOR-1024. The security level for both schemes will be over 256 bits.

We implemented RAPTOR-512 on a typical laptop with an Intel 6600U processor. The performance is shown in Table 1(a) and (b). Our source code is available at [53]. This is a proof-of-concept implementation. We did not take into account potential optimizations such as NTT-based ring multiplication and AVX-2 instructions. We leave those to future work.

References

1. Abe, M., Ohkubo, M., Suzuki, K.: 1-out-of-n signatures from a variety of keys. In: Zheng, Y. (ed.) ASIACRYPT 2002. LNCS, vol. 2501, pp. 415–432. Springer, Heidelberg (2002). https://doi.org/10.1007/3-540-36178-2_26
2. Aguilar Melchor, C., Bettaieb, S., Boyen, X., Fousse, L., Gaborit, P.: Adapting Lyubashevsky's signature schemes to the ring signature setting. In: Youssef, A., Nitaj, A., Hassanien, A.E. (eds.) AFRICACRYPT 2013. LNCS, vol. 7918, pp. 1–25. Springer, Heidelberg (2013). https://doi.org/10.1007/978-3-642-38553-7_1
3. Ajtai, M.: Generating hard instances of lattice problems (extended abstract). In: Proceedings of the Twenty-Eighth Annual ACM Symposium on Theory of Computing, STOC 1996, pp. 99–108. ACM, New York (1996)
4. Alberto Torres, W.A., et al.: Post-quantum one-time linkable ring signature and application to ring confidential transactions in blockchain (lattice RingCT v1.0). In: Susilo, W., Yang, G. (eds.) ACISP 2018. LNCS, vol. 10946, pp. 558–576. Springer, Cham (2018). https://doi.org/10.1007/978-3-319-93638-3_32

5. Albrecht, M.R., et al.: Estimate all the LWE, NTRU schemes!. In: Catalano, D., De Prisco, R. (eds.) SCN 2018. LNCS, vol. 11035, pp. 351–367. Springer, Cham (2018). https://doi.org/10.1007/978-3-319-98113-0_19

6. Alkim, E., Ducas, L., Pöppelmann, T., Schwabe, P.: Post-quantum key exchange - a new hope. In: 25th USENIX Security Symposium, USENIX Security 16, 10–12 August 2016, Austin, TX, USA, pp. 327–343 (2016)

7. Alwen, J., Peikert, C.: Generating shorter bases for hard random lattices. Theory Comput. Syst. **48**(3), 535–553 (2011)

8. Au, M.H., Chow, S.S.M., Susilo, W., Tsang, P.P.: Short linkable ring signatures revisited. In: Atzeni, A.S., Lioy, A. (eds.) EuroPKI 2006. LNCS, vol. 4043, pp. 101–115. Springer, Heidelberg (2006). https://doi.org/10.1007/11774716_9

9. Au, M.H., Liu, J.K., Susilo, W., Yuen, T.H.: Certificate based (linkable) ring signature. In: Dawson, E., Wong, D.S. (eds.) ISPEC 2007. LNCS, vol. 4464, pp. 79–92. Springer, Heidelberg (2007). https://doi.org/10.1007/978-3-540-72163-5_8

10. Au, M.H., Liu, J.K., Susilo, W., Yuen, T.H.: Secure id-based linkable and revocable-iff-linked ring signature with constant-size construction. Theor. Comput. Sci. **469**, 1–14 (2013)

11. Baum, C., Lin, H., Oechsner, S.: Towards practical lattice-based one-time linkable ring signatures. In: Naccache, D., et al. (eds.) Information and Communications Security, pp. 303–322. Springer International Publishing, Cham (2018)

12. Bender, A., Katz, J., Morselli, R.: Ring signatures: stronger definitions, and constructions without random oracles. In: Halevi, S., Rabin, T. (eds.) TCC 2006. LNCS, vol. 3876, pp. 60–79. Springer, Heidelberg (2006). https://doi.org/10.1007/11681878_4

13. Boneh, D., Dagdelen, Ö., Fischlin, M., Lehmann, A., Schaffner, C., Zhandry, M.: Random oracles in a quantum world. In: Lee, D.H., Wang, X. (eds.) ASIACRYPT 2011. LNCS, vol. 7073, pp. 41–69. Springer, Heidelberg (2011). https://doi.org/10.1007/978-3-642-25385-0_3

14. Bootle, J., Cerulli, A., Chaidos, P., Ghadafi, E., Groth, J., Petit, C.: Short accountable ring signatures based on DDH. In: Pernul, G., Ryan, P.Y.A., Weippl, E. (eds.) ESORICS 2015. LNCS, vol. 9326, pp. 243–265. Springer, Cham (2015). https://doi.org/10.1007/978-3-319-24174-6_13

15. Brakerski, Z., Kalai, Y.T.: A framework for efficient signatures, ring signatures and identity based encryption in the standard model. Cryptology ePrint Archive, Report 2010/086 (2010). https://eprint.iacr.org/2010/086

16. Camenisch, J., Stadler, M.: Efficient group signature schemes for large groups. In: Kaliski, B.S. (ed.) CRYPTO 1997. LNCS, vol. 1294, pp. 410–424. Springer, Heidelberg (1997). https://doi.org/10.1007/BFb0052252

17. Chandran, N., Groth, J., Sahai, A.: Ring signatures of sub-linear size without random oracles. In: Arge, L., Cachin, C., Jurdziński, T., Tarlecki, A. (eds.) ICALP 2007. LNCS, vol. 4596, pp. 423–434. Springer, Heidelberg (2007). https://doi.org/10.1007/978-3-540-73420-8_38

18. Chaum, D., van Heyst, E.: Group signatures. In: Davies, D.W. (ed.) EUROCRYPT 1991. LNCS, vol. 547, pp. 257–265. Springer, Heidelberg (1991). https://doi.org/10.1007/3-540-46416-6_22

19. Chen, Y., Nguyen, P.Q.: BKZ 2.0: better lattice security estimates. In: Lee, D.H., Wang, X. (eds.) ASIACRYPT 2011. LNCS, vol. 7073, pp. 1–20. Springer, Heidelberg (2011). https://doi.org/10.1007/978-3-642-25385-0_1

20. Dodis, Y., Kiayias, A., Nicolosi, A., Shoup, V.: Anonymous identification in *ad hoc* groups. In: Cachin, C., Camenisch, J.L. (eds.) EUROCRYPT 2004. LNCS, vol. 3027, pp. 609–626. Springer, Heidelberg (2004). https://doi.org/10.1007/978-3-540-24676-3_36

21. Ducas, L., Durmus, A., Lepoint, T., Lyubashevsky, V.: Lattice signatures and bimodal Gaussians. In: Canetti, R., Garay, J.A. (eds.) CRYPTO 2013. LNCS, vol. 8042, pp. 40–56. Springer, Heidelberg (2013). https://doi.org/10.1007/978-3-642-40041-4_3

22. Ducas, L., Lyubashevsky, V., Prest, T.: Efficient identity-based encryption over NTRU lattices. In: Sarkar, P., Iwata, T. (eds.) ASIACRYPT 2014. LNCS, vol. 8874, pp. 22–41. Springer, Heidelberg (2014). https://doi.org/10.1007/978-3-662-45608-8_2

23. Ducas, L., Prest, T.: Fast Fourier orthogonalization. In: Proceedings of the ACM on International Symposium on Symbolic and Algebraic Computation, ISSAC 2016, pp. 191–198. ACM, New York (2016)

24. Dwork, C., Naor, M.: Zaps and their applications. SIAM J. Comput. **36**(6), 1513–1543 (2007)

25. Esgin, M.F., Steinfeld, R., Sakzad, A., Liu, J.K., Liu, D.: Short lattice-based one-out-of-many proofs and applications to ring signatures. Cryptology ePrint Archive, Report 2018/773 (2018). https://eprint.iacr.org/2018/773

26. Fouque, P.-A., et al.: Falcon: Fast-Fourier lattice-based compact signatures over NTRU (2018)

27. Gentry, C., Peikert, C., Vaikuntanathan, V.: Trapdoors for hard lattices and new cryptographic constructions. In: Proceedings of the Fortieth Annual ACM Symposium on Theory of Computing, STOC 2008, pp. 197–206. ACM, New York (2008)

28. Groth, J., Kohlweiss, M.: One-out-of-many proofs: or how to leak a secret and spend a coin. In: Oswald, E., Fischlin, M. (eds.) EUROCRYPT 2015. LNCS, vol. 9057, pp. 253–280. Springer, Heidelberg (2015). https://doi.org/10.1007/978-3-662-46803-6_9

29. Grover, L.K.: A fast quantum mechanical algorithm for database search. In: Proceedings of the Twenty-Eighth Annual ACM Symposium on Theory of Computing, STOC 1996, pp. 212–219. ACM, New York (1996)

30. Hoffstein, J., Howgrave-Graham, N., Pipher, J., Silverman, J.H., Whyte, W.: NTRUSign: digital signatures using the NTRU lattice. In: Joye, M. (ed.) CT-RSA 2003. LNCS, vol. 2612, pp. 122–140. Springer, Heidelberg (2003). https://doi.org/10.1007/3-540-36563-X_9

31. Hoffstein, J., Pipher, J., Silverman, J.H.: NTRU: a ring-based public key cryptosystem. In: Buhler, J.P. (ed.) ANTS 1998. LNCS, vol. 1423, pp. 267–288. Springer, Heidelberg (1998). https://doi.org/10.1007/BFb0054868

32. Krawczyk, H., Rabin, T.: Chameleon signatures. In: Proceedings of the Network and Distributed System Security Symposium, NDSS: San Diego, California, USA, p. 2000 (2000)

33. Laarhoven, T., Mariano, A.: Progressive lattice sieving. In: Lange, T., Steinwandt, R. (eds.) Post-Quantum Cryptography, pp. 292–311. Springer International Publishing, Cham (2018)

34. Libert, B., Ling, S., Nguyen, K., Wang, H.: Zero-knowledge arguments for lattice-based accumulators: logarithmic-size ring signatures and group signatures without trapdoors. In: Fischlin, M., Coron, J.-S. (eds.) EUROCRYPT 2016. LNCS, vol. 9666, pp. 1–31. Springer, Heidelberg (2016). https://doi.org/10.1007/978-3-662-49896-5_1

35. Liu, J.K., Au, M.H., Susilo, W., Zhou, J.: Linkable ring signature with unconditional anonymity. IEEE Trans. Knowl. Data Eng. **26**(1), 157–165 (2014)
36. Liu, J.K., Wei, V.K., Wong, D.S.: Linkable spontaneous anonymous group signature for ad hoc groups. In: Wang, H., Pieprzyk, J., Varadharajan, V. (eds.) ACISP
2004. LNCS, vol. 3108, pp. 325–335. Springer, Heidelberg (2004). https://doi.org/
10.1007/978-3-540-27800-9_28
37. López-Alt, A., Tromer, E., Vaikuntanathan, V.: On-the-fly multiparty computation
on the cloud via multikey fully homomorphic encryption. In: Proceedings of the
Forty-Fourth Annual ACM Symposium on Theory of Computing, STOC 2012, pp.
1219–1234. ACM, New York (2012)
38. Lu, X., Au, M.H., Zhang, Z.: Raptor: A practical lattice-based (linkable) ring
signature. Cryptology ePrint Archive, Report 2018/857
39. Lyubashevsky, V.: Lattice signatures without trapdoors. In: Pointcheval, D.,
Johansson, T. (eds.) EUROCRYPT 2012. LNCS, vol. 7237, pp. 738–755. Springer,
Heidelberg (2012). https://doi.org/10.1007/978-3-642-29011-4_43
40. Lyubashevsky, V., Micciancio, D.: Generalized compact knapsacks are collision
resistant. In: Bugliesi, M., Preneel, B., Sassone, V., Wegener, I. (eds.) ICALP
2006. LNCS, vol. 4052, pp. 144–155. Springer, Heidelberg (2006). https://doi.org/
10.1007/11787006_13
41. Micciancio, D., Peikert, C.: Trapdoors for lattices: simpler, tighter, faster, smaller.
In: Pointcheval, D., Johansson, T. (eds.) EUROCRYPT 2012. LNCS, vol. 7237, pp.
700–718. Springer, Heidelberg (2012). https://doi.org/10.1007/978-3-642-29011-
4_41
42. National Institute of Standards and Technology. Post-Quantum Cryptography
Standardization (2017)
43. Noether, S.: Ring signature confidential transactions for Monero. Cryptology ePrint
Archive, Report 2015/1098 (2015). https://eprint.iacr.org/2015/1098
44. Peikert, C.: An efficient and parallel Gaussian sampler for lattices. In: Rabin, T.
(ed.) CRYPTO 2010. LNCS, vol. 6223, pp. 80–97. Springer, Heidelberg (2010).
https://doi.org/10.1007/978-3-642-14623-7_5
45. Peikert, C., Rosen, A.: Efficient collision-resistant hashing from worst-case assumptions on cyclic lattices. In: Halevi, S., Rabin, T. (eds.) TCC 2006. LNCS, vol. 3876,
pp. 145–166. Springer, Heidelberg (2006). https://doi.org/10.1007/11681878_8
46. Rivest, R.L., Shamir, A., Tauman, Y.: How to leak a secret. In: Boyd, C. (ed.)
ASIACRYPT 2001. LNCS, vol. 2248, pp. 552–565. Springer, Heidelberg (2001).
https://doi.org/10.1007/3-540-45682-1_32
47. Shacham, H., Waters, B.: Efficient ring signatures without random oracles. In:
Okamoto, T., Wang, X. (eds.) PKC 2007. LNCS, vol. 4450, pp. 166–180. Springer,
Heidelberg (2007). https://doi.org/10.1007/978-3-540-71677-8_12
48. Shor, P.W.: Polynomial time algorithms for discrete logarithms and factoring on a
quantum computer. In: Adleman, L.M., Huang, M.-D. (eds.) ANTS 1994. LNCS,
vol. 877, p. 289. Springer, Heidelberg (1994). https://doi.org/10.1007/3-540-58691-
1_68
49. Stehlé, D., Steinfeld, R.: Making NTRU as secure as worst-case problems over ideal
lattices. In: Paterson, K.G. (ed.) EUROCRYPT 2011. LNCS, vol. 6632, pp. 27–47.
Springer, Heidelberg (2011). https://doi.org/10.1007/978-3-642-20465-4_4
50. Sun, S.-F., Au, M.H., Liu, J.K., Yuen, T.H.: RingCT 2.0: a compact accumulator-
based (linkable ring signature) protocol for blockchain cryptocurrency Monero.
In: Foley, S.N., Gollmann, D., Snekkenes, E. (eds.) ESORICS 2017. LNCS, vol.
10493, pp. 456–474. Springer, Cham (2017). https://doi.org/10.1007/978-3-319-
66399-9_25

51. Tsang, P.P., Au, M.H., Liu, J.K., Susilo, W., Wong, D.S.: A suite of non-pairing ID-based threshold ring signature schemes with different levels of anonymity (extended abstract). In: Heng, S.-H., Kurosawa, K. (eds.) ProvSec 2010. LNCS, vol. 6402, pp. 166–183. Springer, Heidelberg (2010). https://doi.org/10.1007/978-3-642-16280-0_11

52. Tsang, P.P., Wei, V.K.: Short linkable ring signatures for e-voting, e-cash and attestation. In: Deng, R.H., Bao, F., Pang, H.H., Zhou, J. (eds.) ISPEC 2005. LNCS, vol. 3439, pp. 48–60. Springer, Heidelberg (2005). https://doi.org/10.1007/978-3-540-31979-5_5

53. Zhang, Z.: Raptor source code. https://github.com/zhenfeizhang/raptor

Parallelizable MACs Based on the Sum of PRPs with Security Beyond the Birthday Bound

Alexander Moch[1(✉)] and Eik List[2]

[1] Universität Mannheim, Mannheim, Germany
moch@uni-mannheim.de
[2] Bauhaus-Universität Weimar, Weimar, Germany
eik.list@uni-weimar.de

Abstract. The combination of universal hashing and encryption is a fundamental paradigm for the construction of symmetric-key MACs, dating back to the seminal works by Wegman and Carter, Shoup, and Bernstein. While fully sufficient for many practical applications, the Wegman-Carter construction, however, is well-known to break if nonces are ever repeated, and provides only birthday-bound security if instantiated with a permutation. Those limitations inspired the community to severals recent proposals that addressed them, initiated by Cogliati et al.'s Encrypted Wegman-Carter Davies-Meyer (EWCDM) construction.

This work extends this line of research by studying two constructions based on the sum of PRPs: (1) a stateless deterministic scheme that uses two hash functions, and (2) a nonce-based scheme with one hash-function call and a nonce. We show up to $2n/3$-bit security for both of them if the hash function is universal. Compared to the EWCDM construction, our proposals avoid the fact that a single reuse of a nonce can lead to a break.

Keywords: Symmetric-key cryptography · Authentication ·
Provable security · Permutation · Beyond-birthday security ·
Pseudorandom function · Universal hashing

1 Introduction

MESSAGE AUTHENTICATION CODES (MACs) aim to guarantee the authenticity and integrity of submitted messages. So, a receiver can successfully determine with high probability whether a given pair (m, t) of message and tag has been generated by the legitimate sender and has been transmitted correctly or not. MACs can be stateless deterministic, randomized, stateful; in general, one also distinguishes nonce-based constructions where the sender is responsible to supply a unique nonce to each message to be authenticated. Since cryptographically secure randomness can be expensive to obtain in various settings, our focus is on stateless and nonce-based constructions, hereafter.

© Springer Nature Switzerland AG 2019
R. H. Deng et al. (Eds.): ACNS 2019, LNCS 11464, pp. 131–151, 2019.
https://doi.org/10.1007/978-3-030-21568-2_7

While the primary goal of a MAC is unforgeability, indistinguishability from random bits can be a valuable replacement goal to evaluate the security. If tags are indistinguishable from random, they are also hard to forge.

THE WEGMAN-CARTER APPROACH [34] is a popular and efficient paradigm for constructing secure MACs. There, a given message is first compressed with a universal hash function before the result is processed by a cryptographically secure random function. The initial approach added the hash $h_{k'}(m)$ of a given message m to a key stream k to create a tag: $t = h_{k'}(m) \oplus k$; in practice, the key stream is supposed to be computed from some secure pseudorandom function $F(\nu)$ from some nonce ν. In [33], Shoup replaced the function F with a permutation, addressing the fact that there exist a number of standardized and well-analyzed block ciphers. Bernstein later proved the security of Shoup's construction, e.g., [3]. Bernstein's well-known bound still ensures that the advantage for any adversary that asks $2^{n/2}$ authentication queries [2] is bounded by $1.7q_v\ell/2^n$, where q_v is the number of verification queries and ℓ is the maximal message length, usually in terms of elements of a ring or field used in h. Throughout this work, we adopt the common way of referring to security bounds that are negligible up to $\mathcal{O}(2^{n/2})$ blocks or queries as $n/2$ bits of security.

Despite its simplicity, there exist two interesting directions of extending the Wegman-Carter construction. First, the nonce requirement is a well-known considerable risk: if a single nonce is repeated, the security of the construction may collapse completely since the hash-function key could leak. Secondly, even if nonces never repeat, its security is inherently limited by Bernstein's birthday-type bound. Recent works showed that Bernstein's bound is tight [21,27], which means that the original construction cannot provide higher security.

AN ONGOING SERIES OF RESEARCH aims to find constructions with higher security guarantees that retained some security also under nonce reuse. As one of the starting points, one could identify the proposal of the Encrypted Davies-Meyer (EDM) and the Encrypted Wegman-Carter Davies-Meyer (EWCDM) modes by Cogliati et al. [9]. While EDM is a PRP-to-PRF conversion method and therefore restricted to inputs of n bits length, EWCDM supports nonce-based authentication for variable-input-length messages as does the original Wegman-Carter construction. In EWCDM, a nonce ν is first processed by the Davies-Meyer construction under a permutation π_1; its result is XORed with the hash of a message m and the sum is encrypted under a second independent permutation: $\pi_2(\pi_1(\nu) \oplus \nu \oplus h_{k'}(m))$. EDM misses the hash and uses ν as the only message input. Its authors showed that both constructions provide at least $2n/3$-bit security. Recently, Cogliati and Seurin [10] showed that one can use the same permutation twice in EDM while retaining $2n/3$-bit security.

Mennink and Neves [23] improved on EWCDM. They proved almost full (i.e., n-bit) security for EDM and EWCDM and further showed full n-bit security of proposed dual constructions EDMD and EWCDMD. As a side effect, they made Patarin's Mirror Theory [29–31] easier to grasp for a broader audience. Although Nandi [26] pointed out a slip in [23], which meant that the security of the nonce-based version of its dual, EWCDMD, is still limited by the birthday

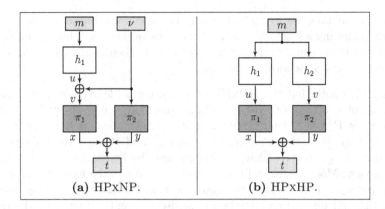

(a) HPxNP.   **(b) HPxHP.**

Fig. 1. Our proposed constructions. π_1 and π_2 represent two permutations over $\{0,1\}^n$, h_1 and h_2 two universal hash functions, m a variable-length message, ν, ν^1, and ν^2 nonces of fixed length, and t the authentication tag.

bound, the work by Mennink and Neves opened the gates for a wider study of possible constructions. At CRYPTO'18, Datta et al. [13] extended this direction by the Decrypted Wegman-Carter Davies-Meyer construction (DWCDM), a single-key variant of EWCDM that employs the permutation in both directions. The maximal security of their construction was capped by $2n/3$ bits by design.

An alternative approach has been taken by Cogliati et al. [8]. They proposed four generic constructions based on the composition of universal hashing and a block cipher: Hash-as-Tweak (HAT), Nonce-as-Tweak (NAT), Hash-as-Key (HAK), and Nonce-as-Key (NAK). They proved n-bit security for all constructions in the ideal-permutation model (assuming a universal hash function). However, the former two constructions require a tweakable primitive, whereas the latter two require message-dependent rekeying.

We can identify four desiderata for interesting MACs based on permutations and universal hashing. In terms of security, the adversary's advantage should remain negligible for $\ell q \gg 2^{n/2}$. In terms of simplicity, the number of calls to the primitive(s) should be minimized. For efficiency, their calls should be parallelizable, and frequent rekeying should be avoided. Last but not least, they should support variable-length messages. So, in spite of recent advances, it remains an interesting question how one can generally achieve those aspects for stateless deterministic and/or nonce-based constructions.

CONTRIBUTION. This work analyzes two constructions based on permutations and universal hashing using the Mirror Theory. Our first construction HPxNP is nonce-based, whereas our second, HPxHP, is stateless deterministic. We name them according to the fact whether they employ a universal hash function (HP) or a nonce (NP) as inputs to the permutation. Figure 1 illustrates them schematically. We show that both modes provide $\mathcal{O}(2n/3)$ bits of security asymptotically.

OUTLINE. Hereupon, we first cover briefly the necessary preliminaries used in this work, including a brief recap of Patarin's Mirror Theory. Thereupon, Sect. 3 proposes our three constructions whose security is then analyzed in the subsequent Sects. 4 and 5. Section 6 concludes.

Remark 1. We note that the HPxHP construction is clearly not novel, but an abstraction of a variety of existing double-lane MACs, e.g., 3KF9 [37], GCM-SIV-2 [18], or PMAC$^+$ [36]. However, in its abstract form, it has been studied by Datta et al. [11] (the same authors already had studied the construction in [12]) from a constructive view, or very recently by Leurent et al. [20] from an attacking view. More precisely, Leurent et al. [20] proposed a forgery attack with data complexity of $\mathcal{O}(2^{3n/4})$ for such constructions. We also take the constructive view, so that our derived security bound is also inherently limited by the result by Leurent et al.; moreover, at the end of each analysis section, we further discuss the effect of using 4-wise independent hash functions for our constructions, with the positive result that the then-obtained security bounds render their result inapplicable and lead to higher security.

2   Preliminaries

GENERAL NOTATIONS. We use calligraphic uppercase letters $\mathcal{X}, \mathcal{Y}$ for sets. We write $\{0,1\}^n$ for the set of bit strings of length n, and denote the concatenation of binary strings x and y by $x \parallel y$ and the result of their bitwise XOR by $x \oplus y$. We write $x \leftarrow \mathcal{X}$ to mean that x is chosen uniformly at random from the set $\mathcal{X}$. We consider $\mathsf{Func}(\mathcal{X}, \mathcal{Y})$ to be the set of all deterministic maps $F : \mathcal{X} \to \mathcal{Y}$ and $\mathsf{Perm}(\mathcal{X})$ to be the set of all permutations over $\mathcal{X}$. Given an event E, we denote by $\Pr[E]$ the probability of E. For two integers n, k with $n \geq k \geq 1$, we denote the falling factorial as $(n)_k \stackrel{\text{def}}{=} \prod_{i=0}^{k-1}(n-i)$.

A (complexity-theoretic) distinguisher $\mathbf{A}$ is an efficient adversary, i.e., an efficient Turing machine that is given access to a number of oracles $\mathcal{O}$ which it can interact with. The task of $\mathbf{A}$ is to distinguish between two worlds of oracles, one of which is chosen at the beginning of the experiment uniformly at random. After its interaction, $\mathbf{A}$ outputs a bit that represents a guess of the world that $\mathbf{A}$ interacted with. The distinguishing advantage between a real world $\mathcal{P}$ and an ideal world $\mathcal{O}$ is given by $\Delta_{\mathbf{A}}(\mathcal{P}, \mathcal{O}) \stackrel{\text{def}}{=} \left|\Pr\left[\mathbf{A}^{\mathcal{P}} \Rightarrow 1\right] - \Pr\left[\mathbf{A}^{\mathcal{O}} \Rightarrow 1\right]\right|$. Throughout this work, we consider information-theoretic distinguishers, i.e., distinguishers that are computationally unbounded, and that are limited only by the number of queries they can ask to their available oracles. We assume that distinguishers do not ask duplicate queries or queries to which they already can compute the answer themselves from earlier queries, as is common. W.l.o.g., we limit our interest to deterministic distinguishers since for each probabilistic distinguisher, there exists a deterministic one with equal advantage that fixed a random tape beforehand (cf. [1,7]). We briefly recall the definitions for the advantage of distinguishing a construction from a random function (PRF) and a random permutation (PRP), respectively.

Definition 1 (PRF Advantage). Let $\mathcal{K}$, $\mathcal{X}$, and $\mathcal{Y}$ be non-empty sets and let $F : \mathcal{K} \times \mathcal{X} \to \mathcal{Y}$ and $\rho \leftarrow \mathsf{Func}(\mathcal{X}, \mathcal{Y})$ and $k \leftarrow \mathcal{K}$. Then, the PRF advantage of $\mathbf{A}$ w.r.t. F is defined as $\mathbf{Adv}_F^{\mathrm{PRF}}(\mathbf{A}) \overset{\mathrm{def}}{=} \Delta_{\mathbf{A}}(F_k, \rho)$.

A keyed permutation $E : \mathcal{K} \times \mathcal{X} \to \mathcal{X}$ is a family of permutations over $\mathcal{X}$ indexed by a key $K \in \mathcal{K}$.

Definition 2 (PRP Advantage). Let $\mathcal{K}$ and $\mathcal{X}$ be non-empty sets, $E : \mathcal{K} \times \mathcal{X} \to \mathcal{X}$ be a keyed permutation, and let $\pi \leftarrow \mathsf{Perm}(\mathcal{X})$ and $k \leftarrow \mathcal{K}$. Then, the PRP advantage of $\mathbf{A}$ w.r.t. F is defined as $\mathbf{Adv}_{E_k}^{\mathrm{PRP}}(\mathbf{A}) \overset{\mathrm{def}}{=} \Delta_{\mathbf{A}}(E_k, \pi)$.

To recall the necessary definitions for universal hashing, let $\mathcal{X}$ and $\mathcal{Y}$ denote two non-empty sets, and $\mathcal{H} = \{h : \mathcal{X} \to \mathcal{Y}\}$ be a family of hash functions h.

Definition 3 (Almost-Universal Hash Function [5]). We say that $\mathcal{H}$ is ε-almost-universal (ε-AU) if, for all distinct $x, x' \in \mathcal{X}$, it holds that $\mathrm{Pr}_{h \leftarrow \mathcal{H}}[h(x) = h(x')] \leq \varepsilon$.

Almost-XOR-universal hash functions were introduced in [19]; the term, however, is due to Rogaway [32].

Definition 4 (Almost-XOR-Universal Hash Function [19,32]). Here, let $\mathcal{Y} \subseteq \{0,1\}^n$ for some positive integer n. We say that $\mathcal{H}$ is ε-almost-XOR-universal (ε-AXU) if, for all distinct $x, x' \in \mathcal{X}$ and arbitrary $\Delta \in \mathcal{Y}$, it holds that $\mathrm{Pr}_{h \leftarrow \mathcal{H}}[h(x) \oplus h(x') = \Delta] \leq \varepsilon$.

Definition 5 (k-wise Independence [35]). We say that $\mathcal{H}$ is k-independent if, for all pair-wise distinct $x_1, \ldots x_k \in \mathcal{X}$ and all $y_1, \ldots, y_k \in \mathcal{Y}^k$, it holds that $\mathrm{Pr}_{h \leftarrow \mathcal{H}}[h(x_i) = y_i, \text{ for } 1 \leq i \leq k] = 1/|\mathcal{Y}|^k$.

2.1 H-Coefficient Technique

The H-coefficients technique is a proof method due to Patarin, where we consider the variant by Chen and Steinberger [7,28]. The results of the interaction of an adversary $\mathbf{A}$ with its oracles are collected in a transcript τ. The oracles can sample randomness prior to the interaction (often a key or an ideal primitive that is sampled beforehand), and are then deterministic throughout the experiment [7]. The task of $\mathbf{A}$ is to distinguish the real world $\mathcal{O}_{\mathrm{real}}$ from the ideal world $\mathcal{O}_{\mathrm{ideal}}$. Let Θ_{real} and Θ_{ideal} denote the distribution of transcripts in the real and the ideal world, respectively. A transcript τ is called *attainable* if the probability to obtain τ in the ideal world – i.e. over Θ_{ideal} – is non-zero. Then, the fundamental Lemma of the H-coefficients technique, the proof to which is given in [7,28], states:

Lemma 1 (Fundamental Lemma of the H-coefficient Technique [28]). Assume, the set of attainable transcripts can be partitioned into two disjoint sets GoodT and BadT. Further assume that there exist $\epsilon_1, \epsilon_2 \geq 0$ such that for any transcript $\tau \in \mathsf{GoodT}$, it holds that

$$\frac{\mathrm{Pr}\left[\Theta_{\mathrm{real}} = \tau\right]}{\mathrm{Pr}\left[\Theta_{\mathrm{ideal}} = \tau\right]} \geq 1 - \epsilon_1, \quad \text{and} \quad \mathrm{Pr}\left[\Theta_{\mathrm{ideal}} \in \mathsf{BadT}\right] \leq \epsilon_2.$$

Then, for all adversaries $\mathbf{A}$, it holds that $\Delta_{\mathbf{A}}(\mathcal{O}_{\mathrm{real}}, \mathcal{O}_{\mathrm{ideal}}) \leq \epsilon_1 + \epsilon_2$.

2.2   Mirror Theory

We will combine the H-coefficient technique with Patarin's Mirror Theory, which allows us to lower bound the amount of good transcripts. The ratio yields then the probability for a good transcript. In the following, we recall the necessary definitions of the Mirror Theory according to [23] that followed Patarin [29,30].

Remark 2. Mirror Theory became popular to a broader audience after its reformulation by Mennink and Neves [23]. While the core ideas are not difficult to understand, the proof by Patarin in [29] employed a recursive argument that has been subject to intensive debates in the past, cf. [13,23]. The correctness of the argument for the first recursion has been established, where Patarin showed $\mathcal{O}(2n/3)$ bits of security for the sum of permutations [29]. Patarin's proof had to approximate the second recursion; a full proof would have to continue on for many further recursions with an exponential number of cases, which seems a highly sophisticated task. Clearly, it is out of scope of this work. Instead of relying on the assumptions of the full Mirror Theory, we follow the line of e.g., [13,22] and consider it not for full n-bit security. In this work, we require only up to $\mathcal{O}(2n/3)$ bits of security, thus, effectively relying only the first recursion.

Mirror theory evaluates the number of possible solutions to a system of affine equations of the form $P_{a_i} \oplus P_{b_i} = \lambda_i$ in a finite group. Let $q \geq 1$ denote a number of equations and $r \geq 1$ a number of unknowns. Let $\mathcal{P} = \{P_1, \ldots, P_r\}$ represent the set of r distinct unknowns and consider an equation system

$$\mathcal{E} = \left\{ P_{a_1} \oplus P_{b_1} = \lambda_1, \ldots, P_{a_q} \oplus P_{b_q} = \lambda_q \right\},$$

where a_i, b_i for $1 \leq i \leq q$ are mapped to $\{1, \ldots, r\}$ by a surjective index map $\varphi : \{a_1, b_1, \ldots, a_q, b_q\} \to \{1, \ldots, r\}$. Given a subset of equations $\mathcal{I} \subseteq \{1, \ldots, q\}$, the multiset $\mathcal{M}_\mathcal{I}$ is defined as $\mathcal{M}_\mathcal{I} = \bigcup_{i \in \mathcal{I}} \{\varphi(a_i), \varphi(b_i)\}$.

Definition 6 (Circle-freeness). An equation system $\mathcal{E}$ is circle-free if there exists no subset of indices $\mathcal{I} \subseteq \{1, \ldots, q\}$ of equations s.t. $\mathcal{M}_\mathcal{I}$ has even multiplicity elements only.

So, no linear combination of equations is independent of the unknowns.

Definition 7 (Block-maximality). Let $\mathcal{Q}_1, \ldots, \mathcal{Q}_s = \{1, \ldots, r\}$ be a partitioning of the r indices into s minimal so-called blocks s.t. for all equation indices $i \in \{1, \ldots, q\}$, there exists a single block index $\ell \in \{1, \ldots, s\}$ s.t. the unknowns of the i-th equation are contained in only this block: $\{\varphi(a_i), \varphi(b_i)\} \subseteq \mathcal{Q}_\ell$. Then, the system of equations $\mathcal{E}$ is called ξ-block-maximal for $\xi \geq 2$ if there exists no $i \in \{1, \ldots, s\}$ s.t. $|\mathcal{Q}_i| > \xi$.

So, the unknowns can be partitioned into blocks of size at most $\xi + 1$ if $\mathcal{E}$ is ξ-block-maximal.

Definition 8 (Non-degeneracy). A system of equations $\mathcal{E}$ is non-degenerate iff there is no $\mathcal{I} \subseteq \{1, \ldots, q\}$ s.t. $\mathcal{M}_\mathcal{I}$ has exactly two odd multiplicity elements and $\bigoplus_{i \in \mathcal{I}} \lambda_i = 0$.

So, an equation system is non-degenerate if there is no linear combination of one or more equations that imply $P_i = P_j$ for distinct i, j and $P_i, P_j \in \mathcal{P}$. The central theorem of Patarin's mirror theorem is then Theorem 2 in [23], which itself is a brief form of Theorem 6 in [29].

Theorem 1 (Mirror Theorem [23]). Let $\xi \geq 2$. Let $\mathcal{E}$ be a system of equations over the unknowns $\mathcal{P}$ that is (i) circle-free, (ii) ξ-block-maximal, and (iii) non-degenerate. Then, as long as $(\xi - 1)^2 \cdot r \leq 2^n/67$, the number of solutions s.t. $P_i \neq P_j$ for all pairwise distinct $i, j \in \{1, \ldots, r\}$ is at least

$$\frac{(2^n)_r}{(2^n)^q}.$$

A proof sketch is given in [23, Appendix A], and the details in [29]. An updated proof had been given in [25].

Mennink and Neves described a relaxation wherein the condition that two unknowns P_a and P_b must differ whenever a and b differ is released to the degree that distinct unknowns must be pairwise distinct only inside their blocks. So, it must hold for $a \neq b$ that $P_a \neq P_b$ when $a, b \in \mathcal{R}_j$ for some $j \in \{1, \ldots, s\}$ for a given partitioning $\{1, \ldots, r\} = \bigcup_{i=1}^{s} \mathcal{R}_i$.

Definition 9 (Relaxed Non-degeneracy). An equation system $\mathcal{E}$ is relaxed non-degenerate w.r.t. the partitioning $\{1, \ldots, r\} = \bigcup_{i=1}^{s} \mathcal{R}_i$ iff there is no $\mathcal{I} \subseteq \{1, \ldots, q\}$ s.t. $\mathcal{M}_{\mathcal{I}}$ has exactly two odd multiplicity elements and $\bigoplus_{i \in \mathcal{I}} \lambda_i = 0$.

In their Theorem 3, [23] extended Theorem 1 to the following relaxed form:

Theorem 2 (Relaxed Mirror Theorem [23]). Let $\xi \geq 2$ and $\mathcal{E}$ be a system of equations over the unknowns $\mathcal{P}$ that is (i) circle-free, (ii) ξ-block-maximal, and (iii) non-degenerate. Then, as long as $(\xi - 1)^2 \cdot r \leq 2^n/67$, the number of solutions s.t. $P_i \neq P_j$ for all pairwise distinct $i, j \in \{1, \ldots, r\}$ is at least

$$\frac{\mathsf{NonEq}(\mathcal{R}_1, \ldots, \mathcal{R}_s; \mathcal{E})}{(2^n)^q},$$

where $\mathsf{NonEq}(\mathcal{R}_1, \ldots, \mathcal{R}_s; \mathcal{E})$ is the number of solutions to $\mathcal{P}$ that satisfy $P_a \neq P_b$ for all $a, b \in \mathcal{R}_j$ for all $1 \leq j \leq s$ as well as all inequalities by $\mathcal{E}$.

Mennink and Neves stress that the relaxed Theorem 2 is equivalent to Theorem 1 for $s = 1$, i.e., when the equation system consists of a single block. Moreover, the number of solutions that are covered in the term $\mathsf{NonEq}(\mathcal{R}_1, \ldots, \mathcal{R}_s; \mathcal{E})$ can be lower bounded by $(2^n)_{|\mathcal{R}_1|} \cdot \prod_{i=2}^{s} (2^n - (\xi - 1))_{|\mathcal{R}_i|}$ since every variable is in exactly one block which imposes at most $\xi - 1$ additional inequalities to the other unknowns in its block.

Remark 3. We consider PRF security in the information-theoretic setting, similar to [23]. The underlying permutations are secret and assumed to be drawn uniformly at random from $\mathsf{Perm}(\{0, 1\}^n)$. Our results generalize to the complexity-theoretic setting where the permutations π_1 and π_2 will be instantiated with a block cipher E under independent random secret keys k_1 and k_2, E_{k_1} and E_{k_2}, respectively. The bounds from this paper can be easily adapted to the complexity-theoretic setting by adding a term of $2 \cdot \mathbf{Adv}_{E_k}^{\mathrm{PRP}}(q)$. The term refers to twice the maximal advantage for an adversary $\mathbf{A}'$ to distinguish $E : \mathcal{K} \times \{0,1\}^n \to \{0,1\}^n$ keyed with a random key $k \leftarrow \mathcal{K}$ from a random permutation π, where $\mathbf{A}$ asks at most q queries. Note that we employ only the forward direction of the permutation; so, PRP security suffices.

3 Constructions

Let $n \geq 1$ be a positive integer, and let $\mathcal{K}$ denote a non-empty set. Let $\pi_1, \pi_2 \leftarrow$ $\mathrm{Perm}(\{0,1\}^n)$ be independently uniformly at random sampled permutations over n-bit strings. Let $\mathcal{H} = \{h \mid h : \{0,1\}^* \to \{0,1\}^n\}$ be a family of ε_1-AXU hash functions; for HPxHP, we will define and use instead $\mathcal{H}_1 = \{h_1 \mid h_1 : \{0,1\}^* \to \{0,1\}^n\}$ as a family of ε_1-AU hash functions, and $\mathcal{H}_2 = \{h_2 \mid h_2 : \{0,1\}^* \to \{0,1\}^n\}$ as a family of ε_2-AU hash functions. We require the hash functions to be sampled independently uniformly at random, which is usually realized by sampling hash keys independently uniformly at random.

Our first, nonce-based construction, HPxNP, is illustrated in Fig. 1a. It shares similarities with Minematsu's Enhanced Hash-then-Mask construction [24] that had been analyzed further in [14,15]; however, Minematsu's construction used a function instead of a permutation and a per-message random IV. In this construction, the message is hashed to an n-bit value $h(m)$. For this construction, we need $\mathcal{H}$ to be an ε-almost-XOR-universal family of hash functions. An n-bit nonce ν is XORed to the hash u to obtain $v := h(m) \oplus \nu$; v and ν serve as inputs to the two calls to a permutation π_1 and π_2, respectively, and yield $x := \pi_1(v)$ and $y := \pi_2(\nu)$. Finally, the outputs of the permutation calls are XORed and released as authentication tag: $t := x \oplus y$.

Our second construction, HPxHP, is illustrated in Fig. 1b. It consists of two parallel invocations of the hash functions on the input message $m \in \{0,1\}^*$ that are hashed using $h_1 \in \mathcal{H}_1$ and $h_2 \in \mathcal{H}_2$, respectively, to two n-bit values u and v. Those serve as inputs to the two calls to a permutation π_1 and π_2, respectively and yield $x := \pi_1(u)$ and $y := \pi_2(v)$. Finally, the outputs of the permutation calls are XORed and released as authentication tag: $t := x \oplus y$.

In practice, the permutations π_1 and π_2 will be instantiated with a secure block cipher E under two independent keys k_1 and k_2. An intuitive choice for the hash function is, for example, polynomial hashing. Let $\mathbb{F}_{2^n}$ be the Galois Field $GF(2^n)$ with a fixed primitive polynomial $p(\mathrm{x})$. For $n = 128$, the GCM polynomial $p(\mathrm{x}) = \mathrm{x}^{128} + \mathrm{x}^7 + \mathrm{x}^2 + \mathrm{x} + 1$ is a usual choice. The hash function is instantiated by sampling a hash key $k \leftarrow \mathbb{F}_{2^n}$. Given k and a message $m \in (\mathbb{F}_{2^n})^\ell$ of ℓ blocks m_i, $1 \leq i \leq \ell$, polynomial hashing is then defined as the sum of

$$h_k(m) \stackrel{\mathrm{def}}{=} \sum_{i=1}^{\ell} k^{\ell+1-i} \cdot m_i,$$

where additions and multiplications are in $\mathbb{F}_{2^n}$. It is well-known that, for messages of at most ℓ blocks (after padding), polynomial hashing is $\ell/2^n$-AXU and $\ell/2^n$-AU. Note that polynomial hashing requires an injective padding to prevent trivial hash collisions; a 10^*-padding works, but may extend messages by a block.

While the sum of a polynomial hash is sequential, computing the individual terms on a few cores in parallel is well-known at the cost of storing multiple powers of the hash key. For instance, optimized instances of GCM parallelize the computations of four (or eight) subsequent blocks $k^4 \cdot m_i$, $k^3 \cdot m_{i+1}$, $k^2 \cdot m_{i+2}$, and $k^4 \cdot m_{i+3}$, before their results are summed, reduced by the modulus, and summed to the sum of the previous blocks $\sum_{j=1}^{i-1} k^j m_j$ [16,17]. Thus, several hash multiplications, or two hash-function calls, or hashing and computing a permutation are efficiently parallelizable as long as the platform is not too resource-restricted. Note that a number of related hash functions exist with similar security properties; pseudo-dot-product hashing, BRW hashing, or combined approaches such as [6] can half the number of necessary multiplications, and provide similar parallelizability. We refer the interested reader to an overview by Bernstein [4].

4   Security Analysis of HPxNP

First, we consider the construction HPxNP. Patarin's approach [29] allows us to obtain a bound of $\mathcal{O}(2n/3)$ bits of security. At the end of this section, we discuss the implications of considering ξ_{average} instead, as was also suggested ibidem.

Theorem 3. Let $n \geq 1, \xi \geq 2$ be integers, and $\mathcal{H} = \{h \mid h : \{0,1\}^* \to \{0,1\}^n\}$ be a family of ε-AXU hash functions with $h \twoheadleftarrow \mathcal{H}$. For any nonce-respecting PRF distinguisher $\mathbf{A}$ that asks at most $q \leq 2^n/(67\xi^2)$ queries, it holds that

$$\mathbf{Adv}^{\mathrm{PRF}}_{\mathrm{HPxNP}[h,\pi_1,\pi_2]}(\mathbf{A}) \leq \frac{2q^2 \cdot \varepsilon}{\xi^2} + \frac{\binom{q}{2} \cdot \varepsilon}{2^n} + \frac{q}{2^n}.$$

Note that in this case, the optimal choice of ξ to obtain the best bound is $2^{n/6}$, assuming that $\varepsilon \in \mathcal{O}(2^{-n})$. Then, the bound in Theorem 3 is dominated by the first term of $\mathcal{O}(q^2/2^{4n/3} + q^2/2^{2n} + q/2^n)$, while the number of queries is allowed to be $q \leq 2^{2n/3}$. Other values for ξ reduce either the security bound or the number of queries.

The remainder of this section is devoted to show Theorem 3. Here, $\mathbf{A}$ makes q construction queries (ν_i, m_i), for $1 \leq i \leq q$, that are stored together with the query results t_i in a transcript $\tau = \{(\nu_i, m_1, t_1), \ldots, (\nu_q, m_q, t_q)\}$. In both worlds, the oracle samples h at the start uniformly at random from all hash instances. $\mathbf{A}$ sees the results t_i after each query. We use a common method to alleviate the proof: after the adversary finished its interaction with the oracle, but before outputting its final decision bit, $\mathbf{A}$ is given the hash-function instance h so that it can compute the values $u_1, \ldots, u_q$ itself. Clearly, this only makes the adversary stronger, but spares a discussion of security internals of the hash function.

Let $1 \leq r \leq 2q$ and consider the set $\mathcal{P} = \{P_1, \ldots, P_r\}$ of r unknowns. We consider a system of q equations

$$\mathcal{E} = \{P_{a_1} \oplus P_{b_1} = t_1, \quad P_{a_2} \oplus P_{b_2} = t_2, \quad \ldots, \quad P_{a_q} \oplus P_{b_q} = t_q\},$$

where $P_{a_i} := x_i = \pi_1(h(m_i) \oplus \nu_i)$ and $P_{b_i} := y_i = \pi_2(\nu_i)$. We further define an index mapping $\varphi : \{a_1, b_1, \ldots, a_q, b_q\} \to \{1, \ldots, r\}$. For all $i, j \in \{1, \ldots, q\}$:

- $\varphi(a_i) \neq \varphi(a_j) \Leftrightarrow h_1(m_i) \oplus \nu_i \neq h_1(m_j) \oplus \nu_j$.
- $\varphi(b_i) \neq \varphi(b_j)$ since $\nu_i \neq \nu_j$.
- $\varphi(a_i) \neq \varphi(b_j)$ since both permutations π_1 and π_2 are independent.

The index mapping φ has a range of size $q_x + q_y$, where $q_x = |\{x_i, \ldots, x_q\}| \leq q$ and $q_y = |\{\nu_1, \ldots, \nu_q\}| = q$.

4.1 Bad Transcripts

φ only exposes collisions of the form $\varphi(a_i) = \varphi(a_j)$ or equivalently $x_i = x_j$. We define the following bad events:

- bad_1: there exist ξ distinct equation indices $i_1, i_2, \ldots, i_\xi \in \{1, \ldots, q\}$ s.t. $x_{i_1} = x_{i_2} = \ldots = x_{i_\xi}$ where ξ is the threshold given in Theorem 3.
- bad_2: There exist query indices $i \neq j$, $i, j \in \{1, \ldots, q\}$ s.t. $(u_i, t_i) = (u_j, t_j)$.

Let us consider bad_1 first. Since h is ε-AXU, the expected amount of collisions is $q^2 \cdot \varepsilon$. Unfortunately ε-AXU is not strong enough to allow for statements regarding multicollisions, i.e. we cannot make a statement on the probability that three or more input values collide. Considering the maximal block size ξ, the worst case would be that all collisions occur in the same hash value. If there exists a block of size $(\xi + 1)$, this block contains ξ^2 collisions. Let $\#\mathsf{Colls}(q)$ be the random variable that counts the collisions in h. By Markov's Inequality, the probability that there are more than $\binom{\xi}{2}$ collisions in h is at most:

$$\Pr\left[\#\mathsf{Colls}_1(q) \geq \binom{\xi}{2}\right] \leq \frac{\mathbb{E}(C)}{\binom{\xi}{2}} = \frac{\binom{q}{2} \cdot \varepsilon}{\binom{\xi}{2}} \leq \frac{2q^2\varepsilon}{\xi^2}.$$

For bad_2, recall that the ideal world samples the tags independently uniformly at random. Since h is ε-AXU, it follows for some distinct pair $i, j \in \{1, \ldots, q\}$:

$$\Pr\left[u_i = u_j \wedge t_i = t_j\right] \leq \frac{\binom{q}{2} \cdot \varepsilon}{2^n}.$$

It follows from the sum of both probability for bad_1 and bad_2 that

$$\Pr\left[\tau \in \mathsf{BadT} \mid \Theta_{\mathrm{ideal}} = \tau\right] \leq \frac{2q^2 \cdot \varepsilon}{\xi^2} + \frac{\binom{q}{2} \cdot \varepsilon}{2^n}.$$

4.2   Ratio of Good Transcripts

Lemma 2. The system of equations is (i) circle-free, (ii) ξ-block-maximal and (iii) relaxed non-degenerate with respect to the partitioning into $\mathcal{R}_1 \sqcup \mathcal{R}_2$, where $\mathcal{R}_1 =^{\text{def}} \{\varphi(a_1), \ldots, \varphi(a_q)\}$ and $\mathcal{R}_2 =^{\text{def}} \{\varphi(b_1), \ldots, \varphi(b_q)\}$.

Proof. The proof relies on the fact that $\varphi(b_i) \neq \varphi(b_j)$ and $\varphi(a_i) \neq \varphi(b_j)$ for any $i \neq j$. For any $\mathcal{I} \subseteq \{1, \ldots, q\}$ the corresponding multiset $M_{\mathcal{I}}$ has at least $|\mathcal{I}|$ odd multiplicity elements and therefore the system of equations $\mathcal{E}$ is (i) circle-free.

(ii) If $\mathcal{E}$ were not ξ-block-maximal, then there must be an ordering $\mathcal{I} = \{i_1, \ldots, i_\xi\}$ s.t. $\varphi(a_{i_1}) = \ldots = \varphi(a_{i_\xi})$. This is equivalent to a ξ-fold collision $x_{i_1} = \ldots = x_{i_\xi}$, which contradicts the assumption that τ is a good transcript.

(iii) Suppose that $\mathcal{E}$ would be relaxed degenerate. Then, there would exist a minimal subset $\mathcal{I} \subseteq 1, \ldots, q$ that has exactly two odd multiplicity elements corresponding to the same oracle and s.t. $\bigoplus_{i \in \mathcal{I}} t_i = 0$. If $|\mathcal{I}| = 1$, $M_{\mathcal{I}}$ would have two elements from different oracles. If $|\mathcal{I}| = 2$ and $t_{i_1} = t_{i_2}$, then we would know that $x_{i_1} \neq x_{i_2}$ since $\nu_{i_1} \neq \nu_{i_2}$, i.e. $y_{i_1} \neq y_{i_2}$. Therefore, we have four odd multiplicity elements. If $|\mathcal{I}| \geq 3$, there would exist at least three odd multiplicity elements. So, $\mathcal{E}$ cannot be relaxed degenerate, which concludes the proof.   □

Lemma 3. Let $\tau \in \mathsf{GoodT}$ and $q \leq 2^n/(67\xi^2)$. Then, it holds that

$$\frac{\Pr[\Theta_{\text{real}} = \tau]}{\Pr[\Theta_{\text{ideal}} = \tau]} \geq 1 - \frac{q}{2^n}.$$

Proof. The probability to obtain a good transcript τ consists of that for obtaining the tags $t_1, \ldots, t_q$, and the hash-function outputs $h(m_i)$. The probability to obtain the latter is given in both worlds by $|\mathcal{H}|^{-1}$. The bound in Lemma 3 is determined by the ratio of the respective probabilities. This term appears in the real world as well as in the ideal world and cancels out eventually. Hence, we ignore it for the remainder of the analysis. The probability of obtaining the rest of the transcript, i.e., the tags t_i, in the ideal world is then given by

$$\Pr[t_1, \ldots, t_q | \Theta_{\text{ideal}}] = \frac{1}{(2^n)^q}$$

since the outputs t_i are sampled independently and uniformly at random from $\{0,1\}^n$ in the ideal world. In the real world, the probability is given by

$$\Pr[\Theta_{\text{real}} = \tau] \geq \frac{\frac{\mathsf{NonEQ}(\mathcal{R}_1, \mathcal{R}_2; \mathcal{E})}{2^{nq}} \cdot (2^n - q_x)! \cdot (2^n - q_y)!}{(2^n!)^2}$$

$$= \frac{\mathsf{NonEQ}(\mathcal{R}_1, \mathcal{R}_2; \mathcal{E})}{2^{nq}(2^n)_{q_x}(2^n)_{q_y}}.$$

Remember that $q_y = q$ since all ν_i are distinct. To lower bound NonEQ $(\mathcal{R}_1, \mathcal{R}_2; \mathcal{E})$, note that we have $(2^n)_{q_x}$ choices for $\{P_j \,|\, j \in \mathcal{R}_1\}$ and at least

$(2^n - 1)_q$ possible choices for $\{P_j \mid j \in \mathcal{R}_2\}$, as every index in $\mathcal{R}_2$ is in a block with exactly one unknown from $\mathcal{R}_1$. Thus

$$\Pr\left[\Theta_{\text{real}} = \tau\right] \geq \frac{(2^n - 1)_q (2^n)_{q_x}}{2^{nq} (2^n)_q (2^n)_{q_x}} = \frac{1}{2^{nq}} \left(1 - \frac{q}{2^n}\right).$$

Hence, we obtain the ratio as in Lemma 3.   □

4.3   Using ξ_{average}

In [29], Patarin suggests that one potentially can consider the average instead of the maximal block size for the sum of permutations in Mirror Theory. More precisely, Generalization 2 of [29, Sect. 6] suggests that:

> "The theorem $P_i \oplus P_j$ is still true if we change the condition $\xi_{\max}\alpha \ll 2^n$ by $\xi_{\text{average}} \ll 2^n$."

The bottleneck in our bound is the event bad_1; bad_2 as well as the good transcripts do not consider ξ at all and the respective terms become significant for $q = 2^n$. Upper bounding the block size is necessary to ensure the condition $q \leq 2^n/(67\xi_{\max}^2)$. Using a universal family of hash functions only allows for a very crude upper bound of the maximal block size which limits us at a security level of around $2^{2n/3}$ queries.

If we could use the average block size as suggested by Patarin, we are limited by the condition $q \leq 2^n/(67\xi_{\text{average}}^2)$; then, bad_1 would no longer be necessary and would significantly improve the bound. The following theorem would yield an upper bound on the expected average block size ξ_{average}.

Theorem 4. For any $q \leq 2^n$ and $\varepsilon \leq 1$, we expect that $\xi_{\text{average}} \leq (q-1)\varepsilon + 2$.

The proof is deferred to the full version of this work, but we will briefly sketch the idea for $\varepsilon = 2^{-n}$: For $q \ll 2^n$, the expected amount of collisions $q^2/2^n$ is in $\mathcal{O}(q)$. For $q = 2^n$, the expected amount of collisions is 2^{n-1}. In the worst case (regarding the average), the collisions are uniformly distributed, i.e. $h(m_1) = h(m_2), h(m_3) = h(m_4), \ldots, h(m_{2^n-1}) = h(m_{2^n})$. This pattern corresponds to the case that every block were of size 3 and hence the average is 3 as well. Any other pattern would not increase the average block size. The proof will consider the more general case for ε. From Theorem 4, we obtain

$$q \leq \frac{2^n}{67((q-1)\varepsilon + 2)^2}.$$

We note that the use of ξ_{average} implies the need to employ the stronger form of the Mirror Theory, that assumes that the iterated proof suggested by Patarin holds. Both the stronger form of the Mirror Theory and the Generalization 2 [29] are subject to their own analysis.

5   Security Analysis of HPxHP

The analysis of HPxHP shares many similarities with that of HPxNP, but differs in certain key points. Regarding the maximum block size, a hash collision (considering the hashes separately) may occur now on one of both sides, i.e., there may be a collision in $h_1(m) = h_1(m')$ or in $h_2(m) = h_2(m')$, which increases the block size and effectively doubles the probability of obtaining a hash collision.[1] Further, since collisions may occur on both sides, it is possible to obtain a circle.

With a universal hash function, we can obtain security up to $\mathcal{O}(2^{2n/3})$ queries, matching the security bound of earlier analyses. With a stronger k-wise independent hash function, it is possible to obtain security up to $\mathcal{O}(2^{\frac{(n-1)k}{k+1}})$ queries. Putting stronger requirements on the family of hash functions increases its size and therefore the length of the key. We still find this result interesting since recent results [20] provided attacks with a query complexity of $\mathcal{O}(2^{3n/4})$. If we demand stronger properties from the hash function, our security level exceeds the complexity by the known attacks. Again, we provide an analysis with a universal hash function and $\xi_{\max}$ first. Thereupon, we will argue about the necessary proof changes to adapt to stronger hash-function families.

Theorem 5. Let $n \geq 1, \xi \geq 2$ be integers and $\mathcal{H}_1$ and $\mathcal{H}_2$ be ε_1 and ε_2-AU families of hash functions, respectively, and let $h_1 \twoheadleftarrow \mathcal{H}_1$ and $h_2 \twoheadleftarrow \mathcal{H}_2$ be sampled independently uniformly at random. Let $\varepsilon \stackrel{\text{def}}{=} \max\{\varepsilon_1, \varepsilon_2\}$. For any PRF distinguisher $\mathbf{A}$ that asks at most $q \leq 2^n/(67\xi^2)$ queries, it holds that

$$\mathbf{Adv}_{\text{HPxHP}[h_1,h_2,\pi_1,\pi_2]}^{\text{PRF}}(\mathbf{A}) \leq \frac{4q^2\varepsilon}{\xi^2} + 3 \cdot (q\varepsilon)^2 + q^3\varepsilon^2 + \frac{\xi \cdot q}{2^n - \xi}.$$

For $\xi = 2^{n/6}$, and assuming an optimal $\varepsilon = \mathcal{O}(2^{-n})$, the bound in Theorem 5 has the form of $\mathcal{O}(q^2/2^{4n/3} + q^2/2^{2n} + q^3/2^{2n} + q/2^{5n/6})$ for $q \in \mathcal{O}(2^{2n/3})$ queries. So, it is dominated by the first term. The remainder of this section contains the proof of Theorem 5. Consider a deterministic distinguisher $\mathbf{A}$ that has access to either HPxHP$[h_1, h_2, \pi_1, \pi_2]$ or ρ, which chooses the outputs given to $\mathbf{A}$ uniformly at random. $\mathbf{A}$ makes q construction queries m_i that are stored together with the query results t_i in a transcript $\tau = \{(m_1, t_1), \ldots, (m_q, t_q)\}$. In both worlds, the oracle samples h_1 and h_2 at the beginning independently and uniformly at random from their hash families. $\mathbf{A}$ sees the results t_i after each query. Again, we make the adversary stronger by defining that the hash keys are revealed to the adversary after it finished its interaction with the oracle, but before outputting its final decision bit.

Let $1 \leq r \leq 2q$ and consider the set $\mathcal{P} = \{P_1, \ldots, P_r\}$ of r unknowns. Again, we consider a system of q equations

$$\mathcal{E} = \{P_{a_1} \oplus P_{b_1} = t_1, \quad P_{a_2} \oplus P_{b_2} = t_2, \quad \ldots, \quad P_{a_q} \oplus P_{b_q} = t_q\},$$

---

[1] Technically speaking, there is a total of $q(q-1)/2$ of input pairs. When bounding the probability of a collision we used q^2 instead, ignoring the factor $1/2$.

where $P_{a_i} := x_i = \pi_1(h_1(m_i))$ and $P_{b_i} := y_i = \pi_2(h_2(m_i))$. We further define an index mapping $\varphi : \{a_1, b_1, \ldots, a_q, b_q\} \rightarrow \{1, \ldots, r\}$; φ maps equal permutation outputs $x_i = x_j$ that occur for any $i \neq j$ (from equal hash values $u_i = u_j$) to the same unknown P_k; similarly, φ maps equal permutation outputs $y_i = y_j$ that occur for any $i \neq j$ (from equal hash values $v_i = v_j$) to the same unknown P_ℓ. For all $i, j \in \{1, \ldots, q\}$, it holds that

- $\varphi(a_i) \neq \varphi(a_j) \Leftrightarrow h_1(m_i) \neq h_1(m_j)$.
- $\varphi(b_i) \neq \varphi(b_j) \Leftrightarrow h_2(m_i) \neq h_2(m_j)$.
- $\varphi(a_i) \neq \varphi(b_j)$ since both permutations π_1 and π_2 are independent.

In the real world, the transcript has collisions in the values $x_i = x_j$ or $y_i = y_j$ for $i \neq j$, when the corresponding hash values $u_i = u_j$ or $v_i = v_j$ collide. A collision in x_i and x_j corresponds to a collision in $\varphi(a_i)$ and $\varphi(a_j)$ and a collision in y_i and y_j corresponds to a collision in $\varphi(b_i)$ and $\varphi(b_j)$. Multi-collisions in the range values of π_1 and π_2 correspond to blocks in the mirror theory. To upper bound the size of the largest block $\mathcal{Q}_k$, we need to consider a special type of collision between two queries i and j. In this setting, we say that two queries i and j collide if $h_1(m_i) = h_1(m_j)$ and/or[2] $h_2(m_i) = h_2(m_j)$. The probability for such a collision to happen is $\varepsilon_1 + \varepsilon_2 \leq 2\varepsilon$.

We define an event bad$_1$ if there exists a ξ-multi-collision in any subset of queries $\{i_1, \ldots, i_{\xi+1}\} \subseteq \{1, \ldots, q\}$, where ξ is the threshold in Theorem 5. We need to consider four more events that render a transcript to be bad:

- bad$_1$: There exists a subset $\mathcal{I} \subseteq \{1, \ldots, q\}$ of size $|\mathcal{I}| = \xi$, s.t. for each pair of distinct indices $i, j \in \mathcal{I}$, it holds that $\varphi(a_i) = \varphi(a_j)$ and/or $\varphi(b_i) = \varphi(b_j)$; ξ is the threshold in Theorem 5.
- bad$_2$: There exist $i \neq j$, $i, j \in \{1, \ldots, q\}$ s.t. $(u_i, v_i) = (u_j, v_j)$ and $t_i \neq t_j$.
- bad$_3$: There exist $i \neq j$, $i, j \in \{1, \ldots, q\}$ s.t. $(u_i, t_i) = (u_j, t_j)$ and $v_i \neq v_j$.
- bad$_4$: There exist $i \neq j$, $i, j \in \{1, \ldots, q\}$ s.t. $(v_i, t_i) = (v_j, t_j)$ and $u_i \neq u_j$.
- bad$_5$: There exists a subset $\mathcal{I} \subseteq \{1, \ldots, q\}$ s.t. $\mathcal{M}_\mathcal{I}$ contains only elements of even multiplicity.

If an attainable transcript τ is not bad, we define τ as good. We denote by GoodT and BadT the sets of good and bad transcripts, respectively. In the H-coefficient technique, the probability that a transcript is bad is analyzed solely for the ideal world. The bound in Theorem 5 follows then from Lemma 1 and Lemmas 4, 5 and 6.

5.1 Bad Transcripts

Lemma 4. Let $\xi \geq 1$ denote the threshold from Theorem 5. It holds that

$$\Pr\left[\tau \in \mathsf{BadT} \,|\, \Theta_{\text{ideal}} = \tau\right] \leq \frac{4q^2\varepsilon}{\xi^2} + 3 \cdot (q\varepsilon)^2 + q^3\varepsilon^2.$$

---

[2] To avoid confusion, by 'and/or' we actually mean the logical 'or'.

Proof. In the following, we upper bound the probability that a transcript is bad. Most of the time, we can upper bound the probabilities of the individual bad events to occur and simply take the sum of their probabilities. We will postpone the discussion of the first bad event and begin with the second bad event.

For bad_2, it holds that h_1 and h_2 are both ε-AU and independent. We drop the condition $t_i \neq t_j$ since it only decreases the probability and an upper bound suffices for our purpose. The probability that both hash values collide simultaneously for two queries is at most

$$\Pr[bad_2] \leq \binom{q}{2}\varepsilon^2 \leq \frac{q^2\varepsilon^2}{2}.$$

For the third and fourth bad events, the probabilities can be formulated similarly. To upper bound bad_3, the probability that $u_i = u_j$ is again at most ε for a fixed pair of distinct query indices $i \neq j$. Since the outputs t_i and t_j are sampled uniformly at random and independently from the hash values, we can again neglect the requirement $v_i \neq v_j$ and obtain the same upper bound for bad_3 as for bad_2, when we use $\varepsilon \geq 2^{-n}$. A similar argument holds for bad_4.

When upper bounding the probability of bad_5, we are limited by the hash function. We consider all 3-tuples (m_a, m_b, m_c) such that $h_1(m_a) = h_1(m_b)$ and $h_2(m_b) = h_2(m_c)$. This event can be bounded by $\binom{q}{3}\varepsilon^2$, which also excludes the occurrence of circles. Thus, it holds that $\Pr[bad_5] \leq q^3\varepsilon^2$. Double-collisions that are small circles by themselves are excluded by bad_2.

Now, we consider bad_1. Again, we upper bound the maximal block size for the individual hash functions. Then, we condition bad_1 on $\neg bad_5$ to ensure that no collisions in h_1 are connected to collisions in h_2. Both hash functions are ε-almost-universal. Again, the worst case w.r.t. block maximality is that all collisions occur in the same block of size $\xi + 1$. Such a block would have $\binom{\xi}{2}$ collisions. Let $\#Colls_1(q)$ be a random variable for the number of collisions between $h_1(m_i) = h_1(m_j)$ for $1 \leq i, j \leq q$ and $i \neq j$. Using Markov's Inequality, we obtain

$$\Pr\left[\#Colls_1(q) \geq \binom{\xi}{2}\right] \leq \frac{\mathbb{E}[\#Colls_1(q)]}{\binom{\xi}{2}} \leq \frac{2q^2\varepsilon}{\xi^2}.$$

We can derive a similar argument using a random variable $\#Colls_2(q)$ for the number of collisions between collisions $h_2(m_i) = h_2(m_j)$, So, the probability to obtain a block of size ξ is upper bounded by

$$\Pr[bad_1 | \neg bad_5] \leq \frac{4q^2\varepsilon}{\xi^2}.$$

Our bound in Lemma 4 follows from summing up the obtained terms.   □

5.2   Good Transcripts

It remains to upper bound the ratio of probabilities for a good transcript in both worlds. For the real world, we will use the Relaxed Mirror Theory. We show that a good transcript fulfills all properties needed by the Relaxed Mirror Theorem.

Lemma 5. Let $\tau \in \mathsf{GoodT}$. Let $\mathcal{E}$ be the system of q equations corresponding to $(\varphi^\tau, m_1, \ldots, m_q)$. Then, $\mathcal{E}$ is (i) circle-free, (ii) ξ-block-maximal, and (iii) relaxed non-degenerate w.r.t. the partitioning $\{1, \ldots, r\} = \mathcal{R}_1 \cup \mathcal{R}_2$, where $\mathcal{R}_1 = \{\varphi(a_i), \ldots, \varphi(a_q)\}$ and $\mathcal{R}_2 = \{\varphi(b_i), \ldots, \varphi(b_q)\}$.

Proof. We defined τ to be a good transcript; hence, no bad event has occurred, which implies that the transcript is (i) circle-free since we excluded bad_5 here.

(ii) If $\mathcal{E}$ were not ξ-block-maximal, there would exist a minimal subset $\mathcal{Q} \subseteq \{1, \ldots, r\}$ with $|\mathcal{Q}| \geq \xi + 1$ so that there exists some $i \in \{1, \ldots, q\}$ for which either $\{\varphi(a_i), \varphi(b_i)\} \subseteq \mathcal{Q}$ or $\{\varphi(a_i), \varphi(b_i)\} \cap \mathcal{Q} = \emptyset$. The latter event does not violate the block-maximality, so we can focus on the former statement.

Assuming that $\mathcal{E}$ were not ξ-block-maximal, we can define a subset of indices $\mathcal{I} \subset \{1, \ldots, q\}$ for which it holds that $\{\varphi(a_i), \varphi(b_i)\} \subseteq \mathcal{Q}$ for all $i \in \mathcal{I}$. Then, we can define an ordered sequence of the indices in $\mathcal{I}$ to $i_1, \ldots, i_\xi$ s.t. it would have to hold for all pairs of subsequent indices i_j, i_{j+1}, for $1 \leq j < \xi$ that $\varphi(a_i) = \varphi(a_j)$ and/or $\varphi(b_i) = \varphi(b_j)$. This is equivalent to our definition of bad_1 and would therefore violate our assumption that τ is good. Hence, every good transcript τ is ξ-block-maximal.

(iii) Assume that τ would be relaxed degenerate. This would imply there exists a subset $\mathcal{I} \subseteq \{1, \ldots, q\}$ such that the multiset $M_\mathcal{I}$ has exactly two odd multiplicity elements from a single set $\mathcal{R}_1$ or $\mathcal{R}_2$ and the tags of the elements corresponding to $\mathcal{I}$ sum up to zero, i.e.

$$\bigoplus_{i \in \mathcal{I}} t_i = \bigoplus_{i \in \mathcal{I}} \pi_1(h_1(m_i)) \oplus \pi_2(h_2(m_i)) = 0.$$

Recall that $\varphi(a_i) \neq \varphi(a_j)$ if and only if $h_1(m_i) \neq h_1(m_j)$, $\varphi(b_i) \neq \varphi(b_j)$ if and only if $h_2(m_i) \neq h_2(m_j)$ and $\varphi(a_i) \neq \varphi(b_j)$ for any choice of i and j. An element $\varphi(a_i)$ has even multiplicity in $M_\mathcal{I}$ if there is an even amount of inputs that collide in $h_1(m_i)$. And similarly an element $\varphi(b_i)$ has even multiplicity in $M_\mathcal{I}$ if there is an even amount of inputs that collide in $h_2(m_i)$. If there is an even amount of queries that collide in a hash value, one can easily see that these elements will cancel out in the above sum.

For simplicity, assume, there exists a subset $\mathcal{I} \subseteq \{1, \ldots, q\}$ with exactly two odd multiplicity elements from $\mathcal{R}_1$ and even multiplicity elements only from $\mathcal{R}_2$. All elements from $\mathcal{R}_2$ cancel out in the sum above. and all even multiplicity elements from $\mathcal{R}_1$ cancel out as well. Let the two odd multiplicity elements from $\mathcal{R}_1$ have multiplicity $2n_1 + 1$ and $2n_2 + 1$, where $n_1, n_2 \geq 0$. In total, $2n_1$ and $2n_2$ terms will cancel out and what remains is $\pi_1(h_1(m_i)) \oplus \pi_1(h_1(m_j)) = 0$ where $\varphi(a_i) \neq \varphi(a_j)$. However, this event cannot occur since $\varphi(a_i) \neq \varphi(a_j)$ implies that $h_1(m_i) \neq h_1(m_j)$; thus the system cannot be relaxed degenerate. $\square$

Lemma 6. Let $\tau \in \mathsf{GoodT}$ and $q \leq 2^n/(67\xi^2)$. Then, it holds that

$$\frac{\Pr[\Theta_{\mathrm{real}} = \tau]}{\Pr[\Theta_{\mathrm{ideal}} = \tau]} \geq 1 - \frac{\xi \cdot q}{2^n - \xi}.$$

Proof. The probability to obtain a good transcript τ consists of that for obtaining the tags $t_1, \ldots, t_q$, and the hash-function outputs u_i and v_i. The probability to obtain the latter is given in both worlds by $\Pr\left[(h_1, h_2) \mid (h_1, h_2) \leftarrow \mathcal{H}_1 \times \mathcal{H}_2\right]$. The bound in Lemma 6 is determined by the ratio of the respective probabilities. This term appears in the real world as well as in the ideal world and cancels out eventually. Hence, we ignore it for the remainder of the analysis. The probability for the tags t_i in the ideal world is then given by $\Pr[t_1, \ldots, t_q \mid \Theta_{\text{ideal}}] = 1/(2^n)^q$ since the outputs t_i are sampled independently and uniformly at random from $\{0, 1\}^n$ in the ideal world.

In the real world, the situation is more complex and a little more work is necessary. We denote by $q_x := |\{\pi_1(h_1(m_i)) \mid i \in \{1, \ldots, q\}\}|$ the amount of distinct values for π_1 and similarly we denote by $q_y := |\{\pi_2(h_2(m_i)) \mid i \in \{1, \ldots, q\}\}|$ the amount of distinct values for π_2. The number of solutions to the $q_x + q_y$ unknowns is at least $\mathsf{NonEQ}(\mathcal{R}_1, \mathcal{R}_2; \mathcal{E})/2^{nq}$. There are $(2^n - q_x)!$ possible choices for the remaining output values of π_1 and $(2^n - q_y)!$ possible choices for the remaining output values of π_2. Thus, we can lower bound

$$\Pr\left[\Theta_{\text{real}} = \tau\right] \geq \frac{\frac{\mathsf{NonEQ}(\mathcal{R}_1, \mathcal{R}_2; \mathcal{E})}{2^{nq}} \cdot (2^n - q_x)! \cdot (2^n - q_y)!}{(2^n!)^2} = \frac{\mathsf{NonEQ}(\mathcal{R}_1, \mathcal{R}_2; \mathcal{E})}{2^{nq}(2^n)_{q_x}(2^n)_{q_y}}.$$

We will use the obvious lower bound for $\mathsf{NonEQ}(\mathcal{R}_1, \mathcal{R}_2; \mathcal{E})$ and we obtain

$$\Pr\left[\Theta_{\text{real}} = \tau\right] \geq \frac{(2^n)_{q_x}(2^n - \xi)_{q_y}}{2^{nq}(2^n)_{q_x}(2^n)_{q_y}} = \frac{1}{2^{nq}} \cdot \frac{(2^n - \xi)_{q_y}}{(2^n)_{q_y}}.$$

We can immediately see that

$$\frac{\Pr\left[\Theta_{\text{real}} = \tau\right]}{\Pr\left[\Theta_{\text{ideal}} = \tau\right]} \geq \frac{(2^n - \xi)_{q_y}}{(2^n)_{q_y}}.$$

We can further reformulate the expression $(2^n - \xi)_{q_y}/(2^n)_{q_y}$ to

$$\frac{(2^n - q_y)(2^n - q_y - 1) \cdots (2^n - q_y - (\xi - 1))}{(2^n)(2^n - 1)(2^n - 2) \cdots (2^n - (\xi - 1))} = \prod_{i=0}^{\xi - 1} \frac{2^n - i - q_y}{2^n - i}.$$

This can be reformed to and upper bounded by

$$\prod_{i=0}^{\xi - 1} \left(1 - \frac{q_y}{2^n - i}\right) \geq \left(1 - \frac{q}{2^n - \xi}\right)^{\xi} \geq 1 - \frac{\xi \cdot q}{2^n - \xi},$$

where the final inequality is Bernoulli's. $\square$

5.3   Using k-Wise Independent Hash Functions

In contrast to the analysis of HPxNP, for HPxHP, we find ξ not only in the analysis of bad_1, but also in that of bad_5 plus in the bound for the good transcripts. For the same reasons as in HPxNP, bad_1 and bad_5 cap the bound at around $q = 2^{2n/3}$. Using the average block size would not work here since it would not affect the bound of bad_5. However, we can increase the security bound of HPxHP with stronger, k-wise independent hash functions. For even k, this allows to obtain a bound of $q = 2^{kn/(k+1)}$ since such hash functions yield better bounds for circles of sizes $\geq k$. Since circles always contain an even amount of queries, there would be no benefit of an uneven values k. Leurent et al. required a 4-circle that is expected after $2^{3n/4}$ queries for their attack. Using a 4-independent hash function, the first 4-circle occurs after 2^n queries on average. So, we can obtain a security bound that exceeds the complexity of Leurent et al.'s attack. For simplicity, we will consider 4-wise independent hash functions first and illustrate the changes to the security bound of HPxHP. Thereupon, we extend our analysis to larger values of k. For space limitations, we defer the proofs of Lemmas 7 and 8 to the full version of this work.

Lemma 7. Let $\mathcal{H}_1$ and $\mathcal{H}_2$ be independent 4-wise independent hash functions. Let $\xi \geq 7$. Then

$$\Pr\left[\mathsf{bad}_1 | \neg \mathsf{bad}_2\right] \leq \frac{2\binom{q}{4}}{2^{3n}\binom{\xi}{4}} + \frac{16q^5}{2^{4n}}.$$

We find two interesting points here: (1) Raising the requirement of the hash functions to 4-wise independence yields a 4-circle after 2^n queries on average instead of after $2^{3n/4}$ queries as in the attack by Leurent et al. Thus, a security level of $2^{4n/5}$ can be obtained. (2) We cannot show yet if it is possible to consider ξ_{average} instead of ξ_{max}. If we can consider the average block size instead of the maximum block size, the upper bound of circles is the bottleneck. Vice versa, it seems that attacks on the HPxHP-type of MACs must exploit the occurrence of circles. We can formulate the following lemma to bound the probability of bad_5.

Lemma 8. Let $\mathcal{H}_1$ and $\mathcal{H}_2$ be independent 4-wise independent hash functions. Then $\Pr\left[\mathsf{bad}_5 | \neg \mathsf{bad}_2 \wedge \neg \mathsf{bad}_1\right] \leq q^4/2^{4n}$.

6   Conclusion

We presented two MAC constructions that are provably secure to up to $\mathcal{O}(2^{2n/3})$ queries; HPxHP avoids nonces at the price of two independent hash-function evaluations; HPxNP trades one hash-function call for the use of a nonce.

Our results add to the works that demonstrate the usefulness of Patarin's Mirror Theory for such constructions. We indicated that considering the average instead of the maximal block size in the Mirror Theory would greatly increase the security of one of our constructions. A proof is deferred to the full version of this work. Though, a deeper study of Patarin's theory is required to derive the consequences of this replacement, which is out of the scope of this work.

Leurent et al.'s generic distinguisher on constructions similar to HPxHP with a data complexity of $\mathcal{O}(2^{3n/4})$ queries exploited the occurrence of circles in the underlying hash functions. So, there is still a gap between the best security bound and their attack. We studied that stronger, k-wise independent hash functions decreased the probability of circles in the full version of this work where we indicate that it can raise the security level above the bound of $\mathcal{O}(2^{3n/4})$.

We can imagine that the security level of our constructions is higher than $2n/3$ bits. For example, the bottleneck in our proof of HPxNP is the bound for the maximal block size as long as the hash function family is "only" universal. A stronger hash function helps here; plus, it may as well be possible to consider the average block size and obtain $\mathcal{O}(2^n)$ security. However, this needs to be verified.

Acknowledgments. We would like to thank the anonymous reviewers for their helpful comments.

References

1. Andreeva, E., Daemen, J., Mennink, B., Van Assche, G.: Security of keyed sponge constructions using a modular proof approach. In: Leander, G. (ed.) FSE 2015. LNCS, vol. 9054, pp. 364–384. Springer, Heidelberg (2015). https://doi.org/10.1007/978-3-662-48116-5_18

2. Bernstein, D.J.: Stronger security bounds for wegman-carter-shoup authenticators. In: Cramer, R. (ed.) EUROCRYPT 2005. LNCS, vol. 3494, pp. 164–180. Springer, Heidelberg (2005). https://doi.org/10.1007/11426639_10

3. Bernstein, D.J.: The Poly1305-AES message-authentication code. In: Gilbert, H., Handschuh, H. (eds.) FSE 2005. LNCS, vol. 3557, pp. 32–49. Springer, Heidelberg (2005). https://doi.org/10.1007/11502760_3

4. Bernstein, D.J.: Polynomial evaluation and message authentication, February 2007. https://cr.yp.to/antiforgery/pema-20071022.pdf

5. Carter, L., Wegman, M.N.: Universal classes of hash functions. J. Comput. Syst. Sci. **18**(2), 143–154 (1979)

6. Chakraborty, D., Ghosh, S., Sarkar, P.: A fast single-key two-level universal hash function. IACR Trans. Symmetric Cryptol. **2017**(1), 106–128 (2017)

7. Chen, S., Steinberger, J.: Tight security bounds for key-alternating ciphers. In: Nguyen, P.Q., Oswald, E. (eds.) EUROCRYPT 2014. LNCS, vol. 8441, pp. 327–350. Springer, Heidelberg (2014). https://doi.org/10.1007/978-3-642-55220-5_19

8. Cogliati, B., Lee, J., Seurin, Y.: New constructions of MACs from (tweakable) block ciphers. IACR Trans. Symmetric Cryptol. **2017**(2), 27–58 (2017)

9. Cogliati, B., Seurin, Y.: EWCDM: an efficient, beyond-birthday secure, nonce-misuse resistant MAC. In: Robshaw, M., Katz, J. (eds.) CRYPTO 2016. LNCS, vol. 9814, pp. 121–149. Springer, Heidelberg (2016). https://doi.org/10.1007/978-3-662-53018-4_5

10. Cogliati, B., Seurin, Y.: Analysis of the single-permutation encrypted Davies-Meyer construction. Des. Codes Crypt. **86**(12), 2703–2723 (2018)

11. Datta, N., Dutta, A., Nandi, M., Paul, G.: Double-block hash-then-sum: a paradigm for constructing BBB secure PRF. IACR Trans. Symmetric Cryptol. **2018**(3), 36–92 (2018). Full updated version at https://eprint.iacr.org/2018/804

12. Datta, N., Dutta, A., Nandi, M., Paul, G., Zhang, L.: Building single-key beyond birthday bound message authentication code. Cryptology ePrint Archive, Report 2015/958 (2015). Version: 20160211:123920

13. Datta, N., Dutta, A., Nandi, M., Yasuda, K.: Encrypt or decrypt? To make a single-key beyond birthday secure nonce-based MAC. In: Shacham, H., Boldyreva, A. (eds.) CRYPTO 2018. LNCS, vol. 10991, pp. 631–661. Springer, Cham (2018). https://doi.org/10.1007/978-3-319-96884-1_21

14. Dutta, A., Jha, A., Nandi, M.: Exact security analysis of hash-then-mask type probabilistic MAC constructions. IACR Cryptology ePrint Archive 2016/ 983 (2016)

15. Dutta, A., Jha, A., Nandi, M.: Tight security analysis of EHtM MAC. IACR Trans. Symmetric Cryptol. **2017**(3), 130–150 (2017)

16. Gueron, S., Kounavis, M.E.: Intel carry-less multiplication instruction and its usage for computing the GCM mode - rev 2.02. Intel White Paper. Technical report, Intel corporation, 20 April 2014

17. Gueron, S., Lindell, Y.: GCM-SIV: full nonce misuse-resistant authenticated encryption at under one cycle per byte. In: Ray, I., Li, N., Kruegel, C. (eds.) ACM CCS, pp. 109–119. ACM (2015)

18. Iwata, T., Minematsu, K.: Stronger security variants of GCM-SIV. IACR Trans. Symmetric Cryptol. **2016**(1), 134–157 (2016)

19. Krawczyk, H.: LFSR-based hashing and authentication. In: Desmedt, Y.G. (ed.) CRYPTO 1994. LNCS, vol. 839, pp. 129–139. Springer, Heidelberg (1994). https://doi.org/10.1007/3-540-48658-5_15

20. Leurent, G., Nandi, M., Sibleyras, F.: Generic attacks against beyond-birthday-bound MACs. In: Shacham, H., Boldyreva, A. (eds.) CRYPTO 2018. LNCS, vol. 10991, pp. 306–336. Springer, Cham (2018). https://doi.org/10.1007/978-3-319-96884-1_11

21. Luykx, A., Preneel, B.: Optimal forgeries against polynomial-based MACs and GCM. In: Nielsen, J.B., Rijmen, V. (eds.) EUROCRYPT 2018. LNCS, vol. 10820, pp. 445–467. Springer, Cham (2018). https://doi.org/10.1007/978-3-319-78381-9_17

22. Mennink, B.: Towards tight security of cascaded LRW2. In: Beimel, A., Dziembowski, S. (eds.) TCC 2018. LNCS, vol. 11240, pp. 192–222. Springer, Cham (2018). https://doi.org/10.1007/978-3-030-03810-6_8

23. Mennink, B., Neves, S.: Encrypted davies-meyer and its dual: towards optimal security using mirror theory. In: Katz, J., Shacham, H. (eds.) CRYPTO 2017. LNCS, vol. 10403, pp. 556–583. Springer, Cham (2017). https://doi.org/10.1007/978-3-319-63697-9_19

24. Minematsu, K.: How to thwart birthday attacks against MACs via small randomness. In: Hong, S., Iwata, T. (eds.) FSE 2010. LNCS, vol. 6147, pp. 230–249. Springer, Heidelberg (2010). https://doi.org/10.1007/978-3-642-13858-4_13

25. Nachef, V., Patarin, J., Volte, E.: Feistel Ciphers: Security Proofs and Cryptanalysis. Springer, Cham (2017). https://doi.org/10.1007/978-3-319-49530-9

26. Nandi, M.: Birthday attack on dual EWCDM. IACR Cryptology ePrint Archive 2017/579 (2017)

27. Nandi, M.: Bernstein bound on WCS is tight. In: Shacham, H., Boldyreva, A. (eds.) CRYPTO 2018. LNCS, vol. 10992, pp. 213–238. Springer, Cham (2018). https://doi.org/10.1007/978-3-319-96881-0_8

28. Patarin, J.: The "coefficients H" technique. In: Avanzi, R.M., Keliher, L., Sica, F. (eds.) SAC 2008. LNCS, vol. 5381, pp. 328–345. Springer, Heidelberg (2009). https://doi.org/10.1007/978-3-642-04159-4_21

29. Patarin, J.: Introduction to mirror theory: analysis of systems of linear equalities and linear non equalities for cryptography. IACR Cryptology ePrint Archive 2010/287 (2010)

30. Patarin, J.: Mirror theory and cryptography. IACR Cryptology ePrint Archive 2016/702 (2016)
31. Patarin, J.: Mirror theory and cryptography. Appl. Algebra Eng. Commun. Comput. **28**(4), 321–338 (2017)
32. Rogaway, P.: Bucket hashing and its application to fast message authentication. In: Coppersmith, D. (ed.) CRYPTO 1995. LNCS, vol. 963, pp. 29–42. Springer, Heidelberg (1995). https://doi.org/10.1007/3-540-44750-4_3
33. Shoup, V.: On fast and provably secure message authentication based on universal hashing. In: Koblitz, N. (ed.) CRYPTO 1996. LNCS, vol. 1109, pp. 313–328. Springer, Heidelberg (1996). https://doi.org/10.1007/3-540-68697-5_24
34. Wegman, M.N., Carter, L.: New classes and applications of hash functions. In: FOCS, pp. 175–182. IEEE Computer Society (1979)
35. Wegman, M.N., Carter, L.: New hash functions and their use in authentication and set equality. J. Comput. Syst. Sci. **22**(3), 265–279 (1981)
36. Yasuda, K.: A new variant of PMAC: beyond the birthday bound. In: Rogaway, P. (ed.) CRYPTO 2011. LNCS, vol. 6841, pp. 596–609. Springer, Heidelberg (2011). https://doi.org/10.1007/978-3-642-22792-9_34
37. Zhang, L., Wu, W., Sui, H., Wang, P.: 3kf9: enhancing 3GPP-MAC beyond the birthday bound. In: Wang, X., Sako, K. (eds.) ASIACRYPT 2012. LNCS, vol. 7658, pp. 296–312. Springer, Heidelberg (2012). https://doi.org/10.1007/978-3-642-34961-4_19

Software and Systems Security

DynOpVm: VM-Based Software Obfuscation with Dynamic Opcode Mapping

Xiaoyang Cheng[1], Yan Lin[2], Debin Gao[2(✉)], and Chunfu Jia[1(✉)]

[1] Nankai University, Tianjin, China
chengxiaoyangcxy@outlook.com, cfjia@nankai.edu.cn
[2] Singapore Management University, Singapore, Singapore
{yanlin.2016,dbgao}@smu.edu.sg

Abstract. VM-based software obfuscation has emerged as an effective technique for program obfuscation. Despite various attempts in improving its effectiveness and security, existing VM-based software obfuscators use potentially multiple but *static* secret mappings between virtual and native opcodes to hide the underlying instructions. In this paper, we present an attack using frequency analysis to effectively recover the secret mapping to compromise the protection, and then propose a novel VM-based obfuscator in which each basic block uses a *dynamic* and control-flow-aware mapping between the virtual and native instructions. We show that our proposed VM-based obfuscator not only renders the frequency analysis attack ineffective, but dictates the execution and program analysis to follow the original control flow of the program, making state-of-the-art backward tainting and slicing ineffective. We implement a prototype of our VM-based obfuscator and show its effectiveness with experiments on SPEC benchmarking and other real-world applications.

Keywords: Frequency analysis · Software obfuscation · Virtualization

1 Introduction

Unauthorized code analysis and modification threaten the software industry with more sophisticated program analysis and reverse engineering techniques in recent years [5,8,34,35,37]. Such attacks can lead to undesirable outcomes including unauthorized use of software, cheating in computer games, or bypassing and redirecting payment processes. Program protection and software obfuscation have been key techniques in fighting against such attacks, in which code virtualization using a Virtual Machine (VM) embedded inside an executable is emerging as a promising technique for code obfuscation, e.g., VMProtect[1].

VM-based code obfuscation replaces native instructions in an executable with virtual ones that are uniquely defined by the obfuscator. Such virtual instructions

---

This project is partly supported by the National Natural Science Foundation of China (No. 61772291) and the Science Foundation of Tianjin (No. 17JCZDJC30500).

[1] VMProtect Software protection. http://vmpsoft.com/.

R. H. Deng et al. (Eds.): ACNS 2019, LNCS 11464, pp. 155–174, 2019.
https://doi.org/10.1007/978-3-030-21568-2_8

will then be translated into native ones at runtime for correct execution with the original semantics. VM-based obfuscation is effective in hiding two aspects of the execution, namely the instructions to be executed (controlled by the secret mapping between virtual and native bytecodes and the handlers) and the execution path (controlled by the dispatcher).

In this paper, we first propose a simple yet effective attack exploiting the static mapping between virtual and native instructions. Our attack is inspired by the frequency analysis of symbols widely employed in crypto-analysis techniques. Our observation is that the native and corresponding virtual instructions would present the same frequency profile with the static mapping, even if the mapping is unknown and well protected by the VM—analogous to the relation between plaintext and ciphertext symbols whose mapping could be unknown but their frequency profiles are identical. We show that our frequency attack enables an attacker to recover the mapping between virtual and native instructions, which compromises the handlers in the VM embedded. Note that although more recent and enhanced VM-based protectors use multiple mappings between virtual and native instructions, the statically defined (secret and multiple) mappings only add more complexity to the frequency analysis but do not render it ineffective.

Keeping this effective attack in mind, we propose a novel VM-based software protection called DynOpVm, in which the mapping between virtual and native instructions is *dynamic* and *control-flow aware*. The dynamic nature of the mapping renders frequency attack ineffective since every protected basic block employs a different mapping between the virtual and native instructions. The control-flow-aware protection ensures that the correct mapping can only be recovered by following the correct control flow execution, which dictates the execution and, more importantly, the analysis of the program, to follow the original control flow. This further makes program analysis, in particular, backward tainting [2,9,13,20] and slicing techniques [43], difficult as the instructions cannot be decoded at the middle of any program execution.

We face a number of technical challenges especially in designing the control-flow-aware mapping between virtual and native instructions. One of them is to support basic blocks with *multiple* control flows which could result in *multiple* mappings—a conflict since each basic block can only be encoded using a single mapping. We propose solving this challenge by utilizing the secret sharing algorithm, enabling a *single* mapping to be derived from *multiple* control flows. We also demonstrate the effectiveness of our frequency attack and DynOpVm with experiments with the SPEC benchmarking and other real-world applications.

2   Background and Related Work

2.1   VM-Based Program Protection

Here we take the example of Rewolf virtualizer[2] (due to its available source code for clear understanding and experimentation) and briefly describe how an

---

[2] X86 virtualizer. http://rewolf.pl/.

executable protected by it works (with its add-on layer `Poly` disabled). As shown in Fig. 1, when program execution comes to any protected code, a control transfer directs execution of the program to a dispatcher, which obtains the potential virtual instruction and checks its prefix. All virtual instructions begin with a unique prefix (`0xFFFF` in the case of Rewolf virtualizer) as an indicator to the VM. After confirming the identity of the virtual instruction, the VM invokes a corresponding handler (dictated by the virtual opcode that is the next byte in the virtual instruction) to perform the corresponding operation of the original native instruction.

Following the idea of code virtualization, a number of VM-based code obfuscation approaches have been proposed. These include methods in securing the VM [3, 14, 46] and improving the obfuscation process [15, 42]. Publicly available tools like VMProtect, Code Virtualizer[3] and Themida[4] also employ special protections for runtime environments, e.g., VOT4CS [4].

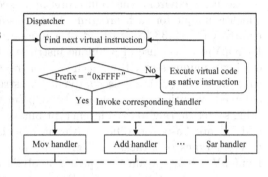

Fig. 1. VM in existing obfuscators

Many of these existing VM-based program obfuscators use a single mapping between virtual and native instructions. Kuang et al. [22] used different ways to interpret the same virtual instructions and obfuscated the atomic handlers. Although the handlers are obfuscated, there still remains only one mapping between native and virtual instructions. Other VM-based obfuscators, e.g., VMProtect, maintain multiple mappings between virtual and native instructions, and randomly choose one of them in each obfuscation instance; however, the multiple available mappings were statically designed with limited variations.

2.2 Attacks on VM-Protected Programs

Rolles proposed to reverse engineer the VM in order to convert virtual bytecode to native instructions [30]. Based on this idea, Rotalumé [33] was further proposed to detect the mapping between virtual bytecode and handlers. Guillot et al. [16] automatically search for patterns of obfuscation. Similarly, VMAttack [19] was presented as an automatic deobfuscation tool to analyze VM structure and to compress instruction sequences. Coogan et al. [11] applied equational reasoning [10] to reconvert the native code. Other proposals [39, 45] utilized taint analysis to reveal the dependency of virtual code and the embedded VM. BinSim [25] attacked the code virtualizer with the help of backward slicing. VMHunt [44]

[3] Code virtualizer. https://oreans.com/codevirtualizer.php.

[4] Themida. https://www.oreans.com/themida.php.

tackled the problem using tracing, symbolic execution, and backward slicing. Our proposed frequency attack works on a different dimension in that it avoids analyzing the semantics of the VM or its corresponding handlers.

2.3   Instruction-Set Randomization and Control-Flow Carrying Code

Instruction-Set Randomization (ISR) can also be seen as a VM-based system, and was proposed as a mitigation against code-injection attacks [6,21,26]. It uses an execution environment to interpret and execute a randomized instruction set which is unique for each program. There has also been proposals to use ISR to enforce CFI [12,36,38]. Instead of a unique instruction set for each program, DynOpVm makes use of a unique instruction set for each basic block by generating a unique secret from each control transfer. Similar to ISR, Control-flow Carrying Code (C^3) [23] uses a dynamic instrumentation system to assist CFI-enforced execution of a program. DynOpVm shares the same idea with C^3 on using secret sharing to encode/encrypt binary instructions; however, DynOpVm and C^3 are based on different threat models, are proposed to fight against different types of attacks, and are implemented in completely different ways. DynOpVm fights against frequency analysis on VM-based obfuscators, while C^3 is to counter Data-Oriented Programming attacks on traditional CFI systems. DynOpVm produces self-contained VM-embedded executables which can execute directly on mainstream Linux systems, whereas C^3 requires a dynamic instrumentation systems for its execution.

3   Frequency Attacks on VM-Based Program Obfuscation

As discussed in Sect. 2.1, existing VM-based program obfuscators, including the original work and subsequent enhancements [3,14,15,22,30,42,46], use a secret but static mapping (potentially multiple ones) between virtual and native instructions for obfuscation. Intuitively, such static mappings, although secret and unknown to an attacker, make frequency analysis possible since native instructions present some unique and specific frequency profile in normal programs.

3.1   Frequency Profile of Native Instructions

A prerequisite of our attack is a unique frequency profile exhibited by native instructions. Related frequency analysis has been conducted on different platforms since the last century [1,17,18,28,29,31], most of which focus on runtime statistics of the instruction set. On the other hand, the objective of our frequency analysis is to collect static profile of instructions for program analysis.

We statically analyze the number of occurrences of native instructions in executables under directory /bin on 64-bit Ubuntu 18.04 and present the 15 instructions with the highest frequencies in Fig. 2. We notice that this frequency profile is uneven while consistent with low standard deviation among the 128 executables. For example, `mov` shows up most often with its frequency more than 3 times of the second most frequent instruction `call`. In addition, `mov` presents a frequency of over 30% while many other instructions have frequencies of lower than 1%. Although these other instructions with low frequency do not stand out in the profile, we comment that the decoding process usually requires only a few instructions to be identified as bootstraps, and other instructions could then be easily recovered by, e.g., frequency analysis of instruction subsequences.

3.2 Frequency Analysis as an Attack

We first implement a virtualizer compatible with 64-bit Linux executables using the same strategy as Rewolf Virtualizer[5], and apply it to protect selected code pieces in SPEC CPU2006 benchmarking programs. We note that other variations of the obfuscator may differ in the implementation details, e.g., the commercial product VMProtect that is closed-source, but we have not noticed evidences that such differences render our frequency attack ineffective, including the fact that it randomly chooses from multiple static handlers.

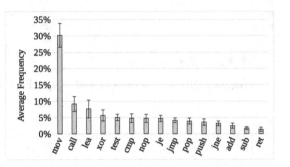

Fig. 2. Freq. analysis of 128 binaries

We intentionally select small code pieces for protection to see if that renders the frequency analysis less accurate. We search for the prefix of 0xFFFF to identify all virtual instructions and their virtual opcode (the byte following the prefix). Note that other obfuscators may employ more complicated ways of encoding the virtual opcodes; however, existing work (e.g., VMHunt [44]) has shown that the beginning of various handlers could be effectively located with analysis of context switch patterns, which clears another prerequisite of our frequency analysis. Here we only present results for 3 programs, `bzip2` (11182 bytes of code protected), `mcf` (3058 bytes of code protected), and `sjeng` (5510 bytes of code protected).

Figure 3 shows the analysis result of 20 instructions with the highest frequency for both the original program and that protected by our virtualizer. It also shows the ground truth mapping between corresponding virtual and native instructions. Results show that frequency analysis attack is accurate even for small code pieces. For example, the top two instructions are always mapped correctly, while the overlapping of top 10 instructions between the original and the protected programs cover 8 instructions or more.

---

[5] We are not aware of any 64-bit VM-based obfuscator that is open source, and therefore decide to make one based on the 32-bit Rewolf virtualizer.

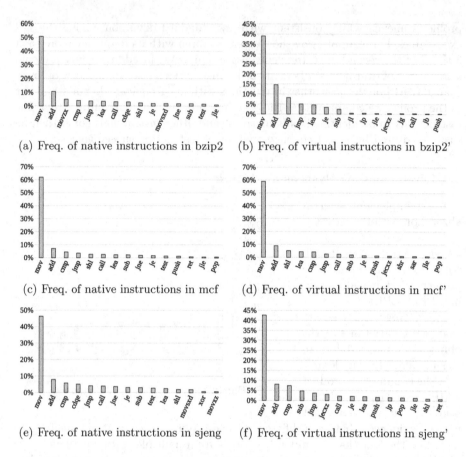

(a) Freq. of native instructions in bzip2   (b) Freq. of virtual instructions in bzip2'

(c) Freq. of native instructions in mcf   (d) Freq. of virtual instructions in mcf'

(e) Freq. of native instructions in sjeng   (f) Freq. of virtual instructions in sjeng'

Fig. 3. Frequency analysis on programs protected by Rewolf virtualizer

When considering a slightly different threat model in which the attacker does not have any information of the protected program (maybe in the event that the entire program is protected) and therefore can only compare the frequency analysis result (Fig. 3(b), (d), and (f)) with the general statistics of native instructions (Fig. 2), we obtain similar results—we can identify the most frequent instruction mov with at least 6 overlappings in the top 10 instructions.

While there are other ways of improving this attack, e.g., by analyzing operands of the instructions and other context information, we believe that the simple demonstration above is sufficient to reveal this fundamental weakness of the existing VM-based program obfuscators, in which static mappings (although secret) are used between virtual and native instructions. To improve the security and to fight against such frequency attacks, we propose a novel technique that employs dynamic and control-flow-aware mappings; see Sect. 4.

3.3   Threat Model and Assumptions

Our objective is to propose a novel VM-based program obfuscator that renders the frequency analysis attack and state-of-the-art program analysis methods, e.g., backward tainting and slicing techniques, ineffective. We assume that the attacker is aware of the details of our technique and has access to the protected binary executable. The attack can be Man-At-The-End (MATE) attack and leverage memory disclosure vulnerabilities in the target application to read and analyze the memory, including data and the code section of the target program.

4   Design and Implementation of DynOpVm

Section 3 presents a simple yet effective attack on existing VM-based program obfuscators using frequency analysis. In this section, we present our novel VM-based obfuscator that is resistant against such attacks. Moreover, to defend against other attacks as discussed in Sect. 2.2, we have a second objective of rendering program analysis techniques, in particular, backward tainting and slicing techniques, ineffective on the protected program (piece).

4.1   Overview of DynOpVm

Defending against frequency analysis is a well-explored problem in cryptography. For example, Vigenère cipher was proposed as a poly-alphabetic substitution system to fight against frequency analysis on English letters [7,40], with the idea that the same plaintext letters can be encrypted to different ciphertext letters. Our proposed solution is inspired by this simple idea to construct different and dynamic mappings between virtual and native instructions for different basic blocks, even if various basic blocks contain the same native instruction.

Fighting against state-of-the-art program analysis tools like backward tainting and slicing is more challenging. What makes such backward analysis possible is the "two-way" nature of control-flow information presented in normal executables, i.e., it is easy to find both the predecessor and successor of an instruction. Essentially we want to make control-flow information in the protected program "one-way", in that even if an attacker manages to decode specific virtual instructions, we want to make it difficult to reveal the caller[6] basic block. We leave it as future work to make even the forward analysis difficult, since the program needs to be able to execute in a forward manner absent from analysis.

Our solution is to make the mapping between virtual and native instructions dependent on control flows, i.e., the addresses of caller and callee instructions. Since both addresses are available in a forward execution (e.g., in executing `call $0x400460` in Fig. 4, the caller and callee addresses are 0x400450 and 0x400460), reconstructing the mapping between virtual and native instructions and decoding the callee is easy. On the other hand, backward analysis to figure

---

[6] In the rest of this paper, we use the words "caller" and "callee" to refer to predecessor and successor basic blocks in a control transfer.

out the caller of `call $0x400460` is difficult since it uses a mapping that is determined by its own caller (address of `jmp $0x400450`).

We design and implement a prototype of our novel VM-based program obfuscator called DynOpVm following this idea. DynOpVm takes as input the original binary executable (without source code), statically encodes each basic block into virtual instructions with a mapping uniquely determined by the caller and callee addresses in the control transfer, and inserts a VM to decode basic blocks. Control transfers are redirected to the VM which dynamically reconstructs the specific mapping between virtual and native instructions, decodes the next basic block "on-the-fly", and then continues with the valid control transfer. We present our detailed design and implementation in the next subsections.

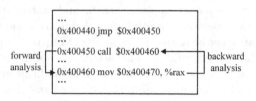

Fig. 4. Forward and backward analyses

4.2 Control-Flow-Aware Encoding of Basic Blocks

As discussed in Sect. 4.1, DynOpVm statically performs binary rewriting. To stay focused in this paper, we make use of existing tools for static analysis and rewriting, and consider general challenges (e.g., distinguishing code from data) out of our scope. At a first glance, such a process isn't overly complicated; however, a basic block could have *multiple* callers, which will result in *multiple* mappings between virtual and native instructions derived for the same callee block. On the other hand, each callee block could only be encoded with one unique mapping. The challenge here is to derive the same mapping from multiple control transfers with multiple callers. Our solution is to introduce an additional layer in deriving the mapping, where each source or destination address of valid control transfer determines a secret share, and multiple secret shares could be used to reconstruct the same mapping—a typical application of Shamir's secret sharing algorithm [32]. In Fig. 5(a), the callers of control transfers CT^1 and CT^2, both of which target BB^A, contribute two different secret shares. Both are used to compute the same secret together with the secret share generated from callee address (the address of BB^A). The secret is then used to encode BB^A. Note that at runtime, only one of the secret shares from the two callers is used to derive the mapping, which is well supported by the secret sharing algorithm.

In applying secret sharing, caller and callee addresses constitute two points on a secret sharing polynomial. We introduce a third point as a master key randomly chosen to defend against information disclosure attacks which could potentially be exploited to reconstruct the mapping. DynOpVm takes a configuration with $t = 3$ (a parabola) to enable reconstruction of the mapping with (potentially multiple) valid control transfers. Figure 5(b) shows two parabolas: one representing a basic block BB^A with two valid callers, and the other representing BB^B with three valid callers. The intersection of the parabola with the

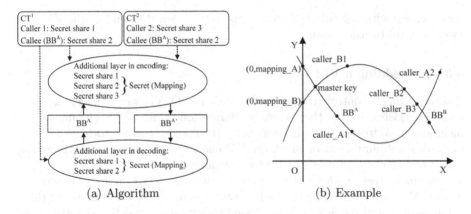

Fig. 5. Secret sharing

y-axis is the secret to determine the mapping between virtual and native instructions for the corresponding callee. DynOpVm obtains the X and Y coordinates (k bits) of a point from the lower-order odd- and even-index bits of an address. The master key (of $2k$ bits long) is randomly chosen. We discuss the security and performance implication of the choice of value k in Sect. 5.

Although this algorithm well supports multiple callers, it introduces constraints on the addresses. For example, once the master key, the address of the callee, and that of one caller are determined, the parabola is fully established and addresses of the remaining callers have to be on the curve. This results in constraints in our binary rewriting to redistribute the basic blocks:

- "Call-preceded" basic blocks (those followed by `call`) cannot be redistributed freely as they are the targets of `ret` instructions. Such additional constraints could result in an unsolvable layout of basic blocks. Our solution is to replace all `call` instructions with `push` followed by `jmp` to remove such additional constraints. A similar challenge arises for conditional jumps and their fall-through instructions, which can be resolved with the same idea.
- Parabolas can have at most two intersections, one of which is the master key. This means that two different callees may only have up to one common caller—an invalid assumption in many applications. To handle this, we add intermediate "stub" blocks to remove the additional common callers.
- Basic blocks with multiple entries would result in multiple mappings derived. We make copies of them to ensure that each basic block has only one entry.

To redistribute basic blocks, we use a look-ahead depth first search algorithm to avoid circular constraints, e.g., when two callers of a to-be-redistributed basic block with fixed addresses make it impossible to find a valid parabola.

DynOpVm encodes and decodes between virtual and native instructions with a simple XOR operation with the secret derived from the secret sharing algorithm. This design of the mapping between virtual and native instructions is mainly due to its simplicity and efficiency. After every basic block is redistributed and encoded with the corresponding mapping, we can then embed the VM and insert control transfers to it.

4.3 Embedding a VM

Before making a control transfer to the VM, DynOpVm saves the `rflag` state and uses registers to pass the necessary information to the VM. Such information includes the address of the caller and callee (two possible callee addresses in case of conditional jumps, out of which the VM chooses one depending on the `rflag` value) and the type of control transfer instruction.

The main task of the VM is to reconstruct the secret and to decode and execute the corresponding basic blocks. Our design of the VM consists of three components—a dispatcher, a decoder, and an actuator—which is slightly different from existing techniques of VM-based program obfuscation as discussed in Sect. 2.1 [3,6,15,24,46]. Our VM dispatcher makes use of information passed to the VM to obtain the address of the callee. After that, the decoder reconstructs the parabola, computes the secret for the callee, and then decodes the instructions into a buffer dynamically allocated, whose address is stored in a segment register. In the end, the VM actuator transfers control to the decoded (native) instructions and executes them. Figure 6 shows this process. Note that the VM has two potential control flows from the dispatcher—d-f-g and b-c—for control transfers to protected and unprotected code, respectively. We discuss more details of our support of this in Sect. 4.4.

The unknown length of the callee basic block makes it tricky for it to be decoded. DynOpVm uses an optimization to decode a fixed size of 128 bytes at a time and repeats the decoding routine in cases of larger basic blocks. `nop` instructions are inserted for alignment purposes for efficient execution. Another challenge is the conflict with

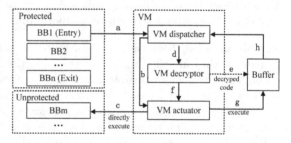

Fig. 6. VM dispatcher, decoder, and actuator

original program code if our code added and VM execution use the stack. DynOpVm uses the `fs` register instead to avoid this conflict.

4.4 Supporting Partial Protection

The key challenge in supporting partial protection of an executable is to make control transfers between protected and unprotected code. This can be achieved by adding control transfers to the VM only in protected basic blocks. However, such a simple solution may potentially allow dedicated attackers to reconstruct the parabola for a protected entry block that has multiple unprotected callers, since these callers are all on the parabola curve. Combining multiple instances of such attacks could even allow recovery of the secret master key.

We introduce a more secure way to support partial protection to fight against such attacks. The basic idea is to reduce the number of unprotected callers with code cloning and inlining. DynOpVm makes a copy of the chosen unprotected code to be inlined into the protected region to reduce the number of control transfers between protected and unprotected code. In this way, attackers will find fewer points on the parabola curve to reconstruct the secret. DynOpVm also maintains a list of valid exit targets in the VM to allow/disallow transfers to unprotected code at runtime. We further propose two potential solutions that could avoid the need of cloning and inlining, since inlining may not be a practical solution in interfacing with, e.g., system libraries. Assuming that the protected code P_{vt} transfers control to a system library function lib with a basic block BB^{call}, and control returns to P_{vt} at basic block BB^{ret}, the two solutions are:

1. Leaving BB^{ret} and lib unprotected (with BB^{call} protected) while adding the address of BB^{ret} as a valid exit target maintained by the VM.
2. Leaving lib unprotected while having BB^{ret} protected with a parabola that passes though the origin, which means that BB^{ret} is encoded with key 0.

Both solutions allow proper execution of the program with more basic blocks exposed in plaintext, although it is non-trivial for an attacker to differentiate them from those encoded with nonzero keys. Solution (1) allows BB^{ret} to be the target of control transfers from any protected basic block. Solution (2) restricts control transfers to BB^{ret}, but potentially allows an attacker with the capability of launching memory disclosure attacks to recover the master secret by reconstructing the parabola, since an additional point (the origin) and the plaintext instruction inside BB^{ret} is given to the attacker.

DynOpVm assumes a strong threat model where memory disclosure attacks are assumed possible, and therefore uses the solution of code cloning and inlining for better security. We comment that the above two solutions could be useful under a different threat model.

4.5   Implementation

We implemented a prototype of DynOpVm for Linux x64 platform. DynOpVm takes as input a 64-bit ELF binary and outputs a modified binary executable with selected basic blocks encoded into virtual instructions and VM embedded. The static instrumentation component is implemented as 8,200 lines of python code with the help of Capstone [27] for disassembling and Type-armor [41] for constructing the CFG. The VM interpretation and execution component is implemented as 900 lines of assembly instructions inserted into the executable file.

Besides executing the design presented in earlier subsections, DynOpVm makes use of gaps among redistributed protected basic blocks to host unprotected functions, and fills the remaining gaps with nop instructions. Finally, DynOpVm patches the new binary file with the text segment extended and corresponding addresses (code pointers, function pointers, data pointers, jump tables and virtual tables) and section information updated.

One challenge is to deal with instructions with PC-relative addressing since the execution will be in the buffer dynamically allocated and the program counter (%rip) at runtime is unknown at static instrumentation. Our solution is to remove PC-relative addressing mode during binary rewriting. To support multi-threaded programs, we use a new memory page for decoding basic blocks for each thread by checking the value in `fs:0x158` where we store the buffer address.

5   Evaluation

In this section, we evaluate the security of DynOpVm with regards to frequency analysis and Shannon entropy, and apply backward slicing attacks presented by Ming et al. [25,44] to evaluate its resistance to such analysis. Besides that, we measure the performance overhead of DynOpVm with real-world applications.

5.1   Security Evaluation

Frequency Attack. As shown in Sect. 3, existing VM-based program obfuscators like Rewolf virtualizer suffer from frequency analysis which allows an attacker to easily figure out the mapping between virtual and native instructions. Intuitively, DynOpVm encodes each basic block with a different mapping determined by the control transfer, and is resistant to such attacks.

Moreover, the use of XOR operation in encoding instructions effectively removes any obvious patterns as in some existing VM-based program obfuscators, e.g., `0xFFFF` in the Rewolf virtualizer. Lack of the capability of identifying each virtual instructions, attackers could not even perform the frequency analysis on them. Here, we want to see how far the frequency analysis could go even if attackers could identify the start of every virtual instruction, and present the results of such frequency analysis[7] on the same SPEC benchmarking programs as used in Sect. 3; see Fig. 7.

Comparing graphs in Fig. 7 and those in Fig. 3 reveals two observations. First, the shape is very different in the sense that the frequency values decay a lot faster in unprotected programs and those protected by the Rowolf virtualizer, while they decay a lot more slowly in programs protected by DynOpVm. Second, the peak frequency value for unprotected programs and those protected by Rowolf virtualizer is at 40% or more, while that for programs protected by DynOpVm is at most one tenth at 4%. This suggests that programs protected by DynOpVm present a much more even distribution in frequency analysis with many virtual instructions at a non-negligible frequency, making recovering the mapping between virtual and native instructions difficult.

---

[7] Our frequency analysis here is on the first byte of the virtual instructions, since the length of them is unknown to attackers.

Entropy and Randomness Analysis. To gain an even more intuitive understanding and to consider the entire virtual instruction (as opposed to just the opcode in the frequency analysis), we calculate the Shannon entropy of the SPEC CPU2006 benchmarking programs unprotected, protected by Rewolf, and protected by DynOpVm, which is shown in Fig. 8. Shannon entropy estimates the randomness in the binary information streams—the higher the entropy, the more random the byte stream is.

Figure 8 shows that programs protected by DynOpVm have more random byte streams and therefore are harder to analyze in terms of the frequency distribution or differentiation among virtual instructions. Interestingly, Rewolf virtualizer produces less random byte streams than the unprotected programs, likely due to the prefix 0xFFFF inserted for every virtual instruction. Note that in this experiment, DynOpVm uses the smallest secret size that makes redistribution of basic blocks possible, with $k \in [8, 10]$.

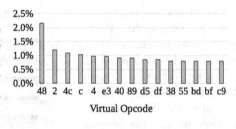

(a) Freq. of virtual opcodes in bzip2"

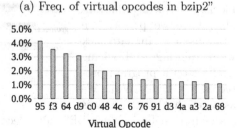

(b) Freq. of virtual opcodes in mcf"

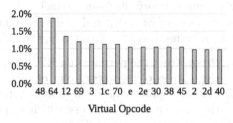

(c) Freq. of virtual opcodes in sjeng"

Fig. 7. Frequency analysis of DynOpVm virtual code

Backward Tainting/Slicing Analysis. Due to the relatively strong threat model used (Sect. 3.3), we admit that it is not impossible for an attacker to decode a specific basic block without dynamically executing it. However, an effective attack would require that sufficient information about predecessors of the basic block be known, e.g., addresses of the control transfer instructions of *multiple* predecessor blocks. It could be possible to obtain such information for one of the predecessor blocks, if, e.g., the predecessor block has been successfully decoded or if it is in an unprotected component; however, obtaining such information for multiple predecessor blocks would require that many protected blocks have been previously decoded successfully. Not arming with information of predecessor blocks, an attacker would face the decoding task of the basic block that has been XOR'ed with a key of size k, where $k \in [8, 10]$ in our experiments.

We stress that our objective in DynOpVm is to make program analysis starting from the middle of an execution difficult, e.g., in backward tainting and slicing analysis, where information of the predecessor blocks is typically unavailable. Here we perform an experiment to simulate backward tainting and slicing analysis on a program protected by DynOpVm. We assume that the analysis

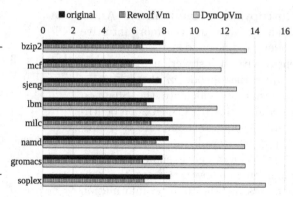

Fig. 8. Shannon entropy

starts from a basic block BB^0 fully decoded with K^0 (e.g., one that contains an interesting sink instruction). We also assume that it is a strong attacker who had previously obtained the master key used in protecting this binary (probably via some memory disclosure attack). The objective of the attack is to find the predecessor of BB^0, denoted as BB^{-1}, and to have it decoded (find K^{-1}) to reveal its native instructions. Intuitively, the steps involved are as follows.

1. Reconstruct the parabola for BB^0 with three points on it: the master key, K^0, the address of the entry point of BB^0.
2. For every point on the parabola constructed (a total of $2^k - 2$ points), derive the corresponding address which is potentially the address of the control transfer instruction of BB^{-1}.
3. For every potential control transfer instruction of BB^{-1}, and for every possible block size of BB^{-1} (we tried all numbers in $[50, 150]$), reconstruct K^{-1} by XORing the virtual and native instructions (assuming that DynOpVm uses a single dedicated native instruction for control transfers).
4. Use the derived K^{-1} to decode the other instructions in BB^{-1} and see if they are valid native instructions.

We follow this strategy to analyze the protected program `bzip2` with a desktop computer with i7-6700 CPU running at 3.40 GHz and 16 GB of RAM running Ubuntu 64-bit kernel 4.4. Results show that even if DynOpVm uses a dedicated `jmp` instruction for all control transfers, the total number of valid BB^{-1} found per BB^0 on average is 437.03; while, in fact, basic blocks in `bzip2` have on average 1.32 predecessor basic blocks. Moreover, the time it takes to try all possible callers of a single BB^0 is 996.51 s on average.

Results show that such an attack is imprecise and inefficient in decoding the predecessor blocks. We note that the experiment above was performed on `bzip2` protected with DynOpVm on a setting of $k=8$. When k is 9 or 10, the average numbers of valid predecessor blocks jump to 2,362.79 and 7,258.40, respectively, and the average time it takes to try all predecessor blocks of a single BB^0 is 4,415.07 and 18,268.28 s, respectively.

5.2   Performance Evaluation

In the performance evaluation, we expand the target set of programs from SPEC benchmarking programs to include an image processing tool `convert` from `ImageMagicks`, two web servers `httpd` and `lighttpd`, a distributed memory caching system `Memcached`, and an FTP server `Pure-FTPd`. We randomly select a few functions in these programs and apply DynOpVm to protect them. Experiments are performed on a desktop computer with Intel Core2 Duo CPU at 3.16 GHz and 8 GB of RAM running Ubuntu 64-bit kernel 4.4.

For the SPEC benchmarking programs and `convert`, we execute them with standard input data `train` and test cases bundled with the source code, respectively. To benchmark the web servers, we configure Apache Benchmark[8] to issue 2,000 requests with 100 concurrent connections. To benchmark `Memcached`, we use `memslap` benchmark[9] with its default configuration. For the FTP server, we configure `pyftpbench` benchmark[10] to open 20 connections and request 100 files per connection with over 100 MB of data requested. We run each experiment 10 times, ensure that the CPUs are fully loaded throughout the tests, and report the median. Table 1 shows the details of these programs where data is collected dynamically at run time. Note that we intentionally have a program (`bzip2`) with more than 99% of the (runtime) instructions protected and other programs with less than 0.1% instructions protected.

Table 1. Details of programs in our performance evaluation set

	# of instructions	# of instructions protected by DynOpVm	Percentage of code protected	# of context switches from unprotected to protected code	# of branching instructions protected by DynOpVm
bzip2	311,200,698	310,963,079	99.92%	12,563	11,632,308
mcf	6,822,420,892	193,631,839	2.84%	118,645	22,755,914
sjeng	27,751,560,742	287,456,204	1.04%	3,169,096	14,012,972
convert	18,875,392	16,967	0.09%	187	2,372
httpd	292,300,296	864,936	0.30%	3,958	80,843
lighttpd	135,150,518	1,825,473	1.35%	16,377	116,225
memcached	1,806,983,275	14,789,569	0.82%	456,924	1,341,456
Pure-ftpd	710,390,558	505,940	0.07%	2,133	27,262

---

[8] Apache benchmark. http://httpd.apache.org/docs/2.0/programs/ab.html.

[9] Memslap: load testing and benchmarking a server. http://docs.libmemcached.org/bin/memslap.html.

[10] Extremely fast and scalable Python FTP server library. https://github.com/giampaolo/pyftpdlib.

Since Rewolf virtualizer has limitations in supporting multi-threaded execution, we compare performance overhead of DynOpVm with another VM-based program obfuscator VMProtect[11].

To evaluate the overhead in execution time, we use the default key size $k = 8$ with exception in `httpd` as the `ap_getparents` function has a complicated CFG and requires a key size of 9 for its protection. We expect two main contributing factors to the performance overhead. First is for the VM to allocate memory and to free up memory resources. Second is the reconstruction of the secret and decoding of the target basic blocks. To gain a detailed understanding of the overhead introduced by either factor, we report the execution time of the original programs unprotected, programs protected by DynOpVm with encoding/decoding disabled and enabled, and programs protected by VMProtect with and without packing; see Fig. 9.

Our first observation is that programs with more protected code (i.e., the SPEC benchmarking programs) incur higher overhead, which is as expected. Although such overhead could go up to 10 times for DynOpVm when almost 100% of the code is protected, the overhead is negligible when only specific and small amount of code needs to be protected. We comment that this makes DynOpVm practically usable in real-world

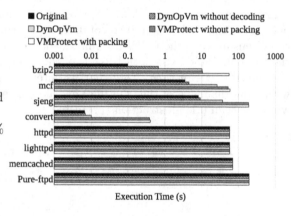

Fig. 9. Overhead in execution time

scenarios. Recent studies [44] also report that most existing VM-based obfuscators target the protection of a small portion of the code only.

We also notice that the runtime overhead of DynOpVm mainly comes from the decoding of basic blocks, as evidenced by the substantial difference between DynOpVm with and without decoding for the three SPEC benchmarking programs. This is also not surprising as decoding involves reconstructing the parabola and performing the XOR operation, which are heavy in computation.

Our third observation is that the overhead of DynOpVm is noticeably lower than that of VMProtect especially when more code needs to be protected, and this is true even with packing disabled on VMProtect, which makes a fair comparison since DynOpVm does not support packing in its current prototype.

Overhead in File Size. Since DynOpVm needs to redistribute basic blocks according to the secret sharing function, it may incur considerable overhead in

---

[11] We could not use VMProtect in our frequency analysis and security evaluation due to its close-source nature.

terms of the file sizes. Moreover, this overhead in space may vary according to the different settings of k. For example, when $k = 12$, the address of an instruction can be any value in the range of $(0, 2^{24})$ as both x and y are 12 bits long.

Figure 10(a) shows the file sizes of the original programs, programs protected by DynOpVm (with $k = 9$ for `httpd` and $k = 8$ for all other programs), and the programs protected by VMProtect (with and without packing enabled). We see that this default setting of k results in DynOpVm having significantly smaller overhead in file size compared to VMProtect when packing is disabled. We stress that the packing option is also potentially possible for DynOpVm, although it is not implemented in our current prototype.

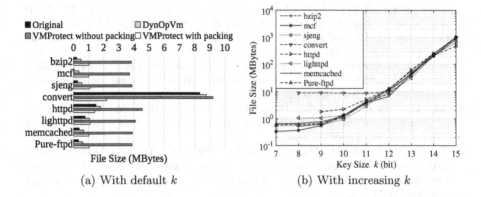

(a) With default k (b) With increasing k

Fig. 10. Overhead of file sizes

When k increases, DynOpVm gains better protection due to the bigger space in possible mappings between virtual and native instructions. However, it also results in higher overhead in file sizes; see Fig. 10. A closer inspection shows that it increases exponentially rather than linearly with increase in k. This demonstrates the trade off in configuring k, and it may favor smaller values in the range of $[8, 12]$ to avoid excessive disk and memory usage.

6   Limitations and Conclusion

Besides the limitation of code cloning and inlining to support partial program protection (note our alternative designs discussed in Sect. 4.4), the current prototype of DynOpVm stores the master key within the protected executable for its simplicity of implementation. This can be improved with a networked component embedded to retrieve the master key during program execution. Our current prototype also reconstructs the mapping for every basic block at runtime, which could be improved with a cache mechanism.

In this paper, we first present a simple yet effective attack using frequency analysis to recover the mapping between virtual and native instructions, and then design and implement a novel VM-based program obfuscation technique called DynOpVm which employs dynamic mapping between virtual and native instructions that is determined by individual control transfers. DynOpVm is resistant to not only the frequency analysis attack but also state-of-the-art backward taint and slicing program analysis techniques. Our evaluation with real-world applications shows that DynOpVm renders frequency attacks ineffective.

References

1. Adams, T.L., Zimmerman, R.E.: An analysis of 8086 instruction set usage in MS DOS programs. ACM SIGARCH Comput. Archit. News **17**(2), 152–160 (1989)
2. Arzt, S., et al.: FlowDroid: precise context, flow, field, object-sensitive and lifecycle-aware taint analysis for Android apps. ACM SIGPLAN Not. **49**(6), 259–269 (2014)
3. Averbuch, A., Kiperberg, M., Zaidenberg, N.J.: An efficient VM-based software protection. In: Proceedings of the 5th International Conference on Network and System Security (NSS), pp. 121–128. IEEE (2011)
4. Banescu, S., Lucaci, C., Krämer, B., Pretschner, A.: VOT4CS: a virtualization obfuscation tool for C. In: Proceedings of the 2016 ACM Workshop on Software Protection, pp. 39–49. ACM (2016)
5. Bao, T., Burket, J., Woo, M., Turner, R., Brumley, D.: BYTEWEIGHT: learning to recognize functions in binary code. In: Proceedings of the 23rd USENIX Security Symposium, pp. 845–860 (2014)
6. Barrantes, E.G., Ackley, D.H., Palmer, T.S., Stefanovic, D., Zovi, D.D.: Randomized instruction set emulation to disrupt binary code injection attacks. In: Proceedings of the 10th ACM Conference on Computer and Communications Security, pp. 281–289. ACM (2003)
7. Bruen, A.A., Forcinito, M.A.: Cryptography, Information Theory, and Error-Correction: A Handbook for the 21st Century, vol. 68. Wiley, Hoboken (2011)
8. Brumley, D., Jager, I., Avgerinos, T., Schwartz, E.J.: BAP: a binary analysis platform. In: Gopalakrishnan, G., Qadeer, S. (eds.) CAV 2011. LNCS, vol. 6806, pp. 463–469. Springer, Heidelberg (2011). https://doi.org/10.1007/978-3-642-22110-1_37
9. Clause, J., Li, W., Orso, A.: Dytan: a generic dynamic taint analysis framework. In: Proceedings of the 2007 International Symposium on Software Testing and Analysis, pp. 196–206. ACM (2007)
10. Coogan, K., Debray, S.: Equational reasoning on x86 assembly code. In: Proceedings of the 11th IEEE International Working Conference on Source Code Analysis and Manipulation (SCAM), pp. 75–84. IEEE (2011)
11. Coogan, K., Lu, G., Debray, S.: Deobfuscation of virtualization-obfuscated software: a semantics-based approach. In: Proceedings of the 18th ACM Conference on Computer and Communications Security, pp. 275–284. ACM (2011)
12. De Clercq, R., et al.: SOFIA: software and control flow integrity architecture. In: Proceedings of the 2016 Design, Automation & Test in Europe Conference & Exhibition (DATE), pp. 1172–1177. IEEE (2016)
13. Egele, M., Kruegel, C., Kirda, E., Vigna, G.: PiOS: detecting privacy leaks in iOS applications. In: Proceedings of the 2011 Network and Distributed System Security Symposium (NDSS), pp. 177–183 (2011)
14. Fang, H., et al.: VMGuard: an integrity monitoring system for management virtual machines. In: Proceedings of the 16th International Conference on Parallel and Distributed Systems (ICPADS), pp. 67–74. IEEE (2010)

15. Fang, H., Wu, Y., Wang, S., Huang, Y.: Multi-stage binary code obfuscation using improved virtual machine. In: Lai, X., Zhou, J., Li, H. (eds.) ISC 2011. LNCS, vol. 7001, pp. 168–181. Springer, Heidelberg (2011). https://doi.org/10.1007/978-3-642-24861-0_12
16. Guillot, Y., Gazet, A.: Automatic binary deobfuscation. J. Comput. Virol. **6**(3), 261–276 (2010)
17. Huang, J., Peng, T.C.: Analysis of x86 instruction set usage for dos/windows applications and its implication on superscalar design. IEICE Trans. Inf. Syst. **85**(6), 929–939 (2002)
18. Ibrahim, A.H., Abdelhalim, M., Hussein, H., Fahmy, A.: Analysis of x86 instruction set usage for Windows 7 applications. In: Proceedings of the 2nd International Conference on Computer Technology and Development (ICCTD), pp. 511–516. IEEE (2010)
19. Kalysch, A., Götzfried, J., Müller, T.: VMAttack: deobfuscating virtualization-based packed binaries. In: Proceedings of the 12th International Conference on Availability, Reliability and Security, p. 2. ACM (2017)
20. Kang, M.G., McCamant, S., Poosankam, P., Song, D.: DTA++: dynamic taint analysis with targeted control-flow propagation. In: Proceedings of the 2011 Network and Distributed System Security Symposium (NDSS) (2011)
21. Kc, G.S., Keromytis, A.D., Prevelakis, V.: Countering code-injection attacks with instruction-set randomization. In: Proceedings of the 10th ACM Conference on Computer and Communications Security, pp. 272–280. ACM (2003)
22. Kuang, K., et al.: Exploit dynamic data flows to protect software against semantic attacks (2017)
23. Lin, Y., Gao, D., Cheng, X.: Control-flow carrying code. In: Proceedings of the 14th ACM Asia Conference on Information, Computer and Communications Security (AsiaCCS) (2019)
24. Maude, T., Maude, D.: Hardware protection against software piracy. Commun. ACM **27**(9), 950–959 (1984)
25. Ming, J., Xu, D., Jiang, Y., Wu, D.: BinSim: trace-based semantic binary diffing via system call sliced segment equivalence checking. In: Proceedings of the 26th USENIX Security Symposium (2017)
26. Portokalidis, G., Keromytis, A.D.: Fast and practical instruction-set randomization for commodity systems. In: Proceedings of the 26th Annual Computer Security Applications Conference, pp. 41–48. ACM (2010)
27. Quynh, N.A.: Capstone: next-gen disassembly framework. Black Hat USA (2014)
28. Rico, R.: Proposal of test-bench for the x86 instruction set (16 bits subset). Technical report TR-UAH-AUT-GAP-2005-21-en (2005). http://atc2.aut.uah.es/~gap/
29. Rico, R., Pérez, J.I., Frutos, J.A.: The impact of x86 instruction set architecture on superscalar processing. J. Syst. Archit. **51**(1), 63–77 (2005)
30. Rolles, R.: Unpacking virtualization obfuscators. In: Proceedings of the 3rd USENIX Workshop on Offensive Technologies (WOOT) (2009)
31. Schwartz, R.J.: The design and development of a dynamic program behavior measurement tool for the Intel 8086/88. ACM SIGARCH Comput. Archit. News **17**(4), 82–94 (1989)
32. Shamir, A.: How to share a secret. Commun. ACM **22**(11), 612–613 (1979)
33. Sharif, M., Lanzi, A., Giffin, J., Lee, W.: Automatic reverse engineering of malware emulators. In: Proceedings of the 30th IEEE Symposium on Security and Privacy (SP), pp. 94–109. IEEE (2009)

34. Shoshitaishvili, Y., Wang, R., Hauser, C., Kruegel, C., Vigna, G.: Firmalice-automatic detection of authentication bypass vulnerabilities in binary firmware. In: Proceedings of the 2015 Network and Distributed System Security Symposium (NDSS) (2015)

35. Shoshitaishvili, Y., et al.: SOK: (state of) the art of war: offensive techniques in binary analysis. In: Proceedings of the 37th IEEE Symposium on Security and Privacy (SP), pp. 138–157. IEEE (2016)

36. Sinha, K., Kemerlis, V.P., Sethumadhavan, S.: Reviving instruction set randomization. In: Proceedings of the 2017 IEEE International Symposium on Hardware Oriented Security and Trust (HOST), pp. 21–28. IEEE (2017)

37. Song, D., et al.: BitBlaze: a new approach to computer security via binary analysis. In: Sekar, R., Pujari, A.K. (eds.) ICISS 2008. LNCS, vol. 5352, pp. 1–25. Springer, Heidelberg (2008). https://doi.org/10.1007/978-3-540-89862-7_1

38. Sullivan, D., Arias, O., Gens, D., Davi, L., Sadeghi, A.R., Jin, Y.: Execution integrity with in-place encryption. arXiv preprint arXiv:1703.02698 (2017)

39. Tang, Z., et al.: SEEAD: a semantic-based approach for automatic binary code de-obfuscation. In: Proceedings of the 2017 Trustcom/BigDataSE/ICESS, pp. 261–268. IEEE (2017)

40. Toemeh, R., Arumugam, S.: Applying genetic algorithms for searching key-space of polyalphabetic substitution ciphers. Int. Arab J. Inf. Technol. (IAJIT) 5(1) (2008)

41. van der Veen, V., et al.: A tough call: mitigating advanced code-reuse attacks at the binary level. In: Proceedings of the 37th IEEE Symposium on Security and Privacy (SP), pp. 934–953. IEEE (2016)

42. Wang, H., Fang, D., Li, G., Yin, X., Zhang, B., Gu, Y.: NISLVMP: improved virtual machine-based software protection. In: Proceedings of the 9th International Conference on Computational Intelligence and Security (CIS), pp. 479–483. IEEE (2013)

43. Weiser, M.: Program slicing. In: Proceedings of the 5th International Conference on Software Engineering, pp. 439–449. IEEE Press (1981)

44. Xu, D., Ming, J., Fu, Y., Wu, D.: VMHunt: a verifiable approach to partially-virtualized binary code simplification. In: Proceedings of the 2018 ACM SIGSAC Conference on Computer and Communications Security, pp. 442–458. ACM (2018)

45. Yadegari, B., Johannesmeyer, B., Whitely, B., Debray, S.: A generic approach to automatic deobfuscation of executable code. In: Proceedings of the 36th IEEE Symposium on Security and Privacy (SP), pp. 674–691. IEEE (2015)

46. Yang, M., Huang, L.: Software protection scheme via nested virtual machine. J. Chin. Comput. Syst. 32(2), 237–241 (2011)

Hide and Seek: An Architecture for Improving Attack-Visibility in Industrial Control Systems

Jairo Giraldo[1], David Urbina[1], Alvaro A. Cardenas[2]([⊠]),
and Nils Ole Tippenhauer[3]

[1] The University of Texas at Dallas, Richardson, TX 75080, USA
{jairo.giraldo,david.urbina}@utdallas.edu
[2] University of California Santa Cruz, Santa Cruz, CA 95064, USA
alvaro.cardenas@ucsc.edu
[3] CISPA Helmholtz Center for Information Security, Saarbrücken, Germany
tippenhauer@cispa.saarland

Abstract. In the past years we have seen an emerging field of research focusing on using the "physics" of a Cyber-Physical System to detect attacks. In its basic form, a security monitor is deployed somewhere in the industrial control network, observes a time-series of the operation of the system, and identifies anomalies in those measurements in order to detect potentially manipulated control commands or manipulated sensor readings. While there is a growing literature on detection mechanisms in that research direction, the problem of *where* to monitor the physical behavior of the system has received less attention.

In this paper, we analyze the problem of where should we monitor these systems, and what attacks can and cannot be detected depending on the location of this network monitor. The location of the monitor is particularly important, because an attacker can bypass attack-detection by lying in some network interfaces while reporting that everything is normal in the others. Our paper is the first detailed study of what can and cannot be detected based on the devices an attacker has compromised and where we monitor our network. We show that there are locations that maximize our visibility against such attacks. Based on our analysis, we design a low-level security monitor that is able to directly observe the field communication between sensors, actuators, and Programmable Logic Controllers (PLCs). We implement that security monitor in a realistic testbed, and demonstrate that it can detect attacks that would otherwise be undetected at the supervisory network.

1 Introduction

One of the recent research trends for the security of Industrial Control Systems (ICS) is to monitor the sensor and control signals being exchanged between different components of the system to verify that the system is operating as intended [5,7,12,23]. For example, if we have a sensor that monitors the height of

© Springer Nature Switzerland AG 2019
R. H. Deng et al. (Eds.): ACNS 2019, LNCS 11464, pp. 175–195, 2019.
https://doi.org/10.1007/978-3-030-21568-2_9

a bouncing ball, then we know that this height follows the differential equations from Newton's laws of mechanics. Thus, if a sensor reports a trajectory that is not plausible given the laws of physics, we can immediately identify that something has gone wrong with the sensor (a fault or an attack).

While previous research has contributed greatly to the literature, we have found that most papers working on this topic do not explicitly describe the trust assumptions for all parts of a control loop—controllers, actuators, and sensors.

In this paper, we show that without explicit trust assumptions, attacker models proposed in related work are ambiguous. In particular, we analyze the implicit assumptions made in previous works, and then use a logical attack-detection architecture to elucidate hidden assumptions, limitations, and possible improvements. Then, we develop and implement an architecture to maximize the visibility of attacks.

We summarize our main contributions in this work as follows:

- We review and classify different classes of attacks on a control loop, and map them to real-wold network topologies for industrial control systems.
- We show how implicit trust in subsets of the components in a real system can lead to attacks that deny visibility of the physical process to the control logic or SCADA.
- We provide a table articulating in detail the trust assumptions needed to be able to detect attacks when monitoring at the supervisory layer and at the field layer. As far as we are aware, we are the first to justify why monitoring at the field layer minimizes the number of devices we need to trust in order to detect attacks.
- We design and implement a *deep monitoring* system at the field layer and demonstrate the feasibility of our proposed system through a series of experiments. As far as we are aware, we are the first to illustrate the practical differences between implementing a security monitor at the supervisory layer vs. the field layer.

The remainder of this paper is organized as follows: In Sect. 2, we provide background on ICS networks, and related work. We then propose our new security monitoring architecture in Sect. 3. Based on that concept, we design and implement a deep ICS monitor in Sect. 4. Finally, we present the results of our prototype in Sect. 5.

2   Background

In this section, we first briefly summarize industrial control system networks, and then review related work on attack detection in ICS networks.

2.1   ICS Network Layers

Control systems have a layered hierarchy [24]. The two layers closest to the physical process are Layer 1 and Layer 0:

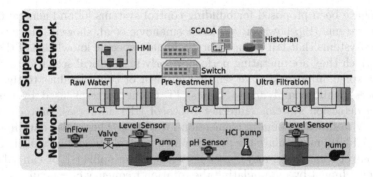

Fig. 1. A supervisory control network (SCN) enables communications between a central control server and embedded controllers. Field communication networks (FCN) enable controllers to contact sensor, actuators and remote IO terminals.

Layer 1 is where Supervisory Control and Data Acquisition (SCADA) Systems and other servers communicate with remote control equipment like Programmable Logic Controllers (PLCs) and Remote Terminal Units (RTUs). The communication between servers in a control room and these control equipment is done via a Supervisory Control Network **(SCN)**;

Layer 0 is where PLCs or RTUs interface with sensors (thermometers, tachometers, etc.) and actuators (pumps, valves, etc.) in the field. While traditionally this interface has been analog (e.g., 4–20 mA), the growing numbers of sensors and actuators as well as their increased intelligence and capabilities, has given rise to new Field Communication Networks **(FCN)** where the PLCs and other types of controllers interface with remote Input/Output boxes or directly with sensors and actuators using new Ethernet-based industrial protocols like EtherNet/IP and Profinet, and wireless networks like WirelessHART. Several ring topologies have also been proposed to avoid a single point of failure for these networks, such as the use of Device Level Ring (DLR) over EtherNet/IP.

Figure 1 illustrates these two networks in the ICS we analyze later in the paper.

SCN and FCN networks have different communication requirements and different industrial network protocols. While SCN can tolerate delays of up to the order of seconds, FCN typically require an order of magnitude of lower communication delays, typically enabling communications between devices with a period of 400 μs.

2.2 Previous Work

In this paper we focus on *network intrusion detection* for ICS. One of the first papers to consider network intrusion detection in industrial control networks was Cheung et al. [8]. Their work articulated that network anomaly detection might be more effective in control networks where communication patterns are more regular and stable than in traditional IT networks. Similar intrusion detection systems have been proposed for building control systems [6] and general cyber-physical systems [19]; however, as Hadžiosmanović et al. showed [11], intrusion detection systems that fail to incorporate domain-specific knowledge of the context in which they are operating perform poorly in practical scenarios.

Even worse, an attacker can send false sensor or control values to the physical process while complying to typical IT traffic patterns used by classical intrusion detection systems (Internet Protocol (IP) addresses, protocol specifications with finite automata, connection logs, etc.). These false data injection attacks [5,10,16] manipulate the process under control by sending malicious sensor or control commands, and can cause waste water spills [1], or can sabotage nuclear enrichment by manipulating the rotation frequency of centrifuges [9,13]. To detect these types of attacks we need to monitor the sensor and control algorithms in the systems; i.e., the *semantic* information of the ICS [2,5,12,23].

Previous efforts on semantic monitoring for ICS, however, have been vague in describing the specific types of attacks their proposals can and cannot detect. In particular, previous work implicitly assumes certain elements in a control loop are not compromised in order for their system to work, and this lack of specificity leads to potential threat vectors not previously anticipated.

Before we describe the vulnerabilities of previous work, notice that an attacker can compromise different devices in its goal to physically attack an ICS. In particular the adversary can compromise and launch attacks from (1) SCADA servers [15], (2) controllers/PLCs [14], (3) sensors [16], and (4) actuators [22]. As we will show, it is important to understand where the adversary is launching attacks because it can have a drastic effect in attack-detection systems.

For example, McLaughlin [18] focuses on the field layer of a control system; specifically it tackles the problem of how to verify that control signals u_k sent by the PLC to the actuators do not drive the system to an unsafe state. The proposed approach, C^2, mediates all control signals u_k sent by PLCs to the physical system. McLaughlin mentions that "C^2 mitigates all control channel attacks against devices, and only requires trust in process engineers and physical sensors." This is, however, not true, as **an attacker that has compromised an actuator or a Remote I/O, can bypass C^2**: a PLC can send correct control signals, but if the actuators are compromised they do not need to follow the orders from the PLC, and can discard them to continue attacking the system.

Similarly Hadžiosmanović et al. [12] use network traces from an industrial site using Modbus/TCP to detect attacks by monitoring the state variables of the system, including constants, attribute data, and continuous data. Their network data was captured at the supervisory network, and this means that they are *implicitly trusting the PLCs to tell the truth to the supervisory network*. However, **if a PLC is compromised, it can lie to the supervisory network interface stating that everything is working properly, while at the same time sending erroneous commands via the field communications interface, and this attack would not be detected by monitoring the supervisory network.**

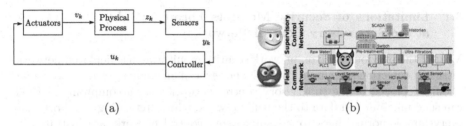

(a)   (b)

Fig. 2. (a) A control loop at time k, with sensor values y_k, control values u_k, actuator action v_k, and state of the system z_k. (b) A compromised PLC can send manipulated control commands to devices in the field while reporting an incorrect status of the system to the supervisory layer.

In another example, Carcano et al. [4] propose a safety monitoring system and raise alerts whenever it is in a critical state (or approaching a critical state). In order to detect that they are approaching an unsafe state, they *implicitly assume trusted sensors*. **If an attacker compromises the sensors, or the PLCs, it can lie to the network security monitor located in the supervisory network and bypass the system.**

The work of Carcano and C^2 rely on having sensors that haven't been compromised. It seems reasonable to assume that if the sensors are trustworthy, we should be able to detect if the system is approaching an anomalous or dangerous state and react accordingly. *Zero-dynamics attacks* [20–22] are examples of attacks where **even if we assume the sensors and the PLCs are not compromised, attackers with compromised actuators can mislead state estimation algorithms.**

In summary, attackers have many vectors for attacks, and none of the previous we analyzed has considered a detection architecture that can prevent an attacker from launching attacks while remaining hidden.

3   An Architecture to Reveal Hidden Attacks

Physical processes are regulated by a control loop, consisting of the following components: (1) the physical phenomena of interest (sometimes called the process), (2) sensors to observe the physical system and send a time series y_k denoting the value of the physical measurement at time k (e.g., the voltage at 3 a.m is 120 KV), (3) based on the sensor measurements received y_k, the controller/PLC sends control commands u_k (e.g., open a valve by 10%) to actuators, and (4) actuators that change the control command to an actual physical change (the device that opens the valve). To differentiate between the real state of the system and the sensor reading, let z_k denote the real value and y_k the one reported by sensors. Similarly, actuators might implement a different control action v_k than the one received from the PLC u_k. A summary is shown in Fig. 2a.

3.1 Limitations of Security Monitors Located (Only) at the Supervisory Control Network

Most of the previous work on network security monitoring has deployed network intrusion detection systems at the SCN; however, if an anomaly detection system is only deployed in the supervisory control network then a compromised PLC can send manipulated data to the field network, while pretending to report that everything is normal back to the supervisory control network, as illustrated in Fig. 2b. In the Stuxnet attack, the attacker compromised a PLC (Siemens 315) and sent a manipulated control signal u^a (which was different from the original u, i.e., $u^a \neq u$). Upon reception of u^a, the frequency converters periodically increased and decreased the rotor speeds well above and below their intended operation levels. While the status of the frequency converters y was then relayed back to the PLC, the compromised PLC reported a manipulated value $y_a \neq y$ to the control center (claiming that devices were operating normally). A similar attack was performed against the Siemens 417 controller [14], where attackers captured 21 s of valid sensor variables at the PLC, and then replayed them continuously for the duration of the attack, ensuring that the data sent to the SCADA monitors would appear normal [14].

If the network monitor is deployed at the supervisory control layer, it will not able to detect compromised PLCs, unless it is able to correlate information from other trusted PLCs, or unless it receives (trusted) sensor data directly (e.g., wireless sensors sending measurements directly to the control center). If the control center in the Stuxnet case had monitored the frequency converters directly through an independent channel, it could have detected the attack.

Another difference in the data visibility between FCN and SCN layers is that the request-and-respond communication generally implemented by SCN layers might miss some important data exchanges in the FCN layer: without a specific request-and-response exchange, the data of interest may not be present during the deep-packet inspection session. For example, if a specific data item request/response exchange occurs with a low frequency or under special circumstances, the data exchanged will be missed. For example, configuration files for field devices can be set so that they only to send data if some specific circumstances arise. Even if the PLC is trustworthy, this delay can prevent an anomaly detector at the SCN from detecting the onset of an attack.

3.2 Detectability of Attacks

In the previous section we saw how attackers can bypass intrusion detection systems when they have compromised a PLC and our monitor is in the supervisory network. If our intrusion detection system is in the field network, the attacker of the previous section cannot remain hidden as we can see the false commands coming out of the PLC and the incorrect sensor measurements from the sensors. But what if the attacker also compromises these other parts of the system?

We now systematically analyze what can be detected and what cannot be detected when we have access to data from the field devices (from the FCN) and when the attacker compromises different parts of the control loop, as illustrated in Fig. 3a. Attack 1 in Fig. 3a shows an attack on the actuator(s) $v_k \neq u_k$, the attack modifies the control command send to the plant. We note that the controller is not aware of the communication interruption. On the other hand, attack 2 in Fig. 3a shows an attack on the sensor(s) $y_k \neq z_k$, which allows the attacker to deceive the controller about the real state of the plant. The controllers can be compromised as well, as illustrated by attack 3 in Fig. 3a, $u_k \neq \mathcal{K}(y_k)$, where $\mathcal{K}$ is the logic the control algorithm should have implemented.

We also capture attacks coming from a compromised SCADA server as illustrated in Fig. 3b, as malicious control commands from the SCADA server or a malicious change of parameters to the controller will generate a false control command equivalent to $u_k \neq \mathcal{K}(y_k)$.

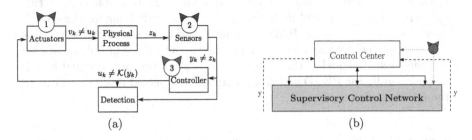

Fig. 3. (a) Different attack points in a control system: (1) Attack on the actuators, (2) Attack on the sensors, (3) Attack on the controller. (b) Attacks on central control or supervisory control network translate to attack $u_k \neq \mathcal{K}(y_k)$ in (a).

We now discuss the detectability of each attack.

1. If we trust the controller (e.g., the PLC) but do not trust sensors or actuators then, it is *game over*: the attacker can change the physical world with bad actuation actions while at the same time using the sensors to report that everything is working normally.
2. If we trust the actuators but not the controller or the sensors then it is also game over: the attacker can use the controller to send false control signals u_k^a to the actuator, while false sensor measurements can be generated to justify the false control action.
3. If we trust the sensors but not the controller or the actuators, then for most practical cases we can detect an attack using a Physics-Based Anomaly Detection (PBAD) as proposed e.g., by Urbina et al. [23]. A PBAD will work because the goal of the attack is to affect the physical system, and we assume we can monitor changes done by the attacker through the sensor time series y_k. Having said that, zero-dynamic attacks [22] are examples where even when we trust sensor measurements, we cannot detect attacks caused by a compromised actuator. Zero-dynamic attacks are rare and depend heavily on the properties of the process and the sensors we have deployed.

4. If we trust the actuator and the controller, then we know the control signal u_k will have the expected intended effect on the physical system. Any false data injected by the sensors will cause a control command u_k to be sent in response to these false measurements, and in turn, any implausible combination of control and sensor signals might be an indicator of an attack and can be detected by a PBAD.

5. If we trust the controller and the sensors, then we again have implausible combinations of control actions and sensor measurements that can be detected by a PBAD because we can see that the control command that was sent to the process did not have the expected result. With the possible exception of zero-dynamic attacks.

6. Finally, we can detect a compromised controller by identifying if a control action is the correct response to the current state of the system. This detection method is not PBAD, but it requires a Redundant Controller (RC) that can verify that the control action is indeed the intended one for the specific operation. Notice that a PBAD has limited use in this case as the physical evolution of the process with a compromised controller will still satisfy the "physics-based" model of the system because the false control signal u_k^a will be observed by the PBAD and it will match the expected result y^a caused by the attacker of the system.

Table 1. Detectability of attacks depending on which devices are compromised

Device status			Detection possible	Comment
PLC	Sensor	Actuator		
✓	×	×	×	False sensing hides bad actuation
×	×	✓	×	False sensing justifies bad controls
×	✓	×	∼	PBAD detectable except zero-dynamics
✓	×	✓	✓	PBAD detectable
✓	✓	×	✓	PBAD detectable
×	✓	✓	✓	RC-detectable
✓	✓	✓	✓	No attack possible

✓ = trusted/detection possible, × = compromised/detection not possible, ∼ = can detect most attacks except for zero-dynamics attacks

Summary and Takeaways. Table 1 summarizes our contributions. Based on our discussion, we can see that by monitoring FCN networks we can improve the number of attacks that we can detect (via PBAD or RC); however when more than one set of devices is compromised (e.g., sensors and actuators) detection is impossible, even at the FCN layer. Finally, while most previous work uses physics-based anomaly detection (PBAD) for detecting false data injection attacks, we showed in our analysis that PBAD is not enough; in particular we described why need to have a redundant controller (RC)-based detection.

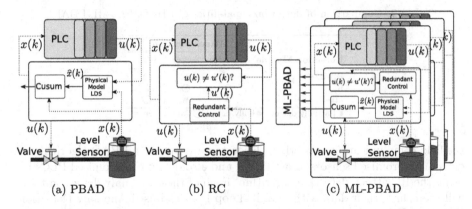

Fig. 4. (a) Illustration of physics-based anomaly detection (PBAD) algorithm. (b) Redundant control (RC) architecture to detect a compromised PLC. (c) Proposed attack detection architecture

Figure 4a illustrates a general Physics-Based Anomaly Detection (PBAD) system where the security monitor takes the control signal sent to the field and the sensor measurement received to see if its compatible to the predicted behavior of the system (a time-series anomaly detection algorithm like the CUSUM then performs statistical tests to see if the anomaly is persistent) [23]. Figure 4b on the other hand shows the RC detector, where a redundant (software-based) controller verifies that given the same sensor inputs, it obtains the same result as the controller.

3.3   Attack Detection Architecture

In the last section we saw that by monitoring the field communications of a control loop we can get better detection results than by monitoring the supervisory network; however, we still get limited attack-detection when an adversary has compromised more than one set of devices as summarized in Table 1.

Real-world industrial systems, however, are far larger than a single control loop. They contain multiple stages controlling interdependent parts of a complex system. For example, the process illustrated at the beginning of this paper in Fig. 1 has three stages of a water purification process, each controlled by a different set of PLCs, sensors, and actuators. These different parts of the process can be used to try to identify the attacks that are not detected in Table 1. For example, if the attacker compromises both sensors and actuators in one control loop, then it can take complete control of the system without being detected; however the effects on one loop will have other evident side-effects on another system and we can hope to detect the attack there. This will need coordination between different anomaly detection systems in each loop, so they can verify with each other what each of them is currently "seeing".

Our proposed anomaly detection architecture is illustrated in Fig. 4c. As described in the previous subsection, by deploying network security monitors in

Table 2. Comparison of detection capabilities of PBAD, RC, ML-PBAD.

	Attack location		
Detection Module	Actuator	Sensor	PLC
PBAD	◐	◐	○
RC	○	○	●
ML-PBAD	●	●	○

◐Partially detect ●Fully detect ○Cannot detect

the field communication network of the system we can use a PBAD algorithm to detect compromised sensors or actuators, and also detect compromised PLCs by using the RC attack-detection algorithm. Each of these anomaly detection tools will then share their data with a Multi-Loop Physics-Based Anomaly Detection (ML-PBAD) algorithm that will detect if the reports from a control loop in one subsystem are consistent with the other control loops. Table 2 summarizes this.

In the next section we will discuss the development and implementation of our architecture in an industrial system.

4   Implementation of Our Security Monitor

In this section, we present the design and implementation of a security monitor that is explicitly placed as *deep* in the ICS network hierarchy as possible—in the field network immediately next to sensors and actuators, and which reports data to a supervisory ML-PBAD algorithm. As such, the monitor is expected to reliably obtain information from the sensors and actuators, without the risk of obtaining manipulated data from intermediate PLCs or SCADA.

4.1   Testbed Description

The testbed we use for our experiments is a water treatment plant consisting of 6 main stages to purify raw water. The testbed is described in more detail in [17]. The testbed has a total of 12 PLCs (6 main PLCs and 6 in backup configuration to take over if the main PLC fails). *Raw water storage* is the part of the process where raw water is stored and it acts as the main water buffer supplying water to the water treatment system. It consists of one tank, an on/off valve that controls the inlet water, and a pump that transfers the water to the ultra filtration (UF) tank. In *Pre-treatment* the Conductivity, pH, and Oxidation-Reduction Potential (ORP) are measured to determine the activation of chemical dosing to maintain the quality of the water within some desirable limits. *Ultra Filtration* is used to remove the bulk of the feed water solids and colloidal material by using fine filtration membranes that only allow the flow of small molecules. The accumulated contaminants are removed by back-washing away the membrane surface depending on the measure of a differential pressure sensor located at the two ends of the UF. After the small residuals are removed by the UF system, the remaining chlorines are destroyed in the *Dechlorinization* stage, using ultraviolet chlorine destruction unit and by dosing a solution of sodium bisulphite. *Reverse*

Osmosis (RO) system is designed to reduce inorganic impurities by pumping the filtrated and dechlorinated water with a high pressure through reverse osmosis membranes. Finally, in *RO final product* stage stores the RO product (clean water).

Each stage has two PLCs (one primary and one redundant in hot-standby mode). The field devices, i.e. sensors/actuators, send and receive sensor information and control actions, respectively, to/from the PLCs through Remote I/O modules (digital input and output, and analog input) in a EtherNet/IP ring topology (EtherNet/IP is a popular industrial control protocol).

4.2   Challenges for Parsing the FCN Layer

Implementing a FCN monitor is more challenging than implementing one at the SCN level. The network of the testbed illustrated in Fig. 1 uses the Common Industrial Protocol (CIP) stack [3] for device communications at the SCN and FCN layers. This is a common industrial protocol and is representative of a wide variety of industry sectors. There a variety of differences between the FCN and SCN layers, as illustrated in Fig. 5.

One difference in the data visibility between FCN and SCN layers is that the request-and-respond communication implemented by SCN layers might miss some important data exchanges in the FCN layer: without a specific request-and-response exchange, the data of interest may not be present during the deep-packet inspection session. For example, if a specific data item request/response exchange occurs with a low frequency or under special circumstances, the data exchanged will be missed.

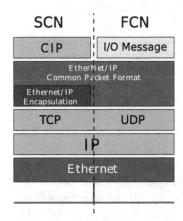

Fig. 5. Differences between the SCN and the FCN network stacks.

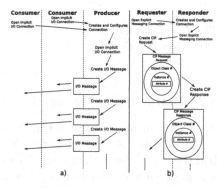

Fig. 6. (a) FCN's multicast implicit I/O connections, and (b) SCN's request/response-oriented explicit messaging connections.

In addition, at the SCN layer, devices communicate through *point-to-point* connections over the Transmission Control Protocol (TCP) and exchange **explicit** CIP messages—see Fig. 7; these explicit messages are standard and openly accessible formats defining a clear semantic of the messages exchanged between devices. As shown in Fig. 6(b), each *Messaging Connection* (MC) provides generic, multi-purpose communication paths by carrying well-known and semantically-rich explicit CIP Messages between two devices. Creating a protocol parser to extract the sensor and actuation commands in this setting is straightforward because we only need to follow the standard specification and all the data types and their interpretation can be understood by the parser.

On the other hand, at the FCN layer, devices communicate through *multicast* connections over User Datagram Protocol (UDP) and exchange **implicit** *I/O Connections* between a producer device and one or more consuming devices (See Fig. 6(a)). The semantic and structure of the data inside the I/O Message is implicitly known by the communicating devices, and is device and vendor dependent (Allen-Bradley in this deployment). In particular, these I/O Messages in the FCN layer follow a flat structure (stream of bits), of fixed size and of untyped data. Therefore we need to work with low-level data where values are exchanged without standard units of measurement, and where the protocol is not publicly available. In order to develop a parser for this layer, we require extra information provided by the electrical drawings of the equipment, illustrating how each field device (e.g. sensor or actuator) is wired to the specific modules of the PLC.

Structure	Field Name	Data Type	Field Value
Encapsulation header	Command	UINT	Encapsulation command
	Length	UINT	Length, in bytes, of the data portion of the message, i.e., the number of bytes following the header
	Session handle	UDINT	Session identification (application dependent)
	Status	UDINT	Status code
	Sender Context	ARRAY of octet	Information pertinent only to the sender of an encapsulation command. Length of 8.
	Options	UDINT	Options flags
Command specific data	Encapsulated data	ARRAY of 0 to 65511 octet	The encapsulation data portion of the message is required only for certain commands

I/O Message	Signal size (bits)	# signals	Avg. Freq. (ms)
Digital Input	1	32	50
Digital Output	1	16	60
Analog Input	16	12	80

Fig. 7. Explicit CIP message encapsulation over EtherNet/IP.

Fig. 8. Modules for each PLC.

4.3   Extracting the Semantics of FCN Data

After implementing the parser in Python, we now need to interpret the data we see in the wire. According to the electrical drawings, we found that each PLC had three modules: a digital input module (to receive on/off status reports from senors or fault alarms from devices in the field), an analog input module (to receive fine-grain information from sensors in the field such as the height of the water level in a tank, or the pH level of the water), and a digital output (to turn on/off actuators in the field). None of the PLCs in this testbed had an analog output module (analog outputs are used to control continuous variables such as the speed of a motor or the partial valve opening).

The number of signals available per module are summarized in Fig. 8. For example, a digital input module for the PLC consists of a stream of 32 bits, corresponding to each of the digital inputs signals. The *spare* channels are those not in use by the current deployment. The digital outputs are grouped in 16-bit stream (1 bit per signal), while the analog inputs are grouped in a 24-byte stream with 16 bits per signal 2's complement.

Electrical drawings of the plant tell us which specific bit (or word) in the PLC module corresponds to each signal. For example, Fig. 9 shows the electrical diagram indicating the description of each bit in the stream for a digital input module (the top part of the figure is our own illustration showing how these sensors connect to the PLC).

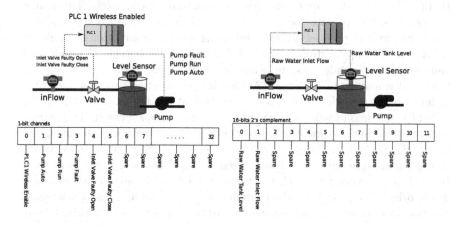

Fig. 9. Digital input module with 32 input signals (1-bit signals) for the raw water storage stage PLC.

Fig. 10. Analog input module with 12 input signals (16-bits signals) for the raw water storage stage PLC.

The I/O Messages containing the analog signals are sent by the field devices to the PLC with an average frequency of 80 ms. They transport the numeric representation of the 4–20 mA analog electrical signals measured by the analog sensors and converted to their raw digital version using an Analog-Digital Converter (ADC). For example the analog inputs for the first stage of the testbed are shown in Fig. 10.

In order to scale back and forth between the 4–20 mA analog signal and the real measurement with standard units, we use Eq. (1). In this equation, *EUMax* and *EUMin* are the desired maximum and minimum limits of the specific *Engineering Unit* (e.g. millimeters (mm), *pH*, cubic meters per hour (m^3/h), etc.) to which the Raw signal is being scaled; RawMax and RawMin are the maximum and minimum possible limits for the original Raw signal. These constant values depend on the type of sensors and the physical property being measured.

$$Out = (In - RawMin) * \frac{EUMax - EUMin}{RawMax - RawMin} + EUMin \qquad (1)$$

By looking at packet captures between the PLC and the field devices we found that each packet represented a specific exchange between a module in the PLC and the field devices. Therefore by simply looking at the packet payload size (32 bits for the digital input module, 16 bits for the digital output module, and 192 bits for analog inputs) we were able to identify the type of communication.

Based on this information, we developed parsers for the three types of packets for all PLCs, and a command-line interpreter (CLI) application which includes a library of attacks and a network monitoring module implementing attack-detection mechanisms. The attack modules are capable of launching diverse spoofing and bad-data-injection attacks against the sensor and actuator signals of the testbed. The attack modules can be loaded, configured, and run independently of each other, allowing to attack sensors/actuators separately. The attack modules can also be orchestrated in teams in order to force more complex behaviors over the physical process, while maintaining a normal operational profile on the HMI. The CLI application consists of 632 lines of Python [26] 2.7 code and the only external dependencies are Scapy and NetFilterQueue.

Specifically, making use of Scapy [27], we developed a new protocol parser for the Allen-Bradley proprietary I/O Messages used at the FCN layer, and for the EtherNet/IP Common Packet Format wrapper that encapsulates it. This parser allows us to sniff, in real-time, the sensor readings and actuation commands, and to inject fake packets in the network. When injecting fake data, our software calculates the data integrity checksums used by the Transport Layer protocol.

Instead of injecting fake packets crafted from scratch, our attack modules catch the original packets from the communication stream and insert fake sensing/control data, before sending the packets to their original destination. Inserting fake packets may result in race conditions when the original and the fake packet are both process by the PLC. We employed the NetFilterQueue [25] Python bindings for libnetfilter queue to redirect all the I/O Messages between PLC and the field devices to a handling queue defined on the PREROUTING table of the Linux firewall *iptables*. The queued packets can be modified using Scapy and the previously mentioned message parser, and finally released to reach their original destination e.g., PLC or field devices. Likewise, this technique allowed us to avoid disruptions on the sequence of EtherNet/IP counters, and injection of undesirable perturbations in the EtherNet/IP connections established between field devices. Our final security monitor is inserted in the EtherNet/IP ring between the PLCs and the field devices.

5   Experiments

We now illustrate how our monitor system can be used to launch and detect attacks at the FCN in the testbed. In the following experiments, the goal of the attacker is to deviate the water level in a tank as much as possible until the tank overflows, without being detected. We assume an attacker who has complete knowledge of the physical behavior of the system and can manipulate EtherNet/IP field communications or has compromised the PLC.

Our network monitoring module was setup to use a stateful CUmulative SUM (CUSUM) anomaly detection on the residuals, with a LDS model of the process. In particular, we use a mass balance equation that relates the change in the water level h with respect to the inlet water flow Q^{in} and outlet water flow Q^{out} volume of water, given by $Area\frac{dh}{dt} = Q^{in} - Q^{out}$, where $Area$ is the cross-sectional area of the base of the tank. Note that in this process the control actions for the valve and pump are On/Off. Hence, Q^{in} or Q^{out} remain constant if they are open, and zero otherwise. Using a time-discretization of 1 s, we obtain an estimated model of the form

$$\hat{h}_{k+1} = h_k + \frac{Q_k^{in} - Q_k^{out}}{Area} \tag{2}$$

where h_k represents the received sensor measurement for the water level at time k, Q_k^{in} represents the on/off variable of the state of the inlet valve at time k, and Q_k^{out} represents the on/off variable of the state of the pump that takes water off the tank. Given these variables, we can predict the height of the tank at the next time step $\hat{h}_{k+1}$.

A residual statistic keeps track of the difference between the height of the tank received at time $k+1$ and the expected height $r_k = |h_k - \hat{h}_k|$. A cumulative sum of these errors (minus a forgetting factor δ) is then computed as part of the CUSUM anomaly detection test: $S_{k+1} = \max(0, S_k + r_k - \delta)$, see [23]. If this statistic is greater than a user-specified threshold τ (usually selected to maintain a low false alarm rate) then we raise an alarm; i.e., if $S_k > \tau$ then we send an alert to the operator.

We now show how our field-level implementation has enough visibility to detect a variety of attacks to the system.

5.1   Sensor Attack (Water Level)

We assume the adversary has gained access to the communication link between the sensor and the PLC and she is able to manipulate the sensor information as we described above. At the moment of the attack, the valve was open and the pump was off, so the water level in the tank starts increasing. This attack corresponds to attack 2 in Fig. 3a. The sensor information is used by the PLC to determine the control action; therefore, if the attacker lies and tells the PLC that the water height is increasing at a slower rate it actually is increasing, the PLC will keep the valve open and the tank overflows before the valve closes. Figure 11a illustrates how the compromised water level increases at a slower rate than the real one, and as a consequence, when the sensor information reaches 0.8 m and the PLC closes the valve, the real water is already overflowing (the height of the tank is 1 m). However, our proposed detection mechanism detects that the sensor measurement received h_k does not match the rate $\hat{h}_k$ at which the water should be increasing. The consecutive differences between h_k and $\hat{h}_k$ form the residual r_k (i.e., $r_k = |h_k - \hat{h}_k|$). Taking a CUSUM detection statistic over r_k triggers an alarm a few seconds after the attacked is launched.

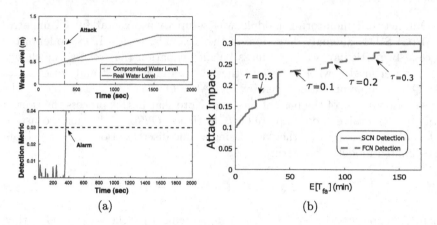

Fig. 11. (a) Sensor attack (water level). (b) Impact of a stealthy sensor attack with detection strategies in SCN and FCN.

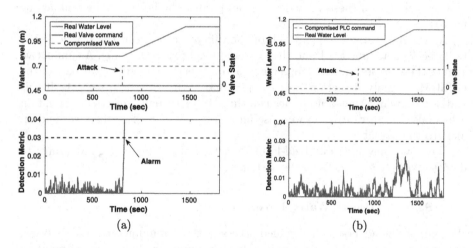

Fig. 12. (a) Actuator attack (inlet valve). (b) Controller attack (PLC/SCADA).

In this case it does not matter if the security monitor is at the FCN layer or at the SCN layer, the attack can be detected at any layer because both layers have visibility into the false sensor data. However, to illustrate the problem of relying only in supervisory networks when a PLC is compromised, we ran the same attack, but this time the PLC reported the reading the anomaly detector was expecting to the supervisory network. The anomaly detector in the field network on the other hand, was able to see the raw sensor measurements being produced and how they did not match with the control commands of having the inlet valve open and the pump extracting water closed. Motivated by the performance metric proposed by Urbina et al. [23], we compute the trade-off between attack impact and frequency of false alarms that a stealthy attacker (one that does not raise any alarms) causes to both systems: an PBAD at the

SCN, and a PBAD at the FCN (see Fig. 11b). In the figure it is clear that if the attacker wants to remain hidden, it has better chances to cause damages to the system if the defender only monitors the SCN.

5.2   Actuator Attack (Inlet Water Valve)

Now we turn our attention to attacks against the actuators, as illustrated in Fig. 3(a). In this scenario, our security monitor observes the intended control command by the PLC to the actuator, but then notices that the sensor measurement does not correspond to the intended control command.

We consider a state of the system where the water in the tank is at 0.8 m and the PLC intends to keep that level by having the intake valve closed, and the pump taking water out of the tank off. Figure 12a shows how a false actuation command to open the valve increases the height of the water in the tank. Again, our anomaly detection system detects that the predicted height (0.8 m) based on the current control commands (both the inlet valve and the pump are off) should remain constant, so the increase of the water level is detected as anomaly.

As in the previous case (sensor attack), if the only attacked device in the system is the intake valve position, then it doesn't matter if the security monitor is at the FCN layer or at the SCN layer, the attack can be detected at any layer because both layers have visibility into the truthful sensor data and notice that it does not correspond to the control commands sent to the field.

5.3   PLC Attack (RC-Detection)

In this attack the logic of the PLC is modified so that it sends a false control command, but reports that everything is fine to the SCN as in Fig. 2b. In particular, the PLC sees that the water is at the high level of 0.8 m (so it shouldn't open the intake valve); however, our change of logic in the PLC instead asks it to open the intake valve to allow more water into the tank, while reporting to the supervisory control layer that the intake valve is closed and that the water level is still 0.8 m.

As discussed before, this attack cannot be detected with a security monitor at the supervisory control layer, because it does not have visibility to the field control commands sent by the PLC. As discussed before, this attack cannot even be detected using PBAD at the FCN because there is no discrepancy between the observed control commands, and their effect on sensor measurements. Figure 12b shows how a command from a compromised PLC cannot be detected by our physics-based anomaly detection statistic as our FCN monitoring tool observes the command to open a valve, and then predictably, the height of the tank begins increasing at the appropriate rate.

To detect this attack we require a redundant control architecture in this case is illustrated in Fig. 4b. In this case the RC attack detection algorithm notices the compromised PLC sends a signal that is not authorized to send in its current state, thus detecting the compromised PLC.

5.4   Multi-loop Anomaly Detection (ML-PBAD)

The worst type of attack corresponds to the case when the sensors and actuators are attacked simultaneously. To show the generality of our ML-PBAD architecture originally presented in Fig. 4c, we implemented it in two different systems; we now present the results for the water system we have been considering.

Here we assume the adversary has compromised both the actuators and the sensors, and therefore is able to send arbitrary actuator control signals (e.g. open the intake valve when the water in the tank is 0.8 m) while at the same time, lie about the sensor readings (i.e., tell our security monitor that the water in the system is constant at 0.8 m).

Now, recall that the testbed has multiple stages controlled by various PLCs, each of them receiving different field signals from the physical process. We focus our attention on the water level of two consecutive stages with two tanks, each of which is controlled by hysteresis switched controls that depend on those levels. We want to show how attacks over sensors and actuators affect the performance of the system, and it is even possible to lead the water level to overflow.

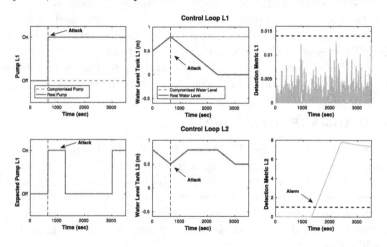

Fig. 13. Sensor and actuator attack in stage 1. The attack cannot be detected by the detection algorithm in process 1, but it can be observed in the other stage.

In particular, we assume our attacker has compromised both the pump actuator and the water level sensor in the first stage of the testbed. As result, if the attacker wants to damage the pump, it can turn on the pump directly from the actuator command. As our security monitor will not see that command, it will assume the pump is off. The attacker then can lie about the water in the system, and tell the PLC (and thus the security monitor) that the water remains at 0.8 m, while in reality the water level in tank one is decreasing.

From the point of view of the security monitor however, the pump is off, and the water level is stable (the security monitor sees the red lines in Fig. 13 (top)) and therefore, the anomaly detection statistic for stage 1 does not increase. However, from the point of view of the field security monitor in stage two of the plant monitoring the control loop of the second PLC, the water level for the second tank will appear to rise without any apparent reason, and this will raise an alarm, as illustrated in Fig. 13 (bottom).

We found that without our proposed ML-PBAD scheme, the attacker is able to raise the water level of the tank to the point of overflow (0.4 m above the setpoint) without being detected by the single loop PBAD. In contrast, the attacker can only raise the water level to 0.1 m above the setpoint without detection if ML-PBAD is used

6 Conclusions

In this paper we have presented a detailed discussion of the lack of missing trust models in previous work, and why specifically looking where to deploy physics-based anomaly detectors is of high importance. In particular we show why deploying security monitors in the field level of industrial control systems has several advantages over deploying only at the supervisory control layer.

We then implemented a field security monitor. We showed the differences between implementing a detector in the field level versus at the supervisory control layer, and then showed its effectiveness to detect more attacks than what is possible at the supervisory control layer.

Finally, by experimenting with attacks to all components of the system, we were able to identify new tools to mitigate some corner cases that cannot be addressed solely with PBAD-anomaly detection algorithms [23]. We then presented a new holistic detection architecture that covers detection of attacks not previously discussed in the literature.

A limitation of a field monitor is that if both, sensor and actuators are compromised, then an attacker can still bypass this detection. To mitigate this problem we proposed the integration from multiple field monitors at different stages in a large process. Our work in this distributed architecture improves the visibility of our system, and makes the work of an attacker who wants to remain stealthy much harder. Powerful attackers will always be able to bypass the system, but our architecture will raise the bar in the amount of effort and knowledge required by attackers to be successful.

Acknowledgements. We would like to thank SUTD for giving us access to their SWaT testbed to conduct our experiments. This material is based on research sponsored by the National Science Foundation with award number CNS-1718848, by the National Institute of Standards and Technology with award number 70NANB17H282, and by the Air Force Research Laboratory under agreement number FA8750-19-2-0010. The U.S. Government is authorized to reproduce and distribute reprints for Governmental purposes notwithstanding any copyright notation thereon. The views and conclusions contained herein are those of the authors and should not be interpreted as necessarily representing the official policies or endorsements, either expressed or implied, of Air Force Research Laboratory or the U.S. Government.

References

1. Abrams, M., Weiss, J.: Malicious control system cyber security attack case study-Maroochy water services, Australia. The MITRE Corporation, McLean (2008)
2. Ahmed, C.M., et al.: NoisePrint: attack detection using sensor and process noise fingerprint in cyber physical systems. In: Proceedings of the 2018 on Asia Conference on Computer and Communications Security, pp. 483–497. ACM (2018)
3. Brooks, P.: EtherNet/IP: industrial protocol white paper. Technical report, Rockwell Automation (2001)
4. Carcano, A., Coletta, A., Guglielmi, M., Masera, M., Fovino, I.N., Trombetta, A.: A multidimensional critical state analysis for detecting intrusions in SCADA systems. IEEE Trans. Ind. Inform. **7**(2), 179–186 (2011)
5. Cardenas, A.A., Amin, S., Lin, Z.S., Huang, Y.L., Huang, C.Y., Sastry, S.: Attacks against process control systems: risk assessment, detection, and response. In: Proceedings of the 6th ACM Symposium on Information, Computer and Communications Security, pp. 355–366 (2011)
6. Caselli, M., Zambon, E., Amann, J., Sommer, R., Kargl, F.: Specification mining for intrusion detection in networked control systems. In: 25th USENIX Security Symposium (USENIX Security 2016), pp. 791–806 (2016)
7. Cheng, L., Tian, K., Yao, D., Sha, L., Beyah, R.A.: Checking is believing: event-aware program anomaly detection in cyber-physical systems. IEEE Trans. Dependable Secur. Comput. (2019)
8. Cheung, S., Dutertre, B., Fong, M., Lindqvist, U., Skinner, K., Valdes, A.: Using model-based intrusion detection for SCADA networks. In: Proceedings of the SCADA Security Scientific Symposium, vol. 46, pp. 1–12 (2007)
9. Falliere, N., Murchu, L.O., Chien, E.: W32: stuxnet dossier. White paper, symantec corp., security response (2011)
10. Gerdes, R.M., Winstead, C., Heaslip, K.: CPS: an efficiency-motivated attack against autonomous vehicular transportation. In: Proceedings of the 29th Annual Computer Security Applications Conference, pp. 99–108. ACM (2013)
11. Hadžiosmanović, D., Simionato, L., Bolzoni, D., Zambon, E., Etalle, S.: N-gram against the machine: on the feasibility of the N-gram network analysis for binary protocols. In: Balzarotti, D., Stolfo, S.J., Cova, M. (eds.) RAID 2012. LNCS, vol. 7462, pp. 354–373. Springer, Heidelberg (2012). https://doi.org/10.1007/978-3-642-33338-5_18
12. Hadžiosmanović, D., Sommer, R., Zambon, E., Hartel, P.H.: Through the eye of the PLC: semantic security monitoring for industrial processes. In: Proceedings of the 30th Annual Computer Security Applications Conference, pp. 126–135. ACM (2014)
13. Langner, R.: Stuxnet: dissecting a cyberwarfare weapon. IEEE Secur. Priv. **9**(3), 49–51 (2011)
14. Langner, R.: To kill a centrifuge: a technical analysis of what stuxnet's creators tried to achieve. Langner Group, Arlington (2013)
15. Lee, R.M., Assante, M.J., Conway, T.: Analysis of the cyber attack on the ukrainian power grid. Technical report, SANS Industrial Control Systems, March 2016
16. Liu, Y., Ning, P., Reiter, M.K.: False data injection attacks against state estimation in electric power grids. In: Proceedings of the 16th ACM Conference on Computer and Communications Security, pp. 21–32. ACM (2009)

17. Mathur, A., Tippenhauer, N.O.: SWaT: a water treatment testbed for research and training on ICS security. In: Proceedings of Workshop on Cyber-Physical Systems for Smart Water Networks (CySWater), April 2016. https://doi.org/10.1109/CySWater.2016.7469060

18. McLaughlin, S.: CPS: stateful policy enforcement for control system device usage. In: Proceedings of the 29th Annual Computer Security Applications Conference, ACSAC 2013, pp. 109–118. ACM, New York (2013)

19. Mitchell, R., Chen, I.R.: A survey of intrusion detection techniques for cyber-physical systems. ACM Comput. Surv. 46(4), 55:1–55:29 (2014)

20. Pasqualetti, F., Dorfler, F., Bullo, F.: Attack detection and identification in cyber-physical systems. IEEE Trans. Autom. Control 58(11), 2715–2729 (2013)

21. Teixeira, A., Pérez, D., Sandberg, H., Johansson, K.H.: Attack models and scenarios for networked control systems. In: Proceedings of the 1st International Conference on High Confidence Networked Systems, pp. 55–64. ACM (2012)

22. Teixeira, A., Shames, I., Sandberg, H., Johansson, K.H.: Revealing stealthy attacks in control systems. In: 2012 50th Annual Allerton Conference on Communication, Control, and Computing (Allerton), pp. 1806–1813. IEEE (2012)

23. Urbina, D., et al.: Limiting the impact of stealthy attacks on industrial control systems. In: Proceedings of the ACM Conference on Computer and Communications Security (CCS), October 2016. https://doi.org/10.1145/2976749.2978388

24. Williams, T.J.: The purdue enterprise reference architecture. Comput. Ind. 24(2), 141–158 (1994)

25. Python bindings for libnetfilter_queue, February 2017. https://github.com/fqrouter/python-netfilterqueue

26. Python Language: version 2.7.10, February 2017. https://docs.python.org/2/

27. Scapy Packet Manupulation Program: version 2.3.1, February 2017. http://www.secdev.org/projects/scapy/doc/

A Modular Hybrid Learning Approach for Black-Box Security Testing of CPS

John Henry Castellanos$^{(\boxtimes)}$ and Jianying Zhou$^{(\boxtimes)}$

Singapore University of Technology and Design, Singapore, Singapore
john_castellanos@mymail.sutd.edu.sg, jianying_zhou@sutd.edu.sg

Abstract. Evaluating the security of Cyber-Physical Systems (CPS) is challenging, mainly because it brings risks that are not acceptable in mission-critical systems like Industrial Control Systems (ICS). Model-based approaches help to address such challenges by keeping the risk associated with testing low. This paper presents a novel modelling framework and methodology that can easily be adapted to different CPS. Based on our experiments, *HybLearner* takes less than 140 s to build a model from historical data of a real-world water treatment testbed, and *HybTester* can simulate accurately about 60 min ahead of normal behaviour of the system including transitions of control strategies. We also introduce a security metrics (*time-to-critical-state*) that gives a measurement of how fast the system might reach a critical state, which is one of the use cases of the proposed framework to build a model-based attack detection mechanism.

Keywords: Cyber-Physical Systems security ·
Black-box security testing · Model-based attack detection

1 Introduction

Running security tests on Cyber-Physical Systems (CPS) is very challenging, especially in the subset of Industrial Control Systems (ICS). They are mission-critical systems that provide essential products/services in modern societies, for example, water treatment and distribution, power grid and transportation infrastructures. Due to risks associated with security tests over operating ICS, experts suggest to perform tests only at the design phase or during a specific operation window, to minimise the availability issues.

Researchers have proposed various model-based testing approaches to address this challenge [1,5,6,12]. There are two paradigms for model-based security testing, white-box and black-box. A white-box approach is appropriate for security testing in the design phase because it can generate an accurate and precise model of the system [5,6]. Unfortunately, it is not always the case, and it is why a black-box approach might be considered.

Researchers from different fields propose multiple techniques to perform black-box or data-driven modelling. *System identification* [7,15] models a system from control and system engineering disciplines, and *automata learning* [18]

© Springer Nature Switzerland AG 2019
R. H. Deng et al. (Eds.): ACNS 2019, LNCS 11464, pp. 196–216, 2019.
https://doi.org/10.1007/978-3-030-21568-2_10

models a system from experimental data. In this paper, we propose a methodology to perform a black-box modelling that serves as a framework to build model-based security testing on ICS.

The main contributions of this work are as follows:

- A methodology and framework to model a CPS as a hybrid system model, following a black-box approach (see Sects. 2.2 and 3). It requires a minimal initial configuration to build the model automatically, and its modular framework allows to be easily adapted to other complex systems.
- Application of hybrid system models in the study of the security of CPS. It demonstrates how to develop a model-based attack detection mechanism (see Sect. 4).
- Introduction of the concept of *time-to-critical-state* as metrics to get insights into security in CPS (see Sect. 3.3). It can be applied to evaluate attack impacts and resilience of the system.

2   Background

2.1   Hybrid Systems

Hybrid systems are extended-state machines that are composed of inputs, outputs, state variables, locations, events and guards [2,8]. Likewise a cyber-physical system, a control system can be represented as a *hybrid system* (see Fig. 1a), where continuous-time components interact with discrete-time components through Analog-to-Digital converters (ADC) and Digital-to-Analog (DAC). The continuous-time system can be considered as the physical process (*Plant*) or the physical domain in CPS. The discrete-time system refers to the cyber domain in CPS or *Controllers* for ICS, and DAC and ADC converters represent actuators and sensors, respectively.

A cyber-physical system can be divided into a set of subsystems, each of which is composed of controllers, sensors, actuators and section of the plant. Similarly, critical states can be split using the same approach. The subsystems have their critical states related to components functionality and can be monitored by the particular controller. They are called **local critical states**, e.g. a tank reaches an overflow level. On the other hand, there are critical states that are related to the interaction of two or more subsystems' states, and it is only detected from a global monitor. They are called **global critical states**, e.g. a tank with a shallow level while another controller demands liquid provision from it.

A more formal definition of hybrid systems and the theoretical framework we use to build our approach is as follows.

2.2   Definition of CPS as Hybrid Automaton

We use the *Hybrid Automata* [2,8,11,22] as the framework to model cyber-physical systems.

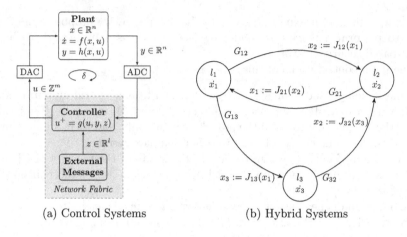

(a) Control Systems   (b) Hybrid Systems

Fig. 1. System models

A hybrid system $\mathbb{H}$ (see Fig. 1b) can be defined as a five-tuple (L, X, E, Inv, Act), where each of the components is defined as follows.

- A set of discrete-time variables L called *locations* (or *modes* [8,11]).
- An n-dimensional manifold X called *states*. The variables $X \in \mathbb{R}^n; X = \{x_1, x_2, \ldots, x_n\}$ in continuous-time t, where $n \in \mathbb{N}$ is known as the dimension of $\mathbb{H}$.
- A set of discrete *events* E depicted as directed edges, each of which connects two *locations* $\{l, l'\}$ to represent a transition $l \rightarrow l'$. (In ICS, it represents a transition between different control strategies.) E has additional parameters such as *edge identifier* e, $Guard_e$, and $Jump_e$. $Guard_e$ is a subset of X. When x reaches a value in this set, $\mathbb{H}$ triggers the transition $l \rightarrow l'$. $Jump_e$ (also known as *Reset* [8,11]) is a function that maps $x \rightarrow x'$ from a state-space in $Guard_e$ to a state-space that belongs to the new *location* l'.
- Inv is known as the *location invariant*. $Inv(l) \subset X$ when $\mathbb{H}$ is in l, x must satisfy $x \in Inv(l)$.
- Act describes a set of first order derivatives $(\dot{x})$, also called *flows* [8], that describes how X evolves during continuous-time t when $\mathbb{H}$ stays at l.

In each location l, there exists inputs $u \in \mathbb{Z}^m$, state variables $x \in \mathbb{R}^n$, and outputs $y \in \mathbb{R}^n$, where $m \in \mathbb{N}$ is known as the dimension of the input set and n, as described above, is the dimension of $\mathbb{H}$. The output depends on the current state variable and the input $y = h_y(x, u)$, and the state variable evolves according to its current state and the input $(\dot{x} = f_x(x, u))$. The system state holds over the interval $[0, \delta]; 0 \leq t \leq \delta$. As described in Fig. 1a, δ is also known as the sampling period and represents a bridge that syncs continuous and discrete time, t and k respectively. Continuous-time components are regulated for t and discrete-time components for k. The control strategy (u^+) is evaluated in each new step $k + 1$ and depends on current values of $u[k]$, $y[k]$ and $z[k]$.

3   Approach

We propose a two-fold methodology, *Learning Phase* (*HybLearner*) and *Evaluation Phase* (*HybTester*). The *learning phase* aims to build a model from experimental data that is a good abstraction of the real system, while the *evaluation phase* aims to test if the produced model is accurate compared with new data.

3.1   Learning Phase - *HybLearner*

HybLearner (Algorithm 1) assumes we have historical data or real-time data and network traffic captures. The model of the system is the composition of all controllers' views (sub-models). The learning phase is split into different stages as depicted in Fig. 2. The process is considered as a controller-based approach, where each controller is responsible for building and maintaining its model.

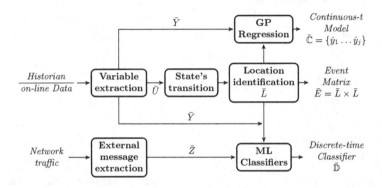

Fig. 2. *HybLearner* framework (*learning phase*)

Variable Classification

As part of the earliest stage, we split raw data into, *plant's inputs, plant's outputs* and *external messages* (u, y, z). *Plant's inputs* are signals that travel from controllers to the plant (actuator signals for ICS, $\bar{U}$ in Sect. 2.2). *Plant's outputs* are feedback signals (set $\bar{Y}$ in Sect. 2.2). *External messages* are selected from analysis to network traffic in each controller (see Algorithm 2). Reading and writing messages to/from other entities, like HMI and supervisory systems, are considered as part of set $\bar{Z}$.

Identifying Locations

For all *plant's inputs* $u \in \mathbb{Z}^m$, we check if there is a transition $v_i : u_i \rightarrow u'_i$, where v_i is a 2-tuple (u_i, u'_i). Location set L is a unique combination of m sets of 2-tuples $L = \{l_1, l_2, \ldots, l_{max}\}$, where $l_1 = v_1 \| v_2 \| \ldots \| v_m$.

Algorithm 1. *HybLearner*

Input : Historian/real-time data *(Raw)*, Network capture *(Net)* and
Configuration file *(CF)*.
Output: Continuous-t model ($\bar{\mathbb{C}}$), Discrete classifier ($\bar{\mathbb{D}}$).

```
1  u, y ←LoadLabel(CF)
2  z = LoadExtLabel(CF,Net)
3  L, F ← Hashtable()
4  c, l_old ← 0, U_old ← {OFF, . . . }, Modelling ← True, Ȳ ← List()
5  while Learning do
6  │   U_i, Y_i, Z_i ← Raw[u, y, z]
7  │   if U_old ≠ U_i then
8  │   │   if Modelling then
9  │   │   │   C[l] ← GPTrain(Ȳ)              // Apply regression technique
10 │   │   │   Modelling ← False
11 │   │   └   Ȳ ← List()         // clear Ȳ for next continuous modelling
12 │   │   if L.contains(U_i) then
13 │   │   └   Modelling ← False
14 │   │   else
15 │   │   │   c ← c + 1
16 │   │   │   L.insert(U_i : c)
17 │   │   └   Modelling ← True
18 │   │   l ← L[U_i]
19 │   │   U_old ← U_i
20 │   │   Ȳ.insert(Y_i)
21 │   │   F[l_old].insert(Y_i, Z_i, l)
22 │   └   l_old ← l
23 D̄ ← TrainClassifier(F)              // Apply classification technique
24 H ← (C̄, D̄)
25 return H
```

Building the Local Finite State Machine Model

We create *locations* as nodes, and each *event* is stored as a directed edge from the source *location* to the destination *location*.

Learning Continuous Dynamics

In each independent *event*, we learn the continuous dynamics of the system's $\dot{x}$. It includes resets *(jumps)* and derivatives *(Act)* in new modes from Sect. 2.2. We manage this as a regression problem in Machine Learning field. We propose to use a non-parametric regression algorithm like Gaussian Processes to learn the continuous dynamics because it can produce high order models.

Inferring Guards and Events

Usually, control strategies are triggered by particular conditions, e.g. close a valve once a tank has reached a certain level. We hypothesise that this transition can be modelled as a multi-class classification problem. To do so, we propose to

---

Algorithm 2. LoadExtLabel

Input : Configuration file *(CF)* and Network capture *(Net)*.
Output: Set of external labels *(z)*.

```
/* This algortihm aims to capture all external interactions from
   other controllers using the network. Control transitions depend
   on state of local and remote variables.                        */
```

1 $myIP \leftarrow$ LoadIP(CF) // Read controller's IP
2 $z =$ List()   // Empty list to store external labels
3 **for** All packets pk in *Net* **do**
4   **if** $pk.srcIP = myIP \land pk.msg$ *is reading* **then**
5   extLabel $\leftarrow$ pk.dstVar
6   **else if** $pk.dstIP = myIP \land pk.msg$ *is writing* **then**
7   extLabel $\leftarrow$ pk.dstVar
8   **if** $extLabel \neq \emptyset \land \neg z.contains(extLabel)$ **then**
9          $z.$insert$(extLabel)$
10     $extLabel \leftarrow \emptyset$
11 **return** z

---

train a classifier per each *location* with ($\bar{Y}$ and $\bar{Z}$) as features. The categorical variables are the possible l' *locations* that an *event* might transit to, it takes the event matrix E (see Fig. 2). To improve classifier accuracy, we include feature-enhancing and feature-selection steps, where only the most relevant features are considered in the training phase.

Boosting Classifier Accuracy
We extend the feature set including a set $\Delta\bar{Y}$. It captures the dynamic behaviour of $\bar{Y}$ (sensor readings) from previous values, i.e. $y[k-5] \rightarrow y[k]$.

A training set composed by $\bar{Y}$, $\Delta\bar{Y}$ and $\bar{Z}$ contain features that bring different relevance in each location. For example, for a location l_1 where a valve is filling a tank the level sensor y_1 is more relevant than a flow sensor y_2 that is connected to another part of the system, then it makes sense to use y_1 instead of y_2 as a feature in the training set. As a feature-selection step, we rank the features using the Gini importance metric (extra-trees classifier) and train the classifier with the most relevant features in that particular location.

Model Composition - The Whole System's View
A system model is composed by the combination of all controllers' views. $\bar{\mathbb{H}} = \mathbb{H}_1\|\mathbb{H}_2\|\dots\|\mathbb{H}_r$ for r number of controllers.

It requires all controllers share information through a common data structure, and synchronise under the same discrete-time scale (k). Then all *HybLearner*'s instances write and read variable states to the same data structure.

3.2   Evaluation Phase - *HybTester*

Algorithm 3. *HybTester*

Input   : Initial conditions: *init*, Discrete classifier: $\bar{\mathbb{D}}$ and Continuous-t
            model: $\bar{\mathbb{C}}$.

Output: Prediction of sensor readings on next step y^+.

1 $u_0, y_0, z_0 \leftarrow init()$ // load initial conditions

2 $l \leftarrow \text{FindLocation}(u_0)$ // Identify current location

3 $c_l \leftarrow \bar{\mathbb{C}}[l]$ // Load the continuous-time model

4 $d_l \leftarrow \bar{\mathbb{D}}[l]$ // Load the discrete-time classifier

5 **while** *Testing* **do**

6 $\quad$ $y^+ \leftarrow c_l(y_0)$ // Predict next step (continuous-time variables)

7 $\quad$ $z^+ \leftarrow \text{GetRemoteValue}()$

8 $\quad$ $l' \leftarrow d_l(y^+, z^+)$ // Predict if an event $l \to l'$ takes place

9 $\quad$ **if** $l \neq l'$ **then**

   $\quad\quad$ /* In case of transition, update model and classifier   */

10 $\quad\quad$ $c_l \leftarrow \bar{\mathbb{C}}[l']$

11 $\quad\quad$ $d_l \leftarrow \bar{\mathbb{D}}[l']$

12 $\quad\quad$ $l \leftarrow l'$

13 $\quad$ $y_0 \leftarrow y^+$

HybTester (Algorithm 3) takes the initial condition (*init*), the discrete-time classifier ($\bar{\mathbb{D}}$) and the continuous-time model ($\bar{\mathbb{C}}$) as input parameters, and produces an estimation of y^+ and u^+ for a period of steps ahead. From *init*, it extracts initial values for set u, y and z. From the initial u_0, it deduces initial location l and loads continuous-time model c_l and discrete-time classifier d_l. *HybTester* predicts next step values of sensor readings y^+ based on continuous-time predictor c_l. On each time step *HybTester*, through classifier d_l, checks if there are conditions that trigger an *event* $l \to l'$ from the current location. If d_l predicts an *event* occurs, new continuous-time model $c_{l'}$ and discrete-time classifier $d_{l'}$ are loaded, and the process continues.

3.3   A Security Metrics: *Time-to-Critical-State* (t_q)

Critical states can be considered as a state where the system operation cannot satisfy minimal safety conditions and threatens product or service quality or human lives. In the literature, *distance to critical states* was proposed as security measurement [3,16,21]. In addition, Krotofil and Cárdenas highlighted the importance of including the time dimension in the resilience analysis of CPS [12].

Contributing in the same direction, we aim to answer two questions regarding security metrics in CPS, how far is the current system state to the nearest critical state, and how fast could the system reach the nearest critical state?

We propose to measure the '*distance*' from the current state to the nearest critical states, not only considering where the critical states are, but how fast the system might get there. We compute this considering the fastest pace of system evolution according to the system's historical registers (worst case scenario).

There are different levels of critical states. One is what we call *local critical states*, and those depend on particular components, e.g. in a water treatment plant, a pump is activated when there is no liquid flowing through it. Others are *global critical states*, where the combination of multiple components states will configure a critical state of the system, even if local components are in a non-critical states, e.g. in transportation systems, a train approaches a station where another train is stationary as each controller only monitors local critical states for each component.

After the learning phase we can identify the set of critical states $\bar{Q}$ and the points from 'normal' operation that are the nearest to them, denoted as x_q. In each location l, states evolve to a different rate $(\dot{x})$, e.g. the filling rate of a tank. Then we compute the ***time-to-critical-state*** (t_q) as the time that the system will take to reach q from x_q under the fastest rate captured during the learning phase (the worst scenario).

$$r_q = \max\{\dot{x}_l : l \in \bar{L}\}$$
$$t_q = \frac{q - x_q}{r_q}; \quad \forall q \in \bar{Q} \tag{1}$$

t_q is expressed in terms of steps (k), the conversion to time units (t) depends on the sampling period (δ), as described in Sect. 2.2, which varies from CPS to CPS, e.g. δ in water treatment plants is in the scale of seconds while in smart grids it is in scale of milliseconds.

4   Use Case: Model-Based Attack Detection

As ***HybLearner*** automatically learns a system's 'normal' behaviour, our hypothesis is that we could detect data-oriented attacks [4,9,21] using a *HybTester-powered* framework. In general, the literature shows that residual analysis is an acceptable practice to detect data-deception attacks [13,17,20]. Cárdenas et al. [4] were one of the first in proposing the use of non-parametric cumulative sum algorithm (CUSUM) to detect data-oriented attacks. We adopt the same approach since it was shown to be appropriate for model-based systems as *HybLearner* and *HybTester*.

The CUSUM detector relies on two parameters (b and τ). b represents the recovery ratio, and it is inversely proportional to the time-to-detection parameter. If b is too small, it might increase the number of false positives. b should be chosen such that

$$\mathbb{E}\|\tilde{y}(k) - \hat{y}(k)\| - b < 0 \tag{2}$$

The CUSUM measurement $S(k)$ in step k is computed as:

$$S(k) = (S(k-1) + \epsilon(k))^+ \tag{3}$$

where

$$S(0) = 0; \epsilon(k) = \|\tilde{y}(k) - \hat{y}(k)\| - b \tag{4}$$

$\hat{y}(k)$ is the value of variable y from the system and $\hat{y}(k)$ is the predicted value of y both evaluated at step k. The optimal b can be chosen by **HybTester** during a period of '*normal*' operation.

The parameter τ is the threshold where a system's behaviour deviates enough to be considered as abnormal, and it can trigger an attack detection. If the threshold increases, the probability of false alarm decreases abruptly. The detection rule is given by:

$$D_\tau := \begin{cases} H_1 & \text{if } S(k) > \tau \\ H_0 & \text{otherwise} \end{cases}$$

To do so, during the *evaluation phase* we automatically compute a threshold τ. In the running phase, a monitoring system will compute the difference between monitored values and predicted ones. If $S(k)$ is greater than the computed τ, it might raise an alarm.

5   Implementation

5.1   Testbed: A Water Treatment Plant

SWaT is a six-stage system built for research purposes in cyber-security of critical infrastructures[1].

A PLC controls each stage of the testbed. Stage one takes raw water from external sources, stores it in a tank, and feeds other stages on-demand. Stage two measures water properties like conductivity and add chemicals (HCl, NaCl and NaOCl) according to a control strategy. Stage three is the ultra-filtration (UF) process, which has a set of pumps to feed a UF membrane filter to remove water solids of a certain size. Stage four is a de-Chlorination system, which uses Ultraviolet (UV) radiation to eliminate residual chlorine and chloramines, and complements the filtering process with a Sodium Bisulfite (NaHSO$_3$) dosing. Stage five is the Reverse Osmosis (RO) process, which operates continuously monitoring the conductivity of the water and executing a pre-configured sequence controlled by a PLC. Stage six stores the resulting product from the previous stage into a tank, and water from this stage is used to clean the RO membrane, and the exceeding product is recycled.

5.2   Toy Example: A Water Tank Filling Subsystem

Figure 3 depicts a simplified version of Stage one of the testbed. We use this subsystem to describe the modelling process, show how to apply the *time-to-critical-state* and implement a detection mechanism.

---

[1] http://itrust.sutd.edu.sg/research/testbeds/secure-water-treatment-swat/.

Control Strategy. The goal of the controller is to keep enough amount of water between H and L levels to guarantee the liquid can be provided for later stages. If the tank level is H, the controller closes MV. When tank level hits L, the controller opens MV and starts filling the tank. The actions on Pumps $P1$, $P2$ depend on the demand of later stages.

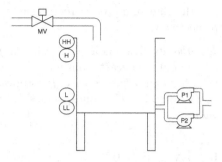

Critical States ($\bar{\mathbb{Q}}$). Stage one has two local *critical states*. q_1 is related to the risk of tank overflow ($HH \leftarrow 1000.0\,\text{mm}$). q_2 is

Fig. 3. Example of a water tank filling system.

associated with the risk of tank underflow because running any of the pumps $P1$ or $P2$ might cause severe damage on any of them ($LL \leftarrow 50.0\,\text{mm}$). Stage one operation can be represented as follows:

$$\text{Stage1 Op} := \begin{cases} q_1 & \text{if } Level \, > \, HH\,(1000) \\ q_2 & \text{if } Level \, < \, LL\,(50) \\ Normal & \text{otherwise} \end{cases}$$

5.3 Infrastructure

As we highlighted before, the framework was developed in a modular manner. It helps to extend the framework to more complex systems. We use *Python 3.6* as the main programming language. Nevertheless, similar approaches can be developed using faster languages like *C++* or *Rust*. They might be considered in the case an on-line modeller is needed, or a system with more strict sampling period δ (e.g. in power grids).

Main infrastructure components are described as follows:

Configuration File. It stores the minimal information that *HybLearn* needs to model a subsystem. It contains Controller's identification (IP address, process), control labels like U = [u1, u2, ...], sensor signal labels, i.e. Y = [y1, y2, ...], and learning period (number of steps).

LoadExtLabel Program. As described in Algorithm 2, we programmed a network traffic parser using the *Scapy*[2] library. The testbed network runs over ethernet/CIP protocol, so we filter TCP/44818 and UDP/2222 traffic, and validate *reading*(0x4c) and *writing*(0x4d) CIP services. The script returns the variable names from remote entities (other controllers or SCADA) that interact with the local controller.

HybLearner and HybTester Programs (Algorithms 1 and 3). They use *neomodel*[3] and *sqlalchemy*[4] libraries to connect to the Databases. The SVM classifier

---

[2] https://scapy.net/.
[3] https://neomodel.readthedocs.io/en/latest/.
[4] Database toolkit for Python (https://www.sqlalchemy.org/).

and the Gaussian process regression were implemented using *sklearn*[5] and *Gpy*[6], respectively.

Databases. The main DB is a Postgres database that stores all records related to raw data, forecast, continuous-time models ($\bar{\mathbb{C}}$) and discrete-time classifiers ($\bar{\mathbb{D}}$). A graph database (*neo4j*[7]) stores locations, events, event matrices, control signal variables ($\bar{U}$: names, values), and sensor signals ($\bar{Y}$: names, min and max values).

6   Evaluation

We used a dataset collected from *SWaT* during 11 days [9]. It contains sensor readings and actuator signals of all six stages of the system as described in Sect. 5.1. We fed *HybLearner* with 25k registers ($\sim$7 h) of normal operation of the testbed. We manually set the initial configuration as $\bar{Y} = \{\text{`lit101'}, \text{`fit101'}\}$ and $\bar{U} = \{\text{`mv101'}, \text{`p101'}, \text{`p102'}\}$.

The *LoadExtLabel* program processed a network capture with 300k packets. It extracted $\bar{Z}$ labels ($\{\text{`fit201'}, \text{`fit301'}, \text{`lit301'}, \text{`mv201'}\}$), which corresponds to variables from Stages two and three of the testbed. We ran *HybLearner* for different stages from the testbed. *HybLearner* took from 18.32 s up to 138.77 s to produce a hybrid model $\mathbb{H}_c$. The execution time varies depending on the number of unique *locations* and *events*.

6.1   Learning the Hybrid Model $\bar{\mathbb{H}}$

HybLearner successfully identified all operational modes of testbed's Stage one. The framework learnt seven *locations*, and nine *events*, Fig. 4 shows all transition and actions taken by actuators in each event.

Continuous-Time Modeller ($\bar{\mathbb{C}}$) and Discrete-Time Classifier ($\bar{\mathbb{D}}$)
HybLearner built nine different models ($\bar{\mathbb{C}}$), they match the nine events in Fig. 4. Figure 12 in Appendix B shows all behaviours for sensor level lit101 during 'normal' operation. Projections of the set of derivatives $\dot{y}$ (*Act*) are used below to compute the *time-to-critical-state* for the system's security evaluation.

As an example, the classification decision for location l_5 is depicted in Fig. 5. After feature selection, the top-2 most relevant features are lit101 and lit301, x-axis and y-axis respectively. It describes conditions the controller triggers a different control strategy for the transition *event* to l_4 or l_6. For example, from Fig. 4 we know that the event $l_5 \rightarrow l_4$ is associated with the change of $P1$:OFF $\rightarrow$ ON, and the event $l_5 \rightarrow l_6$ with the transition MV:ON $\rightarrow$ OFF. If we jointly analyse it with Fig. 5 (Left), we can conclude the decision rule in Fig. 5 (Right).

---

[5] https://scikit-learn.org/stable/.
[6] Gaussian process in Python (https://sheffieldml.github.io/GPy/).
[7] https://neo4j.com/.

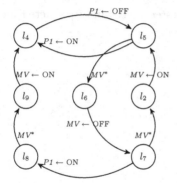

Loc.	Ctrl signals		
	MV	P1	P2
l_2	T	OFF	OFF
l_4	ON	ON	OFF
l_5	ON	OFF	OFF
l_6	T	OFF	OFF
l_7	OFF	OFF	OFF
l_8	OFF	ON	OFF
l_9	T	ON	OFF

Fig. 4. Locations learnt by *HybLearner*. Left: Finite state machine of events. MV^* is a transition state for Valve MV. Right: Location list and description of control signals ($\bar{U}$).

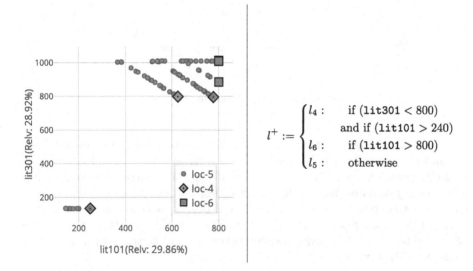

Fig. 5. Left: Top-2 most relevant features for l_5 classification, and boundaries for events $l_5 \rightarrow l_4$ and $l_5 \rightarrow l_6$. Right: Extracted decision rule (control strategy) from l_5-classification analysis.

When we compared against the operational manual of the testbed, we found a strong relationship with the control strategy programmed in the controller's source code. It demonstrates that the control strategy can be automatically learnt from experimental data.

6.2   Simulating the System

We ran *HybTester* for 5k steps (1 h 25 min in real-time) with the initial conditions lit101 = 519.55; mv101 = ON; P101 = ON; P102 = OFF. Figure 6 shows how the system evolves during this period. *HybTester* successfully predicted locations, events and sensor readings.

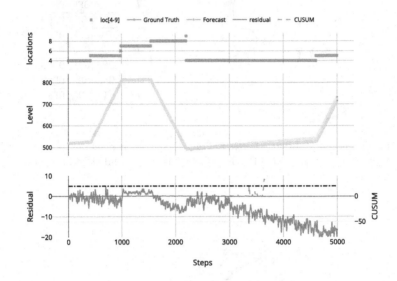

Fig. 6. System simulation for 5k steps.

The residual analysis shows that the difference between the predicted value ($\hat{y}$) and the ground truth ($\tilde{y}$) remains in the range $-10 \leq \epsilon \leq 10$, while the CUSUM value ($S[k]$) holds around 0 for the first 3.5k steps ($\sim$60 min). After 3.5k steps, $\hat{y}$ deviates from $\tilde{y}$, due to error propagation, it causes an avalanche effect in ϵ that produces $S[k]$ exceeds τ and triggers a false positive when the CUSUM detection mechanism is in place. The error propagation issue can be addressed by a periodic synchronisation between $\tilde{y}$ and $\hat{y}$, e.g. every 30 min (1.8k steps) for this scenario.

6.3   Security Metrics: Time-to-Critical-States (t_q)

As mentioned in Sect. 5.2, Stage one has two local critical states associated with lit101. One is linked to tank overflow ($q_1 = 1000.0$) and another with tank underflow ($q_2 = 50.0$) which can cause *P1*, *P2* malfunctioning. After running *HybLearner*, we automatically identify that the nearest points to $\mathbb{Q}$, x_q : $\{815.08, 120.62\}$ respectively. In Fig. 7, we project all *Acts* ($\dot{x}_l$) for all *locations* $l \in \bar{L}$. x_q is placed in the origin of the plot, and the boundaries $\mathbb{Q} - x_q$ (dashed lines) for each critical state. From $\dot{Y}$ set, we choose $\max(\dot{y}) : r_1 = 0.481$ mm/s at l_5 location, and $\min(\dot{y}) : r_2 = -0.474$ mm/s at l_8 location. Using Eq. 1 we get $t_q = \{384, 149\}$.

We can interpret this result as the 'resilience' of Stage one, which means the system can resist any data-oriented attack for at least 149 s without the risk of reaching a critical state ($\bar{\mathbb{Q}}$). The physical properties of the system guarantee it.

6.4 Attack Scenarios

We use three different attacks from the literature [1,9] to test the viability of implementing an attack detection mechanism based on *HybTester*. The attack scenarios assume an malicious actor can inject data-oriented attacks via manipulation of sensor readings y. It can be achieved by attacking the com-

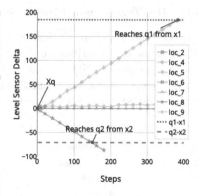

Fig. 7. Shows $\dot{y}$ in different locations for LIT101 (Level sensor). The worst scenarios are for l_5 and l_8.

munication channel sensor-actuator through Man-in-the-Middle attack or compromising sensors directly.

A1. Set Tank Level Above H
The initial conditions before the attack are the following: lit101 = 501.33; mv101 = ON; P101 = ON; P102 = OFF. The attack vector holds the tank level sensor lit101 to 801.0 just above the H label, it should cause the controller to trigger a different control strategy where MV turns OFF, and $P1$ turns ON. The attacker's goal is to bring the system to a critical state q_2 (lit101 < 50.0), attack lasts 437 steps (7 min 12 s).

A2. Set Tank Level Close to L
The initial conditions before the attack begins are: lit101 = 501, 33; mv101 = ON; P101 = OFF; P102 = OFF. The attack vector holds the tank level sensor lit101 to 244.0. It aims to mislead the controller to a different behaviour than what is expected, and the tank might keep filling up while the controller thinks it is stuck at 244.0 level. The attacker's goal is to bring the system to a critical state (q_1) (tank overflow: lit101 > 1000.0). The attack lasts 516 steps (8 min 36 s).

A3. Hold Tank Level and Increase the Level at a Constant Rate
Before the attack begins, initial conditions are: lit101 = 573.87; mv101 = ON; P101 = OFF; P102 = OFF. Attacker implements two attack vectors. The first holds the tank level sensor lit101 to the current value (574.03) for 92 steps. Then the second attack vector increases lit101 to a constant rate of 1.0 mm/s. It aims to deceive the controller into thinking the tank fills faster than usual, trigger control strategies that will help to discharge the container. The attacker's goal is similar to **A1**, brings the system to a critical state (q_2) (lit101 < 50.0). Attack duration: 473 steps (7 min 53 s).

6.5   *HybTester* as a Model-Based Attack Detection Mechanism

We combine *HybTester*'s features to predict 'normal' system operation with CUSUM as we described in Sect. 4. We set CUSUM parameters as $b = 10$, $\tau = 20$, as shown in Fig. 6. This configuration offers a very low false positive rate (1/3.5k steps). With this configuration, the monitor will trigger an alarm only when CUSUM value $S[k]$ exceeds τ (black dotted line at 20).

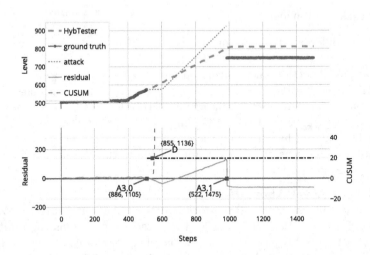

Fig. 8. Attack **A3** with a model-based attack monitor using *HybTester* and CUSUM detector. Attack starts in step $k = 510$ (A3.0) and ends in step $k = 983$ (A3.1). The attack is detected in step $k = 543$ (D).

Figure 8 shows an example of a monitoring mechanism implemented with *HybTester*. The attack corresponds to **A3** described above. The attack starts at $k = 510$ labelled as **A3.0**, and it is detected when $S > 20$ at $k = 543$, which means the monitor takes more than 30 s to detect the attack. Our analysis of *time-to-critical-state* t_q shows that the attacker is far from causing severe damage to the system. With a $t_q[k = 543]$: {855, 1136} at detection point **D**, it means that an operator has at least 855 s to implement a mitigation mechanism before the system reaches q_1.

Atk.	Start		Detect.		Stop	
	k_0	t_{q0}	k_D	t_{qD}	k_1	t_{q1}
A1	48	953	+1	944	+433	527
A2	200	778	+1	777	+518	243
A3	510	886	+33	855	+473	522

Fig. 9. Summary of attacks tested with *HybTester*. Table shows when attacks start (k_0), how many steps *HybTester* takes to detect (k_D), and how long attacks last.

Examples for attacks **A1** and **A2**, and the detection capabilities of *HybTester* are depicted in Appendix A.

Figure 9 summarises results for all attacks (**A1**–**A3**). It shows when attacks start (k_0), how long the mechanism takes to detect the attack (k_D), how long the attack lasts (k_1), and *time-to-critical-state* metrics (t_q) for each of these events. This set of examples supports our hypothesis that the combination of *HybTester* + CUSUM is suitable for building attack detection mechanisms.

Additionally, *time-to-critical-state* metrics at detection point show the buffer of time an operator has to activate response strategies, more than 12 min (>720s) for these cases. And at the point when the attack stops, the *time-to-critical-state* metrics give an approximation of impact measurement of such attack, providing information about how close an attacker could bring the system to a critical state q. These preliminary results open new possibilities to explore open challenges in the study of security of CPS. Challenges like attack quantification or impact measurements can be further explored using *HybLearner*, *HybTester* and *time-to-critical-state* in a more extensive security testing framework.

7   Related Works

Modelling CPS

Model inferring is a classical problem extensively studied in disciplines like control and system theory. Black-box approaches (also called data-driven models) propose diverse techniques like system identification [7,15], and automata learning [18]. The main difference between our approach and these traditional methodologies is that ours aims to model the CPS continuous-time and discrete-time subsystems separately. From Piecewise and Switched systems identification [7], Zimmerschied and Isermann [23] presented a method that uses the LOLIMOT algorithm to identify piecewise systems as a set of local affine models. One of most significant differences is that our approach automatically identifies transitions in actuators' states, and it helps to infer the control strategy programmed in the controllers.

Among recent approaches, we found Crystal [6] as one of the most relevant, it establishes a hybrid model that combines discrete-time and continuous-time. The authors build a model of the physical part of the CPS by combining a neural network and an extended Kalman filter. The produced model predicts next sensor values from current sensor values and the control signals. Additionally, crystal complements the modelling by symbolically executing the controller's source code (discrete part). Although crystal models a hybrid abstraction of the system, as a white-box approach, it requires to have access to the controller's source code which in most cases is inaccessible for critical systems.

Santana et al. [19] present a similar approach to our work. Subtle but remarkable differences are, **HybLearner** automatically identifies *locations*, thus making it easier for deployment in diverse CPS, additionally, its modular core, allows it to model more complex systems.

Security Metrics

In term of security metrics for CPS, most of the previous works propose a concept of *distance-to-critical-states*. For example, Carcano et al. [3] introduce *state proximity* for measuring the distance to a known critical state as the *Manhattan distance* from the current state. From the control and system theory community, Murguia et al. [16] present mathematical tools to quantify the impact of attacker's actions in a system as the distance that an attack deviates a system from its 'normal' operation. Similarly, Urbina et al. [21] introduce the *'impact of undetected attack'* measurement, which is the maximum deviation per unit of time.

Krotofil and Cárdenas [12] highlighted the concept of time as a relevant component for measuring the impact of cyber-attacks, in their process-aware cyber risk assessment for ICS. Crystal [6] presents *just-ahead-of-time analysis* (JAT), which gives a window to respond in case the system leads to a critical state. Our approach can also be used as a model-based safety monitor. More importantly, *HybTester* with *time-to-critical-state* can be implemented as a support tool that helps a system operator to decide a convenient strategy as response to a cyber-attack in the system. Another significant difference with the works in the literature is that our approach considers a measure of 'speed' of how fast the system could reach critical states.

Model-Based Attack Detection Mechanisms

Goh et al. [10] propose an anomaly detection method for a water treatment plant. The method combines Long Short Term Memory Recurrent Neural Network (LSTM-RNN) and Cumulative Sum (CUSUM) to detect anomalies in the system. LSTM-RNN learns the system behaviour from all components, sensors and actuators, and predicts the 'normal behaviour' of all components. Experimental data is compared against predicted behaviour using CUSUM.

Lin et al. [14] propose a model-based approach for attack detection in ICS (TABOR). It uses data-driven techniques to learn a probabilistic timed automata and Bayesian network. Authors applied the *Sliding WIndow based on Differential sEgmentation* (SWIDE) algorithm to extract trends in sensor readings, which is similar to the concept of *locations* applied in our methodology. The sequence and probabilities of these trends are used to evaluate the model and detect anomalies. While TABOR detection capabilities rely mainly on the sequence of events, *HybTester* applies residual analysis and CUSUM to take a decision, and the *time-to-critical-state* metrics bring additional information about the impact of attacks.

8 Conclusion

In this paper, we proposed an automatic way to build a hybrid model of a CPS from experimental data. Due to its modular nature, our approach allows analysing/evaluating components of a CPS separately. It makes computing the *'time-to-critical-state'* metrics (t_q) easier. We also showed that the new modelling framework allows us to deduce the control strategy in the system and helps us to get a more comprehensive view of the system under analysis.

This framework also opens up options for new applications. One of the use cases explored in this paper is to build a model-based detection mechanism. Even though similar ideas appeared in the literature [6,10,14,21], *HybLearner* can build the model automatically, which makes easier to adapt to other CPS, e.g. power grids and smart cars.

As future work, we plan to build an attack simulator using *HybTester* as the core of a model-based security testing framework.

Acknowledgments. This work was partly supported by SUTD start-up research grant SRG-ISTD-2017-124.

A   Model-Based Detection Mechanism

Here we show additional examples how *HybTester* can be used as a model-based detection mechanism for two attacks (**A1** and **A2**) described in Sect. 6.4 (Figs. 10 and 11).

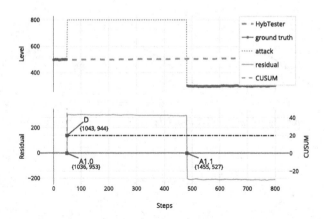

Fig. 10. Attack **A1** which starts in step $k = 48$ (A1.0) and ends in step $k = 481$ (A1.1). The attack is detected in step $k = 49$ (D).

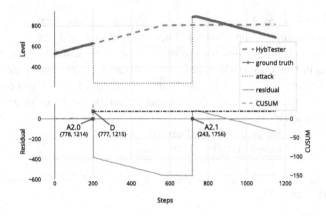

Fig. 11. Attack **A2** which starts in step $k = 200$ (A2.0) and ends in step $k = 718$ (A2.1). The attack is detected in step $k = 201$ (D).

B   Continuous-Time Models for Stage One of $SWaT$

Figure 12 shows all nine derivatives $\dot{y}$ for lit101.

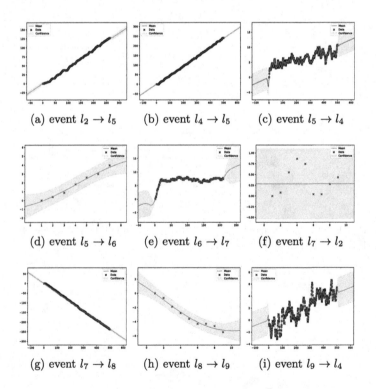

Fig. 12. Continuous-time model $\bar{\mathbb{C}}$.

References

1. Adepu, S., Mathur, A.: An investigation into the response of a water treatment system to cyber attacks. In: 2016 IEEE 17th International Symposium on High Assurance Systems Engineering (HASE) (2016)
2. Alur, R.: Principles of Cyber-Physical Systems. MIT Press, Cambridge (2015)
3. Carcano, A., Coletta, A., Guglielmi, M., Masera, M., Fovino, I.N., Trombetta, A.: A multidimensional critical state analysis for detecting intrusions in SCADA systems. IEEE Trans. Ind. Inform. **7**, 179–186 (2011)
4. Cárdenas, A.A., Amin, S., Lin, Z.S., Huang, Y.L., Huang, C.Y., Sastry, S.: Attacks against process control systems: risk assessment, detection, and response. In: Proceedings of the 6th ACM Symposium on Information, Computer and Communications Security (CCS) (2011)
5. Castellanos, J.H., Ochoa, M., Zhou, J.: Finding dependencies between cyber-physical domains for security testing of industrial control systems. In: Proceedings of the 34th Annual Computer Security Applications Conference (ACSAC) (2018)
6. Etigowni, S., Hossain-McKenzie, S., Kazerooni, M., Davis, K., Zonouz, S.: Crystal (ball): I look at physics and predict control flow! just-ahead-of-time controller recovery. In: Proceedings of the 34th Annual Computer Security Applications Conference (ACSAC) (2018)
7. Garulli, A., Paoletti, S., Vicino, A.: A survey on switched and piecewise affine system identification. In: IFAC Proceedings Volumes (2012)
8. Goebel, R., Teel, A.R., Sanfelice, R.G.: Hybrid Dynamical Systems: Modeling, Stability, and Robustness. Princeton University Press, Princeton (2012)
9. Goh, J., Adepu, S., Junejo, K.N., Mathur, A.: A dataset to support research in the design of secure water treatment systems. In: Havarneanu, G., Setola, R., Nassopoulos, H., Wolthusen, S. (eds.) CRITIS 2016. LNCS, vol. 10242, pp. 88–99. Springer, Cham (2017). https://doi.org/10.1007/978-3-319-71368-7_8
10. Goh, J., Adepu, S., Tan, M., Shan, L.Z.: Anomaly detection in cyber physical systems using recurrent neural networks. In: 2017 IEEE 18th International Symposium on High Assurance Systems Engineering (HASE) (2017)
11. Henzinger, T.A.: The theory of hybrid automata. In: Inan, M.K., Kurshan, R.P. (eds.) Verification of Digital and Hybrid Systems. NATO ASI Series, vol. 170, pp. 265–292. Springer, Heidelberg (2000). https://doi.org/10.1007/978-3-642-59615-5_13
12. Krotofil, M., Cárdenas, A.A.: Resilience of process control systems to cyber-physical attacks. In: Riis Nielson, H., Gollmann, D. (eds.) NordSec 2013. LNCS, vol. 8208, pp. 166–182. Springer, Heidelberg (2013). https://doi.org/10.1007/978-3-642-41488-6_12
13. Kwon, C., Liu, W., Hwang, I.: Security analysis for cyber-physical systems against stealthy deception attacks. In: American Control Conference (ACC) (2013)
14. Lin, Q., Adepu, S., Verwer, S., Mathur, A.: TABOR: a graphical model-based approach for anomaly detection in industrial control systems. In: Proceedings of the 2018 on Asia Conference on Computer and Communications Security (2018)
15. Ljung, L.: System identification. In: Procházka, A., Uhlíř, J., Rayner, P.W.J., Kingsbury, N.G. (eds.) Signal Analysis and Prediction. ANHA, pp. 163–173. Springer, Boston (1998). https://doi.org/10.1007/978-1-4612-1768-8_11
16. Murguia, C., van de Wouw, N., Ruths, J.: Reachable sets of hidden CPS sensor attacks: analysis and synthesis tools. IFAC-PapersOnLine (2017)

17. Pasqualetti, F., Dörfler, F., Bullo, F.: Attack detection and identification in cyber-physical systems. IEEE Trans. Autom. Control **58**, 2715–2729 (2013)
18. Raffelt, H., Steffen, B.: LearnLib: a library for automata learning and experimentation. In: Baresi, L., Heckel, R. (eds.) FASE 2006. LNCS, vol. 3922, pp. 377–380. Springer, Heidelberg (2006). https://doi.org/10.1007/11693017_28
19. Santana, P.H., Lane, S., Timmons, E., Williams, B.C., Forster, C.: Learning hybrid models with guarded transitions. In: Conference on Artificial Intelligence (2015)
20. Teixeira, A., Amin, S., Sandberg, H., Johansson, K.H., Sastry, S.S.: Cyber security analysis of state estimators in electric power systems. In: 49th IEEE Conference on Decision and Control (CDC) (2010)
21. Urbina, D.I., et al.: Limiting the impact of stealthy attacks on industrial control systems. In: Proceedings of the 2016 ACM SIGSAC Conference on Computer and Communications Security (CCS) (2016)
22. Van Der Schaft, A.J., Schumacher, J.M.: An Introduction to Hybrid Dynamical Systems, vol. 251. Springer, London (2000). https://doi.org/10.1007/BFb0109998
23. Zimmerschied, R., Isermann, R.: Nonlinear system identification of block-oriented systems using local affine models. In: IFAC Proceedings Volumes (2009)

PassGAN: A Deep Learning Approach for Password Guessing

Briland Hitaj[1]([✉]), Paolo Gasti[2], Giuseppe Ateniese[1],
and Fernando Perez-Cruz[3]

[1] Stevens Institute of Technology, Hoboken, NJ 07030, USA
{bhitaj,gatenies}@stevens.edu
[2] New York Institute of Technology, New York, NY 10023, USA
pgasti@nyit.edu
[3] Swiss Data Science Center, (ETH Zurich and EPFL), Zürich, Switzerland
fernando.perezcruz@sdsc.ethz.ch

Abstract. State-of-the-art password guessing tools, such as HashCat and John the Ripper, enable users to check billions of passwords per second against password hashes. In addition to performing straightforward dictionary attacks, these tools can expand password dictionaries using password generation rules, such as concatenation of words (e.g., "password123456") and *leet speak* (e.g., "password" becomes "p4s5w0rd"). Although these rules work well in practice, creating and expanding them to model further passwords is a labor-intensive task that requires specialized expertise.

To address this issue, in this paper we introduce PassGAN, a novel approach that replaces human-generated password rules with theory-grounded machine learning algorithms. Instead of relying on manual password analysis, PassGAN uses a Generative Adversarial Network (GAN) to autonomously learn the distribution of real passwords from actual password leaks, and to generate high-quality password guesses. Our experiments show that this approach is very promising. When we evaluated PassGAN on two large password datasets, we were able to surpass rule-based and state-of-the-art machine learning password guessing tools. However, in contrast with the other tools, PassGAN achieved this result without any a-priori knowledge on passwords or common password structures. Additionally, when we combined the output of PassGAN with the output of HashCat, we were able to match 51%–73% more passwords than with HashCat alone. This is remarkable, because it shows that PassGAN can autonomously extract a considerable number of password properties that current state-of-the art rules do not encode.

Keywords: Passwords · Privacy ·
Generative Adversarial Networks (GAN) · Deep learning

An extended version of this paper is available at: https://arxiv.org/abs/1709.00440. A preliminary version of this paper appeared in NeurIPS 2018 Workshop on Security in Machine Learning (SecML'18) [25].

R. H. Deng et al. (Eds.): ACNS 2019, LNCS 11464, pp. 217–237, 2019.
https://doi.org/10.1007/978-3-030-21568-2_11

1   Introduction

Passwords are the most popular authentication method, mainly because they are easy to implement, require no special hardware or software, and are familiar to users and developers [28]. Unfortunately, multiple password database leaks have shown that users tend to choose easy-to-guess passwords [10,14,37], primarily composed of common strings (e.g., `password`, `123456`, `iloveyou`), and variants thereof.

Password guessing tools provide a valuable tool for identifying weak passwords when they are stored in hashed form [50,54]. The effectiveness of password guessing software relies on the ability to quickly test a large number of highly likely passwords against each password hash. Instead of exhaustively trying all possible character combinations, password guessing tools use words from dictionaries and previous password leaks as candidate passwords. State-of-the-art password guessing tools, such as John the Ripper [56] and HashCat [22], take this approach one step further by defining heuristics for password transformations, which include combinations of multiple words (e.g., `iloveyou123456`), mixed letter case (e.g., `iLoVeyOu`), and *leet speak* (e.g., `il0v3you`). These heuristics, in conjunction with Markov models, allow John the Ripper and HashCat to generate a large number of *new* highly likely passwords.

While these heuristics are reasonably successful in practice, they are ad-hoc and based on intuitions on how users choose passwords, rather than being constructed from a principled analysis of large password datasets. For this reason, each technique is ultimately limited to capturing a specific subset of the password space which depends upon the intuition behind that technique. Further, developing and testing new rules and heuristics is a time-consuming task that requires specialized expertise, and therefore has limited scalability.

1.1   Our Approach

To address these shortcomings, in this paper we propose to replace rule-based password guessing, as well as password guessing based on simple data-driven techniques such as Markov models, with a novel approach based on deep learning. At its core, our idea is to train a neural network to determine autonomously password characteristics and structures, and to leverage this knowledge to generate new samples that follow the same distribution. We hypothesize that deep neural networks are expressive enough to capture a large variety of properties and structures that describe the majority of user-chosen passwords; at the same time, neural networks can be trained without any a-priori knowledge or an assumption of such properties and structures. This is in stark contrast with current approaches such as Markov models (which implicitly assume that all relevant password characteristics can be defined in terms of n-grams), and rule-based approaches (which can guess only passwords that match with the available rules). As a result, samples generated using a neural network are not limited to a particular subset of the password space. Instead, neural networks can autonomously encode a wide range of password-guessing knowledge that includes and surpasses what is captured in human-generated rules and Markovian password generation processes.

To test this hypothesis, in this paper we introduce PassGAN, a new approach for generating password guesses based on deep learning and Generative Adversarial Networks (GANs) [18]. GANs are recently-introduced machine learning tools designed to perform density estimation in high-dimensional spaces [18]. GANs perform implicit generative modeling by training a deep neural network architecture that is fed a simple random distribution (e.g., Gaussian or uniform) and by generating samples that follow the distribution of the available data. In a way, they implicitly model the inverse of the cumulative distribution with a deep neural network, i.e., $\mathbf{x} = F_\theta^{-1}(s)$ where s is a uniformly distributed random variable. To learn the generative model, GANs use a cat-and-mouse game, in which a deep generative network (G) tries to mimic the underlying distribution of the samples, while a discriminative deep neural network (D) tries to distinguish between the original training samples (i.e., "true samples") and the samples generated by G (i.e., "fake samples"). This adversarial procedure forces D to leak the relevant information about the training data. This information helps G to adequately reproduce the original data distribution.

PassGAN leverages this technique to generate new password guesses. We train D using a list of leaked passwords (real samples). At each iteration, the output of PassGAN (fake samples) gets closer to the distribution of passwords in the original leak, and therefore more likely to match real users' passwords. To the best of our knowledge, this work is the first to use GANs for this purpose.

1.2   Contributions

PassGAN represents a principled and theory-grounded take on the generation of password guesses. We explore and evaluate different neural network configurations, parameters, and training procedures, to identify the appropriate balance between *learning* and *overfitting*, and report our results. Specifically, our contributions are as follows:

1. We show that a GAN can generate high-quality password guesses. Our GAN is trained on a portion of the RockYou dataset [58], and tested on two different datasets: (1) another (distinct) subset of the RockYou dataset; and (2) a dataset of leaked passwords from LinkedIn [36]. In our experiments, we were able to match 1,350,178 (43.6%) *unique* passwords out of 3,094,199 passwords from the RockYou dataset, and 10,478,322 (24.2%) unique passwords out of 43,354,871 passwords from the LinkedIn dataset. To quantify the ability of PassGAN to generate new passwords, we removed from the testing set all passwords that were present also in the training set. This resulted in testing sets of size 1,978,367 and 40,593,536 for RockYou and LinkedIn, respectively. In this setting, PassGAN was able to match 676,439 (34.6%) samples in the RockYou testing set and 8,878,284 (34.2%) samples in the LinkedIn set. Moreover, the overwhelming majority of passwords generated by PassGAN that did not match the testing sets still "looked like" human-generated passwords,

and thus could potentially match real user accounts not considered in our experiments.

2. We show that PassGAN is competitive with state-of-the-art password generation rules. Even though these rules were specially tuned for the datasets used in our evaluation, the quality of PassGAN's output was comparable to that of password rules.

3. With password generation rules, the number of unique passwords that can be generated is defined by the number of rules and by the size of the password dataset used to instantiate them. In contrast, PassGAN can output a practically unbounded number of password guesses. Crucially, our experiments show that with PassGAN the number of matches increases steadily with the number of passwords generated, Table 1. This is important because it shows that the output of PassGAN is not restricted to a small subset of the password space.

4. PassGAN is competitive with current state of the art password guessing algorithms based on deep neural networks [39], matching the performance of Melicher et al. [39], (indicated as FLA in the rest of the paper).

5. We show that PassGAN can be effectively used to *augment* password generation rules. In our experiments, PassGAN matched passwords that were not generated by any password rule. When we combined the output of Pass-GAN with the output of HashCat, we were able to guess between 51% (case of RockYou) and 73% (case of LinkedIn) additional unique passwords compared to HashCat alone.

We consider this work as the first step toward a fully automated generation of high-quality password guesses. We argue that this work is relevant, important, and timely. *Relevant*, because despite numerous alternatives [13,16,51,64,72], we see little evidence that passwords will be replaced any time soon. *Important*, because establishing the limits of password guessing—and better understanding how guessable real-world passwords are—will help make password-based systems more secure. And *timely*, because recent leaks containing hundreds of millions of passwords [15] provide a formidable source of data for attackers to compromise systems, and for system administrators to re-evaluate password policies.

1.3   Organization

The rest of this paper is organized as follows. In Sect. 2, we briefly overview GANs, and password guessing, and provide a summary of the relevant state of the art. Section 3 provides details regarding our experimental setup, architectural and training choices for PassGAN, and the hyperparameters used in our evaluation. We report on the evaluation of PassGAN, and on the comparison with state-of-the-art password guessing techniques, in Sect. 4. We summarize our findings and discuss their implications, in Sect. 5. We conclude in Sect. 6.

2 Background and Related Work

2.1 Generative Adversarial Networks

Generative Adversarial Networks (GANs) translate the current advances in deep neural networks for discriminative machine learning to (implicit) generative modeling. The goal of GANs is to generate samples from the same distribution as that of its training set $S = \{x_1, x_2, \ldots, x_n\}$. Generative modeling [46] typically relies on closed-form expressions that, in many cases, cannot capture the nuisance of real data. GANs train a generative deep neural network G that takes as input a multi-dimensional random sample z (from a Gaussian or uniform distribution) to generate a sample from the desired distribution. GANs transform the density estimation problem into a binary classification problem, in which the learning of the parameters of G is achieved by relying on a discriminative deep neural network D that needs to distinguish between the "true" samples in S and the "fake" samples produced by G. More formally, the optimization problem solved by GANs can be summarized as follows [24]:

$$\min_{\theta_G} \max_{\theta_D} \sum_{i=1}^{n} \log f(x_i; \theta_D) + \sum_{j=1}^{n} \log(1 - f(g(z_j; \theta_G); \theta_D)), \tag{1}$$

where $f(x; \theta_D)$ and $g(z_j; \theta_G)$, respectively, represent D and G. The optimization shows the clash between the goals of the discriminator and generator deep neural networks. Since the original work by Goodfellow et al. [18], there have been several improvements on GANs [2–5,7,9,11,20,26,27,30,35,40,41,43,44,47,49, 52,55,59,63,67,71,73], where each new paper provides novel improvements in the domain. In this paper, we rely on IWGAN [20] as a building foundation for PassGAN, being that IWGAN [20] is among the first, most stable approaches for text generation via GANs.

2.2 Password Guessing

Password guessing attacks are probably as old as password themselves [45], with more formal studies dating back to 1979 [42]. In a password guessing attack, the adversary attempts to identify the password of one or more users by repeatedly testing multiple candidate passwords.

Two popular modern password guessing tools are John the Ripper (JTR) [56] and HashCat [22]. Both tools implement multiple types of password guessing strategies, including: exhaustive brute-force attacks; dictionary-based attacks; rule-based attacks, which consist in generating password guesses from transformations of dictionary words [60,61]; and Markov-model-based attacks [38,57]. JTR and HashCat are notably effective at guessing passwords. Specifically, there have been several instances in which well over 90% of the passwords leaked from online services have been successfully recovered [53].

Markov models were first used to generate password guesses by Narayanan et al. [48]. Their approach uses manually defined password rules, such as which portion of the generated passwords is composed of letters and numbers. Weir et al. [69] subsequently improved this technique with Probabilistic Context-Free Grammars (PCFGs). With PCFGs, Weir et al. [69] demonstrated how to "learn" these rules from password distributions. Ma et al. [37] and Durmuth et al. [14] have subsequently extended this early work.

To the best of our knowledge, the first work in the domain of passwords utilizing neural networks dates back to 2006 by Ciaramella et al. [8]. Recently, Melicher et al. [39] introduced FLA, a password guessing method based on recurrent neural networks [19,65]. However, the primary goal of these works consists in providing means for password strength estimation. For instance, Melicher et al. [39] aim at providing fast and accurate password strength estimation (thus FLA acronym), while keeping the model as lightweight as possible, and minimizing accuracy loss. By keeping the model lightweight, the reference instantiates a password strength estimator that can be used in browsers through a (local) JavaScript implementation. To achieve this goal, FLA uses weight clipping without significantly sacrificing accuracy. In contrast, PassGAN focuses on the task of password guessing and attempts to do so with no a priori knowledge or assumption on the Markovian structure of user-chosen passwords.

3   Experiment Setup

To leverage the ability of GANs to estimate the probability effectively distribution of passwords from the training set, we experimented with a variety of parameters. In this section, we report our choices on specific GAN architecture and hyperparameters.

We instantiated PassGAN using the *Improved training of Wasserstein GANs* (IWGAN) of Gulrajani et al. [20]. The IWGAN implementation used in this paper relies on the ADAM optimizer [31] to minimize the training error. The following hyper-parameters characterize our model:

- **Batch size**, which represents the number of passwords from the training set that propagate through the GAN at each step of the optimizer. We instantiated our model with a batch size of 64.
- **Number of iterations**, which indicates how many times the GAN invokes its forward step and its back-propagation step [33,34,62]. In each iteration, the GAN runs one generator iteration and one or more discriminator iterations. We trained the GAN using various number of iterations and eventually settled for 199,000 iterations, as further iterations provided diminishing returns in the number of matches.
- **Number of discriminator iterations per generator iteration**, which indicates how many iterations the discriminator performs in each GAN iteration. The number of discriminator iterations per generative iteration was set to 10, which is the default value used by IWGAN.
- **Model dimensionality**, which represents the number of dimensions for each convolutional layer. We experimented using 5 residual layers for both the

generator and the discriminator, with each of the layers in both deep neural networks having 128 dimensions.

- **Gradient penalty coefficient** (λ), which specifies the penalty applied to the norm of the gradient of the discriminator with respect to its input [20]. Increasing this parameter leads to a more stable training of the GAN [20]. In our experiments, we set the value of the gradient penalty to 10.
- **Output sequence length**, which indicates the maximum length of the strings generated by the generator (G). We modified the length of the sequence generated by the GAN from 32 characters (default length for IWGAN) to 10 characters, to match the maximum length of passwords used during training. We padded passwords shorter than 10 characters using accent symbol (i.e., "`") [20]; we then removed it from the output of PassGAN.
- **Size of the input noise vector (seed)**, which determines how many random numbers from a normal distribution are fed as input to G to generate samples. We set this size to 128 floating point numbers.
- **Maximum number of examples**, which represents the maximum number of training items (passwords, in the case of PassGAN) to load. The maximum number of examples loaded by the GAN was set to the size of the entire training dataset.
- **Adam optimizer's hyper-parameters:**
  - **Learning rate**, i.e., how quickly the weights of the model are adjusted
  - **Coefficient** β_1, which specifies the decaying rate of the running average of the gradient.
  - **Coefficient** β_2, which indicates the decaying rate of the running average of the square of the gradient.

  Coefficients β_1 and β_2 of the Adam optimizer were set to 0.5 and 0.9, respectively, while the learning rate was 10^{-4}. These parameters are the default values used by Gulrajani et al. [20].

Our experiments were run using the TensorFlow implementation of IWGAN found at [21]. We used TensorFlow version 1.2.1 for GPUs [1], with Python version 2.7.12. All experiments were performed on a workstation running Ubuntu 16.04.2 LTS, with 64 GB of RAM, a 12-core 2.0 GHz Intel Xeon CPU, and an NVIDIA GeForce GTX 1080 Ti GPU with 11 GB of global memory.

3.1 Training and Testing

To evaluate the performance of PassGAN, and to compare it with state-of-the-art password generation rules, we first trained the GAN, JTR, HashCat, the Markov model, PCFG, and FLA on a large set of passwords from the RockYou password leak [58].[1] Entries in this dataset represent a mixture of common and complex passwords.

---

[1] We consider the use of publicly available password datasets to be ethical, and consistent with security research best practices (see, e.g., [6,10,39]).

RockYou Dataset. The RockYou dataset [58] contains 32,503,388 passwords. We selected all passwords of length 10 characters or less (29,599,680 passwords, which correspond to 90.8% of the dataset), and used 80% of them (23,679,744 total passwords, 9,926,278 unique passwords) to train each password guessing tool. We refer the reader to Sect. 3.2 for further details on the training procedure of each tool. For testing, we computed the (set) difference between the remaining 20% of the dataset (5,919,936 total passwords, 3,094,199 unique passwords) and the training test. The resulting 1,978,367 entries correspond to passwords that were not previously observed by the password guessing tools. This allowed us to count only non-trivial matches in the testing set.

LinkedIn Dataset. We also tested each tool on passwords from the LinkedIn dataset [36], of length up to 10 characters, and that were not present in the training set. The LinkedIn dataset consists of 60,065,486 total unique passwords (43,354,871 unique passwords with length 10 characters or less), out of which 40,593,536 were not in the training dataset from RockYou. (Frequency counts were not available for the LinkedIn dataset.) Passwords in the LinkedIn dataset were exfiltrated as hashes, rather than in plaintext. As such, the LinkedIn dataset contains only plaintext passwords that tools such as JTR and HashCat were able to recover, thus giving rule-based systems a potential edge.

Our training and testing procedures showed: (1) how well PassGAN predicts passwords when trained and tested on the same password distribution (i.e., when using the RockYou dataset for both training and testing); and (2) whether Pass-GAN generalizes across password datasets, i.e., how it performs when trained on the RockYou dataset, and tested on the LinkedIn dataset.

3.2 Password Sampling Procedure for HashCat, JTR, Markov Model, PCFG and FLA

We used the portion of RockYou dataset selected for training, see Sect. 3.1, as the input dataset to HashCat Best64, HashCat gen2, JTR Spiderlab rules, Markov Model, PCFG, and FLA, and generated passwords as follows:

- We instantiated HashCat and JTR's rules using passwords from the training set sorted by frequency in descending order (as in [39]). HashCat Best64 generated 754,315,842 passwords, out of which 361,728,683 were unique and of length 10 characters or less. Note that this was the maximum number of samples produced by Best64 rule-set for the given input set, i.e., RockYou training set. With HashCat gen2 and JTR SpiderLab we uniformly sampled a random subset of size 10^9 from their output. This subset was composed of passwords of length 10 characters or less.
- For FLA, we set up the code from [32] according to the instruction provided in [17]. We trained a model containing 2-hidden layers and 1 dense layer of size 512. We did not perform any transformation (e.g., removing symbols, or transforming all characters to lowercase) on the training set for the sake

of consistency with the other tools. Once trained, FLA enumerates a subset of its output space defined by a probability threshold p: a password belongs to FLA's output if and only if its estimated probability is at least p. In our experiments, we set $p = 10^{-10}$. This resulted in a total of 747,542,984 passwords of length 10 characters or less. Before using these passwords in our evaluation, we sorted them by probability in descending order.

– We generated 494,369,794 unique passwords of length 10 or less using the 3-gram Markov model. We ran this model using its standard configuration [12].
– We generated 10^9 unique passwords of length 10 or less using the PCFG implementation of Weir et al. [68].

4   Evaluation

4.1   PassGAN's Output Space

To evaluate the size of the password space generated by PassGAN, we generated several password sets of sizes between 10^4 and 10^{10}. Our experiments show that, as the number of passwords increased, so did the number of unique (and therefore new) passwords generated. Results of this evaluation are reported in Table 1.

Table 1. Number of passwords generated by PassGAN that match passwords in the RockYou testing set. Results are shown in terms of unique matches.

Passwords generated	Unique passwords	Passwords matched in testing set, and not in training set (1,978,367 unique samples)
10^4	9,738	103 (0.005%)
10^5	94,400	957 (0.048%)
10^6	855,972	7,543 (0.381%)
10^7	7,064,483	40,320 (2.038%)
10^8	52,815,412	133,061 (6.726%)
10^9	356,216,832	298,608 (15.094%)
10^{10}	2,152,819,961	515,079 (26.036%)
$2 \cdot 10^{10}$	3,617,982,306	584,466 (29.543%)
$3 \cdot 10^{10}$	4,877,585,915	625,245 (31.604%)
$4 \cdot 10^{10}$	6,015,716,395	653,978 (33.056%)
$5 \cdot 10^{10}$	7,069,285,569	676,439 (34.192%)

When we increased the number of passwords generated by PassGAN, the rate at which new unique passwords were generated decreased only slightly. Similarly, the rate of increase of the number of matches (shown in Table 1) diminished slightly as the number of passwords generated increased. This is to

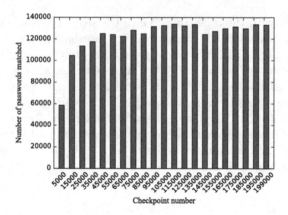

Fig. 1. Number of unique passwords generated by PassGAN on various checkpoints, matching the RockYou testing set. The x axis represents the number of iterations (checkpoints) of PassGAN's training process. For each checkpoint, we sampled 10^8 passwords from PassGAN.

be expected, as the simpler passwords are matched early on, and the remaining (more complex) passwords require a substantially larger number of attempts in order to be matched.

Impact of Training Process on Overfitting. Training a GAN is an iterative process that consists of a large number of iterations. As the number of iterations increases, the GAN learns more information from the distribution of the data. However, increasing the number of steps also increases the probability of overfitting [18,70].

To evaluate this tradeoff on password data, we stored intermediate training checkpoints and generated 10^8 passwords at each checkpoint. Figure 1 shows how many of these passwords match with the content of the RockYou testing set. In general, the number of matches increases with the number of iterations. This increase tapers off around 125,000–135,000 iterations, and then again around 190,000–195,000 iterations, where we stopped training the GAN. This indicates that further increasing the number of iterations will likely lead to overfitting, thus reducing the ability of the GAN to generate a wide variety of highly likely passwords. Therefore, we consider this range of iterations adequate for the RockYou training set.

4.2   Evaluating the Passwords Generated by PassGAN

To evaluate the quality of the output of PassGAN, we generated $5 \cdot 10^{10}$ passwords, out of which roughly $7 \cdot 10^9$ were unique. We compared these passwords with the outputs of length 10 characters or less from HashCat Best64, HashCat gen2, JTR SpiderLab, FLA, PCFG, and Markov model, see Sect. 3.2 for the configuration and sampling procedures followed for each of these tools.

Table 2. Number of matches generated by each password guessing tool against the RockYou testing set, and corresponding number of password generated by PassGAN to outperform each tool. Matches for HashCat Best64 and FLA were obtained by exhaustively enumerating the entire output of each tool. The minimum probability threshold for FLA was set to $p = 10^{-10}$.

Approach	(1) Unique passwords	(2) Matches	(3) Number of passwords required for PassGAN to outperform (2)	(4) PassGAN matches
JTR Spyderlab	10^9	461,395 (23.32%)	$1.4 \cdot 10^9$	461,398 (23.32%)
Markov Model 3-gram	$4.9 \cdot 10^8$	532,961 (26.93%)	$2.47 \cdot 10^9$	532,962 (26.93%)
HashCat gen2	10^9	597,899 (30.22%)	$4.8 \cdot 10^9$	625,245 (31.60%)
HashCat Best64	$3.6 \cdot 10^8$	630,068 (31.84%)	$5.06 \cdot 10^9$	630,335 (31.86%)
PCFG	10^9	486,416 (24.59%)	$2.1 \cdot 10^9$	511,453 (25.85%)
FLA $p = 10^{-10}$	$7.4 \cdot 10^8$	652,585 (32.99%)	$6 \cdot 10^9$	653,978 (33.06%)

In our comparisons, we aimed at establishing whether PassGAN was able to meet the performance of the other tools, *despite its lack of any a-priori knowledge on password structures*. This is because we are primarily interested in determining whether the properties that PassGAN autonomously extracts from a list of passwords can represent enough information to compete with state-of-the-art human-generated rules and Markovian password generation processes.

Our results show that, for each of the tools, PassGAN was able to generate at least the same number of matches. Additionally, to achieve this result, PassGAN needed to generate a number of passwords that was within one order of magnitude of each of the other tools. This holds for both the RockYou and the LinkedIn testing sets. This is not unexpected, because while other tools rely on prior knowledge on passwords for guessing, PassGAN does not. Table 2 summarizes our findings for the RockYou testing set, while Table 3 shows our results for the LinkedIn test set.

Our results also show that PassGAN has an advantage with respect to rule-based password matching when guessing passwords from a dataset different from the one it was trained on. In particular, PassGAN was able to match more passwords than HashCat within a smaller number of attempts ($2.1 \cdot 10^9 - 3.6 \cdot 10^9$ for LinkedIn, compared to $4.8 \cdot 10^9 - 5.06 \cdot 10^9$ for RockYou).

4.3 Combining PassGAN with HashCat

To maximize the number of passwords guessed, the adversary would typically use the output of multiple tools in order to combine the benefits of rule-based

Table 3. Number of matches generated by each password guessing tool against the LinkedIn testing set, and corresponding number of password generated by PassGAN to outperform each tool. Matches for HashCat Best64 and FLA were obtained by exhaustively enumerating the entire output of each tool. The minimum probability threshold for FLA was set to $p = 10^{-10}$.

Approach	(1) Unique passwords	(2) Matches	(3) Number of passwords required for PassGAN to outperform (2)	(4) PassGAN matches
JTR Spyderlab	10^9	6,840,797 (16.85%)	$2.7 \cdot 10^9$	6,841,217 (16.85%)
Markov Model 3-gram	$4.9 \cdot 10^8$	5,829,786 (14.36%)	$1.6 \cdot 10^9$	5,829,916 (14.36%)
HashCat gen2	10^9	6,308,515 (15.54%)	$2.1 \cdot 10^9$	6,309,799 (15.54%)
HashCat Best64	$3.6 \cdot 10^8$	7,174,990 (17.67%)	$3.6 \cdot 10^9$	7,419,248 (18.27%)
PCFG	10^9	7,288,553 (17.95%)	$3.6 \cdot 10^9$	7,419,248 (18.27%)
FLA $p = 10^{-10}$	$7.4 \cdot 10^8$	8,290,173 (20.42%)	$6 \cdot 10^9$	8,519,060 (21.00%)

tools (e.g., fast password generation) and ML-based tools (e.g., generation of a large number of guesses).

To evaluate PassGAN in this setting, we removed all passwords matched by HashCat Best64 (the best performing set of rules in our experiments) from the RockYou and LinkedIn testing sets. This led to two new test sets, containing 1,348,300 (RockYou) and 33,394,178 (LinkedIn) passwords, respectively.

Our results show that the number of matches steadily increases with the number of samples produced by PassGAN. In particular, when we used $7 \cdot 10^9$ passwords from PassGAN, we were able to match 51% (320,365) of passwords from the "new" RockYou dataset, and 73% (5,262,427) additional passwords from the "new" LinkedIn dataset. This confirms that combining rules with machine learning password guessing is an effective strategy. Moreover, it confirms that PassGAN can capture portions of the password space not covered by rule-based approaches. With this in mind, a recent version of HashCat [23] introduced a generic password candidate interface called "slow candidates", enabling the use of tools such as PCFGs [69], OMEN [14], PassGAN, and more with HashCat.

4.4 Comparing PassGAN with FLA

In this section, we concentrate on comparing PassGAN with FLA having a particular focus on the probability estimation.FLA is based on recurrent neural networks [19,65], and typically the model is trained on password leaks from several websites, in our case the RockYou training set. During password generation, the neural network generates one password character at a time. Each new character (including a special end-of-password character) is computed based on its probability, given the current output state, in what is essentially a Markov process. Given a trained FLA model, FLA outputs the following six fields: 1. password, 2. the probability of that password, 3. the estimated output guess number, i.e., the strength of that password, 4. the standard deviation of the randomized trial for this password (in units of the number of guesses), 5. the number of measurements for this password and 6. the estimated confidence interval for the guess number (in units of the number of guesses). The evaluation presented in [39] shows that their technique outperforms Markov models, PCFGs and password composition rules commonly used with JTR and HashCat, when testing a large number of password guesses (in the 10^{10} to 10^{25} range).

We believe that one of the limitations of FLA resides precisely in the Markovian nature of the process used to estimate passwords. For instance, 123456; 12345; and, 123456789 are the three most common passwords in the RockYou dataset, being roughly one every 66-passwords. Similarly, the most common passwords produced by FLA start with "123" or use the word "love". In contrast, PassGAN's most commonly generated passwords, tend to show more variability with samples composed of names, the combination of names and numbers, and more. When compared with the RockYou training set, the most likely samples from PassGAN exhibit closer resemblance to the training set and its probabilities than FLA does. We argue that due to the Markovian structure of the password generation process in FLA, any password characteristic that is not captured within the scope of an n-gram, might not be encoded by FLA. For instance, if a meaningful subset of 10-character passwords is constructed as the concatenation of two words (e.g., MusicMusic), any Markov process with $n \leq 5$ will not be able to capture this behavior properly. On the other hand, given enough examples, the neural network used in PassGAN will be able to learn this property. As a result, while password pookypooky was assigned a probability $p \approx 10^{-33}$ by FLA (with an estimated number of guessing attempts of about 10^{29}), it was guessed after roughly 10^8 attempts by PassGAN.

To investigate further on the differences between PassGAN and FLA, we computed the number of passwords in the RockYou testing set for which FLA required at least 10^{10} attempts and that PassGAN was able to guess within its first $7 \cdot 10^9$ samples. These are the passwords to which FLA assigns low probabilities, despite being chosen by some users. Because PassGAN can model them, we conclude that the probabilities assigned by FLA to these passwords are incorrect. Figure 2 presents our result as the ratio between the passwords matched by FLA at a particular number of guessing attempts, and by PassGAN within its first $7 \cdot 10^9$ attempts. Our results show that PassGAN can model a number of passwords more correctly than FLA. However, this advantage decreased as the number of attempts required for FLA to guess a password increased, i.e., as the estimated probability of that password decreased. This shows that, in general, the two tools agree on assigning probabilities to passwords.

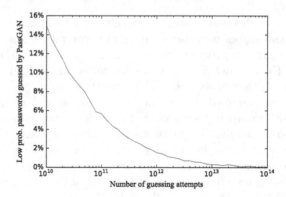

Fig. 2. Percentage of passwords matched by FLA at a particular number of guesses, that are matched by PassGAN in at most $7 \cdot 10^9$ attempts.

4.5   A Closer Look at Non-matched Passwords

We inspected a list of passwords generated by PassGAN that did not match any of the testing sets and determined that many of these passwords are reasonable candidates for human-generated passwords. As such, we speculate that a possibly large number of passwords generated by PassGAN, that did not match our test sets, might still match user accounts from services other than RockYou and LinkedIn. We list a small sample of these passwords in Table 4.

Table 4. Sample of passwords generated by PassGAN that did not match the testing sets.

love42743	ilovey2b93	paolo9630	italyit
sadgross	usa2598	s13trumpy	trumpart3
ttybaby5	dark1106	vamperiosa	~dracula
saddracula	luvengland	albania.	bananabake
paleyoung	@crepess	emily1015	enemy20
goku476	coolarse18	iscoolin	serious003
nyc1234	thepotus12	greatrun	babybad528
santazone	apple8487	1loveyoung	bitchin706
toshibaod	tweet1997b	103tears	1holys01

5   Remarks

In this section, we summarize the findings from our experiments, and discuss their relevance in the context of password guessing.

Character-level GANs are well suited for generating password guesses. In our experiments, PassGAN was able to match 34.2% of the passwords in a testing set extracted from the RockYou password dataset, when trained on a different subset of RockYou. Further, we were able to match 21.9% of the password in the LinkedIn dataset when PassGAN was trained on the RockYou password set. This is remarkable because PassGAN was able to achieve these results with no additional information on the passwords that are present only in the testing dataset. In other words, PassGAN was able to correctly guess a large number of passwords that it did not observe given access to nothing more than a set of samples.

Current rule-based password guessing is very efficient but limited. In our experiments, rule-based systems were able to match or outperform other password guessing tools when the number of allowed guesses was small. This is a testament to the ability of skilled security experts to encode rules that generate correct matches with high probability. However, our experiments also confirmed that the main downside of rule-based password guessing is that rules can generate only a finite, relatively small set of passwords. In contrast, PassGAN was able to eventually surpass the number of matches achieved using password generation rules.

As a result, the best password guessing strategy is to use multiple tools. In our experiments, each password guessing approach has an edge in a different setting. Our results confirm that combining multiple techniques leads to the best overall performance. For instance, by combining the output of PassGAN with the output of the Best64 rules, we were able to match 48% of the passwords in the RockYou testing dataset (which represents a 50.8% increase in the number of matches) and 30.6% of the passwords from the LinkedIn dataset—an increase of about 73.3%. Given the current performance of both PassGAN and FLA, it is not unlikely that tools alone will soon be able to replace rule-based password guessing tools entirely.

GANs are expressive enough to generate passwords from Markovian processes, rules, and to capture more general password structures. Our experiments show that PassGAN is competitive with FLA, which treats password guessing primarily as a Markovian process. Without any knowledge of password rules or guidance on password structure, PassGAN was able to match the performance of FLA within an order of magnitude of guesses by leveraging only knowledge that it was able to extract from a limited number of samples. Further, because GANs are more general tools than Markov models, in our experiment PassGAN was able to generate matching passwords that were ranked as very unlikely by FLA, using a limited number of guesses.

GANs generalize well to password datasets other than their training dataset. When we evaluated PassGAN on a dataset (LinkedIn [36]) distinct from its training set (RockYou [58]), the drop in matching rate was modest, especially compared to other tools. Moreover, when tested on LinkedIn, PassGAN was able to match the other tools within a lower or equal number of guesses compared to RockYou.

State-of-the-art GANs density estimation is correct only for a subset of the space they generate. Our experiments show that IWGAN's density estimation matches the training set for high-frequency passwords. This is important because it allows PassGAN to generate highly-likely candidate passwords early. However, our experiments also show that as the frequency of a password decreases, the quality of PassGAN's density estimation deteriorates. While this becomes less relevant as PassGAN generates more passwords, it shows that the number of passwords that PassGAN needs to output to achieve a particular number of matches could significantly decrease if it is instantiated using a character-level GAN that performs more accurate density estimation. Similarly, a more extensive training dataset, coupled with a more complex neural network structure, could improve density estimation (and therefore PassGAN's performance) significantly.

Final Remarks. GANs estimate the density distribution of the training dataset. As a result, PassGAN outputs repeated password guesses. While a full brute-force guessing attack would have full coverage, learning from the training data distribution allows PassGAN to perform a more efficient attack by generating highly likely guesses. Because password generation can be performed offline, PassGAN could produce several billions of guesses beforehand, and store them in a database. In our experiments, we stored unique password samples, and later used these samples for testing purposes, thus avoiding repetitions. If needed, Bloom filters with appropriate parameters could also be used to discard repeated entries, thus enabling efficient online password guessing.

Clearly, PassGAN can be used in a distributed setting, in which several instances independently output password guesses. While it is possible to avoid local repetitions using, e.g., Bloom filters, coordinating the removal of duplicates among different nodes is more complex and, potentially, more expensive. The appropriate way to address this problem depends primarily on three factors: (1) the cost of generating a password guess; (2) the cost of testing a password guess; and (3) the cost of synchronizing information about previously-generated password between nodes.

If the cost of generating passwords is less than the cost of testing them, and synchronization among nodes is not free, then avoiding repetitions across nodes is not essential. Therefore each model can sample without the need of being aware of other models' generated samples.

If the cost of testing password guesses is less than the cost of generating them, then it might be beneficial to periodically coordinate among nodes to determine which samples have been generated. The synchronization cost dictates the frequency of coordination.

Finally, PassGAN could significantly benefit and improve from new leaked password datasets. The model would improve by learning new rules, and the number of repeated samples could potentially be reduced.

6   Conclusion

In this paper, we introduced PassGAN, the first password guessing technique based on generative adversarial networks (GANs). PassGAN is designed to learn password distribution information from password leaks. As a result, unlike current password guessing tools, PassGAN does not rely on any additional information, such as explicit rules, or assumptions on the Markovian structure of user-chosen passwords. We believe that our approach to password guessing is revolutionary because PassGAN generates passwords with no user intervention—thus requiring no domain knowledge on passwords, nor manual analysis of password database leaks.

We evaluated PassGAN's performance by testing how well it can guess passwords that it was not trained on, and how the distribution of PassGAN's output approximates the distribution of real password leaks. Our results show that PassGAN is competitive with state-of-the-art password generation tools: in our experiments, PassGAN was always able to generate the same number of matches as the other password guessing tools.

However, PassGAN currently requires to output a larger number of passwords compared to other tools. We believe that this cost is negligible when considering the benefits of the proposed technique. Further, training PassGAN on a larger dataset enables the use of more complex neural network structures, and more comprehensive training. As a result, the underlying GAN can perform more accurate density estimation, thus reducing the number of passwords needed to achieve a specific number of matches.

Changing the generative model behind PassGAN to a conditional GAN might improve password guessing in all scenarios in which the adversary knows a set of keywords commonly used by the user (e.g., the names of user's pets and family members). Given this knowledge, the adversary could condition the GAN to these particular words, thus enabling the generator to give special attention to a specific portion of the search space where these keywords reside.

PassGAN can potentially be used in the context of generating Honeywords [29]. Honeywords are decoy passwords that, when mixed with real passwords, substantially reduce the value of a password database for the adversary. Wang et al. [66], raised concerns about the previous techniques proposed by Juels et al. [29] to generate Honeywords: if Honeywords can be easily distinguished from real passwords, then their usefulness is significantly reduced. An extension of PassGAN could potentially address this problem and will be the subject of future work.

References

1. Abadi, M., et al.: TensorFlow: a system for large-scale machine learning. In: OSDI, vol. 16, pp. 265–283 (2016)
2. Arjovsky, M., Chintala, S., Bottou, L.: Wasserstein GAN. CoRR abs/1701.07875 (2017). http://arxiv.org/abs/1701.07875

3. Berthelot, D., Schumm, T., Metz, L.: BEGAN: boundary equilibrium generative adversarial networks. arXiv preprint arXiv:1703.10717 (2017)
4. Binkowski, M., Sutherland, D., Arbel, M., Gretton, A.: Demystifying MMD GANs. In: International Conference on Learning Representations (ICLR) (2018)
5. Cao, Y., Ding, G.W., Lui, Y.C., Huang, R.: Improving GAN training via binarized representation entropy (BRE) regularization. In: International Conference on Learning Representations (ICLR) (2018)
6. Castelluccia, C., Dürmuth, M., Perito, D.: Adaptive password-strength meters from Markov models. In: NDSS (2012)
7. Chen, X., Duan, Y., Houthooft, R., Schulman, J., Sutskever, I., Abbeel, P.: InfoGAN: interpretable representation learning by information maximizing generative adversarial nets. In: Advances in Neural Information Processing Systems, pp. 2172–2180 (2016)
8. Ciaramella, A., D'Arco, P., De Santis, A., Galdi, C., Tagliaferri, R.: Neural network techniques for proactive password checking. IEEE Trans. Dependable Secure Comput. **3**(4), 327–339 (2006)
9. Daskalakis, C., Ilyas, A., Syrgkanis, V., Zeng, H.: Training GANs with optimism. In: International Conference on Learning Representations (ICLR) (2018)
10. Dell'Amico, M., Michiardi, P., Roudier, Y.: Password strength: an empirical analysis. In: Proceedings IEEE INFOCOM, pp. 1–9. IEEE (2010)
11. Denton, E.L., Chintala, S., Fergus, R., et al.: Deep generative image models using a Laplacian pyramid of adversarial networks. In: Advances in Neural Information Processing Systems, pp. 1486–1494 (2015)
12. Dorsey, B.: Markov-chain password generator (2017). https://github.com/brannondorsey/markov-passwords
13. Duc, B., Fischer, S., Bigun, J.: Face authentication with Gabor information on deformable graphs. IEEE Trans. Image Process. **8**(4), 504–516 (1999)
14. Dürmuth, M., Angelstorf, F., Castelluccia, C., Perito, D., Chaabane, A.: OMEN: faster password guessing using an ordered Markov enumerator. In: Piessens, F., Caballero, J., Bielova, N. (eds.) ESSoS 2015. LNCS, vol. 8978, pp. 119–132. Springer, Cham (2015). https://doi.org/10.1007/978-3-319-15618-7_10
15. Fiegerman, S.: Yahoo says 500 million accounts stolen (2017). http://money.cnn.com/2016/09/22/technology/yahoo-data-breach/index.html
16. Frank, M., Biedert, R., Ma, E., Martinovic, I., Song, D.: Touchalytics: on the applicability of touchscreen input as a behavioral biometric for continuous authentication. IEEE Trans. Inf. Forensics Secur. **8**(1), 136–148 (2013)
17. Golla, M.: Password guessing using recurrent neural networks - the missing manual (2017). https://www.password-guessing.org/blog/post/cupslab-neural-network-cracking-manual/
18. Goodfellow, I., et al.: Generative adversarial nets. In: Advances in Neural Information Processing Systems, pp. 2672–2680 (2014)
19. Graves, A.: Generating sequences with recurrent neural networks. arXiv preprint arXiv:1308.0850 (2013)
20. Gulrajani, I., Ahmed, F., Arjovsky, M., Dumoulin, V., Courville, A.C.: Improved training of Wasserstein GANs. In: Advances in Neural Information Processing Systems, pp. 5767–5777 (2017)
21. Gulrajani, I., Ahmed, F., Arjovsky, M., Dumoulin, V., Courville, A.C.: Improved training of Wasserstein GANs - code (2017). https://github.com/igul222/improved_wgan_training
22. HashCat (2017). https://hashcat.net

23. HashCat: HashCat v5.0.0, advanced password recovery (2018). https://hashcat. net/forum/showthread.php?mode=linear&tid=7903&pid=42585

24. Hitaj, B., Ateniese, G., Pérez-Cruz, F.: Deep models under the GAN: information leakage from collaborative deep learning. In: Proceedings of the 2017 ACM SIGSAC Conference on Computer and Communications Security, pp. 603–618. ACM (2017)

25. Hitaj, B., Gasti, P., Ateniese, G., Pérez-Cruz, F.: PassGAN: a deep learning approach for password guessing. In: NeurIPS 2018 Workshop on Security in Machine Learning, SECML 2018, Montreal, CANADA (Co-located with NeurIPS 2018) (2018)

26. Hjelm, R.D., Jacob, A.P., Trischler, A., Che, T., Cho, K., Bengio, Y.: Boundary seeking GANs. In: International Conference on Learning Representations (ICLR) (2018)

27. Hoang, Q., Nguyen, T.D., Le, T., Phung, D.: MGAN: training generative adversarial nets with multiple generators. In: International Conference on Learning Representations (ICLR) (2018)

28. Hunt, T.: Here's why [insert thing here] is not a password killer (2018). https:// www.troyhunt.com/heres-why-insert-thing-here-is-not-a-password-killer/

29. Juels, A., Rivest, R.L.: Honeywords: making password-cracking detectable. In: Proceedings of the 2013 ACM SIGSAC Conference on Computer & Communications Security, pp. 145–160. ACM (2013)

30. Kim, T., Cha, M., Kim, H., Lee, J., Kim, J.: Learning to discover cross-domain relations with generative adversarial networks. arXiv preprint arXiv:1703.05192 (2017)

31. Kingma, D., Ba, J.: Adam: a method for stochastic optimization. arXiv preprint arXiv:1412.6980 (2014)

32. Lab, C.: Fast, lean, and accurate: modeling password guessability using neural networks (source code) (2016). https://github.com/cupslab/neural_network_cracking

33. LeCun, Y., et al.: Backpropagation applied to handwritten zip code recognition. Neural Comput. 1(4), 541–551 (1989)

34. LeCun, Y., et al.: Handwritten digit recognition with a back-propagation network. In: Advances in Neural Information Processing Systems, pp. 396–404 (1990)

35. Li, Y., Swersky, K., Zemel, R.: Generative moment matching networks. In: International Conference on Machine Learning, pp. 1718–1727 (2015)

36. LinkedIn: Linkedin. https://hashes.org/public.php

37. Ma, J., Yang, W., Luo, M., Li, N.: A study of probabilistic password models. In: IEEE Symposium on Security and Privacy (SP), pp. 689–704. IEEE (2014)

38. Hashcat Per Position Markov Chains (2017). https://www.trustwave.com/ Resources/SpiderLabs-Blog/Hashcat-Per-Position-Markov-Chains/

39. Melicher, W., et al.: Fast, lean, and accurate: modeling password guessability using neural networks. In: USENIX Security Symposium, pp. 175–191 (2016)

40. Mirza, M., Osindero, S.: Conditional generative adversarial nets. arXiv preprint arXiv:1411.1784 (2014)

41. Miyato, T., Koyama, M.: cGANs with projection discriminator. In: International Conference on Learning Representations (ICLR) (2018)

42. Morris, R., Thompson, K.: Password security: a case history. Commun. ACM 22(11), 594–597 (1979)

43. Mroueh, Y., Li, C.L., Sercu, T., Raj, A., Cheng, Y.: Sobolev GAN. In: International Conference on Learning Representations (ICLR) (2018)

44. Mroueh, Y., Sercu, T., Goel, V.: McGan: mean and covariance feature matching GAN. In: Proceedings of the 34th International Conference on Machine Learning, ICML 2017, Sydney, NSW, Australia, 6–11 August 2017, pp. 2527–2535 (2017). http://proceedings.mlr.press/v70/mroueh17a.html
45. Murphy, K.P.: Handbook of Information Security, Information Warfare, Social, Legal, and International Issues and Security Foundations. Wiley, Hoboken (2006)
46. Murphy, K.P.: Machine Learning: A Probabilistic Perspective. MIT Press, Cambridge (2012)
47. Nagarajan, V., Kolter, J.Z.: Gradient descent GAN optimization is locally stable. In: Advances in Neural Information Processing Systems, pp. 5585–5595 (2017)
48. Narayanan, A., Shmatikov, V.: Fast dictionary attacks on passwords using time-space tradeoff. In: Proceedings of the 12th ACM Conference on Computer and Communications Security, pp. 364–372. ACM (2005)
49. Nowozin, S., Cseke, B., Tomioka, R.: f-GAN: training generative neural samplers using variational divergence minimization. In: Advances in Neural Information Processing Systems, pp. 271–279 (2016)
50. Percival, C., Josefsson, S.: The scrypt password-based key derivation function. Technical report (2016)
51. Perez, S.: Google plans to bring password-free logins to Android apps by year-end (2017). https://techcrunch.com/2016/05/23/google-plans-to-bring-password-free-logins-to-android-apps-by-year-end/
52. Petzka, H., Fischer, A., Lukovnikov, D.: On the regularization of Wasserstein GANs. In: International Conference on Learning Representations (ICLR) (2018)
53. The Password Project (2017). http://thepasswordproject.com/leaked_password_lists_and_dictionaries
54. Provos, N., Mazieres, D.: Bcrypt algorithm. In: USENIX (1999)
55. Radford, A., Metz, L., Chintala, S.: Unsupervised representation learning with deep convolutional generative adversarial networks. In: 4th International Conference on Learning Representations (2016)
56. John the Ripper (2017). http://www.openwall.com/john/
57. John the Ripper Markov Generator (2017). http://openwall.info/wiki/john/markov
58. RockYou: Rockyou (2010). http://downloads.skullsecurity.org/passwords/rockyou.txt.bz2
59. Roth, K., Lucchi, A., Nowozin, S., Hofmann, T.: Stabilizing training of generative adversarial networks through regularization. In: Advances in Neural Information Processing Systems, pp. 2018–2028 (2017)
60. Hashcat Rules (2017). https://github.com/hashcat/hashcat/tree/master/rules
61. John the Ripper KoreLogic Rules (2017). http://contest-2010.korelogic.com/rules.html
62. Rumelhart, D.E., Hinton, G.E., Williams, R.J.: Learning representations by back-propagating errors. Nature **323**(6088), 533 (1986)
63. Salimans, T., Goodfellow, I., Zaremba, W., Cheung, V., Radford, A., Chen, X.: Improved techniques for training GANs. In: Advances in Neural Information Processing Systems, pp. 2234–2242 (2016)
64. Sitová, Z., et al.: HMOG: new behavioral biometric features for continuous authentication of smartphone users. IEEE Trans. Inf. Forensics Secur. **11**(5), 877–892 (2016)
65. Sutskever, I., Martens, J., Hinton, G.E.: Generating text with recurrent neural networks. In: Proceedings of the 28th International Conference on Machine Learning (ICML 2011), pp. 1017–1024 (2011)

66. Wang, D., Cheng, H., Wang, P., Yan, J., Huang, X.: A security analysis of honey-words. In: NDSS (2018)
67. Wei, X., Gong, B., Liu, Z., Lu, W., Wang, L.: Improving the improved training of Wasserstein GANs: a consistency term and its dual effect. In: International Conference on Learning Representations (ICLR) (2018)
68. Weir, M.: Probabilistic password cracker (2009). https://sites.google.com/site/reusablesec/Home/password-cracking-tools/probablistic_cracker
69. Weir, M., Aggarwal, S., De Medeiros, B., Glodek, B.: Password cracking using probabilistic context-free grammars. In: 30th IEEE Symposium on Security and Privacy, pp. 391–405. IEEE (2009)
70. Wu, Y., Burda, Y., Salakhutdinov, R., Grosse, R.: On the quantitative analysis of decoder-based generative models. arXiv preprint arXiv:1611.04273 (2016)
71. Zhang, H., et al.: StackGAN: text to photo-realistic image synthesis with stacked generative adversarial networks. arXiv preprint arXiv:1612.03242 (2016)
72. Zhong, Y., Deng, Y., Jain, A.K.: Keystroke dynamics for user authentication. In: 2012 IEEE Computer Society Conference on Computer Vision and Pattern Recognition Workshops (CVPRW), pp. 117–123. IEEE (2012)
73. Zhou, Z., et al.: Activation maximization generative adversarial nets. In: International Conference on Learning Representations (ICLR) (2018)

Blockchain and Cryptocurrency

Uncle-Block Attack: Blockchain Mining Threat Beyond Block Withholding for Rational and Uncooperative Miners

Sang-Yoon Chang[1]([✉]), Younghee Park[2], Simeon Wuthier[1],
and Chang-Wu Chen[3]

[1] University of Colorado Colorado Springs, Colorado Springs, CO, USA
schang2@uccs.edu
[2] San Jose State University, San Jose, CA, USA
[3] AMIS, Taipei, Taiwan

Abstract. Blockchain-based cryptocurrency replaces centralized institutions with a distributed network of Internet-based miners to generate currency and process financial transactions. Such blockchain systems reach consensus using proof of work (PoW), and the miners participating in PoW join mining pools to reduce the variance for more stable reward income. Prior literature in blockchain security/game theory identified practical attacks in block withholding attack (BWH) and the state of the art fork-after-withholding (FAW), which have the rational and uncooperative attacker compromise a victim pool and pose as a PoW contributor by submitting shares but withholding the blocks. We advance such threat strategy (creating greater reward advantage to the attackers at the expense of the other miners in the victim pool) and introduce the uncle-block attack (UBA) which exploits uncle blocks for block withholding. We analyze UBA's incentive compatibility and identify and model the critical systems- and environmental- parameters which determine the attack's impacts. Our analyses and simulations results show that a rational attacker is always incentivized to launch the UBA attack strategy (over FAW or protocol compliance) and that UBA is effective even in the unfavorable networking environment (in contrast, in such case, FAW is reduced to the suboptimal BWH attack and does not make use of the withheld block).

Keywords: Blockchain · Cryptocurrencies ·
Distributed consensus protocol · Security · Mining game ·
Block withholding attack

1 Introduction

Blockchain technology builds a distributed ledger comprised of irrevocable transactions and has emerged as the backbone technology for digital cryptocurrencies, which govern, generate, and process the financial transactions in a distributed

© Springer Nature Switzerland AG 2019
R. H. Deng et al. (Eds.): ACNS 2019, LNCS 11464, pp. 241–258, 2019.
https://doi.org/10.1007/978-3-030-21568-2_12

manner (as opposed to relying on a centralized bank), e.g., Bitcoin [17] and Ethereum [5,21]. As of April 2019, the total market cap of the blockchain-based cryptocurrencies is estimated to be more than \$170B [3,8].

Underlying blockchain is the consensus protocol so that all nodes agree on the transactions on the ledger without relying on a trusted third party. The most popular consensus algorithm is based on proof of work (PoW). The miners participate in PoW to generate new currency and process the transactions and are financially incentivized to so by the block rewards, the winnings from solving the probabilistic PoW computational puzzles. To lower the variance of such reward, the miners join and operate as mining pools to share the computational power and the corresponding reward winnings.

PoW consensus protocol is driven by networking, as the found blocks need to get propagated via broadcasting for "timestamping" [17] to determine which block got mined first and will become a part of the blockchain. Because it is in a distributed environment and due to the networking/propagation delays, there can be collisions in the block findings, which results in forking. To improve fairness and decentralization across nodes with varying networking environments, blockchain systems incorporate uncle reward, which are partial rewards for the blocks that got forked but did not become part of the main chain. (We explain the relevant background in blockchain in greater details in Sect. 2.)

According to the consensus protocol, the miner submits a PoW solution *once* it is found. However, previous research identified practical and relevant attacks which have the attacker compromise a victim mining pool and undermine the winnings by posing as a PoW contributor without actually contributing (the attacker also has a different reward channel in its main pool/solo mining, in which it does not need to share the reward with others, unlike the victim pool). In such attacks, the attacker mines the block and controls the timing of the block submission (including possibly permanently withholding the block, which effectively corresponds to discarding the found block) as opposed to following the protocol and immediately submitting the found block. These attacks are in the forms of block-withholding (BWH) attack and fork-after-withholding (FAW) attack. FAW attack, in particular, builds on both selfish mining and BWH and improves the attacker's reward by submitting the block found in the victim mining pool when there is a fork/collision with a third-party miner, making the threat more relevant to the incentive-driven rational miners.

In this paper, we advance the withholding-based attacks and introduce the uncle-block attack (UBA) which extends the block-withholding to uncle blocks. UBA amplifies the state of the art in FAW attack by increasing the attacker reward at the expense of the other miners within the victim pool. UBA not only builds on FAW (inheriting the attacker-desirable properties of FAW) but is also effective independent to the networking environment of the attacker (i.e., effective even when the attacker loses the forking race, in contrast to FAW). While the UBA attack undercuts the rewards of the other miners in the victim pool (and thus corresponds to the strategy which will be taken by a malicious attacker focusing on sabotaging the victims), we extend our threat model further to include the uncooperative and rational attackers and analyze the attacker's incentives in financial rewards for UBA. Our analyses show that the attacker maximizes its reward by launching UBA attack over the state of the art in FAW or the protocol-complying honest mining. Our reward/payout analyses for the attacker uses lower bounds to be conservative in measuring the attacker's performances. Nevertheless, we show significant gains and incentives for launching UBA. While we use formal modeling and analyses to abstract away from the implementation details and deliver fundamental insights about the advanced withholding threat, our model constructions and analyses are driven by the real-world blockchain implementations and our findings are relevant and applicable to the current practice/design of blockchains.

The rest of the paper is organized as follows. Section 2 provides background information about blockchain relevant to our work; Sect. 3 discusses about the prior work in blockchain mining security; and Sect. 4 establishes the threat model and the attack requirements (the same as those for BWH and FAW). We construct our mining game model in Sect. 5 and use it to recap BWH attack and FAW attack. Afterward, we introduce UBA and analyze its reward in Sect. 6. We analyze the attacker's dynamic behaviors (optimizing its infiltration of the victim pool and the computational power use) and its attack payouts/rewards in simulations in Sect. 7. We then discuss about the potential countermeasures in Sect. 8 and conclude the paper in Sect. 9.

2   Background in Blockchain Mining

The PoW consensus comprises of two parts: a probabilistic PoW based on solving a computational puzzle (finding the preimage/input of a one-way hash function) yielding a valid block, and the submission/broadcasting of the block via peer-to-peer (p2p) networking (so that the others update their blockchain ledgers with the block to reach a consensus).

Miners execute the consensus protocol and are incentivized to do so because solving the computational puzzle and consequently registering a block on the blockchain generates financial rewards (new currency and the transaction fees). The consensus protocol is based on a race and only the miner solving the PoW puzzle and submitting/broadcasting the corresponding block the earliest wins the corresponding reward in a round; once that happens, the other miners start a new round of mining by updating the chain with the newly found block. While the PoW consensus is designed to be computationally fair (distributing the reward winning proportionally to the computational power of the miners), the PoW miners experience high variance when finding blocks and winning rewards. Because a miner is competing with a global-scale group of other miners and the mining difficulty gets adjusted accordingly, finding a block is very sporadic and bursty.

To lower the variance and to get a more stable stream of reward income, miners form a pool to combine their computational power to share the power as well as the mining reward winnings. The increased computational power by pooling them together increases the occurrence of winning a block whose reward gets split across the pool miners according to their computational contributions. To estimate each of the miner's contributions, mining pool samples more PoW solutions by introducing *shares*, which correspond to solving the same computational puzzle with the same block header as the block but with easier difficulty; a block solution is a share but a share is not necessarily a block. The reward distribution within a pool using such shares is also designed to be computationally fair. To manage the mining pool, the *pool manager* keeps track of the individual miner members' contributions, registers/broadcasts the block upon its discovery, and distributes the reward to the pool members. Joining the mining pool is popular, e.g., as of July 2018, the computationally-largest mining pool (BTC.com) has 24% of the computational power for the entire Bitcoin mining network, and eight mining pools collectively have greater than 85%.

Forking occurs when two block solution propagations result in a collision (i.e., some nodes receive one block earlier than the other while the other nodes receive the other block first), creating a partition between the miners on which block to use for its impending round of mining. Forking gets resolved by having the miners choose the longest chain, e.g., if one partition finds another new block and propagates that to the other partition, then the miners in the other partition accept that chain which is one block longer than the one that they have been using[1]. The block that causes a fork but does not get registered as the main block is called the *uncle block* (as opposed to the parent block registered on the chain)[2]. Blockchain systems provide partial reward for uncle blocks to increase fairness between the miners, i.e., reduce the effect of the networking discrepancy.

3   Related Work in Mining Security

For uncooperative miners (willing to diverge from the set protocol), sophisticated attacks exist to further increase the mining reward beyond following the protocol of timely block submission. These attacks on the consensus protocol actively

---

[1] In significantly rarer cases, an intentional *hard fork* retains the partition and introduces a new branch/chain. For example, since the launch of the main chain in 2016 ("Homestead"), Ethereum had five hard forks, including three hard forks in 2016 (including the infamous DAO hack incident which split Ethereum and Ethereum Classic), one in 2017, and one in 2019. Intentional *soft forks* are also used for upgrading the blockchain protocols and rules but, in contrast to hard forks, are backward-compatible to the clients running the older softwares. Such intentional forks are out of scope for this paper and we focus on the *accidental forks* caused by the block propagation discrepancy in networking, because the accidental forks occur significantly more frequently than the intentional forks and because the intentional forks are treated differently than the accidental forks which get automatically resolved as described by the longest-chain rule without software updates.

[2] This terminology for the blocks which are valid solutions but did not become the main blocks can differ across implementations, e.g., in Bitcoin, they are called orphan blocks. We uniformly call them *uncle blocks* for simplicity but introduce relevant variables, including the reward amount, to generalize it across implementations.

control the timing of the block submission, including permanently withholding the submission in certain situations. *Selfish mining* withholds a block so that the miner can get a heads-start on computing the next block and have the rest of the miners discard and switch from the blocks that they were mining [10,13, 19]. Blockchain's confirmation mechanism (which waits for multiple blocks to get mined before finalizing the transactions) resists selfish mining because the probability of successful selfish mining decreases exponentially with the number of blocks required for confirmation [17].

There are further attacks in cases of the mining pool. *Block-withholding attack* (BWH) withholds the mined block in mining pools in order to increase the attacker's reward at the expense of the rest of the pool member miners [18]. In BWH, to sabotage the victim mining pool, the attacker simply never submits the found block while submitting the shares. As a consequence, the attacker still reaps the benefits from submitting the share solutions to the victim pool (pretending to contribute and getting the credit for it) while never actually contributing to the pool (since it never submits the actual block solution which will benefit the victim pool). The attacker also increases the expected reward in its main pool by launching BWH on the infiltrated victim pool.

A recent fork-after-withholding (FAW) attack [14] combines selfish mining and BWH. FAW builds on selfish mining and BWH but creates intentional forks in cases when there is a block being broadcasted by another pool with which the attacker has no association. In other words, while always submitting the shares to gain greater payout on the victim pool, the attacker withholds the found block and either discards it (if the attacker's main pool finds another block or if another miner from the victim pool finds a block) or submits it only when there is another competing block that is being propagated by another third-party pool (creating an intentional fork). FAW attack is significant because it forgoes the miner's dilemma (which establishes that the Nash equilibrium between multiple pools is to launch block-withholding attack against each another, which results in suboptimal performances for all the pools, motivating the pools to be cooperative with each other [9]); there is a real incentive (unfair reward gain) for rational miners to launch FAW attack.

Other researchers investigate the emerging security issues as the block reward transitions to only variable transaction-fees (as opposed to also including the base fees that generate new currencies) [6,20]. The variance of the block reward amount incentivizes the attackers to selectively mine the blocks in time (e.g., there are "mining gaps" when the attackers decide not to mine). Although related, our work is orthogonal to these issues since the attacker in our work maximizes its reward advantage *given* the block reward.

4   Threat Model: Uncooperative and Rational Attacker

We distinguish between *honest miners* and *attackers* by whether or not they are cooperative and comply with the consensus protocol. More specifically, while honest miners submit/broadcast the blocks once they are found, attackers control the timing of the consensus-puzzle submissions/blocks by introducing a delay between the time when the block was found and when they are submitted.

We investigate the attacks launched by the miners, as opposed to the pool managers. Compromising the pool as a miner is easier than misbehaving as a mining pool manager (which is trusted by and interact with all the miners within the mining pool and is therefore in constant scrutiny). Compromising the pool as a miner is especially easy in a public blockchain (as opposed to permissioned or private blockchain) and against an open pool, in which registration and Sybil attack (generating/using multiple identities) are easy and even encouraged for anonymity.

The attacker is also rational and driven by the financial incentives of block rewards. Therefore, we study whether the attackers strategies are compatible to such incentives; the attack is irrelevant if it does not increase the attacker's reward because the attacker will choose not to use such the suboptimal strategy. While the attacker is primarily driven by its own self interest, its unfair advantage negatively affects the other miners of the blockchain because the finite reward is shared among the miners (i.e., if a miner wins more, then the other miners win less). Our threat model therefore encompasses the malicious threat model (where the attacker's goal is to sabotage or degrade the performances of the other miners) but can also be extended to the uncooperative and rational miners (who merely want to increase their own rewards without necessarily harming the others).

We assume the threat model of BWH attack and FAW attack, in which the attacker compromises multiple pools and separates the main pool vs. the victim pool. The attacker behaves honestly in the *main pool* while it can launch an attack by diverging from the protocol in the *victim pool*. As a realistic setup, we assume that the main pool is comprised of the attacker only (which is effectively solo mining without joining a pool); the attacker shares the reward winnings in the victim pool while there is no sharing and the attacker takes all the rewards in the main pool. Our model also generalizes to the case of multiple pools, e.g., the main pool or the victim pool can be a collection of mining pools, since the PoW consensus is power-fair, as opposed to identity-fair, as is captured in our mining-game model in Sect. 5.

The attacker setting up main pool vs. victim pool is realistic since setting up a miner account or joining a mining pool are generally easy. This is because public blockchain, such as those used in cryptocurrencies, has loose control of identities and is designed for anonymity (which is in contrast to the permissioned blockchains in other emerging applications), e.g., Nakamoto/Bitcoin suggests using new accounts for new transactions [17]. For example, in 2014, Eligius became a victim pool of the BWH attack and lost 300 BTC, which got detected primarily because the attacker only used two accounts for the attack (which resulted in a detection of abnormal behavior where the accounts submitted only shares but no blocks for too long of a time).

5 Mining Game

5.1 Mining and Computational Power Model

To investigate the incentive compatibility of the attacks, we model the mining game between the miners and quantify the expected reward. We build on the approaches of the prior literature analyzing the withholding-based attacks, e.g., [14,15], but we construct the model to enable the analyses of the novel UBA attack we introduce. The reward distributed depends on the miner's computational power, and we normalize the following variables with respect to the entire mining network's computation power. i.e., the total mining power has a power of 1. The attacker's computation power is α while the victim pool's mining power without the attacker's power is β, so $0 \leq \alpha + \beta \leq 1$. The attacker splits its power between its main pool (honest mining) and the victim pool (willing to launch mining attack strategies to increase the attacker's reward at the expense of the fellow miners in the victim pool), and the fraction of the attacker's power for infiltration of the victim pool is τ (where $0 \leq \tau \leq 1$). Therefore, the attacker's power on the victim pool is $\tau\alpha$, and the total mining power on the victim pool is $\tau\alpha + \beta$ even though the attacker's power may not contribute to the pool earning reward depending on the attack strategies (honest mining is within the attacker's options, and the attacker will do so legitimately contributing to the pool earning if honest mining is the reward-optimal strategy for the attacker). For example, in the simpler BWH attack, the attacker does not submit block at all in the victim pool so the actual power contributing to block earnings of the pool is only β, while the attacker still earns the mining credit and the corresponding reward through share submissions and the reward earning gets split by $\tau\alpha + \beta$ within the victim pool.

In FAW attack, the attacker submits the withheld block on the victim pool only when another block by a third-party pool is submitted and getting propagated. The attacker is motivated to do so and cause a fork because the attacker does not get any reward if a third-party pool wins the block. c denotes the probability that the attacker's block will get rewarded as opposed to the third-party pool's, and c depends on the networking state/topology between the two block submissions.

A miner's expected reward normalized by the reward amount is denoted with R. For example, if an attacker behaves honestly, its expected reward (R_{honest}) is proportional to its computational power by the design of the PoW consensus and the mining pools,

$$R_{\text{honest}} = \alpha \tag{1}$$

The following summarizes the variables used for the reward analyses of the block-withholding threats (more complexity and variables are added as we use them to describe the mining pool game and analyze the uncle-block attack).

α: Attacker's computational power
β: Computational power of the victim pool

τ: Fraction of attacker's power for infiltration of victim
c: Probability that the attacker wins the reward given that there is a fork (collision with another block propagation)

5.2 BWH Attack and FAW Attack Analyses

To provide baselines and examples of the use of our model in Sect. 5.1, we analyze the expected reward of BWH and FAW. This section adapts the prior work in FAW [14], and we only highlight the parts which are the most relevant to our work in this section.

For BWH, the attacker has two possible events for earning a positive reward (in other events, the attacker earns zero reward). The first event is when the attacker finds a block in its honest-mining main pool (the event A) while the second event corresponds to when another miner from the victim pool, not the attacker, finds a block (B). Because the probability of winning a block is proportional to the computational power spent on mining the block and because $1 - \tau\alpha$ amount of power from all miners actually contributes to finding the block (the attacker uses the other $\tau\alpha$ to still compute the PoW but only submit shares while withholding the blocks), the probability of A is $\frac{(1-\tau)\alpha}{1-\tau\alpha}$ and the probability of B is $\frac{\beta}{1-\tau\alpha}$. Assuming negligible probability for natural forking, the expected reward for block-withholding attack normalized by the reward amount (R_{BWH}) is:

$$
\begin{aligned}
R_{\mathrm{BWH}} &= \mathrm{E}[R|A] \cdot \mathrm{Pr}(A) + \mathrm{E}[R|B] \cdot \mathrm{Pr}(B) \\
&= 1 \cdot \frac{(1-\tau)\alpha}{1-\tau\alpha} + \frac{\tau\alpha}{\beta+\tau\alpha} \cdot \frac{\beta}{1-\tau\alpha} \\
&= \frac{(1-\tau)\alpha}{1-\tau\alpha} + \frac{\tau\alpha}{\beta+\tau\alpha} \cdot \frac{\beta}{1-\tau\alpha}
\end{aligned}
\tag{2}
$$

The FAW attack builds on BWH but provides an extra channel for attacker reward. In addition to the events A and B, the attacker can earn reward by broadcasting the withheld block when a third-party miner outside of the attacker-involved main pool and victim pool finds a block, causing a fork and hence the name fork-after-withholding (FAW). This event of the attacker finding a block *and* a third-party miner finding a block is C. The expected reward for FAW attack normalized by the reward amount (R_{FAW}) is:

$$
\begin{aligned}
R_{\mathrm{FAW}} &= \mathrm{E}[R|A] \cdot \mathrm{Pr}(A) + \mathrm{E}[R|B] \cdot \mathrm{Pr}(B) + \mathrm{E}[R|C] \cdot \mathrm{Pr}(C) \\
&= 1 \cdot \frac{(1-\tau)\alpha}{1-\tau\alpha} + \frac{\tau\alpha}{\beta+\tau\alpha} \cdot \frac{\beta}{1-\tau\alpha} + 1 \cdot c \cdot \frac{\tau\alpha}{\beta+\tau\alpha} \cdot \tau\alpha \frac{1-\alpha-\beta}{1-\tau\alpha} \\
&= \frac{(1-\tau)\alpha}{1-\tau\alpha} + \frac{\tau\alpha}{\beta+\tau\alpha} \left(\frac{\beta}{1-\tau\alpha} + c\tau\alpha \frac{1-\alpha-\beta}{1-\tau\alpha} \right)
\end{aligned}
\tag{3}
$$

We summarize and list the three events which yield the attacker positive rewards, as we also use them for our analyses of the rewards for UBA:

A: Attacker's main pool finds a block
B: Another miner from the victim pool finds a block
C: Third-party miner finds a block

6   Uncle-Block Attack

Uncle-block attack (UBA) builds on the FAW attack but exploits the uncle blocks, which are blocks which caused fork but did not eventually get selected as the main block on the blockchain. In UBA, the attacker submits all its withheld blocks at the end of the round (when any block gets propagated). This strategy is different from FAW in that the attacker still submits the withheld block in the events A and B, as opposed to not submitting it as in BWH/FAW attack. This results in the attacker receiving two blocks worth (one main block and one uncle block) of rewards. In addition, uncle-block attack increases the reward in the event C because the block which does not become the main block (corresponding to the $1 - c$ probability in Sect. 5.1) also gets rewarded by the uncle reward.

Uncle block rewards (rewarding multiple blocks in a round) results in greater complexity in the mining game and yields the vulnerability for UBA. For example, one can envision an attacker continue to mine using the same block header until it exhausts the reward in that round (although this turns out to be suboptimal if uncle block has less rewards than the main blocks according to our analyses). In the rest of the section, we introduce the UBA strategy, establish that a non-attacker who does not control/vary the timing of the block submissions is incentivized to move on to the next round (as opposed to staying within the round for uncle rewards), and analyze the optimal miner strategy for the attacker controlling the timing of the submissions. Using these insights, we also quantify the expected reward of UBA and provide a lower bound that is independent of networking conditions (c), which is in contrast to FAW.

6.1   Uncle-Block Model: κ and λ

Suppose the blockchain provides non-zero rewards up to λ uncle blocks and the reward per uncle block is κ. These are blockchain system parameters, for example, $\lambda = 2$ and $\kappa = \frac{7}{8}$ in Ethereum. In practice, these parameters have the following constraints: $\lambda < \infty$ limits the number of rewardable uncle blocks, and $\kappa < 1$ bounds the uncle reward so that the main block is more valuable than the uncle blocks. In each round, the blockchain will provide rewards which can range from 1 (no fork and thus no uncle blocks) to $1 + \lambda\kappa$ (1 main block and λ uncle blocks get rewarded), normalized with respect to the main-block reward.

As a trivial result, UBA reduces to FAW if there is no uncle reward, i.e., $\lambda = 0$ or $\kappa = 0$. Therefore, we focus on the case when there is a positive uncle reward, i.e., $\lambda > 0$ and $\kappa > 0$.

6.2   In Main Pool: Advance with New Block

In this section, we study the miner strategy in its main pool (no infiltration/gaming against other pool members, for example, solo member in the pool). In its main pool, a miner who found a block can still mine from the same block header instead of advancing to the next round with the updated block. Despite the option, the following lemma shows that the miner will be incentivized not to do so and follow the consensus protocol to update the PoW header/execution and move on to the next round if the main block yields greater reward than the uncle blocks. In other words, a miner will choose to advance to the next round rather than mining for the uncle block within the same round if $\kappa < 1$.

Lemma 1. *The optimal miner strategy is the honest mining (following the protocol and advancing to the next round) in its main pool if $\kappa < 1$.*

Proof. The inter-arrival time between the block findings follows an exponential distribution and therefore the block finding process is memoryless, i.e., given that the block is not found, the expected time to find a block is the same as before. Therefore, the miner gains greater reward by mining for the main block and not for the uncle block if $\kappa < 1$, and the reward-optimal mining strategy is to update the block header whenever available.

6.3   Uncle-Block Attack Reward Analyses

We compute the expected reward of UBA, aggregated across the attacker-involved pools and normalized by the reward amount, to show the effectiveness of the attack. Assuming that the attacker updates the round/block header if it finds a block in its honest-mining main pool (as is established to be reward-optimal in Lemma 1), the following theorems provide insights about the reward of UBA.

Theorem 1. *UBA outperforms FAW attack always (i.e., regardless of α, β, τ, c, and κ) and its reward is greater than that in Eq. 4.*

Proof. In all events which provide positive reward to the attacker, A, B, and C, finding an extra block within the same round (using the same block header) only increases the attacker reward if the uncle reward is positive ($\kappa > 0$). The attacker behavior/strategy changes from FAW in events A and B, and UBA increases the reward from FAW (Eq. 3) in all three event cases. In event A (when the attacker finds a block in its honest-mining main pool), the attacker rewards increases from FAW because there is a positive probability of $\tau\alpha \cdot \frac{(1-\tau)\alpha}{1-\tau\alpha}$ that the attacker has been withholding another block in the victim pool (since the main pool mining and the victim pool mining are independent). In such case, the attacker has the control over both blocks and will prioritize the block in the main pool by broadcasting the block in the main pool before the one in the victim pool because, in contrast to the attacker's solo mining in the main pool, the reward in the victim pool gets shared by the other pool members (in which case the uncle

$$R_{\text{UBA}} = E[R|A] \cdot \Pr(A) + E[R|B] \cdot \Pr(B) + E[R|C] \cdot \Pr(C)$$

$$\geq (1 + \kappa \frac{\tau\alpha}{\beta + \tau\alpha} \cdot \tau\alpha) \cdot \frac{(1 - \tau)\alpha}{1 - \tau\alpha} + (1 + \kappa \cdot \tau\alpha) \frac{\tau\alpha}{\beta + \tau\alpha} \cdot \frac{\beta}{1 - \tau\alpha}$$

$$+ [1 \cdot c + \kappa \cdot (1 - c)] \frac{\tau\alpha}{\beta + \tau\alpha} \cdot \tau\alpha \frac{1 - \alpha - \beta}{1 - \tau\alpha}$$

$$= \frac{(1 - \tau)\alpha}{1 - \tau\alpha} + \frac{\tau\alpha}{\beta + \tau\alpha} \left(\kappa \frac{(\tau\alpha)^2}{\beta + \tau\alpha} \cdot \frac{(1 - \tau)\alpha}{1 - \tau\alpha} + (1 + \kappa\tau\alpha) \frac{\beta}{1 - \tau\alpha} + [c + (1 - c)\kappa] \tau\alpha \frac{1 - \alpha - \beta}{1 - \tau\alpha} \right) \quad (4)$$

$$\geq \frac{(1 - \tau)\alpha}{1 - \tau\alpha} + \frac{\tau\alpha}{\beta + \tau\alpha} \left(\kappa \frac{(\tau\alpha)^2}{\beta + \tau\alpha} \cdot \frac{(1 - \tau)\alpha}{1 - \tau\alpha} + (1 + \kappa\tau\alpha) \frac{\beta}{1 - \tau\alpha} + \kappa\tau\alpha \frac{1 - \alpha - \beta}{1 - \tau\alpha} \right) \quad (5)$$

reward is $\kappa \frac{\tau\alpha}{\beta + \tau\alpha}$). In event B (when another miner in the victim pool finds a block), the attacker could have also been withholding a block in the victim pool, which occurs with a probability of $\tau\alpha \cdot \frac{\beta}{1 - \tau\alpha}$, in which case the attacker gets rewarded for both the main block and the uncle block (regardless of which block wins the fork racing) increases to $(1 + \kappa) \frac{\tau\alpha}{\beta + \tau\alpha}$ from just discarding/withholding the found block as in FAW/BWH yielding $\frac{\tau\alpha}{\beta + \tau\alpha}$ in Eq. 3. In the event C (when the attacker has been withholding a block in the victim pool and a third-party miner finds a block), unlike the FAW attack which disregards uncle blocks, even if the attacker's block does not become the main block with a probability of $(1 - c) \cdot \tau\alpha \frac{1 - \alpha - \beta}{1 - \tau\alpha}$, it still gets rewarded by the uncle reward of κ. Putting it together, Eq. 4 presents the expected reward for the UBA attack. The expected reward for launching UBA in Eq. 4 is greater than the FAW reward in Eq. 3 for any α, β, τ, c.

Theorem 1 provides a lower bound of the UBA's reward performance in Eq. 4, which is greater than the FAW reward performance, providing greater unfair reward and incentives for the attackers to conduct the attack. Equation 4 is a lower bound because we ignore the cases when the attacker-controlled victim pool finds multiple blocks before the others do within the same round (which provides positive reward increment if $\lambda > 1$). The bound is rather tight and close to the actual expected reward because the ignored reward cases has exponentially decreasing probabilities; more specifically, the probability of the attacker finding x number of blocks in the victim pool within a round grows by $(\tau\alpha)^x$.

Theorem 2. *UBA's reward is greater than Eq. 5, which is independent of c, if $\kappa \leq 1$.*

Proof. From Eq. 4, by assuming that $\kappa \leq 1$ (i.e., the uncle reward is not greater than the main reward), $c + (1 - c)\kappa \geq c\kappa + (1 - c)\kappa = \kappa$, which yields Eq. 5. The inequality becomes an equality if $\kappa = 1$ (the uncle reward and main reward have the same reward amount) or $c = 0$ (the attacker's fork-causing block always loses to the third-party block submissions).

Theorem 2 presents the UBA's reward performance which is independent of c, which is a critical environmental parameter in FAW and depends on the networking topology and conditions of the attacker. (For example, FAW attack converges to BWH if $c \to 0$.) The magnitude of κ determines how close the approximation is to the actual reward (the greater the κ the tighter the approximation).

We use Eqs. 4 and 5 for our simulation analyses and to quantify the reward performances with actual numerical values. Despite using the lower bound, we show that UBA's effectiveness and impact are significantly superior to the previously known withholding-based attacks, which state of the art is FAW.

To further maximize its reward, an attacker can dynamically control its control parameter τ since if it can know/estimate the rest of the environmental parameters in α, β, and c and the system parameter in κ. The attacker can optimize its τ either by solving it mathematically to check for local maximum ($\frac{dR_{uba}}{d\tau} = 0$) or by using an optimization algorithm (e.g., gradient-descent algorithm). To present a stronger threat, we assume such capability for the attacker, e.g., the attacker can correctly estimate α, β, and c (e.g., α and β are publicly accessible and Eq. 5 enables optimization even if c cannot be estimated) and study the impact of the attacker dynamically adapting its τ to improve its reward in Sect. 7.2; we call the attacker's reward when using the optimal τ τ-capacity.

7   Simulation Analyses

7.1   Simulation Setup and Parameters

We analyze UBA using Monte-Carlo simulations and numerical analyses. Our model introduces environmental parameters (α, β), attacker's control parameters (τ), and the blockchain system control parameters (κ, λ). We focus our analyses from the attacker's perspective (observing the attacker's reward) and thus vary the attacker-controlled parameters (α, τ). This section explains the simulations settings and the parameter choices to characterize the blockchain system and the victim pool system under attack.

Our blockchain system simulation setup is influenced by modern blockchain implementations, e.g., $\kappa = \frac{7}{8}$ as is in Ethereum (the second largest cryptocurrency behind Bitcoin). We set $\lambda = 1$ which is the worse-case for the attacker's reward; any other reward-distribution algorithm supporting $\lambda > 1$, e.g., Ethereum, provides greater reward to the attackers and therefore provides them with greater incentives/impacts to conduct UBA. For the pool system, $\beta = 0.24$, which value corresponds to the strongest mining pool in real-world mining at the time of this writing [2]. The attacker attacking the stronger pool as its victim pool (as opposed to a weaker pool of $\beta \to 0$) provides greater reward and is aligned with its incentive, which we verify in our simulations and agree with previous literature [1,14]. These parameters are fixed unless otherwise noted (we vary the variables to analyze the dependency and the impacts).

We also consider the 51% attack where the attacker can fully control the blockchain if the attacker's computational power exceeds the 50% of the network's. In our context, the 51% attacker can conduct withholding-based selfish mining to reverse the transactions/blocks on the chain and to waste the other miner's computational resources on blocks which the attacker can reverse and make stale. Therefore, we limit our analyses to $0 \leq \alpha \leq 0.5$ (the attacker is capable of 51% attack if $\alpha > 0.5$) in addition to the constraint of $\alpha + \beta \leq 1$ from the definitions of α and β.

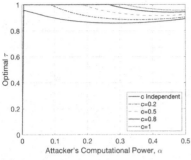

(a) Optimal τ for achieving τ-capacity

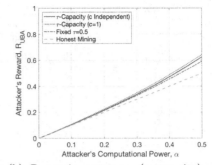

(b) Dynamic strategy (τ-capacity) vs. fixed strategy (no adaptation of τ), including honest mining

Fig. 1. Uncle-block attack (UBA) analyses

7.2   UBA: Dynamic Control and τ-Capacity

In this section, we analyze UBA, which generalizes FAW and BWH. The attacker controls τ and can dynamically adapt it to the environment to maximize its reward. We call such τ the *optimal* τ and the corresponding reward is the τ-*capacity*. Figure 1(a) plots the optimal τ with respect to the attacker's power capability α while varying c. The attacker's optimal τ quickly increases, i.e., the attacker spends more power on infiltration and on the victim pool and less on the honest-behaving main pool, when the attacker has computational power and participates in mining ($\alpha > 0$). With greater c, the attacker's power on the victim pool increases, and there are more α-cases when the attacker's optimal τ is equal to one and the attacker only mines on the victim pool (no power allocated on the main pool). $c = 0$ (i.e., the attacker always loses the forking race against the third-party block submission) represents the worst-case in c and yields the "c independent" reward in Eq. 5. Despite this lower bound and the unfavorable networking condition to the attacker, the attacker still focuses larger amount of its power on the infiltration of the victim pool for maximizing its reward. As long as the attacker has non-zero power ($\alpha > 0$), the attacker spends more than 85.8% of its power on infiltration regardless of c.

Figure 1(b) plots the attacker's reward assuming dynamic τ control (τ-capacity), fixed τ control, and honest mining (no withholding of blocks and shares). The attacker's reward increases with c, and varying c results in reward values between the lowest in $c = 0$ (yielding c-independent reward in Eq. 5) and the highest in $c = 1$; for example, if $\alpha = 0.1$, then the reward increases from 0.101 at $c = 0$ to 0.108 at $c = 1$ and, if $\alpha = 0.24$, then the reward increases from 0.250 at $c = 0$ to 0.278 at $c = 1$ (not shown in the plot). The dynamic strategy choosing the optimal τ and reaching the τ-capacity always outperforms the fixed strategy by definition of τ-capacity; to provide a representative fixed-strategy reward analysis distinguishable in plots, Fig. 1(b) includes data with the suboptimal fixed strategy of $\tau = 0.5$ (half of the power on the main pool and the

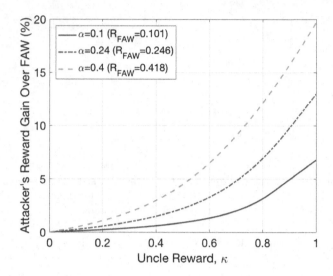

Fig. 2. UBA reward gain over FAW (the legend box includes the FAW reward magnitude corresponding to 0% gain)

other half on the victim pool). Also, the uncle-block attack always outperforms the honest mining, which corresponds to $\tau = 0$ (all computational power in the main pool and no withholding). Moving forward, we assume that the attacker is capable of dynamically adapting τ and achieving the τ-capacity, which requires the correct estimation of α and β (e.g., the hash rate estimations are publicly available, e.g., [2]).

7.3 UBA's Impact Beyond the State of the Art

To compare UBA with FAW, we analyze the *reward gain* of UBA over FAW, which is the difference between the rewards of the two attacks in %. As shown in Fig. 2, the reward gain increases with the uncle reward of κ. As the uncle reward κ increases, UBA provides greater reward to the attacker and the reward gain (the difference from the FAW) also increases; in fact, the UBA's reward converges to that of FAW when $\kappa \to 0$. The reward gain also increases with the attacker's power capability of α both in its magnitude and in the baseline of the FAW attack reward (0% reward gain). In other words, not only the FAW reward itself increases with α but also the UBA's reward gain with respect to the FAW increases; Fig. 2 plots the results when $\alpha = 0.1$, $\alpha = 0.24$ (which is equal to β), and $\alpha = 0.4$.

8   Discussions for Potential Countermeasures

While our work introduces a new vulnerability/threat and sheds negative lights on the uncle block system component of blockchain, we do not recommend blindly discarding the uncle-block mechanism since it serves a useful purpose in increasing fairness among the miners, especially for those experiencing networking discrepancies. Rather, we intend to inform the blockchain researchers and developers for their parameter decisions and future design constructions. Replacement mechanisms and their incorporation to the overall blockchain system remains an open challenge for blockchain research and development. In this section, we list the potential countermeasure ideas, which we consider to be of relatively lower overheads for deployment except for those in Sects. 8.5 and 8.2, to encourage research in preventing and mitigating UBA and other withholding-based threats; the actual development, the system incorporation, and the effective analyses against UBA are outside the scope of this paper.

8.1   Detection Based on Reward Behavior

The withholding-based threats result in abnormal reward behaviors. For example, FAW or UBA increases the forking probability at the blockchain level. Such phenomenon can be sensed and measured for attack detection, which can be then used for mitigation purposes. While we identify behavior-based detection as promising, we do not recommend relying on identity-based detection and mitigation/blacklisting mechanisms, since the identity control is virtually non-existent and it is cheap for the attacker to generate multiple identities/accounts (Sybil attack) by the design of the permissionless blockchains.

8.2   Block Obfuscation and Oblivious Share

Building on the commit-and-reveal/commitment framework in cryptography, *oblivious share* deprives the miner of the knowledge of whether a share is a block (a share fulfilling a harder requirement) or a share until the miner submits the share [11,18]. The attacker (malicious or selfish miner) therefore cannot dynamically adopt the withholding-based threats which require distinguishing the share and the block before submission. While effective against the withholding-based attacks, such approach requires a protocol change (an additional exchange between the mining pool manager and the miners) and is not backward compatible (does not work with the existing system unless the protocol change/update is made) [14,15], causing protocol/communication overheads and making such schemes undesirable for implementation to the blockchain network (which includes closed pools and solo miners, free of withholding vulnerabilities).

8.3   Payout and Reward Function Control

A low-overhead countermeasure is to modify the payout and reward functions, for example, controlling the system parameters of κ and λ in our model. For example, Bag and Sakurai proposes "special reward" for the block submissions [1] to distinguish between block submissions and share submissions (different weights) against block-withholding attack; introducing such parameter can also be useful against UBA.

8.4 Share Timestamping

Timestamping the shares to ensure that the submission order is the same as their finding [7] can help mitigating the withholding-based attacks. Such mechanism can prevent from further share submissions after withholding blocks in UBA and FAW (since the later shares become invalid if they are detected that they have been found after the block) or aid the abnormal-detection mechanisms in Sect. 8.1 by providing crucial timing/order information. SmartPool [16] also uses timestamping to order/sort the shares but for different purpose (for its data structure and to prevent duplicate share submissions).

8.5 Mining Pool Unification

A radical solution to the withholding-based threats is to have one mining pool only so that there is a single mining pool for the miners to join. Having one mining pool for the entire blockchain network eliminates the notion of sabotaging/victimizing a pool. A useful platform for implementing such solution can be distributed mining pools, e.g., SmartPool [16] and P2Pool, which eliminates the centralized mining pool manager and replaces it with a distributed program/computing, motivated to make the blockchain computing more decentralized without the reliance on trusted third party (the mining pool manager in this case) [4,12]. In fact, SmartPool [16] envisions that their platform can be used to unify the mining pools citing that the elimination of the mining pool fee (charged by the centralized mining pool manager for their services) and the reduced variance (compared to independent mining) will provide the incentives for such vision. However, despite such desirable properties, it can be difficult to enforce the change in behaviors in the miners and have all miners mine at the designated pool, especially for an existing blockchain implementation with the existing miners having already joined a pool; enforcing such pool restriction for the miners can also be viewed as a violation of the freedom of the miners and is not backward-compatible to the existing miners.

9 Conclusion

Blockchain uses PoW-based mining and mining pools to achieve consensus in cryptocurrencies. From real-world blockchain and mining pool system implementations, we discover that uncle blocks can be used for exploits by a rational and uncooperative attacker and introduce the uncle-block attack (UBA) strategy. UBA advances and outperforms the prior withholding-based attack strategies in FAW and BWH and is effective even in the case when the attacker has an unfavorable networking environment (which limited the effectiveness of the previous state of the art attack strategy of FAW). Since UBA has the same attack setup requirements as BWH (which already have reported incidents in the real-world implementations), the more impactful UBA presents greater risk against vulnerable blockchain systems.

While our work introducing the novel UBA threat strategy and focusing on the threat/impact analyses raises issues on the current blockchain system components (e.g., mining pool and uncle block), we do not recommend blindly discarding them since they serve useful purposes. Rather, we intend to inform the blockchain researchers and developers for their parameter decisions and future design constructions. Countering UBA and other withholding threats and depriving the rational attackers of the threat incentives remain open challenge for blockchain research and development.

References

1. Bag, S., Sakurai, K.: Yet another note on block withholding attack on bitcoin mining pools. In: Bishop, M., Nascimento, A.C.A. (eds.) ISC 2016. LNCS, vol. 9866, pp. 167–180. Springer, Cham (2016). https://doi.org/10.1007/978-3-319-45871-7_11
2. blockchain.com. Hash rate distribution. https://www.blockchain.com/en/pools
3. blockchain.com. Market capitalization. https://www.blockchain.com/charts/market-cap
4. Bonneau, J., Miller, A., Clark, J., Narayanan, A., Kroll, J.A., Felten, E.W.: SoK: research perspectives and challenges for bitcoin and cryptocurrencies. In: 2015 IEEE Symposium on Security and Privacy, May 2015, pp. 104–121 (2015)
5. Buterin, V.: Ethereum: a next-generation smart contract and decentralized application platform (2014). https://github.com/ethereum/wiki/wiki/White-Paper. Accessed 22 Aug 2016
6. Carlsten, M., Kalodner, H., Weinberg, S.M., Narayanan, A.: On the instability of bitcoin without the block reward. In: Proceedings of the 2016 ACM SIGSAC Conference on Computer and Communications Security, CCS 2016, pp. 154–167. ACM, New York (2016). https://doi.org/10.1145/2976749.2978408
7. Chang, S.-Y., Park, Y.: Silent timestamping for blockchain mining pool security. In: IEEE International Workshop on Computing, Networking and Communications (CNC) (2019)
8. CoinMarketCap. Top 100 cryptocurrencies by market capitalization. https://coinmarketcap.com
9. Eyal, I.: The miner's dilemma. In: Proceedings of the 2015 IEEE Symposium on Security and Privacy, SP 2015, pp. 89–103. IEEE Computer Society, Washington, DC (2015). https://doi.org/10.1109/SP.2015.13
10. Eyal, I., Sirer, E.G.: Majority is not enough: bitcoin mining is vulnerable. CoRR, abs/1311.0243 (2013)
11. Eyal, I., Sirer, E.G.: How to disincentivize large bitcoin mining pools, June 2014
12. Gervais, A., Karame, G.O., Capkun, V., Capkun, S.: Is bitcoin a decentralized currency? IEEE Secur. Priv. 12(3), 54–60 (2014)
13. Gervais, A., Karame, G.O., Wüst, K., Glykantzis, V., Ritzdorf, H., Capkun, S.: On the security and performance of proof of work blockchains. In: Proceedings of the 2016 ACM SIGSAC Conference on Computer and Communications Security, CCS 2016, pp. 3–16. ACM, New York (2016). https://doi.org/10.1145/2976749.2978341
14. Kwon, Y., Kim, D., Son, Y., Vasserman, E., Kim, Y.: Be selfish and avoid dilemmas: fork after withholding (FAW) attacks on bitcoin. In: Proceedings of the 2017 ACM SIGSAC Conference on Computer and Communications Security, CCS 2017, pp. 195–209. ACM, New York (2017). https://doi.org/10.1145/3133956.3134019

15. Luu, L., Saha, R., Parameshwaran, I., Saxena, P., Hobor, A.: On power splitting games in distributed computation: the case of bitcoin pooled mining. In: 2015 IEEE 28th Computer Security Foundations Symposium, July 2015, pp. 397–411 (2015)

16. Luu, L., Velner, Y., Teutsch, J., Saxena, P.: SmartPool: practical decentralized pooled mining. In: 26th USENIX Security Symposium (USENIX Security 2017), pp. 1409–1426. USENIX Association, Vancouver, BC (2017). https://www.usenix.org/conference/usenixsecurity17/technical-sessions/presentation/luu

17. Nakamoto, S.: Bitcoin: a peer-to-peer electronic cash system (2008)

18. Rosenfeld, M.: Analysis of bitcoin pooled mining reward systems. CoRR, abs/1112.4980 (2011). http://arxiv.org/abs/1112.4980

19. Sapirshtein, A., Sompolinsky, Y., Zohar, A.: Optimal selfish mining strategies in bitcoin. In: Grossklags, J., Preneel, B. (eds.) FC 2016. LNCS, vol. 9603, pp. 515–532. Springer, Heidelberg (2017). https://doi.org/10.1007/978-3-662-54970-4_30

20. Tsabary, I., Eyal, I.: The gap game. CoRR, abs/1805.05288 (2018)

21. Wood, G.: Ethereum: a secure decentralised generalised transaction ledger EIP-150 revision (759dccd - 2017–08-07) (2017). https://ethereum.github.io/yellowpaper/paper.pdf. Accessed 12 May 2018

Longitudinal Analysis
of Misuse of Bitcoin

Karim Eldefrawy[1](✉), Ashish Gehani[1], and Alexandre Matton[2]

[1] SRI International, Menlo Park, USA
karim.eldefrawy@sri.com
[2] Stanford University, Stanford, USA

Abstract. We conducted a longitudinal study to analyze the misuse of
Bitcoin. We first investigated usage characteristics of Bitcoin by analyzing how many addresses each address transacts with (from January
2009 to May 2018). To obtain a quantitative estimate of the malicious
activity that Bitcoin is associated with, we collected over 2.3 million
candidate Bitcoin addresses, harvested from the dark web between June
2016 and December 2017. The Bitcoin addresses found on the dark web
were labeled with tags that classified the activities associated with the
onions that these addresses were collected from. The tags covered a wide
range of activities, from suspicious to outright malicious or illegal. Of
these addresses, only 47,697 have tags we consider indicative of suspicious or malicious activities.

We saw a clear decline in the monthly number of Bitcoin addresses
seen on the dark web in the periods coinciding with takedowns of known
dark web markets. We also found interesting behavior that distinguishes
the Bitcoin addresses collected from the dark web when compared to
activity of a random address on the Bitcoin blockchain. For example,
we found that Bitcoin addresses used on the dark web are more likely
to be involved in mixing transactions. To identify mixing transactions,
we developed a new heuristic that extends previously known ones. We
found that Bitcoin addresses found on the dark web are significantly
more active, they engage in transactions with 20 times the neighbors
and 4 times the Bitcoin amounts when compared to random addresses.
We also found that just 2,828 Bitcoin addresses are responsible for 99%
of the Bitcoin value used on the dark web.

1 Introduction

Understanding how cryptocurrencies may affect society depends on being able to
analyze their use and misuse. We present a first step in this direction. Our study

This material is based upon work supported by the National Science Foundation (NSF)
under Grant ACI-1547467. Any opinions, findings, and conclusions or recommendations
expressed in this material are those of the authors and do not necessarily reflect the
views of NSF.
A. Matton—Research performed while visiting SRI.

© Springer Nature Switzerland AG 2019
R. H. Deng et al. (Eds.): ACNS 2019, LNCS 11464, pp. 259–278, 2019.
https://doi.org/10.1007/978-3-030-21568-2_13

shows a decline in the level of malicious Bitcoin activity over the years, when measured in terms of the number of addresses involved. The decline of Bitcoin's usage in suspicious and malicious activities is not surprising for those who follow the space closely. There is now an increased awareness about the lack of strong anonymity in Bitcoin, in comparison with other privacy-preserving coins, such as Monero [18] and Zcash [24]. Even though Bitcoin usage in suspicious activities is declining, our study is still useful since it provides a quantitative understanding of the trend. We believe that our findings can benefit other researchers as well as help educate administrators and law enforcement as they create and implement new regulations.

1.1 Cryptocurrency Studies

Analysis of Bitcoin: One of the first attempts to analyze the Bitcoin blockchain was performed in 2012 by Ron and Shamir [21]. They studied Bitcoin's transactions graph and identified interesting patterns in it. The scale and complexity of the graph has exploded in the seven years since that study was performed. Subsequent analyses [1,4,16,19,20,23] have used heuristics to cluster Bitcoin wallets, based on evidence of shared authority, and then perform active re-identification attacks – for example, by purchasing goods and services to classify the operators in clusters [16], and searching for transaction patterns on exchanges [20].

BitRank [3] is a proprietary wallet scoring system developed by the startup Blockchain Intelligence Group (BIG). BIG's website states that the current beta version of BitRank performs real-time risk assessment to determine the relative safety of pending Bitcoin transactions. As of January 2019, the site provides little public information about the technical details of the system. There are several other services that analyze Bitcoin (and other systems such as Ethereum and Litecoin) to aid businesses and law enforcement. These include Chainanalysis [9], CipherTrace [10], and Elliptic [11]. To the best of our knowledge, they have not published analysis that covers the material in our study for the duration we consider.

In parallel to our effort, Lee *et al.* [15] collected 27 million dark web pages and extracted a mix of 10 million unique Bitcoin, Ethereum, and Monero addresses. They classified the usage of the addresses, identified their use in the trade of illicit goods, and traced cryptocurrency flows, to reveal black money activity on the dark web. Their analysis shows that more than 80% of Bitcoin addresses found on the dark web were involved in malicious activities. The monetary value of the associated cryptocurrency activity was estimated to be $180 million.

Other Cryptocurrencies: In recent work [17], some transactions of the privacy-focused cryptocurrency Monero [18] were found to be highly linkable. We do not claim that any of our analysis or results apply to privacy-preserving cryptocurrencies. This paper only considers Bitcoin, with similar analysis of Monero left as challenging future work.

1.2   Contributions

We provide the following:

- A quantitative study on the misuse of Bitcoin in malicious contexts. Such activities are identified by collecting Bitcoin addresses that are advertised as a means of payment on dark web onions associated with a wide range of undertakings, such as selling illegal substances, human trafficking, and ransomware.
- New heuristics to identify *CoinJoin* mixing transactions. We believe that our heuristics are of independent interest.

We emphasize that our study does not claim that Bitcoin has been (or is) used only for malicious or illegal activities. Our aim is to provide a quantitative assessment of the extent of such activities. This is critical for researchers, regulators, law enforcement, and the wider community to understand the magnitude and scope of the problem. We believe that this understanding is necessary for the cryptocurrency ecosystem to mature.

1.3   Summary of Findings

We highlight some of our results below.

1. **Bitcoin Ownership and Use (in Sect.** 3.1**):** Less than 0.06% of all Bitcoin addresses own over 99% of all bitcoins. In particular, that 0.06% consists of 2,266,265 out of 397,301,155 unique addresses observed. Between January 2009 and May 2018 each address participated in at least one of the 316,386,663 transactions that we analyzed. Most addresses were used at most a few times, which is what we expect based on how wallet software is designed and used.
2. **Bitcoin on the Dark Web (in Sect.** 3.3**):** Of the 2,093,568 Bitcoin addresses found on the dark web, 276,549 were from mirrors of the *Blockchain.info* explorer. 82% of the remaining addresses were active – that is, participated in at least one transaction. In particular, there were 1,491,709 active addresses. Of these, only 47,697 had tags that we considered indicative of suspicious or malicious activities. Just 2,828 addresses owned 99% of the bitcoins that were involved in the dark web. There was a clear decline the number of Bitcoin addresses appearing on the dark web in the months in which dark web markets were taken down.
3. **Mixing Transactions (in Sect.** 4**):** The fraction of all Bitcoin addresses that participate in at least one CoinJoin transaction is only 0.4%. However, our analysis found that on the dark web, this fraction was 5 times higher – that is, 2.3% of Bitcoin addresses found here were part of CoinJoin operations.
4. **Transaction Characteristics (in Sects.** 5.1 **and** 5.2**):** When considering all Bitcoin addresses, 340,138,543 (85.7%) of them have transacted with less than 10 other addresses, while only 25,7925 (0.06%) have transacted with more than a 1,000 addresses, and only 6,178 (0.002%) transacted with more than 10,000 addresses. In contrast, 597,744 (40.1%) of Bitcoin addresses found

on the dark web have transacted fewer than 10 other addresses, while 61,330 (4.1%) have transacted with more than 1,000 addresses, and 3,244 (0.2%) have transacted with more than 10,000 addresses. The higher participation in mixers is one reason that the Bitcoin addresses found on the dark web have transacted with more addresses.

1.4   Study Limitations

Given the significant scope of the effort, it had its limitations. We note three in particular:

1. *Coverage of dark web:* The data spans June 2016 to December 2017. No claim is made regarding its completeness. Section 3.2 describes our collection methodology and the resulting data.
2. *Dark web data labeling:* We relied on previous research on (thematic) labeling of dark web onions to describe the activities that they are involved in. An address that is collected from an onion inherits its labels (which we call tags). Note that only a subset of tags are indicative of suspicious or malicious activities. Section 3.2 describes how the labeling was performed in prior work.
3. *Analysis accuracy:* Since we did not have the ground truth for much of the analysis that we performed, we could not cross-check the accuracy of our inferences. The transaction graph is based on publicly available information, ensuring its reliability. There is also a basis for confidence in the labeling of the dark web data since some of it was manually verified. Since our work on detecting mixing transactions depends on heuristics, the results may have both false positives and false negatives. However, we did verify as many mixing transactions as we could.

1.5   Outline

Section 2 covers background on Bitcoin and mixers (especially CoinJoin). Section 3 provides an overview of the data sets used in our study, a characterization of behavior observed in the individual data sets, a description of our modified heuristic for detecting mixing transactions, and the properties of such transactions. Section 5 presents more details of our Bitcoin analysis and our findings. Section 6 concludes with a discussion of future work.

2   Bitcoin Preliminaries

2.1   Identifying Bitcoin Addresses

Bitcoin uses the Elliptic Curve Digital Signature Algorithm (ECDSA). Each user has at least one ECDSA key pair. A user can digitally sign a transaction with their private key. The user's public key can be used to verify that the signature is valid. The user's Bitcoin address is an encoding of the 160-bit hash of the public key [6]. A Bitcoin address contains a built-in checksum. This allows detection of malformed addresses, as may occur if the address is mistyped.

A Bitcoin address can be generated offline using wallet software. Even if it is listed on web pages, it may never be used. We only consider an address active if it has appeared on the public Bitcoin blockchain. When bitcoins are sent to an address that is well-formed but not owned by any user (or if the user has lost the corresponding private key), the bitcoins will be lost. In the latter case, the private key may be recovered by alternate means [5].

To construct a Bitcoin address, the hash of the user's ECDSA public key and checksum are converted to an alphanumeric representation. This is performed using the Base58Check custom encoding scheme. The resulting address can contain all alphanumeric characters except 0, O, I, and l. Normal addresses start with 1, while addresses from script hashes begin with 3. An address that is used on the main Bitcoin network is 25–34 characters long. Most are 33 or 34 characters in length.

Initially, a regular expression was used to extract candidate Bitcoin addresses from the dark web pages. (See Sect. 3.2 for more information.) Of the 2.3 million found, 0.2 million failed to pass the checksum test [7]. It is expected that some addresses that were classified as inactive in the study will subsequently be used.

2.2   Mixing Transactions

A CoinJoin is a specific type of Bitcoin transaction. It enables a participant to increase their anonymity by "mixing" their payment with those of other users. Each participant creates a new Bitcoin address. Next, they construct a fixed size payment to it. This is then sent to an aggregator that collects all the participants' payments. The aggregator constructs a single transaction that includes all of the payments. This transaction is sent to all the participants for them to sign. The security of the CoinJoin depends on the fact that the transaction is not valid till every participant provides a signature. Once all the signatures are received, the transaction can be posted for inclusion in a block by a miner. Since the payments are all the same amount, there is no direct way to connect an output to a specific input. All of these steps are handled by wallet software. See the CoinShuffle paper [22] for more information.

The aggregator can be a centralized service or a peer-to-peer protocol. Some services are available on the public web, such a JoinMarket and CoinShuffle. Other services are only present on the dark web. Since the payment from a participant in a CoinJoin should only be connected to a single output, this class of transactions introduces noise in our analysis. Of equal concern is that all the other participants appear as payees. This motivated us to develop a heuristic to detect CoinJoins so that they can be excluded from selected portions of our analysis. See Sect. 4 for more detail.

3   Bitcoin and Dark Web Data Sets

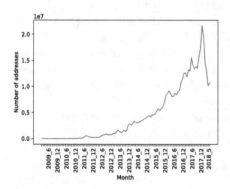

Fig. 1. Monthly used Bitcoin addresses

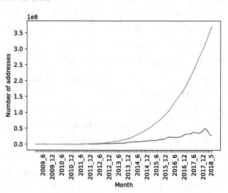

Fig. 2. Active (in last 3 months, blue) and inactive Bitcoin addresses (orange) (Color figure online)

Fig. 3. Bitcoin transactions per month

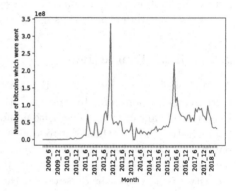

Fig. 4. Amount of bitcoins sent

3.1   Bitcoin's Blockchain

From the genesis of Bitcoin in 2009 to the end of May 2018, the blockchain contains 397,301,155 unique addresses that have participated in at least one of the 316,386,663 transactions that occurred in that timeframe. The number of addresses used in a given month has increased rapidly, as seen in Fig. 1. Since we collected this information using a Bitcoin client, we also cross-checked the numbers with data from the *Blockchain.info* explorer [2]. The number of transactions per month is also increasing, as seen in Fig. 3. However, the quantity of bitcoins transferred each month is significantly more volatile than the number of addresses used or transactions. This can be seen in Fig. 4 (Fig. 2).

Bitcoin addresses behave very differently from each other. Most addresses are only used a few times. This is because the reuse of a single address makes a user more susceptible to deanonymization. A payment from an address must reference and not exceed the sum of past Unspent Transaction Outputs (UTXOs) to that address. To avoid overpayment, a change address is used. In principle, this can be the payer's original address. In practice, it is a different address for the aforementioned reason. The use of wallet software automates the process of using a new address for each transaction and a different change address.

Many addresses participate in several transactions. Some participate in a large number of transactions. For multiple measures, such as the number of transactions per address, or the number of bitcoins received by each address, the resulting graphs can be approximated by a Pareto power-law distribution. For instance, more than 99% of bitcoins used in transactions belong to just 0.06% of the number of addresses that have been used. (The 0.06% set consisted of 2,266,265 addresses.).

3.2   Dark Web Data

Prior work at SRI focused on collecting, labeling, and categorizing information from the dark web [12]. The effort had to first receive approval from SRI's Institutional Review Board (IRB) due to the complex legal and ethical considerations involved. We have not focused on these aspects in our research. Instead, we use data from that study, consisting of labels associated with Bitcoin addresses found on the dark web. Section 1.4 on the limitations of our work identifies this labeling of dark web data as a possible source of error.

For completeness, we briefly discuss the methodology used to collect the data from the dark web. See the description by Ghosh *et al.* [12] for further detail. An acquisition infrastructure was constructed to discover new onion websites, crawl their content, and integrate them into an indexed repository. This leveraged OnionCrawler, a fully automated crawling tool to identify new Tor onion domains. The dark web crawling system was run continuously, twice per day, to address diurnal patterns in onion site availability. If a string that matched the Bitcoin address format was found on a page, the address was associated with the onion (and its labels).

Seed data was used from previously published onion data sets, references to onions in a large collection of DNS resolver logs, and an open repository of (non-onion) web crawl data, called the Common Crawl. The automated categorization was used to label each onion with tags describing the activity found on its pages. We believe the tag provides a clear indication of the activity it refers to. We focused on the following tags in most of our analysis: PONZI, MARKET, HUMAN_TRAFFIC, HACKER, DRUGS, CHILD_P, COUNTERFEIT, RANSOM, CASINO, NATIONALSEC, HOSTING_PROVIDER, PIRAT-EBAY, HITMAN, WEAPONS, JIHAD, EXPLOSIVES, CREDIT_CARD_FRAUD, DISCL-OSURES, ANONYMOUS, PIRATE_BAY, MURDER, DOXBIN, ALPHA_MARKET, ESCORT, WIKILEAKS, DECRYPT_RANSOM.

About 2.3 million candidate Bitcoin addresses were found in the dark web pages. As explained in Sect. 2.1, 0.2 million of these were strings that matched a regular expression for detecting the presence of an address on a web page but subsequently failed the Bitcoin checksum test [7]. After eliminating these false positives, we were left with 2,093,568 Bitcoin addresses. Table 1 shows how many of these addresses were associated with each of the 20 most frequent suspicious tags. More detail is provided next in Sect. 3.3.

Table 1. Number of neighbors and bitcoins owned for active dark web addresses (limited to top 20 dark web tags considered suspicious or malicious)

	Number of addresses	Number of neighbors	Owned Bitcoins
CHILD_P	1,696	Mean = 2,505	Mean = 94.41
		Median = 7	99% = 67.05
HUMAN TRAFFIC	1,876	Mean = 2,350	Mean = 85.52
		Median = 7	99% = 60.16
MARKET	2,604	Mean = 2,023	Mean = 63.2
		Median = 6	99% = 85.52
DRUGS	1,704	Mean = 2,585	Mean = 94.11
		Median = 8	99% = 76.78
HACKER	1,817	Mean = 2,433	Mean = 88.3
		Median = 8	99% = 65.17
PONZI	4,011	Mean = 2,622	Mean = 5.63
		Median = 7	99% = 66.49
RANSOM	1,546	Mean = 210	Mean = 0.12
		Median = 6	99% = 1.41
COUNTERFEIT	1,561	Mean = 2,385	Mean = 68.80
		Median = 9	99% = 80.56
CASINO	1,421	Mean = 2,891	Mean = 112.64
		Median = 7	99% = 89.15
NATIONALSEC	1,415	Mean = 2,951	Mean = 112.56
		Median = 8	99% = 84.55
PIRATE_BAY	1,152	Mean = 2,956	Mean = 7.27
		Median = 8	99% = 87.84
HOSTING_PROVIDER	1,276	Mean = 2,741	Mean = 76.59
		Median = 8	99% = 89.32
CURRENCY	41,883	Mean = 786	Mean = 10.47
		Median = 3	99% = 7.88
BITCOIN WALLET	2,985	Mean = 5,630	Mean = 9.74
		Median = 4	99% = 154.93
FORUM SOFTWARE	1,473	Mean = 1,095	Mean = 5.26
		Median = 3	90% = 52.32
REGISTRATION	1,332	Mean = 3,710	Mean = 80.27
		Median = 11	99% = 88.68
HOSTING PROVIDER	1,317	Mean = 4,041	Mean = 8.75
		Median = 21	99% = 0.0
ELECTRONICS	1,298	Mean = 2,651	Mean = 75.23
		Median = 8	99% = 0.0
BLOG	1,220	Mean = 2,798	Mean = 6.88
		Median = 8	99% = 84.11
NO_TAG	1,440,12	Mean = 234	Mean = 0.8
		Median = 25	99% = 0.19

Table 2. Number of potential and active Bitcoin addresses on the dark web with N tags. Total number of addresses with tags is 296,069. Among them 47,697 are active and have tags we consider suspicious or malicious.

Number of tags (N)	Number of potential addresses with N tags	Number of active addresses with N tags	Number of tags (N)	Number of potential addresses with N tags	Number of active addresses with N tags
1	143,130	41,783	14	696	69
2	45,152	2,319	15	2,210	78
3	24,331	1,519	16	175	30
4	68,236	290	17	76	17
5	4,761	67	18	127	36
6	1,382	32	19	16	3
7	176	57	20	258	53
8	598	151	21	417	344
9	482	60	22	187	13
10	284	44	23	551	41
11	290	66	24	147	33
12	485	31	25	203	65
13	841	75			

3.3 Bitcoin on the Dark Web

About 32% of the Bitcoin addresses that were found on the dark web – that is, 649,556 addresses – were labeled with tags. 1,444,012 addresses did not have any tags. A subset (of size 0.3 million) of the addresses were determined to be from mirrors of *Blockchain.info* explorer pages. These were eliminated from further analysis. The remaining addresses had a total of 49 unique tags associated with them.

We studied the addresses associated withe 20 most frequent suspicious tags. Table 1 reports the number of addresses, neighbors, and bitcoins associated with each of these tags. Though most addresses have few tags, some are labeled with many as seen in Table 2. Since some of the addresses may only be present on a dark web page without ever having been used, we performed the same analysis with active addresses. The results are reported in the same table to facilitate comparison. The histograms in Figs. 5 and 6 depict the data from Table 2.

The 20 most frequently associated tags differ significantly when all Bitcoin addresses are considered versus when only active ones are analyzed, as can be seen from Figs. 5 and 6. The inactive addresses that we eliminated appear to serve as decoys – that is, they are correctly constructed but unused. In the case of active addresses, the most frequently associated tag is "CURRENCY", indicating the prevalence of Bitcoin use in onions. We note that the histograms alone cannot be used to judge the significance of a topic on the dark web.

Of the 1,491,709 Bitcoin addresses found on dark web pages, only 47,697 had tags that we considered suspicious or malicious. The tags are shown in

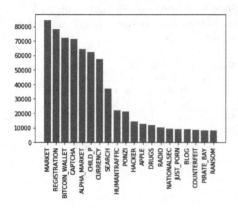 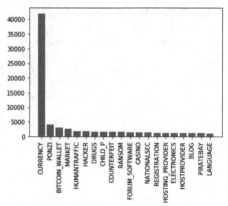

Fig. 5. Number of times a (top 20) tag appears with potential Bitcoin addresses on the dark web

Fig. 6. Number of times a (top 20) tag appears with active Bitcoin addresses on the dark web

Table 1. To gain insight into suspicious activities that involve Bitcoin, our dark web analysis focused on addresses with these tags.

The number of addresses collected from the dark web each month grew initially, but then fell significantly. Figure 7 shows this for all Bitcoin addresses found on the dark web. To better understand usage, Fig. 8 how many addresses appeared in a transaction on the blockchain for the first time in each month. The mid-2017 drops in the graphs may be explained by the seizure and shutdown of the Alphabay and Hansa dark web markets [14]. The final drop in early 2018 is due to our dark web data only extending to the end of 2017.

We note that this data must be interpreted with caution. In particular, there may be suspicious and malicious activity on the dark web that is not captured by the tags we use, creating false negatives. Further, dark web sites may reference benign addresses other than the mirrored *Blockchain.info* explorer pages that we were able to identify and exclude. This would have created false positives.

4   Detecting CoinJoins

CoinJoins are not first class primitives in Bitcoin. Hence, they cannot be definitely identified from inspecting the blockchain. In a minority of cases, a CoinJoin is listed explicitly on a web site, such as a discussion forum. In general, CoinJoin transactions must be detected using a heuristic based on their characteristics.

We build on an algorithm from Goldfeder *et al.* [13] that was designed to identify JoinMarket transactions. First, we identify the most common value (MCV) among the bitcoin amounts in the outputs of a transaction. The number of outputs that have this value is considered to be the number of participants in such a transaction. In addition, the following three conditions must be satisfied:

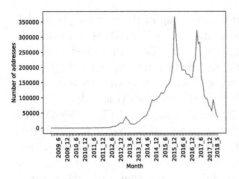 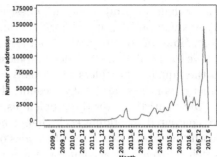

Fig. 7. Number of times a Bitcoin address found on the dark web appears in a transaction on the blockchain

Fig. 8. Number of times a Bitcoin address found on the dark web *first* appears in a transaction on the blockchain

1. The number of participants should be more than half the number of outputs. This is because up to half the outputs could be to change addresses.
2. The number of participants should be less than or equal to the number of inputs. This is because each participant must use at least one address as the source of their payment.
3. There should be at least one possible match between the inputs and the outputs, after considering the Bitcoin transaction fees and a liquidity payment (that is explained below).

Some services, such as JoinMarket, have users that continuously provide their bitcoins for use in CoinJoin transactions. These users serve as liquidity providers so that others who want to perform a CoinJoin can easily find peers with whom they can engage in such transactions. In exchange, such liquidity providers receive a percentage P of the MCV.

Our objective is then to find a set of disjoint input sets (S) so that each one can be matched with an output address (with a **change** address, denoted as $chng$). Each match translates to the following equation, with P being the max percentage of what a CoinJoin user pays for the liquidity provider, n being the number of participants, and MCV is the most common value in the transaction:

$$\forall \ inpt \in \ S : inpt \in [MCV \cdot (1 - P) + chng, \quad MCV \cdot (1 + (n - 1)P) + chng + fees] \tag{1}$$

Since a liquidity provider may receive fees from $n - 1$ other members, the upper limit of the interval contains a factor of $(1 + (n - 1)P)$. In our analysis, the payment P to the liquidity provider is allowed to be up to 2%.

4.1 Algorithm Details

The details of the heuristic used to identify CoinJoin transactions is described in Algorithm 1. The general problem of finding a set S that satisfies Eq. 1 is harder than the problem of variable-sized bin-covering in the unit supply model. Approximation algorithms for generalized and variable-sized bin-covering do exist. However, the intervals in our setting are small enough that most instances can be easily eliminated. Indeed, in most cases the fees and the percentage given to the liquidity providers are usually very low when compared to the inputs. When this fact is taken into account, the problem becomes tractable.

Our heuristic solves the problem using the following steps. First, the outputs are computed by adding each change address to an MCV. Next, we perform a depth-first search of a tree. The nodes of the tree correspond to the output that is being taken into account, and a list of the remaining inputs. At a specific node, we look for all possible sets of remaining inputs that can satisfy Eq. 1 with respect to the output at the node. A new child node with the next output is created for each feasible set.

This approach avoids the exponential explosion that would result from exhaustively generating all possible combinations of sets of inputs. In practice, we found that when a solution exists, the depth-first search usually found it quickly. When there is no solution, the analysis must still traverse the entire tree (i.e., requires and exponential number of steps).

In Algorithm 1, the function *subsets_between_two_values* recursively computes all subsets of the list provided as the first argument, subject to the constraint that their sum must be between the second and third arguments. Computing this function is also very expensive. For instance, if the second argument is 0 and the third is $+\infty$, then it must return all possible combinations of elements of the input list (provided as the first argument). This will be a set of length 2^n.

Finally, we use simple rules to filter cases/transactions that are unlikely to be CoinJoins. One example is checking whether a transaction involves known addresses, such as those of SatoshiDice or other similar services. We also check that the fees are below a threshold fraction of the MCV. These rules allow us to reject many transactions early. These optimizations are not described in Algorithm 1.

4.2 Analysis Results

The heuristic outlined above performs well in practice for CoinJoins with less than 18 inputs. Out of about 400,000 transactions that satisfy the two first conditions, the algorithm requires 180 s of computation time on a 2016 Macbook Pro. The heuristic identified 157 transactions that required deeper analysis.

More than 90% of all CoinJoin transactions have less than 18 inputs [13]. We automatically consider transactions with more than 17 inputs that pass the two first conditions to be CoinJoins (lines 8 and 9 in Algorithm 1). We found that 18% of all transactions considered to be CoinJoins by our heuristic have more than 17 inputs. Among transactions with fewer than 18 inputs, between 25% and 50% of those that satisfy the first two conditions also meet the third criterion. We concluded that between 4.5% and 9% of the CoinJoin transactions have more than 17 inputs. This is close to the result reported by Goldfeder *et al.* [13].

Algorithm 1. CoinJoin Identification Heuristic

---

    input : A transactions T with a list of inputs and a list of outputs (addresses + Bitcoin amounts)

    output: A boolean indicating (if assigned True) that T is classified as a CoinJoin

1   Find the most common value MCV among outputs, and its number of appearance $n\_participants$;

2   **if** $n\_participants < \left\lfloor \frac{length(outputs)+1}{2} \right\rfloor$ **then**

3 | return False;

4   **end**

5   **if** $n\_participants > length(inputs)$ **then**

6 | return False;

7   **end**

8   **if** $length(inputs) > 17$ **then**

9 | return True;

10   **end**

11   $new\_outputs \leftarrow$ array of length n_participants with value MCV in all cases;

12   $i \leftarrow 0$;

13   **for** $value$ in $outputs$ **do**

14 | **if** $value \neq MCV$ **then**

15 | | $new\_outputs[i] \leftarrow new\_outputs[i] + value$;

16 | | $i \leftarrow i + 1$;

17 | **end**

18   **end**

19   Sort inputs and new_outputs in decreasing order; //This does not really change anything, it is just performed for convenience

20   $remaining\_inputs\_list \leftarrow [(new\_inputs, 0)]$; //This list contains sublists. Each one of them is a node in the tree, representing a list of remaining inputs, and the index of the output which has to be considered. We use this as a LIFO list to make the tree search depth-first oriented.

21   $fees\_to\_provider \leftarrow max(2 * MCV/100, 0.0001 BTC)$;

22   **while** $remaining\_inputs\_list$ is not empty **do**

23 | $remaining\_inputs, output\_index \leftarrow remaining\_inputs\_list.pop()$;

24 | $current\_output \leftarrow outputs[output\_index]$;

25 | $lower\_limit \leftarrow current\_output - fees\_to\_provider$;

26 | $upper\_limit \leftarrow$ $current\_output + fees + fees\_to\_provider * (n\_participants - 1)$;

27 | $new\_set\_of\_feasible\_inputs \leftarrow$ $subsets\_between\_two\_values(remaining\_inputs,$

28 | $lower\_limit, upper\_limit)$;

29 | **if** $output\_index = length(new\_outputs) - 1$ and $new\_set\_of\_feasible\_inputs$ is not empty **then**

30 | | return True;

31 | **end**

32 | **for** $remaining\_inputs$ in $new\_set\_of\_feasible\_inputs$ **do**

33 | | $remaining\_inputs\_list.append($

34 | | $(remaining\_inputs, output\_index + 1))$;

35 | **end**

36   **end**

37   return False;

According to the heuristic, 114,925 transactions were CoinJoins. This represents 0.036% of the transactions that were analyzed. A total of 2,035,978 addresses were part of these CoinJoin transactions. This set of addresses was intersected with those found on the dark web, allowing us to conclude that over 2.3% of the addresses on the dark web have been CoinJoin participants. In contrast, this is only true for 0.4% of all Bitcoin addresses. We could not identify a specific dark web category that used more CoinJoins than others.

Dark web addresses appear to be 5 times more likely to participate in Coin-Join transactions. We noted with interest that only 2.3% of addresses appearing on the dark web have participated in CoinJoins, since that is a small fraction. It is conceivable that this is due to the use of alternative mixing approaches.

5   Bitcoin Neighborhood Analysis

We first report our findings from analyzing the activity of all addresses in the Bitcoin blockchain. After this, we focus on the subset of addresses that have participated in transactions as well as appeared on the dark web.

5.1   Across the Blockchain

A wide range of behaviors were exhibited by the 397,016,130 Bitcoin addresses that we analyzed. To characterize them, we studied how many other addresses an address has transacted with, how many transactions it has been involved in, the amount of bitcoin that has flowed into it, from it, and is owned by it. Table 3 reports our findings.

Table 3. Characterization of all addresses in terms of neighbors, transactions, and amount of bitcoin in/out/owned. (BTC = Bitcoin, Tx = transaction)

For all (397,301,155) addresses with at least one transaction	Number of neighbors	BTC in	BTC out	BTC owned	Number of Tx's
Mean	11.92	10.0687	10.03	0.04	3.62
Std	372.26	989.07	987.60	22.55	316.79
Median	3	0.05	0.048	0.00	2
Max	4,586,602	9,351,251	9,356,600	175,236	3,195,815
Min	1	0	0	0	1
Percentile 90%	19	4.37	4.31	0	2
Percentile 99%	137	126.61	126.11	0.03	24
Percentile 99.9%	758	965.99	963.64	1.99	197
Percentile 99.99%	2,846	8,329.38	8,314.63	41.10	1,059
Number of addresses that hold more than 99% of bitcoin: 2,266,265					

Table 4. Breakdown of neighbor count of all (397,301,155) addresses with at least one transaction

Number of addresses with ...		
Less than 10 neighbors	34,013,8543	85.67%
More than 1000 neighbors	257,925	0.06%
More than 10000 neighbors	6,178	0.00156%

To identify the neighbors of addresses we constructed the transaction graph, with one vertex per address, and undirected edges between two addresses if they are both listed in (at least) one transaction, with one as a sender and the other as a receiver. As noted earlier, we excluded CoinJoins before inferring the neighbor relationship. We also do not consider two senders (or receivers) in the same transaction to be neighbors.

The standard deviation of the number of neighbors per address is large, significantly exceeding the 99% percentile. This indicates that the extreme values are located far from the average. This is also confirmed by the fact that the mean is much larger than the median. While 50% of the addresses have transacted with less than 3 other addresses, approximately 6,000 addresses have more than 10,000 neighbors. A few addresses have more than a million neighbors. The latter addresses are probably not manually controlled by humans. Most outliers are addresses that come from exchange services, which are involved in many transactions.

The results for the number of transactions exhibit similar characteristics, with a large standard deviation. The mean and the median are closer. Most addresses are involved in few transactions. Specifically, the number of transactions is smaller than the number of neighbors for most addresses.

The quantity of bitcoin owned by each address also varies widely. The average is 0.04 bitcoin, while the standard deviation is 500 times larger. Most addresses have no bitcoins left. This is explained by the fact that in a transaction the sender needs to use all the bitcoins from each past input referenced. If there is an excess it must either be sent to a change address or it will become part of the fee to the miner.

We found that the addresses that owned the largest quantities of bitcoin corresponded to the ones listed on websites that track wallet addresses with large holdings [8]. Most such addresses belong to exchanges. An exception is "1KAt6STtisWMMVo5XGdos9P7DBNNsFfjx7", which was ranked sixth at the time of writing. Each of the top six addresses own more than 0.5% of the total number of bitcoins.

5.2   Addresses on the Dark Web

The statistics for the addresses used on the dark web differ significantly from those of addresses across the entire blockchain. On the dark web, 90% of the Bitcoin addresses have transacted with up to 400 other addresses, participated in

over 200 transactions, and been involved with 12 bitcoins. Across the entire
blockchain, 90% of the addresses have transacted with fewer than 20 other
addresses and only dealt with amounts totaling 4 bitcoins. The differences can
be seen by comparing Tables 3, 4, 5 and 6.

Table 5. Characterization of Bitcoin addresses found on the dark web, in terms of
neighbors, transactions, and amount of bitcoin in/out/owned. (BTC = Bitcoin, Tx =
transaction)

For (1,491,709) dark-web addresses with at least one transaction	Number of neighbors	BTC in	BTC out	BTC owned	Number of Tx's
Mean	255.09	153.97	152.91	1.12	143.68
Std	3,723.62	14,554.28	1,4536.67	239.37	5,102.65
Median	23	0.10	0.097	0.00	4
Max	2,277,764	9,351,251	9,350,599	175,236	3,195,815
Min	1	0	0	0	1
Percentile 90%	426	12.85	12.61	0.00089	220
Percentile 99%	27,45	375.15	366.29	0.21	1459
Percentile 99.9%	20,891	10577.64	10,287.04	40.00	7,674
Percentile 99.99%	114,947	226,413.71	226,405.41	800.00	8,3299

Number of addresses that hold more than 99% of the bitcoin (limited to addresses
found on the dark web): 2,828

Table 6. Breakdown of transaction neighbor counts for active addresses found on the
dark web

Number of addresses with	Absolute number	Percentage
Less than 10 neighbors	597,744	40.09%
More than 1000 neighbors	61,330	4.11%
More than 10000 neighbors	3,244	0.22%

The same analysis for active addresses found on the dark web indicates that
they transact more than addresses on the Bitcoin blockchain. This can be seen by
comparing Table 3 with Tables 5, 7, and 8. The average amount of bitcoin owned
is also larger for addresses found on the dark web. In addition, 99% of the coins
touched by dark web addresses are owned by just 2,828 dark web addresses.

These results need to be interpreted with caution. The addresses found on the
dark web were publicly accessible. This may have skewed the analysis in favor
of addresses that are more popular and frequently used. This could explain the
significant difference in the characteristics of addresses found on the dark web

in comparison to those across the entire blockchain. This may also account for the fact that 10% of the Bitcoin addresses found on the dark web participate in more than 220 transactions each.

The difference in the number of neighbors per address is even larger, this can be explained by the observation that dark web addresses are more likely to use mixing methods (as our CoinJoin analysis indicated), and those methods will increases the neighbors in our analysis. Also, the sum of the bitcoins owned by these addresses represent less than 10% of all bitcoins. This number is far from exact, and is in fact much smaller, as several of the richest addresses have been cited in forms and discussion on the dark web, so can be found in this set.

Table 7. Characterization of Bitcoin addresses found on the dark web, with at least one CoinJoin transaction, in terms of neighbors, transactions, and amount of bitcoin in/out/owned. (BTC = Bitcoin, Tx = transaction)

For (35,492) dark web addresses with at least one CoinJoin transaction	Number of neighbors	BTC in	BTC out	BTC owned	Number of Tx's
Mean	1,745	2,618	2,612	7.07	1,429
Std	12,726	71,325	71,335	616	28,479
Median	159	1.99	1.97	0	48
Percentile 90%	2341	100	100	0	732

Participation in a CoinJoin is unusual (as can be seen in the statistics reported in Sect. 4). This motivated us to study Bitcoin addresses found on the dark web that have participated in at least one CoinJoin transaction. Table 7 reports the results. In particular, the mean and standard deviation of both the number of neighbors and exchanged Bitcoins are higher than for addresses that do not participate in a CoinJoin.

Assume that the more an address participates in transactions, the higher the chance that it will be part of a CoinJoin. This would explain why the Bitcoin addresses that appear most often on the dark web are likely to be part of Coin-Join transactions. However, we found that even Bitcoin addresses on the dark web that appear at the median frequency are more likely to have participated in CoinJoins. An explanation supported by the data is that transactions associated with Bitcoin addresses found on the dark web involve larger amounts, motivating increased caution.

We stress that the dark web is also used for several legitimate activities. As an additional filter for teasing out real suspicious or malicious activities, we focus on the set of dark web addresses that contained tags associated with what we judged as the most suspicious (and in cases very obvious malicious) activities, i.e., addresses containing at least one tag from the following list: PONZI, MARKET, HUMANTRAFFIC, HACKER, DRUGS, CHILD_P, COUNTERFEIT, RANSOM, CASINO,

Table 8. Characterization of Bitcoin addresses found on the dark web, with at least one malicious tag, in terms of neighbors, transactions, and amount of bitcoin in/out/owned. (BTC = Bitcoin, Tx = transaction)

For (7,713) dark web addresses with at least one malicious tag	Number of neighbors	BTC in	BTC out	BTC owned	Number of Tx's
Mean	1,465	8,234	8,213	22.8	1,527
Std	1,8351	152,755	15,2754	1,269	22,023
Median	6	2.55	2.48	0	3
Percentile 90%	347	295	295	0.004	217

NATIONALSEC, HOSTING_PROVIDER, HITMAN, WEAPONS, JIHAD, EXPLOSIVES, CREDIT_CARD_FRAUD, DISCLOSURES, ANONYMOUS, PIRATE_BAY, WIKILEAKS, MURDER, MARKET, ESCORT, DECRYPT_RANSOM. We note that some addresses associated with some of these tags are not active on the blockchain so not all these tags show up in all our analysis.

We notice that these addresses (see results in Table 8) do not do many more transactions that the whole dark web address set, but these figures remain much bigger than the ones obtained from regular addresses. Moreover, the BTC amounts these dark web addresses handle are even larger. Even the median has a higher value. As the size of the set is small, these addresses are probably among the most well-known addresses used for malicious activities, and a lot of them are used extensively.

6 Future Work

This study provides a quantitative characterization of suspicious and malicious activities involving Bitcoin. In addition to addressing the limitations discussed in Sect. 1.4, we envision the following avenues of research in future work.

1. Similar analyses could be performed for other popular cryptocurrencies, such as Bitcoin forks, Ethereum, and Litecoin. In particular, comparing results from other cryptocurrencies to those from Bitcoin may yield new insights.
2. Augmenting the data sets used in this study with ones that may help attribute malicious activities to geographic location. This could include data mapping addresses to well-known wallets or entities, as well as to IP addresses (for which geolocation data is typically available).
3. Studying cross-cryptocurrency transaction activity could enable detection of synchronized addresses. This may provide a new means for detecting when seemingly unrelated addresses are controlled by the same user or pertain to coordinated activity. Detecting synchronized activity may also offer insight into significant events in the history of cryptocurrencies.

References

1. Androulaki, E., Karame, G.O., Roeschlin, M., Scherer, T., Capkun, S.: Evaluating user privacy in Bitcoin. In: Sadeghi, A.-R. (ed.) FC 2013. LNCS, vol. 7859, pp. 34–51. Springer, Heidelberg (2013). https://doi.org/10.1007/978-3-642-39884-1_4
2. Blockchain.info Bitcoin explorer. https://www.blockchain.com/explorer
3. Blockchain Intelligence Group. https://blockchaingroup.io/
4. Bohr, J., Bashir, M.: Who uses Bitcoin? An exploration of the Bitcoin community. In: 12th International Conference on Privacy, Security, and Trust (2014)
5. Breitner, J., Heninger, N.: Biased nonce sense: lattice attacks against weak ECDSA signatures in cryptocurrencies. In: 23rd International Conference on Financial Cryptography and Data Security (2019)
6. Version 1 Bitcoin Addresses. https://en.bitcoin.it/wiki/Technical_background_of_version_1_Bitcoin_addresses
7. Bitcoin forum: Validating Bitcoin addresses. https://bitcointalk.org/index.php?topic=1026.0
8. Largest bitcoin holdings. https://bitinfocharts.com/top-100-richest-bitcoin-addresses.html
9. Chainanalysis Platform. https://www.chainalysis.com/
10. CipherTrace Platform. https://ciphertrace.com/
11. Elliptic Platform. https://www.elliptic.co/
12. Ghosh, S., Das, A., Porras, P., Yegneswaran, V., Gehani, A.: Automated categorization of onion sites for analyzing the darkweb ecosystem. In: 23rd ACM International Conference on Knowledge Discovery and Data Mining (2017)
13. Goldfeder, S., Kalodner, H., Reisman, D., Narayanan, A.: When the cookie meets the blockchain: privacy risks of web payments via cryptocurrencies. In: 18th Privacy Enhancing Technologies Symposium (2018)
14. Greenberg, A.: Global police spring a trap on thousands of dark web users. Wired, https://www.wired.com/story/alphabay-hansa-takedown-dark-web-trap/. Accessed 20 July 2019
15. Lee, S., et al.: Cybercriminal minds: an investigative study of cryptocurrency abuses in the Dark Web. In: 26th Annual Network and Distributed System Security Symposium (NDSS) (2019)
16. Meiklejohn, S., et al.: A fistful of bitcoins: characterizing payments among men with no names. In: 13th ACM Internet Measurement Conference (IMC) (2013)
17. Miller, A., Moser, M., Lee, K., Narayanan, A.: An empirical analysis of linkability in the Monero blockchain. arXiv:1704.04299 (2017)
18. Monero. https://getmonero.org/
19. Neudecker, T., Hartenstein, H.: Could network information facilitate address clustering in Bitcoin? In: Brenner, M., et al. (eds.) FC 2017. LNCS, vol. 10323, pp. 155–169. Springer, Cham (2017). https://doi.org/10.1007/978-3-319-70278-0_9
20. Ranshous, S., et al.: Exchange pattern mining in the Bitcoin transaction directed hypergraph. In: Brenner, M., et al. (eds.) FC 2017. LNCS, vol. 10323, pp. 248–263. Springer, Cham (2017). https://doi.org/10.1007/978-3-319-70278-0_16
21. Ron, D., Shamir, A.: Quantitative analysis of the full Bitcoin transaction graph. In: Sadeghi, A.-R. (ed.) FC 2013. LNCS, vol. 7859, pp. 6–24. Springer, Heidelberg (2013). https://doi.org/10.1007/978-3-642-39884-1_2
22. Ruffing, T., Moreno-Sanchez, P., Kate, A.: CoinShuffle: practical decentralized coin mixing for Bitcoin. In: Kutyłowski, M., Vaidya, J. (eds.) ESORICS 2014. LNCS, vol. 8713, pp. 345–364. Springer, Cham (2014). https://doi.org/10.1007/978-3-319-11212-1_20

23. Spagnuolo, M., Maggi, F., Zanero, S.: BitIodine: extracting intelligence from the bitcoin network. In: Christin, N., Safavi-Naini, R. (eds.) FC 2014. LNCS, vol. 8437, pp. 457–468. Springer, Heidelberg (2014). https://doi.org/10.1007/978-3-662-45472-5_29
24. Zcash: Privacy-protecting Digital Currency. https://z.cash/

Post Quantum Cryptography

Part One: General Cryptography

Faster Multiplication in $\mathbb{Z}_{2^m}[x]$ on Cortex-M4 to Speed up NIST PQC Candidates

Matthias J. Kannwischer[✉], Joost Rijneveld[✉], and Peter Schwabe[✉]

Radboud University, Nijmegen, The Netherlands
matthias@kannwischer.eu, joost@joostrijneveld.nl, peter@cryptojedi.org

Abstract. In this paper we optimize multiplication of polynomials in $\mathbb{Z}_{2^m}[x]$ on the ARM Cortex-M4 microprocessor. We use these optimized multiplication routines to speed up the NIST post-quantum candidates RLizard, NTRU-HRSS, NTRUEncrypt, Saber, and Kindi. For most of those schemes the only previous implementation that executes on the Cortex-M4 is the reference implementation submitted to NIST; for some of those schemes our optimized software is more than factor of 20 faster. One of the schemes, namely Saber, has been optimized on the Cortex-M4 in a CHES 2018 paper; the multiplication routine for Saber we present here outperforms the multiplication from that paper by 42%, yielding speedups of 22% for key generation, 20% for encapsulation and 22% for decapsulation. Out of the five schemes optimized in this paper, the best performance for encapsulation and decapsulation is achieved by NTRU-HRSS. Specifically, encapsulation takes just over 400 000 cycles, which is more than twice as fast as for any other NIST candidate that has previously been optimized on the ARM Cortex-M4.

Keywords: ARM Cortex-M4 · Karatsuba · Toom · Lattice-based KEMs · NTRU

1 Introduction

In November 2017 the NIST post-quantum project [NIS16b] received 69 "complete and proper" proposals for future standardization of a suite of post-quantum cryptosystems. By December 2018, five of those 69 have been withdrawn. Out of the remaining 64 proposals, 22 are lattice-based public-key encryption schemes or key-encapsulation mechanisms (KEMs). Most of those lattice-based schemes use structured lattices and, as a consequence, require fast arithmetic in a polynomial ring $\mathcal{R}_q = \mathbb{Z}_q[x]/f$ for some n-coefficient polynomial $f \in \mathbb{Z}_q[x]$. Typically the largest performance bottleneck of these schemes is multiplication in $\mathcal{R}_q$.

This work has been supported by the European Commission through the ERC Starting Grant 805031 (EPOQUE) and by COST (European Cooperation in Science and Technology) through COST Action IC1403 (CRYPTACUS). Date: April 30, 2019.

© Springer Nature Switzerland AG 2019
R. H. Deng et al. (Eds.): ACNS 2019, LNCS 11464, pp. 281–301, 2019.
https://doi.org/10.1007/978-3-030-21568-2_14

Many proposals, for example NewHope [ADPS16, AAB+17], Kyber [ABD+17], and LIMA [SAL+17], choose q, n, and f such that multiplication in $\mathcal{R}_q$ can be done via very fast number-theoretic transforms. However, six schemes choose $q = 2^k$ which requires using a different algorithm for multiplication in $\mathcal{R}_q$. Specifically those six schemes are Round2 [GMZB+17], Saber [DKRV17], NTRU-HRSS [HRSS17b], NTRUEncrypt [ZCHW17], Kindi [Ban17], and RLizard [CPL+17]. Round2 recently merged with Hila5 [Saa17] into Round5 [BGML+18] and the Round5 team presented optimized software for the ARM Cortex-M4 processor in [SBGM+18]; the multiplication in Round5 has more structure, allowing for a specialized high-speed routine. In this paper we optimize the other five schemes relying on arithmetic in $\mathcal{R}_q$ with a power-of-two q on the same platform. Note that Saber has previously been optimized on the ARM Cortex-M4 [KMRV18] as well; our polynomial multiplication implementation outperforms the results by 42% which improves the overall performance of key generation by 22%, encapsulation by 20%, and decapsulation by 22%. For the other four schemes the only software that was readily available for the Cortex-M4 was the reference implementation and, unsurprisingly, our carefully optimized code significantly outperforms these implementations. For example, our optimized implementations of RLizard-1024 and Kindi-256-3-4-2 encapsulation and decapsulation are more than a factor of 20 faster. Our implementation of NTRU-HRSS encapsulation and decapsulation solidly outperform the optimized Round5 software presented in [SBGM+18].

We achieve our results by systematically exploring different combinations of Toom-3, Toom-4, and Karatsuba decomposition [Too63, Coo66, KO63] of multiplication in $\mathcal{R}_q$, and by carefully hand-optimizing multiplication of low-degree polynomial multiplication at the bottom of the Toom/Karatsuba decomposition. The exploration of the different approaches is automated through a set of Python scripts that generate optimized assembly given the parameters $q = 2^k$ for $k \leq 16$ and $n \leq 1024$. These Python scripts may be of independent interest for a similar design-space exploration on different architectures.

Organization of This Paper. In Sect. 2 we briefly recall the five NIST candidates that we optimize in this paper and give the necessary background on the target microarchitecture, i.e., the ARM Cortex-M4. In Sect. 3 we first detail our approach to explore different Toom and Karatsuba decomposition strategies for multiplication in $\mathcal{R}_q$ and then explain how we hand-optimized schoolbook multiplications of low-degree polynomials. Finally, Sect. 4 presents performance results for stand-alone multiplication in $\mathcal{R}_q$ for the different parameter sets, and for the five NIST candidates.

Availability of the Software. We place all software presented in this paper, including the Python scripts used for design-space exploration, into the public domain. The software is available at https://github.com/mupq/polymulz2mx-m4 and the implementations have been integrated into the pqm4 framework [KRSS].

Second Round of NISTPQC. Since this paper first appeared online NIST announced the second round candidates of the post-quantum competition. While Kindi and RLizard are no longer under consideration by NIST, Saber, NTRU-HRSS, and NTRUEncrypt made it to the second round. NTRU-HRSS and NTRU-Encrypt were merged into the new scheme NTRU. The optimizations presented in this paper carry over directly to the second round schemes.

2 Preliminaries

In this section, we briefly review the five NIST candidates that we optimize in this paper. Readers interested in the multiplication routine outside the context of NIST submissions are encouraged to skip ahead to Subsect. 2.2, where we introduce the targeted Cortex-M4 platform and give context that is relevant to interpret the benchmark results.

2.1 Cryptosystems Targeted in This Paper

The full specification of each of the five CCA-secure KEMs would take several pages, so for the sake of brevity we leave out various details. In this section, we highlight the relevant aspects; see the full version of this paper for algorithmic descriptions. In particular, all five schemes build a CCA-secure KEM from an encryption scheme; for all but NTRUEncrypt, this encryption scheme is only passively secure. In our descriptions, we focus only on the encryption schemes underlying the KEM and highlight the multiplications in $\mathcal{R}_q$.

RLizard. RLizard is part of the Lizard submission to NIST [CPL+17]. It is a cryptosystem based on the Ring-Learning-with-Errors (Ring-LWE) and Ring-Learning-with-Rounding (Ring-LWR) problems. As the names suggest, these problems are closely related, and efficient reductions exist [BPR12,BGM+16]. The submission motivates the choice for the Learning-with-Rounding problem by stressing its deterministic encryption routine and reduced ciphertext size compared to Learning-with-Errors. RLizard.KEM is a CCA-secure KEM that is constructed by applying Dent's variant of the FO transform [FO99,Den03] to the RLizard CPA-secure PKE scheme.

The main structure underlying RLizard is the ring $\mathcal{R}_q = \mathbb{Z}_q[x]/(x^n + 1)$, but coefficients of the ciphertext are ultimately reduced to $\mathcal{R}_p$, where $p < q$. We consider the parameter set where $n = 1024$, $q = 2048$ and $p = 512$. In the submission the derived KEM is referred to as RING_CATEGORY3_N1024 – for clarity, we denote it as RLizard-1024 from this point onwards. All multiplications in RLizard fit the structure that we target in this work.

NTRU-HRSS-KEM. The NTRU-HRSS scheme [HRSS17a] is based on the 'classic' NTRU cryptosystem [HPS98]. It starts from the CPA-secure NTRU encryption scheme, and, like RLizard, applies Dent's variant of the FO transform [FO99, Den03] to construct a CCA-secure KEM. By restricting the parameter space compared to traditional NTRU, the scheme is simplified and avoids implementation pitfalls such as decryption failures and fixed-weight sampling.

We look at the concrete instance as submitted to NIST [HRSS17b], i.e., fix the parameters to $p = 3$, $q = 8192$ and $n = 701$. NTRU-HRSS relies on arithmetic in a number of different rings. Glossing over the technicalities (see Sects. 2 and 3 of [HRSS17a]), we reuse the notation to define $\Phi_d = 1 + x^1 + x^2 + \cdots + x^{d-1}$, and then define $\mathcal{R}_p = \mathbb{Z}[x]_p/\Phi_n$, $\mathcal{R}'_q = \mathbb{Z}[x]_q/\Phi_n$ and $\mathcal{R}_q = \mathbb{Z}[x]_q/(x^n - 1)$, but abstract away the transitions between rings.

The scheme requires several multiplications and inversions. For this paper, we focus on multiplications in $\mathcal{R}'_q$ and $\mathcal{R}_q$. However, the same routine can be used to perform the multiplication in $\mathcal{R}_p$. Furthermore, as the inversion in $\mathcal{R}'_q$ can be performed using multiplications [HRSS17a], this benefits from the same optimization.

NTRUEncrypt. The NTRUEncrypt scheme [ZCHW17] is also based on the standard NTRU construction [HPS98], but chooses parameters based on a recent revisiting [HPS+17]. NTRUEncrypt builds a CCA-secure KEM from a CCA-secure PKE; this public-key encryption scheme uses the NAEP transform [HGSSW03].

The NIST submission of NTRUEncrypt [ZCHW17] presents several instantiations, but we limit ourselves to the instances where $q = 2^k$. We look at the parameter set NTRU-KEM-743, where $p = 3$, $q = 2048$, and $n = 743$; the arithmetic takes place in the ring $\mathcal{R}_q = \mathbb{Z}_q[x]/(x^n - 1)$, but coefficients are also reduced modulo p when moving to $\mathcal{R}_p$. The optimizations in this work also carry over to the smaller NTRU-KEM-443 parameter set, but not to NTRU-KEM-1024 (which uses a prime q). As before, the relevant multiplication occurs when the noise polynomial r is multiplied with the public key h, but we also utilize our multiplication routine for the other multiplication in Dec.

Saber. Like Lizard and RLizard, Saber [DKRV17] also relies on the Learning-with-Rounding problem. Rather than directly targeting LWR or the ring variant, it positions itself in the middle-ground formed by the Module-LWR problem. The submission conforms to the common pattern of proposing a PKE scheme, and then applying an FO variant [HHK17] to obtain a CCA-secure KEM.

Like RLizard, Saber operates in the ring $\mathcal{R}_q = \mathbb{Z}_q[x]/(x^n + 1)$, and in the smaller $\mathcal{R}_p$. Because of the Module-LWR structure, however, n is fixed to 256 for all parameter sets. Instead of varying the dimension of the polynomial, Saber variants use matrices of varying sizes with entries in the polynomial ring (denoted $\mathcal{R}^{\ell \times k}$). With the fixed $q = 8192$, this ensures that an optimized routine for multiplication in $\mathcal{R}_q$ directly applies to the smaller LightSaber and the larger FireSaber instances as well. Other parameters p and t are powers of 2 smaller than q; for the Saber instance[1], $p = 1024$ and $t = 8$. The vector h is a fixed constant in $\mathcal{R}_q^\ell$.

Note that some of the multiplications in Saber are in $\mathcal{R}_q$ and some are in $\mathcal{R}_p$; in our software both use the same routine. As we will explain in Sect. 3, the smaller value of p would in principle allow us to explore a larger design space for multiplications in $\mathcal{R}_p$; however, for the small value of $n = 256$ there is nothing to be gained in the additional multiplication approaches.

KINDI. In the same vein as Saber, Kindi [Ban17] is based on a matrix of polynomials, relating it to the Module-LWE problem. Somewhat more intricate than the standard approach, however, it relies on a trapdoor construction, and constructs a CPA-secure PKE that is already close to a key-encapsulation mechanism.

Kindi operates in the polynomial ring $\mathcal{R}_q = \mathbb{Z}_q[x]/(x^n + 1)$ with $q = 2^k$, the more general $\mathcal{R}_b = \mathbb{Z}_b[x]/(x^n+1)$ for some integer b, and in the polynomial ring with integer coefficients $\mathcal{R} = \mathbb{Z}[x]/(x^n + 1)$. The relevant arithmetic primarily happens in the ring $\mathcal{R}_q$, though, meaning that the performance of Kindi still considerably improves as a consequence of this work. We consider the parameter set Kindi-256-3-4-2, where $n = 256$ and $q = 2^{14}$.

To obtain a CCA-secure KEM, a slightly simplified version of the modular FO variant [HHK17] is used: as Kindi exhibits a KEM-like structure and already includes re-encryption in Dec, this results in merely adding hash-function calls.

2.2 ARM Cortex-M4

Our target platform is the ARM Cortex-M4 which implements the ARMv7E-M architecture. It has 16 general purpose registers of which 14 are freely usable by the developer. In contrast to smaller architectures like the Cortex-M3, the Cortex-M4 supports the DSP instructions smuad, smuadx, smlad, and smladx, which we use to significantly speed up low-degree polynomial multiplication using the schoolbook method. Those low-degree multiplication routines are used as a core building block for higher-degree polynomial multiplication. The DSP instructions perform two half-word multiplications, accumulate the two products and optionally accumulate another 32-bit word in one clock cycle (as illustrated in Table 1). There is strong synergy between these DSP instructions and the fact that loading a 32-bit word using ldr is as expensive as loading a halfword using ldrh. Related to this, it is important to perform load operations sequentially (i.e., uninterrupted by other instructions) when possible, as this has a pipelining benefit. This shows in the ldm instruction, but also when simply adjoining multiple ldr instructions. While the same behavior occurs for store instructions, combining loads and stores only incurs pipelining benefits when stores follow loads, but not when loads follow stores.

The ARMv7E-M instruction set contains support for 16-bit Thumb instructions, such as simple arithmetic and memory operations with register parameters. Using these instructions has an obvious benefit for code size, but comes at

---

[1] Note that both the scheme and the category 3 parameter set are called Saber.

Table 1. Relevant dual 16-bit multiplication instructions supported by the ARM Cortex-M4

Instruction	Semantics
smuad Ra, Rb, Rc	$Ra \leftarrow Rb_L \cdot Rc_L + Rb_H \cdot Rc_H$
smuadx Ra, Rb, Rc	$Ra \leftarrow Rb_L \cdot Rc_H + Rb_H \cdot Rc_L$
smlad Ra, Rb, Rc, Rd	$Ra \leftarrow Rb_L \cdot Rc_L + Rb_H \cdot Rc_H + Rd$
smladx Ra, Rb, Rc, Rd	$Ra \leftarrow Rb_L \cdot Rc_H + Rb_H \cdot Rc_L + Rd$

the cost of introducing misalignment: instruction fetching is significantly more expensive when instruction offsets are not aligned to multiples of four bytes. To combat this, Thumb instructions can be expanded to full-word width using the .w suffix.

Benchmarking Platform. In our experiments we use the STM32F4-DISCOVERY which features 1 MiB of Flash ROM, 192 KiB of RAM (128 KiB of which are contiguous) running at a maximum frequency of 168 MHz. For benchmarking we use the reduced clock frequency of 24 MHz to not be impacted by wait states caused by slow memory [SS17]. We use the GNU ARM Embedded Toolchain[2] (arm-none-eabi) with arm-none-eabi-gcc-8.3.0. All source files are compiled with the optimization flag -O3.

3   Multiplication in $\mathbb{Z}_{2^m}[x]$

As discussed in the previous sections, we focus on multiplication in $\mathcal{R}_q$, where $q = 2^m$. In particular, we approach this by looking at the non-reduced multiplication in $\mathbb{Z}_{2^m}[x]$, as this is identical across all schemes we investigate. The reduction is done outside of our optimized polynomial multiplication.

Here, we describe the way we break down such a multiplication for a specific number of coefficients n, modulo a specific q. This is done using combinations of Toom-Cook's and Karatsuba's multiplication algorithms. For a given n and q, there are multiple possible approaches; we explore the entire space and select the optimum for each parameter set. We use Python scripts that generate optimized assembly functions for all combinations, for arbitrary-degree polynomials (with degree below 1024). These scripts are parameterized by the degree, the Toom method (see the next subsection; Toom-3, Toom-4, both Toom-4 and Toom-3 or no Toom layer at all), and the threshold at which to switch from Karatsuba to schoolbook multiplication. See Sect. 4.1 for a detailed analysis of these results.

3.1   Toom/Karatsuba Strategies

The naive schoolbook approach to multiply two polynomials with n coefficients results in n^2 multiplications in $\mathbb{Z}_q$. Using well-known algorithms by Karatsuba [KO63] and Toom-Cook [Too63,Coo66], it is possible to trade some of these

---

[2] https://developer.arm.com/open-source/gnu-toolchain/gnu-rm.

multiplications for additions and subtractions. Both algorithms have originally been introduced for the multiplication of large integers, but straight-forwardly translate to polynomial multiplication. Karatsuba's method breaks a multiplication of n-coefficient polynomials into three (instead of four) multiplications of polynomials with $\frac{n}{2}$ coefficients. Toom-Cook is a generalization of this approach. For this work we concern ourselves with Toom-3, which breaks down a multiplication of n-coefficient polynomials into five (rather than nine) multiplications of polynomials with $\frac{n}{3}$ coefficients, and Toom-4, breaking down a multiplication of n-coefficient polynomials into seven multiplications of $\frac{n}{4}$ coefficients.

Toom-Cook. It is important to note that there is a loss in precision when using Toom's method, as it involves division over the integers. While divisions by three and five can be replaced by multiplications by their inverses modulo 2^{16}, i.e., 43691 and 52429, this is not possible for divisions by powers of two. Consequently, Toom-3 loses one bit of precision, and Toom-4 loses three bits. Since our Karatsuba and schoolbook implementations operate in $\mathbb{Z}_{2^{16}}[x]$, this imposes constraints on the values of q for which our implementations can be used; Toom-3 can be used for $q \leq 2^{15}$, Toom-4 can be used for $q \leq 2^{13}$. These losses accumulate, and a combination of both is only possible if $q \leq 2^{12}$. This also rules out higher-order Toom methods. While switching to 32-bit arithmetic would allow using higher order Toom, this slows down Karatsuba and the schoolbooks significantly by increasing load-store overhead and ruling out DSP instructions.

While asymptotically Toom-4 is more efficient than Toom-3 and Karatsuba, in practice the additions and subtractions also impact the run-time. The increased and more complex memory-access patterns also significantly influence performance. Thus, for a given n it is not immediately obvious in general which approach is the fastest. We first evaluate whether to decompose using a layer of Toom-4, Toom-3, both Toom-4 and Toom-3, or no Toom at all. We then repeatedly apply Karatsuba's method to break down the multiplications, up to the threshold at which it becomes inefficient and the "naive" schoolbook method becomes the fastest approach.

Karatsuba. The call to the topmost Karatsuba layer is a function call, but from that point on, we recursively inline the separate layers. Upon reaching the threshold at which the schoolbook approach takes precedence, we jump to the schoolbook multiplication as an explicit subroutine. This provides a trade-off that keeps code size reasonable and is flexible to implement and experiment with, but does imply that the register allocation between the final Karatsuba layer and the underlying schoolbook is disjoint; it may prove worthwhile to look into this for specific n rather than in a general approach.

Note that we only applied Karatsuba's method to split polynomials in two parts (i.e., not more), and did not combine operations across recursive calls. See [WP06] for details on a more general approach.[3]

As we perform several nested layers of Karatsuba multiplication, it is important to carefully manage memory usage. We do not go for a completely in-place approach (as is done in [KMRV18]), but instead allocate stack space for the sums of the high and low limbs, relying on the input and output buffers for all other terms. This leads to effective memory usage without reducing performance.

Assembly-Level Optimizations. For both Toom and Karatsuba, the typical operations require adding and subtracting polynomials of moderate size from a given address. We stress the importance of careful pipelining, loading and storing 16-bit coefficients pairwise into full-word registers, and using `uadd16` and `usub16` arithmetic operations. We rely on offset-based instructions for memory operations, in particular for the more intricate memory access patterns in Toom and Karatsuba. This leads to a slight increase in code size compared to using `ldm` and `stm`, (and some bookkeeping for polynomials exceeding the maximal offset of 4095 bytes), but ensures that addresses are computed during code generation.

For ease of implementation, our code generator for Toom is restricted to dimensions that divide without remainder. For Karatsuba, we do not restrict the dimensions at all: the implementation can work on unbalanced splits, and thus polynomials of unequal length. In order not to waste any memory or cycles here (e.g., by applying common refinement approaches), the Python script becomes a rather complex composition of conditionals; rather than trying to combine pairs of 16-bit additions into `uadd16` operations on the fly, we run a post-processing step over the scheduled instructions to do so.

Rather than considering alignment to 32-bit word boundaries during code generation, we use a post-processing step. After compilation, we disassemble the resulting binary and expand Thumb instructions in the cases where they cause misalignment. This allows using the smaller Thumb instructions where possible, but avoids paying the overhead of misalignment. In particular, this is important when an odd number of Thumb instructions is followed by a large block of 32-bit instructions. The alignment post-processing is done using a Python script that is included in our software package, and may be of independent interest.

3.2   Small Schoolbook Multiplications

We carefully investigate several approaches to perform the small-degree schoolbook multiplications that underlie Karatsuba and Toom-Cook, varying the approaches and implementing distinct generation routines for different n.

---

[3] The approach by Weimerskirch and Paar provides a middle ground between Karatsuba and Toom-Cook. While allowing for a wider range of splits than traditional Karatsuba and a more efficient way of dealing with the newly introduced additions, it does come at the cost of more small-sized multiplications than similarly-sized Toom-Cook instances. A key advantage, though, is the fact that this approach does not introduce divisions that lead to a loss of precision. This could be relevant in particular for multiplications where both n and q are large.

For each approach, we keep the polynomial in packed representation, loading all coefficients into the 32-bit registers in pairs. The ARMv7E-M instruction set provides multiplication instructions that efficiently operate on data in this format: parallel multiplications, but also instructions that operate on a specific halfwords. For $n \leq 10$, all input coefficients can be kept in registers simultaneously, with registers remaining to keep the pointers to the source and destination polynomials around. We first compute all coefficients of terms with odd exponents, before using pkh instructions to repack one of the input polynomials and computing the remaining coefficients. This ensures that the vast majority of the multiplications can be computed using the two-way parallel multiply-accumulate dual instructions. See Fig. 1 for an illustration of this; here, b is repacked to create the dashed pairs. This is somewhat similar to the approach used in [KMRV18], but ends up needing less repacking and memory interaction.

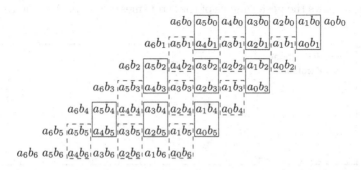

Fig. 1. Pairing coefficients to reduce the number of multiplications, using smladx/-smlad instructions. Dashed boxes represent multiplications involving repacked b.

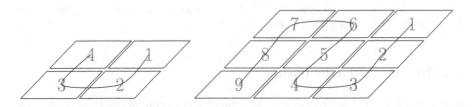

Fig. 2. Decomposing larger schoolbook multiplications

For $n \in \{11, 12\}$, we spill the source pointers to the stack after loading the complete polynomials. At these dimensions, the registers are used to their full potential, and by using the DSP instructions we end up needing only 78 multiplications; 66 combined multiplications, 12 single multiplications, and not a single dedicated addition instruction. This offsets the extra cost of the 6 packing instructions considerably. For $n \in \{13, 14\}$, not all coefficients fit in registers at the same time, leading to spills for the middle columns (i.e., the computation of coefficients around x^n, which are affected by all input coefficients). Even when using the Python abstraction layer, manual register allocation becomes somewhat tedious in the cases that involve many spills to the stack. To remedy this, we use bare-bones register allocation functions akin to the scripts in [HRSS17a].

For larger n, the above strategy leads to an excessive amount of register spills. Instead, we compose the multiplication of a grid of smaller instances. For $15 \leq n \leq 24$, we compose the multiplication out of four smaller multiplications, for $25 \leq n \leq 36$, we use a grid of nine multiplications, etc. Note that we use at most $n = 12$ for the building blocks, given the extra overhead of the register spills for $n \in \{13, 14\}$. We further remark that it is important to carefully schedule the (re)loading and repacking of input polynomials. We illustrate this in Fig. 2.

The approach described above works trivially when n is divisible by $\lceil \frac{n}{12} \rceil$, but leads to a less symmetric pattern for other dimensions. We plug these holes by starting from an n that divides even, and either adding a layer 'around' the parallelogram or nullifying the superfluous operations in a post-processing step.

Figure 3 shows the performance of these routines; see Table 5 for more details.

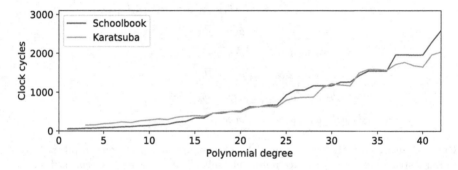

Fig. 3. Runtime of generated optimized polynomial multiplication for small n. For $n < 20$ our hand-optimized schoolbook multiplications are clearly superior, for $n > 36$ first applying at least one layer of Karatsuba is faster.

4   Results and Discussion

In this section we present benchmark results for polynomial multiplication, and for key generation, encapsulation, and decapsulation of the five NIST postquantum candidates Kindi, NTRUEncrypt, NTRU-HRSS, RLizard, and Saber. For each of the schemes we have tried to select the parameter set which targets NIST security category 3. However, NTRU-HRSS only provides a category 1 parameter set, hence we use this. Furthermore, the reference implementations for the category 3 parameter sets of Kindi require more than 128 KiB of RAM and consequently do not trivially fit our platform (STM32F4DISCOVERY). We use Kindi-256-3-4-2 instead, which targets security category 1. For the definition of NIST security categories see [NIS16a, Sect. 4.A.5].

All cycle counts presented in this section were obtained by using an adapted version of the pqm4 benchmarking framework [KRSS], which uses the built-in

24-bit hardware timer. Stack measurements were also also obtained using the method implemented in pqm4, i.e., by writing a canary to the entire memory available for the stack, running the scheme under test and subsequently checking how much of the canary was overwritten.

4.1 Multiplication Results

We first present results for polynomial multiplication as a building block. We report benchmarks for the multiplication for all possible $n < 1024$, using different approaches to evaluate which strategy is optimal.

Figure 3 shows the run-time of our hand-optimized schoolbook implementations and the generated optimized Karatsuba code for small n. For the Karatsuba benchmarks, we have selected the optimal schoolbook threshold, e.g., for $n = 32$ one could either apply one layer of Karatsuba and then use the schoolbook method for $n = 16$ or, alternatively, use two layers of Karatsuba and use schoolbook multiplications for $n = 8$. The former variant is faster in this scenario, which leads to a schoolbook threshold of 16. For each n, we simply iterated over all schoolbook thresholds and selected the fastest variant. The graph shows that directly applying the schoolbook method is superior for $n < 20$, and for $n > 36$ Karatsuba outperforms schoolbook. However, for values in between, the plot is inconclusive. A large cause of this is the amount of hand-optimization that went into some of our schoolbook implementations, but it is also strongly determined by register pressure: there is a large performance hit in the step from $n = 14$ to $n = 15$, which then propagates to dimensions that break down to these schoolbook multiplications using Karatsuba. For cryptographically relevant values we found that the cross-over point is at $n = 22$, i.e., for values $n > 22$ one should use an additional layer of Karatsuba.

Figure 4 shows the performance of the different multiplication approaches for larger n. While that general trend is visible, one still observes a jagged line. We speculate that the main cause for this is similar to the irregularities in Fig. 3: the variance in the increasing cost of the schoolbooks is magnified as n grows larger and specific schoolbook sizes are repeated in the decomposition of large multiplications. Because of the difference in decomposition between Toom-3 and Toom-4, this favors each method for different ranges for n, resulting in alternating optimality. Another factor that is impacted by specific decomposition is the resulting memory access pattern, and, by extension, data alignment, resulting in a large performance penalty. In practice, comparing benchmarks for specific n seems to be the only way to come to conclusive results. In particular, we observe that the lines are not even monotonically increasing; note that it is trivially possible to pad a smaller-degree polynomial and use a larger multiplication routine to benefit of a more efficient decomposition.

As Fig. 4 does not allow us to identity which method performs best for clear bounds on n, we instead focus on individual n as relevant for the five cryptographic schemes we intend to cover. This restricts n to $\{256, 701, 743, 1024\}$. In Table 2, we report the cycle counts alongside the required additional stack space

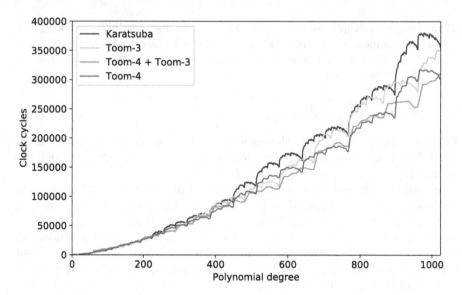

Fig. 4. Runtime of different decomposition variants for large-degree multiplications.

for each of the multiplication methods. All cycle counts are for polynomial multiplication *excluding* subsequent reduction required to obtain an n-coefficient polynomial; additional cost for reduction differs depending on the specific choice of ring. While there is some performance benefit to performing the reduction inline, the main gain is in stack usage. For the Toom variants, this allows for in-place recomposition, reducing stack usage by roughly $2n$ coefficients. This is not trivial for Karatsuba, though, introducing some additional complexity. We leave this for future work.

For the rather small $n = 256$ (Saber, Kindi), we already see that Toom-4 (followed by two layers of Karatsuba) is slightly faster than directly applying Karatsuba. As the difference is small, however, one might decide to not use a Toom layer at all, at the benefit of a much simpler implementation and considerably reduced stack usage. Toom-4 is not suitable for Kindi ($n = 256, q = 2^{14}$), as q is too large. Again the impact is marginal, though, as Karatsuba is only a few percent slower at this dimension, also performing just above Toom-3. For larger $n \in \{701, 743, 1024\}$ (NTRU-HRSS, NTRUEncrypt, RLizard) applying Toom-4 is most efficient. The second layer ends up in the same range of small n, where it is a close competition between applying Toom-3 or directly switching to recursive Karatsuba.

4.2   Encapsulation and Decapsulation Results

In this section we present our performance results for RLizard, Saber, Kindi, NTRUEncrypt, and NTRU-HRSS. All the software presented in this section started from the reference implementations submitted to NIST but went consid-

Table 2. Benchmarks for polynomial multiplication excluding reduction. Fastest approach is highlighted in **bold**. The 'Toom-4 + Toom-3' and 'Toom-4' approaches are not applicable to all parameter sets, as q may be too large.

	Approach	Schoolbook	Clock cycles	Stack usage [bytes]
Saber ($n = 256$, $q = 2^{13}$)	Karatsuba only	16	38 000	2 020
	Toom-3	11	39 043	3 480
	Toom-4	**16**	**36 274**	**3 800**
	Toom-4 + Toom-3	-	-	-
Kindi-256-3-4-2 ($n = 256$, $q = 2^{14}$)	**Karatsuba only**	**16**	**38 000**	**2 020**
	Toom-3	11	39 043	3 480
	Toom-4	-	-	-
	Toom-4 + Toom-3	-	-	-
NTRU-HRSS ($n = 701$, $q = 2^{13}$)	Karatsuba only	11	202 889	5 676
	Toom-3	15	205 947	9 384
	Toom-4	**11**	**172 882**	**10 596**
	Toom-4 + Toom-3	-	-	-
NTRU-KEM-743 ($n = 743$, $q = 2^{11}$)	Karatsuba only	12	217 130	6 012
	Toom-3	16	211 588	9 920
	Toom-4	**12**	**186 639**	**11 208**
	Toom-4 + Toom-3	16	192 503	12 152
RLizard-1024 ($n = 1024$, $q = 2^{11}$)	Karatsuba only	16	356 046	8 188
	Toom-3	11	352 770	13 756
	Toom-4	**16**	**302 504**	**15 344**
	Toom-4 + Toom-3	11	310 712	16 816

erably further than just replacing the multiplication routines with the optimized routines described in Sect. 3. For Saber, we considered starting from the already optimized implementation by Karmakar, Bermudo Mera, Sinha Roy, and Verbauwhede [KMRV18], but achieved marginally better performance starting from the reference code. We start by describing the changes that apply to the reference implementations; some of these changes might be more generally advisable as updates to reference software.

Memory Allocations. The reference implementations of Kindi, RLizard, and NTRUEncrypt make use of dynamic memory allocation on the heap. The RLizard implementation does not free all the allocated memory, which results in memory leaks; also it misinterprets the NIST API and assumes that the public key is always stored right behind the secret key. This may result in reads from uninitialized (or even unallocated) memory. Luckily none of the implementations *require* dynamically allocated memory; the size of all allocated memory is reasonably small and known at compile time. We eliminated all dynamic memory allocations and our software thus only relies on the stack to store temporary data. Our benchmarks show that this significantly improves performance.

Hashing. The five NIST candidates we optimize in this paper make use of variants of SHA-3 and SHAKE [NIS15b] and of SHA-512 [NIS15a]. For SHA-3 and SHAKE we use the optimized assembly implementation from pqm4 [KRSS], which makes use of the optimized Keccak-permutation from the Keccak Code Package [DHP+]. For SHA-512, we use a C implementation from SUPERCOP [BL].

Comparison to Reference Code. Table 3 contains the performance benchmarks for the optimized implementations as well as the reference implementations with the modifications described above. For all schemes targeted in this paper we dramatically increase the performance; the improvements go up to a factor of 49 for the key generation of RLizard-1024. Since both Karatsuba and Toom-Cook require storing additional intermediate polynomials on the stack, we increase stack usage for all schemes except Kindi-256-3-4-2. The reference implementations of Kindi-256-3-4-2 already contained optimized polynomial multiplication methods, which were implemented in a stack-inefficient manner.

Side-Channel Resistance. While side-channel resistance was not a focus of this work, we ensured that our polynomial multiplication is protected against timing attacks. More specifically, in the multiplication routines we avoid all data flow from secrets into branch conditions and into memory addresses. The special multiplication routine in [SBGM+18] is less conservative and *does* use secret-dependent lookup indices with a reference to [ARM12] saying that the Cortex-M4 does not have internal data caches. However, it is not clear to us that really all Cortex-M4 cores do not have any data cache; [ARM12] states that the *"Cortex-M0, Cortex-M0+, Cortex-M1, Cortex-M3, and Cortex-M4 processors do not have any internal cache memory. However, it is possible for a SoC design to integrate a system level cache."* Also, it *is* clear that some ARMv7E-M processors (for example, the ARM Cortex-M7) have data caches and our multiplication code is timing-attack protected also on those devices.

Key-Generation Performance. The focus of this paper is to improve performance of encapsulation and decapsulation. All KEMs considered in this paper are CCA-secure, so the impact of a poor key-generation performance can in principle be minimized by caching ephemeral keys for some time. Such caching of ephemeral keys makes software more complex and in some cases also requires changes to higher level protocols; we therefore believe that key-generation performance, also for CCA-secure KEMs, remains an important target of optimization. The key generation of RLizard, Saber, and Kindi is rather straight-forwardly

Table 3. Benchmarks for reference implementations and optimized implementations using fastest multiplication approach. Reporting run time (cycle count) and stack usage (bytes) for key generation (K), encapsulation (E), and decapsulation (D).

KEMs optimized in this paper					
	Implementation	Clock cycles		Stack usage [bytes]	
Saber	Reference	K:	6 530k	K:	12 616
		E:	8 684k	E:	14 896
		D:	10 581k	D:	15 992
	[KMRV18]	K:	1 147k	K:	13 883
		E:	1 444k	E:	16 667
		D:	1 543k	D:	17 763
	This work	K:	895k	K:	13 248
		E:	1 161k	E:	15 528
		D:	1 204k	D:	16 624
Kindi-256-3-4-2	Reference	K:	21 794k	K:	59 864
		E:	28 176k	E:	71 000
		D:	37 129k	D:	84 096
	This work	K:	969k	K:	44 264
		E:	1 320k	E:	55 392
		D:	1 517k	D:	64 376
NTRU-HRSS	Reference	K:	205 156k	K:	10 020
		E:	5 166k	E:	8 956
		D:	15 067k	D:	10 204
	This work	K:	145 963k	K:	23 396
		E:	404k	E:	14 492
		D:	819k	D:	22 140
NTRU-KEM-743	Reference	K:	59 815k	K:	14 148
		E:	7 540k	E:	13 372
		D:	14 229k	D:	18 036
	This work	K:	5 198k	K:	25 320
		E:	1 601k	E:	23 808
		D:	1 881k	D:	28 472
RLizard-1024	Reference	K:	26 423k	K:	4 272
		E:	32 156k	E:	10 532
		D:	53 181k	D:	12 636
	This work	K:	525k	K:	27 720
		E:	1 345k	E:	33 328
		D:	1 716k	D:	35 448
Other KEMs submitted to the NIST PQC project					
	Implementation	Clock cycles		Stack usage	
R5ND_1PKEb	[SBGM+18]	K:	658k	K:	?
		E:	984k	E:	?
		D:	1 265k	D:	?
R5ND_3PKEb	[SBGM+18]	K:	1 032k	K:	?
		E:	1 510k	E:	?
		D:	1 913k	D:	?
NewHopeCCA1024	[KRSS, AJS16]	K:	1 244k	K:	11 152
		E:	1 963k	E:	17 448
		D:	1 979k	D:	19 648
Kyber768	[KRSS]	K:	1 200k	K:	10 544
		E:	1 446k	E:	13 720
		D:	1 477k	D:	14 880

optimized by integrating our fast multiplication. The key generation of NTRU-Encrypt and NTRU-HRSS also requires inversions, which we did not optimize in this paper; we believe that further research into efficient inversions for those two schemes will significantly improve their key-generation performance.

Comparison to Previous Results. To the best of our knowledge, Saber is the only scheme of those considered in this paper that has been optimized for the ARM Cortex-M family in previous work [KMRV18]. Table 3 contains the performance result on the same platform as ours. Our optimized implementation outperforms the CHES 2018 implementation by 22% for key generation, 20% for encapsulation, and 22% for decapsulation. Karmakar, Bermudo Mera, Sinha Roy, and Verbauwhede report 65 459 clock cycles for their optimized 256-coefficient polynomial multiplication, but we note that their polynomial multiplication includes the reduction. Including the reduction, our multiplication requires 38 215 clock cycles, which is 42% faster. On a more granular level, they claim 587 cycles for 16-coefficient schoolbook multiplication, while we require only 343 cycles (see Table 5; this includes approximately 50 cycles of benchmarking overhead).

Several other NIST candidates have been evaluated on the Cortex-M4 family. We also list the performance results in Table 3 for comparison. Most recently, record-setting results were published for Round5[4] on Cortex-M4 [SBGM+18]. The fastest scheme described in our work, targeting NIST security category 1, NTRU-HRSS, is 59% faster for encapsulation and 35% faster for decapsulation compared to the corresponding CCA variant of Round5 at the same security level. The key generation of NTRU-HRSS is considerably slower, but its inversion is not optimized yet. The fastest scheme implementation described here that targets NIST security category 3, Saber, is 13% faster for key generation, 23% faster for encapsulation, and 37% faster for decapsulation There are also optimized implementations for NewHopeCCA1024 [KRSS, AJS16] and Kyber768 [KRSS]. Both implementations are outperformed by NTRU-HRSS and Saber.

4.3   Profiling of Optimized Implementations

The speed up achieved by optimizing polynomial multiplication clearly shows that it vastly dominates the runtime of reference implementations. Having replaced this core arithmetic operation with highly optimized assembly, we analyze how much time the optimized implementations still spend in non-optimized code to capture how much performance could still be gained by hand-optimizing scheme-specific procedures. We achieve this by measuring the clock cycles spent in polynomial multiplication, hashing, and random number generation. Table 4 shows that still a considerable proportion of encapsulation and decapsulation is spent in polynomial multiplication. However, cycles consumed by hashing and randomness generation become more prominent. In the following we briefly discuss these results and emphasize how one could further speed-up those schemes.

---

[4] R5ND_{1,3,5}PKEb are the CCA-variants of Round5, whereas R5ND_{1,3,5}KEMb are CPA-secure.

Table 4. Time spent in polynomial multiplication, hashing, and sampling randomness for optimized implementations. Still considerable time is spent in polynomial multiplication, but hashing is more apparent.

Scheme		Total [cycles]	Polýmul [cycles]	Hashing [cycles]	Randombytes [cycles]
Saber	K:	895k	327k (37%)	475k (53%)	2.0k (<1%)
	E:	1 161k	435k (38%)	615k (53%)	0.6k (<1%)
	D:	1 204k	544k (45%)	500k (42%)	0
Kindi-256-3-4-2	K:	969k	342k (35%)	409k (42%)	1.2k (<1%)
	E:	1 320k	456k (35%)	604k (46%)	0.6k (<1%)
	D:	1 517k	570k (38%)	603k (40%)	0
NTRU-HRSS	K:	145 963k	1 556k (1%)	80k (<1%)	0.6k (<1%)
	E:	404k	173k (43%)	107k (26%)	0.6k (<1%)
	D:	819k	519k (63%)	67k (8%)	0
NTRU-KEM-743	K:	5 198k	1 680k (32%)	0	85k (2%)
	E:	1 601k	187k (12%)	1 171k (73%)	46k (3%)
	D:	1 881k	373k (20%)	1 172k (63%)	0
RLizard-1024	K:	525k	303k (58%)	0	123k (23%)
	E:	1 345k	605k (45%)	628k (47%)	2.2k (<1%)
	D:	1 716k	908k (53%)	628k (36%)	0

Hashing. For encapsulation, hashing (SHA-3 and SHA-2) dominates the runtime of Kindi-256-3-4-2, NTRU-KEM-743, and Saber. We have replaced these primitives with the fastest implementations available. Still, all schemes spend a substantial number of clock cycles computing hashes. This is partly due to the Fujisaki-Okamoto transformation required to achieve CCA security. Further hash function calls are required to sample pseudo-random numbers from a seed, which most schemes implement using the SHAKE XOF. Having a hardware accelerator for these hash function would highly benefit all of the examined schemes. While ARM Cortex-M4 platforms with SHA-2 hardware support exist, there are (at the time of writing) none available which have SHA-3 hardware support.

Randomness Generation. Kindi-256-3-4-2, NTRU-HRSS, and Saber do not make use of randombytes extensively, but sample a small seed and then expand this using SHAKE. RLizard-1024 and NTRU-KEM-743 directly sample their randomness randombytes. As we implement randombytes using the hardware RNG on the STM32F4Discovery, it is more efficient than using SHAKE to expand a seed. There are, however, important caveats to consider when only using the hardware number generator. It is unclear what the cryptographic properties of such an RNG are, and how this affects the security of the various schemes, in particular since most reveal randomness as part of the CCA transform.

A   Schoolbook Multiplication Benchmarks

Table 5. Benchmarks for small schoolbook multiplication routines. The cycle counts include an overhead of approximately 50 cycles for benchmarking.

n	Cycles	n	Cycles	n	Cycles	n	Cycles
1	56	13	232	25	926	37	1 965
2	59	14	252	26	1 057	38	1 966
3	69	15	341	27	1 057	39	1 963
4	74	16	343	28	1 168	40	1 965
5	85	17	467	29	1 167	41	2 294
6	92	18	466	30	1 170	42	2 588
7	107	19	508	31	1 264	43	2 595
8	114	20	510	32	1 266	44	2 594
9	131	21	626	33	1 431	45	2 824
10	140	22	626	34	1 547	46	2 825
11	168	23	670	35	1 546	47	2 822
12	177	24	672	36	1 549	48	2 824

References

[AAB+17] Alkim, E., et al.: Newhope: algorithm specification and supporting documentation. Submission to the NIST Post-Quantum Cryptography Standardization Project (2017). https://cryptojedi.org/papers/#newhopenist

[ABD+17] Avanzi, R., et al.: CRYSTALS-Kyber: algorithm specification and supporting documentation. Submission to the NIST Post-Quantum Cryptography Standardization Project (2017). https://pq-crystals.org/kyber

[ADPS16] Alkim, E., Ducas, L., Pöppelmann, T., Schwabe, P.: Post-quantum key exchange - a new hope. In: Holz, T., Savage, S. (eds.) Proceedings of the 25th USENIX Security Symposium. USENIX Association (2016). https://eprint.iacr.org/2015/1092

[AJS16] Alkim, E., Jakubeit, P., Schwabe, P.: NewHope on ARM Cortex-M. In: Carlet, C., Hasan, M.A., Saraswat, V. (eds.) SPACE 2016. LNCS, vol. 10076, pp. 332–349. Springer, Cham (2016). https://doi.org/10.1007/978-3-319-49445-6_19

[ARM12] ARM Cortex-M programming guide to memory barrier instructions (2012). https://static.docs.arm.com/dai0321/a/DAI0321A_programming_guide_memory_barriers_for_m_profile.pdf

[Ban17] El Bansarkhani, R.: KINDI: algorithm specification and supporting documentation. Submission to the NIST Post-Quantum Cryptography Standardization Project (2017). http://kindi-kem.de

[BGM+16] Bogdanov, A., Guo, S., Masny, D., Richelson, S., Rosen, A.: On the hardness of learning with rounding over small modulus. In: Kushilevitz, E., Malkin, T. (eds.) TCC 2016. LNCS, vol. 9562, pp. 209–224. Springer, Heidelberg (2016). https://doi.org/10.1007/978-3-662-49096-9_9

[BGML+18] Bhattacharya, S., et al.: Round5: compact and fast post-quantum public-key encryption. Cryptology ePrint Archive, Report 2018/725 (2018). https://eprint.iacr.org/2018/725

[BL] Bernstein, D.J., Lange, T.: eBACS: ECRYPT benchmarking of cryptographic systems. http://bench.cr.yp.to. Accessed 14 Oct 2018

[BPR12] Banerjee, A., Peikert, C., Rosen, A.: Pseudorandom functions and lattices. In: Pointcheval, D., Johansson, T. (eds.) EUROCRYPT 2012. LNCS, vol. 7237, pp. 719–737. Springer, Heidelberg (2012). https://doi.org/10.1007/978-3-642-29011-4_42

[Coo66] Cook, S.: On the minimum computation time of functions. Ph.D. thesis, Harvard University (1966)

[CPL+17] Cheon, J.H., et al.: Lizard: algorithm specification and supporting documentation. Submission to the NIST Post-Quantum Cryptography Standardization Project (2017). https://csrc.nist.gov/projects/post-quantum-cryptography/round-1-submissions

[Den03] Dent, A.W.: A Designer's guide to KEMs. In: Paterson, K.G. (ed.) Cryptography and Coding 2003. LNCS, vol. 2898, pp. 133–151. Springer, Heidelberg (2003). https://doi.org/10.1007/978-3-540-40974-8_12

[DHP+] Daemen, J., Hoffert, S., Peeters, M., Van Assche, G., Van Keer, R.: eXtended Keccak Code Package. https://github.com/XKCP/XKCP. Accessed 14 Oct 2018

[DKRV17] D'Anvers, J.-P., Karmakar, A., Roy, S.S., Vercauteren, F.: Saber: algorithm specification and supporting documentation. Submission to the NIST Post-Quantum Cryptography Standardization Project (2017). https://csrc.nist.gov/projects/post-quantum-cryptography/round-1-submissions

[FO99] Fujisaki, E., Okamoto, T.: Secure integration of asymmetric and symmetric encryption schemes. In: Wiener, M. (ed.) CRYPTO 1999. LNCS, vol. 1666, pp. 537–554. Springer, Heidelberg (1999). https://doi.org/10.1007/3-540-48405-1_34

[GMZB+17] Garcia-Morchon, O., Zhang, Z., Bhattacharya, S., Rietman, R., Tolhuizen, L., Torre-Arce, J.-L.: Round2: algorithm specification and supporting documentation. Submission to the NIST Post-Quantum Cryptography Standardization Project (2017). https://www.onboardsecurity.com/nist-post-quantum-crypto-submission

[HGSSW03] Howgrave-Graham, N., Silverman, J.H., Singer, A., Whyte, W.: NAEP: provable security in the presence of decryption failures. Cryptology ePrint Archive, Report 2003/172 (2003). https://eprint.iacr.org/2003/172

[HHK17] Hofheinz, D., Hövelmanns, K., Kiltz, E.: A modular analysis of the fujisaki-okamoto transformation. In: Kalai, Y., Reyzin, L. (eds.) TCC 2017. LNCS, vol. 10677, pp. 341–371. Springer, Cham (2017). https://doi.org/10.1007/978-3-319-70500-2_12

[HPS98] Hoffstein, J., Pipher, J., Silverman, J.H.: NTRU: a ring-based public key cryptosystem. In: Buhler, J.P. (ed.) ANTS 1998. LNCS, vol. 1423, pp. 267–288. Springer, Heidelberg (1998). https://doi.org/10.1007/BFb0054868

[HPS+17] Hoffstein, J., Pipher, J., Schanck, J.M., Silverman, J.H., Whyte, W., Zhang, Z.: Choosing parameters for NTRUEncrypt. In: Handschuh, H. (ed.) CT-RSA 2017. LNCS, vol. 10159, pp. 3–18. Springer, Cham (2017). https://doi.org/10.1007/978-3-319-52153-4_1

[HRSS17a] Hülsing, A., Rijneveld, J., Schanck, J., Schwabe, P.: High-speed key encapsulation from NTRU. In: Fischer, W., Homma, N. (eds.) CHES 2017. LNCS, vol. 10529, pp. 232–252. Springer, Cham (2017). https://doi.org/10.1007/978-3-319-66787-4_12

[HRSS17b] Hülsing, A., Rijneveld, J., Schanck, J.M., Schwabe, P.: NTRU-KEM-HRSS: algorithm specification and supporting documentation. Submission to the NIST Post-Quantum Cryptography Standardization Project (2017). https://ntru-hrss.org

[KMRV18] Karmakar, A., Mera, J.M.B., Roy, S.S., Verbauwhede, I.: Saber on ARM. IACR Trans. Cryptogr. Hardware Embed. Syst. **2018**(3), 243–266 (2018). https://eprint.iacr.org/2018/682

[KO63] Karatsuba, A., Ofman, Y.: Multiplication of multidigit numbers on automata. Sov. Phys. Doklady **7**, 595–596 (1963). Translated from Doklady Akademii Nauk SSSR, vol. 145, no. 2, pp. 293–294, July 1962. http://cr.yp.to/bib/1963/karatsuba.html

[KRSS] Kannwischer, M.J., Rijneveld, J., Schwabe, P., Stoffelen, K.: PQM4: post-quantum crypto library for the ARM Cortex-M4. https://github.com/mupq/pqm4. Accessed 14 Oct 2018

[NIS15a] FIPS PUB 180-4: Secure hash standard (2015). http://nvlpubs.nist.gov/nistpubs/FIPS/NIST.FIPS.180-4.pdf

[NIS15b] FIPS PUB 202 – SHA-3 standard: Permutation-based hash and extendable-output functions (2015). http://nvlpubs.nist.gov/nistpubs/FIPS/NIST.FIPS.202.pdf

[NIS16a] Submission requirements and evaluation criteria for the post -quantum cryptography standardization process (2016). https://csrc.nist.gov/csrc/media/projects/post-quantum-cryptography/documents/call-for-proposals-final-dec-2016.pdf

[NIS16b] NIST Computer Security Division. Post-Quantum Cryptography Standardization (2016). https://csrc.nist.gov/Projects/Post-Quantum-Cryptography

[Saa17] Saarinen, M.-J.O.: Hila5: algorithm specification and supporting documentation. Submission to the NIST Post-Quantum Cryptography Standardization Project (2017). https://mjos.fi/hila5

[SAL+17] Smart, N.P., et al.: Lima: algorithm specification and supporting documentation. Submission to the NIST Post-Quantum Cryptography Standardization Project (2017). https://lima-pq.github.io

[SBGM+18] Saarinen, M.-J.O., Bhattacharya, S., Garcia-Morchon, O., Rietman, R., Tolhuizen, L., Zhang, Z.: Shorter messages and faster post-quantum encryption with Round5 on Cortex M. Cryptology ePrint Archive, Report 2018/723 (2018). https://eprint.iacr.org/2018/723. Version: 13 Oct 2018 08:50:18 UTC

[SS17] Schwabe, P., Stoffelen, K.: All the AES you need on Cortex-M3 and M4. In: Avanzi, R., Heys, H. (eds.) SAC 2016. LNCS, vol. 10532, pp. 180–194. Springer, Cham (2017). https://doi.org/10.1007/978-3-319-69453-5_10

[Too63] Toom, A.L.: The complexity of a scheme of functional elements realizing the multiplication of integers. Sov. Math. Doklady **3**, 714–716 (1963). www.de.ufpe.br/~toom/my-articles/engmat/MULT-E.PDF

[WP06]   Weimerskirch, A., Paar, C.: Generalizations of the Karatsuba algorithm for efficient implementations (2006). https://eprint.iacr.org/2003/172

[ZCHW17] Zhang, Z., Chen, C., Hoffstein, J., Whyte, W.: NTRUEncrypt: algorithm specification and supporting documentation. Submission to the NIST Post-Quantum Cryptography Standardization Project (2017). https://csrc.nist.gov/projects/post-quantum-cryptography/round-1-submissions

Generic and Practical Key Establishment from Lattice

Zhengzhong Jin[1,2] and Yunlei Zhao[3(✉)]

[1] School of Mathematics, Fudan University, Shanghai, China
[2] Department of Computer Science, Johns Hopkins University, Baltimore, USA
[3] School of Computer Science, Fudan University, Shanghai, China
ylzhao@fudan.edu.cn

Abstract. In this work, we abstract some key ingredients in previous key establishment and public-key encryption schemes from LWE and its variants. Specifically, we explicitly formalize the building tool, referred to as key consensus (KC) and its asymmetric variant AKC. KC and AKC allow two communicating parties to reach consensus from close values, which plays the fundamental role in lattice-based cryptography. We then prove the upper bounds on parameters for any KC and AKC, which reveal the inherent constraints on the parameters among security, bandwidth, error probability, and consensus range. As a conceptual contribution, this simplifies the design and analysis of these cryptosystems in the future. Guided by the proved upper bounds, we design and analyze both generic and highly practical KC and AKC schemes, which are referred to as OKCN and AKCN respectively for presentation simplicity. We present a generic protocol structure for key establishment from learning with rounding (LWR), which can be instantiated with either KC or AKC. We then provide an analysis breaking the correlation between the rounded deterministic noise and the secret, and design an algorithm to calculate the error probability numerically. When applied to LWE-based key establishment, OKCN and AKCN can result in more practical or well-balanced schemes, compared to existing LWE-based protocols in the literature.

1 Introduction

Most public-key cryptosystems currently in use, based on the hardness of solving (elliptic curve) discrete logarithm or factoring large integers, will be broken, if large-scale quantum computers are ever built. The arrival of such quantum computers is now believed by many scientists to be merely a significant engineering

This work is supported in part by National Key Research and Development Program of China under Grant No. 2017YFB0802000, National Natural Science Foundation of China under Grant Nos. 61472084 and U1536205, Shanghai Innovation Action Project under Grant No. 16DZ1100200, Shanghai Science and Technology Development Funds under Grant No. 6JC1400801, and Shandong Provincial Key Research and Development Program of China under Grant Nos. 2017CXG0701 and 2018CXGC0701.

R. H. Deng et al. (Eds.): ACNS 2019, LNCS 11464, pp. 302–322, 2019.
https://doi.org/10.1007/978-3-030-21568-2_15

challenge, and is estimated to be within the next two decades or so. Historically, it has taken almost two decades to deploy the modern public key cryptography infrastructure. Therefore, regardless of whether we can estimate the exact time of the arrival of the quantum computing era, we should begin now to prepare our information security systems to be able to resist quantum computing. In addition, for the content we want to protect over a period of 15 years or longer, it becomes necessary to switch to post-quantum cryptography today. In the majority of contexts, *ephemeral* key establishment (KE), which plays a central role in modern cryptography, is among the most critical asymmetric primitives to upgrade to post-quantum security.

Lattice-based cryptography is one of the promising mathematical approaches to achieving security resistant to quantum attacks. For cryptographic usage, compared with the classic hard lattice problems such as SVP and CVP, the learning with errors (LWE) problem is proven to be much more versatile [Reg09]. One of the main technical contributions in recent years on achieving practical key establishment based on LWE and its variants is the improvement and generalization of the key reconciliation mechanisms [Reg09, DXL12, LPR10, LP10]. But the key reconciliation mechanisms were only previously used and analyzed, for both KE and PKE, in a *non-black-box* way. This means, for new key reconciliation mechanisms developed in the future to be used for constructing lattice-based cryptosystems, we need to analyze their security from scratch. Moreover, for the various parameters involved in key reconciliation, the bounds on what could or couldn't be achieved are unclear. As a consequence, we lack basic criteria to evaluate various reconciliation mechanisms and to indicate whether they can be further improved.

Abstraction/generalization is fundamental to natural science (mathematics, physics), and is particularly important to cryptography. For example, in the area of signature, Schnorr signature is generalized via Fiat-Shamir transformation [FS86], with abstraction of Σ-protocol [CDS94]. The similar abstraction and generalization also plays a fundamental role in CCA-secure PKE, and in many more areas of modern cryptography. Abstraction and generalization is particularly helpful and expected for lattice-based cryptography, as they are usually less easy to understand and evaluate, and are related to the ongoing NIST post-quantum cryptography standardization [NIST].

1.1 Our Contributions

In this work, we abstract the key ingredients in previous key establishment and PKE schemes based on LWE and its variants, by introducing and formalizing the building tool, referred to as key consensus (KC) and its asymmetric variant AKC. KC and AKC allow two communicating parties to reach consensus from close values obtained by some secure information exchange, such as exchanging their LWE samples. We then discover upper bounds on parameters for any KC and AKC. As a conceptual contribution, this simplifies the design and analysis of these cryptosystems in the future. We then design and analyze both generic and highly practical KC and AKC schemes, which are referred to as *symmetric key consensus with noise* (OKCN) and *asymmetric key consensus with noise* (AKCN) respectively for presentation simplicity.

We propose the first construction of key establishment *merely* based on the LWR problem with concrete analysis and evaluation, to the best of our knowledge. We use the randomness lifting technique to present a unified protocol structure that can be instantiated with either KC or AKC. We provide an analysis breaking the correlation between the rounded deterministic noise and the secret, and design an algorithm to calculate the error probability numerically. When applied to LWE-based key establishment, OKCN and AKCN can result in more practical or well-balanced schemes, compared to the related LWE-based protocols in the literature. The protocols developed in this work are implemented. The code and scripts, together with those for evaluating concrete security and failure rates, are (anonymously) available from Github http://github.com/OKCN.

1.2 Related Work

AKC (resp., KC) was pioneered by the works on lattice-based PKE [LP10, LPR10] (resp., the work on key establishment [DXL12]). LWR-based key establishment was pioneered by the Lizard protocol [CKLS16]. The Lizard protocol is AKC-based, and is based on (special variants of) both LWE and LWR. To the best our knowledge, key establishment protocol *merely* from the LWR problem was first achieved in an early version of our work [JZ16].[1] The works [BBG+17,DKRV17,BGL+18] considered AKC-based key transport protocols from some variants of LWR (some of which use sparse-ternary secret keys), and show that randomness lifting is not necessary for AKC-based protocol from LWR. But these protocols do not support KC-based instantiations. We remark that, for the recommended parameters in all the works, randomness lifting corresponds to uniform sampling from $[-2^k, 2^k - 1]$ for some positive integer k, which is fast and easy.

2 Preliminaries

A string or value α means a binary one, and $|\alpha|$ is its binary length. For any real number x, $\lfloor x \rfloor$ denotes the largest integer that less than or equal to x, and $\lfloor x \rceil = \lfloor x + 1/2 \rfloor$. For any positive integers a and b, denote by $\mathrm{lcm}(a, b)$ the least common multiple of them. For any $i, j \in \mathbb{Z}$ such that $i < j$, denote by $[i, j]$ the set of integers $\{i, i+1, \cdots, j-1, j\}$. For any positive integer t, we let $\mathbb{Z}_t$ denote $\mathbb{Z}/t\mathbb{Z}$. The elements of $\mathbb{Z}_t$ are represented, by default, as $[0, t-1]$. Nevertheless, sometimes, $\mathbb{Z}_t$ is explicitly specified to be represented as $[-\lfloor (t-1)/2 \rfloor, \lfloor t/2 \rfloor]$.

If S is a finite set then $|S|$ is its cardinality, and $x \leftarrow S$ is the operation of picking an element uniformly at random from S. For two sets $A, B \subseteq \mathbb{Z}_q$, define

---

[1] Our work appeared in the literature since November 2016 [JZ16], and the construction and analysis of LWR-based protocol are presented in the update of February 2017.

$A + B \triangleq \{a + b | a \in A, b \in B\}$. For an addictive group $(G, +)$, an element $x \in G$ and a subset $S \subseteq G$, denote by $x + S$ the set containing $x + s$ for all $s \in S$. For a set S, denote by $\mathcal{U}(S)$ the uniform distribution over S. For any discrete random variable X over $\mathbb{R}$, denote $\mathsf{Supp}(X) = \{x \in \mathbb{R} \mid \Pr[X = x] > 0\}$.

We use standard notations and conventions below for writing probabilistic algorithms, experiments and interactive protocols. If $\mathcal{D}$ denotes a probability distribution, $x \leftarrow \mathcal{D}$ is the operation of picking an element according to $\mathcal{D}$. If α is neither an algorithm nor a set then $x \leftarrow \alpha$ is a simple assignment statement. If A is a probabilistic algorithm, then $A(x_1, x_2, \cdots ; r)$ is the result of running A on inputs $x_1, x_2, \cdots$ and coins r. We let $y \leftarrow A(x_1, x_2, \cdots)$ denote the experiment of picking r at random and letting y be $A(x_1, x_2, \cdots ; r)$. By $\Pr[R_1; \cdots ; R_n : E]$ we denote the probability of event E, after the ordered execution of random processes $R_1, \cdots, R_n$.

2.1   The LWE and LWR Problems

Given positive *continuous* $\alpha > 0$, define the real Gaussian function $\rho_\alpha(x) \triangleq \exp(-x^2/2\alpha^2)/\sqrt{2\pi\alpha^2}$ for $x \in \mathbb{R}$. Let $D_{\mathbb{Z},\alpha}$ denote the one-dimensional *discrete* Gaussian distribution over $\mathbb{Z}$, which is determined by its probability density function $D_{\mathbb{Z},\alpha}(x) \triangleq \rho_\alpha(x)/\rho_\alpha(\mathbb{Z}), x \in \mathbb{Z}$. Finally, let $D_{\mathbb{Z}^n,\alpha}$ denote the n-dimensional *spherical* discrete Gaussian distribution over $\mathbb{Z}^n$, where each coordinate is drawn *independently* from $D_{\mathbb{Z},\alpha}$.

Given positive integers n and q that are both polynomials in the security parameter λ, an integer vector $\mathbf{s} \in \mathbb{Z}_q^n$, and a probability distribution χ on $\mathbb{Z}_q$, let $A_{q,\mathbf{s},\chi}$ be the distribution over $\mathbb{Z}_q^n \times \mathbb{Z}_q$ obtained by choosing $\mathbf{a} \in \mathbb{Z}_q^n$ uniformly at random, and an error term $e \leftarrow \chi$, and outputting the pair $(\mathbf{a}, b = \mathbf{a}^T\mathbf{s} + e) \in \mathbb{Z}_q^n \times \mathbb{Z}_q$. The error distribution χ is typically taken to be the discrete Gaussian probability distribution $D_{\mathbb{Z},\alpha}$ defined previously; However, as suggested in [BCD+16], other alternative distributions of χ can be taken. Briefly speaking, the (decisional) *learning with errors* (LWE) assumption [Reg09] says that, for sufficiently large security parameter λ, no probabilistic polynomial-time (PT) algorithm can distinguish, with non-negligible probability, $A_{q,\mathbf{s},\chi}$ from the uniform distribution over $\mathbb{Z}_q^n \times \mathbb{Z}_q$. This holds even if $\mathcal{A}$ sees polynomially many samples, and even if the secret vector $\mathbf{s}$ is drawn randomly from χ^n [ACPS09].

The LWR problem [BPR12] is a "decarbonized" variant of the LWE problem. Let $\mathcal{D}$ be some distribution over $\mathbb{Z}_q^n$, and $\mathbf{s} \leftarrow \mathcal{D}$. For integers $q \geq p \geq 2$ and any $x \in \mathbb{Z}_q$, denote

$$\lfloor x \rceil_p = \lfloor \frac{p}{q}x \rceil. \tag{1}$$

Then, for positive integers n and $q \geq p \geq 2$, the LWR distribution $A_{n,q,p}(\mathbf{s})$ over $\mathbb{Z}_q^n \times \mathbb{Z}_p$ is obtained by sampling $\mathbf{a}$ from $\mathbb{Z}_q^n$ uniformly at random, and outputting $\left(\mathbf{a}, \lfloor \mathbf{a}^T\mathbf{s} \rceil_p\right) \in \mathbb{Z}_q^n \times \mathbb{Z}_p$. Briefly speaking, the (decisional) LWR assumption says that, for sufficiently large security parameter, no PT algorithm $\mathcal{A}$ can distinguish, with non-negligible probability, the distribution $A_{n,q,p}(\mathbf{s})$ from the distribution $(\mathbf{a} \leftarrow \mathbb{Z}_q^n, \lfloor u \rfloor_p)$ where $u \leftarrow \mathbb{Z}_q$. This holds even if $\mathcal{A}$ sees poly-nomially many samples. An efficient reduction from the LWE problem to the LWR problem, for super-polynomial large q, is provided in [BPR12]. Let B denote the bound for any component in the secret $\mathbf{s}$. It is recently shown that, when $q \geq 2mBp$ (equivalently, $m \leq q/2Bp$), the LWE problem can be reduced to the (decisional) LWR assumption with m independently random samples [BGM+16]. Moreover, the reduction from LWE to LWR is actually independent of the distribution of the secret $\mathbf{s}$.

3   Key Consensus with Noise

Before presenting the definition of key consensus (KC) scheme, we first introduce a new function $|\cdot|_t$ relative to arbitrary positive integer $t \geq 1$: $|x|_t = \min\{x \bmod t, t - x \bmod t\}$, $\forall x \in \mathbb{Z}$, where the result of modular operation is represented in $\{0, ..., (t-1)\}$. For instance, $|-1|_t = \min\{-1 \bmod t, (t+1) \bmod t\} = \min\{t-1, 1\} = 1$. In the following description, we use $|\sigma_1 - \sigma_2|_q$ to measure the distance between two elements $\sigma_1, \sigma_2 \in \mathbb{Z}_q$.

Definition 1. *A KC scheme* $KC = (\text{params}, \text{Con}, \text{Rec})$ *is specified as follows.*

- *params* $= (q, m, g, d, aux)$ *denotes the system parameters, where* q, m, g, d *are positive integers satisfying* $2 \leq m, g \leq q, 0 \leq d \leq \lfloor \frac{q}{2} \rfloor$, *and aux denotes some auxiliary values that are usually determined by* (q, m, g, d) *and could be set to be a special symbol* $\emptyset$ *indicating "empty".*
- $(k_1, v) \leftarrow \text{Con}(\sigma_1, \text{params})$: *On input of* $(\sigma_1 \in \mathbb{Z}_q, \text{params})$, *the probabilistic polynomial-time conciliation algorithm* Con *outputs* (k_1, v), *where* $k_1 \in \mathbb{Z}_m$ *is the shared-key, and* $v \in \mathbb{Z}_g$ *is a hint signal that will be publicly delivered to the communicating peer to help the two parties reach consensus.*
- $k_2 \leftarrow \text{Rec}(\sigma_2, v, \text{params})$: *On input of* $(\sigma_2 \in \mathbb{Z}_q, v, \text{params})$, *the deterministic polynomial-time reconciliation algorithm* Rec *outputs* $k_2 \in \mathbb{Z}_m$.

Correctness: *A KC scheme is correct, if for any* $\sigma_1, \sigma_2 \in \mathbb{Z}_q$ *such that* $|\sigma_1 - \sigma_2|_q \leq d$, $(k_1, v) \leftarrow \text{Con}(\sigma_1, \text{params})$ *and* $k_2 \leftarrow \text{Rec}(\sigma_2, v, \text{params})$, *it holds* $k_1 = k_2$.

Security: *A KC scheme is secure, if* k_1 *and* v *are independent, and* k_1 *is uniformly distributed over* $\mathbb{Z}_m$, *whenever* $\sigma_1 \leftarrow \mathbb{Z}_q$ *and* k_1 *is the output of* $\text{Con}(\sigma_1, \text{params})$. *The probability is taken over the sampling of* σ_1 *and the random coins used by* Con.

3.1   Efficiency Upper Bound of KC

The following theorem reveals an upper bound on the parameters q (dominating security and efficiency), m (parameterizing range of consensus key), g (parameterizing bandwidth), and d (parameterizing error rate), which allows us to take balance on these parameters according to different priorities. Due to space limitation, the proof is given in the full version [JZ16].

Algorithm 1. OKCN: Symmetric KC with Noise

1: **params** $= (q, m, g, d, aux)$, $aux = \{q' = \mathsf{lcm}(q, m), \alpha = q'/q, \beta = q'/m\}$
2: **procedure** $\mathrm{CON}((\sigma_1, \mathsf{params}))$ $\triangleright \sigma_1 \in [0, q-1]$
3:     $e \leftarrow [-\lfloor(\alpha-1)/2\rfloor, \lfloor\alpha/2\rfloor]$
4:     $\sigma_A = (\alpha\sigma_1 + e) \bmod q'$
5:     $k_1 = \lfloor\sigma_A/\beta\rfloor \in \mathbb{Z}_m$
6:     $v' = \sigma_A \bmod \beta$
7:     $v = \lfloor v'g/\beta\rfloor$ $\triangleright v \in \mathbb{Z}_g$
8:     **return** (k_1, v)
9: **end procedure**
10: **procedure** $\mathrm{REC}(\sigma_2, v, \mathsf{params})$ $\triangleright \sigma_2 \in [0, q-1]$
11:     $k_2 = \lfloor\alpha\sigma_2/\beta - (v + 1/2)/g\rceil \bmod m$
12:     **return** k_2
13: **end procedure**

Theorem 1. If $KC = (\mathsf{params}, \mathsf{Con}, \mathsf{Rec})$ is a correct and secure key consensus scheme, and $\mathsf{params} = (q, m, g, d, aux)$, then $2md \leq q\left(1 - \frac{1}{g}\right)$.

3.2 Construction and Analysis of OKCN

The key consensus scheme, named *symmetric key consensus with noise* (OKCN)", is presented in Algorithm 1. The following fact is direct from the definition of $|\cdot|_t$.

Fact 1. For any $x, y, t, l \in \mathbb{Z}$ where $t \geq 1$ and $l \geq 0$, if $|x - y|_q \leq l$, then there exists $\theta \in \mathbb{Z}$ and $\delta \in [-l, l]$ such that $x = y + \theta t + \delta$.

Theorem 2. Suppose that the system parameters satisfy $(2d+1)m < q\left(1 - \frac{1}{g}\right)$ where $m \geq 2$ and $g \geq 2$. Then, the OKCN scheme is correct.

Proof. Suppose $|\sigma_1 - \sigma_2|_q \leq d$. By Fact 1, there exist $\theta \in \mathbb{Z}$ and $\delta \in [-d, d]$ such that $\sigma_2 = \sigma_1 + \theta q + \delta$. From line 4 and 6 in Algorithm 1, we know that there is a $\theta' \in \mathbb{Z}$, such that $\alpha\sigma_1 + e + \theta'q' = \sigma_A = k_1\beta + v'$. And from the definition of α, β, we have $\alpha/\beta = m/q$. Taking these into the formula of k_2 in Rec (line 11 in Algorithm 1), we have

$$k_2 = \lfloor\alpha\sigma_2/\beta - (v + 1/2)/g\rceil \bmod m \tag{2}$$

$$= \lfloor\alpha(\theta q + \sigma_1 + \delta)/\beta - (v + 1/2)/g\rceil \bmod m \tag{3}$$

$$= \left\lfloor m(\theta - \theta') + \frac{1}{\beta}(k_1\beta + v' - e) + \frac{\alpha\delta}{\beta} - \frac{1}{g}(v + 1/2)\right\rceil \bmod m \tag{4}$$

$$= \left\lfloor k_1 + \left(\frac{v'}{\beta} - \frac{v + 1/2}{g}\right) - \frac{e}{\beta} + \frac{\alpha\delta}{\beta}\right\rceil \bmod m \tag{5}$$

Algorithm 2. OKCN simple

1: params : $q = 2^{\bar{q}}, g = 2^{\bar{g}}, m = 2^{\bar{m}}, d$, where $\bar{g} + \bar{m} = \bar{q}$
2: **procedure** CON(σ_1, params)
3:    $k_1 = \left\lfloor \frac{\sigma_1}{g} \right\rfloor$
4:    $v = \sigma_1 \bmod g$
5:    **return** (k_1, v)
6: **end procedure**
7: **procedure** REC(σ_2, v, params)
8:    $k_2 = \left\lfloor \frac{\sigma_2 - v}{g} \right\rceil \bmod m$
9:    **return** k_2
10: **end procedure**

Notice that $|v'/\beta - (v + 1/2)/g| = |v'g - \beta(v + 1/2)|/\beta g \leq 1/2g$. So

$$\left| \left(\frac{v'}{\beta} - \frac{v + 1/2}{g} \right) - \frac{e}{\beta} + \frac{\alpha \delta}{\beta} \right| \leq \frac{1}{2g} + \frac{\alpha}{\beta}(d + 1/2).$$

From the assumed condition $(2d + 1)m < q(1 - \frac{1}{g})$, we get that the right-hand side is strictly smaller than $1/2$; Consequently, after the rounding, $k_2 = k_1$.   □

Theorem 3. *OKCN is secure. Specifically, when $\sigma_1 \leftarrow \mathbb{Z}_q$, k_1 and v are independent, and k_1 is uniform over $\mathbb{Z}_m$, where the probability is taken over the sampling of σ_1 and the random coins used by Con.*

Proof. Recall that $q' = \text{lcm}(q, m), \alpha = q'/q, \beta = q'/m$. We first demonstrate that σ_A is subject to uniform distribution over $\mathbb{Z}_{q'}$. Consider the map $f : \mathbb{Z}_q \times \mathbb{Z}_\alpha \to \mathbb{Z}_{q'}$; $f(\sigma, e) = (\alpha \sigma + e) \bmod q'$, where the elements in $\mathbb{Z}_q$ and $\mathbb{Z}_\alpha$ are represented in the same way as specified in Algorithm 1. It is easy to check that f is an one-to-one map. Since $\sigma_1 \leftarrow \mathbb{Z}_q$ and $e \leftarrow \mathbb{Z}_\alpha$ are subject to uniform distributions, and they are independent, $\sigma_A = (\alpha \sigma_1 + e) \bmod q' = f(\sigma_1, e)$ is also subject to uniform distribution over $\mathbb{Z}_{q'}$.

In the similar way, defining $f' : \mathbb{Z}_m \times \mathbb{Z}_\beta \to \mathbb{Z}_{q'}$ such that $f'(k_1, v') = \beta k_1 + v'$, then f' is obviously a one-to-one map. From line 6 of Algorithm 1, $f'(k_1, v') = \sigma_A$. As σ_A is distributed uniformly over $\mathbb{Z}_{q'}$, (k_1, v') is uniformly distributed over $\mathbb{Z}_m \times \mathbb{Z}_\beta$, and so k_1 and v' are independent. As v only depends on v', k_1 and v are independent.   □

Special Parameters, and Performance Speeding-Up. The first and the second line of Con (line 3 and 4 in Algorithm 1) play the role in transforming a uniform distribution over $\mathbb{Z}_q$ to a uniform distribution over $\mathbb{Z}_{q'}$. If one chooses q, g, m to be power of 2, i.e., $q = 2^{\bar{q}}, g = 2^{\bar{g}}, m = 2^{\bar{m}}$ where $\bar{q}, \bar{g}, \bar{m} \in \mathbb{Z}$, then such transformation is not necessary, and the random noise e used in calculating σ_A in Algorithm 1 is avoided. If we take $\bar{g} + \bar{m} = \bar{q}$, it can be further simplified into the variant depicted in Algorithm 2, with the constraint on parameters is further relaxed.

Corollary 1. *If m, g are power of 2, $q = m \cdot g$, and $2md < q$, then the KC scheme described in Algorithm 2 is* correct *and* secure. *Notice that the constraint on parameters is further simplified to $2md < q$ in this case.*

To the best of our knowledge, OKCN is the first multi-bit reconciliation mechanism, and the first that can be instantiated to tightly match the upper-bound proved in Theorem 1.

4   Asymmetric Key Consensus with Noise

Definition 2. *An asymmetric key consensus scheme $AKC = ($params, Con, Rec$)$ is specified as follows:*

- *params $= (q, m, g, d, aux)$ denotes the system parameters, where q, $2 \le m, g \le q$, $1 \le d \le \lfloor \frac{q}{2} \rfloor$ are positive integers, and aux denotes some auxiliary values that are usually determined by (q, m, g, d) and could be set to be empty.*
- *$v \leftarrow$ Con$(\sigma_1, k_1,$ params$)$: On input of $(\sigma_1 \in \mathbb{Z}_q, k_1 \in \mathbb{Z}_m,$ params$)$, the probabilistic polynomial-time conciliation algorithm Con outputs the public hint signal $v \in \mathbb{Z}_g$.*
- *$k_2 \leftarrow$ Rec$(\sigma_2, v,$ params$)$: On input of $(\sigma_2, v,$ params$)$, the deterministic polynomial-time algorithm Rec outputs $k_2 \in \mathbb{Z}_m$.*

Correctness: *An AKC scheme is* correct, *if for any $\sigma_1, \sigma_2 \in \mathbb{Z}_q$ such that $|\sigma_1 - \sigma_2|_q \le d$, and $v \leftarrow$ Con$(\sigma_1, k_1,$ params$)$, $k_2 \leftarrow$ Rec$(\sigma_2, v,$ params$)$, it holds $k_1 = k_2$.*

Security: *An AKC scheme is* secure, *if v is independent of k_1 whenever σ_1 is uniformly distributed over $\mathbb{Z}_q$, and v is the output of Con$(\sigma_1, k_1,$ params$)$. Specifically, for arbitrary $\tilde{v} \in \mathbb{Z}_g$ and arbitrary $\tilde{k}_1, \tilde{k}'_1 \in \mathbb{Z}_m$, it holds that $\Pr[v = \tilde{v}|k_1 = \tilde{k}_1] = \Pr[v = \tilde{v}|k_1 = \tilde{k}'_1]$, where the probability is taken over $\sigma_1 \leftarrow \mathbb{Z}_q$ and the random coins used by Con.*

Theorem 4. *Let AKC be an asymmetric key consensus scheme with* params $= (q, m, d, g, aux)$. *If AKC is correct and secure, then $2md \le q\left(1 - \frac{m}{g}\right)$.*

The proof of Theorem 4 is given in the full version [JZ16]. Comparing the formula $2md \le q(1 - m/g)$ in Theorem 4 with the formula $2md \le q(1 - 1/g)$ in Theorem 1, we see that the only difference is a factor m in g. This indicates that, on the same values of (q, m, d), an AKC scheme has to use a bigger bandwidth parameter g compared to KC.

4.1   Construction and Analysis of AKCN

The AKCN scheme, referred to as *asymmetric key consensus with noise*, is depicted in Algorithm 3. For AKCN, we can offline compute and store k_1 and $g\lfloor k_1 q/m \rceil$ in order to accelerate online performance.

Algorithm 3. AKCN: Asymmetric KC with Noise

1: **params** $= (q, m, g, d, aux)$, where $aux = \emptyset$.
2: **procedure** CON$(\sigma_1, k_1, \mathsf{params})$ $\triangleright \sigma_1 \in [0, q-1]$
3:     $v = \lfloor g\left(\sigma_1 + \lfloor k_1 q/m \rfloor\right)/q \rceil \bmod g$
4:     **return** v
5: **end procedure**
6: **procedure** REC$(\sigma_2, v, \mathsf{params})$ $\triangleright \sigma_2 \in [0, q-1]$
7:     $k_2 = \lfloor m(v/g - \sigma_2/q) \rceil \bmod m$
8:     **return** k_2
9: **end procedure**

The design of AKCN was guided by, and motivated for, the upper-bound for AKC proved in this work. In designing AKCN, we combine all the existing optimizations in the literature in order to almost meet the upperbound proved in Theorem 4. AKCN is a generalization of the basic reconciliation mechanisms proposed in [LPR10,LP10], and its design was also inspired by the design of our OKCN and the works [BPR12,PG13]. But AKCN and the underlying reconciliation mechanism of [PG13] could be viewed as incomparable in general. In particular, the reconciliation mechanisms proposed in [LPR10,LP10] correspond to the special case of AKCN when $g = q$ and $m = 2$. Note that, with AKCN, we use Eq. 1 described in the definition of LWR [BPR12], which may also be derived implicitly from [Pei09].

Theorem 5. *Suppose the parameters of AKCN satisfy* $(2d+1)m < q\left(1 - \frac{m}{g}\right)$. *Then, the AKCN scheme described in Algorithm 3 is* correct.

Proof. From the formula generating v, we know that there exist $\varepsilon_1, \varepsilon_2 \in \mathbb{R}$ and $\theta \in \mathbb{Z}$, where $|\varepsilon_1| \leq 1/2$ and $|\varepsilon_2| \leq 1/2$, such that

$$v = \frac{g}{q}\left(\sigma_1 + \left(\frac{k_1 q}{m} + \varepsilon_1\right)\right) + \varepsilon_2 + \theta g$$

Taking this into the formula computing k_2 in Rec, we have

$$k_2 = \lfloor m(v/g - \sigma_2/q) \rceil \bmod m$$

$$= \left\lfloor m\left(\frac{1}{q}(\sigma_1 + k_1 q/m + \varepsilon_1) + \frac{\varepsilon_2}{g} + \theta - \frac{\sigma_2}{q}\right) \right\rceil \bmod m$$

$$= \left\lfloor k_1 + \frac{m}{q}(\sigma_1 - \sigma_2) + \frac{m}{q}\varepsilon_1 + \frac{m}{g}\varepsilon_2 \right\rceil \bmod m$$

By Fact 1 (page 6), there exist $\theta' \in \mathbb{Z}$ and $\delta \in [-d, d]$ such that $\sigma_1 = \sigma_2 + \theta' q + \delta$. Hence,

$$k_2 = \left\lfloor k_1 + \frac{m}{q}\delta + \frac{m}{q}\varepsilon_1 + \frac{m}{g}\varepsilon_2 \right\rceil \bmod m$$

Since $|m\delta/q + m\varepsilon_1/q + m\varepsilon_2/g| \leq md/q + m/2q + m/2g < 1/2$, $k_1 = k_2$. $\qquad\square$

Theorem 6. *The AKCN scheme is secure. Specifically, v is independent of k_1 when $\sigma_1 \leftarrow \mathbb{Z}_q$.*

Proof. For arbitrary $\tilde{v} \in \mathbb{Z}_g$ and arbitrary $\tilde{k}_1, \tilde{k}_1' \in \mathbb{Z}_m$, we prove that $\Pr[v = \tilde{v}|k_1 = \tilde{k}_1] = \Pr[v = \tilde{v}|k_1 = \tilde{k}_1']$ when $\sigma_1 \leftarrow \mathbb{Z}_q$.

For any $(\tilde{k}, \tilde{v})$ in $\mathbb{Z}_m \times \mathbb{Z}_g$, the event $(v = \tilde{v} \mid k_1 = \tilde{k})$ is equivalent to the event that there exists $\sigma_1 \in \mathbb{Z}_q$ such that $\tilde{v} = \lfloor g(\sigma_1 + \lfloor \tilde{k}q/m \rceil)/q \rceil \bmod g$. Note that $\sigma_1 \in \mathbb{Z}_q$ satisfies $\tilde{v} = \lfloor g(\sigma_1 + \lfloor \tilde{k}q/m \rceil)/q \rceil \bmod g$, if and only if there exist $\varepsilon \in (-1/2, 1/2]$ and $\theta \in \mathbb{Z}$ such that $\tilde{v} = g(\sigma_1 + \lfloor \tilde{k}q/m \rceil)/q + \varepsilon - \theta g$. That is, $\sigma_1 = (q(\tilde{v} - \varepsilon)/g - \lfloor \tilde{k}q/m \rceil) \bmod q$, for some $\varepsilon \in (-1/2, 1/2]$. Let $\Sigma(\tilde{v}, \tilde{k}) = \{\sigma_1 \in \mathbb{Z}_q \mid \exists \varepsilon \in (-1/2, 1/2] \text{ s.t. } \sigma_1 = (q(\tilde{v} - \varepsilon)/g - \lfloor \tilde{k}q/m \rceil) \bmod q\}$. Defining the map $\phi : \Sigma(\tilde{v}, 0) \to \Sigma(\tilde{v}, \tilde{k})$, by setting $\phi(x) = \left(x - \lfloor \tilde{k}q/m \rceil\right) \bmod q$. Then ϕ is obviously a one-to-one map. Hence, the cardinality of $\Sigma(\tilde{v}, \tilde{k})$ is irrelevant to $\tilde{k}$. Specifically, for arbitrary $\tilde{v} \in \mathbb{Z}_g$ and arbitrary $\tilde{k}_1, \tilde{k}_1' \in \mathbb{Z}_m$, it holds that $\left|\Sigma(\tilde{v}, \tilde{k}_1)\right| = \left|\Sigma(\tilde{v}, \tilde{k}_1')\right| = |\Sigma(\tilde{v}, 0)|$.

Now, for arbitrary $\tilde{v} \in \mathbb{Z}_g$ and arbitrary $\tilde{k} \in \mathbb{Z}_m$, when $\sigma_1 \leftarrow \mathbb{Z}_q$ we have that $\Pr[v = \tilde{v} \mid k_1 = \tilde{k}] = \Pr\left[\sigma_1 \in \Sigma(\tilde{v}, \tilde{k}) \mid k_1 = \tilde{k}\right] = |\Sigma(\tilde{v}, \tilde{k})|/q = |\Sigma(\tilde{v}, 0)|/q$. The right-hand side only depends on $\tilde{v}$, and so v is independent of k_1. □

4.2   Discussions on KC vs. AKC

Key establishment (KE) schemes based upon KC and AKC have different performances and features.

- KC-based KE corresponds to Diffie-Hellman key establishment in the lattice world, while AKC-based to El Gamal key transport.
- When deploying AKC-based KE in practice, if the randomness used by the responder (e.g., a low-power device like smart card) is poor, it will significantly ruin the session-key security. Or, if the responder is just lazy (or for economic reasons), who may re-use session-keys across multiple sessions, as demonstrated with some deployed TLS implementations in reality. In comparison, with KC-based KE, the two players play a symmetric role in generating the session-key, and thus the damage caused by poor randomness can be alleviated. In addition, symmetry is usually a desirable feature for cryptographic schemes in practice.
- On the same parameters (q, m, g) (which imply the same bandwidth), OKCN-based KE has lower error probability than AKCN-based. Or, on the same parameters (q, m, d) (which imply the same error probability), OKCN-based KE has smaller bandwidth than AKCN-based. This comparison is enabled by the upper-bounds on these parameters proved in Theorems 1 and 4.
- KC-based KE is more versatile, in the sense that it can also be straightforwardly adapted into a key transport protocol or a CPA-secure PKE scheme. Moreover, in another work [CGZ18], we show that the deterministic version of OKCN is also a fundamental building tool for lattice-based signature.

$$\begin{array}{ll}
\underline{\text{Initiator}} & \underline{\text{Responder}} \\
\text{seed} \leftarrow \{0,1\}^{\kappa} & \\
\mathbf{A} = \text{Gen(seed)} \in \mathbb{Z}_q^{n\times n} & \\
\mathbf{X}_1 \leftarrow \chi^{n\times l_A} & \\
\mathbf{Y}_1 = \lfloor \mathbf{A}\mathbf{X}_1 \rceil_p &
\end{array}$$

$$\xrightarrow{\text{seed}, \mathbf{Y}_1 \in \mathbb{Z}_p^{n\times l_A}}$$

$$\begin{array}{l}
\mathbf{A} = \text{Gen(seed)} \\
\mathbf{X}_2 \leftarrow \chi^{n\times l_B} \\
\mathbf{Y}_2 = \lfloor \mathbf{A}^T\mathbf{X}_2 \rceil_p \\
\epsilon \leftarrow [-q/2p, q/2p - 1]^{n\times l_A} \\
\Sigma_2 = \mathbf{Y}_1^T\mathbf{X}_2 + \lfloor \epsilon^T\mathbf{X}_2 \rceil_p \\
(\mathbf{K}_2, \mathbf{V}) \leftarrow \text{Con}(\Sigma_2, \text{params})
\end{array}$$

$$\xleftarrow{\mathbf{Y}_2 \in \mathbb{Z}_p^{n\times l_B}, \mathbf{V} \in \mathbb{Z}_g^{l_A\times l_B}}$$

$$\begin{array}{l}
\Sigma_1 = \mathbf{X}_1^T\mathbf{Y}_2 \\
\mathbf{K}_1 \leftarrow \text{Rec}(\Sigma_1, \mathbf{V}, \text{params})
\end{array}$$

Fig. 1. LWR-based key establishment from KC, where $\mathbf{K}_1, \mathbf{K}_2 \in \mathbb{Z}_m^{l_A\times l_B}$ and $|\mathbf{K}_1| = |\mathbf{K}_2| = l_A l_B |m|$.

- KC-based KE is more appropriate for incorporating into the existing standards like IKE and TLS that are based on Diffie-Hellman via the SIGMA mechanism [Kra03]. We note that key transport is explicitly abandoned with TLS1.3.
- For the parameters proposed in this work, OKCN is actually (slightly) more efficient than AKCN.

For the above reasons, we focus more on KC-based key establishment (specifically, key exchange) than AKC-based in this work. Still, we aim for a unified protocol structure that can be instantiated with either KC or AKC, in order to simplify system complexity.

5   LWR-Based Key Establishment

The KC-based key establishment (KE) from the LWR problem is depicted in Fig. 1. Denote by $(n, l_A, l_B, q, p, KC, \chi)$ the system parameters, where $p|q$, and p and q are chosen to be power of 2. Let $KC = (\text{params} = (p, m, g, d, aux), \text{Con}, \text{Rec})$ be a *correct* and *secure* key consensus scheme, χ be a small noise distribution over $\mathbb{Z}_q$, and Gen be a pseudo-random generator (PRG) generating the matrix $\mathbf{A}$ from a small seed. In the actual implementation, we use OKCN-simple as the underlying KC mechanism. For presentation simplicity, we assume $\mathbf{A} \in \mathbb{Z}_q^{n\times n}$ to be square matrix. The length of the random seed, i.e., κ, is typically set to be 256. The actual session-key is derived from $\mathbf{K}_1$ and $\mathbf{K}_2$ via some key derivation function KDF. For presentation simplicity, the functions Con and Rec are applied to matrices, meaning that they are applied to each of the coordinates respectively. For presentation simplicity, we describe the LWR-based key establishment protocol from any KC scheme. But it can be trivially adapted to work on any *correct* and *secure* AKC scheme. In this case, the responder user Bob simply chooses $\mathbf{K}_2 \leftarrow \mathbb{Z}_m^{l_A \times l_B}$, and the output of $\mathsf{Con}(\boldsymbol{\Sigma}_2, \mathbf{K}_2, \text{params})$ is simply defined to be $\mathbf{V}$. The security proof of the LWR-based KE protocol is analogous to that in [Pei14, BCD+16], and is given in the full version.

5.1 Analysis of Correctness and Failure Rate

For any integer x, let $\{x\}_p$ denote $x - \frac{q}{p}\lfloor x\rceil_p$, where $\lfloor x\rceil_p = \lfloor \frac{p}{q}x\rceil$. Then, for any integer x, $\{x\}_p \in [-q/2p, q/2p - 1]$, hence $\{x\}_p$ can be naturally regarded as an element in $\mathbb{Z}_{q/p}$. In fact, $\{x\}_p$ is equal to $x \bmod q/p$, where the result is represented in $[-q/2p, q/2p - 1]$. When the notation $\{\cdot\}_p$ is applied to a matrix, it means $\{\cdot\}_p$ applies to every element of the matrix respectively.

We have $\boldsymbol{\Sigma}_2 = \mathbf{Y}_1^T\mathbf{X}_2 + \lfloor \boldsymbol{\varepsilon}^T\mathbf{X}_2\rceil_p = \lfloor \mathbf{AX}_1\rceil_p^T\mathbf{X}_2 + \lfloor \boldsymbol{\varepsilon}^T\mathbf{X}_2\rceil_p = \frac{p}{q}(\mathbf{AX}_1 - \{\mathbf{AX}_1\}_p)^T\mathbf{X}_2 + \lfloor \boldsymbol{\varepsilon}^T\mathbf{X}_2\rceil_p$. And $\boldsymbol{\Sigma}_1 = \mathbf{X}_1^T\mathbf{Y}_2 = \mathbf{X}_1^T\lfloor \mathbf{A}^T\mathbf{X}_2\rceil_p = \frac{p}{q}(\mathbf{X}_1^T\mathbf{A}^T\mathbf{X}_2 - \mathbf{X}_1^T\{\mathbf{A}^T\mathbf{X}_2\}_p)$. Hence,

$$\boldsymbol{\Sigma}_2 - \boldsymbol{\Sigma}_1 = \frac{p}{q}(\mathbf{X}_1^T\{\mathbf{A}^T\mathbf{X}_2\}_p - \{\mathbf{AX}_1\}_p^T\mathbf{X}_2) + \lfloor \boldsymbol{\varepsilon}^T\mathbf{X}_2\rceil_p \quad \bmod p$$

$$= \left\lfloor \frac{p}{q}(\mathbf{X}_1^T\{\mathbf{A}^T\mathbf{X}_2\}_p - \{\mathbf{AX}_1\}_p^T\mathbf{X}_2 + \boldsymbol{\varepsilon}^T\mathbf{X}_2)\right\rceil \quad \bmod p$$

The general idea is that $\mathbf{X}_1, \mathbf{X}_2, \boldsymbol{\varepsilon}, \{\mathbf{A}^T\mathbf{X}_2\}_p$ and $\{\mathbf{AX}_1\}_p$ are small enough, so that $\boldsymbol{\Sigma}_1$ and $\boldsymbol{\Sigma}_2$ are close. If $|\boldsymbol{\Sigma}_1 - \boldsymbol{\Sigma}_2|_p \leq d$, the *correctness* of the underlying *KC* guarantees $\mathbf{K}_1 = \mathbf{K}_2$. For given concrete parameters, we numerically derive the probability of $|\boldsymbol{\Sigma}_2 - \boldsymbol{\Sigma}_1|_p > d$ by numerically calculating the distribution of $\mathbf{X}_1^T\{\mathbf{A}^T\mathbf{X}_2\}_p - (\{\mathbf{AX}_1\}_p^T\mathbf{X}_2 - \boldsymbol{\varepsilon}^T\mathbf{X}_2)$ for the case of $l_A = l_B = 1$, then applying the *union bound*. The independency between variables indicated by the following Theorem 7 can greatly simplify the calculation.

Let $\mathsf{Inv}(\mathbf{X}_1, \mathbf{X}_2)$ denote the event that there exist invertible elements of ring $\mathbb{Z}_{q/p}$ in both vectors $\mathbf{X}_1$ and $\mathbf{X}_2$. We claim that $\mathsf{Inv}(\mathbf{X}_1, \mathbf{X}_2)$ happens with *overwhelming* probability. This claim follows from $\Pr[\mathsf{Inv}(\mathbf{X}_1, \mathbf{X}_2)] = 1 - \Pr[\text{all entries of } \mathbf{X}_1, \mathbf{X}_2 \text{ are non-invertible in } \mathbb{Z}_{q/p}] = 1 - \Pr[x \leftarrow \chi : x \text{ is non-}invertible]^{n\cdot(l_A + l_B)}$. In our application, $\Pr[x \leftarrow \chi : x \text{ is non-invertible}]$ is far from one, hence, $\mathsf{Inv}(\mathbf{X}_1, \mathbf{X}_2)$ holds with overwhelming probability.

Lemma 1. *Consider the case of* $l_A = l_B = 1$. *For any* $a \in \mathbb{Z}_{q/p}, \mathbf{x} \in \mathbb{Z}_{q/p}^n$, *denote* $S_{\mathbf{x},a} = \{\mathbf{y} \in \mathbb{Z}_{q/p}^n \mid \mathbf{x}^T\mathbf{y} \bmod (q/p) = a\}$. *For any fixed* $a \in \mathbb{Z}_{q/p}$, *conditioned on* $\mathsf{Inv}(\mathbf{X}_1, \mathbf{X}_2)$ *and* $\mathbf{X}_1^T\mathbf{A}^T\mathbf{X}_2 \bmod (q/p) = a$, *the random vectors* $\{\mathbf{A}^T\mathbf{X}_2\}_p$ *and* $\{\mathbf{AX}_1\}_p$ *are independent, and are subjected to uniform distribution over* $S_{\mathbf{X}_1,a}, S_{\mathbf{X}_2,a}$ *respectively.*

Proof. Under the condition of $\mathsf{Inv}(\mathbf{X}_1, \mathbf{X}_2)$, for any fixed $\mathbf{X}_1$ and $\mathbf{X}_2$, define the map $\phi_{\mathbf{X}_1,\mathbf{X}_2}: \mathbb{Z}_q^{n \times n} \rightarrow \mathbb{Z}_{q/p}^n \times \mathbb{Z}_{q/p}^n$, such that $\mathbf{A} \mapsto (\{\mathbf{AX}_1\}_p, \{\mathbf{A}^T\mathbf{X}_2\}_p)$.

We shall prove that the image of $\phi_{\mathbf{X}_1,\mathbf{X}_2}$ is $S = \{(\mathbf{y}_1, \mathbf{y}_2) \in \mathbb{Z}_{q/p}^n \times \mathbb{Z}_{q/p}^n \mid \mathbf{X}_2^T\mathbf{y}_1 = \mathbf{X}_1^T\mathbf{y}_2 \bmod (q/p)\}$. Denote $\mathbf{X}_1 = (x_1, \mathbf{X}_1'^T)^T$ and $\mathbf{y}_2 = (y_2, \mathbf{y}_2'^T)^T$.

Without loss of generality, we assume x_1 is invertible in the ring $\mathbb{Z}_{q/p}$. For any $(\mathbf{y}_1, \mathbf{y}_2) \in S$, we need to find an $\mathbf{A}$ such that $\phi_{\mathbf{X}_1, \mathbf{X}_2}(\mathbf{A}) = (\mathbf{y}_1, \mathbf{y}_2)$.

From the condition $\mathsf{Inv}(\mathbf{X}_1, \mathbf{X}_2)$, we know that there exists an $\mathbf{A}' \in \mathbb{Z}^{(n-1) \times n}$ such that $\{\mathbf{A}'\mathbf{X}_2\}_p = \mathbf{y}_2'$. Then, we let $\mathbf{a}_1 = x_1^{-1}(\mathbf{y}_1 - \mathbf{A}'^T\mathbf{X}_1') \bmod (q/p)$, and $\mathbf{A} = (\mathbf{a}_1, \mathbf{A}'^T)$. Now we check that $\phi_{\mathbf{X}_1, \mathbf{X}_2}(\mathbf{A}) = (\mathbf{y}_1, \mathbf{y}_2)$.

$$\{\mathbf{AX}_1\}_p = \left\{ (\mathbf{a}_1 \ \mathbf{A}'^T) \begin{pmatrix} x_1 \\ \mathbf{x}_1' \end{pmatrix} \right\}_p = \{x_1 \mathbf{a}_1 + \mathbf{A}'^T \mathbf{X}_1'\}_p = \mathbf{y}_1$$

$$\{\mathbf{A}^T\mathbf{X}_2\}_p = \left\{ \begin{pmatrix} \mathbf{a}_1^T \\ \mathbf{A}' \end{pmatrix} \mathbf{X}_2 \right\}_p = \left\{ \begin{pmatrix} \mathbf{a}_1^T \mathbf{X}_2 \\ \mathbf{A}' \mathbf{X}_2 \end{pmatrix} \right\}_p = \left\{ \begin{pmatrix} x_1^{-1}(\mathbf{y}_1^T - \mathbf{X}_1'^T \mathbf{A})\mathbf{X}_2 \\ \mathbf{A}' \mathbf{X}_2 \end{pmatrix} \right\}_p$$

$$= \left\{ \begin{pmatrix} x_1^{-1}(\mathbf{X}_1^T \mathbf{y}_2 - \mathbf{X}_1'^T \mathbf{y}_2') \\ \mathbf{y}_2' \end{pmatrix} \right\}_p = \left\{ \begin{pmatrix} y_2 \\ \mathbf{y}_2' \end{pmatrix} \right\}_p = \mathbf{y}_2$$

Hence, if we treat $\mathbb{Z}_q^{n \times n}$ and S as $\mathbb{Z}$-modules, then $\phi_{\mathbf{X}_1, \mathbf{X}_2} : \mathbb{Z}_q^{n \times n} \to S$ is a surjective homomorphism. Then, for any fixed $(\mathbf{X}_1, \mathbf{X}_2)$, $(\{\mathbf{AX}_1\}_p, \{\mathbf{A}^T\mathbf{X}_2\}_p)$ is uniformly distributed over S. This completes the proof. $\square$

Theorem 7. *Under the condition* $\mathsf{Inv}(\mathbf{X}_1, \mathbf{X}_2)$, *the following two distributions are identical:*

- $(a, \mathbf{X}_1, \mathbf{X}_2, \{\mathbf{AX}_1\}_p, \{\mathbf{A}^T\mathbf{X}_2\}_p)$, *where* $\mathbf{A} \leftarrow \mathbb{Z}_q^{n \times n}$, $\mathbf{X}_1 \leftarrow \chi^n$, $\mathbf{X}_2 \leftarrow \chi^n$, *and* $a = \mathbf{X}_1^T \mathbf{A}^T \mathbf{X}_2 \bmod (q/p)$.
- $(a, \mathbf{X}_1, \mathbf{X}_2, \mathbf{y}_1, \mathbf{y}_2)$, *where* $a \leftarrow \mathbb{Z}_{q/p}, \mathbf{X}_1 \leftarrow \chi^n$, $\mathbf{X}_2 \leftarrow \chi^n$, $\mathbf{y}_1 \leftarrow S_{\mathbf{X}_2, a}$, *and* $\mathbf{y}_2 \leftarrow S_{\mathbf{X}_1, a}$.

Proof. For any $\tilde{a} \in \mathbb{Z}_{q/p}$, $\tilde{\mathbf{X}}_1, \tilde{\mathbf{X}}_2 \in \mathsf{Supp}(\chi^n)$, $\tilde{\mathbf{y}}_1, \tilde{\mathbf{y}}_2 \in \mathbb{Z}_{q/p}^n$, we have

$$\Pr[a = \tilde{a}, \mathbf{X}_1 = \tilde{\mathbf{X}}_1, \mathbf{X}_2 = \tilde{\mathbf{X}}_2, \{\mathbf{AX}_1\}_p = \tilde{\mathbf{y}}_1, \{\mathbf{A}^T\mathbf{X}_2\}_p = \tilde{\mathbf{y}}_2 \mid \mathsf{Inv}(\mathbf{X}_1, \mathbf{X}_2)]$$
$$= \Pr[\{\mathbf{AX}_1\}_p = \tilde{\mathbf{y}}_1, \{\mathbf{A}^T\mathbf{X}_2\}_p = \tilde{\mathbf{y}}_2 \mid a = \tilde{a}, \mathbf{X}_1 = \tilde{\mathbf{X}}_1, \mathbf{X}_2 = \tilde{\mathbf{X}}_2, \mathsf{Inv}(\mathbf{X}_1, \mathbf{X}_2)]$$
$$\Pr[a = \tilde{a}, \mathbf{X}_1 = \tilde{\mathbf{X}}_1, \mathbf{X}_2 = \tilde{\mathbf{X}}_2 \mid \mathsf{Inv}(\mathbf{X}_1, \mathbf{X}_2)]$$

From Lemma 1, the first term equals to $\Pr[\mathbf{y}_1 \leftarrow S_{\tilde{\mathbf{X}}_2, \tilde{a}}; \mathbf{y}_2 \leftarrow S_{\tilde{\mathbf{X}}_1, \tilde{a}} : \mathbf{y}_1 = \tilde{\mathbf{y}}_1, \mathbf{y}_2 = \tilde{\mathbf{y}}_2 \mid a = \tilde{a}, \mathbf{X}_1 = \tilde{\mathbf{X}}_1, \mathbf{X}_2 = \tilde{\mathbf{X}}_2, \mathsf{Inv}(\mathbf{X}_1, \mathbf{X}_2)]$.

For the second term, we shall prove that a is independent of $(\mathbf{X}_1, \mathbf{X}_2)$, and is uniformly distributed over $\mathbb{Z}_{q/p}$. Under the condition of $\mathsf{Inv}(\mathbf{X}_1, \mathbf{X}_2)$, the map $\mathbb{Z}_q^{n \times n} \to \mathbb{Z}_{q/p}$, such that $\mathbf{A} \mapsto \mathbf{X}_1^T \mathbf{A}^T \mathbf{X}_2 \bmod (q/p)$, is a surjective homomorphism between the two $\mathbb{Z}$-modules. Then, $\Pr[a = \tilde{a} \mid \mathbf{X}_1 = \tilde{\mathbf{X}}_1, \mathbf{X}_2 = \tilde{\mathbf{X}}_2, \mathsf{Inv}(\mathbf{X}_1, \mathbf{X}_2)] = p/q$. Hence, under the condition of $\mathsf{Inv}(\mathbf{X}_1, \mathbf{X}_2)$, a is independent of $(\mathbf{X}_1, \mathbf{X}_2)$, and is distributed uniformly at random. So the two ways of sampling result in the same distribution. $\square$

We design and implement the following algorithm to numerically calculate the distribution of $\boldsymbol{\Sigma}_2 - \boldsymbol{\Sigma}_1$ efficiently. For any $c_1, c_2 \in \mathbb{Z}_q, a \in \mathbb{Z}_{q/p}$, we numerically calculate $\Pr[\mathbf{X}_1^T \{\mathbf{A}^T\mathbf{X}_2\}_p = c_1]$ and $\Pr[\{\mathbf{AX}_1\}_p^T \mathbf{X}_2 - \boldsymbol{\varepsilon}^T \mathbf{X}_2 = c_2, \mathbf{X}_1^T \mathbf{A}^T \mathbf{X}_2 \bmod (q/p) = a]$, then derive the distribution of $\boldsymbol{\Sigma}_2 - \boldsymbol{\Sigma}_1$.

As $\mathsf{Inv}(\mathbf{X}_1, \mathbf{X}_2)$ occurs with *overwhelming* probability, for any event E, we have $|\Pr[E] - \Pr[E|\mathsf{Inv}(\mathbf{X}_1, \mathbf{X}_2)]| < negl$. For simplicity, we ignore the effect of $\mathsf{Inv}(\mathbf{X}_1, \mathbf{X}_2)$ in the following calculations. By Theorem 7, $\Pr[\mathbf{X}_1^T\{\mathbf{A}^T\mathbf{X}_2\}_p = c_1] = \Pr[\mathbf{X}_1 \leftarrow \chi^n, \mathbf{y}_2 \leftarrow \mathbb{Z}_{q/p}^n; \mathbf{X}_1^T\mathbf{y}_2 = c_1]$. This probability can be numerically calculated by computer programs. The probability $\Pr[\{\mathbf{A}\mathbf{X}_1\}_p^T\mathbf{X}_2 - \varepsilon^T\mathbf{X}_2 = c_2, \mathbf{X}_1^T\mathbf{A}^T\mathbf{X}_2 \bmod (q/p) = a]$ can also be calculated by the similar way. Then, for arbitrary $c \in \mathbb{Z}_q$,

$$\Pr[\mathbf{\Sigma}_1 - \mathbf{\Sigma}_2 = c] = \Pr[\mathbf{X}_1^T\{\mathbf{A}^T\mathbf{X}_2\}_p - \{\mathbf{A}\mathbf{X}_1\}_p^T\mathbf{X}_2 + \varepsilon^T\mathbf{X}_2 = c]$$

$$= \sum_{\substack{c_1-c_2=c \\ a\in\mathbb{Z}_{q/p}}} \Pr[\mathbf{X}_1^T\{\mathbf{A}^T\mathbf{X}_2\}_p = c_1, \{\mathbf{A}\mathbf{X}_1\}_p^T\mathbf{X}_2 - \varepsilon^T\mathbf{X}_2 = c_2 | \mathbf{X}_1^T\mathbf{A}^T\mathbf{X}_2 \bmod (q/p)=a] \cdot \Pr[\mathbf{X}_1^T\mathbf{A}^T\mathbf{X}_2 \bmod (q/p)=a]$$

$$= \sum_{\substack{c_1-c_2=c \\ a\in\mathbb{Z}_{q/p}}} \Pr[\mathbf{X}_1^T\{\mathbf{A}^T\mathbf{X}_2\}_p = c_1 | \mathbf{X}_1^T\mathbf{A}^T\mathbf{X}_2 \bmod (q/p)=a] \cdot \Pr[\{\mathbf{A}\mathbf{X}_1\}_p^T\mathbf{X}_2 - \varepsilon^T\mathbf{X}_2 = c_2 | \mathbf{X}_1^T\mathbf{A}^T\mathbf{X}_2 \bmod (q/p)=a] \Pr[\mathbf{X}_1^T\mathbf{A}^T\mathbf{X}_2 \bmod (q/p)=a]$$

$$= \sum_{\substack{a\in\mathbb{Z}_{q/p} \\ c_1-c_2=c}} \frac{\Pr[\mathbf{X}_1^T\{\mathbf{A}^T\mathbf{X}_2\}_p = c_1, c_1 \bmod (q/p)=a] \Pr[\{\mathbf{A}\mathbf{X}_1\}_p^T\mathbf{X}_2 - \varepsilon^T\mathbf{X}_2 = c_2, \mathbf{X}_1^T\mathbf{A}^T\mathbf{X}_2 \bmod (q/p) = a]}{\Pr[\mathbf{X}_1^T\mathbf{A}^T\mathbf{X}_2 \bmod (q/p) = a]}$$

$$= \sum_{\substack{a\in\mathbb{Z}_{q/p} \\ c_1-c_2=c \\ c_1 \bmod (q/p)=a}} \frac{\Pr[\mathbf{X}_1^T\{\mathbf{A}^T\mathbf{X}_2\}_p = c_1] \Pr[\{\mathbf{A}\mathbf{X}_1\}_p^T\mathbf{X}_2 - \varepsilon^T\mathbf{X}_2 = c_2, \mathbf{X}_1^T\mathbf{A}^T\mathbf{X}_2 \bmod (q/p) = a]}{\Pr[\mathbf{X}_1^T\mathbf{A}^T\mathbf{X}_2 \bmod (q/p) = a]}$$

By Theorem 7, conditioned on $\mathsf{Inv}(\mathbf{X}_1, \mathbf{X}_2)$ and $\mathbf{X}_1^T\mathbf{A}^T\mathbf{X}_2 \bmod (q/p) = a$, $\mathbf{X}_1^T\{\mathbf{A}^T\mathbf{X}_2\}_p$ is independent of $\{\mathbf{A}\mathbf{X}_1\}_p^T\mathbf{X}_2 - \varepsilon^T\mathbf{X}_2$, which implies the second equality. The scripts are available from http://github.com/OKCN.

5.2   Parameter Selection and Evaluation

It is suggested in [ADPS16, BCD+16] that rounded Gaussian distribution can be replaced by discrete distribution that is very close to rounded Gaussian in the sense of Rényi divergence [BLL+15] (Table 1).

Table 1. Discrete distributions of every component in the LWR secret. We choose the standard variances "var." large enough to prevent potential combinational attacks.

dist.	Bits	var.	Probability of							Order	Divergence
			0	±1	±2	±3	±4	±5	±6		
D_R	16	2.00	18110	14249	6938	2090	389	44	3	500.0	1.0000270
D_P	16	1.40	21456	15326	5580	1033	97	4	0	500.0	1.0000277

Security Estimation. The dual attack tries to distinguish the distribution of LWE samples and the uniform distribution. Suppose $(\mathbf{A}, \mathbf{b} = \mathbf{As} + \mathbf{e}) \in \mathbb{Z}_q^{m\times n} \times \mathbb{Z}_q^m$ is an LWE sample, where $\mathbf{s}$ and $\mathbf{e}$ are drawn from discrete Gaussian of variance σ_s^2 and σ_e^2 respectively. Then we choose a positive real $c \in \mathbb{R}, 0 < c \le q$, and construct $L_c(\mathbf{A}) = \{(\mathbf{x}, \mathbf{y}/c) \in \mathbb{Z}^m \times (\mathbb{Z}/c)^n \mid \mathbf{x}^T\mathbf{A} = \mathbf{y}^T \mod q\}$, which is a

Table 2. Parameters for LWR-Based key establishment with OKCN-simple. "bw." refers to the bandwidth in kilo-bytes. "err." refers to the overall error rate that is calculated by the algorithm developed in Sect. 5.1. "$|\mathbf{K}|$" refers to the length of consensus bits.

	n	q	p	l	m	g	distr.	bw.	err.	$|\mathbf{K}|$
Recommended	672	2^{15}	2^{12}	8	2^4	2^8	D_R	16.19	2^{-30}	256
Paranoid	832	2^{15}	2^{12}	8	2^4	2^8	D_P	20.03	2^{-34}	256

lattice with dimension $m+n$ and determinant $(q/c)^n$. For a short vector $(\mathbf{x}, \mathbf{y}) \in L_c(\mathbf{A})$ found by the BKZ algorithm, we have $\mathbf{x}^T \mathbf{b} = \mathbf{x}^T (\mathbf{A}\mathbf{s} + \mathbf{e}) = c \cdot \mathbf{y}^T \mathbf{s} + \mathbf{x}^T \mathbf{e}$ mod q. If $(\mathbf{A}, \mathbf{b})$ is an LWE sample, the distribution of the right-hand side will be very close to a Gaussian of standard deviation $\sqrt{c^2 \|\mathbf{y}\|^2 \sigma_s^2 + \|\mathbf{x}\|^2 \sigma_e^2}$, otherwise the distribution will be uniform. $\|(\mathbf{x}, \mathbf{y})\|$ is about $\delta_0^{m+n}(q/c)^{\frac{n}{m+n}}$, where δ_0 is the root Hermite factor. We heuristically assume that $\|\mathbf{x}\| = \sqrt{\frac{m}{m+n}} \|(\mathbf{x}, \mathbf{y})\|$, and $\|\mathbf{y}\| = \sqrt{\frac{n}{m+n}} \|(\mathbf{x}, \mathbf{y})\|$. Then we can choose $c = \sigma_e/\sigma_s$ that minimizes the standard deviation of $\mathbf{x}^T \mathbf{b}$. The advantage of distinguishing $\mathbf{x}^T \mathbf{b}$ from uniform distribution is $\varepsilon = 4 \exp(-2\pi^2 \tau^2)$, where $\tau = \sqrt{c^2 \|\mathbf{y}\|^2 \sigma_s^2 + \|\mathbf{x}\|^2 \sigma_e^2}/q$. This attack must be repeated $R = \max\{1, 1/(2^{0.2075b} \varepsilon^2)\}$ times to be successful.

The primal attack reduces the LWE problem to the unique-SVP problem. Let $\Lambda_w(\mathbf{A}) = \{(\mathbf{x}, \mathbf{y}, z) \in \mathbb{Z}^n \times (\mathbb{Z}^m/w) \times \mathbb{Z} \mid \mathbf{A}\mathbf{x} + w\mathbf{y} = z\mathbf{b} \mod q\}$, and a vector $\mathbf{v} = (\mathbf{s}, \mathbf{e}/w, 1) \in \Lambda_w(\mathbf{A})$. $\Lambda_w(\mathbf{A})$ is a lattice of $d = m + n + 1$ dimensions, and its determinant is $(q/w)^m$. From geometry series assumption, we can derive $\|\mathbf{b}_i^*\| \approx \delta_0^{d-2i-1} \det(\Lambda_w(\mathbf{A}))^{1/d}$. We heuristically assume that the length of projection of $\mathbf{v}$ onto the vector space spanned by the last b Gram-Schmidt vectors is about $\sqrt{\frac{b}{d}} \|(\mathbf{s}, \mathbf{e}/w, 1)\| \approx \sqrt{\frac{b}{d} (n\sigma_s^2 + m\sigma_e^2/w^2 + 1)}$. If this length is shorter than $\|\mathbf{b}_{d-b}^*\|$, this attack can be successful. Hence, the successful condition is $\sqrt{\frac{b}{d} (n\sigma_s^2 + m\sigma_e^2/w^2 + 1)} \leq \delta_0^{2b-d-1} \left(\frac{q}{w}\right)^{m/d}$. We know that the optimal w balancing the secret $\mathbf{s}$ and the noise $\mathbf{e}$ is about σ_e/σ_s.

We aim at providing parameter sets for long term security, and estimate the concrete security *in a more conservative way* than [APS15] from the defender's point of view. We first consider the attacks of LWE whose secret and noise have different variances. Then, we treat the LWR problem as a special LWE problem whose noise is uniformly distributed over $[-q/2p, q/2p - 1]$. In our security estimation, we simply ignore the difference between the discrete distribution and the rounded Gaussian, on the following grounds: the dual attack and the primal attack only concern about the standard deviation, and the Rényi divergence between the two distributions is very small (Table 3).

Table 3. Security estimation of the parameters described in Table 2. "C, Q, P" stand for "Classical, Quantum, Plausible" respectively.

Scheme	Attack	m'	b	C	Q	P
Recommended	Primal	665	459	143	**131**	104
	Dual	633	456	142	**130**	103
Paranoid	Primal	768	584	180	164	**130**
	Dual	746	580	179	163	**129**

Initiator

seed $\leftarrow \{0,1\}^\kappa$

$\mathbf{A} = \mathsf{Gen}(\mathsf{seed}) \in \mathbb{Z}_q^{n \times n}$

$\mathbf{X}_1, \mathbf{E}_1 \leftarrow \chi^{n \times l_A}$

$\mathbf{Y}_1 = \mathbf{A}\mathbf{X}_1 + \mathbf{E}_1$

$$\xrightarrow{\mathsf{seed}, \mathbf{Y}_1 \in \mathbb{Z}_q^{n \times l_A}}$$

Responder

$\mathbf{A} = \mathsf{Gen}(\mathsf{seed})$

$\mathbf{X}_2, \mathbf{E}_2 \leftarrow \chi^{n \times l_B}$

$\mathbf{Y}_2 = \mathbf{A}^T \mathbf{X}_2 + \mathbf{E}_2$

$\mathbf{E}_\sigma \leftarrow \chi^{l_A \times l_B}$

$\mathbf{\Sigma}_2 = \mathbf{Y}_1^T \mathbf{X}_2 + \mathbf{E}_\sigma$

$(\mathbf{K}_2, \mathbf{V}) \leftarrow \mathsf{Con}(\mathbf{\Sigma}_2, \mathsf{params})$

$$\xleftarrow{\mathbf{Y}_2' = \lfloor \mathbf{Y}_2/2^t \rfloor \in \mathbb{Z}_{\lceil q/2^t \rceil}^{n \times l_B}, \mathbf{V} \in \mathbb{Z}_g^{l_A \times l_B}}$$

$\mathbf{\Sigma}_1 = \mathbf{X}_1^T(2^t \mathbf{Y}_2' + 2^{t-1}\mathbf{1})$

$\mathbf{K}_1 \leftarrow \mathsf{Rec}(\mathbf{\Sigma}_1, \mathbf{V}, \mathsf{params})$

Fig. 2. LWE-based key establishment from KC and AKC, where $\mathbf{K}_1, \mathbf{K}_2 \in \mathbb{Z}_m^{l_A \times l_B}$ and $|\mathbf{K}_1| = |\mathbf{K}_2| = l_A l_B |m|$. **1** refers to the matrix which every elements are 1.

6   LWE-Based Key Establishment

In this section, following the protocol structure in [Pei14, ADPS16, BCD+16], we present the applications of OKCN and AKCN to key establishment protocols based on LWE. Denote by $(\lambda, n, q, \chi, KC, l_A, l_B, t)$ the underlying parameters, where λ is the security parameter, $q \geq 2$, n, l_A and l_B are positive integers that are polynomial in λ (for protocol symmetry, l_A and l_B are usually set to be equal and are actually small constant). To save bandwidth, we cut off t least significant bits of $\mathbf{Y}_2$ before sending it to Alice.

Let $KC = (\mathsf{params}, \mathsf{Con}, \mathsf{Rec})$ be a *correct* and *secure* KC scheme, where params is set to be (q, g, m, d). The KC-based key establishment protocol from LWE is depicted in Fig. 2, and the actual session-key is derived from $\mathbf{K}_1$ and $\mathbf{K}_2$ via some key derivation function KDF. There, for presentation simplicity, the Con and Rec functions are applied to matrices, meaning they are applied to each of the coordinates separately. Note that $2^t \mathbf{Y}_2' + 2^{t-1}\mathbf{1}$ is an approximation of $\mathbf{Y}_2$, so we have $\mathbf{\Sigma}_1 \approx \mathbf{X}_1^T \mathbf{Y}_2 = \mathbf{X}_1^T \mathbf{A}^T \mathbf{X}_2 + \mathbf{X}_1^T \mathbf{E}_2$, $\mathbf{\Sigma}_2 = \mathbf{Y}_1^T \mathbf{X}_2 + \mathbf{E}_\sigma =$

$\mathbf{X}_1^T \mathbf{A}^T \mathbf{X}_2 + \mathbf{E}_1^T \mathbf{X}_2 + \mathbf{E}_\sigma$. As we choose $\mathbf{X}_1, \mathbf{X}_2, \mathbf{E}_1, \mathbf{E}_2, \mathbf{E}_\sigma$ according to a small noise distribution χ, the main part of $\boldsymbol{\Sigma}_1$ and that of $\boldsymbol{\Sigma}_2$ are the same $\mathbf{X}_1^T \mathbf{A}^T \mathbf{X}_2$. Hence, the corresponding coordinates of $\boldsymbol{\Sigma}_1$ and $\boldsymbol{\Sigma}_2$ are close in the sense of $|\cdot|_q$, from which some key consensus can be reached. The failure probability depends upon the number of bits we cut t, the underlying distribution χ and the distance parameter d, which will be analyzed in detail in subsequent sections. In the following security definition and analysis, we simply assume that the output of the PRG Gen is truly random. For presentation simplicity, we have described the LWE-based key establishment protocol from a KC scheme. But it can be straightforwardly adapted to work on any correct and secure AKC scheme, as clarified in Sect. 5.

6.1   Noise Distributions and Correctness

For a *correct* KC with parameter d, if the distance of corresponding elements of $\boldsymbol{\Sigma}_1$ and $\boldsymbol{\Sigma}_2$ is less than d in the sense of $|\cdot|_q$, then the scheme depicted in Fig. 2 is correct. Denote $\varepsilon(\mathbf{Y}_2) = 2^t \lfloor \mathbf{Y}_2/2^t \rfloor + 2^{t-1}\mathbf{1} - \mathbf{Y}_2$. Then

$$
\begin{aligned}
\boldsymbol{\Sigma}_1 - \boldsymbol{\Sigma}_2 &= \mathbf{X}_1^T(2^t \mathbf{Y}_2' + 2^{t-1}\mathbf{1}) - \mathbf{Y}_1^T \mathbf{X}_2 - \mathbf{E}_\sigma \\
&= \mathbf{X}_1^T(\mathbf{Y}_2 + \varepsilon(\mathbf{Y}_2)) - \mathbf{Y}_1^T \mathbf{X}_2 - \mathbf{E}_\sigma \\
&= \mathbf{X}_1^T(\mathbf{A}^T \mathbf{X}_2 + \mathbf{E}_2 + \varepsilon(\mathbf{Y}_2)) - (\mathbf{A}\mathbf{X}_1 + \mathbf{E}_1)^T \mathbf{X}_2 - \mathbf{E}_\sigma \\
&= \mathbf{X}_1^T(\mathbf{E}_2 + \varepsilon(\mathbf{Y}_2)) - \mathbf{E}_1^T \mathbf{X}_2 - \mathbf{E}_\sigma
\end{aligned}
$$

We consider each pair of elements in matrix $\boldsymbol{\Sigma}_1, \boldsymbol{\Sigma}_2$ separately, then derive the overall error rate by *union bound*. Now, we only need to consider the case $l_A = l_B = 1$. In this case, $\mathbf{X}_i, \mathbf{E}_i, \mathbf{Y}_i, (i = 1, 2)$ are column vectors in $\mathbb{Z}_q^n$, and $\mathbf{E}_\sigma \in \mathbb{Z}_q$.

If $\mathbf{Y}_2$ is independent of $(\mathbf{X}_2, \mathbf{E}_2)$, then we can directly calculate the distribution of $\sigma_1 - \sigma_2$. But now $\mathbf{Y}_2$ depends on $(\mathbf{X}_2, \mathbf{E}_2)$. To overcome this difficulty, we show that $\mathbf{Y}_2$ is independent of $(\mathbf{X}_2, \mathbf{E}_2)$ under a condition of $\mathbf{X}_2$ that happens with very high probability.

Proposition 1. *For any positive integer q, n, and a column vector $\mathbf{s} \in \mathbb{Z}_q^n$, let $\phi_{\mathbf{s}}$ denote the map $\mathbb{Z}_q^n \to \mathbb{Z}_q : \phi_{\mathbf{s}}(\mathbf{x}) = \mathbf{x}^T \mathbf{s}$. If there exits a coordinate of $\mathbf{s}$ which is not zero divisor in ring $\mathbb{Z}_q$, then map $\phi_{\mathbf{s}}$ is surjective.*

For a column vector $\mathbf{s}$ composed by random variables, denote by $F(\mathbf{s})$ the event that $\phi_{\mathbf{s}}$ is surjective. The following proposition gives a lower bound of probability of $F(\mathbf{s})$, where $\mathbf{s} \leftarrow \chi^n$. In our application, this lower bound is very close to 1.

Proposition 2. *Let p_0 be the probability that e is a zero divisor in ring $\mathbb{Z}_q$, where e is subject to χ. Then $\Pr[\mathbf{s} \leftarrow \chi^n : F(\mathbf{s})] \geq 1 - p_0^n$*

Theorem 8. *If $\mathbf{s}, \mathbf{e} \leftarrow \chi^n, \mathbf{A} \leftarrow \mathbb{Z}_q^{n \times n}, \mathbf{y} = \mathbf{As} + \mathbf{e} \in \mathbb{Z}_q^n$, then under the condition $F(\mathbf{s})$, $\mathbf{y}$ is independent of $(\mathbf{s}, \mathbf{e})$, and is uniformly distributed over $\mathbb{Z}_q^n$.*

Proof. For all $\tilde{\mathbf{y}}, \tilde{\mathbf{s}}, \tilde{\mathbf{e}}$, $\Pr[\mathbf{y} = \tilde{\mathbf{y}} \mid \mathbf{s} = \tilde{\mathbf{s}}, \mathbf{e} = \tilde{\mathbf{e}}, F(\mathbf{s})] = \Pr[\mathbf{A}\tilde{\mathbf{s}} = \tilde{\mathbf{y}} - \tilde{\mathbf{e}} \mid \mathbf{s} = \tilde{\mathbf{s}}, \mathbf{e} = \tilde{\mathbf{e}}, F(\mathbf{s})]$. Let $\mathbf{A} = (\mathbf{a}_1, \mathbf{a}_2, \ldots, \mathbf{a}_n)^T$, $\tilde{\mathbf{y}} - \tilde{\mathbf{e}} = (c_1, c_2, \ldots, c_n)^T$, where $\mathbf{a}_i \in \mathbb{Z}_q^n$, and $c_i \in \mathbb{Z}_q$, for every $1 \le i \le n$. Since $\phi_{\mathbf{s}}$ is surjective, the number of possible choices of $\mathbf{a}_i$, satisfying $\mathbf{a}_i^T \cdot \tilde{\mathbf{s}} = c_i$, is $|\mathrm{Ker}\phi_{\mathbf{s}}| = q^{n-1}$. Hence, $\Pr[\mathbf{A}\tilde{\mathbf{s}} = \tilde{\mathbf{y}} - \tilde{\mathbf{e}} \mid \mathbf{s} = \tilde{\mathbf{s}}, \mathbf{e} = \tilde{\mathbf{e}}, F(\mathbf{s})] = (q^{n-1})^n/q^{n^2} = 1/q^n$. Since the right-hand side is the constant $1/q^n$, the distribution of $\mathbf{y}$ is uniform over $\mathbb{Z}_q^n$, and is irrelevant of $(\mathbf{s}, \mathbf{e})$. □

We now begin to analyze the error rate of the scheme presented in Fig. 2.

Denote by E the event $|\mathbf{X}_1^T(\mathbf{E}_2 + \varepsilon(\mathbf{Y}_2)) - \mathbf{E}_1^T\mathbf{X}_2 - \mathbf{E}_\sigma|_q > d$. Then $\Pr[E] = \Pr[E|F(\mathbf{S})] \Pr[F(\mathbf{S})] + \Pr[E|\neg F(\mathbf{S})] \Pr[\neg F(\mathbf{S})]$. From Theorem 8, we replace $\mathbf{Y}_2 = \mathbf{A}^T\mathbf{X}_2 + \mathbf{E}_2$ in the event $E|F(\mathbf{S})$ with uniformly distributed $\mathbf{Y}_2$. Then,

$$\Pr[E] = \Pr[\mathbf{Y}_2 \leftarrow \mathbb{Z}_q^n : E|F(\mathbf{S})] \Pr[F(\mathbf{S})] + \Pr[E|\neg F(\mathbf{S})] \Pr[\neg F(\mathbf{S})]$$
$$= \Pr[\mathbf{Y}_2 \leftarrow \mathbb{Z}_q^n : E|F(\mathbf{S})] \Pr[F(\mathbf{S})] + \Pr[\mathbf{Y}_2 \leftarrow \mathbb{Z}_q^n : E|\neg F(\mathbf{S})] \Pr[\neg F(\mathbf{S})]$$
$$+ \Pr[E|\neg F(\mathbf{S})] \Pr[\neg F(\mathbf{S})] - \Pr[\mathbf{Y}_2 \leftarrow \mathbb{Z}_q^n : E|\neg F(\mathbf{S})] \Pr[\neg F(\mathbf{S})]$$
$$= \Pr[\mathbf{Y}_2 \leftarrow \mathbb{Z}_q^n : E] + \varepsilon$$

where $|\varepsilon| \le \Pr[\neg F(\mathbf{S})]$. In our application, p_0 is far from 1, and n is very large, by Theorem 2, ε is very small, so we simply ignore ε. If $\mathbf{Y}_2$ is uniformly distributed, then $\varepsilon(\mathbf{Y}_2)$ is a centered uniform distribution. Then, the distribution of $\mathbf{X}_1^T(\mathbf{E}_2 + \varepsilon(\mathbf{Y}_2)) - \mathbf{E}_1^T\mathbf{X}_2 - \mathbf{E}_\sigma$ can be directly computed by programs.

Discrete Distributions. In this work, for LWE-based key establishment, we use the following discrete distributions, which are specified in Table 4, where "bits" refers to the number of bits required to sample the distribution and "var." means the standard variation of the Gaussian distribution approximated.

Table 4. Discrete distributions proposed in this work, and their Rényi divergences.

dist.	Bits	var.	Probability of						Order	Divergence
			0	±1	±2	±3	±4	±5		
D_1	8	1.10	94	62	17	2			15.0	1.0015832
D_2	12	0.90	1646	992	216	17			75.0	1.0003146
D_3	12	1.66	1238	929	393	94	12	1	30.0	1.0002034
D_4	16	1.66	19794	14865	6292	1499	200	15	500.0	1.0000274
D_5	16	1.30	22218	15490	5242	858	67	2	500.0	1.0000337

Instantiations, and Comparisons with Frodo. For "OKCN simple" proposed in Algorithm 2, it achieves a tight parameter constraint, specifically, $2md < q$. In comparison, the parameter constraint achieved by Frodo is $4md < q$. As we shall see, such a difference is one source that allows us to achieve better trade-offs among error probability, security, (computational and bandwidth) efficiency, and consensus range. In particular, it allows us to use q that is one bit shorter than that used in Frodo. Beyond saving bandwidth, employing a one-bit shorter q also much improves the computational efficiency (as the matrix $\mathbf{A}$ becomes shorter, and consequently the cost of generating $\mathbf{A}$ and the related matrix operations are more efficient), and can render stronger security levels simultaneously. Here, we briefly highlight one performance comparison: OKCN-T2 (resp., Frodo-recommended) has 18.58kB (resp., 22.57kB) bandwidth, 887.15kB (resp., 1060.32kB) matrix $\mathbf{A}$, at least 134-bit (resp., 130-bit) quantum security, and error rate 2^{-39} (resp., $2^{-38.9}$) (Table 5).

Table 5. Parameters proposed for OKCN-LWE with t least significant bits cut off.

	q	n	l	m	g	t	d	dist.	err.	bw. (kB)	$|A|$ (kB)	$|K|$	pq-sec
OKCN-T2	2^{14}	712	8	2^4	2^8	2	509	D_5	$2^{-39.0}$	18.58	887.15	256	134
OKCN-T1	2^{14}	712	8	2^4	2^8	1	509	D_5	$2^{-52.3}$	19.29	887.15	256	134

6.2   CCA-Secure AKCN-LWE, and Comparison with FrodoKEM

FrodoKEM [FrodoKEM] in submission to NIST PQC standardization is AKC-based and is a CCA-secure key encapsulation mechanism (KEM). The underlying AKC mechanism of FrodoKEM corresponds to the special case of AKCN for the parameters params $= (q, m, g, d)$ where $g = q$ and $m = 4$ or $m = 8$. In addition, FrodoKEM chooses $t_2 = 0$, i.e., without compression of $\mathbf{Y}_2$. This means that, on the same parameters, AKCN-LWE outperforms FrodoKEM in bandwidth. We also note that the discrete distributions proposed by FrodoKEM, referred to as $\chi_{\text{Frodo-640}}$ and $\chi_{\text{Frodo-976}}$, are different from those of KC-based Frodo [BCD+16]. By replacing the underlying AKC mechanism of FrodoKEM with our AKCN, we get an AKCN-based CCA-secure KEM scheme. Two set of parameters for our AKCN-based CCA-secure KEM, referred to as AKCN-640 and AKCN-976 respectively, are briefly summaried in Table 6.

Table 6. Brief comparison between CCA-secure AKCN-LWE and FrodoKEM. The ciphertext size is the total length of bytes sent by Bob. For AKCN-640, its ciphertext is 7% smaller than Frodo-640. While its error probability is larger than Frodo-640, it's still under 2^{-130} that is sufficiently smaller for 103-bit pq-security. For AKCN-976, its ciphertext is 12.8% smaller than Frodo-976, and its error probability is still under 2^{-160} that is sufficiently smaller for 150-bit pq-security.

	n	q	m	g	t	dist	ciphertext	err.	$|K|$	C	Q
Frodo-640	640	2^{15}	2^2	2^{15}	0	$\chi_{\text{Frodo-640}}$	9720	$2^{-148.8}$	128	144	103
AKCN-640	640	2^{15}	2^2	2^{10}	1	$\chi_{\text{Frodo-640}}$	9040	$2^{-132.7}$	128	144	103
Frodo-976	976	2^{16}	2^3	2^{16}	0	$\chi_{\text{Frodo-976}}$	15744	$2^{-199.6}$	192	209	150
AKCN-976	976	2^{16}	2^3	2^8	2	$\chi_{\text{Frodo-976}}$	13728	$2^{-164.1}$	192	209	150

References

[APS15] Albrecht, M.R., Player, R., Scott, S.: On the concrete hardness of learning with errors. J. Math. Cryptol. **9**(3), 169–203 (2015)

[ADPS16] Alkim, E., Ducas, L., Pöppelmann, T., Schwabe, P.: Post-quantum key exchange — a new hope. USENIX Security, pp. 327–343 (2016)

[ACPS09] Applebaum, B., Cash, D., Peikert, C., Sahai, A.: Fast cryptographic primitives and circular-secure encryption based on hard learning problems. In: Halevi, S. (ed.) CRYPTO 2009. LNCS, vol. 5677, pp. 595–618. Springer, Heidelberg (2009). https://doi.org/10.1007/978-3-642-03356-8_35

[BLL+15] Bai, S., Langlois, A., Lepoint, T., Stehlé, D., Steinfeld, R.: Improved security proofs in lattice-based cryptography: using the Rényi divergence rather than the statistical distance. In: ASIACRYPT, pp. 3–24 (2015)

[BPR12] Banerjee, A., Peikert, C., Rosen, A.: Pseudorandom functions and lattices. In: Pointcheval, D., Johansson, T. (eds.) EUROCRYPT 2012. LNCS, vol. 7237, pp. 719–737. Springer, Heidelberg (2012). https://doi.org/10.1007/978-3-642-29011-4_42

[BGL+18] Bhattacharya, S., et al.: Round5: compact and fast post-quantum public-key encryption. Cryptology ePrint Archive, 2018/725

[BBG+17] Baan, H., et al.: Round2: KEM and PKE based on GLWR. Cryptology ePrint Archive, 2017/1183

[BGM+16] Bogdanov, A., Guo, S., Masny, D., Richelson, S., Rosen, A.: On the hardness of learning with rounding over small modulus. In: Kushilevitz, E., Malkin, T. (eds.) TCC 2016. LNCS, vol. 9562, pp. 209–224. Springer, Heidelberg (2016). https://doi.org/10.1007/978-3-662-49096-9_9

[BCD+16] Bos, J., et al.: Frodo: take off the ring! Practical, quantum-secure key exchange from LWE. In: ACM CCS, pp. 1006–1018 (2016)

[CN11] Chen, Y., Nguyen, P.Q.: BKZ 2.0: better lattice security estimates. In: Lee, D.H., Wang, X. (eds.) ASIACRYPT 2011. LNCS, vol. 7073, pp. 1–20. Springer, Heidelberg (2011). https://doi.org/10.1007/978-3-642-25385-0_1

[CGZ18] Cheng, L., Gong, B., Zhao, Y.: Lattice-based signature from key consensus. Cryptology ePrint Archive, Report 2018/1180

[CKLS16] Cheon, J.H., Kim, D., Lee, J., Song, Y.: Lizard: cut off the tail! practical post-quantum public-key encryption from LWE and LWR. Cryptology ePrint Archive, Report 2016/1126

[CW90] Coppersmith, D., Winograd, S.: Matrix multiplication via arithmetic progressions. J. Symb. Comput. **9**(3), 251–280 (1990)

[CDS94] Cramer, R., Damgård, I., Schoenmakers, B.: Proofs of partial knowledge and simplified design of witness hiding protocols. In: Desmedt, Y.G. (ed.) CRYPTO 1994. LNCS, vol. 839, pp. 174–187. Springer, Heidelberg (1994). https://doi.org/10.1007/3-540-48658-5_19

[DKRV17] D'Anvers, J., Karmakar, A., Roy, S.S., Vercauteren, F.: SABER: Mod-LWR based KEM. Proposal to NIST PQC Standardization

[DXL12] Ding, J., Xie, X., Lin, X.: A simple provably secure key exchange scheme based on the learning with errors problem. Cryptology ePrint Archive, Report 2012/688 (2012)

[DTV15] Duc, A., Tramèr, F., Vaudenay, S.: Better algorithms for LWE and LWR. In: Oswald, E., Fischlin, M. (eds.) EUROCRYPT 2015. LNCS, vol. 9056, pp. 173–202. Springer, Heidelberg (2015). https://doi.org/10.1007/978-3-662-46800-5_8

[FS86] Fiat, A., Shamir, A.: How to prove yourself: practical solutions to identification and signature problems. In: Odlyzko, A.M. (ed.) CRYPTO 1986. LNCS, vol. 263, pp. 186–194. Springer, Heidelberg (1987). https://doi.org/10.1007/3-540-47721-7_12

[JZ16] Jin, Z., Zhao, Y.: Optimal key consensus in presence of noise. CoRR abs/1611.06150 (2016). https://arxiv.org/abs/1611.06150

[Kra03] Krawczyk, H.: SIGMA: the 'SIGn-and-MAc' approach to authenticated Diffie-Hellman and its use in the IKE protocols. In: Boneh, D. (ed.) CRYPTO 2003. LNCS, vol. 2729, pp. 400–425. Springer, Heidelberg (2003). https://doi.org/10.1007/978-3-540-45146-4_24

[LP10] Lindner, R., Peikert, C.: Better key sizes (and attacks) for LWE-based encryption. In: Kiayias, A. (ed.) CT-RSA 2011. LNCS, vol. 6558, pp. 319–339. Springer, Heidelberg (2011). https://doi.org/10.1007/978-3-642-19074-2_21

[LPR10] Lyubashevsky, V., Peikert, C., Regev, O.: On ideal lattices and learning with errors over rings. In: Gilbert, H. (ed.) EUROCRYPT 2010. LNCS, vol. 6110, pp. 1–23. Springer, Heidelberg (2010). https://doi.org/10.1007/978-3-642-13190-5_1

[FrodoKEM] Naehrig, M., et al.: Supporting documentation: frodokem. Technical report, National Institute of Standards and Technology (2017). https://csrc.nist.gov/CSRC/media/Projects/Post-Quantum-Cryptography/Round-1-Submissions

[NIST] NIST: Post-Quantum Cryptography Standardization. https://csrc.nist.gov/Projects/Post-Quantum-Cryptography/Post-Quantum-Cryptography-Standardization

[Pei09] Peikert, C.: Public-Key Cryptosystems from the worst-case shortest vector problem. In: STOC, pp. 333–342 (2009)

[Pei14] Peikert, C.: Lattice cryptography for the internet. In: Mosca, M. (ed.) PQCrypto 2014. LNCS, vol. 8772, pp. 197–219. Springer, Cham (2014). https://doi.org/10.1007/978-3-319-11659-4_12

[PG13] Pöppelmann, T., Güneysu, T.: Towards practical lattice-based public-key encryption on reconfigurable hardware. In: Lange, T., Lauter, K., Lisoněk, P. (eds.) SAC 2013. LNCS, vol. 8282, pp. 68–85. Springer, Heidelberg (2014). https://doi.org/10.1007/978-3-662-43414-7_4

[Reg09] Regev, O.: On lattices, learning with errors, random linear codes, and cryptography. J. ACM 56(6), 34–72 (2009)

One Sample Ring-LWE with Rounding and Its Application to Key Exchange

Jintai Ding[1], Xinwei Gao[2], Tsuyoshi Takagi[3,4], and Yuntao Wang[3(✉)]

[1] University of Cincinnati, Cincinnati, USA
jintai.ding@gmail.com
[2] Beijing Jiaotong University, Beijing, China
xinwei.gao.7@yandex.com
[3] The University of Tokyo, Tokyo, Japan
{takagi,y-wang}@mist.i.u-tokyo.ac.jp
[4] CREST, Japan Science and Technology Agency, Kawaguchi, Japan

Abstract. In this paper, we introduce a new provably secure ephemeral-only RLWE+Rounding-based key exchange protocol and a proper approach to more accurately estimate the security level of the RLWE problem with only one sample. Since our scheme is an ephemeral-only key exchange, it generates only one RLWE sample from protocol execution. We carefully analyze how to estimate the practical security of the RLWE problem with only one sample, which we call the ONE-sample RLWE problem. Our approach is different from existing approaches that are based on estimation with multiple RLWE samples. Though our analysis is based on some recently developed techniques in Darmstadt, our type of practical security estimate was never done before and it produces security estimates substantial different from the estimates before based on multiple RLWE samples. We show that the new design improves the security and reduce the communication cost of the protocol simultaneously by using one RLWE+Rounding sample technique. We also present two parameter choices ensuring 2^{-60} key exchange failure probability which cover security of AES-128/192/256 with concrete security analysis and implementation. We believe that our construction is secure, simple, efficient and elegant with wide application prospects.

Keywords: Key exchange · Post-quantum · Diffie-Hellman · RLWE · Lattice · One sample

1 Introduction

1.1 The Post-quantum World

Key exchange is a very important cryptographic primitive which allows communicating parties to agree on same keys over insecure network. In 1976, the first key exchange primitive – Diffie-Hellman key exchange protocol was proposed in [20]. This ground-breaking work is a key part of public key cryptography and it inspires cryptographers to build new public key cryptosystems and

© Springer Nature Switzerland AG 2019
R. H. Deng et al. (Eds.): ACNS 2019, LNCS 11464, pp. 323–343, 2019.
https://doi.org/10.1007/978-3-030-21568-2_16

key exchange protocols. With properly chosen parameters and implementations, Diffie-Hellman key exchange and its variants are hard to break with current computing resources.

However, such cryptosystems are no longer secure against sufficiently large quantum computers. In 1994, Shor proposed a quantum algorithm which can solve discrete logarithm problem (DLP) and integer factorization problem (IFP) on a quantum computer [32] in polynomial time. Therefore, if a sufficient large quantum computer is built, Shor's algorithm is expected to break cryptosystems which are constructed based on DLP, IFP and their elliptic curve variants etc., including RSA, DSA, ElGamal etc. It is vital to develop secure and practical post-quantum alternatives for the upcoming post-quantum world.

During recent years, various works are focusing on the lattice-based Ring Learning With Errors (RLWE) problem [25], which is the ring variant of Learning With Errors (LWE) problem [27]. They enjoy high efficiency as well as strong security, making them very promising towards the post-quantum world.

In 2015, NSA announced that it is planning the transition to quantum-resistant cryptography suites in near future. In 2016, NIST formally published calls for new post-quantum cryptography algorithms [19]. This stresses importance and urgency to develop post-quantum alternatives for near future. NIST focused on three primitives: public key encryption, digital signature and key establishment.

1.2 Quantum-Resistant RLWE+Rounding Key Exchange with One Sample

The first complete key exchange solution appeared in the LWE & RLWE-based key exchange protocols proposed by Ding et al. in 2012 [21]. There are various similar works that construct LWE/RLWE-based key exchange protocols, including BCNS [14], NewHope [6], Frodo [13], NewHope-Simple [5], HILA5 [28], Kyber [15] etc. Also there are various new protocols in NIST's round 1 submissions [19].

[11] proposed the Learning With Rounding (LWR) problem, which can reduce communication cost of LWE problem through rounding. Since rounding and recovering algorithms generate deterministic errors, [11] suggests that error term in LWE problem can be discarded with properly chosen parameters. Till now, concrete security of LWR and its ring variant – RLWR problem is not well understood. In LWR and RLWR, "error" on the term $\mathbf{a} \cdot \mathbf{s}$ is only generated by deterministic rounding and recovering algorithm, and this brings security concerns over LWR and RLWR problems. This is also the reason why we prefer the "RLWE+Rounding" approach, instead of using RLWR directly.

Inspired by the notion of RLWR and RLWE-based key exchange, we introduce a new rounding technique dedicated to our key exchange design to reduce the communication cost and increase the security simultaneously. Unlike LWR/RLWR-based cryptosystems, we keep the freshly generated and secret error term $2\mathbf{e}$ in our RLWE instance $\mathbf{a} \cdot \mathbf{s} + 2\mathbf{e}$, then we apply our new rounding technique. We call this a RLWE+Rounding sample. By designing new rounding and recovering techniques, we reduce communication cost substantially and further improve the practical efficiency of our key exchange protocol. Moreover, it actually adds larger perturbation – "error" on $\mathbf{a} \cdot \mathbf{s}$ compared to standard RLWE instance, which helps to improve security of our protocol even further.

In addition, we give two flexible parameter choices and implementation that ensure low key exchange failure probability and cover security of AES-128/192/256 using our new security analysis technique for only one sample case.

1.3   Parameter Settings for ONE-Sample RLWE Case

It is very clear that for an RLWE-based ephemeral key exchange, an attack can only get one sample. And each RLWE sample can be expanded to n LWE samples by rotating elements in the convolution polynomial ring. Recently a work of [29] developed techniques in solving standard LWE instances with a restricted number of samples. However, it is not adapted in practical security analysis of RLWE key exchanges directly. Especially we can not adopt the LWE-estimator [4] directly because of the perturbations from the rounding/recovering functions in our key exchange scheme. We developed the security analysis of the dual embedding attack (we call "SIS attack" in this work) on solving ONE-sample RLWE case.

Further, in Table 1 we show the complexity of solving the standard LWE instance using SIS attack given n and $2n$ samples. We use Regev's parameter settings $(n, \alpha = \frac{1}{\sqrt{2\pi n} \log^2 n}, q \approx n^2)$ in the original LWE paper [27]. We estimate the hardness of standard LWE for $n = \{128, 512, 1024, 2048\}$ using the LWE-estimator [4] and restrict the number of given samples to n and $2n$. From the table we can see that the gap of complexities is distinctly larger with n increasing. Note that the n and $2n$ samples here can be seen as extracted from ONE-sample RLWE case and TWO-samples RLWE case respectively. Hence for the security analysis of RLWE instance, the available number of samples may lead a big gap for high dimensions.

Table 1. Hardness estimation for restricted number of LWE samples with Regev's parameter settings from LWE-estimator.

n	128		512		1024		2048	
#{given samples}	128	256	512	1024	1024	2048	2048	4096
#{used samples}	128	228	512	919	1024	1853	2048	3821
logarithmic complexity (clock cycles)	66.8	57.7	241.4	201.6	497.3	410.2	1043.8	851.5

1.4   Contribution

In this paper, we introduce an appropriate method to estimate the security of only one RLWE sample. Complexity of various practical attacks on having only one sample and multiple samples are very different. We discuss such differences carefully. We apply the one sample model to construct an ephemeral-only RLWE-based key exchange protocol. Our construction is an ephemeral

RLWE+Rounding variant of the classic Diffie-Hellman key exchange protocol, which can be regarded as a direct drop-in replacement for current widely-deployed Diffie-Hellman key exchange protocol and its variants. We use the new RLWE+Rounding technique instead of RLWR to improve the security of our scheme and reduce communication cost simultaneously. We note that multiple key reuse attacks targeting RLWE-based key exchange protocols do not work for our protocol. Moreover, we study the practical SIS attack on the only one-sample RLWE case. We give secure parameter settings for AES-128/192/256 security levels, which are based on the progressive BKZ simulator as a practical reference and using the sieving-BKZ estimation as a lower bound, taking the impact of exponential memory requirement of sieving subroutine into account. We present protocol specifications, parameter choices, security analysis and performance analysis of our protocol.

Advantages. Here we briefly summarize advantages of our construction as follows: (1) one RLWE sample and flexible parameter choices. Attackers can only use **one** RLWE sample for lattice attacks since our construction is an ephemeral-only key exchange; (2) reduced Communication Cost. Our rounding technique gives at least 10% smaller communication cost compared with similar RLWE-based ones at similar security level; (3) longer Final Shared Keys. Our protocol generates a 512 or 1024 bits key, while most similar works generate 256-bit key. We believe long shared key is extremely important for real-world applications, e.g. the master key in TLS protocol is 384 bits; (4) forward Secure. Our protocol is an ephemeral Diffie-Hellman-like schemes instead of KEM, where in practice, the latter approach reuses public key. If the secret key is leaked, then all previous captured traffic can be decrypted.

2   Ephemeral-Only RLWE+Rounding Key Exchange

2.1   Preliminaries

Let $R_q = \mathbb{Z}_q[x]/f(x)$ be the quotient ring of integer polynomials with $f(x) = x^n + 1$, q a prime number, and n a number as a power of 2. A polynomial $\mathbf{a}$ in R_q is represented as $\mathbf{a} = a_1 + a_2 x + \cdots + a_n x^{n-1}$. Coefficients of a polynomial $\mathbf{a}$ can also denoted by a vector $\mathbf{a} = (a_1, ..., a_n)$.

Let Λ be a discrete subset of $\mathbb{Z}^n$. For any vector $\mathbf{c} \in \mathbb{R}^n$ and any positive parameter $\sigma > 0$, let $\rho_{\sigma,\mathbf{c}}(\mathbf{x}) = e^{-\pi \|\mathbf{x}-\mathbf{c}\|^2/\sigma^2}$ be the Gaussian function on $\mathbb{R}^n$ with the center $\mathbf{c}$ and the parameter σ. Denote $\rho_{\sigma,\mathbf{c}}(\Lambda) = \sum_{x \in \Lambda} \rho_{\sigma,\mathbf{c}}(x)$ be the discrete integral of $\rho_{\sigma,\mathbf{c}}$ over Λ, and $D_{\Lambda,\sigma,\mathbf{c}}$ be the discrete Gaussian distribution over Λ with the center $\mathbf{c}$ and the parameter σ. For all $\mathbf{y} \in \Lambda$, we have $D_{\Lambda,\sigma,\mathbf{c}}(\mathbf{y}) = \frac{\rho_{\sigma,\mathbf{c}}(\mathbf{y})}{\rho_{\sigma,\mathbf{c}}(\Lambda)}$. In this paper, we fix Λ to be $\mathbb{Z}^n$ and $\mathbf{c}$ to be zero vector. For ease of notation, we denote $D_{\mathbb{Z}^n,\sigma,0}$ as $D_{\mathbb{Z}^n,\sigma}$. Let $U[a,b]$ be the uniform distribution over discrete set $\{a, a+1, \cdots, b-1, b\}$ over integers. Let $\xleftarrow{\$} \chi$ denote a random sampling according to the distribution χ. Here we represent $\mathbb{Z}_q$ as $\{-\frac{q-1}{2}, \cdots, \frac{q-1}{2}\}$. However, on occasion, we treat elements in $\mathbb{Z}_q$ as elements in $\{0, \cdots, q-1\}$ for convenience, but we will remark the switch clearly.

Let $||\cdot||_1$ be the l_1-norm, $||\cdot||_2$ be the l_2-norm, $||\cdot||_\infty$ be the l_∞-norm. Let $\lfloor x \rfloor$ be the floor function which outputs the greatest integer that is less than or equal to x, $\lceil x \rceil$ be ceiling function which outputs the least integer that is greater than or equal to x, $\lfloor x \rceil$ be the rounding function which rounds x to nearest integer. Let "$a \| b$" denotes the concatenation of a and b. Function log denotes the natural logarithm, $\log_2$ denotes logarithm with base 2.

First we recall and introduce useful lemmas.

Lemma 1 ([34], Lemma 2.5). *For $\sigma > 0$, $r \geq 1/\sqrt{2\pi}$, $\Pr[\|\mathbf{x}\|_2 > r\sigma\sqrt{n}; \mathbf{x} \xleftarrow{\$} D_{\mathbb{Z}^n,\sigma}] < (\sqrt{2\pi e r^2} \cdot e^{-\pi r^2})^n$.* $\qquad \square$

Lemma 2. *For $\mathbf{a}, \mathbf{b} \in R_q$, $\|\mathbf{a} \cdot \mathbf{b}\|_\infty \leq \|\mathbf{a}\|_2 \cdot \|\mathbf{b}\|_2$.*

Proof. Denote the coefficient vector of polynomial $\mathbf{a}(x) = a_1 + a_2 x + a_3 x^2 + \cdots + a_{n-1}x^{n-2} + a_n x^{n-1} \in R_q$ as $(a_1, a_2, a_3, \cdots, a_{n-1}, a_n)$.

For $\mathbf{c} = \mathbf{a} \cdot \mathbf{b} \in R_q$, c_n equals the inner product of $(a_1, a_2, \cdots, a_{n-1}, a_n)$ and $(b_n, b_{n-1}, \cdots, b_2, b_1)$. Similar computations can be applied to coefficients $c_{n-1}, \cdots, c_2, c_1$ as well. By applying Cauchy-Schwarz inequality and property of norm (i.e. for any vector $\mathbf{x}$, $\|\mathbf{x}\|_\infty \leq \|\mathbf{x}\|_2 \leq \|\mathbf{x}\|_1$), we have $\|\mathbf{c}\|_\infty \leq \|\mathbf{a}\|_2 \cdot \|\mathbf{b}\|_2$. $\qquad \square$

2.2 Core Functions

In this section, we define several functions which are crucial to construct our RLWE-based key exchange protocols.

Hint Function. Hint functions $\sigma_0(x)$, $\sigma_1(x)$ from $\mathbb{Z}_q$ to $\{0, 1\}$ are defined as:

$$\sigma_0(x) = \begin{cases} 0, x \in [-\lfloor \frac{q}{4} \rfloor, \lfloor \frac{q}{4} \rfloor] \\ 1, otherwise \end{cases} , \sigma_1(x) = \begin{cases} 0, x \in [-\lfloor \frac{q}{4} \rfloor + 1, \lfloor \frac{q}{4} \rfloor + 1] \\ 1, otherwise \end{cases}$$

Signal Function. A signal function Sig() is defined as:

For any $y \in \mathbb{Z}_q$, $\text{Sig}(y) = \sigma_b(y)$, where $b \xleftarrow{\$} \{0, 1\}$. If $\text{Sig}(y) = 1$, we say y is in the outer region, otherwise y is in the inner region.

Signal function is defined for an integer $x \in \mathbb{Z}_q$. Signal function for $\mathbf{a} \in R_q$ is computed by applying Sig() for each coefficient $a_i \in \mathbb{Z}_q$. In this document, we use the same notation "Sig()" for both signal functions over $\mathbb{Z}_q$ and R_q.

Reconciliation Function. $\text{Mod}_2()$ is a deterministic function with error tolerance δ. $\text{Mod}_2()$ is defined as: for any x in $\mathbb{Z}_q$ and $w = \text{Sig}(x)$, $\text{Mod}_2(x, w) = (x + w \cdot \frac{q-1}{2} \mod q) \mod 2$. Here we treat elements in $\mathbb{Z}_q$ as elements in $\mathbb{Z}$ before we perform the modulo 2 operation.

We define the error tolerance δ, as the largest integer such that for any $x, y \in \mathbb{Z}_q$, if $\|x - y\|_\infty \leq \delta$, then $\text{Mod}_2(x, w) = \text{Mod}_2(y, w)$, where $w = \text{Sig}(y)$. Error tolerance δ is $\frac{q}{4} - 2$, which is the key to ensure correctness of key exchange over RLWE with overwhelming probability.

Reconciliation function is defined for an integer $x \in \mathbb{Z}_q$. The function for $\mathbf{a} \in R_q$ is computed by applying $\text{Mod}_2()$ for each coefficient $a_i \in \mathbb{Z}_q$. We use the same notation "$\text{Mod}_2()$" for reconciliation functions over $\mathbb{Z}_q$ and R_q.

Lemma 3. *Let $q > 8$ be an odd integer. Function $Mod_2()$ as defined above is a robust extractor with respect to signal function $Sig()$ with error tolerance $\delta = \frac{q}{4} - 2$.*

For concrete proofs of Lemma 3, please refer to [21].

Rounding Function. For $x \in \mathbb{Z}_q$, $q > p > 0$ be integers. x is a coefficient of polynomial in R_q, q, p are parameters of our protocol.

For the convenience of notation, we change the representation of $x \in \{-\frac{q-1}{2}, \cdots, \frac{q-1}{2}\}$ to $x \in \{0, \cdots, q-1\}$ before Round() runs. Function Round(x, p, q) is defined in Algorithm 1.

Algorithm 1. Round(x, p, q)

Input: $x \in \mathbb{Z}_q, p, q$
Output: Rounded value x' of x
1: $t \leftarrow \lfloor 2q/p \rfloor, k \leftarrow \lfloor x/t \rfloor$
2: **if** x is odd number **then**
3:     $x' \leftarrow 2k + 1$
4: **else if** x is even number **then**
5:     $x' \leftarrow 2k$
6: **end if**

7: **if** $x' = p$ **then**
8:     $rnd \xleftarrow{\$} U[0, 1]$
9:     **if** $rnd = 1$ **then**
10:         $x' \leftarrow x' - 2$
11:     **else**
12:         $x' \leftarrow (x' + 2) \mod (p + 1)$
13:     **end if**
14: **end if**

Rounding function is defined for an integer $x \in \mathbb{Z}_q$. Rounding function for $\mathbf{a} \in R_q$ is computed by applying Round() for each coefficient $a_i \in \mathbb{Z}_q$ of $\mathbf{a} \in R_q$. In this document, we use the same notation Round() for both rounding functions over $\mathbb{Z}_q$ and R_q.

Recovering Function. Recover() is a deterministic function. $q > p > 0$ be integers. x' is one coefficient of rounded polynomial, q, p are parameters of our protocol. Function Recover(x', p, q) is defined in Algorithm 2.

Algorithm 2. Recover(x', p, q)

Input: x', p, q
Output: Recovered value x'' of x'
1: $t \leftarrow \lfloor q/p \rfloor$
2: **if** x' is odd number **then**
3:     $x'' \leftarrow x' \cdot t + 1$
4: **else if** x' is even number **then**
5:     $x'' \leftarrow (x' + 1) \cdot t$
6: **end if**

In order to be consistent with theoretical analysis, we change representation of $x'' \in \{0, \cdots, q-1\}$ to $x'' \in \{-\frac{q-1}{2}, \cdots, \frac{q-1}{2}\}$ after Recover() runs.

Recovering function is defined for an integer x'. Recovering function for vector $\mathbf{a}$ is computed by applying Recover() for each coefficient a_i in vector $\mathbf{a}$. In this document, we use the same notation "Recover()" for both recovering functions over integer x' and vector $\mathbf{a}$.

Lemma 4. *For parameter p and q, let $t = \lceil \log_2 q \rceil - \lceil \log_2 p \rceil$, $\boldsymbol{x} = (x_1, x_2, \cdots, x_n)$ be a vector whose each coefficient is uniformly random sampled integer in $\mathbb{Z}_q$, $\boldsymbol{x}'$ be a vector whose each coefficient $x_i' = Recover(Round(x_i, p, q), p, q)$. Let $\boldsymbol{d} = \boldsymbol{x} - \boldsymbol{x}'$ be a vector whose each coefficient $d_i = x_i - x_i'$ ($i \in [1, n]$). Then d_i is an even number with possible values in set $\{-2^t, -2^t + 2, \cdots, 2^t - 2\}$. $\Pr[d_i = -2^t] = \Pr[d_i = -2^t + 2] = \cdots = \Pr[d_i = 2^t - 2] = \frac{1}{2^t}$* $\square$

Note that our rounding and recovering algorithm is very different from Kyber [15]. Our algorithms round and recover integers with same parity in order to meet the need of our reconciliation mechanism, while Kyber directly rounds and recovers to nearest integer with same or different parity.

A Derivation Function. In each key exchange execution, we use a 128-bit *seed* to generate fresh **a**. Set *seed* to pseudorandom number generator. Each coefficient $a_i \in \mathbb{Z}_q$ ($i \in [1, n]$) of $\mathbf{a} \in R_q$ is derived as follows:

Algorithm 3. Derive_a(*seed*)

Output: Coefficient a_i of polynomial $\mathbf{a} \in R_q$

1: $a_i \overset{\$}{\leftarrow} U[0, q-1]$

2.3   Protocol Specification

In this section, we present our RLWE-based key exchange protocol.

2.3.1 Specification. We give the description of key exchange between party i and party j. In our protocol, users share following parameters: n, σ, q, p. The protocol is illustrated in Fig. 1.

Initiate. Party i instantiates key exchange by generating 128-bit random *seed*, computes fresh $\mathbf{a} = \text{Derive\_a}(seed)$ and public key $\mathbf{p_i} = \mathbf{a} \cdot \mathbf{s_i} + 2\mathbf{e_i} \in R_q$, where $\mathbf{s_i}$ and $\mathbf{e_i}$ are sampled from $D_{\mathbb{Z}^n, \sigma}$. Round $\mathbf{p_i}$ as $\mathbf{p_i'} = \text{Round}(\mathbf{p_i}, p, q)$, send $\mathbf{p_i'}$ and *seed* to party j.

Response. Party j computes fresh $\mathbf{a} = \text{Derive\_a}(seed)$, public key $\mathbf{p_j} = \mathbf{a} \cdot \mathbf{s_j} + 2\mathbf{e_j} \in R_q$, where $\mathbf{s_j}$ and $\mathbf{e_j}$ are sampled from $D_{\mathbb{Z}^n, \sigma}$. Round $\mathbf{p_j}$ as $\mathbf{p_j'} = \text{Round}(\mathbf{p_j}, p, q)$. Recover public key received from party i as $\mathbf{p_i''} = \text{Recover}(\mathbf{p_i'}, p, q)$. Computes key exchange material $\mathbf{k_j} = \mathbf{p_i''} \cdot \mathbf{s_j} \in R_q$, signal value $w_j = \text{Sig}(\mathbf{k_j})$ and final shared key $sk_j = \text{Mod}_2(\mathbf{k_j}, w_j)$. Send $\mathbf{p_j'}$ and w_j to party i.

Finish. Party i recovers public key received from party j as $\mathbf{p_j''} = \text{Recover}(\mathbf{p_j'}, p, q)$. Compute key exchange material $\mathbf{k_i} = \mathbf{p_j''} \cdot \mathbf{s_i} \in R_q$ and final shared key $sk_i = \text{Mod}_2(\mathbf{k_i}, w_j)$.

Party i Party j

$seed \xleftarrow{\$} \{0,1\}^{128}$

$\mathbf{a} = \text{Derive\_a}(seed) \in R_q$ $\mathbf{a} = \text{Derive\_a}(seed) \in R_q$

Public key: $\mathbf{p_i} = \mathbf{a} \cdot \mathbf{s_i} + 2\mathbf{e_i} \in R_q$ Public key: $\mathbf{p_j} = \mathbf{a} \cdot \mathbf{s_j} + 2\mathbf{e_j} \in R_q$

Private key: $\mathbf{s_i} \in R_q$ $\xrightarrow{\quad \mathbf{p_i'}, seed \quad}$ Private key: $\mathbf{s_j} \in R_q$

where $\mathbf{s_i}, \mathbf{e_i} \xleftarrow{\$} D_{\mathbb{Z}^n,\sigma}$ where $\mathbf{s_j}, \mathbf{e_j} \xleftarrow{\$} D_{\mathbb{Z}^n,\sigma}$

$\mathbf{p_i'} = \text{Round}(\mathbf{p_i}, p, q)$ $\mathbf{p_j'} = \text{Round}(\mathbf{p_j}, p, q)$

                                                               $\mathbf{p_i''} = \text{Recover}(\mathbf{p_i'}, p, q) \in R_q$

$\mathbf{p_j''} = \text{Recover}(\mathbf{p_j'}, p, q) \in R_q$ $\mathbf{k_j} = \mathbf{p_i''} \cdot \mathbf{s_j} \in R_q$

$\mathbf{k_i} = \mathbf{p_j''} \cdot \mathbf{s_i} \in R_q$ $\xleftarrow{\quad \mathbf{p_j'}, w_j \quad}$ $w_j = \text{Sig}(\mathbf{k_j}) \in \{0,1\}^n$

$sk_i = \text{Mod}_2(\mathbf{k_i}, w_j) \in \{0,1\}^n$ $sk_j = \text{Mod}_2(\mathbf{k_j}, w_j) \in \{0,1\}^n$

Fig. 1. The proposed RLWE key exchange protocol

2.3.2 Correctness. With above protocol, we have

$$\begin{aligned} \mathbf{k_i} = \mathbf{p_j''s_i} &= (\mathbf{as_j} + 2\mathbf{e_j} + \mathbf{d_j})\mathbf{s_i} \\ &= \mathbf{as_js_i} + 2\mathbf{e_js_i} + \mathbf{d_js_i} \end{aligned} \tag{1}$$

$$\begin{aligned} \mathbf{k_j} = \mathbf{p_i''s_j} &= (\mathbf{as_i} + 2\mathbf{e_i} + \mathbf{d_i})\mathbf{s_j} \\ &= \mathbf{as_is_j} + 2\mathbf{e_is_j} + \mathbf{d_is_j} \end{aligned} \tag{2}$$

$\mathbf{k_i} - \mathbf{k_j} = 2(\mathbf{e_js_i} - \mathbf{e_is_j}) + (\mathbf{d_js_i} - \mathbf{d_is_j})$. In order to achieve key exchange with overwhelming success probability, $\|\mathbf{k_i} - \mathbf{k_j}\|_\infty \leq$ error tolerance δ of error reconciliation mechanism, i.e. $\|\mathbf{k_i} - \mathbf{k_j}\|_\infty \leq \frac{q}{4} - 2$. Since the elements in $\mathbf{d}_i$ and $\mathbf{d}_j$ are all even, we have

$$\begin{aligned} \|\mathbf{k_i} - \mathbf{k_j}\|_\infty &= \|2(\mathbf{e_js_i} - \mathbf{e_is_j}) + (\mathbf{d_js_i} - \mathbf{d_is_j})\|_\infty \\ &\leq 4\|\mathbf{se}\|_\infty + 2\|\mathbf{d's}\|_\infty \end{aligned} \tag{3}$$

where $\mathbf{s}, \mathbf{e} \in R_q \xleftarrow{\$} D_{\mathbb{Z}^n,\sigma}$. Definition of $\mathbf{d'}$ is consistent with Lemma 4.

With Lemmas 1 and 2, we have $4\|\mathbf{se}\|_\infty \leq 4\|\mathbf{s}\|_2 \cdot \|\mathbf{e}\|_2 \leq 4(r\sigma\sqrt{n})^2 = 4r^2\sigma^2 n$, where $r \geq 1/\sqrt{2\pi}$ is defined in Lemma 1 and n is the degree of polynomial. With Lemma 4, we have $2\|\mathbf{d's}\|_\infty \leq 2\|\mathbf{d'}\|_2 \cdot \|\mathbf{s}\|_2 = 2\|\mathbf{d'}\|_2 \cdot r\sigma\sqrt{n}$. Recall that error tolerance $\delta = \frac{q}{4} - 2$. Therefore as long as $q \geq 4 \cdot [2 + (4r^2\sigma^2 n) + (2\|\mathbf{d'}\|_2 \cdot r\sigma\sqrt{n})]$, key exchange failure probability is estimated to be $(\sqrt{2\pi e r^2} \cdot e^{-\pi r^2})^n$.

2.3.3 Parameter Choice. Parameter choices covering security of AES-128/192/256 are given in Table 2.

Note that for parameter choice $(n, \sigma, q, p) = (1024, 2.6, 120833, 7552)$, it is enough to cover security of AES-128/192/256. We will elaborate this in Sect. 3.4. Modulus $q = 120833$ can instantiate NTT efficiently as $q \equiv 1 \mod 2n$. A failed key exchange implies that at least one bit in sk_i and sk_j mismatches.

Table 2. Our parameter choice

n	σ	q	p	Claimed security level	Failure probability
512	4.19	120833	7552	AES-128	2^{-60}
1024	2.6	120833	7552	AES-192/256	2^{-60}

For Lemma 4 and above parameter choices, let $t = \lceil \log_2 q \rceil - \lceil \log_2 p \rceil$. We have $\Pr[d_i = -2^t] = \Pr[d_i = -2^t + 2] = \cdots = \Pr[d_i = 2^t - 2] = \frac{1}{2^t}$. Therefore, $n = 512, t = 4, \|d\|_2 = 32\sqrt{43}$, $n = 1024, t = 4, \|d\|_2 = 32\sqrt{86}$.

2.4 Passive Security

We define the passive security of our Diffie-Hellman-like ephemeral-only RLWE-based key exchange protocol in Sect. 2.3. Notations are consistent with Sect. 2.3. We start with the security of our key exchange protocol without rounding and recovering public key. Our proof refers to the methodology in [13]. Then we discuss the hardness of our protocol.

Definition 1. *We say a key exchange protocol is secure under passive adversary, if for any PPT adversary the advantage is negligible.*

Note that even if the secret information is involved in signal function computation, intuitively it is infeasible for adversary $\mathcal{A}$ to recover secret from the binary signal w_j. Thus the signal w_j can not be seen as a RLWE sample from the perspective of both security proof and real attacks (on key exchange itself and RLWE problem) in our setting, i.e. keys from key exchange execution are not reused.

Intuitively, any probabilistic polynomial time (PPT) adversary should not distinguish a real shared key ($sk \in \{0,1\}^n$) from a random one ($rand \xleftarrow{\$} \{0,1\}^n$) even if he gets the transcripts (public key and signal value) of the protocol. We define the advantage of an passive adversary $\mathcal{A}$ as:

$$\mathbf{Adv}_{\mathcal{A}} = |\Pr(\mathcal{A}(\mathbf{a}, \mathbf{p_i}, \mathbf{p_j}, w_j, sk) = 1) - \Pr(\mathcal{A}(\mathbf{a}, \mathbf{p_i}, \mathbf{p_j}, w_j, rand) = 1)|.$$

Then we want the adversary to distinguish the final shared key $sk \in \{0,1\}^n$ from uniformly random one ($rand \xleftarrow{\$} \{0,1\}^n$) within negligible probability.

Lemma 5. *For any odd $q > 2$, if x is uniformly random in $\mathbb{Z}_q$, then $Mod_2(x, w)$ is uniformly random conditioned on signal $w \in \{0,1\}$.*

Please refer to [21] for concrete proofs of Lemma 5. In addition, we give the following lemma for the security proof of our protocol.

Lemma 6. $\mathbf{k_j}$ *can be seen as a RLWE sample in the security proof, when $\mathbf{p_i}$ is computed as RLWE instance.*

Proof. Due to the proposition of multiplication distribution, the multiplication of two Gaussians is itself a Gaussian [16]. In our protocol, both $\mathbf{s}$ and $\mathbf{e}$ are sampled from Gaussian distribution $D_{\mathbb{Z}^n,\sigma}$ with small standard deviation. Hence the secret polynomial can be computed as $\mathbf{k_j} = \mathbf{p_i} \cdot \mathbf{s_j} = \mathbf{a} \cdot \mathbf{s_i} \cdot \mathbf{s_j} + 2\mathbf{s_j} \cdot \mathbf{e_i}$. Since $\mathbf{s_j}$ and $\mathbf{e_i}$ are sampled from $D_{\mathbb{Z}^n,\sigma}$, due to the proposition that the product of two Gaussian PDFs is proportional to Gaussian PDF with a standard deviation that is the square root of half of the denominator, i.e. $\sigma_{\mathbf{s_j} \cdot \mathbf{e_i}} = \sqrt{\frac{\sigma_{\mathbf{s_j}}^2 \cdot \sigma_{\mathbf{e_i}}^2}{\sigma_{\mathbf{s_j}}^2 + \sigma_{\mathbf{e_i}}^2}} = \frac{\sqrt{2}}{2}\sigma$.

If we denote by $\mathbf{a}' = \mathbf{a} \cdot \mathbf{s_i}$, $\mathbf{e_i}' = \mathbf{s_j} \cdot \mathbf{e_i}$, we can get a RLWE instance $(\mathbf{a}', \mathbf{e_i}')$ with parameters $(n, q, \sigma_{\mathbf{e_i}'})$. Namely, $\mathbf{k_j}$ can be seen as an RLWE instance with parameters $(n, q, \frac{\sqrt{2}}{2}\sigma)$ if $\mathbf{p_i}$ is RLWE itself.

In the following Theorem and its proof, we rewrite $\mathbf{k_j}$ as $\mathbf{k_j} = \mathbf{a}' \cdot \mathbf{s_j} + 2\mathbf{e_i}'$ for the sake of convenience. As discussed above that essentially $\mathbf{k_j}$ can not be used as an RLWE instance in real attack since the secret key can not be recovered from the published signal ω_j. □

Theorem 1. *The construction above is secure against passive PPT adversaries, if the pseudorandom function Derive_a() is secure and the decision RLWE hardness assumption holds.*

Proof. Theorem 1 can be stated in this way: Let n, q, σ be parameters in our proposed key exchange protocol and let $D_{\mathbb{Z}^n,\sigma}$ be the Gaussian distribution defined in Sect. 2.1. If the pseudorandom function *Derive_a()* is secure against PPT adversary $\mathcal{B}_0$ and the decision RLWE problem is hard for (n, q, σ), then the key exchange protocol in Fig. 1 guarantees keys indistinguishable from uniform random. Namely,

$$\mathbf{Adv}_{\mathcal{A}} \leq \mathbf{Adv}_{Derive\_a}(\mathcal{B}_0) + \mathbf{Adv}_{n,q,D_{\mathbb{Z}^n,\frac{\sqrt{2}}{2}\sigma}}(\mathcal{A} \circ \mathcal{B}_1) + \mathbf{Adv}_{n,q,D_{\mathbb{Z}^n,\sigma}}(\mathcal{A} \circ \mathcal{B}_2). \quad (4)$$

holds where $\mathcal{B}_1$ and $\mathcal{B}_2$ are assumed PPT adversaries who can distinguish the RLWE samples from uniform random.

We prove the security by a sequence of games and lemmas. Let S_i be the challenge where the adversary guesses b in game i. The first game **Game₀** is the real game which the adversary gets all of the original published information, while in the last game **Game₄** the adversary gets uniformly random parameters without RLWE information. We show that the views of **Game₀** and **Game₄** are computational indistinguishable for any PPT adversaries, under the decision RLWE hardness assumption.

Game₀. This is the original game between the protocol challenger and the passive adversary $\mathcal{A}$. That is, the adversary obtains $\mathbf{a}, \mathbf{p_i}, \mathbf{p_j}, w_j, \mathbf{k_b}$, where $\mathbf{p_i} = \mathbf{a} \cdot \mathbf{s_i} + 2\mathbf{e_i}$ and $\mathbf{p_j} = \mathbf{a} \cdot \mathbf{s_j} + 2\mathbf{e_j}$. Then $\mathcal{A}$ outputs a guess b'. Note that there are three RLWE pairs in **Game₀**: $(\mathbf{a}, \mathbf{p_i})$ with secret vector $\mathbf{s_i}$, and $(\mathbf{a}, \mathbf{p_j})$ and $(\mathbf{a}', \mathbf{k_j})$ both with secret vector $\mathbf{s_j}$. Here we can rewrite $\mathbf{Adv}_{\mathcal{A}}$ as

$$\mathbf{Adv}_{\mathcal{A}} = |\Pr(S_0) - 1/2|. \quad (5)$$

Game₁. This game is identical to **Game₀** except that instead of generating $\mathbf{a}$ pseudorandomly from *seed* using function Derive_a(), the challenger samples $\mathbf{a}$ uniformly at random.

Lemma 7. *Any PPT passive adversary cannot distinguish* **Game₀** *and* **Game₁**, *if the assumption holds that the pseudorandom function Derive_a() is secure.*

Proof. It is obvious that the two games are indistinguishable under our assumption that the pseudorandom function Derive_a() is secure, i.e.

$$|\Pr(S_0) - \Pr(S_1)| \leq \mathbf{Adv}_{Derive\_a}(\mathcal{B}_0). \tag{6}$$

$\square$

Game₂. This game is identical to **Game₁** except that instead of setting $\mathbf{p}_i = \mathbf{a} \cdot \mathbf{s}_i + 2\mathbf{e}_i$, the challenger sets $\mathbf{p}_i = \mathbf{r}_i$, where $\mathbf{r}_i \xleftarrow{\$} R_q$.

Lemma 8. *Any PPT passive adversary cannot distinguish* **Game₁** *and* **Game₂**, *if the decision RLWE assumption holds.*

That is to say, in **Game₁**, the challenge $(\mathbf{a}, \mathbf{p}_i)$ is sampled honestly from RLWE oracle. In **Game₂**, $(\mathbf{a}, \mathbf{p}_i)$ is uniformly sampled from $R_q \times R_q$ at random. These two distributions are computationally indistinguishable under the assumption that the decision RLWE problem is hard for parameter set (n, q, σ).

Proof. We prove the lemma by showing that if there exists an adversary $\mathcal{A}$ who can distinguish **Game₁** and **Game₂**, then we can construct another adversary $\mathcal{B}_1$ to distinguish the RLWE samples from uniform random. $\mathcal{B}_1$ works as follows. Once obtaining challenges $(\mathbf{a}, \mathbf{b}_i) \in R_q \times R_q$ from the RLWE oracle, where $\mathbf{b}_i$ is either $\mathbf{a} \cdot \mathbf{s}_i + 2\mathbf{e}_i$ or random $\mathbf{r}_i$ in R_q, $\mathcal{B}_1$ samples $\mathbf{s}_j \xleftarrow{\$} D_{\mathbb{Z}^n, \sigma}$ and sets $\mathbf{k}_j = \mathbf{b}_i \cdot \mathbf{s}_j$. $\mathcal{B}_1$ also computes $\mathbf{p}_j = \mathbf{a} \cdot \mathbf{s}_j + 2\mathbf{e}_j$. Finally $\mathcal{B}_1$ sends $(\mathbf{a}, \mathbf{p}_i = \mathbf{b}_i, \mathbf{p}_j, w_j, \mathbf{k}_j)$ to $\mathcal{A}$. $\mathcal{B}_1$ outputs whatever $\mathcal{A}$ outputs. We note that $\mathcal{B}_1$ can compute w_j by himself. If $\mathbf{b}_i$ is an RLWE sample, then what $\mathcal{A}$ obtains are exactly the same as in **Game₁**, if $\mathbf{b}_i$ is uniformly random in R_q, then what $\mathcal{A}$ obtains are exactly the same as in **Game₂**. This implies that if $\mathcal{A}$ can distinguish **Game₁** and **Game₂** with noticeable advantage, then $\mathcal{B}$ can distinguish RLWE samples from uniformly random with the same advantage. Simultaneously, the adversary $\mathcal{B}_1$ sets $\mathbf{k}_j = \mathbf{u}_j$ by $\mathbf{u}_j = \mathbf{b}_i \cdot \mathbf{s}_j$, where $\mathbf{b}_i$ is either sampled from RLWE or uniformly random $\mathbf{r}_i$ in R_q.

Intuitively it leads to $\mathbf{u}_j = \mathbf{b}_i \cdot \mathbf{s}_j$ is RLWE or uniformly random $\mathbf{r}_j$, according to the analysis under Lemma 6. Hence indeed what $\mathcal{B}_1$ sends to $\mathcal{A}$ can be rewritten as $(\mathbf{a}, \mathbf{p}_i = \mathbf{b}_i, \mathbf{p}_j, w_j, \mathbf{k}_j = \mathbf{u}_j)$ to $\mathcal{A}$. Thus we have two RLWE samples $(\mathbf{a}, \mathbf{p}_i = \mathbf{b}_i)$ and $(\mathbf{a}', \mathbf{k}_j = \mathbf{u}_j)$ in **Game₂** where under the RLWE assumption, RLWE sample $(\mathbf{a}, \mathbf{p}_i)$ with $D_{\mathbb{Z}^n, \sigma}$ is indistinguishable with random sample $(\mathbf{a}, \mathbf{r}_i)$, and RLWE sample $(\mathbf{a}', \mathbf{k}_j)$ with $D_{\mathbb{Z}^n, \frac{\sqrt{2}}{2}\sigma}$ is indistinguishable with $(\mathbf{p}_i, \mathbf{r}_j)$ respectively. This finishes the proof and simultaneously we can get the following inequation:

$$|\Pr(S_1) - \Pr(S_2)| \leq \mathbf{Adv}_{n, q, D_{\mathbb{Z}^n, \frac{\sqrt{2}}{2}\sigma}}(\mathcal{A} \circ \mathcal{B}_1). \tag{7}$$

$\square$

Game₃. This game is identical to **Game₂** except that instead of setting $\mathbf{p_j} = \mathbf{a} \cdot \mathbf{s_j} + 2\mathbf{e_j}$, the challenger sets $\mathbf{p_j} = \mathbf{r_j}$, where $\mathbf{r_j} \overset{\$}{\leftarrow} R_q$.

Lemma 9. *Any PPT passive adversary cannot distinguish* **Game₂** *and* **Game₃**, *if the decision RLWE assumption holds.*

Proof. The proof for Lemma 9 is analogous to the proof for Lemma 8, i.e. we should show if there exists an adversary $\mathcal{A}$ who can distinguish **Game₂** and **Game₃**, then we can construct another adversary $\mathcal{B}_2$ to distinguish the RLWE samples from uniform random. $\mathcal{B}_2$ works as follows. Once obtaining challenges $(\mathbf{a}, \mathbf{b_j})$ where $\mathbf{b_j}$ is either RLWE instance or random $\mathbf{r_j}$ in R_q, $\mathcal{B}_2$ sets $\mathbf{p_j} = \mathbf{b_j}$. Finally $\mathcal{B}_2$ sends $(\mathbf{a}, \mathbf{p_i}, \mathbf{p_j} = \mathbf{b_j}, w_j, \mathbf{k_j})$ to $\mathcal{A}$. $\mathcal{B}_2$ outputs whatever $\mathcal{A}$ outputs. Hence we have

$$|\Pr(S_2) - \Pr(S_3)| \leq \mathbf{Adv}_{n,q,D_{\mathbb{Z}^n,\sigma}}(\mathcal{A} \circ \mathcal{B}_2). \tag{8}$$

□

Furthermore, in **Game₃**, the adversary is given $(\mathbf{a}, \mathbf{b_j})$ which is either sampled uniformly at random. However, when $\mathbf{p_i}$ is uniformly sampled, elements of $\mathbf{k_j} = \mathbf{p_i} \cdot \mathbf{s_j} \in R_q$ is also uniformly distributed. Thus the elements in w_j can be seen uniformly distributed owing to the construction of signal function. Due to Lemma 5, sk_j computed by the reconciliation function from $\mathbf{k_j}$ and w_j is also distributed uniformly at random. Namely, there is no RLWE information in **Game₃** so the adversary can not distinguish the key is generated from the key exchange protocol or just uniformly sampled. Hence, we have the following equation in **Game₃**.

$$|\Pr(S_3)| = 1/2. \tag{9}$$

Consequently, we can get in Eq. (4) (and finish the proof for Theorem 1) by combining the formulas from (5) to (9). □

Now we deal with the security regarding to rounding and recovering $\mathbf{a} \cdot \mathbf{s} + 2\mathbf{e}$ in the next lemma.

Lemma 10. *For following two key exchange protocols:*

1. $\mathbf{p_i} = \mathbf{a} \cdot \mathbf{s_i} + 2\mathbf{e_i}, \mathbf{p_j} = \mathbf{a} \cdot \mathbf{s_j} + 2\mathbf{e_j}, \mathbf{k_i} = \mathbf{p_j} \cdot \mathbf{s_i}, \mathbf{k_j} = \mathbf{p_i} \cdot \mathbf{s_j}, w_j = Sig(\mathbf{k_j}), sk_i = Mod_2(\mathbf{k_i}, w_j), sk_j = Mod_2(\mathbf{k_j}, w_j)$
2. $\mathbf{p_i} = \mathbf{a} \cdot \mathbf{s_i} + 2\mathbf{e_i}, \mathbf{p_j} = \mathbf{a} \cdot \mathbf{s_j} + 2\mathbf{e_j}, \mathbf{p_i'} = Round(\mathbf{p_i}, p, q), \mathbf{p_i''} = Recover(\mathbf{p_i'}, p, q), \mathbf{p_j'} = Round(\mathbf{p_j}, p, q), \mathbf{p_j''} = Recover(\mathbf{p_j'}, p, q), \mathbf{k_i} = \mathbf{p_j''} \cdot \mathbf{s_i}, \mathbf{k_j} = \mathbf{p_i''} \cdot \mathbf{s_j}, w_j = Sig(\mathbf{k_j}), sk_i = Mod_2(\mathbf{k_i}, w_j), sk_j = Mod_2(\mathbf{k_j}, w_j)$

The hardness of computing final shared key of second protocol is at least as hard as computing final shared key of first protocol.

Proof. With publicly known algorithm Round() and Recover(), publicly known parameters and public terms $\mathbf{p_i'}, \mathbf{p_j'}$, any adversary can compute $\mathbf{p_i''} \approx \mathbf{p_i}$ and $\mathbf{p_j''} \approx \mathbf{p_j}$. However, $\mathbf{p_i''} \neq \mathbf{p_i}$, $\mathbf{p_j''} \neq \mathbf{p_j}$, Round() and Recover() function generate additional errors, which makes recovering private key $\mathbf{s_i}$ or $\mathbf{s_j}$ using transcripts from our key exchange at least no easier than using $\mathbf{p_i}, \mathbf{p_j}$ or $\mathbf{k_i}, \mathbf{k_j}$ to solve RLWE problem. □

3 Estimating Security of One RLWE Sample

Before showing the analysis in this section, we stress that only ONE sample can be used in the real attack for our ephemeral protocol settings. It is infeasible for attacker to recover secret key or apply lattice attacks given the binary signal vector from our ephemeral key exchange. Hence the signal w can not be used as another RLWE sample in the real attack (and also the security proof in Sect. 2.4).

3.1 Prerequisites

Lattice Theory. A *lattice* L is defined as an infinite space expanded by *basis* $\mathbf{B} = \{\mathbf{b}_1, \ldots, \mathbf{b}_n\}$, where $\mathbf{b}_i$ $(i = 1, \ldots, n)$ are a set of linearly independent vectors in $\mathbb{R}^m$. Here n is the dimension of L. The n-dimensional *volume* of L is denoted by $\mathrm{Vol}(L)$, which is computed by the *determinant* of basis B, i.e. $\mathrm{Vol}(L) = \det(B)$. We denote $V_n(R) = R^n \cdot \frac{\pi^{n/2}}{\Gamma(n/2+1)}$ as the volume of n-dimensional Euclidean ball of radius R.

Ring LWE (RLWE) Problem. Let $m \geq 1$ be a power of 2 and $q \geq 2$ be an integer, let $R_q = \mathbb{Z}_q[x]/\Phi_m(x)$, where $\Phi_m(x) = x^n + 1$ is the m-th cyclotomic polynomial with $n = m/2$. Let χ be a β-bounded distribution. For secret polynomial $\mathbf{s} \xleftarrow{\$} \chi$ and error polynomial $\mathbf{e} \xleftarrow{\$} \chi$, choosing $\mathbf{a} \in R_q$ uniformly random, output $(\mathbf{a}, \mathbf{b} = \mathbf{a} \cdot \mathbf{s} + \mathbf{e} \in R_q)$. Search version of RLWE problem is: for $\mathbf{s} \xleftarrow{\$} \chi$, given $poly(n)$ number of samples of $(\mathbf{a}, \mathbf{b} = \mathbf{a} \cdot \mathbf{s} + \mathbf{e}) \in (R_q, R_q)$, find $\mathbf{s}$ (and $\mathbf{e}$ simultaneously).

Proposition. Let $\mathbf{z} = \mathrm{Recover}(\mathrm{Round}(\mathbf{a} \cdot \mathbf{s} + 2\mathbf{e}, p, q), p, q) = \mathbf{as} + 2\mathbf{e} + \mathbf{d} = \mathbf{as} + 2\mathbf{f} \in R_q$, where $\mathbf{s}, \mathbf{e} \xleftarrow{\$} D_{\mathbb{Z}^n, \sigma}$ and $2\mathbf{f} = 2\mathbf{e} + \mathbf{d}$ (elements in $\mathbf{d}$ are even). Hence we can regard $\mathbf{f}$ as error term $\mathbf{e}$ in the definition of RLWE above. The attack on our protocol is given $\mathbf{z}$ and $\mathbf{a}$, output private key $\mathbf{s}$. This problem is equivalent to:

$$\mathbf{z} = \mathbf{a} \cdot \mathbf{s} + 2\mathbf{f} \mod q$$
$$\Leftrightarrow 2^{-1}\mathbf{z} = 2^{-1}\mathbf{a} \cdot \mathbf{s} + \mathbf{f} \mod q$$
$$\Leftrightarrow \mathbf{z}'' = \mathbf{a}'' \cdot \mathbf{s} + \mathbf{f} \mod q$$

Standard deviation of term $\mathbf{f}$ is denoted as σ_f. Note that σ_f is different from σ notation in Sect. 2.1 as f no longer follows discrete Gaussian distribution (histogram shows similar shape as Gaussian distribution), therefore σ_f is computed as the square root of variance.

Shortest Vector Problem. Given an input basis $B = (\mathbf{b}_1, \ldots, \mathbf{b}_n)$ of a lattice L, *Shortest Vector Problem* (SVP) is to find a non-zero shortest vector in L. We introduce the following two variants of the SVP to be used in this section.

Short Integer Solution Problem. Given an integer q and a matrix $\mathbf{A} \in \mathbb{Z}_q^{n \times m}$, *Short Integer Solution problem* (SIS) is to compute a short vector $\mathbf{y} \in \mathcal{B}$ s.t. $\mathbf{Ay} \equiv \mathbf{0} \mod q$, where $\mathcal{B}$ is a set of short vectors with some norm bound.

Unique Shortest Vector Problem. *Unique SVP problem* (uSVP) is for a given lattice L which satisfies $\lambda_1(L) \ll \lambda_2(L)$, find the shortest vector in L. Here $\lambda_i(L)$ means the length of i-th linear independent shortest vector for $i = 1, 2$.

Root Hermite Factor. To evaluate the performance of lattice algorithms for solving SVP, we use the *root Hermite Factor* (rHF) defined in [22] as:

$$\delta = \text{rHF}(\mathbf{b}_1, \ldots, \mathbf{b}_n) = (\|\mathbf{b}_1\|_2 / \text{Vol}(L)^{1/n})^{1/n}.$$

Geometric Series Assumption (GSA). The *Geometric Series Assumption* [31] indicates the quality of an LLL-type reduced basis. It says l_2 norm of GSO vectors $\|\mathbf{b}_i^*\|$ in the reduced basis decrease geometrically with a constant r as $\|\mathbf{b}_i^*\|_2^2 / \|\mathbf{b}_1\|_2^2 = r^{i-1}$ ($i = 1, \ldots, n$ and $r \in [3/4, 1)$).

Lattice Algorithms. There are some lattice algorithms such as BKZ and sieving to solve SVP and its variants. *BKZ algorithm* was originally proposed in [30], which computes basis that are almost β-reduced, namely the projected lengths of each basis vectors are the shortest ones in the relative β-sized local blocks. BKZ algorithm runs in exponential time and there are some efficient improvements for BKZ algorithms [18,38]. In 2016, Aono et al. proposed a precise simulator to estimate runtime of progressive BKZ algorithm (pBKZ), which processes given basis by increasing block size with some strategy [8]. When dimension n is large ($n \geq 100$), runtime TimeBKZ(n, β_t) of pBKZ with target blocksize β_t is estimated by Eq. (18) in [8]. Further details may be found in [8] and a reference implementation is freely available at [9].

In 2001, Ajtai et al. proposed a sieving algorithm to solve SVP, which requires a runtime of $2^{0.52n+o(n)}$ in n dimension lattice and simultaneously requires exponential storage of $2^{0.2n+o(n)}$ [1]. According to recent research results, for a n-dimensional lattice L and fixed blocksize β in BKZ, the runtime of sieving algorithm can be estimated in $2^{0.292\beta+o(\beta)}$ clock cycles for a β-dimensional subroutine [4], and totally BKZ-β costs $8n \cdot 2^{0.292\beta+16.4}$ operations [12]. The phase transition of time cost and memory cost is considered in our work. Namely, we assume that practically the exponential large memory ($\beta \cdot 2^{0.292*\beta+o(\beta)}$) cost of sieve will increase the computation cost by at least one magnitude (x10).

3.2 Algorithms for Solving RLWE

In this work we use the adapted SIS attack algorithm on solving RLWE, which is an adaptation of the dual-embedding method mentioned in [29] and [10]. Note that the SIS attack with "rescaling technique" is also called as "Bai-Galbraith's" embedding attack in [3], which is developed by Bai and Galbraith to improve the attack on binary LWE in [10]. In the adapted SIS algorithm, we do not introduce the rescaling technique but just enlarge the lattice dimension. There are also some analysis to the embedding attack and its variants in previous articles [35–37,39].

3.3 Significance of Number of Samples in Practical Attack

At first we claim that because of the setting of our key exchange protocol: only one RLWE instance $(\mathbf{a}, \mathbf{b} = \mathbf{a} \cdot \mathbf{s} + \mathbf{e} \bmod q) \in (R_q, R_q)$ is given, Kannan's embedding technique [23] and Liu-Nguyen's decoding attack [24] cannot be adopted since the lattice $L_{(\mathbf{A}, q)} = \{\mathbf{v} \in \mathbb{Z}_q^m \mid \mathbf{v} \equiv \mathbf{A}\mathbf{x} \pmod{q}, \mathbf{x} \in D_\sigma^n\}$ is trivial when $m \leq n$. Therefore our estimator should be different from some other key exchange schemes as NewHope [6] and Albrecht's estimator [3] etc. which regard RLWE and normal LWE problem as having the same difficulty without considering the number of available RLWE samples. From the discussion in Sect. 1.3 and the estimations in Table 1, we observe that there is a big gap of hardness estimations between ONE-sample RLWE and multiple-samples RLWE. Note that indeed the lowest number m of required LWE samples from the 2016 estimate (Section 3.4) are as follows: m is 576 for $(n, q, \sigma_f) = (512, 120833, 4.92)$ and m is 1097 for $(n, q, \sigma_f) = (1024, 120833, 4.72)$. Therefore, the optimal number in the 2016 estimate can be obtained only from "more than one RLWE samples" ($m = 576 > n = 512$ and $m = 1097 > n = 1024$). Hence in practical attack, we can get only one n-dimensional RLWE instance, which can be amplified to $2n + 1$ without changing the distribution of error vectors. Therefore the lattice dimension of solving RLWE in our case is $d = 2n + 1$.

3.4 Our Simulator

At AsiaCrypt 2017 [3], Albrecht et al. re-estimated the hardness of LWE problem using Kannan's embedding and Bai-Gal's embedding respectively under estimation in NewHope [6] (denoted as "2016 estimate"). 2016 estimate states that if the Gaussian Heuristic and the GSA [31] hold for BKZ-β reduced basis and

$$\sqrt{\beta/d} \cdot \|(\mathbf{e}|1)\|_2 \approx \sqrt{\beta}\sigma \leq \delta^{2\beta - d} \cdot \mathrm{Vol}(L_{(\mathbf{A}, q)})^{1/d}. \tag{10}$$

Then error $\mathbf{e}$ can be found by BKZ-β with root Hermite Factor δ. In our case, we assume $\mathbf{f}$ is the Gaussian distributed error vector plus the uniformly distributed perturbation sampled from a bounded set due to Rounding-Recovering functions and $(\mathbf{s}|\mathbf{f}|1)$ is the target vector in our attack. So there is a gap between the distribution of $\mathbf{f}$ and the Gaussian distribution. However, given a same standard deviation σ_f, the expected length of vectors sampled from the hybrid distribution is bigger than the one sampled from Gaussian distribution on average, by a simple computation using the center limit theorem. Hence in our estimation we assume $\mathbf{f}$ is Gaussian distributed. We adapt the left side of the inequality (10) as $\sqrt{\beta/d} \cdot \|(\mathbf{s}|\mathbf{f}|1)\|_2 \approx \sqrt{\beta \cdot (\sigma_e^2 + \sigma_f^2)}$. For BKZ reduction runtime estimation, we will give the result of progressive BKZ and Albrecht's BKZ with sieving estimator.

Step 1. A short vector $\|\mathbf{b}_1\|_2 = \delta^d \cdot \det(\mathbf{B})$ is assumed to be inside of the BKZ-β reduced basis $\mathbf{B}$ of dimension d [17], where the root Hermite Factor is

$$\delta = \left(\left((\pi\beta)^{1/\beta}\beta\right)/(2\pi e)\right)^{\frac{1}{2(\beta - 1)}}. \tag{11}$$

Since σ_f can be experimentally derived from σ_e, we can compute lower bound of σ_f in RLWE(n, q, σ_f) which covers security of AES-128/192/256 using Eqs. (11) and (12). Note that f no longer follows discrete Gaussian distribution (histogram shows similar shape as Gaussian distribution). Therefore we take a heuristic approach to estimate σ_f.

In our case, $d = 2n + 1$ is the dimension of lattice and also Vol($L_{(\mathbf{A},q)}$) = q^n. Therefore we can pre-compute the expected root Hermite factor δ for $\beta = 10, \cdots, n$ and adapt inequality (10) to

$$\sqrt{\beta \cdot (\sigma_e^2 + \sigma_f^2)} \leq \delta^{2\beta - 2n - 1} \cdot q^{n/(2n+1)}. \tag{12}$$

To compute the target β in the progressive BKZ simulator, we use the correspondence between δ and the GSA constant r: Given a d-dimensional basis, in order to use progressive BKZ simulator, we need target β_t for our parameter choice. At this stage, we can get the target GSA constant $r_t = \delta^{-4d/(d-1)}$. Therefore we can compute the terminating blocksize β_t in progressive BKZ corresponding to r_t by equations (10) and (11) given in [8].

Step 2. We compute the complexity of BKZ-β with sieving SVP oracle estimated as $8d \cdot 2^{0.292\beta + 16.4}$ double precision floating point operations [2,12]. we translate this to complexity of bit unit by $T_{sieving-BKZ} = 8d \cdot 2^{0.292\beta + 16.4} \cdot 64$ (bits).

Simultaneously, T_{BKZ} can also be replaced by progressive BKZ simulator explained in Sect. 3.1. We run the progressive BKZ simulator for both $n = 512$ and $n = 1024$ cases. Considering the number of iterations for each fixed blocksize in BKZ, we get following two fitting functions to estimate the runtime of two cases respectively.

$$\log_2(Time_{pBKZ}(secs)) = \begin{cases} 0.003924 \cdot \beta^2 - 0.568 \cdot \beta + 41.93 \ (n = 512) \\ 0.004212 \cdot \beta^2 - 0.6886 \cdot \beta + 55.49 \ (n = 1024) \end{cases} \tag{13}$$

Then we compute the complexity of bit unit by $T_{pBKZ} = Time_{pBKZ} \times 2.7 \times 10^9 \times 64$ (bits). on our Intel(R) Xeon(R) CPU E5-2697 v2 @ 2.70GHz server.

We generate 1,000 and 2,000 **as + 2e** samples for parameter choice $(n, \sigma, q, p) = (1024, 2.6, 120833, 7552)$ and $(n, \sigma, q, p) = (512, 4.19, 120833, 7552)$. For each sample, we apply Round() and Recover() functions, giving us

$$\mathbf{z} = \text{Recover}(\text{Round}(\mathbf{a} \cdot \mathbf{s} + 2\mathbf{e}, p, q), p, q) = \mathbf{a} \cdot \mathbf{s} + 2\mathbf{f}.$$

With $\frac{\mathbf{z} - \mathbf{as}}{2} = \mathbf{f}$, we compute standard deviation σ_f. Results are given in Table 3, where the parameter settings can ensure 2^{-60} failure probability.

Due to the uncertainty simulation for runtime with large dimension and large β (>1000 and >200 respectively), we are not sure about the simulation results for our key exchange protocol. We will leave it as future work. However, our parameter choices can cover results from pBKZ simulator. Therefore we show results from pBKZ simulator in Table 3 as well.

The 2016 estimate for AES-128 and AES-192/256 security gives 142.27 and 279.05 bit operations respectively. Practically the exponential memory's access

Table 3. Our simulation data and parameter settings covering security of AES-128/192/256

Security level (n, q, σ)	AES-128 (512,120833,4.19)		AES-192 and AES-256 (1024,120833,2.6)	
Method	pBKZ	2016 estimate	pBKZ	2016 estimate
Logarithmic computational complexity	319.14	142.27	1473.09	279.05
Blocksize	330	366	660	831
GSA Const.	0.983		0.991	
σ (for **s** and **e**) of our parameter choice	4.19		2.6	
σ_f	4.92		4.72	

of sieving algorithm will increase the computation cost by at least one magnitude (x10), therefore we conclude that our parameter choices with $n = 512$ can achieve at least 145.59 bits security, $n = 1024$ can achieve at least 282.37 bits security. With results given in Table 3, we claim that parameter choices given in Table 2 cover security of AES-128/192/256.

Furthermore, Aono et al. proposed a method to compute the lower bound N on the cost of extreme-pruning enumeration algorithm, for a certain pruning success probability α' to find a shortest vector, which bases on a simulated HKZ-reduced basis [7]. We use the formula (17) in [7] and set $\alpha' = 1$. Analogous to the sieving-BKZ model in 2016 estimate, we compute the complexity of BKZ with enumeration subroutine by $T_{enum-BKZ} = 8d \cdot N$ (bits). When we compute $T_{enum-BKZ}$ using the blocksizes 366 and 831 given in Table 3, we get 194 bit security and 596 bit security respectively. It means that our parameter settings are safe under the BKZ with enumeration subroutine model.

4 Implementation and Performance

In this section, we introduce our implementation and performance of our key exchange scheme in Sect. 2.3. Note that in our implementation, a number in $\mathbb{Z}_q$ is represented as $[0, q-1]$. One can convert the regions defined for hint and signal functions from $\{-\frac{q-1}{2}, \cdots, \frac{q-1}{2}\}$ to corresponding regions in $[0, q-1]$.

We use Victor Shoup's NTL library [33] in our implementation, where the fast Number Theoretic Transformation (NTT) technique with adapted butterfly operation is applied, for doing polynomial operations as multiplication, division, GCD, factoring and so on. Simultaneously, we use the Discrete Gaussian Sampler (DGS) based on Cumulative Distribution Table (CDT) in [26].

4.1 Experimental Results

Our implementation uses C++ language. We run 100,000 times experiments for each parameter choice on a computer with Intel Xeon E5-2697 v2 @ 2.70 GHz

Table 4. Runtime (millisecond) of our implementation

Security level	TimeDGS	TimePM	TimeKeyPair	TimeP_i	TimeP_j
AES-128	0.05	0.40	0.48	0.92	0.74
AES-192/256	0.09	0.83	1.00	1.90	1.55

CPU, running CentOS Linux release 7.4.1708, g++ version 6.3.0. We evaluate the average runtime for discrete Gaussian sampling (TimeDGS), polynomial multiplication (TimePM), key generation (TimeKeyPair), party i timing (TimeP_i) and party j timing (TimeP_j) respectively. We show the experimental results in Table 4 with two decimal precision.

Rounding, recovering and error reconciliation are extremely efficient. Most expensive ones are discrete Gaussian sampling and polynomial multiplication.

4.2   Communication Cost Comparison

We show the communication cost of our work with several similar RLWE-based key exchange or KEM protocols in Table 5. Our construction has smallest communication cost compared with rest of the RLWE-based protocols. Thus, we believe that our construction provides better trade-off between security and communication cost.

Table 5. Communication cost comparison between several Diffie-Hellman-like key exchange and KEM constructions from RLWE problem

Name	Type	n	q	Claimed security	Public key (Bytes)	Total (Bytes)
This work	DH	512	120833	AES-128 145-bit	832	1744
	DH	1024	120833	AES-192/256 282-bit	1664	3472
BCNS [14]	DH	1024	$2^{32} - 1$	128-bit	4096	8320
NewHope [6]	DH	1024	12289	281-bit	1792	3872
NewHope-Simple [5]	KEM	1024	12289	281-bit	1792	4000
HILA5 [28]	KEM	1024	12289	255-bit	1792	3836

5   Conclusion

It is crucial to build secure and practical post-quantum cryptography primitives for the upcoming post-quantum world. We believe that our new ephemeral-only Diffie-Hellman-like RLWE+Rounding key exchange gives a new solution. We also apply a proper approach to estimate the security of only one RLWE sample, which is closely related to our key exchange protocol design. We also take the overwhelming memory requirement of sieving algorithm into consideration. Our elegant and simple design gives better security and smaller communication cost.

Acknowledgement. Jintai Ding is partially supported by NSF grant DMS-1565748 and US Air Force grant FA2386-17-1-4067. Tsuyoshi Takagi and Yuntao Wang are supported by JST CREST Grant Number JPMJCR14D6 and JSPS KAKENHI Grant Number JP17J01987, Japan. Xinwei Gao is supported by China Scholarship Council.

References

1. Ajtai, M., Kumar, R., Sivakumar, D.: A sieve algorithm for the shortest lattice vector problem. In: Proceedings of the Thirty-Third Annual ACM Symposium on Theory of Computing, STOC 2001, pp. 601–610 (2001)
2. Albrecht, M.R.: On dual lattice attacks against small-secret LWE and parameter choices in HElib and SEAL. In: Coron, J.-S., Nielsen, J.B. (eds.) EUROCRYPT 2017. LNCS, vol. 10211, pp. 103–129. Springer, Cham (2017). https://doi.org/10.1007/978-3-319-56614-6_4
3. Albrecht, M.R., Göpfert, F., Virdia, F., Wunderer, T.: Revisiting the expected cost of solving uSVP and applications to LWE. In: Takagi, T., Peyrin, T. (eds.) ASIACRYPT 2017. LNCS, vol. 10624, pp. 297–322. Springer, Cham (2017). https://doi.org/10.1007/978-3-319-70694-8_11
4. Albrecht, M.R., Player, R., Scott, S.: On the concrete hardness of learning with errors. J. Math. Cryptol. 9(3), 169–203 (2015)
5. Alkim, E., Ducas, L., Pöppelmann, T., Schwabe, P.: NewHope without reconciliation. IACR Cryptology ePrint Archive 2016, 1157 (2016). http://eprint.iacr.org/2016/1157
6. Alkim, E., Ducas, L., Pöppelmann, T., Schwabe, P.: Post-quantum key exchange-a new hope. In: USENIX Security Symposium, pp. 327–343 (2016)
7. Aono, Y., Nguyen, P.Q., Seito, T., Shikata, J.: Lower bounds on lattice enumeration with extreme pruning. In: Shacham, H., Boldyreva, A. (eds.) CRYPTO 2018. LNCS, vol. 10992, pp. 608–637. Springer, Cham (2018). https://doi.org/10.1007/978-3-319-96881-0_21
8. Aono, Y., Wang, Y., Hayashi, T., Takagi, T.: Improved progressive BKZ algorithms and their precise cost estimation by sharp simulator. In: Fischlin, M., Coron, J.-S. (eds.) EUROCRYPT 2016. LNCS, vol. 9665, pp. 789–819. Springer, Heidelberg (2016). https://doi.org/10.1007/978-3-662-49890-3_30
9. Aono, Y., Wang, Y., Hayashi, T., Takagi, T.: The progressive BKZ code (2017). http://www2.nict.go.jp/security/pbkzcode/
10. Bai, S., Galbraith, S.D.: Lattice decoding attacks on binary LWE. In: Susilo, W., Mu, Y. (eds.) ACISP 2014. LNCS, vol. 8544, pp. 322–337. Springer, Cham (2014). https://doi.org/10.1007/978-3-319-08344-5_21
11. Banerjee, A., Peikert, C., Rosen, A.: Pseudorandom functions and lattices. In: Pointcheval, D., Johansson, T. (eds.) EUROCRYPT 2012. LNCS, vol. 7237, pp. 719–737. Springer, Heidelberg (2012). https://doi.org/10.1007/978-3-642-29011-4_42
12. Becker, A., Ducas, L., Gama, N., Laarhoven, T.: New directions in nearest neighbor searching with applications to lattice sieving. In: Proceedings of the Twenty-Seventh Annual ACM-SIAM Symposium on Discrete Algorithms, SODA 2016, pp. 10–24 (2016)
13. Bos, J., et al.: Frodo: take off the ring! practical, quantum-secure key exchange from LWE. In: Proceedings of the 2016 ACM SIGSAC Conference on Computer and Communications Security, pp. 1006–1018. ACM (2016)

14. Bos, J.W., Costello, C., Naehrig, M., Stebila, D.: Post-quantum key exchange for the TLS protocol from the ring learning with errors problem. In: 2015 IEEE Symposium on Security and Privacy (SP), pp. 553–570. IEEE (2015)

15. Bos, J.W., et al.: CRYSTALS - kyber: a CCA-secure module-lattice-based KEM. IACR Cryptology ePrint Archive 2017, 634 (2017). http://eprint.iacr.org/2017/634

16. Bromiley, P.A.: Products and convolutions of Gaussian distributions, vol. 3 (2003)

17. Chen, Y.: Lattice reduction and concrete security of fully homomorphic encryption. Dept. Informatique, ENS, Paris, France, Ph.D. thesis (2013)

18. Chen, Y., Nguyen, P.Q.: BKZ 2.0: better lattice security estimates. In: Lee, D.H., Wang, X. (eds.) ASIACRYPT 2011. LNCS, vol. 7073, pp. 1–20. Springer, Heidelberg (2011). https://doi.org/10.1007/978-3-642-25385-0_1

19. Computer Security Division, Information Technology Laboratory, N.I.O.S., Technology, U.D.O.C.: Post-quantum cryptography—CSRC (2017). https://csrc.nist.gov/projects/post-quantum-cryptography

20. Diffie, W., Hellman, M.: New directions in cryptography. IEEE Trans. Inf. Theory **22**(6), 644–654 (1976)

21. Ding, J., Xie, X., Lin, X.: A simple provably secure key exchange scheme based on the learning with errors problem. IACR Cryptology ePrint Archive 2012, 688 (2012). http://eprint.iacr.org/2012/688

22. Gama, N., Nguyen, P.Q.: Predicting lattice reduction. In: Smart, N. (ed.) EUROCRYPT 2008. LNCS, vol. 4965, pp. 31–51. Springer, Heidelberg (2008). https://doi.org/10.1007/978-3-540-78967-3_3

23. Kannan, R.: Minkowski's convex body theorem and integer programming. Math. Oper. Res. **12**(3), 415–440 (1987)

24. Liu, M., Nguyen, P.Q.: Solving BDD by enumeration: an update. In: Dawson, E. (ed.) CT-RSA 2013. LNCS, vol. 7779, pp. 293–309. Springer, Heidelberg (2013). https://doi.org/10.1007/978-3-642-36095-4_19

25. Lyubashevsky, V., Peikert, C., Regev, O.: On ideal lattices and learning with errors over rings. In: Gilbert, H. (ed.) EUROCRYPT 2010. LNCS, vol. 6110, pp. 1–23. Springer, Heidelberg (2010). https://doi.org/10.1007/978-3-642-13190-5_1

26. Peikert, C.: An efficient and parallel Gaussian sampler for lattices. In: Rabin, T. (ed.) CRYPTO 2010. LNCS, vol. 6223, pp. 80–97. Springer, Heidelberg (2010). https://doi.org/10.1007/978-3-642-14623-7_5

27. Regev, O.: On lattices, learning with errors, random linear codes, and cryptography. J. ACM (JACM) **56**(6), 34 (2009)

28. Saarinen, M.-J.O.: HILA5: On reliability, reconciliation, and error correction for ring-LWE encryption. In: Adams, C., Camenisch, J. (eds.) SAC 2017. LNCS, vol. 10719, pp. 192–212. Springer, Cham (2018). https://doi.org/10.1007/978-3-319-72565-9_10

29. Schmidt, M., Bindel, N.: Estimation of the hardness of the learning with errors problem with a restricted number of samples. IACR Cryptology ePrint Archive 2017, 140 (2017). http://eprint.iacr.org/2017/140

30. Schnorr, C.P., Euchner, M.: Lattice basis reduction: improved practical algorithms and solving subset sum problems. Math. Program. **66**(1), 181–199 (1994)

31. Schnorr, C.P.: Lattice reduction by random sampling and birthday methods. In: Alt, H., Habib, M. (eds.) STACS 2003. LNCS, vol. 2607, pp. 145–156. Springer, Heidelberg (2003). https://doi.org/10.1007/3-540-36494-3_14

32. Shor, P.W.: Polynomial-time algorithms for prime factorization and discrete logarithms on a quantum computer. SIAM Rev. **41**(2), 303–332 (1999)

33. Shoup, V.: NTL, a library for doing number theory (2017). http://www.shoup.net/ntl/

34. Stephens-Davidowitz, N.: Discrete Gaussian sampling reduces to CVP and SVP. In: Proceedings of the Twenty-Seventh Annual ACM-SIAM Symposium on Discrete Algorithms, pp. 1748–1764. Society for Industrial and Applied Mathematics (2016)

35. Wang, W., Wang, Y., Takayasu, A., Takagi, T.: Estimated cost for solving generalized learning with errors problem via embedding techniques. In: Inomata, A., Yasuda, K. (eds.) IWSEC 2018. LNCS, vol. 11049, pp. 87–103. Springer, Cham (2018). https://doi.org/10.1007/978-3-319-97916-8_6

36. Wang, Y., Aono, Y., Takagi, T.: An experimental study of Kannan's embedding technique for the search LWE problem. In: Qing, S., Mitchell, C., Chen, L., Liu, D. (eds.) ICICS 2017. LNCS, vol. 10631, pp. 541–553. Springer, Cham (2018). https://doi.org/10.1007/978-3-319-89500-0_47

37. Wang, Y., Aono, Y., Takagi, T.: Hardness evaluation for search LWE problem using progressive BKZ simulator. IEICE Trans. **101–A**(12), 2162–2170 (2018)

38. Wang, Y., Takagi, T.: Improving the BKZ reduction algorithm by quick reordering technique. In: Susilo, W., Yang, G. (eds.) ACISP 2018. LNCS, vol. 10946, pp. 787–795. Springer, Cham (2018). https://doi.org/10.1007/978-3-319-93638-3_47

39. Wang, Y., Wunderer, T.: Revisiting the sparsification technique in Kannan's embedding attack on LWE. In: Su, C., Kikuchi, H. (eds.) ISPEC 2018. LNCS, vol. 11125, pp. 440–452. Springer, Cham (2018). https://doi.org/10.1007/978-3-319-99807-7_27

Masking Dilithium

Efficient Implementation and Side-Channel Evaluation

Vincent Migliore[1], Benoît Gérard[2,3(✉)], Mehdi Tibouchi[4],
and Pierre-Alain Fouque[2]

[1] LAAS–CNRS, Univ. Toulouse, CNRS, INSA, Toulouse, France
vincent.migliore@laas.fr
[2] Univ. Rennes, CNRS, IRISA, Rennes, France
{benoit.gerard,pierre-alain.fouque}@irisa.fr
[3] Direction Générale de l'Armement, Bruz, France
[4] NTT Corporation, Musashino, Japan
mehdi.tibouchi.br@hco.ntt.co.jp

Abstract. Although security against side-channel attacks is not an explicit design criterion of the NIST post-quantum standardization effort, it is certainly a major concern for schemes that are meant for real-world deployment. In view of the numerous physical attacks that have been proposed against post-quantum schemes in recent literature, it is in particular very important to evaluate the cost and effectiveness of side-channel countermeasures in that setting.

For lattice-based signatures, this work was initiated by Barthe et al., who showed at EUROCRYPT 2018 how to apply arbitrary order masking to the GLP signature scheme presented at CHES 2012 by Güneysu, Lyubashevsky and Pöppelman. However, although Barthe et al.'s paper provides detailed proofs of security in the probing model of Ishai, Sahai and Wagner, it does not include practical side-channel evaluations, and its proof-of-concept implementation has limited efficiency. Moreover, the GLP scheme has historical significance but is not a NIST candidate, nor is it being considered for concrete deployment.

In this paper, we look instead at Dilithium, one of the most promising NIST candidates for postquantum signatures. This scheme, presented at CHES 2018 by Ducas et al. and based on module lattices, can be seen as an updated variant of both GLP and its more efficient sibling BLISS; it comes with an implementation that is both efficient and constant-time.

Our analysis of Dilithium from a side-channel perspective is three-fold. We first evaluate the side-channel resistance of an ARM Cortex-M3 implementation of Dilithium without masking, and identify exploitable side-channel leakage. We then describe how to securely mask the scheme, and verify that the masked implementation no longer leaks. Finally, we show how a simple tweak to Dilithium (namely, replacing the prime modulus by a power of two) makes it possible to obtain a considerably more efficient masked scheme, by a factor of 7.3 to 9 for the most time-consuming masking operations, without affecting security.

© Springer Nature Switzerland AG 2019
R. H. Deng et al. (Eds.): ACNS 2019, LNCS 11464, pp. 344–362, 2019.
https://doi.org/10.1007/978-3-030-21568-2_17

1   Introduction

Post-quantum Cryptography and Lattice-Based Signatures. As the threat of quantum computers becomes increasingly concrete, the need for public-key cryptography to transition away from legacy schemes based on factoring and discrete logarithms and towards post-quantum secure primitives gets more pressing. In particular, there is a growing push to make post-quantum cryptography, which was of somewhat theoretical interest for some time, ready for real-world deployment. At the forefront of that push is NIST's post-quantum standardization process [1], which aims at selecting post-quantum secure schemes for encryption and signatures that can practically replace RSA and elliptic curve cryptography. The first round includes 69 candidates across encryption and signatures, based on codes, lattices, multivariate cryptography, hash functions and more.

Among them, lattice-based schemes stand out as particularly attractive, thanks to their strong security foundations and their high level of efficiency, often comparable to RSA and elliptic curves both in terms of key and ciphertext/signature size, and of computational complexity. However, they present a unique set of challenges from an implementation perspective, due to the reliance on new types of operations such as Gaussian sampling, polynomial arithmetic, number-theoretic transforms and rejection sampling.

Such new operations are a concern, in particular, from the standpoint of fault and side-channel analysis. A number of implementation attacks have been proposed against lattice-based schemes, including fault attacks [4, 11], cold boot attacks [2], cache timing attacks [13,18] and more standard power/electromagnetic analysis [12], taking advantage of vulnerabilities of the implementation of those new operations in order to mount key recovery attacks. Lattice-based signatures have notably been the target of multiple such attacks. It is therefore of prime importance to study how to securely and efficiently protect implementations against those attacks.

Masking Lattice-Based Signatures. Regarding side-channels, a generic and provable countermeasure is known: masking, in which all sensitive variables in the signing algorithm is stored and processed as several shares, typically using some linear secret sharing scheme. The two most common approaches are *boolean masking*, where a secret bitstring x is represented as the bitwise XOR $x = x_1 \oplus \cdots \oplus x_t$ of uniformly random shares x_i's, and *arithmetic masking*, where a secret element x of $\mathbb{Z}/m\mathbb{Z}$ is represented as the sum $x = x_1 + \cdots + x_t$ modulo m of uniformly random elements of $\mathbb{Z}/m\mathbb{Z}$. Boolean masking is better suited to mask logical operations, whereas arithmetic masking is convenient for operations than can be represented in a simple way as arithmetic circuits (i.e., multivariate polynomials modulo m).

Applying masking countermeasures to lattice-based signatures is a challenging task, mainly due to the overall structure of the corresponding signing algorithm, which typically involve sampling some sensitive randomness, combining it with the secret key, and then carrying out some form of rejection sampling on the resulting value. The random sampling and rejection sampling are complicated operations which are better suited for boolean masking, whereas the main part of the signing algorithm involving the secret key is linear modulo some prime p, and therefore convenient for arithmetic masking. Protecting the entire algorithm therefore requires conversions between arithmetic and boolean masking, targeted unmasking of provably non-sensitive variables, and the design of novel masked gadgets to support the new sampling and rejection operations.

This was all first tackled recently by Barthe et al. [3] in a EUROCRYPT 2018 paper providing a complete, arbitrary order masking of the (relatively simple) lattice-based signature scheme of Güneysu, Lyubashevsky and Pöppelman (GLP). The paper addresses all the issues above in the case of GLP to construct a provably secure masked implementation of the key generation and signing algorithms of GLP. It suffers from several limitations, however. First, the GLP scheme itself has the advantage of being relatively simple compared to later lattice-based signatures like BLISS and the current NIST candidates, but it is of limited practical relevance, due to a level of efficiency that falls short of the state of the art, and more lax security guarantees. Second, the masked implementation of Barthe et al. incurs a rather severe overhead compared to the (already not that efficient) unmasked scheme. And finally, although the paper comes with security proofs, it does not include a practical side-channel evaluation: this can be a problem in practice due to discrepancies between formal specifications and compiled code, unexpected data dependencies introduced at the CPU-level, and other hardware issues like glitches.

Our Contributions. As a result, it is desirable to consider the application of the masking countermeasure to a more up-to-date lattice-based signature scheme (preferably a NIST candidate), hopefully achieving better performance than the masked implementation of Barthe et al., and with a concrete validation of side-channel resistance.

This is the goal pursued in this work, where we examine in particular the Dilithium signature scheme of Ducas et al. [10], a NIST candidate that can be seen as a descendant of both GLP and BLISS. It comes with an implementation that emphasizes both efficiency and constant running time (so as to achieve security against timing attacks and simple power analysis). In particular, like GLP but unlike BLISS, its main variant excludes Gaussian distribution and only relies on random numbers that are sampled uniformly from small intervals.

Our main contributions are as follows:

1. we carry out a side-channel evaluation of the reference design of Dilithium when implemented on an ARM Cortex-M3 micro-controller (the STM32F1), and identify exploitable side-channel leakage, which underscores the need for suitable countermeasures;
2. we propose an efficient masking of Dilithium at any order, partially leveraging the work carried out by Barthe et al. on GLP (in particular, we reuse their formally verified masked gadgets);

3. we describe a simple variant of Dilithium that lends itself to a considerably more efficient masking while preserving security, using the key idea of switching from a prime modulus to a power of two[1];
4. we implement these masked schemes on the same ARM Cortex-M3 microcontroller, we manage to remove unexpected leakages due to some microarchitectural features and evaluate both the efficiency and side-channel resistance of the implementation, with satisfactory results on both counts.

The paper is organized as follows. Section 2 recalls the key generation and the signing algorithms of Dilithium. Section 3 evaluates the side-channel leakage of sensitive operations on our STM32F1 target micro-controller. Section 4 proposes an efficient masking of the Dilithium reference design, as well as that of our proposed variant (using a power-of-two modulus) which greatly improves masking efficiency. Section 5 provides implementation results, both in terms of performance and of side-channel resistance.

2   The Dilithium Signature Scheme

Dilithium is a signature scheme based on Lyubashevsky's Fiat–Shamir with aborts framework and is based on hard problems in module lattices. Its core functions are *KeyGen* for the key generation, *Sign* to produce a signature of a message, and *Verify* to verify the signature.

One of the main features of Dilithium (aside from its module lattice approach) is the key compression mechanism to reduce public key size. The compression is performed at two different levels. First, Module matrices are constructed with an extendable output function (XOF), which generates a (deterministic) pseudorandom string from a small seed. Thus, the public only requires the seed and not the full matrix. Second, the public key size is reduced using a truncation on its second component. This truncation is performed coefficient-wise and is associated to an error-correcting code mechanism to recover truncated bits[2].

In addition, Dilithium does not instantiate Module with discrete Gaussian sampling, but with bounded coefficients. This approach greatly simplifies the arithmetic of Dilithium (and at the same time masking) since discrete Gaussian sampling is much more complex than a simple bound check.

In this paper, we mainly focus on the key generation and the signature generation algorithms (which will respectively be called DILITHIUM.KeyGen and DILITHIUM.Sign) since the verification algorithm does not handle sensitive data and hence does not require masking.

DILITHIUM.KeyGen. The DILITHIUM.KeyGen algorithm, described in Algorithm 1, generates the secret key S_{key} and public key P_{key} required to respectively sign and verify a message.

---

[1] This statement is discussed later on in Sect. 4.4.
[2] For a formal description of the different truncation procedures used in Dilithium (namely $Decompose_q$, $HighBits_q$, $LowBits_q$ and Power2Round) the reader can refer to the original Dilithium paper [9].

Algorithm 1. DILITHIUM.KeyGen()

1: $\rho, \rho' \leftarrow \{0,1\}^{256}$
2: $A\ \ =\ \mathrm{Sam}(\rho)$ $\in R_q^{k \times \ell}$
3: $(S_1, S_2) = \mathrm{Sam}(\rho')$ $\in R_\eta^{\ell \times 1} \times R_\eta^{k \times 1}$
4: $T\ \ =\ A \cdot S_1 + S_2$ $\in R_q^{k \times 1}$
5: $T_1\ \ =\ \mathrm{Power2Round}(T, d) \in R_q^{k \times 1}$
6: $P_{key} = (\rho, T_1)$
7: $S_{key} = (\rho', S_1, S_2, T)$
8: return (P_{key}, S_{key})

The randomness is obtained using an extendable output function (XOF) called Sam which takes a random seed as input and returns an extendable pseudo-random string. The Sam function is used to compute the matrix A (which is part of the public key) and matrices (S_1, S_2) (which are part of the secret key). Unlike coefficients of A, the coefficients of S_1 and S_2 are *small* ones.

Regarding arithmetic complexity, the Sam function and the polynomial multiplication line 4 are the most time-consuming part of the computation. For the implementation provided for the NIST competition, the Sam function is implemented using SHAKE-256, and polynomial multiplications with NTT algorithm.

DILITHIUM.Sign. The DILITHIUM.Sign algorithm is described in Algorithm 2. It is constructed by a rejection sampling loop where a fresh signature is generated until it satisfies some security properties. First of all, a uniformly sampled matrix Y in $R_{\gamma_1 - 1}$ is secretly generated, and multiplied by the public value A to produce W (lines 6 and 7). Then a challenge $C \in B_{60}$ is generated as the output of a hash function H with (ρ, T_1, W_1, μ) as input, where W_1 is composed by the high order bits of W and μ is the message to sign.

Algorithm 2. DILITHIUM.Sign(S_{key}, μ)

1: $A\ \ =\ \mathrm{Sam}(\rho)$ $\in R_q^{k \times \ell}$
2: $T_1 = \mathrm{Power2Round}(T, d) \in R_q^{k \times 1}$
3: $T_0 = T - T_1 \cdot 2^d$ $\in R_q^{k \times 1}$
Rejection sampling loop
4: $\rho'' \leftarrow \{0,1\}^{256}$
5: $Y\ \ =\ \mathrm{Sam}(\rho'')$ $\in R_{\gamma_1 - 1}^{\ell \times 1}$
6: $W\ =\ A \cdot Y$ $\in R_q^{k \times 1}$
7: $W_1 = \mathrm{HighBits}_{q, 2\gamma_2}(W) \in R_q^{k \times 1}$
8: $C\ \ =\ \mathrm{H}(\rho, T_1, W_1, \mu)$ $\in \{0,1\}^{256}$
9: $Z\ \ =\ Y + CS_1$ $\in R_q^{\ell \times 1}$
10: $R_0 = \mathrm{LowBits}_{q, 2\gamma_2}(W - CS_2)$
11: if $||Z||_\infty \geq \gamma_1 - \beta$ or $||R_0||_\infty \geq \gamma_2 - \beta$ or $||CT_0||_\infty \geq \gamma_2$ goto 4
12: $H = \mathrm{MakeHint}_{q, 2\gamma_2}(-CT_0, W - CS_2 + CT_0)$
13: return (Z, H, C)

To ensure that the signature does not leak information about the key, line 11 executes some bound checks. If this verification fails, a new signature is generated. One of the most important parameter is β, because it will determine the number of rounds required before a valid signature is produced. For recommended parameters, an average of 5 rounds are needed before producing a good set of parameters. Eventually, the $MakeHint_{q,2\gamma_2}$ procedure line 12 will generate some hints for the public key reconstruction (bits are due to its truncation.).

3   Side-Channel Evaluation of Unmasked Dilithium

In this section we report the results we obtained evaluating the potential side-channel weaknesses of an unprotected implementation of Dilithium. We performed Welch's t-test to localize potential leakages and single-bit DPA on secret variables to confirm that actually correspond to exploitable leakages.

Operation Choice Motivation. We limited the unprotected-case study to three operations namely, the rejection, $LowBits_{q,2\gamma_2}$ and $HighBits_{q,2\gamma_2}$. We detail now the motivations that led to this choice.

The rejection is one of the most critical operations as it is both used for secret data generation and for rejection sampling during the signature computation. A successful attack on the rejection will leak information on S_1, S_2 during the key generation, on Y during the signature or on a rejected Z (which leaks information about S_1 as stated by the designers). Regarding decomposition operations, $LowBits_{q,2\gamma_2}(W - C \cdot S_2)$ in line 10 of Algorithm 2 and $HighBits_{q,2\gamma_2}$ which is part of the computation of $MakeHint_{q,2\gamma_2}(-CT_0, W - CS_2 + CT_0)$ (line 12) have been chosen because $W - C \cdot S_2$ is a sensitive variable since, together with the public value, Z it would allow the attacker to recover the secret key T.

We did not studied the Sam function. Although it is a good candidate for an attack as it is used to generate S_1, S_2 and Y, its actual implementation can vary from a Dilithium implementation to another. Indeed, designers of Dilithium state that *different implementations are free to use whichever pseudo-random generator is offering the best performance and security on their respective platform.* The situation is similar for the random oracle H as its actual implementation from the NIST submission relies on SHAKE256 what is not mandatory. Studying the resistance of these primitives is indeed of great importance before deploying a solution but is out of the scope of this paper where we aim at considering intrinsic security properties of DILITHIUM.

Note that the polynomial multiplications used to compute $T = A \cdot S_1 + S_2$ during the key generation (line 4 of Algorithm 1) and $W = A \cdot Y$ during the signature is also a sensitive step of the algorithm. Since this classical operation has already been shown to be sensitive to side-channel attacks and is easy to mask (due to its linearity) we did not evaluate its unprotected version.

Experimental Setup and Methodology. Our workbench were composed of an STM32F1 micro-controller from a discovery platform (referred as the DUT in the rest of the section) running sensitive operations, an H 2.5-2 near-field probe

coupled with a 20dB pre-amplifier to measure electromagnetic leaks, an instru-
mented RTO2014 oscilloscope from Rohde & Schwarz (with 1 GHz bandwidth)
to capture traces and a desktop computer for performing trace analysis.

The oscilloscope was configured with a sample rate ensuring 8 samples per
DUT clock cycle (that is a bit more than 160 MHz). The data was sent to the
DUT through a serial connection, then before the computation a trigger helped
the synchronization of the oscilloscope and the DUT (using a GPIO pin of the
board). A python script was used to perform t-test and DPA on the captured
traces. For the t-test we used the fixed vs random approach and took care of
randomly mix requests from both populations. The single-bit DPA has been
performed on each bit of the sensitive data in the input of the target operations.

Evaluation Results. We present here the results obtained. For the t-test
(Fig. 1), the threshold use is the classical 4.5 one (red lines).

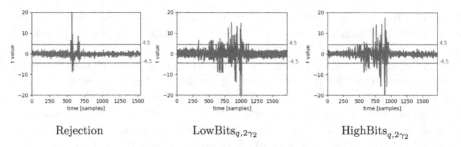

Fig. 1. T-Test evaluation for targeted operations (using 500 traces). (Color figure
online)

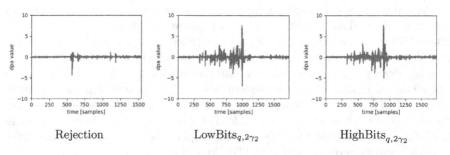

Fig. 2. Single-bit DPA curves on bit 0 of sensitive data (using 5000 traces).

As can be seen in Fig. 1, basic implementation are highly leaking (we observe
clear peaks using only 500 traces). In all cases, we confirmed the threat induced
by those leakages by computing single-bit DPA curves for all sensitive inputs.
Results can be seen in Fig. 2 and show that t-test peaks are actual leakages. We
obtain similar results for other target bits even if for some bits the signal has a
smaller magnitude.

Note that the point is to consider the presence of exploitable first order leakages in the sense that they provide information about sensitive variables. We do not claim any attack here. The exploitation of these leakages to recover any secret is out of the scope of the paper but our experiments show that a lot of information is available.

4 Masking Dilithium

Results of Sect. 3 confirm that an attacker having a physical access to a device can easily perform a side-channel key-recovery on a standard Dilithium implementation. In this section, we propose some guidelines to efficiently protect the Dilithium algorithm.

First, we provide some information about the leakage model adopted for the determination of masking operations. Second, we present a high-level strategy for masking. Third, we detail the implementation of secured operations.

4.1 Leakage Model

The first introduced side-channel security model was the noisy leakage model in which the attacker obtains sensitive information mixed with noise [5,19]. The main limitation of this approach is the deep knowledge of the noise it requires which is strongly device-dependent.

A more generic approach is the probing model [14]. In the t-probing model, the attacker observes t intermediate noise-free variables of the algorithm (as if she was directly probing the bus). In [8], a reduction have been obtained proving that security in the t-probing model implies security in the noisy leakage one.

This last model is the one to consider in the case a designer wants to totally remove leakages up to a given order. To achieve probing security, operations on secret variables are computed over shared values, i.e. variables which are split into shares containing partial information of the initial variable mixed with noise. Masking variables at order d requires at least $d+1$ shares. The threshold probing model introduces the notion of t-probing secure gadget.

Definition 1. *A circuit G is a t-probing secure gadget if and only if every tuple composed of t of its intermediate variables is independent from any sensitive variables it manipulates.*

In the following, we expose our masking strategy and describe the secure gadgets used for our implementation.

4.2 Presentation of the Masked Key Generation and Signature

We provide here design considerations on securing DILITHIUM.Keygen and DILITHIUM.Sign in the t-probing model. The sensitive operations performed are of different natures which implies using both arithmetic and Boolean masking.

In the following, we help the reader by disambiguating the used masking using the prefixes `arith::` for arithmetic (the sensitive variable is the sum of the shares) and `bool::` for Boolean masked operations (the sensitive variable is the exclusive or of the shares).

Masking of DILITHIUM.Keygen. Basically, DILITHIUM.KeyGen can be split into 3 phases: the sampling of uniform matrices A, S_1 and S_2; the computation of $T = A \cdot S_1 + S_2$; and the computation of high-order bits of T using the PowerToRound function. Variables S_1 and S_2 are clearly sensitive data because they are part of the secret key what is not the case of variable $T = A \cdot S_1 + S_2$ since it is part of the public key. Consequently, only lines 3 and 4 of Algorithm 1 require masking, i.e. the sampling of S_1 and S_2, usage of these secrets in the computation of T and the secured reconstruction of T. The high-level description of the masked version of DILITHIUM.Keygen is proposed in Fig. 3.

The first masked operation is `arith::generate` which provides a secured uniform sampling algorithm within a given bound. The choice of arithmetic masking will ease the following computations: the multiplication of A with masked S_1 can be performed independently on each share of S_1 due to the linearity of the operation with respect to the masking. The second masked operation is `arith::unmask` which securely reconstructs an integer from its shares.

Masking of DILITHIUM.Sign. The most sensitive data used in the signature is Y because it is directly linked with the secret S_2 by the equation $Z = Y + C \cdot S_1$. Since both Z and C are public when a valid signature is produced, the attacker just need to solve a linear system of equations to extract S_2. Variable Z is also critical because in case of a rejection, Z leaks partial information about the secret S_1 as stated in the original security proof of Dilithium. Thus, intermediate Z must be protected. Function H however does not need to be protected. Its inputs ρ, T_1, μ and its output C are public and W_1 is not sensitive (W_1 is reconstructed from public data in the signature verification).

In Fig. 4, we present the masked version of DILITHIUM.Sign. Additional gadgets must be introduced namely:

- **arith::to::bool::lowbits** which securely computes the LowBits$_{q,2\gamma_2}$ from arithmetic masked shares, and provides the result as boolean masked shares;

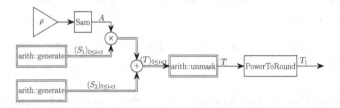

Fig. 3. Masked implementation of DILITHIUM.Keygen. Masked functions are represented with a double lined box.

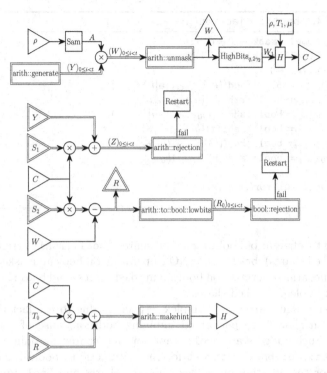

Fig. 4. Masked implementation of DILITHIUM.Sign. Masked functions are represented with a double-lined box.

- **arith::rejection** and **bool::rejection** which check if the infinity norm of polynomial A is below a constant β for respectively arithmetic and boolean masked shares;
- **arith::makehint** which securely performs the $\text{MakeHint}_{q,2\gamma_2}$ operation on arithmetic masked inputs and returns an unmasked value.

4.3 Description of Secured Gadgets of Dilithium with Prime Modulus

In this section, we provide the description of the different masked gadgets for Dilithium with prime modulus. The decomposition and the MakeHint_q operations are newly introduced gadget while others were introduced in [3].

4.3.1 Description of Standard Gadgets. Gadgets are basically split into to categories: linear and non-linear gadgets. Algorithmic definitions of non-linear gadgets can be found in the full version of this paper [17].

Linear gadgets can be straightforwardly masked as they are implemented by applying the related instruction separately on each share. Linear gadgets used for the masking of Dilithium are `arith::add` (addition of arithmetic masked shares),

---

Algorithm 3. $\texttt{bool::rejection}((\mathbf{a})_{0 \leq i < t}, \text{len}, \beta)$

1: $(k_0)_{0 \leq i < t} \Leftarrow \texttt{bool::mask}(-\beta - 1)$
2: $(k_1)_{0 \leq i < t} \Leftarrow \texttt{bool::mask}(q - \beta - 1)$
3: for i in 0 to $len - 1$
4:       $(b_0)_{0 \leq i < t} \Leftarrow \texttt{bool::add}((k_0)_{0 \leq i < t}, (\mathbf{a}[i])_{0 \leq i < t})$
5:       $(b_0)_{0 \leq i < t} \Leftarrow \texttt{bool::rshift}((b_0)_{0 \leq i < t}, 31)$
6:       $(b_1)_{0 \leq i < t} \Leftarrow \texttt{bool::add}((k_1)_{0 \leq i < t}, (\mathbf{a}[i])_{0 \leq i < t})$
7:       $(b_1)_{0 \leq i < t} \Leftarrow \texttt{bool::rshift}((b_1)_{0 \leq i < t}, 31)$
8:       $(b_0)_{0 \leq i < t} \Leftarrow \texttt{bool::xor}((b_0)_{0 \leq i < t}, (b_1)_{0 \leq i < t})$
9:       $(r)_{0 \leq i < t} = \texttt{bool::and}((r)_{0 \leq i < t}, (b_0)_{0 \leq i < t})$
10: end for
11: return $\texttt{bool::fullxor}((r)_{0 \leq i < t})$

$\texttt{bool::lshift}$ (left shift of boolean masked shares), $\texttt{bool::rshift}$ (right shift of boolean masked shares), $\texttt{bool::not}$ (NOT operation on boolean masked shares), $\texttt{bool::neg}$ (negation operation on boolean masked shares) and $\texttt{bool::xor}$ (XOR operation on boolean masked shares).

Non-linear gadgets are more complex, especially due to the fact that operations between shares are performed implying additional use of randomness (refreshing). Such gadgets are $\texttt{bool::mask}$ for the secured masking of a given integer, $\texttt{arith::to::bool::convert}$ for the arithmetic to boolean conversion, $\texttt{bool::add}$ for the addition on boolean masked shares and $\texttt{bool::and}$ for the AND operation on boolean masked shares. These standard gadgets are not a contribution of this paper: for the reader's convenience, a description is given in the full version of this paper [17].

4.3.2 Description of arith::generate. The $\texttt{arith::generate}$ gadget generates uniformly sampled integers in a given interval. For the non-masked version of Dilithium, this operation is performed in two steps: a first step which uses the XOF function Sam to generate random values; and a second step which checks that the coefficient lies in the target interval and rejects it if not. As stated before, we did not considered the Sam function since the used algorithm may depend on the developers' choice. Since the processing of the generation is analogous to Algorithm 15 of [3] we did not provide full details in these proceedings, but a description can be found in the full version of this paper [17].

4.3.3 Description of arith::rejection and bool::rejection. The gadget performing the rejection operation on a vector of boolean masked shares called $\texttt{bool::rejection}$ is presented in Algorithm 3. For coefficient a, bound β and modulo q, the algorithm checks if $\beta \leq a \leq q - \beta$. The algorithm is constructed by a loop which iterates on all masked coefficients, and evaluates if any coefficient is out of bound by checking both lower and higher bounds.

To do so, the two bound checks are performed by subtracting the given bound to the coefficient and checking the sign bit. It is a similar approach to

Algorithm 4. `arith:makeint`$((r)_{0\leq i<t}, (z)_{0\leq i<t}, \beta)$. Masked algorithm of MakeHint$_{q,2\gamma_2}$ with a prime modulus q. w is the word base (usually 32 or 64).

1: $(r_1)_{0\leq i<t} \gets$ `arith::to::bool::highbits`$((r)_{0\leq i<t}, \beta)$
2: $(a)_{0\leq i<t} =$ `arith::addmodq`$((r)_{0\leq i<t}, (z)_{0\leq i<t})$
3: $(a_1)_{0\leq i<t} \gets$ `arith::to::bool::highbits`$((a)_{0\leq i<t}, \beta)$
4: $(t)_{0\leq i<t} =$ `bool::xor`$((r_1)_{0\leq i<t}, (a_1)_{0\leq i<t})$
6: return `bool::fullxor`$((t)_{0\leq i<t}) \gg (w-1)$

`arith::generate` at the except that during generation, we only need to check one bound (namely $2 \cdot \beta$) and shift the result by $-\beta$.

The gadget `arith::rejection` is simply implemented as the composition of `arith::to::bool:convert` and `bool::rejection`.

4.3.4 Description of Decomposition Operations.

Decomposition operations are by far the most complex operations regarding masking. The cornerstone is the function Decompose$_{q,2\gamma_2}$ which takes an integer r as input and returns (r_0, r_1) such that $r = 2r_1\gamma_2 + r_0$. The value r_0 (reps. r_1) is precisely LowBits$_{q,2\gamma_2}(r)$ (resp. HighBits$_{q,2\gamma_2}(r)$). Both functions are actually computed using a call to Decompose$_{q,2\gamma_2}$ then returning the relevant part of r since no relevant optimization can be made when only one of the r_i's is needed.

To illustrate the complexity of this computation, a constant time implementation of Decompose$_{q,2\gamma_2}$ is provided in the full version of this paper [17]. This algorithm leverages the specific form of both the modulus q and the base used to perform the Euclidean division so that only some shifts and integer additions are used. However, even with these optimizations, Decompose$_{q,2\gamma_2}$ requires numerous non-linear operations (addition of Boolean shares or Boolean AND). The masked version of Decompose$_{q,2\gamma_2}$ is also provided in the full version of this paper [17].

4.3.5 Description of arith::makehint.

The computation of MakeHint$_{q,2\gamma_2}$ strongly relies on decomposition gadgets thus its masking is straightforward as soon as there exists a masked version of HighBits$_{q,2\gamma_2}$. The masked algorithm for computing MakeHint$_{q,2\gamma_2}$ is proposed in Algorithm 4.

4.4 Optimization of Dilithium Masking for Power of Two Modulus

The main drawback of the prime modulus used in the standard version of Dilithium is the number of non-linear operations required during decomposition operations. As an example, the computation of LowBits$_{q,2\gamma_2}(W - C \cdot S_2)$ in line 10 of Algorithm 2 requires 12,288 `bool::add` and 4,608 `bool::and` operations.

The choice of a prime modulus q of a specific form is mainly made for efficiency reasons, as it makes number-theoretic transform (NTT)-based polynomial multiplications possible. However, when it comes to the masked scheme, using a

---

Algorithm 5. arith::generate(β). Generates an uniformly sampled integer in the bounds $[-\beta, +\beta]$.

1: mask $= 1 << (\text{NumberOfBits}(\beta) + 1) - 1$
2: do
3:        for i in 0 to $t - 1$
4:                $(x)_i$ $= \text{rand}() \wedge \text{mask}$
5:        end for
6:        $(x)_0$ $= (x)_0 - 2 \cdot \beta - 1$
7:        $(b)_{0 \leq i < t} = \text{arith::to::bool::convert}((x)_{0 \leq i < t})$
8: while $\text{bool::recompose}((b)_{0 \leq i < t}) = 0$
9:        $(x)_0$ $= (x)_0 + \beta + 1$
10: return $(x)_{0 \leq i < t}$

---

power of two modulus q instead speeds up almost all masked gadgets and greatly simplifies the masking of $\text{Decompose}_{q, 2\gamma_2}$. Polynomial multiplications then have to be carried out using non-Fourier techniques like Karatsuba, but such techniques turn out to be quite competitive for the parameters of Dilithium.

From a security standpoint, one expects the security level of Dilithium using a power-of-two modulus to be essentially the same as that of the original prime modulus scheme. Indeed, the asymptotic security arguments for the underlying lattice problems Module-LWE and Module-SIS are known to hold for moduli of an arbitrary arithmetic form. This was established by Langlois and Stehlé in their paper on worst-case to average-case reductions for module lattices [15], specifically as Theorem 3.6 for Module-SIS, and Theorem 4.8 (using a modulus switching argument) for Module-LWE. In addition, while in practice parameters are set to match the best concrete lattice attacks on the scheme rather than using security reductions, using a power-of-two modulus does not appear to make any known concrete attack faster compared to the prime modulus case. We also note that power-of-two moduli are commonly used by designers of practice-oriented lattice-based constructions, including the NIST-submitted encryption scheme Saber [7].

Consequently, we propose this power-of-two variant of Dilithium as a relevant alternative insofar as side-channel resistance is a concern.

4.4.1 Simplification of arith::generate. The new arith::generate is proposed in Algorithm 5. As q is a power of two, and due to the fact that computer units perform two's complement arithmetic, the integer modular reduction after the rejection sampling can be skipped. Moreover, even if the size of the modulus is different from the computer base arithmetic (usually 32-bit of 64-bit), the modular reduction is almost a truncation of high-order bits so we do not need to take into account modular reduction during intermediate computations.

We also found that for the power of two case, it is faster to generate input random integers with arithmetic masked shares (see Sect. 5). It is not a trivial

---

Algorithm 6. $\text{Decompose}_{q,2\gamma_2}(r)$.

Parameters: b such that $2^b = 2\gamma_2$ and w the processor word size.

1: m $= (1 \ll b) - 1$
2: d $= 1 \ll (b-1)$

Computation of r_0

3: r_0 $= r \ll (w - b)$
4: m_0 $= \text{MaskFromSign}(r_0)$
5: m_0 $= m_0 \ll b$
6: r_0 $= r_0 \gg (w - b)$
7: r_0 $= r_0 \oplus m_0$

Computation of r_1

8: r_1 $= (r + d) \gg b$
9: return (r_0, r_1)

---

result because the bound check loop now requires a conversion from arithmetic to boolean masking, and this operation is known to be expensive.

4.4.2 Adaptation of bool::rejection. The bool::rejection operation is almost unchanged. The only difference is the fact that because the integer modular reduction with a power of two modulus is a truncation of high order bits, the implementation of the rejection sampling does not require the exact exponent of the modulus q (see the full version of this paper [17]).

4.4.3 Simplification of Decomposition Operations. In the Dilithium specification, the decomposition operations are performed in base $2\gamma_2 = \gamma_1 = (q-1)/16$ ($q-1$ is divisible by 16). Using q a power of two, we have to decompose using a base $2\gamma_2 = 2^b$. Therefore, the decomposition operations become straightforward and are close to a truncation (at the except that the remainder must be zero centered).

Algorithm 6 provides the new constant time implementation of $\text{Decompose}_{q,2\gamma_2}$ with a power of two modulus q (hence a power of two base). As one can see, it is now possible to separate computations of the low order bits and high order bits. This is directly correlated with the fact that q is divisible by 16 (and not $q - 1$) so there is no need to check the border case where $r - r_0 = q - 1$.

An explanation of Algorithm 6 is provided in the full version of this paper [17]. The masked versions of $\text{LowBits}_{q,2\gamma_2}$ (referred as arith::to::bool::lowbits), $\text{HighBits}_{q,2\gamma_2}$ (referred as arith::to::bool::highbits) and $\text{MakeHint}_{q,2\gamma_2}$ (referred as arith::makehint) are presented in the full version of this paper [17] as well.

5 Implementation Results

In this section, we provide details on the implementation of masking for Dilithium, along with execution times and a side-channel leakage evaluation.

The followed approach is similar to the one used for the evaluation of the unprotected implementation in Sect. 3.

5.1   Challenges of the Masked Implementation

We faced several challenges for the implementation of side channel countermeasures on the ARM Cortex-M3.

The first challenge was the complexity of masking itself. Top level Dilithium gadgets are constructed by calls of common sub-gadgets (which are also possibly large ones). Thus, inlining all procedures were not a relevant approach. Instead, we have evaluated the trade-off between function calls and inlining to reduce memory footprint with a limited impact on performances.

The second challenge was the limitation of the processor micro-architecture. Even with a program following the theoretical t-probing model, the processor micro-architecture itself can possibly leak additional information not covered by the initial model. In the case of the ARM Cortex-M3 micro-architecture, such sensitive components are intermediate registers r_a and r_b which are located between standard registers and arithmetic units (and thus not directly accessible). These registers are not erased between instructions and consequently they leak the transient state of successively manipulated values. Our first implementation in C was actually subject to such leakages and turned out to be unsafe. Thus, we implemented the library in assembly language to control the scheduling of instructions thus overcoming this phenomenon. In addition, since Dilithium gadgets are composed of function calls, we adapted calls to only manipulate addresses of sensitive data instead of the data itself.

A third issue was the complexity of tracking leaky instructions. We first directly evaluated real traces captured with our workbench. However, this approach is time consuming due to trace acquisition and processing. Moreover, the correspondence between timing and assembly instructions is not trivial due to pipelining (it is tractable but takes a lot of time if not automatized). Our final approach was the exploitation of ARM simulators that also evaluate side-channel leakages. We evaluated two of the most recent ones: ELMO [16] and MAPS [6]. Each simulator has some idiosyncrasies but for both, the main idea is to simulate the number of bit flips during computations as it is directly correlated to the power consumption. At the time of our experiments, ELMO was only supporting the ARM Cortex-M0 while MAPS was only supporting Cortex-M3. We discuss the relevance of both tools for our particular needs in the full version of this paper [17]. To take into account the optimization provided by the Cortex-M3, we finally based our simulations on MAPS and brought some modifications to its core to manage some specific instructions.

5.2   Evaluation of Execution Times

We focused on the most costly masked operations of Dilithium and calculated computation times for both power of two and prime arithmetic. In particular,

Table 1. Execution times of main gadgets for both prime and power of two modulus q on STM32F1 (order-1 masking, computation on 1 coefficient).

	$q = 8380417$	$q = 2^{23}$	speedup
arith::to::bool::lowbits	331 μs/7,944 cycles	38 μs/912 cycles	8
arith::to::bool::highbits	275 μs/6,600 cycles	37 μs/888 cycles	7
arith::makehint	560 μs/13,440 cycles	79 μs/1,896 cycles	7
bool::rejection	66 μs/1,584 cycles	66 μs/1,584 cycles	1

we have evaluated arith::to::bool::lowbits, arith::to::bool::highbits, arith::makehint and bool::rejection. Results are summarized in Table 1.

We can observe that the computation times of decomposition operations are greatly improved with power of two modulus, with a speed-up from 7× (for arith::makehint) to 8× (for arith::to::bool::lowbits). This is due to the fact that only shifts are used for the decomposition when q is a power of two while an Euclidean division is required if q is prime.

We also evaluated the overhead of the masking of Dilithium (power of two implementation) compared to the non-masked version on the full implementation on a general purpose processor. Computation results are summarized in Table 2.

Table 2. Execution times of DILITHIUM.KeyGen and DILITHIUM.Sign on an Intel Core i7-7600U CPU running at 2.80 GHz (10,000 runs).

	Unmasked	Order-1	Order-2	Order-3
DILITHIUM.KeyGen	323 μs	1.83 ms	2.52 ms	4.32 ms
	(reference)	(5.66×)	(7.8×)	(13.4×)
DILITHIUM.Sign	992 μs	5.64 ms	11.68 ms	28.08 ms
	(reference)	(5.68×)	(11.77×)	(28.3×)

First order masking is 5× slower than unmasked implementation. The complexity of masking is limited due to the possibility of partially masking Dilithium.

5.3   Evaluation of Side-Channel Security

We have evaluated masked gadgets separately due to the limited size on the STM32F1 micro-controller. We focused on the power-of-two modulus version since it corresponds to the main contribution of this paper. To speed up the evaluation phase, we first used MAPS simulator to reduce the majority of leakages. Then, we addressed remaining leakages with our side-channel workbench.

In Fig. 5, we provide the t-test evaluation of arith::to::bool::lowbits, arith::to::bool::highbits, arith::makehint and arith::rejection. We did not detected leakage using 10,000 traces on the first-order protected implementation which is to compare with the high leakages observed using only 500 curves for an unprotected implementation.

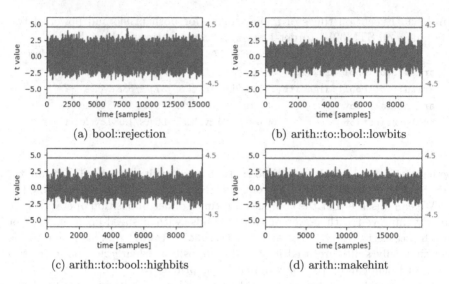

(a) bool::rejection

(b) arith::to::bool::lowbits

(c) arith::to::bool::highbits

(d) arith::makehint

Fig. 5. Evaluation of the t-test on masked gadgets after 10.000 traces.

6   Conclusion

In this paper, we described how to efficiently mask the Dilithium signature scheme. Our approach is based on a slight modification of the reference implementation of Dilithium by setting a power of two modulus instead of prime.

This optimization greatly reduces the complexity of decomposition operations such as $LowBits_q$ or $HighBits_q$, reducing computation times by a factor up to 8. Regarding the overhead compared to a non-masked implementation, the order-1 masking is slower by approximately a factor of 5.6, 11.6 for order-2 masking and 28 for order-3 masking.

We also provided a side-channel leakage analysis for both non-masked and masked of version of Dilithium on STM32F1 micro-controller. We were able to successfully found some leakages on decomposition functions and the rejection operation after no more than 500 traces for the non-masked version while our protected implementation did not show first-order leakage for 10.000 traces.

The implementation and evaluation of a full protected implementation of the scheme is of great interest. We provided figures on a standard CPU that would be interestingly completed by results on an embedded device. However, this requires some memory usage optimization or the use of a larger targeted chip than the STM32F1 (which in turns implies a harder evaluation process). This is a valuable work in itself and would make an interesting extension to this paper.

References

1. NIST Post-Quantum Cryptography. http://csrc.nist.gov/groups/ST/post-quantum-crypto/
2. Albrecht, M.R., Deo, A., Paterson, K.G.: Cold boot attacks on ring and module LWE keys under the NTT. IACR Cryptology ePrint Archive **2018**, 672 (2018)
3. Barthe, G., et al.: Masking the GLP lattice-based signature scheme at any order. In: Nielsen, J.B., Rijmen, V. (eds.) EUROCRYPT 2018. LNCS, vol. 10821, pp. 354–384. Springer, Cham (2018). https://doi.org/10.1007/978-3-319-78375-8_12
4. Bindel, N., Buchmann, J., Krämer, J.: Lattice-based signature schemes and their sensitivity to fault attacks. In: FDTC (2016)
5. Chari, S., Jutla, C.S., Rao, J.R., Rohatgi, P.: Towards sound approaches to counteract power-analysis attacks. In: Wiener, M. (ed.) CRYPTO 1999. LNCS, vol. 1666, pp. 398–412. Springer, Heidelberg (1999). https://doi.org/10.1007/3-540-48405-1_26
6. Le Corre, Y., Großschädl, J., Dinu, D.: Micro-architectural power simulator for leakage assessment of cryptographic software on ARM Cortex-M3 processors. In: Fan, J., Gierlichs, B. (eds.) COSADE 2018. LNCS, vol. 10815, pp. 82–98. Springer, Cham (2018). https://doi.org/10.1007/978-3-319-89641-0_5
7. D'Anvers, J.-P., Karmakar, A., Sinha Roy, S., Vercauteren, F.: Saber: module-LWR based key exchange, CPA-secure encryption and CCA-secure KEM. In: Joux, A., Nitaj, A., Rachidi, T. (eds.) AFRICACRYPT 2018. LNCS, vol. 10831, pp. 282–305. Springer, Cham (2018). https://doi.org/10.1007/978-3-319-89339-6_16
8. Duc, A., Dziembowski, S., Faust, S.: Unifying leakage models: from probing attacks to noisy leakage. In: Nguyen, P.Q., Oswald, E. (eds.) EUROCRYPT 2014. LNCS, vol. 8441, pp. 423–440. Springer, Heidelberg (2014). https://doi.org/10.1007/978-3-642-55220-5_24
9. Ducas, L., et al.: Crystals-Dilithium: a lattice-based digital signature scheme. IACR Trans. Cryptogr. Hardw. Embed. Syst. **2018**(1), 238–268 (2018)
10. Ducas, L., Kiltz, E., Lepoint, T., Lyubashevsky, V., Seiler, G., Stehlé, D.: CRYSTALS-DILITHIUM, algorithm specifications and supporting documentation (2017)
11. Espitau, T., Fouque, P.-A., Gérard, B., Tibouchi, M.: Loop-abort faults on lattice-based fiat-shamir and hash-and-sign signatures. In: Avanzi, R., Heys, H. (eds.) SAC 2016. LNCS, vol. 10532, pp. 140–158. Springer, Cham (2017). https://doi.org/10.1007/978-3-319-69453-5_8
12. Espitau, T., Fouque, P., Gérard, B., Tibouchi, M.: Side-channel attacks on BLISS lattice-based signatures. In: ACM CCS, pp. 1857–1874 (2017)
13. Groot Bruinderink, L., Hülsing, A., Lange, T., Yarom, Y.: Flush, Gauss, and reload. In: Cryptographic Hardware and Embedded Systems - CHES 2016 (2016)
14. Ishai, Y., Sahai, A., Wagner, D.: Private circuits: securing hardware against probing attacks. In: Boneh, D. (ed.) CRYPTO 2003. LNCS, vol. 2729, pp. 463–481. Springer, Heidelberg (2003). https://doi.org/10.1007/978-3-540-45146-4_27
15. Langlois, A., Stehlé, D.: Worst-case to average-case reductions for module lattices. Des. Codes Cryptogr. **75**(3), 565–599 (2015)
16. McCann, D., Whitnall, C., Oswald, E.: ELMO: emulating leaks for the ARM Cortex-M0 without access to a side channel lab. IACR Cryptology ePrint Archive **2016**, 517 (2016)
17. Migliore, V., Gérard, B., Tibouchi, M., Fouque, P.A.: Masking Dilithium: efficient implementation and side-channel evaluation. IACR Cryptology ePrint Archive (2019)

18. Pessl, P., Groot Bruinderink, L., Yarom, Y.: To BLISS-B or not to be–attacking Strongswan's implementation of post-quantum signatures. In: ACM CCS (2017)
19. Prouff, E., Rivain, M.: Masking against side-channel attacks: a formal security proof. In: Johansson, T., Nguyen, P.Q. (eds.) EUROCRYPT 2013. LNCS, vol. 7881, pp. 142–159. Springer, Heidelberg (2013). https://doi.org/10.1007/978-3-642-38348-9_9

Proxy Re-Encryption and Re-Signatures from Lattices

Xiong Fan[1]($\boxtimes$) and Feng-Hao Liu[2]

[1] Cornell University, Ithaca, NY, USA
xfan@cs.cornell.edu
[2] Florida Atlantic University, Boca Raton, FL, USA
fenghao.liu@fau.edu

Abstract. Proxy re-encryption (PRE) and Proxy re-signature (PRS) were introduced by Blaze, Bleumer and Strauss [Eurocrypt '98]. Basically, PRE allows a semi-trusted proxy to transform a ciphertext encrypted under one key into an encryption of the same plaintext under another key, without revealing the underlying plaintext. Since then, many interesting applications have been explored, and constructions in various settings have been proposed. On the other hand, PRS allows a semi-trusted proxy to transform Alice's signature on a message into Bob's signature on the same message, but the proxy cannot produce new valid signature on new messages for either Alice or Bob.

In this work, we first point out a subtle mistake in the security proof of the work by Kirshanova (PKC '14), who proposed a lattice-based CCA1 PRE. Thus, this reopens the direction of lattice-based CCA1-secure constructions, even in the single-hop setting. Then we construct a single-hop PRE scheme that is proven secure in our new tag-based CCA-PRE model. Next, we construct the *first* multi-hop PRE construction. Lastly, we also construct the *first* PRS scheme from lattices that is proved secure in our proposed unified security model.

1 Introduction

Proxy re-encryption (PRE) allows a (semi-trusted) proxy to transform an encryption of m under Alice's public key into another encryption of the same message under Bob's public key. The proxy, however, cannot learn the underlying message m, and thus both parties' privacy can be maintained. This primitive (and its variants) have various applications ranging from encrypted email forwarding [8], to securing distributed file systems [6]. In addition application-driven purposes, various works have shown connections between re-encryption (and its variants) with other cryptographic primitives, such as program obfuscation [13,14,23] and fully-homomorphic encryption [3,11]. Thus studies along this line are both important and interesting for theory and practice.

Another primitive, called proxy re-signature (PRS), allows a semi-trusted proxy to transform Alice's signature σ_A on a message μ into Bob's signature σ_B on the same message μ, but the proxy cannot produce new valid signature on

© Springer Nature Switzerland AG 2019
R. H. Deng et al. (Eds.): ACNS 2019, LNCS 11464, pp. 363–382, 2019.
https://doi.org/10.1007/978-3-030-21568-2_18

new messages for either Alice or Bob. PRS is employed in various applications, such as providing a proof that a certain path in a graph is taken.

Both concepts of PRE and PRS were introduced by Blaze, Bleumer, and Strauss [8], who also gave the first construction of a CPA (i.e. chosen-plaintext attacks) secure *bi-directional multi-hop* PRE scheme under the Decisional Diffie-Hellman assumption, and a restricted PRS construction. Later on, Ateniese and Hohenberger [7] formalized security notions for PRS, and gave two PRS constructions (one is bi-directional, and the other one is uni-directional) based on bilinear maps in the random oracle model. Ateniese et al. [6] constructed the first CPA secure *uni-directional* scheme based on bilinear maps, yet their construction can only support a *single-hop* re-encryption. Hohenberger et al. [23] and Chandran et al. [14] used an obfuscation-based approach and constructed CPA secure uni-directional single-hop PRE scheme (and its variants). Chandran et al. [13], using the obfuscation-based approach, constructed the first CPA secure uni-directional multi-hop PRE scheme based on lattices assumptions.

For the PRE part, as argued that CPA security can be insufficient for some useful scenarios, Canetti and Hohenberger [10] considered a natural stronger security notion — chosen-ciphertext attacks (CCA) security where the adversary has access to a decryption oracle. Intuitively, this security notion guarantees that the underlying message of the challenge ciphertext remains hidden even if the adversary can somehow obtain decryptions of other ciphertexts. They give a meaningful security formulation of CCA secure PRE, and then constructed the first CCA-secure bidirectional multi-hop PRE scheme. Later, Shao et al. [33] constructed a CCA-secure uni-directional single-hop PRE, and Chow et al. [16] proposed another CCA-secure uni-directional scheme in random oracle model. Libert and Vergnaud [26] improved the result by constructing a CCA uni-directional single-hop PRE without random oracles, and this remains the state of the art of the current construction (for the setting of uni-directional CCA-PRE under the definition of [10]). We note that it is unclear how to extend security of the previous obfuscation-approach [13,14,23] (that are only CPA-secure) to the CCA setting. One particular technical challenge is that the re-encryption key output by the simulator might be distinguishable given the CCA decryption oracle, and thus the previous security analyses cannot go through. For CPA security, our understanding is quite well—we know how to construct PRE schemes that are uni-directional and multi-hop in the standard model. However, for CCA security, our understanding in the standard model is much limited in the following sense. First, there is no known scheme that achieves both uni-directional and multi-hop at the same time. Moreover, all currently known constructions [4,6,8,10,16,26,33] are based on Diffie-Hellman-style assumptions. Then Kirshanova [24] proposed a single-hop construction based on lattices, and argued that it is CCA1 secure[1]. However, after a careful examination of her security proof, we found a subtle mistake in the security proof. As the

---

[1] CCA1 security is weaker in the sense that the attacker does not have the decryption oracle after receiving the challenge ciphertext.

mistake is not easily fixable, how to construct a lattice-based PRE that achieves CCA1-security, (even for the single-hop case) remains open.

For the PRS part, Ateniese and Hohenberger [7] left some open problems such as how to construct uni-directional PRS where the proxy can only translate signatures in one direction. Can we avoid the random oracle analysis? Libert and Vergnaud [25] answered these questions positively by constructing the first *multi-use* unidirectional PRS in standard model relying on a new computational assumption in bilinear group.

In this paper, we study lattice-based PRE and PRS constructions. In particular, we make contributions in the following four folds:

- First, we point out a subtle mistake in the security proof of the work [24] (the CCA1 construction), and argue that this is not easy to fix. Briefly speaking, the re-encryption key from the challenge user to another honest user generated in the security proof is distinguishable from the real, and thus the analysis breaks down. Therefore, the construction of [24] does not achieve the CCA1 notion considered in most prior work and this paper.
- Second, we propose a new model called tag-based CCA that lies in between the CCA1 and CCA2 model. Our tag-based CCA allows the attacker to query the decryption oracle before and after the challenge ciphertext, and the honest re-encryption oracle who only re-encrypts honestly generated ciphertexts. This is a combination of CCA and a new notion – honest re-encryption (HRA) attacks proposed recently by Cohen [17].

  We then construct a lattice-based PRE scheme that achieves our tag-based CCA notion. We also describe a generic transformation from the relaxed functionality to the full-fledged one using know techniques (i.e., zero-knowledge proofs). Using a recent work that constructs NIZK from circularly secure FHE [12], we are able to achieve the full-fledged CCA-security if we further assume the required circular security on LWE.
- Third we define a selective notion of tag-based CCA security for multi-hop PRE where the attacker needs to commit to a tree structure for the challenging ciphertext at the beginning. Then we prove that our basic single-hop construction, with a slight modification, can be extended to the multi-hop setting and achieve such a security notion. This is, to our knowledge, the *first* construction of multi-hop PRE that achieves a relaxed yet meaningful notion of CCA security.
- Lastly, we propose a simpler and unified security model for PRS which captures more dynamic settings. We show that the idea of our multi-hop PRE model and the construction can be extended to construct PRS that achieves the security notion. This is the *first* (to our knowledge) multi-hop unidirectional PRS from lattices.

1.1   Technique Highlights

In the following, we highlight our technical ideas for the four contributions as described above.

Part I: The Subtle Mistake in the Work [24]. The subtle mistake comes in the security proof where the work [24] constructs two adjacent hybrids that are distinguishable. For clarification of exposition, we first briefly present the main idea of the construction [24]. Then we will point out where the subtlety is and explain why the problem cannot be easily fixed.

Basically, the PRE construction can be regarded as an extension of CCA-secure public key encryption scheme in [28]. For concreteness, we consider two users: User 1 has public key $\mathsf{pk}_1 = (\mathbf{A}_0, \mathbf{A}_1, \mathbf{A}_2, \mathbf{H})$, and User 2 has public key $\mathsf{pk}_2 = (\mathbf{A}_0', \mathbf{A}_1', \mathbf{A}_2', \mathbf{H}')$, where each public key consists of four matrices. The secret key of User 1 consists of low-norm matrices $\mathbf{R}_1, \mathbf{R}_2$ satisfying $\mathbf{A}_1 = -\mathbf{A}_0\mathbf{R}_1, \mathbf{A}_2 = -\mathbf{A}_0\mathbf{R}_2$, and it is similar for the case of User 2. We note that the readers here do not need to worry about the dimensions. To encrypt under pk_1, we consider an encryption matrix $\mathbf{A}_u = [\mathbf{A}_0|\mathbf{A}_1 + \mathbf{HG}|\mathbf{A}_2 + \mathbf{H}_u\mathbf{G}]$, where $\mathbf{H}_u$ is a random invertible matrix (as a tag to the ciphertext), then encrypt messages using the dual-Regev style encryption [22], i.e. $\mathsf{ct} = \boldsymbol{s}^\mathsf{T}\mathbf{A}_u + \boldsymbol{e} + \mathsf{encode}(m)$. Similarly, we can encrypt under pk_2 with the same structure.

To generate a re-encryption key from User 1 to User 2, the work [24] considers a short matrix $\mathbf{X}$ satisfying the following relation:

$$[\mathbf{A}_0|\mathbf{A}_1 + \mathbf{HG}|\mathbf{A}_2 + \mathbf{H}_u\mathbf{G}] \begin{bmatrix} \mathbf{X}_{00} & \mathbf{X}_{01} & \mathbf{X}_{02} \\ \mathbf{X}_{10} & \mathbf{X}_{11} & \mathbf{X}_{12} \\ 0 & 0 & \mathbf{I} \end{bmatrix} = [\mathbf{A}_0'|\mathbf{A}_1' + \mathbf{H}'\mathbf{G}|\mathbf{A}_2' + \mathbf{H}_u\mathbf{G}].$$

In particular, for the last column of the re-encryption key matrix, it holds that

$$[\mathbf{A}_0|\mathbf{A}_1 + \mathbf{HG}] \begin{bmatrix} \mathbf{X}_{02} \\ \mathbf{X}_{12} \end{bmatrix} = \mathbf{A}_2' - \mathbf{A}_2. \tag{1}$$

It is not hard to see that $\mathsf{ct} \cdot \mathbf{X} = \boldsymbol{s}^\mathsf{T} \cdot \mathbf{A}_u' + \tilde{\boldsymbol{e}} + \mathsf{encode}(m)$, a ciphertext of m under pk_2, so the correctness property is guaranteed.

To prove security, the work [24] uses a standard reduction argument based on the LWE assumption: suppose there exists an adversary that can break the PRE scheme, then there exists a reduction, with oracle access to the adversary, who can break the underlying LWE assumption. For this type of proofs, typically the reduction needs to embed the hard instance (LWE instance for this case), then simulates a scheme (PRE) to the adversary, and finally the reduction can use the adversary to break the underlying hardness assumption. It is **crucially important** that the simulated scheme cannot be distinguished by the adversary; otherwise, the adversary can always output $\perp$ if he detects the scheme is different from the real scheme, and such adversary is useless to the reduction. The security proof in the work [24] missed this point. At a high level, her reduction simulated a PRE scheme that *can* be distinguishable by the adversary easily, so the whole argument breaks down. Below we further elaborate on the details.

For simplicity we consider a simple case where there are only two honest users, Users 1 and 2 and the adversary only gets one re-encryption key from User 1 to User 2. The challenge ciphertext comes from an encryption of User 1, i.e. pk_1. For such case, the reduction of the work [24] pre-selects a tag matrix $\mathbf{H}_{u^*}$ (for the challenge ciphertext), matrices $\mathbf{R}_1^*, \mathbf{R}_2^*$, and then embeds an LWE instance $\mathbf{A}^*$ in the encryption matrix: $\mathbf{A}_u^* = [\mathbf{A}^* | - \mathbf{A}^* \mathbf{R}_1^* | - \mathbf{A}^* \mathbf{R}_2^* + (\mathbf{H}_u - \mathbf{H}_{u^*})\mathbf{G}]$. In this case, the reduction sets $\mathsf{pk}_1 = (\mathbf{A}_0, \mathbf{A}_1, \mathbf{A}_2, \mathbf{H})$ to be $(\mathbf{A}^*, -\mathbf{A}^* \mathbf{R}_1^* - \mathbf{H}^* \mathbf{G}, -\mathbf{A}^* \mathbf{R}_2^* - \mathbf{H}_{u^*} \mathbf{G}, \mathbf{H}^*)$ for some random invertible $\mathbf{H}^*$.

To generate re-encryption key from the challenge user 1 to User 2, the reduction first pre-samples small matrices $\mathbf{X}_{00}, \mathbf{X}_{01}, \mathbf{R}_1', \mathbf{R}_2'$, and a random invertible matrix $\mathbf{H}'$. Then it computes:

$$\mathbf{A}_0' = [\mathbf{A}^* | - \mathbf{A}^* \mathbf{R}_1^*] \begin{bmatrix} \mathbf{X}_{00} \\ \mathbf{X}_{10} \end{bmatrix}, \quad \mathbf{A}_i' = [\mathbf{A}^* | - \mathbf{A}^* \mathbf{R}_1^*] \begin{bmatrix} \mathbf{X}_{00} \\ \mathbf{X}_{10} \end{bmatrix} \cdot \mathbf{R}_i', \forall i = 1, 2$$

The reduction sets

$$\mathsf{pk}_2 = (\mathbf{A}_0', \mathbf{A}_1', \mathbf{A}_2', \mathbf{H}'), \quad \mathsf{rk}_{1 \to 2} = \begin{bmatrix} \left(\begin{smallmatrix} \mathbf{X}_{00} \\ \mathbf{X}_{10} \end{smallmatrix}\right) \left(\begin{smallmatrix} \mathbf{X}_{00} \\ \mathbf{X}_{10} \end{smallmatrix}\right) \mathbf{R}_1' \left(\begin{smallmatrix} \mathbf{X}_{00} \\ \mathbf{X}_{10} \end{smallmatrix}\right) \mathbf{R}_2' \\ 0 \qquad 0 \qquad \mathbf{I} \end{bmatrix}$$

generated as above. Then obviously the matrices $\mathbf{A}_1', \mathbf{A}_2'$ can be expressed as $\mathbf{A}_1' = \mathbf{A}_0' \mathbf{R}_1', \mathbf{A}_2' = \mathbf{A}_0' \mathbf{R}_2'$, where $\mathbf{R}_1', \mathbf{R}_2'$ are small matrices and still act as secret key for User 2. Therefore, the reduction can still use the same algorithm in the real scheme to answer decryption queries for User 2.

However, if $\mathbf{A}_2'$ is generated in this way, then it is easy to check and compare with Eq. (1):

$$[\mathbf{A}_0 | \mathbf{A}_1 + \mathbf{H}\mathbf{G}] \begin{bmatrix} \mathbf{X}_{02} \\ \mathbf{X}_{12} \end{bmatrix} = [\mathbf{A}^* | - \mathbf{A}^* \mathbf{R}_1^*] \begin{bmatrix} \mathbf{X}_{00} \\ \mathbf{X}_{10} \end{bmatrix} \cdot \mathbf{R}_2' \neq \mathbf{A}_2' - \mathbf{A}_2. \tag{2}$$

This means adversary, given the simulated $\mathsf{pk}_1, \mathsf{pk}_2, \mathsf{rk}_{1 \to 2}$, can easily tell whether they are from the real scheme or the simulated scheme. Thus, the security proof in this way [24] is not correct.

A straightforward fix would be to set $\mathbf{A}_2' = [\mathbf{A}^* | - \mathbf{A}^* \mathbf{R}_1^*] \begin{bmatrix} \mathbf{X}_{00} \\ \mathbf{X}_{10} \end{bmatrix} \cdot \mathbf{R}_2' + \mathbf{A}_2 = \mathbf{A}_0' \cdot \mathbf{R}_2' + \mathbf{A}_2$ so that Eqs. (1) and (2) match. But in this way it is not clear how to express $\mathbf{A}_2$ as $\mathbf{A}_0' \mathbf{R}$ for some small matrix $\mathbf{R}$, because it is not clear how to express $\mathbf{A}_2$ as $\mathbf{A}_0' \tilde{\mathbf{R}}$ for some small $\tilde{\mathbf{R}}$. Note that $\mathbf{R}$ serves as the secret key of pk_2 to simulate decryption queries. Consequently, it is not clear how the reduction can answer decryption queries as the previous approach. It seems that this construction/proof is facing a dilemma: either the reduction can answer the decryption queries but the re-encryption key can be distinguished, or the reduction can generate an indistinguishable re-encryption key but cannot answer the decryption queries.

Part II: Our New Construction for Single-Hop PRE. To overcome the dilemma, we consider a new matrix structure: the setup algorithm outputs a public matrix $\mathbf{A}$, and each user extends the previous matrix structure to be $\mathbf{A}_u = [\mathbf{A} | \mathbf{A}_1 + \mathbf{H}\mathbf{G} | \mathbf{A}_2 + \mathbf{H}_u \mathbf{G}]$, where $\mathbf{A}_1 = -\mathbf{A}\mathbf{R}_1, \mathbf{A}_2 = -\mathbf{A}\mathbf{R}_2$ and the matrices $\mathbf{R}_1, \mathbf{R}_2$ are the corresponding secret key. The shared matrix $\mathbf{A}$ offers a significant advantage for the simulation: the reduction can embed the LWE instance $\mathbf{A}^*$ as the public shared matrix, and then sets

$$\mathbf{A}_2' = [\mathbf{A}^* | - \mathbf{A}^* \mathbf{R}_1^*] \begin{bmatrix} \mathbf{X}_{00} \\ \mathbf{X}_{10} \end{bmatrix} \cdot \mathbf{R}_2' - \mathbf{A}^* \mathbf{R}_2^*.$$

This allows the reduction to express $\mathbf{A}_2'$ as $\mathbf{A}^*\mathbf{R}$ for some small and known matrix $\mathbf{R}$. Then the reduction can use this to simulate the decryption queries, while the Eq. (1) will match for the real scheme and the simulated scheme. Our modified construction achieves a relaxed re-encryption functionality in comparison to the construction proposed in [26], i.e. the re-encryption key can only transform well-formed ciphertexts into indistinguishable re-encrypted ciphertexts, but transformation of maliciously chosen cihpertexts can be distinguished if the adversary has the secret key of the target user. In Sect. 3, we present more detailed discussions and a simple transformation from the relaxed functionality to the "full-fledged" functionality using zero-knowledge proofs[2].

Part III: Extension to Multi-hop PRE. We further observe that the matrix structure in our construction can be extended to the multi-hop case with a slight modification. Interestingly, our scheme itself can support general network structures (for functionalities), yet our security proof (for CCA security), however, requires the structure of tree-structured networks (i.e. the adversary can only query re-encryption keys that form a tree among the users). If the adversary's queries form a general graph, then security of our scheme becomes unclear: we are not able to prove security under the current techniques, but there is no known attack, either. We leave it as an interesting open problem to determine whether our construction is secure under general network structures.

A technical reason for this phenomenon comes from the order of sampling for the simulation. We give a simple example for illustration: let there be three parties in the network, Users one, two, and three. It is easy for the reduction to simulate in the following order pk_1, $\mathsf{rk}_{1\to 2}$, pk_2, $\mathsf{rk}_{2\to 3}$, and then pk_3 *without* knowing a trapdoor of the LWE instance $\mathbf{A}^*$. The reduction, however, would get stuck if he needs to further generate $\mathsf{rk}_{1\to 3}$, which should be consistent with the already sampled pk_1 and pk_3. We recall that the reduction is able to check whether $\mathsf{rk}_{1\to 3}$ is consistent with pk_1 and pk_3 in both the real scheme and the simulated scheme (as Eq. (1)). Thus, the reduction must simulate such consistency as the real scheme. Even though there are techniques from the Ring-LWE [21,27] that allows sampling in the *reverse* order of pk_3, $\mathsf{rk}_{2\to 3}$, pk_2, $\mathsf{rk}_{1\to 2}$, pk_1, it does not help to solve the problem because the reduction still does not know how to generate $\mathsf{rk}_{1\to 3}$ after pk_1 and pk_3 are sampled, without a trapdoor of $\mathbf{A}^*$.

Part IV: Unified Model and Construction for Multi-hop PRS. An interesting observation from our multi-hop CCA-PRE construction is that it is also compatible with the lattice signature structure in the work of Boyen [9]. In particular, in that work, the signature scheme has the following structure: $[\mathbf{A}|\mathbf{B}_\mu]$, where is an encoded matrix for message μ. This message-dependent matrix can be extended to a similar structure similar to that in multi-hop PRE construction. Recall that prior PRS work [7,25] consider four scenarios for the security requirement. In each scenario, the adversary has access to a subset of oracles (signing, re-signing, re-key generation), and security requires that the adversary

---

[2] Under current techniques, zero knowledge proof systems based on pure lattices assumptions either require interactions or random oracles.

cannot forge a signature on behalf of honest users (whose secret keys are not at the adversary's hand). Our unified security model is based on the approach of multi-hop PRE model with necessary modifications to fit into the signature framework.

1.2 Related Works

Proxy Re-Encryption. As mentioned above, in recent years, there has been multiple PRE constructions achieving different security notions from different assumptions. In addition to the bi-directional PRE-CPA constructions [8,10], there is also some work [6,23] about building uni-directional PRE-CPA from various assumptions. For CCA-PRE construction, we only know how to construct single-hop scheme from bilinear group assumption as shown in work [26], and single-hop scheme from LWE assumption in the random oracle model as shown in [4]. Besides the above mentioned work, recently Nuñez et al. [31] proposed a nice framework capturing more fine-grained CCA-security of PRE, corresponding to the adversary's ability in the security experiment. Our multi-hop tag-based CCA-secure PRE construction described in the full version [19] can be categorized as $CCA_{1,2}$ model in their paper regarding a special structure (trees).

Proxy Re-Signature. Bi-directional PRS was considered in the literature [7, 15]. The generation of re-key algorithm needs to take inputs both users' secret key. The more fine-grained notion, uni-directional PRS scheme was proposed in [25]. Shao et al. [34] cooked up a bilinear group based scheme (in random oracle model) that is insecure but proven secure in prior PRS model [7,25], but their result cannot be extended to the lattice setting.

2 Preliminaries

Notations. Let PPT denote probabilistic polynomial time. We use bold uppercase letters to denote matrices, and bold lowercase letters for vectors. We let λ be the security parameter and $[n]$ denote the set $\{1, ..., n\}$. We use $[\cdot||\cdot]$ to denote the concatenation of vectors or matrices, and use ℓ_∞ norm for the norms of all vectors and matrices used in our paper. We say a function $f(n)$ is *negligible* if it is $O(n^{-c})$ for all $c > 0$, and we $\mathsf{negl}(n)$ to denote a negligible function of n. Let X and Y be two random variables taking values in Ω. Define the statistical distance, denoted as $\Delta(X, Y)$ as

$$\Delta(X, Y) := \frac{1}{2} \sum_{s \in \Omega} |\mathbf{Pr}[X = s] - \mathbf{Pr}[Y = s]|$$

Let $X(\lambda)$ and $Y(\lambda)$ be ensembles of random variables. We say that X and Y are statistically close if $d(\lambda) := \Delta(X(\lambda), Y(\lambda))$ is a negligible function of λ. We say two ensembles $X(\lambda)$ and $Y(\lambda)$ are computationally indistinguishable (denoted as $X(\lambda) \approx Y(\lambda)$) if for every PPT distinguisher D, it holds that

$$|\mathbf{Pr}[D(X(\lambda)) = 1] - \mathbf{Pr}[D(Y(\lambda)) = 1]| = \mathsf{negl}(\lambda)$$

Lemma 2.1 ([1]). *Regarding the norm defined above, we have the following bounds:*

- *Let* $\mathbf{R} \in \{-1, 1\}^{m \times m}$ *be chosen at random, then* $\mathbf{Pr}[\|\mathbf{R}\| > 12\sqrt{2m}] < e^{-2m}$.
- *Let* $\mathbf{R}$ *be sampled from* $\mathcal{D}_{\mathbb{Z}^{m \times m}, \sigma}$, *then we have* $\mathbf{Pr}[\|\mathbf{R}\| > \sigma\sqrt{m}] < e^{-2m}$.

Randomness Extraction. We will use the following lemma to argue the indistinguishability of two different distributions, which is a generalization of the leftover hash lemma proposed by Dodis et al. [18].

Lemma 2.2 ([1]). *Suppose that* $m > (n + 1) \log q + w(\log n)$. *Let* $\mathbf{R} \in \{-1, 1\}^{m \times k}$ *be chosen uniformly at random for some polynomial* $k = k(n)$. *Let* $\mathbf{A}, \mathbf{B}$ *be matrix chosen randomly from* $\mathbb{Z}_q^{n \times m}, \mathbb{Z}_q^{n \times k}$ *respectively. Then, for all vectors* $\boldsymbol{w} \in \mathbb{Z}^m$, *the distribution* $(\mathbf{A}, \mathbf{AR}, \mathbf{R}^\mathsf{T}\boldsymbol{w})$ *is statistically close to distribution* $(\mathbf{A}, \mathbf{B}, \mathbf{R}^\mathsf{T}\boldsymbol{w})$.

Learning with Errors. The LWE problem was introduced by Regev [32], who showed that solving it *on the average* is as hard as (quantumly) solving several standard lattice problems *in the worst case*, when the error distribution is instantiated as discrete Gaussian distribution with proper parameters.

Definition 2.3 (LWE). *For an integer* $q = q(n) \geq 2$, *and an error distribution* $\chi = \chi(n)$ *over* $\mathbb{Z}_q$, *the learning with errors problem* $\mathsf{LWE}_{n,m,q,\chi}$ *is to distinguish between the distribution* $\{\mathbf{A}, \mathbf{A}^\mathsf{T}\boldsymbol{s} + \boldsymbol{x}\}$ *from distribution* $\{\mathbf{A}, \boldsymbol{u}\}$, *where* $\mathbf{A} \xleftarrow{\$} \mathbb{Z}_q^{n \times m}$, $\boldsymbol{s} \xleftarrow{\$} \mathbb{Z}_q^n$, $\boldsymbol{u} \xleftarrow{\$} \mathbb{Z}_q^m$, *and* $\boldsymbol{x} \leftarrow \chi^m$.

Small Integer Solution. The SIS problem was first suggested to be hard on average by Ajtai [2] and then formalized by Micciancio and Regev [30]. It is known to be as hard as certain worst-case problems (e.g., SIVP) in standard lattices [2,22,29,30].

Definition 2.4 (SIS). *For any* $n \in \mathbb{Z}$, *and any functions* $m = m(n), q = q(n), \beta = \beta(n)$, *the average-case Small Integer Solution problem* $(\mathsf{SIS}_{q,n,m,\beta})$ *is: Given an integer* q, *a matrix* $\mathbf{A} \in \mathbb{Z}_q^{n \times m}$ *chosen uniformly at random and a real* $\beta \in \mathbb{R}$, *find a non-zero integer vector* $\boldsymbol{z} \in \mathbb{Z}^m - \{\mathbf{0}\}$, *such that* $\mathbf{A}\boldsymbol{z} = 0$ $\mod q$ *and* $\|\boldsymbol{z}\| \leq \beta$.

G-Trapdoors and Sampling Algorithms. We briefly describe the main results in [28]: the definition of **G**-trapdoor and the algorithms $\mathsf{Invert}^{\mathcal{O}}$ and $\mathsf{Sample}^{\mathcal{O}}$. Roughly speaking, a **G**-trapdoor is a transformation, represented by a matrix $\mathbf{R}$ from a public matrix $\mathbf{A}$ to a special matrix $\mathbf{G}$. The formal definition is as follows:

Definition 2.5 ([28]). *Let* $\mathbf{A} \in \mathbb{Z}_q^{n \times m}$ *and* $\mathbf{G} \in \mathbb{Z}_q^{n \times w}$ *be matrices with* $m \geq w \geq n$. *A* **G***-trapdoor for* $\mathbf{A}$ *is a matrix* $\mathbf{R} \in \mathbb{Z}^{m-w} \times w$ *such that* $\mathbf{A}\begin{bmatrix} \mathbf{R} \\ \mathbf{I} \end{bmatrix} = \mathbf{HG}$ *for some invertible matrix* $\mathbf{H} \in \mathbb{Z}_q^{n \times n}$. *We refer to* $\mathbf{H}$ *as the tag or label of the trapdoor. The quality of the trapdoor is measured by its largest singular value* $s_1(\mathbf{R})$.

In order to embed matrix $\mathbf{G}$ into a uniformly looking matrix $\mathbf{A}$ together with a transformation $\mathbf{R}$, we should start with a uniform matrix $\mathbf{A}_0$ and a matrix $\mathbf{R}$, and construct $\mathbf{A} = [\mathbf{A}_0| - \mathbf{A}_0\mathbf{R} + \mathbf{H}\mathbf{G}]$. For an appropriate chosen dimensions $(\mathbf{A}, \mathbf{A}\mathbf{R})$ is negligible from uniformly random distribution by the Lattice-based Leftover Hash Lemma.

Following the work of Micciancio and Peikert [28], our scheme uses a special collection of elements defined over ring $\mathcal{R} = \mathbb{Z}_q[x]/(f(x))$, where $f(x) = x^n + f_{n-1}x^{n-1} + \cdots + f_0$ is a irreducible modulo every p dividing q. Since $\mathcal{R}$ is a free $\mathbb{Z}_q$-module of rank n, thus elements of $\mathcal{R}$ can be represented as vectors in $\mathbb{Z}_q$ relative to standard basis of monomials $1, x, ..., x^{n-1}$. Multiplication by any fixed element of $\mathcal{R}$ then acts as a linear transformation on $\mathbb{Z}_q^n$ according to the rule

$$x \cdot (a_0, ..., a_{n-1})^\mathsf{T} = (0, a_0, ..., a_{n-2})^\mathsf{T} - a_{n-1}(f_0, f_1, ..., f_{n-1})^\mathsf{T}$$

and so can be represented by an matrix in $\mathbb{Z}_q^{n\times n}$ relative to the standard basis. In other words, there is an injective ring homomorphism $h : \mathcal{R} \rightarrow \mathbb{Z}_q^{n\times n}$ that maps any $a \in \mathcal{R}$ to matrix $\mathbf{H} = h(a)$ representing multiplication by a. As introduced in [28], we need a very large set $\mathcal{U} = \{u_1, ..., u_l\}$ with the "unit differences" property: for any $i \neq j$, the difference $u_i - u_j \in \mathcal{R}^*$, and hence $h(u_i - u_j) = h(u_i) - h(u_j) \in \mathbb{Z}_q^{n\times n}$ is invertible.

Lemma 2.6 ([28]). *There is an efficient algorithm* $\mathsf{Sample}^{\mathcal{O}}(\mathbf{R}, \mathbf{A}', \mathbf{H}, \mathbf{u}, s)$, *where* $\mathbf{R}$ *is a* $\mathbf{G}$-*trapdoor for matrix* $\mathbf{A}$ *with invertible tag* $\mathbf{H}$, *a vector* $\mathbf{u} \in \mathbb{Z}^n$ *and an oracle* $\mathcal{O}$ *for Gaussian sampling over a desired coset* $\Lambda_q^v(\mathbf{G})$. *It will output a vector drawn from a distribution within negligible statistical distance of* $\mathcal{D}_{\Lambda^u(\mathbf{A}),s}$, *where* $\mathbf{A} = [\mathbf{A}'| - \mathbf{A}'\mathbf{R} + \mathbf{H}\mathbf{G}]$.

In the following, we provide two extensions of the LWE inversion algorithms proposed by Micciancio and Peikert [28], which would be used in the security proof and scheme respectively.

- $\mathsf{Invert}^{\mathcal{O}}(\mathbf{R}_1, \mathbf{R}_2, \mathbf{A}, \boldsymbol{b})$: On input a vector $\boldsymbol{b} = \boldsymbol{s}^\mathsf{T}\mathbf{A} + \boldsymbol{e}^\mathsf{T}$, a matrix $\mathbf{A} = [\mathbf{A}_0| - \mathbf{A}_0\mathbf{R}_1 + \mathbf{H}_1\mathbf{G}| - \mathbf{A}_0\mathbf{R}_2 + \mathbf{H}_2\mathbf{G}]$ and its corresponding $\mathbf{G}$-trapdoor $\mathbf{R}_1, \mathbf{R}_2$ with invertible tag $\mathbf{H}_1, \mathbf{H}_2$, the algorithm first computes $\boldsymbol{b}' = \boldsymbol{b}^\mathsf{T}\left[\begin{smallmatrix}\mathbf{R}_1+\mathbf{R}_2\\\mathbf{I}\\\mathbf{I}\end{smallmatrix}\right]$, and then run the oracle $\mathcal{O}(\boldsymbol{b}')$ to get $(\boldsymbol{s}', \boldsymbol{e}')$. The algorithm outputs $\boldsymbol{s} = (\mathbf{H}_1 + \mathbf{H}_2)^{-1}\boldsymbol{s}'$ and $\boldsymbol{e} = \boldsymbol{b} - \boldsymbol{s}^\mathsf{T}\mathbf{A}$.
- $\mathsf{Invert}'^{\mathcal{O}}(\mathbf{R}_1, \mathbf{R}_2, \mathbf{A}, \boldsymbol{b})$: On input a vector $\boldsymbol{b} = \boldsymbol{s}^\mathsf{T}\mathbf{A} + \boldsymbol{e}^\mathsf{T}$, a matrix $\mathbf{A} = [\mathbf{A}_0| - \mathbf{A}_0\mathbf{R}_1| - \mathbf{A}_0\mathbf{R}_2 + \mathbf{H}_2\mathbf{G}]$ and its corresponding $\mathbf{G}$-trapdoor $\mathbf{R}_1, \mathbf{R}_2$ with invertible tag $\mathbf{H}_1, \mathbf{H}_2$, the algorithm first computes $\boldsymbol{b}' = \boldsymbol{b}^\mathsf{T}\left[\begin{smallmatrix}\mathbf{R}_1+\mathbf{R}_2\\\mathbf{I}\\\mathbf{I}\end{smallmatrix}\right]$, and then run the oracle $\mathcal{O}(\boldsymbol{b}')$ to get $(\boldsymbol{s}', \boldsymbol{e}')$. The algorithm outputs $\boldsymbol{s} = \mathbf{H}_2^{-1}\boldsymbol{s}'$ and $\boldsymbol{e} = \boldsymbol{b} - \boldsymbol{s}^\mathsf{T}\mathbf{A}$.

3 Proxy Re-Encryption: Syntax and Security Definitions

In this section, we first recall the syntax of single-hop PRE [26], and then we define a new variant of CCA-PRE security, i.e. tag-based CCA-PRE security that captures constructions associated with tags. However, for lattice-based constructions, our current technique cannot achieve the full-fledged PRE construction in that the re-encryption algorithm does not provide the full-fledged functionality in that it does not fully implement the regular re-encryption oracle which decrypts first, outputs $\perp$ if the decrypted value is invalid, and outputs a fresh ciphertext of the same message, otherwise. Our re-encryption algorithm guarantees the functionality when the input ciphertexts are well-formed, but if the input ciphertexts are not well-formed, the re-encryption algorithm is not able output $\perp$, yet it can only output re-encrypted ciphertexts that will be decrypted to $\perp$. This security notion is also known as security against *honest re-encryption attacks* (HRA), where the re-encryption oracle only re-encrypts honestly generated ciphertexts. The HRA model was defined in a recent work by Cohen [17], and it also identified many interesting scenarios captured by the HRA security. The work by Cohen [17] achieves the CPA + HRA security, and this work achieves a stronger notion – CCA + HRA security.

In fact, our relaxed functionality is not far from the full-fledged functionality if the input-ciphertext provider is required to prove the validity of the ciphertexts. We note that there exists an efficient lattice-based Σ protocol [5] with interaction, and we can further use the Fiat-Shamir transform [20] to achieve a NIZK proof system if a random oracle is assumed. Very recently, the work [12] constructed NIZK from FHE with circular security, which can be based on LWE with a certain circular security. Using this lattice-based NIZK, we can upgrade our security to the full-fledge CCA-PRE security. Therefore, if we further assume the required circular security on LWE, we are able to achieve the full-fledge CCA-PRE. We leave it as an interesting open problem to determine whether the circular security is inherent in achieving the full-fledge CCA-PRE.

The relaxed PRE security notion has already provided meaningful security guarantees and allowed a modular design to achieve the full-fledged functionality, e.g., the proxy additionally requests a proof of well-formness of the input ciphertexts. We believe that this notion deserves attention for the community.

3.1   Single-Hop PRE Syntax

We recall the syntax of uni-directional PRE, which can be regarded as a natural extension of bi-directional case defined in [10] and later studied in uni-directional scenario by Libert and Vergnaud [26]. The PRE scheme consists a tuple of PPT algorithms (Setup, KeyGen, Enc, Dec, ReKeyGen, ReEnc), which can be defined as follows:

- pp $\leftarrow$ Setup(1^λ) generates the public parameters pp.
- (pk, sk) $\leftarrow$ KeyGen(pp) generates (pk, sk) for each user.
- ct $\leftarrow$ Enc(pk, μ, i) encrypts a message μ at level $i \in \{1, 2\}$. The re-encryption can only operate on ciphertexts that are at level 1.
- $\mu' =$ Dec(sk, (ct, i)) decrypts a ciphertext ct.
- rk$_{i \rightarrow j}$ $\leftarrow$ ReKeyGen(pk$_i$, sk$_i$, pk$_j$) computes the re-encryption key rk$_{i \rightarrow j}$.

- $(\mathsf{ct}', 2) \leftarrow \mathsf{ReEnc}(\mathsf{rk}_{i \to j}, (\mathsf{ct}, 1))$ computes the re-encrypted ciphertext ct'. If the well-formedness of ciphertext ct is publicly verifiable, the algorithm should output "invalid" when ct is ill-formed.

Correctness. For correctness, we consider two cases for the PRE scheme: one for "fresh" ciphertexts generated by encryption algorithm, and the other for re-encryption ciphertexts generated by the re-encryption algorithm. We say that a single-hop PRE scheme is correct if the following holds.

- For any $\mathsf{pp} \leftarrow \mathsf{Setup}(1^\lambda)$, any $(\mathsf{pk}, \mathsf{sk}) \leftarrow \mathsf{KeyGen}(\mathsf{pp})$, any message μ and level $i \in \{1, 2\}$, it holds that

$$\mathbf{Pr}[\mathsf{Dec}(\mathsf{sk}, \mathsf{Enc}(\mathsf{pk}, \mu, i)) = \mu] = 1 - \mathsf{negl}(\lambda)$$

- For any $\mathsf{pp} \leftarrow \mathsf{Setup}(1^\lambda)$, any $(\mathsf{pk}_i, \mathsf{sk}_i), (\mathsf{pk}_j, \mathsf{sk}_j) \leftarrow \mathsf{KeyGen}(\mathsf{pp})$, any message μ, it holds that

$$\mathbf{Pr}[\mathsf{Dec}(\mathsf{sk}_j, \mathsf{ReEnc}(\mathsf{rk}_{i \to j}, \mathsf{ct})) = \mu] = 1 - \mathsf{negl}(\lambda)$$

where $\mathsf{ct} \leftarrow \mathsf{Enc}(\mathsf{pk}_i, \mu, 1), \mathsf{rk}_{i \to j} \leftarrow \mathsf{ReKeyGen}(\mathsf{pk}_i, \mathsf{sk}_i, \mathsf{pk}_j)$.

3.2 Single-Hop PRE Security Definitions

In the security part, we first present the CCA-PRE definition proposed in [26] with minor modifications – in particular the definition of derivative in security model. Next, we describe a weaker security model considered in [24], whose restriction is: the re-encryption queries submitted by the adversary are only allowed between honest users. Then we propose an intermediate model, where the capability of re-encryption oracle is slightly weaker than its counterpart in [26]. Intuitively, we say a ciphertext is well-formed if it is an encryption of a message under the claimed public key. In the re-encryption oracle in [26], the well-formedness of ciphertext is public verifiable, i.e the verification only needs public keys. However, in our intermediate model, the verification needs the assistance of secret keys. Let $\mathcal{A}$ denote any PPT adversary, and $\varPi$ be a PRE scheme. We define the notion of CCA-secure PRE in the uni-directional setting using the following experiment $\mathbf{Expt}_{\mathcal{A}}^{\mathsf{CCA-PRE}}(1^\lambda)$, which describes the interaction between several oracles and an adversary $\mathcal{A}$. As we discussed before, we include public parameters pp in each user's public key pk and secret key sk, so we will omit pp in the description for simplicity. The experiment $\mathbf{Expt}_{\mathcal{A}}^{\mathsf{single}}(1^\lambda)$ consists of an execution of $\mathcal{A}$ with the following oracles with detail as follows:

- The challenger runs setup algorithm $\mathsf{pp} \leftarrow \mathsf{Setup}(1^\lambda)$ and initializes two empty sets $\mathcal{H} = \emptyset, \mathcal{C} = \emptyset$. Then he sends pp to adversary $\mathcal{A}$.
- Proceeding adaptively, adversary $\mathcal{A}$ has access to the following oracles:

Uncorrupted key generation oracle: Obtain a new key pair $(\mathsf{pk}_i, \mathsf{sk}_i) \leftarrow \mathsf{KeyGen}(\mathsf{pp})$. Send pk_i back to adversary $\mathcal{A}$, set the honest user set $\mathcal{H} = \mathcal{H} \cup \{i\}$ and pass the the tuple $(i, \mathsf{pk}_i, \mathsf{sk}_i)$ to re-encryption key generation oracle $\mathcal{O}_{\mathsf{ReKeyGen}}$ and decryption oracle $\mathcal{O}_{\mathsf{Dec}}$.

Corrupted key generation oracle: Obtain a new key pair $(\mathsf{pk}_i, \mathsf{sk}_i) \leftarrow$ KeyGen(pp). Send the key pair $(\mathsf{pk}_i, \mathsf{sk}_i)$ back to adversary $\mathcal{A}$, set the corrupted user set $\mathcal{C} = \mathcal{C} \cup \{i\}$ and pass the tuple $(i, \mathsf{pk}_i, \mathsf{sk}_i)$ to re-encryption key generation oracle $\mathcal{O}_{\mathsf{ReKeyGen}}$ and decryption oracle $\mathcal{O}_{\mathsf{Dec}}$.

Re-encryption key generation oracle $\mathcal{O}_{\mathsf{ReKeyGen}}$: On input an index pair (i, j) from the adversary, if the query (i, j) is made after accessing the challenge oracle, then output $\perp$ if $i = i^*$ and $j \in \mathcal{C}$. Otherwise, do the following:

- If the pair (i, j) is queried for the first time, the oracle returns a re-encryption key $\mathsf{rk}_{i \rightarrow j} \leftarrow \mathsf{ReKeyGen}(\mathsf{pk}_i, \mathsf{sk}_i, \mathsf{pk}_j)$;
- else (the pair (i, j) has been queried before), the oracle returns the re-encryption key $\mathsf{rk}_{i \rightarrow j}$.

Re-encryption oracle $\mathcal{O}_{\mathsf{ReEnc}}$: On input $(i, j, (\mathsf{ct}, k))$, the oracle returns a special symbol $\perp$ if (ct, k) is not a well-formed first level ciphertext, or $j \in \mathcal{C}$ and $(i, \mathsf{ct}) = (i^*, \mathsf{ct}^*)$. Otherwise, it computes re-encrypted ciphertext $\mathsf{ct}' \leftarrow \mathsf{ReEnc}(\mathsf{rk}_{i \rightarrow j}, \mathsf{ct})$ and sends back $(\mathsf{ct}', 2)$.

Decryption oracle $\mathcal{O}_{\mathsf{Dec}}$: On input (i, ct), if $i \notin \mathcal{C} \cup \mathcal{H}$ or ct is not a valid ciphertext, then return a special symbol $\perp$. It also outputs a special symbol $\perp$ if (i, ct) is a *Derivative* (c.f. Definition 3.2) of the challenge pair (i^*, ct^*). Otherwise, it returns $\mathsf{Dec}(\mathsf{sk}_i, \mathsf{ct})$ to adversary $\mathcal{A}$.

Challenge oracle: This oracle can be queried only once. On input (i^*, μ_0, μ_1), where $i^* \in \mathcal{H}$ and no re-encryption key from i^* to corrupted users $\mathcal{C}$ has been queried by adversary, the oracle chooses a bit $b \in \{0, 1\}$ and returns $\mathsf{ct}^* \leftarrow \mathsf{Enc}(\mathsf{pk}_{i^*}, \mu_b, 1)$ as the challenge ciphertext, and passes i^* to re-encryption key generation oracle $\mathcal{O}_{\mathsf{ReKeyGen}}$, and (i^*, ct^*) to re-encryption oracle $\mathcal{O}_{\mathsf{ReEnc}}$.

Decision oracle: This oracle can be queried only once. On input b' from adversary $\mathcal{A}$, the oracle outputs 1 if $b' = b$, and 0 otherwise.

The advantage of an adversary in the above experiment $\mathbf{Expt}_{\mathcal{A}}^{\mathsf{single}}(1^\lambda)$ is defined as $|\mathbf{Pr}[b' = b] - \frac{1}{2}|$.

Definition 3.1 (CCA-PRE Model). *A uni-directional PRE scheme is CCA-PRE secure if all PPT adversaries have at most a negligible advantage in experiment* $\mathbf{Expt}_{\mathcal{A}}^{\mathsf{single}}(1^\lambda)$.

In our PRE construction, every ciphertext is associated with a tag u chosen randomly in the encryption algorithm, thus we call our security model *tag-based CCA security*. In [26], a pair (i, ct) is called *derivative* of the challenge ciphertext pair (i^*, ct^*) if $\mathsf{Dec}(\mathsf{ct}, \mathsf{sk}_i) \in \{\mu_0, \mu_1\}$, where $\{\mu_0, \mu_1\}$ are the challenge message pair. We achieve a slightly stronger notion of derivative as defined in the following

Definition 3.2 (Derivative). *A pair $(i, (\mathsf{ct}, u))$ is called derivative of the challenge ciphertext pair $(i^*, (\mathsf{ct}^*, u^*))$ if $u = u^*$.*

Remark 3.3. It is obvious to see that tag-based CCA security is stronger than CCA1 security (where the adversary cannot access the decryption oracle after the challenge ciphertext), and is slightly weaker than CCA2 security. This relaxation is meaningful and can be nearly the best we can achieve if we further require the property of *unlinkability* for re-encrypted ciphertexts. That is, if we want the re-encrypted algorithm to produce statistically indistinguishable ciphertexts, i.e. the re-encrypted ciphertexts are almost identically distributed as fresh ones, then arguably it is not possible to achieve CCA2 security, because the decryption oracle cannot distinguish a re-encryption of challenge ciphertext from a fresh ciphertext, so an adversary can easily break the security game by querying the decryption oracle with a re-encrypted ciphertext of the challenge ciphertext. For tag-based schemes, where the tag remains the same for re-encrypted ciphertexts, we can ensure that the challenge ciphertext will not be decrypted by the decryption oracle due to derivative definition (see Definition 3.2). The tag-based CCA security guarantees the challenge ciphertext remains hidden, even if the adversary can obtain decryptions of ciphertexts with other tags.

Remark 3.4. Our re-encryption oracle only re-encrypts well-form ciphertexts. This is explicitly defined as honest re-encryption attacks (HRA) by Cohen [17]. The formulation of this work is slightly different from that of the work by Cohen [17], but the two formulations have the same spirit.

The above security model only captures the CCA security of ciphertexts on the first level. We also present the CCA security of ciphertexts on the second level. Since the challenge ciphertext is on the second level, which means it cannot be further re-encrypted to ciphertext under other public keys, so there is no need to restrict the re-encryption queries regarding the challenge ciphertext. We highlight the difference comparing to security model of first level ciphertexts in the following definition.

Definition 3.5. (Second-Level Security). *The difference of experiment between second-level security and the security definition in Definition 3.1 are below:*

- *In challenge oracle: the oracle returns* $ct^* \leftarrow \mathsf{Enc}(pk_{i*}, \mu_b, 2)$ *as the challenge ciphertext.*
- *The re-encryption oracle* $\mathcal{O}_{\mathsf{ReEnc}}$ *does not need to check whether the queried tuple is the same as challenge ciphertext.*

Definition 3.6. (PRE with Relaxed Functionality). *A PRE scheme with a relaxed functionality if the re-encryption algorithm outputs statistically close to the distribution of fresh ciphertexts of the second level when the input ciphertexts are well-formed. That is, if* $(ct, 1)$ *is a well-formed ciphertext, then* $\mathsf{ReEnc}(rk_{i \to j}, (ct, 1))$ *is statistically close to* $(ct', 2) \leftarrow \mathsf{Enc}(pk_j, \mathsf{Dec}(ct, 1), 2)$. *If the input ciphertexts are not well-formed, then only* $\mathsf{Dec}(sk_j, (ct', 2)) = \perp$ *is guaranteed.*

Remark 3.7. *As we argued above, the relaxed functionality does not completely implement the re-encryption oracle* $\mathcal{O}_{\mathsf{ReEnc}}$ *as in the above definition. The difference can be bridged by a crypto proof system, (either interactively or* *non-interactively) assuming the input ciphertext is associated with a proof. We present the formal description of this idea in the full version of this paper.*

In our construction, we do not allow querying the relaxed functionality directly with arbitrary input ciphertexts re-encrypted to a corrupted party, e.g., invalid input ciphertexts chosen by the adversary to some corrupted Party j. As the transformation can leak the re-encryption key, if the adversary corrupts Party j and can obtain a re-encryption key $\mathsf{rk}_{i \to j}$, then he can easily break the security of pk_i.

We note that the the CCA model of [24] is weaker than the model considered in this paper. In particular, the model [24] has the following restrictions: the re-encryption key queries (or re-encryption queries) submit by adversary $\mathcal{A}$ are restricted among honest users (we ignore the re-encryption queries within corrupted users, since adversary can generate by himself).

4   Single-Hop Tag-Based CCA-Secure PRE Construction

In this section, we present our construction of single-hop PRE. The PRE system has message space $\{0,1\}^{nk}$, which we map bijectively to the cosets of $\Lambda/2\Lambda$ for $\Lambda = \Lambda(\mathbf{G}^t)$ via some encoding function encode that is efficient to evaluate and invert. In particular, letting $\mathbf{S} \in \mathbb{Z}^{nk \times nk}$ be any basis of Λ, we can map $\boldsymbol{\mu} \in \{0,1\}^{nk}$ to $\mathsf{encode}(\boldsymbol{\mu}) = \mathbf{S}\boldsymbol{\mu} \in \mathbb{Z}^{nk}$. The PRE scheme (Setup, KeyGen, Enc, Dec, ReKeyGen, ReEnc) can be described as follows:

- Setup($1^\lambda, 1^N$): The global setup algorithm set the lattice parameter (n, k, q, s). Then it randomly selects a matrix $\mathbf{A} \in \mathbb{Z}_q^{n \times nk}$, and outputs the public parameter $\mathsf{pp} = (\mathbf{A}, n, m, q, s)$.
- KeyGen(pp): The key generation algorithm for i-th user chooses random matrices $\mathbf{R}_{i1}, \mathbf{R}_{i2} \leftarrow \mathcal{D}_{\mathbb{Z}^{nk \times nk}, s}$, letting $\mathbf{A}_{i1} = \mathbf{A}\mathbf{R}_{i1} \bmod q$ and $\mathbf{A}_{i2} = \mathbf{A}\mathbf{R}_{i2} \bmod q$. The public key is $\mathsf{pk}_i = \mathbf{A}_i = [\mathbf{A}| - \mathbf{A}_{i1}| - \mathbf{A}_{i2}]$, and the secret key is $\mathsf{sk}_i = [\mathbf{R}_{i1}|\mathbf{R}_{i2}]$.
- Enc($\mathsf{pk}_i, \boldsymbol{\mu}, \ell$): The encryption algorithm does
  - If $\ell = 1$, choose non-zero $u \leftarrow \mathcal{U}$ and let the message/level-dependent matrix
  $$\mathbf{A}_{i,u,l} = [\mathbf{A}| - \mathbf{A}_{i1} + h(\ell)\mathbf{G}| - \mathbf{A}_{i2} + h(u)\mathbf{G}]$$
  Choose $s \leftarrow \mathbb{Z}_q^n, \boldsymbol{e}_0, \boldsymbol{e}_1, \boldsymbol{e}_2 \leftarrow \mathcal{D}_{\mathbb{Z},s}^{nk}$. Let
  $$\boldsymbol{b}^\mathsf{T} = (\boldsymbol{b}_0, \boldsymbol{b}_1, \boldsymbol{b}_2) = 2(\boldsymbol{s}^\mathsf{T}\mathbf{A}_{i,u,\ell} \bmod q) + \boldsymbol{e}^\mathsf{T} + (0, 0, \mathsf{encode}(\boldsymbol{\mu})^\mathsf{T}) \bmod 2q$$
  where $\boldsymbol{e} = (\boldsymbol{e}_0, \boldsymbol{e}_1, \boldsymbol{e}_2)$. Output the ciphertext $\mathsf{ct} = (u, \boldsymbol{b}, 1)$.
  - If $\ell = 2$, the algorithm uses the same procedure to encrypt the message, except it chooses error $\boldsymbol{e}_0, \boldsymbol{e}_1, \boldsymbol{e}_2 \leftarrow \mathcal{D}_{\mathbb{Z},s'}^{nk}$, and outputs $\mathsf{ct} = (u, \boldsymbol{b}, 2)$.

- Dec($\mathsf{sk}_i, \mathsf{ct}$): The decryption algorithm
  1. If ct does not parse or $u = 0$, output $\bot$. Otherwise, reconstruct the message/level-dependent matrix $\mathbf{A}_{i,u,\ell}$

$$\mathbf{A}_{i,u,l} = [\mathbf{A} | - \mathbf{A}_{i1} + h(\ell)\mathbf{G}| - \mathbf{A}_{i2} + h(u)\mathbf{G}]$$

  Call $\mathsf{Invert}^{\mathcal{O}}([\mathbf{R}_{i1}|\mathbf{R}_{i2}], \mathbf{A}_u, \mathbf{b} \bmod q)$ to get values $\mathbf{z} \in \mathbb{Z}_q^n$ and $\mathbf{e} = (\mathbf{e}_0, \mathbf{e}_1, \mathbf{e}_2)$ for which $\mathbf{b} = \mathbf{z} + \mathbf{e} \bmod q$. If the algorithm Invert fail for any reason, output $\bot$.
  2. Check the length of the obtained error vectors, namely if $\|\mathbf{e}_0\| \geq s'\sqrt{m}$ or $\|\mathbf{e}_i\| \geq s'^2 m$, for $i = 1, 2$, output $\bot$.
  3. Let $\mathbf{v} = \mathbf{b} - \mathbf{e}$, and parse $\mathbf{v} = (\mathbf{v}_0, \mathbf{v}_1, \mathbf{v}_2)$. If $\mathbf{v}_0 \notin 2\Lambda(\mathbf{A}^\mathsf{T})$, output $\bot$. Finally, output

$$\mathsf{encode}^{-1}(\mathbf{v}^\mathsf{T} \begin{bmatrix} \mathbf{R}_{i1} & \mathbf{R}_{i2} \\ \mathbf{I} & 0 \\ 0 & \mathbf{I} \end{bmatrix} \bmod 2q) \in \{0,1\}^{nk}$$

  if it exists, otherwise output $\bot$.
- ReKeyGen($\mathsf{pk}_i, \mathsf{sk}_i, \mathsf{pk}_j$): The re-encryption key generation algorithm does:
  1. Use $\mathsf{sk}_i = [\mathbf{R}_{i1}|\mathbf{R}_{i2}]$ to run extended sampling algorithm $\mathsf{Sample}^{\mathcal{O}}$ to sample $\mathbf{X}_{01}, \mathbf{X}_{02}, \mathbf{X}_{11}, \mathbf{X}_{12} \in \mathbb{Z}^{nk \times nk}$ such that

$$[\mathbf{A}| - \mathbf{A}_{i1} + h(1)\mathbf{G}| - \mathbf{A}_{i2} + \mathbf{B}] \begin{bmatrix} \mathbf{I} & \mathbf{X}_{01} & \mathbf{X}_{02} \\ 0 & \mathbf{X}_{11} & \mathbf{X}_{12} \\ 0 & 0 & \mathbf{I} \end{bmatrix} = [\mathbf{A} - \mathbf{A}_{j1} + h(2)\mathbf{G}| - \mathbf{A}_{j2} + \mathbf{B}]$$

  for any matrix $\mathbf{B} \in \mathbb{Z}^{n \times nk}$.
  2. Output the re-encryption key

$$\mathsf{rk}_{i \to j} = \{\mathbf{X}_{01}, \mathbf{X}_{02}, \mathbf{X}_{11}, \mathbf{X}_{12}\}$$

- ReEnc($\mathsf{rk}_{i \to j}, \mathsf{ct}$): First the re-encryption algorithm parses $\mathsf{ct} = (u, b, \ell)$ outputs a special symbol $\bot$ if $\ell = 2$. Otherwise, it computes

$$\mathbf{b}^\mathsf{T} \cdot \mathsf{rk}_{i \to j} = \mathbf{s}^\mathsf{T}[\mathbf{A}| - \mathbf{A}_{j1} + h(1)\mathbf{G}| - \mathbf{A}_{j2} + h(u)\mathbf{G}] + \mathbf{e}'^\mathsf{T} + \widetilde{\mathbf{e}}^\mathsf{T} + (0, 0, \mathsf{encode}(\mu)^\mathsf{T})$$

where $\mathbf{e}' = (\mathbf{e}_0', \mathbf{e}_1', \mathbf{e}_2')$, $\widetilde{\mathbf{e}} \leftarrow \mathcal{D}_{\mathbb{Z}^{3nk}, s'}$, and

$$\mathbf{e}_0' = \mathbf{e}_0, \qquad \mathbf{e}_1' = \mathbf{e}_0\mathbf{X}_{01} + \mathbf{e}_1\mathbf{X}_{11}, \qquad \mathbf{e}_2' = \mathbf{e}_0\mathbf{X}_{02} + \mathbf{e}_1\mathbf{X}_{12} + \mathbf{e}_2 \qquad (3)$$

Then, it outputs $\mathsf{ct}' = (u, \mathbf{b}', 2)$.

Parameter Setting. In this part, we set the lattice parameters used in our construction. The correctness proof of our construction can be found in full version [19]. $\mathbf{G} \in \mathbb{Z}_q^{n \times nk}$ is a gadget matrix for $q = \mathsf{poly}(n), n = \mathsf{poly}(\lambda)$ and $k = O(\log q) = O(\log n)$. For matrix $\mathbf{A} \in \mathbb{Z}_q^{n \times m}$ in the public parameters and secret keys $\mathbf{R} \leftarrow \mathcal{D}$, we set $m = O(nk)$ and $\mathcal{D} = \mathcal{D}_{\mathbb{Z}, w(\sqrt{\log n})}^{m \times nk}$ respectively. We set the deviation s for discrete Gaussian distribution used in security proof to be $s = w(\sqrt{\log n})\sqrt{m}$, and parameter for level 2 error is $s' = s\sqrt{m}$. For the error rate α in the LWE assumption, we set sufficiently large $1/\alpha = O(nk) \cdot w(\sqrt{\log n})$.

5 Proxy Re-Signature with Selectively Chosen Tag

In this section, we present the syntax and our construction of PRS.

5.1 Syntax and Correctness Definition

We first recall the syntax and security definition of PRS in [7,25], then propose a simpler and unified security model that captures the security requirements. Our model adapts the same spirit of the prior security model of proxy re-encryption [10,26], with necessary modifications to fit into the signature framework. We also compare our new notion with the previous security model in [7,25].

Let $L = L(\lambda)$ denotes the maximum level the PRS system supports. The scheme $\Sigma = (\mathsf{Setup}, \mathsf{KeyGen}, \mathsf{Sign}, \mathsf{Verify}, \mathsf{ReKeyGen}, \mathsf{ReSign})$ is described as follows:

- $\mathsf{pp} \leftarrow \mathsf{Setup}(1^\lambda, 1^L)$ generates the public parameter pp for the whole system.
- $(\mathsf{pk}, \mathsf{sk}) \leftarrow \mathsf{KeyGen}(\mathsf{pp}, i)$ generates $(\mathsf{pk}_i, \mathsf{sk}_i)$ for user i.
- $\sigma \leftarrow \mathsf{Sign}(\mathsf{sk}_i, \mu, \kappa)$ computes a signature σ for μ at level κ.
- $\mathsf{Verify}(\mathsf{pk}_i, \sigma, \mu, \kappa)$ outputs 1 (accept) or 0 (reject).
- $\mathsf{rk}_{i \to j}^\kappa \leftarrow \mathsf{ReKeyGen}(\mathsf{pk}_i, \mathsf{pk}_j, \mathsf{sk}_j, \kappa)$ computes a re-signing key from the i-th user at level κ to the j-th user at level $\kappa + 1$.
- $\mathsf{ReSign}(\mathsf{rk}_{i \to j}^\kappa, \mu, \sigma, \kappa)$ computes a re-signature σ' under pk_j if $\mathsf{Verify}(\mathsf{pk}_i, \sigma, \mu, \kappa) = 1$, or $\perp$ otherwise.

Correctness. For all security parameter λ, any $\mathsf{pp} \leftarrow \mathsf{Setup}(1^\lambda, 1^L)$, all couples of secret/public key pairs $(\mathsf{sk}_i, \mathsf{pk}_i), (\mathsf{sk}_j, \mathsf{pk}_j)$ generated by $\mathsf{KeyGen}(\mathsf{pp})$, for any message μ and $\kappa \in [L]$, it holds that

$$\mathsf{Verify}(\mathsf{pk}_i, \mu, \kappa, \mathsf{Sign}(\mathsf{sk}_i, \mu, \kappa)) = 1$$

$$\mathsf{Verify}(\mathsf{pk}_j, \kappa + 1, \mu, \sigma) = 1$$

where $\sigma = \mathsf{ReSign}(\mathsf{rk}_{i \to j}^\kappa, \mu, \kappa, \mathsf{Sign}(\mathsf{sk}_i, \mu, \kappa))$ and $\mathsf{rk}_{i \to j}^\kappa \leftarrow \mathsf{ReKeyGen}(\mathsf{pk}_i, \mathsf{pk}_j, \mathsf{sk}_j, \kappa)$.

5.2 Our PRS Construction

Now we present our PRS construction and its security proof sketch. For simplicity, we first present the scheme with security regarding a selective chosen tag, where in the security experiment, the adversary needs to commit to the challenge tag before obtaining public parameters and public keys. In the full version, we also describe how to modify our construction, slightly, to achieve security for adaptively chosen tags. Let the message space be $\mathcal{M} = \mathbb{Z}_q$, and the tag space be $\mathcal{T} = \mathbb{Z}_q$. The description is the following:

- $\mathsf{Setup}(1^\lambda, 1^L)$: The setup algorithm sets the lattice parameters (n, q, m, s), then randomly chooses a matrix $\mathbf{A} \in \mathbb{Z}_q^{n \times m}$ and vectors $\boldsymbol{b}, \boldsymbol{v} \in \mathbb{Z}_q^n$. Output the public parameter $\mathsf{pp} = (\mathbf{A}, \boldsymbol{b}, \boldsymbol{v}, q, n, m)$.

- KeyGen(pp): The key generation algorithm computes $(\mathsf{pk}_i, \mathsf{sk}_i)$ as follows:
  1. Sample two small matrices $\mathbf{R}_{i1}, \mathbf{R}_{i2}$ from discrete Gaussian distribution $\mathcal{D}_{\mathbb{Z}^{m \times m}, s}$.
  2. Compute $\mathbf{A}_i = \mathbf{A} \cdot \mathbf{R}_{i1} \bmod q$ and $\mathbf{A}_i' = \mathbf{A} \cdot \mathbf{R}_{i2} \bmod q$.
  3. The public key pk_i and secret key sk_i for i-th user is

$$\mathsf{pk}_i = (\mathbf{A}_i, \mathbf{A}_i'), \qquad \mathsf{sk}_i = (\mathbf{R}_{i1}, \mathbf{R}_{i2})$$

- Sign(pp, $\mathsf{sk}_i, \mu, \kappa$): The signing algorithm does:
  1. Randomly select a non-zero tag $t \in \mathbb{Z}_q^*$, and define the signing matrix to be

$$\mathbf{F}_{t,i,\kappa} = [\mathbf{A}|\mathbf{A}_i + h(\kappa)\mathbf{G}|\mathbf{A}_i' + t\mathbf{G}]$$

  2. Sample a vector $\mathbf{r}_1 \leftarrow \mathcal{D}_{\mathbb{Z}^m, s}$, then sample vector $(\mathbf{r}_0, \mathbf{r}_2) \in \mathbb{Z}^{2m}$, using

$$(\mathbf{r}_0, \mathbf{r}_2) \leftarrow \mathsf{Sample}^{\mathcal{O}}(\mathbf{A}, t\mathbf{G}, \mathbf{R}_{i2}, \mathbf{T_G}, \mathbf{b} + \mu\mathbf{v} - (\mathbf{A}_i' + h(\kappa)\mathbf{G})\mathbf{r}_1, s)$$

  Therefore, it holds that $\mathbf{F}_{t,i,\kappa} \cdot \sigma = \mathbf{b} + \mu\mathbf{v} \bmod q$, where $\sigma = (\mathbf{r}_0, \mathbf{r}_1, \mathbf{r}_2)$.
  3. Output the signature (σ, t, i, κ).
- Verify(pp, $\mathsf{pk}_i, \mu, (\sigma, t, i, \kappa)$): The verification algorithm dose:
  1. Parse the signature tuple as $\sigma = (\mathbf{r}_0, \mathbf{r}_1, \mathbf{r}_2)$, tag t, user index i and level index κ, then first check the norm of $|\sigma| = |(\mathbf{r}_0, \mathbf{r}_1, \mathbf{r}_2)|$. Output 0 if $|\sigma| \geq B$.
  2. Reconstruct the signing matrix

$$\mathbf{F}_{t,i,\kappa} = [\mathbf{A}|\mathbf{A}_i + h(\kappa)\mathbf{G}|\mathbf{A}_i' + t\mathbf{G}]$$

  and output 1 if $\mathbf{F}_{t,i,\kappa} \cdot \sigma = \mathbf{b} + \mu\mathbf{v}$, otherwise output 0.
- ReKeyGen($\mathsf{pk}_i, (\mathsf{sk}_j, \mathsf{pk}_j), \kappa$): The re-signing key generation:
  1. Sample small matrices $(\mathbf{X}_{01}, \mathbf{X}_{11}, \mathbf{X}_{02}, \mathbf{X}_{12})$, using

$$(\mathbf{X}_{01}, \mathbf{X}_{11}) \leftarrow \mathsf{Sample}^{\mathcal{O}}(\mathbf{A}, h(\kappa+1)\mathbf{G}, \mathbf{R}_{j1}, \mathbf{T_G}, \mathbf{A}_i + h(\kappa)\mathbf{G}, s),$$

$$(\mathbf{X}_{02}, \mathbf{X}_{12}) \leftarrow \mathsf{Sample}^{\mathcal{O}}(\mathbf{A}, h(\kappa+1)\mathbf{G}, \mathbf{R}_{j1}, \mathbf{T_G}, \mathbf{A}_i' - \mathbf{A}_j', s)$$

  Therefore it holds that

$$[\mathbf{A}|\mathbf{A}_j + h(\kappa+1)\mathbf{G}|\mathbf{A}_j' + t\mathbf{G}] \begin{bmatrix} \mathbf{I} & \mathbf{X}_{01} & \mathbf{X}_{02} \\ 0 & \mathbf{X}_{11} & \mathbf{X}_{12} \\ 0 & 0 & \mathbf{I} \end{bmatrix} = [\mathbf{A}|\mathbf{A}_i + h(\kappa)\mathbf{G}|\mathbf{A}_i' + t\mathbf{G}]$$

  2. Output the re-signing key $\mathsf{rk}_{i \to j}^\kappa = (\mathbf{X}_{01}, \mathbf{X}_{02}, \mathbf{X}_{11}, \mathbf{X}_{12})$.
- ReSign($\mathsf{rk}_{i \to j}^\kappa, (\sigma, t, i, \kappa), \mu, \mathsf{pk}_i$): The re-signing algorithm does:
  1. First parse $\sigma = (\mathbf{r}_0, \mathbf{r}_1, \mathbf{r}_2)$. Output $\perp$ if Verify(pp, $\mathsf{pk}_i, \mu, (\sigma, t, i, \kappa)) = 0$.
  2. Otherwise, output the re-signature tuple $(\sigma', t, j, \kappa + 1)$, where $\sigma' = \mathsf{rk}_{j \to j}^\kappa \cdot \sigma$.

5.3   Parameter Setting

Let λ be the security parameter. For $L = \mathsf{polylog}(\lambda)$ maximum allowed re-signing, we set the parameters of our scheme based on standard SIS assumption as $q = n^{O(L)}, n = \mathsf{poly}(\lambda), L = \mathsf{polylog}(\lambda), m = O(n \log q)$. To ensure the SIS instance has a worst-case lattice reduction as shown in [30], i.e. $q \geq \beta \omega(\sqrt{n \log n})$, we set $\beta = \mathsf{polylog}(n)$. In order to achieve indistinguishability between real execution and reduction, the Gaussian parameter is set to be $s = \omega(\sqrt{\log n})$. As a signature produced by algorithm Sign has the size of $O(s\sqrt{m})$, and after each re-signing, the size grows at the rate of $O(sm)$, so we set parameter used in verification to be $B = \omega(2^L)$. Our PRS construction can support $L = \mathsf{poly}(\lambda)$-hop using subexponential SIS assumption.

6   Conclusion

In this work, we first point out a subtle error in work [24] and then showed how to construct single-hop PRE that is secure in our new model, tag-based CCA security. We then extend our security definition and construction to the multi-hop scenario, as elaborated in the full version [19]. Lastly, we propose a simpler and unified security model for PRS which captures more dynamic settings, then give a construction based on SIS assumption. Due to the space constrain, the security definition and proof of PRS are in the full version of this paper [19].

Acknowledgement. Xiong Fan is supported by NSF Award CNS-1561209. Feng-Hao Liu is supported by the NSF Award CNS-1657040. Any opinions, findings, and conclusions or recommendations expressed in this material are those of the author(s) and do not necessarily reflect the views of the sponsors.

References

1. Agrawal, S., Boneh, D., Boyen, X.: Efficient lattice (H)IBE in the standard model. In: Gilbert, H. (ed.) EUROCRYPT 2010. LNCS, vol. 6110, pp. 553–572. Springer, Heidelberg (2010). https://doi.org/10.1007/978-3-642-13190-5_28
2. Ajtai, M.: Determinism versus non-determinism for linear time RAMs (extended abstract). In 31st ACM STOC, pp. 632–641. ACM Press, May 1999
3. Alwen, J., et al.: On the relationship between functional encryption, obfuscation, and fully homomorphic encryption. In: Stam, M. (ed.) IMACC 2013. LNCS, vol. 8308, pp. 65–84. Springer, Heidelberg (2013). https://doi.org/10.1007/978-3-642-45239-0_5
4. Aono, Y., Boyen, X., Phong, L.T., Wang, L.: Key-private proxy re-encryption under LWE. In: Paul, G., Vaudenay, S. (eds.) INDOCRYPT 2013. LNCS, vol. 8250, pp. 1–18. Springer, Cham (2013). https://doi.org/10.1007/978-3-319-03515-4_1
5. Asharov, G., Jain, A., López-Alt, A., Tromer, E., Vaikuntanathan, V., Wichs, D.: Multiparty computation with low communication, computation and interaction via threshold FHE. In: Pointcheval, D., Johansson, T. (eds.) EUROCRYPT 2012. LNCS, vol. 7237, pp. 483–501. Springer, Heidelberg (2012). https://doi.org/10.1007/978-3-642-29011-4_29

6. Ateniese, G., Fu, K., Green, M., Hohenberger, S.: Improved proxy re-encryption schemes with applications to secure distributed storage. In: NDSS 2005. The Internet Society, February 2005
7. Ateniese, G., Hohenberger, S.: Proxy re-signatures: new definitions, algorithms, and applications. In: Atluri, V., Meadows, C., Juels, A. (eds.) ACM CCS 2005, pp. 310–319. ACM Press, November 2005
8. Blaze, M., Bleumer, G., Strauss, M.: Divertible protocols and atomic proxy cryptography. In: Nyberg, K. (ed.) EUROCRYPT 1998. LNCS, vol. 1403, pp. 127–144. Springer, Heidelberg (1998). https://doi.org/10.1007/BFb0054122
9. Boyen, X.: Lattice mixing and vanishing trapdoors: a framework for fully secure short signatures and more. In: Nguyen, P.Q., Pointcheval, D. (eds.) PKC 2010. LNCS, vol. 6056, pp. 499–517. Springer, Heidelberg (2010). https://doi.org/10.1007/978-3-642-13013-7_29
10. Canetti, R., Hohenberger, S.: Chosen-ciphertext secure proxy re-encryption. In: Ning, P., De Capitani di Vimercati, S., Syverson, P.F. (eds.) ACM CCS 2007, pp. 185–194. ACM Press, October 2007
11. Canetti, R., Lin, H., Tessaro, S., Vaikuntanathan, V.: Obfuscation of probabilistic circuits and applications. In: Dodis, Y., Nielsen, J.B. (eds.) TCC 2015. LNCS, vol. 9015, pp. 468–497. Springer, Heidelberg (2015). https://doi.org/10.1007/978-3-662-46497-7_19
12. Canetti, R., Lombardi, A., Wichs, D.: Non-interactive zero knowledge and correlation intractability from circular-secure FHE. Cryptology ePrint Archive, Report 2018/1248 (2018). https://eprint.iacr.org/2018/1248
13. Chandran, N., Chase, M., Liu, F.-H., Nishimaki, R., Xagawa, K.: Re-encryption, functional re-encryption, and multi-hop re-encryption: a framework for achieving obfuscation-based security and instantiations from lattices. In: Krawczyk, H. (ed.) PKC 2014. LNCS, vol. 8383, pp. 95–112. Springer, Heidelberg (2014). https://doi.org/10.1007/978-3-642-54631-0_6
14. Chandran, N., Chase, M., Vaikuntanathan, V.: Functional re-encryption and collusion-resistant obfuscation. In: Cramer, R. (ed.) TCC 2012. LNCS, vol. 7194, pp. 404–421. Springer, Heidelberg (2012). https://doi.org/10.1007/978-3-642-28914-9_23
15. Chow, S.S.M., Phan, R.C.-W.: Proxy re-signatures in the standard model. In: Wu, T.-C., Lei, C.-L., Rijmen, V., Lee, D.-T. (eds.) ISC 2008. LNCS, vol. 5222, pp. 260–276. Springer, Heidelberg (2008). https://doi.org/10.1007/978-3-540-85886-7_18
16. Chow, S.S.M., Weng, J., Yang, Y., Deng, R.H.: Efficient unidirectional proxy re-encryption. In: Bernstein, D.J., Lange, T. (eds.) AFRICACRYPT 2010. LNCS, vol. 6055, pp. 316–332. Springer, Heidelberg (2010). https://doi.org/10.1007/978-3-642-12678-9_19
17. Cohen, A.: What about Bob? the inadequacy of CPA security for proxy reencryption. In: Lin, D., Sako, K. (eds.) PKC 2019. LNCS, vol. 11443, pp. 287–316. Springer, Cham (2019). https://doi.org/10.1007/978-3-030-17259-6_10
18. Dodis, Y., Reyzin, L., Smith, A.: Fuzzy extractors: how to generate strong keys from biometrics and other noisy data. In: Cachin, C., Camenisch, J.L. (eds.) EUROCRYPT 2004. LNCS, vol. 3027, pp. 523–540. Springer, Heidelberg (2004). https://doi.org/10.1007/978-3-540-24676-3_31
19. Fan, X., Liu, F.-H.: Proxy re-encryption and re-signatures from lattices. IACR Cryptology ePrint Archive **2017**, 456 (2017)

20. Fiat, A., Shamir, A.: How to prove yourself: practical solutions to identification and signature problems. In: Odlyzko, A.M. (ed.) CRYPTO 1986. LNCS, vol. 263, pp. 186–194. Springer, Heidelberg (1987). https://doi.org/10.1007/3-540-47721-7_12

21. Garg, S., Gentry, C., Halevi, S.: Candidate multilinear maps from ideal lattices. In: Johansson, T., Nguyen, P.Q. (eds.) EUROCRYPT 2013. LNCS, vol. 7881, pp. 1–17. Springer, Heidelberg (2013). https://doi.org/10.1007/978-3-642-38348-9_1

22. Gentry, C., Peikert, C., Vaikuntanathan, V.: Trapdoors for hard lattices and new cryptographic constructions. In: Ladner, R.E., Dwork, C. (eds.) 40th ACM STOC, pp. 197–206. ACM Press, May 2008

23. Hohenberger, S., Rothblum, G.N., Shelat, A., Vaikuntanathan, V.: Securely obfuscating re-encryption. In: Vadhan, S.P. (ed.) TCC 2007. LNCS, vol. 4392, pp. 233–252. Springer, Heidelberg (2007). https://doi.org/10.1007/978-3-540-70936-7_13

24. Kirshanova, E.: Proxy re-encryption from lattices. In: Krawczyk, H. (ed.) PKC 2014. LNCS, vol. 8383, pp. 77–94. Springer, Heidelberg (2014). https://doi.org/10.1007/978-3-642-54631-0_5

25. Libert, B., Vergnaud, D.: Multi-use unidirectional proxy re-signatures. In: Ning, P., Syverson, P.F., Jha, S. (eds.) ACM CCS 2008, pp. 511–520. ACM Press, October 2008

26. Libert, B., Vergnaud, D.: Unidirectional chosen-ciphertext secure proxy re-encryption. In: Cramer, R. (ed.) PKC 2008. LNCS, vol. 4939, pp. 360–379. Springer, Heidelberg (2008). https://doi.org/10.1007/978-3-540-78440-1_21

27. Lyubashevsky, V., Peikert, C., Regev, O.: On ideal lattices and learning with errors over rings. In: Gilbert, H. (ed.) EUROCRYPT 2010. LNCS, vol. 6110, pp. 1–23. Springer, Heidelberg (2010). https://doi.org/10.1007/978-3-642-13190-5_1

28. Micciancio, D., Peikert, C.: Trapdoors for lattices: simpler, tighter, faster, smaller. In: Pointcheval, D., Johansson, T. (eds.) EUROCRYPT 2012. LNCS, vol. 7237, pp. 700–718. Springer, Heidelberg (2012). https://doi.org/10.1007/978-3-642-29011-4_41

29. Micciancio, D., Peikert, C.: Hardness of SIS and LWE with small parameters. In: Canetti, R., Garay, J.A. (eds.) CRYPTO 2013. LNCS, vol. 8042, pp. 21–39. Springer, Heidelberg (2013). https://doi.org/10.1007/978-3-642-40041-4_2

30. Micciancio, D., Regev, O.: Worst-case to average-case reductions based on Gaussian measures. In: 45th FOCS, pp. 372–381. IEEE Computer Society Press, October 2004

31. Nunez, D., Agudo, I., Lopez, J.: A parametric family of attack models for proxy re-encryption. In: 2015 IEEE 28th Computer Security Foundations Symposium (CSF), pp. 290–301. IEEE (2015)

32. Regev, O.: On lattices, learning with errors, random linear codes, and cryptography. In: Gabow, H.N., Fagin, R. (eds.) 37th ACM STOC, pp. 84–93. ACM Press, May 2005

33. Shao, J., Cao, Z., Liu, P.: CCA-Secure PRE scheme without random oracles. Cryptology ePrint Archive, Report 2010/112 (2010). http://eprint.iacr.org/2010/112

34. Shao, J., Feng, M., Zhu, B., Cao, Z., Liu, P.: The security model of unidirectional proxy re-signature with private re-signature key. In: Steinfeld, R., Hawkes, P. (eds.) ACISP 2010. LNCS, vol. 6168, pp. 216–232. Springer, Heidelberg (2010). https://doi.org/10.1007/978-3-642-14081-5_14

Public Key and Commitment

DL-Extractable UC-Commitment Schemes

Behzad Abdolmaleki[1], Karim Baghery[1], Helger Lipmaa[1(✉)], Janno Siim[1], and Michał Zając[2]

[1] University of Tartu, Tartu, Estonia
helger.lipmaa@gmail.com
[2] Clearmatics, London, UK

Abstract. We define a new UC functionality (DL-extractable commitment scheme) that allows committer to open a commitment to a group element g^x; however, the simulator will be able to extract its discrete logarithm x. Such functionality is useful in situations where the secrecy of x is important since the knowledge of x enables to break privacy while the simulator needs to know x to be able to simulate the corrupted committer. Based on Fujisaki's UC-secure commitment scheme and the Damgård-Fujisaki integer commitment scheme, we propose an efficient commitment scheme that realizes the new functionality. As another novelty, we construct the new scheme in the weaker RPK (registered public key) model instead of the CRS model used by Fujisaki.

Keywords: CRS model · Extractable commitment · RPK model · Universal composability · UC commitment

1 Introduction

A commitment scheme is one of the most basic primitives in cryptography. Essentially, it implements a digital safe: in the commitment phase, the committer puts her message to the safe, locks it, and hands it to the receiver. In the open phase, the committer uses her key to open the safe. Thus, a commitment scheme satisfies at least the following two properties: it is binding (the committer cannot change the committed message) and hiding (before the opening, the receiver does not know which message was committed to).

In many applications, commitment schemes must satisfy stronger properties. In the case of *UC-security* [8], one first defines an ideal functionality (e.g., the functionality of the commitment scheme) and then constructs a protocol that UC-realizes this functionality. Such protocol is said to be UC-secure. Due to Canetti's composition theorem [8], a UC-secure protocol enjoys secure composability with arbitrary protocols, without the need to reprove its security. Importantly, UC-secure protocols do not have to be modified to be secure in a specific software environment and thus can be used as a black-box by practitioners. As such, UC is the recommended best practice in cryptographic engineering.

R. H. Deng et al. (Eds.): ACNS 2019, LNCS 11464, pp. 385–405, 2019.
https://doi.org/10.1007/978-3-030-21568-2_19

The first UC-commitment scheme was proposed by Canetti and Fischlin [9]. A UC-commitment scheme was shown to be complete for the construction of UC-secure zero knowledge protocols [9,14] and two-party and multi-party computations [10]. UC-commitment schemes have to satisfy the properties of extractability (the simulator can unambiguously extract the committed message) and equivocability (the simulator can open a commitment to an arbitrary value) at the same time, and thus they cannot be constructed without an additional setup assumption [9]. The most widely known setup assumption is the common reference string (CRS, [6]) model that allows for a *universally trusted* entity that generates the CRS from the correct distribution without revealing its trapdoor.

Many different CRS-model UC-commitment schemes are known, starting with [7,9,10,14]. Lindell [21] proposed the first efficient scheme based on an ordinary prime-order group. Blazy *et al.* [5] corrected a bug in Lindell's scheme and proposed a new scheme with additional optimizations. Fujisaki [16] further optimized the scheme of Blazy *et al.*, obtaining the most efficient currently known UC-commitment scheme Fuj in an ordinary prime-order group.

The main idea of the UC-commitment schemes of [5,16,21] is that the committer C encrypts a message m. During the open phase, C outputs m together with an interactive proof (a Σ-protocol) that she encrypted m. She also erases the used randomizer (hence, these commitments schemes assume secure erasure). The UC simulator simulates the Σ-protocol using the CRS trapdoor; to achieve UC-security, the Σ-protocol has to be straight-line extractable. Due to the use of a Σ-protocol, [5,16,21] have either an interactive commit phase (resulting in adaptive security) or an interactive open phase (resulting in static security). Within this paper, we will concentrate on adaptively secure variants. Fischlin, Libert, and Manulis [15] used a Groth-Sahai proof [19] instead of a Σ-protocol to construct a non-interactive adaptive UC-commitment scheme; however, their scheme is computationally less efficient and uses bilinear pairings.

An important question, often asked by practitioners, is how to implement the CRS model. More precisely, how can one guarantee the existence of a *single* party $\mathcal{R}$ that can be trusted by *everybody* to choose the CRS from the correct distribution without leaking its trapdoors? Fortunately, weaker setup models are known. Barak, Canetti, Nielsen, and Pass [2] introduced the weaker registered public key (RPK) model where it is essentially required that each party $\mathcal{G}_i$ must trust *some* key registration authority $\mathcal{R}_i$ who registers his key. The authorities $\mathcal{R}_i$ can coincide or be different, depending on the application. They do not need to trust each other. In particular, the CRS model is a very strong case of the RPK model where there is only one authority $\mathcal{R}$ whom all parties have to trust. Barak *et al.* [2] proposed a UC-commitment scheme that is secure in the RPK model: in fact, they used the property of a known UC-commitment scheme in the CRS model that its CRS can be divided into two parts: a binding part (trusted by the receiver R) and a hiding part (trusted by the committer C). Thus, the binding part can be registered by the authority of R and the hiding part can be registered by the authority of C. Unfortunately, their scheme is quite inefficient.

Moreover, the functionality of UC-commitments is not always sufficient. E.g., consider the following generic class of (UC-secure) pairing-based multiplicative public key generation protocols. (This protocol is motivated by a non-UC-secure CRS-generation protocol for SNARKs [17,18,22] from [4] that can be used also to generate the CRS of UC-secure SNARKs like [20].) Let $\mathsf{p} = (p, \mathbb{G}_1, \mathbb{G}_2, \mathbb{G}_T, \hat{e}, g_1, g_2, g_T)$ be an (asymmetric) prime-order bilinear group where g_i is a generator of $\mathbb{G}_i$. Different parties $\mathcal{G}_i$, $i \in [1 .. \nu]$, sample their one-time public keys $(g_1^{\sigma_i}, g_2^{\sigma_i})$, for secret key σ_i, and UC-commit to them. After all parties have committed, everybody opens commitments to their public keys. Next, they enact a sequential protocol where the ith party computes $g_1^{\sigma_i^*} := g_1^{\prod_{j=1}^{i} \sigma_j}$ as $g_1^{\sigma_i^*} \leftarrow \left(g_1^{\sigma_{i-1}^*} \right)^{\sigma_i}$, by using a public group element $g_1^{\sigma_{i-1}^*}$ and a secret integer σ_i. Under the minimal assumption that at least one $\mathcal{G}_i$ is honest, it is required that the joint public key $g_1^{\sigma_\nu^*}$ is uniformly random and that no coalition of less than ν knows the corresponding secret key σ_ν^*. Due to this, σ_i should not be leaked while opening to $g_2^{\sigma_i}$ is needed for public verification of the correctness of the operation of $\mathcal{G}_i$. Namely, for this, one needs to check that $\hat{e}(g_1^{\sigma_i^*}, g_2) = \hat{e}(g_1^{\sigma_{i-1}^*}, g_2^{\sigma_i})$; thus, avoiding the use of costly zero-knowledge protocols.

On the other hand, in the security proof, the UC simulator Sim needs to recover σ_i (and not only $(g_1^{\sigma_i}, g_2^{\sigma_i})$) to be able to simulate the operation of a corrupted party. Hence, we have arrived to the requirement that after the committer commits to a message m, it should be opened to (g_1^m, g_2^m) while the simulator must be able to extract m from the functionality.

Similar functionality is needed to achieve security in other UC protocols, especially in the setting where one uses a DL-based cryptosystem (or a commitment scheme) to encrypt the witness yet needs to extract the witness for simulation purposes. It can be implemented by encrypting the witness (that has to be extractable) bitwise, and then giving a NIZK argument that each ciphertext encrypts a Boolean value $m \in \{0, 1\}$. Protocols using such a technique have obviously huge communication.

Finally, non-falsifiable assumptions (e.g., knowledge assumptions [12,23]) are usually used to (i) extract a unique long message from a succinct commitment, one can avoid such use of non-falsifiable assumptions by having a linearly-long commitment (as done, say, in [20]), and (ii) extract the exponent from a group element, for example, in the case one uses the Groth-Sahai commitment scheme for scalars [19]. To avoid using non-falsifiable assumptions in this case, one can use a DL-extractable commitment scheme that we define in the current paper.

Our Contributions. Let $\mathbb{G}$ be a prime-order group with generator g. We will define the new ideal functionality $\mathcal{F}_{\mathsf{mcomdl}}$ of a *DL-extractable commitment scheme*. Intuitively, the main difference between $\mathcal{F}_{\mathsf{mcomdl}}$ and the standard functionality $\mathcal{F}_{\mathsf{mcom}}$ of UC-commitment schemes [9] is that in $\mathcal{F}_{\mathsf{mcomdl}}$, the committer sends m to the functionality who stores m. When opening the commitment, the functionality $\mathcal{F}_{\mathsf{mcomdl}}$ only sends $g^m \in \mathbb{G}$ (while $\mathcal{F}_{\mathsf{mcom}}$ sends m itself) to the receiver. Since the functionality stores m, it means that after the committer is corrupted, the UC simulator will get to know m.

We seem to be the first to formalize $\mathcal{F}_{mcomdl}$ as a separate functionality (see Remark 1 in Sect. 3 for a comparison to the notion of P-extractability of Belenkiy et al. [3]); such a formalization creates a common language and enables other researchers to use our implementation of $\mathcal{F}_{mcomdl}$ as a black-box. At this moment it is even difficult to search for papers that implicitly use this functionality due to lack of agreed-upon language and notation. We expect there to be more applications after the current work establishes the common language.

After that, we construct a commitment scheme Γ_{dl} that UC-realizes $\mathcal{F}_{mcomdl}$ in the $\mathcal{F}_{rpk}$-hybrid model, i.e., assuming availability of a UC-secure realization of the RPK model. Essentially, Γ_{dl} is based on Fujisaki's CRS-model UC-commitment scheme Fuj [16] with the following important modifications. First, [5,16,21] all work in the CRS model. We crucially observe that the commitment key of Fuj consists of two independent parts, one guaranteeing hiding and another one guaranteeing binding. Relying on this separation, we will lift Fuj (and also its DL-extractable version) to the weaker RPK model. Since the RPK model seems to be relatively unknown in the community, reintroducing it and constructing an efficient commitment scheme in this model can be seen as another major contribution of the current work.

Second, to guarantee DL-extractability, we proceed as follows. One of the optimizations of Fujisaki compared to [5,21] is the use of the efficient IND-PCA secure Short Cramer-Shoup (SCS, [1]) public-key cryptosystem. We couple an SCS encryption of g^m with an additively homomorphic Paillier encryption [24] of m, an integer commitment [13] to m, and a straight-line extractable Σ-protocol showing that these three encryptions/commitments of m are mutually consistent. The UC simulator uses the Paillier encryption (importantly, the simulator does not rewind the Σ-protocol) to extract m from a corrupted committer. Thus, the Paillier encryption is needed for extraction while the integer commitment is needed to prove that the SCS plaintext g^{m_1} and the Paillier plaintext m_2 satisfy $m_1 \equiv m_2 \pmod{p}$ where p is the order of $\mathbb{G}$.

The construction of Γ_{dl} and its security proof are somewhat subtle due to the use of three different algebraic/number-theoretic settings (prime-order bilinear groups, Paillier encryption modulo $N = PQ$, and an integer commitment scheme). However, most of this subtlety is needed to construct the Σ-protocol and to prove its security.

Finally, the functionality of a DL-extractable commitment scheme can be straightforwardly generalized to that of a preimage-extractable commitment scheme where the map $m \mapsto g^m$ is replaced by $m \mapsto F(m)$ for any one-way permutation F. We leave study of such a generalization to the future work.

2   Preliminaries

Let PPT denote probabilistic polynomial-time. Let $\lambda \in \mathbb{N}$ be the information-theoretic security parameter, in practice, e.g., $\lambda = 128$. All adversaries will be stateful. For an algorithm $\mathcal{A}$, let $\mathsf{RND}(\mathcal{A})$ denote the random tape of $\mathcal{A}$, and let $r \leftarrow_\$ \mathsf{RND}(\mathcal{A})$ denote sampling of a randomizer r of sufficient length for $\mathcal{A}$'s needs. By $y \leftarrow \mathcal{A}(x; r)$ we denote that $\mathcal{A}$, given an input x and a randomizer r, outputs y. We denote by $\mathsf{negl}(\lambda)$ an arbitrary negligible function, and by $\mathsf{poly}(\lambda)$ an arbitrary polynomial function. $\mathcal{D}_1 \approx_c \mathcal{D}_2$ means that the distributions $\mathcal{D}_1$ and $\mathcal{D}_2$ are computationally indistinguishable.

Functionality $\mathcal{F}_{\mathsf{rpk}}^{f}$

$\mathcal{F}_{\mathsf{rpk}}^{f}$ proceeds as follows, given function f and security parameter λ, running with parties $\mathcal{G}_i$ and an adversary Sim. Initially, a set R of strings is set to be empty.

Registration: When receiving a message $(\mathtt{register}, \mathsf{sid})$ from a party $\mathcal{G}_i$ (either corrupted or uncorrupted) send $(\mathtt{register}, \mathsf{sid}, \mathcal{G}_i)$ to Sim and receive p' from Sim. If $p' \in R$ then let $p \leftarrow p'$. Otherwise, $r \leftarrow_\$ \{0,1\}^\lambda$, let $p \leftarrow f(r)$, and add p to R. Record $(\mathcal{G}_i, p)$ and return (sid, p) to $\mathcal{G}_i$ and to Sim.

Registration by a corrupted party: When receiving a message $(\mathtt{register}, \mathsf{sid}, r)$ from a corrupted party $\mathcal{G}_i$, record $(\mathcal{G}_i, f(r))$. In this case, $f(r)$ is not added to R.

Retrieval: When receiving a message $(\mathtt{retrieve}, \mathsf{sid}, \mathcal{G}_i)$ from party $\mathcal{G}_j$, send $(\mathtt{retrieve}, \mathsf{sid}, \mathcal{G}_i, \mathcal{G}_j)$ to Sim, and obtain a value p from Sim. If $(\mathcal{G}_i, p)$ is recorded then return $(\mathsf{sid}, \mathcal{G}_i, p)$ to $\mathcal{G}_j$. Else, return $(\mathsf{sid}, \mathcal{G}_i, \bot)$ to $\mathcal{G}_j$.

Functionality $\mathcal{F}_{\mathsf{crs}}^{\mathcal{D}}$

$\mathcal{F}_{\mathsf{crs}}^{\mathcal{D}}$ is parametrized by a distribution $\mathcal{D}$. It proceeds as follows, running with parties $\mathcal{G}_i$ and an adversary Sim.

CRS generation: Sample $\mathsf{crs} \leftarrow_\$ \mathcal{D}$.

Retrieval: upon receiving $(\mathtt{retrieve}, \mathsf{sid})$ from $\mathcal{G}_i$, send $(\mathtt{CRS}, \mathsf{sid}, \mathsf{crs})$ to $\mathcal{G}_i$.

Fig. 1. Functionalities $\mathcal{F}_{\mathsf{rpk}}^{f}$ and $\mathcal{F}_{\mathsf{crs}}^{\mathcal{D}}$

UC Security. We work in the standard universal composability framework of Canetti [8] with static corruptions of parties. For consistency, we use the definition of computational indistinguishability, denoted by $\approx_c$, from that work. The UC framework defines a PPT environment machine $\mathcal{Z}$ that oversees the execution of a protocol in one of two worlds. The "ideal world" execution involves "dummy parties" (some of whom may be corrupted by an ideal adversary/simulator Sim) interacting with a functionality $\mathcal{F}$. The "real world" execution involves PPT parties (some of whom may be corrupted by a PPT real world adversary $\mathcal{A}$) interacting only with each other in some protocol π. We refer to [8] for a detailed description of the executions, and a definition of the real world ensemble $\mathsf{EXEC}_{\pi,\mathcal{A},\mathcal{Z}}$ and the ideal world ensemble $\mathsf{IDEAL}_{\mathcal{F},\mathsf{Sim}^{\mathcal{A}},\mathcal{Z}}$.

A protocol π *UC-securely computes* $\mathcal{F}$ if there exists a PPT Sim such that for every non-uniform PPT $\mathcal{Z}$ and PPT $\mathcal{A}$, $\{\mathsf{IDEAL}_{\mathcal{F},\mathsf{Sim}^{\mathcal{A}},\mathcal{Z}}(\lambda, \mathsf{x})\}_{\lambda \in \mathbb{N}, \mathsf{x} \in \{0,1\}^*} \approx_c \{\mathsf{EXEC}_{\pi,\mathcal{A},\mathcal{Z}}(\lambda, \mathsf{x})\}_{\lambda \in \mathbb{N}, \mathsf{x} \in \{0,1\}^*}$.

The importance of this definition is a composition theorem that states that any protocol that is universally composable is secure when run concurrently with many other arbitrary protocols; see [8,10] for discussions and definitions.

In the registered public key (RPK, [2]) model, it is assumed that each party $\mathcal{G}_i$ trusts *some* key-registration authority $\mathcal{R}_i$ and has registered her key with $\mathcal{R}_i$. (The same $\mathcal{R}_i$ can be used by several parties, or each party can choose to trust a separate authority.) If $\mathcal{G}_i$ is honest, then the secret key exists and the public key comes from correct distribution (in this case, the public key is said to be *"safe"*). If $\mathcal{G}_i$ is dishonest, the secret key still exists (and the public key has been computed from it honestly) but there is no guarantee about its distribution (in this case, the public key is said to be *"well-formed"*). See Fig. 1 for the description of the functionality of the key registration from [2].

Several different variants (most importantly, the "traditional proof-of-knowledge" version where the secret key and the public key are generated by $\mathcal{G}_i$ who then sends the public key to $\mathcal{R}_i$ and proves the knowledge of the secret key to $\mathcal{R}_i$ by using a stand-alone zero-knowledge proof) of the RPK model are known. The new commitment can be implemented in any of such variants of the RPK model; in particular the definition of the $\mathcal{F}_{\mathsf{rpk}}$-hybrid model does not depend on the variant. We assume that each party knows the identities of all other parties and their key-registration authorities, see [2] for discussion.

In the CRS model [6], there is a single, universally trusted, third party (TTP) that picks a common reference string crs from a well-defined probability distribution and makes it available to all parties. An ideal functionality realizing the CRS model is presented on Fig. 1. In a usual implementation, crs comes with a secret trapdoor td, such that td is sampled from a well-defined distribution $\mathcal{D}_{\mathsf{td}}$, and for some public function f, we have $\mathsf{crs} \leftarrow f(\mathsf{td})$. In the case of a NIZK argument system, the knowledge of td allows the simulator to prove statements outside of the language. Here, it is assumed that TTP only provides td to the simulator but not to the adversary. The CRS model can be seen as a very strong version of the RPK model where all parties $\mathcal{G}_i$ trust the same TTP $\mathcal{R}$.

We denote an execution of π in the RPK-hybrid (the CRS-hybrid case is similar) model by $\mathsf{HYBRID}_{\pi,\mathcal{A},\mathcal{Z}}^{\mathcal{F}_{\mathsf{rpk}}^f}(\lambda, \mathsf{x})$. A protocol π *UC-securely computes* $\mathcal{F}$ in the $\mathcal{F}_{\mathsf{rpk}}^f$-hybrid model if there exists a PPT Sim such that every non-uniform PPT $\mathcal{Z}$ and PPT $\mathcal{A}$, $\{\mathsf{IDEAL}_{\mathcal{F},\mathsf{Sim}^{\mathcal{A}},\mathcal{Z}}(\lambda, \mathsf{x})\}_{\lambda \in \mathbb{N}, \mathsf{x} \in \{0,1\}^*} \approx_c$ $\{\mathsf{HYBRID}_{\pi,\mathcal{A},\mathcal{Z}}^{\mathcal{F}_{\mathsf{rpk}}^f}(\lambda, \mathsf{x})\}_{\lambda \in \mathbb{N}, \mathsf{x} \in \{0,1\}^*}$.

Root Assumption. An integer is $C(\lambda)$-*smooth* if all its prime factors are at most $C(\lambda)$, and $C(\lambda)$-*rough* [13] if all its prime factors are larger than $C(\lambda)$.

Let $\tilde{\mathbb{G}} = \mathbb{U} \times \mathbb{H}$ be a multiplicative abelian group such that $\mathbb{H}$ has order divisible only by large primes. That is, let $C(\lambda)$ and $l(\lambda)$ be two functions from $\mathbb{Z}^+$ to $\mathbb{Z}^+$, such that $C(\lambda)$ is superpolynomial and $l(\lambda)$ is polynomial. Let 2^B be an efficiently computable upperbound on $|\tilde{\mathbb{G}}|$, $2^B \geq \mathrm{ord}(\tilde{\mathbb{G}})$. Denote $l_{\tilde{\mathbb{G}}} := \mathrm{ord}(\mathbb{U})$. We assume $l_{\tilde{\mathbb{G}}} \leq l(\lambda)$, the description $\mathrm{descr}(\tilde{\mathbb{G}})$ of $\tilde{\mathbb{G}}$ includes $l_{\tilde{\mathbb{G}}}$, and that it is easy to verify whether some bitstring represents an element of $\tilde{\mathbb{G}}$. Let $\mathcal{G}(1^\lambda)$ generate $\mathrm{descr}(\tilde{\mathbb{G}})$ that has the mentioned properties. In the following instantiation, the root assumption is the same as the well-known Strong RSA assumption. (Another known instantiation [13] is based on class groups.)

Note that if $\tilde{\mathbb{G}} = \mathbb{U} \times \mathbb{H}$ is the multiplicative group modulo $N = PQ$ where $P = 2P' + 1$ and $Q = 2Q' + 1$ are safe primes, then $\mathrm{ord}(\tilde{\mathbb{G}}) = \varphi(N) = 4P'Q'$. (This setting is often recommended if one uses the RSA or the Paillier cryptosystem [24].) In this case, $\mathbb{U} \cong \mathbb{Z}_2 \times \mathbb{Z}_2$ is a group of order $l_{\tilde{\mathbb{G}}} = 4$ and $\mathbb{H}$ is a group of order $P'Q'$. Here, $\mathrm{descr}(\tilde{\mathbb{G}}) = \{N, l_{\tilde{\mathbb{G}}}\}$.

Consider the following experiment:

$\mathsf{Expt}^{\mathsf{root}}_{\Pi,\mathcal{A}}(\lambda)$
$\mathrm{descr}(\tilde{\mathbb{G}}) \leftarrow \mathcal{G}(1^\lambda); Y \leftarrow_{\$} \tilde{\mathbb{G}}; (e, X, \mu) \leftarrow \mathcal{A}(\mathrm{descr}(\tilde{\mathbb{G}}), Y);$ **if** $e \in \mathbb{Z} \wedge e > 1 \wedge X \in \tilde{\mathbb{G}} \wedge \mu \in \mathbb{U} \wedge Y = \mu X^e$ **then return** $1;$ **else return** $0;$ **fi**

The *root assumption* [13] holds relative to $\mathcal{G}$, if for all λ and PPT $\mathcal{A}$, $\Pr[\mathsf{Expt}^{\mathsf{root}}_{\Pi,\mathcal{A}}(\lambda) = 1] = \mathsf{negl}(\lambda)$.

Commitment Schemes. A *commitment scheme* $\Gamma = (\Gamma.\mathsf{Gen}, \Gamma.\mathsf{Com}, \Gamma.\mathsf{Vf})$ is defined by three PPT algorithms: (i) $\Gamma.\mathsf{Gen}(1^\lambda)$ generates a public key (CRS) $\Gamma.\mathsf{ck}$ and a secret key (trapdoor) $\Gamma.\mathsf{td}$; (ii) $\Gamma.\mathsf{Com}(\Gamma.\mathsf{ck}; m; r)$ commits to m under the CRS ck, using the random coins r. It outputs commitment c and opening information op; (iii) $\Gamma.\mathsf{Vf}(\Gamma.\mathsf{ck}; \mathsf{c}, m, \mathsf{op})$ verifies that c is a commitment to m.

It is required that for any $(\Gamma.\mathsf{ck}, \Gamma.\mathsf{td}) \leftarrow \Gamma.\mathsf{Gen}(1^\lambda)$ (where $\Gamma.\mathsf{td}$ is unused unless Γ has a trapdoor property), message m, randomizer r, and $(\mathsf{c}, \mathsf{op}) \leftarrow \Gamma.\mathsf{Com}(\Gamma.\mathsf{ck}; m; r)$, it holds that $\Gamma.\mathsf{Vf}(\Gamma.\mathsf{ck}; \mathsf{c}, m, \mathsf{op}) = 1$. Γ is *statistically hiding*, if the distributions of commitment c, corresponding to any two values of m, are statistically indistinguishable. Γ is *computationally binding*, if given ck and c, no PPT adversary $\mathcal{A}$ can create two different messages m_i with corresponding openings op_i, such that $\Gamma.\mathsf{Vf}(\Gamma.\mathsf{ck}; \mathsf{c}, m_1, \mathsf{op}_1) = \Gamma.\mathsf{Vf}(\Gamma.\mathsf{ck}; \mathsf{c}, m_2, \mathsf{op}_2) = 1$ with a non-negligible probability.

A commitment scheme Γ is *trapdoor* if there exists a PPT algorithm $\Gamma.\mathsf{tdOpen}$, such that given the trapdoor $\Gamma.\mathsf{td}$ (corresponding to commitment key $\Gamma.\mathsf{ck}$), two messages m_1 (with opening op_1) and m_2, and any commitment c: if $\Gamma.\mathsf{Vf}(\Gamma.\mathsf{ck}; m_1, \mathsf{c}, \mathsf{op}_1) = 1$ then $\Gamma.\mathsf{tdOpen}(\Gamma.\mathsf{td}; m_1, \mathsf{op}_1, m_2) = \mathsf{op}_2$, such that $\Gamma.\mathsf{Vf}(\Gamma.\mathsf{ck}; m_2, \mathsf{c}, \mathsf{op}_2) = 1$. The Pedersen trapdoor commitment scheme $\mathsf{Ped} = (\mathsf{Ped.Gen}, \mathsf{Ped.Com}, \mathsf{Ped.Vf}, \mathsf{Ped.tdOpen})$ [25] in cyclic group $\mathbb{G}$, with generator g, is defined as follows:

$\mathsf{Ped.Gen}(1^\lambda)$: sample $\mathsf{td} \leftarrow_{\$} \mathbb{Z}_p$, set $h \leftarrow g^{\mathsf{td}}$, and output $(\mathsf{Ped.ck} = (g, h), \mathsf{Ped.td} \leftarrow \mathsf{td})$.

$\mathsf{Ped.Com}(\mathsf{Ped.ck}; m; r)$ for $m \in \mathbb{Z}_p$, $r \leftarrow_{\$} \mathbb{Z}_p$: output $(\mathsf{c}, \mathsf{op}) = (g^m h^r, r)$.

$\mathsf{Ped.Vf}(\mathsf{Ped.ck}; m, \mathsf{c}, \mathsf{op} = r)$: output 1 if $\mathsf{c} = g^m h^r$ and 0 otherwise.

$\mathsf{Ped.tdOpen}(\mathsf{Ped.td}; m_1, \mathsf{op}_1 = r_1, m_2)$: output $\mathsf{op}_2 = r_2 \leftarrow (m_1 - m_2)/\mathsf{td} + r_1$.

It is well-known that Ped is perfectly hiding, computationally binding under the discrete logarithm assumption, and trapdoor.

A commitment scheme is an ICS if the messages come from domain $\mathbb{Z}$. Thus, statistical hiding means that it is intractable to compute two different *integers* $m_1, m_2 \in \mathbb{Z}$ and corresponding openings op_1 and op_2, such that

$\mathsf{Vf}(\mathsf{ck};\mathsf{c},m_1,\mathsf{op}_1) = \mathsf{Vf}(\mathsf{ck};\mathsf{c},m_2,\mathsf{op}_2) = 1$. In the case of Pedersen, m and $m+p$ have the same commitments and thus Ped is not an ICS. Let $\tilde{\mathbb{G}}$ be a group where the root assumption holds. The Damgård-Fujisaki ICS [13] over $\tilde{\mathbb{G}}$ works as follows:

$\mathsf{DF.Gen}(1^\lambda)$: V chooses an $\tilde{h} \in \tilde{\mathbb{G}}$ s.t. $\mathrm{ord}(\tilde{h})$ is $C(\lambda)$-rough, and sets $\tilde{g} \leftarrow \tilde{h}^\alpha$ where $\alpha \leftarrow_\$ \mathbb{Z}_{2^{2B+\lambda}}$. V sends $\mathsf{DF.ck} = (\tilde{g}, \tilde{h})$ to P and proves that $\tilde{g} \in \langle \tilde{h} \rangle$.
$\mathsf{DF.Com}(\mathsf{DF.ck};m;r)$ for $m \in \mathbb{Z}$, $r \leftarrow_\$ \mathbb{Z}_{2^{B+\lambda}}$: output $\mathsf{c} \leftarrow \tilde{g}^m \tilde{h}^r$, $\mathsf{op} = (1,r)$.
$\mathsf{DF.Vf}(\mathsf{DF.ck};m,\mathsf{c},\mathsf{op} = (\mu,r))$: check that $\mathsf{c} = \mu \tilde{g}^m \tilde{h}^r$ and $\mu^{l_{\tilde{\mathbb{G}}}} = 1$.

See [13] for a discussion on μ and other details. As proven in [13], DF is statistically hiding and computationally binding under the root assumption.

A (multi-use) UC-commitment scheme [9] implements the functionality $\mathcal{F}_{\mathsf{mcom}}$ (see Fig. 2). The $\mathcal{F}_{\mathsf{mcom}}$ functionality takes as an additional input another unique "commitment identifier" cid, which is used if a sender commits to the same receiver multiple times within a session. We assume that the combination of (sid, cid) is globally unique, [9]. UC-commitment schemes have to satisfy the properties of extractability (the simulator can unambiguously extract the committed message) and equivocability (the simulator can open a commitment to an arbitrary value) at the same time, and thus they cannot be constructed without an additional setup assumption [9].

Functionality $\mathcal{F}_{\mathsf{mcom}}$

$\mathcal{F}_{\mathsf{mcom}} = \mathcal{F}_{\mathsf{mcom}}^{\mathcal{M}}$ interacts with parties $\mathcal{G}_i$ and adversary Sim as follows.
- **Upon receiving** (commit, sid, cid, $\mathcal{G}_i, \mathcal{G}_j, m \in \mathcal{M}$) **from** $\mathcal{G}_i$: if a tuple (sid, cid, ...) with the same (sid, cid) was previously stored, do nothing. Otherwise, store (sid, cid, $\mathcal{G}_i, \mathcal{G}_j, m$) and send (rcpt, sid, cid, $\mathcal{G}_i, \mathcal{G}_j$) to $\mathcal{G}_j$ and Sim.
- **Upon receiving** (open, sid, cid) **from** $\mathcal{G}_i$: if a tuple (sid, cid, $\mathcal{G}_i, \mathcal{G}_j, m$) was previously stored then send (open, sid, cid, $\mathcal{G}_i, \mathcal{G}_j, m$) to $\mathcal{G}_j$ and Sim. Otherwise, ignore.

Fig. 2. Functionality $\mathcal{F}_{\mathsf{mcom}}$ for committing multiple messages

---

Cryptosystems. A *labelled public-key cryptosystem* Π is defined by three PPT algorithms: (i) $\Pi.\mathsf{KGen}(1^\lambda)$ generates a public key $\Pi.\mathsf{pk}$ and a secret key $\Pi.\mathsf{sk}$; (ii) $\Pi.\mathsf{Enc}_{\Pi.\mathsf{pk}}^{\mathsf{lbl}}(m;r)$ encrypts the message m under the key $\Pi.\mathsf{pk}$ with label lbl, using the random coins r; (iii) $\Pi.\mathsf{Dec}_{\Pi.\mathsf{sk}}^{\mathsf{lbl}}(\mathsf{c})$ decrypts the ciphertext c, using the secret key $\Pi.\mathsf{sk}$ with label lbl. It is required that for all $(\Pi.\mathsf{pk}, \Pi.\mathsf{sk}) \in \Pi.\mathsf{KGen}(1^\lambda)$, all labels lbl, all random coins r and all messages m, $\Pi.\mathsf{Dec}_{\Pi.\mathsf{sk}}^{\mathsf{lbl}}(\Pi.\mathsf{Enc}_{\Pi.\mathsf{pk}}^{\mathsf{lbl}}(m;r)) = m$.

IND-CPA (indistinguishability under the chosen plaintext attack) and IND-PCA (indistinguishability under the plaintext checking attacks, [1]) are defined by using the following experiments:

$\mathsf{Expt}^{\mathsf{pca}}_{\Pi,\mathcal{A}}(\lambda) \ / \ \mathsf{Expt}^{\mathsf{cpa}}_{\Pi,\mathcal{A}}(\lambda)$

$\mathcal{Q} \leftarrow \emptyset; (\Pi.\mathsf{pk}, \Pi.\mathsf{sk}) \leftarrow \Pi.\mathsf{KGen}(1^\lambda); (\mathsf{lbl}^*, m_0, m_1) \leftarrow \mathcal{A}^{\mathcal{O}(\cdot,\cdot,\cdot)}(\Pi.\mathsf{pk});$
$b \leftarrow_\$ \{0,1\}; r \leftarrow_\$ \mathsf{RND}(\Pi); \mathsf{c}^* \leftarrow \Pi.\mathsf{Enc}^{\mathsf{lbl}^*}_{\Pi.\mathsf{pk}}(m_b; r); b' \leftarrow \mathcal{A}^{\mathcal{O}(\cdot,\cdot,\cdot)}(\mathsf{c}^*);$
if $(\mathsf{lbl}^*, \mathsf{c}^*) \notin \mathcal{Q}$ **then return** $b = b';$ **fi** ;

The experiment-dependent oracle is defined as follows: (i) in $\mathsf{Expt}^{\mathsf{cpa}}_{\Pi,\mathcal{A}}(\lambda)$, $\mathcal{O}(\cdot,\cdot,\cdot)$ returns always 0. (ii) in $\mathsf{Expt}^{\mathsf{pca}}_{\Pi,\mathcal{A}}(\lambda)$, $\mathcal{O}(\mathsf{lbl}, \mathsf{c}, m)$ adds $(\mathsf{lbl}, \mathsf{c})$ to $\mathcal{Q}$. It returns 1 if the decryption of c under the label lbl is m. Otherwise, it returns 0.

Π is *IND-CPA secure* if for any PPT adversary $\mathcal{A}$, $\mathsf{Adv}^{\mathsf{cpa}}_{\Pi,\mathcal{A}}(\lambda) := |\Pr[\mathsf{Expt}^{\mathsf{cpa}}_{\Pi,\mathcal{A}}(\lambda) = 1] - 1/2| = \mathsf{negl}(\lambda)$. Π is *IND-PCA secure* if for any PPT adversary $\mathcal{A}$, $\mathsf{Adv}^{\mathsf{pca}}_{\Pi,\mathcal{A}}(\lambda) := |\Pr[\mathsf{Expt}^{\mathsf{pca}}_{\Pi,\mathcal{A}}(\lambda) = 1] - 1/2| = \mathsf{negl}(\lambda)$.

The IND-PCA-secure Short Cramer-Shoup (SCS) labelled cryptosystem $\mathsf{SCS} = (\mathsf{SCS.KGen}, \mathsf{SCS.Enc}, \mathsf{SCS.Dec})$ [1] works as follows:

$\mathsf{SCS.KGen}(1^\lambda)$: $g \leftarrow_\$ \mathbb{G}^*$; $x_1, x_2, y_1, y_2, z \leftarrow_\$ \mathbb{Z}_p$; $h \leftarrow g^z$, $c \leftarrow g^{x_1} h^{x_2}$, $d \leftarrow g^{y_1} h^{y_2}$. Choose H from a collision-resistant hash function family $\mathcal{H}$. Return $\mathsf{SCS.pk} = (g, h, c, d, \mathsf{H})$ and $\mathsf{SCS.sk} = (x_1, x_2, y_1, y_2, z)$.

$\mathsf{SCS.Enc}^{\mathsf{lbl}}_{\mathsf{SCS.pk}}(g^m \in \mathbb{G}; \cdot)$: sample $r \leftarrow_\$ \mathbb{Z}_p$; set $(u, e, v) \leftarrow (g^r, g^m h^r, (cd^\tau)^r)$, where $\tau \leftarrow \mathsf{H}(\mathsf{lbl}, u, e)$. Return the ciphertext $(u, e, v)^\top$.

$\mathsf{SCS.Dec}^{\mathsf{lbl}}_{\mathsf{SCS.sk}}((u, e, v)^\top \in \mathbb{G}^3)$: set $\tau \leftarrow \mathsf{H}(\mathsf{lbl}, u, e)$, $g^m \leftarrow e/u^z$; if $u^{x_1+y_1\tau}(e/g^m)^{x_2+y_2\tau} \neq v$ then abort. Otherwise, output g^m.

Abdalla *et al.* [1] proved that SCS is IND-PCA secure given $\mathcal{H}$ is a collision-resistant hash function family and DDH is hard in $\mathbb{G}$.

An additively homomorphic public-key cryptosystem has plaintext space equal to $\mathbb{Z}_N$ for integer N, s.t. the product of two ciphertexts decrypts to the sum of the two corresponding plaintexts. We will use the Paillier cryptosystem Pai [24]. It encrypts plaintexts from $\mathbb{Z}_N$, where N is a well-chosen RSA modulus, and outputs ciphertexts from $\mathbb{Z}_{N^2}$: $\mathsf{Pai.Enc}_{\mathsf{Pai.pk}}(m \in \mathbb{Z}_N; r \in \mathbb{Z}_N^*) = (1+N)^m r^N \equiv (1+mN)r^N \pmod{N^2}$. See [24] for more details, including the decryption algorithm. Pai is IND-CPA secure under the DCRA assumption [24].

Σ-Protocols [11] *in the RPK Model.* Let $\mathbf{R} = \{\mathsf{x}, \mathsf{w}\}$ be an NP-relation. A Σ-protocol $\Sigma = (\Sigma.\mathsf{P}_1, \Sigma.\mathsf{P}_2, \Sigma.\mathsf{Vf}, \Sigma.\mathsf{Sim})$ is a three-round protocol between the prover P and the verifier V, such that the first and the third messages are by the prover, and the second message is by the verifier. Let rpk_V be the public key of the verifier. P has input $(\mathsf{rpk}_\mathsf{V}; \mathsf{x}, \mathsf{w})$ and V has input $(\mathsf{rpk}_\mathsf{V}; \mathsf{x})$. The first message is denoted as $a \leftarrow \Sigma.\mathsf{P}_1(\mathsf{rpk}_\mathsf{V}; \mathsf{x}, \mathsf{w}; s)$, where $s \leftarrow_\$ \mathsf{RND}(\Sigma)$ is sampled from the randomizer space of the protocol. The second message e is chosen uniformly at random from $\{0,1\}^\lambda$, $e \leftarrow_\$ \{0,1\}^\lambda$. The third message is denoted as $z \leftarrow \Sigma.\mathsf{P}_2(\mathsf{rpk}_\mathsf{V}; \mathsf{x}, \mathsf{w}; e; s)$. The verifier accepts iff $\Sigma.\mathsf{Vf}(\mathsf{rpk}_\mathsf{V}; \mathsf{x}; a, e, z) = 1$.

A Σ-protocol is *complete* for $\mathbf{R}$ if an honest verifier always accepts an honest prover. A Σ-protocol is *specially sound* for $\mathbf{R}$ if given an input x and two acceptable views (a, e_1, z_1) and (a, e_2, z_2), $e_1 \neq e_2$, one can efficiently extract a witness w, such that $(\mathsf{x}, \mathsf{w}) \in \mathbf{R}$. A Σ-protocol is *statistically special honest-verifier zero-knowledge (SSHVZK)* for $\mathbf{R}$ if for any rpk_V, x and e, $\Sigma.\mathsf{Sim}(\mathsf{rpk}_\mathsf{V}; \mathsf{x}, e)$ can first choose a z and then a, such that the simulated view (a, e, z) and the real view, given the same e, have negligible statistical distance.

3   New Functionality $\mathcal{F}_{\text{mcomdl}}$ and Instantiation

In a DL-extractable UC-commitment scheme, one commits to an *integer* m from $\mathbb{Z}_p$ but the opening is to a *group element* $g^m \in \mathbb{G}$. (In particular, m should stay secret from other participants even after the opening.) Nevertheless, we require that there exists an efficient extraction algorithm that can retrieve the discrete logarithm (i.e., the committed *integer*) $m \in \mathbb{Z}_p$ of g^m. That is, while opening returns g^m, the extraction returns m. See Fig. 3 for the corresponding functionality $\mathcal{F}_{\text{mcomdl}}$ that is parametrized by $\mathbb{Z}_p$ and $\mathbb{G}$ (this means that $\mathbb{Z}_p$ and $\mathbb{G}$ are "hard-coded" into the functionality). We formalize our goal by letting parties to commit to an integer m (which will be stored by the functionality and thus can be extracted) but opening the commitment to g^m. Hence, any commitment scheme that implements $\mathcal{F}_{\text{mcomdl}}$ must necessarily be DL-extractable.

Functionality $\mathcal{F}_{\text{mcomdl}}$

$\mathcal{F}_{\text{mcomdl}}$, parametrized by $\mathcal{M} = \mathbb{Z}_p$ and $\mathbb{G}$, interacts with $\mathcal{G}_1, \ldots, \mathcal{G}_\nu$ as follows.
- Upon receiving $(\text{commit}, \text{sid}, \text{cid}, \mathcal{G}_i, \mathcal{G}_j, m)$ from $\mathcal{G}_i$, where $m \in \mathbb{Z}_p$: if a tuple $(\text{sid}, \text{cid}, \cdots)$ with the same (sid, cid) was previously recorded, do nothing. Otherwise, record $(\text{sid}, \text{cid}, \mathcal{G}_i, \mathcal{G}_j, m)$ and send $(\text{rcpt}, \text{sid}, \text{cid}, \mathcal{G}_i, \mathcal{G}_j)$ to $\mathcal{G}_j$ and Sim.
- Upon receiving $(\text{open}, \text{sid}, \text{cid})$ from $\mathcal{G}_i$, proceed as follows: if a tuple $(\text{sid}, \text{cid}, \mathcal{G}_i, \mathcal{G}_j, m)$ was previously recorded then send $(\text{open}, \text{sid}, \text{cid}, \mathcal{G}_i, \mathcal{G}_j, y \leftarrow g^m)$ to $\mathcal{G}_j$ and Sim. Otherwise do nothing.

Fig. 3. DL-extractable functionality $\mathcal{F}_{\text{mcomdl}}$ for committing multiple messages

---

Remark 1. Belenkiy *et al.* [3] defined P-extractable commitment scheme, for an *efficient* function P, as a commitment scheme where one commits to m and opens to m but where the extractor is able to extract $P(m)$. DL-extractable commitment is a variant of P-extractable commitment for $P = $ DL being an intractable function. If $P(m) = g^m =: \exp_g(m)$ then one obtains a functionality, dual to $\mathcal{F}_{\text{mcomdl}}$. (However, [3] did not consider UC-security and thus did not use the language of functionalities.) Compared to DL-extractability, $\exp_g$-extractability is trivial to implement: indeed, the notion of $\exp_g$-extractability was motivated by the fact that well-known commitment schemes like the Groth-Sahai commitment scheme for scalars [19] had this property. (The extractor of this commitment scheme obtains g^m by Elgamal-decrypting the commitment. Since computing DL is intractable, one arrives to the notion of a $\exp_g$-extractable commitment.) Obtaining DL-extractability is non-trivial since DL is a hard function and thus one has to take special care about making the DL of a message extractable. □

The functionality $\mathcal{F}_{\text{mcomdl}}$ can be straightforwardly generalized to the functionality $\mathcal{F}_{\text{mcom-}F^{-1}}$ for an arbitrary one-way permutation F, where the opening message includes $y \leftarrow F(m)$ instead of $y \leftarrow g^m$. Since we are interested in the applications of $\mathcal{F}_{\mathsf{mcomdl}}$, we will omit further discussion.

We implement $\mathcal{F}_{\mathsf{mcomdl}}$ as follows: for $m \in \mathbb{Z}_p$, we encrypt the group element g^m by using the Short Cramer-Shoup encryption [1], encrypt the integer m by using the Paillier [24] additively homomorphic public-key cryptosystem, and finally commit to the integer m by using the Damgård-Fujisaki [13] ICS. We add a Σ-protocol Σ_{eq} proving the knowledge of m that was used in all cases; importantly, only g^m can be extracted from Σ_{eq} and in particular, m will remain secret. Since UC-security does not permit to use rewinding to retrieve m, we use straight-line extraction techniques from [16]. The Σ-protocol is started during the commit phase, and after that the committer C erases the used random coins. In the open phase, C opens the commitment to g^m by finishing Σ_{eq}. When simulating an honest committer, the UC simulator Sim first commits to 0; Sim uses the properties of a trapdoor commitment scheme and the SSHVZK property to simulate Σ_{eq}. (This guarantees equivocability.) If C is corrupted then Sim uses the knowledge of the Paillier secret key to decrypt the Paillier encryption of m and thus obtains m. (This guarantees extractability.) Thus, we obtain a DL-extractable commitment scheme.

3.1 Σ-Protocol Σ_{eq}

Let SCS be the SCS cryptosystem and Pai be the Paillier cryptosystem. Recall that the plaintext space of SCS is $\mathbb{G}$ (of order p) and the plaintext space of Pai is $\mathbb{Z}_N$ for an $N > p$. (The case $N = p$ is straightforward to handle.) Let

$$
\mathbf{R}_{\mathsf{eq}} = \left\{
\begin{array}{l}
(\mathsf{x} = (\mathsf{p}, \mathsf{SCS.pk_P}, \mathsf{Pai.pk_P}, g^m, \mathsf{c}_1, \mathsf{c}_2, \mathsf{lbl}), \mathsf{w} = (m', r_1, r_2)): \\
\mathsf{c}_1 = \mathsf{SCS.Enc}^{\mathsf{lbl}}_{\mathsf{SCS.pk_P}}(g^m; r_1) \wedge \mathsf{c}_2 = \mathsf{Pai.Enc}_{\mathsf{Pai.pk_P}}(m'; r_2) \wedge \\
m \equiv m' \pmod{p} \wedge m' < N
\end{array}
\right\},
$$

where $\mathsf{p} \leftarrow \mathsf{Pgen}(1^\lambda)$. Let $\mathbf{L}_{\mathsf{eq}} = \{\mathsf{x} : \exists \mathsf{w}, (\mathsf{x}, \mathsf{w}) \in \mathbf{R}_{\mathsf{eq}}\}$ be the corresponding language. Thus, $\mathsf{x} \in \mathbf{L}_{\mathsf{eq}}$ iff the two ciphertexts encrypt g^m and m' respectively, such that $m \equiv m' \pmod{p}$. Note that g^m is public while m is not; this corresponds to the use of g^m in the new DL-extractable UC-commitment scheme.

The proof of the following theorem uses ideas from the proof given in Sect. 5.1 of [13]. Note that in the next theorem, we actually do not need the public key to be registered. We will assume it here for the sake of convenience since registration is needed in the new DL-extractable UC-commitment scheme.

Theorem 1 (Security of Σ_{eq}). *Let* H *be sampled from a collision-resistant hash function family,* SCS *be the SCS cryptosystem,* Pai *be the Paillier cryptosystem, and* DF *be the Damgård-Fujisaki ICS. Assume* V *has registered her public key* $\mathsf{rpk_V} = \mathsf{DF.ck_V}$. *Let* T *be a public constant such that* $m < T$, *e.g.* $T = p$; *let* $C(\lambda) = 2^\lambda$ *and let* 2^B *be a close upperbound on* $\mathrm{ord}(\tilde{\mathbb{G}})$. *Assume* $2^{2\lambda+1}p < N$. *The* Σ-*protocol* Σ_{eq} *in Fig. 4 (where* $\Sigma_{\mathsf{eq}}.\mathsf{Sim}$ *will be defined in the SSHVZK proof) is complete and SSHVZK for* $\mathbf{R}_{\mathsf{eq}}$. *The protocol* Σ_{eq} *is computationally specially sound under the root assumption in* $\tilde{\mathbb{G}}$.

1. Denote $\mathsf{RND}(\Sigma_{eq}) := \mathbb{Z}_{2^{B+\lambda}} \times \mathbb{Z}_p \times [0 .. \max(2^{2\lambda}p, T \cdot C(\lambda) \cdot 2^\lambda) - 1] \times \mathbb{Z}_{N^2}^* \times [0 .. C(\lambda)2^{B+2\lambda} - 1]$. P samples $\boldsymbol{s} := (s_1, s_2, s_3, s_4, s_5) \leftarrow_\$ \mathsf{RND}(\Sigma_{eq})$.
   P sets $\tilde{a}_1 \leftarrow \mathsf{DF.Com}(\mathsf{DF.ck_V}; m; s_1)$, $\boldsymbol{a}_2 \leftarrow (g^{s_2}, h^{s_2}, (cd^\tau)^{s_2})^\top$, $a_3 \leftarrow g^{s_3}$, $a_4 \leftarrow (1 + s_3 N)s_4^N \bmod N^2$, $\tilde{a}_5 \leftarrow \tilde{g}^{s_3}\tilde{h}^{s_5}$.
   P sends $a \leftarrow \Sigma_{eq}.\mathsf{P}_1(\mathsf{rpk_V}; \mathsf{x}, \mathsf{w}; \boldsymbol{s}) := (\tilde{a}_1, \boldsymbol{a}_2, a_3, a_4, \tilde{a}_5)$ to V.
2. V sends $e \leftarrow_\$ \{0,1\}^\lambda$ to P.
3. P sets $z_1 \leftarrow r_1 e + s_2$, $z_2 \leftarrow me + s_3$, $z_3 \leftarrow r_2^e s_4 \bmod N^2$, $z_4 \leftarrow s_1 e + s_5$. Let $\boldsymbol{z} := (z_1, z_2, z_3, z_4)$. P sends $\Sigma_{eq}.\mathsf{P}_2(\mathsf{rpk_V}; \mathsf{x}, \mathsf{w}; e; \boldsymbol{s}) := \boldsymbol{z}$ to V.
4. V outputs 1 iff the following holds (otherwise, V outputs 0):
   (a) $\boldsymbol{c}_1^e \boldsymbol{a}_2 = (g^{z_1}, g^{em}h^{z_1}, (cd^\tau)^{z_1})^\top$,
   (b) $g^{em} \cdot a_3 = g^{z_2}$,
   (c) $c_2^e a_4 \equiv (1 + N)^{z_2} z_3^N \pmod{N^2}$,
   (d) $\tilde{a}_1^e \tilde{a}_5 = \tilde{g}^{z_2} \tilde{h}^{z_4}$, and
   (e) $z_2 \in [-T \cdot C(\lambda) .. T \cdot C(\lambda)(2^\lambda + 1)]$.
   Denote this check by $\Sigma_{eq}.\mathsf{Vf}(\mathsf{rpk_V}; \mathsf{x}; a, e, \boldsymbol{z}) \in \{0,1\}$.

Fig. 4. Σ-protocol Σ_{eq} for $\mathbf{R}_{eq}$, where in the honest case, $\mathbf{c}_1 = (c_{11}, c_{12}, c_{13})^\top \leftarrow \mathsf{SCS.Enc}_{\mathsf{SCS.pkp}}^{\mathsf{lbl}}(g^m; r_1) = (g^{r_1}, g^m h^{r_1}, (cd^\tau)^{r_1})^\top$ and $\mathbf{c}_2 \leftarrow \mathsf{Pai.Enc}_{\mathsf{Pai.pkp}}(m; r_2) = (1 + N)^m r_2^N \equiv (1 + mN)r_2^N \bmod N^2$. Here, $r_1 \leftarrow_\$ \mathbb{Z}_p$, $\tau = \mathsf{H}(\mathsf{lbl}, c_{11}, c_{12})$, and $r_2 \leftarrow_\$ \mathbb{Z}_N^*$.

Proof. ☐Special soundness:☐ consider two accepting views $(a, e, \boldsymbol{z})$ and $(a, e', \boldsymbol{z}')$ with $e \neq e'$. Let $m^* \leftarrow (z_2' - z_2)/(e' - e) \bmod p$ and $r^* \leftarrow (z_1' - z_1)/(e' - e) \bmod p$. We get from the first four verification equations respectively that

$$\mathbf{c}_1 = (g^{r^*}, g^m h^{r^*}, (cd^\tau)^{r^*})^\top = \mathsf{SCS.Enc}_{\mathsf{SCS.pk_p}}(g^m; r^*),$$
$$m \equiv m^* \pmod{p},$$
$$c_2^{e'-e} \equiv (1 + N)^{z_2' - z_2}(z_3'/z_3)^N \pmod{N^2} \tag{1}$$

$$\tilde{a}_1^{e'-e} = \tilde{g}^{z_2' - z_2}\tilde{h}^{z_4' - z_4}. \tag{2}$$

For example, from (b) we get $g^{em} \cdot a_3 = g^{z_2}$ and $g^{em'} \cdot a_3 = g^{z_2'}$. It follows that $g^{(e'-e)m} = g^{z_2 - z_2'}$ and thus $g^m = g^{(z_2 - z_2')/(e'-e)} = g^{m^*}$.

First, consider Eq. (2). Since $\tilde{g} = \tilde{h}^\alpha$, $\tilde{a}_1^{e'-e} = \tilde{h}^\delta$ for $\delta := \alpha(z_2' - z_2) + (z_4' - z_4)$. We will next consider three possible cases. Let bad be the event that we either have the case (i) or the case (ii).

(i) $(e' - e) \nmid \delta$ *as an integer.*
Write $\gamma = \gcd(\delta, e' - e)$. By the Extended Euclidean algorithm, there exist i and j (where $j < |e' - e| < C(\lambda)$), such that $j\delta + i(e' - e) = \gamma$. Thus, $\tilde{h}^\gamma = \tilde{h}^{j\delta + i(e'-e)} = \tilde{a}_1^{j(e'-e)}\tilde{h}^{i(e'-e)} = (\tilde{a}_1^j \tilde{h}^i)^{e'-e}$. Set now $\mu \leftarrow (\tilde{a}_1^j \tilde{h}^i)^{(e'-e)/\gamma}/\tilde{h}$. Thus, $\mu^\gamma = 1$. Since $\gamma < C(\lambda)$, $\mathrm{ord}(\mu)$ is $C(\lambda)$-smooth and thus $\mu^{l_{\tilde{\mathbb{G}}}} = 1$. Since $\tilde{h} = \mu^{-1}(\tilde{a}_1^j \tilde{h}^i)^{(e'-e)/\gamma}$, $((e' - e)/\gamma, \tilde{a}_1^j \tilde{h}^i, \mu^{-1})$ is a solution to the root problem.

(ii) $(e' - e) \mid \delta$ *as an integer, but either* $(e' - e) \nmid (z_2' - z_2)$ *or* $(e' - e) \nmid (z_4' - z_4)$. Let q be a prime factor of $e' - e$, such that q^j is the highest power of q dividing $e' - e$ and at least one of $z_2' - z_2$ or $z_4' - z_4$ is non-zero modulo q^j (such q exists due to the assumption of non-divisibility). If $q^j \mid (z_2' - z_2)$ then (due to the definition of δ and q^j) also $q^j \mid (z_4' - z_4)$, a contradiction. Thus, $z_2' - z_2 \not\equiv 0 \pmod{q^j}$.

Write $\alpha = a + b \cdot \mathrm{ord}(\tilde{h})$ for some $a < \mathrm{ord}(\tilde{h})$ and b. The adversary only has information about α via the value $\tilde{g}$; moreover, $\tilde{g}$ completely determines a while it contains no information about b. Since $q^j \mid \delta$,

$$\delta = b(z_2' - z_2) \cdot \mathrm{ord}(\tilde{h}) + a(z_2' - z_2) + (z_4' - z_4) \equiv 0 \pmod{q^j}. \qquad (3)$$

Because q is a prime factor of $e' - e$ and $e' - e < C(\lambda)$, $q < C(\lambda)$ and thus $\mathrm{ord}(\tilde{h}) \not\equiv 0 \pmod{q}$. From the adversary's viewpoint, b is chosen uniformly at random from a set of at least $2^{B+\lambda}$ values, and it must satisfy Eq. (3) for bad to be true. Equation (3) has at most $\eta := \gcd((z_2' - z_2) \cdot \mathrm{ord}(\tilde{h}), q^j)$ solutions. Clearly, η is a power of q but it is at most q^{j-1}. Since $2^{B+\lambda} > 2^\lambda q^j$, the distribution of $b \bmod q^j$ is statistically close to uniform in $\mathbb{Z}_{q^j}$, with the probability that b satisfies Eq. (3) being at most $1/q - 2^{-\lambda} \le 1/2 - 2^{-\lambda}$. Thus, given the event bad, the case (i), where we *can* solve the root problem, happens with high probability.

(iii) $(e' - e) \mid (z_2' - z_2)$ *and* $(e' - e) \mid (z_4' - z_4)$ *as an integer.*
Let $m^\dagger \leftarrow (z_2' - z_2)/(e' - e) \in \mathbb{Z}$ and $r^\dagger \leftarrow (z_4' - z_4)/(e' - e) \in \mathbb{Z}$. Let $\mu \leftarrow \tilde{g}^{m^\dagger} \tilde{h}^{r^\dagger}/\tilde{a}_1$. W.l.o.g., assume $e' > e$. By Eq. (2), $\mu^{e'-e} = (\tilde{g}^{m^\dagger} \tilde{h}^{r^\dagger}/\tilde{a}_1)^{e'-e} = \tilde{g}^{z_2'-z_2} \tilde{h}^{z_4'-z_4}/\tilde{a}_1^{e'-e} = 1$. Since $e' - e < C(\lambda)$ then $\mathrm{ord}(\mu)$ is $C(\lambda)$-smooth and hence $\mu^{l_{\tilde{G}}} = 1$. Thus, we can open $\tilde{a}_1$ to $(m^\dagger, r^\dagger, \mu)$.

Since $z_2 < T \cdot C(\lambda)(2^\lambda + 1) < 2^{2\lambda+1} p$ by the last verification equation (Item 4e), we get that $|m^\dagger| < 2^{2\lambda+1} p < N$.

Next, Assume that (iii) Holds and Consider Eq. (1). Since N and $e' - e \in [-2^\lambda + 1 .. 2^\lambda - 1]$ are coprime, there exist integers α and β, such that $\alpha N + \beta(e' - e) = 1$. Let $r_2 \leftarrow c_2^\alpha (z_3'/z_3)^\beta \bmod N^2$. Thus, due to Eq. (1), $c_2^{1-\alpha N} = c_2^{\beta(e'-e)} \equiv (1 + N)^{\beta(z_2'-z_2)}(z_3'/z_3)^{\beta N} \pmod{N^2}$, and thus $c_2 \equiv (1 + N)^{\beta(z_2'-z_2)} r_2^N \pmod{N^2}$. Clearly, $\beta(z_2' - z_2) = \beta(e' - e)m^\dagger$ as an integer. Thus, due to the definition of β, $\beta(z_2' - z_2) = \beta(e' - e)m^\dagger = (1 - \alpha N)m^\dagger \equiv m^\dagger \pmod{N}$ and thus $c_2 \equiv (1+N)^{m^\dagger} r_2^N \pmod{N^2}$. Since directly by the definition of m^* and $m^\dagger$, $m^* \equiv m^\dagger \pmod{p}$, we get that c_1 and c_2 encrypt the same element m^* modulo p.

$\boxed{\text{SSHVZK:}}$ $\Sigma_{\mathrm{eq}}.\mathsf{Sim}(\Sigma_{\mathrm{eq}}.\mathsf{rpk}_V; x, e)$ sets $s_1 \leftarrow_{\$} \mathbb{Z}_{2^{B+\lambda}}$, $s_5 \leftarrow_{\$} [0 .. C(\lambda)2^{B+2\lambda} - 1]$, $z_1 \leftarrow_{\$} \mathbb{Z}_p$, $z_2 \leftarrow_{\$} \mathbb{Z}_{2^{2\lambda} p}$ (thus, Σ_{eq} is statistically but not perfectly zero knowledge), $z_3 \leftarrow_{\$} \mathbb{Z}_{N^2}^*$, $z_4 \leftarrow s_1 e + s_5$, $\tilde{a}_1 \leftarrow \mathsf{DF.Com}(\mathsf{ck}_V; 0; s_1)$ (this is indistinguishable from a commitment to m since DF is statistical hiding), $a_2 \leftarrow ((g^{z_1}, g^{em} h^{z_1}, (cd^\tau)^{z_1})/c_1)^\top$, $a_3 \leftarrow g^{z_2 - em}$, $a_4 \leftarrow (1 + z_2 N) z_3^N c_2^{-e} \bmod N^2$, $\tilde{a}_5 \leftarrow \tilde{g}^{z_2} \tilde{h}^{z_4} \tilde{a}_1^{-e}$. The simulator outputs (a, z). The claim follows. $\qquad \square$

3.2   New DL-Extractable UC-Commitment Scheme

The following DL-extractable UC-commitment scheme Γ_{dl} (see Fig. 5) is similar to Fujisaki's UC-commitment scheme Fuj [16], with the following two key differences. (i) Based on our observation that the CRS of Fuj can be divided into two parts, one guaranteeing binding and the second one guaranteeing hiding, we redefine it in the (weaker) RPK model instead of the CRS model. Importantly, the RPK model can also be used after the modification in the next step. (ii) We replace the Σ-protocol (a proof of the knowledge of the SCS-encrypted message g^m) from [16] with Σ_{eq}, interpreted as *the proof of knowledge of the discrete logarithm m of the SCS-encrypted message*. As explained above, Σ_{eq} achieves this by additionally encrypting m by using Pai; hence, the UC simulator, knowing the secret key Pai.sk, decrypts c_2 to get m, and returns $m \bmod p$. (See the beginning of Sect. 3 for a longer intuition behind the construction of Γ_{dl}.)

Due to this, if one assumes the security of Σ_{eq} then the security proof of Γ_{dl} is similar to that given in [16]. Hence, we refer the reader to [16] for any additional intuition about Fujisaki's commitment scheme. While the description of Γ_{dl} in Fig. 5 looks long, it is mainly so because of the use of three different encryptions/commitments which means that certain steps in the Fujisaki's commitment scheme are tripled.

We divide the public key rpk_i of $\mathcal{G}_i$ in Γ_{dl} into the binding part (used when $\mathcal{G}_i$ acts as the receiver R) and the hiding part (used when $\mathcal{G}_i$ acts as the committer C). C and R use $rpk_C^h = (\mathsf{Pai.pk}_C = N, \mathsf{SCS.pk}_C = (g, h, c, d, H_C^h))$ from C's public key rpk_C and $rpk_R^b = (\mathsf{Ped.ck}_R, \mathsf{DF.ck}_R, H_R^b)$ from R's public key rpk_R. Obviously, C knows rpk_C while she has to retrieve rpk_R from $\mathcal{R}_R$.

See Fig. 5 for the full description of Γ_{dl}. Here, Γ_{dl}.Gen for party $\mathcal{G}_i \in \{C, R\}$ is executed by the key registration authority $\mathcal{R}_i$ as usual in the RPK model, Γ_{dl}.Com and Γ_{dl}.Open are executed by C, and Γ_{dl}.Vf is executed by R. The algorithms Γ_{dl}.tdOpen and Γ_{dl}.Ext are only executed within the security proof. To get straight-line simulation, we use the same method as [16]. Finally, note we have included $(|bl|, c_3, e)$ to op mainly to simplify the notation.

Theorem 2. *Assume that* SCS *is an IND-PCA secure and* Pai *is an IND-CPA secure additively homomorphic cryptosystem,* Ped *is a computationally binding and perfectly hiding trapdoor commitment scheme and* DF *is a computationally binding and statistically hiding ICS. Assume secure erasure. Then* Γ_{dl} *from Fig. 5 UC-realizes* $\mathcal{F}_{mcomdl}$ *in the* $\mathcal{F}_{rpk}$-*hybrid model against adaptive attackers, i.e., it is a secure DL-extractable UC-commitment scheme in the RPK model.*

The proof of Theorem 2 follows closely the security proof of Fujisaki's UC-commitment scheme [16], with a few notable differences (the use of the RPK model instead of the CRS model, and the use of a different Σ-protocol, which causes us to use one more game to handle Paillier encryption).

Proof. As usual, we consider a sequence of hybrid games in which we change the rules of games step by step. We denote the changes by using gray background .

Game$_0$ = **HYBRID**$^{\mathcal{F}_{rpk}}$: This is the *real world* game in the RPK model (HYBRID$^{\mathcal{F}_{rpk}}$). In Game$_0$, the real protocol is executed between the committer C and the receiver R. The environment $\mathcal{Z}$ adaptively chooses the input for honest committer C and receives the output of honest parties. Adversary $\mathcal{A}$ attacks the real protocol in the real world, i.e., she can see the interactions between the honest parties or interact with the honest parties as playing the role of some

$\Gamma_{dl}.\mathsf{Gen}(1^\lambda)$: Generate new keys $(\mathsf{SCS.pk}, \mathsf{SCS.sk})$ for SCS, $(\mathsf{Pai.pk}, \mathsf{Pai.sk})$ for Pai, $(\mathsf{DF.ck}, \mathsf{DF.td})$ for DF, and $(\mathsf{Ped.ck}, \mathsf{Ped.td})$ for Ped. Choose collision-resistant hash functions $\mathsf{H}^h, \mathsf{H}^b$. Let $\mathsf{p} \leftarrow \mathsf{Pgen}(1^\lambda)$. Let $\mathsf{rpk} = (\mathsf{rpk}^h, \mathsf{rpk}^b)$ where $\mathsf{rpk}^h = (\mathsf{p}, \mathsf{SCS.pk}, \mathsf{Pai.pk}, \mathsf{H}^h)$ and $\mathsf{rpk}^b = (\mathsf{p}, \mathsf{Ped.ck}, \mathsf{DF.ck}, \mathsf{H}^b)$. Let $\mathsf{td} = (\mathsf{td}^h, \mathsf{td}^b)$, where $\mathsf{td}^h = (\mathsf{SCS.sk}, \mathsf{Pai.sk})$ and $\mathsf{td}^b = (\mathsf{Ped.td}, \mathsf{DF.td})$.

Return $(\mathsf{rpk}, \mathsf{td})$. // The equivocability td is Ped.td; The extraction td is Pai.sk;

$\Gamma_{dl}.\mathsf{Com}(\mathsf{rpk}_\mathsf{C}; \mathsf{lbl}, m)$ **where** $\mathsf{lbl} = (\mathsf{sid}, \mathsf{cid}, \mathsf{C}, \mathsf{R})$: to commit to $m \in \mathbb{Z}_p$ for R upon receiving $(\mathsf{commit}, \mathsf{lbl}, m)$, C does the following.

1. Obtain $\mathsf{rpk}_\mathsf{R} = (\mathsf{rpk}_\mathsf{R}^h, \mathsf{rpk}_\mathsf{R}^b)$ from $\mathcal{R}_\mathsf{R}$;
   $\mathsf{ck}_\mathsf{CR} \leftarrow (\mathsf{rpk}_\mathsf{C}^h, \mathsf{rpk}_\mathsf{R}^b)$; $\Sigma_\mathsf{eq}.\mathsf{rpk}_\mathsf{R} \leftarrow \mathsf{DF.ck}_\mathsf{R}$;
   $r_1 \leftarrow_\$ \mathsf{RND}(\mathsf{SCS})$; $r_2 \leftarrow_\$ \mathsf{RND}(\mathsf{Pai})$;
   $c_1 \leftarrow \mathsf{SCS.Enc}_{\mathsf{SCS.pk}_\mathsf{C}}^{\mathsf{lbl}}(g^m; r_1)$; $c_2 \leftarrow \mathsf{Pai.Enc}_{\mathsf{Pai.pk}_\mathsf{C}}(m; r_2)$;
   $c \leftarrow (c_1, c_2)$;
   $x \leftarrow (\mathsf{p}, \mathsf{SCS.pk}_\mathsf{C}, \mathsf{Pai.pk}_\mathsf{C}, g^m, c, \mathsf{lbl})$; $w \leftarrow (m, r_1, r_2)$;
   $s \leftarrow_\$ \mathsf{RND}(\Sigma_\mathsf{eq})$; $a \leftarrow \Sigma_\mathsf{eq}.\mathsf{P}_1(\Sigma_\mathsf{eq}.\mathsf{rpk}_\mathsf{R}; x, w; s)$; $h_x \leftarrow \mathsf{H}_\mathsf{R}^b(\mathsf{lbl}, x, a)$;
   (*) $r_3 \leftarrow_\$ \mathsf{RND}(\mathsf{Ped})$; $c_3 \leftarrow \mathsf{Ped.Com}(\mathsf{Ped.ck}_\mathsf{R}; h_x; r_3)$;
   Send (lbl, c_3) to R;
2. After obtaining (lbl, c_3), R fetches $\mathsf{rpk}_\mathsf{C} = (\mathsf{rpk}_\mathsf{C}^h, \mathsf{rpk}_\mathsf{C}^b)$ from $\mathcal{R}_\mathsf{C}$, sets ck_CR as above, and checks that c_3 is a valid ciphertext. If yes, he sets $e \leftarrow_\$ \{0, 1\}^\lambda$ and sends (lbl, e) to C. Otherwise, R ignores it.
3. After receiving (lbl, e), C does the following.
   $z \leftarrow \Sigma_\mathsf{eq}.\mathsf{P}_2(\Sigma_\mathsf{eq}.\mathsf{rpk}_\mathsf{R}; x, w; e; s)$;
   Securely delete $(w = (m, r_1, r_2), s)$;
   $\mathsf{op} \leftarrow (\mathsf{lbl}, c_3, e; a, z, r_3)$; Store $\mathsf{st}_\mathsf{C} = (c, g^m, \mathsf{op})$;
   Output (c, op) (privately); Send $(\mathsf{com}, \mathsf{lbl}, c)$ to R;
4. R checks that $c = (c_1, c_2) \in \mathbb{G}^3 \times \mathbb{Z}_{N^2}$. If yes, R outputs $(\mathsf{rcpt}, \mathsf{lbl})$, and stores $\mathsf{st}_\mathsf{R} \leftarrow (\mathsf{lbl}, c_3, e, c = (c_1, c_2))$. Otherwise, R ignores it.

$\Gamma_{dl}.\mathsf{Open}(\mathsf{st}_\mathsf{C})$: upon receiving $(\mathsf{open}, \mathsf{sid}, \mathsf{cid})$, C sends (g^m, op) to R.

$\Gamma_{dl}.\mathsf{Vf}(\mathsf{ck}_\mathsf{CR}; c, g^m, \mathsf{op})$ **where** $c = (c_1, c_2)$: upon receiving $(g^m, \mathsf{op} = (\mathsf{lbl}, c_3, e; a, z, r_3))$ where $\mathsf{lbl} = (\mathsf{sid}, \mathsf{cid}, \mathsf{C}, \mathsf{R})$, R does the following.

1. $x \leftarrow (\mathsf{p}, \mathsf{SCS.pk}_\mathsf{C}, \mathsf{Pai.pk}_\mathsf{C}, g^m, c, \mathsf{lbl})$; $h_x \leftarrow \mathsf{H}_\mathsf{R}^b(\mathsf{lbl}, x, a)$;
2. If cid has not been used with C, (lbl, c_3, e) are the same as in the commit phase, $c_3 = \mathsf{Ped.Com}(\mathsf{Ped.ck}_\mathsf{R}; h_x; r_3)$, and $\Sigma_\mathsf{eq}.\mathsf{Vf}(\Sigma_\mathsf{eq}.\mathsf{rpk}_\mathsf{R}; x; a, e, z) = 1$, then output $(\mathsf{open}, \mathsf{lbl}, g^m)$. Otherwise, ignore the message.

$\Gamma_{dl}.\mathsf{tdOpen}(\mathsf{rpk}_\mathsf{C}, \mathsf{td}_\mathsf{R}^b; c, g^m, \mathsf{op}, g^{m'})$:
   $x \leftarrow (\mathsf{p}, \mathsf{SCS.pk}_\mathsf{C}, \mathsf{Pai.pk}_\mathsf{C}, g^m, c, \mathsf{lbl})$; $x' \leftarrow (\mathsf{p}, \mathsf{SCS.pk}_\mathsf{C}, \mathsf{Pai.pk}_\mathsf{C}, g^{m'}, c, \mathsf{lbl})$;
   $(a', z') \leftarrow \Sigma_\mathsf{eq}.\mathsf{Sim}(\Sigma_\mathsf{eq}.\mathsf{rpk}_\mathsf{R}; x', e)$;
   $\mathsf{op}' \leftarrow \mathsf{Ped.tdOpen}(\mathsf{Ped.td}_\mathsf{R}; \mathsf{H}_\mathsf{R}^b(\mathsf{lbl}, x, a), r_3, \mathsf{H}_\mathsf{R}^b(\mathsf{lbl}, x', a'))$;
   return op';

$\Gamma_{dl}.\mathsf{Ext}(\mathsf{td}_\mathsf{C}^h; c)$: Return $\mathsf{Pai.Dec}_{\mathsf{Pai.sk}}(c_2) \mod p$;

Fig. 5. The commitment scheme Γ_{dl} in the RPK model

parties after they are corrupted. When a party is corrupted, $\mathcal{A}$ can read her current inner state and $\mathcal{A}$ also fully controls her. $\mathcal{Z}$ can control $\mathcal{A}$ and see the inside of the execution of the protocol (the interactions between the honest parties or between the honest parties and the adversary) via the view of $\mathcal{A}$.

$\boxed{\text{Game}_1\text{:}}$ In Game_1, Sim simulates the authorities $\mathcal{R}_C, \mathcal{R}_R$ generating the registered public keys rpk_C and rpk_R used by C and R. Sim stores $\text{td}_{CR} = (\text{td}_C^h, \text{td}_R^b)$. Sim simulates honest parties as in Game_0, **except for the case where R is honest but C is corrupted**. After obtaining $(\text{lbl}, c_3; e; c)$ from the view of the protocol between C and R in the commit phase, where $\text{lbl} = (\text{sid}, \text{cid}, C, R)$, Sim stores $m^* \leftarrow \text{Pai.Dec}_{\text{Pai.sk}_C}(c_2)$ as a part of the state. In the open phase, when C successfully opens to g^m, Sim sends $\left(\text{open}, \text{lbl}, g^{m^*}\right)$ to $\mathcal{Z}$.

In the case of adaptive corruption of R before the open phase, Sim simply reveals $\text{st}_C = (c, g^{m^*}, \text{op})$ to $\mathcal{A}$. Honest R has no secret.

Lemma 1. *If Σ_{eq} is specially sound, Ped is computationally binding, and H_R^b is collision-resistant then $\mathcal{Z}$ distinguishes Game_0 and Game_1 with a negligible probability.*

Proof (Proof of Lemma 1). The only difference from Game_0 is that in Game_1, Sim (playing as honest R) outputs g^{m^*} instead of g^m at the open phase. Sim opens g^{m^*} after C decommits to g^m in a verifiable way. If not, Sim outputs nothing. Denote by bad the event that $m^* \not\equiv m \pmod{p}$ where g^m is the value successfully opened by C. We claim that bad occurs only with a negligible probability; otherwise, either the soundness of Σ_{eq}, the binding of Ped, or the collision resistance of H_R^b is broken.

Assume that $m^* \not\equiv m \pmod{p}$ at least in one of such executions. In the first such execution, we rewind the adversary at the step (*) in the commit phase and send a new random challenge e'. Assume, by contradiction, that C returns $c' = (c_1', c_2')$ such that $c' \neq c$ but still successfully decommits to some value m' with a'. Then it implies breaking of the binding of Ped or the collision-resistancy of H_R^b, because we can simulate it without knowing the trapdoor key. For the same reason, $x' = x$ (and thus $m' = m$) holds except with a negligible probability. Thus, rewinding the commit phase, C outputs the same $\text{st}_C = (c, g^m, \text{op})$ except with a negligible probability when it can successfully decommit. Note that $m^* \not\equiv m \pmod{p}$ implies that $x \notin \mathbf{L}_{\text{eq}}$. Since x (and thus m) is now fixed with an overwhelming probability, C can convince R on false instance x only with probability $2^{-\lambda}$ (this follows from the special soundness of Σ_{eq}), which is negligible in λ. Hence, bad occurs only with a negligible probability and the views of $\mathcal{Z}$ in the two games are computationally indistinguishable. We stress that we rewind just in the proof of binding, but not in the simulation. $\square$

$\boxed{\text{Game}_2\text{:}}$ identical to Game_1 except following cases.

Honest C: In the open phase, upon receiving $(\text{open}, \text{sid}, \text{cid})$ from $\mathcal{Z}$, Sim sets $(a^*, e, z^*) \leftarrow \Sigma_{\text{eq}}.\text{Sim}(\Sigma_{\text{eq}}.\text{rpk}_R; x, e)$ and sends $(g^m, \text{op} = (\text{lbl}, c_3, e; a^*, z^*, r_3))$ to R; *Importantly, in the simulation of honest C in the open phase, Sim does not have to know w.*

C was adaptively corrupted before receiving e: in the commit phase, Sim sets $r_3^* \leftarrow \text{Ped.tdOpen}(\text{Ped.td}_R; h_x, r_3, h_x^*)$ and then reveals the current secret state $(w = (m, r_1, r_2), s, r_3^*)$ to $\mathcal{Z}$.

C was adaptively corrupted after receiving e but before the open phase: Sim simulates C honestly. Note that (w, s) is supposed to be erased by honest C before sending c, and thus, Sim does not need to reveal it. The proof of the following lemma is straightforward.

Lemma 2. *If Σ_{eq} is SHVZK and Ped is trapdoor, then $\mathcal{Z}$ distinguishes Game$_1$ and Game$_2$ with negligible probability.*

$\boxed{\text{Game}_3:}$ In this game, we do the following changes.

Honest C: In the commit phase, after receiving $(\text{commit}, \text{lbl}, m)$ from $\mathcal{Z}$, when it receives e, Sim computes $\mathbf{c}_1^* \leftarrow \text{SCS.Enc}_{\text{SCS.pk}_C}^{\text{lbl}}(1; r_1)$ and sends $\mathbf{c}^* \leftarrow (\mathbf{c}_1^*, c_2)$ to R. In the open phase, upon receiving input $(\text{open}, \text{sid}, \text{cid})$ from $\mathcal{Z}$, Sim first sets $\mathbf{x}^* \leftarrow (p, \text{SCS.pk}_C, \text{Pai.pk}_C, g^m, \mathbf{c}^*, \text{lbl})$ where $\mathbf{x}^* \notin \mathbf{L}_{eq}$ because $\mathbf{c}_1^* = \text{SCS.Enc}_{\text{SCS.pk}_C}^{\text{lbl}}(1; r_1)$.

In the case of adaptive corruption of C: Sim simulates C as in Game$_2$.

Security analysis. The only difference from the previous game is that in Game$_3$, the simulator Sim (playing as honest C) computes $\mathbf{c}_1^* \leftarrow \text{SCS.Enc}_{\text{SCS.pk}_C}^{\text{lbl}}(1; r_1)$ encrypting 1 instead of g^m. As in [16], we run the (multi-message) IND-PCA game to show this game is indistinguishable from the previous game. Denote by bad_i the event in Game$_i$ that $m^* \not\equiv m \pmod{p}$ where m is the value successfully opened by C. As analysed above, $\Pr[\text{bad}] = \Pr[\text{bad}_1] = \text{negl}(\lambda)$. In addition, Game$_1$ is statistically close to Game$_2$ and so, $\Pr[\text{bad}_1] \approx \Pr[\text{bad}_2] = \text{negl}(\lambda)$. We use this fact to prove the following lemma.

Lemma 3. *If SCS is IND-PCA secure then $\mathcal{Z}$ distinguishes Game$_2$ and Game$_3$ with only a negligible probability.*

Proof (Proof of Lemma 3). The proof is a variant of the proof in [16], App. A. We define the multi-message IND-PCA security for a public-key cryptosystem Π. Let $\text{Expt}_{\Pi,\mathcal{B}}^{\text{mpca}}(\lambda)$ be the following experiment:

$$
\begin{array}{|l|}
\hline
\text{Expt}_{\Pi,\mathcal{B}}^{\text{mpca}}(\lambda) \\
\hline
\mathcal{Q}_{\text{Enc}} \leftarrow \emptyset; \mathcal{Q}_{\text{pca}} \leftarrow \emptyset; (\Pi.\text{pk}, \text{sk}) \leftarrow \Pi.\text{KGen}(1^\lambda); \\
b \leftarrow_{\$} \{0,1\}; b' \leftarrow \mathcal{B}^{\text{Enc}_{\Pi.\text{pk}}^b(\cdot,\cdot,\cdot), O_{\Pi.\text{sk}}^{\text{pca}}(\cdot,\cdot,\cdot)}(\Pi.\text{pk}); \\
\text{if } b = b' \text{ then return } 1; \text{else return } 0; \text{fi} \\
\hline
\end{array}
$$

Here, the oracles are defined as follows:

- $\text{Enc}_{\Pi.\text{pk}}^b(\text{lbl}^*, g^{m_0}, g^{m_1})$ rejects it if $\text{lbl}^* \in \mathcal{Q}_{\text{pca}}$. Otherwise, it adds lbl^* to $\mathcal{Q}_{\text{Enc}}$ and returns $\mathbf{c} \leftarrow \Pi.\text{Enc}_{\Pi.\text{pk}}^{\text{lbl}^*}(g^{m_b})$.
- $O_{\Pi.\text{sk}}^{\text{pca}}(\text{lbl}, g^m, \mathbf{c})$ rejects it if $\text{lbl} \in \mathcal{Q}_{\text{Enc}}$. Otherwise, it adds lbl to $\mathcal{Q}_{\text{pca}}$, and returns 1 iff $\mathbf{c}$ is a proper ciphertext of g^m on label lbl.

Π is *multi-message indistinguishable against the plaintext checkable attacks* (mIND-PCA secure) if $\text{Adv}_{\Pi,\mathcal{B}}^{\text{mpca}}(\lambda) := |\Pr[\text{Expt}_{\Pi,\mathcal{B}}^{\text{mpca}}(\lambda) = 1] - 1/2| = \text{negl}(\lambda)$ for all non-uniform PPT $\mathcal{B}$.

By using the standard hybrid argument, for any mIND-PCA adversary $\mathcal{B}$ against Π with at most $q = q(\lambda)$ queries to the encryption oracle, there exists an IND-PCA adversary $\mathcal{B}'$ against Π, s.t. $\mathsf{Adv}_{\Pi,\mathcal{B}}^{\mathrm{mpca}}(\lambda) \leq q(\lambda) \cdot \mathsf{Adv}_{\Pi,\mathcal{B}'}^{\mathrm{pca}}(\lambda)$, where the running time of $\mathcal{B}'$ is roughly bounded by the running time of $\mathcal{B}$ plus $q - 1$ encryption operations. We construct mIND-PCA adversary $\mathcal{B}$ using $\mathcal{Z}$ and the adversary $\mathcal{A}$ as follows. W.l.o.g., assume that $\Pr[\mathsf{Game}_2(\mathcal{A}) = 1] \leq \Pr[\mathsf{Game}_3(\mathcal{A}) = 1]$, where $\mathsf{Game}_i(\mathcal{A})$ is the random variable assigning the output bit of the environment $\mathcal{Z}$ in Game_i. $\mathcal{B}$ is given $\mathsf{SCS.pk}_\mathsf{C}$ as an instance in the mIND-CPA game. $\mathcal{B}$ sets up rpk_C and rpk_R by picking the remaining parameters. Here, she knows $\mathsf{Ped.td}_\mathsf{R}$ but does not know $\mathsf{SCS.sk}_\mathsf{C}$. $\mathcal{B}$ runs $\mathcal{Z}$ and $\mathcal{A}$ and plays the role of simulator Sim as in Game_2 (or Game_3), except for the following two cases:

(i) If C is honest and $\mathcal{A}$ receives (lbl, c_3) from $\mathcal{Z}$, $\mathcal{B}$ submits $(\mathsf{lbl}, g^m, 1)$ to the oracle $\mathsf{Enc}_{\mathsf{SCS.pk}_\mathsf{C}}^b$ and receives $\mathbf{c}$. Then, $\mathcal{B}$ plays the role of the simulator in Game_2 (or equivalently, in Game_3).

(ii) If R is honest but C is corrupted, after receiving all three messages in the commit phase with C, $\mathcal{B}$ simply stores it. In the open phase, when C successfully decommits to g^m, $\mathcal{B}$ submits $(\mathsf{lbl}, g^m, \mathbf{c}_1)$ to the oracle $O_{\mathsf{sk}_\mathsf{C}}^{\mathrm{pca}}$ and receives the answer bit. If the answer bit is 1, then $\mathcal{B}$ outputs $(\mathbf{open}, \mathsf{lbl}, g^m)$ to the environment. **Otherwise, she halts and outputs 1 (break point).**

If such an event does not occur, $\mathcal{B}$ proceeds the game with $\mathcal{Z}$ and $\mathcal{A}$ as playing the role of Sim. When $\mathcal{Z}$ outputs a bit b', $\mathcal{B}$ outputs b' in the mIND-PCA game.

Security Analysis. Above, $\mathcal{B}$ perfectly simulates Game_2 when $b = 0$ just before the break point. Recall that bad_i denotes the event in Game_i that $m^* \not\equiv m \pmod{p}$ where g^m is the value successfully decommitted to by corrupted C. The probability that the break occurs is equal to the probability that bad_2 occurs, which is negligible. Similarly, $\mathcal{B}$ perfectly simulates Game_3 when $b = 1$ just before the break point. We do not know $\Pr[\mathsf{bad}_3]$. However, since $\Pr[\mathsf{bad}_2] = \mathsf{negl}(\lambda)$, we can conclude $b = 1$ if the break happens. If the break never happens, $\mathcal{B}$ perfectly simulates either Game_2 or Game_3 according to b. Thus, the difference of the output of $\mathcal{Z}$ is bounded by the advantage of $\mathcal{B}$: $\mathsf{Adv}_{\mathsf{SCS},\mathcal{B}}^{\mathrm{mcpa}}(\lambda) = |\Pr[\mathsf{Game}_3(\mathcal{Z}) = 1 \wedge \neg\mathsf{bad}_3] + \Pr[\mathsf{bad}_3] - (\Pr[\mathsf{Game}_2(\mathcal{Z}) = 1 \wedge \neg\mathsf{bad}_2] + \Pr[\mathsf{bad}_2])|$. Thus, $\Pr[\mathsf{Game}_3(\mathcal{Z}) = 1] - \Pr[\mathsf{Game}_2(\mathcal{Z}) = 1] \leq \mathsf{Adv}_{\mathsf{SCS},\mathcal{B}}^{\mathrm{mcpa}}(\lambda) + \Pr[\mathsf{bad}_2] - \Pr[\mathsf{Game}_2(\mathcal{Z}) = 1 \wedge \mathsf{bad}_2] \leq \mathsf{Adv}_{\mathsf{SCS},\mathcal{B}}^{\mathrm{mcpa}}(\lambda) + \mathsf{negl}(\lambda)$. $\square$

$\boxed{\mathsf{Game}_4\text{:}}$ In this game, Sim enacts the following changes compared to Game_3.

If C is honest: upon receiving input $(\mathtt{commit}, \mathsf{lbl}, m)$ from $\mathcal{Z}$, after receiving e, Sim computes $c_2^* = \mathsf{Pai.Enc}_{\mathsf{Pai.pk}_\mathsf{C}}(0; r_2)$ and returns $\mathbf{c}^* \leftarrow (\mathbf{c}_1^*, c_2^*)$ to R.

In the open phase, upon receiving input $(\mathtt{open}, \mathsf{sid}, \mathsf{cid})$ from $\mathcal{Z}$, Sim first sets $\mathsf{x} = (p, \mathsf{SCS.pk}_\mathsf{C}, \mathsf{Pai.pk}_\mathsf{C}, g^m, \mathbf{c}, \mathsf{lbl})$ where $\mathsf{x} \notin \mathbf{L}_{\mathsf{eq}}$ because $\mathbf{c}_1^* = \mathsf{SCS.Enc}_{\mathsf{SCS.pk}_\mathsf{C}}^{\mathsf{lbl}}(1; r_1)$ and $c_2^* = \mathsf{Pai.Enc}_{\mathsf{Pai.pk}_\mathsf{C}}(0; r_2)$.

If C is adaptively corrupted: Sim simulates C identically as in Game_3.

Security Analysis. The only difference from Game_3 is that in Game_4, the simulator Sim (playing as honest C) computes $c_2^* \leftarrow \mathsf{Pai.Enc}_{\mathsf{Pai.pk}_\mathsf{C}}(0; r_2)$ instead of

$c_2 \leftarrow \mathsf{Pai.Enc}_{\mathsf{Pai.pk}_C}(m; r_2)$. We run the (multi-message) IND-CPA game to show Game_4 is indistinguishable from Game_3.

Lemma 4. *If* Pai *is IND-CPA secure then* $\mathcal{Z}$ *distinguishes* Game_3 *and* Game_4 *with only a negligible probability.*

Proof. The proof is a variation of the proof of Lemma 3. We now analyse Pai, and define CPA-related security games (like mIND-CPA) instead of PCA-related security games. □

$\boxed{\mathsf{Game}_5\!:}$ In the ideal world, there additionally exists an ideal functionality $\mathcal{F}_{\mathsf{mcomdl}}$ and the task of the honest parties in the ideal world is simply to convey inputs from $\mathcal{Z}$ to the ideal functionalities and vice versa (the ideal honest parties communicate only with $\mathcal{Z}$ and the ideal functionalities).

Initialization step: Sim generates rpk_R and rpk_C and saves the trapdoors.
Simulating communication with $\mathcal{Z}$**:** Every input value that Sim receives from $\mathcal{Z}$ is written on $\mathcal{A}$'s input tape (as if coming from $\mathcal{Z}$) and vice versa.

Simulating the commit phase when C **is honest:** Upon receiving $(\mathsf{rcpt}, \mathsf{lbl} = (\mathsf{sid}, \mathsf{cid}, C, R))$ from $\mathcal{F}_{\mathsf{mcomdl}}$, Sim sets $m^* \leftarrow 0$ and uses it instead of m in what follows. Unless explicitly said otherwise, we will denote any variable X that uses m^* instead of m as X^* without making all the details explicit. For example, $\mathsf{c}_1^* \leftarrow \varPi.\mathsf{Enc}_{\mathsf{SCS.pk}_R}^{\mathsf{lbl}}(g^{m^*}; r_1)$, $\mathsf{c}^* \leftarrow (\mathsf{c}_1^*, \mathsf{c}_2)$, $a^* \leftarrow \Sigma_{\mathsf{eq}}.\mathsf{P}_1(\Sigma_{\mathsf{eq}}.\mathsf{rpk}_R; x^*, w^*; s)$, $h_x^* \leftarrow \mathsf{H}_R^b(\mathsf{lbl}, x^*, a^*)$, and Sim reveals $(\mathsf{lbl}, \mathsf{c}_3^*)$.
Simulating the commit phase when C **is corrupted and** R **is honest:** After receiving $(\mathsf{lbl}, \mathsf{c}_3, e, \mathsf{c})$ from C in the commit phase, Sim sets $m^* \leftarrow \mathsf{Pai.Dec}_{\mathsf{Pai.sk}_C}(\mathsf{c}_2)$ and uses m^* instead of m after that.

Simulating adaptive corruption of C **before receiving** e **in the commit phase:** When C is corrupted, Sim immediately reads C's inner state and obtains m. Sim uses m to compute all variables as in the real protocol, except setting $r_3 \leftarrow \mathsf{Ped.tdOpen}(\mathsf{Ped.td}_R; h_x^*, r_3^*, h_x)$ and revealing (m, w, s, r_3).
Simulating adaptive corruption of C **after the commit phase but before the open phase:** When C is corrupted, Sim immediately reads ideal committer C's inner state and obtains m. Sim sets all variables as in the real protocol, except $(a, z) \leftarrow \Sigma_{\mathsf{eq}}.\mathsf{Sim}(\Sigma_{\mathsf{eq}}.\mathsf{rpk}_R; x, e)$. Sim sets $r_3 \leftarrow \mathsf{Ped.tdOpen}(\mathsf{Ped.td}_R; h_x^*, r_3^*, h_x)$ and reveals st_C.
Simulating adaptive corruption of R **after the commit phase but before the open phase:** Sim stores $\mathsf{st}_R = (\mathsf{lbl}, \mathsf{c}_3, e, \mathsf{c})$ as if it comes from R.

Simulating the open phase when C **is honest:** Upon receiving input $(\mathsf{open}, \mathsf{lbl}, g^m)$ from $\mathcal{F}_{\mathsf{mcomdl}}$, Sim uses g^m to compute all variables as in the real protocol, except $(a, z) \leftarrow \Sigma_{\mathsf{eq}}.\mathsf{Sim}(\Sigma_{\mathsf{eq}}.\mathsf{rpk}_R; x, e)$. Sim sets $r_3 \leftarrow \mathsf{Ped.tdOpen}(\mathsf{Ped.td}_R; h_x^*, r_3^*, h_x)$. Sim reveals (g^m, op).
Simulating the open phase when C **is corrupted and the receiver** R **is honest:** Upon receiving (g^m, op) from C, Sim sends $(\mathsf{open}, \mathsf{sid}, \mathsf{cid})$ to $\mathcal{F}_{\mathsf{mcomdl}}$. $\mathcal{F}_{\mathsf{mcomdl}}$ follows its code: if a tuple $(\mathsf{sid}, \mathsf{cid}, C, R, g^{m^*})$ with the same $(\mathsf{sid}, \mathsf{cid})$

was previously stored by $\mathcal{F}_{\mathsf{mcomdl}}$, $\mathcal{F}_{\mathsf{mcomdl}}$ sends $(\mathsf{open}, \mathsf{sid}, \mathsf{cid}, \mathsf{C}, \mathsf{R}, g^{m^*})$ to the ideal receiver R and Sim. Then, R conveys it to $\mathcal{Z}$.

By construction, this game is identical to the previous game.   □

Acknowledgement. The authors were supported by the European Union's Horizon 2020 research and innovation programme under grant agreement No. 780477 (project PRIViLEDGE), and by the Estonian Research Council grant PRG49. The work was done while Zając was working at the University of Tartu.

References

1. Abdalla, M., Benhamouda, F., Pointcheval, D.: Public-key encryption indistinguishable under plaintext-checkable attacks. In: Katz, J. (ed.) PKC 2015. LNCS, vol. 9020, pp. 332–352. Springer, Heidelberg (2015). https://doi.org/10.1007/978-3-662-46447-2_15
2. Barak, B., Canetti, R., Nielsen, J.B., Pass, R.: Universally composable protocols with relaxed set-up assumptions. In: 45th FOCS, pp. 186–195 (2004)
3. Belenkiy, M., Chase, M., Kohlweiss, M., Lysyanskaya, A.: P-signatures and non-interactive anonymous credentials. In: Canetti, R. (ed.) TCC 2008. LNCS, vol. 4948, pp. 356–374. Springer, Heidelberg (2008). https://doi.org/10.1007/978-3-540-78524-8_20
4. Ben-Sasson, E., Chiesa, A., Green, M., Tromer, E., Virza, M.: Secure sampling of public parameters for succinct zero knowledge proofs. In: 2015 IEEE Symposium on Security and Privacy, pp. 287–304 (2015)
5. Blazy, O., Chevalier, C., Pointcheval, D., Vergnaud, D.: Analysis and improvement of Lindell's UC-secure commitment schemes. In: Jacobson, M., Locasto, M., Mohassel, P., Safavi-Naini, R. (eds.) ACNS 2013. LNCS, vol. 7954, pp. 534–551. Springer, Heidelberg (2013). https://doi.org/10.1007/978-3-642-38980-1_34
6. Blum, M., Feldman, P., Micali, S.: Non-interactive zero-knowledge and its applications (extended abstract). In: 20th ACM STOC, pp. 103–112 (1988)
7. Camenisch, J., Shoup, V.: Practical verifiable encryption and decryption of discrete logarithms. In: Boneh, D. (ed.) CRYPTO 2003. LNCS, vol. 2729, pp. 126–144. Springer, Heidelberg (2003). https://doi.org/10.1007/978-3-540-45146-4_8
8. Canetti, R.: Universally composable security: a new paradigm for cryptographic protocols. In: 42nd FOCS, pp. 136–145 (2001)
9. Canetti, R., Fischlin, M.: Universally composable commitments. In: Kilian, J. (ed.) CRYPTO 2001. LNCS, vol. 2139, pp. 19–40. Springer, Heidelberg (2001). https://doi.org/10.1007/3-540-44647-8_2
10. Canetti, R., Lindell, Y., Ostrovsky, R., Sahai, A.: Universally composable two-party and multi-party secure computation. In: 34th ACM STOC, pp. 494–503 (2002)
11. Cramer, R., Damgård, I., Schoenmakers, B.: Proofs of partial knowledge and simplified design of witness hiding protocols. In: Desmedt, Y.G. (ed.) CRYPTO 1994. LNCS, vol. 839, pp. 174–187. Springer, Heidelberg (1994). https://doi.org/10.1007/3-540-48658-5_19
12. Damgård, I.: Towards practical public key systems secure against chosen ciphertext attacks. In: Feigenbaum, J. (ed.) CRYPTO 1991. LNCS, vol. 576, pp. 445–456. Springer, Heidelberg (1992). https://doi.org/10.1007/3-540-46766-1_36

13. Damgård, I., Fujisaki, E.: A statistically-hiding integer commitment scheme based on groups with hidden order. In: Zheng, Y. (ed.) ASIACRYPT 2002. LNCS, vol. 2501, pp. 125–142. Springer, Heidelberg (2002). https://doi.org/10.1007/3-540-36178-2_8

14. Damgård, I., Nielsen, J.B.: Perfect hiding and perfect binding universally composable commitment schemes with constant expansion factor. In: Yung, M. (ed.) CRYPTO 2002. LNCS, vol. 2442, pp. 581–596. Springer, Heidelberg (2002). https://doi.org/10.1007/3-540-45708-9_37

15. Fischlin, M., Libert, B., Manulis, M.: Non-interactive and re-usable universally composable string commitments with adaptive security. In: Lee, D.H., Wang, X. (eds.) ASIACRYPT 2011. LNCS, vol. 7073, pp. 468–485. Springer, Heidelberg (2011). https://doi.org/10.1007/978-3-642-25385-0_25

16. Fujisaki, E.: Improving practical UC-secure commitments based on the DDH assumption. In: Zikas, V., De Prisco, R. (eds.) SCN 2016. LNCS, vol. 9841, pp. 257–272. Springer, Cham (2016). https://doi.org/10.1007/978-3-319-44618-9_14

17. Gennaro, R., Gentry, C., Parno, B., Raykova, M.: Quadratic span programs and succinct NIZKs without PCPs. In: Johansson, T., Nguyen, P.Q. (eds.) EUROCRYPT 2013. LNCS, vol. 7881, pp. 626–645. Springer, Heidelberg (2013). https://doi.org/10.1007/978-3-642-38348-9_37

18. Groth, J.: Short pairing-based non-interactive zero-knowledge arguments. In: Abe, M. (ed.) ASIACRYPT 2010. LNCS, vol. 6477, pp. 321–340. Springer, Heidelberg (2010). https://doi.org/10.1007/978-3-642-17373-8_19

19. Groth, J., Sahai, A.: Efficient non-interactive proof systems for bilinear groups. In: Smart, N. (ed.) EUROCRYPT 2008. LNCS, vol. 4965, pp. 415–432. Springer, Heidelberg (2008). https://doi.org/10.1007/978-3-540-78967-3_24

20. Kosba, A.E., et al.: C∅C∅: a framework for building composable zero-knowledge proofs. Technical report 2015/1093, IACR (2015). http://eprint.iacr.org/2015/1093. Accessed 9 Apr 2017

21. Lindell, Y.: Highly-efficient universally-composable commitments based on the DDH assumption. In: Paterson, K.G. (ed.) EUROCRYPT 2011. LNCS, vol. 6632, pp. 446–466. Springer, Heidelberg (2011). https://doi.org/10.1007/978-3-642-20465-4_25

22. Lipmaa, H.: Progression-free sets and sublinear pairing-based non-interactive zero-knowledge arguments. In: Cramer, R. (ed.) TCC 2012. LNCS, vol. 7194, pp. 169–189. Springer, Heidelberg (2012). https://doi.org/10.1007/978-3-642-28914-9_10

23. Naor, M.: On cryptographic assumptions and challenges. In: Boneh, D. (ed.) CRYPTO 2003. LNCS, vol. 2729, pp. 96–109. Springer, Heidelberg (2003). https://doi.org/10.1007/978-3-540-45146-4_6

24. Paillier, P.: Public-key cryptosystems based on composite degree residuosity classes. In: Stern, J. (ed.) EUROCRYPT 1999. LNCS, vol. 1592, pp. 223–238. Springer, Heidelberg (1999). https://doi.org/10.1007/3-540-48910-X_16

25. Pedersen, T.P.: Non-interactive and information-theoretic secure verifiable secret sharing. In: Feigenbaum, J. (ed.) CRYPTO 1991. LNCS, vol. 576, pp. 129–140. Springer, Heidelberg (1992). https://doi.org/10.1007/3-540-46766-1_9

A New Encoding Framework for Predicate Encryption with Non-linear Structures in Prime Order Groups

Jongkil Kim[1]([✉]), Willy Susilo[1], Fuchun Guo[1], Joonsang Baek[1], and Nan Li[2]

[1] Institute of Cybersecurity and Cryptology, School of Computing and Information Technology, University of Wollongong, Wollongong, Australia
{jongkil,wsusilo,fuchun,baek}@uow.edu.au
[2] School of Electrical Engineering and Computing,
The University of Newcastle, Newcastle, Australia
nan.li@newcastle.edu.au

Abstract. We present a new encoding framework for predicate encryption (PE) in prime order groups. Our framework captures a broader range of adaptively secure PE schemes by allowing PE schemes to have more flexible (i.e., non-linear) structures. The existing works dealing with adaptively secure PE schemes in prime order groups require strict structural restrictions on PE schemes. In particular, the exponents of public keys and master secret keys of the PE schemes, which are referred to as common variables, must be linear. In this paper, we introduce a modular approach which includes non-linear common variables in PE schemes. First, we formalize non-linear structures by improving Attrapadung's pair encoding framework (Eurocrypt'14). Then, we provide a generic compiler that incorporates encodings under our framework to PE schemes in prime order groups. Notably, we prove the security of our compiler by introducing a new technique that decomposes common variables into two types and makes one of them shared between semifunctional and normal spaces on processes of the dual system encryption. As instances of our new framework, we introduce new attribute-based encryption schemes supporting non-monotone access structures, namely non-monotonic ABE. Our new schemes are adaptively secure in prime order groups and have either short ciphertexts (in the case of KP-ABE) or short keys (in the case of CP-ABE).

Keywords: Pair encoding · Non-monotone access structure ·
Attribute-based encryption · Prime order groups ·
Dual system encryption

1 Introduction

Wee [18] and Attrapadung [3] introduced generic modular frameworks which generalize predicate encryption (PE) using encodings. They extracted common

© Springer Nature Switzerland AG 2019
R. H. Deng et al. (Eds.): ACNS 2019, LNCS 11464, pp. 406–425, 2019.
https://doi.org/10.1007/978-3-030-21568-2_20

properties that PE schemes shared and formalized them under the encoding frameworks. Their encoding frameworks include generic constructions (i.e., compilers) of PE schemes based on encodings and approaches to proofs of adaptive security only using the properties the encodings commonly have. Therefore, these frameworks give a new insight into building PE schemes as the security of PE schemes can be proven by showing that their corresponding encoding schemes satisfy those properties.

Recently, encoding frameworks have been adopted to find a generic construction in prime order groups [1,2,5,11,14]. The benefit of the prime order groups is the efficiency gains that they can bring to encryption schemes. However, the constructions based on the prime order groups commonly impose a more structural restriction on encoding schemes. In particular, they require the exponents of public and master secret keys (which are referred to as common variables) to have a simple linear structure.

For example, if we denote the common variables of an encoding scheme by $h_1, ..., h_m$, the constructions require that public and master secret keys to be set as $g, g^{h_1}, ..., g^{h_m}$ where g is a group generator. Note that they cannot allow encoding schemes to have the parameters of group elements whose exponents are not linear in h_i such as $g^{h_1^2}$ or $g^{h_1 h_2}$. This is because most of the known techniques in prime order groups require parameters in an encryption scheme to be represented using matrices. Hence, the multiplication between parameters cannot be easily handled since those matrices do not commute. It adds more restrictions on the structures of the encoding scheme and limits the usage of encoding frameworks.

1.1 Our Contribution

Framework with Less Structural Requirement. We introduce a modular framework which is applicable to PE schemes having non-linear common variables in prime order groups. Prior to our work, existing frameworks [1,2,5,11,14] in prime order groups covers PE schemes which have a simple linear structure. Our new framework overcomes this barrier by suggesting a new framework and a new proof technique. To mitigate the structural restriction and effectively express non-linearity of PE schemes, we improve Attrapadung's pair encoding framework [3] which is one of the most popular encoding frameworks for PE and provide a new adaptively secure compiler that incorporates an encoding scheme under our improved framework to a PE scheme in prime order groups.

ABEs with a Non-monotone Access Structure. As instances of our new encoding technique, we introduce two new attribute-based encryption (ABE) schemes supporting a non-monotone access structure as follows:

- Non-monotonic CP-ABE (NM-CP-ABE) with short keys (Scheme 1).
- Non-monotonic KP-ABE (NM-KP-ABE) with short ciphertexts (Scheme 2).

Note that although Yamada et al. already introduced selectively secure schemes in [26], no encoding framework was able to achieve adaptive security in prime order groups due to the non-linearity. For the first time, our new schemes achieve non-monotone access structure, short parameters (key or ciphertexts) and adaptive security at the same time. Table 1 summarizes comparison between our schemes and the existing non-monotonic ABE schemes.

Table 1. Comparisons of Non-monotonic ABE schemes in prime order groups

Scheme	Multi-use of Att.	Security	Assumptions	Type	NM-CP-ABE	
					CT	Priv. Key
LSW [16]	Yes	Selective	RO+n-MEBDH	KP	$3n + 1$	$2t + t'$
AHLLPR [6]	Yes	Selective	n-DBDHE	KP	4	$(N + 1)t$
YAHK [26]	Yes	Selective	q-types	CP	$3t + 1$	$4n + 2$
	Yes	Selective	q-types	KP	$4n + 1$	$3t$
OT [23]	No	Adaptive	DLIN	CP	$14t + 5$	$14n\tilde{u} + 5$
	No	Adaptive	DLIN	KP	$14n\tilde{u} + 5$	$14t + 5$
Scheme 1	Yes	Adaptive	Static + q-types	CP	$3(N + 2)t + 6$	21
Scheme 2	Yes	Adaptive	Static + q-types	KP	24	$3(N + 2)t + 9$

t: the number of attributes in an access policy, t': the number of negated attributes in an access policy,

n: the number of attributes in attribute sets, N: the maximum number of attributes in attribute sets

$\tilde{u}$: the maximum number of appearances of an attribute in an access policy.

Static: 'Static' in Assumptions implies that $LW1$, $LW2$ and DBDH

1.2   Overview of Our Technique

Main Idea. Our solution largely adopts the notion of pair encoding framework, which is outlined in Appendix A.1. However, the pair encoding framework cannot properly describe non-linear common variables. Therefore, we modify the syntax of pair encoding to be more flexible. The most significant change in our framework is decomposing common variables in the pair encoding framework into *hidden common variables* and *shared common variables* as we describe below:

- *Hidden Common Variables (HCVs)* are identical to common variables used in existing frameworks [1,5,11,14]. The HCVs must be linear.
- *Shared Common Variables (SCVs)* are variables which are non-linear or cause a non-linearity.

In detail, the exponents of public parameters and master secrets in our encoding framework are the composition of those two types of common variables. We use $\boldsymbol{b}(\boldsymbol{w}, b_0, \boldsymbol{h}) = (b_1, ..., b_\omega)$ to denote the exponents of those parameters and also use $\boldsymbol{w} = (w_1, ..., w_{\omega_1})$ and $\boldsymbol{h} = (h_1, ..., h_{\omega_2})$ to denote SCVs and HCVs, respectively. b_i is defined as a monomial which is $b_i = b_0 f_i(\boldsymbol{w})$ or $f_i(\boldsymbol{w})h_j$ where $f_i(\boldsymbol{w})$ is a monomial consisting of the elements of $\boldsymbol{w}$ and $j \in [\omega_2]$ and b_0 is a variable adopted for a linear operation of monomials where HCVs do not appear. This setting makes $b(w, b_0, h)$ linear in (b_0, h). More formally, by the definition of b, for all $b_0, b_0' \in \mathbb{Z}_p$ and $h, h' \in \mathbb{Z}_p^{\omega_2}$, we have

$$b(w, b_0, h) + b(w, b_0', h') = b(w, b_0 + b_0', h + h').$$

We call this property *linearity in HCVs*.

HCVs and SCVs work differently in the security proof. Encoding frameworks can be considered as generalizations of Waters' dual system encryption [25]. In the dual system encryption, *semi-functional space* is used to partially mimic the construction of an encryption scheme to prove the security more simply, but variables appeared in semi-functional space must not correlate with their original values in the construction, which we call normal space. HCVs are variables which are typically used in the dual system encryption. They are projected from normal space to semi-functional space in the proofs. Their values in semi functional space do not correlate to their original values. However, SCVs are a new type of variables. They are also projected to the semi-functional space, but their projected values are identical to their original values. This is possible since the proof works in a prime order group. In other words, SCVs are shared both in semi-functional and normal spaces, where the construction is defined. We handle these changes by refining the security proof and the property of encodings.

Parameter b_0. Additionally, due to the notational deficiency of the pair encoding to express the linearity of (hidden) common variables, we have adopted a new variable b_0 in our encoding framework as done in Kim et al.'s work [14]. Speaking more precisely, even if HCVs of b are linear form (i.e. the maximum degree of those variables is set to be 1), the linearity in HCVs of b cannot properly be notated if coordinates of b do not have an element of h. Thus, we use a new variable b_0 to denote the change the values during the linear operation and place b_0 where an element of h does not appear. Consequently, all coordinates of b must contain either b_0 or h_i and linear in those variables.

Our Compiler in Prime Order Groups. To construct a new compiler of encodings with a less restrictive structural assumption, we adopt the technique from [14], in which the common variables are projected into semi-functional space. This technique is built upon combining a nested dual system encryption technique and Lewko and Waters' IBE [17]. In particular, the simulator sets a common variable as $d \cdot h' + h''$ where $d \in \mathbb{Z}_p$ is given by g^d using a group generator g and h'' are values generated by the simulator. This setting hides the values of h' using h'' to the adversary. Also, the simulator enables to project h' using g^d, which is indistinguishable from a random value in the assumption to which the security is reduced.

In our framework, the exponents of public parameters are more complex monomials, but the simulator still can hide HCVs before they are projected into semi-functional space. In our proof, we let the simulator set a non-linear monomial $f_i(w)h_j = f_i(w)(dh_j' + h_j'') = d \cdot f_i(w) \cdot h_j' + f_i(w) \cdot h_j''$ where $f_i(w)$ is a monomial consisting only of SCVs, which are denoted as w. In particular, if g^d

Table 2. Comparisons of normal and semi-functional parts in encoding frameworks

		Normal parts	Semi-functional parts
KSGA [14]	Key	$k(\alpha, x, (1, h); r)$	$k(\alpha', x, (1, h'); r')$
	CT	$c(y, (1, h); s, s)$	$c(y, (1, h'); s', s')$
A [4]	Key	$k(\alpha, x, h; r)$	$k(\alpha', x, h'; r)$
	CT	$c(y, h; s, s)$	$c(y, h'; s, s)$
Ours	Key	$k(\alpha, x, b(w, 1, h); r)$	$k(\alpha', x, b(w, 1, h'); r')$
	CT	$c(y, b(w, 1, h); s, s)$	$c(y, b(w, 1, h'); s', s')$

is indistinguishable from a random value (i.e. g^{d+r} where r is a random value), $g^{f_i(w)h_j}$ becomes $g^{d \cdot f_i(w) \cdot h'_j} \cdot g^{r \cdot f_i(w)h'_j} \cdot g^{f_i(w) \cdot h''_j}$. Hence, $g^{r \cdot f_i(w)h'_j}$ can simulate the semi-functional space, where r and h'_j simulates a random variable and a HCV, respectively. $f_i(w)$ appears in the semi-functional space, but its value is the same as that of the normal space as it is defined as SCV.

Refined α Hiding. In our setting, SCVs are not hidden. It means that their projected values in the semi-functional space are identical to their original values as shown in Table 2. Sharing SCVs makes a security proof complex because it means the values must be defined and fixed before receiving any query from the adversary (i.e. when a system sets up). We address this challenge by refining α hiding property of pair encoding framework. We use two oracles which are indistinguishable from each other to simulate the refined α hiding property. In our setting, the oracles output $g^{b(w,1,1)}$ as an initial instance so that the simulator creates public keys and normal parts of private keys using shared common variables w.

It is worth noting that the oracles in the existing techniques [4,14] do not output any value related to common values but only outputs a group generator g as an initial instance. In the pair encoding framework, because the initial instance does not include any public parameters, the α hiding property is proved by selecting public parameters after they obtain the target predicate of the challenge ciphertext (in selective security proof) or the challenge key (in co-selective security proof). However, we observed that, even in selective security proofs, some common variables can be set without using any information about the challenge ciphertext. This makes us use those variables as SCVs. We show that achieving those oracles is feasible by providing new instances.

2   Related Work

Conjunctive schemes of ABE and Identity-based revocation systems were introduced [7,20] to fill the gap between practice and theory. In those schemes, only an identity can be used to revoke users and the other attributes are used to form an access policy. Inner product encryption [8,13,21,22] naturally achieves a non-monotone access structure using polynomials. However, it is well known that expressing a Boolean formula using inner product is inefficient.

A technique to convert encryption schemes in composite order groups into prime order groups were introduced by Lewko [15] using Dual Pairing Vector Spaces (DPVS) [21, 22]. However, their conversion technique is not generic and the size of parameters and the amount of computational work required for encryption/decryption increase linearly with the size of vector it uses. Dual System Groups (DSG) [12] were recently introduced by Chen and Wee. They showed that DSG can be utilized to construct a broad range of encryption schemes in prime order groups. Since then, many generic constructions [1, 4, 11] of encoding schemes in prime order groups have employed DSG except Kim et al.'s work [14]. In Kim et al.'s work, instead of using DSG, they generalized Lewko and Waters' IBE [17] as is done in this paper, but their technique does not cover encryption schemes with non-linear structure.

The compiler for pair encoding in a prime order group is proposed by Attrapadung [5]. In their technique, the common values are defined as a matrix form, which makes the encoding need more structural assumptions. To address this, they redefined the pair encoding to *regular encoding* with additional structural restrictions, which implies the linearity of common values.

Agrawal and Chase also suggested a new way to prove the security of encoding schemes [2]. They proposed a technique where the security of predicate encryption schemes can be proven by showing their encoding satisfy the symbolic property. Namely, if it is shown that the encoding scheme is mapped to a specific format, then the security is proven without any extra efforts. However, the technique still works under the same structural assumptions the pair encoding framework [3] is based on and it is not clear how the symbolic property works with a non-linear structure.

3 Preliminary

3.1 Bilinear Maps

Let $\mathcal{G}$ be a group generator which takes a security parameter λ as input and outputs (p, G_1, G_2, G_T, e), G_1, G_2 and G_T are cyclic groups of prime order p, and $e : G_1 \times G_2 \to G_T$ is a map such that $e(g^a, h^b) = e(g, h)^{ab}$ for all $g \in G_1$ $h \in G_2$ and $a, b \in \mathbb{Z}_p$ and $e(g, h) \neq 1 \in G_T$ whenever $g \neq 1$ and $h \neq 1$. We assume that the group operations in G_1, G_2 and G_T, as well as the bilinear map e, are all computable in polynomial time with respect to λ. It should be noted that the map e is symmetric if $G_1 = G_2$. If $G_1 \neq G_2$, the map e is asymmetric.

3.2 Non-monotone Access Structure

Definition 1 *(Access Structure)* [10]. *Let* $\{P_1, ..., P_n\}$ *be a set of parties. A collection* $\mathbb{A} \subset 2^{\{P_1, ..., P_n\}}$ *is monotone if* $\forall B, C$: *if* $B \in \mathbb{A}$ *and* $B \subset C$, *then* $C \in \mathbb{A}$. *A monotone access structure is a monotone collection* $\mathbb{A}$ *of non-empty* subsets of $\{P_1, ..., P_n\}$, i.e., $\mathbb{A} \subset 2^{\{P_1, ..., P_n\}} \setminus \{\}$. The sets in $\mathbb{A}$ are called the authorized sets, and the sets not in $\mathbb{A}$ are called the unauthorized sets.

Definition 2 *(Linear Secret-Sharing Schemes (LSSS))* [10]. *A secret sharing scheme Π over a set of parties $\mathcal{P}$ is called linear (over $\mathbb{Z}_p$) if (1) The shares for each party form a vector over $\mathbb{Z}_p$. (2) There exists a matrix A called the share-generating matrix for Π. The matrix A has m rows and ℓ columns. For all $i = 1, ..., m$, the ith row of A is labeled by a party $\rho(x)$ (ρ is a function from $\{1, ..., m\}$ to $\mathcal{P}$). When we consider the column vector $v = (s, r_2, ..., r_\ell)$, where $s \in \mathbb{Z}_p$ is the secret to be shared and $r_2, ..., r_\ell \in \mathbb{Z}_p$ are randomly chosen, then Av is the vector of m shares of the secret s according to Π. The share $(Av)_i$ belongs to party $\rho(x)$.*

Moving from Monotone to Non-monotone Access Structures. For a non-monotone access structure, we adopt a technique from Ostrovsky, Sahai and Waters [24]. They assume a family of linear secret sharing schemes $\{\Pi_\mathbb{A}\}_{\mathbb{A} \in \mathcal{A}}$ for a set of monotone access structures $\mathbb{A} \in \mathcal{A}$. For each access structure $\mathbb{A} \in \mathcal{A}$, the set of parties $\mathcal{P}$ underlying the access structures has the following properties: The names of the parties may be of two types: either it is normal (like x) or primed (like x'), and if $x \in \mathcal{P}$ then $x' \in \mathcal{P}$ and vice versa. They conceptually associate primed parties as representing the negation of normal parties.

We let $\tilde{\mathcal{P}}$ denote the set of all normal parties in $\mathcal{P}$. For every set $\tilde{S} \subset \tilde{\mathcal{P}}$, $N(\tilde{S}) \subset \mathcal{P}$ is defined by $N(\tilde{S}) = \tilde{S} \cup \{x' | x \in \tilde{P} \setminus \tilde{S}\}$. For each access structure $\mathbb{A} \in \mathcal{A}$ over a set of parties $\mathcal{P}$, a non-monotone access structure $NM(\mathbb{A})$ over the set of parties $\tilde{\mathcal{P}}$ is defined by specifying that $\tilde{S}$ is authorized in $NM(\mathbb{A})$ iff $N(\tilde{S})$ is authorized in $\mathbb{A}$. Therefore, the non-monotone access structure $NM(\mathbb{A})$ will have only normal parties in its access sets. For each access set $X \in NM(\mathbb{A})$, there will be a set in $\mathbb{A}$ that has the elements in X and primed elements for each party not in X. Finally, a family of non-monotone access structures $\tilde{\mathcal{A}}$ is defined by the set of these $NM(\mathbb{A})$ access structures.

3.3   Computational Assumptions

Our compiler needs three simple static assumptions which are also used in [14, 17]. For the following assumptions, we define $\mathbb{G} = (p, G_1, G_2, G_T, e) \xleftarrow{R} \mathcal{G}$ and let $f_1 \in G_1$ and $f_2 \in G_2$ be selected randomly.

Assumption 1 *(LW1).* Let $a, c, d \in \mathbb{Z}_p$ be selected randomly. Given

$$D := \{f_1, f_1^a, f_1^{ac^2}, f_1^c, f_1^{c^2}, f_1^{c^3}, f_1^d, f_1^{ad}, f_1^{cd}, f_1^{c^2d}, f_1^{c^3d} \in G_1, f_2, f_2^c \in G_2\},$$

it is hard to distinguish between $T_0 = f_1^{ac^2d}$ and $T_1 \xleftarrow{R} G_1$.

Assumption 2 *(LW2).* Let $d, t, w \in \mathbb{Z}_p$ be selected randomly. Given

$$D := \{f_1, f_1^d, f_1^{d^2}, f_1^{tw}, f_1^{dtw}, f_1^{d^2t} \in G_1, f_2, f_2^c, f_2^d, f_2^w \in G_2\},$$

it is hard to distinguish between $T_0 = f_2^{cw}$ and $T_1 \xleftarrow{R} G_2$.

Assumption 3 (*Decisional Bilinear Diffie-Hellman (DBDH) Assumption*). Let $a, c, d \in \mathbb{Z}_p$ be selected randomly. Given

$$D := \{f_1, f_1^a, f_1^c, f_1^d \in G_1, f_2, f_2^a, f_2^c, f_2^d \in G_2\},$$

it is hard to distinguish between $T_0 = e(f_1, f_2)^{acd}$ and $T_1 \xleftarrow{R} G_T$.

3.4 Predicate Encryption

We adopt the definition of PE and its adaptive security of [3].

Definition of Predicate Encryption [3]. A PE for a predicate $R_\kappa : \mathcal{X} \times \mathcal{Y} \rightarrow \{0,1\}$ consists of Setup, Encrypt, KeyGen and Decrypt as follows:

- Setup($1^\lambda, \kappa$) → (PK, MSK): The algorithm takes in a security parameter 1^λ and an index κ which is allocated uniquely for the function R_κ. It outputs a public parameter PK and a master secret key MSK.
- Encrypt(x, M, PK) → CT: The algorithm takes in an attribute $x \in \mathcal{X}$, a public parameter PK and a plaintext M. It outputs a ciphertext CT.
- KeyGen(y, MSK, PK) → SK: The algorithm takes in an attribute $y \in \mathcal{Y}$, MSK and PK. It outputs a private key SK.
- Decrypt(PK, SK, CT) → M: the algorithm takes in SK for y and CT for x. If $R_\kappa(x, y) = 1$, it outputs a message $M \in \mathcal{M}$. Otherwise, it aborts.

Correctness. For all $(x, y) \in \mathcal{X} \times \mathcal{Y}$ such that $R_\kappa(x, y) = 1$, if SK is the output of KeyGen(y, MSK, PK) and CT is the output of Encrypt(x, M, PK) where PK and MSK are the outputs of Setup($1^\lambda, \kappa$), Decrypt(SK, CT) outputs M for all $M \in \mathcal{M}$.

Definition of Adaptive Security of Predicate Encryption [3]. A predicate encryption scheme for a predicate function R_κ is adaptively secure if there is no PPT adversary $\mathcal{A}$ which has a non-negligible advantage in the game between $\mathcal{A}$ and the challenge $\mathcal{C}$ defined below.

- **Setup:** $\mathcal{C}$ runs Setup($1^\lambda, \kappa$) to create (PK, MSK). PK is sent to $\mathcal{A}$.
- **Phase 1:** $\mathcal{A}$ requests a private key for $y_i \in \mathcal{Y}$ and $i \in [q_1]$. For each y_i, $\mathcal{C}$ returns SK_i created by running KeyGen(y_i, MSK, PK).
- **Challenge:** When $\mathcal{A}$ requests the challenge ciphertext of $x \in \mathcal{X}$, for $R_\kappa(x, y_i) = 0$; $\forall i \in [q_1]$, and submits two messages M_0 and M_1, $\mathcal{C}$ randomly selects b from $\{0, 1\}$ and returns the challenge ciphertext CT created by running Encrypt(x, M_b, PK).
- **Phase 2:** This is identical with **Phase 1** except for the additional restriction that $y_i \in \mathcal{Y}$ for $i = q_1 + 1, ..., q_t$ such that $R_\kappa(x, y_i) = 0$; $\forall i \in \{q_1 + 1, ..., q_t\}$.
- **Guess:** $\mathcal{A}$ outputs $b' \in \{0, 1\}$. If $b = b'$, then $\mathcal{A}$ wins.

We define the advantage of an adversary $\mathcal{A}$ as $Adv_{\mathcal{A}}^{PE}(\lambda) := |\Pr[b = b'] - 1/2|$.

4   Our Encoding Framework

We introduce our new encoding framework. We largely take a notion of pair encoding framework to describe our encoding. However, our encoding framework can capture the predicate family that has non-linear common variables.

4.1   Syntax

Our encoding scheme for a predicate function R_κ in prime order p consists of four deterministic algorithms Param, Enc_1, Enc_2 and Pair.

- Param$(\kappa) \rightarrow (\boldsymbol{b} := (b_1, b_2, ..., b_\omega); \omega_1, \omega_2, \omega)$: It takes as input a predicate family κ and outputs integers $\omega_1, \omega_2, \omega \in p$ and a sequence of monomials $\{b_i\}_{i \in [\omega]} \in \mathbb{Z}_p$ with the sequence of variables of $\{b_0, h_j; h_j \in \boldsymbol{h}\}$ and functions f_i where $b_0 \in \mathbb{Z}_p$, $\boldsymbol{h} \in \mathbb{Z}_p^{\omega_2}$ and $f_i(\boldsymbol{w})$ is a monomial consisting of the elements of $\boldsymbol{w} \in \mathbb{Z}_p^{\omega_1}$. That is, for all $i \in [\omega]$, $b_i = b_0 f_i(\boldsymbol{w})$ or $f_i(\boldsymbol{w}) h_j$. $\boldsymbol{b}$ shared by the following two algorithms Enc_1 and Enc_2. We let $\boldsymbol{w} = (w_1, ..., w_{\omega_1})$ denote the SCVs and $\boldsymbol{h} = (h_1, ..., h_{\omega_2})$ denote the HCVs.
- $\mathsf{Enc}_1(x \in \mathcal{X}) \rightarrow (\boldsymbol{k} := (k_1, k_2, ..., k_{m_1}); m_2)$: It takes as inputs $x \in \mathcal{X}$ and outputs a sequence of polynomials $\{k_i\}_{i \in [m_1]}$ with coefficients in $\mathbb{Z}_p$, and $m_2 \in \mathbb{Z}_p$ where m_2 is the number of random variables. Every polynomial k_i is a linear combination of monomials of the form $\alpha, r_i b_0, \alpha b_j, r_i b_j$ in variables $\alpha, r_1, ..., r_{m_2}$ and $b_0, b_1, ..., b_\omega$. In more detail, for $i \in [m_1]$,

$$k_i := \delta_i \alpha + \sum\nolimits_{j \in [m_2]} \delta_{i,j} r_j b_0 + \sum\nolimits_{j \in [m_2], k \in [\omega]} \delta_{i,j,k} r_j b_k$$

where $\delta_i, \delta_{i,j}, \delta_{i,j,k} \in \mathbb{Z}_p$ are constants which define k_i.
- $\mathsf{Enc}_2(y \in \mathcal{Y}) \rightarrow (\boldsymbol{c} := (c_1, c_2, ..., c_{\tilde{m}_1}); \tilde{m}_2)$: It takes as inputs $y \in \mathcal{Y}$ and outputs a sequence of polynomials $\{c_i\}_{i \in [\tilde{m}_1]}$ with coefficients in $\mathbb{Z}_p$, and $\tilde{m}_2 \in \mathbb{Z}_p$ where $\tilde{m}_2$ is the number of random variables. Every polynomial c_i is a linear combination of monomials of the form $sb_0, s_i b_0, sb_j, s_i b_j$ in variables $s, s_1, ..., s_{\tilde{m}_2}$ and $b_0, b_1, ..., b_\omega$. In more detail, for $i \in [\tilde{m}_1]$,

$$c_i := \phi_i s\, b_0 + \sum\nolimits_{j \in [\tilde{m}_2]} \phi_{i,j} s_j b_0 + \sum\nolimits_{j \in [\tilde{m}_2], k \in [\omega]} \phi_{i,j,k} s_j b_k$$

where $\phi_i, \phi_{i,j}, \phi_{i,j,k} \in \mathbb{Z}_p$ are constants which define c_i.
- Pair$(x, y) \rightarrow \boldsymbol{E}$: It takes inputs $x \in \mathcal{X}$ and $y \in \mathcal{Y}$. It outputs $\boldsymbol{E} \in \mathbb{Z}_p^{m_1 \times \tilde{m}_1}$.

Correctness: The correctness holds symbolically when $b_0 = 1$. if $R_\kappa(x, y) = 1$, for every $(x, y) \in \mathcal{X} \times \mathcal{Y}$ such that $R_\kappa(x, y) = 1$, there exists $\boldsymbol{E} \in \mathbb{Z}_p^{m_1 \times \tilde{m}_1}$ satisfying $\boldsymbol{k} \boldsymbol{E} \boldsymbol{c}^\top = \alpha s$ where $\boldsymbol{k} \boldsymbol{E} \boldsymbol{c}^\top = \sum_{i \in [m_1], j \in [\tilde{m}_1]} E_{i,j} k_i c_j$.

4.2 Properties

Our encodings satisfy the following properties.

Property 1 (Linearity in hidden common variables). Suppose w, r, s and s are fixed, our encodings are linear in α and h for all $(\alpha, b_0, h) \in \mathbb{Z}_p \times \mathbb{Z}_p \times \mathbb{Z}_p^{\omega_2}$. That is, for all $\alpha, \alpha', b_0, b_0' \in \mathbb{Z}_p, h, h' \in \mathbb{Z}_p^{\omega_2}$, the followings hold:

$$k(\alpha, x, b(w, b_0, h); r) + k(\alpha', x, b(w, b_0', h'); r) = k(\alpha + \alpha', x, b(w, b_0 + b_0', h + h'); r)$$

$$c(y, b(w, b_0, h); s, s) + c(y, b(w, b_0', h'); s, s) = c(y, b(w, b_0 + b_0', h + h'); s, s)$$

Property 2 (Linearity in random variables). Suppose w and h are fixed, our encodings are linear in α, s, r and s for all $(\alpha, s, r, s) \in \mathbb{Z}_p \times \mathbb{Z}_p \times \mathbb{Z}_p^{m_2} \times \mathbb{Z}_p^{\tilde{m}_2}$. That is, for all $\alpha, \alpha', s, s' \in \mathbb{Z}_p, r, r' \in \mathbb{Z}_p^{\tilde{m}_2}$ and $s, s' \in \mathbb{Z}_p^{\tilde{m}_2}$, the followings hold:

$$k(\alpha, x, b(w, b_0, h); r) + k(\alpha', x, b(w, b_0, h); r') = k(\alpha + \alpha', x, b(w, b_0, h); r + r')$$

$$c(y, b(w, b_0, h); s) + c(y, b(w, b_0, h); s') = c(y, b(w, b_0, h); s + s')$$

where $w, b_0, h \in \mathbb{Z}_p^{\omega_1} \times \mathbb{Z}_p \times \mathbb{Z}_p^{\omega_2}$.

Property 3 (Parameter Vanishing). For all $\alpha, b_0, b_0' \in \mathbb{Z}_p, w, w' \in \mathbb{Z}_p^{\omega_1}, h, h' \in \mathbb{Z}_p^{\omega_2}$, there exists $\mathbf{0} \in \mathbb{Z}_p^{2k+1}$ which makes the distributions of $k(\alpha, x, b(w, b_0, h); \mathbf{0})$ and $k(\alpha, x, b(w', b_0', h'); \mathbf{0})$ are statistically identical.

Property 4 (α hiding). We let $g_1 \xleftarrow{R} G_1$, $g_2 \xleftarrow{R} G_2$, $\alpha, s \xleftarrow{R} \mathbb{Z}_p$, $w \xleftarrow{R} \mathbb{Z}_p^{\omega_1}$, $h \xleftarrow{R} \mathbb{Z}_p^{\omega_2}, r \xleftarrow{R} \mathbb{Z}_p^{w_2}$ and $s \xleftarrow{R} \mathbb{Z}_p^{m_2}$. For all $(x, y) \in \mathcal{X} \times \mathcal{Y}$ such that $R_\kappa(x, y) = 0$, the following two distributions are indistinguishable:

$$\{g_1^{b(w,1,1)}, g_2^{b(w,1,1)}, g_1^{c(y,(b(w,1,h);s,s)}, g_2^{k(\alpha,x,b(w,1,h);r)}\}$$

$$\approx \{g_1^{b(w,1,1)}, g_2^{b(w,1,1)}, g_1^{c(y,(b(w,1,h);s,s)}, g_2^{k(0,x,b(w,1,h);r)}\}.$$

4.3 The Compiler

For a predicate family $R_\kappa : \mathcal{X} \times \mathcal{Y} \to \{0, 1\}$ and its encoding $E(R_\kappa, p)$, A PE scheme $PE(E(R_\kappa, p))$ consists of four algorithms **Setup, KeyGen, Encrypt** and **Decrypt**.

- **Setup($1^\lambda, \kappa$) $\to \langle PK, MSK \rangle$.** The setup algorithm randomly chooses bilinear groups $\mathcal{G} = (p, G_1, G_2, G_T, e)$ of prime order $p > 2^\lambda$. It takes group generators $g_1 \xleftarrow{R} G_1, g_2 \xleftarrow{R} G_2$ from $\mathcal{G}$. It executes $(b, \omega_1, \omega_2, \omega) \leftarrow$ Param and sets $b_0 = 1$. It randomly selects $\alpha, a, y_u, y_v, y_f \in \mathbb{Z}_p, w \in \mathbb{Z}_p^{\omega_1}$ and $h \in \mathbb{Z}_p^{\omega_2}$. It sets $\tau = y_v + a \cdot y_u$. It publishes public parameters (PK) as

$$\{e(g_1, g_2)^\alpha, g_1, g_1^a, g_T, g_1^{b(w,1,h)}, g_1^{a \cdot b(w,1,h)}, g_1^{\tau \cdot b(w,1,h)}\}.$$

It sets MSK as $\{\alpha, g_2, g_2^{b(w,1,h)}, f_2 = g_2^{y_f}, u_2 = f_2^{y_u}, v_2 = f_2^{y_v}\}.$

- **KeyGen**$(x, MSK) \to SK$. The algorithm takes as inputs $x \in \mathcal{X}$ and MSK. To generate SK, it runs $(\boldsymbol{k}; m_2) \leftarrow \mathsf{Enc}_1$ and randomly selects $\boldsymbol{r} \in \mathbb{Z}_p^{m_2}$ and $\boldsymbol{z} \in \mathbb{Z}_p^{|\boldsymbol{k}|}$. It parses α from MSK and outputs $SK := (\boldsymbol{D}_1, \boldsymbol{D}_2, \boldsymbol{D}_3)$ where $\boldsymbol{D}_1 = g_2^{k(\alpha, x, b(w, 1, h); r)} v_2^{\boldsymbol{z}}$, $\boldsymbol{D}_2 = u_2^{\boldsymbol{z}}$, $\boldsymbol{D}_3 = f_2^{-\boldsymbol{z}}$.
- **Encrypt**$(M, y, PK) \to CT$. The algorithm takes as inputs $y \in \mathcal{Y}$, a message M and PK. It runs $(\boldsymbol{c}; \tilde{m}_2) \leftarrow \mathsf{Enc}_2$ and randomly selects $s \in \mathbb{Z}_p$ and $\boldsymbol{s} \in \mathbb{Z}_p^{\tilde{m}_2+1}$. The algorithm sets $C_0 = M \cdot e(g_1, g_2)^{\alpha s}$ and outputs $CT := (C_0, \boldsymbol{C}_1, \boldsymbol{C}_2, \boldsymbol{C}_3)$ where $\boldsymbol{C}_1 = g_1^{c(y, b(w, 1, h); s, \boldsymbol{s})}$, $\boldsymbol{C}_2 = (g_1^a)^{c(y, b(w, 1, h); s, \boldsymbol{s})}$, $\boldsymbol{C}_3 = (g_1^\tau)^{c(y, b(w, 1, h); s, \boldsymbol{s})}$.
- **Decrypt**$(x, y, SK, CT) \to M$. It takes as inputs SK for $x \in \mathcal{X}$ and CT for $y \in \mathcal{Y}$. It runs $\boldsymbol{E} \leftarrow \mathsf{Pair}(x, y)$ and computes

$$A_1 = e(\boldsymbol{C}_1^{\boldsymbol{E}^\top}, \boldsymbol{D}_1), \ A_2 = e(\boldsymbol{C}_2^{\boldsymbol{E}^\top}, \boldsymbol{D}_2), A_3 = e(\boldsymbol{C}_3^{\boldsymbol{E}^\top}, \boldsymbol{D}_3).$$

Suppose $R_\kappa(x, y) = 1$, $A_1 \cdot A_2 \cdot A_3 = e(g_1, g_2)^{\alpha s}$. It outputs $M = C_0 / e(g_1, g_2)^{\alpha s}$.

Correctness. For $(x, y) \in \mathcal{X} \times \mathcal{Y}$ such that $R_\kappa(x, y) = 1$, $\boldsymbol{E}$ is a reconstruction matrix such that $\boldsymbol{c}\boldsymbol{E}^\top \boldsymbol{k}^\top = \alpha s$ when $b_0 = 1$. Hence, we can compute followings:

$$A_1 = e(\boldsymbol{C}_1^{\boldsymbol{E}^\top}, \boldsymbol{D}_1) = e(g_1, g_2)^{\boldsymbol{c}\boldsymbol{E}^\top \boldsymbol{k}^\top} e(g_1, v_2)^{\boldsymbol{c}\boldsymbol{E}^\top \boldsymbol{z}^\top} = e(g_1, g_2)^{\alpha s} e(g_1, v_2)^{\boldsymbol{c}\boldsymbol{E}^\top \boldsymbol{z}^\top}$$

$$A_2 = e(\boldsymbol{C}_2^{\boldsymbol{E}^\top}, \boldsymbol{D}_2) = e(g_1, u_2)^{a \cdot \boldsymbol{c}\boldsymbol{E}^\top \boldsymbol{z}^\top}, \ A_3 = e(\boldsymbol{C}_3^{\boldsymbol{E}^\top}, \boldsymbol{D}_3) = e(g_1, f_2)^{-\tau \cdot \boldsymbol{c}\boldsymbol{E}^\top \boldsymbol{z}^\top}$$

It should be noted that $\tau = y_v + a y_u$ where y_v and y_u are discrete logarithms of v_2 and u_2 to the base f_2, respectively. Therefore, $A_1 \cdot A_2 \cdot A_3 = e(g_1, g_2)^{\alpha s}$.

Theorem 1. *Suppose the assumptions LW1, LW2 and DBDH hold in $\mathcal{G}$, for all encoding $E(R_\kappa, p)$ with a predicate family R_κ and a prime p, $PE(E(R_\kappa, p))$ is adaptively secure. Precisely, for any PPT adversary $\mathcal{A}$, there exist PPT algorithms $\mathcal{B}_1, \mathcal{B}_2, \mathcal{B}_3$ and $\mathcal{B}_4$, whose running times are the same as $\mathcal{A}$ such that, for any λ,*

$$Adv_{\mathcal{A}}^{FE(P)}(\lambda) \leq w_t \cdot Adv_{\mathcal{B}_1}^{LW1}(\lambda) + 2 \cdot m_t \cdot Adv_{\mathcal{B}_2}^{LW2}(\lambda) + Adv_{\mathcal{B}_3}^{DBDH}(\lambda) + q \cdot Adv_{\mathcal{B}_4}^{\alpha\text{-}hd}(\lambda)$$

where (1) q is the number of key queries in phases I/II, (2) m_t is the total number of random variables used to simulate all private keys, (3) w_t is the number of random variables used in the challenge ciphertext and (4) $Adv_{\mathcal{B}_4}^{\alpha\text{-}hd}(\lambda)$ is the advantage of $\mathcal{B}_4$ to breaking α hiding.

5   Security Analysis

We define the semi-functional (SF) algorithms for the security analysis. We let the simulator randomly select $\boldsymbol{h}' \in \mathbb{Z}_p^{\omega_2}$.

SFKeyGen$(x, MSK, \boldsymbol{h}', j, \alpha') \to SK$. The algorithm takes as inputs the master secret key MSK, $x \in \mathcal{X}$ and $j \in \{0, ..., m_2\}$. Then, the algorithm selects $\alpha' \xleftarrow{R}$

$\mathbb{Z}_p$ and $\tilde{r}_j \xleftarrow{R} \mathbb{Z}_p^{m_2}$ of which the first j elements are random variables and the others are 0. It also creates a normal key (D_1, D_2, D_3) using **KeyGen**. It outputs $SK := \langle D_1', D_2', D_3' \rangle$ where $D_1' = D_1 \cdot f_2^{-ak(\alpha', x, b(w,1,h'); \tilde{r}_j)}, D_2' = D_2 \cdot f_2^{-\tau k(\alpha', x, b(w,1,h'); \tilde{r}_j)}, D_3' = D_3$. We define the type of SK as follows:

$$\text{The type of SK}: \begin{cases} \text{Nominally semi-functional (NSF) if } \alpha' = 0 \\ \text{Temporary semi-functional (TSF) if } \alpha' \neq 0 \text{ and } j \neq 0 \\ \text{Semi-functional (SF)} \qquad\qquad \text{if } \alpha' \neq 0 \text{ and } j = 0 \end{cases}$$

In SF keys, $\tilde{r}_0$ equals to the zero vector $\mathbf{0}$ by the definition. Due to the parameter vanishing property, we can rewrite SF keys (SF-SK) as follows:

$$D_1' = D_1 \cdot f_2^{-ak(\alpha', x, b(w,0,0);0)}, D_2' = D_2 \cdot f_2^{-\tau k(\alpha', x, b(w,0,0);0)}.$$

SFEncrypt$(M, y, PK, h', j) \rightarrow CT$. The algorithm takes as inputs a message M, the public key PK and a description $y \in \mathcal{Y}$ and $j \in [\tilde{m}_2 + 1]$. It sets $f_1 = g_1^{y_f}$ and $u_1 = f_1^{y_u}$. It generates a normal ciphertext (C_0, C_1, C_2, C_3). If $j = 1$, it selects $\tilde{s} \xleftarrow{R} \mathbb{Z}_p$. The algorithm sets $C_0' = C_0$ and outputs CT following:

$$C_1' = C_1, \; C_2' = C_2 \cdot f_1^{c(y, b(w,1,h'); \tilde{s}, 0)}, \; C_3' = C_3 \cdot u_1^{c(y, b(w,1,h'); \tilde{s}, 0)}.$$

If $j > 1$, it selects a random value $\tilde{s} \xleftarrow{R} \mathbb{Z}_p$ and a random vector $\tilde{s}_{j-1} \xleftarrow{R} \mathbb{Z}_p^{\tilde{m}_2}$ where the first $j - 1$ elements are random variables and the others are 0. The algorithm then sets $C_0' = C_0$ and outputs $CT := \langle C_0', C_1', C_2', C_3' \rangle$ where

$$C_1' = C_1, \; C_2' = C_2 \cdot f_1^{c(y, b(w,1,h'); \tilde{s}, \tilde{s}_{j-1})}, \; C_3' = C_3 \cdot u_1^{c(y, b(w,1,h'); \tilde{s}, \tilde{s}_{j-1})}.$$

In particular, we call CT a semi-functional (SF) ciphertext if $j = \tilde{m}_2 + 1$.

We summarize the security games that we use for the security proof in Table 3. In the proof, we will show that all games in Table 3 are indistinguishable. The most critical proof among them is the invariance between games $\mathsf{G}_{k,j-1}^N$ and $\mathsf{G}_{k,j}^N$ where $j \in [m_2]$. This shows how we feature the jth random variable in the normal space to the semi-functional space. We provide this proof in Lemma 2. We will show the other proofs (of Lemmas 1, 3, 4 and 5) in the full version of this paper.

Lemma 1. Suppose there exists a PPT $\mathcal{A}$ who can distinguish $\mathsf{G}_{0,i}$ and $\mathsf{G}_{0,i+1}$ with non-negligible advantage ϵ. Then, we can build an algorithm $\mathcal{B}$ which breaks $LW1$ with the advantage ϵ using $\mathcal{A}$.

Lemma 2. Suppose there exists a PPT $\mathcal{A}$ who can distinguish $\mathsf{G}_{k,j-1}^N$ and $\mathsf{G}_{k,j}^N$ for $j \in [m_2]$ with non-negligible advantage ϵ where m_2 is the size of random variables that the kth key uses. Then, we can build an algorithm $\mathcal{B}$ which breaks $LW2$ with the advantage ϵ using $\mathcal{A}$.

Table 3. Games for security analysis

G_{Real}	: This is a real game that all keys and ciphertexts are normal. $(= G_{0,0})$
$G_{0,j}$	: $CT \leftarrow$ **SFEncrypt**(M, y, PK, h', j) for $j = 1, ..., \tilde{m}_2 + 1$
G_0	: $(= G_{0,\tilde{m}_2+1} = G_{1,0}^N$ by the definitions)

$G_{k,j}^N$: $(k \geq 1)$ $\alpha_i' \xleftarrow{R} \mathbb{Z}_p$, $h' \xleftarrow{R} \mathbb{Z}_p^{\omega_2}$

$$SK_i \leftarrow \begin{cases} \textbf{SFKeyGen}(x, MSK, \mathbf{0}, 0, \alpha_i') & \text{if } i < k \text{ (type = SF)} \\ \textbf{SFKeyGen}(x, MSK, h', j, \boxed{0}) & \text{if } i = k \text{ (type = NSF)} \\ \textbf{KeyGen}(x, MSK) & \text{if } i > k \text{ (type = Normal)} \end{cases}$$

G_{k,m_2-j}^T : $(k \geq 1)$ $\alpha_i' \xleftarrow{R} \mathbb{Z}_p$, $h' \xleftarrow{R} \mathbb{Z}_p^{\omega_2}$

$$SK_i \leftarrow \begin{cases} \textbf{SFKeyGen}(x, MSK, \mathbf{0}, 0, \alpha_i') & \text{if } i < k \text{ (type = SF)} \\ \textbf{SFKeyGen}(x, MSK, h', m_2 - j, \boxed{\alpha_i'}) & \text{if } i = k \text{ (type = TSF)} \\ \textbf{KeyGen}(x, MSK) & \text{if } i > k \text{ (type = Normal)} \end{cases}$$

G_k : $(k \geq 1)$ $(= G_{k,0}^T = G_{k+1,0}^N$ by the definitions)

$$\alpha_i' \xleftarrow{R} \mathbb{Z}_p, SK_i \leftarrow \begin{cases} \textbf{SFKeyGen}(x, MSK, h', 0, \alpha_i') & \text{if } i <= k \text{ (type = SF)} \\ \textbf{KeyGen}(x, MSK) & \text{if } i > k \text{ (type = Normal)} \end{cases}$$

G_{Final}	: $M' \xleftarrow{R} \mathcal{M}$, $CT \leftarrow$ **SFEncrypt**(M, y, PK, h', j)

Proof: Using the given instance $\{f_1, f_1^d, f_1^{d^2}, f_1^{tw}, f_1^{dtw}, f_1^{d^2t} \in G_1, f_2,$ $f_2^c, f_2^d, f_2^w, T \in G_2\}$, $\mathcal{B}$ will simulate either $\text{Game}_{k,j-1}^N$ or $\text{Game}_{k,j}^N$ using $\mathcal{A}$ to break $LW2$.

Setup: $\mathcal{B}$ randomly chooses $\alpha \in \mathbb{Z}_p, a, y_v' \in \mathbb{Z}_p, w \in \mathbb{Z}_p^{\omega_1}, h', h'' \in \mathbb{Z}_p^{\omega_2}$. It implicitly sets $y_v = d - aw + y_v'$, $y_u = w$, $b = 1/d$ and $\tau = d - aw + y_v' + aw = d + y_v'$. It sets a public key PK and MSK as follows:

$$PK =: \{e(g_1, g_2)^\alpha = e(f_1^d, f_2^d)^\alpha, g_1 = f_1^d,$$

$$g_1^{b(w,1,h)} = (f_1^d)^{b(w,1,h')} f_1^{b(w,0,h'')}, g_1^a, g_1^{a \cdot b(w,1,h)}, g_1^\tau = f_1^{d^2}(f_1^d)^{y_v'},$$

$$g_1^{\tau \cdot b(w,1,h)} = (f_1^{d^2})^{b(w,1,h')}(f_1^d)^{b(w,0,h'')}(f_1^d)^{y_v' b(w,1,h')}(f_1)^{y_v' b(w,0,h'')}\}.$$

$$MSK := \{g_2 = f_2^d, g_2^\alpha = (f_2^d)^\alpha, g_2^{b(w,1,h)} = (f_2^d)^{b(w,1,h')} f_2^{b(w,0,h'')},$$

$$v_2 = f_2^d(f_2^w)^{-a} f_2^{y_v'}, u_2 = f_2^w, f_2\}.$$

Phase I and II: The algorithm knows all MSK. Therefore, it can create the normal keys for $(> k)$. For the first $k-1$ key $(< k)$, $\mathcal{B}$ first generates a normal key. Then, it randomly selects α' from $\mathbb{Z}_p$ and creates an SF key. This is possible since $\mathcal{B}$ knows a, α', x and f_2.

For the kth key, it randomly selects z' from $\mathbb{Z}_p^{|k|}$ and sets $z = z' + c \cdot k(0, x, b(w, 1, h'); 1_j)$ where 1_j is a vector of which only the jth coordinate is 1 and all other coordinates are 0. Then, it randomly chooses r'' from $\mathcal{R}_r$ and sets $r = r'' - c \cdot 1_j$. z and r are randomly distributed because of z' and r''. It also generates $r_1', ..., r_{j-1}'$ from $\mathbb{Z}_p$ and sets $r_{j-1}' = (r_1', ..., r_{j-1}', 0, 0, 0) \in \mathcal{R}_r$.

$$K_0 = (f_2^d)^{k(\alpha,x,b(w,1,h');r'')} f_2^{k(0,x,b(w,0,h'');r'')} (f_2^c)^{-k(0,x,b(w,0,h''); 1_j)}$$
$$\cdot (f_2^d (f_2^w)^{-a} f_2^{y_v'})^{z'} T^{-ak(0,x,b(w,1,h');1_j)} (f_2^c)^{y_v' k(0,x,b(w,1,h');\cdot 1_j)}$$
$$\cdot f_2^{-ak(0,x,b(w,1,h');r_{j-1}')},$$
$$K_1 = (f_2^w)^{z'} T^{k(0,x,b(w,1,h');1_j)} f_2^{k(0,x,b(w,1,h');r_{j-1}')},$$
$$K_2 = f_2^{-z'} (f_2^c)^{-k(0,x,b(w,1,h'),1_j)}$$

If $T = f_2^{cw}$, then this key is a properly distributed nominally semi-function (NSF) key created using $\mathbf{SFKeyGen}(x, MSK, h', j - 1, 0)$ because

$$K_0 = f_2^{d \cdot k(\alpha',x,b(w,1,h');r'')} \boxed{f_2^{d \cdot k(0,x,b(w,1,h');-c \cdot 1_j)}} f_2^{k(0,x,b(w,0,h'');r'')}$$
$$\cdot f_2^{k(0,x,b(w,0,h'');-c \cdot 1_j)} f_2^{(d-wa+y_v')(z')} \boxed{f_2^{d \cdot k(0,x,b(w,1,h');c \cdot 1_j)}}$$
$$\cdot f_2^{-wa \cdot k(0,x,b(w,1,h');c \cdot 1_j)} f_2^{y_v' \cdot k(0,x,b(w,1,h');c \cdot 1_j)} f_2^{-a \cdot k(0,x,b(w,1,h');r_{j-1}')} \quad (1)$$

$$= f_2^{dk(\alpha',x,b(w,1,h');r)} f_2^{k(0,x,b(w,0,h'');r)} f_2^{(d-wa+y_v')(z'+k(0,x,b(w,1,h');c \cdot 1_j))}$$
$$\cdot f_2^{-ak(0,x,b(w,1,h');r_{j-1}')} \quad (2)$$
$$= f_2^{k(da',x,b(w,d,dh'+h'');r)} f_2^{(d-wa+y_v')(z'+k(0,x,b(w,1,h');c \cdot 1_j))}$$
$$\cdot f_2^{-ak(0,x,b(w,1,h');r_{j-1}')} \quad (3)$$
$$= g_2^{k(\alpha',x,b(w,1,h);r)} v_2^z f_2^{-ak(0,x,b(w,1,h');r_{j-1}')}$$

$$K_1 = (f_2^w)^{z'} (f_2^{cw})^{k(0,x,b(w,1,h');1_j)} f_2^{k(0,x,b(w,1,h');r_{j-1}')} = u_2^z f_2^{k(0,x,b(w,1,h');r_{j-1}')}$$

This implicitly sets $r = r'' - c \cdot 1_j$ and $z = z' + k(0, x, b(w, 1, h'); c \cdot 1_j)$. The equality (1) in above equation holds by the *linearity in random values*. The equality (2) holds because of the definition of r ($= r'' - c \cdot 1_j$) and linearity in random values. The equality (3) holds due to linearity in hidden common variables.

Otherwise, if T is a random and we let $f_2^{cw+\gamma}$ denote T, this is also a properly distributed (NSF) key but it was created using $\mathbf{SFKeyGen}(x, MSK, h', j, 0)$ since this implicitly sets $r_j' = r_{j-1}' + \gamma \cdot 1_j$. It is worth noting that r_j' is uniformly random because γ is randomly distributed.

Challenge: When the adversary requests the challenge ciphertext with two messages M_0 and M_1, $\mathcal{B}$ randomly selects β from $\{0, 1\}$. Then, it randomly selects $s'', \tilde{s} \in \mathbb{Z}_p$ and $s'', \tilde{s} \in \mathcal{R}_s$. Then, it implicitly sets $s = wt\tilde{s} + s''$, $s' = -d^2 t\tilde{s}$, $s' = wt\tilde{s} + s''$ and $s' = -d^2 t\tilde{s}$. Because of $s'', \tilde{s}, s''$ and $\tilde{s}$, they are randomly distributed. $\mathcal{B}$ sets $C = M_\beta \cdot e(f_1^{dwt}, f_2^d)^{\alpha \tilde{s}} e(f_1^d, f_2^d)^{\alpha s''}$ and the others as

$$C_0 = (f_1^{dwt})^{c(y,b(w,1,h');\tilde{s},\tilde{s})} (f_1^d)^{c(y,b(w,1,h');s'',s'')} (f_1^{wt})^{c(y,b(w,0,h'');\tilde{s},\tilde{s})}$$
$$\cdot f_1^{c(y,b(w,0,h'');s'',s'')}$$
$$= g_1^{c(y,b(w,1,h);s,s)}$$

$$C_1 = (C_0)^a (f_1^{d^2 t})^{-c(y,b(w,1,h');\tilde{s},\tilde{s})} = g_1^{ac(y,b(w,1,h);s,s)} f_1^{c(y,b(w,1,h');s',s')}$$

$$C_2 = (f_1^{d^2})^{c(y,b(w,1,h');s'',s'')} (f_1^{dwt})^{c(y,b(w,y_v',h''+y_v'h');\tilde{s},\tilde{s})}$$
$$\cdot (f_1^d)^{c(y,b(w,y_v',h''+y_v'h');s'',s'')} (f_1^{wt})^{c(y,b(w,0,y_v'h'');\tilde{s},\tilde{s})} f_1^{c(y,b(w,0,y_v'h'');s'',s'')}$$
$$= g_1^{\tau \cdot c(y,b(w,1,h);s,s)} u_1^{c(y,b(w,1,h');s',s')}.$$

Therefore, the challenge ciphertext is properly distributed. The equalities in the above equations hold by both *linearity in hidden common variables* and *linearity in random values*. In particular, the last equalities in C_0, C_1 and C_2 hold because of $s' = -d^2 t \tilde{s}$, $s' = -d^2 t \tilde{s}$ and the definitions of public parameters. $\tilde{s}$ and $\tilde{s}$ are randomly distributed to the adversary although they also appear in $s = wt\tilde{s} + s''$, $s = wt\tilde{s} + s''$ since their values are not revealed due to s'' and s'', which are uniquely allocated random values.   □

Lemma 3. *Suppose there exists an $\mathcal{A}$ who can distinguish G_{k,m_2}^N and G_{k,m_2}^T with non-negligible advantage ϵ for any $k < q$. Then, we can build an algorithm $\mathcal{B}$ who can break the α hiding property with ϵ using $\mathcal{A}$.*

Lemma 4. *Suppose there exists a PPT $\mathcal{A}$ who can distinguish $G_{k,j-1}^T$ and $G_{k,j}^T$ for $j \in [m_2]$ with non-negligible advantage ϵ where m_2 is the size of random variables that the kth key uses. Then, we can build an algorithm $\mathcal{B}$ which breaks $LW2$ with the advantage ϵ using $\mathcal{A}$.*

Lemma 5. *Suppose there exists a PPT $\mathcal{A}$ who can distinguish G_{q_t} and G_{Final} with non-negligible advantage ϵ. Then, we can build an algorithm $\mathcal{B}$ which breaks $DBDH$ with the advantage ϵ using $\mathcal{A}$.*

6   Adaptively Secure NM-CP-ABE with Short Keys

We introduce an NM-CP-ABE with short keys. The part of the security proof, co-selective security, is inspired by the selective NM-KP-ABE scheme of [6].

Assumptions for NM-CP-ABE with Short Keys. We define two computational assumptions in an asymmetric pairing. We take (n-A2) from [26] and use n-DBDHE. We modify them to prove α hiding using the technique that Lewko and Waters introduced in [19]. We provide the security of our assumptions in the generic group model in the full version of this paper.

Assumption 4 *(n-A2).* If a group generator $\mathcal{G}$ and a positive integer n are given, we define the following distribution

$$\mathbb{G} = (p, G_1, G_2, G_T, e) \overset{R}{\leftarrow} \mathcal{G}, \quad c, d, a, b_1, ..., b_n \overset{R}{\leftarrow} \mathbb{Z}_p,$$

$$g_1 \xleftarrow{R} G_1, \quad g_2 \xleftarrow{R} G_2, \quad D := \{g_1, g_2, g_1^c, g_2^c\} \cup \{g_1^{z_1}, g_2^{z_2} | z_1 \in Z_1, z_2 \in Z_2\}$$

$$Z_1 = \{ \qquad\qquad \forall (i,j) \in [n,n],\, dc, a, b_j, dcb_j, dcb_i b_j, a^i/b_j^2$$
$$\forall (i,j,j') \in [2n,n,n],\, j \neq j',\, a^i b_j / b_{j'}^2,$$
$$\forall (i,j,j') \in [n,n,n],\, j \neq j',\, dca^i b_j / b_{j'},\, dca^i b_j / b_{j'}^2,$$
$$\forall (i,j,j',j'') \in [n,n,n,n],\, j \neq j',\, j' \neq j''\},\, dca^i b_j b_{j'} / b_{j''}^2 \qquad \},$$
$$Z_2 = \{ \qquad\qquad \forall (i,j) \in [n,n],\, dc, a^i, a^i b_j, a^i/b_j^2$$
$$\forall (i,j) \in [2n,n],\, i \neq n+1,\, a^i/b_j$$
$$\forall (i,j,j') \in [2n,n,n],\, j \neq j',\, a^i b_j / b_{j'}^2 \qquad \}.$$

Given the instances, distinguishing between $T_0 = g_2^{da^{n+1}}$ and $T_1 \xleftarrow{R} G_2$ is hard.

Assumption 5 *(n−DBDHE)*. If a group generator $\mathcal{G}$ and a positive integer n are given, we define the following distribution

$$\mathbb{G} = (p, G_1, G_2, G_T, e) \xleftarrow{R} \mathcal{G}, \quad b, c, d, \xleftarrow{R} \mathbb{Z}_p,$$

$$g_1 \xleftarrow{R} G_1, g_2 \xleftarrow{R} G_2, \quad D := \{g_1, g_2, g_1^c, g_2^c\} \cup \{g_1^{z_1}, g_2^{z_2} | z_1 \in Z_1, z_2 \in Z_2\}$$

where $Z_1 = Z_2 := \{dc, b^i | \forall i \in [2n], i \neq n+1\}$.

Given D, it is hard to distinguish between $T_0 = g_2^{db^{n+1}}$ and $T_1 \xleftarrow{R} G_2$.

We define the advantage of an algorithm $\mathcal{A}$ to break *n-A2* or *n-DBDHE* as

$$Adv_{\mathcal{G},\mathcal{A},n}^{\{A2,\, DBDHE\}}(\lambda) = |Pr[\mathcal{A}(D, T_0) = 1] - Pr[\mathcal{A}(D, T_1) = 1]|$$

Encoding Scheme for NM-CP-ABE with Short Keys. Our encoding scheme for NM-CP-ABE with short keys consists of the following encoding algorithms:

- **Param**(κ): It sets $\omega_1 = 1, \omega_2 = 2N + 3$ and $\omega = 3N + 4$. It selects $\alpha \xleftarrow{R} \mathbb{Z}_p$, $\boldsymbol{w} = \eta \xleftarrow{R} \mathbb{Z}_p$, $\boldsymbol{h} = (\delta, \nu, \zeta, y_1, ..., y_N, y_1', ..., y_N') \xleftarrow{R} \mathbb{Z}_p^{2N+3}$. It sets $\boldsymbol{b}(\boldsymbol{w}, 1, \boldsymbol{h}) = (\delta, \nu, \zeta, \eta, y_1, ..., y_N, y_1', ..., y_N', \eta \cdot y_1', ..., \eta \cdot y_N')$.

- **Enc**$_1(S)$: The algorithm selects $r_0, r_1, r_2 \xleftarrow{R} \mathbb{Z}_p$ and sets $\boldsymbol{r} = (r_0, r_1, r_2)$. It sets $d_1 = \alpha + \delta r_2 + \nu r_0$, $d_2 = -r_0$, $d_3 = r_2$. For all $w_i \in S = \{w_1, ..., w_k\}$ such that S is not an empty set and $k \leq N$. It sets

$$d_4 = -\zeta r_2 + (y_1 a_1 + ... + y_N a_N) r_1, \quad d_5 = r_1,$$

$$d_6' = \eta(y_1' a_1 + ... + y_N' a_N) r_2, \quad d_7' = \eta r_2$$

where a_i is an coefficient of z^{i-1} in $P(z) = \prod_{w \in S}(z - w)$ for $i \in [k+1]$. It defines $\boldsymbol{k}(\alpha, S, \boldsymbol{b}(\boldsymbol{w}, 1, \boldsymbol{h}); \boldsymbol{r}) := (d_1, d_2, d_3, d_4, d_5, d_6', d_7')$.

- **Enc**$_2(\tilde{\mathbb{A}})$: For the non-monotone access structure $\tilde{\mathbb{A}}$, there exists a monotone access structure $\tilde{\mathbb{A}} = NM(\mathbb{A})$ where $\mathbb{A} = (A, \rho)$ and A is an $\ell \times m$ access matrix. The algorithm randomly selects $s, s_2, ..., s_m, t_1, ..., t_\ell \xleftarrow{R} \mathbb{Z}_p$ and sets $\boldsymbol{s} = (s_2, ..., s_m, t_1, ..., t_\ell)$ and $\lambda_i = A_i \cdot \phi$ where A_i is the ith row of A and $\phi = (s, s_2, ..., s_m)$. It sets $c_1 = s$, $c_2 = \nu s$. For all $i \in [\ell]$, it sets $c(\tilde{\mathbb{A}}, b(w, 1, h); s, s) := (c_1, c_2, c_{i,1}, c_{i,2}, ..., c_{i,N+2}; \forall i \in [\ell])$ as follows:

$$c_{i,1} = \delta\lambda_i + \zeta t_i, \quad c_{i,2} = t_i,$$

$$c_{i,3} = -(y_2 - y_1\rho(i))t_i, \quad ..., \quad c_{i,N+1} = -(y_N - y_1\rho(i)^{N-1})t_i \quad \text{if } \rho(i) = x_i;$$

$$c_{i,1} = \delta\lambda_i - \eta y_1' t_i, \quad c_{i,2} = t_i,$$

$$c_{i,3} = -(y_2' - y_1'\rho(i))t_i, \quad ..., \quad c_{i,N+1} = -(y_N' - y_1'\rho(i)^{N-1})t_i \quad \text{if } \rho(i) = x_i';$$

where the attribute corresponding to the ith row of A by the mapping ρ is denoted by x_i (or x_i', if it is a negated attribute).

- **Pair**$(S, \tilde{\mathbb{A}})$: If S satisfies $\tilde{\mathbb{A}}$, there exists $S' = N(S)$ which satisfies an access structure $\mathbb{A} = (A, \rho)$ such that $\tilde{\mathbb{A}} = NM(\mathbb{A})$. We define $I = \{i|\rho(i) \in S'\}$. It computes $\mu = (\mu_1, ..., \mu_{|I|})$ such that $\mu \cdot A_I = (1, 0, ..., 0)$. We set γ the index such that $w_\gamma = x_i$. To compute the share of $i \in I$, for $\Lambda_{i \in I} \forall i \in I$, it computes $a_0, ..., a_N$ which are the coefficient of z^i in $P(z)$. Then, it sets

$$\Lambda_i = c_{i,1} \cdot d_3 + c_{i,2} \cdot d_4 + \Sigma_{j \in [N] \setminus \{1\}} a_j \cdot c_{i,1+j} \cdot d_5 = \lambda_i \delta r_2 \quad \text{if } \rho(i) = x_i;$$

$$\Lambda_i = c_{i,1} \cdot d_3 + \frac{c_{i,2} \cdot d_6' + \Sigma_{j \in [N] \setminus \{1\}} a_j \cdot c_{i,1+j} \cdot d_7'}{\Sigma_{j \in [N]} a_j \cdot \rho(i)^j} = \lambda_i \delta r_2 \quad \text{if } \rho(i) = x_i'.$$

Finally, the algorithm computes $c_1 \cdot d_1 + c_2 \cdot d_2 - \prod_{i \in [I]} \mu_i \Lambda_i = \alpha s$.

We computationally prove the α hiding of our scheme by Lemma 6.

Lemma 6. *Suppose there exists a PPT adversary $\mathcal{A}$ who can break α hiding with non-negligible advantage ϵ. Then, we can build an algorithm $\mathcal{B}$ breaking $n_1 - DBDHE$ or $n_2 - A2$ with ϵ using $\mathcal{A}$ with an attributes set of size $k < n_1, n_2$.*

Proof: We provide this proof in the full version of this paper. $\square$

6.1 Duality

We introduce NM-KP-ABE with short ciphertexts as a dual scheme of our NM-CP-ABE with short keys using the conversion technique in [9]. The following encoding scheme constructs NM-KP-ABE with short ciphertexts:

- **Param**(κ): It runs Param of NM-CP-ABE to get $b(w, 1, h)$ and outputs $b'(w', 1, h') := (\pi, b'(w, 1, h))$ where $\pi \xleftarrow{R} \mathbb{Z}_p$. This sets $w' = w$ and $h' = (\pi, h)$.
- **Enc$_1$**$(\tilde{\mathbb{A}})$: It runs Enc$_2(\tilde{\mathbb{A}})$ of NM-CP-ABE to get $c(\tilde{\mathbb{A}}, b(w, 1, h); s, s)$ and sets $d_1' = \alpha + \pi s$ and $k'(\alpha, \tilde{\mathbb{A}}, b(w', 1, h'); r') := (d_1', c(\tilde{\mathbb{A}}, b(w, 1, h); s, s))$. It is worth noting that s can be parsed from c. It implicitly sets $r' = (s, s)$.
- **Enc$_2$**(S): It creates $s' \xleftarrow{R} \mathbb{Z}_p$ and runs Enc$_1(S)$ of NM-CP-ABE to get $k(\pi s', \tilde{\mathbb{A}}, b(w, 1, h); r)$. It sets $c_1' = s'$ and $c'(S, b(w', 1, h'); s', s') := (c_1', k(\pi s', \tilde{\mathbb{A}}, b(w, 1, h); r))$. It implicitly sets $s' = r$.
- **Pair**$(S, \tilde{\mathbb{A}})$: Pair$(S, \tilde{\mathbb{A}})$ of NM-CP-ABE outputs E such that $kEc^\top = \pi ss'$. The algorithm computes $d_1' \cdot c_1' = \alpha s' + \pi ss'$. Finally, the algorithm computes $\alpha s' = d_1' \cdot c_1' - kEc^\top$.

A Appendix

A.1 Syntax of Pair Encoding Framework

We briefly introduce Attrapadung's pair encoding framework [3]. In pair encoding, instances for a predicate $R_\kappa : \mathcal{X} \times \mathcal{Y} \to \{0,1\}$ consist of four deterministic algorithms which are Param, Enc1, Enc2 and Pair.

- Param$(\kappa) \to \omega$: It takes as input an index κ and outputs the number of common variables ω of $\boldsymbol{b} = (b_1, ..., b_\omega)$. The common variables are shared with Enc1 and Enc2.

- Enc1$(x) \to (\boldsymbol{k} := (k_1, ..., k_{m_1}); m_2)$: It takes as $x \in \mathcal{X}$ and outputs a sequence of polynomials of $\{k_i\}_{i \in [m_1]}$ with coefficient in $\mathbb{Z}_p$ and m_2 which is the number of variables. Every k_i is a linear combination of monomials α, r_k, $b_j r_k$ where $k \in [m_2]$ and $\alpha, r_1, ..., r_{m_2} \in \mathbb{Z}_p$ are variables.
  Enc2$(y) \to (\boldsymbol{c} := (c_1, ..., c_{w_1}); w_2)$ It takes as $y \in \mathcal{Y}$ and outputs a sequence of polynomials of $\{c_i\}_{i \in [1,w_1]}$ with coefficient in $\mathbb{Z}_p$ and w_2 which is the number of variables. Every c_i is a linear combination of monomials s, s_k, $b_j s$, $b_j s_k$ where $k \in [w_2]$ and $s, s_1, ..., s_{w_2} \in \mathbb{Z}_p$ are variables.

- Pair$(x, y) \to \boldsymbol{E}$ takes as inputs x and y and outputs a reconstruction matrix $\boldsymbol{E}$ such that $\boldsymbol{k}\boldsymbol{E}\boldsymbol{c}^\top = \alpha s$.

The instances of the pair encoding framework satisfy multiple properties, namely *linearity in random variables*, *parameter vanishing* and (*computational* or *perfect*) α *hiding* [3].

References

1. Agrawal, S., Chase, M.: A study of pair encodings: predicate encryption in prime order groups. In: Kushilevitz, E., Malkin, T. (eds.) TCC 2016. LNCS, vol. 9563, pp. 259–288. Springer, Heidelberg (2016). https://doi.org/10.1007/978-3-662-49099-0_10

2. Agrawal, S., Chase, M.: Simplifying design and analysis of complex predicate encryption schemes. In: Coron, J.-S., Nielsen, J.B. (eds.) EUROCRYPT 2017. LNCS, vol. 10210, pp. 627–656. Springer, Cham (2017). https://doi.org/10.1007/978-3-319-56620-7_22

3. Attrapadung, N.: Dual system encryption via doubly selective security: framework, fully secure functional encryption for regular languages, and more. In: Nguyen, P.Q., Oswald, E. (eds.) EUROCRYPT 2014. LNCS, vol. 8441, pp. 557–577. Springer, Heidelberg (2014). https://doi.org/10.1007/978-3-642-55220-5_31

4. Attrapadung, N.: Dual system encryption framework in prime-order groups. IACR Cryptology ePrint Archive 2015, 390 (2015)

5. Attrapadung, N.: Dual system encryption framework in prime-order groups via computational pair encodings. In: Cheon, J.H., Takagi, T. (eds.) ASIACRYPT 2016. LNCS, vol. 10032, pp. 591–623. Springer, Heidelberg (2016). https://doi.org/10.1007/978-3-662-53890-6_20

6. Attrapadung, N., Herranz, J., Laguillaumie, F., Libert, B., de Panafieu, E., Ràfols, C.: Attribute-based encryption schemes with constant-size ciphertexts. Theor. Comput. Sci. 422, 15–38 (2012)

7. Attrapadung, N., Imai, H.: Conjunctive broadcast and attribute-based encryption. In: Shacham, H., Waters, B. (eds.) Pairing 2009. LNCS, vol. 5671, pp. 248–265. Springer, Heidelberg (2009). https://doi.org/10.1007/978-3-642-03298-1_16

8. Attrapadung, N., Libert, B.: Functional encryption for inner product: achieving constant-size ciphertexts with adaptive security or support for negation. In: Nguyen, P.Q., Pointcheval, D. (eds.) PKC 2010. LNCS, vol. 6056, pp. 384–402. Springer, Heidelberg (2010). https://doi.org/10.1007/978-3-642-13013-7_23

9. Attrapadung, N., Yamada, S.: Duality in ABE: converting attribute based encryption for dual predicate and dual policy via computational encodings. In: Nyberg, K. (ed.) CT-RSA 2015. LNCS, vol. 9048, pp. 87–105. Springer, Cham (2015). https://doi.org/10.1007/978-3-319-16715-2_5

10. Beimel, A.: Secure schemes for secret sharing and key distribution. Ph.D., thesis, Israel Institute of Technology, Technion, Haifa, Israel (1996)

11. Chen, J., Gay, R., Wee, H.: Improved dual system ABE in prime-order groups via predicate encodings. In: Oswald, E., Fischlin, M. (eds.) EUROCRYPT 2015. LNCS, vol. 9057, pp. 595–624. Springer, Heidelberg (2015). https://doi.org/10.1007/978-3-662-46803-6_20

12. Chen, J., Wee, H.: Fully, (almost) tightly secure IBE and dual system groups. In: Canetti, R., Garay, J.A. (eds.) CRYPTO 2013. LNCS, vol. 8043, pp. 435–460. Springer, Heidelberg (2013). https://doi.org/10.1007/978-3-642-40084-1_25

13. Katz, J., Sahai, A., Waters, B.: Predicate encryption supporting disjunctions, polynomial equations, and inner products. In: Smart, N. (ed.) EUROCRYPT 2008. LNCS, vol. 4965, pp. 146–162. Springer, Heidelberg (2008). https://doi.org/10.1007/978-3-540-78967-3_9

14. Kim, J., Susilo, W., Guo, F., Au, M.H.: Functional encryption for computational hiding in prime order groups via pair encodings. Des. Codes Crypt. 86(1), 97–120 (2018)

15. Lewko, A.: Tools for simulating features of composite order bilinear groups in the prime order setting. In: Pointcheval, D., Johansson, T. (eds.) EUROCRYPT 2012. LNCS, vol. 7237, pp. 318–335. Springer, Heidelberg (2012). https://doi.org/10.1007/978-3-642-29011-4_20

16. Lewko, A., Sahai, A., Waters, B.: Revocation systems with very small private keys. In: IEEE Symposium on Security and Privacy, pp. 273–285. IEEE Computer Society (2010)

17. Lewko, A.B., Waters, B.: New techniques for dual system encryption and fully secure HIBE with short ciphertexts. IACR Cryptology ePrint Arch. 2009, 482 (2009)

18. Lewko, A., Waters, B.: New techniques for dual system encryption and fully secure HIBE with short ciphertexts. In: Micciancio, D. (ed.) TCC 2010. LNCS, vol. 5978, pp. 455–479. Springer, Heidelberg (2010). https://doi.org/10.1007/978-3-642-11799-2_27

19. Lewko, A., Waters, B.: New proof methods for attribute-based encryption: achieving full security through selective techniques. In: Safavi-Naini, R., Canetti, R. (eds.) CRYPTO 2012. LNCS, vol. 7417, pp. 180–198. Springer, Heidelberg (2012). https://doi.org/10.1007/978-3-642-32009-5_12

20. Liu, Z., Wong, D.S.: Practical ciphertext-policy attribute-based encryption: traitor tracing, revocation, and large universe. In: Malkin, T., Kolesnikov, V., Lewko, A.B., Polychronakis, M. (eds.) ACNS 2015. LNCS, vol. 9092, pp. 127–146. Springer, Cham (2015). https://doi.org/10.1007/978-3-319-28166-7_7

21. Okamoto, T., Takashima, K.: Hierarchical predicate encryption for inner-products. In: Matsui, M. (ed.) ASIACRYPT 2009. LNCS, vol. 5912, pp. 214–231. Springer, Heidelberg (2009). https://doi.org/10.1007/978-3-642-10366-7_13

22. Okamoto, T., Takashima, K.: Fully secure functional encryption with general relations from the decisional linear assumption. In: Rabin, T. (ed.) CRYPTO 2010. LNCS, vol. 6223, pp. 191–208. Springer, Heidelberg (2010). https://doi.org/10.1007/978-3-642-14623-7_11

23. Okamoto, T., Takashima, K.: Fully secure unbounded inner-product and attribute-based encryption. In: Wang, X., Sako, K. (eds.) ASIACRYPT 2012. LNCS, vol. 7658, pp. 349–366. Springer, Heidelberg (2012). https://doi.org/10.1007/978-3-642-34961-4_22

24. Ostrovsky, R., Sahai, A., Waters, B.: Attribute-based encryption with non-monotonic access structures. In: Ning, P., di Vimercati, S.D.C., Syverson, P.F. (eds.) ACM CCS, pp. 195–203. ACM (2007)

25. Waters, B.: Dual system encryption: realizing fully secure IBE and HIBE under simple assumptions. In: Halevi, S. (ed.) CRYPTO 2009. LNCS, vol. 5677, pp. 619–636. Springer, Heidelberg (2009). https://doi.org/10.1007/978-3-642-03356-8_36

26. Yamada, S., Attrapadung, N., Hanaoka, G., Kunihiro, N.: A framework and compact constructions for non-monotonic attribute-based encryption. In: Krawczyk, H. (ed.) PKC 2014. LNCS, vol. 8383, pp. 275–292. Springer, Heidelberg (2014). https://doi.org/10.1007/978-3-642-54631-0_16

Unbounded Inner-Product Functional Encryption with Succinct Keys

Edouard Dufour-Sans[1,2] and David Pointcheval[1,2(✉)]

[1] DIENS, École normale supérieure, CNRS,
PSL University, Paris, France
[2] Inria, Paris, France
{edufoursans,david.pointcheval}@ens.fr

Abstract. In 2015, Abdalla *et al.* introduced Inner-Product Functional Encryption, where both ciphertexts and decryption keys are vectors of fixed size n, and keys enable the computation of an inner product between the two. In practice, however, the size of the data parties are dealing with may vary over time. Having a public key of size n can also be inconvenient when dealing with very large vectors.

We define the Unbounded Inner-Product functionality in the context of Public-Key Functional Encryption, and introduce schemes that realize it under standard assumptions. In an Unbounded Inner-Product Functional Encryption scheme, a public key allows anyone to encrypt *unbounded vectors*, that are essentially mappings from $\mathbb{N}^*$ to $\mathbb{Z}_p$. The owner of the master secret key can generate functional decryption keys for other unbounded vectors. These keys enable one to evaluate the inner product between the unbounded vector underlying the ciphertext and the unbounded vector in the functional decryption key, provided certain conditions on the two vectors are met. We build Unbounded Inner-Product Functional Encryption by introducing pairings, using a technique similar to that of Boneh-Franklin Identity-Based Encryption. A byproduct of this is that our scheme can be made Identity-Based "for free". It is also the first Public-Key Inner-Product Functional Encryption Scheme with a constant-size public key (and master secret key), as well constant-size functional decryption keys: each consisting of just one group element.

Keywords: Unbounded vectors · Functional Encryption · Inner product

1 Introduction

Functional Encryption (FE) [8,10,13,17] is a new paradigm for encryption that does away with the "all-or-nothing" requirement of traditional Public-Key Encryption. FE allows users to learn specific functions of the encrypted data: for any function f from a class $\mathcal{F}$, a functional decryption key dk_f can be computed such that, given any ciphertext c with underlying plaintext x, using dk_f, a user can efficiently compute $f(x)$, but does not get any additional information

© Springer Nature Switzerland AG 2019
R. H. Deng et al. (Eds.): ACNS 2019, LNCS 11464, pp. 426–441, 2019.
https://doi.org/10.1007/978-3-030-21568-2_21

about x. This is the most general form of encryption as it encompasses identity-based encryption, attribute-based encryption, broadcast encryption.

FE schemes for general functionalities have been introduced [4,5,12–14,16,19] but have thus far always been based on non-standard assumptions such as indistinguishability obfuscation or multilinear maps.

Inner-Product Functional Encryption. In 2015, Abdalla, Bourse, De Caro, and Pointcheval [1] (ABDP) suggested it might be worthwhile to instead give FE schemes for more restricted functionalities, but with reasonable efficiency and security proofs relying on better understood assumptions. They built FE schemes for the Inner-Product functionality which they proved selectively secure under the Decisional Diffie-Hellman and Learning-with-Errors assumptions. There are now variants with adaptive security [3].

1.1 Motivation

Inner-Product Functional Encryption (IPFE) enables many interesting applications, such as the computation of aggregate statistics or the evaluation of regression models, but, unfortunately, it until now required that the data being processed have a fixed size. The public and secret keys also scale with this size, which can prove an inconvenience. We would like to construct schemes in which the public key is of constant, small size (ideally, a single group element), but where encrypting large vectors—in fact, arbitrarily large vectors—remains possible.

Let us go back to one of the motivating examples of IPFE: that of a school encrypting all the grades of each student, by discipline, as part of a single ciphertext every quarter. An authority can then distribute keys that enable one to compute a specific student's average grade (weighted by coefficients or by class hours), or the average over a class. It can also give keys that reveal the average grade in Mathematics or in Physics, always without jeopardizing the confidentiality of individual data, beyond what one can learn about the individuals from their aggregate. Now assume that a new student joins the school from one quarter to another. We would like to avoid the school having to query the authority for a new, readjusted public key (or for an extension of the current one). Whether the old keys should still work on the new, larger ciphertexts is to be decided on a case by case basis, and justifies our introducing multiple definitions: our *strict* and *permissive* notions.

One may wonder why the new keys could not be derived by a hash function (in the random oracle model, as we will use) in previous IPFE schemes. This would be for the public key, but with no way to derive the private keys required to generate the functional decryption keys.

1.2 Our Results

We introduce the first Unbounded Inner-Product Functional Encryption schemes (UIPFE). Both schemes share the following features:

1. **Unboundedness:** They enable the encryption of, and the generation of functional decryption keys for, unbounded vectors;
2. **Succinct keys:** In both cases the master secret key is a single secret scalar $s \in \mathbb{Z}_p$, and the public key is a corresponding group element $g_1^s \in \mathbb{G}_1$. Furthermore, the functional decryption keys simply consist of a group element $d \in \mathbb{G}_2$, in addition to the public vector describing the function evaluated by the functional decryption key;
3. **Identity-Based Access Control:** We consider both the computation on encrypted data aspect and the access control aspect of FE by letting users specify an identity in their ciphertext. The master authority gives functional decryption keys that limit evaluations of the unbounded inner product to ciphertexts of a given identity. This only expands the possible applications of our schemes, as the naive behavior can always be achieved by using the constant null identity.

Our main scheme is:

1. **Strict:** It only allows decryption when the domain of the ciphertext matches that of the key. In a sense, it may thus be thought of as operating infinitely many IPFE schemes in parallel.
2. **Selectively secure under a standard assumption:** We prove the security of our first scheme under the classical DBDH assumption, in the random oracle model.

We also introduce a scheme which is:

1. **Permissive:** It allows decryption when the support of the key (see Sect. 3.3) is included in the domain of the ciphertext.
2. **Selectively secure:** We prove the security of our second scheme in the random oracle model under ℓeDBDH, an interactive assumption we introduce. It resembles the DBDH assumption, except for the fact that the adversary can query linear combinations that depend on the CDH of the elements of one group, on condition that they never fully reveal it.

1.3   Concurrent Work

In concurrent and independent work, [18] also showed how to build Unbounded Inner-Product Functional Encryption from Bilinear Maps. Remarkably, their constructions do not require random oracles, and they prove full security under the SXDH assumption. Their constructions, however, are significantly less suited to practical use, since public keys require 28 group elements, ciphertexts 7 per coordinate and decryption keys 7 per coordinate (note that our decryption keys only require one group element regardless of the size of the function). Moreover, when decrypting, their schemes require a number of pairing evaluations that scales linearly with the sizes of the vectors, while ours compute a single pairing per decryption. Their constructions (*ct-dominant*) are what we call *permissive*, with the additional strong restriction that indices in the ciphertext must be contiguous (their E:con notion which requires the indices of the ciphertext to be *consecutive*). Moreover, they do not explicitly consider access control, while our schemes operate in the Identity-Based framework.

1.4 Related Work: Private-Key Multi-input Inner-Product Functional Encryption for Unboundedly Many Inputs

Goldwasser *et al.* [11] introduced the notion of Multi-Input Functional Encryption for cases where we want the functions being evaluated on encrypted data to take multiple inputs, with each input corresponding to a different ciphertext. Abdalla *et al.* gave the first construction of Multi Input Functional Encryption for Inner Products [2], and Datta, Okamato and Tomida [9] recently showed how to achieve what they call *Unbounded Private-Key Multi-Input Inner-Product Functional Encryption.* While this is an important result, we must stress that they tackle a problem which significantly differs from ours: they encrypt vectors of constant size, and the Unbounded adjective applies to the number of inputs: they can generate keys which enable the evaluation of an inner product on a number of ciphertexts (inputs) which is not *a priori* bounded, while in our work it is the individual ciphertext (input) which has unbounded length. A perhaps more striking difference is that their scheme is Private-Key, with the encryption procedure requiring the master secret key, while we tackle the Public-Key setting.

1.5 Paper Organization

In Sect. 2, we define unbounded vectors, inner products between them and a pseudo-norm on them. We also recall the setting of pairing groups and the DBDH assumption. Section 3 defines FE, its security, and the different functionalities we are interested in. We build the first Strict Identity-Based Unbounded IPFE from standard assumptions in Sect. 4, and prove it selectively secure in the random oracle model under the DBDH assumption. Finally, in Sect. 5, we give a construction for Permissive Identity-Based Unbounded IPFE which we prove selectively secure in the random oracle model under an interactive variant of DBDH.

2 Notations

2.1 Unbounded Vectors

Both the plaintexts we are encrypting and the functions for which we will be generating keys will be referred to as unbounded vectors or lists. We write them as $\boldsymbol{x} = (x_i)_{i \in \mathcal{D}}$ or $\boldsymbol{y} = (y_i)_{i \in \mathcal{D}'}$, respectively, where both $\mathcal{D}$ and $\mathcal{D}'$ are finite subsets of $\mathbb{N}^*$, and $x_i, y_j \in \mathbb{Z}_p$ for $i \in \mathcal{D}, j \in \mathcal{D}'$. The vectors $\boldsymbol{x}$ and $\boldsymbol{y}$ are thus mappings from $\mathbb{N}^*$ to $\mathbb{Z}_p$, and $\mathcal{D}$ (resp. $\mathcal{D}'$) is the explicit domain of $\boldsymbol{x}$ (resp. $\boldsymbol{y}$). When the context is clear, we will sometimes assimilate the vector space $\{(z_i)_{i \in \mathcal{D}} | z_i \in \mathbb{Z}_p\}$ and the isomorphic space $\mathbb{Z}_p^n$ where $n = |\mathcal{D}|$, the latter being more convenient for discussing changes of bases.

Inner Products. For $\boldsymbol{x} = (x_i)_{i \in \mathcal{D}}$ and $\boldsymbol{y} = (y_i)_{i \in \mathcal{D}'}$ we define the inner product as:

$$\langle \boldsymbol{x}, \boldsymbol{y} \rangle = \sum_{i \in \mathcal{D} \cap \mathcal{D}'} x_i y_i.$$

This comes from the fact that for indices $i \notin \mathcal{D}$, implicitly $x_i = 0$.

2.2   (Pseudo)Norm

Our proofs will require that given $\boldsymbol{x}^b \in \mathbb{Z}_p^n$ for $b \in \{0,1\}$ with $\boldsymbol{x}^0 \neq \boldsymbol{x}^1$ (with the same domain) and $\boldsymbol{y} \in \mathbb{Z}_p^n$, if we pick a basis $(\boldsymbol{z}_1, \ldots, \boldsymbol{z}_{n-1})$ of $(\boldsymbol{x}^0 - \boldsymbol{x}^1)^\perp$ and use ζ to denote the coefficient of $(\boldsymbol{x}^0 - \boldsymbol{x}^1)$ in the decomposition of $\boldsymbol{y}$ in basis $(\boldsymbol{x}^0 - \boldsymbol{x}^1, \boldsymbol{z}_1, \ldots, \boldsymbol{z}_{n-1})$,

$$\langle \boldsymbol{y}, \boldsymbol{x}^0 \rangle = \langle \boldsymbol{y}, \boldsymbol{x}^1 \rangle \implies \zeta = 0.$$

This is not true in general. From $\langle \boldsymbol{y}, \boldsymbol{x}^0 \rangle = \langle \boldsymbol{y}, \boldsymbol{x}^1 \rangle$ we can deduce that $\zeta \cdot \langle \boldsymbol{x}^0 - \boldsymbol{x}^1, \boldsymbol{x}^0 - \boldsymbol{x}^1 \rangle = 0$, but we can only conclude if $\langle \boldsymbol{x}^0 - \boldsymbol{x}^1, \boldsymbol{x}^0 - \boldsymbol{x}^1 \rangle \neq 0 \bmod p$. Previous works achieve this by bounding the individual components of $\boldsymbol{x}^0$ and $\boldsymbol{x}^1$, but this is not sufficient for unbounded vectors since we do not know n *a priori*. Instead, for any $\boldsymbol{x} = (x_i)_{i \in \mathcal{D}}$ we define

$$\|\boldsymbol{x}\| = \min_{\{(x_i')_{i \in \mathcal{D}} \in \mathbb{Z}^\mathcal{D} \mid x_i' \equiv x_i (mod\ p)\ \forall i \in \mathcal{D}\}} \sqrt{\sum_{i \in \mathcal{D}} x_i'^2}$$

where squaring and summation take place in $\mathbb{Z}$. It is easy to verify that for all vectors $\boldsymbol{a}$ and $\boldsymbol{b}$, $\|\boldsymbol{a} - \boldsymbol{b}\| \leq \|\boldsymbol{a}\| + \|\boldsymbol{b}\|$ and $\|\boldsymbol{a}\| = 0 \implies \boldsymbol{a} = \boldsymbol{0}$ in $\mathbb{Z}_p^n$. We will always require that plaintext vectors being encrypted verify $\|\boldsymbol{x}\| < \frac{\sqrt{p}}{2}$, so that

$$\|\boldsymbol{x}^0 - \boldsymbol{x}^1\|^2 \leq (\|\boldsymbol{x}^0\| + \|\boldsymbol{x}^1\|)^2 < (\frac{\sqrt{p}}{2} + \frac{\sqrt{p}}{2})^2 \leq p$$

and since $\langle \boldsymbol{x}^0 - \boldsymbol{x}^1, \boldsymbol{x}^0 - \boldsymbol{x}^1 \rangle = 0 \bmod p \iff \|\boldsymbol{x}^0 - \boldsymbol{x}^1\|^2 = 0 \bmod p$ that would imply $\|\boldsymbol{x}^0 - \boldsymbol{x}^1\|^2 = 0$ and thus $\boldsymbol{x}^0 = \boldsymbol{x}^1$ in $\mathbb{Z}_p^n$, which would contradict our assumption.

2.3   Pairing Group

We use a pairing group generator PGGen, a PPT algorithm that on input 1^λ returns a description $\mathcal{PG} = (\mathbb{G}_1, \mathbb{G}_2, p, P_1, P_2, e)$ of asymmetric pairing groups where $\mathbb{G}_1, \mathbb{G}_2, \mathbb{G}_T$ are additive cyclic groups of order p for a 2λ-bit prime p, P_1 and P_2 are generators of $\mathbb{G}_1$ and $\mathbb{G}_2$, respectively, and $e : \mathbb{G}_1 \times \mathbb{G}_2 \to \mathbb{G}_T$ is an efficiently computable (non-degenerate) bilinear map. Define $P_T := e(P_1, P_2)$, which is a generator of $\mathbb{G}_T$.

We always use implicit representation of group elements. For $s \in \{1, 2, T\}$ and $a \in \mathbb{Z}_p$, define $[a]_s = aP_s \in \mathbb{G}_s$ as the implicit representation of a in $\mathbb{G}_s$.

Note that from a random $[a]_s \in \mathbb{G}_s$ it is generally hard to compute the value a (discrete logarithm problem in $\mathbb{G}_s$). Obviously, given $[a]_s, [b]_s \in \mathbb{G}_s$ and a scalar $x \in \mathbb{Z}_p$, one can efficiently compute $[ax]_s \in \mathbb{G}_s$ and $[a+b]_s = [a]_s + [b]_s \in \mathbb{G}_s$.

More generally, for $s \in \{1, 2, T\}$ and a matrix $\mathbf{A} = (a_{ij}) \in \mathbb{Z}_p^{n \times m}$ we define $[\mathbf{A}]_s$ as the implicit representation of $\mathbf{A}$ in $\mathbb{G}_s$:

$$[\mathbf{A}]_s := \begin{pmatrix} a_{11}P_s & \cdots & a_{1m}P_s \\ & & \\ a_{n1}P_s & \cdots & a_{nm}P_s \end{pmatrix} \in \mathbb{G}_s^{n \times m}$$

Given $[a]_1, [a]_2$, one can efficiently compute $[ab]_T$ using the pairing e. For two matrices $\mathbf{A}, \mathbf{B}$ with matching dimensions define $e([\mathbf{A}]_1, [\mathbf{B}]_2) := [\mathbf{AB}]_T \in \mathbb{G}_T$.

Using these notations, we can recall the seminal Decisional Bilinear Diffie-Hellman Assumption [7], adapted to the asymmetric setting:

Definition 1 (Decisional Bilinear Diffie-Hellman Assumption). *The Decisional Bilinear Diffie-Hellman (DBDH) Assumption in the asymmetric setting states that, in a pairing group $\mathcal{G} \xleftarrow{\$} \mathsf{PGGen}(1^\lambda)$, no PPT adversary can distinguish between the two following distributions with non-negligible advantage, where $a, b, c, r \xleftarrow{\$} \mathbb{Z}_p$:*

$$\{([a]_1, [b]_1, [a]_2, [c]_2, [abc]_T)\} \text{ and } \{([a]_1, [b]_1, [a]_2, [c]_2, [r]_T)\}.$$

3 Definitions and Security Models

3.1 Functional Encryption

We give the definition of Functional Encryption as originally defined in [8,15].

Definition 2 (Functional Encryption). *A functional encryption scheme for a functionality $\mathcal{F} : \mathcal{K} \times \mathcal{X} \to \mathcal{Z}$ (where we require that the key space $\mathcal{K}$ contains the empty key ϵ) is a tuple of PPT algorithms* $\mathsf{SetUp}, \mathsf{KeyGen}, \mathsf{Enc}, \mathsf{Dec}$ *defined as follows.*

$\mathsf{SetUp}(\lambda)$: *takes as input a security parameter 1^λ and outputs a master secret key* msk *and a public key* pk.

$\mathsf{KeyGen}(\mathsf{msk}, k)$: *takes as input the master secret key and a key description $k \in \mathcal{K}$, and outputs a functional decryption key* dk_k.

$\mathsf{Encrypt}(\mathsf{pk}, x)$: *takes as input the public key* pk *and a message $x \in \mathcal{X}$, and outputs a ciphertext c.*

$\mathsf{Decrypt}(\mathsf{dk}_k, c)$: *takes as input a functional decryption key* dk_k *and a ciphertext c, and returns an output $y \in \mathcal{Z} \cup \{\bot\}$, where $\bot$ is a special rejection symbol.*

We implicitly assume that mpk is included in msk and in all the encryption keys ek_i as well as the functional decryption keys dk_k.

Correctness. The correctness property states that, given $(\mathsf{pk}, \mathsf{msk}) \leftarrow \mathsf{SetUp}(\lambda)$, for any key description $k \in \mathcal{K}$ and any message $x \in \mathcal{X}$, if $c \leftarrow \mathsf{Encrypt}(\mathsf{pk}, x)$ and $\mathsf{dk}_k \leftarrow \mathsf{DKeyGen}(\mathsf{msk}, k)$, then $\mathsf{Decrypt}(\mathsf{dk}_k, c) = F(k, x)$.

Security. For any stateful adversary $\mathcal{A}$, and any functional encryption scheme, we define the following advantage.

$$
\mathsf{Adv}_{\mathcal{A}}(\lambda) := \Pr \left[\beta' = \beta : \begin{array}{l} (\mathsf{pk}, \mathsf{msk}) \leftarrow \mathsf{SetUp}(1^\lambda) \\ (x_0, x_1) \leftarrow \mathcal{A}^{\mathsf{KeyGen}(\mathsf{msk}, \cdot)}(\mathsf{pk}) \\ \beta \xleftarrow{\$} \{0, 1\} \\ c \leftarrow \mathsf{Encrypt}(\mathsf{pk}, x_\beta) \\ \beta' \leftarrow \mathcal{A}^{\mathsf{KeyGen}(\mathsf{msk}, \cdot)}(c) \end{array} \right] - \frac{1}{2},
$$

with the restriction that $F(\epsilon, x_0) = F(\epsilon, x_1)$ and that for all key descriptions k queried to $\mathsf{KeyGen}(\mathsf{msk}, \cdot)$, the equation $F(k, x_0) = F(k, x_1)$ must hold. We say the scheme is IND-CPA secure if for all PPT adversaries $\mathcal{A}$, $\mathsf{Adv}_{\mathcal{A}}(\lambda) = \mathsf{negl}(\mathfrak{K})$.

A Weaker Notion. One may define a weaker variant of indistinguishability, called *Selective Security* or `sel-IND` security: the encryption queries are sent before the initialization.

3.2 The Unbounded Inner-Product Functionality

Inner-Product Functional Encryption as defined in [1], and later works, takes messages of fixed length and outputs ciphertexts of the same fixed length. Messages are vectors of n scalars, indexed from 1 to n. We will show how to build Inner-Product Functional Encryption schemes for arbitrary-size vectors.

While bounded message IPFE only considers vectors with contiguous indices we do not require this in our definitions to make them more general.

We give four definitions of Inner-Product Functional Encryption for Unbounded Vectors. The first two differ in their requirement on the domains of the ciphertexts and the keys for encryption to be successful. The last two are Identity-Based variants of the first two.

Definition 3 (Strict Unbounded IPFE).

- $\mathcal{K} = \{\epsilon\} \cup \{(y_i)_{i \in \mathcal{D}'} | \mathcal{D}' \subset \mathbb{N}^* \text{ finite}, y_i \in \mathbb{Z}_p \ \forall i \in \mathcal{D}'\}$;
- $\mathcal{X} = \{\boldsymbol{x} = (x_i)_{i \in \mathcal{D}} | \mathcal{D} \subset \mathbb{N}^* \text{ finite}, x_i \in \mathbb{Z}_p \ \forall i \in \mathcal{D} \text{ and } \|\boldsymbol{x}\| < \frac{\sqrt{p}}{2}\}$;
- $\mathcal{Z} = \mathbb{Z}_p$;
- $F(\epsilon, (x_i)_{i \in \mathcal{D}}) = \mathcal{D}$ and

$$
F((y_i)_{i \in \mathcal{D}'}, (x_i)_{i \in \mathcal{D}}) = \begin{cases} \langle \boldsymbol{y}, \boldsymbol{x} \rangle & \text{if } \mathcal{D}' = \mathcal{D}; \\ \bot & \text{otherwise.} \end{cases}
$$

Definition 4 (Permissive Unbounded IPFE).

- $\mathcal{K} = \{\epsilon\} \cup \{(y_i)_{i \in \mathcal{D}'} | \mathcal{D}' \subset \mathbb{N}^* \text{ finite}, y_i \in \mathbb{Z}_p \ \forall i \in \mathcal{D}'\}$;
- $\mathcal{X} = \{\boldsymbol{x} = (x_i)_{i \in \mathcal{D}} | \mathcal{D} \subset \mathbb{N}^* \text{ finite}, x_i \in \mathbb{Z}_p \ \forall i \in \mathcal{D}\}$;
- $\mathcal{Z} = \mathbb{Z}_p$;
- $F(\epsilon, (x_i)_{i \in \mathcal{D}}) = \mathcal{D}$ and

$$
F((y_i)_{i \in \mathcal{D}'}, (x_i)_{i \in \mathcal{D}}) = \begin{cases} \langle \boldsymbol{y}, \boldsymbol{x} \rangle & \text{if } \mathcal{D}' \subset \mathcal{D}; \\ \bot & \text{otherwise.} \end{cases}
$$

Definition 5 (Strict Identity-Based Unbounded IPFE).

- $\mathcal{K} = \{\epsilon\} \cup \{(id', (y_i)_{i \in \mathcal{D}'}) | id' \in \{0,1\}^*, \mathcal{D}' \subset \mathbb{N}^* \text{ finite}, y_i \in \mathbb{Z}_p \; \forall i \in \mathcal{D}'\};$
- $\mathcal{X} = \{(id, \boldsymbol{x} = (x_i)_{i \in \mathcal{D}}) | id \in \{0,1\}^*, \mathcal{D} \subset \mathbb{N}^* \text{ finite}, x_i \in \mathbb{Z}_p \; \forall i \in \mathcal{D}\};$
- $\mathcal{Z} = \mathbb{Z}_p;$
- $F(\epsilon, (id, (x_i)_{i \in \mathcal{D}})) = (id, \mathcal{D})$ and

$$F((id', (y_i)_{i \in \mathcal{D}'}), (id, (x_i)_{i \in \mathcal{D}})) = \begin{cases} \langle \boldsymbol{y}, \boldsymbol{x} \rangle & \text{if } \mathcal{D}' = \mathcal{D} \text{ and } id = id'; \\ \bot & \text{otherwise.} \end{cases}$$

Definition 6 (Permissive Identity-Based Unbounded IPFE).

- $\mathcal{K} = \{\epsilon\} \cup \{(id', (y_i)_{i \in \mathcal{D}'}) | id' \in \{0,1\}^*, \mathcal{D}' \subset \mathbb{N}^* \text{ finite}, y_i \in \mathbb{Z}_p \; \forall i \in \mathcal{D}'\};$
- $\mathcal{X} = \{(id, \boldsymbol{x} = (x_i)_{i \in \mathcal{D}}) | id \in \{0,1\}^*, \mathcal{D} \subset \mathbb{N}^* \text{ finite}, x_i \in \mathbb{Z}_p \; \forall i \in \mathcal{D}\};$
- $\mathcal{Z} = \mathbb{Z}_p;$
- $F(\epsilon, (id, (x_i)_{i \in \mathcal{D}})) = (id, \mathcal{D})$ and

$$F((id', (y_i)_{i \in \mathcal{D}'}), (id, (x_i)_{i \in \mathcal{D}})) = \begin{cases} \langle \boldsymbol{y}, \boldsymbol{x} \rangle & \text{if } \mathcal{D}' \subseteq \mathcal{D} \text{ and } id = id'; \\ \bot & \text{otherwise.} \end{cases}$$

3.3   An Alternative Security Definition

To prove our permissive scheme secure, we will require a slightly different definition of security than the standard one, so we introduce it here. Like ABDP and later works on practical IPFE, key generation in our scheme is homomorphic: $\mathsf{KeyGen}(msk, \boldsymbol{y}_1) + \mathsf{KeyGen}(msk, \boldsymbol{y}_2) = \mathsf{KeyGen}(msk, \boldsymbol{y}_1 + \boldsymbol{y}_2)$. Moreover, ciphertexts are not required for inactive slots in the key. For instance, from $\mathsf{KeyGen}(msk, \boldsymbol{y})$ where $\boldsymbol{y} = (y_j)_{j \in \mathcal{D}}$ and for some $i \in \mathcal{D}$, $y_i = 0$, one can evaluate $\sum_{j \in \mathcal{D}} x_j y_j$ from $(\mathsf{Encrypt}(pk, (x_j))_{j \in \mathcal{D}, j \neq i}$. The standard security game of Functional Encryption does not take this into account as it only considers the domain of the vector $\boldsymbol{y}$. Let us first define, for any unbounded vector $\boldsymbol{z} = (z_i)_{i \in \mathcal{D}}$, its domain as $\mathsf{Domain}(\boldsymbol{z}) = \mathcal{D}$ and its support as $\mathsf{Support}(\boldsymbol{z}) = \{i \in \mathcal{D} | z_i \neq 0\}$. The support is thus the set of the active slots.

Definition 7 (Homomorphic Key Security). *In Homomorphic Key IND (and* sel*-IND) security, we modify the conditions for ignoring the adversary's guess as follows:*

If for some $m \in \mathbb{N}^*$ and $\boldsymbol{y}^1, ..., \boldsymbol{y}^m$ queried to $\mathsf{KeyGen}(msk, \cdot)$,
there are $\omega_i \in \mathbb{Z}_p$, for all $i \in [m]$ such that, having defined $\boldsymbol{y} \leftarrow \sum_i \omega_i \boldsymbol{y}^i$,
$\mathsf{Support}(\boldsymbol{y}) \subseteq \mathsf{Domain}(\boldsymbol{x}^0) = \mathsf{Domain}(\boldsymbol{x}^1)$ and $\langle \boldsymbol{y}, \boldsymbol{x}^0 \rangle \neq \langle \boldsymbol{y}, \boldsymbol{x}^1 \rangle$,
then, ignore the adversary's guess.

Indeed, if the adversary can find a linear combination of the keys that make an inactive slot critical on the challenge ciphertext, then it can trivially win the game. This is very specific to the permissive constructions that allow any $\mathcal{D}' \subset \mathcal{D}$.

4   A Strict Identity-Based Unbounded IPFE

4.1   Description of the Scheme

We first present a selectively-secure **strict** identity-based UIPFE:

- SetUp(λ): Pick a pairing group $\mathcal{PG} = (\mathbb{G}_1, \mathbb{G}_2, \mathbb{G}_T, g_1, g_2, e)$ of prime order p. Pick a full-domain hash function $\mathcal{H}$ into $\mathbb{G}_2$. Pick $s \xleftarrow{\$} \mathbb{Z}_p$ and publish pk $= [s]_1$. Set msk $= (s, \text{pk})$.
- Encrypt(pk, id, $\boldsymbol{x}$): Take as input an unbounded vector $\boldsymbol{x} = (x_i)_{i \in \mathcal{D}}$ where $\mathcal{D} \subset \mathbb{N}^*$ is finite, an identity id and the public key pk. Pick $r \xleftarrow{\$} \mathbb{Z}_p$, and output $\boldsymbol{C} = ([r]_1, (c_i)_{i \in \mathcal{D}})$ where $c_i = [x_i]_T + e([s]_1, r[u_{\text{id}||\mathcal{D}||i}]_2)$ and $[u_{\text{id}||\mathcal{D}||i}]_2 := \mathcal{H}(\text{id}||\mathcal{D}||i)$ for all $i \in \mathcal{D}$.
- KeyGen(msk, id', $\boldsymbol{y}$): Take as input an unbounded vector $\boldsymbol{y} = (y_i)_{i \in \mathcal{D}'}$ (where $\mathcal{D}' \subset \mathbb{N}^*$ is finite) representing its associated inner-product function, an identity id' and the master secret key msk $= (s, \text{pk})$. Output

$$\text{dk}_{\boldsymbol{y}} = (\boldsymbol{y}, -s \sum_{i \in \mathcal{D}'} y_i [u_{\text{id}'||\mathcal{D}'||i}]_2)$$

  where $[u_{\text{id}'||\mathcal{D}'||i}]_2 := \mathcal{H}(\text{id}'||\mathcal{D}'||i)$ for all $i \in \mathcal{D}'$.
- Decrypt(dk$_{\boldsymbol{y}}$, $\boldsymbol{C}$): Take as input a ciphertext $\boldsymbol{C} = (c_0, (c_i)_{i \in \mathcal{D}})$ and a decryption key dk$_{\boldsymbol{y}} = ((y_i)_{i \in \mathcal{D}} = \boldsymbol{y}, d)$. Compute

$$[\alpha]_T = e(c_0, d) + \sum_{i \in \mathcal{D}} y_i c_i$$

  and recover the discrete logarithm to output α.

We clarify that $\cdot||\cdot$ denotes an efficient injective encoding into the set of binary strings.

Correctness. When id $=$ id' we have:

$$
\begin{aligned}
[\alpha]_T &= e(c_0, d) + \sum_{i \in \mathcal{D}} y_i c_i \\
&= e([r]_1, -s \sum_{i \in \mathcal{D}} y_i [u_{\text{id}||\mathcal{D}||i}]_2)) + \sum_{i \in \mathcal{D}} y_i ([x_i]_T + e([s]_1, r[u_{\text{id}||\mathcal{D}||i}]_2)) \\
&= [\sum_{i \in \mathcal{D}} -s r y_i u_{\text{id}||\mathcal{D}||i} + y_i x_i + s r y_i u_{\text{id}||\mathcal{D}||i}]_T = [\sum_{i \in \mathcal{D}} y_i x_i]_T = [\langle \boldsymbol{y}, \boldsymbol{x} \rangle]_T.
\end{aligned}
$$

4.2   Security Analysis

Theorem 8 (sel-IND Security). *The Strict Identity-Based UIPFE scheme described above is sel-IND-secure under the DBDH assumption, in the random oracle model for $\mathcal{H}$.*

Proof. Given an adversary $\mathcal{A}$ that breaks the sel-IND security of our scheme, we construct an adversary $\mathcal{B}$ that breaks the DBDH assumption.

$\mathcal{B}$ receives a DBDH tuple $([a]_1, [b]_1, [a]_2, [c]_2, [d]_T)$. $\mathcal{B}$'s goal is to guess whether $d = abc$ or d is uniformly random. $\mathcal{A}$ chooses a pair of challenge vectors $(\boldsymbol{x}^0 = (x_i^0)_{i \in \mathcal{D}^*}, \boldsymbol{x}^1 = (x_i^1)_{i \in \mathcal{D}^*})$ to be encrypted under identity id^* and sends them to $\mathcal{B}$.

From now on, we write $|\mathcal{D}^*| = n$ and assimilate $\{(w_i)_{i \in \mathcal{D}^*} | w_i \in \mathbb{Z}_p \; \forall i \in \mathcal{D}^*\}$ with the vector space $\mathbb{Z}_p^n$, where $m : \mathcal{D}^* \to [n]$ maps the original indices to those in $\mathbb{Z}_p^n$.

Then, we follow the proof technique from [1], with a basis $(\boldsymbol{z}_1, \ldots, \boldsymbol{z}_{n-1})$ of $(\boldsymbol{x}^0 - \boldsymbol{x}^1)^\perp$. $\mathcal{B}$ also picks $n - 1$ random scalars $(r_1, \ldots, r_{n-1}) \in \mathbb{Z}_p^{n-1}$. The family $(\boldsymbol{x}^0 - \boldsymbol{x}^1, \boldsymbol{z}_1, \ldots, \boldsymbol{z}_{n-1})$ is a basis of $\mathbb{Z}_p^n$ and we can write the canonical vectors e_i as

$$e_i = \alpha_i \cdot (\boldsymbol{x}^0 - \boldsymbol{x}^1) + \sum_{j \in [n-1]} \lambda_{i,j} \cdot \boldsymbol{z}_j$$

for some $\alpha_i \in \mathbb{Z}_p$, $\lambda_{i,j} \in \mathbb{Z}_p$, for all $i \in [n]$, $j \in [n-1]$. $\mathcal{B}$ can now simulate $\mathcal{A}$'s view:

- **Public Key.** $\mathcal{B}$ simply sets $\mathsf{pk} = [a]_1$ (implicitly setting the master secret key msk to be the unknown scalar a) and sends it to $\mathcal{A}$.
- **Random Oracle Calls.** On any fresh input $str = \mathsf{id}||\mathcal{D}||i$, if $\mathsf{id}||\mathcal{D} \neq \mathsf{id}^*||\mathcal{D}^*$ or $i \notin \mathcal{D}^*$, $\mathcal{B}$ returns a random group element in $\mathbb{G}_2$, *the discrete logarithm of which* it stores as h_{str} and reuses upon a later request for the same input. On input $\mathsf{id}^*||\mathcal{D}^*||i$ for some $i \in \mathcal{D}^*$, $\mathcal{B}$ returns

$$\alpha_{m(i)}[c]_2 + \sum_{j \in [n-1]} \lambda_{m(i),j}[r_j]_2$$

which it doesn't need to store because the above formula is deterministic.
- **Ciphertext.** $\mathcal{B}$ picks $\beta \in \{0, 1\}$ and generates a ciphertext for $\boldsymbol{x}^\beta$ from $[b]_1$, $[a]_2$ and $[d]_T$ as $c_0 = [b]_1$ and:

$$c_i = [x_i^\beta]_T + \alpha_{m(i)}[d]_T + \left(\sum_{j \in [n-1]} \lambda_{m(i),j} r_j \right) e([b]_1, [a]_2)$$

for all $i \in \mathcal{D}^*$.
- **Decryption Keys.** $\mathcal{A}$ will input $\mathsf{id}', \boldsymbol{y} = (y_i)_{i \in \mathcal{D}'}$. Make those calls to the random oracle that haven't been made for inputs $\mathsf{id}'||\mathcal{D}'||i$ for $i \in \mathcal{D}'$. If $\mathsf{id}' \neq \mathsf{id}^*$ or $\mathcal{D}' \neq \mathcal{D}^*$ simply return $(\boldsymbol{y}, -\sum_{i \in \mathcal{D}'} h_{\mathsf{id}'||\mathcal{D}'||i} y_i[a]_2)$. Otherwise write $(y_i)_{i \in \mathcal{D}^*} = \zeta \cdot (\boldsymbol{x}^0 - \boldsymbol{x}^1) + \sum_{i \in [n-1]} \nu_i \cdot \boldsymbol{z}_i$ for $\zeta \in \mathbb{Z}_p$, $\nu_i \in \mathbb{Z}_p$, for all $i \in [n-1]$. Then, return

$$\mathsf{dk}_y = \left(\boldsymbol{y}, - \left(\sum_{i \in [n-1]} \nu_i \left(\sum_{j \in [n-1]} \lambda_{i,j} r_j \right) \right) [a]_2 \right).$$

At the end of the simulation if $\mathcal{A}$ correctly guesses β, $\mathcal{B}$ guesses that $d = abc$ (the tuple is a proper BDH tuple), otherwise it guesses that d is uniformly random. It remains to be verified that $\mathcal{B}$ correctly simulates $\mathcal{A}$'s environment:

- The master public key and the random oracle responses are clearly uniformly random, thus properly distributed, despite the change of basis.
- From Sect. 2.2 we know that the coefficient ζ of $\boldsymbol{x}^0 - \boldsymbol{x}^1$ in the decomposition of a $\boldsymbol{y}$ for which a key has been queried is zero, otherwise the adversary $\mathcal{A}$ will not pass the final condition and its guess will be ignored. Hence, this contribution disappears from the functional key. The simulation of this key is perfect unless the attack is not legitimate;
- Now, notice that when $\mathcal{B}$ receives a true BDH tuple, it properly returns an encryption of $\boldsymbol{x}^\beta$, but when $[d]_T$ is uniformly random, the bit β is perfectly hidden.

Under the DBDH assumption, $\mathcal{A}$ cannot distinguish between these situations and thus, as in the latter, has no information on β. This concludes the proof. □

5   A Permissive Identity-Based Unbounded IPFE

5.1   Description of the Scheme

We now present a selectively-secure **permissive** identity-based UIPFE:

- SetUp(λ): Pick a pairing group $\mathcal{PG} = (\mathbb{G}_1, \mathbb{G}_2, \mathbb{G}_T, g_1, g_2, e)$ of prime order p. Pick a full-domain hash function $\mathcal{H}$ into $\mathbb{G}_2$. Pick $s \xleftarrow{\$} \mathbb{Z}_p$ and publish $\mathsf{pk} = [s]_1$. Set $\mathsf{msk} = (s, \mathsf{pk})$.
- Encrypt($\mathsf{pk}, \mathsf{id}, \boldsymbol{x}$): Take as input an unbounded vector $\boldsymbol{x} = (x_i)_{i \in \mathcal{D}}$ where $\mathcal{D} \subset \mathbb{N}^*$ is finite, an identity id and the public key pk. Pick $r \xleftarrow{\$} \mathbb{Z}_p$, and output $\boldsymbol{C} = ([r]_1, (c_i)_{i \in \mathcal{D}})$ where $c_i = [x_i]_T + e([s]_1, r[u_{\mathsf{id}||i}]_2)$ and $[u_{\mathsf{id}||i}]_2 := \mathcal{H}(\mathsf{id}||i)$ for all $i \in \mathcal{D}$.
- KeyGen($\mathsf{msk}, \mathsf{id'}, \boldsymbol{y}$): Take as input an unbounded vector $\boldsymbol{y} = (y_i)_{i \in \mathcal{D'}}$ (where $\mathcal{D'} \subset \mathbb{N}^*$ is finite) representing its associated inner-product function, an identity id' and the master secret key $\mathsf{msk} = (s, \mathsf{pk})$. Output

$$\mathsf{dk}_{\boldsymbol{y}} = (\boldsymbol{y}, -s \sum_{i \in \mathcal{D'}} y_i [u_{\mathsf{id'}||i}]_2)$$

  where $[u_{\mathsf{id'}||i}]_2 := \mathcal{H}(\mathsf{id'}||i)$ for all $i \in \mathcal{D'}$.
- Decrypt($\mathsf{dk}_{\boldsymbol{y}}, \boldsymbol{C}$): Take as input a ciphertext $\boldsymbol{C} = (c_0, (c_i)_{i \in \mathcal{D}})$ and a decryption key $\mathsf{dk}_{\boldsymbol{y}} = ((y_i)_{i \in \mathcal{D'}} = \boldsymbol{y}, d)$. Compute

$$[\alpha]_T = e(c_0, d) + \sum_{i \in \mathcal{D'}} y_i c_i$$

  and recover the discrete logarithm to output α.

Correctness. When $\mathsf{id} = \mathsf{id}'$ we have:

$$[\alpha]_T = e(c_0, d) + \sum_{i \in \mathcal{D}} y_i c_i$$

$$= e([r]_1, -s \sum_{i \in \mathcal{D}'} y_i[u_{\mathsf{id}||i}]_2)) + \sum_{i \in \mathcal{D}'} y_i([x_i]_T + e([s]_1, r[u_{\mathsf{id}||i}]_2))$$

$$= [\sum_{i \in \mathcal{D}'} -sry_i u_{\mathsf{id}||i} + y_i x_i + sry_i u_{\mathsf{id}||i}]_T = [\sum_{i \in \mathcal{D}'} y_i x_i]_T = [\langle \boldsymbol{y}, \boldsymbol{x} \rangle]_T.$$

5.2 New Assumption

Unfortunately, we will not be able to prove the security of this new scheme under a standard assumption. We thus define a new interactive one, that allows the adversary to see some linear combinations:

Definition 9 (Linearly Extended Decisional Bilinear Diffie-Hellman Assumption). *The Linearly Extended Decisional Bilinear Diffie-Hellman (ℓeDBDH) Assumption states that no PPT adversary $\mathcal{A}$ should be able to win the following game against a challenger $\mathcal{C}$ with non-negligible advantage:*

- *Initialize: $\mathcal{C}$ picks $a, b, c, r \xleftarrow{\$} \mathbb{Z}_p$ and $\delta \xleftarrow{\$} \{0, 1\}$. If $\delta = 0$, $\mathcal{C}$ sends*

$$([a]_1, [b]_1, [a]_2, [c]_2, [abc]_T)$$

to $\mathcal{A}$, otherwise it sends

$$([a]_1, [b]_1, [a]_2, [c]_2, [r]_T).$$

- *Extension Queries: $\mathcal{A}$ has unlimited access to an oracle that, on input $i \in \mathbb{N}^*$:*
  - *if it stored a value h_i for i, reuses it;*
  - *otherwise, picks $h_i \xleftarrow{\$} \mathbb{Z}_p$, sends it to $\mathcal{A}$ and stores it;*
- *Linear Extension Queries: $\mathcal{A}$ has unlimited access to an oracle that, on input $(y_i)_{i \in \mathcal{D}}$ for some finite $S \subset \mathbb{N}$:*
  1. *For each $i \in \mathcal{D} \setminus \{0\}$:*
     - *if it stored a value h_i for i, reuses it;*
     - *otherwise, picks $h_i \xleftarrow{\$} \mathbb{Z}_p$ and stores it;*
  2. *stores $(y_i)_i$ and sends $[y_0 ac + \sum_{i \in \mathcal{D}, i \neq 0} y_i h_i a]_2$ to $\mathcal{A}$.*
- *Finalize: $\mathcal{A}$ provides its guess δ' on $\mathcal{C}$'s bit δ. $\mathcal{C}$ uses the stored $((y_i^{(k)})_i)_k$ to check that $e_0 \notin \boldsymbol{Span}((\boldsymbol{y}^{(k)})_k)$, and if so it outputs $\beta := \delta'$, otherwise it outputs $\beta \xleftarrow{\$} \{0, 1\}$.*

5.3 Security Analysis

Theorem 10 (Homomorphic Key sel-IND Security). *The Permissive Identity-Based UIPFE scheme described above is Homomorphic Key sel-IND-secure under the ℓeDBDH assumption, in the random oracle model for $\mathcal{H}$.*

Proof. Given an adversary $\mathcal{A}$ that breaks the sel-IND security of our scheme, we construct an adversary $\mathcal{B}$ that breaks the ℓeDBDH assumption.

$\mathcal{B}$ receives a DBDH tuple $([a]_1, [b]_1, [a]_2, [c]_2, [d]_T)$ from a ℓeDBDH oracle. $\mathcal{B}$'s goal is to guess whether $d = abc$ or d is uniformly random. $\mathcal{A}$ chooses a pair of challenge vectors $(\boldsymbol{x}^0 = (x_i^0)_{i \in \mathcal{D}^*}, \boldsymbol{x}^1 = (x_i^1)_{i \in \mathcal{D}^*})$ to be encrypted under identity id* and sends them to $\mathcal{B}$.

From now on we write $|\mathcal{D}^*| = n$ and assimilate $\{(w_i)_{i \in \mathcal{D}^*} | w_i \in \mathbb{Z}_p \ \forall i \in \mathcal{D}^*\}$ with the vector space $\mathbb{Z}_p^n$, and define $m : \mathcal{D}^* \to [n]$ which maps the original indices to those in $\mathbb{Z}_p^n$ and $m^\perp : \mathbb{N} \setminus \mathcal{D}^* \to \mathbb{N}^*$ which maps the other indices into $\mathbb{N}^*$.

$\mathcal{B}$ picks a basis $(\boldsymbol{z}_1, \ldots, \boldsymbol{z}_{n-1})$ of $(\boldsymbol{x}^0 - \boldsymbol{x}^1)^\perp$ as well as $n-1$ random scalars $(r_1, \ldots, r_{n-1}) \in \mathbb{Z}_p^{n-1}$. $(\boldsymbol{x}^0 - \boldsymbol{x}^1, \boldsymbol{z}_1, \ldots, \boldsymbol{z}_{n-1})$ is a basis of $\mathbb{Z}_p^n$ and we can write the canonical vectors e_i as

$$e_i = \alpha_i \cdot (\boldsymbol{x}^0 - \boldsymbol{x}^1) + \sum_{j \in [n-1]} \lambda_{i,j} \cdot \boldsymbol{z}_j$$

for some $\alpha_i \in \mathbb{Z}_p$, $\lambda_{i,j} \in \mathbb{Z}_p$, for all $i \in [n]$, $j \in [n-1]$. $\mathcal{B}$ can now simulate $\mathcal{A}$'s view:

- **Public Key.** $\mathcal{B}$ simply sets $\mathsf{pk} = [a]_1$ (implicitly setting the master secret key msk to be the unknown scalar a) and sends it to $\mathcal{A}$.
- **Random Oracle Calls.** On any fresh input $str = \mathsf{id}||i$, if $\mathsf{id} \neq \mathsf{id}^*$, $\mathcal{B}$ returns a random group element in $\mathbb{G}_2$, *the discrete logarithm of which* it stores as h_{str} and reuses upon a later request for the same input. On input $\mathsf{id}^*||i$ for some $i \notin \mathcal{D}^*$, $\mathcal{B}$ makes an Extension Query to the ℓeDBDH oracle with input $m^\perp(i)$ and forwards its output to $\mathcal{A}$. On input $\mathsf{id}^*||i$ for some $i \in \mathcal{D}^*$, $\mathcal{B}$ returns

$$\alpha_{m(i)}[c]_2 + \sum_{j \in [n-1]} \lambda_{m(i),j}[r_j]_2$$

which it doesn't need to store because the above formula is deterministic.
- **Ciphertext.** $\mathcal{B}$ picks $\beta \in \{0, 1\}$ and generates a ciphertext for $\boldsymbol{x}^\beta$ from $[b]_1$, $[a]_2$ and $[d]_T$ as $c_0 = [b]_1$ and:

$$c_i = [x_i^\beta]_T + \alpha_{m(i)}[d]_T + \left(\sum_{j \in [n-1]} \lambda_{m(i),j} r_j \right) e([b]_1, [a]_2)$$

for all $i \in \mathcal{D}^*$.
- **Decryption Keys.** $\mathcal{A}$ will input $\mathsf{id}', \boldsymbol{y} = (y_i)_{i \in \mathcal{D}'}$. Make those calls to the random oracle that haven't been made for inputs $\mathsf{id}'||i$ for $i \in \mathcal{D}'$. If $\mathsf{id}' \neq \mathsf{id}^*$ or $\mathcal{D}' \neq \mathcal{D}^*$ simply return $(\boldsymbol{y}, -\sum_{i \in \mathcal{D}'} h_{\mathsf{id}'||i} y_i [a]_2)$. Otherwise write $\mathcal{D}_1 = \mathcal{D}^* \setminus \{0\} \cap \mathcal{D}'$ and $\mathcal{D}_2 = \mathcal{D}' \setminus \mathcal{D}_1$. Decompose $\boldsymbol{y}$ as $(y_i)_{i \in \mathcal{D}^*} = \zeta(\boldsymbol{x}^0 - \boldsymbol{x}^1) + \sum_{i \in [n-1]} \nu_i \boldsymbol{z}_i$ for $\zeta \in \mathbb{Z}_p$, $\nu_i \in \mathbb{Z}_p$, for all $i \in [n-1]$. Make a Linear Extension Query to the ℓeDBDH oracle for input $(y_i')_{i \in \{0\} \cup m^\perp(\mathcal{D}_2)}$ such that $y_{m^\perp(i)}' = y_i$

for all $i \in \mathcal{D}_2$ and $y'_0 = \zeta$, which returns $D \in \mathbb{G}_2$. Then, return

$$\mathsf{dk}_{\boldsymbol{y}} = \left(\boldsymbol{y}, -D - \left(\sum_{i \in [n-1]} \nu_i \left(\sum_{j \in [n-1]} \lambda_{i,j} r_j \right) \right) [a]_2 \right).$$

At the end of the simulation if $\mathcal{A}$ correctly guesses β, $\mathcal{B}$ guesses that $d = abc$ (the tuple is a proper BDH tuple), otherwise it guesses that d is uniformly random. It remains to be verified that $\mathcal{B}$ correctly simulates $\mathcal{A}$'s environment:

- The master public key, functional decryption key and the random oracle responses are clearly uniformly random, thus properly distributed, despite the change of basis;
- From Sect. 3.3, we know that the span of all queried keys will not contain a key with domain included in $\mathcal{D}^*$ with a non zero component on $\boldsymbol{x}^0 - \boldsymbol{x}^1$, which guarantees that $\mathcal{B}$ does not break the condition that bars trivial victories in the ℓeDBDH game;
- Now, notice that when $\mathcal{B}$ receives a true BDH tuple, it properly returns an encryption of $\boldsymbol{x}^\beta$, but when $[d]_T$ is uniformly random, the bit β is perfectly hidden.

Under the ℓeDBDH assumption $\mathcal{A}$ cannot distinguish between these situations and thus, as in the latter, has no information on β. This concludes the proof. $\square$

6   Open Problems

We have introduced constructions that are quite efficient in terms of size, since every key involved consists of a single group element, and thus the computational load is also much lower than in [18]. In addition, the vector ciphertexts do not need their domain to be a unique interval as in [18]. Still, several interesting problems remain open, and we now list promising directions for future research:

- Building Unbounded IPFE for any behavior without pairings, either groups without multilinearity or from other assumptions.
- Building Unbounded Functional Encryption schemes for different functionalities, such as Quadratic Polynomials (which already require pairings in the bounded setting [6]).
- Achieving adaptive security or removing random oracles with minimal overhead.

Acknowledgments. We would like to thank the anonymous reviewers for detailed comments. This work was supported in part by the European Community's Seventh Framework Programme (FP7/2007-2013 Grant Agreement no. 339563 – CryptoCloud) and the European Community's Horizon 2020 Project FENTEC (Grant Agreement no. 780108).

References

1. Abdalla, M., Bourse, F., De Caro, A., Pointcheval, D.: Simple functional encryption schemes for inner products. In: Katz, J. (ed.) PKC 2015. LNCS, vol. 9020, pp. 733–751. Springer, Heidelberg (2015). https://doi.org/10.1007/978-3-662-46447-2_33
2. Abdalla, M., Gay, R., Raykova, M., Wee, H.: Multi-input inner-product functional encryption from pairings. In: Coron, J.-S., Nielsen, J.B. (eds.) EUROCRYPT 2017. LNCS, vol. 10210, pp. 601–626. Springer, Cham (2017). https://doi.org/10.1007/978-3-319-56620-7_21
3. Agrawal, S., Libert, B., Stehlé, D.: Fully secure functional encryption for inner products, from standard assumptions. In: Robshaw, M., Katz, J. (eds.) CRYPTO 2016. LNCS, vol. 9816, pp. 333–362. Springer, Heidelberg (2016). https://doi.org/10.1007/978-3-662-53015-3_12
4. Ananth, P., Brakerski, Z., Segev, G., Vaikuntanathan, V.: From selective to adaptive security in functional encryption. In: Gennaro, R., Robshaw, M. (eds.) CRYPTO 2015. LNCS, vol. 9216, pp. 657–677. Springer, Heidelberg (2015). https://doi.org/10.1007/978-3-662-48000-7_32
5. Badrinarayanan, S., Goyal, V., Jain, A., Sahai, A.: Verifiable functional encryption. In: Cheon, J.H., Takagi, T. (eds.) ASIACRYPT 2016. LNCS, vol. 10032, pp. 557–587. Springer, Heidelberg (2016). https://doi.org/10.1007/978-3-662-53890-6_19
6. Baltico, C.E.Z., Catalano, D., Fiore, D., Gay, R.: Practical functional encryption for quadratic functions with applications to predicate encryption. In: Katz, J., Shacham, H. (eds.) CRYPTO 2017. LNCS, vol. 10401, pp. 67–98. Springer, Cham (2017). https://doi.org/10.1007/978-3-319-63688-7_3
7. Boneh, D., Franklin, M.K.: Identity based encryption from the Weil pairing. SIAM J. Comput. 32(3), 586–615 (2003)
8. Boneh, D., Sahai, A., Waters, B.: Functional encryption: definitions and challenges. In: Ishai, Y. (ed.) TCC 2011. LNCS, vol. 6597, pp. 253–273. Springer, Heidelberg (2011). https://doi.org/10.1007/978-3-642-19571-6_16
9. Datta, P., Okamoto, T., Tomida, J.: Full-hiding (unbounded) multi-input inner product functional encryption from the k-linear assumption. In: Abdalla, M., Dahab, R. (eds.) PKC 2018. LNCS, vol. 10770, pp. 245–277. Springer, Cham (2018). https://doi.org/10.1007/978-3-319-76581-5_9
10. Garg, S., Gentry, C., Halevi, S., Raykova, M., Sahai, A., Waters, B.: Candidate indistinguishability obfuscation and functional encryption for all circuits. In: 54th FOCS, pp. 40–49. IEEE Computer Society Press, October 2013
11. Goldwasser, S., et al.: Multi-input functional encryption. In: Nguyen, P.Q., Oswald, E. (eds.) EUROCRYPT 2014. LNCS, vol. 8441, pp. 578–602. Springer, Heidelberg (2014). https://doi.org/10.1007/978-3-642-55220-5_32
12. Goldwasser, S., Kalai, Y.T., Popa, R.A., Vaikuntanathan, V., Zeldovich, N.: How to run turing machines on encrypted data. In: Canetti, R., Garay, J.A. (eds.) CRYPTO 2013. LNCS, vol. 8043, pp. 536–553. Springer, Heidelberg (2013). https://doi.org/10.1007/978-3-642-40084-1_30
13. Goldwasser, S., Kalai, Y.T., Popa, R.A., Vaikuntanathan, V., Zeldovich, N.: Reusable garbled circuits and succinct functional encryption. In: Boneh, D., Roughgarden, T., Feigenbaum, J. (eds.) 45th ACM STOC, pp. 555–564. ACM Press, June 2013
14. Gorbunov, S., Vaikuntanathan, V., Wee, H.: Functional encryption with bounded collusions via multi-party computation. In: Safavi-Naini, R., Canetti, R. (eds.) CRYPTO 2012. LNCS, vol. 7417, pp. 162–179. Springer, Heidelberg (2012). https://doi.org/10.1007/978-3-642-32009-5_11

15. O'Neill, A.: Definitional issues in functional encryption. Cryptology ePrint Archive, Report 2010/556 (2010). http://eprint.iacr.org/2010/556
16. Sahai, A., Seyalioglu, H.: Worry-free encryption: functional encryption with public keys. In: Al-Shaer, E., Keromytis, A.D., Shmatikov, V. (eds.) ACM CCS, vol. 10, pp. 463–472. ACM Press, October 2010
17. Sahai, A., Waters, B.: Fuzzy identity-based encryption. In: Cramer, R. (ed.) EUROCRYPT 2005. LNCS, vol. 3494, pp. 457–473. Springer, Heidelberg (2005). https://doi.org/10.1007/11426639_27
18. Tomida, J., Takashima, K.: Unbounded inner product functional encryption from bilinear maps. In: Peyrin, T., Galbraith, S. (eds.) ASIACRYPT 2018. LNCS, vol. 11273, pp. 609–639. Springer, Cham (2018). https://doi.org/10.1007/978-3-030-03329-3_21
19. Waters, B.: A punctured programming approach to adaptively secure functional encryption. In: Gennaro, R., Robshaw, M. (eds.) CRYPTO 2015. LNCS, vol. 9216, pp. 678–697. Springer, Heidelberg (2015). https://doi.org/10.1007/978-3-662-48000-7_33

Password-Authenticated Public-Key Encryption

Tatiana Bradley[1], Jan Camenisch[2], Stanislaw Jarecki[1(✉)], Anja Lehmann[3], Gregory Neven[2], and Jiayu Xu[1]

[1] University of California, Irvine, USA
{tebradle,sjarecki,jiayux}@uci.edu
[2] Dfinity, Palo Alto, Germany
{gregory,jan}@dfinity.org
[3] IBM Research - Zurich, Rüschlikon, Switzerland
anj@zurich.ibm.com

Abstract. We introduce password-authenticated public-key encryption (PAPKE), a new cryptographic primitive. PAPKE enables secure end-to-end encryption between two entities without relying on a trusted third party or other out-of-band mechanisms for authentication. Instead, resistance to man-in-the-middle attacks is ensured in a human-friendly way by authenticating the public key with a shared password, while preventing offline dictionary attacks given the authenticated public key and/or the ciphertexts produced using this key.

Our contributions are three-fold. First, we provide property-based and universally composable (UC) definitions for PAPKE, with the resulting primitive combining CCA security of public-key encryption (PKE) with password authentication. Second, we show that PAPKE implies Password-Authenticated Key Exchange (PAKE), but the reverse implication does not hold, indicating that PAPKE is a strictly stronger primitive than PAKE. Indeed, PAPKE implies a two-flow PAKE which remains secure if either party re-uses its state in multiple sessions, e.g. due to communication errors, thus strengthening existing notions of PAKE security. Third, we show two highly practical UC PAPKE schemes: a generic construction built from CCA-secure and anonymous PKE and an ideal cipher, and a direct construction based on the Decisional Diffie-Hellman assumption in the random oracle model.

Finally, applying our PAPKE-to-PAKE compiler to the above PAPKE schemes we exhibit the first 2-round UC PAKE's with efficiency comparable to (unauthenticated) Diffie-Hellman Key Exchange.

1 Introduction

A well-known Achilles' heel of end-to-end encryption is the distribution and trustworthiness of long-term cryptographic keys [27]. In particular, it is extremely hard for end users to judge the authenticity of public keys. They

---

Full version of this paper appears in [12].

© Springer Nature Switzerland AG 2019
R. H. Deng et al. (Eds.): ACNS 2019, LNCS 11464, pp. 442–462, 2019.
https://doi.org/10.1007/978-3-030-21568-2_22

can therefore easily be tricked into encrypting the data under a wrong key and thereby lose all security. If the exchange of keys is facilitated by a third party such as a certificate authority or a service provider, as is the case for most public-key infrastructures (PKIs) as well as for end-to-end encrypted messengers such as Signal, WhatsApp, or iMessage, users need to trust that third party to provide the correct keys. Indeed, if a service provider is able to substitute its own keys for those of the intended recipients, it can mount a man-in-the-middle (MITM) attack and decrypt all subsequent communication.

An article in The Guardian [18] describes this trust required in the service provider and its capability of striking MITM attacks as a "backdoor" and a "security loophole" in the encryption scheme used by WhatsApp. This characterization was repudiated in an open letter signed by over seventy cryptographers and security experts [26], stating that this is not a "backdoor", but simply how cryptography works. While technically correct, this explanation is not very satisfactory from an end-user's perspective and prompts the question: *should cryptography work like that?* Is there really no way to protect encrypted communication between end users from such MITM and key substitution attacks?

Ad-Hoc Solutions Against MITM Attacks. Many approaches to preventing man-in-the-middle attacks in the context of secure end-to-end communication exist, but they either rely on trusted third parties, or on mostly ad-hoc solutions built on top of conventional encryption schemes, aiming to allow end-users to verify the correctness of public keys. None of these approaches provides the degree of usability and security that one can hope for, and which our solution provides.

Trust-on-first-use, as commonly used by Secure Shell (SSH), reduces the likelihood of MITM attacks, but cannot completely prevent them. The *web of trust* [24] as used e.g. in Pretty Good Privacy (PGP), establishes a distributed trust model via individual vetting: it requires users to endorse associations of public keys to specific people, and to endorse other people as trusted endorsers. Even though this approach was popular in the early days of cryptography, it was never widely adopted, possibly because of the strong level of involvement it requires from users to inspect each others' keys and to issue endorsements.

Today, the most common method to establish trust in end users' public keys is to let users manually verify a hash value of keys, known as a key *fingerprint*, using an out-of-band channel. Fingerprints are often represented in human-friendly formats to ease verification, e.g., as digits [28], pronounceable strings [20], ASCII art [23], or QR codes [28], but they require either physical proximity of communication partners (QR codes) or they are tedious to verify.[1] A crucial problem with key fingerprints is the far-from-optimal trade-off between security and usability: Strong fingerprints with 60 decimal or 32 hexadecimal digits are simply too long to verify by hand. Shorter fingerprints are more human-friendly but are vulnerable to preimage attacks, allowing an adversary to generate a key with the same fingerprint. A recent study comparing different manual key verification

---

[1] Users also struggle with the notion of key fingerprints, e.g. *all* Telegram users in one study [5] believed the fingerprint to be either the encryption key or a ciphertext.

mechanisms found that all were subject to attacks whose success rates ranged between 6% and 72% [25].

Introducing a New Tool. We propose a new cryptographic primitive, *Password-Authenticated Public-Key Encryption (PAPKE)*, which authenticates an encryption public key using human-memorable passwords, but does so in a way which is not subject to offline dictionary attacks given the authenticated public key or the ciphertexts encrypted using that key.

More precisely, PAPKE modifies the notion of public-key encryption so that both the *key generation* and the *encryption* algorithms take as an additional input *a password*, i.e. an arbitrary human-memorable string. The semantics of this password input is that Alice, when generating her public key, implicitly authenticates and "locks" this key with a password, and to encrypt a message, Bob must use a matching password to "unlock" the authenticated public key correctly. The correctness guarantee is that Alice decrypts the message encrypted by Bob *if* Bob encrypted it using the same password that Alice used in key generation. The notion of password-authentication of the public key which PAPKE enforces is the following: If a man-in-the-middle attacker substitutes Alice's public key with its own, the confidentiality of messages which Bob encrypts under this key is guaranteed as long as the adversary fails to guess the password shared by Alice and Bob. Crucially, the attacker must guess this password at the time it creates the substituted public key, and the eventual leakage of the password after generation of the adversarial key has no impact on encryption security.

PAPKE thus enables end-to-end secure communication without relying on a trusted party or exchanging long fingerprints on an out-of-band channel, and instead it bootstraps security from a short human-memorizable password.

PAPKE and Offline Dictionary Attacks. The challenge of password-based schemes is obtaining strong security based on weak secrets. In particular, such a scheme must be resilient against *offline* password attacks. For PAPKE this means that an adversary who receives an authenticated public key and the ciphertexts created using this key cannot use offline computation to find the passwords used to create either object. In other words, the adversary cannot use the public key or the intercepted ciphertexts to locally test password guesses. Otherwise, the low entropy of passwords would hardly provide any extra security: according to NIST [13] even a 16-character human-memorizable password has only 30 bits of entropy on average, and hence can easily be brute-forced.

To illustrate this challenge, consider a few simple but failed attempts at constructing a secure PAPKE scheme. A natural way to password-authenticate any information, including a public key, would be to MAC it using the (hashed) password as a MAC key. This, however, would be subject to an offline dictionary attack, as the attacker can locally test password guesses until it finds the one for which the MAC verifies. More generally, any procedure which allows for *explicit verification* of the authenticated public key under a password would be subject to an offline attack. What if the key was not authenticated itself but the encrypting party included the password in the plaintext? This would be insecure against a man-in-the-middle attack which sends its public key to the encryptor and decrypts it to read the encryptor's password.

Indeed, in a secure PAPKE the authenticated public key must commit the receiver Alice to the password used in the key generation, and the sender Bob cannot verify this commitment explicitly, but it can create a ciphertext such that (1) it is correct if Bob's and Alice's passwords match, (2) the plaintext is undecryptable if the two passwords differ, (3) the encryptor cannot tell which is the case, and (4) if the two passwords do not match then no one, including Alice who created the public key, can learn anything about Bob's password beyond the fact that it does not match the unique password she used to generate her public key.

We stress that PAPKE uses passwords to strictly enhance encryption security, i.e., for non-substituted keys, PAPKE provides standard CCA security that does not depend on the strength of the user's password. Thus the purpose of the password is solely to hedge security in case the encryptor uses a substituted key, but we stress that this hedging is applicable only if the encryptor shares a password with the party who generates the public key.

Our Contribution. We provide a thorough study of the proposed PAPKE primitive, and our contributions fall into the following three categories:

(Ia) Strong Security Notions for PAPKE. First, we formally introduce the concept of password-authenticated public key encryption, and define the desired security properties both via a universally composable (UC) functionality [14] and a set of property-based definitions. While property-based definitions are often more intuitive, a formalization in the UC framework provides stronger and more realistic security guarantees because it does not require any assumptions on the password distribution and correctly models real-world phenomena such as password reuse and making typing mistakes when entering the password. We prove that our UC security definition implies our property-based ones, hence proving a scheme secure in the UC setting implies its security under the more intuitive property-based notions.

(Ib) Relation to PAKE. To better understand the strength of the PAPKE primitive we compare it to the well-studied primitive of Password-Authenticated Key Exchange (PAKE) [7,11,15] The relation between PAPKE and PAKE is two-fold. First, PAPKE immediately implies a two-round PAKE: Alice and Bob can perform password-authenticated key exchange if Alice sends to Bob a PAPKE public key authenticated by her password, and Bob encrypts a session key using the received key and his password. Indeed, we show that if this simple protocol is instantiated with any scheme satisfying our UC PAPKE notion then the resulting protocol satisfies the strong UC notion of PAKE [15].

Regarding the other direction it might seem at first glance that any 2-round PAKE protocol, e.g. [4,7,8], can generically imply a PAPKE scheme as follows: The PAKE requester's flow can define a PAPKE public key, and the PAKE responder's flow, together with an encryption of the plaintext under the established session key, can define a PAPKE ciphertext. However, we show that this intuition is in fact *incorrect*, as the non-interactive usage of encryption that is required by PAPKE is not compatible with standard PAKE security notions. Indeed, as we discuss below, the two-round PAKE implied by PAPKE has stronger security than what is implied by standard PAKE notions because it remains secure (and robust) even if either party re-uses its state. Summing up, the relation of PAPKE and PAKE is that PAPKE implies a 2-round PAKE with a (novel) property of security under session state re-use.

(II) Efficient PAPKE Constructions. We show two very practical constructions that securely realize the UC PAPKE functionality. Our first construction generically builds a PAPKE scheme from a public-key encryption (PKE) scheme and an ideal cipher: The authenticated public key is an encryption of the PKE public key under the password, with the encryption implemented using an ideal cipher over the space of PKE public keys. To obtain the desired UC-security, the PKE scheme must satisfy a number of properties beyond standard CCA security, such as key-anonymity [6] and strong robustness [1]. We show a concrete instantiation of this scheme using a variant of DHIES [2] which satisfies these properties under the so-called Oracle Diffie-Hellman (ODH) assumption. This results in a highly-efficient construction secure under ODH in the Ideal Cipher model, which uses 1 exponentiation for key generation, 2 for encryption, and 1 for decryption.

However, ideal ciphers over arbitrary cyclic groups, e.g. an elliptic curve, are not so easy to implement. While generic constructions for ideal ciphers from random oracles exist [16,19], implementing ideal ciphers over a specific algebraic group is not straightforward, and if not done carefully can result in timing and/or offline password guessing attacks. Thus we also provide an alternative concrete construction that does not rely on ideal ciphers and therefore might be easier to implement. It uses the Fujisaki-Okamoto transform [17] of a twisted "twin-key" ElGamal construction of independent interest. This construction uses 2 exponentiations for key generation, 2 multi-exponentiations for encryption, and 1 exponentiation and 1 multi-exponentiation in decryption, and relies on the Decisional Diffie-Hellman (DDH) assumption in the Random Oracle Model.

(IIIa) Efficient 2-Round UC PAKE Schemes. Our generic PAPKE-to-PAKE compiler discussed above implies two highly efficient UC PAKE protocols when instantiated with the above two PAPKE schemes. To the best of our knowledge these are the first two-round UC-secure PAKE's which rely on standard cyclic groups, i.e., do not use groups with bilinear maps or other trapdoor structure, and which resort instead to either the Ideal Cipher (IC) or the Random Oracle Model (ROM) to achieve practical efficiency. Specifically, our results imply a UC PAKE which uses 2 expentiations per party but relies on an ideal cipher over a group, and a UC PAKE which uses 4 (multi)-exponentiations for the requester and 2 exponentiations for the responder and relies on a random oracle model for hash functions. Note that the first scheme matches and the second scheme comes very close to the 2 exponentiations/party cost of *unauthenicated* Diffie-Hellman Key Exchange, with is the minimum cost for PAKE one can reasonably expect. The closest efficiency-wise UC PAKE we know of is by Abdalla et al. [3], which

was shown secure under comparable assumptions, but which requires 3 message flows while our UC PAKE's use only 2 flows.

(IIIb) PAKE's with Session Re-use Security. As we argued in (Ib) above, the PAPKE-to-PAKE compiler results in a 2-round PAKE which has novel security and reliability properties which follow from the fact that PAPKE enforces ciphertext security when the same public key is used to encrypt multiple messages. Recall that the PAKE requester message is a PAPKE public key, and the PAKE responder message is a PAPKE ciphertext encrypting a random session key under this public key, and both the public key and the ciphertext are created using the passwords of resp. the requester and the responder. (See Sect. 3 for the full description of this PAKE.) The novel security property of this PAKE is that each of these keys is secure even though all sessions re-use the same session state and the first message flow of the requester. The standard model of PAKE security does not guarantee security in this case, but a PAKE which is secure in this way can be beneficial to higher-level applications. For example it can help handle communication faults: A responder session which believes that its response has not been delivered correctly can safely respond to the same requester message again, and a requester who gets multiple responses can securely spin off a subprocess for each of them without re-starting a new session from scratch.

Roadmap. In Sect. 2 we define PAPKE as a strengthened version of public-key encryption. Section 3 discusses the relation between PAKE and PAPKE, and shows a generic compiler from any UC PAPKE to UC PAKE. Section 4 presents our two highly efficient UC PAPKE schemes. In Appendix A we exemplify one highly-efficient concrete 2-round UC PAKE protocol obtained via the generic compiler of Sect. 3 applied to one of the PAPKE schemes of Sect. 4.

2   Security Model for **PAPKE**

In this section we introduce our security models for password-authenticated encryption. A peculiarity of formal security definitions for *password-based* primitives is that they must model the inherent probability of an adversary correctly guessing the low-entropy password. Property-based definitions [7] (sometimes also called game-based definitions) typically do so by requiring that the adversary's probability of winning the security game is negligibly more than a (non-negligible) threshold determined by its number of online queries and the entropy of the distribution from which the password is chosen. Composable security definitions [15] such as those in Canetti's Universal Composability (UC) framework [14], on the other hand, model the possibility of guessing the password directly into the ideal behavior of the primitive.

As argued by Canetti et al. [15], composable definitions provide stronger and more realistic security guarantees than property-based ones, because they do not make any implicit assumptions about the password distribution and correctly model real-world phenomena such as password reuse and typos while entering the password. Nevertheless, property-based definitions are often more intuitive and easier to understand than UC definitions. Below we present the property-based PAPKE security notions, and in the full version [12] we define UC notion of PAPKE and show that it implies the property-based notion.

Definition 1 (PAPKE). *Let $\mathcal{D}$ be a dictionary of possible passwords, and $\mathcal{M}$ be a message space. A password-authenticated public-key encryption scheme is a tuple of algorithms* PAPKE = (KGen, Enc, Dec) *with the following behavior:*

KGen$(\kappa, pwd) \to_R (apk, sk)$: *on input a security parameter κ and password $pwd \in \mathcal{D}$, output an authenticated public key apk and a secret key sk.*

Enc$(apk, pwd, m) \to_R c$: *on input an authenticated public key apk, password pwd and a message $m \in \mathcal{M}$, output a ciphertext c.*

Dec$(sk, c) \to m$: *on input a secret key sk and ciphertext c, output a message $m \in \mathcal{M} \cup \{\bot\}$ where $\bot$ indicates that the ciphertext is invalid.*

For correctness we require that for any password $pwd \in \mathcal{D}$, key pair $(apk, sk) \leftarrow_R$ KGen(κ, pwd), and ciphertexts $c \leftarrow_R$ Enc(apk, pwd, m), we have that $m = $ Dec(sk, c). Informally, the desired security properties of PAPKE schemes are:

Resistance against Offline-Attacks: None of the values that are (partially) derived from a password allows offline dictionary attacks on the passwords that were used to generate them: The authenticated public key apk does not leak anything about the setup password pwd, and ciphertexts c formed under apk do not leak any information about the password attempt pwd' that was used in the encryption. The only and inevitable information leaked is that the party who holds the secret key sk corresponding to apk learns whether $pwd' = pwd$, because that holds if and only if Dec$(sk, c) \neq \bot$.

CCA Security: Ciphertexts encrypted under an *honestly* generated authenticated public key apk hide the encrypted message from any adversary who doesn't know the secret key. This property is modeled in the standard CCA setting, and it holds even if the adversary knows all passwords used.

Security against Man-in-the-Middle (MITM) Attacks: The choice of an authenticated public key apk^* commits the adversary to some single password guess pwd^*, and all ciphertexts encrypted under apk^* using any password $pwd \neq pwd^*$ hide the encrypted message. The only available attack is an *online* attack, where the adversary guesses password pwd used by the honest encryptor and generates apk^* so that it commits to $pwd^* = pwd$. Thus the MITM attack gains effectively one password guess per each adversarial public key apk^* which the honest party uses in encryption.

Long-Term Security: The security of encryptions under an adversarially chosen key apk^* is preserved in a forward-secure manner because it holds even if the adversary (eventually) learns the encryptor's password $pwd \neq pwd^*$.

Ciphertext Authenticity: The password also guarantees authenticity of ciphertexts. That is, an adversary who knows an honestly generated key apk, but not the password pwd (or the secret key sk), cannot create valid ciphertexts, i.e., ciphertexts that decrypt under sk into some message $m \neq \bot$.

2.1 Property-Based Security Definition

We formalize the above intuitive security requirements using two game-based definitions, namely indistinguishability against chosen-ciphertext and chosen-key attack (IND-CCKA), and ciphertext authenticity (AUTH-CTXT). For the sake of brevity, we will refer to property IND-CCKA as the *privacy* property. The privacy experiment formalizes the first four properties listed above:

> **Experiment** $\mathsf{Exp}_{\mathcal{A},\mathsf{PAPKE}}^{\mathsf{IND\text{-}CCKA}}(\kappa)$:
> $pwd \leftarrow_R \mathcal{D}$, $\mathbf{L} \leftarrow \emptyset$, $(apk, sk) \leftarrow_R \mathsf{KGen}(\kappa, pwd)$
> $b \leftarrow_R \{0,1\}$, $\mathtt{revealed} \leftarrow 0$
> $b' \leftarrow_R \mathcal{A}^{\mathsf{LoR}(b,pwd,\cdot,\cdot,\cdot),\mathsf{Dec}(sk,\cdot),\mathsf{Reveal}(pwd)}(apk)$
>   oracle LoR on input a public key apk^* and
>   two messages m_0 and m_1 where $|m_0| = |m_1|$
>   if $apk^* \neq apk$ and $\mathtt{revealed} = 1$, return $\perp$
>   else, compute $C \leftarrow_R \mathsf{Enc}(apk^*, pwd, m_b)$,
>   if $apk^* = apk$ add C to $\mathbf{L}$
>   return C
>   oracle Dec on input a ciphertext $C \notin \mathbf{L}$:
>   return $m \leftarrow \mathsf{Dec}(sk, C)$ where $m \in \mathcal{M} \cup \{\perp\}$
>   oracle Reveal: return pwd and set $\mathtt{revealed} \leftarrow 1$
> **return** 1 if $b' = b$

Definition 2 (IND-CCKA). *A PAPKE scheme is called* indistinguishable under chosen-ciphertext and key attacks *if for all efficient adversaries $\mathcal{A}$, and any password space $\mathcal{D}$ it holds that*

$$\Pr[\mathsf{Exp}_{\mathcal{A},\mathsf{PAPKE}}^{\mathsf{IND\text{-}CCKA}}(\kappa) = 1] \leq \frac{1}{2} + \frac{1}{2} \cdot \frac{q_{apk^*} + q_{\mathsf{Dec}}}{|\mathcal{D}|} + \mathsf{negl}(\kappa)$$

for a negligible function negl, *where q_{apk^*} denotes the number of public keys $apk^* \neq apk$ that $\mathcal{A}$ used in its queries to the* LoR *oracle, and where:*

- *if $q_{apk^*} > 0$, then q_{Dec} is the number of $\mathcal{A}$'s queries to the* Dec *oracle while* $\mathtt{revealed} = 0$ (active/MITM security)
- *if $q_{apk^*} = 0$, then $q_{\mathsf{Dec}} \leftarrow 0$*   (passive/CCA security)

In the IND-CCKA definition above we set $q_{\mathsf{Dec}} = 0$ for passive attacks, i.e. if $q_{apk^*} = 0$, then the security bound is $1/2 + \mathsf{negl}(\kappa)$. In other words, if $\mathcal{A}$ does not stage any MITM attack, i.e. it never substitutes the challenge public key apk with $apk^* \neq apk$, then IND-CCKA is like standard CCA-security of PKE, i.e. $\mathcal{A}$ can make any number of encryption and decryption queries and they will not impact its success probability.

Authenticity (AUTH-CTXT). The ciphertext authenticity property (Definition 3) formalizes that the adversary $\mathcal{A}$, given apk generated for password pwd chosen at random in dictionary $\mathcal{D}$, cannot create a valid ciphertext except for probability $(1+q_{apk^*}+q_{\mathsf{Dec}})/|\mathcal{D}|$, where q_{apk^*} is the number of encryption queries $\mathcal{A}$ makes under bad and distinct keys $apk^* \neq apk$, and q_{Dec} is the number of decryption queries. (See [12] for full discussion of these definitional choices.) Note that here we do not let $\mathcal{A}$ learn pwd because knowing pwd suffices to form a valid ciphertext. The password-guessing count is $q_{apk^*} + q_{\mathsf{Dec}}$ plus 1 because the final ciphertext $\mathcal{A}$ creates can itself be used to guess a password.

The authenticity experiment is defined as follows:

> **Experiment** $\mathsf{Exp}_{\mathcal{A},\mathsf{PAPKE}}^{\mathsf{AUTH\text{-}CTXT}}(\kappa)$:
> $pwd \leftarrow_{\mathrm{R}} \mathcal{D}, \mathbf{L} \leftarrow \emptyset, (apk, sk) \leftarrow_{\mathrm{R}} \mathsf{KGen}(\kappa, pwd)$
> $C^* \leftarrow_{\mathrm{R}} \mathcal{A}^{\mathsf{Enc}(pwd,\cdot,\cdot),\mathsf{Dec}(sk,\cdot)}(apk)$
>   oracle Enc on input a key apk^* and message m :
>   compute $C \leftarrow_{\mathrm{R}} \mathsf{Enc}(apk^*, pwd, m)$
>   if $apk^* = apk$ add C to $\mathbf{L}$
>   return C
>   oracle Dec on input a ciphertext C :
>   return $m \leftarrow \mathsf{Dec}(sk, C)$, where $m \in \mathcal{M} \cup \{\perp\}$
> **return** 1 if $\mathsf{Dec}(sk, C^*) \neq \perp$ and $C^* \notin \mathbf{L}$

Definition 3 (AUTH-CTXT). *A* PAPKE *scheme* *provides* authenticity of ciphertexts *if for all efficient adversaries* $\mathcal{A}$*, and any password space* $\mathcal{D}$ *it holds that*

$$\Pr[\mathsf{Exp}_{\mathcal{A},\mathsf{PAPKE}}^{\mathsf{AUTH\text{-}CTXT}}(\kappa) = 1] \leq \frac{q_{apk^*} + q_{\mathsf{Dec}} + 1}{|\mathcal{D}|} + \mathsf{negl}(\kappa)$$

for a negligible function negl*, where* q_{apk^*} *is the number of bad keys* $apk^* \neq apk$ *in* $\mathcal{A}$*'s* Enc *oracle queries and* q_{Dec} *is the number of* $\mathcal{A}$*'s* Dec *oracle queries.*

3 Relation Between PAPKE and PAKE

PAPKE, the new cryptographic primitive we propose, is closely related to Password Authenticated Key Agreement (PAKE) [7,11,15]. Specifically, we show that it is easy to build a (UC-secure) two-round PAKE scheme from a (UC-secure) PAPKE scheme, but that while the converse looks like it should be true at first sight, it is not true in general, because PAPKE has stricter properties than a standard PAKE. In particular, we give a counterexample of a secure two-round PAKE scheme that, when converted into a PAPKE scheme in the straightforward fashion, yields an insecure PAPKE scheme. Indeed, PAPKE can be thought of as a two-round PAKE with a novel property of security under session state re-use, which to the best of our knowledge has not been observed and provably realized before.

Constructing PAKE from PAPKE. We show that any UC-secure PAPKE can be converted into a two-round UC-secure PAKE. This construction is shown in Fig. 1, and it is fairly simple: The initiator $\mathcal{P}_i$ generates an authenticated public key apk from the input password pwd and sends it to $\mathcal{P}_j$. The responder $\mathcal{P}_j$, given its password pwd' and the received public key apk, picks a random session key $k \leftarrow_\mathrm{R} \{0,1\}^\kappa$, and responds to $\mathcal{P}_i$ with an encryption of k under apk and pwd'. $\mathcal{P}_i$ receives key k by decrypting the received ciphertext, or outputs $\perp$ if the decryption fails. Note that all communication is done over an insecure channel, fully controlled by the adversary. In particular, an adversary can replace $\mathcal{P}_i$'s public key and/or $\mathcal{P}_j$'s ciphertext. However, PAPKE security implies that neither $\mathcal{P}_i$'s public key nor $\mathcal{P}_j$'s ciphertext reveal anything about passwords, resp. pwd and pwd', and the only attack the adversary can stage is an on-line guessing attack, because each substituted public key apk^* or ciphertext c^* commits the adversary to a *single* password guess pwd^*, and is guaranteed to fail (e.g. $\mathcal{P}_j$ fails to encrypt anything useful under apk^* or $\mathcal{P}_i$ fails to decrypt c^*) unless the guessed password pwd^* matches the password of resp. $\mathcal{P}_j$ or $\mathcal{P}_i$.

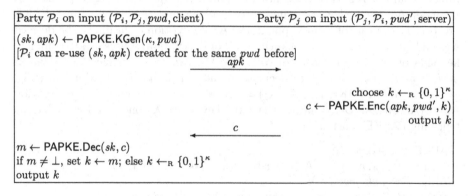

Fig. 1. Two-round PAKE protocol PAPKE-2-PAKE given PAPKE = (KGen, Enc, Dec).

The proof of Theorem 1 is included in the full version [12]. Note that if the PAKE initiator $\mathcal{P}_i$ chooses to re-use its state (sk, apk) across protocol instances which share the same input pwd then $\mathcal{P}_i$ reveals that all these instances share the same input, hence such protocol can only realize functionality $\mathcal{F}_{\mathsf{PAKE}}$ modified so that a party can choose to reveal that two of its sessions run on the same password.

Theorem 1. *If* PAPKE *realizes the UC PAPKE functionality* $\mathcal{F}_{\mathsf{PAPKE}}$, *defined in [12], then the* PAPKE-2-PAKE *scheme shown in Fig. 1 realizes the UC PAKE functionality* $\mathcal{F}_{\mathsf{PAKE}}$ *[15].*

An Intuitive PAKE-2-PAPKE Compiler, and Why It Doesn't Work. It turns out that the intuitive approach of building PAPKE from two-round PAKE does not work due to subtle differences in the security notions of both primitives.

Indeed, PAPKE has some security properties which are stronger than PAKE, and this in particular implies that the PAPKE-to-PAKE compiler shown above adds a new security property to the resulting PAKE. (We discuss that PAKE security property below.) For the ease of exposition, we state our results for the game-based representations of PAKE and PAPKE instead of using their UC variants, and refer to parties $\mathcal{P}_i$ and $\mathcal{P}_j$ as A and B respectively. On a first glance, it seems reasonable to generically build a PAPKE scheme from any two-round PAKE protocol, e.g. [4,7,8]. Specifically, any two-round PAKE protocol $\langle(A_1, A_2) \rightleftharpoons (B_1, B_2)\rangle$ can be abstracted as follows:

Party A (input pwd)		Party B (input pwd')
$(state_A, m_A) \leftarrow_R A_1(\kappa, pwd)$	$\xrightarrow{\quad m_A \quad}$	
	$\xleftarrow{\quad m_B \quad}$	$(state_B, m_B) \leftarrow_R B_1(\kappa, pwd')$
$k_A \leftarrow A_2(state_A, m_B)$		$k_B \leftarrow B_2(state_B, m_A)$

The natural approach to constructing PAPKE would combine a two-round PAKE with an authenticated encryption scheme AE: The PAKE message m_A from A would be A's static authenticated public key apk, and to encrypt message m under A's key $apk = m_A$ any party could complete the two-round PAKE protocol in the role of B and append the AE encryption of m under the derived session key k_B to B's PAKE message m_B. For decryption, A uses m_B to complete her side of the PAKE protocol to derive the same session key $k_A = k_B$ (if $pwd = pwd'$) and uses k_A to decrypt the attached ciphertext. More formally, given a 2-round PAKE $= \langle(A_1, A_2) \rightleftharpoons (B_1, B_2)\rangle$ and authenticated encryption AE $= (AE.Enc, AE.Dec)$ sharing the same key space $\mathcal{K}$, one could consider the following PAPKE construction:

PAPKE.KGen(κ, pwd):
    run $(state_A, m_A) \leftarrow_R A_1(\kappa, pwd)$, return $(sk \leftarrow state_A, apk \leftarrow m_A)$
PAPKE.Enc(apk, pwd', m):
    run $(state_B, m_B) \leftarrow_R B_1(\kappa, pwd')$ and $k_B \leftarrow B_2(state_B, apk)$
    encrypt $c \leftarrow AE.Enc(k_B, m)$ and return $c' \leftarrow (m_B, c)$
PAPKE.Dec(sk, c'):
    parse $c' = (m_B, c)$ and $sk = state_A$
    get $k_A \leftarrow A_2(state_A, m_B)$ and return $m \leftarrow AE.Dec(k_A, c)$

Intuitively, this should yield a secure PAPKE if PAKE is secure. However, this generic construction uses PAKE in a way that is not covered by its security definition: Whenever party A decrypts a PAPKE ciphertext it effectively *re-uses* the same local PAKE session state $state_A$ (and the same first-round message m_A) across multiple PAKE sessions. Indeed, this gap can be exploited to craft special PAKE and AE schemes that are secure by themselves but result in an insecure PAPKE when used in this natural compiler. (The full formal description of this counterexample is included in [12]).

Implications for UC PAKE Protocols. We discuss the main conclusions we draw from the two technical facts above.

First 2-Round UC PAKE's Competitive with Game-Based PAKE's. In Appendix A we include two highly efficient UC PAKE protocols by instantiating the PAPKE-2-PAKE compiler with the PAPKE constructions of Sect. 4. To the best of our knowledge these are the first 2-round UC PAKE's which rely on standard cyclic groups with efficiency comparable to the Diffie-Hellman key exchange in the IC or RO model. While UC PAKE can be achieved using even 1 (simultaneous) round of communication, all 1-round UC PAKEs we know, e.g. [21,22], use groups with bilinear maps and are significantly costlier. Thus practitioners are likely to resort to constructions which require IC or ROM models but give much better concrete efficiency.

Concretely, we show two 2-round UC PAKE protocols: PAKE-IC-DHIES, secure under Oracle Diffie-Hellman (ODH) [2] in the IC model which uses 2 exponentiations per party, and PAKE-FO, secure under DDH in ROM which uses 4 (multi-)exps for the requester and 2 for the responder. The Universally Composable notion of PAKE security [15] has long been recognized as stronger than the game-based notions [7,11], not only because it implies concurrent security and can be used in protocol composition, but also because, unlike the game-based notions, the UC PAKE implies security for non-uniform password distributions, password re-use, correlated passwords, misstyped passwords, and any other forms of information leakage. However, there has been an efficiency and round-complexity gap between UC PAKE's and PAKE's shown secure under game-based notions with the 3-round 2-exp/party UC PAKE of Abdalla et al. [3], which assumes DDH in IC model, coming closest to the 2-round 2-exp/party game-based PAKE of Abdalla-Pointcheval [4], which assumes DDH in ROM. Our UC PAKE constructions match [4] in round complexity, and our IC model construction also matches [4] in the number of exponentiation operations.[2]

PAKE with Security on Session Re-use. As we argued above, the reason the compiler from 2-round PAKE to PAPKE does not work is that a standard PAKE security model does not extend to the case of the requester party, A, re-using the local state $state_A$ of a single PAKE session across many sessions, each of which would derive a session key k_A from same state k_A but potentially different responder messages m_B. By contrast, PAKE created from the secure PAPKE in Fig. 1 does have this property: The requester party $\mathcal{P}_i$ can use the same local state, which is the PAPKE secret key sk, across many sessions, deriving $k_A \leftarrow$ PAPKE.Dec(sk, c) on any number of responder messages c. By the same token, the responder $\mathcal{P}_j$ in this PAKE protocol is free to re-use $\mathcal{P}_i$'s first-round message apk in multiple sessions, because PAPKE ciphertexts created in each such session are all secure, and their plaintexts can all be used as session keys.

Indeed, this shows that protocol PAPKE-2-PAKE is a secure 2-round PAKE with security under re-use of requester's session state across multiple sessions. This can improve efficiency in PAKE applications where the initiator re-uses same password across multiple sessions (and does not mind revealing that fact), and it can also make it easier to handle communication faults, because both

---

[2] However, our local computation cost also includes Ideal Cipher operations.

parties can keep their session information, the session state $state_A = sk$ for $\mathcal{P}_i$ and the requester's first message $m_A = apk$ for $\mathcal{P}_j$, and re-use them in case of communication faults instead of re-starting from scratch.

4   Efficient and UC-Secure PAPKE Constructions

First attempts to construct PAPKE schemes that authenticate public keys and plaintexts with a password would probably involve message authentication codes (MACs) of the public key and/or the encrypted plaintext under a key derived from the password. Such solutions, however, fall prey to offline dictionary attacks, either given just the authenticated public key, or by substituting the real public key with an adversarial one and testing the decrypted MAC. Thus the challenge is to devise schemes that withstand offline attacks and achieve the strong security guarantees formalized in our UC and property-based definitions. We present two very practical PAPKE constructions that achieve this goal.

The first construction, PAPKE-IC in Sect. 4.1, combines any CCA secure public-key encryption and an ideal cipher, using the ideal cipher to encrypt the public key with the password as a key. We prove this PAPKE scheme secure in the ideal-cipher model if the PKE scheme satisfies a number of properties that go beyond the standard CCA security, namely key anonymity, robustness, and the requirement that public keys are uniform in the (ideal) cipher domain.

While the PAPKE-IC construction is conceptually simple, instantiating the combination of ideal ciphers and public-key encryption requires some care, and subtle implementation mistakes could render the PAPKE-IC construction insecure (see the discussion in Sect. 4.1 below). Hence we propose a second PAPKE construction, PAPKE-FO in Sect. 4.2, which is not generic, but it does not need an ideal cipher and therefore might be easier to implement. It is based on a twin-key version of the Fujisaki-Okamoto transform of ElGamal encryption, and it is secure under the DDH assumption in ROM.

4.1   PAPKE-IC: Generic Construction from PKE and Ideal Cipher

Our first construction, protocol PAPKE-IC in Fig. 2, builds PAPKE generically from a public-key encryption PKE and an ideal cipher IC = (IC.Enc, IC.Dec). The basic idea of the construction is simple and similar to the Encrypted Key Exchange (EKE) PAKE of Bellovin and Merritt [8]: The receiver generates a key pair for the PKE scheme and encrypts the public key under the ideal cipher using the password as a key. The resulting encrypted public key is used as PAPKE authenticated public key apk. To encrypt a message, the sender decrypts apk under the ideal cipher using the password as a key, and encrypts the message under the resulting public key. Our PAPKE-IC shares this basic design with EKE, except that we use a CCA-secure encryption while EKE implicitly uses a version of (CPA-secure) ElGamal whose security *as encryption* is less clear.

Protocol PAPKE-IC requires a number of properties of the PKE scheme that go beyond the standard notion of CCA security. First, its public keys must be *uniformly distributed* over the domain of the ideal cipher, because otherwise an attacker can test passwords offline by trying to decrypt *apk*. Second, ciphertexts of the PKE cannot reveal under which public key they were encrypted, as that would allow offline attacks as well. The second property is known as key privacy or *anonymity* [6]. Third, and perhaps a bit harder to see, is that an adversary should be unable to construct ciphertexts that decrypt correctly under multiple secret keys, but such ciphertext would allow the adversary to test multiple password guesses in one query to the decryption oracle. This property is known as *strong robustness* [1]. The latter two properties are formalized as, respectively, AI-CCA and SROB-CCA (see [12]). Finally, PKE and IC have to be "compatible" in the sense that IC is an ideal cipher over the key space $\mathcal{PK}$ of PKE.

Setup: Let PKE = (KGen, Enc, Dec) be a public-key encryption scheme with uniform public-key space $\mathcal{PK}$ and let IC = (IC.Enc, IC.Dec) be an ideal cipher over $\mathcal{PK}$.

PAPKE.KGen(κ, pwd):

Generate $(pk, sk) \leftarrow_R$ PKE.KGen(κ) and $apk \leftarrow$ IC.Enc(pwd, pk) and output (sk, apk).

PAPKE.Enc(apk, pwd', m):

Decrypt the public key, $pk \leftarrow$ IC.Dec(pwd, apk) and output $c \leftarrow_R$ PKE.Enc(pk, m).

PAPKE.Dec(sk, c':

Decrypt $m \leftarrow$ PKE.Dec(sk, c') and output m.

Fig. 2. The generic PAPKE scheme PAPKE-IC.

The proof of the following theorem appears in the full version [12]:

Theorem 2. *Protocol* PAPKE-IC *in Fig. 2 securely realizes functionality* $\mathcal{F}_{\mathsf{PAPKE}}$ *in the* $\mathcal{F}_{\mathsf{IC}}$*-hybrid model, if the public key encryption* PKE *has uniform public-key space* $\mathcal{PK}$ *and is* AI-CCA *and* SROB-CCA*-secure.*

Implementing Ideal Ciphers over Groups. Our PAPKE-IC construction assumes an ideal cipher over a key space $\mathcal{PK}$ that for many PKE schemes will be a cyclic group $\mathbb{G}$. We stress that such an assumption is also used in several PAKE schemes, beginning from the Bellare et al. analysis [7] of the Encrypted Key Exchange (EKE) PAKE scheme of Bellovin and Merritt [8]. Ideal ciphers over variable domains can be implemented for a variety of domains, e.g. [10]. However, for many groups implementing an ideal cipher is somewhat cumbersome and can introduce possibilities for offline and/or timing attacks. Simply applying a block cipher to the public key doesn't work as not all strings of the same length are valid group elements, and an adversary could offline tests by decrypting the authenticated public key under a guessed password and testing if the decryption yields a valid group element. If $\mathcal{PK} = \mathbb{G}$ is any elliptic curve group, there are deterministic methods that map any string onto a group element [9] and hence offline and timing attacks are not a concern. The opposite direction can be implemented as in [9], but that encoding works only for subspace S of roughly $1/2$ of $\mathbb{G}$ elements. This slows down key generation, i.e. pair $(pk, sk) \leftarrow_R$ PKE.KGen has to be chosen s.t. $pk \in S$, but it does not lead to timing attacks on passwords. Still, these mappings complicate key generation and are non-trivial to implement, which motivates searching for alternative solutions that do not rely on ideal ciphers over arbitrary groups.

DHIES-Based Instantiation. In Appendix A, we specify an efficient concrete instantiation of PAPKE-IC, called PAPKE-IC-DHIES, which uses a variant of DHIES as the robust and anonymous PKE. Scheme PAPKE-IC-DHIES is as efficient as one could hope for in a DH-based cryptosystem, i.e. it uses 1 exponentiation in key generation, 2 exponentiations in encryption, and 1 in decryption. The DHIES variant we use (DHIES*) was shown to satisfy the required properties under the Oracle-Diffie-Hellman assumption (ODH), using a collision-resistant hash function and a secure authenticated encryption scheme [1]. The authenticated encryption (or rather the combination of symmetric encryption and a MAC) needs to satisfy some additional, non-standard properties, and the ODH assumption also has an impact on the choice of the hash function. We refer to Appendix A for a more detailed discussion. Thus, similar to the challenges that arise when securely instantiating the ideal cipher, implementing DHIES* also requires some care in the implementation and choice of its underlying primitives.

4.2 PAPKE-FO: Concrete Construction from DDH and ROM

Our second PAPKE construction, protocol PAPKE-FO in Fig. 3, does not require an ideal cipher over a group of PKE public keys, and may thus be easier to implement. It is however slightly more costly, with 2 exponentiations for key generation, 2 multi-exponentiations (with two bases) for encryption, and 1 exponentiation and 1 (two base) multi-exponentiation for decryption. This construction is built using the Fujisaki-Okamoto (FO) transform [17] for ElGamal encryption but with a "twin" Diffie-Hellman key instead of a single key.

The high-level idea is to derive the authenticated public key *apk* by "blinding" the public key g^x of the ElGamal encryption scheme with the hash of the password as $apk \leftarrow g^x \cdot \mathsf{H_0}(pwd)$, where $\mathsf{H_0}$ is a hash function onto $\mathbb{G}$, which can be implemented in deterministic way (to avoid timing attacks) using e.g. [9]. To encrypt message m under password pwd' and key *apk*, the encryptor "unblinds" the public key as $y \leftarrow apk \cdot \mathsf{H_0}(pwd')^{-1}$ and then encrypts m under y using FO-ElGamal, i.e. the Fujisaki-Okamoto transform applied to ElGamal which lifts its security from CPA to CCA, required to achieve the CCA-security and ciphertext authenticity properties of PAPKE.

None of the password-derived values *apk* or c allows an offline attack: Any "unblinding" of *apk* would yield a valid public key g^x for some x, and ElGamal ciphertexts are known to guarantee key anonymity [6], meaning that ciphertexts do not leak information about the public key used in encryption. (Note that the leakage of the unblinded public key $y = g^x$ used in encryption would allow an adversary who sees $apk = y \cdot H_0(pwd)$ to mount an offline attack on pwd.) The scheme is correct because if $pwd' = pwd$ then the hash values cancel and encryption is done under the "original" public key $y = g^x$. However, if the passwords do not match then encryption is done under an effectively random public key $y \leftarrow_R \mathbb{G}$. The latter gives us the desired security against active attacks: If an honest party is tricked into encryption under a malicious apk^* but uses a different password than the one which was used to blind apk^*, then the ciphertext will be indistinguishable from random, even if $\mathcal{A}$ knows the secret key to apk^*. Note, however, that unlike the ideal cipher encryption of apk under pwd used in PAPKE-IC, the method used here to blind key g^x and form the authenticated key apk is essentially a one-time pad over $\mathbb{G}$, and thus is not by itself a commitment to password pwd. Below we discuss how we modify the above sketch and in particular make this blinding password-committing.

Note that in Fig. 3 the message space is $\mathcal{M} = \{0,1\}^n$ for fixed n but it can be extended to arbitrary messages e.g. using $H_2(R)$ as a key in symmetric-key encryption instead of as a one-time pad.

Setup: Let $\mathbb{G}$ be a group of prime order p such that $2^{\kappa-1} < p < 2^{\kappa}$, and let g_1, g_2 be two random generators in $\mathbb{G}$. We use three hash functions modeled as random oracles: $H_0 : \{0,1\}^* \to \mathbb{G}$, $H_1 : \mathbb{G}^3 \times \{0,1\}^n \to \mathbb{Z}_p^2$ and $H_2 : \mathbb{G} \to \{0,1\}^n$.

PAPKE.KGen(κ, pwd):
- Choose $x \leftarrow_R \mathbb{Z}_p$ and compute $y_1 \leftarrow g_1^x$, $y_2 \leftarrow g_2^x$, $Y_2 \leftarrow y_2 \cdot H_0(pwd)$.
- Output (sk, apk) for $sk \leftarrow (x, y_1, y_2)$ and $apk \leftarrow (y_1, Y_2)$.

PAPKE.Enc(apk, pwd', m):
- Abort if $|m| > n$.
- Parse $(y_1, Y_2) \leftarrow apk$, and "unblind" the second public key, $y_2 \leftarrow Y_2 \cdot H_0(pwd)^{-1}$.
- Generate randomness via the RO: compute $(r_1, r_2) \leftarrow H_1(R, y_1, y_2, m)$ for $R \leftarrow_R \mathbb{G}$.
- Encrypt R under y_1 and y_2: $c_1 \leftarrow g_1^{r_1} g_2^{r_2}$, $c_2 \leftarrow y_1^{r_1} y_2^{r_2} \cdot R$, $c_3 \leftarrow H_2(R) \oplus m$.
- Output $c \leftarrow (c_1, c_2, c_3)$.

PAPKE.Dec(sk, c'):
- Parse $(x, y_1, y_2) \leftarrow sk$.
- Decrypt $c = (c_1, c_2, c_3)$: $R \leftarrow c_2/c_1^x$, $m \leftarrow c_3 \oplus H_2(R)$, and $(r_1, r_2) \leftarrow H_1(R, y_1, y_2, m)$.
- Verify the correctness of decryption: if $c_1 = g_1^{r_1} g_2^{r_2}$ set $m' \leftarrow m$, else set $m' \leftarrow \bot$.
- Output m'

Fig. 3. Our DDH-based PAPKE scheme PAPKE-FO.

Achieving UC-Security via "Twin" Keys. To achieve UC security we have to ensure that both the key apk and the ciphertext c commit each party to a well-defined password choice. Technically, the simulator SIM must be able to extract (i) pwd from an adversarial apk^* and (ii) pwd' and m from an adversarial ciphertext c. While (ii) can be realized via the Fujisaki-Okamoto transform, case (i) requires more care. We need (i) for the reasons outlined above, i.e. a ciphertext encrypted by an honest party under an adversarial key apk^* must be decryptable only if apk^* commits to the encryptor's password. In the UC functionality $\mathcal{F}_{\mathsf{PAPKE}}$ this is enforced by SIM having to pass a single password guess pwd^* corresponding to the real-life adversary's choice of apk^*, and if $pwd^* \neq pwd'$, i.e., the guess does not match the encryptor's password pwd', then the encryption must reveal no information on the encrypted plaintext.

We achieve this by generating a "twin" public key using two generators g_1, g_2 in the CRS. The apk then consists of $y_1 \leftarrow g_1^x$ and $Y_2 \leftarrow g_2^x \cdot \mathsf{H}_0(pwd)$, i.e., we keep one public key in the clear and the other one is blinded with the password hash. In the security proof we set $g_2 \leftarrow g_1^s$, which allows the simulator to decrypt $\mathsf{H}_0(pwd)$ from apk, and look up pwd from the random oracle queries. Further, encryption is done under *both* public keys: y_1 and the "unblinded" $y_2 = Y_2 \cdot \mathsf{H}_0(pwd)^{-1}$. This double encryption under the plain and derived key is crucial, as it prevents an adversary $\mathcal{A}$ from providing a malformed apk^* which would allow $\mathcal{A}$ to still decrypt, but from which SIM cannot extract a password. Thus, our "twin" key construction enforces that only a well-formed apk can lead to decryptable ciphertexts (if the passwords match), without requiring heavy tools such as zero-knowledge proofs.

For space-saving reasons the proof of the following theorem is relegated to the full version of the paper. Functionalities $\mathcal{F}_{\mathsf{CRS}}$ and $\mathcal{F}_{\mathsf{RO}}$ are UC models for resp. the CRS string and the RO hash functions we assume in this construction.

Theorem 3. *Protocol* PAPKE-FO *in Fig. 3 securely realizes functionality* $\mathcal{F}_{\mathsf{PAPKE}}$ *under the DDH assumption in group* $\mathbb{G}$ *in the* $\mathcal{F}_{\mathsf{CRS}}, \mathcal{F}_{\mathsf{RO}}$-*hybrid model.*

Acknowledgments. Anja Lehmann was supported by the European Union's Horizon 2020 research and innovation program under Grant Agreement No. 786725 (OLYMPUS). Tatiana Bradley, Stanislaw Jarecki, and Jiayu Xu were supported by the NSF Cybersecurity Innovation for Cyberinfrastructure (CICI) Grant Award No. ACI-1547435.

A   Concrete PAPKE and PAKE Instantiation Example

Here we show particular instantiations of some of our results, a PAPKE scheme PAPKE-IC-DHIES and a PAKE protocol PAKE-IC-DHIES. PAPKE-IC-DHIES is a particular instantiation of the generic PAPKE-IC scheme of Sect. 4.1 based on the DHIES* PKE by Abdalla et al. [1], and protocol PAKE-IC-DHIES is derived via the PAPKE-2-PAKE compiler of Sect. 3 applied to PAPKE-IC-DHIES.

Concrete Instantiation of PAPKE-IC **Using** DHIES. In Sect. 4.1 we show a generic UC-secure PAPKE scheme that relies on an ideal cipher and a public-key encryption scheme that is both AI-CCA and SROB-CCA-secure. Abdalla et al. [1] show that these properties can be realized by DHIES*, a simple modification of DHIES [2] which excludes zero randomness at encryption, i.e., samples r from

---

Setup: $\mathbb{G}$ is a cyclic group of prime order p with generator g; $\mathsf{IC} = (\mathsf{IC.Enc}, \mathsf{IC.Dec})$ is an Ideal Cipher over $\mathbb{G}$ with key space $\{0,1\}^*$; $\mathsf{AE} = (\mathsf{AE.Enc}, \mathsf{AE.Dec})$ is an authenticated encryption with key space $\{0,1\}^\kappa$; $\mathsf{H} : \mathbb{G} \to \{0,1\}^\kappa$ is a collision-resistant hash function.

PAPKE.KGen(κ, pwd):

- Pick $x \leftarrow_{\mathsf{R}} \mathbb{Z}_p$, compute $y \leftarrow g^x$ and $apk \leftarrow \mathsf{IC.Enc}(pwd, y)$.
- Assign $sk \leftarrow x$ and output (sk, apk).

PAPKE.Enc(apk, pwd', m):

- Compute $y \leftarrow \mathsf{IC.Dec}(pwd, apk)$, $r \leftarrow_{\mathsf{R}} \mathbb{Z}_p^*$, $k \leftarrow \mathsf{H}(y^r)$, $c_1 \leftarrow g^r, c_2 \leftarrow \mathsf{AE.Enc}(k, m)$.
- Output $c = (c_1, c_2)$.

PAPKE.Dec(sk, c'):

- Parse $(c_1, c_2) \leftarrow c$, compute $k \leftarrow \mathsf{H}(c_1^x)$.
- If $c_1 = 1$ set $m \leftarrow \bot$ otherwise set $m \leftarrow \mathsf{AE.Dec}(k, c_2)$, and output m.

Fig. 4. Concrete PAPKE instantiation PAPKE-IC-DHIES.

$\mathbb{Z}_p^*$ instead of $\mathbb{Z}_p$, and rejects ciphertexts that have 1 as first component. We specify DHIES* below relying on authenticated encryption AE, a hash function H and a cyclic group $(\mathbb{G}, p, g)$ of prime order p. Scheme PAPKE-IC-DHIES in Fig. 4 is a (semi) concrete instantiation of PAPKE-IC using DHIES*, which uses 2 exponentiations for encryption and 1 for decryption, as well as an ideal cipher over group $\mathbb{G}$ and hashing onto $\mathbb{G}$.

DHIES*.KGen(κ): $x \leftarrow_{\mathsf{R}} \mathbb{Z}_p$, $y \leftarrow g^x$, set $pk \leftarrow y, sk \leftarrow x$ and return (pk, sk)

DHIES*.Enc(pk, m): parse $pk = y$, get $r \leftarrow_{\mathsf{R}} \mathbb{Z}_p^*$, $k \leftarrow \mathsf{H}(y^r)$, $c_1 \leftarrow g^r$, $c_2 \leftarrow \mathsf{AE.Enc}(k, m)$ and return $c = (c_1, c_2)$.

DHIES*.Dec(sk, c): parse $c = (c_1, c_2)$ and $sk = x$, get $k \leftarrow \mathsf{H}(c_1^x)$. If $c_1 = 1$ output $m \leftarrow \bot$ and $m \leftarrow \mathsf{AE.Dec}(k, c_2)$ else.

Concrete PAKE Protocols. We specify an example of a concrete UC PAKE instantiation obtained by applying the generic PAPKE-2-PAKE compiler shown in Fig. 1 to the PAPKE scheme PAPKE-IC-DHIES shown in Fig. 4. In [12] we also specify PAKE protocol PAKE-FO implied by our second PAPKE construction, PAPKE-FO of Fig. 3. To the best of our knowledge, these are the first two-round UC-secure PAKE's which rely on standard groups, i.e. no bilinear maps, but resort to the IC and/or ROM model to achieve practical efficiency. Concretely, PAKE-IC-DHIES uses from 2 exponentiations per party and PAKE-FO uses 4 (multi-)exponentiations for one party and 2 for the other. This *almost* matches the efficiency and assumptions used by two-round PAKE's which were shown secure under only game-based security notions, e.g. [4,7,11], and it reduces from 3 to 2 the rounds of previously known UC PAKE secure under comparable assumptions of Abdalla et al. [3].

Protocol PAKE-IC-DHIES shown in Fig. 5 requires the same setup as the PAPKE scheme PAPKE-IC-DHIES in Fig. 4, i.e. $\mathbb{G}$ is a cyclic group of prime order p with generator g, $\mathsf{IC} = (\mathsf{IC.Enc}, \mathsf{IC.Dec})$ is an ideal cipher over group $\mathbb{G}$ with key space $\{0,1\}^*$, $\mathsf{AE} = (\mathsf{AE.Enc}, \mathsf{AE.Dec})$ is an authenticated encryption with key space $\{0,1\}^\kappa$, and $\mathsf{H} : \mathbb{G} \to \{0,1\}^\kappa$ is a collision-resistant hash. The following security statement for PAKE-IC-DHIES follows from Theorems 1, 2, and the security properties of DHIES* [1]:

Corollary 1. *The* PAKE-IC-DHIES *scheme described in Fig. 5 securely realizes* $\mathcal{F}_{\mathsf{PAKE}}$ *in the* $\mathcal{F}_{\mathsf{CRS}}, \mathcal{F}_{\mathsf{IC}}$-*hybrid model if the Oracle-Diffie-Hellman assumption is hard for* $\mathbb{G}$, H *is a collision-resistant hash, and* AE *is a secure, strongly unforgeable and collision-resistant authenticated encryption scheme.*

Party $\mathcal{P}_i$, upon input (NEWSESSION, $sid', \mathcal{P}_i, \mathcal{P}_j, pwd$, client):	Party $\mathcal{P}_j$, upon input (NEWSESSION, $sid', \mathcal{P}_j, \mathcal{P}_i, pwd'$, server):
get $x \leftarrow_{\mathrm{R}} \mathbb{Z}_p$, $y \leftarrow g^x$ set $apk \leftarrow \mathsf{IC.Enc}(pwd, y)$, store $sk \leftarrow x$ $\xrightarrow{\quad sid', apk \quad}$	wait for message with prefix sid' choose $k \leftarrow_{\mathrm{R}} \{0,1\}^\kappa$ get $y \leftarrow \mathsf{IC.Dec}(pwd', apk)$, $r \leftarrow_{\mathrm{R}} \mathbb{Z}_p^*$, $k' \leftarrow \mathsf{H}(y^r)$, $c_1 \leftarrow g^r$, $c_2 \leftarrow \mathsf{AE.Enc}(k', k)$, set $c \leftarrow (c_1, c_2)$ output (NEWKEY, sid', k)
$\xleftarrow{\quad sid', c \quad}$	
parse $c = (c_1, c_2)$, get $k' \leftarrow \mathsf{H}(c_1^x)$ if $c_1 = 1$ set $m \leftarrow \bot$; else $m \leftarrow \mathsf{AE.Dec}(k', c_2)$ if $m \neq \bot$, set $k \leftarrow m$; else $k \leftarrow_{\mathrm{R}} \{0,1\}^\kappa$ output (NEWKEY, sid', k)	

Fig. 5. Two-round PAKE protocol PAKE-IC-DHIES.

References

1. Abdalla, M., Bellare, M., Neven, G.: Robust encryption. Cryptology ePrint Archive, Report 2008/440 (2008). http://eprint.iacr.org/2008/440
2. Abdalla, M., Bellare, M., Rogaway, P.: The oracle diffie-hellman assumptions and an analysis of DHIES. In: Naccache, D. (ed.) CT-RSA 2001. LNCS, vol. 2020, pp. 143–158. Springer, Heidelberg (2001). https://doi.org/10.1007/3-540-45353-9_12
3. Abdalla, M., Catalano, D., Chevalier, C., Pointcheval, D.: Efficient two-party password-based key exchange protocols in the UC framework. In: Malkin, T. (ed.) CT-RSA 2008. LNCS, vol. 4964, pp. 335–351. Springer, Heidelberg (2008). https://doi.org/10.1007/978-3-540-79263-5_22
4. Abdalla, M., Pointcheval, D.: Simple password-based encrypted key exchange protocols. In: Menezes, A. (ed.) CT-RSA 2005. LNCS, vol. 3376, pp. 191–208. Springer, Heidelberg (2005). https://doi.org/10.1007/978-3-540-30574-3_14
5. Abu-Salma, R., Sasse, M.A., Bonneau, J., Danilova, A., Naiakshina, A., Smith, M.: Obstacles to the adoption of secure communication tools. In: 2017 IEEE Symposium on Security and Privacy, pp. 137–153. IEEE Computer Society Press, May 2017

6. Bellare, M., Boldyreva, A., Desai, A., Pointcheval, D.: Key-privacy in public-key encryption. In: Boyd, C. (ed.) ASIACRYPT 2001. LNCS, vol. 2248, pp. 566–582. Springer, Heidelberg (2001). https://doi.org/10.1007/3-540-45682-1_33

7. Bellare, M., Pointcheval, D., Rogaway, P.: Authenticated key exchange secure against dictionary attacks. In: Preneel, B. (ed.) EUROCRYPT 2000. LNCS, vol. 1807, pp. 139–155. Springer, Heidelberg (2000). https://doi.org/10.1007/3-540-45539-6_11

8. Bellovin, S.M., Merritt, M.: Encrypted key exchange: password-based protocols secure against dictionary attacks. In: 1992 IEEE Symposium on Security and Privacy, pp. 72–84. IEEE Computer Society Press, May 1992

9. Bernstein, D.J., Hamburg, M., Krasnova, A., Lange, T.: Elligator: elliptic-curve points indistinguishable from uniform random strings. In: Sadeghi, A.R., Gligor, V.D., Yung, M. (eds.) ACM CCS 2013, pp. 967–980. ACM Press, November 2013

10. Black, J., Rogaway, P.: Ciphers with arbitrary finite domains. In: Preneel, B. (ed.) CT-RSA 2002. LNCS, vol. 2271, pp. 114–130. Springer, Heidelberg (2002). https://doi.org/10.1007/3-540-45760-7_9

11. Boyko, V., MacKenzie, P., Patel, S.: Provably secure password-authenticated key exchange using Diffie-Hellman. In: Preneel, B. (ed.) EUROCRYPT 2000. LNCS, vol. 1807, pp. 156–171. Springer, Heidelberg (2000). https://doi.org/10.1007/3-540-45539-6_12

12. Bradley, T., Camenisch, J., Jarecki, S., Lehmann, A., Neven, G., Xu, J.: Password-authenticated public key encryption. Cryptology ePrint Archive, Report 2019/199 (2019). http://eprint.iacr.org/2019/199

13. Burr, W.E., et al.: Electronic Authentication Guideline. NIST Special Publication, Gaithersburg (2011)

14. Canetti, R.: Universally composable security: a new paradigm for cryptographic protocols. In: 42nd FOCS, pp. 136–145. IEEE Computer Society Press, October 2001

15. Canetti, R., Halevi, S., Katz, J., Lindell, Y., MacKenzie, P.: Universally composable password-based key exchange. In: Cramer, R. (ed.) EUROCRYPT 2005. LNCS, vol. 3494, pp. 404–421. Springer, Heidelberg (2005). https://doi.org/10.1007/11426639_24

16. Dai, Y., Steinberger, J.: Indifferentiability of 8-round Feistel networks. In: Robshaw, M., Katz, J. (eds.) CRYPTO 2016. LNCS, vol. 9814, pp. 95–120. Springer, Heidelberg (2016). https://doi.org/10.1007/978-3-662-53018-4_4

17. Fujisaki, E., Okamoto, T.: Secure integration of asymmetric and symmetric encryption schemes. In: Wiener, M. (ed.) CRYPTO 1999. LNCS, vol. 1666, pp. 537–554. Springer, Heidelberg (1999). https://doi.org/10.1007/3-540-48405-1_34

18. Guardian: Whatsapp design feature means some encrypted messages could be read by third party (2017). https://www.theguardian.com/technology/2017/jan/13/whatsapp-design-feature-encrypted-messages/

19. Holenstein, T., Künzler, R., Tessaro, S.: The equivalence of the random oracle model and the ideal cipher model, revisited. In: Fortnow, L., Vadhan, S.P. (eds.) 43rd ACM STOC, pp. 89–98. ACM Press, June 2011

20. Huima, A.: The Bubble Babble binary data encoding (2000). http://web.mit.edu/kenta/www/one/bubblebabble/spec/jrtrjwzi/draft-huima-01.txt/

21. Jutla, C.S., Roy, A.: Dual-system simulation-soundness with applications to UC-PAKE and more. In: Iwata, T., Cheon, J.H. (eds.) ASIACRYPT 2015. LNCS, vol. 9452, pp. 630–655. Springer, Heidelberg (2015). https://doi.org/10.1007/978-3-662-48797-6_26

22. Katz, J., Vaikuntanathan, V.: Round-optimal password-based authenticated key exchange. J. Cryptology **26**(4), 714–743 (2013)
23. OpenSSH 5.1 release announcement (2008). https://www.openssh.com/txt/release-5.1/
24. Rivest, R.L., Lampson, B.: SDSI - a simple distributed security infrastructure (1996). http://people.csail.mit.edu/rivest/sdsi10.html/
25. Tan, J., Bauer, L., Bonneau, J., Cranor, L.F., Thomas, J., Ur, B.: Can unicorns help users compare crypto key fingerprints? In: Mark, G., et al. (eds.) CHI Conference on Human Factors in Computing Systems, pp. 3787–3798. ACM (2017)
26. Tufekci, Z.: In response to guardian's irresponsible reporting on whatsapp: a plea for responsible and contextualized reporting on user security (2017). http://technosociology.org/?page_id=1687/
27. Unger, N., et al.: SoK: secure messaging. In: 2015 IEEE Symposium on Security and Privacy, pp. 232–249. IEEE Computer Society Press, May 2015
28. WhatsApp encryption overview: technical white paper (2016). https://www.whatsapp.com/security/WhatsApp-Security-Whitepaper.pdf/

Theory of Cryptographic
Implementations

Public Immunization Against Complete Subversion Without Random Oracles

Giuseppe Ateniese[1], Danilo Francati[1(✉)], Bernardo Magri[2],
and Daniele Venturi[3]

[1] Stevens Institute of Technology, Hoboken, NJ, USA
dfrancat@stevens.edu
[2] Department of Computer Science, Aarhus University, Aarhus, Denmark
[3] Department of Computer Science, Sapienza University of Rome, Rome, Italy

Abstract. We seek constructions of general-purpose immunizers that take arbitrary cryptographic primitives, and transform them into ones that withstand a powerful "malicious but proud" adversary, who attempts to break security by possibly subverting the implementation of *all* algorithms (including the immunizer itself!), while trying not to be detected. This question is motivated by the recent evidence of cryptographic schemes being intentionally weakened, or designed together with hidden backdoors, e.g., with the scope of mass surveillance.

Our main result is a subversion-secure immunizer in the plain model (assuming collision-resistant hashing), that works for a fairly *large class* of *deterministic* primitives, i.e., cryptoschemes where a secret (but *tamperable*) random source is used to generate the keys and the public parameters, whereas all other algorithms are deterministic. The immunizer relies on an additional *independent* source of *public* randomness, which is used to sample a public seed. While the public source is *untamperable*, the subversion of all other algorithms is allowed to depend on it.

Previous work in the area only obtained subversion-secure immunization for very restricted classes of primitives, often in weaker models of subversion and relying on random oracles, or by leveraging a higher number of independent random sources.

1 Introduction

A common trend in modern cryptography is to design cryptographic schemes that come with a proof of security in a well-defined model. The proof is typically by reduction, meaning that violating the security of the scheme implies the existence of an efficient algorithm for solving some well-studied mathematical problem which is believed to be hard (e.g., factoring certain integers, or inverting a one-way function). While having such a security proof is a desirable feature, it is at least as important to make sure that the security model fits reality, as otherwise provably secure schemes are of little use in practice.

B. Magri—The author was supported by the Concordium Blockchain Research Center, Aarhus University, Denmark.

R. H. Deng et al. (Eds.): ACNS 2019, LNCS 11464, pp. 465–485, 2019.
https://doi.org/10.1007/978-3-030-21568-2_23

Unfortunately, security models often make idealized assumptions that are not always fulfilled in the real world. In this paper, we focus on one of those gaps, which is the discrepancy between the *specification* of a cryptographic scheme and its *implementation*. In particular, we consider the extreme case where the implementation is fully adversarial, i.e., the adversary is allowed to subvert or substitute some (or possibly all) algorithms in the original specification, with the purpose of weakening security.

The above scenario recently gained momentum due to the NSA leaks by Edward Snowden [3,18,21], and because of the EC_DUAL PRG[1] incident [9]. These hazards challenge modern cryptographers to design protection mechanisms withstanding subversion and tampering, as it was also highlighted by Phil Rogaway in his 2015 IACR Distinguished Lecture [22].

1.1 Background

To guarantee some form of security in such an adversarial setting, we must put some restrictions on the adversary, as otherwise, it is easy to subvert a cryptographic scheme in a way that becomes insecure (e.g., the subverted scheme could always output the secret key). A natural restriction, which is also inspired by real-world attacks, is to demand that subversion should be *undetectable* by honest users. In other words, the adversary's goal is to tamper with the specification of a cryptographic scheme in such a way that the produced outputs appear indistinguishable from that of a faithful implementation, yet they allow an adversary to break security given some additional pieces of information altogether.

As it turns out, the possibility of such attacks was already uncovered more than twenty years ago by Young and Yung [29,30], who dubbed the field kleptography (a.k.a. "cryptography against cryptography"). At Crypto 2014, Bellare, Paterson, and Rogaway [7] revisited this setting for the concrete case of symmetric encryption. In particular, on the one hand, they showed that it is possible to hide a backdoor in the encryption algorithm of any sufficiently randomized symmetric encryption scheme in such a way that the produced ciphertexts appear indistinguishable from honestly computed ones, yet knowledge of the backdoor allows the adversary to extract the secret key in full; on the other hand, they suggested that deterministic symmetric encryption schemes are secure against all subversion attacks that meet some form of undetectability. Their results were later extended in several ways [6,10], while follow-up work studied similar questions for the case of digital signatures [1], pseudorandom generators [11,12], non-interactive zero knowledge [5], key encapsulation [2], and hash functions [16,25].

Complete Subversion. A common feature of the works above is that only some of the algorithms underlying a given cryptographic scheme are subject to subversion, while the others are assumed to follow the original specification faithfully.

---

[1] The PRG was standardized by NIST in 2006, and later withdrawn in 2014 as it was including a potential backdoor allowing to predict future outputs of the PRG algorithm.

Motivated by this limitation, Russell *et al.* [23] put forward a new framework where the adversary is allowed to subvert *all* algorithms; furthermore, in order to cast undetectability, they introduced a trusted third party, a so-called watchdog, whose goal is to test whether the (possibly subverted) implementation is compliant with the original specification of a cryptographic scheme. In a nutshell, a primitive is subversion secure if there exists a universal watchdog such that either no adversary subverting all algorithms can break the security of the scheme, or, if instead, a subversion attack is successful, the watchdog can detect it with non-negligible probability.

The testing procedure executed by the watchdog is typically performed only once before the (possibly subverted) scheme is used "in the wild". This is known as the *offline* watchdog model. Unfortunately, there are subversion attacks that cannot be detected in an offline fashion. Think, e.g., of a signature scheme where the signature algorithm is identical to the original specification, except that upon input of a special message (that is also hard-wired in the implementation) it compromises security (e.g., it returns the secret key). Now, assuming that the message space is large enough, an offline watchdog has a negligible chance of hitting this hidden trigger, so that the subverted implementation will pass the test phase; yet, the subverted scheme is clearly insecure (in the standard sense of unforgeability against chosen-message attacks).

To cast such attacks, [23] introduces the *online* watchdog model, where the watchdog is essentially allowed to additionally monitor the public interaction between users while the scheme is being used "in the wild" (on top of performing the same offline testing, as before).[2]

Cliptography. The main contribution of Russell *et al.* [23], apart from introducing the model of complete subversion, is to propose a methodology to clip the power of subversion attacks against one-way (trapdoor) permutations. Moreover, they show how to rely on such subversion-secure one-way permutations to derive subversion-secure pseudorandom generators and digital signatures. All their results are in the random oracle model (ROM) of Bellare and Rogaway [8].

In a follow-up paper [24], the same authors show how to obtain public-key chosen-plaintext attack secure encryption resisting complete subversion, again in the ROM. This result (inherently) requires the assumption of two *independent* secret, but tamperable, sources of randomness. They further show that their construction can be instantiated in the standard model (i.e., without random oracles) assuming a super-constant number of *independent* sources.

Open Questions. The works of [23,24] only cover a limited set of cryptographic primitives. Furthermore, the assumption of having a large number of *independent* sources is quite a strong one in practice [28]. Hence, the natural question:

---

[2] One can imagine even more powerful watchdogs monitoring public transcripts while being given the user's secret keys; these are known as *omniscient* watchdogs, but will not be considered in this paper.

Is it possible to protect other primitives against complete subversion, by relying on a single source of secret, but tamperable, randomness, and without assuming random oracles?

1.2 Our Contributions

In this paper, we make significant progress towards answering the above question. Our starting point is a notion of subversion-resistant immunizer Ψ, whose goal is to take an arbitrary primitive Π that is secure w.r.t. some game **G**, and transform it into an immunized primitive $\Pi^* = \Psi(\Pi)$ (for the same cryptographic task) that is secure w.r.t. **G** under complete subversion (in the sense of [23]). The immunizer leverages two *independent* random sources, which we denote by R and S: The source R is an m-bit source which is assumed to be *secret*, but tamperable; the source S is an ℓ-bit source which is assumed to be *public* but *untamperable*. The subversion $\widetilde{\Pi}$ is allowed to depend on the seed s sampled from S and used by the immunized cryptosystem (i.e., first s is sampled and made public, and then the adversary subverts Π^*).

Next, we show how to construct a subversion-secure immunizer tailored to protect *deterministic* primitives Π (secure w.r.t. some game **G**), where the latter means that the original specification of Π consists of a secret random m-bit source R that is sampled in order to generate the public/secret keys of the scheme (via an algorithm K), and the public parameters (via an algorithm P), whereas every other algorithm F_i underlying Π is deterministic. Our immunizer can be instantiated using any collision-resistant hash function, but for certain primitives Π two additional properties are required (more on this later).

Interestingly, our results allow us to protect new cryptographic primitives against complete subversion; examples include: (weak) pseudorandom functions and permutations, message authentication codes, collision/second preimage/pre-image resistant hash functions, deterministic symmetric encryption, and more. Previously to our work, for the primitives mentioned above, it was only known how to obtain security in weaker models of subversion, or with random oracles. We refer the reader to Table 1 for a comparison of our results with state-of-the-art research in the area.

1.3 Techniques

We turn to a high-level description of the techniques behind our results. Let $\Pi = (P, K, R, F_1, \ldots, F_N)$ be a *deterministic* cryptographic scheme. As explained above, algorithms P and K are responsible to generate, respectively, global public parameters ρ and a public/secret key pair (pk, sk) that are taken as input by all other algorithms F_i.[3] Importantly, all algorithms are deterministic, except for P and K which further take as input independent random coins $r \in \{0,1\}^m$ generated by sampling a secret, uniformly random, source R.

---

[3] The string pk might be empty for secret-key primitives.

Table 1. Comparing our constructions with other results for security under subversion. We use the following abbreviations: "Pub" for public, "Sec" for secret, "CPA-SKE/CPA-PKE" for public/secret-key encryption under chosen-plaintext attacks, "PRG" for pseudorandom generator, "OWF/TDF" for one-way (trapdoor) function, "CRH" for collision-resistant hash function, "ROM" for random oracle model, "$\forall$ det-unp" for all deterministic primitives with security w.r.t. an unpredictability game, "$\forall$ det-ind^2" for all deterministic primitives with *square* security w.r.t. an indistinguishability game. The value δ is a small constant. The green color means the source is assumed to be untamperable.

Reference	Primitive	Complete Subversion	# of Sources		Additional Assumptions	Notes
			Pub	Sec		
[7]	CPA-SKE	✗	0	1	–	Unique ciphertexts
[1]	SIG	✗	0	1	–	Unique signatures
[12]	PRG	✗	1	1	ROM	–
[23]	OWF/TDF	✓	0	1	ROM	–
	PRG	✓	0	1	ROM	–
	SIG	✓	0	1	ROM	–
[24]	CPA-PKE	✓	0	2	ROM	–
	CPA-PKE	✓	0	$O(\lambda^\delta/\log\lambda)$	OWF	–
§4	$\forall$ det-unp	✓	1	1	CRH	Public model, Single Instance
	$\forall$ det-ind^2	✓	1	1	CRH	

Our immunization strategy follows the design principle of "decomposition and trusted amalgamation" introduced in [24], by means of hash functions $h_{s_1}, h_{s_2} : \{0,1\}^n \to \{0,1\}^m$ with seeds s_1, s_2 sampled independently from a public source S. More in details, we take $2k \stackrel{\text{def}}{=} 2n/m$ samples $r_1^1, \ldots, r_k^1$ and $r_1^2, \ldots, r_k^2$ from the (possibly subverted) source R, and then we hash the amalgamated strings $r_1 \stackrel{\text{def}}{=} r_1^1 || \cdots || r_k^1$ and $r_2 \stackrel{\text{def}}{=} r_1^2 || \cdots || r_k^2$, respectively, using seeds s_1 and s_2. Finally, the immunized parameter generation algorithm P^* runs $\mathsf{P}(1^\lambda; h_{s_1}(r_1))$, whereas the immunized key generation algorithm K^* runs $\mathsf{K}(1^\lambda; h_{s_2}(r_2))$; the algorithms $(\mathsf{F}_i)_{i \in N}$ are not modified.

Intuitively, the above immunizer tries to sanitize the randomness used for parameters/keys generation in such a way that it is harder for an adversary to generate such values together with a backdoor. We stress that the trick of hashing the random coins for key generation was introduced by [23], although there it was applied only to immunize trapdoor permutations in the ROM, whereas we generalize their approach in such a way that it can be applied to a large class of deterministic primitives (as defined above) in the plain model.

Input Constrained/Unconstrained Games. Recall that for some primitives it is inherently impossible to obtain subversion security in the offline watchdog model. Hence, in our analysis of the above immunizer, we identify a natural property of cryptographic games which allows us to prove security in the *offline* watchdog model; for games not satisfying this property we instead obtain security in the *online* watchdog model.

More in details, a game **G** for some primitive Π consists of an interaction between an adversary A and a challenger C, where C is given oracle access to the algorithms underlying Π in order to answer queries from A, and determine whether A wins the game or not. We call **G** *input constrained*, if the inputs x_i upon which each (deterministic) algorithm F_i is queried during the game are sampled by C via some public distribution D_i that is independent of the adversary. On the other hand, a game that is not input constrained is called *input unconstrained*. Examples of input-constrained games **G** include, e.g., the standard security games for weak pseudorandom functions and one-way permutations. See Sect. 2.2 for more examples.

Security Proof. We prove security of the above immunizer assuming the hash functions h_{s_1}, h_{s_2} are min-entropy condensers for seed-dependent sources. Intuitively, this means that given a uniform ℓ-bit seed s and an n-bit input x coming from a possibly adversarial (but efficiently sampleable) source which might depend on s, and with min-entropy at least k, the output $h_s(x)$ is an m-bit string whose distribution is computationally close to that of an efficiently sampleable source Y with min-entropy at least $m - d$. Such condensers were constructed by Dodis *et al.* [14] using sufficiently strong collision-resistant hash functions.

Fix some primitive Π with input-constrained game **G**. Let us start with the original subversion game, where first the seeds s_1, s_2 are sampled (from the untamperable public source S) and given to the adversary. Then, the attacker specifies a subversion $\widetilde{\Pi}$ for the immunized cryptosystem; hence, the adversary interacts with the challenger, which first samples random strings $r_1 = r_1^1 || \cdots || r_k^1$ and $r_2 = r_1^2 || \cdots || r_k^2$, using the subverted source $\widetilde{R}$ as explained above, and then plays the game **G** for Π, given oracle access to the subverted algorithms $\widetilde{P}, \widetilde{K}, (\widetilde{F}_i)_{i \in [N]}$. By contradiction, assume that there is an adversary A that wins the subversion game, but for which no watchdog W can detect the subversion. We then proceed with a sequence of hybrids, as outlined below:

1. In the 1st hybrid, we replace algorithms $\widetilde{K}$, $\widetilde{P}$, and $\widetilde{F}_i$, with their genuine immunized implementation $K^*(1^\lambda; \cdot) = K(1^\lambda; h_{s_1}(\cdot))$, $P^*(1^\lambda; \cdot) = P(1^\lambda; h_{s_2}(\cdot))$, and $(F_i^*)_{i \in [N]} = (F_i)_{i \in [N]}$. One can show that any distinguisher between the original game and this hybrid can be turned into an efficient offline watchdog W detecting the subversion of A. Thus, the two experiments are computationally close.

2. In the 2nd hybrid, we now generate the public parameters and the keys by running $P(1^\lambda; y_1)$ and $K(1^\lambda; y_2)$, where y_1, y_2 come from the source Y guaranteed by the condenser. To argue indistinguishability, assume for simplicity that the subverted source $\widetilde{R}$ is stateless.[4] First, we show that $\widetilde{R}$ has a nontrivial amount of min-entropy, as otherwise, it is again possible to construct a watchdog W that detects subversion. Second, we argue that since $\widetilde{R}$ is stateless and efficiently sampleable, the strings $r_1 = r_1^1 || \cdots || r_k^1$ and $r_2 = r_1^2 || \cdots || r_k^2$ have min-entropy at least k, so that indistinguishability of the two experiments follows by security of the min-entropy condenser. Note that the last

---

[4] The case of stateful subversion can be reduced to that of stateless subversion if we assume that watchdogs are allowed to reset the state of a tested implementation, a trick due to [23].

step is possible because the public random source S is untamperable, and moreover, the subverted random source $\tilde{\mathsf{R}}$ has non-trivial min-entropy even conditioned on s_1, s_2 sampled from S.

3. Finally, in order to conclude the proof, we exploit the framework of "overcoming weak expectations" by Dodis and Yu [15], who established that for a *large class* of primitives[5] there is a natural trade-off between concrete security and the capacity to withstand a certain entropy deficiency d on the distribution of the key A technical challenge here comes from the fact that this framework only applies to cryptosystems Π where the secret key is uniformly random (and moreover there are no public parameters, or those are generated using uniform randomness). However, we show a similar tradeoff still holds for our specific setting, at least for *single-instance* games where the original random source R is sampled only twice (one for generating the public parameters, and one for sampling the keys).[6]

1.4   Comparison with Russell *et al.* [23, 24]

The trick of splitting a cryptographic algorithm into several sub-components (as we do for P, K, R) was originally introduced in [23], and later refined in [24], under the name of "split-program" methodology. Remarkably, [24] shows that for semantically-secure public-key encryption (an inherently *randomized* primitive) de-coupling the encryption algorithm in a randomized component R (for generating the random coins) and a deterministic component Enc (for computing the ciphertext) is not sufficient to defeat kleptographic attacks. For this reason, they propose a "double-splitting" technique where R is further split into two (tamperable) components $\mathsf{R}_1, \mathsf{R}_2$. In this perspective, our immunization strategy can be thought of as a form of "double splitting", where one of the two sources is assumed to be untamperable but made *public*.

The fact that subversion-secure immunization in the offline watchdog model only works for input-constrained games is reminiscent of a general observation made in [23] stating that an offline watchdog can always detect the subversion of deterministic algorithms with public input distributions (see [23, Lemma 2.3]).

Finally, we would like to stress that our work only covers immunization against complete subversion in the form of algorithm-substitution attacks. In particular, the adversary always specifies an algorithm $\tilde{\mathsf{P}}$ that is used for sampling the public parameters during the security game. Hence, our immunizers do not provide any guarantee in the "adversarially chosen parameters model" considered in [11,12,16,23] (where the adversaries specify the malicious public parameters directly).

---

[5] In particular, the result of [15] applies to all unpredictability primitives, and all indistinguishability primitives meeting so-called *square* security.

[6] Hence, our results do not cover, e.g., multi-instance games where several public parameters and keys might be generated.

1.5 Further Related Work

The original attacks in the kleptographic setting extended previous work on subliminal channels by Simmons [26,27]. This research is also intimately connected to the problem of steganography, whose goal in the context of secret communication is to hide the mere fact that messages are being exchanged [19].

Dodis *et al.* [12], study different immunization strategies for backdoored pseudorandom generators. While they do not consider complete subversion, as the immunizer and the PRG algorithm are assumed to be trusted, they deal with the case where a cryptographic scheme might be subverted "by design" (e.g., because it is standardized with maliciously generated public parameters).

Another line of work suggests defeating subversion attacks employing a cryptographic reverse firewall [1,13,20]. Such a firewall is used to re-randomize the incoming/outgoing messages of a potentially subverted primitive. The firewall itself is assumed to be trusted, and moreover, it relies on a secret, and untamperable, random source. Yet another approach consists of designing self-guarding schemes [17], which allow us to defeat subversion without relying on external parties (such as watchdogs or reverse firewalls), at the price of assuming a secure initialization phase where the primitive to protect was not under subversion.

2 Preliminaries

2.1 Notation

We use the notation $[n] \stackrel{\text{def}}{=} \{1, \ldots, n\}$. Capital letters (such as X) are used to denote random variables, caligraphic letters (such as $\mathcal{X}$) to denote sets, and sans serif letters (such as A) to denote algorithms. All algorithms in this paper are modelled as (possibly interactive) Turing machines.

For a string $x \in \{0,1\}^*$, we let $|x|$ be its length; if $\mathcal{X}$ is a set, $|\mathcal{X}|$ represents the number of elements in $\mathcal{X}$. When x is chosen randomly in $\mathcal{X}$, we write $x \xleftarrow{\$} \mathcal{X}$. If A is an algorithm, we write $y \xleftarrow{\$} A(x)$ to denote a run of A on input x and output y; if A is randomized, then y is a random variable and $A(x; r)$ denotes a run of A on input x and (uniform) randomness r. An algorithm A is *probabilistic polynomial-time* (PPT) if A is randomized and for any input $x, r \in \{0,1\}^*$ the computation of $A(x; r)$ terminates in a polynomial number of steps (in the size of the input). We denote the expected value of a random variable X as $\mathbb{E}[X]$.

Negligible Functions. Throughout the paper, we denote by $\lambda \in \mathbb{N}$ the security parameter. A function $\nu : \mathbb{N} \to [0,1]$ is called *negligible* in the security parameter λ if it vanishes faster than the inverse of any polynomial in λ, i.e. $\nu(\lambda) \in O(1/p(\lambda))$ for all positive polynomials $p(\lambda)$. We sometimes write $\mathsf{negl}(\lambda)$ (resp., $\mathsf{poly}(\lambda)$) to denote all negligiblie functions (resp., polynomial functions) in the security parameter.

Unpredictability and Indistinguishability. The min-entropy of a random variable $X \in \mathcal{X}$ is $\mathbb{H}_\infty(X) \overset{\text{def}}{=} -\log \max_{x \in \mathcal{X}} \mathbb{P}[X = x]$, and intuitively it measures the best chance to predict X (by a computationally unbounded algorithm). For conditional distributions, unpredictability is measured by the conditional average min-entropy $\widetilde{\mathbb{H}}_\infty(X|Y) \overset{\text{def}}{=} -\log \mathbb{E}_y \left[2^{-\mathbb{H}_\infty(X|Y=y)}\right]$.

The statistical distance between two random variables $X \in \mathcal{X}$ and $Y \in \mathcal{Y}$, is defined as $\mathbb{SD}(X; Y) \overset{\text{def}}{=} \frac{1}{2} \sum_{v \in \mathcal{X} \cup \mathcal{Y}} |\mathbb{P}[X = v] - \mathbb{P}[Y = v]|$. Let $X = \{X_\lambda\}_{\lambda \in \mathbb{N}}$ and $Y = \{Y_\lambda\}_{\lambda \in \mathbb{N}}$ be two ensembles of random variables. We say that X and Y are *statistically* indistinguishable, denoted $X \approx_s Y$, as a shortening for $\mathbb{SD}(X_\lambda; Y_\lambda) \in \mathsf{negl}(\lambda)$. Similarly, we say that X and Y are *computationally* indistinguishable, denoted $X \approx_c Y$, if for all PPT distinguishers D we have $\Delta_\mathsf{D}(X_\lambda; Y_\lambda) \in \mathsf{negl}(\lambda)$, where

$$\Delta_\mathsf{D}(X_\lambda; Y_\lambda) \overset{\text{def}}{=} \left|\mathbb{P}\left[\mathsf{D}(1^\lambda, X_\lambda) = 1\right] - \mathbb{P}\left[\mathsf{D}(1^\lambda, Y_\lambda) = 1\right]\right|.$$

An ensemble $X = \{X_\lambda\}_{\lambda \in \mathbb{N}}$ is efficiently sampleable if there exists a PPT algorithm X such that, for each $\lambda \in \mathbb{N}$, the output of $\mathsf{X}(1^\lambda)$ is distributed identically to X_λ.

2.2 Abstract Games

In this work, we deal with abstract cryptographic schemes. Usually, a cryptographic scheme is just a sequence of (possibly randomized) efficient algorithms. However, for our purpose, it will be convenient to specify two special algorithms which are common to any cryptographic scheme; those are the algorithms for generating the public/secret keys and the public parameters (if any). Moreover, our focus will be on *deterministic* schemes (see below).

In this vein, a deterministic cryptographic scheme is a sequence of efficient algorithms $\Pi \overset{\text{def}}{=} (\mathsf{P}, \mathsf{K}, \mathsf{R}, \mathsf{F}_1, \ldots, \mathsf{F}_N)$, where:

- P is a deterministic algorithm that upon input the security parameter 1^λ, and random coins $r \in \mathcal{R}$, outputs public parameters $\rho \in \mathcal{P}$;
- K is a deterministic algorithm that upon input the security parameter 1^λ, and random coins $r \in \mathcal{R}$,[7] outputs a pair of keys $(pk, sk) \in \mathcal{PK} \times \mathcal{SK}$;
- The random coins for (P, K) are obtained via independent calls to algorithm R, which outputs a uniformly random string $r \in \mathcal{R}$ upon each invocation.
- For each $i \in [N]$, algorithm $\mathsf{F}_i : \mathcal{X}_i \to \mathcal{Y}_i$ is deterministic.

We stress that the above syntax is meant to capture both secret-key and public-key primitives; in the former case the public key is simply equal to the empty string $pk = \varepsilon$, and $\mathcal{PK} = \emptyset$. Further, without loss of generality, we assume that all algorithms $\mathsf{F}_1, \ldots, \mathsf{F}_N$ take as input both ρ and (pk, sk); the key generation algorithm also receives ρ as additional input.

---

[7] We assume the amount of randomness to generate the public parameters and the keys is the same; a generalization is straightforward.

Typically, a cryptographic scheme must meet two properties. The first is a *correctness* requirement, which essentially says that Π correctly implements the desired functionality;[8] although we will not define correctness in general, we will later assume Π meets some well-defined correctness property. The second is a *security* requirement, which we model as an interactive process (a.k.a. game) between an adversary and a challenger.

Definition 1 (Cryptographic game). *A cryptographic game $\mathbf{G} \stackrel{def}{=} (\mathsf{C}, \gamma)$ is defined by a challenger C and a constant $\gamma \in [0, 1)$; the game is (implicitly) parametrized by a cryptographic scheme $\Pi = (\mathsf{P}, \mathsf{K}, \mathsf{R}, \mathsf{F}_1, \ldots, \mathsf{F}_N)$, an adversary A, and the security parameter $\lambda \in \mathbb{N}$. In an execution of the game the (efficient) challenger $\mathsf{C}(1^\lambda)$ interacts with the (efficient) adversary $\mathsf{A}(1^\lambda)$, and at the end the challenger outputs a decision bit $d \in \{0, 1\}$. We denote the output of the game as $d \stackrel{\boxplus}{\leftarrow} \langle \mathsf{A}(1^\lambda), \mathsf{C}^{\mathsf{P},\mathsf{K},\mathsf{R},(\mathsf{F}_i)_{i \in [N]}}(1^\lambda)\rangle$; we sometimes also write $(d, \tau) \stackrel{\boxplus}{\leftrightarrows} (\mathsf{A}(1^\lambda) \leftrightarrows \mathsf{C}^{\mathsf{P},\mathsf{K},\mathsf{R},(\mathsf{F}_i)_{i \in [N]}}(1^\lambda))$ for a transcript of the interaction between the adversary and the challenger, C^Π as a shorthand for $\mathsf{C}^{\mathsf{P},\mathsf{K},\mathsf{R},(\mathsf{F}_i)_{i \in [N]}}$, and $\mathbf{G}_{\Pi,\mathsf{A},\mathsf{C}}$ for the random variable corresponding to an execution of game $\mathbf{G}$ with scheme Π, adversary A, and challenger C.*

We say that Π is (t, ϵ)-secure w.r.t. game $\mathbf{G} = (\mathsf{C}, \gamma)$ if the following holds: For all probabilistic attackers A running in time t we have

$$\left| \mathbb{P}\left[d = 1 : \; d \stackrel{\boxplus}{\leftarrow} \langle \mathsf{A}(1^\lambda), \mathsf{C}^{\mathsf{P},\mathsf{K},\mathsf{R},(\mathsf{F}_i)_{i \in [N]}}(1^\lambda)\rangle \right] - \gamma \right| \le \epsilon.$$

Moreover, whenever for all $t \in \mathsf{poly}(\lambda)$ there exists $\epsilon \in \mathsf{negl}(\lambda)$ such that Π is (t, ϵ)-secure w.r.t. game $\mathbf{G}$, we simply say that Π is secure w.r.t. game $\mathbf{G}$.

Input-Constrained Games. An important distinction will be whether the adversary is allowed or not to choose the inputs for the oracle calls made by the challenger. We call games where the latter is not possible *input-constrained* games.

Definition 2 (Input-constrained games). *Let $\Pi = (\mathsf{P}, \mathsf{K}, \mathsf{R}, \mathsf{F}_1, \ldots, \mathsf{F}_N)$ be a cryptographic scheme, and $\mathbf{G} = (\mathsf{C}, \gamma)$ be a security game for Π. We call $\mathbf{G}$ input constrained if the following holds: For each $i \in [N]$, there exists a public and efficiently samplable distribution D_i, such that the challenger chooses the inputs to each oracle F_i by sampling a fresh and independent value from D_i.*

In contrast, games where the above property is not met are called *input unconstrained*. We provide a few clarifying examples below.

One-Way Functions: A one-way function (OWF) is a cryptographic scheme $\Pi = (\mathsf{P}, \mathsf{R}, \mathsf{OWF})$ where $N = 1$, and $\mathsf{OWF} : \mathcal{X} \to \mathcal{Y}$ is a function. Security of Π is characterized by a game $\mathbf{G}^{\mathrm{owf}} = (\mathsf{C}_{\mathrm{owf}}, 0)$ defined as follows: (i) $\mathsf{C}_{\mathrm{owf}}$ picks $\rho = \mathsf{P}(1^\lambda; r)$ (for uniform $r \stackrel{\boxplus}{\leftarrow} \mathsf{R}(1^\lambda)$), samples $x \stackrel{\boxplus}{\leftarrow} \mathcal{X}$, computes

---

[8] For instance, if Π is a signature scheme, correctness demands that honestly computed signatures (w.r.t. a valid secret key) always verify correctly (w.r.t. the corresponding public key).

$y = \mathsf{OWF}(1^\lambda, \rho, x)$, and sends (ρ, y) to the adversary; (ii) A wins iff it returns a values $x' \in \mathcal{X}$ such that $\mathsf{OWF}(1^\lambda, \rho, x') = y$. Notice that $\mathsf{C}_{\mathrm{owf}}$ needs to invoke oracle OWF upon input x' in order to determine the decision bit d, and thus the game is input unconstrained.

One-Way Permutations: A one-way permutation (OWP) is a cryptographic scheme $\Pi = (\mathsf{P}, \mathsf{R}, \mathsf{OWP})$ where $N = 1$, and $\mathsf{OWP} : \mathcal{X} \to \mathcal{X}$ is a permutation. Security of Π is characterized by a game $\mathbf{G}^{\mathrm{owp}} = (\mathsf{C}_{\mathrm{owp}}, 0)$ defined as follows: (i) $\mathsf{C}_{\mathrm{owp}}$ picks $\rho = \mathsf{P}(1^\lambda; r)$ (for uniform $r \xleftarrow{\boxplus} \mathsf{R}(1^\lambda)$), samples $x \xleftarrow{\boxplus} \mathcal{X}$, computes $y = \mathsf{OWP}(1^\lambda, \rho, x)$, and sends (ρ, y) to the adversary; (ii) A wins iff it returns a value $x' \in \mathcal{X}$ such that $x' = x$. Notice that $\mathsf{C}_{\mathrm{owp}}$ does not need to make any oracle call in order to determine the decision bit d, and thus the game is input constrained with public distribution D equal to the uniform distribution over the domain $\mathcal{X}$.

(Weak) Pseudorandom Functions: A pseudorandom function (PRF) is a cryptographic scheme $\Pi = (\mathsf{P}, \mathsf{R}, \mathsf{R}, \mathsf{PRF})$ where $N = 1$, and $\mathsf{PRF} : \mathcal{K} \times \mathcal{X} \to \mathcal{Y}$ is a keyed function. Security of Π is characterized by a game $\mathbf{G}^{\mathrm{prf}} = (\mathsf{C}_{\mathrm{prf}}, 1/2)$ defined as follows: (i) $\mathsf{C}_{\mathrm{prf}}$ samples a bit $b \xleftarrow{\boxplus} \{0,1\}$, picks $\rho = \mathsf{P}(1^\lambda; r_1)$ and $\kappa = \mathsf{K}(1^\lambda, \rho; r_2)$ (where $r_1, r_2 \xleftarrow{\boxplus} \mathsf{R}(1^\lambda)$), and sends ρ to the adversary; (ii) A can ask queries of the form $x \in \mathcal{X}$, upon which $\mathsf{C}_{\mathrm{prf}}$ either replies with $y = \mathsf{PRF}(\kappa, x)$ (in case $b = 0$) or $y \xleftarrow{\boxplus} \mathcal{Y}$ (in case $b = 1$); (iii) A returns a bit b' and wins iff $b = b'$. Notice that $\mathsf{C}_{\mathrm{prf}}$ needs to invoke oracle PRF upon inputs specified by the adversary, and thus the game is input unconstrained.

For *weak* PRFs the game is changed as follows: In step (ii) the queries made by the adversary are empty, and instead $\mathsf{C}_{\mathrm{prf}}$ samples $x \xleftarrow{\boxplus} \mathcal{X}$ and returns (x, y), where y is computed as before. Hence, the game is constrained with public distribution equal to the uniform distribution over $\mathcal{X}$.

Hash Functions: A cryptographic hash function is a cryptographic scheme $\Pi = (\mathsf{P}, \mathsf{R}, \mathsf{Hash})$ where $N = 1$, and $\mathsf{Hash} : \mathcal{X} \to \mathcal{Y}$ is a (typically compressing) function. Security of Π is characterized by a game $\mathbf{G}^{\mathrm{cr}} = (\mathsf{C}_{\mathrm{cr}}, 0)$ defined as follows: (i) C_{cr} picks $\rho = \mathsf{P}(1^\lambda; r)$ (for uniform $r \xleftarrow{\boxplus} \mathsf{R}(1^\lambda)$), and sends ρ to the adversary; (ii) A wins iff it returns a pair of values $(x, x') \in \mathcal{X}^2$ such that $\mathsf{Hash}(1^\lambda, \rho, x) = \mathsf{Hash}(1^\lambda, \rho, x')$ and $x \neq x'$. Notice that C_{cr} needs to invoke oracle Hash upon input x, x' in order to determine the decision bit d, and thus the game is input unconstrained.

Secret-Key Encryption: A deterministic secret-key encryption scheme is a cryptographic scheme $\Pi = (\mathsf{P}, \mathsf{K}, \mathsf{R}, \mathsf{Enc}, \mathsf{Dec})$ where $N = 2$. The (deterministic) encryption algorithm takes as input the secret key $\kappa \in \mathcal{K}$ and a message $m \in \mathcal{M}$, and outputs a ciphertext $c \in \mathcal{C}$. The (deterministic) decryption algorithm takes as input the secret key $\kappa \in \mathcal{K}$ and a ciphertext $c \in \mathcal{C}$, and outputs a message $m \in \mathcal{M}$ (or an error symbol). Security of a deterministic encryption scheme is characterized, e.g., by a game $\mathbf{G}^{\mathrm{cca\text{-}ske}} = (\mathsf{C}_{\mathrm{cca\text{-}ske}}, 1/2)$ specified as follows: (i) $\mathsf{C}_{\mathrm{cca\text{-}ske}}$ picks $\rho = \mathsf{P}(1^\lambda; r_1)$ and $\kappa = \mathsf{K}(1^\lambda, \rho; r_2)$ (where $r_1, r_2 \xleftarrow{\boxplus} \mathsf{R}(1^\lambda)$), and sends ρ to the adversary; (ii) A can specify encryption queries: Upon input a message $m \in \mathcal{M}$, the challenger returns $c = \mathsf{Enc}(1^\lambda, \kappa, m)$; (iii) A can specify decryption queries: Upon input a ciphertext $c \in \mathcal{C}$, the challenger returns $m = \mathsf{Dec}(1^\lambda, \kappa, c)$; (iv) A can specify a challenge query: Upon input $(m_0^*, m_1^*) \in \mathcal{M}^2$, the challenger returns $c^* = \mathsf{Enc}(1^\lambda, \kappa, m_b^*)$ where $b \xleftarrow{\$} \{0,1\}$ is a hidden bit; (v) A can continue to specify encryption/decryption queries, with the restriction that c^* cannot be part of a decryption query; (vi) A returns a bit b' and wins iff $b = b'$. Notice that $\mathsf{C_{cca\text{-}ske}}$ needs to invoke oracles $\mathsf{Enc}, \mathsf{Dec}$ in order to answer encryption/decryption queries, and thus the game is input unconstrained.

Single-Instance Games. As mentioned in the introduction, our results only apply to a sub-class of games where the random source R is sampled only twice, in order to obtain the randomness needed for generating the public parameters and the keys. We call such games *single instance.*

Definition 3 (Single-instance games). *Let* $\Pi = (\mathsf{P}, \mathsf{K}, \mathsf{R}, \mathsf{F}_1, \ldots, \mathsf{F}_N)$ *be a cryptographic scheme, and* $\mathbf{G} = (\mathsf{C}, \gamma)$ *be a security game for* Π. *We call* $\mathbf{G}$ *single instance if during a game execution the challenger invokes the oracle* R *twice, in order to obtain coins* r_1, r_2 *that are later fed to oracles* P, K.

3   Security Model

In this section, we consider a standard-model definition for subversion security, via so-called *immunizers*. An immunizer is a transformation that takes as input a cryptographic scheme (for some task) and transforms it into another scheme for the same task that withstands complete subversion; the immunizer is allowed to leverage a single source of public, but untamperable, randomness. Importantly, we seek security in the standard model (i.e., without random oracles) and in a setting where the immunizer itself is subject to subversion.

We first define our model formally, in Sect. 3.1, for the case of offline watchdogs. Then, in Sect. 3.2, we discuss some definitional choices and compare our definitions with previous work in the area. In the full version, we explain how to extend our framework to the case of online watchdogs.

3.1   Subversion-Secure Immunizers

Let $\Pi = (\mathsf{P}, \mathsf{K}, \mathsf{R}, \mathsf{F}_1, \ldots, \mathsf{F}_N)$ be a cryptographic scheme (as defined in Sect. 2.2), where we assumed that $\mathcal{R} \stackrel{\text{def}}{=} \{0,1\}^m$ (i.e., the source R is a random m-bit source). An immunizer for Π is a transformation $\Psi[\mathcal{H}, \mathsf{S}]$ parameterized by a family of hash functions $\mathcal{H} = \{h_s : \{0,1\}^n \to \{0,1\}^m\}_{s \in \{0,1\}^\ell}$ and a public random source S over $\{0,1\}^\ell$. We write $\Pi^* \stackrel{\text{def}}{=} \Psi(\Pi) \stackrel{\text{def}}{=} (\mathsf{P}^*, \mathsf{K}^*, \mathsf{R}^*, \mathsf{F}_1^*, \ldots, \mathsf{F}_N^*)$ for the specification of the immunized cryptosystem, where:

- $\mathsf{R}^* \equiv \mathsf{R}$ (i.e., the immunized scheme uses the same secret random source as the original scheme);
- P^* and K^* take as input a seed $s \in \{0,1\}^\ell$, and have n-bit random tapes;

Game $\mathbf{G}^{\mathrm{pub}}_{\Pi,\Psi,\mathsf{A},\mathsf{C}}(\lambda)$

$s \xleftarrow{\$} \mathsf{S}(1^\lambda);$

$(\widetilde{\Pi}, \alpha) \xleftarrow{\$} \mathsf{A}_0(1^\lambda, s, \langle \Pi, \Psi \rangle)$

$r_1^1, \ldots, r_k^1, r_1^2, \ldots, r_k^2 \xleftarrow{\$} \widetilde{\mathsf{R}}(1^\lambda);$

$r_1 = r_1^1 || \cdots || r_k^1; r_2 = r_1^2 || \cdots || r_k^2;$

$(d, \widetilde{\tau}) \xleftarrow{\$} (\mathsf{A}_1(1^\lambda, \alpha) \leftrightarrows \mathsf{C}^{\widetilde{\mathsf{P}}(s,\cdot), \widetilde{\mathsf{K}}(s,\cdot), \widetilde{\mathsf{F}}_1(s,\cdot), \ldots, \widetilde{\mathsf{F}}_N(s,\cdot)}(1^\lambda, r_1, r_2))$

return d

Fig. 1. Games defining subversion security of an immunizer $\Psi[\mathcal{H}, \mathsf{S}]$, in the standard model. We use the notation $\mathsf{C}^{\widetilde{\mathsf{P}}(s,\cdot), \widetilde{\mathsf{K}}(s,\cdot), \widetilde{\mathsf{F}}_1(s,\cdot), \ldots, \widetilde{\mathsf{F}}_N(s,\cdot)}(1^\lambda, r_1, r_2)$ to denote a run of the challenger C with random coins r_1, r_2 (that will be used as input of algorithms $\widetilde{\mathsf{P}}, \widetilde{\mathsf{K}}$ during the game).

- $(\mathsf{F}_i^*)_{i \in N}$ take as input a seed $s \in \{0,1\}^\ell$ plus the same inputs as the corresponding algorithm in Π;
- The seed s is obtained by sampling the public random source S (i.e., $s \xleftarrow{\$} \mathsf{S}(1^\lambda)$).

We require an immunizer Ψ to satisfy two properties. The first property is the usual correctness requirement, meaning that the immunized primitive Π^* meets the same correctness condition as that of Π (for every possible choice of the seed for the hash function). The second property is some flavor of security to subversion attacks. More in details, the public source S is assumed to be untamperable and uniform. The adversary A knows a description of the immunizer Ψ and of the original primitive Π, and is allowed to choose $\widetilde{\Pi} = (\widetilde{\mathsf{P}}, \widetilde{\mathsf{K}}, \widetilde{\mathsf{R}}, (\widetilde{\mathsf{F}}_i)_{i \in N})$ depending on the actual seed $s \in \{0,1\}^\ell$ that is sampled from the public source S during a trusted setup phase (which might be run by an external party). Finally, the adversary plays the security game for Π, where the challenger picks $2n/m := 2k$ samples $(r_i^1, r_i^2)_{i \in [k]}$ from $\widetilde{\mathsf{R}}$, amalgamates them into strings $r_1 = r_1^1 || \cdots || r_k^1$ and $r_2 = r_1^2 || \cdots || r_k^2$, and finally interacts with A given black-box access to $\widetilde{\mathsf{P}}(s, \cdot), \widetilde{\mathsf{K}}(s, \cdot), \widetilde{\mathsf{F}}_i(s, \cdot)$ (i.e., to the subversion specified by the adversary using seed $s \in \{0,1\}^\ell$), where r_1 and r_2 are used as inputs for $\widetilde{\mathsf{P}}$ and $\widetilde{\mathsf{K}}$, respectively. Note that $\widetilde{\Pi}$ is completely arbitrary, and thus all algorithms (including the immunizer) are subject to subversion.

We define the advantage of adversary A in the subversion game with primitive Π, immunizer Ψ, and challenger C as:

$$\mathbf{Adv}^{\mathrm{pub}}_{\Pi,\Psi,\mathsf{A},\mathsf{C}}(\lambda) \overset{\mathrm{def}}{=} \left| \mathbb{P}\left[\mathbf{G}^{\mathrm{pub}}_{\Pi,\Psi,\mathsf{A},\mathsf{C}}(\lambda) = 1\right] - \gamma \right|, \tag{1}$$

where the game $\mathbf{G}^{\mathrm{pub}}_{\Pi,\Psi,\mathsf{A},\mathsf{C}}(\lambda)$ is depicted in Fig. 1, and the probability is taken over the randomness of $\widetilde{\mathsf{S}}, \widetilde{\mathsf{R}}, \mathsf{S}, \mathsf{R}$, and over the coin tosses of A.

$$
\begin{array}{ll}
\underline{\text{Game } \mathbf{G}^{\text{det}}_{\Pi,\Psi,\mathsf{W}}(\lambda, \mathsf{aux}, b)} & \underline{\mathbf{G}^{\text{det-on}}_{\Pi,\Psi,\mathsf{W}}(\lambda, \mathsf{aux}, b)} \\[4pt]
\mathsf{aux} \stackrel{\text{def}}{=} (\langle\widetilde{\Pi}\rangle, s) & \mathsf{aux} \stackrel{\text{def}}{=} (\langle\widetilde{\Pi}\rangle, s, \widetilde{\tau}) \\
\textbf{if } b = 0 & \textbf{if } b = 0 \\
\quad \textbf{return } \mathsf{W}^{\widetilde{\Pi}}(1^\lambda, \langle\Pi,\Psi\rangle, s) & \quad \textbf{return } \mathsf{W}^{\widetilde{\Pi}}(1^\lambda, \langle\Pi,\Psi\rangle, s, \widetilde{\tau}) \\
\textbf{elseif } b = 1 & \textbf{elseif } b = 1 \\
\quad \Pi^* = \Psi(\Pi) & \quad \Pi^* = \Psi(\Pi) \\
\quad \textbf{return } \mathsf{W}^{\Pi^*}(1^\lambda, \langle\Pi,\Psi\rangle, s) & \quad \textbf{return return } \mathsf{W}^{\Pi^*}(1^\lambda, \langle\Pi,\Psi\rangle, s, \widetilde{\tau}) \\
\textbf{fi} & \textbf{fi}
\end{array}
$$

Fig. 2. Description of the detection game of an immunizer $\Psi[\mathcal{H}, \mathsf{S}]$ with offline (left) and online (right) watchdogs, in the standard model. The auxiliary information aux is taken from the subversion game (cf. Fig. 1).

Clearly, since the subverted cryptosystem $\widetilde{\Pi}$ specified by the adversary is completely arbitrary, it might be trivial to break security in the above setting. (E.g., consider Π to be a signature scheme and the corresponding subversion to have the signing algorithm return the signing key.) Hence, we need to restrict the adversary in some way. Following previous work, we will consider the adversary to be "malicious-but-proud" in the sense that in order to be successful a subversion attack should also be *undetectable* by the honest user. The latter is formalized by a detection game featuring an efficient algorithm, called the watchdog, whose goal is to detect whether a subversion took place. In particular, given a description of the immunizer and the original scheme, the watchdog has to distinguish the immunized cryptosystem Π^* from the subversion $\widetilde{\Pi}$ used by the adversary in the subversion game. The detect advantage of watchdog W is defined as:[9]

$$
\mathbf{Adv}^{\text{det}}_{\Pi,\Psi,\mathsf{W}}(\lambda) \stackrel{\text{def}}{=} \left| \mathbb{P}\left[\mathbf{G}^{\text{det}}_{\Pi,\Psi,\mathsf{W}}(\lambda, \mathsf{aux}, 0) = 1 \right] - \mathbb{P}\left[\mathbf{G}^{\text{det}}_{\Pi,\Psi,\mathsf{W}}(\lambda, \mathsf{aux}, 1) = 1 \right] \right|, \quad (2)
$$

where the game $\mathbf{G}^{\text{det}}_{\Pi,\Psi,\mathsf{W}}(\lambda, \mathsf{aux}, b)$ is depicted in Fig. 2, and the probability is taken over the randomness of $\widetilde{\mathsf{S}}, \widetilde{\mathsf{R}}, \mathsf{S}, \mathsf{R}$, and over the coin tosses of W; the values in the auxiliary information aux are taken from $\mathbf{G}^{\text{pub}}_{\Pi,\Psi,\mathsf{A},\mathsf{C}}(\lambda)$. Similarly to previous work, we assume that W has rewinding black-box access to its oracles, a feature required in order to detect stateful subversion [23, Remark 2.5].
We are now ready to define subversion security of an immunizer for the offline watchdog.

---

[9] Of course, we could also treat the detection game as an indistinguishability game $\mathbf{G} = (\mathsf{C}, \gamma)$, and thus define the detection advantage as a function of $\gamma = 1/2$. However, we prefer the above formulation in order to be consistent with previous work [23, 24].

Definition 4 (Subversion-resistant immunizer). *Let* $\Pi = (\mathsf{P}, \mathsf{K}, \mathsf{R}, \mathsf{F}_1,$
$\ldots, \mathsf{F}_N)$ *be a cryptographic scheme, and* $\mathbf{G} = (\mathsf{C}, \gamma)$ *be a security game for*
Π. *For a constant* $c^* \geq 1$, *and a family of hash functions* $\mathcal{H} = \{h_s : \{0, 1\}^n \rightarrow$
$\{0, 1\}^m\}_{s \in \{0,1\}^\ell}$, *we say that an immunizer* $\Psi[\mathcal{H}, \mathsf{S}]$ *is* $(t_\mathsf{A}, t_\mathsf{W}, c^*, \epsilon^*)$-*subversion-
resistant with an* offline *watchdog if the following holds: There exists a watchdog*
W *with running time* t_W *such that for all adversaries* A *with running time* t_A *for*
which $\mathbf{Adv}^{\text{pub}}_{\Pi, \Psi, \mathsf{A}, \mathsf{C}}(\lambda) > \epsilon^*$, *we have*

$$\mathbf{Adv}^{\text{det}}_{\Pi, \Psi, \mathsf{W}}(\lambda) \geq \frac{1}{c^*} \cdot \mathbf{Adv}^{\text{pub}}_{\Pi, \Psi, \mathsf{A}, \mathsf{C}}(\lambda).$$

Moreover, for all $s \in \{0, 1\}^\ell$, *we require that the immunized cryptosystem*
with seed s *meets the same correctness requirement as that of* Π.

Remark 1 (On subverting the immunizer). We stress that the subversion $\widetilde{\Pi}$
should be thought of as the subversion of the *immunized* cryptosystem $\Pi^* =$
$\Psi(\Pi)$. In particular, since the subversion is completely arbitrary, the latter means
that the adversary can tamper with (and, in fact, completely bypass) the immunizer itself.

Remark 2 (On including the seed in the auxiliary information). Note that the
seed s sampled during the subversion game is part of the auxiliary information
aux, and later given as additional input to the watchdog in the detection game.

It is easy to see that the latter is necessary. Consider, for instance, a signature
scheme $\Pi = (\mathsf{P}, \mathsf{K}, \mathsf{R}, \mathsf{Sign}, \mathsf{Vrfy})$, and let $\Pi^* = (\mathsf{P}^*, \mathsf{K}^*, \mathsf{R}^*, \mathsf{Sign}^*, \mathsf{Vrfy}^*) = \Psi(\Pi)$
be the immunized version of Π. Since the subversion $\widetilde{\Pi}$ is allowed to depend on
the seed s, the adversary could instruct $\widetilde{\mathsf{K}}$ to output a fixed verification/signature
key pair $(\overline{vk}, \overline{sk})$, known to the adversary, whenever $\widetilde{\mathsf{K}}$ is run upon input s. Now,
if the watchdog W would not be given as input the actual seed s, the above
attack would be undetectable, as W has only a negligible chance of hitting the
seed s while sampling the source S.

3.2 Discussion

On rough terms, Definition 4 says the following. There exists a universal (efficient) watchdog algorithm such that for any adversary that has advantage at
least ϵ^* in the subversion game (cf. Eq. (1)), the probability that the watchdog detects the subversion (cf. Eq. (2)) is at least equal to the advantage of the
adversary in the subversion game divided by some positive constant $c^* \geq 1$.

We observe that there could be a substantial gap between the value of ϵ^* and
the actual advantage of an adversary in the subversion game. In practice, we
would like to obtain Definition 4 for small ϵ^*, c^*, such that either the advantage
in the subversion game is smaller than ϵ^*, or the advantage in the detection
game has a similar magnitude as that in the subversion game (which might be
much larger than ϵ^*).

Looking ahead, the choice to state security of immunizers in the style of concrete security will allow us to lower bound the level of unpredictability in the subverted random source $\widetilde{R}$ with a concrete (rather than asymptotic) value, a feature that will be exploited by our immunizer. One might wonder why Definition 4 considers only a single parameter ϵ^*, instead of having two distinct parameters (i.e., one parameter, say ϵ^*, for the advantage of A in breaking the scheme, and another parameter, say δ^*, for the advantage of W in detecting a subversion). While this might seem like a natural way of phrasing concrete security, it is problematic since such a definition conveys information about a single point over the range of values $\epsilon^*, \delta^* \in [0, 1]$. A similar issue was already observed in [10], who also suggested the approach of relating the advantage in the two games.

4   The Immunizer

4.1   Ingredients: Seed-Dependent Randomness Condensers

We recall the notion of seed-dependent randomness condenser [14]. Intuitively, this corresponds to a family of hash functions indexed by an ℓ-bit seed, and mapping n into m bits. The security guarantee is that when the seed s is uniform, and the input x comes from an adversarial, efficiently sampleable, source which might depend on s, and with min-entropy at least k, the output of the hash function has at least $m - d$ bits of min-entropy, for deficiency parameter $d \geq 1$.

Definition 5 (Seed-dependent condenser). *Let* $\mathcal{G} \overset{def}{=} \{g_s : \{0,1\}^n \to \{0,1\}^m\}_{s \in \{0,1\}^\ell}$ *be a family of efficiently computable functions. We say that* $\mathcal{G}$ *is a family of* $(\frac{k}{n} \to \frac{m-d}{m}, t, \epsilon)$*-seed-dependent condensers if for all probabilistic adversaries* A *running in time* t *who take a seed* $s \xleftarrow{\$} \{0,1\}^\ell$ *and output (using more coins) a distribution* $X \xleftarrow{\$} A(s)$ *of entropy* $\widetilde{\mathbb{H}}_\infty(X|S) \geq k$, *the joint distribution* $(S, g_S(X))$ *is* ϵ*-close to some* (S, Y), *where* $\widetilde{\mathbb{H}}_\infty(Y|S) \geq m - d$ *and* S *is uniform over* $\{0,1\}^\ell$.

4.2   Immunizer Description

We refer the reader to Fig. 3 for a formal description of our immunizer, where we assumed that $\mathcal{R} \overset{def}{=} \{0,1\}^m$. Roughly, the immunizer sanitizes the random coins used to generate the public parameters ρ and the public/secret keys (pk, sk) by first sampling $(r_i^1, r_i^2)_{i \in [k]} \xleftarrow{\$} R(1^\lambda)$ and amalgamating $r_1 = r_1^1 || \cdots || r_k^1$ and $r_2 = r_1^2 || \cdots || r_k^2$, and then using, respectively, $h_{s_1}(r_1)$ and $h_{s_2}(r_2)$ as random coins for P and K, where the seeds $s_1, s_2 \in \{0,1\}^\ell$ are sampled using the public source S. All other algorithms are unchanged.

Subversion-Resistant Immunizer $\Psi[\mathcal{H}, \mathsf{S}]$:

Let $\Pi = (\mathsf{P}, \mathsf{K}, \mathsf{R}, \mathsf{F}_1, \ldots, \mathsf{F}_N)$ be a cryptographic scheme, and define $\Pi^* \stackrel{\text{def}}{=} \Psi(\Pi) \stackrel{\text{def}}{=} (\mathsf{P}^*, \mathsf{K}^*, \mathsf{R}^*, \mathsf{F}_1^*, \ldots, \mathsf{F}_N^*)$ as follows.

- Algorithm P^*: Upon input $(1^\lambda, s_1, r_1)$, return $\rho = \mathsf{P}(1^\lambda; h_{s_1}(r_1))$.
- Algorithm R^*: Upon input 1^λ, return r such that $r \stackrel{\$}{\leftarrow} \mathsf{R}(1^\lambda)$.
- Algorithm K^*: Upon input $(1^\lambda, s_2, \rho, r_2)$, return $(pk, sk) = \mathsf{K}(1^\lambda, \rho; h_{s_2}(r_2))$.
- Algorithm F_i^* (for $i \in [N]$): Upon input $(1^\lambda, \rho, (pk, sk), x)$, return $y = \mathsf{F}_i(1^\lambda, \rho, (pk, sk), x)$.

Fig. 3. Description of our subversion-resistant immunizer; the seeds s_1, s_2 are sampled from the public source S, and correspond to hash functions $h_{s_1}, h_{s_2} \in \mathcal{H}$ mapping n-bit strings into m-bit strings.

4.3   Security Analysis

Here, we analyze the security of the immunizer described in Fig. 3. For input-constrained games, we obtain the following result whose proof appears in the full version. An analogous statement holds for input-unconstrained games, in the online watchdog model.

Theorem 1. *Let $\Pi = (\mathsf{P}, \mathsf{K}, \mathsf{R}, \mathsf{F}_1, \ldots, \mathsf{F}_N)$ be a deterministic cryptographic scheme, with $\mathcal{R} = \{0,1\}^m$, and consider any input-constrained, single-instance game $\mathbf{G} = (\mathsf{C}, \gamma)$ for Π. Then, for any $n, c^* > 4$, the immunizer $\Psi[\mathcal{G}, \mathsf{S}]$ of Fig. 3 is $(t_\mathsf{A}, t_\mathsf{W}, c^*, \epsilon^*)$-subversion-resistant with an offline watchdog, as long as $\mathcal{G} \stackrel{\text{def}}{=} \{g_s : \{0,1\}^n \to \{0,1\}^m\}_{s \in \{0,1\}^\ell}$ is a family of $(\frac{k}{n} \to \frac{m-d}{m}, t_{\text{cond}}, \epsilon_{\text{cond}})$-seed-dependent condensers and Π is either (t, ϵ)-secure w.r.t. game $\mathbf{G}$ (in case of unpredictability games) or (t, ϵ)-square-secure w.r.t. game $\mathbf{G}$ (in case of indistinguishability games), for parameters $t_{\text{cond}}, t, t_\mathsf{W} \approx t_\mathsf{A}$, and*

$$\epsilon \leq \begin{cases} \frac{c^*-1}{c^*} \cdot \frac{\epsilon^*}{2^{2d}} - \frac{2\epsilon_{\text{cond}}}{2^{2d}} & \text{if } \mathbf{G} \text{ is an unpredictability game} \\ \left(\frac{c^*-1}{c^*} \cdot \epsilon^* - 2\epsilon_{\text{cond}}\right)^2 \cdot \frac{1}{2^{2d}} & \text{if } \mathbf{G} \text{ is an indistinguishability game.} \end{cases}$$

Remark 3. Looking ahead, the reason for which Theorem 1 does not work for all deterministic primitives is that its proof crucially relies on the "overcoming weak expectations" framework. In particular, for single-instance indistinguishability games, this theorem requires square security, and it is well known that some primitives such as pseudorandom generators and pseudorandom functions do not have good square security [4,15].

Remark 4. The fact that our immunizer samples $2k$ times from the source R does *not* contradict the assumption that $\mathbf{G}$ is a single-instance game, as the latter condition only concerns the game $\mathbf{G}$ for the original primitive Π.

One can also show that the limitation of Remark 3 is inherent, in the sense that our immunizer is might be insecure for primitives that are not square friendly. Take, for instance, any PRG $\Pi = (\mathsf{R}, \mathsf{K}, \mathsf{PRG})$, where $\mathsf{K}(1^\lambda; r) = r$ outputs directly a seed sampled from the secret source R, and $\mathsf{PRG}(1^\lambda, r)$ stretches the seed to a pseudorandom output. Let $\Pi^* = (\mathsf{R}^*, \mathsf{K}^*, \mathsf{PRG}^*) = \Psi(\Pi)$ be the immunized version of Π. Now, consider the attacker $\mathsf{A}(s)$ that plays the subversion game by specifying the subversion $\widetilde{\Pi}$ where:

- $\widetilde{\mathsf{K}}$ and $\widetilde{\mathsf{PRG}}$ are unchanged (i.e., $\widetilde{\mathsf{K}} \equiv \mathsf{K}^*$, and $\widetilde{\mathsf{PRG}} \equiv \mathsf{PRG}^*$);
- $\widetilde{\mathsf{R}}$ embeds a key κ for a pseudorandom function PRF with one-bit output, and performs the following rejection-sampling procedure:
  - Sample a random r;
  - If $\mathsf{PRF}(1^\lambda, \kappa, y) = 1$, where $\mathsf{PRG}(h_s(r)) = y$, return r;
  - Else, sample a fresh r and start again.

Intuitively, the above subversion allows A to win the subversion game by simply checking whether $\mathsf{PRF}(1^\lambda, \kappa, y) = 1$, where y is the challenge. Moreover, this attack is undetectable as a watchdog not knowing the key κ has a negligible advantage in distinguishing $\widetilde{\mathsf{R}}$ from R^* (by the security of the pseudorandom function). Note that the above attack requires the adversary to choose the subversion depending on the seed.

Instantiating the Immunizer. When instantiating seed-dependent randomness condensers with state-of-the-art constructions [14,15], we obtain the following parameters.

Corollary 1. *For any cryptographic primitive Π that is either* $(\mathsf{poly}(\lambda),, \mathsf{negl}(\lambda))$-*secure (in case of unpredictability games) or* $(\mathsf{poly}(\lambda), \mathsf{negl}(\lambda))$-*square-secure (in case of indistinguishability games) w.r.t. an input-constrained, single-instance game* $\mathbf{G}$, *there exists an immunizer for Π that is* $(\mathsf{poly}(\lambda), \mathsf{poly}(\lambda), 5, \mathsf{negl}(\lambda))$-*subversion-resistant for the* pub-*model with an offline watchdog, with parameters $n, m, \ell \in \omega(\log(\lambda))$.*

Proof. By choosing $t, t_\mathsf{A}, t_\mathsf{W} \in \mathsf{poly}(\lambda)$, $\epsilon, \epsilon^* \in \mathsf{negl}(\lambda)$, $c^* = 5$, and setting $n \in \omega(\log(\lambda))$ in Theorem 1, we need a family of seed-dependent randomness condensers that achieves $t_{\mathrm{cond}} \in \mathsf{poly}(\lambda)$, $\epsilon_{\mathrm{cond}} \in \mathsf{negl}(\lambda)$, $k \in \omega(\log(\lambda))$, and entropy deficiency $d \in O(\log(\lambda))$.

Dodis, Ristenpart, and Vadhan [14] (see also [15]) have shown that any $(\mathsf{poly}(\lambda), \mathsf{poly}(\lambda)/2^m)$-collision-resistant family of hash functions directly yields such a family of condensers. The statement follows. □

5   Conclusions

We have shown how to immunize arbitrary *deterministic* cryptographic primitives against complete subversion, meaning that the adversary is allowed to tamper with all the underlying algorithms, and with the immunizer itself. In the random oracle model, there is a simple immunizer that relies on a single secret, but tamperable, source of randomness [23,24]. In the standard model, instead, we need to assume an additional independent public, and in some case untamperable, random source.

Open problems include, e.g., finding better immunizers, both in terms of computational assumptions and/or the number of assumed trusted random sources. Also, exploring alternative approaches to achieve subversion security in the plain model for larger classes of cryptographic schemes (e.g., randomized ones), while still relying on $O(1)$ independent random sources, is an interesting direction for future research.

References

1. Ateniese, G., Magri, B., Venturi, D.: Subversion-resilient signature schemes. In: CCS, pp. 364–375 (2015)
2. Auerbach, B., Bellare, M., Kiltz, E.: Public-key encryption resistant to parameter subversion and its realization from efficiently-embeddable groups. In: Abdalla, M., Dahab, R. (eds.) PKC 2018. LNCS, vol. 10769, pp. 348–377. Springer, Cham (2018). https://doi.org/10.1007/978-3-319-76578-5_12
3. Ball, J., Borger, J., Greenwald, G.: Revealed: how US and UK spy agencies defeat internet privacy and security. Guardian Weekly, September 2013
4. Barak, B., et al.: Leftover hash lemma, revisited. In: Rogaway, P. (ed.) CRYPTO 2011. LNCS, vol. 6841, pp. 1–20. Springer, Heidelberg (2011). https://doi.org/10.1007/978-3-642-22792-9_1
5. Bellare, M., Fuchsbauer, G., Scafuro, A.: NIZKs with an untrusted CRS: security in the face of parameter subversion. In: Cheon, J.H., Takagi, T. (eds.) ASIACRYPT 2016. LNCS, vol. 10032, pp. 777–804. Springer, Heidelberg (2016). https://doi.org/10.1007/978-3-662-53890-6_26
6. Bellare, M., Jaeger, J., Kane, D.: Mass-surveillance without the state: strongly undetectable algorithm-substitution attacks. In: CCS, pp. 1431–1440 (2015)
7. Bellare, M., Paterson, K.G., Rogaway, P.: Security of symmetric encryption against mass surveillance. In: Garay, J.A., Gennaro, R. (eds.) CRYPTO 2014. LNCS, vol. 8616, pp. 1–19. Springer, Heidelberg (2014). https://doi.org/10.1007/978-3-662-44371-2_1
8. Bellare, M., Rogaway, P.: Random oracles are practical: a paradigm for designing efficient protocols. In: CCS, pp. 62–73 (1993)
9. Checkoway, S., et al.: On the practical exploitability of dual EC in TLS implementations. In: USENIX Security Symposium, pp. 319–335 (2014)
10. Degabriele, J.P., Farshim, P., Poettering, B.: A more cautious approach to security against mass surveillance. In: Leander, G. (ed.) FSE 2015. LNCS, vol. 9054, pp. 579–598. Springer, Heidelberg (2015). https://doi.org/10.1007/978-3-662-48116-5_28
11. Degabriele, J.P., Paterson, K.G., Schuldt, J.C.N., Woodage, J.: Backdoors in pseudorandom number generators: possibility and impossibility results. In: Robshaw, M., Katz, J. (eds.) CRYPTO 2016. LNCS, vol. 9814, pp. 403–432. Springer, Heidelberg (2016). https://doi.org/10.1007/978-3-662-53018-4_15

12. Dodis, Y., Ganesh, C., Golovnev, A., Juels, A., Ristenpart, T.: A formal treatment of backdoored pseudorandom generators. In: Oswald, E., Fischlin, M. (eds.) EUROCRYPT 2015. LNCS, vol. 9056, pp. 101–126. Springer, Heidelberg (2015). https://doi.org/10.1007/978-3-662-46800-5_5

13. Dodis, Y., Mironov, I., Stephens-Davidowitz, N.: Message transmission with reverse firewalls - secure communication on corrupted machines. In: Robshaw, M., Katz, J. (eds.) CRYPTO 2016. LNCS, vol. 9814, pp. 341–372. Springer, Heidelberg (2016). https://doi.org/10.1007/978-3-662-53018-4_13

14. Dodis, Y., Ristenpart, T., Vadhan, S.P.: Randomness condensers for efficiently samplable, seed-dependent sources. In: Cramer, R. (ed.) TCC 2012. LNCS, vol. 7194, pp. 618–635. Springer, Heidelberg (2012). https://doi.org/10.1007/978-3-642-28914-9_35

15. Dodis, Y., Yu, Y.: Overcoming weak expectations. In: Sahai, A. (ed.) TCC 2013. LNCS, vol. 7785, pp. 1–22. Springer, Heidelberg (2013). https://doi.org/10.1007/978-3-642-36594-2_1

16. Fischlin, M., Janson, C., Mazaheri, S.: Backdoored hash functions: immunizing HMAC and HKDF. In: IEEE Computer Security Foundations Symposium, pp. 105–118 (2018)

17. Fischlin, M., Mazaheri, S.: Self-guarding cryptographic protocols against algorithm substitution attacks. In: IEEE Computer Security Foundations Symposium, pp. 76–90 (2018)

18. Greenwald, G.: No place to hide: Edward Snowden, the NSA, and the U.S. surveillance state. Metropolitan Books, May 2014

19. Hopper, N.J., von Ahn, L., Langford, J.: Provably secure steganography. IEEE Trans. Comput. **58**(5), 662–676 (2009)

20. Mironov, I., Stephens-Davidowitz, N.: Cryptographic reverse firewalls. In: Oswald, E., Fischlin, M. (eds.) EUROCRYPT 2015. LNCS, vol. 9057, pp. 657–686. Springer, Heidelberg (2015). https://doi.org/10.1007/978-3-662-46803-6_22

21. Perlroth, N., Larson, J., Shane, S.: N.S.A. able to foil basic safeguards of privacy on web. The New York Times, September 2013

22. Rogaway, P.: The moral character of cryptographic work. IACR Cryptology ePrint Archive 2015, 1162 (2015). http://eprint.iacr.org/2015/1162

23. Russell, A., Tang, Q., Yung, M., Zhou, H.-S.: Cliptography: clipping the power of kleptographic attacks. In: Cheon, J.H., Takagi, T. (eds.) ASIACRYPT 2016. LNCS, vol. 10032, pp. 34–64. Springer, Heidelberg (2016). https://doi.org/10.1007/978-3-662-53890-6_2

24. Russell, A., Tang, Q., Yung, M., Zhou, H.: Generic semantic security against a kleptographic adversary. In: ACM CCS, pp. 907–922 (2017)

25. Russell, A., Tang, Q., Yung, M., Zhou, H.-S.: Correcting subverted random oracles. In: Shacham, H., Boldyreva, A. (eds.) CRYPTO 2018. LNCS, vol. 10992, pp. 241–271. Springer, Cham (2018). https://doi.org/10.1007/978-3-319-96881-0_9

26. Simmons, G.J.: The Prisoners' problem and the subliminal channel. In: Chaum, D. (ed.) Advances in Cryptology, pp. 51–67. Springer, Boston (1984). https://doi.org/10.1007/978-1-4684-4730-9_5

27. Simmons, G.J.: The subliminal channel and digital signatures. In: Beth, T., Cot, N., Ingemarsson, I. (eds.) EUROCRYPT 1984. LNCS, vol. 209, pp. 364–378. Springer, Heidelberg (1985). https://doi.org/10.1007/3-540-39757-4_25

28. Trevisan, L., Vadhan, S.P.: Extracting randomness from samplable distributions. In: FOCS, pp. 32–42 (2000)

29. Young, A.L., Yung, M.: The dark side of "Black-Box" cryptography or: should we trust capstone? In: Koblitz, N. (ed.) CRYPTO 1996. LNCS, vol. 1109, pp. 89–103. Springer, Heidelberg (1996). https://doi.org/10.1007/3-540-68697-5_8

30. Young, A., Yung, M.: Kleptography: using cryptography against cryptography. In: Fumy, W. (ed.) EUROCRYPT 1997. LNCS, vol. 1233, pp. 62–74. Springer, Heidelberg (1997). https://doi.org/10.1007/3-540-69053-0_6

Strong Leakage and Tamper-Resilient PKE from Refined Hash Proof System

Shi-Feng Sun[1,3], Dawu Gu[1(✉)], Man Ho Au[2], Shuai Han[1], Yu Yu[1], and Joseph Liu[3]

[1] Shanghai Jiao Tong University, Shanghai, China
dwgu@sjtu.edu.cn
[2] Hong Kong Polytechnic University, Hung Hom, China
[3] Monash University, Melbourne, Australia

Abstract. We revisit the problem of constructing public key encryption (PKE) secure against both key-leakage and tampering attacks. First, we present an enhanced security against both kinds of attacks, namely *strong leakage and tamper-resilient chosen-ciphertext* (sLTR-CCA) security, which imposes only minimal restrictions on the adversary's queries and thus captures the capability of the adversary in a more reasonable way. Then, we propose a generic paradigm achieving this security on the basis of a refined hash proof system (HPS) called *public-key-malleable HPS*. The paradigm can not only tolerate a large amount of bounded key-leakage, but also resist an arbitrary polynomial of restricted tampering attacks, even depending on the challenge phase. Moreover, the paradigm with slight adaptations can also be proven sLTR-CCA secure with respect to subexponentially hard auxiliary-input leakage. In addition, we instantiate our paradigm under certain standard number-theoretic assumptions, and thus, to our best knowledge, obtain the first efficient PKE schemes possessing the strong bounded/auxiliary-input leakage and tamper-resilient chosen-ciphertext security in the standard model.

Keywords: Public key encryption · Hash proof system ·
Chosen-ciphertext security · Leakage attack · Tampering attack

1 Introduction

Traditionally, cryptographic algorithms are always proven secure under the assumption that the randomness and secrets involved are completely hidden from adversaries. In reality, however, various kinds of physical attacks demonstrated that attackers usually managed to extract partial secret information by observing the physical characteristics of executing cryptographic devices.

In recent years, motivated by the proliferation of key-leakage attacks such as [24,30], a line of research usually called leakage-resilient cryptography [2,8,9,13, 16,29,33,34,36,37], was initiated with the purpose of designing provably secure

© Springer Nature Switzerland AG 2019
R. H. Deng et al. (Eds.): ACNS 2019, LNCS 11464, pp. 486–506, 2019.
https://doi.org/10.1007/978-3-030-21568-2_24

cryptographic primitives against adversaries that can obtain secret information via such kind of attacks. Generally, key-leakage attacks are captured by a leakage oracle, which enables the adversary to get partial secret information by specifying an efficient leakage function chosen by himself, and the property of leakage-resilience stipulates that the cryptographic primitives remain secure even for the adversary that has access to the leakage oracle. Thus, some restrictions should be imposed on the leakage functions, such that it is hard for the adversary to recover the whole secret key. According to the constrains on leakage function f, the main types of leakage we are interested in this work are (1) *bounded-memory leakage* [1], where f is required to be efficiently computable and with output length much less than $|sk|$, and (2) *auxiliary-input leakage* [14], where f is stipulated to be sufficiently hard to invert for all efficient algorithms, but with no limitation on its output. We note that the latter can be seen as a generalization of the former, which captures a larger class of key-leakage attacks.

Although leakage-resilient cryptography provides a promising way for protecting against key-leakage attacks, they are still vulnerable to fault injection and memory tampering attacks [6,22]. The theoretical treatment of such attacks was initiated by Bellare et al. [4], and then a series of research [3,5,32,35,39,40] was conducted for designing various provably secure cryptographic primitives against this kind of attacks. Similarly, tampering attacks are captured by a family of efficiently computable functions $\mathcal{T} : \mathcal{SK} \mapsto \mathcal{SK}$, and the tamper-resilience requires that the cryptographic primitives remain provably secure even for the adversary that can learn partial secret information by observing the output of cryptographic devices executed under a transformed secret state. Take a signature scheme as an example: the adversary given a target verification key vk can observe the signatures of adaptively chosen messages under not only the original secret key sk but also the related keys $f_t(sk)$, where f_t is the tampering function adaptively chosen by the adversary from $\mathcal{T}$; identical to the standard security, the goal of the adversary is to produce a valid signature on a new message under vk. Obviously, tamper-resilience implies the original standard security.

In light of the fact that physical attacks include key-leakage attacks as well as tampering attacks in the real world, another concerned line of research—starting from the seminal work of Kalai et al. [28]—aims at developing cryptographic systems that resist both kinds of attacks. However, it is not an easy task to design cryptographic algorithms resilient to both key-leakage and tampering attacks. As far as we know, there are only few works [11,19–21,28,31,38] considering how to realize leakage and tamper-resilience at the same time. More details about these works will be given in the following section.

1.1 Related Works

In 2011, Kalai et al. [28] initiated the study of designing public key cryptosystems resilient to both key-leakage and tampering attacks. With the support of *key-update mechanism*, they presented a one-bit-message encryption scheme and a digital signature scheme in the *continuous tampering and leakage (CTL) model*, where the adversary is allowed to continuously issue leakage queries and tampering queries. However, their encryption scheme is only chosen-plaintext attack (CPA) secure, meaning that the adversary is not permitted to observe the effect of tampering on the output of decryption oracle. In addition, they presented a more efficient signature scheme without key-update algorithms in the so-called continuous tampering and bounded leakage (CTBL) model by assuming the existence of a protected *self-destruct*.

Following the above framework, Fujisaki et al. [21] further investigated how to construct chosen-ciphertext attack (CCA) secure PKE in the CTL or CTBL model. In particular, they showed that the encryption scheme in [34] can be proven CCA secure against continuous tampering and bounded leakage attacks (CTBL-CCA secure) under the *self-destructive* mechanism. Moreover, they presented a new PKE scheme with a *key-update algorithm*, which is proven CCA secure against continuous tampering and leakage attacks (CTL-CCA secure).

Different from the previous approach, Damgård et al. [11] introduced an alternative path to achieve security against both key-leakage and tampering attacks with neither self-destruction nor key-update mechanism. Note that, as observed by Gennaro et al. [23], it is *impossible* to achieve security against any polynomial number of *arbitrary* (and efficiently computable) tampering attacks without making further assumptions (such as self-destruction). Therefore, they imposed a restriction on the number of allowed tampering attempts made by the adversary, and introduced the so-called *bounded leakage and tampering (BLT) model*. To achieve security in this model, their main idea is to reduce tampering to leakage. By this way, they could achieve tamper-resilience against arbitrary key-relations, but disallowed the adversary to make any "post-challenge" tampering attempts. Moreover, the tamper-resilience is realized at the heavy cost of decreasing the amount of tolerated leakage. Following this attractive work, Faonio et al. further [19] showed that the already existing signature scheme [13] and encryption scheme [34] are proven secure in this model, thus giving the first BLT secure signature without random oracle and the first BLT-CCA secure PKE scheme avoiding non-interactive zero-knowledge proofs.

Recently, motivated by the feasibility of "post-challenge" tampering attacks, [38] studied leakage and tamper-resilient CCA secure PKE from a distinct perspective, where they made a constraint on the type of tampering functions (exactly non-arbitrary tampering attacks) instead of the number of tampering attacks as in BLT model. Precisely, they introduced the *leakage and tamper-resilient (LTR) model*, which is generally parameterized by a family T of tampering functions and a class $\mathcal{F}$ of leakage functions. Apart from having access to bounded-memory or auxiliary-input leakage, the adversary in this model is also allowed to make any polynomial number of both "pre-challenge" and "post-challenge" tampering queries. In contrast to previous models, the tampering functions in LTR model should be *restricted* instead of arbitrary efficiently computable functions. Otherwise, there exists no $(\mathcal{F}, T)$-LTR secure encryption schemes, since it is impossible to realize security against arbitrary post-challenge tampering as proven in [11,23]. Moreover, they proposed a generic construction of pubic key encryption based on the newly introduced (key-homomorphic) HPS and showed its LTR-CCA security in the standard model.

Another relevant line of research is to protect cryptosystems against physical attacks by leveraging (leakage-resilient) non-malleable codes [17,20,27,31]. While this yields a generic way for resisting leakage and/or tampering attacks, it usually relies on certain hardware requirements such as self-destruction, key-update mechanism or split-state model. Moreover, this way might bring certain expansion to the key storage. In this work, we are more interested in designing leakage and tamper-resilient public cryptosystems without such constrains.

1.2 Motivations

It is well-known that properly defining security models is of great importance to provable security. If a security model fails to capture the power of adversary, the cryptographic algorithms proven secure in such model may still suffer from serious security threats. Hence, it is crucial to catch the minimal restrictions on the adversary and then establish the security models as reasonable as possible.

Although the LTR security introduced by [38] is meaningful in practice, there is still an *artificial restriction* on the adversary. More specifically, the adversary in their model is disallowed to ask for any tampering query (f_t, ct) such that $ct = ct^*$, where ct^* is the challenge ciphertext. That is, the adversary is unable to issue *challenge-dependent* tampering queries and thus cannot observe the effect of tampering on the decryption of ct^*, even if the related key $f_t(sk) \neq sk$. In practice, this is an unreasonable constraint since the adversary may launch tampering attacks depending on the target ciphertext, so it is natural to ask whether or not we can *overcome this shortcoming and achieve an improved security that allows the adversary to issue challenge-dependent tampering queries satisfying* $(f_t(sk), ct) \neq (sk, ct^*)$?

On the other hand, it is still unreasonable, as shown in [26], to impose the restriction $(f_t(sk), ct) \neq (sk, ct^*)$ to the adversary since s/he is only capable of choosing tampering functions and without any knowledge of sk in practice, so we ask if we can *further reduce the above constraint to* $(f_t, ct) \neq (I, ct^*)$, where I denotes the identity function?

1.3 Contributions

With these questions in mind, we first present an enhanced security notion for PKE, namely *strong bounded leakage and tamper-resilient chosen-ciphertext security*, i.e., $(\lambda, \mathcal{T})$-sLTR-CCA security. In contrast to the original LTR-CCA security, it only stipulates that $(f_t, ct) \neq (I, ct^*)$ rather than $ct \neq ct^*$, which is obviously the minimal restriction on the adversary's capability and captures the essential constraint on *challenge-dependent* tampering queries since otherwise there exists no provably secure PKE schemes in the LTR model.

To the end, we then introduce a refined HPS named $\mathcal{T}_{pm}$-public-key-malleable HPS ($\mathcal{T}_{pm}$-PM-HPS) and present a generic paradigm for $(\lambda, \mathcal{T})$-sLTR-CCA secure PKE from $\mathcal{T}_{pm}$-PM-HPS and true-simulation extractable NIZK argument system. For our construction, the tamper-resilience captured by $\mathcal{T}$ and the amount λ of leakage depend on the $\mathcal{T}_{pm}$-public-key malleability and leakage-resilience property of the underlying PM-HPS. Particularly, the tampering function family we achieve is $\mathcal{T} = \mathcal{T}_{pm} \cap (\mathcal{F}_{pfp} \cup \{I\})$, where $\mathcal{F}_{pfp}$ denotes a family of functions with poly-fixed points. It means that our construction can obtain tamper-resilience against $\mathcal{F}_{pfp}$ only if $\mathcal{F}_{pfp}$-PM-HPS exists.

Moreover, we present a *strong auxiliary-input and tamper-resilient chosen-ciphertext security*, i.e., $(\alpha, \mathcal{T})$-sLTR-CCA security, where the adversary has access to α-hard-to-invert auxiliary-input leakage but limited to submit tampering queries s.t. $(f_t(sk), ct) \neq (sk, ct^*)$. Then we show that a sightly adapted variant of the paradigm mentioned before can also achieve the $(\alpha, \mathcal{T})$-sLTR-CCA security. We also explain why the proposed construction cannot meet the minimal restriction $(f_t, ct) \neq (I, ct^*)$.

At last, we instantiate the PM-HPS with the DDH and DLIN problems, and get the first efficient PKE schemes in the *strong* bounded/auxiliary-input leakage and tamper-resilient CCA security model. The instantiated scheme from Sect. 3 (resp. Sect. 4) is secure against $(l - 2) \log p - \omega(\log \kappa)$ bits of key-leakage (resp. 2^{-l^δ}-auxiliary input). Unfortunately, the instantiated PM-HPS only support *affine*-public-key malleability, and thus our concrete constructions can only achieve tamper-resilience against affine function class. Therefore, how to construct $\mathcal{F}_{pfp}$-PM-HPS from number-theoretical assumptions is an interesting question.

2   Preliminaries

2.1   Definitions and Lemmas

Definition 1 (Statistical Distance [15]). *For two random variables X, Y over Ω, their statistical distance is defined as $\Delta(X, Y) = \frac{1}{2} \sum_{\omega \in \Omega} |\Pr[X = \omega] - \Pr[Y = \omega]|$. Then, X and Y are called ϵ-close if $\Delta(X, Y) \leq \epsilon$. Particularly, they are called statistically close for some negligible ϵ.*

Definition 2 (Randomness Extractors [15]). *A function $\mathrm{Ext} : \mathcal{K} \times \{0, 1\}^\tau \to \{0, 1\}^\ell$ is called an average-case (v, ε)-strong randomness extractor if for any pair of random variables (X, Z) such that $X \in \mathcal{K}$ and $\tilde{H}_\infty(X|Z) \geq v$, it holds that $\Delta((\mathrm{Ext}(X, R), R, Z), (U_\ell, R, Z)) \leq \varepsilon$, where R and U_ℓ are uniformly and independently distributed over $\{0, 1\}^\tau$ and $\{0, 1\}^\ell$, respectively.*

Definition 3 (Function Family with Poly-Fixed Points). *Suppose that $\mathcal{F}$ is a family of functions onto a finite set $\mathcal{X}$, we call it a function family with poly-fixed points over $\mathcal{X}$, denoted by $\mathcal{F}_{pfp}$, if it holds that $\max_{f \in \mathcal{F}} |\{x \in \mathcal{X} : f(x) = x\}| \leq p(\kappa)$, where $p(\kappa)$ is some polynomial in κ.*

Lemma 1 (Generalized Leftover Hash Lemma [15]). *Let $\mathcal{H} = \{h : \mathcal{X} \to \mathcal{Y}\}$ be a family of universal hash functions. Then, for arbitrarily random variables*

(X, Z) it holds that $\Delta((h(X), h, Z), (U_{\mathcal{Y}}, h, Z)) \leq \frac{1}{2}\sqrt{2^{-\tilde{H}_\infty(X|Z)}|\mathcal{Y}|}$, where $h \leftarrow \mathcal{H}$ and $U_{\mathcal{Y}} \leftarrow \mathcal{Y}$.

This lemma states that a family of universal hash functions gives an average-case (v, ε)-strong randomness extractor as long as $\log|\mathcal{Y}| \leq v - 2\log(1/\varepsilon)$.

Lemma 2 ([25]). Let X, U be two random variables over $\mathcal{X}$, such that $U \leftarrow \mathcal{X}$, and Z be some (correlated) random variable. If for any $\varepsilon \in [0, 1]$, $\Delta((X, Z), (U, Z)) \leq \varepsilon$, then it holds that $\tilde{H}_\infty(X|Z) \geq -\log(\frac{1}{|\mathcal{X}|} + \varepsilon)$.

Lemma 3 ([15]). Let X, Y, Z be arbitrarily correlated random variables assuming Y takes at most 2^λ possible values, then $\tilde{H}_\infty(X|(Y, Z)) \geq \tilde{H}_\infty(X|Z) - \lambda$. Particularly, $\tilde{H}_\infty(X|Y) \geq H_\infty(X) - \lambda$.

2.2 Hardness Assumptions

We let Group be a PPT algorithm that takes a security parameter κ and outputs a tuple $(\mathbb{G}, g, p)$, where $\mathbb{G}$ is a cyclic group of order p with generator g.

DECISIONAL DIFFIE-HELLMAN ASSUMPTION [33]. The decisional Diffie-Hellman (DDH) problem is hard if for all PPT algorithm $\mathcal{A}$, the following advantage

$$Adv_{\mathcal{A}, \mathsf{Group}}^{\mathrm{DDH}}(1^\kappa) = \left| \Pr[\mathcal{A}(\mathbb{G}, g_1, g_2, g_1^x, g_2^x) = 1] - \Pr[\mathcal{A}(\mathbb{G}, g_1, g_2, g_1^{x_1}, g_2^{x_2}) = 1] \right|,$$

is negligible in κ, where $\mathbb{G} = (\mathbb{G}, g, p) \leftarrow \mathsf{Group}(1^\kappa)$, $g_1, g_2 \in \mathbb{G}$ and $x, x_1, x_2 \in \mathbb{Z}_p$ are chosen uniformly at random and independently.

d-LINEAR ASSUMPTION [18,33,41]. The d-linear (d-LIN) problem is called hard if for all PPT algorithm $\mathcal{A}$, the following advantage is negligible in κ:

$$Adv_{\mathcal{A}, \mathsf{Group}}^{\mathrm{d\text{-}LIN}}(1^\kappa) = \left| \Pr[\mathcal{A}(\mathbb{G}, g_1, \cdots, g_d, g_0, g_1^{x_1}, \cdots, g_d^{x_d}, g_0^{\sum_{i=1}^d x_i}) = 1] - \right.$$
$$\left. \Pr[\mathcal{A}(\mathbb{G}, g_1, \cdots, g_d, g_0, g_1^{x_1}, \cdots, g_d^{x_d}, g_0^{x_0}) = 1] \right|,$$

where $\mathbb{G} = (\mathbb{G}, g, p) \leftarrow \mathsf{Group}(1^\kappa)$, the elements $g_0, g_1, \cdots, g_d \in \mathbb{G}$ and $x_0, x_1, \cdots, x_d \in \mathbb{Z}_p$ are chosen uniformly at random and independently.

Alternatively, this assumption can be restated under the algebraic framework of [18], and it is usually named $\mathcal{L}_d$-Matrix Diffie-Hellman ($\mathcal{L}_d$-MDDH) assumption where $\mathcal{L}_d$ is a matrix distribution defined as below. More formally, it is said that the $\mathcal{L}_d$-MDDH assumption holds relative to Group if for all PPT adversaries $\mathcal{A}$, the following advantage is negligible in κ:

$$Adv_{\mathcal{A}, \mathsf{Group}}^{\mathcal{L}_d\text{-}\mathrm{MDDH}}(1^\kappa) = \left| \Pr[\mathcal{A}(\mathbb{G}, g^{\mathbf{A}}, g^{\mathbf{x}^\top \mathbf{A}}) = 1] - \Pr[\mathcal{A}(\mathbb{G}, g^{\mathbf{A}}, g^{\mathbf{r}^\top}) = 1] \right|,$$

where $\mathbb{G} = (\mathbb{G}, g, p) \leftarrow \mathsf{Group}(1^\kappa)$, $\mathbf{x} \leftarrow \mathbb{Z}_p^d$ and $\mathbf{r} \leftarrow \mathbb{Z}_p^{d+1}$. Moreover, $\mathbf{A}$ is sampled according to the distribution $\mathcal{L}_d$ and the distribution is defined as follows:

$$\mathbf{A} = \begin{pmatrix} a_1 & 0 & \cdots & 0 & 0 & 1 \\ 0 & a_2 & \cdots & 0 & 0 & 1 \\ \vdots & \vdots & \ddots & \vdots & \vdots & \vdots \\ 0 & 0 & \cdots & a_{d-1} & 0 & 1 \\ 0 & 0 & \cdots & 0 & a_d & 1 \end{pmatrix} \in \mathbb{Z}_p^{d \times (d+1)}$$

where $a_i \in \mathbb{Z}_p^*$. Notice that $(\mathbf{A}, \boldsymbol{x}^\top \mathbf{A})$ can be compactly written as $(a_1, \cdots, a_d,$ $a_1 x_1, \cdots, a_d x_d, \sum_{i=1}^d x_i)$ with $a_i \leftarrow \mathbb{Z}_p^*$ (Precisely, a_i can be seen as the implicit representatoin of g_i in $\mathbb{Z}_p^*$, i.e., $a_i = \log_{g_0} g_i$.) and $x_i \leftarrow \mathbb{Z}_p$ for all $i \in [d]$.

2.3   Public-Key-Malleable HPS

Inspired by [26], we present a new variant of HPS, called public-key malleable HPS. Precisely, it is refined from the regular one by introducing some new properties, such as public-key malleability and public-key collision resistance. For simplicity, we present it similarly as in [33,38], by viewing it as a key encapsulation mechanism. For clarity, we follow the notations of [38] in the following.

Public-Key-Malleable Projective Hashing. Suppose $\mathcal{G}$ be the set of system parameters, such as the underlying algebraic groups, and let $\mathcal{HK}, \mathcal{PK}$ and $\mathcal{K}$ be the sets of secret hash keys, public keys and encapsulated symmetric keys, respectively. Besides, we let $\mathcal{C}$ be the set of all ciphertexts and $\mathcal{V}$ the set of all valid ones. Also, we assume that there are efficient algorithms for sampling $hk \leftarrow \mathcal{HK}$, $c \leftarrow \mathcal{V}$ (together with a corresponding witness w) and $c \leftarrow \mathcal{C} \backslash \mathcal{V}$.

Let $\Lambda = \{\Lambda_{hk} : \mathcal{C} \to \mathcal{K}\}$ be a family of hash functions indexed with $hk \in \mathcal{HK}$ and $\mu : \mathcal{HK} \to \mathcal{PK}$ be a projection function. We call Λ ϵ-smooth, $\mathcal{T}$-public-key-malleable and projective if it satisfies the following properties:

Projectivity: Λ is said to be projective if for all $c \in \mathcal{V}$, $hk_1 \neq hk_2$ but $\mu(hk_1) = \mu(hk_2)$, it holds that $\Lambda_{hk_1}(c) = \Lambda_{hk_2}(c)$, meaning that the action of $\Lambda_{hk}(\cdot)$ on $\mathcal{V}$ is completely determined by $\mu(hk)$ and c.

$\mathcal{T}_{pm}$–Public-Key Malleability: Λ is said to be $\mathcal{T}_{pm}$–public-key-malleable if for all $hk \in \mathcal{HK}$ and $f_t \in \mathcal{T}_{pm}$, there exists a polynomial-time algorithm, called $\mathcal{T}_{pm}$-public-key transformer $\texttt{Trans} : \mathcal{T}_{pm} \times \mathcal{PK} \to \mathcal{PK}$, such that

$$\mu(f_t(hk)) = \texttt{Trans}(f_t, \mu(hk)).$$

Smoothness: Λ is said to be ϵ-smooth if the action of $\Lambda_{hk}(\cdot)$ on $\mathcal{C} \backslash \mathcal{V}$ is completely undetermined. That is, the following distributions are ϵ-close:

$$\Delta\big((c, pk, \Lambda_{hk}(c)), (c, pk, K)\big) \leq \epsilon$$

where $hk \leftarrow \mathcal{HK}$, $pk = \mu(hk)$, $c \leftarrow \mathcal{C} \backslash \mathcal{V}$ and $K \leftarrow \mathcal{K}$.

Public-Key-Malleable HPS. Generally, a public-key-malleable HPS comprises three polynomial-time algorithms PM-HPS = (Param, Pub, Priv): on input a security parameter κ, $\texttt{Param}(1^\kappa)$ generates a parameterized instance $params = (\mathcal{G}, \mathcal{C}, \mathcal{V}, \mathcal{HK}, \mathcal{PK}, \mathcal{K}, \Lambda, \mu)$; on input a public key $pk = \mu(hk)$, a valid ciphertext c and a witness w of the fact that $c \in \mathcal{V}$, $\texttt{Pub}(pk, c, w)$ outputs an encapsulated key $K = \Lambda_{hk}(c)$; with a secret key hk and a ciphertext $c \in \mathcal{C}$ as input, the algorithm $\texttt{Priv}(hk, c)$ returns the encapsulated key $K = \Lambda_{hk}(c)$.

In addition, we assume that $\mu(\cdot)$ is efficiently computable and so is $\Lambda_{hk}(\cdot)$ for each $hk \in \mathcal{HK}$. For all $hk \in \mathcal{HK}, pk = \mu(hk)$ and $c \in \mathcal{V}$ with witness w, it is obvious that we have $\texttt{Pub}(pk, c, w) = \texttt{Priv}(hk, c) = \Lambda_{hk}(c)$.

Subset Membership Problem: A subset membership (SMP) problem associated with a PM-HPS is hard if for any PPT adversary $\mathcal{A}$, its advantage

$$Adv^{\text{SMP}}_{\text{PM-HPS},\mathcal{A}}(1^\kappa) = \big|\Pr[\mathcal{A}(\mathcal{C},\mathcal{V},c_0) = 1 : c_0 \leftarrow \mathcal{V}] - \Pr[\mathcal{A}(\mathcal{C},\mathcal{V},c_1) = 1 : c_1 \leftarrow \mathcal{C}\backslash\mathcal{V}]\big|,$$

is negligible in κ, which means it is difficult for all $\mathcal{A}$ to distinguish a random valid ciphertext $c_0 \in \mathcal{V}$ from a random invalid ciphertext $c_1 \in \mathcal{C}\backslash\mathcal{V}$.

Public-Key Collision Problem: A public-key collision (PKC) problem associated with a PM-HPS is called hard if for any PPT adversary $\mathcal{A}$, the following advantage is negligible in κ,

$$Adv^{\text{PKC}}_{\text{PM-HPS},\mathcal{A}}(\kappa) = \left|\Pr\left[hk \neq hk' \wedge \mu(hk) = \mu(hk') : \begin{array}{l} params \leftarrow \mathsf{Param}(1^\kappa), \\ (hk, hk') \leftarrow \mathcal{A}(params) \end{array}\right]\right|,$$

which means it is difficult for all $\mathcal{A}$ to find a collision of μ. For a PM-HPS, it is called public-key collision resistant if the associated PKC problem is hard.

Definition 4. *A PM-HPS is called a smooth HPS with $\mathcal{T}_{pm}$-public-key malleability and public-key collision resistance, if for all $\kappa \in \mathbb{N}$ and outcomes of Param(1^κ): (1) the underling projective hash is $\epsilon(\kappa)$-smooth and $\mathcal{T}_{pm}$-public-key malleable for some negligible $\epsilon(\kappa)$; (2) both the SMP and PKC problems are hard.*

2.4 True-Simulation Extractability

The notion of true-simulation extractability is proposed by Dodis et al. [13]. More formally, for an NP relation R with corresponding language $\mathsf{L} = \{y : \exists x \ s.t. \ (y,x) \in \mathsf{R}\}$, a tSE-NIZK proof system for R generally consists of a triple of polynomial-time algorithms (Gen, Prov, Verf):

Gen(1^κ): on input a security parameter κ, the algorithm generates a common reference string crs together with a trapdoor tk and an extraction key ek.

Prov(y, x)[1]: on input a valid pair $(y,x) \in \mathsf{R}$, the algorithm outputs an argument π proving that $\mathsf{R}(y,x) = 1$.

Verf(y, π): on input a pair (y, π), the algorithm verifies whether or not the argument π w.r.t. y is true and outputs $0/1$.

For such a proof system $\Pi = (\mathsf{Gen}, \mathsf{Prov}, \mathsf{Verf})$, it is called true simulation extractable (tSE) if it satisfies all the following properties:

Completeness. For all (y,x) s.t. $\mathsf{R}(y,x) = 1$ and $(crs, tk, ek) \leftarrow \mathsf{Gen}(1^\kappa)$, it holds

$$\Pr[\mathsf{Verf}(y,\pi) = 1 : \pi \leftarrow \mathsf{Prov}(y,x)] = 1.$$

Composable Non-interactive Zero Knowledge. There exists an efficient simulator $\mathcal{S}$ such that, for all PPT algorithm $\mathcal{A}$ in the following game, it holds that

$$\left|\Pr\left[b' = b : \begin{array}{l} (crs, tk, ek) \leftarrow \mathsf{Gen}(1^\kappa); (y,x) \leftarrow \mathcal{A}(crs); b \leftarrow \{0,1\} \\ \pi_0 = \mathsf{Prov}(y,x); \pi_1 = \mathcal{S}(y,tk); b' \leftarrow \mathcal{A}(crs, \pi_b) \end{array}\right] - \frac{1}{2}\right| \leq negl(\lambda).$$

---

[1] Note that the algorithm Prov (as well Verf) also takes crs as implicit input. Unless otherwise stated, we don't give it explicitly henceforth.

Strong True Simulation Extractability. There is an efficient algorithm $\mathsf{Ext}(y, \pi, ek)$ such that for all PPT algorithm $\mathcal{A}$ in the following game, it holds that

$$
\Pr\left[
\begin{array}{c}
(y^*, x^*) \in \mathsf{R} \vee (y^*, \pi^*) \in Q \\
\vee\ \mathsf{Verf}(y^*, \pi^*) = 0
\end{array}
:
\begin{array}{l}
(crs, tk, ek) \leftarrow \mathsf{Gen}(1^\kappa) \\
(y^*, \pi^*) \leftarrow \mathcal{A}^{\mathcal{O}_{tk}(\cdot,\cdot)}(crs) \\
x^* \leftarrow \mathsf{Ext}(y^*, \pi^*, ek).
\end{array}
\right] \geq 1 - negl(\lambda).
$$

where Q denotes the set of all (y, π) that $\mathcal{A}$ obtained via the oracle $\mathcal{O}_{tk}(\cdot, \cdot)$.

Specifically, if $\mathcal{A}$ asks only for a single query to the simulation oracle, then Π is called one-time strong true simulation extractable. From the above, we know that Ext succeeds to extract a valid witness for y^* with an overwhelming probability, if $\mathcal{A}$ could output a fresh and valid pair (y^*, π^*) at the end.

2.5   Public Key Encryption

A PKE is a tuple of polynomial time algorithms (Setup, KeyGen, Enc, Dec) with the following syntax: given a security parameter κ, $\mathsf{Setup}(1^\kappa)$ generates the public parameters pp; given pp, $\mathsf{KeyGen}(pp)$ outputs a public and secret key pair $(pk, sk) \in \mathcal{PK} \times \mathcal{SK}$; given a public key pk and a message $m \in \mathcal{M}$, $\mathsf{Enc}(pk, m)$ outputs a ciphertext $c \in \mathcal{C}$; given a secret key sk and a ciphertext c, $\mathsf{Dec}(sk, c)$ returns a plaintext or $\bot$ which indicates that the ciphertext is invalid.

The public parameters pp are system-wide and implicitly taken as part of the inputs of all algorithms. In an implementation, these parameters could be hardwired into the algorithm code and stored in a tamper-proof way. For the standard correctness, it is required that $m = \mathsf{Dec}(sk, \mathsf{Enc}(pk, m))$ for any message $m \in \mathcal{M}$, $pp \leftarrow \mathsf{Setup}(1^\kappa)$ and $(pk, sk) \leftarrow \mathsf{KeyGen}(pp)$.

2.6   Security Definitions

In this part, we present two enhanced security notions against the leakage and tampering attacks, both of which are stronger than that in [38]. Similarly, the definitions are parameterized by a key-leakage bound λ (or a class $\mathcal{F}$ of computationally uninvertible functions) and a class $\mathcal{T}$ of restricted tampering functions.

First, we give the formal definition of CCA security against bounded-memory leakage and tampering attacks (i.e., $(\lambda, \mathcal{T})$-sLTR-CCA Security), as follows.

Definition 5 ($(\lambda, \mathcal{T})$-sLTR-CCA Security). *Let PKE = (Setup, KeyGen, Enc, Dec) be a PKE scheme, it is $(\lambda, \mathcal{T})$-strong leakage and tamper-resilient CCA (sLTR-CCA) secure if for any PPT adversary $\mathcal{A} = (\mathcal{A}_1, \mathcal{A}_2)$, its advantage*

$$
Adv_{\mathcal{A}, PKE, \mathcal{T}}^{\lambda\text{-sLTR-CCA}}(\kappa) = \left| \Pr[\mathbf{Expt}_{\mathcal{A}, PKE, \mathcal{T}}^{\lambda\text{-sLTR-CCA}}(\kappa) = 1] - 1/2 \right| \leq negl(\kappa),
$$

is negligible in κ, where the experiment $\mathbf{Expt}_{\mathcal{A}, PKE, \mathcal{T}}^{\lambda\text{-sLTR-CCA}}(\kappa)$ is defined as:

$$\boxed{\begin{array}{l} \textbf{Expt}^{\lambda\text{-sLTR-CCA}}_{\mathcal{A},\mathsf{PKE},\mathcal{T}}(\kappa): \\ \hline pp \leftarrow \mathsf{Setup}(1^\kappa),\ (pk, sk) \leftarrow \mathsf{KeyGen}(pp) \\ (m_0, m_1, st) \leftarrow \mathcal{A}_1^{\mathcal{O}^\lambda_{sk}(\cdot), \mathcal{O}^{\mathcal{T}}_{sk}(\cdot,\cdot)}(pp, pk) \text{ s.t. } |m_0| = |m_1| \\ b \leftarrow \{0,1\}, ct^* \leftarrow \mathsf{Enc}(pk, m_b) \\ b' \leftarrow \mathcal{A}_2^{\mathcal{O}^{\mathcal{T}}_{sk}(\cdot,\cdot)}(st, ct^*) \\ \textbf{return } (b' = b). \end{array}}$$

In the experiment, $\mathcal{O}^\lambda_{sk}(\cdot)$ denotes a leakage oracle, by which $\mathcal{A}$ is allowed to learn at most λ-bit secret information. Particularly, whenever receiving the i-th leakage query $f_i(\cdot)$, the oracle returns $f_i(sk)$ if $\sum_{j=1}^i |f_j(sk)| \leq \lambda$; otherwise, outputs $\perp$. $\mathcal{O}^{\mathcal{T}}_{sk}(\cdot,\cdot)$ denotes a tampering oracle, by which $\mathcal{A}$ can observe the effect of decryption under a transformed key. Specifically, given a tampering query $(f_t(\cdot), ct)$ s.t. $f_t \in \mathcal{T}$, the oracle returns $\mathsf{Dec}(f_t(sk), ct)$. After seeing ct^*, $\mathcal{A}$ is disallowed to ask for any leakage query, but sill permitted to issue tampering queries only if $(f_t, ct) \neq (I, ct^*)$, where I denotes the identity function.

Notice that, this notion is parameterized by a leakage bound λ and a class $\mathcal{T}$ of tampering functions, where each $f_t \in \mathcal{T}$ has the form of $f_t : \mathcal{SK} \to \mathcal{SK}$ and the leakage bound indicates that the whole lifetime of the system leaks at most λ-bit secret information. Specially, if $\mathcal{T} = \{I\}$, $\mathcal{O}^{\mathcal{T}}_{sk}(\cdot,\cdot)$ is the standard decryption oracle, and the above defines λ-leakage resilient CCA (LR-CCA) security. Moreover, when $\mathcal{O}^{\mathcal{T}}_{sk}(\cdot,\cdot)$ is completely omitted from the experiment, it is exactly the definition of λ-LR-CPA security.

Remark 1. The sole limitation on tampering query is $(f_t, ct) \neq (I, ct^*)$, which means that $\mathcal{A}$ is allowed to obtain the decryption of ct^* under the tampered secret key $f_t(sk)$ only if $f_t \neq I$. Clearly, this definition is much stronger than that in [38] where (f_t, ct) is subject to $ct \neq ct^*$. On the other hand, $(f_t, ct) \neq (I, ct^*)$ is the minimal restriction on tampering queries, since otherwise there is no PKE achieving the above security, thus our definition captures the essential constraint on tampering queries. Note that the challenger in above game needs to check if $f_t = I$ when $ct = ct^*$, so it is necessary for $\mathcal{A}$ to give a clear description of f_t, like in related-key attack security [5,40] where the description of key-derivation function should be known by the challenger. Otherwise (e.g., f_t is obfuscated), it may be difficult to verify f_t belongs to the targeted function class and to simulate the tampering query.

Next, we introduce the definition of CCA security against auxiliary-input leakage and tampering attacks (i.e., $(\alpha, \mathcal{T})$-sLTR-CCA Security). In contrast to bounded-memory leakage, auxiliary-input initialized by [14], may *information-theoretically* reveal the whole secret key, but still hard for any *efficient* algorithm to recover it. Hence, it captures a wider class of physical attacks and can be seen a generalization of bounded-memory leakage. Before presenting the formal security definition, we first recall the hardness of inverting a function family given in [38].

Definition 6 (Hard to Invert Function). *A family of functions $\mathcal{F} = \{f : \mathcal{PK} \times \mathcal{SK} \to \mathcal{SK}\}$ is said to be α-hard to invert, denoted by $\mathcal{F}(\alpha)$, if for any*

PPT algorithm $\mathcal{A}$, $\alpha = \alpha(k) \geq 2^{-k}$ and $f \in \mathcal{F}$, the probability of $\mathcal{A}$ inverting f is no more than α. That is,

$$Adv_{\mathcal{A}}^{f}(k) = \Pr[\mathcal{A}(1^{\kappa}, f(pk, sk)) = sk : (pk, sk) \leftarrow \mathsf{KeyGen}(1^{\kappa})] \leq \alpha,$$

where k denotes the min-entropy of sk. If the probability $Adv_{\mathcal{A}}^{f}(k) \leq \alpha$ holds even for the adversary that also takes pk as input, the function family $\mathcal{F}$ is called α-strongly hard to invert.

Definition 7 ($(\alpha, \mathcal{T})$-sLTR-CCA Security). *Let PKE = (Setup, KeyGen, Enc, Dec) be a PKE scheme, it is said to be $(\alpha, \mathcal{T})$-strong leakage and tamper-resilient CCA (sLTR-CCA) secure if for any PPT adversary $\mathcal{A} = (\mathcal{A}_1, \mathcal{A}_2)$ and α-hard to invert function $f \in \mathcal{F}(\alpha)$, its advantage*

$$Adv_{\mathcal{A},PKE,\mathcal{T}}^{\alpha\text{-sLTR-CCA}}(\kappa) = \left| \Pr[\mathbf{Expt}_{\mathcal{A},PKE,\mathcal{T}}^{\alpha\text{-sLTR-CCA}}(\kappa) = 1] - 1/2 \right| \leq negl(\kappa),$$

where the experiment $\mathbf{Expt}_{\mathcal{A},PKE,\mathcal{T}}^{\alpha\text{-sLTR-CCA}}(\kappa)$ is defined as:

$\mathbf{Expt}_{\mathcal{A},PKE,\mathcal{T}}^{\alpha\text{-sLTR-CCA}}(\kappa)$:

$pp \leftarrow \mathsf{Setup}(1^{\kappa})$, $(pk, sk) \leftarrow \mathsf{KeyGen}(pp)$

$(m_0, m_1, st) \leftarrow \mathcal{A}_1^{\mathcal{O}_{sk}^{\mathcal{T}}(\cdot, \cdot)}(pp, pk, f(pk, sk))$ s.t. $|m_0| = |m_1|$

$b \leftarrow \{0, 1\}$, $ct^* \leftarrow \mathsf{Enc}(pk, m_b)$

$b' \leftarrow \mathcal{A}_2^{\mathcal{O}_{sk}^{\mathcal{T}}(\cdot, \cdot)}(st, ct^*)$

return $(b' = b)$.

The experiment above is almost the same as $\mathbf{Expt}_{\mathcal{A},PKE,\mathcal{T}}^{\lambda\text{-sLTR-CCA}}(\kappa)$, except that the leakage query $f \in \mathcal{F}(\alpha)$ is now an α-hard to invert function rather than a function with bounded output-length. Furthermore, the tampering oracle $\mathcal{O}_{sk}^{\mathcal{T}}(\cdot, \cdot)$ in this experiment imposes a slightly stricter restriction on tampering queries $(f_t(\cdot), ct)$. In fact, the adversary after seeing ct^* is only allowed to submit tampering queries s.t. $(f_t(sk), ct) \neq (sk, ct^*)$. Obviously, this limitation is not so reasonable as before since the adversary has no knowledge of sk, but it is still much weaker than [38] where $(f_t(\cdot), ct)$ is required to satisfy $ct \neq ct^*$. Therefore, this new definition is much stronger than the previous.

3   Construction of $(\lambda, \mathcal{T})$-sLTR-CCA Secure PKE

In this section, we present a generic construction of $(\lambda, \mathcal{T})$-sLTR-CCA secure PKE from a smooth HPS (with $\mathcal{T}_{pm}$-public-key malleability and public-key collision resistance) PM-HPS = (Param, Pub, Priv), where Param on input 1^{κ} generates a parameterized instance $(\mathcal{G}, \mathcal{C}, \mathcal{V}, \mathcal{HK}, \mathcal{PK}, \mathcal{K}, \Lambda, \mu)$. In addition, we need an average-case $(\log |\mathcal{K}| - \lambda, \varepsilon)$-strong extractor $\mathsf{Ext} : \mathcal{K} \times \{0,1\}^{\tau} \rightarrow \{0,1\}^{\ell}$ and a tSE-NIZK proof system $\Pi = (\mathsf{Gen}, \mathsf{Prov}, \mathsf{Verf})$ for the language

$$\mathsf{L} = \{(pk, c_0, c_1, s) : \exists\, (m, w) \text{ s.t. } \mathsf{Ext}(\mathsf{Pub}(pk, c_0, w), s) \oplus m = c_1 \wedge (c_0, w) \in \mathsf{R}_{\mathcal{V}}\},$$

where $pk \in \mathcal{PK}$, $m \in \{0,1\}^\ell$, w is the witness of $c_0 \in \mathcal{V}$ (i.e., (c_0, w) belongs to the relation $R_\mathcal{V}$ defined by $\mathcal{V}$) and s is a random seed from $\{0,1\}^\tau$.

More concretely, our construction with message space $\{0,1\}^\ell$ consists of four efficient algorithms PKE = (Setup, KeyGen, Enc, Dec):

Setup(1^κ): given a security parameter κ, the algorithm runs Param(1^κ) and Gen(1^κ) to generate $params = (\mathcal{G}, \mathcal{C}, \mathcal{V}, \mathcal{HK}, \mathcal{PK}, \mathcal{K}, \Lambda, \mu)$ and the common reference string crs. It then outputs $pp = (params, crs)$.

KeyGen(pp): given parameters pp, the algorithm samples a uniform secret hash key hk and outputs the public and secret key pair $(pk, sk) = (\mu(hk), hk)$.

Enc(pk, m): on input pk and a message $m \in \{0,1\}^\ell$, the algorithm samples $c_0 \in \mathcal{V}$ with witness w, chooses $s \leftarrow \{0,1\}^\tau$, and outputs the ciphertext $ct = (c_0, c_1, s, \pi)$, where $c_1 = \text{Ext}(\text{Pub}(pk, c_0, w), s) \oplus m$, $\pi = \text{Prov}((pk, c_0, c_1, s); (m, w))$.

Dec(sk, ct): given secret key sk and a ciphertext $ct = (c_0, c_1, s, \pi)$, the algorithm first checks if $\text{Verf}((\mu(sk), c_0, c_1, s), \pi) = 1$ (Note that pk here is computed from secret key sk, which is important for achieving the enchanced security). If not, returns $\perp$. Otherwise, it recovers the message by computing $m = \text{Ext}(\text{Priv}(sk, c_0), s) \oplus c_1$.

We recall that the algorithm $\text{Priv}(sk, c)$ computes the (public-key-malleable) projective hash function $\Lambda_{sk}(c)$ with secret hash key $sk = hk$ for any $c \in \mathcal{C}$ and $\text{Pub}(pk, c_0, w)$ evaluates $\Lambda_{sk}(c_0)$ with public key $pk = \mu(sk)$ and the witness w of $c_0 \in \mathcal{V}$. Regarding the correctness, it follows easily from the fact that $\text{Pub}(pk, c_0, w) = \Lambda_{sk}(c_0) = \text{Priv}(sk, c_0)$ for any $c_0 \in \mathcal{V}$ with witness w as well as the completeness of the tSE-NIZK proof system Π.

Remark 2. We remark that the generic construction is similar to [38] from a high level, but the underlying HPS needs to be carefully refined for our purpose. More precisely, the main differences of this construction from [38] are reflected in the following aspects: (1) it is built upon a refined HPS with some extra properties, e.g., $\mathcal{T}$-public-key malleability and public-key collision resistance; (2) the consistency of ciphertext is verified with sk instead of pk, which is crucial for achieving our security; (3) its security analysis in the stronger model is much more complicated, although the framework seems similar. A high-level idea of the proof is shown below, whereas the details are given in the full version due to the limited pages.

Theorem 1. *Assuming that PM-HPS is a $\epsilon(\kappa)$-smooth HPS with $\mathcal{T}_{pm}$-public-key malleability and public-key collision resistance, Ext is an average-case ($\log|\mathcal{K}| - \lambda, \varepsilon(\kappa)$)-strong extractor and Π is a tSE-NIZK proof system, then the proposed construction is $(\lambda, \mathcal{T})$-sLTR-CCA secure for any $\lambda \leq \log|\mathcal{K}| - \ell - \omega(\log\kappa)$ and $\mathcal{T} \subseteq (\mathcal{T}_{pm} \cap \widetilde{\mathcal{F}}_{pfp})$, where ℓ is the length of encrypted message, $\varepsilon(\kappa)$ and $\epsilon(\kappa) \leq (2^\ell - 1)/|\mathcal{K}|$ are negligible in κ, and $\widetilde{\mathcal{F}}_{pfp} = \mathcal{F}_{pfp} \cup \{I\}$. Particularly, for all parameter κ and PPT adversary $\mathcal{A}$, it holds that*

$$Adv_{\mathcal{A},PKE,\mathcal{T}}^{\lambda\text{-}sLTR\text{-}CCA}(\kappa) \leq 2(Adv_{PM\text{-}HPS,\mathcal{B}}^{SMP}(\kappa) + \epsilon(\kappa) + \varepsilon(\kappa)) + Adv_{PM\text{-}HPS,\mathcal{B}'}^{PKC}(\kappa)$$
$$+ Q_t \cdot p(\kappa) \cdot 2^\lambda \cdot (1/|\mathcal{K}| + \epsilon) + negl(\kappa).$$

Proof (Sketch). In an overview, the leakage oracle could be perfectly simulated since the simulator always possesses the secret key. Moreover, the $\mathcal{T}$-type tampering queries could be properly answered by exploiting the public-key malleability together with the tSE property of NIZK. Thus, once all the tampering queries are well processed, the leakage-resilience of the construction can be easily reduced to the underlying CPA secure PKE directly derived from HPS.

4   Construction of $(\alpha, \mathcal{T})$-sLTR-CCA Secure PKE

In this part, we show that a slightly adapted version of the previous construction (in Sect. 3) can achieve $(\alpha, \mathcal{T})$-sLTR-CCA security. In particular, the strong extractor Ext will never be used. For simplicity, we just present the different algorithms, exactly the encryption and decryption algorithms, in the following:

Enc(pk, m): on input pk and $m \in \mathcal{M}$, it samples $c_0 \in \mathcal{V}$ with witness w, chooses a random seed s, and computes $c_1 = \mathsf{Pub}(pk, c_0, w) \cdot m$ and $\pi = \mathsf{Prov}((pk, c_0, c_1); (m, w))$. Finally, it outputs the ciphertext $ct = (c_0, c_1, \pi)$.

Dec(sk, ct): on input sk and $ct = (c_0, c_1, \pi)$, the algorithm first verifies whether $\mathsf{Verf}((\mu(sk), c_0, c_1), \pi) = 1$. If not, returns $\perp$. Otherwise, it recovers the message by computing $m = c_1/\mathsf{Priv}(sk, c_0)$.

The correctness holds as analyzed before. Like the previous scheme, there is also a similar underlying PKE w.r.t. this adapted version. Similar to the proof given in the previous section, the leakage-resilience property of this construction essentially inherits from the underlying PKE'. Therefore, if PKE' is CPA-secure against auxiliary-input leakage, then the construction can be proven secure against both the auxiliary-input and tampering attacks with a similar proof idea. However, it cannot realize tamper-resilience w.r.t. the minimal restriction, i.e., $(f_t, ct) \neq (I, ct^*)$, the reason for which will be explained as below.

Theorem 2. *Assuming that PM-HPS is a $\epsilon(\kappa)$-smooth HPS with $\mathcal{T}_{pm}$-public-key malleability and public-key collision resistance, and Π is a tSE-NIZK proof system, if the underlying PKE' constructed only from PM-HPS is α-LR-CPA secure, then the above construction is $(\alpha, \mathcal{T})$-sLTR-CCA secure for α-hard to invert functions and tampering functions $\mathcal{T} = \mathcal{T}_{pm}$, where $\epsilon(\kappa)$ is negligible in κ. Particularly, for all parameter κ and PPT adversary $\mathcal{A}$, it holds that*

$$Adv_{\mathcal{A},PKE,\mathcal{T}}^{\alpha\text{-}sLTR\text{-}CCA}(\kappa) \leq 2Adv_{PKE',\mathcal{A}}^{\alpha\text{-}LR\text{-}CPA}(\kappa) + Adv_{PM\text{-}HPS,\mathcal{B}'}^{PKC}(\kappa) + negl(\kappa).$$

The proof idea is similar to the previous scheme, except that (1) the leakage-resilience of this construction is reduced to a PKE scheme resilient to auxiliary-input and (2) we need not to process all queries (f_t, ct) s.t. $ct = ct^*, f_t \neq I$ and $f_t(sk) = sk$ since the definition of $(\alpha, \mathcal{T})$-sLTR-CCA security requires that $(f_t(sk), ct) \neq (sk, ct^*)$ for each allowed tampering query (f_t, ct). In fact, the main point of achieving tamper-resilience w.r.t. the restriction $(f_t, ct) \neq (I, ct^*)$ (rather than $(f_t(sk), ct) \neq (sk, ct^*)$) is that $f_t \neq I$ implies $f_t(sk) \neq sk$ with an overwhelming probability. For the $(\lambda, \mathcal{T})$-sLTR-CCA security, this is possible as sk may still have high min-entropy even conditioned on the λ-bit leakage. In the context of auxiliary input leakage, however, the leakage may reveal the whole entropy of sk, thus we cannot derive $f_t(sk) \neq sk$ from $f_t \neq I$. This is why we have to restrict $(f_t(sk), ct) \neq (sk, ct^*)$ for each tampering query (f_t, ct) in the definition of $(\alpha, \mathcal{T})$-sLTR-CCA security.

5 Instantiations

In this section, we present some instantiations based on the standard assumptions such as DDH and d-LIN assumption, which shows that the enhanced security notions can be achieved on basis of well-known hardness assumptions.

5.1 PM-HPS from DDH Assumption

The public-key-malleable HPS PM-HPS $= (\mathrm{Param}, \mathrm{Pub}, \mathrm{Priv})$ based on the DDH assumption is described as below. In fact, it is the same as the HPS presented in [10,38], then we further show it also satisfies the extended properties for our applications. First, we recall the description of PM-HPS as follows:

Param(1^κ): on input a security parameter κ, it generates $(\mathbb{G}, g, p) \leftarrow$ Group(1^κ), and then chooses $g_1, g_2 \leftarrow \mathbb{G}$ and outputs $params = (\mathcal{G}, \mathcal{C}, \mathcal{V}, \mathcal{HK}, \mathcal{PK}, \mathcal{K}, \Lambda, \mu)$:

- $\mathcal{G} = (\mathbb{G}, p, g_1, g_2), \mathcal{C} = \mathbb{G} \times \mathbb{G}, \mathcal{V} = \{(g_1^w, g_2^w) : w \in \mathbb{Z}_p\}, \mathcal{HK} = \mathbb{Z}_p \times \mathbb{Z}_p, \mathcal{PK} = \mathbb{G}, \mathcal{K} = \mathbb{G}.$
- $pk = \mu(hk) = g_1^{x_1} g_2^{x_2}, \Lambda_{hk}(c) = c_1^{x_1} c_2^{x_2}$ for any $hk = (x_1, x_2) \in \mathcal{HK}$ and $c = (c_1, c_2) \in \mathcal{C}.$

Pub(pk, c, w): given public key pk and ciphertext $c = (c_1, c_2) \in \mathcal{V}$ with witness $w \in \mathbb{Z}_p$, the algorithm computes the hash value as pk^w.

Priv(hk, c): on input secret key $hk = (x_1, x_2) \in \mathcal{HK}$ and any ciphertext $c = (c_1, c_2) \in \mathcal{C}$, this algorithm computes the hash value on c as $c_1^{x_1} c_2^{x_2}$.

The projectiveness and smoothness of this construction could be readily analyzed as in [10,33]. In the following, we mainly show that it satisfies the properties of $\mathcal{T}$-*public-key malleability* and *public-key collision resistance*. Before going ahead, we first define the class $\mathcal{T}$ of functions associated with the former property, which is exactly a family of restricted affine functions on $\mathcal{HK}$ defined as $\mathcal{T}_{raff} = \{f_{(a,b)}(hk) = (ax_1 + b_1, ax_2 + b_2) : a \in \mathbb{Z}_p, hk = (x_1, x_2), b = (b_1, b_2) \in \mathcal{HK}\}$. Now we proceed to show the properties mentioned above:

$\mathcal{T}_{raff}$-*public-key malleability*: For all $hk = (x_1, x_2) \in \mathcal{HK}$ and $f_{(a,b)}(\cdot) \in \mathcal{T}_{raff}$ with $a \in \mathbb{Z}_p$ and $b = (b_1, b_2) \in \mathcal{HK}$, it is easy to observe that

$$\mu(f_{(a,b)}(hk)) = \mu(ax_1 + b_1, ax_2 + b_2) = g_1^{ax_1 + b_1} g_2^{ax_2 + b_2} = (g_1^{x_1} g_2^{x_2})^a \cdot g_1^{b_1} \cdot g_2^{b_2}.$$

Then for all $pk = \mu(hk) \in \mathcal{PK}$ and $f_{(a,b)} \in \mathcal{T}_{raff}$ with $a \in \mathbb{Z}_p$ and $b = (b_1, b_2) \in \mathcal{HK}$, the $\mathcal{T}_{raff}$-public-key transformer $\mathrm{Trans} : \mathcal{T}_{raff} \times \mathcal{PK} \to \mathcal{PK}$ is defined as: $\mathrm{Trans}(f_{(a,b)}, \mu(hk)) = \mu(hk)^a \cdot g_1^{b_1} \cdot g_2^{b_2}$. Now due to $\mu(hk) = g_1^{x_1} g_2^{x_2}$, we have that $\mu(f_{(a,b)}(hk)) = \mathrm{Trans}(f_{(a,b)}, \mu(hk))$.

Public-Key Collision Resistance: Under the discrete logarithm (DL) assumption, the PKC problem associated with the above PM-HPS is hard. Suppose for contradiction that there exists an adversary $\mathcal{A}$ that can break the property of public-key collision resistance, i.e., finding $hk = (x_1, x_2) \neq (x_1', x_2') = hk'$ s.t. $\mu(hk) = \mu(hk')$, then we can construct an efficient algorithm $\mathcal{B}$ that can solve the DL problem by invoking $\mathcal{A}$.

Given a random DL instance $(\mathbb{G}, p, g, h)$, the algorithm $\mathcal{B}$ aiming at computing $\alpha = \log_g h$ sets $g_1 = g$ and $g_2 = h$, and then produces and returns the public parameters *params* to $\mathcal{A}$. After that, if $\mathcal{A}$ eventually outputs a collision $hk = (x_1, x_2) \neq (x_1', x_2') = hk'$ of μ s.t. $\mu(hk) = \mu(hk')$, then we have $g_1^{x_1 + \alpha x_2} = g_1^{x_1' + \alpha x_2'}$ and can get from the equation that $\alpha = \frac{x_1 - x_1'}{x_2' - x_2}$. Hence, the PKC problem associated with PM-HPS is as hard as the DL problem.

As to the hardness of SMP problem, it is directly from the hardness of DDH problem, the detailed analysis of which can be found in [10,33].

The preceding PM-HPS is constructed directly from the DDH problem. Next, we present its generalized version, as shown in [33,38]. More concretely, the generalized construction is depicted as follows:

Param(1^κ): on input a security parameter κ, the algorithm generates $(\mathbb{G}, g, p) \leftarrow$ Group(1^κ), and then chooses $\boldsymbol{g} = (g_1, \cdots, g_l) \in \mathbb{G}^l$ where $l \geq 2 \log p + \omega(\log \kappa)$, and sets *params* $= (\mathcal{G}, \mathcal{C}, \mathcal{V}, \mathcal{HK}, \mathcal{PK}, \mathcal{K}, \Lambda, \mu)$ as:

- $\mathcal{G} = (\mathbb{G}, p, \boldsymbol{g}), \mathcal{C} = \mathbb{G}^l = \{(g_1^{r_1}, \cdots, g_l^{r_l}) : r_1, \cdots, r_l \in \mathbb{Z}_p\}, \mathcal{V} = \{(g_1^w, \cdots, g_l^w) : w \in \mathbb{Z}_p\}, \mathcal{HK} = \mathbb{Z}_2^l, \mathcal{PK} = \mathbb{G}, \mathcal{K} = \mathbb{G}$.
- $pk = \mu(hk) = \prod_{i=1}^{l} g_i^{x_i}, \Lambda_{hk}(c) = \prod_{i=1}^{l} c_i^{x_i}$ for any $hk = (x_1, \cdots, x_l) \in \mathcal{HK}$ and $c = (c_1, \cdots, c_l) \in \mathcal{C}$.

Pub(pk, c, w): given pubic key pk and ciphertext $c = (c_1, \cdots, c_l) \in \mathcal{V}$ with witness $w \in \mathbb{Z}_p$, the algorithm computes the hash value as pk^w.

Priv(hk, c): given $hk = (x_1, \cdots, x_l) \in \mathcal{HK}$ and $c = (c_1, \cdots, c_l) \in \mathcal{C}$, the algorithm evaluates the hash value on c as $\prod_{i=1}^{l} c_i^{x_i}$.

The projectiveness and smoothness could be analyzed similarly to [38]. We notice that smoothness holds only if $l \geq 2 \log p + \omega(\log \kappa)$, due to the generalized leftover hash lemma. In the following, we mainly demonstrate that the construction satisfies both the $\mathcal{T}$-*public-key malleability* and *public-key collision resistance* property. With respect to the function class $\mathcal{T}$ associated with the former property, it is formalized in a similar way as before. Specifically, it is defined as $\mathcal{T}_{raff} = \{f_{(a,b)}(hk) = (ax_1 + b_1, \cdots, ax_l + b_l) : a \in \mathbb{Z}_p, hk = (x_1, \cdots, x_l), \boldsymbol{b} = (b_1, \cdots, b_l) \in \mathcal{HK}\}$. Now we continue to show the properties as desired:

$\mathcal{T}_{raff}$-*Public-Key Malleability*: For all $hk = (x_1, \cdots, x_l) \in \mathcal{HK}$ and $f_{(a,b)}(\cdot) \in \mathcal{T}_{raff}$ with $a \in \mathbb{Z}_p$ and $\boldsymbol{b} = (b_1, \cdots, b_l) \in \mathcal{HK}$, it is easy to observe that

$$\mu(f_{(a,b)}(hk)) = \mu(ax_1 + b_1, \cdots, ax_l + b_l) = \prod_{i=1}^{l} g_i^{ax_i + b_i} = (\prod_{i=1}^{l} g_i^{x_i})^a \cdot \prod_{i=1}^{l} g_i^{b_i}.$$

Then for all $pk = \mu(hk) \in \mathcal{PK}$ and $f_{(a,b)} \in \mathcal{T}_{raff}$ with $a \in \mathbb{Z}_p$ and $\boldsymbol{b} = (b_1, \cdots, b_l) \in \mathcal{HK}$, we define the $\mathcal{T}_{raff}$-public-key transformer **Trans** : $\mathcal{T}_{raff} \times$

$\mathcal{PK} \rightarrow \mathcal{PK}$ as: $\mathtt{Trans}(f_{(a,b)}, \mu(hk)) = \mu(hk)^a \cdot \prod_{i=1}^{l} g_i^{b_i}$. Following from $\mu(hk) = \prod_{i=1}^{l} g_i^{x_i}$, we have $\mu(f_{(a,b)}(hk)) = \mathtt{Trans}(f_{(a,b)}, \mu(hk))$.

Public-Key Collision Resistance: Under the DL assumption, the PKC problem associated with the above PM-HPS is hard. Suppose that there exists an efficient adversary $\mathcal{A}$ that can break the property of public-key collision resistance, i.e., finding $hk = (x_1, \cdots, x_l) \neq (x_1', \cdots, x_l') = hk'$ s.t. $\mu(hk) = \mu(hk')$, then we can design an efficient algorithm $\mathcal{B}$ to solve the DL problem by invoking $\mathcal{A}$.

Given a random DL instance $(\mathbb{G}, p, g, h)$, the algorithm $\mathcal{B}$ aiming at computing $\alpha = \log_g h$ randomly picks $j \in [l], \beta_i \in \mathbb{Z}_p$ for all $i \in [l] \setminus \{j\}$, and sets $\boldsymbol{g} = (g_1, \cdots, g_l)$ as $g_i = g^{\beta_i}$ for $i \neq j$ and $g_j = h$.

Then, it produces the public parameters *params* and sends them to the adversary $\mathcal{A}$. After that, if $\mathcal{A}$ eventually outputs a collision $hk = (x_1, \cdots, x_l) \neq (x_1', \cdots, x_l') = hk'$ s.t. $\mu(hk) = \mu(hk')$, then we have that $\prod_{i=1}^{l} g_i^{x_i} = \prod_{i=1}^{l} g_i^{x_i'}$ which is equivalent to $h^{x_j - x_j'} = \prod_{i \neq j} g^{\beta_i(x_i' - x_i)}$. Furthermore, we get that $\alpha = \frac{\sum_{i \neq j} \beta_i(x_i' - x_i)}{x_j - x_j'}$ conditioned on $x_j \neq x_j'$.

For analyzing $\mathcal{B}$'s success probability, we denote by coll the event that $\mathcal{A}$ outputs $hk \neq hk'$ but $\mu(hk) = \mu(hk')$. Then the probability of $\mathcal{B}$ solving the DL problem is $\Pr[\mathcal{B}(\mathbb{G}, p, g, h) = \alpha] \geq \Pr[\mathcal{B}(\mathbb{G}, p, g, h) = \alpha \wedge \text{coll} \wedge x_j \neq x_j'] \geq \frac{2}{l} Adv_{\text{PM-HPS}, \mathcal{A}}^{\text{PKC}}(\kappa)$.

Hence, the PKC problem associated with PM-HPS is hard as long as the DL assumption holds. As to the hardness of SMP problem, it follows readily from the hardness of the (generalized) DDH problem [12].

5.2 PM-HPS from d-LIN Assumption

The public-key malleable HPS PM-HPS = (Param, Pub, Priv) based on d-LIN assumption is described below, which is in fact the same as the HPS in [38].

Param(1^κ): on input parameter κ, it generates $(\mathbb{G}, g, p) \leftarrow \mathsf{Group}(1^\kappa)$, then randomly chooses $\mathbf{A} \in \mathbb{Z}_p^{d \times (d+1)}$ and outputs *params* $= (\mathcal{G}, \mathcal{C}, \mathcal{V}, \mathcal{HK}, \mathcal{PK}, \mathcal{K}, \Lambda, \mu)$:

- $\mathcal{G} = (\mathbb{G}, g, p, g^{\mathbf{A}}), \mathcal{C} = \{g^{r^\top} : r \in \mathbb{Z}_p^{d+1}\}, \mathcal{V} = \{g^{w^\top \mathbf{A}} : w \in \mathbb{Z}_p^d\}, \mathcal{HK} = \mathbb{Z}_p^{d+1}, \mathcal{PK} = \mathbb{G}^{d \times 1}, \mathcal{K} = \mathbb{G}$.
- $pk = \mu(hk) = g^{\mathbf{A}x}, \Lambda_{hk}(c) = g^{r^\top x}$ for $hk = \boldsymbol{x} \in \mathcal{HK}$ and $c = g^{r^\top} \in \mathcal{C}$.

Pub($pk, c, \boldsymbol{w}$): given $pk = g^{\mathbf{A}x}$ and $c = g^{w^\top \mathbf{A}} \in \mathcal{V}$ with witness $\boldsymbol{w} \in \mathbb{Z}_p^d$, the algorithm computes $g^{w^\top \mathbf{A}x}$.

Priv(hk, c): given $hk = \boldsymbol{x} \in \mathcal{HK}$ and $c = g^{r^\top} \in \mathcal{C}$, it computes $g^{r^\top x}$.

The projectiveness and smoothness could be shown as in [38], and the hardness of SMP problem follows readily from that of $\mathcal{L}_d$-MDDH problem. What remains to do is to show this construction satisfies both the $\mathcal{T}$-*public-key malleability* and *public-key collision resistance* property as well. As to the function class $\mathcal{T}$ associated with the malleability property, it is defined similarly as before.

More precisely, $\mathcal{T}_{raff} = \{f_{(a,b)}(hk) = a\boldsymbol{x} + \boldsymbol{b} : a \in \mathbb{Z}_p, hk = \boldsymbol{x}, \boldsymbol{b} \in \mathcal{HK}\}$. Now we continue to show the desired properties below:

$\mathcal{T}_{raff}$-*Public-Key Malleability*: For all $hk = \boldsymbol{x} \in \mathcal{HK}$ and $f_{(a,b)} \in \mathcal{T}_{raff}$ with $a \in \mathbb{Z}_p$ and $\boldsymbol{b} \in \mathcal{HK}$, it is easy to observe that

$$\mu(f_{(a,b)}(hk)) = \mu(a\boldsymbol{x} + \boldsymbol{b}) = g^{\mathbf{A}(a\boldsymbol{x}+\boldsymbol{b})} = (g^{\mathbf{A}\boldsymbol{x}})^a \cdot g^{\mathbf{A}\boldsymbol{b}}.$$

Then for all $pk = \mu(hk) \in \mathcal{PK}$ and $f_{(a,b)} \in \mathcal{T}_{raff}$ with $a \in \mathbb{Z}_p$ and $\boldsymbol{b} \in \mathcal{HK}$, we define the $\mathcal{T}_{raff}$-public-key transformer $\mathtt{Trans} : \mathcal{T}_{raff} \times \mathcal{PK} \to \mathcal{PK}$ as: $\mathtt{Trans}(f_{(a,b)}, \mu(hk)) = \mu(hk)^a \cdot g^{\mathbf{A}\boldsymbol{b}}$. Following from that $\mu(hk) = g^{\mathbf{A}\boldsymbol{x}}$, we get $\mu(f_{(a,b)}(hk)) = \mathtt{Trans}(f_{(a,b)}, \mu(hk))$.

Public-Key Collision Resistance: Under the $\mathcal{L}_d$-MDDH assumption, the PKC problem associated with the above construction is intractable. Suppose for contradiction that there exists a PPT adversary $\mathcal{A}$ that can find two different secret key $hk = (x_1, x_2) \neq (x_1', x_2') = hk'$ s.t. $\mu(hk) = \mu(hk')$, then we can construct an efficient algorithm $\mathcal{B}$ that can use $\mathcal{A}$ to solve the $\mathcal{L}_d$-MDDH problem.

Given $(\mathbb{G}, p, g, g^{\mathbf{A}}, g^{\boldsymbol{u}^{\top}})$, where $\boldsymbol{u}^{\top} = \boldsymbol{w}^{\top}\mathbf{A}$ or $\boldsymbol{r}^{\top}$ with $\boldsymbol{w} \leftarrow \mathbb{Z}_p^d$ and $\boldsymbol{r} \leftarrow \mathbb{Z}_p^{d+1}$, the algorithm $\mathcal{B}$ sets $\mathcal{G} = (\mathbb{G}, p, g, g^{\mathbf{A}})$ and generates the public parameters $params$. After receiving $params$, $\mathcal{A}$ outputs a pair of secret keys $(hk, hk') = (\boldsymbol{x}, \boldsymbol{x}')$. If they are distinct but satisfies $\mu(hk) = \mu(hk')$, i.e., $g^{\mathbf{A}\boldsymbol{x}} = g^{\mathbf{A}\boldsymbol{x}'}$, we get $g^{\mathbf{A}(\boldsymbol{x}-\boldsymbol{x}')} = g^{\boldsymbol{0}}$. Then $\mathcal{B}$ sets $\boldsymbol{v} = \boldsymbol{x} - \boldsymbol{x}'$ and distinguishes $\boldsymbol{u}^{\top} = \boldsymbol{w}^{\top}\mathbf{A}$ from $\boldsymbol{u}^{\top} = \boldsymbol{r}^{\top}$ by checking if $g^{\boldsymbol{u}^{\top}\boldsymbol{v}} = g^{\boldsymbol{0}}$. Obviously, $\mathcal{B}$ successfully solves the $\mathcal{L}_d$-MDDH problem as long as $\mathcal{A}$ breaks the public-key collision resistance property.

At last, with respect to efficient constructions of tSE-NIZKs, they could be built in a generic and efficient way from any standard CCA-secure encryption scheme and NIZK argument system, just as shown and argued in [11,13].

6   Comparison with Related Works

Next we give a brief comparison of our schemes with those works [11,19,38] that rely not on hardware assumptions. CCA security against both key-leakage and tampering attacks was initially studied by Damgård et al. [11], where they introduced the notion of BLT-CCA security. Their main idea is to reduce tampering to leakage. Although this enables to achieve tamper-resilience against arbitrary tampering attacks (or arbitrary key-relations), the total number of tampering attacks, due to the limited amount of key-leakage, must be strictly bounded and no post-tampering attempts are permitted (i.e., tampering attacks launched after observing challenge ciphertext). Moreover, this method leads to a significant reduction of the amount of leakage tolerated by the construction. In contrast, [38] revisited the problem from an alternative perspective and introduced the notion of LTR-CCA security, where the adversary is allowed to issue an arbitrary polynomial of tampering queries even after challenge phase. Furthermore, it can be realized in a more flexible way without any dependence between tampering and leakage. However, there is still a restriction on their

Table 1. Brief comparison with related works

Schemes	Leakage		Tampering			sLTR	Inst.	Assum.
	BML*	AIL	C.-Dep.	$\mathcal{T}$	Unb.			
[11]	$(l - t - 2)\log p - \omega(\log \kappa)$	×	×	$\mathcal{T}_{all}$	×	×	L	DDH
[19]	$\mathcal{O}(\xi\kappa - (t+1)\kappa - \ell)$	×	×	$\mathcal{T}_{all}$	×	×	L	RSI
[38]	$(l - 2)\log p - \omega(\log \kappa)$	√	×	$\mathcal{T}_{raff}$	√	×	F	DDH
Section 3	$(l - 2)\log p - \omega(\log \kappa)$	×	√	$\mathcal{T}_{raff}$	√	√	F	DDH/DLIN
Section 4	—	√	√	$\mathcal{T}_{raff}$	√	√	F	DDH

∗: the amount of leakage tolerated by the related constructions based on BHHO [7], except for FV [19] that are instantiated with [34]; t: the number of tampering attacks permitted by [11] and [19]; ξ: a parameter specified in the instantiation of [19]; l: the length of message encrypted in [19]; Inst.: instantiation; Unb.: unbounded; L: limited; F: flexible; $\mathcal{T}_{all}$: the class of all kinds of tampering functions; $\mathcal{T}_{raff}$: the class of all restricted affine functions

security that the adversary is not allowed to issue any challenge-dependent (for short, C.-Dep.) tampering query. Instead, our enhanced security notion called sLTR-CCA security only stipulates that $(f_t, ct) \neq (I, ct^*)$, instead of $ct \neq ct^*$.

As to efficiency, our constructions are similar to [11,38], which are all built upon tSE-NIZK proof system, but they can achieve a better leakage-resilience than [11] and a higher security level than [38]. Recently, Faonio et al. [19] showed that the already existing scheme [34] can also achieve BLT security, and thus obtained the first direct, pairing free IND-CCA BLT secure PKE without relying on tSE-NIZK. However, we do not know how to realize sLTR-CCA security without using tSE-NIZK yet, and we leave it as an interesting future work. The results and comparison with related works is summarized in Table 1.

7 Conclusion

We introduced an enhanced security against both key-leakage and tampering attacks. Then, we show that our new security is achievable by presenting a generic construction on the basis of public-key-malleable HPSs. Our construction can tolerate a large amount of key-leakage and resist an arbitrary polynomial number of restricted tampering attempts. Moreover, we show that the construction with slight modifications can also achieve chosen-ciphertext security against both auxiliary-input leakage and tampering attacks. However, our instantiations based on DDH/DLIN assumption only achieve security against affine-tampering attacks, due to the restricted public-key malleability of the PM-HPS. We left open the constructions of PM-HPS with more general public-key malleability and sLTR-CCA secure PKE against more wider tampering function classes. In addition, designing CCA-secure PKE against both challenge-dependent leakage and tampering attacks is very meaningful, which is left as future work.

Acknowledgements. The authors would like to thank all anonymous reviewers for their valuable comments. This work is supported by the National Key R&D Program of China (No. 2016YFB0801201), the Natural Science Foundation of China (No. 61802255, 61602396, U1636217) and the China Postdoctoral Science Foundation (No. 2017M621472).

References

1. Akavia, A., Goldwasser, S., Vaikuntanathan, V.: Simultaneous hardcore bits and cryptography against memory attacks. In: Reingold, O. (ed.) TCC 2009. LNCS, vol. 5444, pp. 474–495. Springer, Heidelberg (2009). https://doi.org/10.1007/978-3-642-00457-5_28
2. Alwen, J., Dodis, Y., Naor, M., Segev, G., Walfish, S., Wichs, D.: Public-key encryption in the bounded-retrieval model. In: Gilbert, H. (ed.) EUROCRYPT 2010. LNCS, vol. 6110, pp. 113–134. Springer, Heidelberg (2010). https://doi.org/10.1007/978-3-642-13190-5_6
3. Bellare, M., Cash, D., Miller, R.: Cryptography secure against related-key attacks and tampering. In: Lee, D.H., Wang, X. (eds.) ASIACRYPT 2011. LNCS, vol. 7073, pp. 486–503. Springer, Heidelberg (2011). https://doi.org/10.1007/978-3-642-25385-0_26
4. Bellare, M., Kohno, T.: A theoretical treatment of related-key attacks: RKA-PRPs, RKA-PRFs, and applications. In: Biham, E. (ed.) EUROCRYPT 2003. LNCS, vol. 2656, pp. 491–506. Springer, Heidelberg (2003). https://doi.org/10.1007/3-540-39200-9_31
5. Bellare, M., Paterson, K.G., Thomson, S.: RKA security beyond the linear barrier: IBE, encryption and signatures. In: Wang, X., Sako, K. (eds.) ASIACRYPT 2012. LNCS, vol. 7658, pp. 331–348. Springer, Heidelberg (2012). https://doi.org/10.1007/978-3-642-34961-4_21
6. Biham, E., Shamir, A.: Differential fault analysis of secret key cryptosystems. In: Kaliski, B.S. (ed.) CRYPTO 1997. LNCS, vol. 1294, pp. 513–525. Springer, Heidelberg (1997). https://doi.org/10.1007/BFb0052259
7. Boneh, D., Halevi, S., Hamburg, M., Ostrovsky, R.: Circular-secure encryption from decision Diffie-Hellman. In: Wagner, D. (ed.) CRYPTO 2008. LNCS, vol. 5157, pp. 108–125. Springer, Heidelberg (2008). https://doi.org/10.1007/978-3-540-85174-5_7
8. Brakerski, Z., Goldwasser, S.: Circular and leakage resilient public-key encryption under subgroup indistinguishability. In: Rabin, T. (ed.) CRYPTO 2010. LNCS, vol. 6223, pp. 1–20. Springer, Heidelberg (2010). https://doi.org/10.1007/978-3-642-14623-7_1
9. Chen, Y., Wang, Y., Zhou, H.-S.: Leakage-resilient cryptography from puncturable primitives and obfuscation. In: Peyrin, T., Galbraith, S. (eds.) ASIACRYPT 2018. LNCS, vol. 11273, pp. 575–606. Springer, Cham (2018). https://doi.org/10.1007/978-3-030-03329-3_20
10. Cramer, R., Shoup, V.: Universal hash proofs and a paradigm for adaptive chosen ciphertext secure public-key encryption. In: Knudsen, L.R. (ed.) EUROCRYPT 2002. LNCS, vol. 2332, pp. 45–64. Springer, Heidelberg (2002). https://doi.org/10.1007/3-540-46035-7_4
11. Damgård, I., Faust, S., Mukherjee, P., Venturi, D.: Bounded tamper resilience: how to go beyond the algebraic barrier. In: Sako, K., Sarkar, P. (eds.) ASIACRYPT 2013. LNCS, vol. 8270, pp. 140–160. Springer, Heidelberg (2013). https://doi.org/10.1007/978-3-642-42045-0_8

12. Dodis, Y., Goldwasser, S., Tauman Kalai, Y., Peikert, C., Vaikuntanathan, V.: Public-key encryption schemes with auxiliary inputs. In: Micciancio, D. (ed.) TCC 2010. LNCS, vol. 5978, pp. 361–381. Springer, Heidelberg (2010). https://doi.org/10.1007/978-3-642-11799-2_22

13. Dodis, Y., Haralambiev, K., López-Alt, A., Wichs, D.: Efficient public-key cryptography in the presence of key leakage. In: Abe, M. (ed.) ASIACRYPT 2010. LNCS, vol. 6477, pp. 613–631. Springer, Heidelberg (2010). https://doi.org/10.1007/978-3-642-17373-8_35

14. Dodis, Y., Kalai, Y.T., Lovett, S.: On cryptography with auxiliary input. In: STOC 2009, pp. 621–630 (2009)

15. Dodis, Y., Ostrovsky, R., Reyzin, L., Smith, A.: Fuzzy extractors: how to generate strong keys from biometrics and other noisy data. SIAM J. Comput. **38**(1), 97–139 (2008)

16. Dziembowski, S., Pietrzak, K.: Leakage-resilient cryptography. In: FOCS 2008, pp. 293–302 (2008)

17. Dziembowski, S., Pietrzak, K., Wichs, D.: Non-malleable codes. In: ICS 2010, pp. 434–452 (2010)

18. Escala, A., Herold, G., Kiltz, E., Ràfols, C., Villar, J.L.: An algebraic framework for Diffie-Hellman assumptions. J. Cryptol. **30**(1), 242–288 (2017)

19. Faonio, A., Venturi, D.: Efficient public-key cryptography with bounded leakage and tamper resilience. In: Cheon, J.H., Takagi, T. (eds.) ASIACRYPT 2016. LNCS, vol. 10031, pp. 877–907. Springer, Heidelberg (2016). https://doi.org/10.1007/978-3-662-53887-6_32

20. Faust, S., Mukherjee, P., Nielsen, J.B., Venturi, D.: Continuous non-malleable codes. In: Lindell, Y. (ed.) TCC 2014. LNCS, vol. 8349, pp. 465–488. Springer, Heidelberg (2014). https://doi.org/10.1007/978-3-642-54242-8_20

21. Fujisaki, E., Xagawa, K.: Public-key cryptosystems resilient to continuous tampering and leakage of arbitrary functions. In: Cheon, J.H., Takagi, T. (eds.) ASIACRYPT 2016. LNCS, vol. 10031, pp. 908–938. Springer, Heidelberg (2016). https://doi.org/10.1007/978-3-662-53887-6_33

22. Gandolfi, K., Mourtel, C., Olivier, F.: Electromagnetic analysis: concrete results. In: Koç, Ç.K., Naccache, D., Paar, C. (eds.) CHES 2001. LNCS, vol. 2162, pp. 251–261. Springer, Heidelberg (2001). https://doi.org/10.1007/3-540-44709-1_21

23. Gennaro, R., Lysyanskaya, A., Malkin, T., Micali, S., Rabin, T.: Algorithmic tamper-proof (ATP) security: theoretical foundations for security against hardware tampering. In: Naor, M. (ed.) TCC 2004. LNCS, vol. 2951, pp. 258–277. Springer, Heidelberg (2004). https://doi.org/10.1007/978-3-540-24638-1_15

24. Halderman, J.A., et al.: Lest we remember: cold boot attacks on encryption keys. In: USENIX Security 2008, pp. 45–60 (2008)

25. Halevi, S., Lin, H.: After-the-fact leakage in public-key encryption. In: Ishai, Y. (ed.) TCC 2011. LNCS, vol. 6597, pp. 107–124. Springer, Heidelberg (2011). https://doi.org/10.1007/978-3-642-19571-6_8

26. Han, S., Liu, S., Lyu, L.: Super-strong RKA secure MAC, PKE and SE from tag-based hash proof system. Des. Codes Cryptogr. **86**, 1411–1449 (2017)

27. Jafargholi, Z., Wichs, D.: Tamper detection and continuous non-malleable codes. In: Dodis, Y., Nielsen, J.B. (eds.) TCC 2015. LNCS, vol. 9014, pp. 451–480. Springer, Heidelberg (2015). https://doi.org/10.1007/978-3-662-46494-6_19

28. Kalai, Y.T., Kanukurthi, B., Sahai, A.: Cryptography with tamperable and leaky memory. In: Rogaway, P. (ed.) CRYPTO 2011. LNCS, vol. 6841, pp. 373–390. Springer, Heidelberg (2011). https://doi.org/10.1007/978-3-642-22792-9_21

29. Katz, J., Vaikuntanathan, V.: Signature schemes with bounded leakage resilience. In: Matsui, M. (ed.) ASIACRYPT 2009. LNCS, vol. 5912, pp. 703–720. Springer, Heidelberg (2009). https://doi.org/10.1007/978-3-642-10366-7_41

30. Kocher, P., Jaffe, J., Jun, B.: Differential power analysis. In: Wiener, M. (ed.) CRYPTO 1999. LNCS, vol. 1666, pp. 388–397. Springer, Heidelberg (1999). https://doi.org/10.1007/3-540-48405-1_25

31. Liu, F.-H., Lysyanskaya, A.: Tamper and leakage resilience in the split-state model. In: Safavi-Naini, R., Canetti, R. (eds.) CRYPTO 2012. LNCS, vol. 7417, pp. 517–532. Springer, Heidelberg (2012). https://doi.org/10.1007/978-3-642-32009-5_30

32. Lu, X., Li, B., Jia, D.: Related-key security for hybrid encryption. In: Chow, S.S.M., Camenisch, J., Hui, L.C.K., Yiu, S.M. (eds.) ISC 2014. LNCS, vol. 8783, pp. 19–32. Springer, Cham (2014). https://doi.org/10.1007/978-3-319-13257-0_2

33. Naor, M., Segev, G.: Public-key cryptosystems resilient to key leakage. In: Halevi, S. (ed.) CRYPTO 2009. LNCS, vol. 5677, pp. 18–35. Springer, Heidelberg (2009). https://doi.org/10.1007/978-3-642-03356-8_2

34. Qin, B., Liu, S.: Leakage-resilient chosen-ciphertext secure public-key encryption from hash proof system and one-time lossy filter. In: Sako, K., Sarkar, P. (eds.) ASIACRYPT 2013. LNCS, vol. 8270, pp. 381–400. Springer, Heidelberg (2013). https://doi.org/10.1007/978-3-642-42045-0_20

35. Qin, B., Liu, S., Yuen, T.H., Deng, R.H., Chen, K.: Continuous non-malleable key derivation and its application to related-key security. In: Katz, J. (ed.) PKC 2015. LNCS, vol. 9020, pp. 557–578. Springer, Heidelberg (2015). https://doi.org/10.1007/978-3-662-46447-2_25

36. Sun, S.F., Gu, D., Liu, S.: Efficient chosen ciphertext secure identity-based encryption against key leakage attacks. Secur. Commun. Netw. 9(11), 1417–1434 (2016)

37. Sun, S.-F., Gu, D., Liu, S.: Efficient leakage-resilient identity-based encryption with CCA security. In: Cao, Z., Zhang, F. (eds.) Pairing 2013. LNCS, vol. 8365, pp. 149–167. Springer, Cham (2014). https://doi.org/10.1007/978-3-319-04873-4_9

38. Sun, S., Gu, D., Parampalli, U., Yu, Y., Qin, B.: Public key encryption resilient to leakage and tampering attacks. J. Comput. Syst. Sci. 89, 142–156 (2017)

39. Sun, S.-F., Parampalli, U., Yuen, T.H., Yu, Y., Gu, D.: Efficient completely non-malleable and RKA secure public key encryptions. In: Liu, J.K., Steinfeld, R. (eds.) ACISP 2016. LNCS, vol. 9723, pp. 134–150. Springer, Cham (2016). https://doi.org/10.1007/978-3-319-40367-0_9

40. Wee, H.: Public key encryption against related key attacks. In: Fischlin, M., Buchmann, J., Manulis, M. (eds.) PKC 2012. LNCS, vol. 7293, pp. 262–279. Springer, Heidelberg (2012). https://doi.org/10.1007/978-3-642-30057-8_16

41. Wee, H.: KDM-security via homomorphic smooth projective hashing. IACR Cryptology ePrint Archive 2015, 721 (2015)

Privacy Preserving Techniques

Benchmarking Privacy Preserving Scientific Operations

Abdelrahaman Aly[1] and Nigel P. Smart[1,2]

[1] Imec-COSIC, KU Leuven, Leuven, Belgium
abdelrahaman.aly@esat.kuleuven.be, nigel.smart@kuleuven.be
[2] University of Bristol, Bristol, UK

Abstract. In this work, we examine the efficiency of protocols for secure evaluation of basic mathematical functions (`sqrt`, `sin`, `arcsin`, amongst others), essential to various application domains. e.g., Artificial Intelligence. Furthermore, we have incorporated our code in state-of-the-art Multiparty Computation (MPC) software, so we can focus on the algorithms to be used as opposed to the underlying MPC system. We make use of practical approaches that, although, some of them, theoretically can be regarded as less efficient, can, nonetheless, be implemented in such software libraries without further adaptation. We focus on basic scientific operations, and introduce a series of data-oblivious protocols based on fixed point representation techniques. Our protocols do not reveal intermediate values and do not need special adaptations from the underlying MPC protocols. We include extensive computational experimentation under various settings and MPC protocols.

1 Introduction

Secure Multiparty Computation (MPC) allows a set of parties to compute an arbitrary function of their inputs without revealing anything about them, except for what can be deduced from the output of the function. Standard MPC protocols usually provide secure basic operations, such as additions, multiplications and logic gates, from which more complex functionalities can be built. In many data processing applications one requires access to standard scientific operations, and thus to an approximation of what in the C language is represented by the data types `float` and `double`. There are two techniques for performing this approximation in the literature: fixed point representations and floating point representations. Both of which have been implemented in various MPC systems; for example [2,6,10].

Efficient algorithms for fixed point representations were introduced in a series of works by Catrina et al. (see [8] for a detailed summary). Typically, fixed point arithmetic uses a publicly available, predefined precision to which all data values are kept. This is more efficient than a floating point representation, as examined in [1] for example, where the operations are closer to what one would expect for the equivalent C data types. However, the increased cost of using floating point

© Springer Nature Switzerland AG 2019
R. H. Deng et al. (Eds.): ACNS 2019, LNCS 11464, pp. 509–529, 2019.
https://doi.org/10.1007/978-3-030-21568-2_25

representations makes their use highly problematic in practice. In addition, it is sufficient, in many applications, to work with a fixed point precision, for example in various statistical or machine learning applications.

Despite many prior works on fixed point operations in MPC, there has been little work on benchmarking these operations. In this work we provide a number of benchmarks of simple scientific operations on fixed point numbers in a variety of cases. In particular, we focus on standard mathematical operations such as $\mathtt{sqrt}(x), \sin(x), \cos(x), \arcsin(x), \exp(x), \log_a(x)$, etc, in both the full threshold setting with two and three players, and in the honest majority three party setting. We build our protocols on top of the actively-secure-with-abort MPC protocols available in the SCALE-MAMBA system [2]. This system is chosen as it is publicly available and allows different access structures to be utilized for the same input program.

A number of previous works have looked at *algorithms* to implement these operations [1,3,4,11,21,22]; however our paper concentrates on investigating practical performance and in addition looks at optimizations to such protocols in the case of MPC systems which allow a certain amount of pre-processing (for example in SCALE-MAMBA shared random bits are produced in the pre-processing, and so come for free in the 'online' phase).

One can consider the current state of the art of MPC development as mirroring the development of standard computer programming and architectures. Thus, one often needs to go an revisit earlier works to understand simple ways of implementing functions which might be taken for granted. In this work we make extensive use of the methods used in the 1960s and 1970s to build mechanisms to evaluate scientific operations on fixed and floating point data. In particular we use the work on function approximation by Taylor and Padé approximations provided in the seminal work of Hart [16].

In our work a secret fixed point value is represented by a secret integer v in the range $[-2^{k-1}, \ldots, 2^{k-1}]$ (k is fixed and public) and a public precision value f. The fixed point number represented by v is $v/2^f$. In the kind of MPC systems we consider (i.e. those based on linear secret sharing) the value v is embedded in a finite field $\mathbb{F}_q$. We shall denote by $[\![v]\!]$ the fact that v is shared over $\mathbb{F}_q$. To represent a fixed point number x, whose sharing we denote by $\langle x \rangle$, we take an integer v in the above range such that $x \approx v/2^f$. Thus we can write $\langle x \rangle = \{[\![v]\!], k, f\}$.

Given secure protocols for addition and multiplication of $\mathbb{F}_q$ elements, one can construct secure protocols for addition and multiplication of fixed point values, see [8] for the precise protocols. These protocols will be secure as long as the underlying protocols for addition and multiplication of $\mathbb{F}_q$ elements are also secure.

The addition and multiplication protocols of [8] often require one to open 'masked' values of fixed point values. To do this, there is a statistical security parameter κ, and we require that $\kappa + 2 \cdot k < \log_2 q$. The statistical security parameter measures the statistical distance of certain opened values in the protocol from a uniform distribution. In particular, when we want to open a masked k or $2\cdot k$ bit integer value, we use a mask of $k+\kappa$ or $2\cdot k+\kappa$ bits. This ensures that the distribution of the masked output is within statistical distance of $2^{-\kappa}$ from the uniform distribution. In our implementation we take $(\log_2 q, \kappa, k) = (128, 40, 41)$ and $f = 20$.

We emphasize that our work is centered around MPC based on secret sharing based-MPC, as opposed to systems based on Garbled Circuits or Homomorphic Encryption. More specifically, our works is aimed at any set of individuals that want to perform these operations, whilst using some LSSS based system. Clearly, on this regard, there are different tradeoffs and algorithms if the underlying MPC system chosen is one based on, say Garbled Circuits, however, this falls outside the scope of this work.

Square Root Function: The problem of computing securely the sqrt has been studied by several authors in both the floating point and fixed point settings e.g., [1,18,21,22]. The collection of work that addressed this problem before, approached it by either expressing the output as a Taylor series, or via some other kind of numerical approximation (e.g. via Goldschmidt or Newton-Raphson approximation).

Liedel's [22] method at first glance seems to be the most efficient. This method assumes a fixed point representation in line to what is expressed in [8], produces (given private input $\langle x \rangle$) first an initial approximation of $\sqrt{\langle x \rangle}$. This initial approximation is then improved by performing iterations of Goldschmidt and Newton-Raphson. Liedel offers a way to calculate the initial approximation by solving a system of equations over normalized inputs. However, there is a hidden assumption in the method, which turns out to be very restrictive in practice. This makes the applicability of Liedel's method less useful, and has motivated modern multiparty frameworks, such as Sharemind to use Taylor series based protocols [18]. In our method we use the spirit of Liedel's method, i.e. we use Goldshmidt and Newton-Raphson to perform the final approximation, however we produce the initial approximation to the $\sqrt{(\langle x \rangle)}$ by computing its closest power of two.

Trigonometric Functions: There are a number of works that explore alternatives to build trigonometric functions [3,4]. All use numerical approximations or series evaluations, but restrict the values to specific ranges (i.e. angle reduction is not performed before the trigonometric function is computed). We on the other hand, offer an angle reduction protocol that is designed to take advantage of the fixed point representation of [8]. This would naively utilize a division with remainder operation which is usually a more expensive primitive [1,21], than a multiplication. Instead, we make an intelligent use of the fixed point representation of our inputs and a series of more basic operations. We then utilize, as do the two prior works, the numerical methods of Hart [16] to produce the final approximation to $\sin(x)$ and $\cos(x)$. Our method is then extended to $\tan(x)$.

Inverse Trigonometric Functions: In the same direction as our other contributions in this paper, we propose an approach to build oblivious inverse trigonometric functions, by using numerical approximations. We again use the methods of Hart here. Bayatbabolghani et al. [4], introduced a protocol based on the work of Medina [24], using a sequence of polynomials to obtain the $\texttt{arctan}(\langle x \rangle)$ of a secret shared input x. In their work, they provided secure protocols to achieve this, and some discussion about complexity and performance, comparing it with [16]. However no specific implementation details were provided, except for the usage of these operations within spectrum fingerprint detection algorithms. Their experimentation was performed using the PICCO compiler [27].

The Functions Exp and Log: Following the same methodology, we present protocols for algorithms such as exponentiation (considering the base and exponent as secret shared inputs) and log (to a public available base). We achieve this, by numerically approximating to We both operations using the methods of Hart [16] (base two), and then making use of standard logarithmic identities, with the aim of computing both functions. Previous work on exponentiation algorithms, initially used binary expansions and utilized existing work on bit-decomposition for field elements. The basic relevant work in this regard was introduced by Damgård et al. [11], where the authors hide both the exponent and the base by evaluating the binary expansion of the exponent. Further works have centered on reducing the influence of the binary expansion [25, 26]. For logarithmic functions, there is virtually no prior work on fixed point MPC variants, although there has been some work on floating point variants. For instance, Kamm [17] makes use of Taylor series to obtain the natural logarithm of a given floating point input.

In summary we provide methods to securely compute various scientific operations, and we evaluate their performance in practice using an off-the-shelf MPC system. We hope our work stimulates others to investigate improvements to our methods. Our choice of fixed point representation is to enable fast secure evaluation of the scientific functions, clearly it would be better to use floating point representations.

2 Preliminaries

In this section we outline the necessary details to understand the following contributions. In particular, how we perform fixed point arithmetic, numerical approximation, our arithmetic black box, as well as our experimental setup.

Notation for Fixed Point Arithmetic: We make use of the square bracket notation from [13], where $[\![a]\!]$ denotes a secret shared value $a \in \mathbb{F}_q$. Note that our protocols are designed to work regardless of the underlying Linear Secret Sharing Scheme (LSSS). We assume all our inputs are elements of some field elements $\mathbb{F}_q$, where q is a prime of bit-size ℓ. We use typical assumptions while encoding integer values in $\mathbb{F}_q$. That is to say that we consider half of the input domain to represent positive numbers, and the other half negative. Let P be the set of all parties of size $|P|$.

We follow a representation proposed by Catrina and Saxena [8], which is common in the MPC literature and libraries [2–4]. We define $\mathbb{Z}_{\langle k \rangle}$ as the set of integers $\{x \in \mathbb{Z} : -2^{k-1} \leq x \leq 2^{k-1} - 1\}$, which we embed into $\mathbb{F}_q$ via the map $x \mapsto x \pmod{q}$. We define $\mathbb{Q}_{\langle k,f \rangle}$ as the set of rational numbers $\{x \in \mathbb{Q} : x = \overline{x} \cdot 2^{-f}, \overline{x} \in \mathbb{Z}_{\langle k \rangle}\}$. We represent $x \in \mathbb{Q}$ as the integer $x \cdot 2^f = \overline{x} \in \mathbb{Z}_{\langle k \rangle}$, which is then represented in $\mathbb{F}_q$ via the mapping used above. Thus $x \in \mathbb{Q}$ is in the range $[-2^e, 2^e - 2^{-f}]$ where $e = k - f$. As we are working with fixed point numbers we assume that the parameters f and k are public. For our following algorithms to work (in particular fixed point multiplication and division) we require that $q > 2^{2 \cdot k}$. We can then imagine a minimal representation of a secret shared fixed point number x, as $\langle x \rangle$ to be a tuple composed by $\{[\![v]\!], k, f\}$. We extend the notation in [13], encoding secret shared field elements as $[\![x]\!]$ and fixed-point inputs as $\langle x \rangle$. Note that operations with public fixed-point operations are possible by using the same basic encoding. Vectors of secret shared inputs are also denoted by $[\![Y]\!]$ or $\langle Y \rangle$, and its size is $|Y|$, with the context being implicitly clear.

Experimental Setup: All experiments in this paper were run using a LAN network test-bed (10 Gb switch and connections), with dedicated machines. Each machine had the same hardware and software configuration, namely 32 GB RAM, 256 SSD storage, Intel Core i7-770 3.6 GHZ processor, and were running Ubuntu 16.04.5 LTS. The machines ran the SCALE-MAMBA system [2] for their base MPC protocols. This is an MPC framework which runs in the offline-online paradigm, namely work is performed in two distinct phases: a function independent offline phase (used to generate correlated randomness) and an online phase (where the function is evaluated). More specifically, the former phase is dedicated to generating Beaver Triples [5] and random shared bits.

SCALE-MAMBA allows us to test our protocols in an actively secure environment (in particular active security with abort) for various access structures. For comparison purposes we looked at three setups;

- A two and three party full-threshold access structure which uses (essentially) the SPDZ protocol from [12,14,19],
- A three party honest majority setting using Shamir secret sharing. This variant uses Maurer's protocol [23] to generate offline data, which is then processed as in [20].

SCALE-MAMBA has built in protocols for performing fixed point arithmetic based on the methodology of [8] described above. We made use of the default configuration of SCALE-MAMBA to run all our experiments, except for those for the exponentiation and logarithm functions. This implies that we used a 128-bit modulus for $\mathbb{F}_q$. Additionally, fixed point inputs are $k = 41$ bits in length of which $f = 20$ bits are dedicated to its fixed point precision. This implies an implicit statistical security parameter κ for the fixed point arithmetic emulation of 40 bits.

We note that the implementation of SCALE-MAMBA optimizes execution times by running parallel threads to create offline data "just-in-time". However, for the cases where the offline phase can be executed in advance, we also run experiments to measure exclusively the online phase and to estimate the execution time of any associated offline phase. Communication cost greatly influences the overall running times of the system; and because of this the compiler will try to optimize execution times so as to maximize throughput. This is done by executing multiple operations in a single round. Our experiments include configurations for cases when compilation is optimized in this way, and when is not. Thus, we get estimates for when one wants to maximize throughput, and when one wants to minimize latency.

In all our experimental reports in what follows we present three figures.

- **Offline Phase.** We measure the average time it takes to produce enough triples during the offline phase for a single execution of the functionality (e.g., a single $\langle \sin(x) \rangle$ or $\langle \tan(x) \rangle$ call).
- **Latency Measurement.** In this setting we evaluate the online phase of our protocol executing a single operation at a time (i.e. sequential as opposed to parallel execution). We then present the average run time for the online phase only. This gives an estimate of the expected latency a user can expect if latency of computation is the main performance issue.
- **Throughput Maximization.** We also measured when we run several instances of the functionality (in our case 50) in parallel. Thus this enables us to give a *lower bound* for the expected throughput, i.e. how many operations can be performed per second, if throughput is the main performance issue.

Note that computational costs for the offline phase dominate on overall performance, and that in SCALE-MAMBA, the offline phase works on the same way regardless of whether the online phase is configured to maximise throughput or minimize latency.

Arithmetic Black Box: To facilitate the understanding of the implications of using functionalities that are as secure as the underlying MPC protocols that implement them, we follow literature on the field by describing an *arithmetic blackbox* ($\mathcal{F}_{ABB}$). This was originally introduced by [13], in the context of abstracting away finite field operations in $\mathbb{F}_q$ via shares $[\![x]\!]$, but one can also extend it to operations on our fixed point sharing $\langle x \rangle$, as well as more complex operations which have already been proved to be secure under composition.

The $\mathcal{F}_{ABB}$ works as an idealized functionality, capable to store secret values over $\mathbb{F}_q$ (input) and make them public under request (output). A stored $x \in \mathbb{F}_q$ will be denoted by $[\![x]\!]$. Furthermore, it can perform a series of operations under request by the computational parties, for example addition and multiplication of such elements. Hence, it can be asked to compute any function, by constructing the associated functionality as an arithmetic circuit. This allows our protocols to abstract themselves from the specific details of how the MPC system implements them. The basic functionality, which includes addition and multiplication of field elements as well as fixed-point inputs and is detailed in Table 1. With the protocols used to implement these functions, in our experiments, being taken from the underlying protocols in SCALE-MAMBA described above. In the same table, we also present the number of rounds needed to execute each function in the online phase of the SCALE-MAMBA system. Additionally, we make occasional use of high level functionalities which have been given and proven secure by various other authors. These protocols are given by Table 2.

Table 1. Secure arithmetic operations provided by the $\mathcal{F}_{ABB}$.

Operation	Purpose	Rounds
$x \leftarrow [\![x]\!]$	Opening/outputting a secret field element	1
$[\![x]\!] \leftarrow x$	Inputting secret a field element	1
$[\![z]\!] \leftarrow [\![x]\!] + [\![y]\!]$	Adds secret field elements	0
$[\![z]\!] \leftarrow [\![x]\!] + y$	Adds secret field and public element	0
$[\![z]\!] \leftarrow [\![x]\!] \cdot y$	Multiplies secret field and public element	0
$[\![z]\!] \leftarrow [\![x]\!] \cdot [\![y]\!]$	Multiply secret elements	1
$\langle z \rangle \leftarrow \langle x \rangle + \langle y \rangle$	Adds secret fixed point numbers	0
$\langle z \rangle \leftarrow \langle x \rangle + y$	Adds secret and public fixed point numbers	0
$\langle z \rangle \leftarrow \langle x \rangle \cdot \langle y \rangle$	Multiplies secret fixed point numbers	1
$\langle z \rangle \leftarrow \langle x \rangle \cdot y$	Multiplies secret and public fixed point numbers	0
$\langle z \rangle \leftarrow [\![x]\!] + \langle y \rangle$	Adds secret fixed point number with secret field element	0
$\langle z \rangle \leftarrow [\![x]\!] \cdot \langle y \rangle$	Multiplies secret fixed point number with secret field element	1

Table 2. Secure complex functionalities derived from the $\mathcal{F}_{ABB}$.

Operation	Purpose	Rounds	Protocol
$[\![b]\!] \leftarrow [\![x]\!] < [\![y]\!]$	Compares a secret and field elements	$1 + \log_2(\ell)$	[7]
$[\![b]\!] \leftarrow [\![x]\!] < y$	Compares a secret and public field elements	$1 + \log_2(\ell)$	[7]
$[\![b]\!] \leftarrow \langle x \rangle < \langle y \rangle$	Compares a secret and fixed point numbers	$1 + \log_2(\ell)$	[7]
$[\![b]\!] \leftarrow \langle x \rangle < y$	Compares a secret and public fixed point numbers	$1 + \log_2(\ell)$	[7]
$\langle z \rangle \leftarrow \langle x \rangle / \langle y \rangle$	Divides secret fixed point numbers	$2 \cdot \log_2(\frac{k}{3.5}) + 8$	[8]
$\langle z \rangle \leftarrow \text{choose}([\![b]\!], \langle x \rangle, \langle y \rangle)$	MUX. Returns $\langle x \rangle$ or $\langle y \rangle$ depending on bit $[\![b]\!]$ s.t. $(\langle y \rangle - \langle x \rangle) \cdot [\![b]\!] + \langle x \rangle$	1	[11]
$\langle z \rangle \leftarrow \text{choose}(b, \langle x \rangle, \langle y \rangle)$	MUX. Returns $\langle x \rangle$ or $\langle y \rangle$ depending on bit b s.t. $(\langle y \rangle - \langle x \rangle) \cdot b + \langle x \rangle$	1	[11]
$[\![b]\!]_0, \ldots, [\![b]\!]_{\ell-1} \leftarrow \text{bit\_decompose}([\![x]\!])$	Bit decomposition of secret field element	$\log_2(q)$	[11,26]
$[\![b]\!]_0, \ldots, [\![b]\!]_{k-1} \leftarrow \text{pre\_OR}([\![x]\!]_0, .., [\![x]\!]_{k-1})$	fan-in or	1	[11]
$[\![z]\!] \leftarrow \text{trunc}(\langle x \rangle)$	$\text{trunc}(x)$ so that returns x's integral magnitude	2	[8]

On Mixed Type Operations: In some cases, and as denoted by Table 1, we may need to either add or multiply secret share fixed point with a standard shared modulo p value. In this case we are assumed to know a bound on the number of bits in the shared modulo p value; i.e. it is never a general element in $\mathbb{F}_p$ but one of bounded size when reduced to a centre around zero. As described by Catrina and Saxena [8] we need to scale the integer inputs by 2^f. This way, integer operands share the same encoding than their fixed point counterparts. This process is called "scaling", and can be achieved by shifting the input to the left by $|f|$ bits. We refer the reader to [8], for a more complete explanation of this process.

Note that subtractions, can be trivially derived from the functionality described by Table 1. Given that we can encode negative numbers, subtractions can be seen as a special case of addition, where the substracted input is multiplied by -1.

On Numerical Approximation: As it was previously mentioned, our protocols are based on the results outlined by Hart in his work, *Computer Approximations* [16]. We make use of numerical methods that, through the use of Polynomial and Padé approximants, can obtain "good enough" approximations to transcendental functions, over a given input interval. To be able to operate, we reduce (normalize) our inputs to such intervals and keep track of their cyclic position. Throughout this work, polynomials are referred in the same way as in the original work by Hart; that is to say a polynomial is described as capital P_i and Q_i where i, refers to the index of table, taken directly from Hart's work [16]. In the case of a polynomial approximation to a function f we have $f(x) \approx P_i(x)$, whilst in the case of a Padé approximation we have $f(x) \approx P_i(x)/Q_i(x)$. We have included, an appendix with all the polynomials used in this work, as well as their precision.

3   Approximated Square Root

In this section, we introduce our results, with respect to the oblivious computation of the square root. The intuition of our work is as follows, given a shared fixed point number $\langle x \rangle = \{[\![v]\!], k, f\}$; we create an initial approximation of the form $\langle v \rangle / 2^{\frac{[\![m]\!]}{2}}$, where $[\![m]\!]$ is the secret shared location of the most significant bit in $[\![v]\!]$. Following Liedel [22], we then improve our approximation by using a number of Newton-Raphson and Goldschmidt iterations. However, the initial approximation to the square root presented by Liedel does not work on all possible input numbers. In particular the approximation algorithm requires a fixed point division by the number $2^{3 \cdot k - 2 \cdot f} = 2^t$. To perform this we create the clear fixed point representation of the value $1/2^t$ and then perform a multiplication between a clear and a shared value. However, to represent $1/2^t$ in our fixed point representation we require there to be a value $i \in [0, \ldots, k]$ such that $i - f = -t$, i.e. $t = f - i < f$. Thus there are some inputs for which Liedel's method to produce the first approximation would require us to increase our precision, and hence our costs, and potentially the underlying prime size. However, we will see that a more crude initial approximation suffices.

Most Significative Bit: Our protocols require us to identify the Most Significative Bit (MSB) from any $\mathbb{F}_q$ element. To achieve this, we adapt the results from [11,22], in such a way that we can isolate it. Our adapted construction makes use of the following inputs:

- $[\![v]\!]$: Integer input value.
- k: Represents a bound on the size of v as an integer. In particular $|v| < 2^k$.

Our protocol will return the most significant bit, which is less than k, but encoded as an index vector. Protocol 1, encompass the method used to achieve this. Note that, to improve the understanding (implementation-wise) of the protocols in this section (and, in particular Protocol 2), the output index vector will be of size k when k is even and $k + 1$ when k is odd. This is needed to enable the indexing in our parity extraction step in Protocol 2 to be correct.

Protocol 1. Most Significative Bit Extraction

Input: Secret shared integer input$[\![v]\!]$. Bit-wise upper bound k
Output: Returns secret shared vector $[\![z]\!]$ with $z \in \{0,1\}^k$ or $\{0,1\}^{k+1}$, which
        is all zero except for the location of the MSB of v.
1 $[\![V]\!]_b \leftarrow$ bit_decompose$([\![v]\!])$;
2 $[\![V']\!]_b \leftarrow \{0_1, ..., 0_{|V_b|}\}$;
3 **for** $i \leftarrow k$ **to** 1 **do**
4 | $[\![V']\!]_{l-i+1} \leftarrow [\![V]\!]_i$;   //invert its order
5 $[\![Y]\!] \leftarrow$ pre_OR$([\![V']\!]_b)$;
6 $[\![Y']\!] \leftarrow \{0_1, ..., 0_{|Y|}\}$;
7 **for** $i \leftarrow k$ **to** 1 **do**
8 | $[\![Y']\!]_{k-i+1} \leftarrow [\![Y]\!]_i$;   //restore its order
9 $[\![z]\!] \leftarrow \{0_1, ..., 0_{k+1-(k \mod 2)}\}$;
10 **for** $i \leftarrow 1$ **to** $k - 1$ **do**
11 | $[\![z]\!]_i \leftarrow [\![Y']\!]_i - [\![Y']\!]_{i+1}$;
12 $[\![z]\!]_k \leftarrow [\![Y']\!]_k$;
13 **return** $[\![z]\!]$;

The protocol works by first obtaining the bit decomposition of our field element, we then obtain the fan-in OR (pre_OR$([\![x]\!])$) of the binary expansion of the input, in inverse order. Note that, without loss of generality, our protocol is explained by using full integers of size k, however it can be used to select the MSB of any substring of size smaller than k. We then simply proceed to obliviously identify the point where, the pre_OR$([\![a]\!])$ stop returning $[\![0]\!]$ and become $[\![1]\!]$. Finally, we adjust the return vector size depending on k.

Initial Square Root Approximation: By extracting the MSB of the input we can obtain our initial approximation via $[\![w]\!] \leftarrow 2^{\frac{[\![m]\!]}{2}}$ if $[\![m]\!]$ is even, or $\langle w \rangle \leftarrow 2^{\frac{[\![m-1]\!]}{2}}$ if odd, where $[\![m]\!]$ is the MSB of $[\![v]\!]$. Note, this needs to be done without disclosing the parity of m, as explained in Protocol 2. This would suffice to obtain the desired approximation. Additionally, we have to deal with the effects of the parity of f (by making minor changes depending on whether f is even or odd).

Protocol 2. Approximation of the Square Root (app_sq)

Input: Secret shared integer input $[\![v]\!]$, and bit-wise upper bound k.
Output: MSB index position $[\![m]\!]$, its parity $[\![o]\!]$ and a power of 2
approximation for $\langle\sqrt{x}\rangle$ in $[\![w]\!]$

1 $[\![z]\!] \leftarrow \text{MSB}([\![v]\!], k)$; (i.e. Protocol 1)
2 $[\![m]\!] \leftarrow [\![0]\!]$;
3 $[\![o]\!] \leftarrow [\![0]\!]$;   //is odd
4 **for** $i \leftarrow 1$ **to** k **do**
5 $\quad$ $[\![m]\!] \leftarrow [\![m]\!] + (i) \cdot [\![z]\!]_{i-1}$;
6 $\quad$ **if** $(i \bmod 2) = 1$ **then**
7 $\quad\quad$ $[\![o]\!] \leftarrow [\![o]\!] + [\![z]\!]_i$;
8 $[\![W]\!] \leftarrow \{[\![0]\!]_1, ..., [\![0]\!]_{\lceil\frac{k}{2}+1\rceil}\}$;   //size is $\lceil\frac{k}{2}\rceil + 1$
9 $[\![W]\!] \leftarrow [\![0]\!]$;
10 **for** $i \leftarrow 1$ **to** $\frac{k}{2} + 1$ **do**
11 $\quad$ $[\![w]\!] \leftarrow [\![w]\!] + (2^{i-1}) \cdot [\![W]\!]_i$;
12 **return** $[\![o]\!], [\![m]\!], [\![w]\!]$;

The protocol converts the sharing of the $\{0,1\}^k$ vector in $[\![z]\!]$ produced by Protocol 1 into an integer sharing $[\![m]\!]$ with $m \in \{1, \ldots, k\}$. At the same time we identify the parity of m, and we then calculate $[\![w]\!]$ by evaluating the binary expansion of the index encoding vector.

Privacy Preserving Square Root: Once, we have obtained our initial approximation, following Liedel [22] results, which we present in Protocol 3. We fix the maximum number of iterations for the Goldshmidt Newton-Raphson combination, just as in Liedel [22], and assign it to θ. The precision of our construction is tied to θ and, has to be tunned in according to the application at hand. Our experiments yielded an accuracy of around six digits after six repetitions. We first obtain $[\![w]\!]$ by invoking Protocol 2 and then proceed to build an instance of $[\![w]\!]$ as a fixed point number, in accordance to the parity of f, $[\![m]\!]$ and Protocol 2. The protocol works by executing a Goldschmidt's iteration followed by a final Newton iteration.

Results: To provide a comparison with the previous work of Liedel, we also present run-times for his results as well. However, we stress again that Liedel's method is not as general as the method we propose, as we can cope with a much larger set of input parameters. In Table 3 we present the required offline data, per single square root operation. Then in Table 4 we present the execution times for the offline phase (for a single square root operation), plus the minimum latency

Table 3. Offline data needed for a single fixed point square root operation

Protocol	Liedel	This work
Multiplication triples	197	684
Square tuples	1	0
Shared bits	2598	4049

Table 4. Performance figures for full threshold (2 and 3 parties) and Shamir with 3 parties for the fixed point square root calculation.

Protocol	Full threshold 2 parties		Full threshold 3 parties		Shamir 3 parties	
	Liedel	This work	Liedel	This work	Liedel	This work
Offline (sec)	2.49	3.90	2.905	4.708	0.065	0.088
Latency (sec)	0.0034	0.0048	0.0043	0.0060	0.0039	0.0062
Throughput (ops/sec)	1042	491	795	313	785	308

Protocol 3. Optimized Approximated $\langle\sqrt{x}\rangle$ for fixed point

---

Input: Secret shared fixed point input $\langle x \rangle = \{[\![v]\!], k, f\}$.
Output: Square root of input $\langle\sqrt{x}\rangle$.
1 $\theta \leftarrow \max(\lceil \log_2(x_k)\rceil, 6)$;
2 $[\![o]\!], [\![m]\!], [\![w]\!] \leftarrow$ app_sq($[\![x_v]\!], x_k$);
3 $[\![o]\!] \leftarrow$ choose($(f \mod 2), 1 - [\![o]\!], [\![o]\!]$);
4 $[\![w]\!] \leftarrow$ choose($(1 - [\![o]\!]) \cdot (f \mod 2), 2 \cdot [\![w]\!], [\![w]\!]$);
5 $t \leftarrow (f - (f \mod 2))/2$;
6 $\langle w' \rangle \leftarrow ([\![w]\!] \cdot 2^t, k - f, f)$;
7 $\langle w' \rangle \leftarrow$ choose($[\![o]\!], \langle w' \rangle \cdot \sqrt{2}, \langle w' \rangle$);
8 $\langle y \rangle \leftarrow \langle w' \rangle^{-1}$;
9 $\langle g \rangle \leftarrow \langle x \rangle \cdot \langle y \rangle$;
10 $\langle h \rangle \leftarrow \langle y \rangle/2$;
11 **for** $i \leftarrow 1$ **to** θ **do**
12 $\quad\Big|\quad \langle r \rangle \leftarrow \frac{3}{2} - \langle g \cdot h \rangle$;
13 $\quad\Big|\quad \langle g \rangle \leftarrow \langle g \rangle \cdot \langle r \rangle$;
14 $\quad\Big|\quad \langle h \rangle \leftarrow \langle h \rangle \cdot \langle r \rangle$;
15 $\langle r \rangle \leftarrow \frac{3}{2} - \langle g \cdot h \rangle$;
16 $\langle h \rangle \leftarrow \langle h \rangle \cdot \langle r \rangle$;
17 $\langle H \rangle \leftarrow 3 - 4 \cdot \langle x \rangle \cdot \langle h \rangle^2$;
18 $\langle H \rangle \leftarrow \langle h \rangle \cdot \langle H \rangle$;
19 $\langle\sqrt{x}\rangle \leftarrow \langle x \rangle \cdot \langle H \rangle$;

---

and maximum throughput we obtained in the three different configurations we tested. We see that, when Liedel's method can be applied then the performance is better, but the extra cost of our method in dealing with general inputs is only about a factor of two.

Discussion: A recent implementation, with regards to the secure evaluation of square root functions on distributed environments, was introduced by Dimitrov et al. [15]. These implementations where part of their work on alternative representations for real numbers. Their results make use of a golden number encoding, as well as some logarithmic based representation for real numbers. The authors followed the Liedel line of work for their implementation, and used (the passively secure) Sharemind [6] system as their test-bed. They made use of a similar configuration (3 parties) on high-end machines, except for the fact they ran their experiments using Intel Xeon microprocessor series. For comparison reasons, they included experimentation against 32 and 64 bit long fixed point representations included in Sharemind. Their work however only gives estimations on the number of operations per second, but no mention on whether these are batched together. The fastest implementation is their logarithmic representation using a low bit-size for the inputs and a somewhat small precision. Direct comparison is hard to make as they target only passively secure MPC, whereas we focus on actively secure MPC.

4   Trigonometric Functions

We introduce a series of adaptations of the numerical approximations given by Hart [16] for the basic trigonometric functions, and then implement them in an oblivious fashion. The approximations have been chosen to balance accuracy and low degree (i.e. efficiency).

Angle Reduction: We first introduce a mechanism, Protocol 4, to map any input $\langle x \rangle$ to the range $[0, \frac{\pi}{2}]$, and the quadrant which $\langle x \rangle$ lies in (given by b_1 and b_2). The quadrant is a byproduct of the process of the initial mapping. Protocol 4 requires a $\texttt{trunc}(x)$ operation call, and a low number of fundamental operations. The outputs of the operation, are as follows:

- $\langle w \rangle$: $w = x \pmod{\pi/2}$.
- $[\![b_1]\!]$: $b_1 = (x \pmod{2 \cdot \pi}) > \pi$.
- $[\![b_2]\!]$: $b_2 = (x \pmod{\pi}) > \pi/2$.

Sine, Cosine and Tangent Functions: First, the input $\langle x \rangle$ has to be mapped to the correct interval. We then can obtain the sin of any angle by using the polynomial approximation $\sin(x) = \nu \cdot P_{3307}(\nu^2)$ where $\nu = w \cdot 2/\pi$ for $w = x$ (mod $\pi/2$), with the polynomial P_{3307} from Hart [16] given in the Appendix. We can produce the cosine function, by evaluating $P_{3508}(w^2)$ from [16] (again details in Appendix). Given the cyclic nature of both sin and cos, we adjust the sign of the outputs by b_1 and b_2 accordingly. Finally, using the standard identity, $\tan(x) = \sin(x)/\cos(x)$ we can then give the tangent function.

Protocol 4. Angle reduction protocol

Input: Secret shared fixed point input $\langle x \rangle = \{[\![v]\!], p, f\}$.
Output: Secret shared reduced angle $\langle w \rangle$ such that $0 \leq \langle w \rangle \leq \frac{\pi}{2}$, and flags
$\qquad [\![b_1]\!]$ and $[\![b_2]\!]$.

1 $\langle d \rangle \leftarrow \langle x \rangle \cdot \frac{1}{2 \cdot \pi}$; //This is a scalar mult.
2 $[\![d]\!] \leftarrow \mathtt{trunc}(\langle d \rangle)$;
3 $\langle y \rangle \leftarrow \langle x \rangle - [\![d]\!] \cdot (2 \cdot \pi)$;
4 $[\![b_1]\!] \leftarrow \langle y \rangle > \pi$;
5 $\langle w \rangle \leftarrow \mathtt{choose}([\![b_1]\!], (2 \cdot \pi) - \langle y \rangle, \langle y \rangle)$;
6 $[\![b_2]\!] \leftarrow \langle w \rangle > \frac{\pi}{2}$;
7 $\langle w \rangle \leftarrow \mathtt{choose}([\![b_2]\!], (\pi - w) - \langle w \rangle, \langle w \rangle)$;
8 **return** $\langle w \rangle, [\![b_1]\!], [\![b_2]\!]$;

Inverse Trigonometric Functions: Inverse trigonometric functions can be built directly, from an approximation to the arctan function via

$$\mathtt{arcsin}(x) = \arctan\left(\frac{x}{\sqrt{1 - x^2}}\right) \text{ and } \mathtt{arccos}(x) = \frac{\pi}{2} - \mathtt{arcsin}(x).$$

For arctan we have to perform a somewhat similar input reduction procedure as was done for the main trigonometric functions above; as is also the case in [4]. We first simplify the process by operating on positive values only, since $\arctan(-x) = -\arctan(x)$. Thus, we first need to identify the sign of $\langle x \rangle$ sign. We then can reduce $\langle x \rangle$ value to the interval $[0, 1]$, by using the formula $\arctan(x) = \frac{\pi}{2} - \arctan\left(\frac{1}{x}\right)$. From this point, it suffices to obtain an approximation for $\mathtt{arctan}(x)$ in the interval $x \in [0, 1]$. Which we again do via a Padé approximation $P_{5102}(X)/Q_{5102}(X)$ from [16] (see the Appendix). Protocol 5 shows how we obtain this value, by using the building blocks, enumerated in previous sections.

Protocol 5. Approximated $\mathtt{arctan}(\langle x \rangle)$

Input: Secret shared fixed point input $\langle x \rangle = \{[\![v]\!], k, f\}$.
Output: Approximation for $\langle \mathtt{arctan}(\langle x \rangle) \rangle$

1 $[\![s]\!] \leftarrow \langle x \rangle < 0$;
2 $\langle \mathtt{abs}(x) \rangle \leftarrow \mathtt{choose}([\![s]\!], -1 \cdot \langle x \rangle, \langle x \rangle)$;
3 $[\![b]\!] \leftarrow \langle \mathtt{abs}(x) \rangle > 1$;
4 $\langle \nu \rangle \leftarrow \mathtt{choose}([\![b]\!], \frac{1}{\langle \mathtt{abs}(x) \rangle}, \langle \mathtt{abs}(x) \rangle)$;
5 $\langle y \rangle \leftarrow P_{5102}(\langle \nu \rangle^2)/Q_{5102}(\langle \nu \rangle^2)$;
6 $\langle \mathtt{arctan}(\langle x \rangle) \rangle \leftarrow \langle x \rangle \cdot \langle y \rangle$;

Results: Just as in the case of the square root function we present our results in two tables. To calculate $\langle \mathtt{arccos}(x) \rangle$, trivially follows from solving $\langle \mathtt{arcsin}(x) \rangle$, hence, running times are essentially the same and thus ignored. The first table, Table 5, gives the offline cost per function call, whereas the second, Table 6, gives the actual measured costs using our programs.

Table 5. Offline data needed for a single fixed point trigonometric operation

Protocol	$\langle\texttt{sin()}\rangle$	$\langle\texttt{cos()}\rangle$	$\langle\texttt{tan()}\rangle$
Multiplication Triples	267	266	680
Square Tuples	1	1	1
Shared Bits	3806	3562	8018

Protocol	$\langle\texttt{arcsin()}\rangle$	$\langle\texttt{arctan()}\rangle$
Multiplication Triples	2053	967
Square Tuples	0	0
Shared Bits	13431	7732

Discussion: There are some related works that explore similar results but differ in regards to the underlying method to compute on encrypted data. The problem of computing trigonometric functions using Homomorphic Encryption was most recently addressed by Cheon et al. [9]. In their work they tackle various topics related to fixed point representation in the homomorphic encryption domain. The authors included results for several operations related to statistical functions. Amongst them, the authors provided timings for sigmoids, using Taylor series. Their test-bed (a single machine) was fairly similar to the set-up of our own machines, but they have used Intel i5 processors instead. On their timings themselves, they were slightly slower than what it was achieved by this work. Namely, their variant of the HEEAN protocol, was capable of evaluating sigmoid functions in around 167 ms (non-amortized cost), whereas our most common set-up, which considers three parties using Shamir's secret sharing such a function could be evaluated in 4 ms. As a final note, it has to be taken into account that Homomorphic Encryption and MPC are often targetted at different scenarios, thus making difficult to establish direct comparison, given that the protocol selection does not exclusively depends on their performance.

Table 6. Performance figures for full threshold (2 and 3 parties) and Shamir with 3 parties for the fixed point trigonometric operations.

	Full Threshold 2 Parties			Full Threshold 3 Parties			Shamir 3 Parties		
Protocol	$\langle\texttt{sin()}\rangle$	$\langle\texttt{cos()}\rangle$	$\langle\texttt{tan()}\rangle$	$\langle\texttt{sin()}\rangle$	$\langle\texttt{cos()}\rangle$	$\langle\texttt{tan()}\rangle$	$\langle\texttt{sin()}\rangle$	$\langle\texttt{cos()}\rangle$	$\langle\texttt{tan()}\rangle$
Offline (sec)	3.78	3.37	7.89	4.62	4.24	9.49	0.084	0.084	0.18
Latency (sec)	0.0042	0.0035	0.0053	0.0050	0.0043	0.0076	0.0044	0.0045	0.0078
Throughput (ops/sec)	617	561	289	542	724	301	446	467	239

	Full Threshold 2 Parties		Full Threshold 3 Parties		Shamir 3 Parties	
Protocol	$\langle\texttt{arcsin()}\rangle$	$\langle\texttt{arctan()}\rangle$	$\langle\texttt{arcsin()}\rangle$	$\langle\texttt{arctan()}\rangle$	$\langle\texttt{arcsin()}\rangle$	$\langle\texttt{arctan()}\rangle$
Offline (sec)	15.43	7.36	18.3	8.70	0.56	0.18
Latency (sec)	0.024	0.0068	0.028	0.0082	0.030	0.0089
Throughput (ops/sec)	41	275	57	218	40	191

5   Exponentiation and Logarithms

In this section, we explore how to obtain the power and the logarithm of any base, to any exponent. This can be achieved by the use of standard logarithmic identities and numerical approximations; namely $\log_b(x) = \log_2(b) \cdot \log_2(x)$ and $\exp(x, y) = x^y = \exp(2, y \cdot \log_2(x))$.

Logarithmic Function: To calculate $\langle \log_2(x) \rangle$, we first need to express $\langle x \rangle$ using the secret shared floating point notation used in [1]. This is to enable us to extract the normalized value of x in the range $[0.5, 1]$, to enable the calculation of the function via numerical approximation. We denote this operation as follows:

$$(\llbracket v_f \rrbracket, \llbracket f_f \rrbracket, \llbracket s \rrbracket, \llbracket z \rrbracket) \leftarrow \texttt{f\_cast}(\langle x \rangle),$$

which produces the elements to encode the shared fixed point number $\langle x \rangle$ as a shared floating point number. The details of these elements is as follows:

- $\llbracket s \rrbracket$ is a sharing of the sign of x.
- $\llbracket z \rrbracket$ is a sharing determining whether x is zero or not.
- $\llbracket f_f \rrbracket$ is the secret shared significand for the representation.
- $\llbracket v_f \rrbracket$ is the mantissa, namely an integer value which is normalized to be in the range $[2^{k-1}, \ldots, 2^k)$.

The underlying floating point number can thus be expressed as $(1 - 2 \cdot s) \cdot (1 - z) \cdot v_f \cdot 2^{f_f}$. To compute $\texttt{f\_cast}(\langle x \rangle)$ we make use of the method introduced by Aliasgari et al. [1]. Internally, this functionality determines the position of the MSB in $\llbracket v \rrbracket$, this enables us to obtain the number of bit shifts needed to compute $\llbracket v_f \rrbracket$ and, hence, $\langle f_f \rangle$ from the $\llbracket v \rrbracket$ and f values used to represent $\langle x \rangle$. We direct the reader to [1] for a more complete explanation of this conversion routine.

Let us define $\llbracket e_f \rrbracket = k + \llbracket f_f \rrbracket$. To obtain the $\langle \log_2(x) \rangle$ we map $\langle x \rangle$ to the range $[0.5, 1]$, by computing $\langle \nu \rangle = \langle \frac{1}{2^k} \rangle \cdot \llbracket v_f \rrbracket$. Then we can use it to compute $\langle \log_2(x) \rangle = \llbracket e_f \rrbracket + \langle \log_2(\nu) \rangle$. The approximation to $\langle \log_2(\nu) \rangle$ can then be produced by a Padé approximation, calculated by the means of the P_{2524}/Q_{2524} polynomials, introduced by [16] (and given in the Appendix). Note that we define for this function $\log_2(x) = 0$ when $x \leq 0$. The motivation behind this behaviour is given because, including any abort would signal, when the answer is opened, information related to the input.

Exponentiation Functions: We are left with deriving $\langle \exp(2, x) \rangle$, for a secret shared input $\langle x \rangle$. Due to standard identities, this can be obtained from a polynomial approximation to $\exp(2, x)$ in the interval $[0, 1]$. In this regard, we first need to isolate the integral part $\llbracket i \rrbracket$ and fractional remainder $\langle r \rangle$ of the input value $\langle x \rangle$ such that $\langle x \rangle = \llbracket i \rrbracket + \langle r \rangle$. We can then calculate $2^{\llbracket i \rrbracket}$, using conventional techniques for bit-decomposition and exponentiation e.g., [11]. We can obtain $2^{\langle r \rangle}$ using a polynomial approximation, by means of $P_{1045}(\langle r \rangle)$, as given in the Appendix. From that point on, it suffices to follow the identities outlined at the beginning of this section to obtain $\langle \exp(x, y) \rangle$.

Protocol 6. Approximated $\langle \exp(2, x) \rangle$

Input: Secret shared fixed point input $\langle x \rangle = \{[\![v]\!], k, f\}$.
Output: Approximation for $\langle \exp(2, x) \rangle$

1 $[\![s]\!] \leftarrow \langle x \rangle < 0$;
2 $\langle x \rangle \leftarrow \mathtt{choose}([\![s]\!], -1 \cdot \langle x \rangle, \langle x \rangle)$; //Convert input to positive number
3 $[\![i]\!] \leftarrow \mathtt{trunc}(x)$; //extract integer component of x
4 $\langle r \rangle \leftarrow \langle x \rangle - [\![i]\!]$; //Extract fractional component of x
5 $([\![i]\!]_0, ..., [\![i]\!]_{\ell-1}) \leftarrow \mathtt{bit\_decompose}([\![i]\!])$;
6 $[\![d]\!] \leftarrow \prod_{j=0}^{\ell-1}([\![i_j]\!] \cdot 2^{2^j} + 1 - [\![i_j]\!])$;
7 $\langle u \rangle \leftarrow P_{1045}(\langle r \rangle)$;
8 $\langle g \rangle \leftarrow \langle u \rangle \cdot [\![d]\!]$;
9 $\langle \exp(2, x) \rangle \leftarrow \mathtt{choose}(1 - [\![s]\!], \langle g \rangle, \frac{1}{\langle g \rangle})$;

Table 7. Offline data needed for a single fixed point exp/log operation

Protocol	$\langle \log_2(x) \rangle$	$\langle \exp(2, x) \rangle$
Multiplication triples	1880	1337
Square tuples	0	1
Shared bits	5937	7688

Results: Under default precision parameters of the SCALE-MAMBA system, and because of the size of the polynomials used for our approximations of both base two functions i.e., $\langle \log_2(x) \rangle$ and $\langle \exp(2, x) \rangle$, numerical results become less accurate and numerically unstable. Thus, to run our experiments in this example, we doubled the size of our inputs and their precision i.e. we use $k = 81$, $f = 40$, $\kappa = 80$. This, of course, influences the field size on which we operate, which has to be of at least 245 bits, instead of the 128 bits modulus used on our other experiments. Bigger field sizes also imply an increase on communication cost given that the size of the shares increases accordingly. Note that, as we use some level of bit decomposition in our protocols, the number of triples required also increases with the size of k and κ. Our results are presented in Tables 7 and 8.

Table 8. Performance figures for full threshold (2 and 3 parties) and Shamir with 3 parties for the fixed point exp/log operations.

Protocol	Full threshold 2 parties		Full threshold 3 parties		Shamir 3 parties	
	$\langle \log_2(x) \rangle$	$\langle \exp(2, x) \rangle$	$\langle \log_2(x) \rangle$	$\langle \exp(2, x) \rangle$	$\langle \log_2(x) \rangle$	$\langle \exp(2, x) \rangle$
Offline (s)	14	18	15.89	19.83	0.27	0.35
Latency (s)	0.015	0.015	0.018	0.016	0.021	0.18
Throughput (ops/s)	66	76	56	66	50	64

Discussion: Just as for the trigonometric functions we can compare our work to that of Cheon et al. [9] using homomorphic encryption. They perform can perform exponentiation operations in about 164 ms (not amortized), whereas we can perform an exponentiation, with a known public base, in about 2.5 ms (under our 3 parties Shamir based setting). It is worth noting that Dimitrov et al. [15] also provided implementations for the exponent function, using alternative ways to represent these rational numbers, using MPC. However, it is difficult to draw direct comparisons with this later work as they target passively secure MPC, whereas we focus on actively secure MPC.

Acknowledgements. This work has been supported in part by ERC Advanced Grant ERC-2015-AdG-IMPaCT, by the Defense Advanced Research Projects Agency (DARPA) and Space and Naval Warfare Systems Center, Pacific (SSC Pacific) under contract No. N66001-15-C-4070, and by the FWO under an Odysseus project GOH9718N.

A   Polynomial and Padé Approximations

Tables in this appendix provide the concrete polynomials for the Polynomial/Padé approximations used by our protocols. The tables were extracted from Hart's Computer Approximations [16]. We follow the same nomenclature as the book's author. That is to say, scientific notation where each of the polynomial coefficients, is given by its Significand (s) and its coefficient Magnitude (m). Let c_i, be the coefficient of term i, for all $i \in P(x)$. Then c_i can be obtained by calculating $m_i \cdot 10^{s_i}$. This is true for all polynomials in this Appendix.

$P_{3307}(X)$: The polynomial that is used to approximate the function $\sin(x)$ on the interval $[0, \frac{\pi}{2}]$. The absolute error of the approximation is given by:

$$\left| \sin(x) - x \cdot P_{3307}(x^2) \right| < 10^{-20.19} \text{ for } x \in [0, \frac{\pi}{2}].$$

	s	Magnitudes (m) of P_{3307}
0	1	+0.15707 96326 79489 66192 31314 989
1	0	−0.64596 40975 06246 25365 51665 255
2	−1	+0.79692 62624 61670 45105 15876 375
3	−2	−0.46817 54135 31868 79164 48035 89
4	−3	+0.16044 11847 87358 59304 30385 5
5	−5	−0.35988 43235 20707 78156 5727
6	−7	+0.56921 72920 65732 73962 4
7	−9	−0.66880 34884 92042 33722
8	−11	+0.60669 10560 85201 792
9	−13	−0.43752 95071 18174 8
10	−15	+0.25002 85418 9303

$P_{3508}(X)$: The polynomial that is used to approximate the function $\cos(x)$ on the interval $[0, \frac{\pi}{2}]$. The absolute error, for this polynomial is given by:

$$\left|\cos(x) - P_{3508}(x^2)\right| < 10^{-23.06} \text{ for } x \in [0, \frac{\pi}{2}].$$

s		Magnitudes (m) of P_{3508}
0	0	+0.99999 99999 99999 99999 99914 771
1	0	−0.49999 99999 99999 99999 91637 437
2	−1	+0.41666 66666 66666 66653 10411 988
3	−2	−0.13888 88888 88888 88031 01864 15
4	−4	+0.24801 58730 15870 23300 45157
5	−6	−0.27557 31922 39332 25642 1489
6	−8	+0.20876 75698 16541 25915 59
7	−10	−0.11470 74512 67755 43239 4
8	−13	+0.47794 54394 06649 917
9	−15	−0.15612 26342 88277 81
10	−18	+0.39912 65450 7924

$P_{5102}(X)$ and $Q_{5102}(X)$: These are the polynomials we use to calculate the Padé approximation for the function $\arctan(x)$ on the $[0, \tan(\pi/4)]$ interval. Note that, $\tan(\pi/4) = 1$. We can express the relative error for this approximation as:

$$\left| \frac{\arctan(x) - x \cdot \frac{P_{5102}(x^2)}{Q_{5102}(x^2)}}{\arctan(x)} \right| < 10^{-22.69}. \text{ for } x \in [0, \tan \pi/4].$$

s	Magnitudes (m) of P_{5102}	s	Magnitudes (m) of Q_{5102}
0	5 +0.21514 05962 60244 19331 93254 468	5	+0.21514 05962 60244 19331 93298 234
1	5 +0.73597 43380 28844 42408 14980 706	5	+0.80768 78701 15592 48851 76713 209
2	6 +0.10027 25618 30630 27849 70511 863	6	+0.12289 26789 09278 47762 98743 322
3	5 +0.69439 29750 03225 23370 59765 503	5	+0.97323 20349 05355 56802 60434 387
4	5 +0.25858 09739 71909 90257 16567 793	5	+0.42868 57652 04640 80931 84006 664
5	4 +0.50386 39185 50126 65579 37791 19	5	+0.10401 13491 56689 00570 05103 878
6	3 +0.46015 88804 63535 14711 61727 227	4	+0.12897 50569 11611 09714 11459 55
7	2 +0.15087 67735 87003 09877 17455 528	2	+0.68519 37831 01896 80131 14024 294
8	−1 +0.75230 52818 75762 84445 10729 539	1	+0.1

$P_{2524}(X)$ and $Q_{2523}(X)$: These are the polynomials that are used to calculate the Padé approximation for the function $\log_2(x)$ on the interval $[0.5, 1]$. The relative error for this approximation is given by:

$$\left| \frac{\log_2(x) - \frac{P_{2524(x)}}{Q_{2524(x)}}}{\log_2(x)} \right| < 10^{-8.32} \text{ for } x \in [0.5, 1].$$

	s	Magnitudes (m) of P_{2524}	s	Magnitudes (m) of Q_{2524}
0	1	$-0.20546\ 66719\ 51$	0	$+0.35355\ 34252\ 77$
1	1	$-0.88626\ 59939\ 1$	1	$+0.45451\ 70876\ 29$
2	1	$+0.61058\ 51990\ 15$	1	$+0.64278\ 42090\ 29$
3	1	$+0.48114\ 74609\ 89$	1	$+0.1$

$P_{1045}(X)$: We use this polynomial, to calculate the Padé approximation for the function $\exp(2, x)$ on the interval $[0, 1]$. The relative error of the approximation is given by:

$$\left| \frac{\exp(2, x) - P_{1045}(x)}{\exp(2, x)} \right| < 10^{-12.11} \text{ for } x \in [0, 1].$$

	s	Magnitudes (m) of P_{1045}
0	1	$+0.10000\ 00077\ 44302\ 1686$
1	0	$+0.69314\ 71804\ 26163\ 82779\ 5756$
2	0	$+0.24022\ 65107\ 10170\ 64605\ 384$
3	-1	$+0.55504\ 06862\ 04663\ 79157\ 744$
4	-2	$+0.96183\ 41225\ 88046\ 23749\ 77$
5	-2	$+0.13327\ 30359\ 28143\ 78193\ 29$
6	-3	$+0.15510\ 74605\ 90052\ 57397\ 8$
7	-4	$+0.14197\ 84739\ 97656\ 06711$
8	-5	$+0.18633\ 47724\ 13796\ 7076$

References

1. Aliasgari, M., Blanton, M., Zhang, Y., Steele, A.: Secure computation on floating point numbers. In: NDSS 2013. The Internet Society, February 2013
2. Aly, A., et al.: SCALE and MAMBA documentation (2018). https://homes.esat. kuleuven.be/~nsmart/SCALE/
3. Bayatbabolghani, F., Blanton, M., Aliasgari, M., Goodrich, M.: Secure computations of trigonometric and inverse trigonometric functions. In: IEEE Symposium on Security and Privacy (IEEE S&P 2017), San Jose, May 2017
4. Bayatbabolghani, F., Blanton, M., Aliasgari, M., Goodrich, M.: Secure fingerprint alignment and matching protocols. arXiv preprint arXiv:1702.03379 (2017)

5. Beaver, D.: Foundations of secure interactive computing. In: Feigenbaum, J. (ed.) CRYPTO 1991. LNCS, vol. 576, pp. 377–391. Springer, Heidelberg (1992). https://doi.org/10.1007/3-540-46766-1_31

6. Bogdanov, D., Laur, S., Willemson, J.: Sharemind: a framework for fast privacy-preserving computations. In: Jajodia, S., Lopez, J. (eds.) ESORICS 2008. LNCS, vol. 5283, pp. 192–206. Springer, Heidelberg (2008). https://doi.org/10.1007/978-3-540-88313-5_13

7. Catrina, O., de Hoogh, S.: Improved primitives for secure multiparty integer computation. In: Garay, J.A., De Prisco, R. (eds.) SCN 2010. LNCS, vol. 6280, pp. 182–199. Springer, Heidelberg (2010). https://doi.org/10.1007/978-3-642-15317-4_13

8. Catrina, O., Saxena, A.: Secure computation with fixed-point numbers. In: Sion, R. (ed.) FC 2010. LNCS, vol. 6052, pp. 35–50. Springer, Heidelberg (2010). https://doi.org/10.1007/978-3-642-14577-3_6

9. Cheon, J.H., Han, K., Kim, A., Kim, M., Song, Y.: A full RNS variant of approximate homomorphic encryption. In: Cid, C., Jacobson Jr., M. (eds.) SAC 2018. LNCS, vol. 11349, pp. 347–368. Springer, Cham (2018). https://doi.org/10.1007/978-3-030-10970-7_16

10. Cybernetica SA: Sharemind (2018). https://sharemind.cyber.ee

11. Damgård, I., Fitzi, M., Kiltz, E., Nielsen, J.B., Toft, T.: Unconditionally secure constant-rounds multi-party computation for equality, comparison, bits and exponentiation. In: Halevi, S., Rabin, T. (eds.) TCC 2006. LNCS, vol. 3876, pp. 285–304. Springer, Heidelberg (2006). https://doi.org/10.1007/11681878_15

12. Damgård, I., Keller, M., Larraia, E., Pastro, V., Scholl, P., Smart, N.P.: Practical covertly secure MPC for dishonest majority – or: breaking the SPDZ limits. In: Crampton, J., Jajodia, S., Mayes, K. (eds.) ESORICS 2013. LNCS, vol. 8134, pp. 1–18. Springer, Heidelberg (2013). https://doi.org/10.1007/978-3-642-40203-6_1

13. Damgård, I., Nielsen, J.B.: Universally composable efficient multiparty computation from threshold homomorphic encryption. In: Boneh, D. (ed.) CRYPTO 2003. LNCS, vol. 2729, pp. 247–264. Springer, Heidelberg (2003). https://doi.org/10.1007/978-3-540-45146-4_15

14. Damgård, I., Pastro, V., Smart, N., Zakarias, S.: Multiparty computation from somewhat homomorphic encryption. In: Safavi-Naini, R., Canetti, R. (eds.) CRYPTO 2012. LNCS, vol. 7417, pp. 643–662. Springer, Heidelberg (2012). https://doi.org/10.1007/978-3-642-32009-5_38

15. Dimitrov, V., Kerik, L., Krips, T., Randmets, J., Willemson, J.: Alternative implementations of secure real numbers. In: Weippl, E.R., Katzenbeisser, S., Kruegel, C., Myers, A.C., Halevi, S. (eds.) ACM CCS 2016, pp. 553–564. ACM Press, October 2016

16. Hart, J.F.: Computer Approximations. Krieger Publishing Co. Inc., Melbourne (1978)

17. Kamm, L.: Privacy-preserving statistical analysis using secure multi-party computation. Ph.D. thesis, University of Tartu, Estonia (2015)

18. Kamm, L., Willemson, J.: Secure floating-point arithmetic and private satellite collision analysis. Cryptology ePrint Archive, Report 2013/850 (2013). http://eprint.iacr.org/2013/850

19. Keller, M., Pastro, V., Rotaru, D.: Overdrive: making SPDZ great again. In: Nielsen, J.B., Rijmen, V. (eds.) EUROCRYPT 2018. LNCS, vol. 10822, pp. 158–189. Springer, Cham (2018). https://doi.org/10.1007/978-3-319-78372-7_6

20. Keller, M., Rotaru, D., Smart, N.P., Wood, T.: Reducing communication channels in MPC. In: Catalano, D., De Prisco, R. (eds.) SCN 2018. LNCS, vol. 11035, pp. 181–199. Springer, Cham (2018). https://doi.org/10.1007/978-3-319-98113-0_10

21. Kerik, L., Laud, P., Randmets, J.: Optimizing MPC for robust and scalable integer and floating-point arithmetic. In: Clark, J., Meiklejohn, S., Ryan, P.Y.A., Wallach, D., Brenner, M., Rohloff, K. (eds.) FC 2016. LNCS, vol. 9604, pp. 271–287. Springer, Heidelberg (2016). https://doi.org/10.1007/978-3-662-53357-4_18

22. Liedel, M.: Secure distributed computation of the square root and applications. In: Ryan, M.D., Smyth, B., Wang, G. (eds.) ISPEC 2012. LNCS, vol. 7232, pp. 277–288. Springer, Heidelberg (2012). https://doi.org/10.1007/978-3-642-29101-2_19

23. Maurer, U.: Secure multi-party computation made simple. Discret. Appl. Math. **154**(2), 370–381 (2006)

24. Medina, H.A.: A sequence of polynomials for approximating arctangent. Am. Math. Mon. **113**(2), 156–161 (2006). http://www.jstor.org/stable/27641866

25. Ning, C., Xu, Q.: Multiparty computation for modulo reduction without bit-decomposition and a generalization to bit-decomposition. In: Abe, M. (ed.) ASIACRYPT 2010. LNCS, vol. 6477, pp. 483–500. Springer, Heidelberg (2010). https://doi.org/10.1007/978-3-642-17373-8_28

26. Ning, C., Xu, Q.: Constant-rounds, linear multi-party computation for exponentiation and modulo reduction with perfect security. In: Lee, D.H., Wang, X. (eds.) ASIACRYPT 2011. LNCS, vol. 7073, pp. 572–589. Springer, Heidelberg (2011). https://doi.org/10.1007/978-3-642-25385-0_31

27. Zhang, Y., Steele, A., Blanton, M.: PICCO: a general-purpose compiler for private distributed computation. In: Sadeghi, A.R., Gligor, V.D., Yung, M. (eds.) ACM CCS 2013, pp. 813–826. ACM Press, November 2013

Turbospeedz: Double Your Online SPDZ! Improving SPDZ Using Function Dependent Preprocessing

Aner Ben-Efraim[1], Michael Nielsen[2], and Eran Omri[1(✉)]

[1] Department of Computer Science, Ariel University, Ariel, Israel
`anermosh@post.bgu.ac.il`, `omrier@gmail.com`
[2] Uber, Aarhus, Denmark
`michael@cryptax.com`

Abstract. Secure multiparty computation allows a set of mutually distrusting parties to securely compute a function of their private inputs, revealing only the output, even if some of the parties are corrupt. Recent years have seen an enormous amount of work that drastically improved the concrete efficiency of secure multiparty computation protocols. Many secure multiparty protocols work in an "offline-online" model. In this model, the computation is split into two main phases: a relatively slow "offline phase", which the parties execute before they know their input, and a fast "online phase", which the parties execute after receiving their input.

One of the most popular and efficient protocols for secure multiparty computation working in this model is the SPDZ protocol (Damgård et al., CRYPTO 2012). The SPDZ offline phase is function independent, i.e., does not require knowledge of the computed function at the offline phase. Thus, a natural question is: can the efficiency of the SPDZ protocol be improved if the function is known at the offline phase?

In this work, we answer the above question affirmatively. We show that by using a function dependent preprocessing protocol, the online communication of the SPDZ protocol can be brought down significantly, almost by a factor of 2, and the online computation is often also significantly reduced. In scenarios where communication is the bottleneck, such as strong computers on low bandwidth networks, this could potentially almost double the online throughput of the SPDZ protocol, when securely computing the same circuit many times in parallel (on different inputs).

We present two versions of our protocol: Our first version uses the SPDZ offline phase protocol as a black-box, which achieves the improved online communication at the cost of slightly increasing the offline communication. Our second version works by modifying the state-of-the-art

A. Ben-Efraim and E. Omri—Research supported by ISF grant 152/17 and the Ariel Cyber Innovation Center.
M. Nielsen—Partially supported by the European Research Council (ERC) under the European Unions's Horizon 2020 research and innovation programme under grant agreement No. 669255 (MPCPRO).

R. H. Deng et al. (Eds.): ACNS 2019, LNCS 11464, pp. 530–549, 2019.
https://doi.org/10.1007/978-3-030-21568-2_26

SPDZ preprocessing protocol, Overdrive (Keller et al., Eurocrypt 2018). This version improves the overall communication over the state-of-the-art SPDZ.

Keywords: Secure multiparty computation · SPDZ · Concrete efficiency · Offline/online

1 Introduction

Secure multiparty computation allows a set of mutually distrusting parties to securely compute a function of their private inputs, revealing only the output, even if some of the parties are corrupt. Secure computation was introduced by Yao [41] for 2 parties and by Goldreich et al. [26] for the multiparty case. Soon afterwards strong feasibility results were established, e.g., [9,13,15,26,34,38]. Establishment of feasibility led to research of efficiency, and a long series of works, [1,4,19,20,22,29,30] and others, reduced the asymptotic communication and computational complexity of secure computation to almost optimal. In this work and in the following, we focus on the setting of dishonest majority with active security, in which all parties except one can be dishonest, and dishonest players may deviate from the protocol description.

However, many of these asymptotically efficient protocols perform poorly when it comes to real world applications. For example, secure multiparty protocols based on fully-homomorphic encryption, e.g., [4], have almost optimal communication and computational complexity, but their concrete efficiency (i.e., their run-time in practice on real world problems) makes them somewhat impractical. The necessity of secure computation in real-world applications has therefore encouraged the study of concretely efficient protocols. Recent years have seen an enormous amount of work in this direction, and the concrete efficiency of secure multiparty computation protocols has also been significantly improved, e.g., [11,16,23,24,35,40].

Real world scenarios have also led to the study of the "preprocessing" or "offline-online" model. In this model, the parties run a relatively expensive "offline" phase, i.e., a preprocessing protocol, before they know their inputs. After receiving their inputs, the parties then run a very efficient "online" protocol that uses the computations made at the offline phase. Such protocols can be used to make "real-time" secure computations, when it is known well in advance that these computations would take place.

Some of the works in the offline-online model, most notably SPDZ [23,24], have a function independent offline phase, i.e., they assume the parties do not know the function to be computed during the preprocessing. Other works, such as most concretely efficient constant round secure multiparty protocols [11,28, 36,40], have a function dependent offline phase, i.e., they assume the parties already know the function at the expensive offline phase.

Both function independent offline and function dependent offline make sense in different real world applications. For example, assume a set of parties wish to securely compute an online auction at a specific date. On the one hand, a function dependent offline phase might allow the parties to run the auction more quickly. On the other hand, a function independent preprocessing would allow the parties more flexibility, such as changing the auction details up to the last minute. Therefore, it is important to study both of these models. In fact, several recent works in concretely efficient secure multiparty protocols, e.g., [28, 36, 40], separate the offline phase into two parts: a function independent preprocessing phase and a function dependent preprocessing phase.

Despite the SPDZ protocol being one of the most popular and efficient secure multiparty computation protocols, we observe that all previous works on the SPDZ protocol, e.g., [6, 18, 23, 24, 39], have only a function independent preprocessing phase. Thus, a natural question arises:

Question 1. Can the famous SPDZ protocol profit from using a function dependent preprocessing protocol?

1.1 Our Contribution and Techniques

In this work we answer Question 1 affirmatively. We present a new "SPDZ-like" protocol for secure computation against malicious adversaries, which requires approximately only half the communication in the online phase compared to the current state-of-the-art SPDZ online [23]. Furthermore, our protocol requires approximately only half the computation in the online MACCheck protocol, which is one of the main computational costs of the SPDZ online phase. Thus, we expect that our protocol could almost double the online throughput compared to SPDZ in some scenarios, e.g., strong machines on low-bandwidth networks that securely compute the same function multiple times in parallel on different inputs. We remark that these scenarios are of interest in real world applications; for example, increasing the throughput of secure multiple parallel AES computations has been discussed in [2] for Kerberos.

For semi-honest security, Beaver [8] showed how to randomize circuits. Our technique can be seen as compiling the original circuit randomization technique to tolerate active security. Compared to protocols based on so-called "multiplication triples", e.g., [14, 23, 24], we correlate the randomness across gates throughout the circuit, which in turn allows us to save roughly half the communication in the online phase. Our protocols show that such techniques are useful for arithmetic circuits with a dishonest majority, which we present through an improvement of the well-studied SPDZ protocol.

More specifically, in our preprocessing protocol, the parties compute at each output wire of a multiplication gate an additional secret-shared random value. At the online phase, the parties reveal the sum of the real value and this random value. Then, using this revealed sum and additional information revealed at our preprocessing protocol, the parties can *locally* compute the shares for the output wires of the multiplication gates of the following layer in the circuit. Therefore, the only communication in the online phase for multiplication gates is revealing a single secret-shared value – the sum of the real value and a random value

– whereas in [23] they reveal two values at each multiplication gate. However, our preprocessing protocol requires knowledge of the computed function. So in contrast to previous works on SPDZ, such as [6,18,23,24,39], our protocol's offline phase is function dependent.

For intuition, one could see this as follows: the extra randomness allows "shifting" the revealed values from corresponding to the input wires of multiplication gates (2 input wires for each gate) to corresponding to the output wires of the multiplication gates (1 output wire per gate) in the previous layer of the circuit. This "shift" is made possible because we know the function at the offline phase. Thus, our online protocol requires only half the amount of revealed values per multiplication gate compared to the improved online SPDZ [23], and additionally, we also save revealing values for input wires by observing that random values used for input distribution, which are "thrown out" in SPDZ, can be reused securely in our protocol. Since almost all the online communication comes from the revealing of these values, our online protocol requires almost half the amount of communication required by the online protocol in [23].[1] We further observe that the number of revealed values directly affects the amount of computation in the SPDZ MACCheck protocol, which is run at the end of the online phase to verify that no cheating has occurred.

We present two versions of a protocol that achieve an improved online phase. In the first version, we work on top of the SPDZ offline phase; that is, we first run the SPDZ offline preprocessing protocol (with values as detailed below), and then run another preprocessing protocol. This additional preprocessing protocol is constant-round and its communication and computation is comparable to the SPDZ online phase, i.e., relatively small compared to the main cost of the SPDZ offline phase.

The number of Beaver triples (see Sect. 2 for the definition of Beaver triples) we need for our protocol is exactly the same as in SPDZ. In this version of our protocol, we also require generating an additional (in comparison with SPDZ) random shared value for each multiplication gate at the function independent preprocessing. However, we note that generating a random shared value is significantly cheaper than generating a Beaver triple. Thus, in total, our offline phase, including both our new function dependent preprocessing protocol and the SPDZ preprocessing with additional random shared values, should not be significantly worse than the SPDZ offline phase.

The second version for the protocol achieving an improved online phase is obtained by modifying the state-of-the-art SPDZ preprocessing protocol, Overdrive [33]. In this version of our protocol, we "align" randomness generated in Overdrive with the randomness needed for our online protocol. As a result, this version of the protocol requires at most the same amount of offline communication as Overdrive, and in some cases (depending on the computed circuit) even

---

[1] Additional online communication includes squaring gates and communication in the MACCheck protocol, where we do not improve over [23]. However, this communication is relatively small, especially in large circuits. Therefore, our online communication is only slightly more than half the online communication of [23].

less. In order to "align" the randomness, the new offline phase requires some extra computation (compared to Overdrive), but this computation consists of simple additions. Experiments in Overdrive suggest that communication is often the bottleneck also in the offline phase. Therefore, we expect our offline to improve the offline time in many instances (since we save communication), and even in circuits where we do not save offline communication, the extra additions needed for our protocol should not significantly increase the offline time.

To summarize, our protocol significantly improves over the SPDZ protocol in the online phase. If we modify the state-of-the-art Overdrive, we also improve the overall communication, while if we use the SPDZ offline phase as a black-box our offline phase is only slightly worse (which is still desirable in accordance with the spirit of the offline-online model). Thus, in cases where the computed function is known in advance, our protocol should be preferred over SPDZ.

1.2 Related Works

Works that focus on the preprocessing phase of the SPDZ protocol, such as MASCOT [31], Overdrive [33], and others, e.g., [7], are somewhat complementary to our work, since we use them for our offline phase. In the first version of our protocol we use these protocols as a black-box. In the second version of our protocol, we show that if the function is known at the offline phase, Overdrive can be slightly modified to "align" with our online protocol, increasing the efficiency (of the overall time) even further.[2]

There have also been several works that modified the SPDZ online phase in order to achieve additional properties, such as public auditability [6], efficient cheater detection [39], and extension to the integers modulo 2^k [18]. It is interesting to check if our ideas can also be used to improve the online phase in these protocols.

Another line of related works is secure computation based on lookup-tables, e.g., [17,25,32]. Similarly to our work, these protocols require a function dependent offline phase, and further require sending only a single field element to each other party per gate at the online phase. Furthermore, protocols based on lookup-tables can have significantly more sophisticated gates, whereas we only have addition and multiplication gates. However, known protocols based on lookup-tables in the malicious setting, e.g., [25,32], require memory that grows linearly with the size of the field, per gate. Therefore, in contrast to our protocol (and SPDZ), protocols based on lookup-tables are useful mainly over small fields.[3] We note that in the semi-honest setting, Couteau [17] showed an

---

[2] We note that our "aligning" method works even better with the SPDZ preprocessing of [23], but the overall improvement would still probably not surpass using Overdrive. In contrast, due to a randomization technique used in MASCOT [31] triple generation, it is not clear if this "alignment" can also be applied to MASCOT preprocessing.

[3] To be more precise, these protocols perform best over small characteristic fields. However, they can be somewhat efficiently extended to arithmetic computations over the integers using the Chinese Remainder Theorem, e.g., [5,10], and to extension fields with small characteristic using multiplication embedding.

extension of the lookup-table approach to arbitrarily large fields, where only a constant number of field elements is stored per gate per party.

A different approach to secure multiparty computation is based on garbled circuits. In the garbled circuit approach, the parties in some sense encrypt the function circuit at the offline phase. Then, at the online phase, the parties reveal keys for the inputs and locally compute the output of the circuit. This approach, for the multiparty setting, was originally proposed by Beaver et al. [9], and has recently received significant attention for concrete efficiency in several works, e.g., [10,11,28,36,40]. In contrast to SPDZ and protocols based on look-up tables, these protocols are constant round. Thus, the main advantage of secure multiparty protocols based on garbled circuits is to reduce the online time of deep circuits over high-latency networks. However, due to their large online computation complexity (for a large number of parties) they are generally not suitable for a high-throughput online goal, which is the main advantage of our protocol. Furthermore, it was shown (e.g., [11]) that in low-latency networks (e.g., LAN), protocols based on garbled circuits perform relatively poorly. And last, similarly to protocols based on lookup-tables, protocols based on garbled circuits require memory that is linear in the field size per gate, and are therefore impractical over large fields (See footnote 3).

We remark that there are also secure computation protocols which are specialized for restricted scenarios such as a semi-honest adversary, an honest majority, and/or a small number of parties, e.g., [2,3,21,27]. We cannot compete with these protocols since achieving malicious security for any number of corrupt parties is significantly harder.

Regarding technique, our method can be seen as optimizing the computation by computing the gates on random values revealed on the wires. Similar ideas have been considered in previous works in various scenarios, such as Beaver's original circuit randomization in the semi-honest setting [8], the point-and-permute technique for garbled circuits [9] (that this technique implies computing the gates on revealed random values is seen more clearly in arithmetic garbled circuits [5,10,37]), in protocols based on look-up tables [25,32], in protocols for an honest majority, e.g., [21], and recently for an extremely efficient protocol for 4 parties with an honest majority [27]. Our protocols show that this technique can also be used to improve the well studied SPDZ protocol.

Organization. In Sect. 2 we recall the ideas of the SPDZ protocol and Overdrive. In Sect. 3 we describe our function dependent offline protocols that uses SPDZ offline as a black-box, and our new online protocol. In Sect. 4 we explain how to improve the overall time of our protocol when using Overdrive. In Sect. 5 we prove correctness and state our security theorems; the proof of security can be found in [12].

Notation and Conventions. Similarly to SPDZ, throughout this paper we assume the computation is performed by n parties over some finite field $\mathbb{F}$. We also assume that $|\mathbb{F}|$ is exponential in the security parameter κ. When we refer to the computed function, we assume it is encoded as an arithmetic circuit C over $\mathbb{F}$.

2   Review of the SPDZ Protocol and Overdrive

In this section, we briefly review the (improved) SPDZ protocol presented in [23]. Then we partially explain how Overdrive [33] generates multiplication triples using a public-key semi-homomorphic encryption. We follow [23] for SPDZ because it has the currently most efficient online phase. Overdrive [33] is currently the state-of-the-art protocol for generating multiplication triples. The results in this section are given only as a preliminary to our work in the following sections, and are taken mainly from [23] and [33].

The SPDZ protocol executes a relatively expensive "offline" preprocessing phase in order to achieve a very efficient online phase, which is secure against any number of corruptions (in the model of security with abort). Before giving an overview of the SPDZ protocol, we recall Beaver multiplication triples [8], which is one of the main building blocks of the SPDZ protocol.

Definitions of $[[\cdot]]$-*Shared Elements and Beaver Multiplication Triples.* Assume each party has a uniform additive share $\alpha_i \in \mathbb{F}$ of a secret global MAC value $\alpha = \Sigma_{i=1}^n \alpha_i$. An element $a \in \mathbb{F}$ is $[[\cdot]]$-shared if each party holds a pair $(a_i, \gamma(a)_i)$, where a_i is an additive secret-sharing of a, i.e., $a = \Sigma_{i=1}^n a_i$, and $\gamma(a)_i$ is an additive secret-sharing of $\gamma(a) = \alpha \cdot a$, i.e., $\gamma(\alpha) = \Sigma_{i=1}^n \gamma(a)_i$. For an element $a \in \mathbb{F}$ we denote $[[a]] \stackrel{\text{def}}{=} ((a_1, \ldots, a_n), (\gamma(a)_1, \ldots, \gamma(a)_n))$.

A nice feature of $[[\cdot]]$-shared elements is that addition of 2 $[[\cdot]]$-shared elements, addition of a public scalar, and multiplication by a public scalar can be computed locally.

Property 1. For $a, b, e \in \mathbb{F}$ with $[[a]], [[b]]$ being $[[\cdot]]$-shares of a,b respectively and e a public value

- $[[a]] + [[b]] \stackrel{\text{def}}{=} ((a_1 + b_1, \ldots, a_n + b_n), (\gamma(a)_1 + \gamma(b)_1, \ldots, \gamma(a)_n + \gamma(b)_n))$ is a $[[\cdot]]$-share of $a + b$,
- $e \cdot [[a]] \stackrel{\text{def}}{=} ((e \cdot a_1, \ldots, e \cdot a_n), (e \cdot \gamma(a)_1, \ldots, e \cdot \gamma(a)_n))$ is a $[[\cdot]]$-share of $e \cdot a$,
- $e + [[a]] \stackrel{\text{def}}{=} ((e + a_1, a_2, \ldots, a_n), (\gamma(a)_1 + e \cdot \alpha_1, \ldots, \gamma(a)_n + e \cdot \alpha_n))$ is a $[[\cdot]]$-share of $e + a$.

However, to perform multiplication of 2 $[[\cdot]]$-shared elements in the SPDZ protocol, the parties require interaction and a Beaver multiplication triple [8].

A Beaver multiplication triple is a triple, $([[a]], [[b]], [[c]])$, of $[[\cdot]]$-shared values such that $c = a \cdot b$. Similarly, a squaring pair is a pair, $([[a]], [[c]])$, of $[[\cdot]]$-shared values such that $c = a^2$; squaring pairs are used in [23] to compute the square of a $[[\cdot]]$-shared value more efficiently.

MACCheck Protocol. During both the offline and the online phase of the SPDZ protocol, certain $[[\cdot]]$-shared values are (partially) revealed to some or all of the parties. I.e., the parties learn the shared value (but not the MAC). A malicious adversary may attempt to manipulate its shares to reveal different values than the ones actually shared. Thus, some procedure must be run to ensure such a cheating does not occur.

This procedure is the MACCheck protocol of [23], which receives a set of revealed $[[\cdot]]$-shared values and efficiently verifies, with failure probability $\leq \frac{2}{|\mathbb{F}|}$ ($|\mathbb{F}|$ being the size of the field), that no cheating has occurred. Note that in this paper we discuss only large fields (i.e., $\mathbb{F}$ is exponential in the security parameter), so MACCheck verifies that the adversary did not cheat except with negligible probability. The details of this protocol can be found in [23, Fig. 10]. We will need only the following claim:

Claim 1 (Informal) [23, Lemma 1]. *Given a set of partially revealed $[[\cdot]]$-shared values, if the revealed values do not match the $[[\cdot]]$-shared values, MACCheck aborts except with probability $\leq \frac{2}{|\mathbb{F}|}$. Furthermore, if the adversary does not cheat, MACCheck leaks no information on the queried values, the global MAC α, and the honest parties' shares.*

The SPDZ Offline Phase. The main part of the SPDZ offline phase is a preprocessing protocol that securely generates Beaver triples and additional random $[[\cdot]]$-shared values. There have been several works that significantly improved the original SPDZ preprocessing protocol, e.g., [7,31,33]. The current state-of-the-art protocols are Overdrive [33] for large prime fields, which is based on semi-homomorphic encryption, and MASCOT [31] for large fields of characteristic 2, which is based on oblivious transfer.

In Sect. 3 we assume black-box access to the SPDZ offline functionality (which in practice would probably be implemented using Overdrive). I.e., we assume that the parties can access a functionality $\mathcal{F}_{\text{Prep}}$ that gives the parties the shares of the requested number of Beaver triples $([[a]], [[b]], [[c]])$, square pairs $([[a]], [[c]])$, random $[[\cdot]]$-shared elements $[[r]]$, and input maskings $(r_i, [[r_i]])$.[4] The functionality $\mathcal{F}_{\text{Prep}}$ can be found in [23, Fig. 16]. For concrete protocols, one should look at [7,23,31,33].

In Sect. 4 we show how to modify Overdrive (SPDZ offline protocol) so that the values generated at the offline are "aligned" with the values needed in our online protocol. A partial overview of Overdrive, in particular of the triple generation protocol and the SPDZ sacrifice step, is given at the end of this section, and the modification is explained in Sect. 4.

The SPDZ Online Phase. As mentioned, one of the highlights of the SPDZ protocol is its very efficient online protocol that is secure against any number of corruptions (in the model of security with abort), which is achieved using the relatively expensive preprocessing protocol. In the online protocol, the parties first compute $[[\cdot]]$-shares of their inputs as follows: party i shares its input x_i by revealing $x_i - r_i$, where r_i is an input masking that was generated at the offline phase. The parties then locally compute $[[x_i]] \leftarrow [[r_i]] + (x_i - r_i)$ using Property 1.

Addition gates are computed locally: let the input wires be x, y and the output wire be z. The parties locally compute $[[z]] \leftarrow [[x]] + [[y]]$ using Property 1.

---

[4] An input masking $(r_i, [[r_i]])$ is a random $[[\cdot]]$-shared element, where the value r_i is known to party i.

In order to compute multiplication gates, the parties use a Beaver triple $([[a]], [[b]], [[c]])$ as follows: let the input wires be x, y and the output wire be z. The parties locally compute $[[\epsilon]] \leftarrow [[x]] - [[a]]$ and $[[\rho]] \leftarrow [[y]] - [[b]]$, and then communicate to partially reveal ϵ and ρ. Then, the parties use Property 1 to locally compute

$$[[x \cdot y]] \leftarrow [[c]] + \epsilon \cdot [[b]] + \rho \cdot [[a]] + \epsilon \cdot \rho \tag{1}$$

Squaring gates are computed in a similar but slightly simpler way, using a square pair.

At the end of the protocol, before outputting the result, the parties run a MACCheck protocol to verify that the corrupt parties did not cheat. If the corrupt parties did attempt to cheat, the cheating is detected with overwhelming probability, and the honest parties abort. Note that fairness is not guaranteed, i.e., the adversary can learn the output while the honest parties do not.

Triple Generation Using Overdrive. Overdrive [33] (and previously [14]) construct multiplication triples using a public-key semi-homomorphic encryption Enc. For efficiency, Overdrive uses the BGV encryption that introduces noise, which needs to be "drowned" for security reasons. Furthermore, the parties need to prove that some encryptions are generated correctly using zero-knowledge proofs. Due to space constraints we do not go into the details here, and encourage the reader to read [33] for the details.

The multiplication scheme is as follows: assume the parties hold additive shares $a = \Sigma_i a_i, b = \Sigma_i b_i$, then $ab = (\Sigma_i a_i \cdot \Sigma_i b_i) = \Sigma_i a_i b_i + \Sigma_{i \neq j} a_i b_j$. Each $a_i b_i$ can be computed locally by party i, and (shares of) $a_i b_j$ are computed using the following two party protocol: Party i sends $\text{Enc}(a_i)$ encrypted under its own public key. Party j, using Party i's public key and the received $\text{Enc}(a_i)$, responds with $C_i = b_j \cdot \text{Enc}(a_i) - \text{Enc}(c_j)$, where c_j is a randomly chosen share. Then party i decrypts $c_i = \text{Dec}(C_i)$ and by the homomorphic property $c_i + c_j = a_i b_j$, so (c_i, c_j) is a secret-sharing of $a_i b_j$.

The above multiplication is used in two places in Overdrive: (**1**) To compute the shares of $c = ab$ in the multiplication triple, and (**2**) To generate the MACed shares $[[a]], [[b]], [[c]]$; we shall assume the latter is done by calling the functionality $\mathcal{F}_{[[]]}$. Due to space constraints we do not include the implementation of $\mathcal{F}_{[[]]}$ or the original Overdrive triple generation protocol, which can be found in [33, Figs. 4 and 7]. Our modified version of the triple generation protocol, used for our protocol in Sect. 4, is given in Fig. 3.

One issue that arises is that the adversary might attempt to cheat in the triple generation. For efficiency reasons, only some of this is captured in Overdrive using zero-knowledge proofs. In particular, the adversary is able to create triples $(a, b, ab + \mathsf{e})$ for some error e of her choice. This is solved in Overdrive using the "SPDZ sacrifice" – triples are generated in pairs, and one is "sacrificed" to ensure the other triple is correct. The SPDZ sacrifice was slightly improved in [31], showing that it suffices to use correlated triple pairs $(([[a]], [[b]], [[c]]), ([[a]], [[\hat{b}]], [[\hat{c}]]))$.

The (improved) SPDZ sacrifice works roughly as follows: a random element r is chosen *after* the triples are (possibly incorrectly) generated. Then, $\rho = rb - \hat{b}$ is partially opened. Using ρ, the parties compute (using Property 1) and partially reveal $\tau = rc - \hat{c} - \rho a$, and abort if $\tau \neq 0$. It can be shown that if the adversary cheated in generating the triples, i.e., $c = ab + e$ and $\hat{c} = a\hat{b} + \hat{e}$ with $e \neq 0$ and/or $\hat{e} \neq 0$, then $\tau \neq 0$ with overwhelming probability. If the adversary tries to cheat in the revealing of ρ and/or τ, she is later be caught by the MACCheck protocol with overwhelming probability. It is easy to see that if the adversary does not cheat then the parties do not abort. And because $\hat{b}$ and $\hat{c}$ are "sacrificed" (i.e., not used elsewhere in the protocol), ρ does not leak any information on $([[a]], [[b]], [[c]])$.

3 Our New Protocol, Using SPDZ Offline as Black-Box

In this section we describe our two new protocols – our added function dependent offline protocol and our new "SPDZ-like" online protocol. The offline protocol in this section uses the SPDZ preprocessing protocol as a black-box. A more efficient version of our protocol, which is achieved by modifying the state-of-the-art SPDZ preprocessing protocol, Overdrive, is given in Sect. 4.

We use slightly different notation and equations than the ones explained in Sect. 2, so we first give the details of our notation and equations.

3.1 Notation and Equations

Similarly to the online phase of the SPDZ protocol, in our online protocol the parties compute (in topological order on the circuit) for each wire a $[[\cdot]]$-shared value that corresponds to the real value on the wire. We denote the real value on wire ω by v_ω and correspondingly its $[[\cdot]]$-shared value by $[[v_\omega]]$.[5] Observe that the real values depend on the inputs, and are thus determined only at the online phase.

In our online protocol, the parties additionally hold at each wire ω shares of a random field element, which we term the *permutation element* and denote by λ_ω (and its $[[\cdot]]$-share by $[[\lambda_\omega]]$). The shares of these permutation elements are generated and computed in the offline phase. Note that these permutation elements are independent of the real values. It is also important that the permutation elements are independent of the multiplication triples.

At the online phase, after computing the shares corresponding to the real value, the parties open the sum of the real value and the permutation element. We call this sum the *external value*, and denote it by $e_\omega \overset{\text{def}}{=} v_\omega + \lambda_\omega$. The important observation is that since the permutation element is independently random and unknown, the external value reveals no information on the real value; similar observations are implicitly used in SPDZ, e.g., when revealing ϵ, ρ of multiplication input wires.

---

[5] In [23,24] they do not distinguish between the wire and its value – there v_ω and $[[v_\omega]]$ are denoted ω and $[[\omega]]$, respectively. Our notation is similar to notations used for multiparty garbled circuits, e.g., [9,11].

For addition gates with input wires x, y, we let the permutation element of the output wire z be the sum of the permutation elements on the input wires, i.e., $\lambda_z = \lambda_x + \lambda_y$. Thus, the shares of λ_z can be computed locally by the parties from the shares of λ_x and λ_y. Furthermore, we observe that during the online phase, the external value on the output wire can also be computed locally by the parties, since the above implies that the external value of the output wire is the sum of the external values of the input wires:

$$e_z = v_z + \lambda_z = (v_x + v_y) + (\lambda_x + \lambda_y) = (v_x + \lambda_x) + (v_y + \lambda_y) = e_x + e_y \quad (2)$$

For a multiplication gate with input wires x and y and output wire z, assume the beaver triple $([[a]], [[b]], [[c]])$ is associated with the multiplication gate. We denote the *input offsets* by

$$\widetilde{\lambda_x} \overset{\text{def}}{=} a - \lambda_x \quad (3)$$

and

$$\widetilde{\lambda_y} \overset{\text{def}}{=} b - \lambda_y. \quad (4)$$

We further denote the *adjusted external values* on the input wires by

$$\widehat{e}_x \overset{\text{def}}{=} e_x + \widetilde{\lambda_x} = (v_x + \lambda_x) + (a - \lambda_x) = v_x + a, \quad (5)$$

$$\widehat{e}_y \overset{\text{def}}{=} e_y + \widetilde{\lambda_y} = (v_y + \lambda_y) + (b - \lambda_y) = v_y + b. \quad (6)$$

Then, we have the following resulting equation:

$$v_x v_y = (v_x + a)(v_y + b) - a(v_y + b) - b(v_x + a) + ab = \widehat{e}_x \widehat{e}_y - \widehat{e}_y a - \widehat{e}_x b + c \quad (7)$$

Equation (7) is used in our online protocol in order to compute the shares of the multiplication. For the output wire, we set the permutation element on the output wire to be $\lambda_z = c + r$, where r is a fresh random $[[\cdot]]$-shared value.[6]

Remark 1. Note that Eq. (7) we use is slightly different than Eq. (1) used in [23, 24] – Eq. (1) uses the values $\epsilon = v_x - a$ and $\rho = v_y - b$ instead of the values $\widehat{e}_x = v_x + a$ and $\widehat{e}_y = v_y + b$. However, this change is only semantic.

Similarly to [23] we observe that squaring gates can be computed using a square pair, i.e., a pair $([[a]], [[c]])$ such that $c = a^2$, instead of a multiplication triple. Squaring gates are computed using the following equation:

$$(v_x)^2 = (v_x + a)^2 - 2a(v_y + a) + a^2 = (\widehat{e}_x)^2 - 2\widehat{e}_x a + c \quad (8)$$

Remark 2. In [23] squaring requires partially revealing only a single value, and therefore we do not have any saving over [23] for squaring gates. Due to space constraints and the similarity with regular multiplication gates, we omit further discussion on squaring gates.

---

[6] It might be tempting to naïvely set $\lambda_z = c$, but this would not be secure, because λ_z must be independently random. However, in Sect. 4 we show that by modifying Overdrive, this part can be optimized.

3.2   Function Dependent Offline Protocol

In this section we describe our new function dependent offline protocol and the functionality it implements. Our offline protocol and its functionality and simulator use the SPDZ offline protocol, functionality, and simulator. For clarification, we denote the SPDZ offline of [23] using "Prep" and the new offline using "FDPrep", i.e.,

- The protocols are denoted Π_{Prep} and Π_{FDPrep}.
- The functionalities are denoted $\mathcal{F}_{\text{Prep}}$ and $\mathcal{F}_{\text{FDPrep}}$.
- The simulators are denoted $\mathcal{S}_{\text{Prep}}$ and $\mathcal{S}_{\text{FDPrep}}$.

Our function dependent offline protocol is formally described in Fig. 1. Our offline protocol runs the original SPDZ offline as a sub-protocol, and implements a very similar functionality to the SPDZ offline functionality. The main differences of our new offline from the original SPDZ offline are:

1. The new offline protocol/functionality receives the circuit as input. The original SPDZ protocol/functionality is then run with the number of multiplication gates, squaring gates, and input wires as in the circuit. For each multiplication and squaring gate, the SPDZ offline also generates an additional random $[[\cdot]]$-shared element.
2. Each generated multiplication triple is associated with a specific multiplication gate. Similarly each square pair is associated with a specific squaring gate, and each input wire is assigned a specific random $[[\cdot]]$-shared element revealed only to Party i.
3. For each multiplication and squaring gate, the protocol/functionality also associates a random $[[\cdot]]$-shared element, called the permutation element.
4. The protocol/functionality reveals specific "offset values", where an "offset value" is the difference between 2 random $[[\cdot]]$-shared elements. The protocol runs a MACCheck on these revealed values to ensure the adversary did not cheat on any of these values.

Notice that all the offsets can be revealed in parallel. Therefore, we added only a constant number of communication rounds to the SPDZ preprocessing protocol.

3.3   New Online Protocol

In this section we explain our new online protocol, which is formally given in Fig. 2. As explained in the introduction, the main difference of our new online protocol from previous SPDZ online protocols, e.g., [23,24], is that the parties have at each wire more values, which helps them compute the output values more efficiently. Concretely, in the SPDZ online phase only the real value on the wire is secret-shared amongst the parties. In our protocol, another random field element, the permutation element, is secret-shared amongst the parties. Furthermore, in our protocol the *external value*, i.e., the sum of the real value and the permutation element, is revealed to all the parties.

Protocol $\Pi_{\mathbf{FDPrep}}$

Initialize: The parties call $\Pi_{\mathbf{Prep}}$ (i.e., a secure implementation of $\mathcal{F}_{\mathbf{Prep}}$) with the number of multiplication gates, squaring gates, and input wires to receive the desired number of input maskings, multiplication triples, squaring pairs, and random $[[\cdot]]$-shared elements.[a] The parties then perform the following local computations in topological order on the gates of the circuit:

Input Wires: For every $i \in [n]$, for each input wire of party i the parties associate an available masking $(r_i, [[r_i]])$ (i.e., a random $[[\cdot]]$-shared element revealed to party i).

Addition gates: On an addition gate with input permutation element shares $[[\lambda_x]]$ and $[[\lambda_y]]$ the parties locally compute the output permutation element shares $[[\lambda_z]] \leftarrow [[\lambda_x]] + [[\lambda_y]]$.

Multiplication gates: On a multiplication gate with input permutation element shares $[[\lambda_x]]$ and $[[\lambda_y]]$ the parties assign to the gate the next available multiplication triple $([[a]], [[b]], [[c]])$ and the next available $[[\cdot]]$-shared random element $[[r]]$, and locally compute:

- $[[\cdot]]$-shares of the offset values $[[\widetilde{\lambda_x}]] \leftarrow [[a]] - [[\lambda_x]]$ and $[[\widetilde{\lambda_y}]] \leftarrow [[b]] - [[\lambda_y]]$.
- $[[\cdot]]$-shares of the permutation element on the output wire $[[\lambda_z]] \leftarrow [[c]] + [[r]]$.

Output: After performing all the above local computation, the parties partially reveal the offset values $\widetilde{\lambda_x}, \widetilde{\lambda_y}$ for every multiplication gate and $\widetilde{\lambda_x}$ for every squaring gate.

Output verification: This procedure is entered once the parties have finished the above function dependent preprocessing phase.

The parties call the MACCheck protocol with the input being all the opened values so far. If MACCheck fails, they output ϕ and abort, otherwise they accept the partially opened offset values.

---

[a]Recall that we require an additional $[[\cdot]]$-shared element for each multiplication/squaring gate.

Fig. 1. Our new function dependent preprocessing protocol

These external values, after certain adjustment, help in computing $[[\cdot]]$-shares of the output value of multiplication gates: In order to connect the shared and revealed values on the output wire to the input wires of the following multiplication gates, the parties use the revealed offsets from the function dependent preprocessing, to compute the adjusted external values on the input wires. The permutation elements that correspond to these adjusted external values match the shared values of the multiplication triples, which allows the parties to use Eq. (7). Thus, the $[[\cdot]]$-shares of the product and the $[[\cdot]]$-shares of the output external value are in fact computed *locally*, and all that remains (to continue this process to the following gates) is to partially reveal the output external value.

We observe that we also save communication on input wires compared to [23] because we "reuse" the shares used for distribution of the input (r_i in **Input** part of Fig. 2) by letting r_i be equal to the permutation element on that wire.

The main advantage of our new protocol over the SPDZ protocol of [23] is that it requires opening only a single value for each multiplication gate at the online phase. However, notice that in the function dependent preprocessing we open 2 additional values, so in total we open 1.5 times more values than SPDZ. To counter this undesirable side-effect, we present in Sect. 4 a more efficient version of our protocol that works by modifying Overdrive.

Protocol Π_{Online}

Initialize: The parties call $\mathcal{F}_{\text{FDPrep}}$ with the circuit to receive the masking values at each of the input wires and the random elements, the Beaver triples/squaring pairs, and the revealed offsets at each of the multiplication/squaring gates.

Input: To share his input v_{x_i}, party i takes the associated mask value $(r_i, [[r_i]])$ and does the following:

- Broadcast $e_{x_i} = v_{x_i} + r_i$.
- The parties compute $[[v_{x_i}]] \leftarrow e_{x_i} - [[r_i]]$.
- The parties store e_{x_i} as the external value on the wire, and $[[r_i]]$ as shares of the permutation element, λ_{x_i}.

Add: On an addition gate with input wires x, y, input shared values $([[v_x]], [[v_y]])$, input shared permutation elements $([[\lambda_x]], [[\lambda_y]])$, and input external values (e_x, e_y), the parties locally compute the following for the output wire z:

1. $[[v_z]] \leftarrow [[v_x]] + [[v_y]]$
2. $[[\lambda_z]] \leftarrow [[\lambda_x]] + [[\lambda_y]]$[a]
3. $e_z \leftarrow e_x + e_y$

Multiply: On a multiplication gate with input shared values $([[v_x]], [[v_y]])$ and input external values (e_x, e_y), the parties take the associated multiplication triple $([[a]], [[b]], [[c]])$, the partially opened offsets $\widetilde{\lambda}_x, \widetilde{\lambda}_y$, and the associated random $[[\cdot]]$-shared value $[[r]]$ and perform the following steps:

1. Locally compute:
   - $\widehat{e_x} \leftarrow e_x + \widetilde{\lambda}_x$ and $\widehat{e_y} \leftarrow e_y + \widetilde{\lambda}_y$.
   - $[[v_z]] \leftarrow \widehat{e_x}\widehat{e_y} - \widehat{e_y}[[a]] - \widehat{e_x}[[b]] + [[c]]$.[b]
   - $[[\lambda_z]] \leftarrow [[c]] + [[r]]$.[a]
2. Partially open $[[e_z]] \leftarrow [[v_z]] + [[\lambda_z]]$.

Output: This procedure is entered once the parties have finished the circuit evaluation, but still the final output v_z has not been opened.

1. The parties call the MACCheck protocol with the input being all the opened values so far in the online phase. If MACCheck fails, they output ϕ and abort.[c]
2. The parties open v_z and call MACCheck with input v_z, to verify its MAC. If the check fails, they output ϕ and abort, otherwise they accept v_z as a valid output.

---

[a]This computation was performed at the function dependent offline phase.

[b]By Equation (7), v_z holds the value $v_x \cdot v_y$.

[c]ϕ represents that the corrupted parties remain undetected.

Fig. 2. Our new online phase protocol

4 Improvement via Modification in Overdrive

In this section we explain how to improve the overall time of our protocol, by modifying Overdrive (SPDZ offline protocol), instead of using it as a black-box. The main benefit of this optimization is that (1) It avoids creating more random elements in the offline phase than in SPDZ, and (2) It avoids partially opening more elements in the offline phase than in SPDZ.

A first naïve attempt might be to set the permutation element of the output wire to equal c of the multiplication triple, but this would be insecure, because the proof of security requires the permutation of the output wire to be independently random. In contrast, if the output wire is an input to a multiplication gate, then setting the permutation element to equal a of the multiplication triple of the following gate is secure. It turns out that by a slight tweak, this can also be extended to general arithmetic circuits.

Furthermore, the efficiency can be even further improved by setting all a's corresponding to the same wire to be equal. Clearly, this cannot be done using

---

Protocol Π_{FDTriple}

Initialize: Each party P_i randomly chooses $\lambda_{\omega,i} \leftarrow \mathbb{F}$ for every wire ω that is an input wire of the circuit[a] or an output wire of a multiplication gate. Then, in topological order on the circuit, for each addition gate with input wires x, y and output wire z, party P_i computes $\lambda_{z,i} = \lambda_{x,i} + \lambda_{y,i}$.

Multiplication: For each multiplication gate with input wires x, y

1. Each party P_i sets $a_i = \lambda_{x,i}, b_i = \lambda_{y,i}$ and randomly selects $\hat{b}_i \leftarrow \mathbb{F}$.
2. Every unordered pair (P_i, P_j) executes the following 2-party multiplication as in [33]:
   (a) P_i sends P_j the encryption $\text{Enc}_i(a_i)$.[b]
   (b) P_j responds with $C^{(ij)} = b_j \cdot \text{Enc}_i(a_i) - \text{Enc}_i(e^{(ij)})$ for a random $e^{(ij)} \leftarrow \mathbb{F}$.[b]
   (c) P_i decrypts $d^{(ij)} = \text{Dec}_i(C^{(ij)})$.
   (d) The last two steps are repeated with $\hat{b}_j$ to get $\hat{e}^{(ij)}$ and $\hat{d}^{(ij)}$.
3. Each party P_i computes $c_i = a_i b_i + \Sigma_{i \neq j}(e^{(ji)} + d^{(ij)})$, and $\hat{c}_i$ similarly.

Authentication: Each party P_i inputs to $\mathcal{F}_{[[]]}$ the shares $\lambda_{\omega,i}$ for each wire ω that is an input wire of the circuit or an output wire of a multiplication gate, and additionally the shares $c_i, \hat{b}_i$, and $\hat{c}_i$ for each multiplication gate; for each such value the functionality outputs to the parties $[[\lambda_\omega]], [[c]], [[\hat{b}]],$ or $[[\hat{c}]]$, respectively, where $\lambda_\omega = \Sigma_i \lambda_{\omega,i}$, etc.

Sacrifice: The parties do the following for each multiplication triple pair $([[a]], [[b]], [[c]]), ([[a]], [[\hat{b}]], [[\hat{c}]])$:

1. Call $r \leftarrow \mathcal{F}_{\text{RAND}}$.
2. Compute and partially open $[[\rho]] = r[[b]] - [[\hat{b}]]$.[c]
3. Compute and partially open $[[\tau]] = r \cdot [[c]] - [[\hat{c}]] - \rho \cdot [[a]]$.[c] If $\tau \neq 0$ then abort.

MACCheck and Output: Run MACCheck on all opened values. If the check fails then abort. Otherwise, output all non-sacrificed computed triples $([[a]], [[b]], [[c]])$.

---

[a]The value $\lambda_\omega = \Sigma_i \lambda_{\omega,i}$ is the random value used in Π_{Online} for the input distribution, and therefore is later partially revealed to the relevant party.

[b]For simplicity, the details of the zero-knowledge proofs and of the noise drowning have been omitted; the complete details of this 2-party protocol can be found at [33, Figure 7].

[c]Note that a and b are linear combinations of the permutation elements λ_ω input to $\mathcal{F}_{[[]]}$, and thus $[[a]]$ and $[[b]]$ can be locally computed by the parties.

Fig. 3. Our modified triple generation protocol

SPDZ offline in a black-box fashion, since SPDZ offline generates independently random multiplication triples. Therefore, it is not clear that this optimization can be achieved for every SPDZ offline protocol. Nevertheless, we show that it is possible to achieve this optimization securely by modifying some SPDZ offline protocols, and in particular Overdrive, which is currently the state-of-the-art SPDZ preprocessing protocol. The formal details of creating these correlated triples are given in Fig. 3.

The result of this optimization is that $\widetilde{\lambda_x}, \widetilde{\lambda_y}$ in Eqs. (3) and (4) always equal 0, implying that during the online phase the adjusted external values $\hat{e}$ are equal to the external values e on the gates' input wires. Thus, this optimization also slightly simplifies and improves our online protocol.

Additionally, depending on the circuit, in some cases the same encryptions $\text{Enc}(a_i)$ in Step 2a could be used in several multiplications. For example, this may be possible when the same wire is input to several gates[7] (or even using the semi-homomorphic property $\text{Enc}(a + a') = \text{Enc}(a) + \text{Enc}(a')$). Reusing the

---

[7] Note that due to the asymmetry in the multiplication, this is not possible if the value plays b in the other multiplication.

same encryption reduces both the computation and communication, and choosing which wires should play a and b in the 2-party protocol to gain maximal reduction can be computed based solely on the circuit.

Since the only operations we perform in addition to those already necessary in Overdrive are additions corresponding to addition gates, we do not increase communication and only slightly increase computation in the worst case. Furthermore, due to reusing the encryptions, in many circuits our offline protocol will even have less computation and communication then using Overdrive for generating independent triples.

Note that since we changed the triple generation, it implies that in the SPDZ sacrifice step the shares of a and b in the multiplication step now correspond to a linear combination of shares input to $\mathcal{F}_{[[]]}$. Therefore, we must show that this change maintains the security. Recall that the security requirements from the SPDZ sacrifice are that **(1)** If the adversary cheats and sets $c = ab + \mathsf{e}$ or $\hat{c} = a\hat{b} + \hat{\mathsf{e}}$ with $\mathsf{e} \neq 0$ and/or $\hat{\mathsf{e}} \neq 0$ then the honest parties abort with overwhelming probability, and **(2)** If $\hat{b}$ and $\hat{c}$ are "sacrificed" (not used later in the protocol) then no information is leaked on $([[a]], [[b]], [[c]])$.

The proof is similar to the proof of the original SPDZ sacrifice. Two crucial points are that **(1)** a and b are linear combinations of the permutation elements (which are input into $\mathcal{F}_{[[]]}$) and thus so are rb and ρa (when ρ is treated as a constant), and that **(2)** $\hat{b}$ is independently and randomly chosen for each sacrifice, and therefore $\rho = tb - \hat{b}$ revels nothing even if some of the b's in different multiplications are correlated (or even equal).

5 Correctness and Security

In this section we explain the correctness and state our security theorem. Due to space constraints, the proof of security is deferred to full version.

Correctness. Assuming no party tries to cheat, the correctness follows from observing that at each wire

- The parties hold shares of the correct real value,
- The revealed external value corresponds to the sum of the real value and the shared permutation element.

This statement is proved by induction in topological order on the wires:

- For input wires this follows from the Input part in Protocol Π_{online}.
- For output wires of addition gates, the claim on the real values follows from Property 1, and the claim on the external value follows from Eq. (2).
- For output wires of multiplication and squaring gates the claim on the real value follows from Eqs. (7) and (8), respectively, and the claim on the external value follows immediately from the protocol.

Security. We now state our security theorems. The proofs and the functionalities can be found in [12]. We first state following security theorem for our function dependent offline protocol in Sect. 3,

Theorem 2. *In the $\mathcal{F}_{\text{Prep}}$-hybrid model, Protocol Π_{FDPrep} securely computes $\mathcal{F}_{\text{FDPrep}}$ in the presence of a static malicious adversary corrupting up to $n-1$ of the parties.*

For the online phase protocol, we prove the following theorem,

Theorem 3. *In the $\mathcal{F}_{\text{FDPrep}}$-hybrid model, the protocol Π_{Online} securely computes the function in the presence of a static malicious adversary corrupting up to $n-1$ of the parties.*

Regarding our protocol in Sect. 4, we need to show that the triples are correctly generated, i.e., $c = ab$ for every output triple (note that the fact that a and b are computed correctly from the permutation elements is captured in the MACCheck) and that no information is leaked on the permutation elements (again, note that this implies no non-trivial information is leaked on the triples).[8]

Theorem 4. *If Enc is a public-key semi-homomorphic encryption, then in Protocol Π_{FDTriple} in every output triple $c = ab$, where a and b are as defined in Π_{FDTriple}. Furthermore, assuming $\hat{b}, \hat{c}$ are not used outside Π_{FDTriple}, at the end of the offline protocol the value λ_ω is uniformly random in the view of the adversary, for every wire ω that is either an input wire of an honest party or an output wire of a multiplication gate.*

Acknowledgements. We would like to thank Amos Beimel for helpful discussions. Special thanks to Ivan Damgård and Marcel Keller for helping us to understand SPDZ and Overdrive better.

References

1. Applebaum, B., Ishai, Y., Kushilevitz, E., Waters, B.: Encoding functions with constant online rate or how to compress garbled circuits keys. In: Canetti, R., Garay, J.A. (eds.) CRYPTO 2013. LNCS, vol. 8043, pp. 166–184. Springer, Heidelberg (2013). https://doi.org/10.1007/978-3-642-40084-1_10
2. Araki, T., Furukawa, J., Lindell, Y., Nof, A., Ohara, K.: High-throughput semi-honest secure three-party computation with an honest majority. In: ACM CCS, pp. 805–817 (2016)
3. Araki, T., et al.: Optimized honest-majority MPC for malicious adversaries - breaking the 1 billion-gate per second barrier. In: IEEE SP, pp. 843–862 (2017)

---

[8] Of course a full proof would also require including the details of the zero-knowledge proofs, noise drowning, etc., as done in [33]. But these are beyond the scope of this paper and therefore left to the full version.

4. Asharov, G., Jain, A., López-Alt, A., Tromer, E., Vaikuntanathan, V., Wichs, D.: Multiparty computation with low communication, computation and interaction via threshold FHE. In: Pointcheval, D., Johansson, T. (eds.) EUROCRYPT 2012. LNCS, vol. 7237, pp. 483–501. Springer, Heidelberg (2012). https://doi.org/10.1007/978-3-642-29011-4_29

5. Ball, M., Malkin, T., Rosulek, M.: Garbling gadgets for boolean and arithmetic circuits. In: ACM CCS, pp. 565–577 (2016)

6. Baum, C., Damgård, I., Orlandi, C.: Publicly auditable secure multi-party computation. In: Abdalla, M., De Prisco, R. (eds.) SCN 2014. LNCS, vol. 8642, pp. 175–196. Springer, Cham (2014). https://doi.org/10.1007/978-3-319-10879-7_11

7. Baum, C., Damgård, I., Toft, T., Zakarias, R.: Better preprocessing for secure multiparty computation. In: Manulis, M., Sadeghi, A.-R., Schneider, S. (eds.) ACNS 2016. LNCS, vol. 9696, pp. 327–345. Springer, Cham (2016). https://doi.org/10.1007/978-3-319-39555-5_18

8. Beaver, D.: Efficient multiparty protocols using circuit randomization. In: Feigenbaum, J. (ed.) CRYPTO 1991. LNCS, vol. 576, pp. 420–432. Springer, Heidelberg (1992). https://doi.org/10.1007/3-540-46766-1_34

9. Beaver, D., Micali, S., Rogaway, P.: The round complexity of secure protocols. In: STOC, pp. 503–513 (1990)

10. Ben-Efraim, A.: On multiparty garbling of arithmetic circuits. In: Peyrin, T., Galbraith, S. (eds.) ASIACRYPT 2018. LNCS, vol. 11274, pp. 3–33. Springer, Cham (2018). https://doi.org/10.1007/978-3-030-03332-3_1

11. Ben-Efraim, A., Lindell, Y., Omri, E.: Optimizing semi-honest secure multiparty computation for the internet. In: ACM CCS, pp. 578–590 (2016)

12. Ben-Efraim, A., Nielsen, M., Omri, E.: Turbospeedz: double your online SPDZ! Improving SPDZ using function dependent preprocessing. On ePrint: Report 2019/080

13. Ben-Or, M., Goldwasser, S., Wigderson, A.: Completeness theorems for non-cryptographic fault-tolerant distributed computations. In: STOC, pp. 1–10 (1988)

14. Bendlin, R., Damgård, I., Orlandi, C., Zakarias, S.: Semi-homomorphic encryption and multiparty computation. In: Paterson, K.G. (ed.) EUROCRYPT 2011. LNCS, vol. 6632, pp. 169–188. Springer, Heidelberg (2011). https://doi.org/10.1007/978-3-642-20465-4_11

15. Chaum, D., Crépeau, C., Damgård, I.: Multiparty unconditionally secure protocols. In: STOC, pp. 11–19 (1988)

16. Choi, S.G., Hwang, K.-W., Katz, J., Malkin, T., Rubenstein, D.: Secure multiparty computation of boolean circuits with applications to privacy in on-line marketplaces. In: Dunkelman, O. (ed.) CT-RSA 2012. LNCS, vol. 7178, pp. 416–432. Springer, Heidelberg (2012). https://doi.org/10.1007/978-3-642-27954-6_26

17. Couteau, G.: A note on the communication complexity of multiparty computation in the correlated randomness model. In: EUROCRYPT (2019, to appear)

18. Cramer, R., Damgård, I., Escudero, D., Scholl, P., Xing, C.: SPDZ$_{2^k}$: efficient MPC mod 2^k for dishonest majority. In: Shacham, H., Boldyreva, A. (eds.) CRYPTO 2018. LNCS, vol. 10992, pp. 769–798. Springer, Cham (2018). https://doi.org/10.1007/978-3-319-96881-0_26

19. Damgård, I., Ishai, Y.: Constant-round multiparty computation using a black-box pseudorandom generator. In: Shoup, V. (ed.) CRYPTO 2005. LNCS, vol. 3621, pp. 378–394. Springer, Heidelberg (2005). https://doi.org/10.1007/11535218_23

20. Damgård, I., Ishai, Y.: Scalable secure multiparty computation. In: Dwork, C. (ed.) CRYPTO 2006. LNCS, vol. 4117, pp. 501–520. Springer, Heidelberg (2006). https://doi.org/10.1007/11818175_30

548   A. Ben-Efraim et al.

21. Damgård, I., Nielsen, J.B.: Scalable and unconditionally secure multiparty computation. In: Menezes, A. (ed.) CRYPTO 2007. LNCS, vol. 4622, pp. 572–590. Springer, Heidelberg (2007). https://doi.org/10.1007/978-3-540-74143-5_32

22. Damgård, I., Ishai, Y., Krøigaard, M.: Perfectly secure multiparty computation and the computational overhead of cryptography. In: Gilbert, H. (ed.) EUROCRYPT 2010. LNCS, vol. 6110, pp. 445–465. Springer, Heidelberg (2010). https://doi.org/10.1007/978-3-642-13190-5_23

23. Damgård, I., Pastro, V., Smart, N., Zakarias, S.: Multiparty computation from somewhat homomorphic encryption. In: Safavi-Naini, R., Canetti, R. (eds.) CRYPTO 2012. LNCS, vol. 7417, pp. 643–662. Springer, Heidelberg (2012). https://doi.org/10.1007/978-3-642-32009-5_38

24. Damgård, I., Keller, M., Larraia, E., Pastro, V., Scholl, P., Smart, N.P.: Practical covertly secure MPC for dishonest majority – or: breaking the SPDZ limits. In: Crampton, J., Jajodia, S., Mayes, K. (eds.) ESORICS 2013. LNCS, vol. 8134, pp. 1–18. Springer, Heidelberg (2013). https://doi.org/10.1007/978-3-642-40203-6_1

25. Damgård, I., Nielsen, J.B., Nielsen, M., Ranellucci, S.: The TinyTable protocol for 2-party secure computation, or: gate-scrambling revisited. In: Katz, J., Shacham, H. (eds.) CRYPTO 2017. LNCS, vol. 10401, pp. 167–187. Springer, Cham (2017). https://doi.org/10.1007/978-3-319-63688-7_6

26. Goldreich, O., Micali, S., Wigderson, A.: How to play any mental game. In: STOC, pp. 218–229 (1987)

27. Gordon, S.D., Ranellucci, S., Wang, X.: Secure computation with low communication from cross-checking. In: Peyrin, T., Galbraith, S. (eds.) ASIACRYPT 2018. LNCS, vol. 11274, pp. 59–85. Springer, Cham (2018). https://doi.org/10.1007/978-3-030-03332-3_3

28. Hazay, C., Scholl, P., Soria-Vazquez, E.: Low cost constant round MPC combining BMR and oblivious transfer. In: Takagi, T., Peyrin, T. (eds.) ASIACRYPT 2017. LNCS, vol. 10624, pp. 598–628. Springer, Cham (2017). https://doi.org/10.1007/978-3-319-70694-8_21

29. Hirt, M., Nielsen, J.B.: Robust multiparty computation with linear communication complexity. In: Dwork, C. (ed.) CRYPTO 2006. LNCS, vol. 4117, pp. 463–482. Springer, Heidelberg (2006). https://doi.org/10.1007/11818175_28

30. Hirt, M., Maurer, U., Przydatek, B.: Efficient secure multi-party computation. In: Okamoto, T. (ed.) ASIACRYPT 2000. LNCS, vol. 1976, pp. 143–161. Springer, Heidelberg (2000). https://doi.org/10.1007/3-540-44448-3_12

31. Keller, M., Orsini, E., Scholl, P.: MASCOT: faster malicious arithmetic secure computation with oblivious transfer. In: ACM CCS, pp. 830–842 (2016)

32. Keller, M., Orsini, E., Rotaru, D., Scholl, P., Soria-Vazquez, E., Vivek, S.: Faster secure multi-party computation of AES and DES using lookup tables. In: Gollmann, D., Miyaji, A., Kikuchi, H. (eds.) ACNS 2017. LNCS, vol. 10355, pp. 229–249. Springer, Cham (2017). https://doi.org/10.1007/978-3-319-61204-1_12

33. Keller, M., Pastro, V., Rotaru, D.: Overdrive: making SPDZ great again. In: Nielsen, J.B., Rijmen, V. (eds.) EUROCRYPT 2018. LNCS, vol. 10822, pp. 158–189. Springer, Cham (2018). https://doi.org/10.1007/978-3-319-78372-7_6

34. Kilian, J.: Basing cryptography on oblivious transfer. In: STOC, pp. 20–31 (1988)

35. Larraia, E., Orsini, E., Smart, N.P.: Dishonest majority multi-party computation for binary circuits. In: Garay, J.A., Gennaro, R. (eds.) CRYPTO 2014. LNCS, vol. 8617, pp. 495–512. Springer, Heidelberg (2014). https://doi.org/10.1007/978-3-662-44381-1_28

36. Lindell, Y., Pinkas, B., Smart, N.P., Yanai, A.: Efficient constant round multi-party computation combining BMR and SPDZ. In: Gennaro, R., Robshaw, M. (eds.) CRYPTO 2015. LNCS, vol. 9216, pp. 319–338. Springer, Heidelberg (2015). https://doi.org/10.1007/978-3-662-48000-7_16
37. Malkin, T., Pastero, V., Shelat, A.: An algebraic approach to garbling (Unpublished manuscript)
38. Rabin, T., Ben-Or, M.: Verifiable secret sharing and multiparty protocols with honest majority. In: STOC, pp. 73–85 (1989)
39. Spini, G., Fehr, S.: Cheater detection in SPDZ multiparty computation. In: Nascimento, A.C.A., Barreto, P. (eds.) ICITS 2016. LNCS, vol. 10015, pp. 151–176. Springer, Cham (2016). https://doi.org/10.1007/978-3-319-49175-2_8
40. Wang, X., Ranellucci, S., Katz, J.: Global-scale secure multiparty computation. In: ACM CCS, pp. 39–56 (2017)
41. Yao, A.C.: Protocols for secure computations. In: FOCS, pp. 160–164 (1982)

pRate: Anonymous Star Rating
with Rating Secrecy

Jia Liu[1]($\boxtimes$) and Mark Manulis[2]

[1] Thales UK Ltd., Cambridge, UK
jia.liu@thalesgroup.com
[2] Surrey Centre for Cyber Security,
University of Surrey, Guildford, UK
mark@manulis.eu

Abstract. We introduce pRate, a novel reputation management scheme with strong security and privacy guarantees for the users and their reputation scores. The reputation scores are computed based on the (aggregated) number(s) of stars that users receive from their raters. pRate allows users to advertise privacy-friendly statements about their reputation when searching for potential transaction partners. Ratings can only be submitted by partners who have been initially authorised by the ratee and issued a rating token. The scheme is managed by a possibly untrusted reputation manager who can register users and assist ratees in updating their reputation scores, yet without learning these scores. In addition to ensuring the secrecy of the ratings, a distinctive feature of pRate over prior proposals, is that it hides the identities of raters and ratees from each other during the transaction and rating stages. The scheme is built from a number of efficient cryptographic primitives; its security is formally modeled and proven to hold under widely used assumptions on bilinear groups.

Keywords: Reputation management · Star rating · Anonymity · Rating secrecy

1 Introduction

Establishing trust between prospective transaction partners on online platforms is a major challenge for today's digital economy. Reputation systems have gained popularity as an important risk assessment mechanism for measuring and managing the trustworthiness of involved parties and a variety of reputation systems is already deployed across many online marketplaces, e.g., eBay, Yelp!, BlaBlaCar, Airbnb, etc. Reputation is one of the most important assets of an individual and has its special market value [19, 35]. Online reviews are extremely influential for businesses. Studies have shown that 90% of customers read reviews before making a purchase decision and 94% of customers would use a business with a four-star rating [1].

© Springer Nature Switzerland AG 2019
R. H. Deng et al. (Eds.): ACNS 2019, LNCS 11464, pp. 550–570, 2019.
https://doi.org/10.1007/978-3-030-21568-2_27

In a reputation system, typically provided and managed by an online platform (reputation manager), each user is associated with a reputation score and transaction partners can rate each other, leave feedback and recommendations. The concern of repercussions thereby often deters users from providing honest ratings. It is particularly hard to get honest opinions when users are not anonymous, e.g., over 95% of Airbnb listings and almost all of the ratings of the BlaBlaCar rides are above 4.5-star scores which are overwhelmingly positive [35,36]. The fear of retaliation is considered as a major factor for users to withhold truthful feedback after having some negative experience [32,35]. Retaliation can be in any form such as unfairly low ratings, refusal of future transactions, or even physical assault. There is also fear that shared personal information can create racial and/or gender bias among users when choosing transaction partners. For example, Airbnb had to face racial discrimination complaints from African-American and Latino would-be renters. Moreover, the great amount of information shared on the online platform poses a serious threat to personal privacy and security. Take for instance car sharing or riding services where booked trips and travel patterns can be misused for person abductions or car thefts. The reputation score itself is also a potential threat to privacy as it can possibly be used to link users across transactions. The linkage between user activities and ratings can also de-anonymise users [29,30].

Another point of concern is a potential bias from the service provider that manages the online reputation system. For many years, the online rating site Yelp! has been accused of removing positive reviews and highlighting negative ones, thus causing a massive downgrading of businesses in an attempt to force them to purchase advertisements [2–4,19]. Hence protecting honest users and the integrity of their ratings from a potentially biased reputation manager is another important requirement in the design of the reputation systems. One way to achieve this is to prevent the reputation manager from learning the individual scores obtained by the users.

Various privacy-preserving reputation schemes [5,6,9–11,15,20–22] (see also Sect. 7 for more discussion) have been proposed to protect anonymity of raters and ratees to some extent, but none of these aims to hide reputation scores against the reputation manager. As far as we know, only [27,31,37] discuss the protection of reputation scores. The scheme in [27] hides rating scores from the users but not from the reputation manager and does not provide anonymity of the users. The scheme in [31] only supports unidirectional rating, i.e., a buyer can use pseudonyms to anonymously rate a service provider but not vice versa. Also, this system lacks accountability on users since users can arbitrarily create uncertified pseudonyms. AnonRep [37] is an anonymous reputation system designed for evaluating the quality of messages posted on a public board. Since any posted message can be rated by arbitrary users, AnonRep cannot be used to rate transactions where only transaction partners are allowed to rate each other.

Our Contribution. We propose a star rating scheme called pRate that provides strong privacy and security guarantees for the users and their reputation scores. In our scheme, a reputation manager issues and updates reputation credentials for the users without learning the actual scores. Users can advertise their reputation scores anonymously and selectively to other parties. Two users are able to transact and rate each other without leaking any identity information to each other. Despite being anonymous, transaction partners are held accountable for their behaviours. This is achieved by enabling the reputation manager to learn the identities of transacting partners (but not the details of their transaction) when they submit their ratings, i.e., misbehaving users can thus be reported to and identified by the reputation manager. We also describe a batch accumulation mechanism which enables the reputation manager to aggregate multiple ratings, hiding the link between the transaction and the rating sessions, and preventing the ratee from learning individual rating values. Our construction is based on BBS+ signature [17], Bulletproofs [14], Chaum-Pedersen-Signed ElGamal Encryption [34], and several standard (non-interactive) zero-knowledge proofs of knowledge. We formally model and prove the security properties of pRate under well-known assumptions on bilinear maps in the random oracle model.

Organisation. The rest of this paper is organised as follows: Sect. 2 gives an overview of pRate. Section 3 presents formal definitions of its functionality and security. Section 4 describes the cryptographic assumptions and building blocks. The construction of pRate is specified in Sect. 5. Section 6 provides its security analysis. Section 7 describes other related work. The paper concludes in Sect. 8.

2   Overview of the pRate Scheme

pRate is a star rating system that provides strong security guarantees for protecting reputation scores and user privacy. pRate is managed by the *reputation manager (RM)* who issues and updates reputation credentials for the users without learning their reputation scores. Users can advertise their reputation scores and exchange rating tokens enabling them to rate each other anonymously by submitting their (encrypted) ratings to the RM. A user i who submits a rating for another user j is called the *rater*, whereas user j is called the *ratee*.

In pRate each user's reputation is measured by a v-star score $(n_1, \cdots, n_v)$, where v is fixed and each n_i represents the number of received i-stars. For example, $v = 5$ implies that a single rating can contain up to five stars and a score $(10, 20, 30, 40, 50)$ in this case would mean that the user has received a total of ten 1-star, twenty 2-star, thirty 3-star, forty 4-star and fifty 5-star individual ratings. A user's reputation score is aggregated in a reputation credential which is blindly signed by the RM. Using the reputation credential, a user can publish an anonymous advertisement for their current reputation score. Instead of revealing the exact reputation score in the advertisement, the user can show that it satisfies some predicate P, e.g., that the average score is higher than four stars or that 90% of ratings are above three stars. Based on their advertisements, two anonymous users can establish an authenticated and confidential communication channel over which they exchange their rating tokens. These rating tokens encrypt the identities of the two transaction partners which can only be decrypted by the RM. Hence, both user identities are kept anonymous and unlinkable from each other during the transaction and rating phases. In order to rate each other, each transaction partner would use the received rating token to encrypt the rating value (which can only be decrypted by the ratee), sign and submit his encrypted rating to the RM. This phase does not require any online presence of the ratee and can be performed at any time. Each rating token has a unique serial number and can be used only once. Upon receiving the submitted (encrypted) rating, the RM extracts the identities of the rater and the ratee, aggregates the ratee's rating, and sends an update to the ratee enabling the latter to update his reputation credential. The rating tokens make users accountable for their behaviour and can also be used to directly report misbehaving users in case of wrongdoings. The fact that the RM is able to retrieve the identities of the rater and the ratee during the rating accumulation phase prevents a number of conventional attacks against reputation systems, such as Sybil attacks, self-promotion attacks, ballot stuffing attacks, whitewashing attacks and bad mouthing attacks [25]. Furthermore, pRate offers the following security and privacy properties:

- *Anonymity:* This property allows users to advertise their reputation scores and rate each other in an anonymous and unlinkable way. More specifically, a user can prove statements about his reputations score without revealing his identity and the actual score. Moreover, the link between the advertisements and ratings of transaction partners based on these advertisements remains unknown to the RM and any other users in the system. Multiple advertisements by the same user also remain unlinkable against other users and the RM. Different ratings submitted by the same user also remain unlinkable from the ratee's perspective.
- *Rating-secrecy:* Only the user knows the exact values from his reputation score. The submitted ratings are encrypted and thus remain hidden from the RM and other users. The RM can aggregate a newly submitted rating for some user into that user's reputation credential without learning the actual value of the rating.
- *Unforgeability:* This property ensures that none of the advertisements, rating tokens, or submitted rating values can be forged. In particular, any valid advertisement can only be generated by a user with a valid reputation credential which ensures that each user is accountable for their behaviours. It is impossible to forge a rating token exchanged during the transaction or to submit a forged rating for an honest user, even if the attacker corrupts the RM and other users. When a rater submits a new (encrypted) rating to the RM, the latter can check that the rater has been previously authorised by the ratee and that the rating is well-formed. A ratee can verify that updates for the reputation score received from the RM are correctly formed and were received from raters who have been previously authorised by the ratee. This ensures that the RM is not able to introduce fake ratings nor forge or modify ratings received from authorised honest raters.

In pRate, users publish anonymous advertisements to remain unlinkable across multiple transactions and use temporary public keys to set up independent secure communication channels for each transaction. Although the use of temporary keys preserves users' anonymity during the transaction and rating submission, we note that in real-world applications the identities of transacting users can be leaked due to some side-channel information. For example, in Airbnb, guests would meet home owners in person. For these applications, we provide a batch accumulation mechanism which enables the RM to aggregate multiple ratings for the same user prior to sending its reputation score update. This accumulation can be used to break the link between a single transaction session and the submitted rating for that transaction. The ratee would thus learn only the aggregated rating value from multiple transactions.

In addition to the above security properties, pRate is highly non-interactive and efficient. pRate allows users to publish and verify the reputation advertisements published by other users without any interaction with other users or the RM. Submission of ratings to the RM does not require online presence of the ratee, while the update of a rating by the ratee does not require interaction with the rater. The scheme provides short reputation credentials and utilises a number of efficient cryptographic mechanisms, including short and computationally efficient zero-knowledge proofs.

3 Syntax and Security Properties of pRate

In this section, we formalise the syntax of our pRate scheme and define its main security and privacy properties. A pRate scheme consists of the following polynomial-time algorithms and protocols:

- $(\mathsf{ik}, \mathsf{ok}, \mathsf{pp}) \leftarrow \mathsf{Setup}(1^\lambda)$: With this algorithm the RM initialises the rating scheme. On input of a security parameter λ, it outputs a master issuing key ik, a master opening key ok, and a set of public parameters pp.
- $((\mathsf{urep}[i], \mathsf{scr}[i]) \leftarrow \mathsf{Join}(\mathsf{pp}, i), \mathsf{reg}[i] \leftarrow \mathsf{Issue}(\mathsf{pp}, \mathsf{ik}, i))$: This is a registration protocol between a new user i and the RM, modeled as a pair of interactive algorithms, Join executed by i, and Issue executed by the RM. Upon successful completion, the protocol outputs a *reputation credential* $\mathsf{urep}[i]$ and an initial *reputation score* $\mathsf{scr}[i]$ to the user, and a *registration record* $\mathsf{reg}[i]$ to the RM which is stored in the registration database.
- $(\mathsf{aid}, \pi_{\mathsf{rep}}) \leftarrow \mathsf{RepAds}(\mathsf{pp}, \mathsf{urep}[i], \mathsf{scr}[i], m, P)$: With this algorithm any registered user i can anonymously advertise its reputation. The algorithm takes some message m and a predicate P as an additional input and outputs a reputation advertisement consisting of an *advertisement identifier* aid and a *reputation proof* π_{rep}. We consider m as a placeholder for any additional information about the advertised transaction. Moreover, since the advertiser is anonymous, we assume that m includes information on how the advertiser can be securely contacted by prospective transaction partners, e.g., by including some temporary public key for establishing a secure channel. With predicate P as an input to the algorithm we enable advertisements proving statements about user's $\mathsf{scr}[i]$, i.e. $P(\mathsf{scr}[i]) = 1$, without disclosing the score.

- $1/0 \leftarrow \mathsf{RepVer}(\mathsf{pp}, \mathsf{aid}, \pi_{\mathsf{rep}}, m, P)$: This algorithm verifies the validity of a published reputation advertisement, in particular of the reputation proof π_{rep} in relation to the predicate P. It outputs 1 if π_{rep} is valid and 0 otherwise.
- $((\mathsf{sn}_0, \mathsf{sn}_1, \mathsf{RT}_0, \mathsf{UT}_0) \leftarrow \mathsf{Token}(\mathsf{pp}, \mathsf{urep}[i_0], \mathsf{aid}_0, \mathsf{aid}_1), (\mathsf{sn}_1, \mathsf{sn}_0, \mathsf{RT}_1, \mathsf{UT}_1) \leftarrow$ $\mathsf{Token}(\mathsf{pp}, \mathsf{urep}[i_1], \mathsf{aid}_1, \mathsf{aid}_0))$: This is an interactive protocol for the exchange of rating tokens between two users i_0 and i_1. Upon successful execution, the interactive algorithm $\mathsf{Token}(\mathsf{pp}, \mathsf{urep}[i_b], \mathsf{aid}_b, \mathsf{aid}_{1-b})$ run by each user i_b $(b \in \{0, 1\})$ outputs unique *serial numbers* $\mathsf{sn}_b, \mathsf{sn}_{1-b}$, a *rating token* RT_b that user i_b will use to rate i_{1-b}, and an *update token* UT_b that i_b will retain and use later to update its own reputation credential.
- $\delta \leftarrow \mathsf{RateGen}(\mathsf{pp}, \mathsf{urep}[i], \mathsf{RT}, x)$: This algorithm enables a user i to generate a rating. On input of the public parameters pp, a reputation credential $\mathsf{urep}[i]$, a rating token RT received from the transaction partner, and a chosen rating value $x \in [1, v]$, it outputs a *rating* δ. This algorithm may fail and output $\perp$ if the process could not be completed successfully, e.g., $x \notin [1, v]$.
- $(i, j, \mathsf{aux})/\perp \leftarrow \mathsf{RateAcc}(\mathsf{pp}, \mathsf{ok}, \mathsf{reg}, \delta)$: Using this algorithm the RM accumulates received ratings into the reputation credential of the ratee. Upon successful execution, the algorithm outputs the extracted rater's identity i, ratee's identity j, and an update information aux, which the RM sends to the ratee j. As part of this algorithm, the RM may also update the record $\mathsf{reg}[j]$ of the ratee. This algorithm may fail and output $\perp$ if the accumulation process could not be completed successfully, e.g., if the rating δ submitted by the rater is invalid.
- $1/0 \leftarrow \mathsf{Upd}(\mathsf{pp}, \mathsf{urep}[j], \mathsf{scr}[j], \mathsf{UT}, \mathsf{aux})$: With this algorithm a rated user j after receiving the update information aux from the RM and in possession of the matching update token UT can update its own reputation credential $\mathsf{urep}[j]$ and score $\mathsf{scr}[j]$. The algorithm outputs 1 if the update is successful and 0 otherwise.

A secure pRate scheme must possess the anonymity, rating-secrecy and unforgeability properties that were introduced informally in Sect. 2. In the full version of this paper [28], we formalise these properties using game-based security definitions which are loosely based on security models for group signatures [8,13]. For unforgeability, we model three different aspects: (i) *advertisement-unforgeability* to ensure that only users in possession of a valid reputation credential urep can create valid advertisements for their reputations scores, (ii) *ratee-unforgeability* to ensure that only users in possession of a valid reputation credential urep can issue rating tokens during the execution of the Token protocol that can then be used to produce ratings, (iii) *rater-unforgeability* to ensure that only users in possession of rating tokens issued to them by some other user can submit valid ratings for that user.

4   Cryptographic Building Blocks and Assumptions

In the following we recall some well-known assumptions on bilinear maps and cryptographic building blocks used in our scheme.

Bilinear Maps. Let $\mathbb{G}_1, \mathbb{G}_2$ and $\mathbb{G}_T$ be multiplicative groups of prime order p. A function $\hat{e} : \mathbb{G}_1 \times \mathbb{G}_2 \to \mathbb{G}_T$ is a bilinear map if it satisfies the following three properties:

1. Bilinear: $\hat{e}(g^a, h^b) = \hat{e}(g, h)^{ab}$ for all $g \in \mathbb{G}_1, h \in \mathbb{G}_2$ and $a, b \in \mathbb{Z}_p^*$.
2. Non-degenerate: there exists $g \in \mathbb{G}_1, h \in \mathbb{G}_2$ such that $\hat{e}(g, h) \neq 1$.
3. Computable: $\hat{e}(g, h)$ is efficiently computable for all $g \in \mathbb{G}_1, h \in \mathbb{G}_2$.

Our scheme can be implemented using both Type 2 and Type 3 pairings [24], as long as the XDH and q-SDH assumptions described below are supported.

EXternal Diffie-Hellman (XDH) Assumption [16]. Given groups $\mathbb{G}_1, \mathbb{G}_2$, $\mathbb{G}_T$ associated with a bilinear pairing $\hat{e} : \mathbb{G}_1 \times \mathbb{G}_2 \to \mathbb{G}_T$. The XDH assumption holds if the Decision Diffie-Hellman (DDH) problem is hard in $\mathbb{G}_1$.

q-SDH Assumption [12]. The q-Strong Diffie-Hellman (SDH) assumption states that given two multiplicative groups $\mathbb{G}_1$ and $\mathbb{G}_2$ of prime order p with generators g_1 for $\mathbb{G}_1$ and g_2 for $\mathbb{G}_2$, for any PPT adversary $\mathcal{A}$, the following advantage is negligible in λ: $\mathsf{Adv}_{\mathcal{A}}^{\mathsf{q\text{-}SDH}}(1^\lambda) = \Pr[\mathcal{A}(g_1, g_1^\gamma, \cdots, g_1^{\gamma^q}, g_2, g_2^\gamma) = (g_1^{\frac{1}{\gamma+x}}, x) : \gamma \xleftarrow{\$} \mathbb{Z}_p^*]$.

BBS+ Signature [7,17]. The BBS+ signature allows a signer to issue and update a signature on a tuple of messages in a blind way, i.e., without learning the values of the messages. In pRate these techniques are used to construct reputation credentials. A user in possession of a BBS+ signature can selectively disclose some messages and produce zero-knowledge proofs for statements about other messages.

Zero-Knowledge Proofs. Following the notations in [18], we use $\mathsf{PoK}\{(x) : h = g^x\}$ to denote a non-interactive zero-knowledge proof of knowledge of x that satisfies $h = g^x$ and use $\mathsf{SoK}[m]\{(x) : h = g^x\}$ to refer to a signature of knowledge on m. A *range proof* is a special zero-knowledge proof which shows that a committed value lies within a certain interval. Recent Bulletproofs [14] that do not require a trusted setup are used in our scheme to produce privacy-preserving statements about reputation scores. A proof that some secret lies within an interval statement $v \in [0, 2^n - 1]$ requires only $2\lceil \log n \rceil + 4$ group elements and 5 elements in $\mathbb{Z}_p$. Bulletproofs support aggregation, i.e., k range proofs, possibly over different intervals, can be combined into a single proof with only $2 \log k$ additional group elements.

Chaum-Pedersen-Signed ElGamal Encryption (CPS-EG) [34]. The CPS-EG scheme is a modified version of the Schnorr-Signed ElGamal encryption that achieves IND-CCA2-security in the random oracle model. pRate uses the techniques from CPS-EG in generation of rating tokens and ratings. Its IND-CCA2 security provides decryption oracle that is used in the proof of anonymity of pRate.

5 Our pRate Scheme

5.1 Specifications of pRate Algorithms and Protocols

In the following we provide detailed specifications of the algorithms and protocols behind the proposed pRate scheme which allows users to advertise their reputation, to rate and be rated by other users in a privacy-friendly way. The scheme is managed by the reputation manager RM. The communication between a user and the RM is assumed to be over secure channels.

Initialisation of the Scheme. The algorithm $\mathsf{Setup}(1^\lambda)$ executed by the RM performs the following steps. Choose $\gamma, \xi \xleftarrow{\$} \mathbb{Z}_p^*$, $g_0, g_1, \cdots, g_{v+3}, g, u \xleftarrow{\$} \mathbb{G}_1, w \xleftarrow{\$} \mathbb{G}_2$, compute $W = w^\gamma$ and $U = u^\xi$. Output the master issuing key $\mathsf{ik} = \gamma$, the master opening key $\mathsf{ok} = \xi$, and the public parameters $\mathsf{pp} = (g_0, g_1, \cdots, g_{v+3}, g, w, W, u, U)$.

Registration of New Users. The interactive protocol $(\mathsf{Join}(\mathsf{pp}, i), \mathsf{Issue}(\mathsf{pp}, \mathsf{ik}, i))$ executed between a new user i and the RM is specified below.

– $\mathsf{Join}(\mathsf{pp}, i)$:
  - User i chooses randoms $k, s_1 \xleftarrow{\$} \mathbb{Z}_p^*$. Compute $K = g_{v+2}^k, S_1 = g_{v+3}^{s_1}$ and a proof $\pi_{\mathsf{id}} = \mathsf{PoK}\{(k, s_1) : K = g_{v+2}^k \wedge S_1 = g_{v+3}^{s_1}\}$ (see Fig. 2 for details). User i sends $(K, S_1, \pi_{\mathsf{id}})$ to the RM.
  - Upon receiving $(n_1, \cdots, n_v, t, e, s_2, C)$ from RM, user i computes $s = s_1 + s_2$ and $R = g_0 g_1^{n_1} \cdots g_v^{n_v} g_{v+1}^t g_{v+2}^k g_{v+3}^s$. Verify if $\hat{\mathsf{e}}(C, W \cdot w^e) \stackrel{?}{=} \hat{\mathsf{e}}(R, w)$. If successful, set $\mathsf{urep}[i] = (k, s, e, R, C)$ and $\mathsf{scr}[i] = (n_1, n_2, \cdots, n_v, t)$.
– $\mathsf{Issue}(\mathsf{pp}, \mathsf{ik}, i)$: Upon receiving $(K, S_1, \pi_{\mathsf{id}})$ from user i, RM verifies if π_{id} is valid using the verification algorithm in Fig. 2. If successful, select initial values $n_1, \cdots, n_v$ and a timestamp t. Choose $e, s_2 \xleftarrow{\$} \mathbb{Z}_p^*$. Compute $T = g_{v+1}^t, S_2 = g_{v+3}^{s_2}, R = g_0 g_1^{n_1} \cdots g_v^{n_v} T K S_1 S_2$ and $C = R^{\frac{1}{\gamma+e}}$. Set $\mathsf{reg}[i] = (K, e, t, R, C)$ and send $(n_1, \cdots, n_v, t, e, s_2, C)$ to user i.

We remark that the algorithm Join executed by the user i outputs the initial reputation credential $\mathsf{urep}[i] = (k, s, e, R, C)$ and score $\mathsf{scr}[i] = (n_1, n_2, \cdots, n_v, t)$ where the star values $n_1, \cdots, n_v$ can all be set to 0 or any other fixed values, which the system assigns to its new users. The timestamp t initially represents the time at which the reputation credential was issued. The secret key k stored in the reputation credential is the long-term key of the user i and is chosen by the user as part of the protocol. Its knowledge is proven in π_{id} along with the knowledge of randomness s_1. The randomness $s = s_1 + s_2$ which is used to seal the information stored in C is generated jointly by the user and the RM to ease the proof of advertisement-unforgeability. The algorithm Issue executed by the RM outputs the registration record $\mathsf{reg}[i] = (K, e, t, R, C)$ where $K = g_{v+2}^k$ represents the identity of the new user within the system. Some information from the user's reputation credential, i.e., (e, R, C), are stored by the RM and will be used later to compute reputation updates.

Reputation Advertisements and Their Verification. The algorithm RepAds(pp, urep[i], scr[i], m, P) outputs a reputation advertisement (aid, π_{rep}) by computing its identifier aid $= (d, d^k)$ using some random $d \xleftarrow{\$} \mathbb{G}_1$, and the reputation proof $\pi_{\text{rep}} = \text{SoK} [m] \{(\text{urep}[i], \text{scr}[i]) : C = (g_0 g_1^{n_1} \cdots g_v^{n_v} g_{v+1}^t g_{v+2}^k g_{v+3}^s)^{\frac{1}{\gamma+e}} \wedge P(\text{scr}[i]) = 1 \wedge \text{aid} = (d, d^k)\}$ that shows the current user's score scr[i] satisfies some predicate P. In our specification P is left general to show support for arbitrary predicates with corresponding zero-knowledge proofs. Nonetheless, in the full version of this paper [28], we show an example on how to create proofs for predicates $P = \bigwedge_{i=1}^{\zeta} (\psi_i \in [0, 2^{\ell_i}))$ involving interval statements computed from the number of stars $n_1, \cdots, n_v$ and timestamp t in the reputation score, using Bulletproofs [14], a recent zero-knowledge protocol for range proofs. Note that aid $= (d, d^k)$ is computed using the long-term secret key k in urep[i] and will be used in the token exchange protocol below to generate a ciphertext ct that encrypts the user's identity $K = g_{v+2}^k$.

The algorithm RepVer(pp, aid, π_{rep}, m, P) performs verification of the reputation proof π_{rep} and outputs 1 if the proof is valid, otherwise it outputs 0. Clearly, verification of π_{rep} involves verification of the zero-knowledge proof for $P(\text{scr}[i]) = 1$ which depends on P.

Exchange of Rating Tokens. The detailed specification of the Token protocol in which two prospective transaction partners i_0 and i_1 exchange their rating tokens is given in Fig. 1 with the details of underlying zero-knowledge proofs π_{enc} and π_{tok} provided in Fig. 2. It is assumed that both users have already obtained and verified their respective advertisements and have setup a secure channel prior to engaging in the Token protocol (cf. Sect. 5.2 for the discussion on anonymous advertisements and secure channels). We observe that the protocol is symmetric. User i_0 obtains the rating token RT and the update token UT whereas user i_1 obtains the rating-token RT' and the update-token UT'. Note that aid$_b$ with $b = 0, 1$ are used to generate ciphertexts ct, ct' that encrypt the identities K, K' of the users. Only RM can decrypt ct, ct' with the opening key. The serial number sn $= g^r$ resp. sn' $= g^{r'}$ is used to ensure that each rating token can only be used once. The rating token computed by each user further includes randomness r resp. r' which corresponds to the update token retained by the other user.

Rating Generation. A user in possession of a rating token received from another user can act as a rater for that user and prepare their own rating that will be submitted to the RM. The rating generation algorithm RateGen(pp, urep[i], RT, x) executed by user i with reputation credential urep[i] $= (k, s, e, R, C)$ and the chosen rating value g_x with $x \in [1, v]$ performs the following steps. Parse RT $= (\text{sn}, r, a, \text{ct}, \text{ct}', \text{sn}', \pi'_{\text{tok}})$. Verify π'_{tok} using the algorithm from Fig. 2 to check whether RT is a valid rating token. Compute $V = g_x g_{v+3}^r$ and a proof $\pi_{\text{sub}} = \text{PoK}\{(r, a, x, k) : V = g_x g_{v+3}^r \wedge g_x \in \{g_1, \cdots, g_v\} \wedge \text{sn} = g^r \wedge \text{ct} = (u^a, g_{v+2}^k \cdot U^a)\}$ using the algorithm from Fig. 2. V serves as an encryption of the rating value g_x under the random r, and the proof π_{sub} guarantees that the rating encrypted in V is valid, i.e., $g_x \in \{g_1, \cdots, g_v\}$, and that user i is authorised to rate. Finally, output a rating $\delta = (\text{sn}, V, \text{ct}, \text{ct}', \text{sn}', \pi'_{\text{tok}}, \pi_{\text{sub}})$.

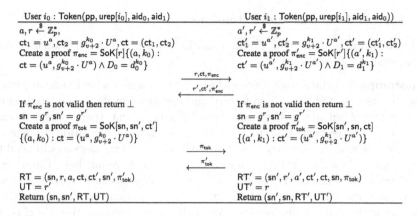

Fig. 1. Exchange of rating tokens. $\mathsf{urep}[i_b] = (k_b, s_b, e_b, R_b, C_b)$, $\mathsf{aid}_b = (d_b, D_b)$, $b \in \{0, 1\}$.

Rating Accumulation. Upon receiving a new rating δ, the RM can check its validity, identify the rater and the ratee, and accumulate the new rating by issuing an update information to the ratee. The algorithm $\mathsf{RateAcc}(\mathsf{pp}, \mathsf{ok}, \mathsf{reg}, \delta)$ run by the RM proceeds as follows. Parse $\delta = (\mathsf{sn}, V, \mathsf{ct}, \mathsf{ct}', \mathsf{sn}', \pi'_{\mathsf{tok}}, \pi_{\mathsf{sub}})$ with $\mathsf{ct} = (\mathsf{ct}_1, \mathsf{ct}_2)$ and $\mathsf{ct}' = (\mathsf{ct}'_1, \mathsf{ct}'_2)$. Check that the serial number sn has not been used before. Verify π'_{tok} and π_{sub} using the algorithms in Fig. 2 to check the validity of δ. In the last step of verification of π_{tok} and π_{sub}, the opening key $\mathsf{ok} = \xi$ is used to compute $K = \mathsf{ct}_2/\mathsf{ct}_1^{\xi}$ and $K' = \mathsf{ct}'_2/\mathsf{ct}_1'^{\xi}$. Find registration records $\mathsf{reg}[i]$ and $\mathsf{reg}[j]$ such that $K_i = K$ and $K_j = K'$ to identify the user i who is rating user j. To accumulate δ into $\mathsf{reg}[j] = (K_j, e, t, R, C)$ with current time $\tilde{t}$, choose $\tilde{s} \xleftarrow{\$} \mathbb{Z}_p^*$ and compute $\tilde{R} = R \cdot g_{v+1}^{\tilde{t}-t} \cdot V \cdot g_{v+3}^{\tilde{s}}$. Create a new reputation credential for user j by choosing a new random $\tilde{e} \xleftarrow{\$} \mathbb{Z}_p^*$ and computing $\tilde{C} = \tilde{R}^{\frac{1}{\gamma+\tilde{e}}}$. Update the registration record $\mathsf{reg}[j] \leftarrow (Z_j, \tilde{e}, \tilde{t}, \tilde{R}, \tilde{C})$, send $\mathsf{aux} = (\delta, \tilde{e}, \tilde{t}, \tilde{s}, \tilde{C})$ to user j, and output (i, j, aux).

Rating Update. Upon receiving the update information from the RM users can update their own reputation credential and score. The algorithm $\mathsf{Upd}(\mathsf{pp}, \mathsf{urep}[j], \mathsf{scr}[j], \mathsf{UT}, \mathsf{aux})$ executed by user j to update own reputation credential and score performs the following steps. Parse $\mathsf{urep}[j] = (k, s, e, R, C)$, $\mathsf{scr}[j] = (n_1, \cdots, n_v, t)$, $\mathsf{aux} = (\delta, \tilde{e}, \tilde{t}, \tilde{s}, \tilde{C})$ with $\delta = (\mathsf{sn}, V, \mathsf{ct}, \mathsf{ct}', \mathsf{sn}', \pi'_{\mathsf{tok}}, \pi_{\mathsf{sub}})$, and $\mathsf{UT} = r$. Verify validity of the update information aux by checking the proofs π'_{tok} and π_{sub}, checking $g^{\mathsf{UT}} \stackrel{?}{=} \mathsf{sn}$ and ensuring that UT hasn't been used in any previous update. If all successful, compute $g_x = V/g_{v+3}^r$ and $\tilde{R} = R \cdot g_{v+1}^{\tilde{t}-t} \cdot V \cdot g_{v+3}^{\tilde{s}}$. Check if $\hat{\mathsf{e}}(\tilde{C}, W \cdot w^{\tilde{e}}) \stackrel{?}{=} \hat{\mathsf{e}}(\tilde{R}, w)$. If successful, update $\mathsf{urep}[j] \leftarrow (k, s+r+\tilde{s}, \tilde{e}, \tilde{R}, \tilde{C})$ and $\mathsf{scr}[j] \leftarrow (n_1, \cdots, n_x+1, \cdots, n_v, \tilde{t})$ and output 1, otherwise output 0.

5.2 Further Remarks and Extensions

In the following we provide several remarks regarding the functionality and design rationale of our scheme.

Timestamps. In pRate, each score includes a timestamp t which indicates when the score was updated last. Upon advertising the user can choose not to disclose the exact time t but to provide a zero-knowledge proof that their score is recent. We do not enforce each user to have the most recent reputation credential, otherwise it would significantly limit the flexibility on when users would need to submit and update their ratings. However, users who have not been rated for a longer period of time could possibly be disadvantaged because of that. In that case, these users can ask the RM to update the timestamp in their reputation credential without disclosing or changing their scores. For this, the RM chooses a fresh timestamp $\tilde{t}$, picks $\tilde{e}, \tilde{s} \overset{\$}{\leftarrow} \mathbb{Z}_p^*$, computes $\tilde{C} = (R \cdot g_{v+1}^{\tilde{t}-t} \cdot g_{v+3}^{\tilde{s}})^{\frac{1}{\gamma + \tilde{e}}}$ and sends $(\tilde{e}, \tilde{t}, \tilde{s}, \tilde{C})$ to the corresponding user.

Anonymous Advertisements. The one-time advertisements published by users prior to each new transaction are anonymous and cannot be linked to the same publisher. Although this provides strong privacy protection, a malicious user may generate a large amount of advertisements to consume resources of online platforms. The RM can restrict users to publish no more than n advertisements in some period of time (e.g., one day) by publishing a set of generators $\{d_1, \cdots, d_n\}$ that would be valid for that period and requiring users to use these d_i for generation of their advertising identifiers aid $= (d_i, d_i^k)$ during that period. Note that any user who generates more advertisements than allowed by the RM would become linkable.

Secure Channels for Token Exchange. We require that rating tokens are exchanged over a secure channel that must be setup between the two prospective transaction partners. Note that these partners do not know each other identities since their reputation advertisements are anonymous. For this purpose we can let each user choose a temporary private-public key pair and include the corresponding public key as part of the published advertisement information m. These temporary keys can then be used to execute any standard secure channel establishment protocol to create an authenticated and confidential channel (see [26] for the property of such channels) over which parties would exchange their tokens. The authentication property in this case would imply that the channel is established between the two original yet anonymous advertisers. Communication between two anonymous users can be established through the platform on which the advertisements are published and to which users could connect anonymously via Tor [23] or with the help of distributed ledger techniques as in [33].

Accountability. In the rating accumulation algorithm RateAcc, the RM learns the identities of the rater and ratee (without being able to link them to the advertisements containing transaction details). This can be useful in the detection of conventional attacks against reputation systems [25] such as Sybil attacks, self-promotion attacks where a dishonest user arbitrarily creates rating tokens to

$\pi_{\mathsf{id}} = \mathsf{PoK}\left\{(k, s_1) : K = g_{v+2}^k \wedge S_1 = g_{v+3}^{s_1}\right\}$

- $\mathsf{Prv}(k, s_1, g_{v+2}, g_{v+3}, K, S_1)$:
  - $r_k, r_s \xleftarrow{\$} \mathbb{Z}_p^*$
  - $R_1 = g_{v+2}^{r_k}, R_2 = g_{v+3}^{r_s}$
  - $c = \mathcal{H}(K, S_1, R_1, R_2)$
  - $\varrho_k = r_k + c \cdot k, \varrho_s = r_s + c \cdot s_1$
  - Return $\pi_{\mathsf{id}} = (c, \varrho_s, \varrho_k)$
- $\mathsf{Ver}(g_{v+2}, g_{v+3}, K, S_1, \pi_{\mathsf{id}})$:
  - Parse $\pi_{\mathsf{id}} = (c, \varrho_s, \varrho_k)$
  - $\hat{R}_1 = g_{v+2}^{\varrho_k}/K^c, \hat{R}_2 = g_{v+3}^{\varrho_s}/S_1^c$
  - $\hat{c} = \mathcal{H}(K, S_1, \hat{R}_1, \hat{R}_2)$
  - If $\hat{c} = c$ then return 1 else 0

$\pi_{\mathsf{enc}} = \mathsf{SoK}[r]\{(a, k) : \mathsf{ct} = (u^a, g_{v+2}^k \cdot U^a)$
$\wedge D = d^k\}$

- $\mathsf{Prv}(a, k, u, g_{v+2}, U, \mathsf{ct}, d, D)$:
  - $r_a, r_k \xleftarrow{\$} \mathbb{Z}_p^*$
  - $R_1 = u^{r_a}, R_2 = g_{v+2}^{r_k} U^{r_a}, R_3 = d^{r_k}$
  - $c = \mathcal{H}(\mathsf{ct}, D, R_1, R_2, R_3)$
  - $\varrho_a = r_a + c \cdot a, \varrho_k = r_k + c \cdot k$
  - Return $\pi_{\mathsf{enc}} = (c, \varrho_a, \varrho_k)$
- $\mathsf{Ver}(u, g_{v+2}, U, \mathsf{ct}, d, D, \pi_{\mathsf{enc}})$:
  - Parse $\mathsf{ct} = (\mathsf{ct}_1, \mathsf{ct}_2)$ and $\pi_{\mathsf{enc}} = (c, \varrho_a, \varrho_k)$
  - $\hat{R}_1 = u^{\varrho_a} \mathsf{ct}_1^{-c}, \hat{R}_2 = g_{v+2}^{\varrho_k} U^{\varrho_a} \mathsf{ct}_2^{-c}, \hat{R}_3 = d^{\varrho_k} D^{-c}$
  - $\hat{c} = \mathcal{H}(\mathsf{ct}, D, \hat{R}_1, \hat{R}_2, \hat{R}_3)$
  - If $\hat{c} = c$ then return 1 else 0

$\pi_{\mathsf{tok}} = \mathsf{SoK}[\mathsf{sn}, \mathsf{sn}', \mathsf{ct}']\left\{(a, k) : \mathsf{ct} = (u^a, g_{v+2}^k \cdot U^a)\right\}$

- $\mathsf{Prv}(a, u, U, \mathsf{ct}, \mathsf{sn}, \mathsf{sn}', \mathsf{ct}')$:
  - $r_a, r_k \xleftarrow{\$} \mathbb{Z}_p^*, R_1 = u^{r_a}, R_2 = U^{r_a}, R_3 = g_{v+2}^{r_k}, Z = U^a$
  - $c = \mathcal{H}(\mathsf{ct}, Z, R_1, R_2, R_3, \mathsf{sn}, \mathsf{sn}', \mathsf{ct}'), \varrho_a = r_a + c \cdot a, \varrho_k = r_k + c \cdot k$
  - Return $\pi_{\mathsf{tok}} = (\mathsf{ct}, c, \varrho_a, \varrho_k)$
- $\mathsf{Ver}(\xi, u, U, \pi_{\mathsf{tok}}, \mathsf{sn}, \mathsf{sn}', \mathsf{ct}')$:
  - Parse $\pi_{\mathsf{tok}} = (\mathsf{ct} = (\mathsf{ct}_1, \mathsf{ct}_2), c, \varrho_a, \varrho_k)$
  - $\hat{R}_1 = u^{\varrho_a} \mathsf{ct}_1^{-c}, \hat{R}_2 = \hat{R}_1^\xi, \hat{R}_3 = g_{v+2}^{\varrho_k} U^{\varrho_a} \hat{R}_2^{-1} \mathsf{ct}_2^{-c}, \hat{Z} = \mathsf{ct}_1^\xi$
  - $\hat{c} = \mathcal{H}(\mathsf{ct}, \hat{Z}, \hat{R}_1, \hat{R}_2, \hat{R}_3, \mathsf{sn}, \mathsf{sn}', \mathsf{ct}')$
  - If $c \neq \hat{c}$ or $U^{\varrho_a} \neq \hat{R}_2 \hat{Z}^{\hat{c}}$ return $\perp$
  - Return $m = \mathsf{ct}_2/\hat{Z}$

$\pi_{\mathsf{dec}} = \mathsf{PoK}\{(r') : H = h^{r'}\}$

- $\mathsf{Prv}(r')$:
  - $\theta \xleftarrow{\$} \mathbb{Z}_p^*, R = h^\theta$
  - $c = \mathcal{H}(H, R), \varrho = \theta + c \cdot r'$
  - Return $\pi_{\mathsf{dec}} = (c, \varrho)$
- $\mathsf{Ver}(H, \pi_{\mathsf{dec}})$:
  - Parse $\pi_{\mathsf{dec}} = (c, \varrho)$
  - $\hat{R} = h^\varrho/H^c$
  - $\hat{c} = \mathcal{H}(H, \hat{R})$
  - If $\hat{c} = c$ then return 1 else 0

$\pi_{\mathsf{sub}} = \mathsf{PoK}\{(r, a, g_x, k) : V = g_x g_{v+3}^r \wedge g_x \in \{g_1, \cdots, g_v\} \wedge \mathsf{sn} = g^r \wedge \mathsf{ct} = (u^a, g_{v+2}^k \cdot U^a)\}$

- $\mathsf{Prv}(r, a, g_x)$:
  - $r_a, r_k \xleftarrow{\$} \mathbb{Z}_p^*, R_1 = u^{r_a}, R_2 = U^{r_a}, R_3 = g_{v+2}^{r_k}, Z = U^a$
  - $\theta_x, \{e_j, \theta_j\}_{j=1, j \neq x}^v \xleftarrow{\$} \mathbb{Z}_p^*$
    * $A_x = g_{v+3}^{\theta_x}, B_x = g^{\theta_x}$
    * For $j \neq x, \varrho_j = \theta_j + e_j \cdot r, A_j = g_{v+3}^{\varrho_j}(g_j/V)^{e_j}$ and $B_j = g^{\theta_j}$
  - $c = \mathcal{H}(\mathsf{ct}, Z, R_1, R_2, R_3, A_1, \cdots, A_v, B_1, \cdots, B_v)$
  - $\varrho_a = r_a + c \cdot a, \varrho_k = r_k + c \cdot k, e_x = c - \sum_{j \neq x} e_j, \varrho_x = \theta_x + e_x \cdot r$
  - Return $\pi_{\mathsf{sub}} = (\mathsf{ct}, \varrho_a, \varrho_k, \{e_j, \varrho_j\}_{j=1}^v)$
- $\mathsf{Ver}(\xi, V, \mathsf{sn}, \pi_{\mathsf{sub}})$:
  - Parse $\pi_{\mathsf{sub}} = (\mathsf{ct} = (\mathsf{ct}_1, \mathsf{ct}_2), \varrho_a, \varrho_k, \{e_j, \varrho_j\}_{j=1}^v)$
  - $c = \sum_{j=1}^v e_j, \hat{R}_1 = u^{\varrho_a} \mathsf{ct}_1^{-c}, \hat{R}_2 = \hat{R}_1^\xi, \hat{R}_3 = g_{v+2}^{\varrho_k} U^{\varrho_a} \hat{R}_2^{-1} \mathsf{ct}_2^{-c}, \hat{Z} = \mathsf{ct}_1^\xi$
  - $\hat{A}_j = g_{v+3}^{\varrho_j}(g_j/V)^{e_j}$ and $\hat{B}_j = g^{\varrho_j} \mathsf{sn}^{-e_j}$ for $j = [1, v]$
  - $\hat{c} = \mathcal{H}(\mathsf{ct}, \hat{Z}, \hat{R}_1, \hat{R}_2, \hat{R}_3, \hat{A}_1, \cdots, \hat{A}_v, \hat{B}_1, \cdots, \hat{B}_v)$
  - If $c \neq \hat{c}$ or $U^{\varrho_a} \neq \hat{R}_2 \hat{Z}^{\hat{c}}$ then return $\perp$
  - Return $m = \mathsf{ct}_2/\hat{Z}$

$\pi_{\mathsf{upd}} = \mathsf{PoK}\{(r, r', x) : V' = g_x g_{v+3}^r h^{r'} \wedge g_x \in \{g_1, \cdots, g_v\}\}$

- $\mathsf{Prv}(r, r', x)$:
  - $\theta_x, \theta_x', \{e_j, \theta_j, \theta_j'\}_{j=1, j \neq x}^v \xleftarrow{\$} \mathbb{Z}_p^*$
    * $A_x = g_{v+3}^{\theta_x} h^{\theta_x'}$
    * For $j \neq x, \varrho_j = \theta_j + e_j \cdot r, \varrho_j' = \theta_j' + e_j \cdot r'$ and $A_j = g_{v+3}^{\varrho_j} h^{\varrho_j'}(g_j/V')^{e_j}$
  - $c = \mathcal{H}(V', A_1, \cdots, A_v), e_x = c - \sum_{j \neq x} e_j, \varrho_x = \theta_x + e_x \cdot r, \varrho_x' = \theta_x' + e_x \cdot r'$
  - Return $\pi_{\mathsf{upd}} = (\{e_j, \varrho_j, \varrho_j'\}_{j=1}^v)$
- $\mathsf{Ver}(V', \pi_{\mathsf{upd}})$:
  - Parse $\pi_{\mathsf{upd}} = (\{e_j, \varrho_j, \varrho_j'\}_{j=1}^v)$
  - $c = \sum_{j=1}^v e_j$
  - $\hat{A}_j = g_{v+3}^{\varrho_j} h^{\varrho_j'}(g_j/V')^{e_j}$ for $j \in [1, v]$
  - $\hat{c} = \mathcal{H}(V', \hat{A}_1, \cdots, \hat{A}_v)$
  - If $c = \hat{c}$ then return 1 else return 0

Fig. 2. Specifications of zero-knowledge proofs utilised in pRate.

increase their own reputation score, and ballot stuffing attacks where dishonest users collude to conduct fake transactions and ratings to improve their reputation scores. The RM can detect such malicious behaviours heuristically, for example, when a user gets an unusual large amount of ratings within a short time period or submits too many ratings. If the RM notices any suspicious activity, the RM can investigate, e.g., request users to provide supporting documents to show that these ratings are based on real transactions, and punish misbehaving users.

Batch Accumulation and Unlinkability. In the rating accumulation algorithm RateAcc, the RM updates user's j reputation credential and sends a update aux to the corresponding user j. We observe that the rating accumulation part does not have to be performed immediately for each new rating that the RM receives for user j. In our scheme this process can be delayed and performed in a batch in order to reduce the overhead from the reputation update. More precisely, the RM can accumulate multiple ratings in a batch by multiplying all ciphertexts into a single product $V = \prod_\ell V_\ell$ and produce a single update information.

When updating a single rating $V_\ell = g_{x_\ell} g_{v+3}^{r_\ell}$, the ratee uses the update token $\mathsf{UT}_\ell = r_\ell$ to extract g_{x_ℓ} from V_ℓ. The update token UT_ℓ is linked to the serial number $\mathsf{sn}_\ell = g^{r_\ell}$ from the token exchange session. We stress that this link does not compromise rater's anonymity because of the anonymous (one-time) advertisement that was used in the token exchange session. Therefore, the ratee is not able to link any previous or future ratings produced by the same rater. In practice, there might be scenarios where some side channel information could leak the identity of the user, e.g., in Airbnb, a guest would meet the home owner in person. For these applications, we can break the link between the token exchange session and the submitted rating by using a more sophisticated batch accumulation technique that applies additional randomisation as described in the following.

The basic idea is to let the RM randomly blind the ratings and give the ratee a decryption key to remove this randomness from the aggregated ratings. The ratee will no longer be able to learn that a rating value x_ℓ is linked to the serial number sn_ℓ and only learn their aggregated value of $\{x_\ell\}_\ell$. Below we describe how the RM randomises the ratings and how the ratee removes this randomness prior to updating its reputation score. The part for updating $\mathsf{reg}[j], C, R$ is the same as before and is omitted here.

- When a user i submits a rating $\delta_\ell = (\mathsf{sn}_\ell, V_\ell, \mathsf{ct}_\ell, \mathsf{ct}'_\ell, \mathsf{sn}'_\ell, \pi'_{\mathsf{tok},\ell}, \pi_{\mathsf{sub},\ell})$ to the RM, the user additionally picks a randomiser $r'_\ell \xleftarrow{\$} \mathbb{Z}_p^*$, computes $V'_\ell = V_\ell \cdot h^{r_\ell}$ and a proof $\pi_{\mathsf{upd},\ell} = \mathsf{PoK}\{(r_\ell, r'_\ell, x_\ell) : V'_\ell = g_{x_\ell} g_{v+3}^{r_\ell} h^{r'_\ell} \wedge g_{x_\ell} \in \{g_1, \cdots, g_v\}\}$ and sends $(r'_\ell, V'_\ell, \pi_{\mathsf{upd},\ell})$ to the RM. The details of $\pi_{\mathsf{upd},\ell}$ are given in Fig. 2.
- After the RM receives n ratings (possibly from different raters) for some user j, it can accumulate these ratings together and update user's j reputation credential once. For this, the RM computes $r' = \sum_\ell r'_\ell$, $H = h^{r'}$, $\pi_{\mathsf{dec}} = \mathsf{PoK}\{(r') : H = h^{r'}\}$, and sends $(\{V'_\ell, \pi_{\mathsf{upd},\ell}\}_\ell, \{\mathsf{sn}_\ell\}_\ell, H, \pi_{\mathsf{dec}})$ to user j. The details of π_{dec} are given in Fig. 2.

– User j computes $V' = \prod_\ell V'_\ell$ and eliminates the randomisers $\{r'_\ell\}_\ell$ by computing $V = V'/H(= \prod_\ell V_\ell)$. Further, user j finds a set of update tokens $\{\mathsf{UT}_\ell = r_\ell\}_\ell$ corresponding to the serial numbers $\{\mathsf{sn}_\ell\}_\ell$ and removes the randomisers $\{r_\ell\}_\ell$ by computing $r = \sum_\ell r_\ell$ and $M = V/g_{v+3}^r(= \prod_\ell g_{x_\ell})$. User j can then use a brute-force approach to find $(m_1, \cdots, m_v)$ s.t. $M = g_1^{m_1} \cdots g_v^{m_v}$ and $n = m_1 + \cdots + m_v$, and, finally, update own reputation score as $\mathsf{scr}[j] = (n_1 + m_1, \cdots, n_v + m_v, \hat{t})$.

We remark that the total number of possible combinations for $(m_1, \cdots, m_v)$ is C_{n+v-1}^{v-1} which is a polynomial of degree v and is feasible to brute-force. For example, if $n = 20$ and $v = 5$, then $C_{n+v-1}^{v-1} = 10626$. Since generators $g_1, \cdots, g_v$ are randomly chosen, the tuple $(m_1, \cdots, m_v)$ that satisfies the above conditions is unique with overwhelming probability. Otherwise, if there is another tuple $(m'_1, \cdots, m'_v)$ for which $M = g_1^{m'_1} \cdots g_v^{m'_v}$ then the equation $g_1^{m_1-m'_1} \cdots g_v^{m_v-m'_v} = 1$ can be used to find a non-trial relation between $g_1, \cdots, g_v$ and break the DL assumption.

The above technique achieves unlinkability between the token exchange sessions and submitted ratings based on the following argument: Let $T_b = (\mathsf{pp}, x_0, x_1, r_0, r_1, V'_0 = g_{x_b} g_{v+3}^{r_0} h^{r'_0}, V'_1 = g_{x_{1-b}} g_{v+3}^{r_1} h^{r'_1}, H = h^{r'_0+r'_1})$ with $r'_0, r'_1 \xleftarrow{\$} \mathbb{Z}_p^*$ for $b = 0, 1$. In T_0, V'_0 encrypts the rating value x_0 and V'_1 encrypts the rating value x_1, while in T_1, V'_0 encrypts the rating value x_1 and V'_1 encrypts the rating value x_0. We can easily see that $H = V'_0 V'_1/(g_{x_0} g_{x_1} g_{v+3}^{r_0} g_{v+3}^{r_1})$ holds for both T_0 and T_1. Since r'_0, r'_1 are chosen uniformly at random, T_0 and T_1 have the same distribution.

5.3 Performance Analysis

In the following we evaluate the computational costs of pRate algorithms and sizes of utilized zero-knowledge proofs. We start with the latter.

Size of Zero-Knowledge Proofs. All zero-knowledge proofs used in pRate are short as can be observed based on the summary in Table 1, where v is the rating score and $\ell = \sum_i \ell_i$ is the size of the intervals in predicate $P = \wedge_i(\psi_i \in [0, 2^{\ell_i}))$, and both can be seen as small constants. Furthermore, the size of the proof π_{rep} in the advertisement can be further reduced to $(v + 11)\mathbb{Z}_p + (2\lceil \log \ell \rceil + 5)\mathbb{G}_1$ using an inner-product proof according to [14].

We illustrate with a concrete example based on a five-star rating scheme, i.e. $v = 5$. Suppose, Alice has a reputation score $\mathsf{scr} = (n_1, n_2, n_3, n_4, n_5, t) = (9, 2, 11, 30, 328, 6940)$ where $t = 6940$ is the number of days elapsed from 1 Jan 2000 to 1 Jan 2019. Alice can prove the following statements about her score:

– The number of 1-star, 2-star and 3-star ratings is less than 16, i.e., $n_1, n_2, n_3 \in [0, 2^4)$. The average score is higher than 4.6, i.e., $(n_1 + 2n_2 + 3n_3 + 4n_4 + 5n_5)/(n_1 + n_2 + n_3 + n_4 + n_5) > 4.6$ which can be proved by showing $n_4, n_5 \in [0, 2^{10})$ and $(-18n_1 - 13n_2 - 8n_3 - 3n_4 + 2n_5) \in [0, 2^{10})$.

– The score was updated no earlier than 1 Oct 2018, i.e., $t > 6848$ where 6848 is the number of days elapsed from 1 Jan 2000 to 1 Oct 2018. This can be proved using $t \in [0, 2^{13})$ and $t - 6848 \in [0, 2^{13})$.

This leads to $\ell = 4 * 3 + 10 * 3 + 13 * 2 = 68$ and $\lceil \log \ell \rceil = 7$.

Computational Costs. We summarize the amount of computations for each pRate algorithm in Table 2, where $mul_{\mathbb{G}_1}$ and $mul_{\mathbb{G}_T}$ denote scalar multiplications in $\mathbb{G}_1$ and $\mathbb{G}_T$, respectively; $exp_{\mathbb{G}_1}$ and $exp_{\mathbb{G}_T}$ are exponentiations in $\mathbb{G}_1$ and $\mathbb{G}_T$, respectively; RepAds and RepVer denote time-consuming pairing operations which can be optimized further (details can be found in the full version of this paper [28]).

Table 1. Sizes of zero-knowledge proofs in pRate.

Zero-knowledge proofs	Numbers of group elements
π_{id}	$3\mathbb{Z}_p$
π_{enc}	$3\mathbb{Z}_p$
π_{dec}	$2\mathbb{Z}_p$
π_{tok}	$3\mathbb{Z}_p + 2\mathbb{G}_1$
π_{sub}	$(2v + 2)\mathbb{Z}_p + 2\mathbb{G}_1$
π_{upd}	$(3v)\mathbb{Z}_p$
π_{rep}	$(v + 2\ell + 9)\mathbb{Z}_p + 3\mathbb{G}_1$

Table 2. Computational costs of pRate algorithms.

Operations	Numbers of group operations
Join	$(v + 4)mul_{\mathbb{G}_1} + (v + 8)exp_{\mathbb{G}_1} + 2pairing$
Issue	$(v + 6)mul_{\mathbb{G}_1} + (v + 7)exp_{\mathbb{G}_1} + 2pairing$
RepAds	$(4\ell + 1)mul_{\mathbb{G}_1} + (4\ell + 3)exp_{\mathbb{G}_1} + (v + 4)mul_{\mathbb{G}_T} + (v + 5)exp_{\mathbb{G}_T}$
RepVer	$(v + 2\ell + 6)mul_{\mathbb{G}_1} + (v + 2\ell + 10)exp_{\mathbb{G}_1} + 1mul_{\mathbb{G}_T} + 2pairing$
Token	$12mul_{\mathbb{G}_1} + 28exp_{\mathbb{G}_1}$
RateGen	$9mul_{\mathbb{G}_1} + (2v + 15)exp_{\mathbb{G}_1}$
RateAcc	$18mul_{\mathbb{G}_1} + (4v + 21)exp_{\mathbb{G}_1}$
Upd	$20mul_{\mathbb{G}_1} + (4v + 23)exp_{\mathbb{G}_1} + 2pairing$

6   Security Analysis of pRate

pRate is designed to minimize the trust put on the RM. In particular, to ensure that (1) the RM cannot learn any rating values submitted by the users, (2) the

RM cannot link submitted ratings to the published anonymous advertisements, and (3) all data sent by the RM to the intended recipients is verifiable. The security of our pRate scheme is established formally in Theorems 1, 2, 3, 4 and 5 based on the properties of anonymity, rating secrecy, and the three flavours of unforgeability from Sect. 3. The assumptions on the capabilities of each party vary for different security properties. In the following we provide only high-level intuition for the security of pRate. Due to the space limitation, the formal proofs of all theorems are provided in the full version of this paper [28]. We note that all security properties hold in the random oracle model due to the use of non-interactive zero-knowledge proofs based on the well-known Fiat-Shamir transformation.

Theorem 1. *The pRate scheme is anonymous under the XDH assumption.*

Following [8], the anonymity is defined in a way that an adversary does not need to recover a user's identity but only distinguish which of the two users of its choice produced an advertisment, engaged in a token generation session and generated a rating. The adversary can learn the RM's master issuing key and any user's reputation credential and score except for the two users in the challenge. An advertisement $(\mathsf{aid}, \pi_{\mathsf{rep}})$ created by a user is fully anonymous due to the use of randomly chosen one-time identifiers $\mathsf{aid} = (d, d^k)$ and the zero-knowledge property of π_{rep}. The token exchange protocol is performed over a secure channel so that the RM cannot link the exchanged tokens to the ratings that it receives. The ciphertexts ct and ct' encrypting the identities of participating users can only be decrypted by the RM so that users remain anonymous to each other. The anonymity holds even when the RM's issuing key ik becomes compromised. However, the adversary cannot learn the RM's master opening key ok; otherwise it is trivial to decrypt $\mathsf{ct}, \mathsf{ct}'$ and learn the identities of the users. The proofs π_{tok} used in rating tokens and π_{sub} used in ratings are constructed based on techniques from CPS-EG which allow us to create a decryption oracle without knowing the RM's opening key ok.

Theorem 2. *The pRate scheme is rating-secret under the XDH assumption.*

Rating-secrecy is defined in a way that an adversary does not need to recover the rating value in a rating but needs to distinguish which of two rating values of its choice is encrypted in the rating. The adversary can learn the RM's master issuing key and the master opening key. Each rating is encrypted in $V = g_x g_{v+3}^r$ using random r that is only known to the rater and the ratee. The zero-knowledge proof π_{sub} ensures that V is correctly formed without leaking any information about x. The RM accumulates ciphertexts V to the ratee's reputation credential without learning the value of x. Of course, if RM colludes with the rater, RM can find out the rating value, but this case is trivial because a rater can reveal his rating to whomever he wants. Our design guarantees that as long as the corresponding rater and ratee are honest, their rating stays confidential. This holds even if the RM's issuing and opening keys become compromised.

566   J. Liu and M. Manulis

Theorem 3. *The pRate scheme is advertisement-unforgeable under the q-SDH assumption.*

Advertisement-unforgeability ensures that an adversary cannot produce an advertisement that cannot be traced back to a valid user. The adversary can learn the RM's master opening key. Note that only users in possession of valid reputation credentials issued to them by the RM can generate verifiable advertisements. The unforgeability of advertisements relies on the unforgeability of the BBS+ signature scheme and holds for honest users, even if the RM's opening key becomes compromised. Note that this property would be trivially broken when the RM's master issuing key was compromised because the adversary could then create fake users using the key.

Theorem 4. *The pRate scheme is ratee-unforgeable under the DL assumption.*

Ratee-unforgeability ensures that an adversary cannot forge a valid rating token that involves an honest user as ratee unless this user does produce it. The adversary can compromise both the RM's master issuing key and the master opening key. Unforgeability of rating tokens RT, computed using the long-term secret key k of the ratee, relies on the zero-knowledge and soundness properties of the proofs π_{tok} used in the token exchange protocol and π_{id} used in the registration protocol. Note that in case of successful forgery, the forking lemma can be used to extract k. The ratee-unforgeability property holds for honest ratees, in presence of the possibly corrupted RM.

Theorem 5. *The pRate scheme is rater-unforgeable under the DL assumption.*

Rater-unforgeability ensures that an adversary cannot forge a valid rating that involves an honest user as rater unless this user does produce it. The adversary can compromise both the RM's master issuing key and the master opening key. Unforgeability of ratings δ, computed using the long-term secret key k of the rater, relies on the zero-knowledge and soundness properties of the proofs π_{sub} used in the rating generation algorithm and π_{id} used in the registration protocol. Note that in case of successful forgery, the forking lemma can be used to extract k. The rater-unforgeability property holds for honest raters, in presence of the possibly corrupted RM.

7 Other Related Work

In terms of privacy, pRate is superior to a number of existing reputation schemes where anonymity of users is provided without considering the secrecy of their reputation scores. The scheme in [22] adopts controlled anonymity and cluster filtering to leverage against the effects of unfair ratings and discriminating seller. The system relies on a trusted third party called marketplace to publish the estimated reputation of buyers and sellers and assigns them pseudonyms to perform transactions. PERM [6] provides reputation-based blacklisting which enables a service provider to score users' anonymous sessions and deny access to users with insufficient reputation. A user's reputation score is uniquely identified with a serial number which will be revealed after the service provider updates the score and generates a new serial number. Therefore the rating by the service provider must be performed sequentially, i.e., one session after another. The work in [21] studies relations on several privacy definitions for reputation systems and presents a reputation function that can satisfy k-anonymity and rating secrecy. An anonymous reputation system based on pseudonymous system and e-cash is described in [5]. An authority called Bank keeps the record of each user's reputation score. Two users communicate with each other under their one-time pseudonyms where one user can rate the other user by transferring a certain amount of repcoins assigned by the Bank via e-cash. This system lacks accountability since users can create an arbitrary number of pseudonyms which are not registered with any authority. A reputation framework for participatory sensing applications is proposed in [20], where a user reports sensor readings to an application server and the server computes a score by evaluating the accuracy of the readings. Each user uses a pseudonym for reporting readings within a certain period and transfers the gained score to the next pseudonym when the next time period starts while preventing attackers from linking these pseudonyms. Reputation systems proposed in [9–11] allow each user to anonymously rate a product at most once. If a user rates the same product multiple times, his anonymity will be broken because these ratings are linkable. The system in [11] is based on group signatures with linkability while the scheme in [9] combines anonymous credentials with a reputation system. These systems focus on protecting anonymity for the rater but not for the ratee and they do not consider how to manage and protect reputation scores. Similar considerations apply to the scheme in [10] which provides a Universal Composability Framework for reputation systems. An anonymous reputation system which gives users rewards for submitting useful comments is presented in [15]. Users can publish their assessment opinions which can then be endorsed by other users such that the original rater receives some reward upon receiving a threshold number of endorsements.

8   Conclusion

In this paper we introduced pRate, a novel privacy-preserving reputation system, where scores are computed based on the (aggregated) number(s) of stars that users receive from their raters. The scheme is managed by a possibly untrusted reputation manager who can register users and assist ratees in updating their reputation scores, yet without learning these scores. In addition to ensuring the secrecy of the ratings, a distinctive feature of pRate over prior proposals, is that it hides the identities of raters and ratees from each other during the transaction and rating stages. pRate can be extended with a randomised batch accumulation technique that will further prevent the ratee from linking the received ratings to the corresponding transactions, thus offering even stronger privacy protection for the ratee. We note that pRate is widely independent of the actual transactions that occur between users and eventual payments associated with these transactions. As such pRate can be used in combination with many other approaches for anonymous transaction processing and payment.

References

1. How online reviews will impact your practice in 2018. https://virayo.com/online-reputation-management/importance-of-online-reviews/
2. Yelp accused of bullying businesses into paying for better reviews. http://www.cbc.ca/news/business/yelp-accused-of-bullying-businesses-into-paying-for-better-reviews-1.2899308
3. Yelp accused of extortion. https://www.wired.com/2010/02/yelp-sued-for-alleged-extortion/
4. Yelp accused of hiding positive reviews for non-advertiser. https://dfw.cbslocal.com/2018/01/09/yelp-accused-hiding-positive-reviews-non-advertiser/
5. Androulaki, E., Choi, S.G., Bellovin, S.M., Malkin, T.: Reputation systems for anonymous networks. In: Borisov, N., Goldberg, I. (eds.) PETS 2008. LNCS, vol. 5134, pp. 202–218. Springer, Heidelberg (2008). https://doi.org/10.1007/978-3-540-70630-4_13
6. Au, M.H., Kapadia, A.: PERM: practical reputation-based blacklisting without TTPS. In: CCS 2012, pp. 929–940 (2012)
7. Au, M.H., Susilo, W., Mu, Y.: Constant-size dynamic k-TAA. In: De Prisco, R., Yung, M. (eds.) SCN 2006. LNCS, vol. 4116, pp. 111–125. Springer, Heidelberg (2006). https://doi.org/10.1007/11832072_8
8. Bellare, M., Micciancio, D., Warinschi, B.: Foundations of group signatures: formal definitions, simplified requirements, and a construction based on general assumptions. In: Biham, E. (ed.) EUROCRYPT 2003. LNCS, vol. 2656, pp. 614–629. Springer, Heidelberg (2003). https://doi.org/10.1007/3-540-39200-9_38
9. Bemmann, K., et al.: Fully-featured anonymous credentials with reputation system. In: ARES (2018)
10. Blömer, J., Eidens, F., Juhnke, J.: Practical, anonymous, and publicly linkable universally-composable reputation systems. In: Smart, N.P. (ed.) CT-RSA 2018. LNCS, vol. 10808, pp. 470–490. Springer, Cham (2018). https://doi.org/10.1007/978-3-319-76953-0_25
11. Blömer, J., Juhnke, J., Kolb, C.: Anonymous and publicly linkable reputation systems. In: Böhme, R., Okamoto, T. (eds.) FC 2015. LNCS, vol. 8975, pp. 478–488. Springer, Heidelberg (2015). https://doi.org/10.1007/978-3-662-47854-7_29
12. Boneh, D., Boyen, X., Shacham, H.: Short group signatures. In: Franklin, M. (ed.) CRYPTO 2004. LNCS, vol. 3152, pp. 41–55. Springer, Heidelberg (2004). https://doi.org/10.1007/978-3-540-28628-8_3
13. Bootle, J., Cerulli, A., Chaidos, P., Ghadafi, E., Groth, J.: Foundations of fully dynamic group signatures. In: Manulis, M., Sadeghi, A.-R., Schneider, S. (eds.) ACNS 2016. LNCS, vol. 9696, pp. 117–136. Springer, Cham (2016). https://doi.org/10.1007/978-3-319-39555-5_7
14. Bünz, B., Bootle, J., Boneh, D., Poelstra, A., Wuille, P., Maxwell, G.: Bulletproofs: short proofs for confidential transactions and more. In: IEEE S&P, pp. 319–338 (2018)
15. Busom, N., Petrlic, R., Sebé, F., Sorge, C., Valls, M.: A privacy-preserving reputation system with user rewards. J. Netw. Comput. Appl. **80**, 58–66 (2017)

16. Camenisch, J., Hohenberger, S., Lysyanskaya, A.: Compact E-cash. In: Cramer, R. (ed.) EUROCRYPT 2005. LNCS, vol. 3494, pp. 302–321. Springer, Heidelberg (2005). https://doi.org/10.1007/11426639_18

17. Camenisch, J., Lysyanskaya, A.: Signature schemes and anonymous credentials from bilinear maps. In: Franklin, M. (ed.) CRYPTO 2004. LNCS, vol. 3152, pp. 56–72. Springer, Heidelberg (2004). https://doi.org/10.1007/978-3-540-28628-8_4

18. Camenisch, J., Stadler, M.: Efficient group signature schemes for large groups (extended abstract). In: Kaliski, B.S. (ed.) CRYPTO 1997. LNCS, vol. 1294, pp. 410–424. Springer, Heidelberg (1997). https://doi.org/10.1007/BFb0052252

19. Cheung, A.S.Y., Schulz, W.: Reputation protection on online rating sites. Stanf. Technol. Law Rev. **21**, 310 (2018)

20. Christin, D., Roßkopf, C., Hollick, M., Martucci, L.A., Kanhere, S.S.: IncogniSense: an anonymity-preserving reputation framework for participatory sensing applications. Pervasive Mobile Comput. **9**(3), 353–371 (2013)

21. Clauß, S., Schiffner, S., Kerschbaum, S.: K-anonymous reputation. In: ASIA CCS (2013)

22. Dellarocas, C.: Immunizing online reputation reporting systems against unfair ratings and discriminatory behavior. In: EC 2000, pp. 150–157 (2000)

23. Dingledine, R., Mathewson, N., Syverson, P.: Tor: the second-generation onion router. In: 13'th USENIX Security (2004)

24. Galbraith, S.D., Paterson, K.G., Smart, N.P.: Pairings for cryptographers. Discrete Appl. Math. **156**(16), 3113–3121 (2008)

25. Hasan, O.: A Survey of privacy preserving reputation systems. Technical report, LIRIS UMR 5205CNRS (2017)

26. Jager, T., Kohlar, F., Schäge, S., Schwenk, J.: On the security of TLS-DHE in the standard model. In: Safavi-Naini, R., Canetti, R. (eds.) CRYPTO 2012. LNCS, vol. 7417, pp. 273–293. Springer, Heidelberg (2012). https://doi.org/10.1007/978-3-642-32009-5_17

27. Kerschbaum, F.: A verifiable, centralized, coercion-free reputation system. In: WPES 2009, pp. 61–70 (2009)

28. Liu, J., Manulis, M.: pRate: anonymous star rating with rating secrecy. Cryptology ePrint Archive: Report 2019/378 (2019). https://eprint.iacr.org/2019/378

29. Minkus, T., Ross, K.W.: I know what you're buying: privacy breaches on eBay. In: De Cristofaro, E., Murdoch, S.J. (eds.) PETS 2014. LNCS, vol. 8555, pp. 164–183. Springer, Cham (2014). https://doi.org/10.1007/978-3-319-08506-7_9

30. Narayanan, A., Shmatikov, V.: Robust de-anonymization of large sparse datasets. In: 2008 IEEE Symposium on Security and Privacy (S&P 2008), pp. 111–125 (2008)

31. Petrlic, R., Lutters, S., Sorge, C.: Privacy-preserving reputation management. In: SAC 2014, pp. 1712–1718 (2014)

32. Resnick, P., Zeckhauser, R.: Trust among strangers in internet transactions: empirical analysis of eBay's reputation system. In: Advances in Applied Microeconomics, vol. 11, pp. 127–157 (2002)

33. Sasson, E.B., et al.: Zerocash: decentralized anonymous payments from bitcoin. In: 2014 IEEE Symposium on Security and Privacy, pp. 459–474 (2014)

34. Seurin, Y., Treger, J.: A robust and plaintext-aware variant of signed ElGamal encryption. In: Dawson, E. (ed.) CT-RSA 2013. LNCS, vol. 7779, pp. 68–83. Springer, Heidelberg (2013). https://doi.org/10.1007/978-3-642-36095-4_5

35. Teubner, T., Hawlitschek, F., Dann, D.: Price determinants on Airbnb: how reputation pays off in the sharing economy. J. Self-Gov. Manage. Econ. **5**(4), 53–80 (2017)

36. Zervas, G., Proserpio, D., Byers, J.: A first look at online reputation on Airbnb, where every stay is above average. In: SSRN Working Paper 2554500 (2015)
37. Zhai, E., Wolinsky, D.I., Chen, R., Syta, E., Teng, C., Ford, B.: Anonrep: towards tracking-resistant anonymous reputation. NSDI 2016 pp. 583–596 (2016)

Masking Fuzzy-Searchable Public Databases

Alexandra Boldyreva[1], Tianxin Tang[1(✉)], and Bogdan Warinschi[2]

[1] Georgia Institute of Technology, Atlanta, USA
{sasha,ttang}@gatech.edu
[2] University of Bristol, Bristol, UK
csxbw@bristol.ac.uk

Abstract. We introduce and study the notion of *keyless fuzzy search* (KlFS) which allows to mask a publicly available database in such a way that any third party can retrieve content *if and only if* it possesses some data that is "close to" the encrypted data – no cryptographic keys are involved. We devise a formal security model that asks a scheme not to leak any information about the data and the queries except for some well-defined *leakage* function if attackers cannot guess the right query to make. In particular, our definition implies that recovering high entropy data protected with a KlFS scheme is costly. We propose two KlFS schemes: both use locality-sensitive hashes (LSH), cryptographic hashes and symmetric encryption as building blocks. The first scheme, is generic and works for abstract plaintext domains. The second scheme is specifically suited for databases of images. To demonstrate the feasibility of our KlFS for images, we implemented and evaluated a prototype system that supports image search by object similarity on masked database.

Keywords: Keyless searchable encryption · LSH · Image search

1 Introduction

Motivation. Consider an app for finding lookalikes. (This is mostly to gain intuition, we discuss more interesting applications further in the paper.) Using this app, people can post their photos and emails and are willing to be contacted by users who look very similar. Nowadays, image similarity search can be fully automated using modern image recognition/retrieval techniques. The downside is the obvious privacy concerns associated to posting personal information online. As the public is increasingly privacy-cautious, it is strongly desirable to reveal pictures and contact information *only* to lookalikes and not everybody else.

It is not clear how, if at all, existing cryptographic techniques can strengthen privacy of data in the application above. Multiparty computation techniques are not appropriate for this setting. The users are not likely to be all available at the same time to run the protocol. The (public) repository where data is held should neither have access to the raw data. Other cryptographic techniques which rely

© Springer Nature Switzerland AG 2019
R. H. Deng et al. (Eds.): ACNS 2019, LNCS 11464, pp. 571–591, 2019.
https://doi.org/10.1007/978-3-030-21568-2_28

on secret keys are also not suitable since people who should be able to access the data are not known a-priory and we want to avoid a completely trusted third party in our de-centralized setting.

We propose and rigorously study solutions to this problem. In short, we show how to mask publicly-accessible databases to allow users who know (some information about) what they are looking for to get that information, yet ensure that mass-harvesting or data mining is prohibitive. From here on, we use "masking" and "encrypting" interchangeably: our methods do not use keys but use (unstructured) data to protect privacy of some content, and the desired hiding properties are somewhat reminiscent of those of encryption.

Narayanan and Shmatikov [32] have proposed obfuscated databases to tackle the same general problem. They treat the case of exact match queries and is not suitable for applications where the match does not have to be exact, such as in the applications we consider. In this paper, we treat the general case of fuzzy queries.

Our Results. We propose the concept of *keyless fuzzy search* (KlFS), where a user can query a masked database, retrieve its parts and unmask the content *if only if* it possesses some data "close to" the masked data. We introduce syntax and security models for this primitive and present constructions. We give constructions for the general case (where the structure of the masked data is arbitrary) and for the specific case of image data and show that even without secret keys useful levels of security are possible.

SYNTAX AND SECURITY. The masking algorithm of a KlFS scheme takes inputs *access data* I (e.g. an image of a face) and an auxiliary message M to return a ciphertext C. To query a database of such ciphertexts, a user executes the query algorithm that takes input some access data I' (e.g. an image) and outputs the query. Given the database and the query, the server can efficiently find and return the ciphertexts of all data that have been created with access data "similar" to I' (e.g. all images containing the face in the query). The user can then decrypt and recover the auxiliary message M and optionally the original data I. The formal definition is in Sect. 3.

For security, we want to capture the idea the attacker obtains information only if it makes the "right" query to retrieve the information. In our formal definition (found in Sect. 3) we measure if an adversary can compute some useful information about the queries and the underlying with significantly better probability than a simulator who only has access to a *leakage function* of the data. Such definitions (with leakage functions) are common for primitives like searchable encryption and property-preserving encryption [18–20,28,29].

DISCUSSION. Since in our setting there are no keys or trusted parties, security depends on how hard it is for the adversary to come up with data that is close to the one in the masked database. Unlike prior definitions from which we draw inspiration, e.g. those for public-key deterministic encryption [4] and message-lock encryption [7], we do not require this task be computationally infeasible. For the type of applications we envision, message unpredictability is a strong assumptions which is often not true (though later in the paper we discuss a method to improve unpredictability for image encryption). We therefore take a more flexible approach and define security for an arbitrary data set with some (not necessarily negligible) min entropy which we leave as an unspecified parameter, and the difficulty of coming up with an "interesting" query will be reflected by the advantage of the adversary.

This hardness is tightly related to the application domain (how much entropy is there in the stored data) and the closeness threshold which allows unmasking protected data. A KlFS would allow an easy check to see if a specific license plate occurs in a surveillance video recording of an airport parking lot yet, determining all license plates that occur in the video would require exhaustive search. While feasible, it complicates the adversary's goal. Similarly, if KlFS is used to mask a database containing fingerprint readings, then harvesting it would require brute-forcing all possible fingerprints, which could be prohibitive.

The above suggests that in some scenarios KlFS should provide reasonable levels of security, yet it also indicates that the precise level of security may be difficult to assess. Empirical studies for particular datasets could be useful.

We note that it is extremely important that if our schemes get deployed, the users understand that their data is not getting a very strong level of security. The goal is not to hide the data, but to mask it to prevent easy harvesting of information. In other words, we do not show that adversaries do not exist; we show that adversaries can be *tethered*.

As such, we envision KlFS as an additional layer of protection to be used in conjunction with other mechanisms. For example, the cloud server may be trusted to protect its data storage against malicious compromises with traditional crypto and security tools, but it may not be trusted enough to not mine the data. In this case, the use of a KlFS scheme will protect the data from mass harvesting by the server.

BASIC CONSTRUCTION. All our constructions use, as a building block, a family of *locality-sensitive hash (LSH)* functions. A randomly chosen LSH function has the property that it collides with high probability when applied to "close" messages, and "far" messages are likely to yield distinct hash values. There are various constructions of LSH families known for different closeness metrics such as Hamming and Euclidean distances, etc. [3,22,26]. Most schemes employ the so-called And-Or construction, where a hash value is actually a vector of independent hashes applied to the same input.

The idea behind our Basic KlFS scheme is simple. To mask with access data I a message M we first apply an LSH to I to compute a hash vector $\mathbf{G}$. From $\mathbf{G}$ we compute a vector of tags $\mathbf{T}$ by applying a cryptographic hash function to each entry in $\mathbf{G}$. In addition, we encrypt M (and optionally I) using a standard symmetric encryption scheme under the keys $H(\mathbf{G}[i])$, where $1 \leq i \leq |\mathbf{G}|$ and H is a cryptographic hash function. In practice we recommend to use a slow hash as those used to slow down offline dictionary attacks on passwords, such as a repeated hash. To query I' a user computes the tag vector $\mathbf{T}'$ the same way using the LSH. The server (who indexed the database by the tags) can then efficiently find the required records by the common tags. The user can unmask as the common tag will yield one of the keys used for masking.

KlFS FOR IMAGE SEARCH. Since KlFS may be particularly suited to support search on images, we further focus on such data. Existing algorithms for such (unencrypted) search use of *feature* vectors. An image is characterized by a set of such vectors and two images are close if sufficiently many features of the two images are close. What "sufficient" and "close" means is defined by the search algorithm.

Our generic KlFS scheme is not immediately suitable since it cannot take advantage of structured information about the images such as feature vectors. Our high-level idea for an extension is as follows. First, we encode the LSH tags of all extracted feature vectors, so that only their equality is leaked. This way the search algorithm can still identify close feature vectors of database pictures and queried images. Next we encrypt database pictures using the standard symmetric encryption scheme under a key K that can be computed only if one knows a threshold number of feature vectors close to those in the picture or, in other words, possesses an image close to that included in the picture. Technically, we achieve this by secret-sharing the key K (one share per LSH tag) and then encrypting each share with a key deterministically derived from each LSH tag. To unmask, one would need to have an image that shares sufficiently many tags with the image used to mask. We define the scheme in detail and analyze its security (again, in the random oracle model) in Sect. 5.

REFINEMENTS. The security of the scheme described above depends tightly on the closeness unpredictability of masking data. While some images are reasonably unpredictable, our empirical experiments on some common image datasets showed that feature vectors are likely to be quite predictable. I.e., after trying several images, an attacker will likely have a feature overlap with that of the masked image, and hence will be able to unmask. Another implication is that our search would yield many false positives (approx. 4%), in the sense that each query would receive a fraction of ciphertexts of images that are "technically" close via a common feature, but visually not close. This is a general observation regarding the primitive which we propose: devising KlFS schemes requires careful analysis to ensure that "closeness" as implemented by the schemes corresponds, to the largest extent possible, to "closeness" as desired by applications.

We show how to alleviate this problem for image search. We adapt an "entropy-filling" technique used by Dong et al. [24] to eliminate false positives in image search to work with masked data. We show that it is possible to extract features in a way that best characterizes the images. The technique filters out the most common features therefore making overlaps between distinct images unlikely. In addition, to improve the true-positive rate while keeping the false-positive rate significantly low, we modify the search algorithm to rely on the PageRank-Nibble algorithm derived from [2] and also used in [24] to improve precision in (unencrypted) image search with very few false positives. We provide more intuition in Sect. 6 and more details in the full version [10].

IMPLEMENTATION. We realized our findings about KlFS for images as a working prototype system that adds privacy to image search. We describe our implementation and its evaluation in Sect. 6 and in the full version [10].

Applications. In [10] we discuss application domains where KlFS may be useful. These include image classification, 3D model storage, vision-based navigation of Unmanned Aerial Vehicles (UAV), self-driving cars and network fault detection. We omit the details here because of lack of space.

More Related Work. Our work is related to the vast literature on efficient searchable encryption, e.g., [9,18,20,21,28] and especially to fuzzy searchable encryption [8,29], and to the related areas of property-preserving [34] and structured encryption [19], but all these works are for the symmetric key setting, where a user possesses a secret key. Our focus is on the keyless setting.

Our work is also related to fuzzy vaults [27] and fuzzy extractors [11,16, 23], even though their main applications are authorization and key generation based on biometrics. These primitives, however, do not permit efficient search on encrypted data in a remote storage setting, as this would require the users to share a state (helper data).

The works on privacy-preserving data mining, e.g. [30,31], provide solutions for mining data while preserving hiding privacy of the users. Our goal is different, we want to restrict access to the data for those who do not know what to look for.

Security in the keyless setting has also been considered by the work on message-locked encryption (MLE) [7], which is a generalization of convergent encryption [25]. The main use of these primitives is for secure file de-duplication. KlFS can be viewed as *fuzzy* MLE (MLE ciphertexts leak equality of the underlying plaintexts and KlFS ciphertexts leak their closeness).

From this perspective, KlFS is related to the idea of obfuscation for (fuzzy) point function (PFO) [14], i.e. the task of obfuscating the function which returns the result of the comparison $x \stackrel{?}{=} a$ for some fixed a. A fuzzy PFO (which only reveals closeness of x and a) can be used in the obvious way to implement linear (therefore inefficient) search over encrypted data. The added ability to decrypt can be obtained using (a fuzzy variant of the) multibit output point function obfuscation with auxiliary information (MB-APFO) [15] and refined in later works [13]. While to explore these connections may be theoretically interesting, it is unclear if this would yield efficient enough constructions of KlFS.

2   Preliminaries

Due to lack of space we provide the notation and recall some basic primitives, such as symmetric encryption and secret sharing, in the full version [10].

CLOSENESS DOMAINS. We adopt the definitions from [8]. We say that $\Lambda = (\mathcal{D}, \mathrm{Cl})$ is a *closeness domain* if

1. $\mathcal{D}$ is a finite or an infinite set;

2. Cl is the (partial) *closeness function* that takes any $x, y \in \mathcal{D}$ and outputs a member of $\{\texttt{close}, \texttt{far}\}$, so that Cl is symmetric (i.e., $\mathrm{Cl}(x, y) = \mathrm{Cl}(y, x)$).

For example, for a metric space $(\mathcal{D}, d)$ and closeness parameters δ^{C} and δ^{F} we define the closeness domain $(\mathcal{D}, \mathrm{Cl})$ as follows. For $V, V' \in \mathcal{D}$,

$$\mathrm{Cl}(V, V') = \begin{cases} \texttt{close}, & \text{if } d(V, V') \leq \delta^{\mathrm{C}} \\ \texttt{far}, & \text{if } d(V, V') > \delta^{\mathrm{F}} \end{cases}$$

There are no requirements on the output of close for pairs that are "near" (i.e. points that neither close nor far).

LOCALITY SENSITIVE HASHING (LSH). All of our constructions utilize locality-sensitive hashing (LSH), so we start with recalling the LSH primitive introduced in [26]. Below, we give definitions for an arbitrary metric space $(\mathcal{D}, d)$.

Definition 1 (Locality-sensitive Hashing). *A family $\mathcal{H}$ is called $(\delta^{\mathrm{C}}, \delta^{\mathrm{F}}, p_1, p_2)$-sensitive if for any two points $x, y \in \mathcal{D}$ [35].*

- *if $d(x, y) \leq \delta^{\mathrm{C}}$ then $\Pr_{\mathcal{H}}[h(x) = h(y)] \geq p_1$,*
- *if $d(x, y) > \delta^{\mathrm{F}}$ then $\Pr_{\mathcal{H}}[h(x) = h(y)] \leq p_2$.*

In this paper we use an extension of LSH which amplifies the accuracy of the parameters via the following construction. The construction, known in the literature as the And-Or construction, is the following.

Definition 2 (Extended LSH (eLSH)). *Let $\mathcal{H}$ be an $(\delta^{\mathrm{C}}, \delta^{\mathrm{F}}, p_1, p_2)$-sensitive hash family. For positive integers k, L, choose random $h_{i,j} \in \mathcal{H}$ for all $i \in [L]$, all $j \in [k]$ and define the hash functions $g_i(\cdot)$ by*

$$g_i(x) = (h_{i,1}(x), h_{i,2}(x), \ldots, h_{i,k}(x)) \qquad \text{for all } i \in [L].$$

We refer to the set of functions g as the (L, k)-eLSH extension of $\mathcal{H}$.

One can think of (L, k)-eLSH extension of $\mathcal{H}$ as an LSH function with improved parameters. The parameters $(\delta^{\mathrm{C}}, \delta^{\mathrm{F}}, P_1, P_2)$ are established by [26] which we recall in the full version [10].

One construction of an LSH scheme that we use in this paper is for the *Hamming distance* on the set of binary strings of length l, i.e. $\mathcal{D} = \{0,1\}^l$. Starting from a simple LSH function which simply projects on a single bit of its input, i.e. to sample a function from this family simply select a random index $j \in \{1, \ldots, l\}$ and define $h_j(x) = x_j$ (where $x \in \mathcal{D}$ and x_j is the j'th bit of x). It follows that for any two points $p, q \in \mathcal{D}$ collide with probability $1 - \frac{d(p,q)}{l}$, where $d(p, q)$ is the Hamming distance on $\mathcal{D}$. The parameters for the corresponding (L, k)-eLSH are derived using the formulas from [26].

3   Keyless Fuzzy Search (KlFS)

SYNTAX FOR A KLFS SCHEME. A *Keyless Fuzzy Search (KlFS) scheme* KlFS is defined for a closeness domain $(\mathcal{D}, \mathrm{Cl})$ and message space $\mathcal{MS}$ by six algorithms KlFS = (Init, Mask, Unmask, Query, CreateDS, FuzzyS), where,

- Init is a randomized algorithm which outputs a public parameter $P \in \{0, 1\}^*$;
- Mask is randomized. It takes P, an element $I \in \mathcal{D}$, and an element $M \in \mathcal{MS}$ and outputs a ciphertext C; We abuse notation and for any subset $\mathbf{D} \subseteq \mathcal{D} \times \mathcal{MS}$ we write $\mathbf{C} \leftarrow \mathsf{Mask}(P, \mathbf{D})$ for the set of ciphertexts obtained by encrypting each $(I, M) \in \mathbf{D}$ using parameters P. We call the elements of $\mathcal{D}$ the *access data* and those of $\mathcal{MS}$ the *auxiliary message*, or simply the message;
- Unmask is deterministic. It takes P, C, an access data $I' \in \mathcal{D}$, and outputs either message M or $\bot$;
- CreateDS, takes a set of ciphertexts $\mathbf{C}$, which we call an (encrypted) database, and outputs a data structure DS;
- Query is deterministic. It takes parameters P, *query data* $I \in \mathcal{D}$, and outputs a query T; notice that access data used in encryption and query data live in the same domain;
- FuzzyS is deterministic. On input a database $\mathbf{C}$, data structure DS, and query T it outputs a set of ciphertexts.

Notice that we mask messages $M \in \mathcal{MS}$ under access data $I \in \mathcal{D}$ and demand that unmasking returns M (see below). We do not preclude that M contains some, or even all of the information about I.

CORRECTNESS AND EFFICIENCY: We split the correctness requirement of a KlFS scheme in two parts. The first part is concerned with the masking/unmasking algorithms. It demands that unmasking a ciphertext with query data far from the access data used to mask will fail whereas decrypting with data that is close to the original access data will succeed (i.e. return the auxiliary message used to encrypt). Note that the former is needed for filtering out the false positives.

The second part deals with the results returned by a search query. We demand that, searching using some query data I' will not return ciphertexts created with access data that is not close to I; conversely, we demand that the search returns all ciphertexts created with access data that is close to I. All of these requirements need to hold with sufficiently high probability, which is a parameter of the scheme.

ϵ-*Correct Decryption:* Let $P \xleftarrow{\$} \mathsf{Init}$ be parameters and $(I, M) \in \mathcal{D} \times \mathcal{MS}$ and $I' \in \mathcal{D}$ be arbitrary. Let $C \xleftarrow{\$} \mathsf{Mask}(P, I, M)$. Then for all $I, I' \in \mathcal{D}$, all $M \in \mathcal{MS}$

- if $\mathrm{Cl}(I, I') = \mathtt{close}$ then

$$\Pr[\mathsf{Unmask}(P, I', C) = M] \geq 1 - \epsilon,$$

– if $\mathrm{Cl}(I, I') = \texttt{far}$

$$\Pr[\mathsf{Unmask}(P, I', C) = \bot] \geq 1 - \epsilon.$$

The probabilities are over the choice of P and the coins used by the algorithms involved.

ϵ-*Correct Fuzzy Search:* Let $P \xleftarrow{\$} \mathsf{Init}$ be parameters, $\mathbf{D} \subseteq \mathcal{D} \times \mathcal{MS}$ be arbitrary and let $\mathbf{C} \xleftarrow{\$} \mathsf{Mask}(P, \mathbf{D})$. Consider the associate data structure $\mathsf{DS} = \mathsf{CreateDS}(\mathbf{C})$, an arbitrary $I' \in \mathcal{D}$ and $T \leftarrow \mathsf{Query}(P, I')$.

We require that:

– For any $(I, M) \in \mathbf{D}$; let C be the resulting ciphertext in $\mathbf{C}$. Then, if $\mathrm{Cl}(I, I') = \texttt{close}$ then
$$\Pr[C \in \mathsf{FuzzyS}(\mathbf{C}, \mathsf{DS}, T)] \geq 1 - \epsilon,$$

– For any $(I, M) \in \mathbf{D}$; let C be the resulting ciphertext in $\mathbf{C}$. Then, if $\mathrm{Cl}(I, I') = \texttt{far}$ then
$$\Pr[C \notin \mathsf{FuzzyS}(\mathbf{C}, \mathsf{DS}, T)] \geq 1 - \epsilon.$$

The probabilities are over the choice of P and any coins used by subsequent algorithms. We do not impose a specific bound on ϵ; the correctness analysis for each scheme would need to determine the best value for ϵ, and, of course, one may be able to derive different bounds for each of the four aspects of the correctness definition.

We say that a KlFS scheme is ϵ-*correct* if it satisfies ϵ-correct decryption and ϵ-correct fuzzy search.

We say KlFS is an *efficiently keyless fuzzy-searchable encryption* (EKlFS) scheme if for any P generated by Init, (sufficiently large) database $\mathbf{C}$, data structure $\mathsf{DS} = \mathsf{CreateDS}(\mathbf{C})$, and query T with $|\mathsf{FuzzyS}(\mathbf{C}, \mathsf{DS}, T)|$ sub-linear in the size of $\mathbf{C}$, the running time of FuzzyS is sub-linear in the size of $\mathbf{C}$. Notice this condition on the running time limits the number of false positives for a fuzzy query.

KLFS SECURITY. We define security of a KlFS scheme using the semantic security approach. As common with such simulation-based definitions for searchable encryption, the definition requires a *leakage function*, which describes whatever the adversary can (unavoidably) glean from the encrypted database, the search data structure and the queries. Since we cannot (and do not want to) fix a one-size-fits-all leakage function, our definition is parametrized by a function leak which takes as input the parameters of the scheme P, the access data $\mathbf{I}$, the auxiliary messages $\mathbf{M}$ and the search queries $\mathbf{Q}$ and outputs some information to be passed to the simulator. Ideally, this information should be as benign as possible, and a scheme designer/user should understand the consequences entailed by leaking this information. Notice that the function depends on the parameters of the scheme which essentially means that the information leaked may vary as a function of the parameters of the scheme.

Our definition can be seen as a non-trivial extension of the semantic-security-based definition for deterministic asymmetric encryption by Bellare et al. [6]. We compare two executions, a real one and an idealized one. In the real execution a database $\mathbf{D}$ and search queries $\mathbf{Q}$ are sampled according to some source $\mathcal{M}$. In addition, we let the source sample some target information target that models any possible information about the data and the queries the attacker can guess. The adversary is provided with the parameters of the scheme, an encryption of the database the search queries and attempts to guess the target information. We compare this execution with that of an adversary (simulator) who needs to guess the same information but only having as input the information which is allowed to be leaked.

If an ideal adversary exists, then the real adversary cannot learn more from the system beyond the information passed to the simulator. Unlike the traditional security definitions, we do not ask that the ideal adversary perform negligibly close to the real one, as this may not be achievable for some classes of sources. Instead, we let the advantage of the attacker (the difference between its and the ideal adversary's performances) be an arbitrary function of the given resources and the data source. We leave it to applications to estimate whether the given bounds are acceptable.

Experiment $\mathbf{Exp}^{\text{prv-real}}_{\text{K1FS},\mathcal{M}}(A)$	Experiment $\mathbf{Exp}^{\text{prv-ideal}}_{\text{K1FS},\mathcal{M},\text{leak}}(S)$

$P \xleftarrow{\$} \text{Init}$; $(\mathbf{I}, \mathbf{M}, \mathbf{Q}, \text{target}) \xleftarrow{\$} \mathcal{M}$
 For $j = 1, \dots, \|\mathbf{I}\|$ do
 $\quad \mathbf{C}[j] \xleftarrow{\$} \text{Mask}(P, \mathbf{I}[j], \mathbf{M}[j])$
 For $j = 1, \dots, \|\mathbf{Q}\|$ do
 $\quad \mathbf{T}[j] \leftarrow \text{Query}(\mathbf{Q}[j])$
 $\text{info} \xleftarrow{\$} A(P, \mathbf{C}, \mathbf{T})$
 Return $\text{info} \stackrel{?}{=} \text{target}$
	$P \xleftarrow{\$} \text{Init}$; $(\mathbf{I}, \mathbf{M}, \mathbf{Q}, \text{target}) \xleftarrow{\$} \mathcal{M}$
	 $\quad \text{info} \xleftarrow{\$} S(P, \text{leak}(P, \mathbf{I}, \mathbf{M}, \mathbf{Q}))$
	 $\quad$ Return $\text{info} \stackrel{?}{=} \text{target}$;

Fig. 1. The PRV real (left) and ideal (right) experiments.

Definition 3. *For a* K1FS *scheme, closeness domain* $(\mathcal{D}, Cl)$, *source* $\mathcal{M}$, *leakage function* leak, *an adversary* A *with given resources, simulator* S *we define the prv-advantage as* $\mathbf{Adv}^{prv}_{\text{K1FS},\mathcal{M},\text{leak}}(A, S)$ *as the difference*

$$\Pr\left[\mathbf{Exp}^{\text{prv-real}}_{\text{K1FS},\mathcal{M}}(A) = 1 \right] - \Pr\left[\mathbf{Exp}^{\text{prv-ideal}}_{\text{K1FS},\mathcal{M},\text{leak}}(S) = 1 \right],$$

where the experiments are defined on Fig. 1.

REMARKS. Note that the above definition is achievable only if the adversary cannot come up with data that is close to the data stored in the database (otherwise, it will be entitled to get the relevant data). This is similar to the requirements of data unpredictability for deterministic and message-lock encryption. We could formally define closeness unpredictability and consider only the sources with such a property. However, our constructions will rely on stronger assumptions so we do not define the minimal assumption for the source and instead define the assumptions required for each scheme.

It is likely that the data set of an application contains data of variable degree of unpredictability. For example, a database of names would have very common names like Adam Smith, somewhat common names like Brent Waters, and rare names like Muthukrishnan Venkitasubramaniam. In this case it makes sense to use the bound on the advantage separately to estimate security for each group, by considering several sources. This would require that there is no correlation between groups (correlations within each group are fine).

We note that our security definition is for a particular source but it is possible to extend the definition to consider a class of sources.

Two remarks are in order regarding the public parameters in the security game. First, our definition only captures security of messages that do not depend on public parameters. This is almost always a reasonable assumption in practice, and is an assumption which is also required in other settings like deterministic and hedged encryption [5] and MLE. Secondly, in our definition the simulator needs to work with honestly generated parameters. One could consider a more permissive definition with a simulator that generates the public parameters of the scheme.

Note that our security notion does capture (though only implicitly) the intuitive goal that it should be harder to extract the entire database than to extract a single entry. The definition demands that the attacker who does not know the right query, gets no information. This means that getting information reduces to coming up with the right queries. Each of these may take time, depending on the underlying message. This brings us back to the essential goal of hardness of retrieving records and tethering the attacker.

4   Basic KlFS

The idea behind the scheme is as follows. The parameters of the scheme consist of an (L, k)-eLSH family. To mask with data I some message M we calculate $g_i(I)$ for each $i \in [L]$ and use these values in two different ways. First, for each i we derive a key for a standard symmetric encryption scheme by using a hash function H and encrypt M under each of these keys. If the information to be encrypted is large, one may use a "hybrid" scheme where M is encrypted once under a random key K and K is encrypted under each $H(g_i(I))$. As mentioned in the Introduction, in practice we recommend to use a slow hash function to slow down the exhaustive search. In addition, we calculate L tags by applying a (different) hash function G to each $g_i(I)$. The ciphertext of M under I consists of the list of ciphertexts together with the set of tags.

The scheme can support search in a masked database as follows. Given some query data I' one can compute the tags associated to I' (i.e. $G(g_i(I'))$ for each i) to form a query. The server (who can index the database by the tags) can then efficiently locate and return all of the ciphertexts with at least one overlapping tag. The user who is given some data I' close enough to I can then recover at least one of the keys used to mask M by calculating $g_i(I')$ (for all i) and decrypt the ciphertext.

BASIC KLFS SCHEME. We now define a basic KlFS for any closeness domain $(\mathcal{D}, \mathrm{Cl})$ for which there exists an extended (L, k)-eLSH scheme $\mathcal{H}$ with parameters $(\delta^C, \delta^F, P_1, P_2)$ that are "compatible" with the closeness function, that is for any $I, I' \in \mathcal{D}$ if $\mathrm{Cl}(I, I') = \texttt{close}$ then $d(I, I') \leq \delta^C$ and if $\mathrm{Cl}(I, I') = \texttt{far}$ then $d(I, I') \geq \delta^F$. Given a standard symmetric encryption scheme $\mathcal{SE} = (\mathcal{K}, \mathcal{E}, \mathcal{D})$ we define the Basic KlFS scheme as shown in Fig. 2. The initialization algorithm picks two additional hash functions H, G (which we model as random oracles).

Note that although we present search as a linear operation on the database in practice this search is sublinear due to the use of data structures such as K-D trees [12]. In addition, we remark that although the decryption algorithm computes the tags associated to the access data I' used for decryption, in practice this computation is not needed: these tags were computed as part of creating the search query for I' and could be saved to be used in decryption. Moreover, only the "matching" tags could be sent by the server as part of each returned ciphertext.

CORRECTNESS AND SECURITY. The following theorem establishes the correctness of the basic scheme. Its proof is in the full version [10].

Theorem 1. *If $\mathcal{H}$ is an (L, k)-eLSH with parameters $(\delta^C, \delta^F, P_1, P_2)$ then the basic scheme defined above is ϵ-correct, with $\epsilon = \max((1 - P_1) + \frac{L}{2^h}, P_2 + \frac{L}{2^h})$, where h is the output length of the random oracle G.*

Next, we analyze the security of the basic scheme. Each ciphertext consists of a symmetric encryption and a set of tags, each tag is of the form $G(g_i(I))$ (for $1 \leq i \leq L$) and each search query is a collection of tags. We show that the only information that is leaked is the overlap between tags and nothing more, provided a minimal requirement on the interplay between this leakage and the keys used for symmetric encryption.

In our analysis, first we formalize the unavoidable leakage of the scheme, and then spell out and discuss the assumption that the source needs to satisfy.

Given some parameters $P = k||L||g_L(\cdot)$, random oracles G and H and $\mathbf{I}, \mathbf{M}, \mathbf{Q}, \texttt{target} \xleftarrow{\$} \mathcal{M}$ let T be the set of all tags (both associated to ciphertexts and to search queries) that are computed in the experiment. Clearly, the size of T is at most $L \cdot (|\mathbf{I}| + |\mathbf{Q}|)$: each entry in $\mathbf{I}$ and $\mathbf{Q}$ (has at most L associated tags). We can then formalize the information leaked $\mathsf{leak}(P, (\mathbf{I}, \mathbf{Q}))$ as a map $\mathbf{L} : [|T|] \to \mathcal{P}([|\mathbf{I}| + |\mathbf{Q}|]) \times [L]$ which for each tag indicates (the indexes of) the ciphertexts and the queries in which that tag occurs, and the position in the list of tags where it does.

Assume that T is ordered (i.e. lexicographically) and let $T[t]$ be the t'th tag in this order. By abusing notation we write $T[t] \in \mathbf{I}[i]$ to indicate that tag $T[t]$ occurs in the ciphertext associated to $\mathbf{I}[i]$ and we write $T[t] \in \mathbf{Q}[j]$ to indicate that tag occurs in the query associated to $\mathbf{Q}[j]$. We can then define the information leaked as

---

Algorithm Init$_\mathcal{H}$

  For $i = 1, \ldots, L$ do
    For $j = 1, \ldots, k$ do
      $h_{i,j}(.) \xleftarrow{\$} \mathcal{H}; \; g_i[j] \leftarrow h_{i,j}(.)$
    $\mathbf{g} = (g_1(\cdot), g_2(\cdot), \ldots, g_L(\cdot))$
    $P \leftarrow k\|L\|\mathbf{g}$; set random oracles G, H
    Return P

Algorithm Mask(P, I, M)

  Parse P as $k\|L\|\mathbf{g}$
  Tags $\leftarrow \emptyset$
  For $i = 1, \ldots, L$ do
    $\mathbf{C}[i] \xleftarrow{\$} \mathcal{E}(H(g_i(I)), M)$
    Tags $\leftarrow$ **Tags** $\cup \{\langle i, G(g_i(I))\rangle\}$
  Return $\mathbf{C}\|$**Tags**

Algorithm Unmask$(P, I', \mathbf{C}\|$Tags$)$

  Parse P as $k\|L\|\mathbf{g}$
  For $i = 1, \ldots, L$ do
    $T \xleftarrow{\$} G(g_i(I'))$
    If $\langle i, T \rangle \in$ **Tags** then
      $M \leftarrow \mathcal{D}(H(g_i(I')), \mathbf{C}[i])$
      Return M
  Return $\perp$

Algorithm Query(P, I)

  Parse P as $k\|L\|\mathbf{g}$
  Tags $\leftarrow \emptyset$
  For $i = 1, \ldots, L$ do
    Tags $\leftarrow$ **Tags** $\cup \{\langle i, G(g_i(I))\rangle\}$
  Return **Tags**

Algorithm FuzzyS$(\mathbf{DB}, \text{DS}, \mathbf{Tags^*})$

  $\mathbf{C_{close}} \leftarrow \emptyset$
  For every $i = 1, \ldots, |\mathbf{DB}|$ do
    Parse $\mathbf{DB}[i]$ as $\mathbf{C}\|$**Tags**
    If **Tags** $\cap$ **Tags*** $\neq \emptyset$ then
      then add $\mathbf{DB}[i]$ to $\mathbf{C_{close}}$
  Return $\mathbf{C_{close}}$

Fig. 2. Algorithms defining Basic KIFS.

$$\mathbf{L}(t) = \{(i, u) \mid \langle u, T[t]\rangle \in \mathbf{I}[i]\} \cup \{\langle j + |\mathbf{I}|, u\rangle \mid \langle u, T[t]\rangle \in \mathbf{Q}[j]\}.$$

Notice that we expressly do not pass $\mathbf{M}$ as input to the leakage function leak since its output $\mathbf{L}$ is independent of $\mathbf{M}$ – this indicates that the scheme leaks no information on the underlying plaintexts.

Next, we identify and explain the assumption on the interplay between the source $\mathcal{M}$ and the parameters of the scheme. Recall that, sensitive data is encrypted under keys of the form $H(g_i(I))$, where H is a random oracle and $g_i(\cdot)$ are hash functions form the extended LSH function $\mathcal{H}$, part of the parameters of the scheme. For security, we need that these keys are unpredictable, even given the information unavoidably leaked by the scheme. That is, for any $g_i(\cdot)$ (sampled from $\mathcal{H}$) and for any index $j \in [|\mathbf{I}|]$ and any index $k \in [|\mathbf{Q}|]$ we have that $\widetilde{H}_\infty(g_i(\mathbf{I}[j]) \mid \text{leak}(P, \mathbf{I}, \mathbf{Q}))) \geq l$ for some sufficiently large l. To simplify notation, and avoid the multiple quantifiers we write $\widetilde{H}_\infty(\mathcal{H}(\mathcal{M}) \mid \mathbf{L}(\mathcal{M})) \geq l$ for this requirement. Notice that this requirement is strictly stronger than closeness-unpredictability of $\mathcal{M}$.

The next theorem (which we prove in the full version [10]) establishes the security of the basic scheme, namely that it leaks no information beyond the tag overlap, unless the attacker can predict the tags. This holds under the assumption that the symmetric encryption scheme used in the implementation hides the plaintext and is *key-private*. This latter assumption is needed since otherwise, ciphertexts will leak information about equality of keys which translates to more specific information about equality of tags than leaked by $\mathbf{L}$: an adversary could tell not only that there are tag overlaps, but can tell to which keys these tags correspond.

Theorem 2. *Let $(\mathcal{D}, Cl)$ be a closeness domain. Let $\mathcal{M}$ be an arbitrary source and let $\mathcal{H}$ be a compatible (L, k)-eLSH scheme with parameters $(\delta^{C}, \delta^{F}, P_1, P_2)$ such that $\widetilde{H}_{\infty}(\mathcal{H}(\mathcal{M}) \mid \mathbf{L}(\mathcal{M})) \geq l$. Let $\mathcal{SE} = (\mathcal{E}, \mathcal{D})$ be a symmetric encryption scheme. We assume that keys for the scheme are bitstrings length l selected uniformly at random. Let Π be the Basic KlFS and let leak be the leakage function defined above. Then for any adversary A, we construct a simulator S such that there exist adversaries B and C so that, in the random oracle model, $\mathbf{Adv}^{prv}_{\Pi, \mathcal{M}, \mathsf{leak}}(A, S)$ is upperbounded by*

$$\mathbf{Adv}^{kh}_{\mathcal{SE}}(B) + \mathbf{Adv}^{ind\text{-}cpa}_{\mathcal{SE}}(C) + \frac{L \cdot (q_G + q_H) \cdot (|\mathbf{I}| + |\mathbf{Q}|))}{2^l},$$

where q_G is the number of queries that A makes to oracle G. Furthermore, the running times of S, B and C are essentially that of A; the number of encryption queries that B and C make is $|\mathbf{I}|$.

DISCUSSION. As the theorem above states, evaluating security requires estimating unpredictability of LSH tags, and we understand this is a difficult task. Evaluation of this property has to be done for the specific LSH instantiation. For example, for the aforementioned random-bit-projection LSH construction for Hamming distance, it is known [16,36] that the rate of source unpredictability is preserved by random random projections (or *samples*, using the terminology of [16]). It is shown in [16] that for some specific sources it is possible to preserve more entropy. In addition, one still has to estimate the unpredictability of the data (empirically or otherwise).

Similarly, it may not be easy to evaluate the implications of the leak function, a key challenge in studying property-preserving encryption in general. Hopefully future works will bring novel methods that facilitate such analysis. For our case, further work is needed to understand how leakage about tags translates into leakage about the data, but this requires a case by case analysis, depending on the use of a particular LSH and closeness domain.

For the case of random-bit-projection LSH, leak implies leaking the "overlap pattern" of LSH tags. In particular, each LSH tag (for eLSH construction) is a list of k bits. The attacker will learn to which data each tag corresponds to, but it does not learn what each tag is or what random bit positions each tag corresponds to (the latter is due to keeping tags as sets as opposed to lists, and by employing key-private encryption). An interesting challenge would be to see empirical inference attacks in the style of [17,33] which may rely on domain specific knowledge.

Also recall that the definition of the source implies that we only ensure security for messages that do not depend on public parameters. This is a rather reasonable assumption in practice and moreover, it is possible future research will remove this assumption, similarly to the case of MLE [1].

As we explained in Sect. 3, the bound can be used to estimate security of data with different entropy, if we consider several independent sources and assume that the data produced by different sources is not correlated across different sources.

5   KIFS for Fuzzy Image Search

FEATURE VECTORS. Most algorithms for image search deal with image *feature vectors*. Feature vectors are small pieces of data containing information about the image or parts of the image, such as color, shape, object boundaries, etc. Some applications may need to work with several types of features. For simplicity, in this work we focus on feature vectors of the same type. We remark that our definitions could easily be extended to handle multiple types of feature vectors. E.g., one could assign a specific index to indicate which type the feature vector belongs to.

We consider a domain of feature vectors $\mathcal{V}$ and assume that there exists an efficient deterministic algorithm extractV that takes an image $I \in \mathcal{D}$ and outputs a set of feature vectors $\mathbf{V} \subset \mathcal{V}$ (such algorithms are well-documented in the computer vision and graphics literature).

INTUITION FOR THE SCHEME. We aim to add security to the existing image search applications. In one such application, a user can search a database of pictures by an image of a face. The user is able to retrieve the pictures containing the person in question. More generally, a user holding an image I should be able to find database pictures that contain (as part of the picture) an image close to I in some metrics. As we discussed in the Introduction, the existing algorithms for unencrypted search work roughly by determining how many features are close between those for query and database data and this is done by comparing equality of LSH tags.

Our goal is to let such algorithms work on masked data. I.e., we want to hide information about the database and the queries besides the information necessary for efficient search, such as similarity of underlying feature vectors. And again, since we are working in the keyless setting, security depends on how hard it is to predict the images. Of course, we want to state and prove the exact security guarantees for our construction, even though we do not expect the security guarantees to be very strong (as we also have functionality and efficiency considerations on the other side of the scale).

Since our general KLFS scheme from Sect. 4 is not immediately suitable (mainly because it does not consider feature vectors), we propose a scheme tailored for the task. First, we encode the LSH tags of all extracted feature vectors, so that only their equality is leaked. This way the search algorithm can still identify close feature vectors of database pictures and queried images. Next we encrypt database pictures using the standard symmetric encryption scheme under a key K that can be computed only if one knows a threshold number of feature vectors close to those in the picture or, in other words, possesses an image close to that included in the picture. We achieve this by secret-sharing the key K and for each feature encrypting the corresponding share with a key deterministically derived from each LSH tag. We now provide the details.

THE CONSTRUCTION. We consider closeness domain $\Lambda = (\mathcal{D}, \mathrm{Cl})$, where $\mathcal{D}$ is a domain of images and Cl determines when two images are close for a match. The latter can depend on the application. (See Sect. 6 for a concrete example.) We assume the existence of deterministic algorithm extractV that takes an image in $\mathcal{D}$ and outputs a set of feature vectors $\mathbf{V}$. We also assume that Cl defines the parameter thr which is the number of close features needed to determine a match (closeness) between two images. The construction will use a $(\delta^{\mathsf{C}}, \delta^{\mathsf{F}}, p_1, p_2)$-sensitive hash family $\mathcal{H}_{L,k}$ with parameters L and k, matching the closeness domain as defined for the general schemes, cryptographic hashes H, G (will be treated as random oracles in the security analysis), a symmetric encryption scheme $\mathcal{SE} = (\mathcal{K}, \mathcal{E}, \mathcal{D})$ and a secret sharing scheme (KS, KR). We remark that in the secret sharing scheme, the parameter n (from t-out-of-n) will vary and will be determined in the construction.

The parameter generation algorithm is as of the Basic KlFS scheme. The rest of the algorithms are defined in Fig. 3. Similarly to the Basic KlFS description, we do not specify in Fig. 3 how FuzzyS makes use of the data structure DS or that the server could only return the matched tags. And in practice unmasking can be sped up if the user stores the tags (and their corresponding indices) so they are not re-computed during decryption.

CORRECTNESS AND SECURITY. The correctness of fuzzy search is as of the Basic KlFS. Correctness of decryption is similar to that of the Basic KlFS, but it also relies on correctness and security of the key sharing scheme. Specifically, correctness of the latter ensures that the threshold number of shares are sufficient to reconstruct the key, which in turn will ensure that decryption using an image close to the one used to encrypt will be correct. Decryption with a "far" image fails due to the use of the key sharing scheme: in this case the decryptor will not have enough shares. We observe that security of key sharing is actually stronger than what we need here (failure of key reconstruction with insufficient number of shares), as correctness is not an adversarial notion.

Before we specify the security of the scheme, we formalize the information that we expect that the scheme leaks. Given some parameters $P = k\|L\|g_L(\cdot)$, random oracles G and H and $(\mathbf{I}, \mathbf{M}, \mathbf{Q}, \mathsf{aux}) \xleftarrow{\$} \mathcal{M}$ we define the leakage function $\mathsf{leak}(P, (\mathbf{I}, \mathbf{Q}))$ as follows. (As for the previous scheme we do not pass $\mathbf{M}$ as input to the leak function to indicate that the information revealed by the scheme does

---

Algorithm Mask(P, I, M)

> Parse P as $k\|L\|\mathbf{g}$
> $\mathbf{V} \leftarrow \mathsf{extractV}(I)$
> $\mathbf{CT} \leftarrow \emptyset$
> $K \xleftarrow{\$} \mathcal{K}$
> $C \xleftarrow{\$} \mathcal{E}(K, M)$
> $(s_1, \dots, s_n) \xleftarrow{\$} \mathsf{KS}(K)$,
>   where $n = |\mathbf{V}|$
> For every feature $V_i \in \mathbf{V}$
> $\mathbf{Tags} \leftarrow \emptyset$
>   For $j = 1, \dots, L$ do
> $\mathbf{EncSh}[j] \leftarrow \mathcal{E}(H(g_j(V_i)), s_i)$
> $\mathbf{Tags} \leftarrow \mathbf{Tags} \cup \{\langle j, G(g_j(V_i)) \rangle\}$
> $\mathbf{CT} \leftarrow \mathbf{CT} \cup \mathbf{EncSh}\|\mathbf{Tags}$
> Return $C\|\mathbf{CT}$

Algorithm Unmask(P, I', C^*)

> Parse P as $k\|L\|\mathbf{g}$
> Parse C^* as $C\|\mathbf{CT}$
> Shares $\leftarrow \emptyset$
> $\mathbf{V}' \leftarrow \mathsf{extractV}(I')$
> For every feature $V_i' \in \mathbf{V}'$
> Parse $\mathbf{CT}_i$ as $\mathbf{EncSh}\|\mathbf{Tags}$
>   For $j = 1, \dots, L$ do
> $T' \leftarrow \langle j, G(g_j(V_i')) \rangle$
>   If $T' \in \mathbf{Tags}$ then
> $s_i \leftarrow \mathcal{D}(H(g_j(V_i')), \mathbf{EncSh}[j])$
>   Add s_i to Shares
> $K \leftarrow \mathsf{KR}(\text{Shares})$
> If $K = \perp$ then return $\perp$
> Else $M \leftarrow \mathcal{D}(K, C)$
> Return M

Algorithm Query(P, I)

> Parse P as $k\|L\|\mathbf{g}$; $\mathbf{V} \leftarrow \mathsf{extractV}(I)$
> For every $V_i \in \mathbf{V}$
> $\mathbf{Tags} \leftarrow \emptyset$
>   For $j = 1, \dots, L$ do
> $\mathbf{Tags} \leftarrow \mathbf{Tags} \cup \{\langle j, G(g_j(V_i)) \rangle\}$
> $\mathbf{T}[i] \leftarrow \mathbf{Tags}$
> Return $\mathbf{T}$

Algorithm FuzzyS($\mathsf{DB}, \mathsf{DS}, \mathbf{T}^*$)

> $match \leftarrow 0$; $\mathbf{C}_{\mathsf{close}}(T) \leftarrow \emptyset$
> For every $C_i \in \mathbf{DB}$
>   Parse C_i as $C\|\mathbf{CT}$
>   For each $\mathbf{CT}_i$
>   Parse $\mathbf{CT}_i$ as $\mathbf{EncSh}\|\mathbf{Tags}$
>   For every $\mathbf{T}^*[l]$ if $\mathbf{Tags} \cap \mathbf{T}^*[l] \neq \emptyset$
>   then $match \leftarrow match + 1$; break
>   If $match > \mathtt{thr}$ then
>   add C_i to $\mathbf{C}_{\mathsf{close}}(T)$
> Return $\mathbf{C}_{\mathsf{close}}(T)$

Fig. 3. Algorithms defining the KIFS for images.

not depend on $\mathbf{M}$.) We let F be the (lexicographically ordered) set of features associated to the images in $\mathbf{I}, \mathbf{Q}$; we write $F[i]$ for the i'th feature in F and let $f = |F|$. Let T be the (lexicographically ordered) set of tags associated to the features above; we let $T[i]$ be the i'th tag and let $n = |T|$. Define the matrix M of $|\mathbf{I}| + |\mathbf{Q}|$ rows, and f columns where the entry on row i and column j of matrix M is the list of tags associated to feature $F[j]$ if $F[j]$ is a feature of $\mathbf{I}[i]$. In other words l is part of the list $M(i, j)$ if $F[j]$ is a feature of $\mathbf{I}[i]$ and $T[l]$ is a tag derived from $F[j]$. The leakage function $\mathbf{L} : [n] \rightarrow \mathcal{P}((|\mathbf{I}| + |\mathbf{Q}|) \times [f] \times [L]))$ is defined by $\mathbf{L}(t) = \{(i, j, u) \mid \langle u, T[t] \rangle \in M(i, j)\}$. Informally, the function reveals for each tag (identified by an index $t \le n$) all access data or query entries (identified by $i \in [|\mathbf{I}| + |\mathbf{Q}|]$) and all features (identified by some $j \le f$) for which the tag was derived from feature j belong to access data (or query) i.

The security theorem below (proved in the full version [10]) establishes that unless the attacker guesses successfully some tag, provided the unavoidable leakage of the scheme, no information is leaked about the data that is masked. Specifically, we assume that we know l such that for any fixed g_i of $\mathcal{H}$, and $j \in [|\mathbf{I}|]$ if we let $V_k(\mathbf{I}[i])$ be the k'th feature extracted by extractV from $\mathbf{I}[i]$, then $\widetilde{H}_\infty(g_i(V_k(\mathbf{I}[j])) \mid \mathsf{leak}(P, \mathbf{I}, \mathbf{Q}))) \geq l$: that is there is sufficient entropy left in the (LSH projection) of each feature vector, even given the inherent leakage of the scheme (i.e. the different feature vector overlaps). We make the analogous requirement for $\mathbf{Q}$ by abuse of notation we write $\widetilde{H}_\infty(\mathcal{H}(\mathsf{extractV}(\mathcal{M})) \mid \mathbf{L}(\mathcal{M})) \geq l$ for the resulting condition.

Theorem 3. *Let $(\mathcal{D}, Cl)$ be a closeness domain. Let $\mathcal{M}$ be an arbitrary source and let $\mathcal{H}$ be a (L, k)-eLSH scheme with parameters $(\delta^C, \delta^F, P_1, P_2)$ such that $\widetilde{H}_\infty(\mathcal{H}(\mathsf{extractV}(\mathcal{M})) \mid \mathbf{L}(\mathcal{M})) \geq l$. Let $\mathcal{SE}$ be a symmetric encryption scheme, let $\Pi\text{-}IM$ be the KlFS described above Then for any adversary A, we construct a simulator S and adversaries B and C so that $\mathbf{Adv}^{prv}_{\Pi\text{-}IM,\mathcal{M},\mathsf{leak}}(A, S)$ is upper-bounded by*

$$\mathbf{Adv}^{kh}_{\mathcal{SE}}(B) + 2\mathbf{Adv}^{ind\text{-}cpa}_{\mathcal{SE}}(C) + \frac{L \cdot f \cdot (q_G + q_H) \cdot (|\mathbf{I}| + |\mathbf{Q}|)}{2^l},$$

where leak *is as defined above, and q_H and q_G are the number of random oracle calls to H and G. Furthermore, the running time of S, B and C are essentially that of A; the number of queries that B and C make to the encryption oracle is $|\mathbf{I}| \cdot f \cdot L$ (where f is the maximum number of features per image).*

DISCUSSION. As we discussed in Sect. 4, it is important to provide general means to further understand the extent and implications of leakage. Meanwhile, to gain more intuition about the leakage function, assume that the database contains 2 similar images I_1, I_2, so that I_1 and I_2 have close features V_1, V_2, V_3. Further assume that V_1, V_2 share LSH tags t_1, t_2; V_1, V_3 share LSH tags t_1, t_3; and V_1, V_3 share t_4. Then, according to leak function we defined, the adversary learns exactly that, namely the Venn diagram of the set of tags overlaps.

One could strengthen our theorem by relaxing the tag unpredictability requirement. Instead, one could require that only the threshold (from the key sharing scheme) tags be unpredictable as opposed to each individual one. In this case, the security of the scheme will also rely on security of the key sharing scheme.

6   Experimental Results and the Revised Scheme

EMPIRICAL STUDY OF THE BASIC KLFS FOR IMAGES. We implemented the KlFS for images from the previous section. We implemented the random bit projection LSH. We used the feature extraction algorithm from OpenCV 2.4.13. We limited the number of extracted features to 200 for each image and considered images close if they have at least two close ORB features (have an overlapping tag).

We experimentally evaluated the security of our scheme and found that it does not provide reasonable security, without any contradiction with the theoretical results. The problem is not with the scheme or its analysis. The problem is that the assumption on which security relies on is not true for the data sets we have experimented with. I.e., the feature vectors and hence the tags are predictable, in that images that are not visually close end up being "technically" close since their feature vectors overlap. An attacker can try several images until one of the features will match a feature from the masked image, and then the attacker will succeed.

MODIFIED KLFS FOR IMAGES. To alleviate the problem, we revise the scheme to incorporate two important modifications. First, to eliminate false positives during image search, we change the feature extraction extractV by adopting the "entropy-filling" technique used by Dong et al. [24]. Specifically, we extract and keep only features that best characterize the images; the common ones are filtered out. This technique significantly reduces the rate of (visually) false positives, which implies much improved closeness unpredictability of the feature vectors and tags.

However, the true-positive rate also reduces. To improve the true-positive rate while keeping the false-positive rate significantly low, one could try to extend the basic scheme to perform multiple search rounds by querying every returned result following the initial query, and then outputting the union of the results. However, this basic extension has two major drawbacks, one is to determine how many recursive calls should we enforce on every query, which seems to be a tough problem on its own. Second, if some images contain features that are close to the initial query, and lead to other large clusters that are not close to the initial query they will inevitably lead to a large number of false-positives. A better way, used in [24] is to incorporate a customized PageRank algorithm (PR-Nibble) derived from [2] as part of the image search scheme. We adapt it for search on masked data. We provide more details on our new KlFS for images in full version [10].

IMPLEMENTATION AND EVALUATION OF MODIFIED KLFS FOR IMAGES. In the full version [10] we present the results of evaluating our implementation. We used the same database as in [24]. In total, 81 groups of famous paintings and CD covers were chosen and manually checked that they were visually close. The test database consists of 10839 images in total. We implemented the masking scheme with cryptographic library Crypto++6.5.4 in C++ on Ubuntu 16.04 with 6-core processor (Intel® Core™ i7-8750H CPU @ 2.20 GHz ×12) with 16 GB RAM and demonstrated that the masking scheme was efficient and the number of false-positives is very low.

The true-positive rate is not very high, but this is as expected, given the necessity for almost no false positives and inability to execute advanced search techniques on unencrypted images use because the data is masked (such as, for example, feeding images into the trained deep neural networks). Still, for data domains where similar images are closely clustered together and clusters are reasonably far apart low true-positive rate may be sufficient. For example, for applications which needs to check for the presence of a specific and highly distinct image in a database where the multiples variations of that picture are present (and therefore does not need to recover all occurrences of that image). This is the case, for example, when determining if a particular human face, license plate number, animal, or logo appears in a collection of frames of a given video. Similarly, in machine learning applications, if an image (with objects or scenes) needs to be classified using a database of labeled images, then it is enough to match the image with the most likely class, and it is not necessary to match all close images.

Acknowledgements. We thank Dima Damen, Walterio Mayol Cuevas, Hugo Krawczyk, Leo Reyzin, Tom Ristenpart and Dan Shepard for useful comments and suggestions. We also thank the anonymous reviewers. Alexandra Boldyreva and Tianxin Tang were supported in part by NSF 1422794 and 1749069 awards.

References

1. Abadi, M., Boneh, D., Mironov, I., Raghunathan, A., Segev, G.: Message-locked encryption for lock-dependent messages. In: Canetti, R., Garay, J.A. (eds.) CRYPTO 2013. LNCS, vol. 8042, pp. 374–391. Springer, Heidelberg (2013). https://doi.org/10.1007/978-3-642-40041-4_21
2. Andersen, R., Chung, F.R.K., Lang, K.J.: Local graph partitioning using PageRank vectors. In: FOCS, pp. 475–486. IEEE Computer Society (2006)
3. Andoni, A., Indyk, P.: Near-optimal hashing algorithms for approximate nearest neighbor in high dimensions. In: FOCS, pp. 459–468. IEEE Computer Society (2006)
4. Bellare, M., Boldyreva, A., O'Neill, A.: Deterministic and efficiently searchable encryption. In: Menezes, A. (ed.) CRYPTO 2007. LNCS, vol. 4622, pp. 535–552. Springer, Heidelberg (2007). https://doi.org/10.1007/978-3-540-74143-5_30
5. Bellare, M., et al.: Hedged public-key encryption: how to protect against bad randomness. In: Matsui, M. (ed.) ASIACRYPT 2009. LNCS, vol. 5912, pp. 232–249. Springer, Heidelberg (2009). https://doi.org/10.1007/978-3-642-10366-7_14
6. Bellare, M., Fischlin, M., O'Neill, A., Ristenpart, T.: Deterministic encryption: definitional equivalences and constructions without random oracles. In: Wagner, D. (ed.) CRYPTO 2008. LNCS, vol. 5157, pp. 360–378. Springer, Heidelberg (2008). https://doi.org/10.1007/978-3-540-85174-5_20
7. Bellare, M., Keelveedhi, S., Ristenpart, T.: Message-locked encryption and secure deduplication. In: Johansson, T., Nguyen, P.Q. (eds.) EUROCRYPT 2013. LNCS, vol. 7881, pp. 296–312. Springer, Heidelberg (2013). https://doi.org/10.1007/978-3-642-38348-9_18
8. Boldyreva, A., Chenette, N.: Efficient fuzzy search on encrypted data. In: Cid, C., Rechberger, C. (eds.) FSE 2014. LNCS, vol. 8540, pp. 613–633. Springer, Heidelberg (2015). https://doi.org/10.1007/978-3-662-46706-0_31
9. Boldyreva, A., Chenette, N., O'Neill, A.: Order-preserving encryption revisited: improved security analysis and alternative solutions. In: Rogaway, P. (ed.) CRYPTO 2011. LNCS, vol. 6841, pp. 578–595. Springer, Heidelberg (2011). https://doi.org/10.1007/978-3-642-22792-9_33
10. Boldyreva, A., Tang, T., Warinschi, B.: Masking fuzzy-searchable public databases. Full version of this paper (2019). ePrint archive https://eprint.iacr.org/2019/434

11. Boyen, X.: Reusable cryptographic fuzzy extractors. In: ACM Conference on Computer and Communications Security, pp. 82–91. ACM (2004)

12. Brown, L., Gruenwald, L.: Tree-based indexes for image data. J. Vis. Commun. Image Represent. **9**(4), 300–313 (1998)

13. Brzuska, C., Mittelbach, A.: Indistinguishability obfuscation versus multi-bit point obfuscation with auxiliary input. In: Sarkar, P., Iwata, T. (eds.) ASIACRYPT 2014. LNCS, vol. 8874, pp. 142–161. Springer, Heidelberg (2014). https://doi.org/10.1007/978-3-662-45608-8_8

14. Canetti, R.: Towards realizing random oracles: hash functions that hide all partial information. In: Kaliski, B.S. (ed.) CRYPTO 1997. LNCS, vol. 1294, pp. 455–469. Springer, Heidelberg (1997). https://doi.org/10.1007/BFb0052255

15. Canetti, R., Dakdouk, R.R.: Obfuscating point functions with multibit output. In: Smart, N. (ed.) EUROCRYPT 2008. LNCS, vol. 4965, pp. 489–508. Springer, Heidelberg (2008). https://doi.org/10.1007/978-3-540-78967-3_28

16. Canetti, R., Fuller, B., Paneth, O., Reyzin, L., Smith, A.: Reusable fuzzy extractors for low-entropy distributions. In: Fischlin, M., Coron, J.-S. (eds.) EUROCRYPT 2016. LNCS, vol. 9665, pp. 117–146. Springer, Heidelberg (2016). https://doi.org/10.1007/978-3-662-49890-3_5

17. Cash, D., Grubbs, P., Perry, J., Ristenpart, T.: Leakage-abuse attacks against searchable encryption. In: ACM Conference on Computer and Communications Security, pp. 668–679. ACM (2015)

18. Cash, D., et al.: Dynamic searchable encryption in very-large databases: data structures and implementation. In: NDSS. The Internet Society (2014)

19. Chase, M., Kamara, S.: Structured encryption and controlled disclosure. In: Abe, M. (ed.) ASIACRYPT 2010. LNCS, vol. 6477, pp. 577–594. Springer, Heidelberg (2010). https://doi.org/10.1007/978-3-642-17373-8_33

20. Chenette, N., Lewi, K., Weis, S.A., Wu, D.J.: Practical order-revealing encryption with limited leakage. In: Peyrin, T. (ed.) FSE 2016. LNCS, vol. 9783, pp. 474–493. Springer, Heidelberg (2016). https://doi.org/10.1007/978-3-662-52993-5_24

21. Curtmola, R., Garay, J.A., Kamara, S., Ostrovsky, R.: Searchable symmetric encryption: improved definitions and efficient constructions. In: ACM Conference on Computer and Communications Security, pp. 79–88. ACM (2006)

22. Datar, M., Immorlica, N., Indyk, P., Mirrokni, V.S.: Locality-sensitive hashing scheme based on p-stable distributions. In: Symposium on Computational Geometry, pp. 253–262. ACM (2004)

23. Dodis, Y., Ostrovsky, R., Reyzin, L., Smith, A.D.: Fuzzy extractors: how to generate strong keys from biometrics and other noisy data. SIAM J. Comput. **38**(1), 97–139 (2008)

24. Dong, W., Wang, Z., Charikar, M., Li, K.: High-confidence near-duplicate image detection. In: ICMR, p. 1. ACM (2012)

25. Douceur, J.R., Adya, A., Bolosky, W.J., Simon, D., Theimer, M.: Reclaiming space from duplicate files in a serverless distributed file system. In: ICDCS, pp. 617–624 (2002)

26. Indyk, P., Motwani, R.: Approximate nearest neighbors: towards removing the curse of dimensionality. In: STOC, pp. 604–613. ACM (1998)

27. Juels, A., Sudan, M.: A fuzzy vault scheme. Des. Codes Crypt. **38**(2), 237–257 (2006)

28. Kamara, S., Papamanthou, C., Roeder, T.: Dynamic searchable symmetric encryption. In: ACM Conference on Computer and Communications Security, pp. 965–976. ACM (2012)

29. Kuzu, M., Islam, M.S., Kantarcioglu, M.: Efficient similarity search over encrypted data. In: ICDE, pp. 1156–1167. IEEE Computer Society (2012)
30. Lindell, Y., Pinkas, B.: Privacy preserving data mining. In: Bellare, M. (ed.) CRYPTO 2000. LNCS, vol. 1880, pp. 36–54. Springer, Heidelberg (2000). https:// doi.org/10.1007/3-540-44598-6_3
31. Matwin, S.: Privacy-preserving data mining techniques: survey and challenges. In: Custers, B., Calders, T., Schermer, B., Zarsky, T. (eds.) Discrimination and Privacy in the Information Society. SAPERE, vol. 3, pp. 209–221. Springer, Heidelberg (2013). https://doi.org/10.1007/978-3-642-30487-3_11
32. Narayanan, A., Shmatikov, V.: Obfuscated databases and group privacy. In: ACM Conference on Computer and Communications Security, pp. 102–111. ACM (2005)
33. Naveed, M., Kamara, S., Wright, C.V.: Inference attacks on property-preserving encrypted databases. In: ACM Conference on Computer and Communications Security, pp. 644–655. ACM (2015)
34. Pandey, O., Rouselakis, Y.: Property preserving symmetric encryption. In: Pointcheval, D., Johansson, T. (eds.) EUROCRYPT 2012. LNCS, vol. 7237, pp. 375–391. Springer, Heidelberg (2012). https://doi.org/10.1007/978-3-642-29011-4_23
35. Shakhnarovich, G., Darrell, T., Indyk, P.: Nearest-Neighbor Methods in Learning and Vision: Theory and Practice (Neural Information Processing). The MIT Press, Cambridge (2006)
36. Vadhan, S.P.: Constructing locally computable extractors and cryptosystems in the bounded-storage model. J. Cryptol. 17(1), 43–77 (2004)

Homomorphic Training of 30,000 Logistic Regression Models

Flavio Bergamaschi[1(✉)], Shai Halevi[2], Tzipora T. Halevi[3], and Hamish Hunt[1]

[1] IBM Research, Winchester, UK
{flavio,hamishhun}@uk.ibm.com
[2] IBM Research, Albany, NY, USA
shaih@alum.mit.edu
[3] Brooklyn College, Brooklyn, NY, USA
thalevi@nyu.edu

Abstract. In this work, we demonstrate the use the CKKS homomorphic encryption scheme to train a large number of logistic regression models simultaneously, as needed to run a genome-wide association study (GWAS) on encrypted data. Our implementation can train more than 30,000 models (each with four features) in about 20 min. To that end, we rely on a similar iterative Nesterov procedure to what was used by Kim, Song, Kim, Lee, and Cheon to train a single model [14]. We adapt this method to train many models simultaneously using the SIMD capabilities of the CKKS scheme. We also performed a thorough validation of this iterative method and evaluated its suitability both as a generic method for computing logistic regression models, and specifically for GWAS.

Keywords: Approximate numbers · Homomorphic encryption · GWAS · Implementation · Logistic regression

1 Introduction

In the decade since Gentry's breakthrough [9] we saw rapid improvement in homomorphic encryption (HE) techniques. What started as a mere theoretical possibility is now a promising technology on its way from the lab to the field. Many of the real-world problems to which this technology was applied originated in the yearly competitions that are organized by the iDASH center [12]. These competitions, organized annually since 2014, pose specific technical problems related to privacy preserving analysis of medical data and ask for solutions using specific technologies. Some of the problems posed in the 2017 and 2018 instalments dealt with training logistic regression (LR) models on encrypted data.

In 2017, the task was to devise a single model. Many solutions were suggested that perform this task in a matter of a few minutes to a few hours [1,6,8,11,14, 15]. In particular, the winning entry in the 2017 competition was due to Kim et al. [14], using the HE scheme due to Cheon et al. [7] (which we call below

© Springer Nature Switzerland AG 2019
R. H. Deng et al. (Eds.): ACNS 2019, LNCS 11464, pp. 592–611, 2019.
https://doi.org/10.1007/978-3-030-21568-2_29

the CKKS scheme). For 2018, the goal was to train a very large number of models, as needed for a Genome-Wide Association Study (GWAS). In GWAS a large number of markers are simultaneously tested for their association with some condition (such as a specific disease). The modus operandi in GWAS is to devise a large number of LR models at once, each model using only a handful of markers, then test these models to see which of them have good predictive power. For the 2018 competition, the iDASH organizers provided a dataset with over 10,000 markers, noting that "implementation of linear or logistic regression based GWAS would require building one model for each SNP, which requires a lot of time." (SNP is a single genomic marker). Instead they suggested to use the *semi-parallel algorithm* of Sikorska et al. [18] for that purpose.

1.1 Our Work

The goal of the current work was to show that "building one model for each SNP" can actually be accomplished with reasonable resources, by a careful adaptation of the techniques used in the iDASH competition from 2017. Specifically, we implemented a solution along the same lines as the procedure used by Kim et al. [14] with some corrections and optimizations. Our implementation is able to compute more than 30,000 LR models in parallel taking only about 20 min.

This work consists of two parts: In one part, we adapted the iterative procedure of Kim et al. [14] to the setting of GWAS, using the SIMD capabilities of the CKKS HE scheme, to compute a large number of models simultaneously. In the other part, we performed a thorough validation of this iterative method, evaluating its suitability both as a generic method for computing LR models and specifically for GWAS.

Adapting and Validating the Iterative Procedure. The iterative procedure of Kim et al. [14] applies Nesterov's accelerated gradient descent [16] with a very small number of iterations (and uses the CKKS cryptosystem to run it on encrypted data). While Kim et al. evaluated the accuracy of their method, the GWAS setting raises some other demands that were not evaluated in [14]. For one thing, in [14] they only devised a handful of models on data with a rather strong signal, whereas in GWAS we need to devise many thousands of models on data that ranges from having very strong to very weak signal (and many in between). Moreover, for GWAS we had to train the model on encrypted data, and also *evaluate it homomorphically* by computing the log-likelihoods ratio.

We found that some details of the iterative procedure had to be adapted to this setting. One notable issue was that when the data was not balanced (e.g., with more 0's than 1's), as the signal weakens the model tends to degenerate to the constant predictor that always says zero (hence getting a *recall value* of zero). In our tests, we found that sub-sampling the training data to ensure that it is balanced resulted in much better recall values with almost no effect on the accuracy of the model. We also found and fixed a few minor mistakes and inconsistencies in the procedure from [14] and its evaluation, see Sect. 3.

In the tests ran, we compared the adequacy of the iterative procedure (in terms of ordering the genomic markers by relevance) to that of the semi-parallel algorithm. We concluded that the ordering in both methods are mostly equivalent, but the iterative procedure often provided better model parameters. We also compared the approximate LR models of the iterative procedure to the LR models computed by Matlab's `glmfit` function. Surprisingly, even when we use very few iterations, the resulting LR models are just as predictive as the ones produced by Matlab, see Sect. 3.1.

We used several datasets of very different characteristics for testing. One was the genome dataset provided by the iDASH team. Others include the Edinburgh myocardial infarction dataset [13] (also used by Kim et al.), a credit-card fraud dataset [2,17], and the dataset related to the sinking of the RMS Titanic [3].[1]

Homomorphic Implementation. Like many contemporary homomorphic encryption schemes, the CKKS approximate number scheme of Cheon et al. [7] supports Single-Instruction-Multiple-Data (SIMD) operations: ciphertexts in CKKS encrypt vectors of numbers and each homomorphic operation induces element-wise operations on the corresponding vectors. This provides the basis of our GWAS procedure: simply pack the parameters of the different models in different entries of these vectors, then use the SIMD structure to run the iterative procedure on all of them in parallel. Specifically in our setting, we used ciphertexts that can pack upto $2^{15} = 32768$ numbers, so we can compute that many models in parallel.

Implementing this approach requires some care, particularly with regards to RAM consumption. We need to ensure that the computation fits in the available RAM as packed ciphertexts are typically large. A notable optimization described in Sect. 4.2 takes advantage that CKKS ciphertexts can pack a vector of *complex numbers* (not just real numbers). Our optimization uses that fact to reduce the number of operations by almost a factor of two by packing twice as many real numbers in each ciphertext, but paying some price in larger noise accumulation.

We also mention that our CKKS implementation, done over the HElib engine [10], differs from other implementations in some details (which makes working with it a little easier). These details are described in Sect. 4. As mentioned above, using this implementation we can compute all the LR models for a GWAS with upto 2^{15} markers and three clinical variables in about twenty minutes.

We note that the running time would grow nearly quadratically with the number of clinical variables: since to train models with more variables we also need more records, then the size of the input matrix grows quadratically with the number of variables. With three clinical variables we were able to train the models in under 20 min, and a back-of-an-envelope calculation indicates that we could handle 8–10 clinical variables in about an hour.

Organization. In Sect. 2, we provide some background on LR, GWAS, and Nesterov's Accelerated Gradient Descent [16]. In Sect. 3, we provide details on our variant of the iterative procedure, and our testing methodology and results.

---

[1] The last three datasets are much smaller than we would like. Nonetheless, they contain features with strong signal and others with very weak signal, so we can still use them to evaluate the GWAS setting.

In Sect. 4, we describe the implementation of this procedure on encrypted data and provide various runtime measurements.

2 Background

2.1 Logistic Regression

Logistic regression (LR) is a machine-learning technique trying to predict one attribute (condition) from other attributes. In this work, we only deal with the case where the condition that we want to predict is binary (e.g., sick or healthy). The data that we get consists of n records (rows) of the form (y_i, x_i) with $y_i \in \{0,1\}$ and $x_i \in \mathbb{R}^d$. We would like to predict the value of $y \in \{0,1\}$ given the attributes x, and the logistic regression technique postulates that the distribution of y given x is given by

$$\Pr[y = 1|x] = \frac{1}{1 + \exp\left(-w_0 - \sum_{i=1}^{n} x_i w_i\right)} = \frac{1}{1 + \exp\left(-x'^T w\right)},$$

where w is some fixed $(d+1)$-vector of real weights that we need to find, and $x'_i = (1|x_i) \in \mathbb{R}^{d+1}$. Given the training data $\{(y_i, x_i)\}_{i=1}^{n}$, we thus want to find the vector w that best matches this data, where the notion of "best match" is typically maximum likelihood. Using the identity $1 - \frac{1}{1+\exp(-z)} = \frac{1}{1+\exp(z)}$, we therefore want to compute (or approximate)

$$w^* = \arg\max_{w} \left\{ \prod_{y_i=1} \frac{1}{1 + \exp\left(-x_i'^T w\right)} \cdot \prod_{y_i=0} \frac{1}{1 + \exp\left(x_i'^T w\right)} \right\}.$$

The last condition can be written more compactly: let $y'_i = 2y_i - 1 \in \{\pm 1\}$ and $z_i = y'_i \cdot x'_i$, then our goal is to compute/approximate

$$w^* = \arg\max_{w} \left\{ \prod_{i=1}^{n} \frac{1}{1 + \exp\left(-z_i^T w\right)} \right\} = \arg\min_{w} \left\{ \sum_{i=1}^{n} \log\left(1 + \exp(-z_i^T w)\right) \right\}.$$

For a candidate weight vector w, we denote the (normalized) *loss function* for the given training set by

$$J(w) \stackrel{\text{def}}{=} \frac{1}{n} \cdot \sum_{i=1}^{n} \log\left(1 + \exp(-z_i^T w)\right), \tag{1}$$

and our goal is to find w that minimizes that loss.

Gradient Descent and Nesterov's Method. In this work, we use a variant of the iterative method used by Kim et al. in [14] based on Nesterov's accelerated gradient descent [16]. Let σ be the sigmoid function $\sigma(x) \stackrel{\text{def}}{=} 1/(1 + e^{-x})$, it can be shown that the gradient of the loss function with respect to w is

$$\nabla J(w) = -\frac{1}{n} \sum_{i=1}^{n} \frac{1}{1 + \exp(z_i^T w)} \cdot z_i = -\frac{1}{n} \sum_{i=1}^{n} \sigma\left(-z_i^T w\right) \cdot z_i. \tag{2}$$

Nesterov's method initializes two evolving vectors (e.g., to the average of the input records), then in each iteration it computes

$$w^{(t+1)} = v^{(t)} - \alpha_t \cdot \nabla J(v^{(t)}),$$
$$v^{(t+1)} = (1 - \gamma_t) \cdot w^{(t+1)} + \gamma_t \cdot w^{(t)}, \tag{3}$$

where α_t, γ_t are scalar parameters that change from one iteration to the next. (α is the learning rate and γ is called the moving average smoothing parameter, see section 3 for how they are set).

Approximating the Sigmoid. As in [14], we use low-degree polynomials to approximate the sigmoid function in a bound range around zero. We use the same degree-3 and degree-7 approximation polynomials in the interval $[-8, +8]$, namely

$$SIG3(x) \stackrel{\text{def}}{=} 0.5 - 1.2 \left(\frac{x}{8}\right) + 0.81562 \left(\frac{x}{8}\right)^3 \text{ and} \tag{4}$$

$$SIG7(x) \stackrel{\text{def}}{=} 0.5 - 1.734 \left(\frac{x}{8}\right) + 4.19407 \left(\frac{x}{8}\right)^3 - 5.43402 \left(\frac{x}{8}\right)^5 + 2.50739 \left(\frac{x}{8}\right)^7$$

2.2   Genome-Wide Association Study (GWAS)

In genetic studies, LR is often used for Genome-Wide Association Study (GWAS). Such studies take a large set of genomic markers (SNPs) and determine which of them are associated with a given trait. A GWAS typically considers one condition variable (e.g., sick or healthy), a small number of clinical variables (such as age, gender, etc.) and a large number of SNPs. For each SNP separately, the study builds a LR model that tries to predict the condition from the clinical variables and that one SNP, then tests how good that model is at predicting the condition. (The clinical variables are sometimes called covariates, below we use these terms almost interchangeably).

Assessing a Model: Likelihood Ratio, p-values, Accuracy, Recall. One way to evaluate the quality of a LR model is to compute its loss function $J(w)$, Eq. (1). We note that this number has a semantic meaning, it is the logarithm of the likelihood of the training data according to the LR model (with parameters w). This number can then be used to compute the likelihood-ratio-test (LRT)[2] which is sometimes called the "p-value" of the model. We note that Eq. (1) is not the only formula used for computing p-values (indeed the iDASH competition organizers used a different formula for it). However, at least according to Wikipedia, the LRT is "the recommended method to calculate the p-value for logistic regression" (cf. [19]).

---

[2] The LRT measures how much more likely we are to observe the training data if the true probability distribution of the y_i's is what we compute in the model vs. the probability to observe the same training data according to the null hypothesis in which the y_i's are independent of the x_i's.

Another way to evaluate the model is to use it for prediction and test how well it performs. Typically, you would divide your dataset into training and test data, devise the model on the training data, then use it on the test data to predict the value of the y_i's (predicting $y_i = 1$ if $\Pr[y = 1 | x_i] > 1/2$ and $y_i = 0$ otherwise). The fraction of correct predictions is called the *accuracy* of the model. It is common to use *five-fold testing* where the procedure above is repeated five times, each time choosing 80% of the records for training and the rest for testing, then averaging the accuracy values of the five runs.

Overall accuracy may not always be a good measure of performance. For example, if 90% of the records in our dataset have $y_i = 0$ then even the constant predictor $y = 0$ will have 90% accuracy. We therefore also test the *recall* of the model, which is its success probability over *only the records with* $y_i = 1$. This too is typically measured with a five-fold testing.

3   The Logistic Regression Iterative Procedure

The LR procedure that we used is similar to the one used by Kim et al. [14], but we had to make some changes and correct a few inaccuracies:

Balancing the Input. We observed that when the input dataset is unbalanced, the model obtained from the iterative procedure is highly biased as well, sometimes to the point of having recall value of zero. Our program therefore trains the model always on a random subset of the input dataset where 50% of the records have $y_i = 0$ and 50% have $y_i = 1$. This simple solution corrects the recall values of the resulting models and in our tests it only has a very minor effect on their accuracy.

We remark that this solution can be applied even when the data is encrypted, for example, by storing the $y = 0$ encrypted records separately from the $y = 1$ records. This of course will reveal the y value of all the records, but nothing else about them. If we want to hide also the y value of the records and if we know *a priori* the fraction p of records with $y = 1$, then we could just choose at random which records to use in the study during encryption. For example, if $p < 1/2$ we can choose each $y = 1$ record with probability one and each $y = 0$ record with probability $p/(1 - p)$.

The Number of Iterations. The number of iterations that we can perform is very limited as we are using a somewhat-homomorphic encryption scheme to implement the procedure on encrypted data. We denote this number by τ, and in our implementation and tests we used $\tau = 7$ iterations.

Initializing the Evolving State. Since we need to use a small number of iterations, the initial values of v, w is important to the convergence of the weights. Our tests show that setting them as the average of the inputs (i.e., $v^{(0)} = w^{(0)} = \frac{1}{n} \sum_{i=1}^{n} z_i$) yields better results than choosing them at random.[3]

---

[3] This form of initialization differs from the description in [14], but it is consistent with the code shared online by the authors.

The α and γ Parameters. The learning-rate parameter α was set just as in [14], namely in iteration $t = 1, \ldots, \tau$ we used $\alpha_t = 10/(t + 1)$.

For the moving average smoothing parameter γ, Kim et al. stated in [14] that they used $\gamma \in [0, 1]$, but positive γ values result in bad performance of the Nesterov algorithm. Instead, we used negative values for gamma as suggested in [5]: Setting $\lambda_0 = 0$, we compute for $t = 1, \ldots, \tau$

$$\lambda_t = \frac{1 + \sqrt{1 + 4\lambda_{t-1}^2}}{2} \text{ and } \gamma_t = \frac{1 - \lambda_{t-1}}{\lambda_t}.$$

The values of γ for the first few steps are therefore $\gamma \approx (1, 0, -0.28, -0.43, -0.53, -0.6, -0.65, \ldots)$.

Precision. We tested our procedure in order to decide how much precision is needed since the CKKS scheme only offers limited precision. Our tests found no significant difference in performance, even with only six bits of precision (i.e. error of upto 2^{-7} per operation). We therefore decided to set the precision parameter for the homomorphic scheme at $r = 8$, corresponding to 2^{-8} error. As there was no real effect, we ran most of our plaintext tests below with full precision.

Computing the Log-Likelihood. In addition to computing the model parameters, we extended the procedure from above to also compute the loss function (i.e., the log-likelihood of the resulting model). For this purpose, we needed to approximate also the log-sigmoid function using a low-degree polynomial, in particular we used the degree-4 approximation in the range $[-8, 8]$ (obtained using Python's `numpy.polyfit`):

$$LOGSIG4(x) \stackrel{\text{def}}{=} 0.000527x^4 - 0.0822x^2 + 0.5x - 0.78 \approx \log(\sigma(x)) \quad (5)$$

We then approximate the log-likelihood of each model $\boldsymbol{w}$ as $LOSS(\boldsymbol{w}) \approx -\sum_{i=1}^{n} LOGSIG4(\boldsymbol{z}_i^T \boldsymbol{w})$.

3.1   Experimental Evaluation

We evaluated our procedure across multiple parameters and settings, and compared it to alternative procedures. When attempting such evaluation, it is important to ensure that the procedure is not over-engineered to fit just one type of data, so we run our tests against four different datasets with very different characteristics (though not every test was run on every dataset). These datasets included the iDASH 2018 dataset for correlating cancer with genomic markers, a credit-card fraud dataset, the Edinburgh dataset for correlating heart attacks with various tests and symptoms, and a dataset for correlating various passenger characteristics with the rate of survival in the Titanic disaster. See Appendix B for more details on these datasets.

Sorting the Columns in Order of Relevance. One focus of this work is GWAS-like procedures where we want to filter out the irrelevant columns. Hence, many of our tests examined *the order of relevance* of the different columns rather than the actual model parameters for their respective models. In these tests, we computed all the LR models, one model per SNP (all models containing the clinical variables), approximated the log-likelihood for each, and ordered the SNPs in decreasing order of their log-likelihood. This order is our procedure's estimate of the order of relevance of the different SNPs to the condition. We then used the following methodology to evaluate the "quality" of this ordering:

- We applied the Matlab implementation of LR to re-compute the LR model on the same data, using the `glmfit` function. The resulting LR models (one per SNP) could be different than those produced by our iterative procedure;
- Next, we ran a five-fold test on the data using Matlab's `glmval` to compute the predicted condition values, and computed the accuracy and recall for each model;
- Finally, we plotted the accuracy and recall values against the order of columns from our iterative procedure.

If the procedure works well, we expect a decreasing order of accuracy and recall, since the first models in the order are supposed to correspond to the most relevant SNPs, and hence to the highest accuracy and recall values.

We compared the column ordering from our iterative procedure to the ordering generated by the p-values of the semi-parallel algorithm of Sikorska et al. [18]. (We used the R implementation provided by the iDASH organizers for that purpose). We also tested the column ordering using the accuracy and recall results as produced by the Matlab LR models (using `glmfit` and `glmval`), plotting them against the column ordering of the semi-parallel algorithm.

We stress that for both orderings, we plot the exact same accuracy and recall numbers, i.e. the ones corresponding to the Matlab LR models. The only difference is the order in which we plot these numbers.

Evaluating the Model Parameters. Since our procedure yields not only the log-likelihood (a.k.a. p-value) for each model but also the model parameters themselves, we ran a few tests to examine how well these models perform. Namely, we compared the accuracy and recall of our models with those of the Matlab LR models on the same data. Again, we plotted all the accuracy and recall results in the order of columns of our iterative procedure.

Different Approximations of the Sigmoid Function. We tested our iterative procedure in two settings, one using nine iterations with the degree-3 approximation of the sigmoid, and the other using seven iterations with the degree-7 approximation. While there were no significant differences in the order of SNPs produced by the two variants, the model parameters produced by the degree-7 approximation were often improved than those produced by the degree-3 approximation. We therefore ran most of our tests using only the seven-step degree-7 approximation.

3.2   Accuracy and Recall Results

Here, we summarize the test results. All of these tests were run with our iterative procedure using the degree-7 approximation of the sigmoid function and $\tau = 7$ iterations. All accuracy and recall results below were obtained using five-fold testing (described in Sect. 2.2). One point that needs care when running a five-fold test, is ensuring that the test data has similar characteristics to the training data: Some datasets are collected from multiple sources, hence the first records may have very different characteristics than the last ones. (In particular the data provided for the iDASH competition had that problem). Randomizing the order of the records in the dataset before running the test fixes this.

Comparing the Column Ordering, Iterative vs. Semi-parallel. As we explained above, we run our iterative procedure and the semi-parallel algorithm from [18] side by side on the same data, computing the p-values from each and ordering the SNPs according to these p-values. We then used the Matlab implementation of LR to compute the accuracy and recall values of the model corresponding to each SNP (with the same clinical variable), and plotted these accuracy and recall values in the two orders.

The results for the iDASH dataset are depicted in Fig. 2. For that dataset, the two orders more or less coincide for the most relevant 1500 columns or so (out of 10643). For the next 1500 columns, the orders are no longer the same. Moreover, while the accuracy results are very similar, the iterative ordering yields better recall values than the semi-parallel ordering. The last 8000 columns no longer contain much information on the condition variable, hence the ordering of these columns is essentially random. We also ran the same test for the credit-card fraud dataset, which contains only 30 columns. Here while the two orders identify the same top nine, middle seven, and bottom fourteen columns, the ordering within each of the first two groups was somewhat more accurate for the semi-parallel algorithm than for the iterative method.

Comparing the Iterative vs. Matlab Models. Next, we tried to evaluate the quality of the models generated by the iterative method to the standard LR models of Matlab. Since the iterative method with so few steps is only a crude approximation, we expected the Matlab model to perform better, but wanted to check by how much. We therefore computed for each column the accuracy and recall values of both models (iterative vs. Matlab), and plotted them against the p-value ordering from our procedure. (See the full version for a plot of the results).

To our surprise, the crude approximated model computed by the iterative method performed at least as well (and sometimes better) than the LR model that Matlab computed for the same data. We can see that the iterative model has some bias for outputting $y = 1$, resulting in better recall and somewhat worse accuracy values. For example, notice that around the 1000'th SNP the iterative model has recall value of 1, while the Matlab model's recall values are capped around 0.9 (with essentially the same accuracy). We ran the same test also on the Titanic dataset, and again the iterative models did about as well (and sometimes better) than the Matlab models.

The Edinburgh Dataset. We also ran our iterative procedure on the Edinburgh datasets computing the accuracy/recall for the Matlab model for each column and plotting these values against the p-value ordering of the columns as produced by the iterative procedure.

3.3 Conclusions and Some Comments

Summarizing the tests above, the iterative procedure that we used produces models which are competitive to what we get from Matlab, and that the relevance order that we get from our p-values is just as reasonable as the one obtained by the semi-parallel algorithm. While the semi-parallel algorithm is faster (especially when there are many covariates), for a small number of covariates the iterative procedure has reasonable performance. A reasonable conclusion to draw is that one should still run the semi-parallel algorithm in the context of GWAS, but use the iterative model if it is desired to also get the actual LR models (in addition to ordering the columns by relevance).

In this context, the semi-parallel algorithm assumes that the model weights for the covariates are more or less the same when you devise a model for just the covariates as when you devise a model for the covariates and a single SNP. For the iDASH dataset, this was true for most SNPs (since most SNPs were not correlated with the condition at all), but our tests showed that it seems to **not** be true for the most relevant SNPs. This observation implies that while the semi-parallel algorithm is a good screening tool to filter out the irrelevant SNPs (for which the assumption on the covariates should hold), it probably should not be used to compute the model parameters for the more relevant SNPs.

Finally, during our work we encountered two minor bugs/inconsistencies in the literature, notified the relevant authors, and document them in Appendix A.

4 Homomorphic Evaluation of the LR Procedure

To evaluate the procedure from Sect. 3 on encrypted data, we used the CKKS approximate-number HE scheme of Cheon et al. [7], which we implemented in the HElib library [10]. The underlying plaintext space of this scheme are complex numbers (with limited precision), and the scheme can pack many such complex numbers in a single ciphertext. In Sect. 4.3 below, we briefly describe some details of our HElib-based implementation, see the original work [7] for details about the scheme itself. The API provided by our implementation is as follows:

Parameters. Security parameter λ, plus two functionality parameters: The packing parameter ℓ determines how many complex numbers can be encoded in a single ciphertext, and the accuracy parameter r determines the supported precision. Operations of the scheme are accurate up to additive noise of magnitude bounded by 2^{-r}. We refer to entries in the encrypted vectors as *plaintext slots*.

Noisy Encoding. The native objects manipulated in the CKKS scheme belong to an algebraic ring (specifically algebraic integers in cyclotomic number fields). The scheme provides routines to encode and decode plaintext complex vector $v \in \mathbb{C}^\ell$ into and out of that ring. However the encoding is noisy, which introduces additive errors of magnitude up to 2^{-r} in each entry.

Encryption, Decryption, and Homomorphic Operations. Once encoded in the "native ring," data can be encrypted and decrypted using the public and secret keys, respectively.

- The scheme supports addition and multiplication operations, both plaintext-to-ciphertext and ciphertext-to-ciphertext, including element-wise addition/multiplication on the underlying complex vectors. Providing $w_t = u_t + v_t$ for every entry t for addition, and similarly $w_t = u_t \cdot v_t$ for multiplication.
- There are procedures (which are essentially free) for multiplying and dividing ciphertexts by real numbers, namely setting $v_t = u_t \cdot x$ or $v_t = u_t/x$ for all t.
- Included is the support for "homomorphic automorphisms". Our application uses automorphisms for computing complex conjugates. Namely, given an encoded (or encrypted) vector u, the conjugate operation outputs a similarly encoded/encrypted vector v such that $v_t = \bar{u}_t$ for every entry t. Used to homomorphically extract the real and imaginary parts, via $\mathrm{im}(x) = (x - \bar{x})/2i$ and $\mathrm{re}(x) = (x + \bar{x})/2$ (with i denoting the imaginary square root of -1).

All the operations above (including encoding and encryption) accrue additive errors. Namely, an operation can return a vector v' that differs from the intended result v, with the guarantee that for every entry t we have $|v_t - v'_t| \leq 2^{-r}$.

4.1 The Homomorphic LR Procedure

The input to the LR procedure consists of n records, each containing k covariates (i.e., clinical variables such as age or gender), N genomic markers (or SNPs), and a single binary condition variable (sick or healthy). Our solution is tailored for the case where k is small (up to five), N is large (many thousands) and the number of records is moderate (hundreds to a few thousands).

Our goal is to compute N (approximate) LR models, one per SNP, where the t'th model includes parameters for all the k clinical variables and the (single) t'th SNP. As described in Sect. 3, our approach follows the approach by Kim et al. [14]. Namely, we run an iterative method using Nesterov's algorithm and a low-degree approximation of the sigmoid function implemented on top of the CKKS approximate-number homomorphic encryption scheme [7].

The main difference is that we use the inherent SIMD properties of CKKS to compute all the N models at once: We run the LR computation in a *bitslice mode*, where we pack the data into a number of N-vectors with the t'th entry in each vector corresponds to the t'th model. Each input record has $k + 2$ input ciphertexts: One for the condition variable (with all the slots holding the same

Input(n-by-$(k+2)$ matrix C)		
1. $\boldsymbol{w} := \boldsymbol{v} := \frac{1}{n}\sum_{i=1}^{n} C_{i-}$	// initialize evolving state to average of the rows in C	
2. Repeat for τ steps:	// run the iterative process	
3. $\quad \boldsymbol{x} := C \times \boldsymbol{v}^T$	// $\boldsymbol{x}$ is a dimension-n column vector	
4. $\quad \boldsymbol{y} := SIG7(\boldsymbol{x})$	// approximate the sigmoid on each entry of $\boldsymbol{x}$	
5. $\quad \boldsymbol{g} := -\boldsymbol{y}^T \times C$	// the gradient $\boldsymbol{g}$ is a dimension-$(k+2)$ row vector	
6. $\quad$ Compute $\alpha, \gamma \in \mathbb{R}$ for this step // see details in section 3		
7. $\quad \boldsymbol{w}' := \boldsymbol{v} + \alpha \cdot \boldsymbol{g}$		
8. $\quad \boldsymbol{v} := \gamma \cdot \boldsymbol{w} + (1-\gamma)\cdot \boldsymbol{w}'$	$// = \gamma\boldsymbol{w} + (1-\gamma)\boldsymbol{v} + \alpha(1-\gamma)\boldsymbol{g}$	
9. $\quad \boldsymbol{w} := \boldsymbol{w}'$		
10. $\boldsymbol{x} := C \times \boldsymbol{v}^T$	// compute the log likelihood of the model	
11. $\boldsymbol{y} := LOGSIG4(\boldsymbol{x})$	// approximate the log-sigmoid on each entry of $\boldsymbol{x}$	
12. $u = \sum_{i=1}^{n} y_i$	// the log-likelihood	
13. output $\boldsymbol{w}$ and u	// output the resulting model weights and log likelihood	

Fig. 1. The homomorphic logistic regression procedure

condition bit), one for each of the covariates (with all the slots holding the same covariate value), and one more ciphertext for all the SNPs (with the different SNPs in the different slots).

We denote by C the $n \times (k+2)$ matrix of input ciphertexts, where each row i corresponds to an input record and each column j corresponds to a model parameter.[4] Given the input matrix C, we evaluate homomorphically the iterative Nesterov-based procedure described in Sect. 3 for as many steps as our parameters allow. Our main solution uses seven iterations, each employing a degree-seven approximation of the sigmoid function. The homomorphic procedure is described on a high-level in Fig. 1 with details discussed below.

Fitting the Computation in RAM. Note that as described in Fig. 1, each iteration of the main loop requires two passes over the input matrix C, one for computing $C \times \boldsymbol{v}$ in Line 3 and another to compute $\boldsymbol{y} \times C$ in Line 5. If C does not fully fit in memory, then each iteration would require swapping it twice in and out of main memory. Instead, partitioning C into bands that fit in RAM requires a single pass over it in each iteration. Let $I_1, I_2, \ldots, I_b$ be a partition of the row indexes $[n]$ and let $C_{I_1}, \ldots, C_{i_b}$ be the corresponding partition of the rows of C (and similarly $\boldsymbol{x}_{I_1}, \ldots, \boldsymbol{x}_{i_b}$ be the partition of the entries of $\boldsymbol{x}$, and the same for $\boldsymbol{y}$). We replace lines 3–5 by the following computation:

---

[4] Another "hidden" dimension are the slots $t = 1, \ldots, N$ in each ciphertext, but since our computation is completely SIMD then we can ignore that dimension.

[...]

2. Repeat for τ steps: // run the iterative process
2a. $g := 0$
2.   For $h = 1$ to b // go over the bands of C
3'. $x_{I_h} := C_{I_h} \times v^T$ // x_{I_h} is part of x
4'. $y_{I_h} := SIG7(x_{I_h})$ // approximate the sigmoid on each entry of x
5'. $g := g - y_{I_h}^T \times C_{I_h}$ // the contribution of C_{I_h} to the gradient
6.   [...]   // continue with the update of v, w as before

Computing the Log Likelihood. As we explained in Sect. 2.2, after computing the model parameters w we need to also evaluate this model by computing its p-value, i.e, the loss function from Eq. (1). This computation is very similar to the computation of the gradient, but here we use the approximation of the log-sigmoid $LOGSIG4$ instead of the $SIG7$ approximation of the sigmoid itself. Namely we first compute $x := C \times w$, then $y := LOGSIG4(x)$, and finally sum up (or average) the entries in the vector y.

4.2   Fewer Multiplications via Complex Packing

We implemented a second variant of our solution, which is faster and uses half the number of ciphertexts, but adds more noise per iteration. This was done by packing the data more tightly, utilizing both the real part and the imaginary part of each plaintext slot, thus encrypting two input records in each ciphertext (one in the real part of all the slots and the other in the imaginary parts). Specifically, let $z_{2i-1,j}, z_{2i,j}$ be the two real values that were encrypted in the two ciphertexts $C_{2i-1,j}, C_{2i,j}$ in the matrix C from above. In the new variant we instead use a single ciphertext $C'_{i,j}$, encrypting the complex value $z'_{i,j} = z_{2i-1,j} + i \cdot z_{2i,j}$ (with i the imaginary square root of -1). Let $C' = [C'_{i,j}]$ be the resulting ciphertext matrix, and $N' = \lceil N/2 \rceil$ be the number of rows in the matrix C'.

During the computation we maintain the evolving state vectors v, w as *real vectors* (i.e., their imaginary part is zero). This sometimes requires splitting the encrypted complex numbers into their real and imaginary parts (using the conjugate operation mentioned above). For example, we initialize the evolving state by computing the average of the (complex) rows of C'. Then we split the result into its real and complex parts and average the two.

Similarly, we sometimes also need to assemble two real values into a complex one, just by computing $z_c = z_r + i \cdot z_i$ homomorphically. These split and assemble operations cause this variant to accrue more noise than before. However, it uses half as many input ciphertexts and roughly half as many operations per iteration of the Nesterov algorithm.

Computing the Gradient. The most interesting aspect of this complex-packed procedure is the computation of the gradient in Steps 3–5 from Fig. 1. The multiplication in Step 3 is quite straightforward: since v encrypts a real vector, we can compute $\boldsymbol{x}' := C' \times \boldsymbol{v}^T$ just as before and the multiplication by $\boldsymbol{v}$ operates separately on the real and imaginary parts of C'.

To apply the sigmoid function, requires spliting the resulting $\boldsymbol{x}'$ into its real and imaginary components and compute the sigmoid approximation on each of them separately. Namely, we set $\boldsymbol{x}_r := \mathsf{re}(\boldsymbol{x})$ and $\boldsymbol{x}_\mathsf{i} := \mathsf{im}(\boldsymbol{x})$, then $\boldsymbol{y}_r := SIG7(\boldsymbol{x}_r)$ and $\boldsymbol{y}_\mathsf{i} := SIG7(\boldsymbol{x}_\mathsf{i})$. To save on noise, we fold into the sigmoid computation some of the multiply-by-constant operations from splitting $\boldsymbol{x}'$.

More interesting is how to compute the product $\boldsymbol{y} \times C'$ from Step 5 with our tightly packed version of the ciphertext matrix. Here we use the happy coincidence that for complex numbers we have $(a + ib)(a' - ib') = aa' + bb' + \mathsf{i} \cdot$ something, giving us the inner product $\langle (a, b), (a', b') \rangle$ in the real part. We therefore pack $\boldsymbol{y}' := \boldsymbol{y}_r - \mathsf{i} \cdot \boldsymbol{y}_\mathsf{i}$, compute $\boldsymbol{g}' = -\boldsymbol{y} \times C'$, and the real part of $\boldsymbol{g}'$ turns out to be exactly the gradient vector that we need. To see this, recall that for all i, j we have $y'_j = y_{2j-1} - \mathsf{i} \cdot y_{2j}$ and $C'_{i,j} = z_{2j-1} + \mathsf{i} \cdot z_{2j}$, and therefore

$$g'_j = \sum_{i=1}^{N'} y'_i \cdot C'_{i,j} = \sum_{i=1}^{N/2} \left(y_{2i-1} - \mathsf{i} \cdot y_{2i}\right) \cdot \left(z_{2i-1,j} + \mathsf{i} \cdot z_{2i,j}\right)$$

$$= \sum_{i=1}^{N/2} \left(y_{2i-1} \cdot z_{2i-1,j} + y_{2i} \cdot z_{2i,j} + \mathsf{i} \cdot \text{something}\right) = \left(\sum_{i=1}^{N} y_i \cdot z_{i,j}\right) + \mathsf{i} \cdot \text{something}'.$$

We complete the gradient computation just by extracting the real part, $\boldsymbol{g} := \mathsf{re}(\boldsymbol{g}')$. This new gradient calculation performs half as many multiplications in the inner-product steps (3 and 5), the same number of operations in the sigmoid step 4, and a few more operations to split and recombine complex vectors from real and imaginary parts. Since the inner product operations are by far the most expensive parts of each Nesterov computation, this saves nearly half of the overall number of multiplications. However, in our tests it only saved about 20% of the running time. (We think that this discrepancy is partially because we worked harder on optimized the standard procedure than the complex packed one).

4.3 Implementing CKKS in HElib

The CKKS scheme from [7] is a Regev-type cryptosystem, with a decryption invariant of the form $[\langle \mathsf{sk}, \mathsf{ct} \rangle]_q = \tilde{\mathsf{pt}}$, where sk, ct are the secret-key and ciphertext vectors, respectively, $[\cdot]_q$ denotes reduction modulo q into the interval $[-q/2, q/2]$, and $\tilde{\mathsf{pt}}$ is an element that encodes the plaintext and includes also some noise.

The CKKS scheme is similar in many ways to the BGV scheme from [4]: both schemes use an element $\tilde{\mathsf{pt}}$ of low norm, $|\tilde{\mathsf{pt}}| \ll q$, and the homomorphic operations are implemented almost exactly the same in both. The difference between these schemes lies in the way they interpret the element $\tilde{\mathsf{pt}}$, i.e., how it is decoded into plaintext pt and noise e: We tend to think in the BGV of the low-order bits of $\tilde{\mathsf{pt}}$ as pt and the high-order bits as e, and in CKKS it is the other way around. Specifically, the BGV decodes $\tilde{\mathsf{pt}} = \mathsf{pt} + p \cdot \mathsf{e}$, where p is the plaintext space modulus and $|\mathsf{pt}| < p$, whereas CKKS decodes $\tilde{\mathsf{pt}} = \mathsf{e} + \Delta \cdot \mathsf{pt}$ where Δ is some scaling factor and (hopefully) $|\mathsf{e}| < \Delta$.

This difference in interpretation of $\tilde{pt}$ implies very different plaintext algebras for the two schemes: While BGV deals with integral plaintext elements modulo p, in CKKS the plaintext elements are complex numbers with limited precision. Some other (rather small) differences between the homomorphic operations in BGV and CKKS are related to the way the scaling factor Δ is handled:

– The plaintext modulus p in BGV typically does not change throughout the computation, but the scaling factor Δ in CKKS does vary: Specifically, Δ is squared on multiplication and is scaled via modulus switching.
– In both CKKS and BGV, ciphertexts can only be added when they are defined relative to the same modulus q. However, it is also important for CKKS addition that they have the same scaling factor Δ.

Our CKKS implementation in HElib relies on the same chassis as the BGV cryptosystem that supports the required homomorphic operations and handles any cyclotomic field.[5] Differently from the way it is described in [7], the HElib implementation does not rely on the application to use explicit scaling, instead the library can automatically scale all the ciphertexts as needed. Each ciphertext in our implementation is tagged with both a noise estimate and the scaling factor Δ and the library uses these tags to decide how and when to scale these ciphertexts using modulus-switching. These scaling decisions balance the need to scale the ciphertexts down before multiplication to keep the noise small with the need to keep the scaling factor Δ sufficiently larger than the noise element e.

The cryptosystem is initialized with an accuracy parameter r that from the application perspective roughly means the additive noise terms in the various operations is bounded by 2^{-r} in magnitude. The library tries to ensure that operations with added noise term η will only be applied to ciphertexts with scaling factors $\Delta \geq \eta \cdot 2^r$. Note, that this logic only "does the right thing" when the complex values throughout the computation are close to one in magnitude. For smaller values, the requested accuracy bound will typically not be enough, while for larger values the implementation will spend too much resources trying to keep the precision way too high. The logic works quite well for the LR procedure (Sect. 3) where indeed all the encrypted quantities are kept at size $\Theta(1)$.

4.4   Performance of the Homomorphic Procedure

We tested the running time and memory consumption in a few different settings, depending on the number of available threads, and the number of bands in the matrix C. (As we explained in Sect. 4.1, using more bands is useful when the machine has limited RAM and cannot fit all the encrypted input ciphertexts in memory at once.) We also tested the complex packing optimization from Sect. 4.2 vs. the "standard" way of packing only real numbers in the slots.

These tests were run on a machine with Intel E5-2640 CPU running at 2.5 GHz, with 2×12 cores, 64 GB memory (split 32 GB for each chip in a NUMA configuration), and 15 MB cache. The software configurations (on

---

[5] Our logistic regression procedure uses a power of two cyclotomic field for efficiency.

Ubuntu 16.04.5) included HElib commit `dbaa108b66c5` from Sep 2018, NTL version 11.3.2, GMP version 6.1.2, and Armadillo version 9.200.7. All compiled with gcc 8.1.0 including our LR code.

Parameters. The parameters were chosen so as to get at least 128 security level while having enough levels to complete seven iterations (followed by computing the log likelihood of the resulting model). Specifically, the largest modulus in the chain had $|q| = 900$ bits, and the scheme was instantiated over the m'th cyclotomic field with $m = 2^{17} = 131072$ (so the dimension of the relevant lattice was $\phi(m) = 65536$). This setting gave us estimated security level of 142 bits. These parameters give us $\phi(m)/2 = 32768$ slots in which to pack data, so we could compute up to 32768 LR models in parallel.

The results that we describe below were measured on the iDASH 2018 dataset, where each model has three clinical variables and a single SNP. This dataset had only 10643 SNPs, so we only packed that many numbers in the slots, but the performance numbers are not affected by the number of "empty slots," we would have identical results even if all 32767 slots were filled.

On the other hand, the number of records in the training set does influence the running time (as well as the memory consumption). Here we used the fact that small LR models can be computed accurately by sub-sampling the data. The common "one in ten" rule of thumb states that a model with k features requires at least $10k$ records with 0 and $10k$ records with 1. Since in these tests we had four features in each model (three clinical variables and one SNP), and since we sub-sampled the data to get 50% 0's and 50% 1's, then we needed at least 80 total record, and we run all our tests on 100 records in the training test.

Without the complex-packing optimization, each iteration of the Nesterov procedure took four levels in the modulus chain. This is a little surprising, as each iteration includes a degree-7 polynomial sandwiched between two vector-matrix multiplications so we expect it to take five levels rather than four. The reason is that we used 44 bits "wide" levels, and the noise management logic of HElib performed two consecutive operations at the same level. This indicates some waste in the HElib noise management. With complex packing, we could only perform six iterations with the same parameters as each iteration of the Nesterov procedure used an average six levels.

Results. The results are described in Tables 1 and 2. The optimization of using complex packing cuts the input-reading time in half (as there are half as many ciphertexts), but only reduces the running time by about 20% (for the same number of iterations). There is approximately a linear speedup when the number of threads is increased from one to twelve, but not more due to cache contention on the testing server architecture. The memory requirements grow slowly with the number of threads, twelve threads consumed 1.5× to 2× more memory than a single threads.

Table 1. CPU time and RAM consumption of the "standard packing" method with seven iterations and a single band, vs. number of threads

Parallelization vs. run-time, seven iterations			
# threads	Read input time	Training time	RAM consumption
1	435 s	8847 s	24 GB
2	220 s	4190 s	26 GB
6	78 s	1673 s	28 GB
12	44 s	1202 s	30 GB
24	44 s	1128 s	33 GB

Table 2. CPU time and RAM consumption with six iterations and a single band, both complex and standard packing, vs. number of threads

Standard vs. complex packing, six iterations				
Packing	# threads	Read input time	Training time	RAM consumption
Standard	1	464 s	7620 s	24 GB
	2	223 s	3677 s	26 GB
	6	79 s	1449 s	28 GB
	12	44 s	1128 s	30 GB
	24	40 s	1016 s	33 GB
Complex	1	223 s	5960 s	13 GB
	2	111 s	2998 s	14 GB
	6	42 s	1242 s	16 GB
	12	25 s	859 s	18 GB
	24	23 s	818 s	24 GB

5   Conclusions

In this work, we demonstrated that the CKKS cryptosystem [7] can be used to implement homomorphic training of a very large number of logistic regression models simultaneously in a reasonable amount of time.

For that purpose, we adopted the iterative method used by Kim et al. [14] based on Nesterov's accelerated gradient descent. Our implementation can train simultaneously over 30,000 small models, each with four variables, in about 20 min. We estimate that the same number of models with 8–10 variables can be trained in about an hour. We also provided extensive evaluation of this iterative procedure, testing it on a number of different datasets and comparing its predictive power with a few alternatives. Our tests show that this method is competitive.

A   Corrections in the Literature

During our work we encountered two minor bugs/inconsistencies in the literature. We have notified the relevant authors and document these issues here:

- The Matlab code used in the iDASH **2017** competition had a bug in the way it computed the recall values, computing it as $\frac{false\ positive+true\ positive}{false\ negative+true\ positive}$ instead of $\frac{true\ positive}{false\ negative+true\ positive}$.
- Some of the mean-squared-error (MSE) results reported in [14] seem inconsistent with their accuracy values: For the Edinburgh dataset, they report accuracy value of 86%, but MSE of only 0.00075. We note that 86% accuracy implies MSE of at least $0.14 \cdot (0.5)^2 = 0.035$ (likely a typo).

B   The Datasets that We Used

Recall that we tested the iterative procedure against a few different datasets, to ensure that it is not "tailored" too much to the characteristics of just one type of data. We had some difficulties finding public datasets that we could use for this evaluation, eventually we converged on the following four:

- The iDASH 2018 dataset, as provided by the organizers of the competition, is meant to correlate various genetic markers with the risk of developing cancer. It consists of 245 records, each with a binary condition (cancer or not), three covariates (age, weight, and height), and 10643 markers (SNPs). The last 120 records were missing the covariates, so we ran our procedure by replacing each missing covariate by the average of the same covariate in the other records.
- A credit card dataset [2] attempts to correlate credit-card fraud with observed characteristics of the transaction. This dataset has 984 records each with thirty columns.
- The Edinburgh dataset [13] correlates the condition of Myocardial Infarction (heart attack) in patients who presented to the emergency room in the Edinburgh Royal Infirmary in Scotland with various symptoms and test results (e.g., ST elevation, New Q waves, Hypoperfusion, depression, vomiting, etc.). The same dataset was also used to evaluate the procedure of Kim et al. [14]. The data includes 1253 records, each with nine features.
- The Titanic dataset [3], consisting of 892 records with sixteen features, correlating passenger's survival in that disaster with various characteristics such as gender, age, fare, etc.

The first dataset comes with a distinction between SNPs and clinical variables, but the other three have just the condition variable and all the rest. We had to decide which of the features (if any) to use for covariates. We note that whatever feature we designate as covariate will be present in all the models, so choosing a feature with very high signal will make the predictive power of all the models very similar. We therefore typically opted to choose for a covariate the features which is *least correlated* with the condition. We also ran the same test with no covariates, and the results were very similar.

C   Model Evaluation Figures

iDASH data column ordering: iterative vs. semi-parallel

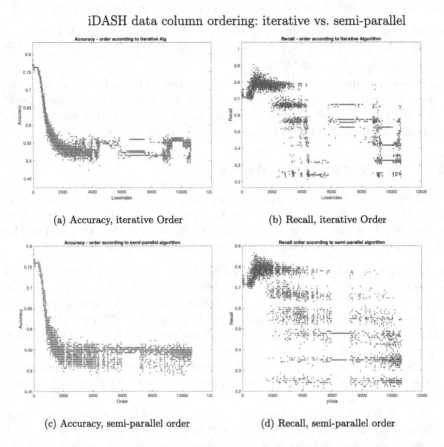

(a) Accuracy, iterative Order   (b) Recall, iterative Order

(c) Accuracy, semi-parallel order   (d) Recall, semi-parallel order

Fig. 2. Accuracy/recall of the Matlab LR models for the iDASH 2018 dataset ordered according to the p-value order of the iterative procedure (top) or the semi-parallel algorithm (bottom).

References

1. Bonte, C., Vercauteren, F.: Privacy-preserving logistic regression training. BMC Medi. Genom. **11**(Suppl 4), 86 (2018). https://doi.org/10.1186/s12920-018-0398-y
2. Bontempi, G., Pozzolo, A.D., Caelen, O., Johnson, R.A.: Credit card fraud detection. Technical report, Université Libre de Bruxelles (2015)
3. Bootwala, A.: Titanic for Binary logistic regression. https://www.kaggle.com/azeembootwala/titanic/home

Homomorphic Training of 30,000 Logistic Regression Models   611

4. Brakerski, Z., Gentry, C., Vaikuntanathan, V.: Fully homomorphic encryption without bootstrapping. In: Innovations in Theoretical Computer Science (ITCS 2012) (2012). http://eprint.iacr.org/2011/277

5. Bubeck, S.: ORF523: Nesterov's accelerated gradient descent. https://blogs. princeton.edu/imabandit/2013/04/01/acceleratedgradientdescent. Accessed January 2019, 2013

6. Chen, H., et al.: Logistic regression over encrypted data from fully homomorphic encryption. BMC Med. Genom. **11**(Suppl 4), 81 (2018). https://doi.org/10.1186/s12920-018-0397-z

7. Cheon, J.H., Kim, A., Kim, M., Song, Y.: Homomorphic encryption for arithmetic of approximate numbers. In: Takagi, T., Peyrin, T. (eds.) ASIACRYPT 2017. LNCS, vol. 10624, pp. 409–437. Springer, Cham (2017). https://doi.org/10.1007/978-3-319-70694-8_15

8. Crawford, J.L.H., Gentry, C., Halevi, S., Platt, D., Shoup, V.: Doing real work with FHE: the case of logistic regression. In: Brenner, M., Rohloff, K. (eds.) Proceedings of the 6th Workshop on Encrypted Computing and Applied Homomorphic Cryptography, WAHC@CCS 2018, pp. 1–12. ACM (2018). https://eprint.iacr.org/2018/202

9. Gentry, C.: Fully homomorphic encryption using ideal lattices. In: Proceedings of the 41st ACM Symposium on Theory of Computing - STOC 2009, pp. 169–178. ACM (2009)

10. Halevi, S., Shoup, V.: HElib - an implementation of homomorphic encryption. https://github.com/shaih/HElib/, Accessed January 2019

11. Han, K., Hong, S., Cheon, J.H., Park, D.: Efficient logistic regression on large encrypted data. Cryptology ePrint Archive, Report 2018/662 (2018). https://eprint.iacr.org/2018/662

12. Integrating Data for Analysis, Anonymization and SHaring (iDASH). https://idash.ucsd.edu/

13. Kennedy, R.L., Fraser, H.S., McStay, L.N., Harrison, R.F.: Early diagnosis of acute myocardial infarction using clinical and electrocardiographic data at presentation: derivation and evaluation of logistic regression models. Eur. Heart J. **17**(8), 1181–1191 (1996). https://github.com/kimandrik/IDASH2017/tree/master/IDASH2017/data/edin.txt

14. Kim, A., Song, Y., Kim, M., Lee, K., Cheon, J.H.: Logistic regression model training based on the approximate homomorphic encryption. BMC Med. Genom. **11**(4), 83 (2018)

15. Kim, M., Song, Y., Wang, S., Xia, Y., Jiang, X.: Secure logistic regression based on homomorphic encryption: design and evaluation. JMIR Med. Inf. **6**(2), e19 (2018). https://doi.org/10.2196/medinform.8805. https://eprint.iacr.org/2018/074

16. Nesterov, Y.: Introductory Lectures on Convex Optimization: A Basic Course. Applied Optimization, vol. 87. Springer, New York (2004). https://doi.org/10.1007/978-1-4419-8853-9

17. Pozzolo, A.D., Caelen, O., Johnson, R.A., Bontempi, G.: Calibrating probability with undersampling for unbalanced classification. In: 2015 IEEE Symposium Series on Computational Intelligence, pp. 159–166, December 2015

18. Sikorska, K., Lesaffre, E., Groenen, P.J., Eilers, P.H.: GWAS on your notebook: fast semi-parallel linear and logistic regression for genome-wide association studies. BMC Bioinf. **14**, 166 (2013)

19. Logistic regression. https://en.wikipedia.org/wiki/Logistic_regression#Discussion. Accessed January 2017

Author Index

Printed in the United States
By Bookmasters